SHIP ISLAND, MISSISSIPPI

ALSO BY TERRY G. SCRIBER AND
THERESA ARNOLD-SCRIBER

*The Fourth Louisiana Battalion in the Civil War:
A History and Roster* (McFarland, 2008)

Ship Island, Mississippi

Rosters and History of the Civil War Prison

Theresa Arnold-Scriber *and* Terry G. Scriber

McFarland & Company, Inc., Publishers
Jefferson, North Carolina, and London

The present work is a reprint of the illustrated case bound edition of Ship Island, Mississippi: Rosters and History of the Civil War Prison, *first published in 2008 by McFarland.*

LIBRARY OF CONGRESS CATALOGUING-IN-PUBLICATION DATA

Arnold-Scriber, Theresa, 1961–
Ship Island, Mississippi : rosters and history of the Civil War prison / Theresa Arnold-Scriber and Terry G. Scriber.
p. cm.
Includes bibliographical references and index.

ISBN 978-0-7864-6899-7
softcover : acid free paper ∞

1. United States—History—Civil War, 1861–1865—Prisoners and prisons. 2. Military prisons—Mississippi—Ship Island—History—19th century. 3. Ship Island (Miss.)—History. 4. United States. Army—Prisons—Mississippi—Ship Island. 5. Prisoners of war—Mississippi—Ship Island—Registers. 6. Registers of births, etc.—Mississippi—Ship Island. 7. Confederate States of America. Army—Registers. 8. United States—History—Civil War, 1861–1865—Registers. I. Scriber, Terry G. II. Title.
E616.S55A76 2012   973.7'462—dc22   2007030053

BRITISH LIBRARY CATALOGUING DATA ARE AVAILABLE

© 2008 Theresa Arnold-Scriber and Terry G. Scriber. All rights reserved

No part of this book may be reproduced or transmitted in any form or by any means, electronic or mechanical, including photocopying or recording, or by any information storage and retrieval system, without permission in writing from the publisher.

On the cover: Major General Benjamin F. Butler directed the first Union expedition to Ship Island in December 1861 (photograph courtesy National Archives); original watercolor detail of "Ship Island—Black Sand" by Bruce Repei, www.brucerepei.com

Manufactured in the United States of America

McFarland & Company, Inc., Publishers
Box 611, Jefferson, North Carolina 28640
www.mcfarlandpub.com

To my wonderful son, Michael Edward Metz, Jr.,
and beautiful granddaughter, Hailei Faith Metz,
in the hope that this book will inspire each of them
to accomplish their dreams and goals in life.
With love always.

Theresa Arnold-Scriber

To my mother, Helen M. Scriber,
for all of her support, love and encouragement
over the years. With love always.

Terry G. Scriber

Contents

Preface and Acknowledgments 1
Introduction 5

I. History

One. Isle de Surgeres to Ship Island 9
Two. The Federals Arrive 30
Three. The Prisoner-of-War Camp 55
Four. Post-War Ship Island 79

II. Rosters

Guide to Using the Rosters 101
Union Dead 106
Alabama Prisoners of War 121
Arkansas Prisoners of War 224
Florida Prisoners of War 225
Georgia Prisoners of War 233
Louisiana Prisoners of War 234
Mississippi Prisoners of War 291
Missouri Prisoners of War 343
North Carolina Prisoners of War 371
South Carolina Prisoners of War 382
Tennessee Prisoners of War 388
Texas Prisoners of War 401

Confederate Navy Prisoners of War 407
Confederate Staff and Regular Prisoners of War 417
Citizen Prisoners of War 426

Chapter Notes 433
Bibliography 439
Index 441

Preface and Acknowledgments

I (Theresa Arnold-Scriber) first became interested in genealogy as a teenager when my dad told me that my family was related to the ever-interesting and controversial figure Benedict Arnold, who served in the Revolutionary War with our soon-to-be nation's first president George Washington. My parents both had a great sense of humor, so upon receiving this information, I basically shrugged it off as a joke and never pursued any further proof of whether it was accurate or not. Later in life, my curiosity piqued, and I decided to pursue proof of this lifelong mystery, which remained in my subconscious thoughts as would a haunting ghost. Years later, through persistent research, I discovered that my dad was not joking and the ancestor lines say it is so, that in fact my family is related to the historical Continental Army general. After confirming that my family's ancestry did include the man history so often referred to as a traitor, I decided to move on to my husband's family history, which is where Terry and I discovered the inspiration for our first Civil War book, *Twenty-Seventh Louisiana Volunteer Infantry*. Digging deep into his family roots, we discovered that his great-great-grandfather, Burlin Moore Scriber, had served during the Civil War in the Confederate army as a corporal in the Twenty-Seventh Louisiana Volunteer Infantry, which led to our interest and curiosity to learn more about one of the most brutal wars in American history. As we persisted to find information relating to Burlin Scriber, we became frustrated that family members knew nothing about the man who volunteered his services to the Confederacy at age 17 and amazingly survived the brutalities, inhumanities, and atrocities associated with war that he experienced at such an impressionable age.

While researching the Civil War, we were surprised to learn that a picturesque tropical island, situated in the Gulf of Mexico a little more than ten miles from the beautiful Mississippi coast, once held prisoners of war in a military stockade during the conflict between the North and the South. Even more surprising was that a military fort was built on this sliver of land. It was hard to believe that civilians, Confederate soldiers, politicians, and even Federal soldiers accused of crimes, suffered sickness, terrifying emotions, and humiliations at the hands of the Union army at such a tranquil site that would attract any vacationer.

When I discovered that the man most associated with Ship Island during the Civil War was a New England native, lawyer, politician, and Union major-general named Benjamin F. Butler, my interest intensified, leading me to learn all I could about the man the South would refer to as "The Beast" and also the island that had played such an important role in

American history. It seemed the more I delved into unraveling the events that took place on this island, the more I realized that the information was all too scattered. There were very few books on the library shelves to educate us about Ship Island. Terry and I both felt this was an injustice to the many people who suffered and died on that island. We decided that a book was needed to honor these people for the tribulations they experienced at a time in our history when food, clothing, and shelter were luxuries to most of those brave individuals who endured the hardships of the Civil War as best they could.

This book is divided into two sections. The first section contains the chapters that will explain the history of the island first discovered in the seventeenth century and up to the present day. The second section is a roster of Confederate soldiers who were imprisoned on the island; they were from Alabama, Arkansas, Florida, Georgia, Louisiana, Mississippi, Missouri, North Carolina, South Carolina, Tennessee and Texas. The roster also contains the names of the soldiers and sailors from the Confederate Regular Army and the Confederate Navy, the citizens who were imprisoned on the island, and the Union soldiers who died at Ship Island while performing garrison duty or who were held there as military convicts. Readers will find more detail about the roster in the "Guide to Using the Rosters." One hundred and fifty-three Confederate soldiers and sailors had been identified as perishing on Ship Island in the past, but many more humans would be buried nameless, unidentified, their remains lying beneath the hot silky sand under the sizzling rays of the Mississippi sun, until their remains washed away into the murky green Gulf of Mexico waters. By April 1865, it was reported that 4,356 prisoners were being held at Ship Island, which inspired us to list as many of those prisoners as possible here. We have also attempted to give the reader a better insight to the circumstances surrounding the imprisonment of some of the citizens who were either captured or sent to the island by order of Union Major-General Butler.

Although it may sound cliché to say that this book has been a "work of love," the fact is that an immense amount of work had to be accomplished due to the fact that so many people imprisoned at Ship Island, Mississippi, were from Northern and Southern states. Terry's wisdom, experience, and encouragement to begin and complete this project was very much appreciated by me and I was thrilled to have his assistance as coauthor of this work. There are so many people to thank and to whom we are very much indebted for their assistance. Many of the descendants of these brave soldiers refused to be acknowledged for their contribution to honor the memory of their brave ancestors.

First of all, a great library is always essential to conducting the necessary research and to gathering the necessary materials to compile a massive book such as this. There is no greater library that we have found than the Calvin M. McClung Historical Collection at the East Tennessee History Center. For anyone who plans to visit Tennessee, it is well worth the time and energy to stop by and see their museum and collections in Knoxville. We would like to thank Jenny Ball and Jamie Osborn of the McClung Historical Library for their assistance in getting us the needed books and microfilm to make this project possible. Also, from the Lawson-McGhee Public Library in Knoxville, Willa Reister and Kevin Mallory of the Inter-Library Loan Department were very helpful in obtaining hard to find resources. Historical institutions such as individual state archives and historical libraries are important to researchers everywhere, and we were fortunate enough to get exceptional assistance from Mary Jo Scott, Bob Bradley, and Debbie Pendleton of the Alabama Department of Archives and History, Sergio Velasco from the Texas State Library and Archives, Adam Watson from the Florida State Archives and State Library, Jeffrey Brown from the Maine Archives, and Nancy Milner of the Connecticut Historical Society Museum.

We would like to thank David Ogden, park ranger and historian, and park rangers Don Holifield and Terry Wildy from the Gulf Islands National Seashore.

A very special thank you goes out to New England historian A. Dean Sergeant, of Rockland, Massachusetts, for contributing his time, energy, and hard work to see this project to fruition and whose enthusiasm for Ship Island never waned. We'd also like to thank his wife, Ruthie, for her patience while he assisted us from afar. They brought some much needed laughter to an exhausting but rewarding project and we were elated to meet such great people whom we now call friends.

Others to thank for their help and contributions to this work are Dale Cox of Florida; Dr. Ken Jones of Stephenville, Texas; Alan Pitts of the History-Sites.com Civil War Message Boards; Dr. Arthur W. Bergeron, Jr.; C. P. Weaver; Robert Larkin of Connecticut; Kermit Breed; Northeast Louisiana historian and good friend Robert "Bob" Archibald; April Rose; Ben Hudson; William "Bill" Boggess and Roy Hammett, Jr., of Louisiana; Tom Normand and T. J. Buckner from OfficeMax of Knoxville, Tennessee.

We would also like to thank teacher Paul LaRue and his student Mary Huff, of the Washington High School Senior Research Class in Ohio, for their assistance with the Union roster. Thanks also to Civil War naval enthusiast Terry Foenander for his gracious assistance with the Confederate Navy prisoner of war roster.

We would like to thank the following people for contributing photos and information: The James R. Box family, and two gentlemen, who preferred to remain anonymous, from Alabama and Virginia for their generosity in opening their private collections to us, as well as Timothy Harrison, editor and publisher of *Lighthouse Digest* magazine.

During our correspondence with Jeff M. Thomson, it was discovered that his great-great-grandfather, Jefferson Winston Williams, who had served in Cowan's Artillery Battery of Mississippi, had named his son — Jeff's great-grandfather — Eugene Cowan Williams. Jeff, who is a member of the Sons of Confederate Veterans Col. Egbert Jones Camp #357, made the following statement regarding his ancestor: "There were clearly some strong sentiments concerning his beliefs in his service." Nicely put, and echoes the reasons we feel so passionately about honoring the citizen-soldiers of the Civil War. They possessed a "tenacious spirit" that could not be broken in times of strife, hardships, and suffering. In the end, it was "patriotism" displayed throughout the North and the South that brought these people face-to-face in a war that was fought with determination, pride, and vigor, without modern technologies and conveniences that spoil us today. How sad that many individuals witnessed blood and gore, pains of hunger, and the agony of loved ones lost forever to the madness of war.

We appreciate the assistance of Rhode Island natives Debra Arnold Clark, Theresa's sister, and Kenneth F. Arnold, Jr., her brother, for their help with this project, and Dorothy Adamo, a close family friend, for her support and kind words about all of our projects. We are hugely indebted to Helen Scriber of Louisiana, Terry's mom, who is a special mother, mother-in-law, and supporter of all our projects. We would also like to thank Theresa's one and only wonderful son, Michael Metz, Jr., of Rhode Island, and her beautiful granddaughter Hailei Faith Metz, without whose love, patience, and support this project could never have been completed. Although Theresa's parents, Kenneth F. Arnold, Sr., and Elaine T. Arnold, are no longer with us, we know in our hearts they also deserve a thank you, as they were both always loving and generous with words of encouragement for us. Most of all, we would like to thank God for all of the blessings in our life.

From the Union and the Confederacy, we sincerely hope future generations of historians find our efforts to be a worthwhile addition to the volumes regarding American history, as well as honoring the memory of those who were imprisoned or died on Ship Island, Mississippi, during the Civil War. Peace and love to all.

Thanks also to Uncle George and Aunt Paula Arnold for their support, laughter and joy during this exhausting work.

Theresa Arnold-Scriber

Introduction

It is difficult to imagine that a small island in the Gulf of Mexico could play such a significant role in the history of the United States of America, but the importance of Ship Island, Mississippi, to the story of our great country is immeasurable. Beginning in 1699 with the French explorer Pierre Lemoyne d'Iberville, who used the island as a base for his operations surrounding the Gulf Coast, continuing with the British and their occupation of the island as a staging point for the disastrous Battle of New Orleans during the War of 1812, and ending in the late nineteenth century with the U.S. military occupation of the island, this small strip of sandy white beach has been largely ignored by modern day historians. This work will attempt to remedy this oversight in American history, and explore the impact of the island as related to what some consider the defining moment of our country, the American Civil War.

At the outbreak of the war in 1861, both North and South realized that gaining control of the mighty Mississippi River was imperative to their individual war efforts. The great prize at the southern end of the river was the Confederacy's largest city, New Orleans, Louisiana, with her many factories and shipbuilding capabilities, as well as the large population base centered in and around the city. The Southern government in Richmond thought Ship Island was protected from invasion by the Northern navy due to the placement of Fort Jackson and Fort St. Phillip at the mouth of the Mississippi, but committed the largest blunder of the war by abandoning Ship Island as a military outpost. The government in Washington immediately seized the island for use as a staging area for its intended push up the river to capture New Orleans and as a base of operations in the Gulf against blockade runners. The strategic advantage to whomever held Ship Island would soon become glaringly apparent to the participants in the conflict, as New Orleans and Baton Rouge, Louisiana, and Natchez, Mississippi, all fell like dominos to the Union fleet that ascended the river, denying their usage to the Confederate war effort effectively for the remainder of the war.

Some historians have described the fall of New Orleans as "the night the war was lost." This is a fairly accurate assessment of the consequences of the city's capture held for the Confederacy. If only Ship Island had been retained by the Confederacy and the invasion of New Orleans delayed, or conceivably even prevented, the possible benefits to the South would have been immeasurable. The unfinished gunboat *Mississippi* was burned in its drydock to prevent its capture by the Federals, an incalculable loss to a country with no navy of its own save converted paddlewheelers and transport ships. The loss of the southern Louisiana population base from which to draw troops and supplies would also be felt later in the conflict as the North played out a war of attrition against Southern manpower and resources. And the harm done to the South's attempts to gain recognition from the European powers, who viewed the loss of a city containing many consuls of their governments as evidence of Confederate weakness, is also a result of the lack of foresight in the abandonment of Ship Island to the Federals.

Once the conquest of the Louisiana river cities was complete, Ship Island would play a much more sinister role in the Union war effort, as many of the citizens and soldiers of the Gulf Coast states would become all too familiar with the island. Utilized first as a prison by Major-General Benjamin F. Butler for the citizens of Union-held south Louisiana who dared to question his rule, it was later used as a prisoner of war camp for Confederate soldiers. The harsh conditions of the island are attested to by the deaths of over 200 Union troops who at various times garrisoned the island, or who were held there as military convicts. The Confederate prisoners fared even worse, dying by the hundreds while guarded by Negro troops whose harsh treatment of the prisoners was sanctioned by Ship Island's commanders. A combination of the blistering sun, a lack of fresh water, and rampant disease all contributed to sending the death rates of the prisoners to frightening levels. Though the original burial locations of the soldiers who perished on the island are recorded as Ship Island Cemetery, along with a corresponding grave number, the final resting places of these men have long since been claimed by the shifting of the island's sands and the Gulf of Mexico's lapping waves. Today, all of the Confederate graves have been washed into the Gulf. As a testimonial to those, North and South, who perished on the island, a roster of both the Union dead and the Confederate prisoners is included in this work.

The Negro troops that were used as a garrison for Ship Island were some of the first black soldiers to serve in the Union army. The prejudices they experienced, and displayed, as freedmen is an interesting study in humanity. The Second Louisiana Native Guards, the first Negro troops in uniform at the outbreak of the war, initially offered their services to the Confederacy, only to be rebuffed by the Confederate government. This prompted the men to become Union soldiers after the fall of New Orleans, serving on Ship Island until being merged into various United States Colored Troops regiments.

One can only wonder, as the Confederacy's only president, Jefferson Davis, whiled away his postwar years in the Gulf Coast city of Biloxi, Mississippi, whether his thoughts turned to the island that lay some 12 miles away in the Gulf and the disasters that its abandonment had wrought on his dream of Southern independence. Memoirs of the former Confederates who had been held on the island and survived to recount its horrors describe it as a true "hell in the Gulf." Adding further insult to the Union deaths that occurred on the island was the scandalous June 21, 1885, exposé by a New Orleans newspaper correspondent and a subsequent cover-up by the Federal government of the supposed disinterred remains of the soldiers who perished on Ship Island, an account which is included in this work.

Today, Ship Island welcomes thousands of Gulf Coast tourists and locals to visit its white sandy beaches, a far cry from its more infamous days as a place of confinement. Though it was divided into two islands by the destructive force of Hurricane Camille in 1969, the island is currently under the care and protection of the National Park Service as part of the Gulf Islands National Seashore. Visitors can walk the shores and climb the dunes of West Ship Island, as well as visit the masonry Fort Massachusetts, with its massive 15-inch Rodman gun. In the July 2001 edition of *Condé Nast Traveler* magazine, the Ship Island beach was named among the 10 best in the country. Swimming, fishing, and exploring are all available, by taking the one hour ferry ride from the Mississippi coast at Gulfport, not to mention the chance to learn more about the little island in the Gulf that played such a major role in American history.

I. History

Isle de Surgeres to Ship Island

Ship Island, Mississippi — February 10, 1699
Twelve or fourteen leagues westward, we found a place, sheltered by islands and the mainland, where there is good anchorage and refuge against storms.
— *Pierre Lemoyne d'Iberville, upon discovering Ship Island*

Situated in the north central Gulf of Mexico, about 12 miles off the Mississippi Gulf Coast, is Ship Island, first sighted over three hundred years ago by French explorers in 1699. Considered a barrier island, the narrow seashore is blanketed with smooth white sand and is vastly surrounded by blue Gulf water. Barrier islands serve as a blockade to ocean waves and violent storms that would otherwise strike the mainland coast with much greater force, causing the islands' sand to shift. Upon Ship Island's discovery in 1699, it was approximately seven miles long and a half-mile wide, stretching east to west, and consisted of 1,350 acres. (For decades, plants, wildlife, and migratory birds on the wind-swept island have provided a wonderful sightseeing adventure to those who have visited the uninhabited landscape.) The west end of the island was a coastal marshy area filled with wildlife such as snakes, pelicans, raccoons, nutria, and osprey. The island, as a whole, was clustered with tall pine trees, where bald eagles, hawks, and owls built their nested incubators to nurture their young. Located behind the island were bays and bayous filled with less salty water where turtles, alligators, and other reptiles flourished and reproduced. Seagulls often lined the seashore until ready to feast, taking flight by steadily flapping their wings before plunging into the sea, snatching up a small fish or crab, then screeching with delight as they flew away with their tasty morsel.[1]

Ship Island lies approximately six miles from Cat Island and twenty miles north of the Chandeleur Islands, and is conveniently located about midway between New Orleans, Louisiana, and Mobile, Alabama. Throughout the years, this paradise island, rich in natural and cultural resources, has provided a safe harbor for those who wish to anchor their ships in the open gulf seas, offering shelter from fierce howling winds during many destructive Gulf storms.

Prior to the Civil War in 1859, a fort was built on the island that was later used as a Federal prison, where captives were often subjected to harsh treatment at the hands of soldiers of the Federal army. Many of the former prisoners described the isolated sandy oasis as hell on earth. The military fortification remained active until the end of World War II, when modern weapons antiquated traditional coastal defenses.[2]

It is strongly suspected that prior to the arrival of the Europeans, Indians were the first to navigate the Mississippi Sound islands, which is evident by the European's interaction with several native tribes who roamed the lower Mississippi Valley territory during the seventeenth century and beyond. The Frenchmen allied themselves with the natives for political, military, and informational gains, whereas the Spanish were considered uncompassionate and thus feared by the natives. Ship Island, in addition to some of the surrounding islands, was used as a base for defensive operations and European adventures, as well as providing a water route to the lakes and river systems connected with the Gulf of Mexico. The available fresh water on the island appealed to the thirsty and weary explorers. For decades, the French, English, and Spanish nations competitively struggled to dominate the Mississippi River and Gulf Coast region, though it was the French who were the first to take advantage of the strategic benefits Ship Island offered. Each foreign country aspired to assert exclusive dominion of the lower Mississippi Valley. The explorers were under specific orders from the rulers in France to guard the entrance of the Mississippi Sound whenever they suspected English or Spanish encroachment. Motivated by the fur trade, gold, and aspirations of colonization, all three countries desperately strived to acquire the wealth they believed the new country, America, offered.[3]

Seventeenth century French explorers, such as the team of Louis Joliet and Père Jacques Marquette, drifted down the Mississippi River and made it as far as Arkansas; and in 1682, explorer Rene Robert Cavalier La Salle descended the River Colbert, the name he gave to the Mississippi River in honor of the French minister of finance. Neither made a lasting impression on the land they so bravely explored, fighting against mother nature, wild beasts and savages. During La Salle's second journey to the New World, he strived to achieve two main goals. He attempted to locate the mouth of the Mississippi River from the Gulf of Mexico, and he also planned to colonize his newfound territory, Louisiana, which he had discovered and laid claim to in the name of His Majesty Louis XIV on April 9, 1682. Unfortunately for La Salle, neither goal was realized and he would eventually encounter tragedy during his exploration. He and his crew sailed too far westward on the Gulf seas and wrecked their ship along the coast of St. Bernard, Texas, entirely missing the mouth of the river. Left without a vessel, the determined La Salle trod the forests of Texas on foot for nearly three years, until his journey came to an abrupt end in March of 1687 when he was shot in the head by one of his own men at Trinity River, Texas.[4]

Pierre Le Moyne d'Iberville, one of thirteen children, was born at Montreal, New France, on July 20, 1661, to Charles Le Moyne, a provincial nobleman, and Catherine Thierry Primot. He later became an accomplished naval officer, soldier, and trader. During the colonial wars battling the English, d'Iberville became known as a cruel fighter and heroic figure in the name of his country. His deeds did not go unrecognized, as he was chosen by Louis Pontchartrain, the minister of marine of New France (Canada), to resume La Salle's efforts to locate the mouth of the Mississippi River and to colonize Louisiana. The Gulf Coast region had been of particular interest to King Louis XIV of France for nearly twenty years prior to when the king granted a letter patent to La Salle on May 12, 1678, permitting him to endeavor to the western part of New France. The king stated in the letter patent, "There is nothing we have more at heart than the discovery of this country," referring to the continent of America.[5] The explorer attempted a different route from La Salle, ascending the river from the Gulf of Mexico in an attempt to reach its northern mouth. Prior to his departure from France, the French minister of marine, Louis Pontchartrain, gave d'Iberville the following orders: "Go to the Gulf of Mexico, locate the mouth of the Mississippi River, select a good site that can be defended with a few men and block entry to the river by other nations."[6]

Preparing for their long journey, ships were equipped with the necessary supplies for the adventurers at LaRochelle, France, before they set sail on October 24, 1698, from Brest, France, located on the eastern side of the country. D'Iberville commanded the thirty-gun frigate *Le Badine,* and M. le Compte de Surgere commanded the thirty-gun frigate *Le Marin,* and two store ships also joined the journey. Upon their arrival at Santo Domingo, their ships were united with the fifty-gun frigate *Le Francois,* commanded by the M. Marqueis de Chateaumerant, who was ordered to escort and assist in defending d'Iberville's vessels. Chateaumerant was accompanied by a pirate of Dutch origin, Captain Lawrence de Graff, who was employed due to his knowledge of the Gulf ports. Aboard the *Le Badine* was d'Iberville's brother, Jean Baptiste LeMoyne, Sieur Bienville, who served as midshipman at age 20; M. de Sauvolle de la Villantray; two-hundred colonists; and one-hundred soldiers, including a company of marines. Priests also accompanied d'Iberville on his long voyage, one of whom was Father Anastase Douay, who had previously been a part of La Salle's expedition to the Mississippi River. They also took along agriculturists, carpenters, mechanics, clothing, food, and various supplies needed to establish a settlement. They sailed on the immense sea north to Florida, arriving at Pensacola on January 26, where they observed two ships anchored in the deep Gulf water. The thickened fog prevented them from sailing any further and they were forced to anchor their ships. Later that afternoon, upon observing a white flag on shore, a longboat came out to identify them, followed by the sound of cannon shots from the mainland. The next day, d'Iberville sent a small group of men ashore to survey the activities of the Spanish post, and to request some wood and water. Although the Spaniards received them cordially, the post commander refused to permit anyone to enter the harbor, and with that news, d'Iberville and his crew weighed anchor and departed.[7]

French explorer Pierre LeMoyne d'Iberville and his fleet (courtesy of the Alabama Department of Archives and History).

On January 31, 1699, while the French fleet was anchored at Mobile Bay, M. de Chateaumerant sounded part of the channel in search of deeper water. The next day, d'Iberville and part of

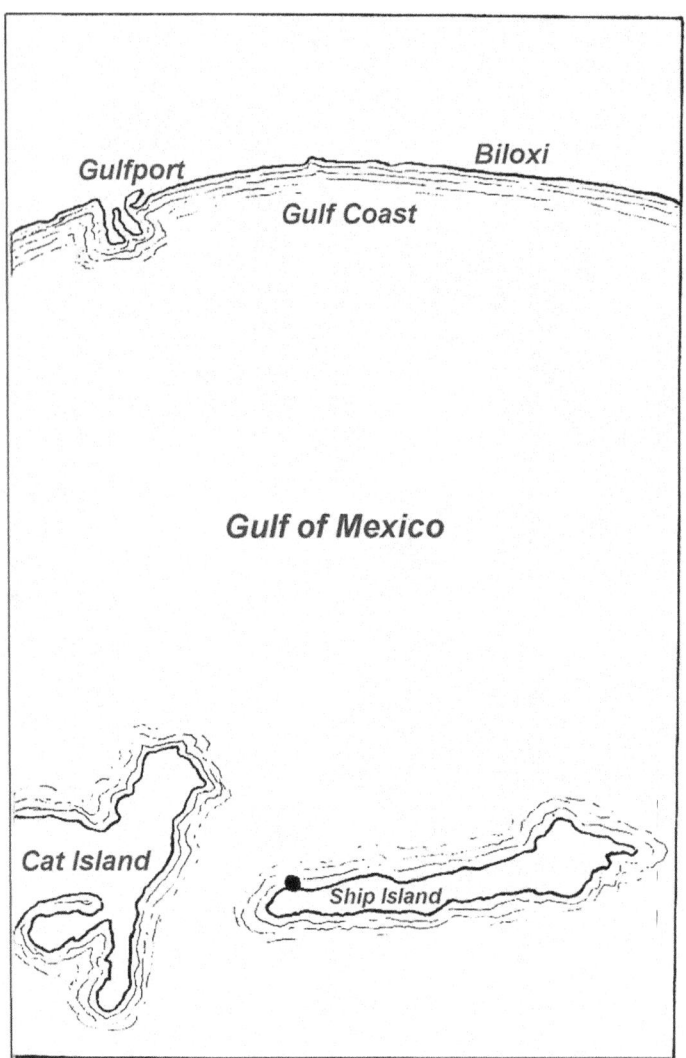

Relation of Ship Island and Cat Island to the Mississippi Gulf Coast (modified by Terry G. Scriber from an illustration at the Library of Congress).

his group rowed ashore with plans to reconnoiter the neighboring islands, and made the decision to sleep overnight. D'Iberville named the land Massacre Island, due to the many skulls and skeleton bones discovered there, along with some earthen pots. Based on their discovery of the bones, they deduced the slaying occurred three or four years prior to their arrival. During that same day, stormy weather prevented further soundings of the channel but when the storms abated d'Iberville continued his search for the deepest water he could find. The exhausted seamen, too tired to row, remained on the island for several days, amusing themselves by hunting for geese, ducks, and raccoons. Later, they boarded their ships and sailed further west, where they encountered a chain of islands running parallel to the coastline. From Massacre Island they were Petit Bois, Horn, Ship, and Cat islands.[8]

Horn Island is very flat, narrow, and fairly wooded. The first Canadians who settled on Dauphin Island had put most of their great number of cattle on Horn Island. It has been said that the island was named for one of Bienville's men who left his horn there. Cat Island is very small, not above a half league in diameter, and its forests were overrun with underbrush. M. de Bienville put some hogs there to breed for food, which multiplied to such numbers that in 1722 it was suspected that the hogs had destroyed the cats that inhabited the island from which it drew its name. In 1711, the name Massacre Island was changed to Dauphin Island by d'Iberville's brother Bienville, who became concerned when several people advised him the name *Massacre* sounded too unpleasant. It is not clear why it was named Dauphin, but it has been suggested that the French word for dolphin is dauphin.[9]

On February 10, 1699, their three ships arrived on the waters in the Mississippi Sound, where they found a place on the Gulf seas that provided good anchorage and refuge against violent storms. This safe haven became known as Ship Island, but was originally called Isle Surgeres, in honor of one of d'Iberville's men, the Compte de Surgere, who first sighted the island. It was also called Isle aux Vassieux by the French explorers, which translated to English means "ship island." It has also been noted that Ship Island was named for its silhouette shape. On February 13, while their ships were safely anchored in the dependable harbor, d'Iberville reported to the Minister of Marine: "Leaving my ships here (Ship Island), we set out on the 21st for Malbouchia (the name given by the savages on this coast to the Mississippi) with two long boats, some bark canoes, and fifty-three men. We entered the river March 2, 1699. I found it obstructed by mud banks and logs of wood, partially petrified. There was about twelve feet of water...."[10]

A few days later, d'Iberville, Bienville, and a group of men set out to search for the mouth of the Mississippi in two biscayans and some bark canoes in the misty rain. Traveling quietly along the river, so as not to frighten the Indians, d'Iberville and Father Douay crossed over to the mainland. They approached a small band of Indians who became startled and fled, leaving behind their ailing elderly chief, who was unable to stand. The chief and the Frenchmen communicated by means of signs, and the elderly chief expressed he wanted a fire built. D'Iberville obliged, also giving him food and tobacco before building a shelter for him. On the mainland, they observed a mixed variety of trees, including many plum trees, the tracks of turkeys, partridges, and rabbits, and also discovered oysters in the water, which would later serve their hearty appetites. Several days later, d'Iberville and his brother met at an Indian village where the Bayogoulas and Mougoulachas were domiciled together on the west bank of the river. Amicable to one another, the group smoked an iron calumet that d'Iberville had made in the shape of a ship with a white flag adorned with the fleurs-de-lis, ornamented with glass beads, which he gave to them along with other presents. He persuaded them that by smoking the calumet together they were united and allied as friends.[11]

The men entered the Mississippi River on March 2, reconnoitered the land and banks of the river and twelve days later reached the village of the Mougoulachas tribe, who received them kindly. D'Iberville noticed the chief wearing a hooded cloak of blue serge, such as the French wore, and inquired about the garment. The Indian chief told him it was a gift presented by Tonti when he visited, and the chief talked a great deal about him. Henry de Tonti was an Italian soldier who lost his hand in battle to a bursting grenade while in the service of France. Tonti accompanied the fearless La Salle on his first journey to the New World, becoming his faithful companion. When La Salle vanished, Tonti became alarmed and made several searches for the friend he had come to love.[12]

While journeying along the river, d'Iberville heard conflicting stories from the natives and began to doubt that the water he was traveling on was the same grand Mississippi River La Salle had traversed many years before. D'Iberville began a search for concrete evidence that this was the same river. A proud man, he did not want it to appear in France that he had been deceived by anyone. His proof finally arrived when his brother Bienville returned from a visit with the Mougoulachas tribe, who were located on the west bank of the river. Bienville presented d'Iberville with a letter the Indian chief called "Speaking Bark." He had exchanged an axe for the valuable letter that Tonti left for La Salle after his unsuccessful search to find him. The letter was dated April 20, 1685, at the village of the Quinnipesas and contained this message from Tonti: "It gives me great uneasiness to be obliged to return under the misfortune of not having found you."[13]

The Mougoulachas tribe also displayed a prayer book, *L'Imitation de Notre Seigneur*, on which the name of La Salle, a Canadian, was inscribed, and some bottles they claimed Tonti gave them as gifts. D'Iberville was satisfied this was the conclusive proof he had sought, removing from his mind all doubt that it was the same Mississippi River La Salle had located. When Tonti began his searches for La Salle, he was unaware that his loyal friend had died at the hands of his own men, as this act of treachery was kept secret for many years. Members of La Salle's party agreed to hide the death from the Indians to keep them under submission, but the secret was kept from Tonti and the French court as well.[14]

On March 3, to celebrate d'Iberville's discovery of the Mississippi River, a Mass was performed, a Te Deum sung, and the party dined on a modest breakfast in order to spare their provisions, which consisted of 2 casks of biscuit, a small quantity of peas, and a quarter of flour for each longboat. D'Iberville named a point not far from the river Mardi Gras, as it was Shrove Tuesday when they held their celebration. After conducting their festivities, they decided to explore more of the Mississippi River, in search of an appropriate site to establish a colony.[15]

On March 16, d'Iberville came to a point on the river where there was a decorated pole that marked the boundary between two native tribes. The Indians called the marker "Istrouma," which the French translated as Baton Rouge, meaning Red Stick. D'Iberville descended the river farther, reaching the mouth of Manchac (modern day Iberville), and after much difficulty the party made their way through Amite, Lake Maurepas, and Lake Pontchartrain, all three of which d'Iberville named. Amite was named for the Indians, and both lakes were named in honor of the French ministers. Upon reaching their ships in the harbor at Ship Island on March 31, d'Iberville and his men enjoyed a short rest and some of the crew were sent in two feluccas to make soundings in present-day Biloxi Bay. D'Iberville needed to determine if his boats would be able to dock in the bay in order to establish a colony there quickly due to a lack of provisions. He needed a safe shelter for his men, as he was about to leave them behind while he journeyed back to France to report his discoveries. He met some friendly Indians, who called themselves *Biloxi*, which inspired him to name the town in honor of them.[16]

D'Iberville examined the banks of the Mississippi in search of a suitable place to establish a colony, but failing to locate one he chose a sandy glade of elevated coast on the eastern shore of a little back bay, known as Biloxi Bay, Mississippi, now known as Ocean Springs. The first colony d'Iberville established was named after the local Biloxi Indians who had received d'Iberville warmly. A wooden four bastioned fort built at this site was named Fort Maurepas in recognition of the French minister of marine. Deer Island (originally called Isle-aux-Chevreuil) is to the left of the bay, about one length off the mainland with plenty of trees to shade the bay area, and received its name for the abundance of deer found on it. This particular site appealed to the exhausted sea travelers for the privacy, comfort, and safety it provided, as well as its proximity to Ship Island. The location allowed small vessels to easily pass through the roadstead. Passing another beautiful bay, Bienville named the arm of the sea Bay St. Louis, in honor of the king of France, due to their arrival there on the day of St. Louis.[17]

Sixty men arrived at the Biloxi site, which was described as having sand as white as silver and many tall pine trees, majestic oaks, and fragrant magnolias where beautifully colored birds sang incessantly amid the boughs. The men immediately began logging oak and hickory trees to prepare for the construction of the fort at Biloxi, though many were inexperienced at construction. They worked vigorously until the fort was completed and because none of the men knew how to use an axe it made the process difficult for the French-Canadians. Everything was taken from the ships that could be spared, including guns, ammunition, cows, hogs, fowls, and a bull that were sent to the new fort. By April 26, the men had unloaded the boats, taken inventory, and inspected their provisions. On the ships, they left only those supplies absolutely necessary for their return trip to France. Biloxi was the first capital of Louisiana and d'Iberville enjoyed his brief duty as governor-general of the newly established territory. On May 3, d'Iberville sailed for France to secure reinforcements and left Fort Maurepas garrisoned with 80 men under the command of his appointed governor, Sauvolle de la Villantray, with his brother Bienville detailed as lieutenant-governor. While in France, d'Iberville was knighted the Cross of the Order of St. Louis for his eminent services, becoming the first man of Canadian birth to receive such an acknowledgement.[18] D'Iberville stated in his report to the marine minister of France:

> After visiting several places well adapted for settlements, I fixed on the bay of Biloxi, four leagues north of the place where the ships were anchored. We made choice of this point on account of the sheltered bay or roadstead where small vessels can come and go in safety, at all times. A place for permanent settlement can be selected at leisure. I erected a wooden fort with four bastions; two are made of hewn timber, placed together on foot and a half thick, nine feet high; the other two of double palisades. It is mounted with fifty-four pieces of cannon, and has a good outfit of ammunition. I left M. de Sauvolle in command; De Beinville, King's Lieutenant; Levasseur, Major; Debordenac, Chaplain; Care, Surgeon; two Captains, two Pilots, four sailors, eighteen filibusters, thirteen Canadians, ten mechanics, six masons, thirty subofficers and soldiers.[19]

Andre Penicaut (aka Perricaul), a young carpenter and officer of the frigate *Le Marin*, commanded by Compte de Surgere, gave the following details of his arrival at Ship Island:

> The first lands we discovered on arriving happened to be two islands, to one of which the Count de Surgere gave his own name, as he had been the first to see it. This island is five leagues long and a quarter of a league wide. We anchored in a roadstead that runs between this island and another which took the name Isle-aux-Chats because of the great number of cats we found on it. Similar in size, it is seven leagues wide and is one league west of Isle Surgere. We went ashore at Isle Surgere and killed a prodigious quantity of wild geese, locally called bustards, which are once again bigger than the geese we have in France. We took there also such an abundance of fish and of oysters in the shell that the crews of the two ships became upset from over-indulgence. On neither of these two islands did we notice any sign of mark that a man had ever been there. We found fresh water good enough to drink, although these two islands are five leagues distant from the mainland. Sixty of us set out in longboats to follow the mainland in an east-west direction, because all the Florida coast lies that way. We found a bay some two leagues in circumference situated five leagues off Isle Surgere. At the head of this bay there is a high ground, where M. d'Hyberville planned to have a fort built. We worked on this fort without stopping until it was finished. Before the embouchure of this bay there is an island about one league long and an eighth of a league wide which is a quarter of a league off the mainland. To this day, it is called Isle-aux-Chevreuils because of the great quantity of deer to be found on it.[20]

On January 8, 1700, d'Iberville and M. de Surgere arrived back at the Biloxi colony from France, bringing much needed supplies and reinforcements for the newborn struggling settlement. The colonists, weak and suffering from fevers and poverty, were reduced to sharing the fort they called home with alligators, snakes, and other native wildlife. Their provisions were meager, as they were dependent on France for supplies and forced to share their limited stores with large groups of Indians and Canadian voyagers, which depleted their already scant resources.[21] A month later, Governor Sauvolle recorded in his journal: "We heard firing of cannon from Surgeres Island 5 leagues distant from our fort, announcing the arrival of M. d'Iberville in command of the *Renommee* of 50 guns and M. de Surgeres of the *Gironde* of 46 guns."[22]

Immediately, the governor gave orders to announce d'Iberville's arrival to the colony. The guns and musketry of the fort were discharged, creating a cloud of smoke, as cheers echoed loudly with excitement, greeting the men who had arrived with food and other necessities. D'Iberville also brought the good news to M. de Sauvolle that he was appointed governor.

The following day, d'Iberville arrived in Biloxi. M. de Sauvolle informed him that in his absence Bienville and a group of men in 2 bark canoes ascending the Mississippi River observed an English corvette of ten guns, commanded by Captain Louis Banc, enter the Mississippi River and proceed twenty-five leagues upstream. Their anticipated competitors had finally arrived, but Bienville wasted no time in sending two of his men with instructions to alert the English captain that he must leave the area immediately, for it was in the possession of the king of France. They also warned the commander that if he did not leave, they would have no choice but to force him. The captain of the corvette explained the reason for the English presence: they desired to colonize on the Mississippi. The French explained they were too late. After speaking to Bienville a third time, the captain threatened to come back and settle the river with superior quality boats constructed for river travel.[23]

The Spanish, who were less of a threat to the French, had come in force to drive the English away, but when the Spanish commander found two well-armed French frigates at Ship Island, he immediately set sail. Unfortunately, on April 30, the main Spanish ship with one hundred and forty men aboard was wrecked on Chandeleur Island, losing all supplies onboard, including clothing and food. The men and their commandant made their escape safely to the island in a longboat. They eventually were carried to their ships in a felucca, biscayan, bilander, and pinnace and headed back to Pensacola. Many of the Spanish survivors had deserted for lack of food, but d'Iberville graciously aided the Spaniards by providing them with clothes, food, and other provisions.[24]

Until August of 1700, the men examined the Mississippi lands and mingled with the Indians, before d'Iberville again departed for France. He spent over a year attempting to convince French authorities there was a much needed commitment to Louisiana. He suggested an active Indian policy which would enforce anti-British sentiments, as well as the need for a strong naval base at Mobile on the Gulf Coast. King Louis XIV supported his suggestions and approved a third expedition to proceed back to the southern lands. He told d'Iberville to commence with the construction of a fort at Mobile, and to enforce his Indian policy to protect the Mississippi basin west of the Appalachians from English aggression. On September 29, 1701, d'Iberville sailed from La Rochelle, France, with three vessels; during his travels, he was forced by an abscess on his side to land at Pensacola in Florida. The Spaniards, fearing the French were attempting to encroach on their territory, treated them unkindly. D'Iberville found the Pensacola base in a deplorable condition, but needing a place to recover from his illness, he accepted the Spaniards' offer to allow him two months recovery time aboard his vessel at their base, all the while under their watchful eyes.[25]

Due to Massacre Island's inability to grow crops, the colonists suffered severely. The island produced only grass, and there were but few trees to provide shelter from the sizzling sun rays. Summertime heat on the Gulf Coast was fiery and physically draining for those who drifted about on the hot white sand. The small amount of maize produced was not enough to fill the bellies or provide the necessary energy of the population, and many colonists were overcome with illness and famine. D'Iberville had instructions to move the colony at Fort Maurepas and to place the new fort 26 leagues north of Massacre Island on the high ground overlooking the Mobile River, at Twenty-Seven Mile Bluff. He brought four families back with him from France to further populate the new fort at Mobile. It was about this time that he renamed Isle Surgere to Ship Island, due to the safe shelter the harbor provided for the ships arriving from France. On August 22, M. de Sauvolle died and Bienville succeeded him in command of Fort Maurepas in Biloxi until December 17, when he received orders from his brother to remove everything from his fort, including artillery, to Massacre Island, for the anticipated new fort at Mobile. In August of 1701, Ship Island was partially destroyed when a hurricane forced its way through the Gulf of Mexico, and its two lagoons, where there was a supply of fresh water, was more like a salt-water pond.[26]

By December 31, Bienville alerted his brother that, although he was well, half of his crew was sick or convalescing, which was unwelcome news for d'Iberville due to the fact he needed workers to establish his new fort. On January 3, 1702, d'Iberville sent a pilot's ketch loaded with provisions and eighty workmen, including Spanish workers lent to him by their commandant, to assist in completing his settlement at Mobile. D'Iberville ordered a warehouse and magazine to be built on Dauphin Island to hold the supplies of his forts, and although his abscess kept him in bed with great pain, he managed to supervise and issue orders to his men. (Some sources record there was also a warehouse built on Ship Island at this time, and d'Iberville oversaw that project; however, d'Iberville does not substantiate this claim in his journal.) When the ketch returned from Massacre Island and the small boat arrived back from Biloxi, the crafts were unloaded there and the provisions put in tents while waiting for Bienville, his brother de Serigny, and over 40 men to complete the warehouse. Another brother, de Chateague, and 10 men completed the roof and were ordered to guard the warehouse and magazine on the island. Once well, d'Iberville joined the efforts to establish their settlement and inspected the completed warehouse and magazine. The Mobile fort was named Fort St. Louis de la Mobile and was the official headquarters of the province until the government was removed almost two decades later.[27]

D'Iberville once again departed from the harbor at Ship Island for France on April 27, 1702, never to return to the Gulf Coast; Bienville was confirmed governor of Louisiana about this time. Prior to his departure, he was offered the assistance of Henry de Tonti, La Salle's companion, who knew the Indians and Mississippi basin well. Tonti felt confident that he could persuade the hostile Indians to join the European efforts to prevent English intrusion. In 1704, the ship *Pelican* arrived with sixty Canadians, food, and supplies, and the colonists reacted with extreme jubilation. There was much sickness and scarcity of provisions on the island. Aboard this ship were also twenty-three young women, certified by the minister of France and chaperoned by four Ursuline nuns who carefully supervised these young ladies. The young women were intended by the French government to mingle with the soldiers and colonists in order to steer the men away from relationships with the Indian maidens, and eventually to marry the European men. The young women became known as the "Casket Girls," because each female was given a small chest, or casket, containing clothing, linens, and jewelry. They were not allowed to marry without the consent of the nuns, though all of the girls did later marry except one, whom no one would engage in a courtship. Many of the women initially sent to the settlement were recruited from the prisons and brothels of Paris, and the fallen women were not received cordially by the Frenchmen. It later inspired the churches to more carefully select women from convents and orphanages for future shipments to the European men, in lieu of the less desirable females.[28]

After spending several years in France, d'Iberville was assigned to assault the British island of Nevis. That same year, he died from yellow fever aboard his flagship on July 9, 1706, at Havana, Cuba, never again to return to the colonies he founded on the Gulf Coast. The shocking news of his death was revealed in 1707 to Bienville and the colonists, inspiring an outpouring of grief from the eyes and hearts of the many settlers who had come to adore him. He left behind his wife, Marie Therese Pollet, and five children.[29]

In 1712, King Louis XIV, realizing the colony was struggling and there was a lack of profit from the settlement, signed the colony over to Antoine Crozat, Marquis du Chatel, a merchant who thought he could successfully extract riches from the settlement. On September 14, the King gave the financier the exclusive right to the internal and external trade of the province, as well as manufacturing rights. From 1712 until 1721, the efforts at colonization and commerce through trading corporations established by Antoine Crozat and John Law had been fruitless, and the control of the colony soon reverted back to the King, who transferred it to a new business, the Western, or India, Company, for a term of twenty-five years. In May of 1713, the frigate *de la Fosse* arrived off Dauphin Island from France, bringing fifty-five year old Antoine de la Motte Cadillac, a French officer, and his family. Crozat appointed Cadillac governor and demoted Bienville to lieutenant-governor in 1713. Two years later, Cadillac died and Jean-Michel de L'Epinay was his successor and, while awaiting his arrival, Bienville became acting governor.[30]

On March 9, 1717, M. L'Epinay arrived at Fort St. Louis de la Mobile and was appointed the new governor at Dauphin Island, and Hubert St. Malo became the new commissary general.

Although Bienville was disappointed about losing his prominent position, L'Epinay did present him with the Cross of the Order of the St. Louis and a royal patent granting him Horn Island as a reward for his services. Three ships containing three companies of infantry, laborers, provisions, merchandise, and military stores were ordered to the island to fortify it, but by late August fierce hurricane winds swept over the island and the harbor became choked with sand, ceasing the fortification plans. That same year, a fort and warehouse were built on Ship Island, which became the new point of anchorage and deposit, and Biloxi was the reestablished site of the officials headquarters. That same month, Crozat surrendered Louisiana to the king, who promptly turned the colony over to John Law and his Mississippi Company.[31] Commissary General St. Malo recommended that Ship Island replace the battered Dauphin Island in his report to the council in 1717: "It is regrettable to see ships depart without one's being able to give definite opinions about the projects to be proposed. M. Artus, commandant of Dauphin Island, could have visited the roadstead of Ship Island which is at present the only port on which one can count.... It would then at present be at Ship Island that those that come from France could unload onto brigatines what they bring for the colony and they would take it to the storehouses intended to receive it."[32]

In February of 1718, Bienville received a commission naming him "Commandant General" of the colony. In March of 1718, Bienville founded a colony near the mouth of the Mississippi River and named it New Orleans, in honor of Prince Philip of Orleans, regent of France. Bienville had fifty laborers, many of them galley slaves, clear away the woods and quickly erect houses; however, it would not become the seat of the government until 1722. During the winter of 1719, while France and Spain were at war, the majority of the council decided to return the seat of the government from Mobile to Old Biloxi. It has been noted that Bienville did not care to remain in Mobile because of its proximity to the old haunts of Spain at Havana. Old Biloxi, a bluff or little mountain on the mainland, was the new post.

In October of 1719, Sieur de Valdeterre arrived at Ship Island after a hazardous journey in the French vessel *Two Brothers*, and was chosen to prepare the new fort at Old Biloxi. Aboard his ship he brought farmers, labor men, about 12,000 German soldiers and agriculturists for the purpose of establishing the settlement. The German workers were purchased by the Mississippi Company from a German prince to colonize Louisiana. Although it was only 38 leagues by water from Dauphin Island to Ship Island, the ship was grounded but refloated and reached the Ship Island anchorage not far from shore. They constructed small boats and utilized canoes that provided them access to the mainland from their anchored ships at Ship Island. They cleared the land and built cabins and warehouses for shelter and storage. Ship Island was now ready to replace the silt-clogged harbor at Dauphin Island as the principal port of anchorage for the colony. In April of 1720, a ship named *St. Louis* arrived from La Habana with numerous prisoners onboard that were to be used for menial labor. The Council of Commerce of Louisiana made the decision to leave the poorly conditioned vessel anchored at Ship Island to serve as a floating warehouse, where it could assist in accelerating the unloading of the cargo vessels in the harbor. The former keeper of a warehouse located at Pensacola, Sieur Thopin, was chosen to command the *St. Louis*. About this time, rum was made available to those who did not abstain from the liquid pleasure. (During the year 1720, two infantry officers stationed at Ship Island, McCarty and La Maisonnoeruve, drank excessive amounts of rum that tragically resulted in their deaths.[33])

In late 1720, because of the unhealthy air and land at Old Biloxi, the decision was made by the council to move the colony of Old Biloxi to New Biloxi, directly opposite Ship Island on the other side of the bay. Ship Island was much closer to New Biloxi, more convenient for anchorage purposes, taking less time to transport supplies from the vessels to the new colony, and the environment was healthier for the colonists. One could make two trips to New Biloxi in the time it would take for one trip to Old Biloxi. The only disadvantage to the new site was that any boat over 8 feet in height needing repair had to be sent to Old Biloxi until adequate facilities could be established at Ship Island.[34]

In January of 1721, the ship *Seine* arrived with only 58 workers, as half of them had perished on account of the bad treatment of their captain on the voyage. New Biloxi was built, temporarily enclosed with good posts, strengthened with timbers inside and loopholes, until they were able to construct it in such a way that the parapets and the ramparts would be as thick as the forts of France. New Biloxi would become known as Fort Louis, a very common name during that time period. New Biloxi would become the capital of the colony and continued as a garrisoned post until 1730.[35]

On January 3, 1721, the ships *La Gironde* and *La Volage* arrived at Ship Island from France with almost 300 young women, and two days later, the ship *La Baleine* arrived with approximately 80 young women; it was hoped they would be possible wives for the colonists and soldiers. These young ladies had been chosen by the bishop from Paris, Salpetriere, to come to the New World. The three chaperone nuns, Sister Gertrude, Sister Louise, and Sister Bergere, were charged with supervising the women until they were ready for marriage. These young women were also provided with a small chest and marriage outfit, but none were permitted to marry without the consent of the nuns. They were brought from France to establish the colonies in the lower Mississippi Valley and Louisiana. The male settlers were less than thrilled with earlier efforts to provide wives for them, as the jails of France were swept and the inmates sent West. The Company of the Indies had an agreement to continue to bring more women from time to time as late as 1727–1728 to permanently reside in the Deep South.[36]

Bienville possessed foresight that he himself may not have recognized, as he was the first known person to fully comprehend the advantages of Ship Island. The island cradled the ships in its harbor, like a mother holding her baby close to her bosom, protecting and saving many vessels from destruction upon the crashing waves of the pounding seas during violent storms and hurricanes. When nature's fury stormed through the Gulf of Mexico in August of 1721, it sunk many ships along the Gulf Coast, but those ships located in the Ship Island harbor incredibly rode the storm out in safety. Two years later, another hurricane ripped apart the hospital, church, and over two dozen buildings in New Orleans, destroying farmer's crops along the Mobile and Pearl rivers, while Ship Island once again kept the ships anchored in her deep waters out of danger.[37]

On December 15, 1721, Bienville wrote to the Naval Council, resolved to protect the harbor at Ship Island: "It would be advisable in my opinion to begin fortifying the point at the entrance of Ship Island rather than Biloxi in order to support in time of war the vessels that might be in that roadstead in which the least privateer can carry them off without its being possible to bring assistance from Biloxi since it is 4 leagues distant. There are always 20 to 21 feet of water in the pass." By mid–January 1722, several engineers prepared drawings and plans for a Ship Island fort for the defense of Ship Island and Cat Island. On April 21, 1722, the Superior Council designated Sieur Villette as keeper of the warehouse at Ship Island, paying him a salary of 1,200 livres per year. His appointed assistant, Sieur Gouint, received a salary of 600 livres per year. Four days later, Bienville urged the Navy Council to dredge one of the passes and documented the disadvantages of Ship Island as a port of entry: "The shallowness of the mouth of the Mississippi will delay the establishment of this colony and is making us incur great expense because of the distance from Ship Island which is five leagues from the mainland where we are established, and to unload them we are obligated to send small vessels there which on their return can approach to within only three quarters of a league of the land. We then send ship's boats to unload these musket shot off shore."[38]

Recognizing the importance of New Orleans as a future strategic location, Bienville transferred the capital from Biloxi to New Orleans in 1723. With the main port being New Orleans, Ship Island was becoming less important and the warehouse on the island obsolete.

France and England were at war from 1754 to 1763, and control of the Gulf area passed to England. In 1763, all of the area east of the Mississippi River, with the exception of the Isle of Orleans, was granted to Great Britain. On October 7, 1763, Ship Island was included in the area signified as West Florida, by His Majesty George II, and in 1781, during the revolutionary war with the Spanish, the region, including Ship Island, was relinquished to Spain by the Treaty of Paris in 1783. In 1810, the United States claimed West Florida as a part of the Louisiana Purchase of 1803 and occupied the area until 1813, when control of Ship Island finally passed to the United States, becoming part of the Mississippi Territory. Ship Island was abandoned until 1814, when the British attacked New Orleans during the War of 1812.[39]

President James Madison declared hostilities against Great Britain on June 1, 1812, and Ship Island was once again to become a point of strategic military importance. In August of 1814, British soldiers captured and burned the White House and other buildings in Washington, D.C. One month after the Washington destruction, the United States retaliated, thrashing the British forces and driving them back at Lake Champlain and at Fort McHenry in Baltimore, Maryland. On September 18, 1814, a 4,400-man expedition under Major-General John Keane had sailed from Plymouth, England, and at Negril Bay, Jamaica, on November 25, the force was increased by 3,100 men, the same British soldiers who had burned Washington. In total, nearly 7,500 soldiers sailed for the Gulf Coast, destination Ship Island, which was the selected site by English Major-General Sir Edward Pakenham as a base of anchorage for his nearly sixty British ships. The thousands of British soldiers roamed Ship Island while strategically planning their attack. As the English general's mind contemplated the best tactical moves against the United States forces, he mapped his military plans while aboard his vessel during the winter months in 1814. Commodore Daniel T. Patterson, commanding the New Orleans post, had received a letter from Pensacola, dated December 5, notifying him of the presence of the British fleet. By mid–December, Admiral Sir Alexander Cochran had the entire British fleet, between 50 and 60 ships, anchored in the channel between Ship and Cat islands. Two American patrol boats located the British fleet and alerted U.S. commanders of their existence in the Gulf. The War of 1812 finally came to an end at Ghent, Belgium, with the signing of a peace treaty between Britain and the United States on Christmas Eve. However, news of the signing of the treaty would not arrive in time to prevent one of the greatest battles in U.S. military history.[40]

The Battle of New Orleans occurred two weeks after the peace treaty was signed, ending the War of 1812. While the British forces stationed at Ship Island prepared to launch their ill-fated assault on the Crescent City, success seemed imminent until Andrew Jackson took control of the city's defenses in December of 1814. With a ragtag army consisting of citizens, slaves, and pirates, Jackson surprised the British positions outside the city with a fierce attack on December 23. The British counterattacked the Americans just four days later, and though the British silenced the United States gunboats, they failed to break through Jackson's defensive line on the plains of Chalmette. On January 8, 1815, the British initiated a frontal assault on the Americans guarding New Orleans. Using the fire of artillery and musketry, the United States artillery demolished the British fighters, curdling the blood of the brightly clad redcoats. Suffering only 21 American casualties, Jackson claimed victory in the name of the Unites States, avenging the burning of the White House. The British invaders suffered 2,000 casualties and withered away from the region in late January of 1815. From the end of the War of 1812 into the 1840s, Ship Island remained abandoned aside from an occasional fisherman and the wildlife lurking about the sand dunes, creeks, and bayous.[41]

In July 1840, U.S. Secretary of War Jefferson Davis, a Mississippian, pressured Congress for a coastal defense system consisting of masonry forts, and the final approval came from President Franklin Pierce consenting to the construction of a fort on Ship Island. On May 19, 1846, a board of engineers reiterated the recommendation of such a fort and on August 30, 1847, the island was finally declared a military reservation by executive order, though work would begin much later.[42]

During the nineteenth century, lighthouses were designated by the United States Lighthouse Board to guide the ships sailing on the Gulf of Mexico waters. James E. Saunders, superintendent of lights in Mobile, Alabama, suggested that a lighthouse of 45 feet in height be built on Ship Island to give ample warning to the ships sailing against the current blowing from the east. In 1853, the first tower was constructed with brick, along with an adjoining station which resembled a one-story home. In late fall of the same year, the light began directing ships as they plied their courses on the rolling Gulf waters. Work upon a permanent brick fortification at the western end of the island, commanding the pass into the Mississippi Sound between Ship Island and Cat Island, was begun in 1859, though progress was slow due to a lack of funds.[43]

The site of the fort was inspired by the deepwater harbor, its usage as a major shipping route, and its previous military history record. The design of the fort was to consist of sturdy arches to support heavy artillery in the event of any military attacks. In 1859, when construction of the fort was begun by the United States Army Engineers, they were faced with a multitude of problems, including the death of the first superintendent, who perished from yellow fever. Another obstacle was the raging storms that destroyed partially finished sections of the fort. After two years of construction, only eight feet of the outer walls were completed. The workers lived in isolation on the narrow secluded island, which looked miniscule surrounded by the enormous body of Gulf water.[44]

On October 16, 1859, the same year the fort was erected on Ship Island, the over-zealous abolitionist John Brown, son of Owen and Ruth (Mills) Brown, natives of Torrington, Connecticut, organized a raid on the federal arsenal at Harper's Ferry, Virginia, along with twenty-one men, in an attempt to arm a slave revolt. Brown, born in 1800 to a deeply religious family, was impacted by his father's strong opposition to slavery and would emerge as one of America's leading ardent abolitionists. In an attempt to ensure success of his maniacal plan in Virginia, he and his outlaws took 60 prominent citizens hostage, but his self-destructive attempt ended within just thirty-six hours when Federal troops led by Robert E. Lee and Lieutenant J.E.B. Stuart soon arrived and attacked the armory engine house, killing ten of the outlaws, including two of Brown's sons, Watson and Oliver. Brown himself was wounded and transferred by the Federal troops to Charlestown, Virginia, to be tried and sentenced for his crimes. The vehement abolitionist, who thought his actions justified in the name of the extinction of slavery, met his fate on a Charlestown gallows on December 2, 1859. Brown's actions were viewed favorably by many Northerners, particularly his fellow abolitionists, who hailed him as a martyr, while Southerners were outraged and began fearing intrusion on their homes and institutions. The acts of violence committed by Brown provoked sentiments of a coming war that was to be anything but civil.[45]

By the nineteenth century, slavery entered a new phase, as slaves were considered valuable property necessary for economic security; slavery became especially prominent in the South. Amidst the controversy surrounding the slavery issue, the Democratic National Convention assembled first at Charleston, South Carolina, in April of 1860, prompting delegates from seven Southern states—South Carolina, Alabama, Georgia, Louisiana, Florida, Texas, and Mississippi—to walk out, refusing to support the Presidential Democratic nominee, Stephen Arnold Douglas, because of his position regarding slavery. Douglas adopted the formula known as "popular sovereignty," which left the United States federal territories to decide whether to allow slavery within their borders. The majority of Southerners were infuriated by his doctrines.[46]

On November 21, 1860, John Jones Pettus was inaugurated as Governor of Mississippi, and in his address the governor exclaimed with great emphasis: "The Scene at Harper's Ferry is not the end, but in my opinion, only the beginning of the end of this conflict." In conclusion, Pettus announced that if the Republican party elected its president in 1860, that he shall "regard the institution of slavery so seriously threatened as to justify Mississippi in asking for a convention of all the states interested in its perpetuation."[47]

It began to look for the first time as if a completed fort on the Mississippi Gulf Coast would be a probable necessity in a conflict that seemed increasingly imminent to the state. The fort was viewed as a potential asset, as it was situated along a shipping route which could deliver needed supplies, ammunition and reinforcements. It could also serve for military purposes as a base of blockade, interrupting entrance to the Mississippi and to the powerful Southern city of New Orleans. On December 20, 1860, South Carolina took the initiative to free herself from the bonds with the Union, and their adopted declaration read: "The Union now subsisting between South Carolina and other states, under the name of 'The United States of America' is hereby dissolved."[48]

Mississippi, following South Carolina's lead, was the second state to leave the Union, and on January 7, 1861, a convention was called to order at Jackson by Samuel Jameson Gholson, a prominent Mississippi attorney. The majority of members were pro-secessionists, leaving little doubt as to whether the act of secession would pass; as expected, the vote was overwhelmingly in favor 85 to 15. Just eight days later, the drafters of the ordinance of secession had come forward to sign the official document. By February 1, 1861, five additional Southern states had followed South Carolina and Mississippi's decision to become an independent nation: Florida, Alabama, Georgia, Louisiana and Texas. On November 13, 1860, following the election of Abraham Lincoln to the presidency, Governor Pettus issued a proclamation calling upon the Mississippi legislature to provide "surer and better safeguards for the lives, liberty and property of her citizens that have been found or are to be hoped for in Black Republican oaths."[49]

In February 1861, Abraham Lincoln, now U.S. president, warned the South in his inaugural address:

> In your hands, my dissatisfied fellow country men and not in mine, is the monumentous issue of the Civil War. The government will not assail you unless you first assail it. You have no conflict, without being yourselves the aggressors. You have no oath registered in heaven to destroy the government, while I shall have the most solemn one to preserve, protect and defend it. You can forebear the assault upon it; I can not shrink from the defense of it. With you, and not with me, is the solemn question of Shall it be peace, or a sword?[50]

On February 9, 1861, Jefferson Davis was selected as the first, and only, president of the Confederate States of America. On February 18, 1861, at the State Capitol in Montgomery, Alabama, he delivered his inaugural address, in which he stated: "As a necessity, not a choice, we have resorted to the remedy of separation and henceforth our energies must be directed to the conduct of our own affairs and the perpetuity of the Confederacy which we have formed...."[51]

As the new year unfolded in January of 1861, (Union) Lieutenant-Colonel Joseph Gilbert Totten reported to the U.S. secretary of war on January 8 that a working force was in place on Ship Island, but that it would be months before the first tier of guns could be completed, due to a lack of funds. Then on January 13, a party of armed Mississippi militiamen arrived on the island and informed the construction supervisor that they had come on their own responsibility to take possession of the fort, though they did not intend to interfere with the construction, and left soon thereafter. Later that same afternoon, a second armed party appeared on the island, removed the U.S. flag and hoisted and waved the independent Mississippi flag from the flagpole. It was Captain Howard's Biloxi Rifle Guard who became the first infantry regiment in Mississippi to initiate offensive action against the United States. Most of the Biloxi Rifle

Guard soldiers went home, while ten men were left occupying a vacant engineer building, but they also did not impede the construction or workers. The January 18, 1861, edition of the *Natchez Daily-Courier* reported:

> The Fort at Ship Island, Mississippi Taken.
>
> We are informed from the New Orleans Delta that the United States fort in course of construction at Ship Island, Mississippi, some twelve miles from Biloxi, was taken possession of on Sunday night, by Captain Howard and about 50 men from Biloxi. There were at the fort several U.S. officers and about 50 laborers, who offered no resistance. This is the only fort in Mississippi and was designed to be one of the strongest on the Southern coast. Of course all work on the fort has ceased.[52]

On the morning of January 20, a final and larger group of armed Southerners arrived at Ship Island, taking possession of all the property, including the fort, and ordering all work to cease, causing the frustrated First Lieutenant Frederick Edward Prime of the United States Corps of Engineers, in command at Ship Island, to report, "I considered myself relieved from all connection with those works...." He then collected his belongings and vacated the island.[53] That same day, Colonel John McCabe, Pettus' newly appointed commandant of the unarmed fort, sent a letter to Governor Pettus from Handsboro, Mississippi:

> Dear Sir:
> I arrived in Biloxi this morning at 2 o'clock A.M. and had the Biloxi Rifle Guards, who were awaiting my arrival, immediately convened. They had been hoping that material aid would have been furnished them and their garrison on Ship Island. My explanation of affairs at the seat of government and the impossibility of your furnishing them an efficient armament for the fort, although satisfactory, was by no means agreeable. They, however, immediately dispatched a schooner to Ship Island to bring home the young men garrisoned there and will obey the instructions of your letter to myself.
> I had an interview with Lieutenant Frederick E. Prime, U.S. Corps of Engineers, this morning relative to assuming the work on the fort. He assures me that he is about winding up the affairs of the Federal Government on the Island, which he could have done in any event in consequence of the U.S. Treasury being empty, and of his unwillingness to make contracts which he believes he could not carry out. So that the works on the fort are suspended not because of the seizure of the Island by Mississippi volunteers but because of the inability of the Government to meet its engagements.... We deeply regret the inability of the constituted authorities to equip the fort in a manner commensurate with its importance to us and the whole state but we are fully conscious of the desire of your Excellency to give us the required aid were it in your power, and fully appreciate the compliment implied in your instruction to call on us when necessary to take and occupy the fort.[54]

Though it seemed the actions on the island could have initiated a war, the actual Civil War didn't officially begin until the first shot was fired by the Confederates against Fort Sumter, South Carolina, in April of 1861.

On May 13, 1861, Confederate Secretary of War Leroy Pope Walker telegraphed Brigadier General James Trudeau of Louisiana, instructing him to occupy Ship Island as quickly as possible. The month of May was a busy one, as there was much confusion and plenty of accusations going around concerning Trudeau, Walker, and Louisiana Governor Thomas Overton Moore, whose communications resembled that of a three-ring circus. Trudeau claimed to have 2,000 men at Camp Walker in New Orleans and expressed he could also provide the needed materiel within four days to occupy Ship Island. Two days later, Trudeau wrote to Walker and accused Governor Moore of refusing to supply him the necessary troops and arms to occupy the island. Governor Moore immediately and forcibly replied, denying Trudeau's accusation and then offering any assistance necessary to effect the occupation of the island. Trudeau was offered command of Ship Island by President Davis, on Trudeau's assurances that he had troops ready for service. The governor of Louisiana then informed Adjutant-General Samuel Cooper that he saw Trudeau's advertisement in the evening newspaper calling for a regiment of soldiers for twelve months' service, which no doubt must have embarrassed Trudeau, as the evidence indicated he did not have the necessary troops to occupy the island as he had previously suggested. The conclusion to the saga came on May 15, when General Trudeau was notified by the secretary of war that the command he was assigned at Ship Island was revoked. Two days later, Moore informed Walker that he would send the Fourth Louisiana Infantry Regiment to garrison Ship Island, and also believed he was able to send the Donaldsonville Cannoneers for a twelve month service with uniforms and 2 six-pounders.[55]

At the beginning of May, Cooper informed William Joseph Hardee, commanding at Mobile, Alabama, that his command had been extended to include Grand Bay, Horn Island, Ship Island, and all the approaches in any way connected with the defense of Mobile. On May 24, Brigadier-General Hardee informed Secretary of War Walker that he had ordered the buildings at Ship Island burned. The island was not occupied at the time, but his decision was based on the fear that the Federals might seize the island and use Confederate materiel found there against them.[56]

On May 25, President Davis sent the following letter to General David Emanuel Twiggs, commanding at New Orleans:

> I wish particularly to call your attention to the Mississippi Sound, the channel of communication between New Orleans and Mobile, for which we have attempted to make provision by the occupation of Ship Island, and by fitting out the steam-tug to run upon the sound. Hoping that your health will enable you to perform this service with an ability equal to your zeal in the cause of the South and that the reputation you have acquired in a long service will gain from the performance of this duty additional luster.[57]

Twiggs, born in Georgia, was an aged man of seventy-one, and a veteran of the War of 1812 and the Mexican War. Although some doubted his military capabilities due to his age, he was a very intelligent and capable officer. A month after Hardee ordered the destruction of the buildings at Ship Island, Major-General Twiggs expressed his deep regret in a written letter dated June 25, 1861 to Secretary of War Walker: "It was a great mistake to burn the buildings, &c., there. Not less than $100,000 worth of property was destroyed."[58] For a state already suffering economic despair, the wise old Twiggs had a valid point.

Ship Island was not garrisoned and although troops were ready at Mississippi City, Twiggs' ammunition was scarce and he needed two or more good engineers. He was hardly ready for a Northern invasion. Twiggs applied to the Confederate navy for a loan of heavy guns, but was initially denied before being offered some guns on loan. He was concerned that if the Valley of Mississippi fell into the hands of the Federals, New Orleans would be in a very critical condition.[59]

Lincoln's declaration of a blockade of the Confederate states, previously issued on April 19, 1861, was put in force, and just two months later, hostile ships began exploring the Mississippi Sound. In late June of 1861, Melancton Smith, a cigar smoking fifty-two-year-old military veteran who detested vulgarity, commander of the five-gun USS *Massachusetts,* an iron steamer, reported capturing five schooners in the Mississippi Sound carrying flour, guns, salt, oats, liquor, turpentine, railroad iron, along with twenty-five men. The commander also stated in his report that he interrupted mail being communicated between New Orleans and Mobile that same day, when he turned back the smaller steamboat *Oregon,* which regularly ran with the mail. On July 4, the USS *Massachusetts,* sailed from Pensacola Bay, Florida, to an area near the mouth of the Mississippi River. Four days later, Smith found the Ship Island light had been extinguished and he reported the rebels were occupying the island. Twiggs ordered the lights on Ship Island and Cat Island to be extinguished and the buoys to be removed but afterwards decided to countermand the order because he realized the lights and buoys would benefit the Confederate vessels attempting to run the blockade. Ship Island was crucial to block any advance made by the Federal navy on the blockaded cities of the Gulf Coast.[60]

Captain Edward Higgins, formerly of the navy and now aide-de-camp to Twiggs, organized his own expedition in the Sound. With two lake steamers, the *Oregon*, commanded by Captain A.L. Myers and armed with an 8-inch Columbiad, and the CSS *Swain*, commanded by Lieutenant Alexander F. Warley and armed with a thirty-two pounder and two howitzers, sailed on the high seas in July, seeking to destroy the enemy; but by the time they reached the Mississippi Sound, the Union navy had departed. The *Oregon* landed two guns and one hundred men that included thirty soldiers of the Fourth Louisiana Infantry with their sergeant, over fifty marines with their captain, and a number of sailors on the island, under the command of A.F. Warley.[61] Captain Charles W. Read described the scene in his diary:

> While the *McRae* was getting ready for sea, Captain Higgins, formerly of the navy, but at that time on the staff of General Twiggs, proposed an expedition to capture the Launches of the enemy that were raiding in the Mississippi Sound, and called on Captain Huger for volunteers, which were readily furnished. So taking one thirty two pounder, one eight inch gun and two howitzers, we armed and manned two of the lake steamers. We went through the Sound but did not find the boats of the enemy. It was decided by Captain Higgins that we would land our guns on Ship Island and hold on there until troops could be brought from New Orleans. We commenced landing about 4 P.M., and after very hard work got our guns through the soft sand, up to the highest point of the island, and parapets around them before dark. Our steamers left as soon as the guns were on shore.
>
> About dark a steamer was made out coming in from seaward, and it was evident to all that she was a gunboat of the enemy. The light on the island had been kept burning as usual since the war commenced, but on this night it was extinguished. After dark the gunboat fired a couple of guns, as it seemed, to let the light keeper know that a light was needed. However, the gunboat came in and anchored within a mile of our position. The next morning at dawn of day Lieutenant Warley, who commanded us, directed me to open fire on the steamer with the eight inch gun. As soon as the first shot had been fired, some one on lookout on the lighthouse reported that the steamer had up a white flag.
>
> As it was rather misty, it was believed by the commanding officer that the enemy had surrendered. Smoke was seen issuing from his funnel however, and some of us suspected that he meant anything else than striking his colors. In a few minutes all doubts were dispelled by a thirty two pound shell, which came whizzing from the steamer, knocking the sand in our faces and exploding amongst us. We now opened with all of our guns, but with what effect we could not ascertain. The gunboat replied briskly, but fired wildly. In about an hour, the steamer having raised steam, withdrew out of range and proceeded out to sea. That afternoon our steamers returned, bringing the Fourth Louisiana Regiment, in charge of Colonel Allen. Our sailors embarked and went back to the city.[62]

Confederate occupation of Ship Island began on that hot Saturday afternoon of July 6, 1861. The *Oregon*, after depositing the men on the island, returned to New Orleans to obtain the provisions and munitions needed to supply the fortification. Lieutenant-Colonel Henry Watkins Allen assumed command of the three companies of the Fourth Louisiana Infantry, and instructed the soldiers to set up their tents on the sandy beach and prepare for a defense against the Federals. The following day, the *Oregon* returned with the CSS *Grey Cloud*, finding the Confederates under fire by the New England ship USS *Massachusetts*. The Confederate defenders dug out the enemy's round shot from the sand for reuse, until the much needed supplies finally arrived from the *Oregon*.[63] Lieutenant Warley stated in his report:

> On Monday evening a sail was discovered standing in, and came to anchor to the westward of the Chandeleur Light. At about 9 P.M. she fired a gun, and apparently made signals with white lights, and the "beat to quarters" was distinctly heard. We were on the alert throughout the night. In the morning we discovered that she was a two-masted steam-propellor, at anchor, supposed to be the *Massachusetts*, with a tender stern. She having no flag flying, I waited until sunrise, when I ordered Midshipman Read to open fire on her with the 8-inch gun, which was followed immediately by Midshipman Comstock with the 32-pounder, which compelled the enemy to show his colors. They

proved to be those of the invader. In consequence of her distance the host, which was in direct line, fell short. She immediately got under way and stood in for our batteries at uncertain range opened with her broadside guns, firing wild mostly, and doing no harm.[64]

That same month, the secretary of war alerted Twiggs that if any planters offered their slaves without charge, he was to secure their services for work on the defenses at the fort, and the war department would supply the provisions. Also, seventy-five men were sent to reinforce the garrison on the island.

On July 8, Melancton Smith of the USS *Massachusetts* reported that he witnessed the rebel forces occupying Ship Island, their light extinguished, and at daylight on July 9, he saw three secession flags, thirty-nine tents, four batteries in the process of erection, and bales of cotton being used as materials in the construction of four batteries. The Rebel garrison at Ship Island, operating from shore batteries commanded by Lieutenant Warley, opened fire on the *Massachusetts* from two batteries of one gun each, though fortunately for the steamer, the missiles fell short. Smith then immediately steamed his ship within range of the Confederate guns, returning their fire with his pivot guns that were loaded with round shot and 15 second shells from the gun deck, though with distant firing charges his shots fell short. Meanwhile, the Confederate fire from the shore passed over the forecastle and engine house of the *Massachusetts*, striking the water several yards from the vessel. After exhausting all of his 15 second shells, he proceeded to disengage from the contest. The Confederates expended twenty-six shots, while the *Massachusetts* discharged seventeen blasts. The shots fired by both sides did little harm to one another due to the ones from the Federal ship falling short, and the Confederate fire overpassing the Union vessel, though it did cause minor damage to the ship's rig. Deeming it injudicious to leave for Mobile before dark, Smith proceeded to Chandeleur Island where, upon arriving, he removed the lens and secured the lighting apparatus at the station located on the island to prevent it from falling into the hands of the Confederates in his absence.[65]

Smith stated in his report to William M. Mervine, commander of the Gulf Blockading Squadron: "I am of opinion that the rebels have 1 rifled cannon, 2 guns of heavy caliber, one 12-pounder and a force of 300 to 400 men, in which opinion, the officers of this vessel fully concur, some estimating the force as high as 800."[66]

On July 13, while the *Massachusetts* was anchored within a few miles of Ship Island, two armed steamers, the CSS *Oregon* and the CSS *Arrow*, were discovered under full steam heading for the Federal gunboat. Melancton Smith again reports: "The first shot thrown caused both boats to open fire, but their ammo was uselessly expended and I threw an occasional shot and shell knowing their objective was not to engage, but to toll me up in range of the batteries on shore."[67]

One week later, Twiggs wrote Secretary of War Walker, advising him that Ship Island was now strong enough to resist any force that was likely to be sent against it, and that there were five companies of volunteers on the island. Twiggs had repeatedly complained that he was unable to obtain sufficient guns to protect the fortification. He did not fail to mention, however, that Ship Island could possibly become a *liability* in the near future, due to the burden of defending it. In early August, Twiggs informed Walker: "We require a force of efficient gun boats to cooperate with the Ship Island fort."[68]

On August 8, 1861, the Federals captured the sloop *Charles Henry* of Mobile. Melancton Smith reported off Ship Island the following account:

> The telegraph line that I am ordered to destroy cannot be approached in this vessel at any point nearer than 20 miles and then only by entering the Ship Island passage, which channel is now guarded by a very formidable fortification and corresponding force. The boats of this vessel are not constructed for such hazardous service not having the capacity for carrying a gun while the steamers in Mississippi Sound are all swift and armed with ordnance of long range.[69]

Smith reported as having on board the *Massachusetts*, after filling vacancies caused by the men previously sent with the capture of prizes: one deserter, one man recommended for medical survey and discharge, six men transferred to prize recently captured, four seamen, five ordinary seamen, and three landsmen.[70]

On August 23, U.S. Secretary of the Navy Gideon Welles sent the following communication to U.S. Navy Flag Officer W. M. Mervine, expressing mortification that: "So important a position such as Ship Island should not have been permitted to be fortified and retained by the insurgents.... You have large ships, heavy batteries, and young and willing officers, with men sufficient to dispossess the insurgents from Ship Island. They might have been prevented entirely from entrenching themselves upon it.... There is a great uneasiness in the public mind, as well as anxiety in the Department, on the apparent inactivity of the squadron."[71]

Secretary Welles, unhappy with the lack of activity in the Mississippi Sound area around Ship Island, decided to remove Flag-Officer Mervine, replacing him with Flag-Officer William W. McKean and ordering that the fort on Ship Island be captured or demolished.[72] The fort was named Fort Twiggs, in honor of General Twiggs.

On September 3, 1861, Colonel Johnson Kelly Duncan of the First Louisiana Heavy Artillery was ordered by Twiggs to take temporary command of Ship Island during the absence of Lieutenant-Colonel Allen. Duncan had been a lieutenant in the Third United States Artillery and had been commissioned a captain in the Confederate regular Corps of Artillery. Appointed major of the First Louisiana Heavy Artillery, he was promoted to colonel in July. He was accompanied by four officers of his regiment and ordered to take charge of drilling and heavy gun crews. Colonel Duncan, after thoroughly examining the island, fort, and troops, described the fort as "Semi-circular or horseshoe-like, closed at the gorge with a half bastion front," providing a defense against the enemy by land. When Colonel Duncan made his assessment of the fort, the walls had been carried up only as high as the soles of the embrasures.[73] The Confederates built brick piers and covered the whole structure with heavy timbers and a three-inch plank roof, in turn covered with sandbags, to make the fort as defensible as possible. Duncan reported the armament of the fort as:

> 2 twenty-four pounders in flanking position, 1 eight-inch shell on the front, 8 thirty-two pounders within the circular inside perimeter of the fort, and 1 thirty-two pounder and one 9 inch Dahlgren shell gun outside the fort and behind sandbag parapets.... To have much strength or to be able to or to maintain anything like a determined attack, this fort must be completed after its original plans. If progressed with after the present method of temporarily completing, a few heavy men of war will pelt it to ruins in a very short space of time. I regard it as affording the least possible protection to the men and guns, and totally incapable of resisting any formidable force.
>
> If the island must be fortified, and if possible be held at all hazards, I would earnestly suggest that Fort Twiggs and all work upon it be abandoned at once, and that the only attempt made at fortification be the ordinary resort to sand-bag batteries.[74]

Duncan's dissenting comments regarding his observations of the fort seemed unrelenting and he insisted tenaciously that the island and garrison needed to be abandoned. He noted that enemy gunboats could pass unharmed between Ship Island, the mainland, and any of the channels in and around the island. He also stated that it would be very easy for the enemy to capture the small Confederate steamers and other small boats sailing around the Sound. He suggested that the fort on Ship Island was incapable of resisting a combined Federal land and water attack, and that if troops consisting of 4,000 to 8,000 bombarded the fort by land and sea that the attack would not last more than an hour. He also stressed that the best of guns on Ship Island could not defend the channel between it and Cat Island. To sum up his report, he considered the works on Ship Island anything but impressive. He thought the expense unnecessary and would not support such an impracticable project. Therefore, he strongly urged the immediate abandonment of the island, as he considered it a useless occupation. He suggested the smaller guns be placed in entrenchments near the mouths of the Dog and Pascagoula rivers.[75]

On September 11, a letter opposing the abandonment of Ship Island was sent to General Twiggs from Major Martin Luther Smith of the Confederate Corps of Engineers, who once held the title Captain of U.S. Topographical Engineers. He did, however, remark that the work on Ship Island had progressed rather slowly, that there was still much work to be done, and that a lack of funds was hampering progress on the island. He also stated, in regard to armament, that every available gun of any size had been sent to the island. He was in favor of continuing the Confederate occupation of the island, and believed the garrison there was better sheltered there than at any other point in the area, though he recommended that a gunboat squadron be provided for support.[76]

Twiggs forwarded both reports to the Confederate War Department in Richmond, Virginia, but agreed more with Duncan's observations than Smith's. He insisted he would hold the island until told to do so otherwise. On September 12, Twiggs reported to Secretary of War Walker that within two or three weeks he hoped to have a powder mill in operation on Ship Island, though he explained that the success of the powder mill strongly depended on the promise he received for a supply of saltpeter. He also had 120 rounds of ammunition for each gun on Ship Island, whereas he had only 40 rounds at other fortifications. He also suggested a camp be established near the city closest to Ship Island as a rendezvous point for the troops, as it took considerable time to assemble the soldiers for a furlough from the island.[77]

On September 13, Twiggs received official notification of Richmond's policy regarding Ship Island from Samuel Cooper, the adjutant-general and ranking general of the Confederacy: "Take the immediate measures to evacuate Ship Island, and cause the guns to be removed at once."[78]

Twiggs hastily responded upon receipt of the communication with Cooper, at once issuing Special Order Number 91, ordering Colonel Duncan to evacuate Ship Island. On September 14, Colonel Duncan arrived at Ship Island onboard the CSS *Oregon* and was accompanied by the CSS *Grey Cloud*, *A. G. Brown* and *Ocean Springs*. By the night of September 16, Colonel Duncan removed all the personnel, guns, carriages, equipment, implements, ammunition, commissary and quartermaster's stores, engineers' tools, and all other public and private property except lumber. He loaded its garrison on ships provided for that purpose and before departing, he ordered the stairs in the lighthouse set ablaze, first removing the Fresnal lamp.[79] Commander Melancton Smith alerted Flag-Officer McKean that Lieutenant-Colonel Henry Allen left the following letter, "posted on the fort bulletin," addressed to him at Ship Island:

> Fort Twiggs
> September 17, 1861
>
> By order of my government I have this day evacuated Ship Island. This my brave soldiers under command do with much reluctance and regret. For three long months your good ship has been our constant companion.
>
> We have not exactly, "lived and loved together," but we have been intimately acquainted, having exchanged cards on the 8th day of July last.
>
> In leaving you to-day we beg you accept our best wishes for your health and happiness while sojourning on this pleasant, hospitable shore.
>
> That we may have another exchange of courtesies before the war closes, and that we may meet face to face in closer quarters, is the urgent prayer of very truly, your obedient servant
>
> H.W. Allen
> Lieutenant-Colonel Commanding
> Ship Island[80]

The note led to an advertisement being placed in a New Orleans newspaper by Frank Merriam, an officer on the *Massachusetts*, challenging Allen to a duel. Allen accepted his offer, with an agreement that it was to be fought with double-barreled shotguns on Cat Island, though there has been no documentation found to confirm the duel ever took place.[81]

General Twiggs had concurred with Duncan's strong opposition to holding Ship Island, despite Twiggs' own admission that he had never stepped foot on the island. On September 17, Twiggs alerted the War Department that Ship Island had been evacuated. The next day, Twiggs reported to the secretary of war that the enemy's fleet did considerable shelling at the masked battery on Ship Island. The Confederate abandonment of the island has long been debated by historians as to whether it was a major factor in the Confederate defeat in the war. Though it may not have been the cause of the loss of the war by the Confederates, if they had recognized the strategic military importance of the position of the island, such as the French and British did over almost two centuries before, they would have been able to prevent the capture of the city of New Orleans, or at a minimum seriously delay its capture. Major Martin L. Smith must be commended for his demonstrances with the Confederate War Department to hold such a valuable port and staging area so close to New Orleans, and it is understandable why he would advance to the rank of major-general. It is difficult to understand why Twiggs, an experienced military man, would choose to agree with Duncan's assessment of the island, and not Smith's. General Twiggs was notified in September of 1861 that he was relieved of active duty and replaced in command at New Orleans by Major-General Mansfield Lovell, a native of Maryland and a veteran of the Mexican War. Approximately a year prior to this, Lovell had resigned his employment as deputy street commissioner in New York City to join the Confederate army. Whatever Twiggs' reasoning, the Confederates had lost Ship Island forever, and it was a loss that the struggling new nation could ill afford, as time would soon prove, and from which it would not recover.[82]

Flag-Officer McKean, who was commanding the Gulf Blockading Squadron, had recommended in September of 1861 that the fort on Ship Island be destroyed unless it was the intention of the government to finish and garrison it.[83] In mid–October 1861, Commander-Lieutenant Charles W. Hays explored the open Gulf in the Mississippi Sound, aboard the CSS *Florida*, searching for any blockading vessels. When he proceeded westward of Horn Island, he discovered four enemy ships at anchor under the batteries at Ship Island. A naval engagement soon commenced between the *Florida* and the USS *Cuyler*. Hays had reported the U.S. ship as weighing 1,200 tons, very fast and carrying an armament of about ten guns, one of which he reported was capable of great range. The firing continued on both sides for over an hour, until the *Cuyler* had ceased firing and returned to her consorts under the battery at Ship Island. Hays happily reported that the vessel and the crew escaped without injury, and he could not say if the enemies or their vessel had been harmed.[84] That same month, based on information McKean had received from two of his U.S. commanders, Smith and Lieutenant Winslow, McKean advised Secretary of the Navy Welles that it was now essential to hold the fort on Ship Island. He also said he would strengthen the fort as best he could and garrison it with a number of seamen and marines. He was concerned that the Rebels might land in force on the east end of the island and attack the fort in the rear, so he strongly recommended keeping a steam force of vessels as a defensive strategy in the Mississippi Sound.[85] On November 2, 1861, McKean received an order from Welles to retain possession of Ship Island and to expect the vessels *DeSoto*, who would arrive with rifled guns and ordnance stores, and *New London*, a steamer. Welles informed McKean that every exertion would be made to add light-draft vessels to his naval force. The Federals now had the island in their possession and would retain control of it until the end of the Civil War, and beyond. To ensure protection of the island, stores, and assets from the Confederates, the Federal navy stationed the 18-gun sloop-of-war *Vincennes* at Ship Island from October 1862 until July 1865. At this time, no one from the South or the North could foresee the events that would take place during the Civil War on this beautiful little island.[86]

The Federals Arrive

Montgomery, Alabama— May 25, 1861
I wish particularly to call your attention to the Mississippi Sound, the channel of communications between New Orleans and Mobile, for which we have attempted to make provision by the occupation of Ship Island....
— *Confederate President Jefferson Davis, to Major-General David E. Twiggs at New Orleans*

As the Confederate authorities vacillated in regards to their intentions for Ship Island, plans were rapidly unfolding in Washington centered around the barrier island. On September 10, 1861, Union Major-General Benjamin Franklin Butler was authorized by President Lincoln to "raise, organize, arm, uniform, and equip a volunteer force for the War in the New England states, not exceeding six Regiments of the Maximum Standard, of such arms, and in such proportions, and in such manner as he may judge expedient."[1] Butler, a "political general" from Massachusetts known for his ability to rub people the wrong way, immediately set upon his appointed task, and just as quickly found himself at odds with Massachusetts Governor John Albion Andrew regarding his recruiting efforts in the Bay State. The ill feelings between the two men dated back to Butler's unauthorized offer to use Massachusetts troops to quell a slave uprising in Maryland. Though Lincoln attempted to intercede by sending a telegram to the governors of the New England states requesting their aid in Butler's efforts, Governor Andrew responded by advising Lincoln that he did not intend to relinquish one iota of his control over army recruitment in Massachusetts. However, Lincoln's telegram was received favorably by Governors Israel Washburn, Jr., of Maine, William Alfred Buckingham of Connecticut, and Erastus Fairbanks of Vermont, all of whom pledged their cooperation in the endeavor.[2]

For almost a month, Butler deferred his enlistment efforts in Massachusetts, while in the other New England states he opened offices, established camps, addressed legislatures, and made speeches to recruits. In Connecticut, the Ninth Connecticut Infantry was formed from rowdy Irishmen, and Butler promptly moved them to the agricultural fairgrounds at Camp Chase outside of Lowell, Massachusetts. He also persuaded Secretary of War Simon Cameron to create for him the Department of New England, with headquarters in Boston, in an attempt to quell the independent-minded Governor Andrew. In one of his many trips to Washington to bypass Andrew, Butler pointed out that recruitment was a national matter, and accordingly should be subject to a national draft. He remarked, "Suppose the Governors of the states should refuse to raise any volunteers, would not the President have a right to draft men for the service of the United States?"[3]

While the feud between the two strong-willed New Englanders dragged on, Butler missed the opportunity to lead an expedition to the eastern shore of Virginia that he had projected. As a conciliatory move on behalf of the Lincoln Administration to all whose feathers Butler had ruffled, and to rid the east of his acerbic presence, Butler was given command of a secret expedition that was to be carried out in cooperation with the U.S. Navy: The capture of New Orleans. Years later, then–Secretary of the Navy Gideon Welles recalled that "all would be relieved were this restless officer [Butler] sent to Ship Island or the far Southwest, where his energy, activity and impulsive force might be employed in desultory aquatic and shore duty in concert with the Navy."[4]

Originally conceived by the naval authorities, the plan for the conquest of New Orleans was simple, on paper. Since the Confederate evacuation of Ship Island, the Union blockading fleet had occupied its sandy shores as a base from which to enforce the blockade of Southern ports located along the Gulf Coast. The plan called for Ship Island to be used as the staging area for a fleet of warships to pass Forts Jackson and St. Philip, guarding the entrance to the Mississippi River, after a substantial bombardment by a flotilla of mortar schooners. Also to be based on the island would be a contingent of troops, commanded by Butler, that could be used to storm the Confederate forts and garrison New Orleans, after their surrender to Union naval forces. The catch was whether the fleet could survive the passage, and artillery fire, of the forts at all, and, if so, whether it would be in such condition to compel anyone to surrender.

Chosen to command the naval portion of the expedition against New Orleans was Captain David Glasgow Farragut, the adopted brother of Commander David Dixon Porter, who was selected to command the mortar schooners that were to reduce the forts at the mouth of the Mississippi. Porter's father, in command of the frigate *Essex* during the War of 1812, had taken the nine-year-old Farragut into the navy as a midshipman on December 17, 1810. By age twelve he was serving as a prize master, and at age thirteen he participated admirably in the lopsided battle involving the *Essex* and the British frigates *Cherub* and *Phoebe* in the harbor at Valparaiso. A lieutenant at age twenty-one and a commander during the Mexican War, Farragut later became captain in 1855, only to see promotions in the navy slow down considerably in peacetime. But now that peace had been shattered by the spectre of civil war, he was quickly promoted to flag-officer and given control of the newly constituted West Gulf Blockading Squadron by Secretary Welles on January 9, 1862, which the Senate confirmed on March 19. The leaders to conquer the Queen City of the South had now been selected: a career naval man and a political general, and both wasted no time in getting their respective plans underway.[5]

Butler ordered his agent in New York, C.J. Harrison, to charter the Pacific Mail steamer *Constitution* to carry the vanguard of his forces to Ship Island. On November 19, 1861, the Twenty-Sixth Massachusetts Infantry, the Ninth Connecticut Infantry, and the Fourth Massachusetts Light Artillery paraded through Boston Common with a full band and drum corps, where Butler watched from atop a reviewing stand. On November 21, the 1,908 troops boarded the *Constitution* and sailed from Boston Harbor en route to Ship Island, though they did stop at Fortress Monroe long enough to pick up Brigadier-General John Wolcott Phelps, whom Butler had placed in charge of his advance contingent at Ship Island until his arrival.[6] Traveling slowly down the Atlantic coast and along the Florida shoreline, before turning around the tip of the Florida Keys and entering the Gulf of Mexico, the *Constitution* reached Ship Island on December 2, 1861, and anchored offshore. A musician in the Twenty-Sixth Massachusetts, Alfred Parmenter, wrote to his parents back in New England about his first impression of the island: "Well I have just been on deck and taken another look of Ship Island. We have come to anchor within ⅛ of a mile from shore. You may perhaps gather an idea of the place from the remark of the Quartermaster. "What a hell of a place to send 2000 men 3000 miles."[7]

Major-General Benjamin F. Butler and staff in New Orleans, Louisiana, 1862 (courtesy of a private collection).

On December 3, the New Englanders began to disembark from the *Constitution* onto the sandy white beaches of the island, and almost three days later the men and their equipage were finally unloaded at their new home, which Captain Benjamin Warren of the Twenty-Sixth Massachusetts described as "barren enough to deserve the name 'Misery Island' which name it received by some of the men."[8] Colonel Edward F. Jones of the Sixth Massachusetts Infantry immediately proceeded to organize his regiment's camp and drill his men in infantry tactics. Jones made these entries in his journal concerning his thoughts on Ship Island:

> Friday December 6th: Dreary place on shore — all sand — one House and Light House except a few sheds constitutes all buildings.
> Saturday December 7: Two Rebel Gunboats came out from direction of New Orleans. The *New London* and *DeSota* went out to engage them and they Retreated.
> Saturday December 14th: Spent the day in building a Log Stable. At night the *Kingfisher* arrived bad news — all our horses killed in storm — 69 horses died on the passage by improperly stowage. Poor old Billy, peace to his ashes.
> Tuesday January 7, 1862: Made arrangement in AM for the Funeral of Private Goodreau of Co A who died last night. Went with Gen. Phelps and selected a spot for a Grave & propose to arrange it a little for a Regimental burial ground.
> Saturday January 11, 1862: There is room to encamp about 4000 men on the Easterly Point of the Island but they would be much troubled by mosquitos and would have no place for Drill.
> Friday January 17, 1862: Fog-all Fog ... Fog has been so dense all day that we could not see offshore.... I feel all out of sorts, blue. Sad and do not take my usual interest in matters going on. In fact, there is nothing going on.[9]

Jones continued to record his thoughts through the months of February and March 1862 regarding such subjects as rain, cold weather, drill, and the unpleasant task of burying the troops that perished on the island. On April 12, 1862, he recorded a lightning strike during

Two. The Federals Arrive

a storm that struck eleven men on the island, killing three of them. They are recorded in the roster of Union dead in this book.[10]

A member of the Ninth Connecticut Infantry, Private Albert A. Andrews, wrote this letter to his siblings in Connecticut on March 9, 1862, during his stay on Ship Island:

> Dear Brother and Sister,
>
> I thought I would write you a few lines and let you know that I am well now and hope that this will find you all the same. There has nothing of importance happen since I wrote last, that is the 6th, when I wrote and sent my money to your care by express to Waterbury, thinking perhaps you could get it sooner than father would and send it to him when you can handy, and if it is hard times there it may do him some good. I should like to hear from you and our folks at home very much, it begins to be quiet tiresome to watch for news from home and get none, though the mail has come in here every day for a while back bringing in soldiers and other things needed. The Twelfth Conn. Regt. arrived here yesterday with three other regiments and we expect the Thirteenth Regiment here all the time now. I shall expect to see some old acquaintances among them if I stay here long enough, though I do not think we shall stay but one or two days more at the longest, and they say we are going tomorrow but I do not know when we shall go. Perhaps you would like to know where we expect to go, well I will tell you as near as I can. I think it will be Mobile and Mississippi City, in fact, the 26th Mass. regiment went over to Mobile yesterday and landed a force but had to leave and come back in double-quick time, you may depend after the rebels had fired a few grape and cannister shot at them. I believe there was no one killed but some wounded. They will have to wait until the Bloody 9th is ready to go with them, there will be some hard fighting down here very soon now. We had a first-rate spot to stay through the winter but our easy time is nearly through now, as there is a large force of troops collecting here now, so we shall have to move right along when we get started. This month has been the coldest yet since we have arrived here, it was so cold that we saw a very small scum of ice the other morning which was a great curiousity to us here, as we did not expect to see any this winter. Our men here has been very healthy since we have been here, only one has died out of our Regiment since I enlisted, and my health has never been better, not withstanding our poor keep and hard work, and I think I shall live to get back, if I don't get killed with some stray ball or other. I hope we shall all get back all safe and sound before long too, if I could get some letters and papers from home. If you will send me your *Waterbury American* once in a while, I should think a great deal of one, if I could get any. If you can't send me any papers, write as often as you can and tell me all the news there is and not wait for me to write for it is not every day that I have time to write, and I don't know as I shall have as much time as I have had after soon. Tell Mr. Todd folks that I should like to hear from them very much and I think that I should stay quiet if I was back there again, but I think the war will be ended after a while and then I shall be around after a while if I live. We shall march to New Orleans before long and then, old boy, look out for loose shells. There is some things that I like in camp life and some things I do not so well. When we have to stand out on picket guard, as I have had to stand out for the last two days and have just got off now so I don't write very good today and I hope you will excuse this poor writing. You must give my best respects to all inquiring friends, and write as often as you can. Tell them to write to me if they can and I will write back to all that will write to me. I have thought that you had all forgotten me by nobody writing to me. I have sent a number of times to different persons but received no reply yet. I want you to send a letter to me and let me know if you get the money that sent, as I shall feel very uneasy until I hear from home or some of you people.
>
>   Write Soon,
>   and direct to Ship Island
>   A.A. Andrews, Company
>   9th Regt. C.V.
>   Ship Island, Miss.
>   c/o Captain Curtis[11]

It was not long before the arrival of the Northerners was noted in the New Orleans newspapers, as was the inflammatory and totally unauthorized proclamation of General Phelps to the "loyal citizens of the Southwest," in which he denounced the institution of slavery in the strongest terms possible. In his address, Phelps declared that the admission of any new slave state into the Union was a violation of the U.S. Constitution, and that the states in which slavery existed at the adoption of the Constitution were bound, by becoming parties to that compact, to abolish it. Monopolies, he stated, were destructive to national prosperity, and slavery was the greatest of all monopolies. Labor was inherently noble, and the motto of the country should be "Free labor and workingman's rights." This prompted the *New Orleans Daily-Crescent* of December 18, 1861, to comment that Phelps should be promoted at once: "He is evidently as big a fool as Lincoln and as great a scoundrel as Seward."[12] The Confederate commander at New Orleans, Major-General Mansfield Lovell, was amazingly unalarmed by the Union military buildup at Ship Island. On December 29, he sent the following communication to Confederate secretary of war and New Orleans native Judah P. Benjamin in Richmond: "The enemy has now at Ship Island twenty-two vessels, large and small, and is landing troops in large numbers.... They cannot take New Orleans by a land attack with any force they can bring to bear."[13]

Back in the east, Butler was sparing no time or energy in preparing another contingent of troops to embark for Ship Island upon the return of the *Constitution*. The Twelfth Maine Infantry, under the command of George Foster Shepley, a successful attorney from Portland, and the Eastern Bay State Regiment, commanded by Boston lawyer Jonas H. French, were loaded aboard the *Constitution* upon her return from her maiden voyage to Ship Island. An enraged Governor Andrew managed to get the sailing orders of the vessel temporarily canceled, however, by an impromptu appearance in Washington to air his grievances, prompting General-in-Chief George B. McClellan to order Butler, now at Fortress Monroe, by telegraph to "... disembark your troops from the 'Constitution' and report by telegraph the terms of the charter of that steamer."[14] Butler, of course, attempted to stall his superior in his reply telegraph: "Would advise against disembarkation if possible to be prevented. Troops are now comfortable. Will begin preparations for disembarkation, but await orders?" He then sent this dispatch to his aide in Washington, Major George C. Strong: "Get orders to disembark revoked. Save the ship for us. Get connections. Report at length by mail."[15]

Butler then traveled to Washington to obtain the officers' commissions that Governor Andrew had refused to provide for his two Massachusetts regiments, prompting an appeal from President Lincoln to Andrew on January 11, 1862, in which he stated, "I will be greatly obliged if you will arrange somehow with General Butler to officer his two unofficered regiments."[16] Andrew's response, hardly reassuring to the president, was a restatement of his grievances against Butler, though he did offer to provide officers "in the manner in which I have performed it ... exercising my own discretion in all matters in the same manner."[17] Lincoln, by now fed up with the ongoing feud between Butler and Andrew, sided squarely with Butler. On January 16, 1862, Adjutant-General Lorenzo Thomas quietly announced the ranks and commissions of the officers of Butler's regiments, as if they had been approved in the usual manner. Andrew did, however, manage to get the commissions of two of Butler's general officers turned down by the U.S. Senate. These two were Andrew Butler, brother of the general, who had been appointed as his commissary of subsistence, and Paul R. George, his assistant quartermaster, who was also a longtime friend and business associate.[18]

Butler, meanwhile, received a report from McClellan on January 24, 1862, which declared the New Orleans expedition unfeasible, prompting another monotonous routine of interviews and arguments in favor of the undertaking. Adding to the confusion in Washington was the replacement of Cameron as secretary of war with Edwin M. Stanton. On January 29, Butler managed to get verbal orders from McClellan to get the *Constitution*, still at Fortress Monroe, under way for Ship Island. While back in Boston, Butler gathered the remaining necessities required for the operation, such as fuel, medical supplies, ammunition, and food. Farragut got underway with his heavy warships for the Gulf on February 3, 1862, followed by Commander David Porter and the mortar flotilla on February 12.[19] On February 23, Butler received his official orders from McClellan, naming him "to command of the land forces destined to cooperate with the Navy in the attack on New Orleans." His force would comprise 14,400 infantry, 275 cavalry, and 580 artillery, for a total troop strength of 15,255. The infantry would consist of the Ninth, Twelfth, and Thirteenth Connecticut, the Twenty-Sixth, Thirtieth, and Thirty-First Massachusetts, the Twelfth, Thirteenth, Fourteenth, and Fifteenth Maine, the Eighth New Hampshire, the Seventh and Eighth Vermont, the Twenty-First Indiana, the Sixth Michigan, and the Fourth Wisconsin Infantry regiments. He was also authorized to obtain temporary command of two additional regiments, one from Fort Pickens, Florida, and another from Key West, giving him a total aggregate strength of 18,000. McClellan followed up with these orders to Butler:

> The object of your expedition is one of vital importance — the capture of New Orleans. The route selected is up the Mississippi River, and the first obstacle to be encountered [perhaps the only one] is the resistance offered by Forts Saint Philip and Jackson. It is expected that the Navy can reduce these works. In that case you will, after their capture, leave a sufficient garrison in them to render them perfectly secure.... Should the Navy fail to reduce the works, you will land your forces and siege train, and endeavor to breach the works, silence their guns, and carry them by assault....[20]

That same day, in another general order, McClellan created a new U.S. military department, the Department of the Gulf, placing Butler in command and stating that the headquarters of the department would be movable, wherever General Butler might be. Before departing for Ship Island, Butler called on the new secretary of war and found Lincoln with him. Upon advising them of his orders, Butler recalled that "Mr. Stanton was overjoyed. The President did not appear at all elated." On departing from the presence of the two men, Butler stated to Stanton, "I am going to take New Orleans or you will never see me again," to which Stanton replied, "Well, you take New Orleans and you shall be a lieutenant-general."[21]

On February 25, 1862, Butler, his wife, Sarah, several staff officers, and 1,600 soldiers departed for Ship Island aboard the transport steamer *Mississippi*. As Butler sailed away for glory, or possible disaster, many in Washington breathed a sigh of relief at the departure of the abrasive New Englander. Randolph B. Marcy, father-in-law and chief-of-staff of General McClellan, summed up the feelings of some of Butler's less-than-ardent admirers: "I guess we have found a hole to bury this Yankee elephant in."[22]

Though Butler expected to reach Ship Island in less than two weeks, fate raised the Rebel banner during his voyage to the island. Storms followed the *Mississippi* almost from the moment of her departure, and the rough seas of Hatteras Inlet prevented the ship from taking on Brigadier-General Thomas Williams as a passenger. The Maine soldiers onboard the vessel, formerly cod fishermen and whalers, were roused from their bunks to assist the civilian crew in keeping the *Mississippi* afloat. Three days out of Hampton Roads, the storms dissipated and the ship was able to hoist three sails, enabling her to make good speed in her voyage down the Atlantic coast. Bad luck once again reared its ugly head off Wilmington, North Carolina, when the *Mississippi* ran aground on Frying Pan Shoals off Cape Fear. The captain of the ship performed the worst possible maneuver while the sails were filled with wind when he cast loose the port bow anchor, driving her forward against a fluke of the anchor and punching a hole in her hull. As the forward compartments began taking on water, the pumps were started while Butler had soldiers run forward to the prow and back to the stern in a futile attempt to dislodge the vessel. As heavy supplies were dumped overboard in an effort to lighten the ship, the next full tide loosened the grip that the bottom had on the ship and she was floated out to deeper water.

With the *Mississippi* in need of repair, Butler had the captain set a course for Port Royal where he hoped, with the navy's assistance, to have her punctured hull patched. She was escorted by the USS *Mount Vernon,* which provided a young naval officer to act as a pilot for the *Mississippi*. The ship lay in Port Royal Sound from March 2 through the 13th, where her hull was patched with tarred oakum, rosin, canvas, rubber, and boiler iron, while the army troops were drilled onshore. Once most of the leak had been stopped, the vessel once more was readied for her trip to Ship Island. Disregarding the advice of the naval officers present, the captain of the *Mississippi* backed the ship away from the wharf under her own power, and promptly rammed her rudder against a submerged shell bank. This was followed by the parting of her tiller rope, which resulted in the ship running on shore a half a mile from the wharf, where she was once again stuck until the following day, when a team of naval vessels jerked her free at high tide.[23]

By this point in his voyage, Butler had seen, and felt, enough of the dubious abilities of the captain of the *Mississippi*. A board of inquiry was convened and the captain promptly ousted, replaced by a navigator from the navy for the remainder of the journey to Ship Island. As the New England general finally approached the island, he could see above the billowing white sand the tents of his advance contingent fluttering in the Gulf breeze like white caps. Ship Island's harbor was crowded with naval craft when, as if a final insult of the sea to Butler, the *Mississippi* once again proceeded to run amok. Sarah Butler recorded the event of her arrival at Ship Island:

> It is rather funny the trouble we have with the ship. In the first place the pilot undertook to take her up to the wharf, which is, you see, but a little thing, and by the time we were up, the wind was blowing furiously. They did not dare to fasten to it — she would have carried all away, so after holding there a while, she swept away, and in her backward movement caught a brig by the rigging, tangled it all together, knocked some wood from her bow, and held fast. Thus we anchored. The next morning made all clear and they prepared to separate, the wind still blowing. As the brig tried to draw off, it gave a lurch, came in endwise, and ran her bow clear up on to our deck. There it hung, broken and dangling, like an elephant's trunk, hoisted into our rigging. Everybody on deck was in danger, with this great thing striking in all directions, yet nobody could help laughing, and besides we expect anything now. At last, with pulling and cutting, they tore it away, and we started again on our adventures. This time we rushed madly at the "Black Prince," which was anchored a little farther on, knocked her out of her moorings and tore at her rigging. Then we plunged at another ship, the "Wild Gazelle," caught and grazed her, scattered a few splinters, and stood out into the harbor, and anchored apart from the other vessels.[24]

Butler held his troops onboard the *Mississippi* for several days, both because a Gulf storm made landing them difficult and because he was unsure when he would have to proceed to the Louisiana deltas. Butler was relieved when Farragut returned to Ship Island from scouting the approaches to the Mississippi River some three days after his arrival and advised Butler that he had not yet managed to drag his heavy naval ships over the bar into the river, allaying Butler's fears that his own adventures onboard the *Mississippi* had delayed the navy from their part in the expedition. As a gesture of good will and cooperation, Butler loaned Farragut 1,700 tons of coal that he had secretly ballasted onboard his ship to sell at a profit in Boston upon the ship's return, and dispatched his brother Andrew to Havana, Cuba, for a fresh supply. An incredulous Farragut inquired of Butler, "But how can you in the army let the navy have the coal? Your army regulations are against it, are they not?" Butler's response was typical of the old Massachusetts attorney; "I never read the army regulations, and what is more, I shan't, and then I shall never know I am doing anything against them. If the navy uses the coal for the benefit of the government, I, as a lawyer, know that the government will not get the pay for it out of me."[25]

In New Orleans, Major-General Lovell was still feeling as if the Union presence on Ship Island was nothing for him, or the Richmond authorities, to become alarmed about. On February 27, 1862, Lovell sent this dispatch to the Confederate secretary of war regarding a possible land attack on New Orleans by Union forces:

> Raw troops, with double-barreled shotguns, are amply sufficient to hold our intrenchments against such troops as the enemy can send to attack them. Besides, I regard Butler's Ship Island expedition as a harmless menace so far as New Orleans is concerned. A black Republican dynasty will never give

an old Breckinridge Democrat like Butler command of any expedition which they had any idea would result in such a glorious success as the capture of New Orleans. He will not have 10,000 men for a demonstration by land upon any of the Gulf cities.[26]

With Butler's donation of coal paving the way for smooth relations between the army and navy leadership in the expedition, Farragut turned over to the army several small craft for use as lighters. Butler, in turn, sent one of his army engineers who had worked on Forts Jackson and St. Philip for five years prior to Louisiana's secession, U.S. Lieutenant Godfrey Weitzel, to the mouth of the river to provide useful information regarding the construction of the forts that Porter's mortar schooners were preparing to bombard. Butler also had carpenters hard at work on Ship Island preparing small boats and scaling ladders to be used in the event the navy was unable to reduce the forts and a general assault would have to be made by the army. For moving his troops from Ship Island and into the Mississippi River, Butler had counted on the services of the *Constitution*, which had earlier brought the advance contingents of his force to the island. It was with great dismay that Butler learned the frugal General Phelps, alarmed at the discovery that keeping the vessel at Ship Island was costing the government $2,500 per day, had sent her back to New York. To compensate, Butler pulled together the sailing schooners in which Captain Paul George had shipped horses and supplies to the island, and formed them into trains of emergency transports that could be towed by his steamers.[27]

The day of his arrival at the island, Butler appointed his brother-in-law, John M.G. Parker, as the official postmaster of Ship Island. Parker, who was also an officer in a Massachusetts regiment, had served as a postal employee in Massachusetts prior to the war. Operating his post office from a tent, Postmaster Parker soon had a straight-line handstamp made out of type from a printer's case which was used for a small newspaper entitled *Soldier's News-Letter* that the troops stationed on the island were publishing. Several sutlers on the island sold patriotic envelopes and adornments to be used in sending mail back home to loved ones, some bearing eagles, shields, and portraits of the regimental leaders.[28]

If Butler's voyage to Ship Island had been anything but perfect, Farragut had also been confronted with a multitude of problems upon, and since, his arrival at the island on February 20, 1862. The gunboat *Sciota*, which had been detached to Farragut's river squadron, was found to

Flag Officer David Glasgow Farragut (courtesy of the Library of Congress).

be barely serviceable. The mammoth *Colorado* was in need of a new mainmast, and the *Richmond* and *Pensacola* were still en route to join his expedition. Porter, who had been expected since mid–February, had not communicated his whereabouts to Farragut, but instead had contacted Secretary Welles to advise that he was at Key West, Florida, waiting to collect the balance of his mortar flotilla. Worst of all, Farragut had been confronted with what would prove to be a formidable opponent to his goals in the form of that Louisiana staple known to all river navigators in the New Orleans region: mud.[29]

The lower delta of the Mississippi formed a long, watery arm, flanked by mud and swamps that spread out at Head of Passes, dividing into five branches as it entered the Gulf of Mexico: Pass à l'Outre, Northeast Pass, South Pass, Southwest Pass, and Southeast Pass. At the entrance to each pass was a bar formed by the enormous deposits of mud made by the Mississippi River. Farragut soon realized that he had a tremendous job on his hands to get his heavier ships across these bars. Only Pass à l'Outre on the eastern side of the delta and Southwest Pass on the western side could be used by deep-draft vessels, and traveling from one to the other required another forty miles of steaming by way of the Gulf of Mexico. Farragut hoped to use Pass à l'Outre rather than commit his ships to blockading all of the passes. Instead, Farragut ordered Captain Thomas T. Craven to take the *Brooklyn* up Pass à l'Outre, station her at Head of Passes, destroy the telegraphic communication with New Orleans, and send a detail with the Coast Survey to sound out and buoy the bars of the two main branches. Craven was also ordered to capture all the river pilots at the lighthouse stations. Upon Craven's discovery that the *Brooklyn* could not get into Pass à l'Outre, Farragut had departed Ship Island on February 23 to assess the situation in person, returning to the island several days later to await the arrival of Porter, Butler, and much needed coal for his ships. After spending an evening with Mr. and Mrs. Butler after their arrival at Ship Island, Farragut had drawn the conclusion that his army

Soldiers of the 41st Massachusetts Infantry onboard the USS *Northstar,* writing letters upon their arrival at Ship Island, Mississippi (courtesy of the Library of Congress).

counterpart was an intelligent man, but had no "plan of operation, but simply to follow in my wake and hold what I can take."[30]

Butler was also facing difficulties after his arrival at the island. The failure of the U.S. Senate to approve the commissions of his supply and commissary officers resulted in the replacement of Paul R. George with Captain J.W. McKim, but for many months after his arrival at Ship Island there was no replacement for his brother, Andrew. Having sailed to the island with Phelps and the first contingent of troops back in November before the Senate had vetoed his commission, Andrew was filling the two posts of quartermaster and subsistence officer. This, coupled with his brother being the commanding general of the Department of the Gulf, was causing many among the rank-and-file to raise eyebrows at the possibility of improprieties, prompting one captain to vent his feelings on the matter in his private journal:

> It does seem as though the expedition was put on foot to enable knaves and political demagogues in particular to rob the government in the most unscrupulous manner. Such things are truly disheartening. The men who have sacrificed home, friends, business, everything for the cause of their country are compelled to remain silent and see their energy, labor, and patriotism diverted from its true channel and applied to the unholy purpose of building up an old broken-down, worn-out political demagogue. In view of this, I am not surprised that men lose their energy and their devotion, that officers resign, that everybody grows sick and tired of the business.
>
> There are other evidences of lowered morale on Ship Island. Some of the men have absented themselves from drill without leave. Grumbling is widespread because orders to prepare to embark are no sooner given than they are countermanded. One day, recently, the line was formed five times and as many times dismissed. The men keenly resent the indecision and feel that they are being trifled with and as a result are losing much of their interest in the service, and this is not confined to the ranks alone....[31]

Pvt. Edwin B. Lufkin of the Thirteenth Maine Infantry made these recollections in 1898 of his time spent at Ship Island:

> Ship Island, which was used as a rendezvous by the British in the campaign against New Orleans in the winter of 1814, is five or six miles long and about half a mile wide. On the south side is a strip which is overflowed by the highest tides, and midway between the two ends of the island this low tract extends across to the north side. This tract, when dry, is smooth, level, and hard, thus forming an excellent drill-ground. The east end of the island, in 1862, was mostly covered with a forest of pines; while the only vegetation on the west end was a few scattered patches of sweetbrier, rushes and cactus. At the west end of the island, the channel was deep enough for the largest vessels; and near that end on the north side there was deep water so near the shore that only a short wharf was needed. On this desolate spot, where Butler's expedition for the capture of New Orleans was then organizing, our regiment found itself once more united. Drill, both company and battalion, was now practiced with energy and thoroughness; the island affording, to the fullest extent, the facilities which had been lacking in Augusta. There were also occasional brigade drills and frequent inspections; and about April 10th, after all the troops had arrived, there was a grand review.
>
> We soon learned by sad experience, that although the island, as a rendezvous, possessed conspicuous advantages, its only recommendation from a sanitary point of view was its pure air. The only water obtainable could be endured to avoid dying from thirst, but was not an enticing beverage. It was procured by digging wells from three to six feet deep in the sand. The water in these wells rose and fell with the tide; and, although it was called fresh, it had several distinct flavors, among which were those of salt, gunpowder, and creosote. At its best it was only fit for immediate use; for a bucket of it standing over night would develop an odor of such unspeakable vileness as ought to make it a powerful disinfectant. It had, however, the economic advantage that rendered the administration of cathartics by the regimental surgeons a decided superfluity.
>
> Unsuitable diet added to the discomfort of the troops. Owing to the season and to the long sea voyage, it was next to impossible to obtain fresh vegetables. The army rations were probably as good as could be obtained, but they furnished little variety and were sometimes damaged by salt water. During a portion of the time there was issued from the post bakery soft bread that was so excessively sour that but few of the men would eat more than enough of it to barely sustain life. Soon after it

began to be issued there could be seen on the north shore of the island a winnow of loaves which had been thrown away.

To the effects upon the troops of unwholesome water and unsuitable food, was added that of the heat, which during the latter part of the time we spent there, was almost unendurable. The island is not far north of the tropics, and, with an almost vertical June sun shining upon the dazzling white sand, not only was the heat like that of an oven, but the reflection from the sand was torturing to the eyes. In spite of all the efforts of the medical staff, the sick list of the regiment was frightful; and the percentage of deaths, as well as discharges, was large. Diphtheria, scurvy, fever, chronic diarhoea, and general debility, the latter greatly aggravated by homesickness, allowed the surgeons but little spare time.

Insect pests were numerous—individuals, if not species. Ordinary flies were very annoying, especially in the hospitals, where it seemed almost necessary to have an attendant to each patient in order to keep them out of the faces of the helpless invalids. Some of the regiments were badly troubled by fleas; the Thirteenth, fortunately, not among the number. This, however, could not be said concerning the Pediculus vestimenti, familiarly known among the soldiers as the "grayback." The clothing of the four companies which came from Port Royal on the Matanzas, had become populous with these despisable vermin; and from them, or from some other source, they were soon distributed through the regiment. About the only practicable way of destroying them was by boiling; and as, owing to scarcity of fuel, this could not be done as often as was necessary, one or more "skirmishes" became a part of the regular daily routine. The midges, or sand flies, were terribly annoying to the soldiers, especially while on dress-parade. As this ceremony took place at sunset, just when the midges were most active, it is to be feared that the thoughts of the soldiers, while standing at parade-rest, would sometimes need to be represented in point by a long row of dashes. The Great American Mosquito was there, both numerous and bloodthirsty; but they were found so much more numerous at our next station, that some of the old soldiers now cherish the fond delusion that there were no mosquitoes on Ship Island.

The duty required of the men was probably no harder than was necessary, and would not have seemed hard under favorable conditions; but it appeared severe to men enervated by the sudden change of climate and weakened by disease. As there were but few teams, nearly all the fuel had to be "toted" by the men from the upper end of the island. Most of our supplies had also to be carried from the wharf to our camp, a distance of nearly a mile; but a few weeks after our arrival a plank walk was built, which made that work much easier.

Drill usually occupied from four to six hours per day, while the heat and dampness of the climate rendered necessary a large amount of labor to keep the arms and equipments in respectable condition. There was a large amount of guard duty; three different guards being detailed, viz: a camp guard, a picket guard across the middle of the island, and a headquarters guard near the wharf. After about May 20th, when this was all devolved upon the Thirteenth by the departure of the last of the other regiments, each man on duty had to be on guard every other day. The fatigue began at the same time to be excessive, owing to there having been a large amount of stores collected there, all of which our regiment had to reload for forwarding to New Orleans.

For some time the fatigue duty seriously interfered with drill; so much so, that many days there were few men available for drill except those who had been relieved from guard duty in the morning. Several times some emergency required large details of men to work all night. About this time also, for several weeks there were forty men from the Thirteenth detailed on transport steamers, the crews of which were somewhat shorthanded. After most of the stores had been reshipped and the detailed men returned, the amount of fatigue duty was much reduced; and, to some extent, guard duty also, so that the regiment could pay much more attention to drill; and before leaving the island it attained such a state of discipline that Gen. Weitzel, after reviewing and inspecting it without any previous notice of his coming, said he had never seen a better regiment.[32]

Sensing the unrest within his command, Butler began gently prodding Farragut to make his move: "I am now ready to put on board ship six regiments and two batteries and will be able to be in the Passes in twelve hours."[33] By April 8, 1862, Farragut had seventeen of his vessels in the river and began to crystallize his attack plans on Forts Jackson and St. Philip. Years earlier, Farragut had seen the forts in person, on one occasion transporting a shipment of bricks to Fort Jackson. From Brigadier-General John G. Barnard, chief engineer of the Army of the

Potomac, who had worked extensively on the forts in conjunction with P.G.T. Beauregard, came detailed information, including the location of every barbette gun and casemate, right down to the howitzers bearing on the landface. Fort Jackson, a bastioned brick pentagon with scarp walls twenty-two feet high, surrounded by wet ditches, and fronts of one-hundred ten yards, mounted the heaviest guns and posed the greater threat to Farragut's fleet. With both forts being located along a bend in the river, Jackson lay on the southwestern bank with its heavy guns bearing down and across the river. Below a moat and facing directly downriver, a water battery mounting heavy guns had been dug to bear upon ships as they approached a bend in the river. At the heel of the bend, the river was almost seven hundred yards across, and from that point upriver a half-mile lay Fort St. Philip, an irregular quadrilateral building with a scarp wall fifteen feet high fronting the river. The guns of Fort St. Philip also bore mainly on the river and provided a perpendicular cross fire with the guns of Fort Jackson, with the combined fire of both forts covering three and a half miles of river. Though both forts were designed to mount a combined 189 guns, with 177 bearing on the river and 12 covering the flanks, Jackson mounted only 74 pieces, most of which were light 24- and 32-pounder smoothbores. Seven of its better pieces were placed in the water battery, and, along with a mixture of older cannon, several 8- and 10-inch Columbiads had been placed en barbette on the parapets. St. Philip mounted 52 guns, similar to but overall lighter than those of Jackson, bringing the total firepower of both forts to 126 guns, 63 less than they could accommodate. The forts were garrisoned by 1,100 troops that were a part of the coast defenses under newly promoted Brigadier-General Johnson Kelly Duncan, whose headquarters was at Fort Jackson.[34]

While the preparations continued to be made on Ship Island for the army's eventual role in the coming campaign against New Orleans, General Butler had the opportunity to flex his muscles somewhat against the officials at Biloxi, Mississippi. The small blockade runner *Black Joker* had foundered in a storm after sailing from La Habana with a cargo of coffee, sheet copper, paper, oil, and zinc, and the seventeen survivors, including a small 5-year-old girl named Alma Peniston, had been rescued by the armed schooner *Maria A. Wood* near East Pass, Santa Rosa Island. The survivors were first transferred to the blockade vessel *Vincennes*, before being transferred to the *J.P. Jackson*. Upon the arrival of the *J.P. Jackson* at Ship Island, these people were turned over to Butler's provost-marshal, and the young girl was brought to the headquarters of Butler, where Mrs. Butler bathed the child and mended her clothes. The general then had an aide, Major George C. Strong, escort the child to Biloxi under a flag of truce, where she was dropped off with the local postmaster to be reunited with relatives or friends. Upon returning to his boat, Strong discovered that the ebbing tide had stranded him in the town, and soon after nightfall he was confronted by a band of armed Confederates who threatened him with bodily harm by firing into the vessel. Upon hearing of the affront to his flag of truce, Butler issued this order to Strong on April 2:

> Major: Taking with you on board the steamer Lewis the Ninth Regiment of Connecticut Volunteers and a section of Captain Everett's battery, and acting in conjunction with the Navy, you will proceed to Biloxi, and demand and obtain an ample apology for the firing into a flag of truce upon an errand of humanity under your command upon the 1st instant.
>
> The apology must be an ample one, and you will demand and obtain a guarantee against such occurrences in the future, signed by the mayor, the principal inhabitants, and the colonel commanding the forces there.

The next day, Strong landed at Biloxi, escorted onboard the *Lewis* by the gunboats *New London* and *Jackson* and accompanied by the rowdy Irishmen of the Ninth Connecticut Infantry, where he delivered the following message to the mayor:

> Sir: I am directed by Major-General Butler, commanding the Department of the Gulf, to call your attention to the fact that on the 1st instant a party of men under my command, bearing a flag of

truce and on an errand of mercy, were fired into in a most cowardly manner while their schooner was aground and just after they had left your shore.

An apology was made by a person claiming to be an officer of the Third Mississippi Volunteers, but General Butler has ordered that the repetition of such or similiar outrageous action be the signal for the destruction of your town.[35]

Needless to say, Strong received his apology from the mayor, as well as several New Orleans newspapers that he confiscated for the intelligence on Rebel activities that they might contain. The April 5, 1862, edition of the *New Orleans Daily-Picayune* revealed the Confederate belief that New Orleans was impenetrable from attack below the forts:

> The Mississippi is fortified so as to be impassable for any hostile fleet or flotilla. Forts Jackson and St. Philip are armed with one hundred and seventy heavy guns.... The navigation of the river is stopped by a dam of about a quarter of a mile from above the forts. No flotilla on earth could force that dam in less than two hours. In a day or two we shall have ready two iron-cased floating batteries.... Each ironcased battery will mount twenty, sixty-eight-pounders, placed so as to skim the water, and striking the enemy's hull between wind and water. We have an abundant supply of incendiary shells, cupola furnaces for molten iron, congreve rockets and fireships. Between New Orleans and the forts there is a constant succession of earthworks.

After almost a week of final preparations, Farragut began to move his fleet up the Mississippi on April 14, and in two days he had all in position, including Porter's mortar flotilla, below the Confederate defenses. On April 17, the little mortar schooners were towed into position near the western bank of the stream just below the bend, where they were protected from view from Fort Jackson, some 2,850 yards away from the nearest mortar boat, by a thick woodland filled with interwoven vines. Porter's assurances to the Navy some four months previously that his bomb vessels could reduce Forts St. Philip and Jackson in forty-eight hours was now to be put to the test of battle. The next morning at 9:45 A.M., the crews of his flotilla opened their bombardment of the two forts. In conjunction with the mortar vessels, the gunboats *Sciota* and *Kennebec* roared into action, while the *Iroquois, Cayuga,* and *Wissahickon* were moved up

The "Ironclad Battery" CSS *Louisiana* (courtesy of the Department of the Navy, Naval Historical Center, Washington, D.C.).

by Farragut within range of the forts to draw the Confederate return fire away from the mortar boats. At long last, the active push for New Orleans was underway.[36]

While the preliminary bombardment of Forts Jackson and St. Philip was being launched by the mortar flotilla, Butler had most of his Ship Island troops onboard transports in the lower river, waiting in readiness to assault the forts if it became necessary. Farragut soon came to the conclusion that the mortars by themselves would be insufficient to reduce the forts and compel the surrender of the garrisons, as the return fire from Fort Jackson's casemate guns was undiminished in ferocity. On April 20, Farragut was growing impatient and increasingly concerned about the rapidly diminishing ammunition supply of the mortar schooners and decided to issue a general order for the fleet to pass up the river. On April 22, a reconnaissance detail which Butler had sent to scout the swampy area in back of Fort St. Philip returned to report that there were still no guns mounted on the landward side of the fort. This was the information that Butler was looking for, as he was now informed that troops might be brought from the Gulf in small boats through a tidewater channel known as Maunels Canal without being cut into pieces by artillery fire.[37]

At 2:00 A.M. on April 24, Farragut formed seventeen warships into a line of three divisions, with himself in the second onboard the *Hartford*. His ships, with protective chain cables hanging over the sides and their vulnerable internals protected by bags of sand and ashes, set out to run the gauntlet of fire between the two unreduced forts. Suddenly, the inky blackness of the early morning was broken by the flashes of Farragut's broadsides, which were responded to in kind by the guns from the forts while Confederate fire rafts and river steamers joined the melee. From his position on the deck of the *Saxon*, Butler and his staff watched the inferno of flame emanating from the river, which one of his aides described in vivid detail: "Imagine all the earthquakes in the world, and all the thunder and lightning storms together, in a space of two miles, all going off at once; that would be like it."[38] Though several of Farragut's rearmost ships failed to pass the two forts, the passage had been made by his squadron at a cost of 37 killed and 149 wounded, compared to 9 killed and 33 wounded in Fort Jackson and 2 killed and 4 wounded in Fort St. Philip. The Confederate river fleet had lost 73 killed and 73 wounded, though one of the wounded later died. Seventy river miles ahead lay a now defenseless New Orleans.[39]

Butler borrowed from Commander Porter the light-draft steamer *Miami*, in order to transfer the Twenty-Sixth Massachusetts from their transport that was lying inside the river below the forts and send them out into the Gulf behind Fort St. Philip. There they were transferred into thirty rowboats which they paddled into the swamps in back of the fort. Here the men, accompanied by Butler, waded in hip-deep water for the last mile and a half before reaching Quarantine Station, where they discovered that Farragut, after leaving the gunboats *Wissahickon* and *Kineo* near the station, had departed for New Orleans without them. Due to the flood stage of the river for the past month, Butler was able to completely block all communications by land between Fort St. Philip and New Orleans, and after ferrying several companies of troops across the river to the western bank, he cut off Fort Jackson also. The fate of the garrisons of the two battered forts was now sealed.[40]

Fearing for the safety of his troops that were still onboard the wooden transports in the lower river due to the formidable presence of the Confederate ironclad gunboat still at anchor under St. Philip, Butler sent a message to Brigadier-General Shepley at Ship Island instructing him to send all the small water-craft he could locate. Butler then proceeded up the river on the *Wissahickon* to confer with Farragut.[41]

Butler strangely found New Orleans at the mercy of Farragut's menacing warships, which were anchored in midstream with one broadside bearing on the city and the other threatening Algiers to the west, but her citizens boldly defiant. Farragut informed Butler that Mayor John

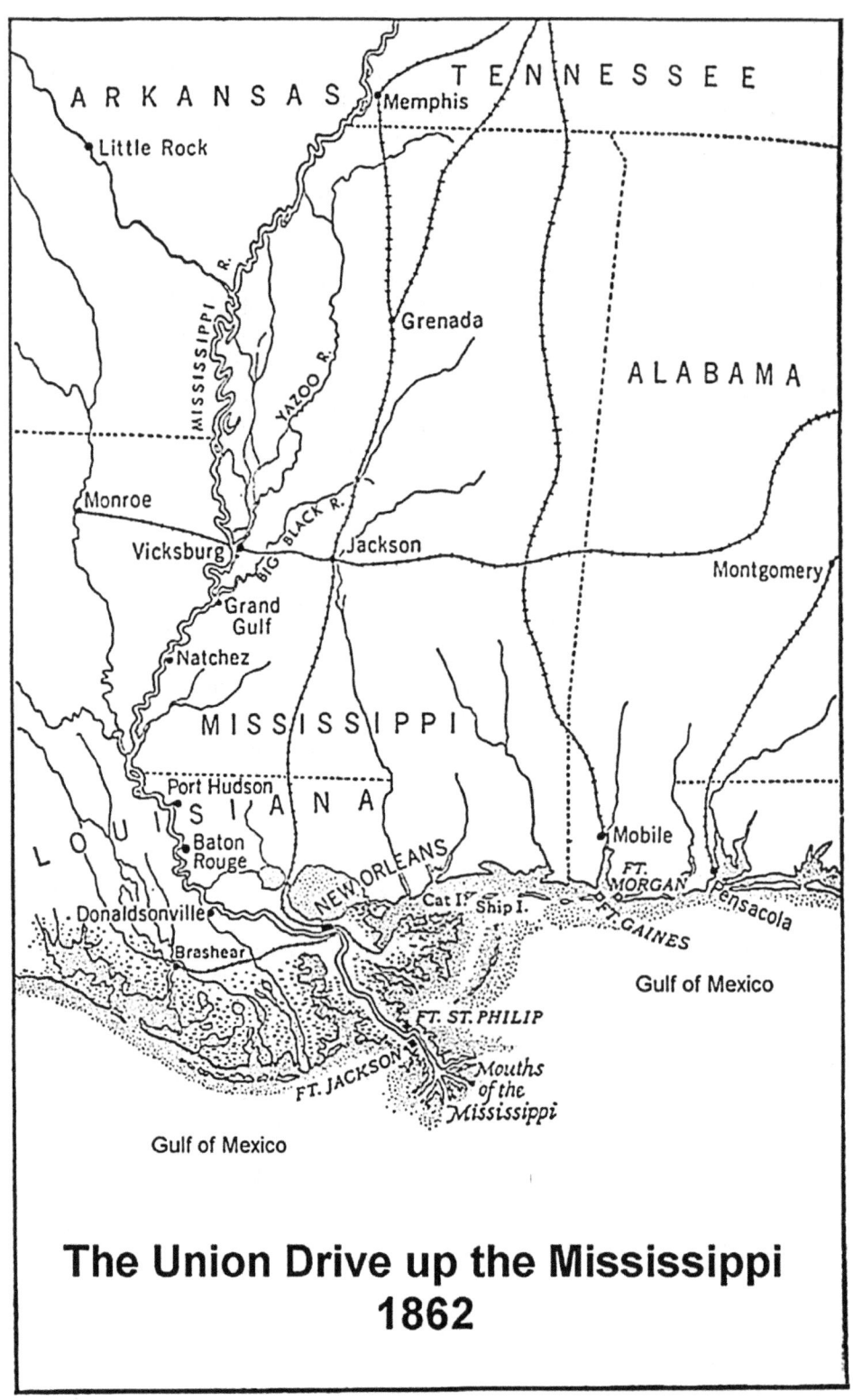

The 1862 Union drive up the Mississippi River (modified by Terry G. Scriber from an illustration at the Library of Congress).

T. Monroe, fearing mob violence and attempting to buy General Lovell time to evacuate Confederate government supplies and troops from the city, had declined to surrender New Orleans or haul down its secessionist flag. On April 26, Farragut sent ashore a contingent of seamen to hoist the Stars and Stripes above the United States Mint, which was located on the fringe of the French Quarter. The following day, a Sunday, while church services were being held throughout the fleet, four New Orleans citizens rushed onto the roof of the Mint and hauled down the flag. The New Orleans newspapers had praised the act, naming one William B. Mumford as the leader of the four.[42]

While this excitement was transpiring in New Orleans, events at the two forts below the city had finally reached a climax. Rebel troops inside Fort Jackson had mutinied, spiking their guns and surrendering to Butler's troops. On April 28, the officers of the two forts formally surrendered to Porter and his mortar flotilla, onboard his flagship, the *Harriet Lane*. Butler hurried downriver the following morning, where he then sent a message to General Shepley at Ship Island, instructing him to embark as many troops onboard the steamer *Tennessee* as she could accommodate and proceed to New Orleans. He was ordered to disembark the Twenty-Sixth Massachusetts at Fort St. Philip to serve as a garrison for the fallen fort, and to leave his most effective colonel in charge at Ship Island. Before departing the island, he was also ordered to organize a 250-man detachment to cooperate with the navy in taking possession of Fort Macomb, and to ensure that appropriate transportation from Ship Island to New Orleans was provided for Mrs. Butler, the horses belonging to the staff officers and artillery, and rations and forage enough to last thirty days. On May 4, the Twelfth Maine Infantry said farewell to Ship Island, followed by the Thirteenth Connecticut Infantry and First Maine Artillery Battery on May 5, and the Eighth Vermont Infantry on May 7.[43]

Back in the Crescent City, Butler had assumed military command of the defeated city that was now under martial law. He had also caught William Mumford, the man responsible for tearing down the Union banner from the U.S. Mint, and had him executed by hanging from a window of the same building. Butler's rule of New Orleans can only be described as ruthless and despotic, and many of the city's citizens would soon become all to familiar with the tiny island located in the Gulf of Mexico, as Butler began to use Ship Island as a place of exile and confinement for those who dared defy his iron-fisted rule, in addition to utilizing the stockade as a prison for Union military convicts.

On May 31, 1862, six Confederate parolees, dubbing themselves the "Monroe Guards," who were captured at the fall of Fort Jackson, were tried and convicted in New Orleans of conspiring to force their way through the Union picket lines in order to travel to Corinth, Mississippi, where they planned to join the forces of (Confederate) General Pierre Gustave Toutant Beauregard. Originally sentenced by Butler to die by firing squad on June 4 for violating their paroles, the six received a last minute commutation of sentence. Instead of being shot to death, the men were ordered "confined at hard labor upon the fortifications at Ship Island," during the pleasure of the President of the United States. The reprieved Louisianans were Edward C. Smith, Patrick Kane, George L. Williams, Abraham McLane, Daniel Doyle, and William Stanley. They were transferred from the Orleans Parish Prison to Ship Island on June 16, becoming the first Confederate prisoners of war to be confined on the island. These men are recorded in the roster of Confederate prisoners in this book.[44]

In the five weeks following the fall of New Orleans to Union forces, the troops on Ship Island had been slashed from sixteen infantry regiments, six artillery batteries, and a cavalry battalion to one regiment of infantry, the Thirteenth Maine, under the command of Colonel Neal Dow, who was now assigned the task of garrison duties on the island. Less than nine hundred officers and troops were forced to man as many posts as normally would be assigned to thousands. Three guard detachments were organized: a camp guard, a headquarters guard near the wharves, and a picket guard across the island midway between the camp and East Point. In addition, the New Englanders were called upon to load tons of stores and supplies that had been stockpiled on the island for shipment to New Orleans, and forty soldiers of the Thirteenth Maine were called upon to travel with the transport ships. During this time, Colonel Dow was promoted to brigadier-general to rank from April 28.[45]

On June 3, the monotonous life of garrison duty was interrupted by an order from General Butler, dated June 1, instructing General Dow to proceed to Pass Christian, Mississippi, located on the coast of the mainland, and arrest five prominent Confederate sympathizers, including the mayor of the town. Butler further ordered that these prisoners were to be taken to Ship Island as hostages, and word spread among their friends and associates that if any of the Union-leaning populace were further harassed in the town, that the five would be summarily hanged. At 2:00 A.M., Dow embarked six companies of the Thirteenth Maine on the steamer *Sallie Robinson*, whereupon, reaching Pass Christian at 7:30 A.M., the men marched into the city and stacked arms, while Dow gave a stern lecture to the available townspeople. Unable to locate the mayor, Dow then led his troops back aboard the steamer, crossing the bay and docking briefly at Shieldsborough wharf before returning to Ship Island.[46]

Despite the stern warnings issued to the citizens of Pass Christian, the Rebel harassment of the Unionists continued unabated, prompting Butler to order a second expedition to the town on June 21. Two hundred troops of the Thirteenth Maine boarded the steamer *Creole* and landed at the town before daybreak the following day, with instructions to seize a Mr. Hearn, who was the town's recorder, a local reverend named Sill, and a Mr. Seal, who were to be held as hostages. The *Creole* was then ordered to enter Bay St. Louis and sweep Confederate shipping from it and its tributaries. Upon arriving at the homes of the designated hostages, none of the three were to be found, prompting the New Englanders to seize Hearn's son-in-law and another man as replacements. The troops then reboarded the *Creole* and moved into Bay St. Louis, where they put a twenty-man patrol, guided by a Choctaw Indian, in small boats to ascend the Wolf River. Their goal was the capture of the captain of a local partisan ranger group who lived some ten miles inland. The *Creole* then proceeded to enter the Jordan River, where she took aboard a large number of refugees and Confederate cattle. She continued upstream until reaching the site of a ferry and, upon observing that the boat had been removed, the steamer reversed course and headed downstream. The crew, in observing a sawmill in the village of Saucier, a stop was made in order to send a party ashore to burn the mill. But before the men even got to land, a group of shotgun-armed partisan rangers fired on the vessel from ambush, delivering a second volley on the unsuspecting Union troops lounging about on the deck of the *Creole* before hastily departing the scene of the ambuscade.[47]

When fired upon, the steamer's helmsman had let go of the wheel while diving for refuge from the shotgun blasts, causing the *Creole* to ground. With no possibility of refloating the vessel before morning, a strong picket was shook out to protect against a night attack by the Confederates. On the morning of June 23, the steamer returned to Bay St. Louis to pick up the twenty-man patrol, where they reported that the object of their expedition had fled before their arrival, though they did destroy a large quantity of Rebel corn, flour, and hospital stores, in addition to liberating twenty head of cattle owned by the partisan ranger captain. By nightfall, the men of the Thirteenth Maine were back at Ship Island, but not for long. Between July 5 and the 11th, the garrison of the island was reduced to two Companies, D and F. The first to depart the island was Company C, which on June 5 was ordered to Fort Pike in the Louisiana Rigolets, followed that same day by Company K, which was ordered to Fort Macomb. They were followed on June 8 by Companies G, H and I, all departing for Fort Jackson, and Company A for the Quarantine Station. On June 11, Companies B and E departed for Fort St. Philip. Ship Island was now garrisoned by a skeleton force.[48]

Though Butler had reduced the Ship Island garrison immensely, he exhibited no inclination to cease populating the island with political prisoners opposed to his rule of the Queen City of the South. On June 28, while the funeral procession of a young Union lieutenant named George DeKay wound its way through the streets of New Orleans, women appeared in the streets wearing Confederate colors. As the procession passed the home of Mrs. Eugenia Phillips, the wife of a former U.S. Congressman from Alabama who had recently been imprisoned, and later

Butler's 1862 order sentencing New Orleans resident Mrs. Burkett to imprisonment on Ship Island (courtesy of a private collection).

> HEADQUARTERS DEPARTMENT OF THE GULF,
> New-Orleans, Aug. 31st 1862.
>
> Lieut Andrews
> Provost Sherriff
>
> The Maj. Genl. Comdg. having remitted the sentence of Mrs. Burkett you are hereby ordered to release her from custody and restore her baggage to her.
>
> By Command of Maj. Gen. Butler
> A. J. Enffer
> Lieut & A.D.C.

Butler's 1862 order releasing Mrs. Burkett from imprisonment on Ship Island (courtesy of a private collection).

banished, from Washington under accusations of being a Confederate sympathizer, she appeared on the piazza of her home, laughing loudly at the sight of the procession. Also emboldened by the news reaching New Orleans of Confederate military victories in the east was local bookseller Fidel Keller, who had displayed a skeleton in his bookshop window that he claimed was a Union soldier, with a sign around its neck reading "Chickahominy," implying he was a casualty of that recent battle. Added to the list of citizens determined to show their defiance to Butler's rule was local judge John W. Andrews, who had exhibited a cross in the Louisiana Club that he boasted was made from the bones of a Yankee soldier that had been killed by Confederate hands. On this day, Butler was upriver at Baton Rouge, Louisiana, though upon his return the following day he promptly ordered the arrests of the three.[49]

On Monday, June 30, 1862, the three made their appearances before Butler to answer the charges brought against them. The first to appear was Eugenia Phillips, who, when asked by the general if she had laughed and mocked Lieutenant DeKay's funeral procession as it had passed her residence, replied contemptuously, "I was in good spirits that day." According to fellow prisoner Marion Southwood, "While denying that her gayety had any reference whatever to the funeral ceremony, Mrs. Phillips refused to make any apologies or concessions to the vulgar tyrant." In a rage, Butler sentenced her as follows:

> Mrs. Phillips, wife of Philip Phillips, having been once imprisoned for her traitorous proclivities and acts at Washington, and released by the clemency of the government, and having been found training her children to spit upon officers of the United States at New Orleans, for which act one of those

children both her husband and herself apologized and were again forgiven, is now found on the balcony of her house during the passage of the funeral procession of Lieutenant DeKay, laughing and mocking at his remains; and, upon being inquired of by the commanding general if this fact were so, contemptuously replies, "I was in good spirits that day," It is therefore ordered: That she be not regarded and treated as a common woman of whom no officer or soldier is bound to take notice, but as an uncommon, bad, and dangerous woman, stirring up strife and inciting to riot. And that, therefore, she be confined at Ship Island, in the state of Mississippi, within proper limits there, till further orders; and that she be allowed one female servant and no more if she so choose. That one of the houses for hospital purposes be assigned her as quarters; and a soldier's rations each day be served out to her, with the means of cooking the same; and that no verbal or written communication be allowed with her except through this office; and that she be kept in close confinement until removed to Ship Island.[50]

Next to face Butler's wrath was Fidel Keller, who was promptly sentenced to two years at hard labor on Ship Island, with the proviso added that he be "allowed to communicate with no person on the island except Mrs. Phillips, who had been sent there for a like offense." Keller, unaware that the Mrs. Phillips to whom Butler was referring was Eugenia Phillips, and assuming he was referring to Mrs. Matilda Phillips, who was the proprietor of a well known local brothel, requested that "so much of it as associated him with 'that woman' might be recalled," to spare his wife's feelings in the event that it became common knowledge that he was associating with such a woman. Butler, unaware of the true motives behind Keller's request, promptly struck out that part of Keller's sentence relating to Mrs. Phillips.[51]

Last to appear in front of Butler that day was Judge Andrews, who Butler sentenced to two years in solitary confinement at hard labor upon the Ship Island fortifications for his crime of "exhibit[ing] a cross, the emblem of the suffering of our blessed Savior, fashioned for a personal ornament" which he had claimed was made from the bones of a Union soldier. He had "shown this too without rebuke in the Louisiana Club which claims to be composed of Chivalric Gentleman."[52]

Mrs. Phillips was accompanied to Ship Island by her white servant, Phoebe. As she stepped ashore from her journey to the island on a small boat, she described the scene that awaited her: "... was all covered with houses and looked comfortable enough. We soon left all evidence of population and came to a stretch of dead white sand and drift, of which pile upon pile looked like waves of sand. In the midst of this on the sand was a railroad passenger car, flat roof, not even a curve that might keep off the perpendicular rays of the sun.... Into this car Lieut. Blodget introduced me as my quarters."[53]

Lieutenant George Blodgett, who had escorted Mrs. Phillips and Phoebe to their quarters, departed after assembling her bed and mosquito bars. The soldier's rations which Butler had ordered to be their fare while imprisoned on the island were described as follows: Breakfast — four rolls, dried apples, and a "horrible mixture" which was called coffee, for which they received two tin cups to consume the beverage; Dinner — crackers and rice cooked together, with four biscuits and salt meat thrown in a tin pan. On July 6, Mrs. Phillips and Phoebe were relocated to a building that had served as the garrison post office, which was considered an improvement over their previous accommodations. Almost four weeks after her arrival on Ship Island, she recorded these thoughts in her journal relating to her incarceration on July 24:

... not been allowed a minute out of my room, no speech with anyone. None of the officers ... are at all anxious as to my existence. The severe storms alarm us, but shut up from the outer world no one would know what our extremities are, for the rain pours in on our bed, bedding and clothes. The sun rises and goes down, and this is all our knowledge of the outer world. The cook puts on the door sill a pan of spoilt beef and some doughy substance three times a day. The coffee being made of beans ... we cannot drink ... and the tea has given out. My only happiness is in looking for the boat to bring me letters. This happens once a week, and is a break in the sad monotony. It seems strange that Gen. Dow with all his inhumanity took away with him the best part of the men here. Since his departure new rules and orders have subjected us to utmost rigor and severity of military rules. For 18 *[days]* no one has come near us and exercise will not be allowed, and I ask no favors. Phoebe is even turned back if she ventures to empty the slops or sweep beyond my door. I dare not allow my mind to dwell any length of time on all these outrages. The amenities of life have certainly never been indulged in by these "Maine gentlemen."[54]

The July 11, 1862, morning edition of the *New Orleans Daily-Picayune* contained this interesting article of an incident that would soon see another citizen of the Crescent City ensconced on Ship Island:

Great Excitement on St. Charles St.

Attempt to Rescue a Female Prisoner — About ½ past 1 o'clock yesterday, St. Charles St. was the centre of an excitement which for a while threatened to become truly serious. It appears that a young and sprightly looking woman, whose name and social position we could not learn, had been arrested by two orderlies near Canal St. and accompanied by a policeman, they were conveying her towards the 1st District Lock-Up. After passing the Bank of New Orleans on their way up St. Charles St., the woman by word or gesture appealed for protection, when one or two persons suddenly attacked the escort, knocking down the policeman and one of the soldiers.

Therupon the cry of murder was raised, pistols were drawn, and Policeman Dunn fired at and thinks he wounded in the shoulder the pugilistic assailant. The man, however, escaped, wounded or unwounded, but several other persons were arrested for manifestations of hostility to the authorities, or approval of the unexpected act of intervention. The woman was in the meantime taken to City Hall — for she did not try to escape. Shortly afterwards she was conveyed down St. Charles St. in a carriage, and finally was lodged in the Parish Prison. It is said that she had a secession badge on her breast, which upon being noticed by a soldier, she threw at him a written slip of paper, announcing that McClellan had been defeated, and 40,000 of his army captured, accompanying the act of greatly insulting remarks.

The female referred to in the article was Anna LaRue, an attractive young lady who was the wife of local gambler John LaRue, who at the time of this incident was incarcerated in Fort Jackson on charges of murder. Mrs. Larue, while wearing a secession badge and dressed in Confederate colors, had begun passing out handbills on St. Charles Street that related the inaccurate information of the capture of (Union) General McClellan during the battles around Richmond, Virginia. Upon insulting a Union soldier, she was promptly arrested by a New Orleans policeman, who attempted to convey her to the mayor's office. Screaming for help, a riot ensued and the policeman was knocked from his feet, and a soldier attempting to intervene on the policeman's behalf was shot. The provost guard of the city hurried to the scene and dispersed the crowd, transporting LaRue to City Hall, where she verbally insulted General Shepley and pulled from her bosom scraps of paper on which were written "insulting epithets" addressed to U.S. government authorities. Upon questioning LaRue, Shepley had her transported to Butler's headquarters, where she was identified as the wife of John LaRue, prompting Butler to send for him. Upon responding, "I play cards for a living" to Butler's question as to his occupation, LaRue was committed to Orleans Parish Prison on charges of vagrancy. Mrs. Larue was sentenced to indefinite confinement on Ship Island, and ordered to be "kept apart from the other women confined there." LaRue was transported to the island to begin her sentence the same day, but was ordered released by Butler on August 3 upon her pledge of good behavior in the future. Upon passing Mrs. Phillips' quarters on her way to the Ship Island landing on August 6, Mrs. Phillips "called to her my 'adieux' and begged her to tell Gen. Butler I ... [am] still in good spirits."[55]

Though Butler relented on the confinement of Anna LaRue, he displayed no inclination during his tenure as commander of the Department of the Gulf to desist from sending unruly citizens to Ship Island. Another notable who was confined on the island was Alexander Walker, the editor of the *New Orleans Daily-Delta*, who was confined there on August 13 for daring to question Butler's policies regarding New Orleans. A month after his arrival, Walker wrote to Confederate President Jefferson Davis outlining his plight of being "consigned with seven other respectable citizens to a small hut fifteen feet by twenty, exposed to sun and rain, without permission to leave except for a bath in the sea once or twice a week." He also stated that as of the date of his writing, there were almost sixty prisoners confined in "portable houses and furnished with the most wretched and unwholesome condemned soldiers rations. Some are kept at hard work on the fort; several in addition to labor are compelled to wear a ball and chain which is never removed."[56]

A correspondent for the *New York Herald* seemed to confirm Walker's assessment of a bleak existence during the long summer months on Ship Island, penning this correspondence that ran in the June 2, 1862, edition: "Ship Island is a barren, sandy, arid waste, as a residence ... the thermometer from 85 deg. to 95 deg. in the shade, with the additional pleasure of having the walls of the wooden houses ornamented by a living cover of flies; reminding a person who is the unfortunate occupant that his house may move off some day by magical wings. There are millions upon millions of flies; men as well as animals are almost devoured by them."

On September 11, Butler ordered the release of Mrs. Phillips, provided that she vowed not to "give aid, comfort or information to the enemies of the United States" and took the U.S. Oath of Allegiance. Lieutenant-Colonel Henry Rust, Jr., who had replaced General Dow as the Ship Island post commander on July 11, reported that Mrs. Phillips "would not admit that her husband had ever asked a favor of Genl. Butler, or interceded in her behalf. She would have died in martyrdom rather than to have had him." When instructed by Rust to raise her right hand so that he might administer the oath, she complied but immediately dropped it to her side. Rust advised her that it would be necessary to keep her hand raised until the ceremony was completed, "and then assent audibly to the oath taken so that there might be no mental reservation." Rust recalled that she did eventually follow his instructions, but with "very bad grace." Nevertheless, on September 18, Mrs. Phillips, Judge Andrews, and another political prisoner named H.S. Traphagen returned to New Orleans onboard the steamer *Ceres*, at long last free of Ship Island.[57]

Though these are some of the more well-known civilians incarcerated on Ship Island during Butler's reign in the Crescent City, many more citizens were consigned to the island due to various infractions. They are recorded in the civilian prisoners section of the roster in this book. Also confined on Ship Island during this time, though in the stockade, were many Union soldiers who had been tried and convicted of a variety of offenses against the military code of conduct.

Butler's command of the Department of the Gulf officially came to an end on November 9, 1862, when Lincoln formally assigned command of the department to Major-General Nathaniel Prentiss Banks, another Massachusetts politician who had served as governor of the Bay State prior to the outbreak of the war. Banks and his staff sailed from New York City on December 4 onboard the *North Star*. They had been preceded by an advance contingent of troops that were to constitute additional forces for Banks' new command, and all were under orders to rendezvous at Ship Island upon reaching the Gulf. On December 11, the transports *Illinois* and *Che Kiang* landed in the Ship Island harbor carrying the men and equipage of the Fifty-Second Massachusetts Infantry, Eighteenth New York Battery, and fourteen companies belonging to the Twenty-Third and Twenty-Eighth Connecticut Infantries.[58] As soon as the soldiers were disembarked, the chaplain of the Twenty-eighth Connecticut, Richard Wheatly, gave this description of Ship Island in a letter home to his family:

Cartoon depicting Major General Benjamin F. Butler as the "Beast of New Orleans" (courtesy of a private collection).

This low sandbank is the creation of the restless Mexican Gulf. It boasts little vegetation. A few grasses, cacti, flowering herbs and shrubs, and some stunted pines, exhaust the list. Nor is the fauna more extensive than the flora. A dilapidated cow and an untimely calf, some splendid horses and refactory mules, ugly alligators, venomous spiders, and spiteful mosquitos would chiefly claim the attention of the naturalist. The encircling waves swarm with fish.[59]

The following day, the Twenty-Fourth Connecticut Infantry arrived onboard the *New Brunswick* at Ship Island, followed soon thereafter by the *S.R. Spaulding*, which disembarked the Twenty-Second Maine Infantry upon the island's sandy shores. On December 13, Banks arrived on the island accompanied by Brigadier-General Cuvier Grover and their respective staffs. After the cursory introductions and formalities were dispensed with, Banks asked Lieutenant-Colonel Rust to arrange a meeting between himself and the political prisoners confined on the island.[60] After the meeting, Banks reboarded the *North Star* and began his journey to New Orleans, where he arrived on December 14 before making his way to the residence of General Butler. It was here that he formally presented the "Beast of New Orleans" with his orders,

Major-General Nathaniel P. Banks (courtesy of the Library of Congress).

which read: "By direction of the President of the United States, Major-General N.P. Banks is assigned to the command of the Department of the Gulf, including the state of Texas."[61]

A bitter Butler lingered in New Orleans for a week to "assist" his successor in the transition in command. In his farewell address to "The Soldiers of the Army of the Gulf," Butler made reference to Ship Island: "Without a murmur, you sustained an encampment on a sand-bar so desolate that banishment to it, with every care and comfort possible, has been the most dreaded punishment inflicted upon your bitterest and most insulting enemies."[62]

At long last, Butler's stay on the Gulf Coast had come to an end, though he did leave an everlasting epitaph to the City of New Orleans that is still in existence today and seen by thousands of citizens and tourists each year. On the granite pedestal of the iconic statue of Andrew Jackson that sits in Jackson Square, in front of St. Louis Cathedral in the French Quarter, Butler had these words chiseled: The Union Must And Shall Be Preserved.[63]

The Prisoner-of-War Camp

> Confederate Veteran Magazine— *July 1930*
> No one could escape the thought of the men who endured the tortures of the damned on that bleak island, where not a single tree offers shade to the weary, and where all day long the hot sun poured its burning rays to the hot white sands that reflected glare and heat until men could endure no longer the agony of thirst and sun.
> — *Mrs. Rogers Winter, reflecting on a Confederate Memorial Service held at Ship Island*

As Banks was settling into his new job as commander of the Department of the Gulf, it was not long before he implemented changes to the Ship Island outpost. On Christmas Eve of 1862, Banks ordered seven companies of the Second Regiment Louisiana Native Guards to Ship Island to serve as the island's garrison, relieving all but companies D and E of the Thirteenth Maine from the tedious duty, who were ordered to remain on the barrier island. The Native Guards, comprised of "free men of color," had been mustered into the U.S. military on October 12, 1862, under Butler's command. Though all of the enlisted men and company officers, save for one, were Negroes, the regiment was commanded by Colonel Nathan W. Daniels, a Caucasian from Pointe Coupée Parish, Louisiana. On January 12, 1863, Colonel Daniels and his seven companies, consisting of B, C, D, F, G, I and K, arrived at Ship Island via the steamer *Morning Light*, where Daniels informed Colonel Rust that he was there to relieve him as post commander of the island. Due to Daniels bearing no official orders stating that he was to assume command, Rust remained on the island until January 20, when he boarded the steamer *Nassan* to depart for New Orleans. Sailing for the mouth of the Mississippi River at 4:00 A.M. the following morning, Rust recorded these thoughts regarding his departure: "Good bye Ship Island. My only regret at leaving is that I must leave my two companies there to the tender mercies of a colonel of Niggers which, if appearances are a true indication, will not be very tender."[1]

Colonel Rust's predictions regarding his Maine troops left behind on the island soon became reality as the New Englanders refused to recognize the black soldiers as equals, prompting Daniels to place most of the two companies under arrest for disobedience of orders on February 12. Daniels stated in a communication to General Banks that as the situation now stood, the Maine troops' services were "useless to the post," and asked that they be transferred to "some place where they thus could be of some avail to the govt.," and estimated that, in his opinion, the seven companies of Native Guards were ample to garrison the island. Banks, himself a New

Englander and no fan of Negroes in uniform, ordered the Maine soldiers to Fort Jackson. On February 13, they at long last departed Ship Island onboard the *New Brunswick*.[2]

Banks also began the process of releasing most of the political prisoners that Butler had imprisoned on the island during his tenure as commander of the department, with the last being released in the summer of 1863. Banks did, however, continue to use the island as a place of confinement for U.S. military personnel convicted of various offenses; it was also used by the U.S. Navy as a station for operations in the Gulf.[3]

The drudgery of garrison duty on the barrier island was interrupted on the morning of April 8, as the steamer *General Banks* arrived from New Orleans and tied up at the Ship Island wharf. They were quickly boarded by Colonel Daniels and a 180-man detachment of companies B and C from the Second Louisiana Native Guards and spent the night anchored off Horn Island before meeting up with the gunboat *John P. Jackson* at daybreak the following morning for a foray to the Mississippi mainland. The two Union vessels then charted course for East Pascagoula, where they arrived sometime in the mid-morning. With the *John P. Jackson* anchoring twelve hundred yards offshore to provide cover to the *General Banks* as she ran in alongside the wharf near the town, twelve troops under the command of Captain Charles Sauvenet secured the wharf while the remainder of the force entered a large frame hotel and unfurled the United States flag from its rooftop. Indignant Confederate infantry and cavalry swarmed the detachment, prompting a four-hour running battle in which the Native Guards repulsed several attempts to cut them off from the *General Banks*. After being apprised that Confederate reinforcements were arriving to annihilate his command, Colonel Daniels ordered his men back to the boat, when, as they were crowded on the wharf, a shell from a six-inch rifled cannon fired from the *John P. Jackson* fell short and exploded among the men, wounding five and killing four as they scrambled aboard the transport. The men also suffered two killed and eight wounded from their battle with the Rebels, but were able to bring off three prisoners and a Confederate flag before retreating in good order. This was one of the first engagements between black Federal troops and Confederate forces during the Civil War, and demonstrated to both sides in the conflict that black soldiers could and would fight, if given the chance.[4]

The euphoria of seeing his command conduct themselves so admirably in battle was short-lived for Colonel Daniels, who on May 3, 1863, was placed under arrest and ordered to face court-martial in New Orleans for "conduct unbecoming an officer and a gentleman, in grossly insulting an officer of the Navy, while in company with a lady." Lieutenant-Colonel Alfred G. Hall, commanding the three remaining companies of the Second Louisiana Native Guards that were stationed at Fort Pike in the Rigolets, was placed in command of Ship Island and its garrison pending the outcome of the court-martial. Daniels and his companion at the time of the incident, First-Lieutenant Elijah K. Prowty, were later convicted of the charges brought against them, and on August 27 the War Department issued a special order announcing they had been discharged from the army for "conduct unbecoming an officer and gentleman."

The incident stemmed from an encounter that Daniels and Prowty had with Lieutenant-Commander A.D. Perkins and his wife while the Perkins' were riding in a carriage in New Orleans. Prowty confronted the two and made the remark, "You say you are riding with a lady, but you are riding with a damned whore. You are a damned shit ass, and I room at 122 St. Charles Hotel and will repeat the same thing tomorrow morning." Daniels was apparently discharged for failing to restrain his adjutant from the verbal abuse heaped upon the Perkins family.[5]

Soon after assuming command of the Department of the Gulf, Banks ordered that the three regiments of Native Guards be reorganized, and a purge of the regimental officers be conducted, replacing most of the Negro officers with Caucasians. On May 1, he unveiled a plan to form a "corps d'armee of colored troops, to be designated as the Corps d'Afrique." The Second Regiment Native Guards was therefore redesignated the Second Regiment, Corps d'Afrique, and still assigned to garrison duty on Ship Island. The island was briefly used during July 1863 as a reception center for 1,376 paroled Union soldiers who had been captured by Confederate forces, though these parolees were transferred to New Orleans in August. On October 23, Banks also issued orders for the transfer of all prisoners held on Ship Island, whether military or civilian, to Fort Jefferson in the Dry Tortugas. Within less than a month, Banks resumed sending military convicts to serve their sentences in the Ship Island stockade, and the Second Regiment, Corps d'Afrique, assigned to provide a guard detail for the stockade.[6]

Andrew Sherman, who had been captured by the Confederates and subsequently paroled, had stopped at Ship Island in June 1863 on his way to rejoin his regiment, the Twenty-Third Connecticut Infantry. He described the island in a letter written during his short time there:

> When I tell you that this island on which we have been encamped since the first part of the month, consists almost entirely of fine, white sand, with scarcely a tree for shade or ornament, and with only here and there a patch of grass, you cannot doubt the propriety of applying the word "barren" to our present quarters. In this sand our tents are pitched, and on this sand, with a mere blanket for a bed, we lie, and sleep as best we can, with the various insects that minister to our discomfort. Our shoes are never free from the irritating presence of this sand. You may find it difficult to believe me when I say that from 10:30 A.M. till about 1:30 P.M. the sand is so hot from the sun's rays that an attempt on our part to walk in it with bare feet, as some of the acclimated natives do, will prove so painful as to deter one from a second attempt.[7]

On October 29, 1863, Colonel William M. Grosvenor was assigned command of the Ship Island garrison and outpost. Arriving from New Orleans on November 3 to relieve Colonel Hall, who was ordered back to Fort Pike, Grosvenor soon came into conflict with several of his subordinate officers. On March 27, 1864, several of the island's garrison were placed in the guardhouse for being intoxicated and disorderly. When they continued to create a disturbance, Grosvenor ordered two of the more rambunctious soldiers tied and gagged with a bayonet. Around midnight, the officer of the guard observed that one of the gagged men had became violently ill, and reported this to Colonel Grosvenor and Assistant-Surgeon John H. Gihon. Grosvenor ordered the soldier to be taken to the barracks, where he was examined by Gihon, who promptly ordered the gag removed from the remaining soldier's mouth. The following morning upon being informed of Gihon's actions, Grosvenor sent for Gihon, and upon his entrance into Grosvenor's quarters, Grosvenor screamed at the medical officer, "Who is commander of the Post?" Gihon's response that he had not intended to question the authority of the Ship Island commander only seemed to enrage Grosvenor even further: "Now you mind! If you, or any other Medical Officer ever again dare to interfere with any punishment that I may order to be inflicted, I will punish you, or him, in the same manner, and that within five minutes after, God damn you Sir, I will let you know that I command this Post!"

This incident was followed by a similiar outburst from Grosvenor on the morning of April 12, 1864, when the roll was beat for battalion drill and Adjutant F. Burchmore sent his orderly to advise the musicians to desist due to the fact there would be no drill this morning. Soon thereafter, Grosvenor entered Burchmore's quarters and demanded, "Adjutant, how is this? What is the reason those drummers don't come along?" Upon explaining his actions to the colonel, Grosvenor fell into a rage, exclaiming, "By what authority do you countermand a standing order, Sir?" Burchmore's response of, "If I have done wrong, it was unintentional" only further inflamed Grosvenor's exploding temper. "By Jesus Christ! I will put you under arrest! God damn you, Sir, I will let you know that I command this post. Damn you! Don't say a word to me! By God you are too God damn lazy to attend to your business!"

Grosvenor's abuse of his subordinates abruptly came to an end on May 4, 1864, when he was formally court-martialed in New Orleans on the charge of verbally abusing Assistant-Surgeon Gihon regarding the March 27 incident, as well as keeping "a woman, not his wife, by the name of Belle Fisher" in his quarters on Ship Island. Grosvenor pleaded guilty to the charge involving Mrs. Fisher, but not guilty to the charges brought by Gihon. Nonetheless, Grosvenor was found guilty on all charges and dismissed from the service, though President Lincoln abrogated the sentence on August 3, 1864. Grosvenor, however, never returned to Ship Island. Once more, Colonel Hall was recalled from Fort Pike to assume command of the Ship Island outpost and garrison, until being relieved by the new post commander, Colonel Ernest Holmstedt, a German immigrant, on June 27, 1864.[8]

The Ship Island garrison was once more reorganized on April 4, 1864, as the Second Regiment, Corps d'Afrique, was redesignated the Seventy-Fourth United States Colored Infantry, in accordance with the policy of the War Department to standardize the designations of the large numbers of African descent regiments that had been organized to serve in the war. Accordingly, all of the regiments were to be designated by a number, followed by their respective branch of service, such as United States Colored Infantry, United States Colored Cavalry, or United States Colored Heavy Artillery. On July 24, 1864, the Seventy-Fourth U.S. Colored Infantry was consolidated with the Ninety-First U.S. Colored Infantry, stationed at Fort Pike, in order to bring the regiment up to its authorized troop numbers. Accordingly, companies F, G, H, I, and K of the Seventy-Fourth were assigned to garrison Ship Island, companies A, B, and C assigned to Fort Pike, and Companies D and E stationed at Fort Macomb.[9]

There was also a reorganization underway of the U.S. Department of the Gulf, following General Banks' disastrous Red River Campaign in the interior of Louisiana that had ended in complete failure. On May 8, 1864, Lincoln appointed Major-General Edward Richard Sprigg Canby to command the newly created Division of West Mississippi, which encompassed the Department of the Gulf and the Department of Arkansas, effectively stripping Banks of his military authority. Banks learned of Lincoln's decision when Canby arrived at Simmesport, Louisiana, on May 19 to assume command.[10]

In response to increasing escapes from the facilities in New Orleans that were designated to hold Confederate prisoners of war, Canby issued orders on October 3, 1864, creating the Union controlled prisoner of war camp on Ship Island. These orders stated that "all prisoners of war, now confined in the city New Orleans, with the exception of those who are too sick to be moved, and those for whose immediate exchange arrangements have already been made, will be transferred, with as little delay as possible, to Ship Island, Mississippi." The prisoners were to be housed in tents until such time that barracks could be erected on the island, though this was never done, and the different classes of prisoners were to be segregated. Captain Matthew Randall Marston was ordered to the island to superintend the arrangements for the reception of the first prisoners, and on October 5, 200 Rebels were moved from the Union Press Building at 28 Carondelet Street in New Orleans to the steamer *Warrior* for the voyage to the barrier island. The fifty tents that had been ordered to accompany the prisoners onboard the *Warrior* to provide shelter on the island were delayed by a combination of bad luck and miscommunication within the Quartermaster Department, prompting the Confederates to be housed in the elements on the sandy beaches upon their arrival on October 7. That same night, a fierce storm descended upon the island, causing the prisoners to spend their inaugural night on the island in miserable conditions. The following day, Colonel Holmstedt had approximately 20 sick prisoners moved into a roofless barracks as a temporary expedient, though Surgeon Gihon warned that many of the Rebels would soon become ill and die if accommodations were not soon provided. Finally, on October 13 the 50 tents, as well as 3 hospital tents, arrived, and the prisoners were able to shelter themselves from the brutal Gulf of Mexico elements.[11]

Ship Island's prisoner population continued to increase throughout October 1864, with the arrival from New Orleans of 817 noncommissioned officers and privates on the 21st and 23rd, followed on the 25th and 28th with 53 noncommissioned officers and privates and 159 petty

Second Louisiana Native Guards at Ship Island, Mississippi (courtesy of C.P. Weaver).

officers seamen from the Confederate navy, bringing the total to 1,292 by the end of October. Orders were given to Colonel Holmstedt by the U.S. Commissary-General of Prisoners that no clothing was to be issued to the Confederates, except in cases of extreme need, as long as the prisoners had clothing sufficient for their "present wants." Prisoners were to be allowed to purchase religious tracts, and ministers loyal to the U.S. were to be permitted to conduct Sunday worship services within the prison camp, provided the men so desired, and any seriously ill men in the camp hospital could, if they so desired, be visited by a member of the clergy. Any prisoners who did not wish to be exchanged or had made an application to take the U.S. Oath of Allegiance were to be allowed to remain on the island.[12]

One of the Confederate prisoners of war transported to Ship Island was John A. Bragg, a landsman onboard the CSS *Selma* that had been captured at Mobile Bay on August 5, 1864. Bragg witnessed the sinking of the USS *Tecumseh* by a Confederate torpedo, and recalled that the crew of the *Selma* took off their hats and cheered at the sight. The *Selma* surrendered to the USS *Metacomet*, and the marines onboard the *Selma* were ordered to be chained hand and foot by the master-at-arms and sent below decks. Upon discovering this act, the commander of the *Metacomet* immediately ordered the chains removed from the marines and that they be brought above decks, and he severely reprimanded the officer who had given the order. The *Metacomet* then moved down to where the U.S. fleet was anchored, where the prisoners of the captured vessel were placed onboard a transport and carried to New Orleans. The captured Confederates were held in a makeshift jail converted from an old cotton press, before again being placed aboard a transport for their journey to Ship Island. Below is Bragg's postwar account of his imprisonment on the island:

> On our landing at the wharf at Ship Island—I can not give the date from memory—we were met by gangs of insolent negro soldiers off of duty, who jeered us with oaths and such remarks as, "Bottom rail on top now." Some even laid their hands upon us, but were thrust back by our white guards, who threatened to run them through with their bayonets if they molested us. We were marched about half a mile to our prison camp, which was prepared for us about half a mile southeast of the wharf. On our way we passed by the headquarters of our prison commandant, which was situated on a ridge, and some three to four hundred yards beyond was our camp, which was a square about

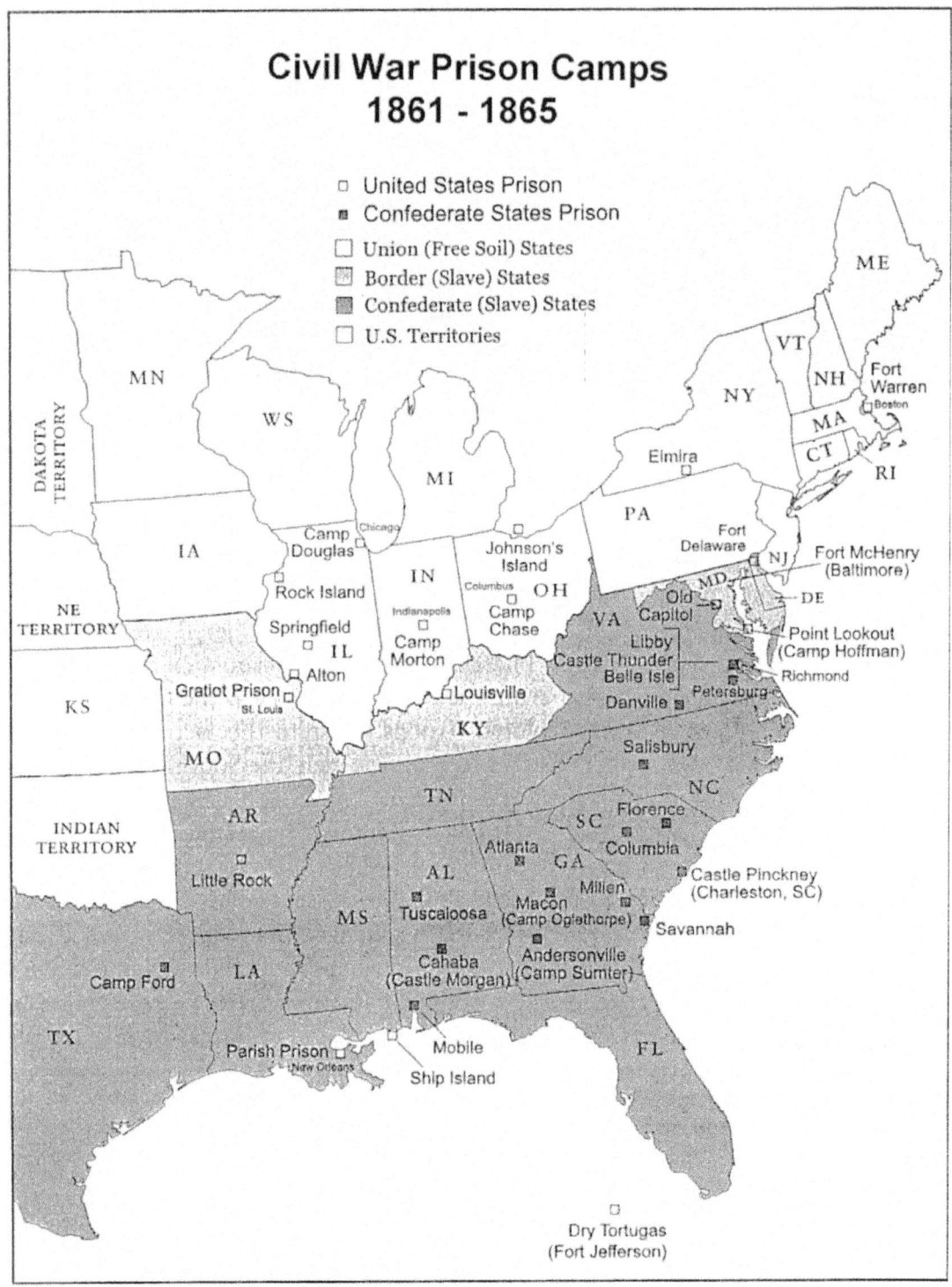

Courtesy of the Library of Congress.

three acres in area. It was enclosed on the four sides by an embankment about 2 feet high, on which our negro prison guards walked and kept watch over us. The dead line was on the inside, a small bank thrown up about a foot high and about twenty feet from the sentinel's walk, about every 20 yards. We were furnished with small A-shaped tents but were given no blankets. Most of us, however, had blankets, which we spread upon the rush grass which we gathered and placed on the ground under our tents. The men of the *Selma* and the *Tennessee* were encamped together, and as we were Navy men, we were better off in the way of clothing than the majority of prisoners on Ship Island.

The tents of all the prisoners were in lines fronting the north. The kitchen was on the south side of the square but subsequently to the northwest corner, and a short distance from it. Our rations were issued twice a day and consisted sometimes of mush made of moldy corn, very bad smelling, sometimes of worm-eaten crackers, with a small amount of boiled beef or bacon, and it of the most unsavory quality. The crackers were so full of worms, that at first I would pick out the worms with my knife, but found that when this was done there was very little left of the crackers. So in my desperate hunger, I finally threw away all my squeamishness, shut my eyes, and ate my crackers regardless of their contents. This is a fact as to our food, which I never think about but with the most revolting sensations of disgust.

We had no fires in our prison camp, and many of the prisoners had no blankets and but little clothing. As the Navy men were better off in the way of clothing, we did not suffer so much. The wood we brought was used exclusively for kitchen purposes. Not being permitted to have fires, we could have no hot water to kill the vermin which swarmed over us and almost ate us up alive. I have often killed the lice by running the blade of my knife over the seams of my clothes, which was the favorite harboring place of these loathsome vermin. Our condition was miserable in the extreme. We moped about all during the day, and passed the cold nights upon our beds of rush grass. Our wretched condition was aggravated by the brutality and insolence of our negro guards. During the night the least noise or movement in any of the tents would invariably draw their fire. We had several miles to go after our wood and it was a task to bring it back, subjected as we were to the coercion of our negro guards. On our return, let a wood-carrier be a little slow, and he would be cursed by a negro guard, who would as likely as not at the same time strike him with his gun.

One of the negro guards at Ship Island, known as Old Frank, was a devil incarnate. He would often push or strike a wood-carrier with his gun, so as to jostle his load against the man in his front. Every time he did this, Old Frank would curse the "damned Rebels, Bottom rail on top now." A white officer sometimes accompanied the guard on these wood-carrying trips. With one solitary exception, these officers made no efforts to check the brutal acts of the negro soldiers. The solitary exception was an Irish lieutenant named Poliet, who whenever he accompanied the wood-carriers, would permit no negro tyranny, but always treated the prisoners with humanity. And he was in fact the only white officer on Ship Island from the Col. commanding down of whom this can be said. So let this be said in memory of at least one generous enemy on Ship Island.

Colonel Holmstedt, the commandant on Ship Island, was certainly not an honorable man, as the circumstances which I am going to relate will prove.

After being on Ship Island for a month or so, I wrote to my father to send me some provisions. He received my letter, and he and my uncle John Southall filled a large box, much larger than a dry goods shoe box, with supplies consisting of two hams, two shoulders, one middling, several bushels of sweet and Irish potatoes, with a considerable amount of cake. The potatoes were in the bottom of the box, separated from the rest by a partition. In course of time, a flag of truce boat arrived and on it was the box for me, besides other boxes and articles sent by parents and friends to other prisoners on Ship Island. The boxes on being landed were carried to Col. Holmstedt's headquarters, and placed on the porch of his house. The next day we were visited by an officer and all having boxes were notified of the fact and ordered to report to Cl. Holmstedt's quarters. As soon as we got there, we saw the colonel sitting on the porch smoking a cigar, with some negro soldiers nearby. One of the negroes was ordered to open my box, which had my name on it. He did so, and took out all the hams, shoulders, the middling, and the cakes, which he laid on the floor, then removing the partition, he began taking out all the largest and best potatoes. Col. Holmstedt now asked to whom the box belonged. On my telling him that I was the owner, he told the negro to give me the box and the potatoes that were left in it, and let me be satisfied with them. I and one of my comrades George Holly filled our hats and bosoms with the potatoes and returned to our quarters, leaving Holmstedt with the lion's share of our property. He acted in a similiar manner with all the other prisoners, appropriating nearly all their supplies, allowing only a small amount to each owner.

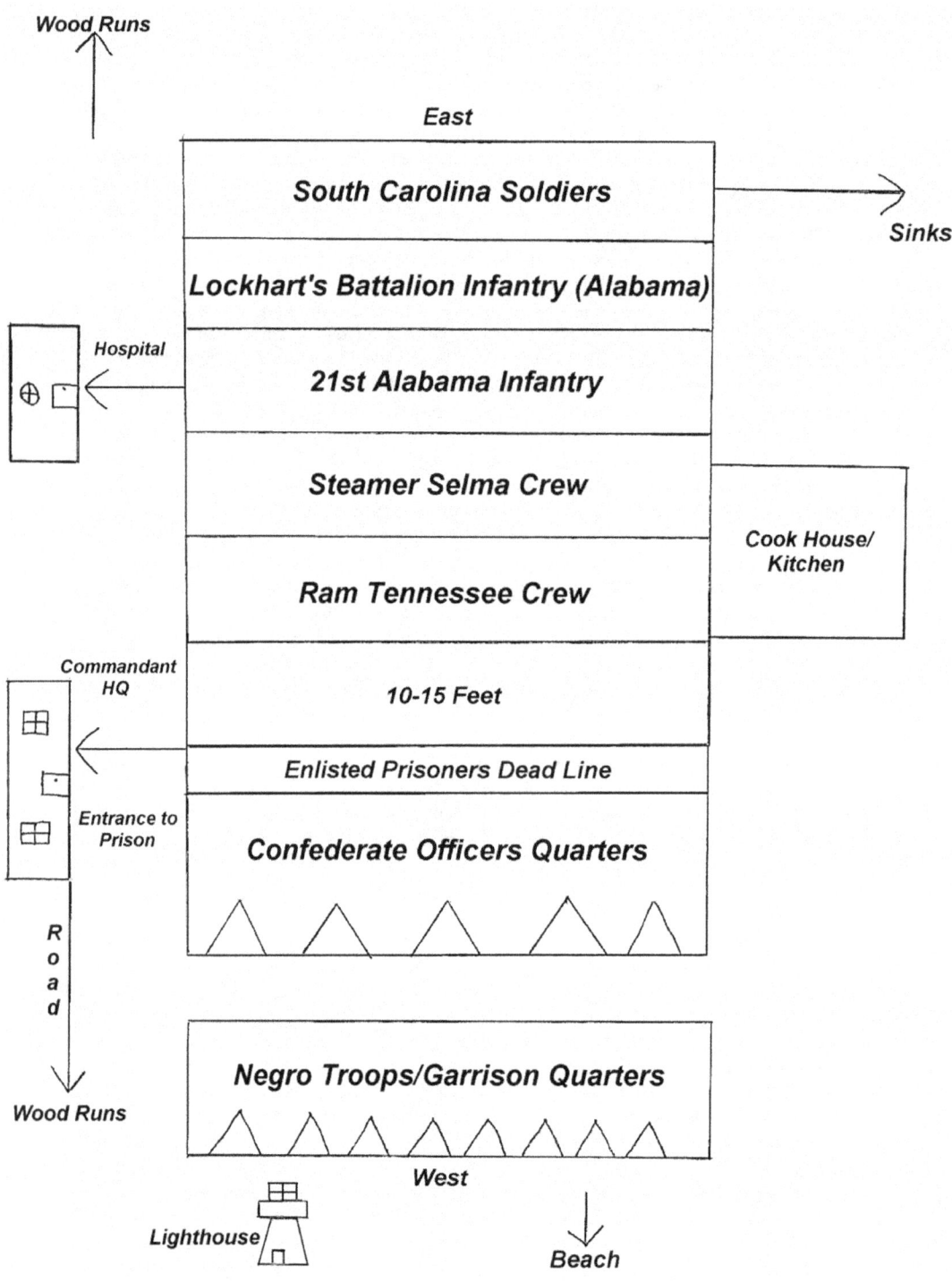

Diagram of the Ship Island prisoner of war camp in late 1864 (modified by Terry G. Scriber from an illustration at the Alabama Department of Archives and History).

Ram *Tennessee* (courtesy of the Department of Navy, Naval Historical Center, Washington, D.C.).

Steamer *Selma* (courtesy of the Department of the Navy, Naval Historical Center, Washington, D.C.).

I remember a boy of sixteen belonging to Lockhart's Battalion to whom his parents had sent a box containing four large cakes and the half of a canvas ham already cooked. When the boy's name was called he stepped forward and the negro opened the box, took out the cakes and ham, and laid them on the porch. Holmstedt ordered the negro to cut one of the cakes in two. When this was done, he said to the negro, "Half it again." He then ordered one of the quarters to be given to the boy. When the disposition of our supplies was ended, we were dismissed to our quarters, whither we went carrying with us the bounty graciously bestowed to us by Col. Holmstedt. The Lockhart boy was so disappointed that he cried bitterly. Such was the infamous action of our prison superintendent, who doubtless supposed robbing prisoners of war no crime, as "Rebels" had no rights which he was bound to respect.[13]

On October 29, the acting medical inspector for the commissary-general of prisoners, Surgeon F.M. Getty, conducted an inspection of Ship Island and its facilities relating to the Confederate prisoners' conditions. Huge deficiencies were noted in some areas, while others were deemed to be satisfactory. Among the deficiencies reported by Getty were the following:

Tents— Kind: canvas— Quality: bad — Condition: much worn.
Vegetables and Pickles— Kind: none.
Men — Morale: not good — Sanitary Condition: not good — Personal Cleanliness: not clean.
Surgeons— none.
Asst. Surgeons— one.
Chaplain — none.
Sick — Condition: not good — Cleanliness: not clean.

Nursing — How performed: indifferent.
Diseases — Prevalent: diarrhea, intermittent fever, scurvy.
Recovery from Diseases or Wounds — tardy.
Hospital Discipline — Bad.
Hospital Washing — How Performed: not attended to.[14]

Upon reviewing Getty's report concerning Ship Island, the U.S. War Department forwarded a copy to Colonel Holmstedt for explanation, with an emphasis on the reports of scurvy among the Rebel prisoners, and calling for him to detail the measures he was taking to bring this dangerous scourge under control. An angry Holmstedt and equally angry Gihon responded that Surgeon Getty had arrived on the island shortly after they had received a large number of prisoners from New Orleans who had arrived without notice and without tents. Until recently, the prisoner meals had been cooked outdoors due to the fact that "not a board of lumber, not even for coffins," could be procured, forcing the prisoners to carry their firewood on their shoulders for a distance of three and a half miles, with only about ten percent physically able to perform this function. Surgeon Gihon was without the means to establish a prison hospital to care for the sick prisoners, as there were no cots, blankets, or bedding available. Only 300 of the prisoners were reported to be in good health, with the remainder afflicted by smallpox, measles, dysentery, diarrhea, rheumatism, and various fevers, with most of the deaths occurring among the prisoners resulting from pneumonia, consumption, and malarial fevers. Holmstedt further responded by pointing out that many of the captured who were imprisoned on the island were men that the manpower-depleted Confederacy had assigned to garrison various forts, and consisted of boys from 11 to 16 years of age all the way to men of 50 to 75 years: "Many of them were so feeble and emaciated that it was necessary to carry them from the boats to the encampment, and it did not require the judgment of a medical officer to foresee a large amount of mortality." Holmstedt assured the War Department that in the three weeks since Getty's inspection, steps had been taken to provide the ill-stricken with bed and blankets, and the scurvy outbreak had been curtailed with the introduction of a vegetable and acid diet.[15]

In mid–October 1864, Lieutenant-Colonel W.D. Smith of the One-Hundred Tenth New York Infantry inspected the Ship Island garrison, consisting of Companies F, G, H, I, and K of the Seventy-Fourth U.S. Colored Infantry, and the Confederate prison camp. Smith found the garrison's discipline, arms, drill, clothing, and equipment to be in good condition. He also found the manner in which the garrison handled their guard and picket duties, with two guards mounted daily and one picket posted, to be satisfactory. Detailed to guard the 200 Confederate prisoners that had been received on October 7 were one officer and 38 enlisted men, while one officer and 43 enlisted men guarded the U.S. military convicts, the two wharves, and the commissary and quartermaster depots. In addition, a picket was established on the eastern end of the island consisting of a sergeant, 3 corporals, and 9 privates who were relieved weekly, with signals in place to communicate with the regimental headquarters.[16]

Upon his return for a follow-up inspection some ten weeks later, Smith found the garrison of the island to still consist of the same companies of the Seventy-Fourth U.S. Colored Infantry, which numbered 15 officers and 405 enlisted men present, though the average daily number on sick call were 2 officers and 40 enlisted men. Also, out of the 420 aggregate were an average total of 1 officer and 60 men on daily detail as teamsters, cooks, carpenters, and harbor crew. The Confederate guard detail consisted of one officer and 59 enlisted men to guard the more than 1,100 prisoners, with three guard shifts commanded by a corporal. The detail was posted with 5 inside the prison camp, 4 on each end of the camp, 2 on the beachside, 1 at the hospital, and 1 stationed at the guard quarters to monitor the arms. In addition, there was an officer-of-the-day, two sergeants-of-the-guard, and the shift corporal. The camp and picket guard consisted of 1 officer and 55 enlisted men, who were designated to detail eleven posts consisting of the guardhouse, the quartermaster wharf, the magazine, the commissary and quartermaster warehouses, the service magazines, the post headquarters, Batteries D, G, E, and F, and the U.S. military convicts in the stockade. The remainder of the men manned a picket line 1 mile east of the Confederate prison camp and 1½ miles from the post headquarters.[17]

In his official report on Ship Island, Smith determined that, in his opinion, the 1,130 Confederate prisoners were allowed too much freedom. Anywhere from 10 to 12 Rebel officers were paroled each day with the "privilege of the middle portion of the island which embraces their own camp officers' quarters and as far as the Sutler establishment." Also, the enlisted prisoners were sent in groups of 10 to 12 to visit the sutler, and were able to learn far too much regarding the island's defenses. At the post headquarters, several prisoners were being used as clerks by Holmstedt, and had "become acquainted with everything relating to the Post." Smith was concerned that in the event the clerks were exchanged, they would be able to detail weaknesses in the island's defenses to the Confederate authorities. The colonel also made a recommendation that, in addition to the 39 U.S. military convicts imprisoned in the stockade that were used to coal and unload ships, an additional 60 to 100 be sent there from Fort Jefferson in the Dry Tortugas and put to work on the island.[18]

Smith also submitted in his report a detailed inspection of the Ship Island sand batteries. Batteries A and B each mounted a 100-pounder Parrott that were positioned as pivot guns and could be brought to bear on any section of the island, as well as its approaches. Battery C boasted a 9-inch Dahlgren that was in a wretched condition, with the eyebolts missing, the shoe riding on the rail, and the platform rotten. As a result, the gun could not be run in and out of battery without a reinforcement of the gun crew. Battery D, also mounting a Dahlgren, was found to be in a similiar state. Battery E also consisted of a 9-inch Dahlgren, with the eyebolts pulled loose from the platform, the shoe resting on a rail, and the traverse wheels bedded into a rotten traverse circle. Batteries F and G, both mounting 9-inch Dahlgrens, were found to be in a similiar state of disrepair. Near Fort Massachusetts, the two 9-inch Dahlgrens in position on rotten platforms had "tipped up side wise."[19]

Prior to Smith's arrival on Ship Island for his second inspection in January 1865, reports had reached U.S. Major-General Gordon Granger, the commander of the U.S. District of South Alabama headquartered at the now conquered Fort Gaines, that the Confederates were constructing a substantial number of flatboats and launches along the Gulf Coast between Cedar Point, Alabama, and East Pascagoula, Mississippi, to possibly invade Ship Island and liberate the Confederate prisoners there. To further heighten Granger's concerns, Commodore James Palmer of the U.S. Navy had informed him that the Rebel prisoners were "guarded by a daily detail from an aggregate force of 240 colored soldiers, without a field battery, with an unfinished fort mounting two heavy guns pointing seaward, and with an old sloop of war [*Vincennes*] in the harbor scarcely available for

Pvt. Joseph Henry Ryan of Tarrant's Alabama Artillery Battery (courtesy of the Friends of the Tarrant Family, Taylorsville Community, Tuscaloosa County, Alabama).

immediate defense." Consequently, Granger voiced his concerns to General Canby's headquarters regarding the "insecurity of Ship Island with its present garrison and insufficient means of defense as a rendezvous for prisoners." Canby responded by ordering his commander at New Orleans, Major-General Stephen Augustus Hurlbut, to reinforce the Ship Island garrison. On January 4, 1865, Hurlbut ordered the Second Ohio Battery of Light Artillery, encamped at Greenville, Louisiana, "to proceed as soon as possible with its guns and a full supply of ammunition" to the barrier island. Departing on January 7, the battery boarded a steamer en route for their new assignment, arriving there the following day. The Ohioans would remain on the island until July 1865, after the conclusion of the war.[20]

On February 1, 1865, the U.S. commissary-general of prisoners ordered that the food ration for the Ship Island Confederate prisoners be decreased to the following allowances daily:

(Pork or Bacon, in Place of Beef)—10 ounces.
(Salt or Fresh Beef)—14 ounces.
(Flour or Soft Bread)—16 ounces.
(Cornmeal, in Place of Flour or Bread)—16 ounces.
(Beans or Peas, in Place of Rice or Hominy)—12½ pounds per 100 rations.
(Rice or Hominy, in Place of Beans or Peas)—8 pounds per 100 rations.
(Soap)—2 pounds per 100 rations.
(Vinegar)—2 quarts per 100 rations.
(Salt)—2 pounds per 100 rations.

The new regulations further stated that coffee, tea, and sugar were to be issued only to the sick and wounded prisoners, at the discretion of the attending surgeon, every other day. The allowance for this was 12 pounds of sugar and 5 pounds of ground coffee, or 7 pounds of unground coffee or 1 pound of tea per 100 rations. Dried potatoes or mixed vegetables could be substituted for the beans, peas, rice, and hominy in the aforementioned quantities, though the vinegar, salt, and soap rations could be altered only by order of the post commander if he deemed them insufficient to prevent disease.[21]

Though tensions were high between the white Confederate prisoners and their black guards on Ship Island, only two shooting deaths resulted at the hands of the Negro troops, with two widely varying accounts of the incidents. The first of these occurred on December 15, 1864, and involved 16-year-old Private Joseph C. Dunklin of Lockhart's Battalion Infantry. In Colonel Holmstedt's December 19, 1864, report to Brigadier-General H.W. Wessels, the commissary-general of prisoners, he furnishes the Union version of events:

> HEADQUARTERS, Ship Island, December 19, 1864
> Brig. Gen. H.W. WESSELS

Commissary-General of Prisoners:
  Sir: I have the honor to report the shooting of Private J.C. Dunclin, of Lockhart's battalion, prisoner of war at this post, by a sentinel, Private George Rice, Company K, Seventy-fourth U.S. Colored Troops, on the 15th of December, 1864. A thorough and immediate investigation was ordered as soon as the case was reported to these headquarters. The cooks for the prisoners of war have repeatedly complained about being unable to attend to their duties if not protected from the annoyances of other prisoners of war, who crowded around the cook-houses in violation of existing orders. On the 15th day of December, 1864, Private J.C. Dunclin, aforesaid, being one of a party who persisted in cooking some victuals for himself at the cook's stove, in spite of repeated warnings from the sentinel whose duty it was to prevent it, the corporal of the guard, Robert Perkins, of Company K, Seventy-fourth U.S. Colored Troops, was called, and for the time caused the annoying parties to leave the stove; but they soon returned, and sentinel Private George Rice left his post and told them he would "waste no more time in telling them to leave," and returned to his post, from where he again ordered them to leave, but Private J.C. Dunclin, of Lockhart's battalion, obstinately persisted

to disobey, when Private George Rice, of Company K, raised his gun and shot him dead. As much as I regret the occurrence of this affair, I can attach no blame to Private George Rice, who only carried out the orders of his superiors in not allowing any resistance to the performance of his duties. George Rice, of Company K, Seventy-fourth U.S. Colored Troops, is a trustworthy soldier, and the shooting of Private J.C. Dunclin, prisoner of war, has had a good effect on the surviving, undisciplined crew.

Very respectfully, your obedient servant,
ERNEST W. HOLMSTEDT
Colonel, Commanding Post[22]

The Confederate version of events differs hugely from the account given by Holmstedt in his official report of Dunklin's shooting. The most prominent was Confederate nurse Kate Cumming's account of the shooting that was related to her by a prisoner who witnessed the killing. The following is her journal entry relating to the incident:

> Joseph Dunklin, a Pvt., of Co. K, Lockhart's Battn., aged 16 years, was shot dead by a Negro soldier, at half-past 3 o'clock P.M., December 15, 1864, on Ship Island, under the following circumstances:
> Dunklin had been sick and was recovering. A lot of sweet potatoes (which were a rarity to us) had been sent by the citizens of Mobile to the prisoners; the little fellow thinking he would like one roasted, asked permission of the sentinel then on duty to cook it on the stove, which permission was granted, (this always being done after regular meals had been served up). The sentinels in the mean time were changed, and he went near the stove, and asked the cook to please give him the potato. As the cook was in the act of handing it to him, he saw the sentinel cocking his gun, and aiming it at the little boy; the cook said to him, "Look out, he is going to shoot!" and immediately the sentinel fired, shooting him through the heart, and killing him instantly. He then loaded his gun again, remarking, "I have killed one of the damned rebels, and I'll kill another if I can get a chance!" Not a word of precaution was given Dunklin before the sentinel fired except by the cook, and all he could do then was to draw his shoulders up and was immediately killed. Dr. Robinson was immediately sent for, and said, "This boy has been brutally murdered, and he intended to report it immediately." He entered the death on his hospital record, "shot dead by a sentinel." The sentinel said that orders were given him by Lt. W.C. Abby, 74th U.S.C.I., then officer of the guard, to allow no one to go to the stove but the cook. Colonel C.D. Anderson, 21st Alabama Regiment, demanded an investigation, but was told by Colonel Holmstedt, commanding the post, that this was a right that "prisoners of war could not demand!!"[23]

The other shooting of a prisoner by a sentinel involved a Texas prisoner, Sergeant Edward H. Inzer of the Ninth Texas Cavalry (Dismounted) on the evening of April 23, 1865, soon after the assassination of President Lincoln. Due to the fact that Holmstedt neglected to file the report required by the commissary-general of prisoners, the only versions of the event are those provided by fellow Confederate prisoners. According to fellow prisoners William A. Gibson and James A.P. Braxley, who claimed to be eyewitnesses to the incident, Inzer went to the door of his tent to shake the sand and dust from his blanket, when the sentinel inquired as to what he was doing. The Texan replied, "I am only shaking the dust out of my blanket." The sentinel then fired his musket, killing Inzer instantly. It is assumed that the sentinel thought the Texan was signaling for an escape attempt.[24]

In Kate Cumming's journal, she continued to record the hardships faced by the Confederate prisoners held on Ship Island. While in Mobile on January 7, 1865, she discovered that the men of the 21st Alabama Infantry who had been captured at the fall of Fort Gaines had been exchanged and were now at their homes recuperating. She was told that while held on the island, the soldiers had "received shocking treatment at the hands of their jailer." She recorded these entries in her journal on January 8 regarding her visit with Sergeant S. Henry Griffing:

> Today I visited a friend, Mr. Henry Griffin, one of the Ship Island prisoners, and a member of the 21st Alabama Regiment. I never saw such an emaciated frame as his. He is completely prostrated from disease and starvation. Many of our men who were captured when the Mobile forts were taken

were sent to New Orleans and then from thence to Ship Island. They were placed under Negro guards, and every possible indignity heaped upon them. They had to walk many miles for every stick of wood they used, and if they showed the least disposition to lay down their load, they had a bayonet stuck into them by the guard. When sick, they were put on straw right on the ground, and Mr. Griffin says, on putting your hand down with a slight pressure, the water would gush up. When I listened to this recital, and thought of the humane treatment I had seen their men receive, my blood boiled with indignation. Our surgeons would not allow a nurse of anyone to say an unbecoming word to them; and many a time while in Chattanooga, I have received the strictest orders concerning what I must prepare for them. Surely these wrongs will benefit our people, and stimulate them to more exertion than ever before. I think that is why they are allowed. I have been told by more than Mr. Griffin, that a lad named Dunklin from Alabama, was shot dead by a Negro guard while putting a potato on the stove to cook.[25]

The harsh conditions of confinement on Ship Island were attested to after the war by James A.P. Braxley, at the age of 60, himself a former prisoner on the island. The following is his statement regarding his experiences after being captured at the fall of Fort Blakely, Alabama:

Early in 1864, I enlisted in Co. B, 63rd Alabama Regt. We first went to West Point, GA, then to Mobile, thence to Spanish Fort, and last to Blakely, where we were captured April 9, 1865. Two days after our capture we were put on board of a boat and carried to Ship Island.

Captain Edward Christopher Columbus Tarrant of Tarrant's Alabama Artillery Battery (courtesy of the Friends of the Tarrant Family, Taylorsville Community, Tuscaloosa County, Alabama).

We were marched out some half a mile or more where our prison camp was made in the form of a square. Here were a large number of Confederate prisoners, some having been there long some time before our arrival. We were surrounded by negro guards, who took an increasing delight in heaping upon us all manner of offensive language. We had no tents. Our rations consisted of 3 crackers and a piece of beef issued to each man in the morning and three crackers and a cup of soup in the afternoon. The crackers were full of worms and the entire ration was insufficient to satisfy the craving of hunger, the meat and soup ill-smelling and badly prepared. This we might have endured for the week we remained upon the island, but the negro brutality was the most unforgivable offense of our prison life, to say nothing of the curses they heaped upon us at all times, in season and out of season. More than all was their murder of the prisoners. While I was there, two prisoners were killed without any cause or provocation. One killed one morning, the other about sunset in the afternoon. I can not recall the particulars of the first, but I was an eyewitness of the killing of the last, who belonged to some command whose camp was immediately next to that of our regiment. This man about sunset, had picked up his blanket, went to the door of his tent, and began to shake the dust out of it, when he was shot dead by one of the negro sentinels. Nothing whatever was done to the negroes for the murder of these two men. The murderous actions of the negro sentinel were always to be dreaded. We never knew at what time they would fire at any of us. There was between our quarters and the sentinel's watch a small slough of water, to which some of the prisoners would report in the morning to wash their hands and faces. One morning, while thus engaged, one of the prisoners was fired at, the ball just missing him. For fear of being shot, we prisoners thence ceased to report to this slough. No action was taken with regard to this murderous action of the negro sentinel.

The sinks for the prisoners were some little distance from the camp, and a prisoner reporting thither was, by the prison regulations, always accompanied by some one of the supernumerary guards. Here was another opening for negro diabolism. It often happened that when a prisoner was going thither accompanied by a guard, amid a volley of oaths, he was called back by a sentinel and cursed for being too slow in going to the sinks. "Now you damned Rebel, you get upon that barrel and mark time till I tell you to get off. Bottom rail on top now, damn you." There were generally a number of empty barrels about the camp. Upon one of these the prisoner was forced to mount and then mark time, often for an hour, or at least until the murderous officer of the negro sentinels was satisfied. Now these are verifiable facts and can be testified to by those still living.

Now all such and similiar facts in regard to the barbarity of negro soldiers on Ship Island can be testified to by surviving Confederate soldiers who served any time of imprisonment on the island. There positively, so far as could be seen, was no effort made by the white officers in charge to control the negroes. They let them do as they pleased to shoot, to kill, to torture, to do anything to gratify their malignant hate of the Southern white man.

At the expiration of a week we were carried to New Orleans, thence put on a boat, went to Vicksburg, thence to Meridian where we were paroled.[26]

Braxley, along with well over 3,000 other Confederate soldiers, was captured in early April 1865 at the fall of Fort Blakely and Spanish Fort along the Alabama Gulf Coast to the forces of General Canby, who had launched a campaign on March 17, 1865, with the goal of capturing Mobile. On April 2, 1865, Colonel Holmstedt logged into the record of prisoners at Ship Island 8 prisoners captured at Fort Gaines. The following day, 281 Confederates were captured by Major-General Frederick Steele's column in its thrust from Pensacola to Pollard, and these men

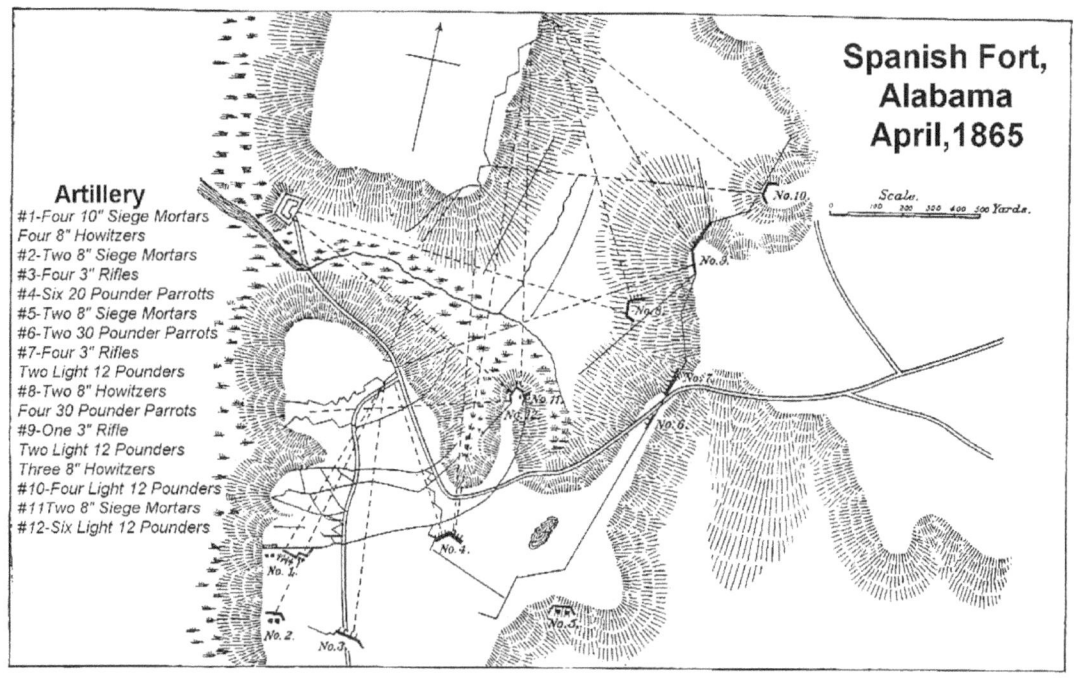

Modified by Terry G. Scriber from an illustration at the Library of Congress.

also were sent to the island, followed the next day by 37 more prisoners. On April 8, the troops of Federal XIII and XVI corps captured Spanish Fort, resulting in 562 prisoners being added to the burgeoning prisoner count on the island. This was nothing compared to the haul made at Blakely on April 9 by the same Union corps of 206 officers and 2,850 enlisted men from the Confederate army, which further swelled the prison population on the island.[27]

Alden McLellan, a lieutenant in the Missouri Brigade, was captured at Blakely and sent to Ship Island also, and recounted his experience after the war:

> On April 9, 1865, my services with the Confederate army terminated at Blakely, Ala., on the Apalachee River, about fifteen miles from Mobile. I was with the 1st Missouri Brigade, under Capt. A.C. Danner, brigade quartermaster. The brigade then was about four hundred men, and was commanded by Col. Elijah Gates, under Brig. Gen. F.M. Cockrell. We left Mobile on March 24, 1865, by boat. After arriving at Blakely, our command went out several times, but did not have any serious engagement. On the 28th of March our works were invested by a strong force of Federals, and the siege was on. During the night of April 7 Spanish Fort was evacuated, the garrison coming to Blakely through the swamps and taking boat to Mobile. Then the whole Federal forces, about twenty thousand, attacked Blakely. Our works extended in a half circle about three thousand yards, each flank on the river. We had about twenty-seven hundred men, many of them the old and young reserves, from Alabama; these last occupied the right of our works. The Missouri and other troops occupied the center and left.
>
> About 5 P.M. on Sunday, April 9, 1865, the attack was general. The Missouri troops were sent to the left on two occasions to help repulse some negro troops attacking there. About this time the Federals came over the works on our right and moved down toward the left. When we saw this, many made their way to the river; but there was little or no means of escape except in a few old boats and on planks, by which means about one hundred and fifty men escaped. About this time I was at the field hospital, being detained by the surgeon in charge (I forget his name) to assist in amputating the leg of a wounded man, which I was required to hold above the knee. The delay was prolonged because of the time it took to get the man under the influence of chloroform.
>
> As soon as I was relieved the hospital steward and I made a run for a wharf to get planks to escape upon, I throwing down four planks. The steward took two, and I ran down to get my planks, but another fellow was floating off on them. By this time the Federals were on the bluffs of the river, about two hundred yards off, and were firing at every object in the river. Some of the shots struck quite near me. I concluded not to take a plank ride just then, and was busy fastening a twenty-dollar gold piece in the lining of my cap and dropping my watch into my bootleg when a Federal called out: "Say, you fellow with a green shirt on, come up or you will get hulled [shot] next time."
>
> I obeyed, making my way to the bluff where others of our men were. In a short while a Federal corporal with one man took another officer and me and started for the rear. When we got to the works, there were several explosions. Some of the incoming victorious troops had got upon the subterra shells that we had placed in front of the works and were more or less injured. They talked very ugly toward us, so our guard had us sit down a little on one side until the troops had passed. On our way to the rear we stopped at a wagon train, and our guard got us some coffee and crackers. While there a Federal abused us for being Rebels, etc. Our guard told him to stop; but he did not until the guard gave him a slap, which rolled him over, and told him to go off and attend to his mules. We were then taken to where the other prisoners were bivouacked for the night. The next morning we started for Greenwood on the east shore of Mobile Bay. After going about three miles, we were countermarched into the abandoned Spanish Fort, which was under fire of one of our batteries in the marsh toward Mobile. (Since I have learned it was Battery Gladden, in charge of our late Maj. Ed Durrive.) After remaining in the fort awhile, we were again started for Greenwood, and the next day were shipped by transport to Ship Island, off the coast of Mississippi.
>
> The troops captured at Blakely were the 1st Missouri Brigade (Col. Elijah Gates), the Alabama Boy Reserves (General Thomas), part of Holtzclaw's Brigade, Barry's Mississippi Brigade, 1st Mississippi Light Artillery, and several light batteries; also Gens. St. John Liddell and F.M. Cockrell — about twenty-seven hundred men. *[After his arrival at Ship Island]* We were corralled on the sand just below the lighthouse and the men next behind us, all under negro guards. When we landed, we were halted, and the men were passing a short distance from us when a tall Arkansan held up his hand and called out to his captain: "The bottom rail is on top." The nigger guard made a lunge at

him with his gun, the bayonet striking the man's hip, and the man jumped, pressing his hand to his hip.

The limit, or "dead line," of our camp was a low ridge made by scraping up the sand. The men had no protection from the sun or rain; the officers had small A tents. The rations were bad and the water bad, as we got only the seepage from barrels sunk in the sand three-fourths of their length. The wood we had to bring two and a half miles from the east end of the island.

While on the island the news came of the assassination of President Lincoln. This was an unfortunate thing for the Southern country, and we felt the effects of it at once, the guards treating us very badly, abusing and shooting us whenever an opportunity offered. One night a man stood up to shake the sand from his blanket and was shot. Capt. J.W. Barklay, of the 1st Missouri Cavalry, and I were preparing a meal by a pile of sand that we had fixed for the purpose, and the Captain was telling of something that had occurred to him before the war. He used the word "niggers," and immediately the guard who was passing and heard the word commenced abusing us for calling them "niggers," and he made such a noise that the officer of the guard and the others of the guard came to him. Then we left and went into our tents and lay down until the fuss was over. I received a box from home containing a pair of pants and a blanket, which I was much in need of, and other small things, some of which were taken before the box reached us.[28]

Private William A. Gibson of the Thirty-fifth Mississippi Infantry–Co. H was also captured at Blakely on April 9, 1865, and recalled his time as a prisoner of war on Ship Island after the war. Below is his account of his imprisonment on the island given from his home in Columbus, Mississippi:

In April, 1861, I enlisted in Company H, 35th Mississippi Regiment, C.S.A, and followed the fortunes of this regiment until, with the entire brigade, was captured at Blakely in April, 1865.

After our capture, we were marched down to the beach, and the next morning were put on board of a ship which landed us the next day on Ship Island.

Upon landing we were marched some hundred yards to a narrow point on the island, surrounded by water on the east, north, and west, where our camp was laid off in the form of a square, of about five or six acres. A small trench, which was the dead line, was made all around the square, and near this dead line at certain intervals, negro guards were stationed. Our sinks were near enough to the beach to be cleansed by the rising of the tide, but the odor was very bad during the day.

In this square for near a month we had to endure our prison life, every day subject to the insults of our negro guards, for negroes were the only kind of Yankee troops stationed on Ship Island. No tents or blankets were issued to us and we had to sleep on the bare ground. The Confederate was indeed fortunate that was the owner of a blanket. Our rations were issued to us every morning, consisting of a few crackers and a small piece of beef to each man; occasionally in lieu of crackers, a small amount of corn mush. For drinking water, we sunk in the sand some empty flour barrels into which the water flowed, but it was so brackish as to be hardly drinkable. We were furnished with no fuel for making fires; consequently we could have no boiling water with which to destroy the vermin which swarmed in our clothes.

During all our stay, as I have said, we were subject to the insults of the negro guards. At dark we all had to lie down, and no one, for any purpose, was permitted to arise during the night, but all had to lie on the ground until daylight. The least infraction of this rule was sure to draw upon the thoughtless offender the fire of some of the negroes.

I remember well an incident that occurred a few days after our arrival on the island. Very early one morning just before day a Texan arose and shook his blanket. A negro sentinel wanted to know what he was doing. The Texan replied, "I am only shaking the dust out of my blanket." The reply to this response was a musket shot from the negro, by which the Texan fell dead. Nothing was ever done to this negro by the Federal authorities for this act.

Every day a detail of us, guarded by negroes, was sent four miles for a supply of wood for our cooks. The detail had to walk in close order, with negro guards on each side and in the rear. The least lagging was met by the jab of a Negro's bayonet, accompanied with the favorite expression, "Keep up dah, my gun loaded at both ends for you."

About a week after our arrival on the island, with these experiences of negro brutality, we were one morning visited by three Federal officers. We were at once ordered into line and one of the officers made a speech to us. He referred to our situation as prisoners of war without the utmost prospect of exchange, and to escape the horrors of prison life, he urged us to come forward and take the oath of allegiance to the Federal Government; that all of us who would do so and pledge themselves not to bear arms against the United States, would be carried north and there be released, and could remain there unmolested until the close of the war. Such is an abstract of the officer's address, which he delivered with the most persuasive effort possible. When he had closed his tempting speech, a Texan in the ranks stepped forth and asked to be allowed to address his comrades. Permission was granted. Stepping forward and taking a stand by the side of the Federal officers, and facing his fellow prisoners, the Texan delivered a most eloquent ovation. I wish I could recall in full all the words uttered by the Texan. He first dwelt upon the bad faith of the United States Government in refusing to exchange prisoners, in violation of the cartel, and then in bitter terms he spoke of the treatment of Confederate prisoners by that government, starving them and placing over them negro guards, whose outrages and insults they were powerless to resent. These negroes were allowed to torment and shoot prisoners at their own option, and all apparently with the approval of the white officer over them. With such an experience, "No Confederate," he said, "will ever take the oath of allegiance to such a government. We will die before we will take such an oath to get out of this place. And should we ever get out of here, we will at once go back into the Confederate ranks and continue to carry on war against this Government. This is our firm resolve — to be true to our cause and never to take the oath of allegiance to the Federal Government."

When the Texan's speech was ended, a most deafening cheer was given by the prisoners, who all firmly resolved that they would endure all the horrors of prison life rather than take the oath!

The Federal officers, be it said, made no effort to check the Texan in his speech, but seeing that their efforts were in vain, they graciously made a miltary salute to the prisoners and took their departure. This was the first, only, and last effort made by the Ship Island authorities to induce the Confederate prisoners to take the oath of allegiance. Their visit to us, with the plain and unpalatable facts given in their presence by the Texan, had however no effect in bringing about any amelioration in our situation. Every day saw the same meager rations, the same brackish water, the same filthy vermin consuming our bodies, and worst of all to endure, the same everlasting insults of the negroes.

Such was our prison life until the Sixth of May. On this day, after six crackers were issued to each man, we were placed on board of a ship and sent to New Orleans; there we were at once placed on boats and carried up the Mississippi to Vicksburg. We were six days on the voyage from Ship Island to Vicksburg. Apart from the crackers issued at Ship Island, we had no other rations until we got to Vicksburg. And when we had eaten up these crackers, we had to dine on the loose grains of corn scattered over the decks of our boats. This statement may seem incredible at this day, nevertheless it is true, whether the Federal authorities were reprehensible or excusable in the matter.

On our arrival in Vicksburg, rations in abundance were issued to us, and we were otherwise well treated by the Federal authorities. We were soon paroled, for the war was over, and with hearts saddened over the downfall of our beloved Confederacy, we all started for our homes.[29]

In mid–April 1865, the commander of the Confederate Department of Alabama, Mississippi, and East Louisiana, Lieutenant-General Richard Taylor, sent a subordinate officer to meet with an agent to be named by General Canby, in regards to securing the early release of the thousands of Confederate prisoners that had been captured in the battles around Mobile for a like number of Union prisoners of war paroled at Vicksburg by the Confederate government. Canby responded by promising Taylor that actions were underway to exchange all Confederates held as prisoners in his command, and that there would be no procrastination in forwarding the captives to Vicksburg, other than the normal paperwork involved in such an undertaking. To expedite the process of exchange, Provost Marshal Brigadier-General George Leonard Andrews ordered Colonel Holmstedt to transfer all the Rebel prisoners held on Ship Island "with as little delay as possible to Vicksburg." Four companies of the Eighteenth New York Cavalry were en route to the island to serve as guards for the prisoners for their voyage to Vicksburg. Holmstedt was also instructed to segregate the officers from the enlisted men, and to forward the proper rolls with each detachment of prisoners. To further accelerate the process,

Canby ordered his chief quartermaster to to have all transport vessels returning from Mobile Bay to anchor at Ship Island and "take as many men aboard as their respective capacities allow."[30]

On April 29, 1865, Holmstedt had 264 army officers, 1 navy officer, and 1 civilian held on Ship Island placed aboard a steamer for the trip to New Orleans, where they landed the following day at Milneburg. The former inmates of the barrier island were then taken to the Elysian Fields Street Depot via train and marched to the Picayune Cotton Press on Press Street, where they were held until May 4. On that day, 200 of them marched to the levee and were placed aboard the steamer *Mollie Able* for their trip to Vicksburg and freedom from captivity. On May 2, 42 civilians, 487 non-commissioned officers, 35 petty officers, and 3,376 privates bid their farewell to the purgatory of Ship Island as well, reaching New Orleans where they were reloaded aboard river steamers for the journey to Vicksburg, leaving 27 citizens and 2 soldiers remaining on the island. On May 6, the *Mollie Able* reached Vicksburg with the 200 officers, where they were reembarked on a train for the journey to Big Black River Bridge, where they were released from captivity.[31]

2nd Lt. Edward William Tarrant of Tarrant's Alabama Artillery Battery (courtesy of the Friends of the Tarrant Family, Taylorsville Community, Tuscaloosa County, Alabama).

Lieutenant Alden McLellan once again offers an insight into his journey from Ship Island to Vicksburg, and the close of the war:

We were on the island about three weeks and then were transported to New Orleans. An amusing thing occurred between the white and colored troops as we left the island. When we went on board the transport, the colored guards who came with us were stopped. They had come prepared to go on the transport, and there were several consultations between officers of white and colored troops before the colored guards were allowed to come on board, and then they were required to keep themselves at the bow of the boat. The white soldiers were not friendly to their colored comrades. At midnight the colored guards went on duty, then all prisoners had to keep inside the boat. The relief that was put on duty near me was very unmilitary. The colored guard approached in proper form, saluted, and asked for instructions. The white guard, who was leaning on his gun, looked at the relief in a very surly manner and said, "Stand there," and walked off, trailing his gun.

We arrived at Milneburg before day and were placed in bath houses until the train took us to Elysian Fields Street Depot. From there we marched to St. Joseph Street, between Carondelet and Baronne Streets, where we stood in the middle of that street for some time until our guards got instructions from some officer quartered in that vicinity where we were to be placed while here. The citizens living near by kindly brought us coffee, bread, cigars, tobacco, etc., which were eagerly scrambled for and thankfully received. While we were on St. Joseph Street there was an old lady in the crowd looking at us who knew me. I spoke to her, but she seemed not to know me and moved away. After a while she approached me and asked if I wanted anything. I asked her to let my family know that I was in the city. She said she did not know where they lived, but would find Mr. Alex McNeil, who did know, and started off to do so.

We then marched to a cotton press on Press Street, Third District, which is now part of the N.O. & N.E. Railroad depot. As we passed down Royal Street, between Elysian Fields and Marigny Street, I saw my aunt, Mrs. George McLellan, and others of her family standing in front of their residence.

I stepped outside of the guard to speak to them. They were astonished, but they greeted me cordially and affectionately. The white guards passed along; but when the colored man came along, he motioned me into the ranks. While in prison my father and mother visited me. The former wished me to remain at home, as he thought that the war was over; but I did not think as he did, and in a few days about two hundred of us marched to the levee in the Third District and were put on the hurricane deck of the steamer *Mollie Able*, Capt. Dan Able, and taken to Vicksburg, Miss., for exchange. The men from Ship Island came by transports via the mouth of the Mississippi River to Vicksburg.

On the march from the prison to the boat I was given more things by my family and friends than I could carry, but my comrades helped me. As the boat was starting off my father was waving his handkerchief to me, when a Federal officer compelled him to stop doing so. Our trip on that boat was very pleasant. Some of the lady passengers played the piano in the cabin. We listened with our heads in the skylight windows, and sang such songs as we knew. The first morning our pilot, Rich Britton, had Capt. J.L. Bradford and myself up in the pilot house taking coffee, but the guard soon sent us down. I found in the stateroom of Pilot Britton a number of things for me, having been placed there by my family.

Through the kindness of Mr. R. Britton, agent of the boat, Lieut. O.F. Gutherie, of the 1st Missouri Cavalry, and I were allowed to get our meals at the table in the cabin, except the night before we arrived in Vicksburg, when we were denied that privilege, because it was rumored that the boat was to be captured by the prisoners and landed, so we could escape. Such was the case, but several of us persuaded Colonel Gates and those in favor of the capture not to do so unless we were taken above Vicksburg.

We landed at Vicksburg about May 6, 1865, and as we passed ashore Captain Able said: "I am very proud of you, but am pleased that you are landing." While standing on the levee at Vicksburg a young Alabama officer was approached by some young negroes, who told him that they had been slaves in his father's family and they wanted to give him some money, but it was declined. Later they brought some vegetables and eatables, which were accepted, at which the colored boys seemed greatly pleased. We were then transported by train to the Big Black River, where we were relieved from guard.

Sgt. Jefferson Winston Williams of the 1st Mississippi Light Artillery, Co. D (courtesy of great-great-grandson Jefferson M. Thomson).

The exchange officer at Vicksburg, as a compliment to us (we being the first batch of exchange prisoners and all officers), had put on the train a ration of sugar and coffee for each of us. Quite a number of us had sampled the sugar before this was known; but the unconsumed portion was returned badly mixed with tobacco, matches, etc., with the proper apologies. When back at Ship Island, we were required to deposit all money and valuables with the Federal quartermaster and were permitted to purchase from the sutler to the value of the money deposited. When we were discharged, the valuables and balance of the moneys due us were returned.

The railroad from Big Black to Jackson, Miss., had not been rebuilt, so we walked to Jackson. When about five miles from Jackson, three of us who were used up by the walk met a colored man with a mule and a wagon, whom we persuaded (much against his will) to haul us to Jackson. I was unable to wear one boot on account of a blistered foot. The next morning I was awakened from my couch in Statehouse Square by the passing of mounted men on their way to cross the Mississippi River. Among them was Charles Crouch, who had been a messmate of mine. When he saw me, he called out, "Go away, drowned man; you were published in the Mobile papers as

Sgt. James R. Box of the 14th Texas (Dismounted) Cavalry, Co. D (courtesy of the James R. Box family).

being shot and drowned at Blakely;" and he rode off, telling me that I had better get to Meridian soon, as our mess was dividing.

It had been agreed by our mess that if anything happened to any of the mess his plunder was to be divided among those left; hence I was anxious to get to Meridian. As I could not get a pass to go by the train, I determined to try my luck; so when Lieutenant Anderson entered the train with a guard and told all that had no passes to get out, half of those in the car left. When my turn came, I held up an old pass, and Anderson shoved it back and passed on. I had told him in the morning why I wanted to get to Meridian. I subsequently learned that the hospital steward who got away on planks from Blakely reported that when he was about halfway across the river and the firing was the worst he heard a splash behind him. On looking back and seeing the two planks floating without anybody on them, he concluded that I was shot and drowned; and so reported it in Mobile, where it was published. The report got to New Orleans, but my mother was not told of it until after I was there as a prisoner.

At Meridian I met my brother-in-law, C.I. Fayssoux, also Sam Rousseau, found my horse and other things all right, stood in line all the afternoon, and got my parole, it being the last one signed that day. It was No. 200, dated May 10, 1865, and signed by Col. W.R. Miles, C.S.A., and Col. Henry Bertram, 20th Wisconsin Volunteers, U.S.A. That evening I got my horse and that of Captain Fayssoux into a freight car and went to Mobile. There I tried several times during the day to get an order for transportation on the boat to New Orleans, but failed. When the boat, the *N.P. Banks*, was about ready to start, the captain of the boat kindly took our paroles, went to the transportation office, and got orders for our transportation. The next morning (May 13, 1865) we arrived at West End. Our baggage was transported to the city over the military railroad, then running alongside the New Basin Canal through St. Joseph Street, Maj. Richard L. Robinson and I riding our horses home. My folks then lived on St. Mary, corner Camp Street. As I passed along the New Basin and up Camp Street several persons waved their hands to me, but most usually looked about and even stepped inside their doors or windows before doing so.

My home-coming was different from what I expected. It was especially sad not only on account of the failure of our cause, but also on account of the absence of my dear brother, Capt. C.W. McLellan, who was killed near Richmond, Va., June 1, 1864. I went to work immediately with my father, William H. McLellan, then of the firm of Nicholson & Co., paving contractors and stone dealers, with yard and office at the corner of Magazine and Robin Streets. They, with Messrs. Henry Hart and John Petit, had a franchise for the street railway subsequently called the St. Charles Street Railroad Company, which they constructed in 1866. I was made secretary and later president and superintendent, where I was continously in service until 1899.[32]

Though Lieutenant McLellan and his fellow officers onboard the *Mollie Able* chose not to make an escape attempt on their voyage from the horrors of confinement on Ship Island, some of the prisoners who were subsequently released did attempt to escape on their trips from the island. Private W.M. Buster, who

Pvt. William Rogers of the 15th Confederate Cavalry (courtesy of the Florida State Library and Archives).

resided in Elmwood, Cass County, Nebraska, after the war, recorded years later his and several fellow prisoners' attempts at escaping from Union hands. Below is Buster's account of what transpired:

> After serving a term in prison, I was exchanged and got back to my command the last of March, 1865. The command was at Blakely, Mobile, Ala. On April 1 we had a "scrap" with General Steele's command, and kept up the skirmishing until the 9th, when Steele charged [and] captured us all, so I was a prisoner again. I resolved to get away, and, putting my wits to work, I walked through the guard line, but was detected and taken back. The next day they took us to Ship Island, and kept us there about two weeks. We were guarded by negroes, who shot several of our boys for nothing. Next we were put on a boat and sent to New Orleans. We lay out in the channel till evening, then started up the river. Several of my company planned to jump off and swim ashore, so about eleven o'clock we jumped into the river just behind the wheel. It was a side-wheeler. Some may think that wasn't hard to do. The boat was loaded down with prisoners, and it looked more like jumping into the grave than anything I had ever done; but we got out all right, and then put in nearly all night trying to wade across the bayou, but had to give it up, and lay down to rest. We heard some talking, and learned that it was more of the boys. We made another attempt to wade the bayou, but failed; so two of us went to a farmhouse to get the man to pilot us across, but he told us we couldn't cross it. He was a friend all right, but said that every place that could be crossed was guarded by Union soldiers. He advised that we give ourselves up, but we wouldn't do that. So we started back, and some negroes saw us and reported to the provost marshal and he got after us, so we had to go right up the river. They chased us about six miles before they caught us.[33]

Upon receiving the news that General Robert E. Lee had surrendered his army at Appomattox Court House in Virginia on April 9, General Joseph E. Johnston had surrendered his command in North Carolina on April 14, and that Confederate President Jefferson Davis was now himself a prisoner of the Union authorities, Lieutenant-General Richard Taylor followed suit and surrendered the troops in his department to General Canby on May 4, 1865. On May 9, 1865, Canby ordered his commander at Vicksburg, Major-General Napoleon Jackson Tecumseh Dana, to parole all prisoners arriving at Vicksburg from Ship Island and send them to their homes, not to be disturbed as long as they honored the terms of their paroles. The exception were those belonging to commands from the border states of Kentucky and Missouri, who would be held at Vicksburg until the U.S. War Department could decide their fate. This was in consequence of the fact that these two states had never formally seceded from the Union, though both had provided many units for both the North and South during the war.[34]

In response to Canby's directive, Dana reported that, prior to receiving the order, all of the prisoners formerly housed on Ship Island had been turned over to the Confederate agent of exchange "on parole in lieu of prisoners delivered by him." In his correspondence of May 14, Dana explained that he had made the assumption that the Ship Island prisoners were an exchange for the Union soldiers delivered to him on parole by the Confederate government, and had accordingly been paroled and a notation entered on the rolls stating: "The officer signing this parole does so in behalf of all the men above his signature and all described on this roll are not to perform any military or constabulary duty until regularly exchanged."[35]

On May 7, 1865, twenty-four citizens were released from Ship Island and transported to New Orleans for the journey to Vicksburg and freedom, leaving one soldier and three civilians still held as prisoners on the island. They were joined four days later by the arrival of one officer and five enlisted men who were transported to the island. The Confederate prison camp was finally emptied permanently in early June following the close of the Civil War, when three citizens and one soldier were shipped to New Orleans for release on June 1, followed by one officer and five enlisted men on June 8. At long last, the hell in the Gulf for the citizens and soldiers of the former Confederacy who were held on the island had come to an end, though the memories of their time spent on the barrier island would remain with many throughout the remainder of their lives. For those who perished during their time of confinement on the island, the relentless Gulf of Mexico would deliver one final indignity after the war, as the Confederate cemetery on the island would be washed into the Gulf's restless waters as a result of the constant shifting of the sand of the barrier island. Finally, they, too, had been freed from their imprisonment on Ship Island.[36]

Post-War Ship Island

> *Ship Island, Mississippi — November 25, 1718*
> That country promises great riches to such as shall inhabit it, from the excellent quality of its lands.
> — *Antoine Simon LePage DuPratz, commenting on the Gulf Coast and Ship Island*

With the close of the great American Civil War, a three company battalion from the Seventy-Eighth United States Colored Infantry, under the command of Major Rufus Paten, remained on Ship Island until December 21, 1865, when it was relieved by Companies F and K of the Tenth United States Colored Heavy Artillery, under the command of Captain Jesse Fettus. Five months later, Company L of the Tenth U.S.C.H.A., under the command of Captain Edwin F. Barstow, arrived from Fort Pike to reinforce the garrison already on the island, and due to the fact that Barstow ranked Captain Fettus he assumed command of the outpost. The garrison remained on the island until February 1, 1867, when they departed for Baton Rouge, Louisiana, to be mustered out of the service of the U.S. military. They were replaced by the Twentieth United States Infantry, who had been ordered to the Department of the Gulf from duty in Richmond, Virginia, and had sailed from Norfolk on January 15, 1867, aboard the steamer *Missouri*, en route to New Orleans. Arriving in the Queen City of the South on January 27, Companies F and I were assigned to duty on Ship Island, landing there before nightfall on January 30 under the command of Captain John J. Huff.[1]

The men of the Twentieth U.S. Infantry remained on the island for ten weeks, when orders were issued on April 6, 1867, from the headquarters of the U.S. Fifth Military District, to relieve the garrison on the island with a two company detachment from the Thirty-Ninth United States Infantry, one of four remaining black regiments in the U.S. Army. Disembarking on Ship Island from Greenville, Louisiana, on April 10, commanded by Captain Thomas H. Reeves, the two companies were soon reinforced by Company H of the regiment, who arrived on the barrier island on July 24. On January 18, 1868, Company I arrived also, accompanied by the regiment's colonel, Joseph Anthony Mower, a distinguished Civil War veteran who had been a major-general of volunteers under William Tecumseh Sherman during the war. Mower immediately established Ship Island as the headquarters for the regiment, and the outpost continued to be staffed by the four companies until June 23, 1868, when Company I was transferred to Fort Pike, though within two days the island garrison resumed its former strength by the arrival of Company A from Fort Pike.[2]

During his stay on the island, Colonel Mower had been ordered to take measures to prevent the Ship Island anchorage from being used by certain individuals as a base from which to outfit an expedition for an invasion of Mexico, in violation of the United States neutrality laws. Unable to control efforts that were out of range of the guns of Fort Massachusetts, Mower requested that the revenue cutter *Wilderness*, or a vessel similiar to the *Ella*, armed with a field gun, be rushed to the island's anchorage.[3]

General Mower and the headquarters of the Thirty-Ninth U.S. Infantry were transferred from Ship Island to New Orleans on January 24, 1869, and the senior officer remaining on the island, Captain D.A. Ward, assumed the role of post commander. This was followed by the arrival on January 30 of Company I from Fort Pike, and Major Zenas Bliss on February 15, who assumed command of the island and garrison. Five weeks later, the garrison was slashed to three companies by the departure of Companies A and I for Jackson Barracks, Louisiana, located in the lower Ninth Ward of New Orleans.[4]

On March 3, 1869, legislation was passed in Washington reorganizing the United States Army from 45 infantry regiments into 25 regiments, and instructing that the enlisted soldiers of two of the regiments were to be composed of black troops. Accordingly, on March 15 orders were issued directing that the new Twenty-Fifth United States Infantry would be formed by the merger of the Thirty-Ninth Infantry, then stationed in North Carolina, and the Fortieth Infantry, on duty in the Department of Louisiana. The field officers of the new regiment were to be Joseph A. Mower, colonel; Edward W. Hincks, lieutenant colonel; and Zenas R. Bliss, major. After the arrival of the Fortieth United States Infantry at Ship Island on April 19, 1869, the merger was completed on April 30, with Companies E, F, and I of the new regiment being designated as the Ship Island garrison. Colonel Mower was in command of the Department of Louisiana at the

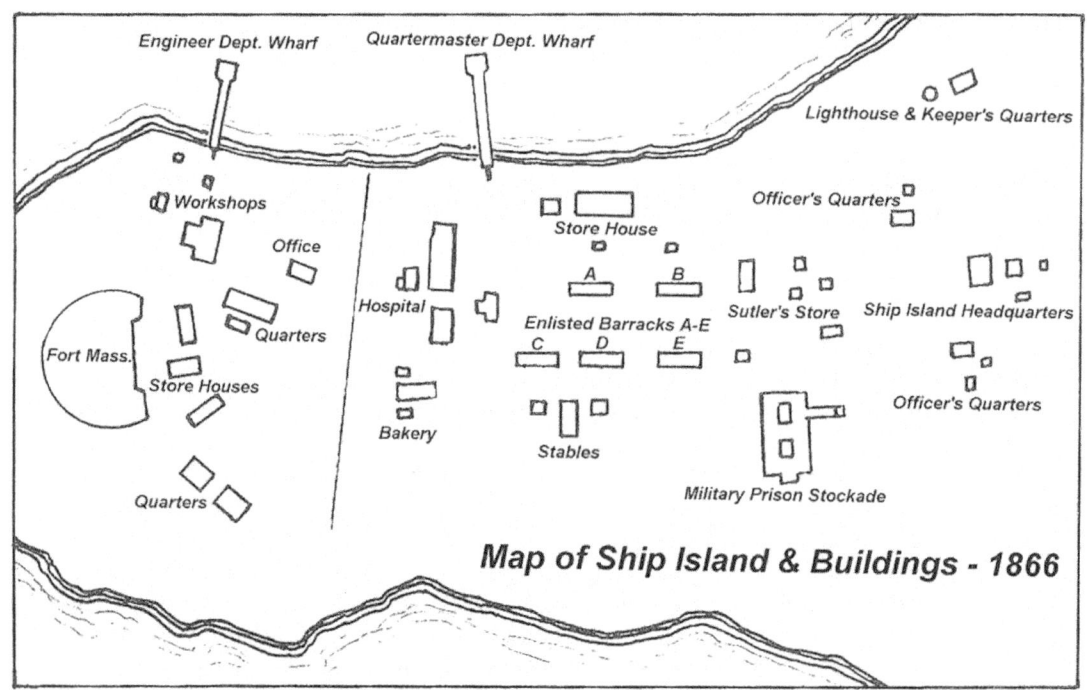

Map of buildings on Ship Island, Mississippi, from a February 13, 1866, diagram prepared by Lieutenant D.W. Payne, U.S. Army Engineers (modified by Terry G. Scriber from an illustration at the Library of Congress).

time of the merger, necessitating Lieutenant-Colonel Hincks to assume command of the new regiment. The Ship Island garrison was enlarged to four companies on February 5, 1870, with the arrival of Company A from Fort Pike, though they later returned to Fort Pike on March 28.[5]

On December 14, 1869, Colonel Mower, in his capacity as commander of the Department of Louisiana, requested authority from the U.S. War Department to "break up the Ship Island military post and prison," and to deploy the garrison currently on the island to other duties within his department, and the U.S. military convicts that were imprisoned on the island forwarded to Forts Jackson and St. Philip, where they would be "profitably employed erecting barracks." Before a decision could be rendered on Mower's request, the Civil War hero succumbed to pneumonia in his Magazine Street home in New Orleans on the evening of January 6, 1870. His successor as commander of the Department of Louisiana, Colonel Charles H. Smith, discovered in a review of Mower's military files that his intentions had been to transfer one of the companies constituting the Ship Island garrison to Jackson Barracks, while the remaining two companies were sent to the two river forts. Smith realized that the Ship Island outpost was expensive to maintain in a time of peace and placed a heavy burden on the quartermaster department in supplying the garrison of the barrier island. He also saw the need to concentrate the Twenty-Fifth U.S. Infantry so as to form a complete regiment, instead of it being assigned piece meal to different military posts. Accordingly, he endorsed Mower's plan for abandoning Ship Island, and made a recommendation that the military convicts currently imprisoned on the island, numbering over 100, be transferred to Forts Pike, St. Philip, and Jackson. The only exceptions to these transfers would be those prisoners currently incarcerated for particularly atrocious crimes, as Smith wished to have those transferred to the state penitentiaries at Baton Rouge, Louisiana, and Little Rock, Arkansas, to serve the remainder of their sentences.[6]

Smith received a communication relating to his proposal on March 19, 1870, authorizing him to proceed with his plan to abandon Ship Island as a garrisoned outpost. The colonel ordered the department quartermaster, Brevet Brigadier-General Calvin H. Frederick, to provide Major Bliss, in charge of the Ship Island garrison, with "suitable shackles and chains" to accommodate 100 military convicts, "to be chained in gangs of from two to five men." He was also instructed to provide transportation for three companies of infantry and 114 prisoners from the island to New Orleans, and to have a stockade and barracks built at Fort Jackson to house the 40 military convicts scheduled to be imprisoned there. Smith's desire to have the more dangerous of the convicts imprisoned in the state penitentiaries was also approved, with 55 men scheduled to be transferred to the Arkansas State Penitentiary. On April 5, Companies E, F, and I of the Twenty-Fifth U.S. Infantry, accompanied by the convicts, bid farewell to Ship Island and boarded a steamer for New Orleans, where they arrived the following day. The prisoners were marched to Jackson Barracks to serve the remainder of their confinement, except those bound for Arkansas and 27 that were transferred to Fort Jackson. During the eight years the military stockade was in operation on the island, 1,132 military convicts, Confederate sympathizers, and parole violators were incarcerated there. In mid–September 1870, Companies C, D, and E, the band, and the regimental headquarters of the Nineteenth United States Infantry were transferred to Ship Island from Jackson Barracks to escape the yellow fever season in New Orleans. The soldiers remained on the island until November 6, when they returned to New Orleans onboard the steamer *Sarah*. These troops became the last U.S. Army combat unit stationed on Ship Island.[7]

The U.S. Army did, however, maintain a presence on Ship Island in the form of an ordnance sergeant who was assigned to maintain the thirteen 10-inch Rodman guns emplaced in the casemates of Fort Massachusetts, the two 100-pounder Parrotts and two 15-inch Rodmans that were dismounted, and a substantial amount of shot and shell for the weaponry. The first to arrive on the island to maintain the guns was Ordnance-Sergeant John Lewis, who assumed responsibility of the guns and ordnance stores, as well as the quartermaster property, upon the withdrawal of the garrison in April 1870. Spending less than a year on the island, he was replaced by Ordnance-Sergeant Charles Hall, whose stay was equally short. Hall was replaced on July 14, 1871, by Ordnance-Sergeant Robert McVey, who was paid a visit by Lieutenant George K. Spencer of the Baton Rouge Arsenal some three days later. Spencer's inspection of the island's guns

15-inch Rodman gun on Ship Island, Mississippi (illustrated by Kenneth F. Arnold, Jr.).

revealed that the 13 Rodman's emplaced in the fort were useless in the event of an assault due to the fact the truck wheels were off the chassis rails, and each gun had only one eccentric socket.[8]

On March 29, 1872, Sergeant James McCabe was promoted to ordnance-sergeant and ordered to Ship Island to relieve McVey in his duties as the keeper of the island's guns. After a careful inventory, McCabe wrote an alarming report to the chief of ordnance describing the conditions of the Ship Island weaponry. In it, he reported that he had found that the thirteen 10-inch Rodman's had been so neglected as to require the outer surfaces of the guns to be cleaned and lacquered, and their carriages cleaned and painted. The two 100-pounder Parrotts and two 15-inch Rodmans were in a wretched condition, with one of the Rodmans being buried in the sand to the point that only a "small part of the upper surface was visible." The ordnance stores were thrown "promiscously over the floor in one of the magazines," and though fourteen of the missing eccentrics for the casemate carriages had been located buried in the sand, twelve were still unaccounted for. McCabe stated in his report that if the guns were to be placed in a condition to provide for the defense of Ship Island, he would require some outside assistance in the undertaking.[9]

The chief of ordnance did dispatch Lieutenant George W. McKee and a work party from the Mount Vernon Arsenal to Ship Island (though they were slow in arriving) in January 1874 to emplace the four weapons lying in the sand, as well as to assist in getting the ordnance stores

Aerial view of Fort Massachusetts (courtesy of Gulf Islands National Seashore, National Park Service, NPS Photo).

Rear of Fort Massachusetts (courtesy of Gulf Islands National Seashore, National Park Service, NPS Photo).

and 10-inch Rodmans in acceptable condition. As the first of February rolled around, the Rodmans in the casemates had been cleaned and painted, the chassis, tubes, and carriages of the four dismounted guns had been dislodged from the sand and brought inside of Fort Massachusetts, where they were in the process of being scraped, cleaned, and painted. By mid–March, the two 15-inch Rodmans and two 100-pounder Parrotts had been mounted en barbette, and upon McKee's departure from the barrier island at the end of March, he reported to the ordnance department that all of the Ship Island ordnance was in "magnificent order." As a prelude of things to come, McKee also reported that the Union soldier cemetery on the island was a "national disgrace," and that while on the island, his work crew had "picked and buried the limbs of soldiers strewn upon the ground." McKee received a response from the chief quartermaster of the Department of the Gulf, Henry Hodges, concerning the condition of the cemetery. Hodges assured McKee that the cemetery would be "put in proper order" as soon as the fiscal appropriation for the year 1875 became available.[10]

The Ship Island Union cemetery was first brought to the attention of the U.S. Army quartermaster-general in mid–May of 1866 by Lieutenant George B. Oldham, who was conducting an inspection of the Ship Island outpost. Oldham found the cemetery, which was located approximately one and a half miles east of Fort Massachusetts and encompassed an area of between two to three acres, to be in a sad state of disrepair, "owing principally to the nature of the ground, which is composed entirely of sand, with the graves almost unnoticeable, having no headboards." To intensify the difficulty in sorting out who was buried where, no records could be found pertaining to the cemetery, and the graves were scattered over the cemetery area, with only 113 buried together and the remaining 150 placed in various areas. As far as Oldham could discern, there were about 225 Union graves in the area. Oldham recommended to Quartermaster-General Montgomery Cunningham Meigs that the bodies be disinterred and reburied, with the grounds of the cemetery enclosed and "laid out in some system," as well as new headstones emplaced to mark the graves.[11]

Captain Charles Barnard, in charge of Union cemetery affairs for the U.S. Fifth Military District, soon began delving into the Ship Island cemetery matter and concluded the island was unsuitable for the location of a national cemetery. The soil of the barrier island consisted of loose sand, and was unable to produce or sustain "vegetation of any value," making it virtually impossible to emplace headstones to mark the graves. In consequence of his findings, Barnard made a recommendation that all of the Union soldiers that had perished on the island be disinterred and reburied in the Chalmette National Cemetery in St. Bernard Parish, Louisiana, located outside of New Orleans. Barnard's suggestions seem to have been received favorably by Meigs, for in December 1867 the bodies of 228 Union soldiers were disinterred and sent to Chalmette National Cemetery for reinterment.[12]

Four years after the removal of the Union bodies to Chalmette, Ordnance-Sergeant McVey reported to the chief quartermaster of the Department of the Gulf that the Ship Island cemetery still held six bodies that were known to be buried inside the grounds, which were enclosed by a rail fence. These included two citizens who had died on the island during their Civil War imprisonment, two children, Private John Williams of Company A of the Thirty-Ninth U.S. Infantry, and an unknown soldier. Approximately 400 yards northeast of the cemetery were seven additional graves of soldiers who had died in 1868 after the war, save for one, C. Preston of Company B of the Twelfth Maine Infantry, who had died on April 5, 1862. McVey also reported that he had been advised that "within a mile or so" of the cemetery were the unmarked graves of Confederate prisoners of war and Corps of Engineers personnel. In April 1878, a request was made of the U.S. War Department from Mrs. Lydia Gould, who was seeking information on the grave of her brother, who had been a soldier in the Fifteenth Maine Infantry before perishing on the island in the Spring of 1862. In the War Department's reply, they assured Mrs. Gould that all of the Union soldiers formerly buried in the Ship Island cemetery had been removed and reinterred in the Chalmette National Cemetery.[13]

On June 18, 1885, a correspondent for the *New Orleans Times-Democrat* who signed himself as "Pap," accepted an invitation from the surgeon-in-charge of the Ship Island Quarantine Station to visit the island. What he discovered during his visit to the island, and his subsequent newspaper article, would soon ignite a firestorm within the War Department. Below is the article that appeared in the June 21, 1885, edition of that newspaper:

SHIP ISLAND
SOMETHING ABOUT THE ISLAND AND ITS INHABITANTS

Shameful Neglect of the Federal Dead — The Graveyard Strewn with Uncovered Skeletons — The Fleet Now in the Harbor

Correspondence of the *Times-Democrat*
Biloxi, Miss., June 18, 1885

Accepting an invitation to visit Dr. R.D. Murray, the courteous and gentlemanly surgeon in charge of the Quarantine Station at Ship Island, I stepped on board the United States Marine Hospital sloop *Annie* one day last week and was soon bounding over the blue billows of Mississippi Sound. The day was lovely, though the wind, to use a nautical phrase, blew a stiff breeze from the south, forcing us to beat against it all the way, consuming several hours more time from constant tacking than if it came from a more favored quarter.

Ship Island, as every one knows, is one of a group of low sandy islands lying off the Mississippi coast, and separating the strong waves of the Gulf from the more placid waters of Mississippi Sound, forming at once a breakwater and safe harbor, with sufficient depth and ample room for the combined navies of the world to ride at anchor in safety. The natural trend of the island is from East to West. It is twelve miles long by a half mile wide at its greatest breadth. The pass through which vessels enter from the Gulf is at the west end, and between this and Cat Island, which is six miles distant.

In 1856 a brick fort was commenced at the west end to command the entrance of the harbor, but work was stopped on it about 1860, when a terrible hurricane occurred, wrecking vessels with materials for its construction. At the commencement of the war, troops from Mobile blew it up, and nothing was done upon it till 1864 or 1865, when it was completed to its present shape. With the present improved ordnance a man-of-war can lay off, out of reach of its guns, and blow it out of existence.

The lighthouse is near by and on the north shore, but its foundation is gradually undermining, and unless something is soon done for its safety, it will succumb to the treacherous waves. A few old tumble-down shanties, built during and after the war, one of them occupied by the inspector of the port and his boatman, the lighthouse-keeper's dwelling, a hospital, storehouse and wharf are all that comprise the west end of Ship Island. Some four miles off the eastward is a lagoon making in from the north shore and extending nearly across the island. Here is situated the quarantine station. The lazaretto is built on the west side of the lagoon, while to the east is the yellow fever hospital and Dr. Murray's house. His lot is a lonely one, though he has his family with him.

All the timber on the island grows back and to the east of the quarantine station, a distance perhaps of three miles, and consists of scrub pine and swamp myrtle, interspersed with palmetto-glades, reeds and rushes mixed with swamp grasses, which constitutes the verdure of the place; all else is a waste of sand.

HISTORY OF THE ISLAND

Ship Island has a historical as well as commercial reputation. It was here, in the month of February, 1699, that Iberville cast anchor and made his first landing, preparatory to colonizing the then wild territory of Louisiana, and from here the indomitable Bienville started on his explorations to the main land, which resulted in establishing the colony at Biloxi and subsequently the founding of Natchez and New Orleans. Then, in the year 1814, a British fleet of seventy sail, consisting of men-of-war and transports, under command of Sir Edward Pakingham, rendezvoused here previous to the attack upon your city and the memorable battle which formed the closing chapter of the war. Again, in 1862, the fleets of Farragut and Butler cast anchor here, and the tents of all New England were pitched upon the sands. Fresh from their Green Mountain homes, most of them young and unused to the hardships of the camp, all unaclimated [sic], transported hither and forced to drink the brackish water of shallow wells, dug by themselves in the hot sand, stung and tormented by mosquitos and sand flies, it is no wonder so many sickened and died, and were buried among the sand dunes of the northern shore. But why they have been so long neglected and forgotten I know not, and must leave the subject to others to explain. Twenty-two years have passed and gone since they were laid away in their shallow graves. Twenty years the smoke of battle has been rolled away by the breeze of peace; the country has grown rich and prosperous, and is again most thoroughly united. National cemeteries have been established at convenient places all over the land, and the dead of a hundred battlefields rest within them, and their names are recorded upon marble tablets. Not so the dead of Ship Island. About a mile east of the light-house, on the north shore, is a range of sand hills, on which was the Federal graveyard, inclosed by a pailing [sic] fence, and here, in rough coffins, were the soldiers buried. Why their bodies were not removed to the National Cemetery at New Orleans, when it was established, I know not. It is a fact, however, that they were neglected and, perhaps, forgotten. The winds and waves of time have demolished the fence that inclosed them. Upward of a hundred feet of their resting place has washed into the sea; the wind has blown the sand from their graves, and left not only their coffins exposed, but

THEIR BLEACHED BONES,

polished by the drifting sand, strew the ground in all directions. The day was fearfully hot as I walked among them and gazed upon their grinning skulls, whose eyeless sockets filled with sand presented a ghastly and horrible sight, and this, too, in a civilized age to the great shame and neglect of a great nation, who has lavished millions upon the resting places of her dead in other localities. At one time head-boards marked these graves, yet I failed to find but one among all these bones, and this bore the following inscription, cut in the wood, no doubt, by some comrade:

E. Miller, Burlington, Me. Age, 20

Long rows of coffins and their fragments are seen in one place, with their heads to the west, undoubtedly as they were originally placed, but the lids are removed and they are filled with sand. I dug down in one of them with my hands, but found no bones, and as there are many hogs on the island, no doubt they have displaced them. Legs of pantaloons, sleeves of coats and portions of vests lie about, with here and there a military button still attached, to show the wearer's avocation.

Some four or five years ago Mr. McCabe, ordnance sergeant at the fort, received an order from the Secretary of War to make a personal examination of the place and write him the condition of the yard and all matters pertaining thereto. This, I understand, the sergeant did, but heard nothing further about it. Of course it is an out of the way place, and few will ever see it, as I saw it the other day, in all its hideousness; but I do hope some United States official may read my statement and report it to the proper authorities, so that hereafter when Decoration Day comes and garlands of sweet flowers adorn the graves of Blue and Gray, no one can point to Ship Island with shame at the human bones that now strew her sands, and who in life wore the uniform of the United States.

THE SHIPPING

There are but few vessels here loading at this time, and they are Norwegian. It seems a fact that all our carring trade is done by foreign vessels. Will our merchant marine service ever have a place among the nations of the earth seems to be a question about as unanswerable as our navy problem, which the last twenty years has failed to produce. This island is apparently washing and wasting away, from the fact that original surveys make it eighteen miles long where now it is only a short twelve, and in breadth it has lost much in the last decade. The water on the north holds a good depth close in shore, and the channel is about as usual, with twenty-three to twenty-five feet at high tide on the bar.

At the east end, which terminates in a low reach of sand as far as the eye can see, the water is much more shallow, and only navigable to small craft during high tide. Looking eastward from this point I see the west end of Horn Island some fifteen miles distant, but in the intervening space I discover two small bars of sand, which I am informed are the Dog Keys, and at certain times of the year are favorite haunts of the gull egg hunter. I don't like to dispute this, but I visited those keys on one occasion and found no gull eggs, though they were there in season.

I found the residents very kind and obliging during my brief visit to Ship Island, and left them with regret. More I must confess at their imprisonment than at my own freedom, but they are all government employees, and their families seem satisfied with the situation, and why not I, since their banishment is voluntary. I returned to Biloxi after a two days trip on the *Annie* much pleased with her officers, Capt. Emile and Fred, alas, thankful for a pleasant visit to Dr. Murray and his cheerful family, Mr. McColl, the lighthouse-keeper, and his aide, Mr. Smith, hospital steward, and his aids, as well as Inspector Cleary and Capt. McCabe, all of whom assisted in making my stay among them pleasant.

There is no one sick upon the island nor in the fleet, and all seem happy with the prospect of a healthy summer. The health officers are very circumspect, always on the alert, and under the careful and guarded eye of Dr. Murray there is no danger of disease spreading from his quarantine.

"Pap"

As a result of "Pap's" article concerning the Ship Island cemetery, the U.S. War Department was deluged with irate correspondence from an indignant populace, forcing Quartermaster-General Samuel Beckley Holabird to order the superintendent of the Chalmette National Cemetery, J.A. Commerford, to proceed to the island and submit a report on what he discovered. Departing from Chalmette on the evening of July 2, Commerford arrived at the barrier island in the afternoon of the following day. On the morning of July 4, the country's Independence Day, he inspected the Ship Island cemetery, which he discovered was located approximately one and a quarter miles from the Ship Island lighthouse, and contained "about 8 acres of white sand which drifts and forms hills from 8 to 10 ft. in height." At one time, he deduced, the cemetery was enclosed by a picket fence, but nothing remained of the enclosure but a few rotten posts. Almost 100 feet from the north shore of the island, Commerford observed "two rows of coffins, 12 in all, on the surface of the ground and partly filled with sand," though upon inspecting them he found no skeletal remains. Several yards to the east, he did observe "quite a number of human bones scattered here and there on the sand, but did not see any skulls." He also reasoned that it would be impossible to provide a correct estimate of "how many bodies are covered up in the sand as there are no marks or signs of graves except those already mentioned," though he did observe the headboard mentioned by "Pap" that bore the inscription of E. Miller.[14]

While proceeding to Ordnance-Sergeant McCabe's quarters to consult with him regarding the cemetery, Commerford discovered two human skulls protruding from the sand in the back of a rundown old building, which he carefully reburied in the sand after marking the spot for exhumation later. Upon arrival at McCabe's quarters, McCabe advised Commerford that, since his arrival on Ship Island in March 1872, in excess of 100 feet of the cemetery "had been washed away ... and that some of the coffins with their contents were washed away by the action of the wind and waves." Commerford reported that he was certain a box in the dimensions of 6 feet by 2 feet by 18 inches could accommodate all the skeletal remains that he had discovered, but due to the conditions of the island such as the action of the waves, the hogs that roamed the island, and the shifting sands "... no grave can be made permanent on Ship Island."[15]

Upon receiving Commerford's report of his visit to Ship Island, Holabird ordered that the skeletal remains be retrieved, boxed for shipment, and forwarded to the Chalmette National Cemetery for reinterrment; he also made arrangements with McCabe to retrieve and transfer to Chalmette any remains that might become exposed in the future. At last, the remaining Union dead of Ship Island would be honored with a burial in a national cemetery, free from the ravages of the Gulf of Mexico elements.[16]

In 1879–1880, Ship Island became the location of the United States' first national quarantine station, as a result of active campaigning by Surgeon-General John Maynard Woodworth of the Marine-Hospital Service. With the increased volume of international shipping in U.S. ports, the need for monitoring possible sources of outbreaks of diseases such as cholera and yellow fever became paramount. On April 29, 1878, Congress passed "An Act to prevent the introduction of contagious or infectious diseases into the United States." This was followed on March 3, 1879, by President Rutherford B. Hayes affixing his signature to "an act to prevent the introduction of infectious and contagious diseases into the United States and to establish a National Board of Health." A second act, passed by Congress on June 2, 1879, did not assign quarantine duties to the Board of Health, but instead authorized it to cooperate with state and local boards of health in enforcing their existing rules and regulations to prevent the spread of infectious diseases. The board did undertake a national survey of the various U.S. ports from Portland, Maine, to the Rio Grande in an effort to determine the requirements and equipage needed for an effective quarantine system, determining that a boarding ship was needed to carry the inspecting officer to a quarantine anchorage, where suspected infectious ships and crew could be detained, as well as the need for an isolation hospital where patients could be treated by medical officers. The board also found that additional requirements needed were a lazaretto to house suspect people not ill but under observation, an officers quarters, a warehouse with sufficient space to store cargoes from infected ships while the proper disinfecting methods were underway, a wharf to land the cargo on, and boats for administration purposes. It was determined that only three or four such quarantine stations with good anchorage and sufficient distance from shipping lanes would be required to effectively establish the national quarantine system.[17]

Toward the end of September 1879, Inspector A.N. Bell of the National Board of Health scouted the areas east of New Orleans in search of a suitable location for the Gulf of Mexico quarantine station. Visiting Ship Island on September 26, Bell discovered "an abundance of water and good anchorage within easy boarding distance of the whole north side of the island." On the island's west end, where the quartermaster's wharf had stood during the Civil War, deep water extended to within several hundred feet of shore, making this an excellent location for a replacement wharf and warehouse. Located between the light station and Fort Massachusetts were the abandoned post quarters used during the war, which were in such condition that a small expenditure could render them as suitable quarters for housing of stevedores, and 4 miles east of the lighthouse at the lagoon, Bell found an ideal location for officers quarters and a hospital. Upon his return to New Orleans, Bell accordingly made his recommendation that Ship Island become the location of the nation's first quarantine station, with responsibility for the Gulf of Mexico shipping traffic, a recommendation which was accepted and endorsed by the board.[18]

While the construction of the appropriate buildings was underway, the man in charge of getting the station up and running, Doctor Samuel M. Bemiss, himself a member of the board, submitted a proposed set of regulations to the Louisiana State Board of Health outlining the mission statement of the Ship Island Quarantine Station. Doctor Bemiss outlined that the goals were to: Diminish the danger of importation of infectious and epidemic diseases by detaining and disinfecting contaminated vessels at a distance sufficiently remote from the coast to prevent communication of diseases from those under quarantine, and provide for passengers and crews of infected vessels good hospital accommodations and treatment for the sick, as well as comfortable and isolated housing for the healthy who may be detained for observation. Additional goals were to provide a suitable warehouse for storing cargo while vessels were being cleaned, and suitable disinfecting rooms and appliances to insure that goods and clothing were promptly and thoroughly disinfected. Ships that would be required to anchor at the quarantine station were those that had infectious diseases aboard or had such diseases aboard while docked at a foreign port, those that had sailed from a foreign harbor where infectious diseases had been prominent, or those ships that were required by the regulations of Mississippi, Louisiana, or Alabama to dock at the station.[19]

The Ship Island Quarantine Station officially opened for the illness season on March 17, 1881, with the arrival of Doctor T.S. Scales, who remained there until October 1. Boarding all ships that arrived at the station for inspections, Doctor Scales placed 10 vessels in quarantine. This was followed in 1882 by a severe outbreak of yellow fever among many of the crews of various vessels, prompting a large number to be placed in quarantine by Doctor Scales and his crew. In 1883, only three vessels were placed in quarantine by Scales before he was relieved of his duties and the responsibility of the quarantine station given to the Marine-Hospital Service on June 30, 1883. Assistant-Surgeon John Godfrey wasted no time in getting the station under the administration of the service, and transferred four employees from the New Orleans Marine-Hospital to Ship Island. On November 1, 1883, Assistant-Surgeon R.D. Murray assumed command of the station and relinquished control of the west end of the island, except as health officer and custodian, though he did maintain control of the quarantine anchorage. During 1884, staff from the station boarded 29 ships, detained 21 for inspection, and treated 265 seamen.[20]

On March 5, 1888, Congress enacted and President Grover Cleveland signed into law a bill authorizing the transfer of the Gulf quarantine station from Ship Island to "some other island" in the Gulf, or "in such pass in the Mississippi Delta as may be designated by a Board named by the Secretary of the Treasury." As a result of this action, on March 7, 1889, the station was relocated from Ship Island to north Chandeleur Island under the direction of Doctor H.R. Carter, the officer-in-charge. During the 1889 and 1890 illness seasons, the Mississippi State Board of Health maintained a quarantine station at Ship Island to protect the interests of the

Gulf Coast communities, under the direction of Doctor A. Parker Champlin. The Mississippi authorities maintained possession of the station until 1893, when a hurricane slammed the Gulf Coast from Pensacola to west of the Mississippi River on October 1, packing winds and waves that "wrecked the Gulf quarantine station, and almost obliterated the island upon which it stood." In this killer storm, 3 staff members of the Chandeleur station and 2 patients lost their lives. The remainder of the staff were transferred to Ship Island to carry on the Gulf quarantine duties and finish out the remainder of quarantine season. To further add to the woes of those charged with enforcing the Gulf quarantine, on November 26, 1893, a severe storm battered Ship Island, virtually wiping out the remaining structures still standing and destroying most of the equipment on the island.[21]

Faced with the prospect of no effective operating Gulf quarantine station, the Marine-Hospital Service reestablished the Ship Island station, and in 1894 a reconstruction project was underway on the island. The Ship Island Quarantine Station would remain in use until December 20, 1916, when the station was moved to Gulfport, Mississippi, and the Ship Island facility placed under the custodianship of two watchmen, to be used only when necessary for the detention and treatment of infectious ships and crew.[22]

During its years in service as a quarantine station, Ship Island saw many hurricanes roar in from the Gulf that wreaked havoc on the island and its inhabitants. Some of the more notable of the storms first occurred on September 26, 1906, when a hurricane roared in that caused horrific damage to the station, all "floating properties," except several small boats, were washed away, and the buildings containing the executive offices, the assistant surgeon and pharmacist quarters, the attendant's housing, the bathhouse and marine ways, and the bridge spanning the lagoon had been destroyed. In addition, the water storage and distribution system had been heavily damaged. This was followed by an extremely active hurricane season in 1915 that saw the first Gulf storm arrive at the island on August 17, causing minimal damage, though it did sweep away several dunes. A second hurricane that swept over the island on October 3 did far more damage, flattening the remaining dunes that afforded protection to the buildings and destroying the approaches to the lagoon bridge and the landing sites along the wharf. The next day Ship Island was invaded by a deluge of marsh animals, water fowl, and snakes that had been flushed out of the flooded wetlands that grounded on the Mississippi Sound side of the island. As the water moccasins, minks, otters, muskrats, and raccoons floated on an immense drift composed of logs, grass, and other debris to the island, "The snakes twined about the boat fittings, wharf timbers, etc., and escaped to the shore in great numbers." At least 300 of the vermin were killed within a span of 7 days, half of them on or near the station on the first day of their arrival on the island. Mercifully, cold weather brought an end to the invasion, but it was reported that for many weeks after the storm it was dangerous to walk about the grounds after sunset. In the months following the storm, the staff of the quarantine station, when not engaged in their official duties, were employed in landscaping, rebuilding walkways and fences, and clearing and burning storm debris. The following year saw the island and quarantine station receive another pounding on July 5, when another hurricane toppled chimneys, tore off several roofs, broke windows, and removed several hundred feet of decking and several pilings from the 1,290 foot wharf. Also, the fumigation barge of the station was driven out into the Gulf of Mexico and lost, and the launch *Hermes* was driven aground and damaged beyond repair. Though repairs were promptly initiated to the station, the continued erosion of the dunes was a more serious problem due to the protection they afforded to the grounds and buildings. September 18, 1916, saw another Gulf hurricane hammer the barrier island, causing additional damage to the buildings and protective dunes, which was a huge factor in the decision to relocate the quarantine station to Gulfport.[23]

Another iconic figure associated with Ship Island was the lighthouse, or lighthouses, the first of which was completed on March 17, 1853. The masonry structure was 45 feet high, the diameter of the base 22 feet, and that at the top 10½ feet. At the footings the walls were 3½ feet thick, graduating to 2 feet at the top. The bricks were laid in Rosendale cement and whitewashed over twice for durability, and the floor of the tower was paved with hard brick. A circular stairway, constructed of 2-inch oak plank with a rise of 8 inches, connected the lower extremity of the tower to within 6 feet of the lantern. The tower contained three windows that could seat twelve 8 × 10 lights, and an arch was turned at the top of the structure on which was laid a stone deck 12 feet in diameter and 4 inches thick. From the deck, 18 × 24 inch scuttle passed into the lantern, with an iron ladder passing from the top of the stairs to the scuttle's entrance. The lantern was constructed of octagonal wrought iron, housing six 20 × 24 inch panes glazed with the best French plate glass, and two 20 × 15 inch copper panes next to the deck. The top of the lantern was a dome formed by 16 iron rafters covered with copper, and a lightning rod extended 2 feet above the vane. The single-level lighthouse keeper's quarters was 34 × 20 feet divided into two rooms, and built of brick also. Attached to the quarters was a 14 × 12 foot kitchen, and outside the residence was a 5 × 4 feet outhouse.[24]

A November 1885 inspection of the lighthouse found that the north beach had eroded to the point where the foundations of the structure and dwelling had been severely undermined. A subsequent inspection by an engineer from the Lighthouse Board revealed that the side wall of the keeper's quarters nearest the beach was positioned to be undercut by flood tides, resulting in a collapse. Upon interviewing lighthouse keeper Dan McColl, who had served in that capacity since February 1875, the engineer learned that during McColl's time on the island, "the beach to a depth of 120 feet fronting the tower had been claimed by the sea," and during strong winds the tower rocked "quite perceptibly." A proposal was submitted to abandon the existing structure, and relocate a new lighthouse further from the effects of the action of the waves. This plan was adopted in February 1886, and plans made for a new tower and keeper's quarters to be located approximately 400 feet southwest of the existing structure. On September 1, 1886, the Lighthouse Board accepted the new station from the contractor who had been charged with its construction. The major difference in this tower and the previous one was that it was of wooden construction, instead of brick. Keeper McColl, an amputee, would stay in his position on Ship Island until June 15, 1899, when the Lighthouse Board reassigned him to less demanding duties at the Cat Island Lighthouse Station, where he would die in June of 1904. He was replaced in his job capacity on Ship Island by Peter Clarisse.[25]

In 1910, the U.S. Congress abolished the Lighthouse Board, replacing it with the newly established Bureau of Lighthouses, and placing it under the guidance of the U.S. Department of Commerce. During the autumn of 1930, the Ship Island Lighthouse Station joined the twentieth century with the introduction of electricity to the island. This resulted in changing the lantern in the lighthouse from oil wick to electric incandescent, a change that saw its candlepower jump from 150 to 200. The new lighting system was powered by a 32-volt kerosene electric generator and storage battery that also powered the keeper's quarters. Under the Reorganization Act of 1939, President Franklin Delano Roosevelt abolished the Lighthouse Service and merged its services into the United States Coast Guard, a move which placed the Ship Island lighthouse under the custodianship of the Coast Guard. During the winter of 1949, the Ship Island lighthouse was automated, the lighthouse keeper reassigned to other duties, and the keeper's quarters dismantled and removed to Biloxi, Mississippi. The Navy Hydrographic Office made the announcement in a Notice to Mariners, that was published on March 11, 1950, to insure that all maritime traffic would be aware that storm warnings would no longer be displayed at the light. The lighthouse was further downgraded on March 11, 1957, when the Coast Guard moved the light to the superstructure of the Gulfport Channel Outer Range Rear Light. The Ship Island Light Station's usefulness as a navigational aid had finally been made obsolete by the advent of new technologies.[26]

First Ship Island, Mississippi, lighthouse (courtesy of *Lighthouse Digest* magazine).

Second Ship Island, Mississippi, lighthouse before being enclosed (courtesy of *Lighthouse Digest* magazine).

As the Ship Island lighthouse was abandoned and had fallen into disrepair, on October 11, 1959, the Coast Guard granted a revocable five year permit to New Orleans native and Pass Christian, Mississippi, resident Philip M. Duvic to use the lighthouse "for private use and occupancy for general recreation purposes." This was done to prevent unmanned Coast Guard property from falling prey to vandalism. The first 12 months after Duvic was granted the permit to use the property, he made a number of improvements to the lighthouse, including a remodeling of the interior of the lighthouse in 1961. On the ground floor, Duvic installed a galley and restroom facility, followed by a ladies' dormitory on the second floor, a men's dormitory on the third floor, and a honeymoon suite on the top deck of the tower. During the summer of 1964, Duvic's permit was not renewed by the Coast Guard, and the lighthouse was declared surplus property and offered for sale on May 5, 1965. A provision of the sale was that the new owner would have to remove the tower from the island within 90 days of purchase. Duvic submitted the winning bid on the property, a sum of $250.

For some unexplained reason, Duvic was never required to fulfill the clause that the tower be removed from Ship Island. Duvic's improvements and usage of the tower came to an end on the evening of August 17, 1969, when the murderous Hurricane Camille sent a wall of water crashing over the island, washing the lower 12 feet of the lighthouse's weather board siding into the Gulf, as well as cracking one of the four concrete piers, though the tower still stood. Duvic, at home with his family at their residence at Pass Christian, barely escaped with their lives, though their home was destroyed. Due to the immense loss of property Duvic experienced at the hands of Camille, he made no further efforts to repair the lighthouse for further usage. Then, on the evening of June 27, 1972, two careless young campers on Ship Island accomplished what war and Mother Nature had been unable to do, when a campfire spread to the tower, quickly reducing it to blackened concrete footings and ashes.[27]

As many of the Gulf Coast residents had fond memories of the old lighthouse, an effort was launched by the Friends of Gulf Islands National Seashore to build a replica of the burned tower on Ship Island. Almost 28 years after the original had been destroyed, a replica was built

Second Ship Island, Mississippi, lighthouse after enclosure (courtesy of *Lighthouse Digest* magazine).

through the efforts of the U.S. Navy Seabees stationed at the local Coast Guard base, with wood furnished from massive trees donated by the United States Forestry Service from which the 64 feet × 12 inch corner beams were hewn. A dedication ceremony was held in May 2000 for the new Ship Island lighthouse, though its time on the island would be short-lived. In August 2005, Hurricane Katrina destroyed the structure as she swept along the Gulf Coast, once again denying a lighthouse to the barrier island. As of this writing, no effort is underway to rebuild the lighthouse.[28]

As for the image most closely associated with Ship Island, the masonry Fort Massachusetts, the old fort still stands despite the ravages of killer hurricanes and time. By the spring of 1901, the fort's ordnance and ordance stores were condemned and advertised for sale by the Ordnance Department. The chosen proposal was one made by A. Marx of 639 Tchoupitoulus Street in New Orleans for $2,054. The bid for the excess weaponry was endorsed by Lieutenant Edward P. Nones, who remarked that due to the inaccessibility of the fort by naval vessels to approach within 200 yards of the site, the expense of breaking up the guns would have to be absorbed by Marx. U.S. Chief of Ordnance Adelbert Buffington ordered that Marx's bid be accepted, and the ensuing months saw Marx's work crews blow up the guns to facilitate their removal in pieces. The exception was the massive 15-inch Rodman mounted on Platform Number 13, which was left in position, where it still commands the approach to the fort today.[29]

With the ordnance now removed from the fort with the exception of the Rodman, plans were put in motion to remove the ordnance-sergeant assigned to oversee the guns and have the

Most recent lighthouse on Ship Island, Mississippi, that was destroyed by Hurricane Katrina, 2005 (courtesy of *Lighthouse Digest* magazine).

lighthouse keeper assume the dual responsibility of fort keeper. On March 26, 1903, Ordnance-Sergeant John E. Barnes was transferred to Fort St. Philip, and lighthouse keeper Peter Clarisse became the official caretaker of Fort Massachusetts, with a per diem of $5.00 per month as compensation, until the position of fort keeper was abolished on April 30, 1904, and Clarisse assumed his original position as lighthouse keeper only.[30]

In November 1922, the U.S. War Department listed several properties as surplus, among which was Fort Massachusetts and the land that comprised the military reservation which encompassed the fort. To allow disposal of these surplus miltary reservations, Congress passed legislation, and President Calvin Coolidge signed into law, an act authorizing the secretary of war to sell the surplus lands. Though several local government proposals were floated, as well as an option given to the State of Mississippi to purchase the fort and land, the Ship Island Military Reservation remained in the hands of the federal government until June 15, 1933, when legislation was signed into law by President Franklin Delano Roosevelt authorizing the sale of the Ship Island Military Reservation to the Joe Graham Post #119 of the American Legion in Harrison County, Mississippi, for the sum of $15,000, payable in annual installments over ten years. This act was initiated at the urging of Luther W. Maples, the Mississippi Department commander of the American Legion and member of the Joe Graham Post, who wrote the War Department that he envisioned "preserving the old fort and making it into a real memorial to the World War veterans and also, a National Playground for the American Legion."[31]

On September 15, 1933, the Joe Graham Post entered into a contract with the War Department to purchase the miltary reservation, with the first payment of $1,500 due on December 11. When the financially strapped post was unable to make the first payment installment, an extension was granted until January 1, 1934, though the post was still unable to make the first installment on the loan. In June 1934, the War Department threatened to repossess the reservation, prompting the post to enlist the help of U.S. Senator Byron Patton "Pat" Harrison of Mississippi to forestall the foreclosure. Legislation that Harrison introduced in the next Congress was signed into law by President Roosevelt on September 4, 1935, authorizing the War Department to have the Ship Island Military Reservation reappraised, and to "accept, in full settlement of the obligation of ... Joe Graham Post under the terms of said contract, such sum, not less than $1,658.22." Upon the reappraisal by the Mobile Real Estate Association, the Joe Graham Post was advised by the War Department that $2,150 would settle the existing amount owed by the post to purchase the reservation. In January 1936, the post paid $2,000 to the U.S. Army chief of finance, and $150 to the Mobile Real Estate Association for the appraisal of the property. With a presence on the island for more than three-quarters of a century, the U.S. War Department had now disposed of its responsibility for Ship Island and Fort Massachusetts. The Joe Graham Post now had title to the historic area and structure.[32]

The American Legion post made a number of improvements to Ship Island over the following decade to create a recreation area on the island, including a restaurant, bathhouse, and other facilities. These improvements were washed away on September 18–19, 1947, when a massive hurricane that was pounding southern Florida changed coordinates and bore down on the Mississippi Gulf Coast. C.E. May, the manager of the Ship Island facilities for the Joe Graham Post, had left the island earlier on September 18 for a trip to Gulfport, planning to return later that day to evacuate three of his employees, Howard Pate, Annie Seals, and her husband, Eugene Seals. As storm warnings were given out along the coast, May was forced to cancel his evacuation trip to the island, and the three were left stranded. As the storm began to unleash its full fury on Ship Island, Pate and the Seals sought shelter inside of Fort Massachusetts in a guardroom, taking with them what was thought to be food and water enough to ride out the storm's fury. The following morning saw the tidal surge begin to sweep through the embrasures and sallyport, driving the three to escape the rising water by moving into a barbette tier service magazine. Upon their return to the guardroom to secure their foodstuffs, they observed that the drum upon which it had been placed had overturned, though they were able to salvage a meager loaf of bread, seven eggs, and a few tomatoes. The three employees then spent a harrowing 24 hours in the service magazine, frying their eggs by burning old magazines and newspapers.[33]

By the morning of September 20, the ferocious winds and waves had subsided enough for the Seals and Pate to venture outside of Fort Massachusetts in an effort to make their way to the badly damaged lighthouse keeper's quarters, where the keeper was glad to see they were still alive. The keeper's quarters had lost its porch and all outside buildings, and the tower itself had been undermined and the floor washed out. The storm had also made the electrical generators inoperable. The following afternoon, Manager May was finally able to make his way to the island, accompanied by Seaman First Class Howard Stone and E.L. King. Of the improvements that the post had made to the island, only the water tank and a few utility poles, minus the electrical cables, were left standing, of which "grass waves from the top of each pole." As to the massive dunes adjacent to the site of the Legionnaire's facilities, all had been practically leveled, and were now just "a few slight mounds." May estimated the loss to the Joe Graham Post at more than $48,000.[34]

With the onset of World War II in the 1940s, the U.S. Coast Guard established on Ship Island an anti-submarine beach patrol in 1942 to counter threats from the Axis to the Gulf Coast. That same year, the Army Air Corps also used the old quarantine station site on the island as a recreational facility for army personnel. Hurricane Camille in 1969 dealt Ship Island its most destructive blow, slicing the island in half and dividing it into East Ship Island and West Ship Island with her 200 mile per hour winds and 30 foot tidal surge. In 1971, the island became part of the Gulf Islands National Seashore, under the protection and care of the National Park Service. Since that time, several other hurricanes have also contributed to the erosion of the barrier island, most notably Georges in 1998 and the massive Katrina in 2005. Still, with all of the destruction that has been wreaked upon her by the ravages of Mother Nature, West Ship Island welcomes thousands of visitors every year to her sandy beaches, brought there via ferry from Gulfport.[35]

In the early summer of 1930, a memorial service was held at Ship Island to honor the Confederate soldiers who had perished there during their imprisonment, as well as those who survived their ordeal as captives. Mrs. Rogers Winter, an attendee at the service, recorded these poignant thoughts about the event that demonstrate the healing effects of time in the aftermath of civil war:

> One of the outstanding events of the recent reunion at Biloxi was the trip to Ship Island to pay tribute to the unknown dead who sleep there in the shifting sands. A selected group of men and women were invited to make the trip to the island in the boats of the Coast Guard ... Capt. S.P. Edmonds, Commander of the U.S. Coast Guard, a graduate of the Naval Academy at Annapolis, was in charge of the government boats which made the trip.
>
> One thought dominated the minds of those who really perceived the meaning of the trip to Ship Island. In the background were so many things that emphasized the historic importance of the changes made by time. As the government boats carried the descendants of the soldiers of the sixties to the scene where the men of the Confederacy suffered such indignity and pain as prisoners of war, a United States battleship appeared on the horizon. It was the ship sent by the government to the harbor at Gulfport as a gesture of admiration for the Confederate heroes gathered at Biloxi, and it was headed back to the Gulf of Mexico just at the time the other boats of the U.S. government were nearing Ship Island for the memorial service. Its low-lying hull was silhouetted in distinct relief against sky and water to the right of the old fort, conceived in the mind of Jefferson Davis as a defence to the South, but completed later by the government to house those in charge of the prisoners at Ship Island. The contrast between the old fort, rendered useless by the progress of modern

warfare, and the slim, powerful, dangerous battleship, whose guns could have demolished the fort in a few moments, could not escape the attentive mind and eye.

Nor could one escape the thought of the men who endured the tortures of the damned on that bleak island, where not a single tree offers shade to the weary, and where all day long the hot sun poured down its burning rays to the hot white sands that reflected glare and heat until men could endure no longer the agony of thirst and sun.

Looking from the white sands of the island during the memorial hour service, one thought how much the men who suffered there must have loved the evening, as it came down about them, and how often to them the jade green waters of the sea must have seemed as the bosom of a friend to which they might creep in silence and in tears, grateful for the soft embraces that gave them rest and death's eternal peace. Many died there in the sea, and many died of hunger and privation and of the scourge of yellow fever. They are listed as "The Unknown Dead," but their memory lives, and on that Friday afternoon of the reunion they received the tribute not only of their own beloved cause, but of the government which survived the conflict of the sixties.

No flowers bloom in the hot, white sands of Ship Island, but twelve army planes covered the graves of the unknown dead with blossoms, and because of Mrs. Kimbrough's devotion to the memory of the heroic Ship Island men, there will stand, in time, a monument there to perpetuate the courage of the men who died, prisoners of war, for the land they loved when they could no longer fight to protect the cause to which they had dedicated their lives. And as they sleep the long, long sleep of the dead, the Ship Island lighthouse stands watch above their graves and signals to the ships in passing, that each may keep safely on its course — a light that burns forever in the darkness, a light symbolic of the men whose devotion to their ideals of honor and patriotism has created a new beacon of light of valor for the generations to come.

And by that beacon light of memory, the youth of the South will set its course, steering always for the safe harbors of a finer citizenship, a deeper devotion to their country which needs today, more than ever before, men who are men, men who are patriots, men who are unafraid to face the issues that confront and menace the government for whose fundamental principles the men of the South fought and died.[36]

II. Rosters

Richmond, VA — June 1, 1861
There is not one true son of the South who is not ready to shoulder his musket to bleed, to die, or to conquer in the cause of liberty here.
— *Confederate States President Jefferson Davis*

Washington, D.C. — February 15, 1861
If all do not join now to save the good old ship of the Union this voyage, nobody will have a chance to pilot her on another voyage.
— *United States President Abraham Lincoln*

Guide to Using the Rosters

These rosters of the Union soldiers who died while serving on Ship Island and the Confederate troops who were held as prisoners of war there have been designed to provide an accurate record of each person's military service and prisoner record, pension application information, veterans census information, and civilian life, spouse(s), children and death/burial information. Please remember that the information for some of the soldiers listed in the rosters is far from complete. Many records of the late Confederacy were destroyed during, and at the close of, the war. In addition, the Union records of Confederates held as prisoners of war were found in a deplorable condition, and whole pages of the Ship Island Prisoner Register were illegible and undecipherable due to the ravages of time before they were microfilmed; some entries that were decipherable are open to wide interpretation as to the correctness of the names listed by the recording Union soldier. By no means do we wish to imply that all records have been located. We encourage the admirers and descendants of these brave men to conduct their own research for further information. However, these rosters are an invaluable tool to assist in your research.

Each soldier is listed by last name in the company in which he served. This is followed by his beginning rank at enlistment, and, if he was promoted, each subsequent rank. His date and place of enlistment follow, along with his muster rolls and date and place of capture, parole, or forwarding to a Northern military prison. If he was paroled and reported for exchange, the date and place will also be listed. Other details that could possibly be listed include the date and place of his 1865 final parole, his military medical history, his physical description, his residences, his occupations, the name of his spouse(s), the number and genders of his children, a listing on enumerations, his service in other units, and his burial location.

In some instances, the U.S. War Department was unable to find a military service record for a particular name. However, this is not definitive proof that the person was not in the military service. As late as February 10, 1932, the Adjutant General of the U.S. War Department stated in correspondence to Louisiana Congressman Bolivar E. Kemp, "The collection of Confederate records in this Department is far from complete, and failure to find the entire record of a person thereon is by no means conclusive proof that he did not serve during some period not covered by the records on file." Hence the inclusion of these men's data.

The removal and consolidation of numerous duplicate names has been accomplished with great care being taken to prevent exclusion. In the event that two names could not definitively be ascertained as the same person, both were left in the roster. If your target subject or ancestor's surname is one which has many varied spellings or pronunciations, you are advised to carefully scrutinize the roster to determine if the person could be listed under an alternative surname spelling. All name variations found in the various records searched are listed next to the name of the person under AKA, or "also known as."

The Union roster is a comprehensive listing of all Federal soldiers who died while stationed on Ship Island, regardless of the state from which they enlisted and served. The Confederate roster of prisoners, due to the vastness of numbers, is broken down by the states from which the soldiers enlisted. Also included in the Confederate section are the Confederate Navy and Confederate Regulars rosters listing the soldiers who were held on the island as prisoners of war, and a citizen roster listing the known individuals who were held on Ship Island as political prisoners by the Union.

Terms used and places referred to in the rosters are defined below. We have also described positions so one will have an idea of what function his ancestor or research subject performed during those turbulent days.

Term Definitions

Acute Diarrhea Different from regular diarrhea in that it was uncontrollable.
Adjutant Principal staff officer, the organ of the commanding officer. Duties included supervising the encampment, transmitting orders, assigning details, and mounting guards. Reported to the colonel of the regiment exclusively.
Anasarca A general accumulation of serious fluid in various tissues and body cavities.
Apoplexy Stroke.
Artificer Performed blacksmith duties, repairing wood and iron parts of the battery carriages.
Ballast Heavy material not listed on a vessel's cargo manifest that was used to stabilize the ship and keep it in proper draft or trim.
Bar The elevated portion of a basin that is usually formed by tidal action, over which a vessel had to pass in order to enter a body of water or harbor.
Battery In the Union army, it consisted of a cluster of six guns of the same caliber. In the Confederate army, it was four guns of the same caliber, though in general practice on both sides the term referred to any number of pieces or the place on which they were placed.
Bayonet An elongated dagger that could be attached to the muzzle of a musket or rifle.
Blockade A system of interdiction of vessel traffic into, and out of, Southern ports.
Blockade Runner A vessel whose mission was to circumvent the blockade of Southern ports and harbors.
Bucked and Gagged A form of punishment consisting of placing the prisoner in a sitting position, tying a bayonet across his open mouth, tying his wrists together and slipping them over his drawn-up knees, and then wedging a longer bayonet beneath his knees and across his forearms. Prisoners were often made to sit in this position for hours.
Camp Chase A prisoner of war camp for captured Confederate soldiers that was located a short distance west of Columbus, Ohio, and named for Ohio native and U.S. Treasury Secretary Salmon P. Chase. Originally built as a training facility for Ohio state troops, by 1863 the camp's prisoner population had swelled to over 8,000.
Camp Douglas Originally a 60-acre Union soldier training base located just south of Chicago, Illinois, the camp was converted into a prison that held as many as 30,000 captured Confederates.
Camp Morton Established on the site of the Indiana State Fairgrounds at Indianapolis and named for the state's wartime governor, Oliver P. Morton, this camp was a model of humane treatment of Confederate prisoners of war by the Union. The camp's commandant, Colonel Richard Owen, became the only commandant to be honored for his ethical treatment of prisoners by having a monument erected in his honor by former inmates after the war.
Captain Responsible for the supervision/direction of a regimental company, and the senior officer in the company. Reported to the regimental major, lieutenant-colonel, and colonel.
Carriage A wheel equipped support for an artillery piece used in casemates of permanent and semi-permanent fortifications.

Casemate A chamber designed to withstand artillery fire.
Cavalry Soldiers armed, trained, and equipped to fight on horseback.
Cholera Caused by unsanitary prison conditions. Symptoms included diarrhea, muscle cramps, dehydration, and vomiting, which often led to death. Often found in human feces. The bacteria was spread by water-supply contamination, flies, and food handling.
Chronic Constant or of long duration.
Citizens Populus of the Confederate States of America who were not enlisted in military service. In this work, they are defined as being held as political prisoners.
Coal Heaver A naval position whose responsibility was to shovel coal into a vessel's boiler in order to produce power to propel the ship.
Commutation Cash paid to a soldier in lieu of such stipulated necessities as food and clothing.
Company A basic military organizational unit comprised ideally of 100 men that was commanded by an officer with the rank of captain.
Confederate Pension Application An application for Confederate soldiers to receive a pension paid through the former Confederate state in which the soldier resided at the time of application. Most Southern states began providing pensions in 1898.
Confederate Regulars Assigned to the army of the Confederate States of America instead of a unit raised in an individual state.
Confederate Widows Pension Application An application from the widow of a Confederate veteran to receive a pension paid by the former Confederate state in which she resided at the time of application.
Conscript A soldier who was drafted or forced to join the military service, rather than volunteering to serve.
Consumption Tuberculosis.
Deadline A line established within the prison camp to mark the limit to which prisoners were allowed to roam within the prison. The violation of crossing this line resulted in instant death, as the guards were instructed to shoot to kill.
Debilitas Illness or a general weakness.
Deserter A soldier or sailor who willfully abandoned his unit or ship with no intention of returning.
Detached Service Formal release of a soldier from his normal duties for a stated period of time in order to allow him to perform other military functions.
Diarrhea In the Civil War era, frequent bowel movements not accompanied by straining.
Dysentery Bloody diarrhea.
Dyspepsia Referred to a wide range of gastrointestinal ailments.
Elmira Originally a training camp for Union soldiers in Chemung County, New York, it was converted into a prison for Confederate prisoners of war in May, 1864. The population escalated to over 12,000, and was known as one of the worst in terms of treatment and conditions utilized by either side during the war.
Embrasure An opening in a casemate that allowed artillery to fire through it.
Engineer Responsible for planning, building and repairing all fortifications and other defensive work. On a naval vessel, the duties included ensuring that the machinery to operate the ship was in working condition.
Erysipelas An infection of the skin, and tissues beneath the skin, that was accompanied by a high fever.
Exchange An agreement between the North and South that consented to exchanging prisoners rather than confining them in prison.
Febris Intermittens A fever that begins and ends at infrequent intervals.
Febris Remittens A fever that will temporarily abate in severity.
Fort Columbus Located on Governor's Island off Manhattan, this facility's prisoner of war population consisted of captured Confederate officers only. At its peak, it reached 300.
Fort Delaware A prisoner of war facility that was located on Pea Patch Island in the Delaware River that was notorious for its strict discipline of Confederate prisoners that bordered on torture. Its population averaged between 7,000 and 8,000, though by the end of the war it held as many as 30,000.
Fort Lafayette Located on a tiny island off the tip of Staten Island, New York, this was another prisoner of war facility for captured Confederates.
Fort McHenry This small prisoner of war camp located at Baltimore, Maryland, held as many as 7,000 captured Confederates at its height.
Fort Pickens Located not far from Pensacola, Florida, this large but poorly defended fort remained under

Union control throughout the war, and was utilized to detain captured Confederates until processing to other prisons.

Fort Warren Located on George's Island in Boston Harbor, Massachusetts, this facility was also a model of sanitary conditions and humane treatment, seeing only 12 Confederate deaths from its prisoner of war population throughout the war.

Furlough A formal leave of absence for a set period of time.

Garrison Military units assigned to occupy an installation with permanent quarters and specific duty areas.

Graybacks Body lice.

Hospital Steward Responsible for the general administration of a regimental hospital, including ventilation, lighting, heating, keeping hospital records, and maintaining hospital supplies, as well as the supervision and discipline of the hospital attendants. A non-commissioned officer who ranked above a first sergeant of a company. In battle, he would assist in the field hospital or a dressing station. On a march, he was responsible for hospital supplies and medicine chests.

Infantry Soldiers armed, trained, and equipped to fight on foot.

Johnson's Island A 300-acre, heavily wooded island in Lake Erie's Sandusky Bay that was located about a mile offshore and a little more than 2 miles from Sandusky, Ohio. The island was leased to the Federal government for usage as a prisoner of war camp, though the actual prison encompassed no more than 40 acres. Meant to hold 1,000 captured Confederates, the prison's population swelled to over 3,000 by the end of the war.

Landsman The lowest ranking member of a naval vessel's crew.

Mess A group of three to twenty prisoners who cooked and ate their rations, and/or sheltered together.

Orderly An aide, typically a private, assigned to perform various tasks for an officer.

Ordnance Sergeant Responsible for maintaining, storing, and transporting the vehicles, guns, ammunition, and equipment of a military unit.

Parole Allowed prisoners taken in battle or surrendered to be released with the stipulation that they would not bear arms again until being exchanged for an equivalent from the opposing side.

Picket A soldier on guard, alone or with others, whose duty was to give warning of an approaching enemy to prevent a surprise attack.

Point Lookout This prisoner of war facility was established after the Battle of Gettysburg on a resort at Point Lookout, Maryland. The 40-acre site came to be the largest prison in the North, with more than 22,000 prisoners. The inmates were housed in tents, and the area was prone to flooding, resulting in 3,584 Confederate prisoners dying there during the war.

Provost Duty Military police duty.

Provost Marshal Secured prisoners charged of criminal crimes of a general nature. They also prevented and pursued deserters.

Pthisis Tuberculosis.

Quarantine Station A landing spot for vessels at which a quarantine officer could inspect the crew and passengers for infectious diseases.

Quartermaster A military officer whose primary duty was to provide quarters, clothing, food, and transportation for troops, as well as forage for animals.

Ram A naval warship that was equipped with a massive iron arm projecting from its prow. It was designed to cripple and sink an enemy vessel by crashing into it.

Rock Island Located on an island 3 miles long and a half-mile wide in the Mississippi River between Davenport, Iowa, and Rock Island, Illinois, this prison opened in December, 1863, and was known for its inhumane conditions and treatment of Confederate prisoners.

Rubeola An acute and highly contagious viral disease marked by distinct red spots that were followed by a rash.

Scorbutic Diathesis Medical term for scurvy.

Scurvy Caused by the lack of ascorbic acid in the body as a result of a deprivation in diet of fresh fruit and vegetables. Advanced stages included spongy gums, loose teeth, and bleeding under the skin and in the mucous membranes.

Sergeant Major The senior enlisted soldier of a regiment, he had absolute, unrestricted access to the commanding officer. All non-commissioned officers were under his command.

Signal Corps A branch of the military whose duties consisted of providing communications between remote locations utilizing a system of flags, torches, rockets, and signal flares.

Sinks Trenches that served as a latrine or toilet.

Substitution A person paid to enlist in the military service on behalf of another.

Surgeon/Assistant Surgeon Responsible for the medical care of all soldiers in a regiment, including treating wounds, injuries, or diseases and prescribing medications. Surgeons were also responsible for the physical evaluation of recruits and the issuance of medical discharges to disabled or ill soldiers. Surgeons usually held the rank of major with the assistant surgeons holding the rank of lieutenant. Assistant surgeons, in the best of situations, were directly out of medical school. They reported to the commanding officer of a regiment.

Typhoid Fever A fever caused as the result of a bacterial intestinal infection.

Variola A highly contagious viral disease characterized by fever, weakness, and skin eruptions with pustules that form scabs. When the scabs slough off the skin, scars are left behind.

Whitworth Gun Manufactured in England, this artillery piece was unique in that it fired a hexagonal, rather than a round, projectile. Available in both a 6-pounder and 12-pounder caliber, it fired both solid shot and shells.

Yellow Fever A disease spread by mosquitoes that destroys the liver and kidneys. Its symptoms included the skin turning yellow. Also known as Yellow Jack.

Union Dead

Aderton, William Pvt., 13th Maine Infantry. Co. B. Enlisted: 11/10/1861 for 3 years. Mustered into service: 12/31/1861 at Augusta, ME. Age at enlistment: 22. Description at enlistment: Eyes: blue. Hair: light. Complexion: light. Height: 5'8". Marital status at enlistment: Single. Occupation at enlistment: Laborer. Residence at enlistment: Canaan, ME. Born: Canaan, ME. Died: 7/17/1862 at Ship Island, MS. Buried: Ship Island, MS, Cemetery; re-interred in 12/1867 at Chalmette, LA, National Cemetery in an unmarked grave.

Allen, Lewis T. Pvt., 13th Maine Infantry. Co. I. Enlisted: 10/31/1861 for 3 years. Mustered into service: 12/12/1861 at Augusta, ME. Age at enlistment: 43. Description at enlistment: Eyes: blue. Hair: brown. Complexion: light. Height: 5'11½". Marital status at enlistment: Single. Occupation at enlistment: Farmer. Residence at enlistment: Centerville, ME. Born: Centerville, ME. Died: 7/12/1862 at Ship Island, MS, due to disease. Buried: Ship Island, MS, Cemetery; re-interred in 12/1867 at Chalmette, LA, National Cemetery in an unmarked grave.

Allen, William Pvt., 6th Michigan Infantry. Co. E. Enlisted: 8/9/1861 for 3 years. Mustered into service: 8/20/1861 at Kalamazoo, MI. Age at enlistment: 19. Residence at enlistment: Calhoun County, MI. Died: 3/30/1862 at Ship Island, MS, due to disease. Buried: Ship Island, MS, Cemetery; re-interred in 12/1867 at Chalmette, LA, National Cemetery in an unmarked grave.

Andrews, Albert A. Pvt., 9th Connecticut Infantry. Co. I. Enlisted: 8/17/1861. Federal Rolls of Prisoners of War: Discharged due to illness on 9/4/1862. Born: 1838. Occupation at enlistment: Farmer. Residence at enlistment: Wolcott, CT.

Andrews, James H. (AKA F.H. John) Pvt., 12th Maine Infantry. Co. D. Enlisted: 10/10/1861 for 3 years. Mustered into service: 11/15/1861 at Cape Elizabeth, ME. Age at enlistment: 22. Description at enlistment: Eyes: blue. Hair: brown. Complexion: light. Height: 5'10½". Marital status at enlistment: Single. Occupation at enlistment: Farmer. Residence at enlistment: Franklin Point, ME. Born: Rumford, ME. Died: 2/12/1862 at Ship Island, MS, due to disease. Buried: Ship Island, MS, Cemetery; re-interred in 12/1867 at Chalmette, LA, National Cemetery in Section 29, Grave #326.

Andrews, John Pvt., 161st New York Infantry. Co. C. (Military Convict). Enlisted: 8/21/1862 at Elmira, NY, for 3 years. Mustered into service: 9/7/1862. Age at enlistment: 21. Sentenced to imprisonment in the Ship Island, MS, stockade. Died: 5/14/1863 at Ship Island, MS, due to disease. Buried: Ship Island, MS, Cemetery; re-interred in 12/1867 at Chalmette, LA, National Cemetery in an unmarked grave.

Andrews, M.J. Seaman, U.S.A. Navy. Buried: Ship Island, MS, Cemetery; re-interred in 12/1867 at Chalmette, LA, National Cemetery in Section 29, Grave #291.

Armstrong, Charles Pvt., 9th New York Infantry. Co. A. (Military Convict). Sentenced to 3 years at hard labor with a ball and chain on Ship Island, MS; Received at Ship Island, MS, on 12/9/1862. Buried: Ship Island, MS, Cemetery; re-interred in 12/1867 at Chalmette, LA, National Cemetery in Section 29, Grave #268.

Bachelder, James P. (AKA Batchelder) Pvt., 8th New Hampshire Infantry. Co. F. Buried: Ship Island, MS, Cemetery; re-interred in 12/1867 at Chalmette, LA, National Cemetery in Section 9, Grave #483.

Balcom, Charles Pvt., 174th New York Infantry. Co. B. (Military Convict). Enlisted: 11/6/1862 at New York City, NY, for 3 years. Mustered into service: 11/13/1862. Age at enlistment: 24. Sentenced to imprisonment in the Ship Island, MS, stockade; Received at Ship Island, MS, on 5/13/1863. Died: 5/27/1863 at Ship Island, MS. Buried: Ship Island, MS, Cemetery; re-interred in 12/1867 at Chalmette, LA, National Cemetery in an unmarked grave.

Barnes, Calvin Pvt., 74th United States Colored Infantry. Co. F. Buried: Ship Island, MS, Cemetery; re-interred in 12/1867 at Chalmette, LA, National Cemetery in an unmarked grave.

Barrett, Alonzo Pvt., 13th Maine Infantry. Co. E. Enlisted: 11/6/1861 for 3 years. Mustered into service: 12/10/1861 at Augusta, ME. Age at enlistment: 43. Description at enlistment: Eyes: blue. Hair: light. Complexion: sandy. Height: 5'3¼". Marital status at enlistment: Single. Occupation at enlistment: Farmer. Residence at enlistment: Weld, ME. Born: Weld, ME. Died: 5/27/1862 at Ship Island, MS. Buried: Ship Island, MS, Cemetery; re-interred in 12/1867 at Chalmette, LA, National Cemetery in an unmarked grave.

Bean, Carlostian J. (AKA Cailoblian, Carlostin, J. Beane) Cpl., 13th Maine Infantry. Co. C. Enlisted: 10/24/1861 for 3 years. Mustered into service: 12/4/1861 at Augusta, ME. Age at enlistment: 23. Description at enlistment: Eyes: light. Hair: light. Complexion: light. Height: 5'6". Marital status at enlistment: Married. Occupation at enlistment: Farmer. Residence at enlistment: Harmony, ME. Born: Athens, ME. Died: 6/16/1862 at Ship Island, MS. Buried: Ship Island, MS, Cemetery; re-interred in 12/1867 at Chalmette, LA, National Cemetery in an unmarked grave.

Berry, James L. Pvt., 13th Maine Infantry. Co. C. Enlisted: 10/26/1861 for 3 years. Mustered into service: 12/4/1861 at Augusta, ME. Age at enlistment: 18. Description at enlistment: Eyes: blue. Hair: dark. Complexion: dark. Height: 5'3". Marital status at enlistment: Single. Occupation at enlistment: Farmer. Residence at enlistment: Pittsfield, ME. Born: Pittsfield, ME. Died: 6/26/1862 at Ship Island, MS. Buried: Ship Island, MS, Cemetery; re-interred in 12/1867 at Chalmette, LA, National Cemetery in an unmarked grave.

Billings, Adonirum J. (AKA A.T.) Cpl., 13th Maine Infantry. Co. F. Enlisted: 11/4/1861 for 3years. Mustered into service: 12/10/1861 at Augusta, ME. Age at enlistment: 32. Description at enlistment: Eyes: blue. Hair: dark. Complexion: dark. Height: 6'0". Marital status at enlistment: Married. Occupation at enlistment: Stonecutter. Residence at enlistment: Brooksville, ME. Born: Bluehill, ME. Died: 8/23/1862 at Ship Island, MS, due to disease. Buried: Ship Island, MS, Cemetery; re-interred in 12/1867 at Chalmette, LA, National Cemetery in Section 19, Grave #500.

Bird, William F. Pvt., 13th Maine Infantry. Co. F. Enlisted: 11/9/1861 for 3 years. Mustered into service: 12/10/1861 at Augusta, ME. Age at enlistment: 28. Description at enlistment: Eyes: black. Hair: dark. Complexion: dark. Height: 5'4". Marital status at enlistment: Married. Occupation at enlistment: Shoemaker. Residence at enlistment: Auburn, ME. Born: Portland, ME. Died: 8/20/1862 at Ship Island, MS, due to disease. Buried: Ship Island, MS, Cemetery; re-interred in 12/1867 at Chalmette, LA, National Cemetery in Section 29, Grave #295.

Black, Oliver Pvt./Musician, 26th Massachusetts Infantry. Co. K. Enlisted: 9/26/1861. Age at enlistment: 16. Residence at enlistment: Lowell, MA. Occupation at enlistment: Farmer. Died: Ship Island, MS. Buried: Ship Island, MS, Cemetery; re-interred in 12/1867 at Chalmette, LA, National Cemetery in Section 29, Grave #255.

Bonney, John Pvt., 12th Connecticut Infantry. Co. K. Enlisted: 12/21/1861 for 3 years. Mustered into service: 12/31/1861 at Camp Lyon, Hartford, CT. Residence at enlistment: Hartford, CT. Died: 9/16/1862 at Ship Island, MS. Buried: Ship Island, MS, Cemetery; re-interred in 12/1867 at Chalmette, LA, National Cemetery in Section 11, Grave #1010.

Borden, Warren L. (AKA Boyden) Pvt., Vermont Light Artillery. 2nd Battery. Enlisted: 12/18/1861 for 3 years. Mustered into service: 12/24/1861. Residence at enlistment: Vergennes, VT. Died: 6/14/1862 at Ship Island, MS, due to disease. Buried: Ship Island, MS, Cemetery; re-interred in 12/1867 at Chalmette, LA, National Cemetery in an unmarked grave.

Bradbury, William S. Pvt., 14th Maine Infantry. Co. F. Enlisted: 11/22/1861 for 3 years. Mustered into service: 1/8/1862 at Augusta, ME. Age at enlistment: 43. Description at enlistment: Eyes: blue. Hair: gray. Complexion: light. Height: 5'7½". Marital status at enlistment: Married. Occupation at enlistment: Farmer. Residence at enlistment: New Sharon, ME. Born: Vienna, ME. Died: 5/24/1862 at Ship Island, MS. Buried: Ship Island, MS, Cemetery; re-interred in 12/1867 at Chalmette, LA, National Cemetery in Section 29, Grave #313.

Bradley, George (AKA Bradford) Pvt., 6th Michigan Heavy Artillery. Co. K. Buried: Ship Island, MS, Cemetery; re-interred in 12/1867 at Chalmette, LA, National Cemetery in Section 29, Grave #281.

Brainard, Herbert T.N. (AKA Rainard, T.W.H.) Pvt., 14th Maine Infantry. Cos. B & C. Enlisted: 12/10/1861; Mustered into service: 12/10/1861. Age at enlistment: 18. Residence at enlistment: Manchester, ME. Died: 3/22/1862 at Ship Island, MS. Buried: Ship Island, MS, Cemetery; re-interred in 12/1867 at Chalmette, LA, National Cemetery in an unmarked grave.

Brant, Lafayette Pvt., 6th Michigan Infantry. Co. B. Enlisted: 8/14/1861 for 3 years. Mustered into service: 8/20/1861 at Kalamazoo, MI. Age at enlistment: 20. Residence at enlistment: Berrien County, MI. Died: 4/2/1862 at Ship Island, MS, due to disease. Buried: Ship Island, MS, Cemetery; re-interred in 12/1867 at Chalmette, LA, National Cemetery in an unmarked grave.

Brooks, John S. Pvt., 8th New Hampshire Infantry. Cos. G & I. Enlisted: 12/13/1861 for 3 years. Mustered into service: 12/23/1861. Age at enlistment: 21. Died: Ship Island, MS. Buried: Ship Island, MS, Cemetery; re-interred in 12/1867 at Chalmette, LA, National Cemetery in Section 29, Grave #247.

Brooks, William E. (AKA W.F.) Pvt., 12th Maine Infantry. Co. B. Enlisted: 10/22/1861 for 3 years. Mustered into service: 11/16/1861 at Cape Elizabeth, ME. Age at enlistment: 23. Description at enlistment: Eyes: black. Hair: brown. Complexion-florid. Height: 5'7". Marital status at enlistment: Single. Occupation at enlistment: Farmer. Residence at enlistment: Gray, ME. Born: Woodstock, ME. Died: 4/5/1862 at Ship Island, MS, due to drowning. Buried: Ship Island, MS, Cemetery; re-interred in 12/1867 at Chalmette, LA, National Cemetery in Section 29, Grave #310.

Brown, George W. Pvt., 14th Maine Infantry. Co. D. Enlisted: 11/28/1861 for 3 years. Mustered into service: 12/11/1861 at Augusta, ME. Age at enlistment: 18. Description at enlistment: Eyes: blue. Hair: light. Complexion: light. Height: 5'9½". Marital status at enlistment: Single. Occupation at enlistment: Farmer. Residence at enlistment: Medford, ME. Born: Exeter, ME. Died: 3/15/1862 at Ship Island, MS, due to disease. Buried: Ship Island, MS, Cemetery; re-interred in 12/1867 at Chalmette, LA, National Cemetery in Section 29, Grave #303.

Butler, Daniel B. (AKA Burton, D.G.) Pvt., 15th Maine Infantry. Co. H. Enlisted: 12/4/1861 for 3 years. Mustered into service: 12/17/1861 at Augusta, ME. Age at enlistment: 19. Description at enlistment: Eyes: blue. Hair: brown. Complexion: light. Height: 5'8½". Marital status at enlistment: Single. Occupation at enlistment: Laborer. Residence at enlistment: Charleston, ME. Born: Orneville, ME. Died: 5/24/1862 at Ship Island, MS, due to disease. Buried: Ship Island, MS, Cemetery; re-interred in 12/1867 at Chalmette, LA, National Cemetery in Section 99, Grave #362.

Buzzell, Solon D. Pvt., 8th Vermont Infantry. Co. K. Enlisted: 1/3/1862 for 3 years. Mustered into service: 2/18/1862 at Camp Holbrook, Brattleboro, VT. Residence at enlistment: Granby, VT. Died: 4/29/1862 at Ship Island, MS, due to disease. Buried: Ship Island, MS, Cemetery; re-interred in 12/1867 at Chalmette, LA, National Cemetery in Section 29, Grave #269.

Cameron, Finaly (AKA Tinley, Finley) Pvt., 14th Maine Infantry. Co. I. Enlisted: 11/25/1861 for 3 years. Mustered into service: 12/14/1861 at Augusta, ME. Age at enlistment: 29. Description at enlistment: Eyes: gray. Hair: black. Complexion: fair. Height: 5'11½". Marital status at enlistment: Single. Occupation at enlistment: Farmer. Residence at enlistment: Stacyville, ME. Born: Mabon, Nova Scotia. Died: 7/18/1862 at Ship Island, MS. Buried: Ship Island, MS, Cemetery; re-interred in 12/1867 at Chalmette, LA, National Cemetery in Section 29, Grave #325.

Camle, G.S. Pvt., 8th Vermont Infantry. Co. G. Buried: Ship Island, MS, Cemetery; re-interred in 12/1867 at Chalmette, LA, National Cemetery in Section 29, Grave #260.

Carpenter, Francis N. (AKA F.A.) Pvt., 14th Maine Infantry. Co. A. Enlisted: 12/18/1861 for 3 years. Mustered into service: 12/28/1861 at Augusta, ME. Age at enlistment: 24. Description at enlistment: Eyes: blue. Hair: light. Complexion: light. Height: 5'7". Marital status at enlistment: Single. Occupation at enlistment: Farmer. Residence at enlistment: Penobscot, ME. Born: Penobscot, ME. Died: 5/4/1862 at Ship Island, MS, due to disease. Buried: Ship Island, MS, Cemetery; re-interred in 12/1867 at Chalmette, LA, National Cemetery in Section 29, Grave #286.

Carson, Levi C. Pvt., 13th Maine Infantry. Co. A. Buried: Ship Island, MS, Cemetery; re-interred in 12/1867 at Chalmette, LA, National Cemetery in Section 29, Grave #299.

Carter, Alden G. Pvt., 14th Maine Infantry. Co. A. Enlisted: 11/20/1861 for 3 years. Mustered into service: 12/3/1861 at Augusta, ME. Age at enlistment: 18. Description at enlistment: Eyes: hazel. Hair: brown. Complexion: light. Height: 5'9". Marital status at enlistment: Single. Occupation at enlistment: Farmer. Residence at enlistment: Bluehill, ME. Born: Sedgwick, ME. Died: 5/23/1862 at Ship Island, ME. Buried: Ship Island, MS, Cemetery; re-interred in 12/1867 at Chalmette, LA, National Cemetery in Section 99, Grave #337.

Cates, Sewell L. (AKA Gates, Oates, Seawall, Sewall) Pvt., 13th Maine Infantry. Co. H. Enlisted: 12/12/1861 for 3 years. Mustered into service: 12/12/1861 at Augusta, ME. Age at enlistment: 21. Description at enlistment: Eyes: blue. Hair: light. Complexion: light. Height: 6'1". Marital status at enlistment: Single. Occupation at enlistment: Lumbering. Residence at enlistment: Berlin Falls, NH. Born: Carroll, ME. Died: 6/27/1862 at Ship Island, MS, due to disease. Buried: Ship Island, MS, Cemetery; re-interred in 12/1867 at Chalmette, LA, National Cemetery in Section 19, Grave #507.

Champlin, George W. (AKA Champlain) Pvt., 114th New York Infantry. Co. F. Enlisted: 8/11/1862 at New Berlin, NY, for 3 years. Mustered into service: 8/12/1862 at Norwich, NY. Age at enlistment: 25. Died: 12/19/1862 at Ship Island, MS, due to disease. Buried: Ship Island, MS, Cemetery; re-interred in 12/1867 at Chalmette, LA, National Cemetery in Section 99, Grave #375.

Chapman, Jacob P. (AKA J.B.) Pvt., 13th Maine Infantry. Co. D. Enlisted: 11/5/1861 for 3 years. Mustered into service: 12/10/1861 at Augusta, ME. Age at enlistment: 25. Description at enlistment: Eyes: blue. Hair: brown. Complexion: dark. Height: 5'7". Marital status at enlistment: Single. Occupation at enlistment: Farmer. Residence at enlistment: Dead River, ME. Born: New Portland, ME. Died: 6/2/1862 at Ship Island, MS, due to disease. Buried: Ship Island, MS, Cemetery; re-interred in 12/1867 at Chalmette, LA, National Cemetery in an unmarked grave.

Chapman, William S. Pvt., 13th Maine Infantry. Co. F. Enlisted: 11/18/1861 for 3 years. Mustered into service: 12/10/1861 at Augusta, ME. Age at enlistment: 21. Description at enlistment: Eyes: blue. Hair: brown. Complexion: light. Height: 5'9". Marital status at enlistment: Single. Occupation at enlistment: Farmer. Residence at enlistment: Athens, ME. Born: Athens, ME. Died: 11/23/1862 at Ship Island, MS, due to disease. Buried: Ship Island, MS, Cemetery; re-interred in 12/1867 at Chalmette, LA, National Cemetery in Section 99, Grave #341.

Chase, Braddock R. Cpl., 30th Massachusetts Infantry. Co. A. Enlisted: 10/1/1861 for 3 years. Mustered into service: 10/18/1861 at Lowell, MA. Age at enlistment: 22. Residence at enlistment: Falmouth, MA. Occupation at enlistment: Painter. Died: 5/20/1862 at Ship Island, MS, due to disease. Buried: Ship Island, MS, Cemetery; re-interred in 12/1867 at Chalmette, LA, National Cemetery in Section 29, Grave #259.

Chase, John Pvt., 12th Maine Infantry. Co. G. Enlisted: 10/15/1861 for 3 years. Mustered into service: 11/15/1861 at Cape Elizabeth, ME. Age at enlistment: 26. Description at enlistment: Eyes: hazel. Hair: dark. Complexion: dark. Height: 6'2". Marital status at enlistment: Single. Occupation at enlistment: Farmer. Residence at enlistment: Upton, ME. Born: Upton, ME. Died: 3/25/1862 at Ship Island, MS, due to disease. Buried: Ship Island, MS, Cemetery; re-interred in 12/1867 at Chalmette, LA, National Cemetery in Section 99, Grave #356.

Church, Morris (AKA Moses) Pvt., 12th Connecticut Infantry. Cos. G & H. Enlisted: 10/30/1861 for 3 years in Co. G; Mustered into service: 11/22/1861 at Camp Lyon, Hartford, CT. Transferred to Co. H on 4/1/1862. Residence at enlistment: Chaplin, CT. Died: 5/21/1862 at Ship Island, MS. Buried: Ship Island, MS, Cemetery; re-interred in 12/1867 at Chalmette, LA, National Cemetery in Section 29, Grave #264.

Clark, Norman Pvt., 31st Massachusetts Infantry. Co. G. Enlisted: 11/18/1861 for 3 years. Mustered into service: 11/18/1861. Age at enlistment: 43. Residence at enlistment: Westfield, MA. Occupation at enlistment: Farmer. Died: 4/15/1862 at Ship Island, MS, due to disease. Buried: Ship Island, MS, Cemetery; re-interred in 12/1867 at Chalmette, LA, National Cemetery in Section 99, Grave #336.

Clark, Stephen B. (AKA Steven) Pvt., 7th Vermont Infantry. Co. F. Enlisted: 1/29/1862 for 3 years. Mustered into service: 2/12/1862. Residence at enlistment: Swanton, VT. Died: 6/26/1862 at Ship Island, MS, due to disease. Buried: Ship Island, MS, Cemetery; re-interred in 12/1867 at Chalmette, LA, National Cemetery in Section 29, Grave #287.

Closson, Joel (AKA Clossom) Pvt., 14th Maine Infantry. Co. A. Enlisted: 11/14/1861 for 3 years. Mustered into service: 12/3/1861 at Augusta, ME. Age at enlistment: 18. Description at enlistment: Eyes: gray. Hair: black. Complexion: dark. Height: 5'6½". Marital status at enlistment: Single. Occupation at enlistment: Farmer. Residence at enlistment: Bluehill, ME. Born: Bluehill, ME. Died: 4/22/1862 at Ship Island, MS. Buried: Ship Island, MS, Cemetery; re-interred in 12/1867 at Chalmette, LA, National Cemetery in Section 29, Grave #324.

Colley, Robert N. (AKA Polley, R.H.) Pvt., 8th New Hampshire Infantry. Co. G. Enlisted: 12/13/1861 for 3 years. Mustered into service: 12/23/1861. Age at enlistment: 27. Residence at enlistment: Manchester, NH. Born: Derry, NH. Died: 5/18/1862 at Ship Island, MS, due to disease. Buried: Ship Island, MS, Cemetery; re-interred in 12/1867 at Chalmette, LA, National Cemetery in Section 19, Grave #486.

Colson, Aaron Pvt., 15th Maine Infantry. Co. A. Enlisted: 11/4/1861 for 3 years. Mustered into service: 12/6/1861 at Augusta, ME. Age at enlistment: 18. Description at enlistment: Eyes: hazel. Hair: brown. Complexion: dark. Height: 5'5". Marital status at enlistment: Single. Occupation at enlistment: Farmer. Residence at enlistment: Trescott, ME. Born: Trescott, ME. Died: 5/10/1862 at Ship Island, MS, due to disease. Buried: Ship Island, MS, Cemetery; re-interred in 12/1867 at Chalmette, LA, National Cemetery in Section 29, Grave #262.

Corson, Levi S. (AKA L.C.) Pvt., 13th Maine Infantry. Co. A. Enlisted: 10/20/1861 for 3 years. Mustered into service: 1/30/1862 at Augusta, ME. Age at enlistment: 18. Description at enlistment: Eyes: blue. Hair: light. Complexion: light. Height: 5'6". Marital status at enlistment: Single. Occupation at enlistment: Farmer. Residence at enlistment: Limerick, ME. Born: Limerick, ME. Died: 6/2/1862 at Ship Island, MS, due to disease. Buried: Ship Island, MS, Cemetery; re-interred in 12/1867 at Chalmette, LA, National Cemetery in an unmarked grave.

Crans, Edward Pvt., 4th Wisconsin Cavalry. Co. K. Enlisted: 7/3/1861 for 3 years in the 4th Wisconsin Infantry; Mustered into service: 7/3/1861 at Racine, WI. Residence at enlistment: Gravesville, WI. Died: 4/2/1862 at Ship Island, MS. Buried: Ship Island, MS, Cemetery; re-interred in 12/1867 at Chalmette, LA, National Cemetery in an unmarked grave.

Cross, Albion P. (AKA Allron) Pvt., 13th Maine Infantry. Co. E. Enlisted: 11/30/1861 for 3 years. Mustered into service: 12/10/1861 at Augusta, ME. Age at enlistment: 24. Description at enlistment: Eyes: black. Hair: dark. Complexion: dark. Height: 5'8". Marital status at enlistment: Single. Occupation at enlistment: Printer. Residence at enlistment: Portland, ME. Born: Portland, ME. Died: 6/25/1862 at Ship Island, MS. Buried: Ship Island, MS, Cemetery; re-interred in 12/1867 at Chalmette, LA, National Cemetery in Section 99, Grave #358.

Crowell, Sanford (AKA Growell, Sandford) Cpl., 13th Maine Infantry. Co. D. Enlisted: 11/14/1861 for 3 years. Mustered into service: 12/10/1861 at Augusta, ME. Age at enlistment: 31. Description at enlistment: Eyes: dark blue. Hair: brown. Complexion: light. Height: 6'4". Marital status at enlistment: Married. Occupation at enlistment: Farmer. Residence at enlistment: Smithfield, ME. Born: Belgrade, ME. Died: 9/1/1862 at Ship Island, MS, due to disease. Buried: Ship Island, MS, Cemetery; re-interred in 12/1867 at Chalmette, LA, National Cemetery in Section 29, Grave #315.

Crowell, Silas T. Pvt., 14th Maine Infantry. Co. G. Enlisted: 11/7/1861 for 3 years. Mustered into service: 12/12/1861 at Augusta, ME. Age at enlistment: 28. Description at enlistment: Eyes: blue. Hair: brown. Complexion: light. Height: 5'9½". Marital status at enlistment: Married. Occupation at enlistment: Shoemaker. Residence at enlistment: Oxford, ME. Born: Danville, VT. Died: 4/11/1862 at Ship Island, MS. Buried: Ship Island, MS, Cemetery; re-interred in 12/1867 at Chalmette, LA, National Cemetery in an unmarked grave.

Currin S. Pvt., 12th Maine Infantry. Co. __. Buried: Ship Island, MS, Cemetery; re-interred in 12/1867 at Chalmette, LA, National Cemetery in an unmarked grave.

Cushing, Ira W. (AKA Cushen, I.A.) Cpl., 15th Maine Infantry. Co. A. Enlisted: 10/19/1861 for 3 years. Mustered into service: 12/6/1861 at Augusta, ME. Age at enlistment: 21. Description at enlistment: Eyes: blue. Hair: brown. Complexion: fair. Height: 5'11¼". Marital status at enlistment: Single. Occupation: Teamster. Residence at enlistment: Pembroke, ME. Born: Pembroke, ME. Died: 5/21/1862 at Ship Island, MS, due to disease. Buried: Ship Island, MS, Cemetery; re-interred in 12/1867 at Chalmette, LA, National Cemetery in Section 99, Grave #345.

Danico, George E. (AKA Damico) Pvt., 15th Maine Infantry. Co. G. Enlisted: 1/9/1862 for 3 years. Mustered into service: 1/25/1862 at Augusta, ME. Age at enlistment: 29. Description at enlistment: Eyes: blue. Hair: light. Complexion: sandy. Height: 5'8". Marital status at enlistment: Single. Occupation at enlistment: Farmer. Residence at enlistment: Fort Fairfield, ME. Born: Ellsworth, ME. Died: 6/1/1862 at Ship Island, MS, due to fever. Buried: Ship Island, MS, Cemetery; re-interred in 12/1867 at Chalmette, LA, National Cemetery in Section 99, Grave #378.

Davis, Josiah R. Sgt., 21st Indiana Infantry. Co. H. Enlisted: 7/24/1861. Died: 4/30/1862 at Ship Island, MS, due to disease. Buried: Ship Island, MS, Cemetery; re-interred in 12/1867 at Chalmette, LA, National Cemetery in Section 29, Grave #278.

Dinsmore, Orin A. (AKA Orrin C.) Pvt., 13th Maine Infantry. Co. I. Enlisted: 1/11/1862 for 3 years. Mustered into service: 1/25/1862 at Augusta, ME. Age at enlistment: 18. Description at enlistment: Eyes: blue.

Hair: light. Complexion: light. Height: 5'6". Marital status at enlistment: Single. Occupation at enlistment: Farmer. Residence at enlistment: Lubec, ME. Born: Lubec, ME. Died: 7/19/1862 at Ship Island, MS, due to disease. Buried: Ship Island, MS, Cemetery; re-interred in 12/1867 at Chalmette, LA, National Cemetery in an unmarked grave.

Dorgan, James Pvt., 159th New York Infantry. Co. D. (Military Convict). Enlisted: 9/10/1862 at Brooklyn, NY, for 3 years. Mustered into service: 11/1/1862 at New York City, NY. Age at enlistment: 37. Sentenced to imprisonment in the Ship Island, MS, stockade; Received at Ship Island, MS, on 10/20/1863. Died: 12/22/1864 at Ship Island, MS. Buried: Ship Island, MS, Cemetery; re-interred in 12/1867 at Chalmette, LA, National Cemetery in an unmarked grave.

Drafton, Harrison Cpl., 14th Maine Infantry. Co. E. Buried: Ship Island, MS, Cemetery; re-interred in 12/1867 at Chalmette, LA, National Cemetery in Section 29, Grave #254.

Duboise, Charles (AKA Dubois) Pvt., 12th Connecticut Infantry. Co. B. Enlisted: 10/1/1861 for 3 years. Mustered into service: 11/23/1861 at Camp Lyon, Hartford, CT. Residence at enlistment: New Haven, CT. Died: 3/18/1865 at Ship Island, MS, due to drowning. Buried: Ship Island, MS, Cemetery; re-interred in 12/1867 at Chalmette, LA, National Cemetery in Section 99, Grave #367.

Durell, Henry E. (AKA E.H.) Pvt., 13th Maine Infantry. Co. K. Enlisted: 11/16/1861 for 3 years. Mustered into service: 12/13/1861 at Augusta, ME. Age at enlistment: 21. Description at enlistment: Eyes: blue. Hair: light. Complexion: light. Height: 5'10". Marital status at enlistment: Single. Occupation at enlistment: Farmer. Residence at enlistment: South Paris, ME. Born: Paris, ME. Died: 4/26/1862 at Ship Island, MS. Buried: Ship Island, MS, Cemetery; re-interred in 12/1867 at Chalmette, LA, National Cemetery in Section 99, Grave #383.

Earle, Joseph W. (AKA Earl) Pvt./Sgt., 4th Wisconsin Cavalry. Co. D. Enlisted: 6/2/1861 in the 4th Wisconsin Infantry for 3 years. Mustered into service: 7/2/1861 at Racine, WI. Residence at enlistment: Springville, WI. Died: 6/21/1862 at Ship Island, MS, due to disease. Buried: Ship Island, MS, Cemetery; re-interred in 12/1867 at Chalmette, LA, National Cemetery in Section 29, Grave #248.

Eastman, Daniel E. Pvt., 30th Massachusetts Infantry. Co. C. Enlisted: 12/6/1861 for 3 years. Mustered into service: 12/19/1861 at Lowell, MA. Age at enlistment: 24. Residence at enlistment: Lowell, MA. Occupation at enlistment: Laborer. Died: 2/27/1862 at Ship Island, MS, due to disease. Buried: Ship Island, MS, Cemetery; re-interred in 12/1867 at Chalmette, LA, National Cemetery in Section 99, Grave #343.

Eggleston, Lewis H. Pvt., 6th Michigan Infantry. Co. G. Enlisted: 8/6/1861 for 3 years. Mustered into service: 8/20/1861 at Kalamazoo, MI. Age at enlistment: 18. Residence at enlistment: Allegan County, MI. Died: 5/28/1862 at Ship Island, MS, due to disease. Buried: Ship Island, MS, Cemetery; re-interred in 12/1867 at Chalmette, LA, National Cemetery in Section 29, Grave #251. Born: 1844 in Ohio.

Fagan, Michael Pvt., 9th Connecticut Infantry. Cos. D & K. Enlisted: 9/27/1861 for 3 years. Mustered into service: 10/30/1861. Residence at enlistment: Bridgeport, CT. Died: 1/30/1862 at Ship Island, MS. Buried: Ship Island, MS, Cemetery; re-interred in 12/1867 at Chalmette, LA, National Cemetery in Section 99, Grave #334.

Fall, Isaac R. (AKA Fale) Pvt., 15th Maine Infantry. Co. H. Enlisted: 11/21/1861 for 3 years. Mustered into service: 12/17/1861 at Augusta, ME. Age at enlistment: 19. Description at enlistment: Eyes: gray. Hair: brown. Complexion: light. Height: 5'11½". Marital status at enlistment: Single. Occupation at enlistment: Laborer. Residence at enlistment: Garland, ME. Born: Garland, ME. Died: 6/26/1862 at Ship Island, MS, due to disease. Buried: Ship Island, MS, Cemetery; re-interred in 12/1867 at Chalmette, LA, National Cemetery in Section 29, Grave #280.

Ferdon, George W. Pvt., 4th Wisconsin Cavalry. Co. K. Enlisted: 6/1/1861 for 3 years. Mustered into service: 7/2/1861 at Racine, WI. Residence at enlistment: Brillion, WI. Died: Ship Island, MS, due to disease. Buried: Ship Island, MS, Cemetery; re-interred in 12/1867 at Chalmette, LA, National Cemetery in an unmarked grave.

Fernald, Joseph Pvt., 13th Maine Infantry. Co. A. Enlisted: 10/7/1861 for 3 years. Mustered into service: 11/20/1861 at Augusta, ME. Age at enlistment: 21. Description at enlistment: Eyes: blue. Hair: black. Complexion: light. Height: 5'9". Marital status at enlistment: Single. Occupation at enlistment: Farmer. Residence at enlistment: Winterport, ME. Born: Frankfort, ME. Died: 6/25/1862 at Ship Island, MS, due to disease. Buried: Ship Island, MS, Cemetery; re-interred in 12/1867 at Chalmette, LA, National Cemetery in Section 29, Grave #321.

Fly, Alfred W. Pvt., 13th Maine Infantry. Co. G. Enlisted: 12/26/1861 for 3 years. Mustered into service: 12/31/1861 at Augusta, ME. Age at enlistment: 19. Description at enlistment: Eyes: hazel. Hair: dark. Complexion: medium. Height: 5'9½". Marital status at enlistment: Single. Occupations at enlistment: Shoemaker and Mechanic. Residence at enlistment: Hiram, ME. Born: Porter, ME. Died: 6/2/1862 at Ship Island, MS, due to disease. Buried: Ship Island, MS, Cemetery; re-interred in 12/1867 at Chalmette, LA, National Cemetery in Section 99, Grave #354.

Follansbee, George R. Pvt., 8th New Hampshire Infantry. Co. B. Enlisted: 10/12/1861 for 3 years. Mustered into service: 12/20/1861. Age at enlistment: 21. Residence at enlistment: Lyndeborough, NH. Born: Merrimack, NH. Died: 4/30/1862 at Ship Island, MS, due to disease. Buried: Ship Island, MS, Cemetery; re-interred in 12/1867 at Chalmette, LA, National Cemetery in Section 19, Grave #497.

Ford, Thomas Seaman, U.S.A. Navy. Buried: Ship Island, MS, Cemetery; re-interred in 12/1867 at Chalmette, LA, National Cemetery in Section 29, Grave #298.

Foss, Samuel F. (AKA Saul T.) Musician/Pvt., 14th Maine Infantry. Co. H. Enlisted: 11/14/1861 for 3 years. Mustered into service: 12/14/1861 at Augusta, ME. Age at enlistment: 16. Description at enlistment: Eyes: black. Hair: brown. Complexion: dark. Height: 5'10½". Marital status at enlistment: Single. Occupation at enlistment: Farmer. Residence at enlistment: Wayne, ME. Born: Wayne, ME. Died: 5/1/1862 at Ship Island, MS, Hospital. Buried: Ship Island, MS, Cemetery; re-interred in 12/1867 at

Chalmette, LA, National Cemetery in Section 19, Grave #498.

Fowler, Orrin (AKA Orin) Pvt., 4th Wisconsin Cavalry. Co. K. Enlisted: 4/27/1861. Residence at enlistment: Brothertown, WI. Died: 4/13/1862 at Ship Island, MS, due to disease. Buried: Ship Island, MS, Cemetery; re-interred in 12/1867 at Chalmette, LA, National Cemetery in Section 29, Grave 282.

French, Charles Hannibal Sgt., 14th Maine Infantry. Co. G. Enlisted: 11/23/1861 for 3 years. Mustered into service: 12/12/1861 at Augusta, ME. Age at enlistment: 22. Description at enlistment: Eyes: gray. Hair: black. Complexion: dark. Height: 5'9". Marital status at enlistment: Single. Occupation at enlistment: Farmer. Residence at enlistment: Oxford, ME. Born: Oxford, ME. Died: 4/16/1862 at Ship Island, MS. Buried: Ship Island, MS, Cemetery; re-interred in 12/1867 at Chalmette, LA, National Cemetery in an unmarked grave.

Gansolus, Abner (AKA Gunsolos, Gunsolm) Pvt., 4th Wisconsin Cavalry. Co. B. Enlisted: 7/2/1861 for 3 years. Mustered into service: 7/2/1861 at Racine, WI. Residence at enlistment: Racine, WI. Died: 4/5/1862 at Ship Island, MS, due to disease. Buried: Ship Island, MS, Cemetery; re-interred in 12/1867 at Chalmette, LA, National Cemetery in Section 99, Grave #355.

Gatchell, Roswell E. (AKA Gaichell, Gitchell, Getchell, Boswell) Pvt., 15th Maine Infantry. Co. F. Enlisted: 11/20/1861 for 3 years. Mustered into service: 12/12/1861 at Augusta, ME. Age at enlistment: 18. Description at enlistment: Eyes: black. Hair: black. Complexion: dark. Height: 5'5". Marital status at enlistment: Single. Occupation at enlistment: Laborer. Residence at enlistment: Brunswick, ME. Born: Brunswick, ME. Died: 5/21/1862 at Ship Island, MS. Buried: Ship Island, MS, Cemetery; re-interred in 12/1867 at Chalmette, LA, National Cemetery in Section 19, Grave #489.

Genine, Patrick (AKA Cenine) Pvt., 21st Indiana Infantry. Co. G. Enlisted: 7/24/1861 for 3 years. Mustered into service: 7/24/1861 at Indianapolis, IN. Died: 4/2/1862 at Ship Island, MS. Buried: Ship Island, MS, Cemetery; re-interred in 12/1867 at Chalmette, LA, National Cemetery in Section 99, Grave #363.

Gibson, Edward M. Pvt., 6th Michigan Infantry. Co. I. Enlisted: 8/13/1861 for 3 years. Mustered into service: 8/20/1861 at Kalamazoo, MI. Age at enlistment: 20. Residence at enlistment: Homer, MI. Died: 3/15/1862 at Ship Island, MS, due to disease. Buried: Ship Island, MS, Cemetery; re-interred in 12/1867 at Chalmette, LA, National Cemetery in Section 19, Grave #505.

Gilbert, William Cpl., 32nd United States Colored Troops. Co. C. Enlisted: 2/20/1864 for 3 years. Mustered into service: 2/20/1864. Buried: Ship Island, MS, Cemetery; re-interred in 12/1867 at Chalmette, LA, National Cemetery in an unknown grave.

Goodhue, John Pvt., 26th Massachusetts Infantry. Co. A. Enlisted: 11/1/1861 for 3 years. Mustered into service: 11/16/1861 at Lowell, MA. Age at enlistment: 18. Residence at enlistment: Lowell, MA. Occupation at enlistment: Manufacturer. Died: 1/6/1862 at Ship Island, MS, due to disease. Buried: Ship Island, MS, Cemetery; re-interred in 12/1867 at Chalmette, LA, National Cemetery in Section 99, Grave #382.

Gordon, E.W. Pvt., 12th Maine Infantry. Co. K. Buried: Ship Island, MS, Cemetery; re-interred in 12/1867 at Chalmette, LA, National Cemetery in Section 29, Grave #308.

Gordon, P.L. Pvt., 14th Maine Infantry. Co. K. Buried: Ship Island, MS, Cemetery; re-interred in 12/1867 at Chalmette, LA, National Cemetery in Section 29, Grave #305.

Grant, George A. Pvt., 12th Maine Infantry. Co. I. Enlisted: 10/9/1861 for 3 years. Mustered into service: 11/16/1861 at Cape Elizabeth, ME. Age at enlistment: 18. Description at enlistment: Eyes: black. Hair: dark. Complexion: dark. Height: 5'9½". Marital status at enlistment: Single. Occupation at enlistment: Farmer. Residence at enlistment: Greenville, ME. Born: Greenville, ME. Died: 2/2/1862 at Ship Island, MS. Buried: Ship Island, MS, Cemetery; re-interred in 12/1867 at Chalmette, LA, National Cemetery in Section 29, Grave #300.

Grant, William F.B. Pvt., 31st Massachusetts Infantry. Co. D. Buried: Ship Island, MS, Cemetery; re-interred in 12/1867 at Chalmette, LA, National Cemetery in Section 29, Grave #306.

Grant, William H. Pvt., 74th United States Colored Troops. Co. H. Buried: Ship Island, MS, Cemetery; re-interred in 12/1867 at Chalmette, LA, National Cemetery in Section 138, Grave #509.

Grass, George Edward (AKA Gross) Pvt., 4th Wisconsin Infantry. Co. K. Buried: Ship Island, MS, Cemetery; re-interred in 12/1867 at Chalmette, LA, National Cemetery in Section 19, Grave #479.

Gray, Reuben Pvt., 13th Maine Infantry. Co. D. Enlisted: 11/20/1861 for 3 years. Mustered into service: 12/10/1861 at Augusta, ME. Age at enlistment: 45. Description at enlistment: Eyes: gray. Hair: dark. Complexion: dark. Height: 6'1". Marital status at enlistment: Married. Occupation at enlistment: Farmer. Residence at enlistment: Starks, ME. Born: Industry, ME. Died: 11/30/1862 at Ship Island, MS, due to disease. Buried: Ship Island, MS, Cemetery; re-interred in 12/1867 at Chalmette, LA, National Cemetery in an unknown grave.

Green R. Pvt., 21st Indiana Infantry. Co. K. Buried: Ship Island, MS, Cemetery; re-interred in 12/1867 at Chalmette, LA, National Cemetery in an unmarked grave.

Griffith, John W. Pvt., 6th Michigan Infantry. Co. I. Enlisted: 7/28/1861 for 3 years. Mustered into service: 8/20/1861 at Kalamazoo, MI. Age at enlistment: 18. Residence at enlistment: Marengo, MI. Died: 4/20/1862 at Ship Island, MS, due to disease. Buried: Ship Island, MS, Cemetery; re-interred in 12/1867 at Chalmette, LA, National Cemetery in Section 99, Grave #373.

Grout, Horace V.B. Pvt., 31st Massachusetts Infantry. Co. D. Enlisted: 10/12/1861 for three years. Mustered into service: 11/20/1861. Age at enlistment: 26. Residence at enlistment: Ware, MA. Occupation at enlistment: Farmer. Died: 4/14/1862 at Ship Island, MS. Buried: Ship Island, MS, Cemetery; re-interred in 12/1867 at Chalmette, LA, National Cemetery in an unmarked grave.

Grover, Adelbert (AKA Gower, Dilbert) Pvt., 12th Maine Infantry. Co. A. Enlisted: 10/9/1861 for 3 years. Mustered into service: 11/15/1861 at Cape Elizabeth, ME. Age at enlistment: 18. Description at enlistment: Eyes: blue. Hair: auburn. Complexion: light. Height: 5'10½". Marital status at enlistment: Single. Occupation at enlistment: Farmer. Residence at enlistment: Bethel, ME. Born: Bethel, ME. Died: 4/4/1862 at Ship Island, MS, due to disease. Buried: Ship Island, MS, Cemetery; re-interred in 12/1867 at Chalmette, LA, National Cemetery in Section 99, Grave #344.

Gunn, Marshall H. Pvt., 13th Maine Infantry. Co. E. (No War Dept. Record)

Hall, Horace Sgt., 78th United States Colored Troops. Co. E. Buried: Ship Island, MS, Cemetery; re-interred in 12/1867 at Chalmette, LA, National Cemetery in Section 138, Grave #512.

Hamilton, Erastus H. (AKA H.E.) Pvt., 14th Maine Infantry. Co. B. Enlisted: 12/9/1861 for 3 years. Mustered into service: 12/17/1861 at Augusta, ME. Age at enlistment: 18. Description at enlistment: Eyes: blue. Hair: light. Complexion: light. Height: 5'5". Marital status at enlistment: Single. Occupation at enlistment: Farmer. Residence at enlistment: Albion, ME. Born: Albion, ME. Died: 3/23/1862 at Ship Island, MS, due to disease. Buried: Ship Island, MS, Cemetery; re-interred in 12/1867 at Chalmette, LA, National Cemetery in an unmarked grave.

Hamilton, L.W. (AKA Lyman, W.L.) Pvt., 14th Maine Infantry. Co. B. Enlisted: 10/3/1861 for 3 years. Mustered into service: 12/4/1861 at Augusta, ME. Age at enlistment: 18. Description at enlistment: Eyes: blue. Hair: dark. Complexion: light. Height: 6'0". Marital Status at enlistment: Single. Occupation at enlistment: Farmer. Residence at enlistment: Albion, ME. Born: Albion, ME. Died: 4/6/1862 at Ship Island, MS, due to disease. Buried: Ship Island, MS, Cemetery; re-interred in 12/1867 at Chalmette, LA, National Cemetery in an unmarked grave.

Hanning, Amos (AKA Honning) Pvt., 15th Maine Infantry. Co. E. Enlisted: 11/11/1861 for 3 years. Mustered into service: 12/14/1861 at Augusta, ME. Age at enlistment: 19. Description at enlistment: Eyes: blue. Hair: dark. Complexion: dark. Height: 5'7". Marital status at enlistment: Single. Occupation at enlistment: Farmer. Residence at enlistment: Houlton, ME. Born: Brighton, N.B. Died: 6/11/1862 at Ship Island, MS, due to disease. Buried: Ship Island, MS, Cemetery; re-interred in 12/1867 at Chalmette, LA, National Cemetery in an unmarked grave.

Hanson, Benjamin Pvt., 6th Michigan Infantry. Co. K. Enlisted: 8/6/1861 for 3 years. Mustered into service: 8/20/1861 at Kalamazoo, MI. Age at enlistment: 20. Residence at enlistment: Edwardsburg, MI. Died: 3/18/1862 at Ship Island, MS, due to disease. Buried: Ship Island, MS, Cemetery; re-interred in 12/1867 at Chalmette, LA, National Cemetery in Section 29, Grave #302.

Hardin, Cuvier G. Pvt., 13th Maine Infantry. Co. H. Enlisted: 10/14/1861 for 3 years. Mustered into service: 12/12/1861 at Augusta, ME. Age at enlistment: 18. Description at enlistment: Eyes: blue. Hair: light. Complexion: light. Height: 5'5½". Marital status at enlistment: Single. Occupation at enlistment: Laborer. Residence at enlistment: Bethel, ME. Born: Bethel, ME. Died: 6/22/1862 at Ship Island, MS, due to disease. Buried: Ship Island, MS, Cemetery; re-interred in 12/1867 at Chalmette, LA, National Cemetery in an unmarked grave.

Harriman, Sylvester Pvt., 8th New Hampshire Infantry. Co. K. Enlisted: 12/9/1861 for 3 years. Mustered into service: 12/20/1861. Age at enlistment: 20. Residence at enlistment: Manchester, NH. Born: Amoskeag, NH. Died: 6/25/1862 at Ship Island, MS. Buried: Ship Island, MS, Cemetery; re-interred in 12/1867 at Chalmette, LA, National Cemetery in Section 29, Grave #284.

Harris, E.H. Pvt., 14th Maine Infantry. Co. B. (No War Dept. Record)

Hatch, Colin C. (AKA Colon, Colson) Pvt., 15th Maine Infantry. Co. B. Enlisted: 10/24/1861 for 3 years. Mustered into service: 12/7/1861 at Augusta, ME. Age at enlistment: 18. Description at enlistment: Eyes: blue. Hair: brown. Complexion: light. Height: 5'6". Marital status at enlistment: Single. Occupation at enlistment: Farmer. Residence at enlistment: Boudoinham, ME. Born: Boudoinham, ME. Died: 5/19/1862 at Ship Island, MS, due to disease. Buried: Ship Island, MS, Cemetery; re-interred in 12/1867 at Chalmette, LA, National Cemetery in Section 19, Grave #501.

Hayford, Rufus S. (AKA Mayford, S.R., R.T.) Pvt., 12th Maine Infantry. Co. G. Enlisted: 10/21/1861 for 3 years. Mustered into service: 11/15/1861 at Cape Elizabeth, ME. Description at enlistment: Eyes: blue. Hair: dark. Complexion: dark. Height: 5'9½". Marital status at enlistment: Single. Occupation at enlistment: Farmer. Residence at enlistment: Salem, ME. Born: Salem, ME. Died: 5/17/1862 at Ship Island, MS. Buried: Ship Island, MS, Cemetery; re-interred in 12/1867 at Chalmette, LA, National Cemetery in Section 99, Grave #351.

Hice, George W. (AKA Hill) Cpl., 6th Michigan Infantry. Co. C. Enlisted: 8/6/1861 for 3 years. Mustered into service: 8/20/1861 at Kalamazoo, MI. Age at enlistment: 26. Residence at enlistment: St. Joseph County, MI. Died: 5/15/1862 at Ship Island, MS, due to disease. Buried: Ship Island, MS, Cemetery; re-interred in 12/1867 at Chalmette, LA, National Cemetery in Section 29, Grave #272.

Hilton, George W. Pvt., 15th Maine Infantry. Co. G. Enlisted: 1/21/1861 for 3 years. Mustered into service: 2/13/1862. Age at enlistment: 21. Description at enlistment: Eyes: blue. Hair: brown. Complexion: light. Height: 6'3". Marital status at enlistment: Single. Occupation at enlistment: Farmer. Residence at enlistment: Jefferson, ME. Born: Jefferson, ME. Died: 6/13/1862 at Ship Island, MS, due to consumption. Buried: Ship Island, MS, Cemetery; re-interred in 12/1867 at Chalmette, LA, National Cemetery in Section 29, Grave #322.

Hitchings, Charles F. (AKA Hitchins) Pvt., 15th Maine Infantry. Co. E. Enlisted: 11/5/1861 for 3 years. Mustered into service: 12/14/1861 at Augusta, ME. Age at enlistment: 18. Description at enlistment: Eyes: dark. Hair: light. Complexion: light. Height: 5'7". Marital status at enlistment: Single. Occupation at enlistment: Farmer. Residence at enlistment: Littleton, ME. Born: Saint David, N.B. Died: 5/25/1862 at Ship Island, MS, due to disease. Buried: Ship Island, MS, Cemetery; re-interred in 12/1867 at Chalmette, LA, National Cemetery in an unmarked grave.

Union Dead

Hoffman, George Seaman, U.S.A. Navy. Buried: Ship Island, MS, Cemetery; re-interred in 12/1867 at Chalmette, LA, National Cemetery in Section 29, Grave #292.

Holdridge, Palmer B. Pvt., 114th New York Infantry. Co. D. Enlisted: 8/9/1862 for 3 years. Mustered into service: 8/13/1862 at Norwich, NY. Age at enlistment: 23. Died: 12/16/1862 at Ship Island, MS, due to disease at age 24. Buried: Ship Island, MS, Cemetery; re-interred in 12/1867 at Chalmette, LA, National Cemetery in Section 29, Grave #267. Adopted son of Levi Keith of Nelson, New York. Married: Kate ___. Children: 1 Son — Freddie Holdridge.

Holmes, Daniel Pvt., 7th Vermont Infantry. Co. E. Buried: Ship Island, MS, Cemetery; re-interred in 12/1867 at Chalmette, LA, National Cemetery in Section 19, Grave #499.

Honipson, T. Pvt., 13th Maine Infantry. Co. I. (No War Dept. Record)

Honning, Amos Pvt., 15th Maine Infantry. Co. E. Enlisted: 12/14/1861. Age at enlistment: 19. Residence at enlistment: Houlton, ME. Died: 6/11/1862 at Ship Island, MS. Buried: Ship Island, MS, Cemetery; re-interred in 12/1867 at Chalmette, LA, National Cemetery in an unmarked grave.

Hooper, Caleb S. (AKA S.C.) Pvt., 13th Maine Infantry. Co. K. Enlisted: 11/12/1861 for 3 years. Mustered into service: 12/28/1861 at Augusta, ME. Age at enlistment: 24. Description at enlistment: Eyes: hazel. Hair: black. Complexion: dark. Height: 5'5". Marital status at enlistment: Single. Occupation at enlistment: House Joiner. Residence at enlistment: Biddeford, ME. Born: Biddeford, ME. Died: 6/19/1862 at Ship Island, MS. Buried: Ship Island, MS, Cemetery; re-interred in 12/1867 at Chalmette, LA, National Cemetery in Section 19, Grave #490.

Hooper, Orlando Pvt., 13th Maine Infantry. Co. K. Enlisted: 12/13/1861 for 3 years. Mustered into service: 12/28/1861 at Augusta, ME. Age at enlistment: 19. Residence at enlistment: Biddeford, ME. Died: 7/2/1862 at Ship Island, MS. Buried: Ship Island, MS, Cemetery; re-interred in 12/1867 at Chalmette, LA, National Cemetery in Section 19, Grave #482.

Hording, Henry Pvt., U.S.A. Regular Army. Co. __. Buried: Ship Island, MS, Cemetery; re-interred in 12/1867 at Chalmette, LA, National Cemetery in Section 29, Grave #297.

Hornipson, S. Pvt., 13th Maine Infantry. Co. I. Buried: Ship Island, MS, Cemetery; re-interred in 12/1867 at Chalmette, LA, National Cemetery in Section 99, Grave #340.

Humphrey, George W. Pvt., 12th Maine Infantry. Co. E. Enlisted: 10/17/1861 for 3 years. Mustered into service: 11/15/1861 at Cape Elizabeth, ME. Age at enlistment: 19. Description at enlistment: Eyes: hazel. Hair: dark. Complexion: light. Height: 5'11". Marital status at enlistment: Single. Occupation at enlistment: Farmer. Residence at enlistment: Temple, ME. Died: 5/3/1862 at Ship Island, MS, due to disease. Buried: Ship Island, MS, Cemetery; re-interred in 12/1867 at Chalmette, LA, National Cemetery in Section 99, Grave #350.

Hutchings, Charles F. Pvt., 15th Maine Infantry. Co. I. Buried at Ship Island, MS, Cemetery; re-interred in 12/1867 at Chalmette, LA, National Cemetery in Section 99, Grave #370.

James, William Pvt., 74th United States Colored Troops. Co. H. (Military Convict). Sentenced to imprisonment in the Ship Island, MS, stockade; Received at Ship Island, MS, on 7/5/1865. Died: 5/19/1866 at Ship Island, MS. Buried: Ship Island, MS, Cemetery; re-interred in 12/1867 at Chalmette, LA, National Cemetery in Section 138, Grave #510.

Johnson, Andrew S. Surgeon, 21st Indiana Infantry. F & S. Buried: Ship Island, MS, Cemetery; re-interred in 12/1867 at Chalmette, LA, National Cemetery in Section 29, Grave #274.

Johnson, Joseph F. Pvt., 8th New Hampshire Infantry. Co. B. Enlisted: 11/11/1861 for 3 years. Mustered into service: 12/30/1861. Age at enlistment: 42. Residence at enlistment: Amherst, NH. Born: Rockingham, VT. Died: 5/29/1862 at Ship Island, MS, due to disease. Buried: Ship Island, MS, Cemetery; re-interred in 12/1867 at Chalmette, LA, National Cemetery in Section 19, Grave #480.

Johnson, Richard Cpl./Sgt., 21st Indiana Infantry. Co. G. Enlisted: 7/24/1861 for 3 years. Mustered into service: 7/24/1861 at Indianapolis, IN. Residence at enlistment: Knox County, IN. Died: 4/3/1862 at Ship Island, MS, due to disease. Buried at Ship Island, MS, Cemetery; re-interred in 12/1867 at Chalmette, LA, National Cemetery in Section 29, Grave #273.

Jordan, Eleazer W. (AKA Eliezer, Elrazer) Pvt., 12th Maine Infantry. Co. K. Enlisted: 10/16/1861 for 3 years. Mustered into service: 11/20/1861 at Cape Elizabeth, ME. Age at enlistment: 22. Description at enlistment: Eyes: light blue. Hair: black. Complexion: florid. Height: 5'8¼". Marital status at enlistment: Single. Occupation at enlistment: Teacher. Residence at enlistment: Durham, ME. Born: Durham, ME. Died: 5/13/1862 at Ship Island, MS, due to disease. Buried at Ship Island, MS, Cemetery; re-interred in 12/1867 in an unmarked grave at Chalmette, LA, National Cemetery.

Jordan, Ralph T. (AKA Randolph) Pvt., 13th Maine Infantry. Co. K. Enlisted: 10/25/1861 for 3 years. Mustered into service: 12/13/1861 at Augusta, ME. Age at enlistment: 18. Description at enlistment: Eyes: blue. Hair: light. Complexion: light. Height: 5'9¾". Marital status at enlistment: Single. Occupation at enlistment: Farmer. Residence at enlistment: Biddeford, ME. Born: Biddeford, ME. Died: 4/7/1862 at Ship Island, MS. Buried: Ship Island, MS, Cemetery; re-interred in 12/1867 at Chalmette, LA, National Cemetery in an unmarked grave.

Kenerson, David C. (AKA Keneson, Kennison, Kennesaw) Pvt., 13th Maine Infantry. Co. H. Enlisted: 11/1/1861 for 3 years. Mustered into service: 12/12/1861 at Augusta, ME. Age at enlistment: 22. Description at enlistment: Eyes: blue. Hair: dark. Complexion: light. Height: 5'8". Marital status at enlistment: Single. Occupation at enlistment: Farmer. Residence at enlistment: Bethel, ME. Born: Bethel, ME. Died: 6/18/1862 at Ship Island, MS, due to disease. Buried: Ship Island, MS, Cemetery; re-interred in 12/1867 at Chalmette, LA, National Cemetery in Section 99, Grave #357.

Knight, Charles M. Pvt., 13th Maine Infantry. Co. D. Enlisted: 1023/1861 for 3 years. Mustered into service: 12/10/1861 at Augusta, ME. Age at enlistment: 20. Description at enlistment: Eyes: blue. Hair: brown. Complexion: light. Height: 5'8". Marital status at enlistment: Single. Occupation at enlistment: Farmer. Residence at enlistment: Skowhegan, ME. Born: Skowhegan, ME. Died: 7/17/1862 at Ship Island, MS, due to disease. Buried: Ship Island, MS, Cemetery; re-interred in 12/1867 at Chalmette, LA, National Cemetery in an unmarked grave.

Knight, Streeter (AKA Sebastian S.) Pvt., 12th Maine Infantry. Co. E. Enlisted: 10/21/1861 for 3 years. Mustered into service: 11/15/1861 at Cape Elizabeth, ME. Age at enlistment: 38. Description at enlistment: Eyes: blue. Hair: sandy. Complexion: light. Height: 5'10". Marital status at enlistment: Single. Occupation at enlistment: Farmer. Residence at enlistment: Sweden, ME. Born: Fryeburg, ME. Died: 6/9/1862 at Ship Island, MS, due to disease. Buried: Ship Island, MS, Cemetery; re-interred in 12/1867 at Chalmette, LA, National Cemetery in Section 29, Grave #276.

Lakin, Newell J. (AKA Larkin, Noel) Pvt., 14th Maine Infantry. Co. H. Enlisted: 11/18/1861 for 3 years. Mustered into service: 12/16/1861 at Augusta, ME. Age at enlistment: 18. Description at enlistment: Eyes: dark. Hair: brown. Complexion: light. Height: 5'6½". Marital status at enlistment: Single. Occupation at enlistment: Farmer. Residence at enlistment: Chesterville, ME. Born: Farmington, ME. Died: 5/24/1862 at Ship Island, MS, Hospital. Buried: Ship Island, MS, Cemetery; re-interred in 12/1867 at Chalmette, LA, National Cemetery in Section 29, Grave #252.

Lamb, Charles S. (AKA G.S.) Pvt., 8th Vermont Infantry. Co. D. Enlisted: 12/17/1861 for 3 years. Mustered into service: 2/18/1862 at Camp Holbrook, Brattleboro, VT. Residence at enlistment: Ryegate, VT. Died: 4/21/1862 at Ship Island, MS, due to disease. Buried: Ship Island, MS, Cemetery; re-interred in 12/1867 at Chalmette, LA, National Cemetery in an unmarked grave.

Lawler, Nicholas Ord. Sgt., U.S.A. Regular Army. Co. __. Buried: Ship Island, MS, Cemetery; re-interred in 12/1867 at Chalmette, LA, National Cemetery in Section 149, Grave #12218.

Lawrence, Robert Pvt., 14th Maine Infantry. Co. A. Enlisted: 2/1/1862 for 3 years. Mustered into service: 2/4/1862 at Augusta, ME. Age at enlistment: 21. Description at enlistment: Eyes: hazel. Hair: brown. Complexion: light. Height: 5'8". Marital status at enlistment: Single. Occupation at enlistment: Seaman. Residence at enlistment: Orland, ME. Born: Orland, ME. Died: 5/22/1862 at Ship Island, MS, due to disease. Buried: Ship Island, MS, Cemetery; re-interred in 12/1867 at Chalmette, LA, National Cemetery in Section 19, Grave #502.

Leely, S.C. Pvt., 13th Maine Infantry. Co. G. Buried: Ship Island, MS, Cemetery; re-interred in 12/1867 at Chalmette, LA, National Cemetery in Section 29, Grave #266.

Libby, Alvarado L. (AKA Libley, Almardo) Pvt., 12th Maine Infantry. Co. G. Enlisted: 10/20/1861 for 3 years. Mustered into service: 11/15/1861 at Cape Elizabeth, ME. Age at enlistment: 18. Description at enlistment: Eyes: hazel. Hair: dark. Complexion: dark. Height: 5'9". Marital status at enlistment: Single. Occupation at enlistment: Farmer. Residence at enlistment: Limerick, ME. Born: Limerick, ME. Died: 6/2/1862 at Ship Island, MS. Buried: Ship Island, MS, Cemetery; re-interred in 12/1867 at Chalmette, LA, National Cemetery in an unmarked grave.

Libby, George H. (AKA Libbey) Pvt., 12th Maine Infantry. Co. C. Enlisted: 10/14/1861 for 3 years. Mustered into service: 11/15/1861 at Cape Elizabeth, ME. Age at enlistment: 18. Description at enlistment: Eyes: hazel. Hair: light. Complexion: light. Height: 5'7½". Marital status at enlistment: Single. Occupation at enlistment: Farmer. Residence at enlistment: Falmouth, ME. Born: Falmouth, ME. Died: 3/17/1862 at Ship Island, MS. Buried: Ship Island, MS, Cemetery; re-interred in 12/1867 at Chalmette, LA, National Cemetery in Section 29, Grave #279.

Lindsley, George J. Pvt., 6th Michigan Infantry. Co. H. Enlisted: 8/6/1861 for 3 years. Mustered into service: 8/20/1861 at Kalamazoo, MI. Age at enlistment: 20. Residence at enlistment: Eaton County, MI. Died: 4/14/1862 at Ship Island, MS, due to disease. Buried: Ship Island, MS, Cemetery; re-interred in 12/1867 at Chalmette, LA, National Cemetery in an unmarked grave.

Littlefield, George W. Pvt., 30th Massachusetts Infantry. Co. I. Enlisted: 11/9/1861 for 3 years. Mustered into service: 11/9/1861 at Lowell, MA. Age at enlistment: 18. Occupation at enlistment: Farmer. Residence at enlistment: Newbury Port, MA. Died: 5/28/1862 at Ship Island, MS, due to disease. Buried: Ship Island, MS, Cemetery; re-interred in 12/1867 at Chalmette, LA, National Cemetery in Section 99, Grave #381.

Long, Marcellus J. Pvt., 6th Michigan Infantry. Co. F. Enlisted: 1/1/1862 for 3 years. Mustered into service: 8/20/1861 at Kalamazoo, MI. Age at enlistment: 21. Residence at enlistment: St. Mary's, MI. Died: 4/20/1862 at Ship Island, MS, due to disease. Buried: Ship Island, MS, Cemetery; re-interred in 12/1867 at Chalmette, LA, National Cemetery in Section 29, Grave #323.

Long, Washburn Pvt., 12th Connecticut Infantry. Co. D. Buried: Ship Island, MS, Cemetery; re-interred in 12/1867 at Chalmette, LA, National Cemetery in Section 99, Grave #371.

Luce, John T. Pvt., 13th Maine Infantry. Co. E. Enlisted: 12/2/1861 for 3 years. Mustered into service: 12/10/1861 at Augusta, ME. Age at enlistment: 19. Description at enlistment: Eyes: blue. Hair: light. Complexion: light. Height: 5'8". Marital status at enlistment: Single. Occupation at enlistment: Farmer. Residence at enlistment: Industry, ME. Born: Industry, ME. Died: 6/8/1862 at Ship Island, MS. Buried: Ship Island, MS, Cemetery; re-interred in 12/1867 at Chalmette, LA, National Cemetery in Section 99, Grave #353.

Madden, John Seaman, U.S.A. Navy. Buried: Ship Island, MS, Cemetery; re-interred in 12/1867 at Chalmette, LA, National Cemetery in Section 29, Grave #290.

Mann, Isaac B. Pvt., 13th Maine Infantry. Co. I. Buried: Ship Island, MS, Cemetery; re-interred in 12/1867 at Chalmette, LA, National Cemetery in Section 99, Grave #348.

Manning, Amos Pvt., 15th Maine Infantry. Co. E. Buried: Ship Island, MS, Cemetery; re-interred in 12/1867 at Chalmette, LA, National Cemetery in Section 99, Grave #352.

Manning, John H. Pvt., 31st Massachusetts Infantry. Co. C. Enlisted: 10/28/1861 for 3 years. Mustered into service: 11/20/1861. Age at enlistment: 20. Occupation at enlistment: Farmer. Residence at enlistment: Goshen, MA. Died: 5/31/1862 at Ship Island, MS, due to disease. Buried: Ship Island, MS, Cemetery; re-interred in 12/1867 at Chalmette, LA, National Cemetery in Section 99, Grave #329.

Mansfield, John Pvt., 21st Indiana Infantry. Co. D. Buried: Ship Island, MS, Cemetery; re-interred in 12/1867 at Chalmette, LA, National Cemetery in Section 99, Grave #339.

Maroney, Thomas Pvt., 38th Massachusetts Infantry. Co. B. (Military Convict). Enlisted: 7/19/1862 for 3 years. Mustered into service: 7/21/1862. Age at enlistment: 35. Residence at enlistment: Boston, MA. Occupation at enlistment: Moulder. Sentenced to imprisonment in the Ship Island, MS, stockade; Received on 2/13/1863. Died: 5/20/1863 at Ship Island, MS. Buried: Ship Island, MS, Cemetery; re-interred in 12/1867 at Chalmette, LA, National Cemetery in an unmarked grave.

Marshall, H.S. Pvt., 13th Maine Infantry. Co. E. Buried: Ship Island, MS, Cemetery; re-interred in 12/1867 at Chalmette, LA, National Cemetery in Section 99, Grave #369.

Mason, Arthur W. Cpl., 4th Wisconsin Cavalry. Co. E. Enlisted: 5/29/1861 for 3 years. Mustered into service: 7/2/1861 at Racine, WI. Residence at enlistment: Clinton, WI. Died: 4/8/1862 at Ship Island, MS, due to disease. Buried: Ship Island, MS, Cemetery; re-interred in 12/1867 at Chalmette, LA, National Cemetery in an unmarked grave.

McDaniels, David (AKA McDonalds) Pvt., 31st Massachusetts Infantry. Co. A. Enlisted: 11/14/1861 for 3 years. Mustered into service: 11/20/1861. Age at enlistment: 23. Residence at enlistment: Lanesborough, MA. Occupation at enlistment: Teamster. Died: 6/24/1862 at Ship Island, MS. Buried: Ship Island, MS, Cemetery; re-interred in 12/1867 at Chalmette, LA, National Cemetery in Section 99, Grave #332.

McDermott, Patrick C. Pvt., 31st Massachusetts Infantry. Co. K. Enlisted: 2/17/1862 for 3 years. Mustered into service: 2/19/1862. Age at enlistment: 18. Residence at enlistment: Cambridge, MA. Occupation at enlistment: Laborer. Died: 4/12/1862 at Ship Island, MS, due to being struck by lightning. Buried: Ship Island, MS, Cemetery; re-interred in 12/1867 at Chalmette, LA, National Cemetery in Section 19, Grave #491.

McFarland, Amos (McFarden) Drummer, 14th Maine Infantry. Co. A. Enlisted: 12/12/1861 for 3 years. Mustered into service: 12/28/1861 at Augusta, ME. Age at enlistment: 40. Description at enlistment: Eyes: blue. Hair: light. Complexion: light. Height: 5'8¾". Marital status at enlistment: Single. Occupation at enlistment: Seaman. Residence at enlistment: Bluehill, ME. Born: Bluehill, ME. Died: 6/21/1862 or 7/12/1862 at Ship Island, MS, due to disease. Buried: Ship Island, MS, Cemetery; re-interred in 12/1867 at Chalmette, LA, National Cemetery in Section 29, Grave #320.

McQuillan, Michael (AKA McQuillen) Pvt., 31st Massachusetts Infantry. Co. K. Enlisted: 1/14/1862 for 3 years. Mustered into service: 2/14/1862. Age at enlistment: 20. Residence at enlistment: Cambridge, MA. Occupation at enlistment: Carpenter. Died: 4/12/1862 at Ship Island, MS, due to being struck by lightning. Buried: Ship Island, MS, Cemetery; re-interred in 12/1867 at Chalmette, LA, National Cemetery in Section 19, Grave #484. Soldier also served for 3 months as a Pvt. with the 3rd Massachusetts Infantry. Co. C.

Merchant, William H. (AKA H.W.) Pvt., 15th Maine Infantry. Co. E. Enlisted: 11/8/1861 for 3 years. Mustered into service: 12/14/1861 at Augusta, ME. Age at enlistment: 19. Description at enlistment: Eyes: blue. Hair: light. Complexion: light. Height: 6'1". Marital status at enlistment: Single. Occupation at enlistment: Farmer. Residence at enlistment: Fort Fairfield, ME. Born: Guilford, ME. Died: 5/22/1862 at Ship Island, MS, due to disease. Buried: Ship Island, MS, Cemetery; re-interred in 12/1867 at Chalmette, LA, National Cemetery in Section 29, Grave #317.

Messerory, Alonzo (AKA Messerve, Meserve) Pvt., 15th Maine Infantry. Co. D. Enlisted: 10/24/1861 for 3 years. Mustered into service: 12/13/1861 at Augusta, ME. Age at enlistment: 18. Description at enlistment: Eyes: hazel. Hair: brown. Complexion: light. Height: 5'4". Marital status at enlistment: Single. Occupation at enlistment: Farmer. Residence at enlistment: Casco, ME. Born: Raymond, ME. Died: 5/24/1862 at Ship Island, MS, due to fever. Buried: Ship Island, MS, Cemetery; re-interred in 12/1867 at Chalmette, LA, National Cemetery in Section 99, Grave #380.

Miller, Eliphalet Pvt., 12th Maine Infantry. Co. F. Enlisted: 10/15/1861 for 3 years. Mustered into service: 11/15/1861 at Cape Elizabeth, ME. Age at enlistment: 20. Description at enlistment: Eyes: gray. Hair: light. Complexion: light. Height: 5'6½". Marital status at enlistment: Single. Occupation at enlistment: Farmer. Residence at enlistment: Burlington, ME. Born: Burlington, ME. Died: 3/8/1862 at Ship Island, MS, due to disease. Buried: Ship Island, MS, Cemetery; re-interred in 12/1867 at Chalmette, LA, National Cemetery in Section 19, Grave #494.

Millett, William E. (E.W.) Pvt., 13th Maine Infantry. Co. K. Enlisted: 10/29/1861 for 3 years. Mustered into service: 12/13/1861 at Augusta, ME. Age at enlistment: 24. Description at enlistment: Eyes: blue. Hair: brown. Complexion: dark. Height: 5'9½". Marital status at enlistment: Single. Occupation at enlistment: Teacher. Residence at enlistment: Hebron, ME. Born: Hartford, ME. Died: 6/2/1862 at Ship Island, MS. Buried: Ship Island, MS, Cemetery; re-interred in 12/1867 at Chalmette, LA, National Cemetery in Section 29, Grave #277.

Montague, Brainard Pvt., 8th New Hampshire Infantry. Co. E. Enlisted: 12/14/1861; Mustered into service: 12/31/1861. Age at enlistment. 21. Residence at enlistment: Sunderland, MA. Died: 5/4/1862 at Ship Island, MS, due to disease. Buried: Ship Island, MS, Cemetery; re-interred in 12/1867 at Chalmette, LA, National Cemetery in an unmarked grave.

Morgan, David Pvt., 31st Massachusetts Infantry. Co. G. Buried: Ship Island, MS, Cemetery; re-interred in 12/1867 at Chalmette, LA, National Cemetery in Section 29, Grave #285.

Morgan, John Seaman, U.S.A. Navy. Buried: Ship

Island, MS, Cemetery; re-interred in 12/1867 at Chalmette, LA, National Cemetery in Section 29, Grave #294.

Morse, Melville W. (AKA Melville, W.H.) Pvt., 12th Maine Infantry. Co. B. Enlisted: 10/5/1861 for 3 years. Mustered into service: 11/16/1861 at Cape Elizabeth, ME. Age at enlistment: 22. Description at enlistment: Eyes: black. Hair: brown. Complexion: florid. Height: 5'6½". Marital Status at enlistment: Single. Occupation at enlistment: Sailor. Residence at enlistment: Livermore Falls, ME. Born: 1/7/1839 in Fayette, ME. Died: 4/5/1862 at Ship Island, MS, due to drowning. Buried: Ship Island, MS, Cemetery; re-interred in 12/1867 at Chalmette, LA, National Cemetery in Section 29, Grave #283.

Needham, George E. (AKA E.G.) Pvt., 14th Maine Infantry. Co. G. Enlisted: 1/18/1862 for 3 years. Mustered into service: 1/23/1862 at Augusta, ME. Age at enlistment: 18. Description at enlistment: Eyes: blue. Hair: light. Complexion: light. Height: 5'9". Marital status at enlistment: Single. Occupation at enlistment: Farmer. Residence at enlistment: Norway, ME. Born: Norway, ME. Died: 4/11/1862 at Ship Island, MS. Buried: Ship Island, MS, Cemetery; re-interred in 12/1867 at Chalmette, LA, National Cemetery in Section 29, Grave #253.

Nokes, Samuel (AKA Moses, Notses, Sherman) Pvt., 119th Illinois Infantry. Co. E. Enlisted: 8/12/1862; Mustered into service: 10/7/1862. Residence at enlistment: Mound Station, IL. Died: 5/12/1865 on board a hospital boat. Buried: Ship Island, MS, Cemetery; re-interred in 12/1867 at Chalmette, LA, National Cemetery in Section 29, Grave #249.

Nunn, John A. Pvt., 74th United States Colored Troops. Cos. H & I. Enlisted: 9/8/1864 for 3 years. Died: Ship Island, MS. Buried: Ship Island, MS, Cemetery; re-interred in 12/1867 at Chalmette, LA, National Cemetery in Section 19, Grave #513.

O'Brien, Daniel (O'Brine) Pvt., 8th New Hampshire Infantry. Co. G. Buried: Ship Island, MS, Cemetery; re-interred in 12/1867 at Chalmette, LA, National Cemetery in Section 99, Grave #331.

O'Donnell, Jeremiah (O'Donald) Pvt., 90th New York Infantry. Co. F. (Military Convict). Enlisted: 10/30/1861; Mustered into service: 10/31/1861. Age at enlistment: 25. Confined at east New York City, NY, due to desertion. Sentenced to imprisonment in the Ship Island, MS, stockade; Received at Ship Island, MS, on 10/9/1863. Died: 8/17/1864 at Ship Island, MS. Buried: Ship Island, MS, Cemetery; re-interred in 12/1867 at Chalmette, LA, National Cemetery in Section 29, Grave #481.

O'Donnell, John Pvt., 24th United States Infantry. Co. H. Buried: Ship Island, MS, Cemetery; re-interred in 12/1867 at Chalmette, LA, National Cemetery in Section 29, Grave #319.

Oliver, David Pvt., 7th Vermont Infantry. Co. K. Buried: Ship Island, MS, Cemetery; re-interred in 12/1867 at Chalmette, LA, National Cemetery in Section 99, Grave #376.

Osgood, Thomas H. (AKA P.H.H.F.) Pvt., 13th Maine Infantry. Co. H. Enlisted: 11/21/1861 for 3 years. Mustered into service: 12/12/1861 at Augusta, ME. Age at enlistment: 18. Description at enlistment: Eyes: blue. Hair: dark. Complexion: dark. Height: 5'6". Marital status at enlistment: Single. Occupation at enlistment: Farmer. Residence at enlistment: Bluehill, ME. Born: Bluehill, ME. Died: 5/7/1862 at Ship Island, MS, due to disease. Buried: Ship Island, MS, Cemetery; re-interred in 12/1867 at Chalmette, LA, National Cemetery in Section 29, Grave #288.

Paine, Eugene (AKA Payne) Pvt., 13th Maine Infantry. Co. D. Enlisted: 10/30/1861 for 3 years. Mustered into service: 12/10/1861 at Augusta, ME. Age at enlistment: 21. Description at enlistment: Eyes: brown. Hair: brown. Complexion: light. Height: 5'8¾". Marital status at enlistment: Single. Occupation at enlistment: Farmer. Residence at enlistment: Anson, ME. Born: Anson, ME. Died: 10/15/1862 at Ship Island, MS, due to disease. Buried: Ship Island, MS, Cemetery; re-interred in 12/1867 at Chalmette, LA, National Cemetery in Section 19, Grave #485.

Parker, Paris Pvt., 13th Maine Infantry. Co. F. Enlisted: 10/30/1861 for 3 years. Mustered into service: 12/10/1861 at Augusta, ME. Age at enlistment: 27. Description at enlistment: Eyes: blue. Hair: dark. Complexion: light. Height: 5'10". Marital status at enlistment: Single. Occupation at enlistment: Dentist. Residence at enlistment: Bucksport, ME. Born: Bluehill, ME. Died: 7/12/1862 at Ship Island, MS, due to disease. Buried: Ship Island, MS, Cemetery; re-interred in 12/1867 at Chalmette, LA, National Cemetery in Section 19, Grave #495.

Peabody, Ansell S. (AKA S.A., Ansel) Pvt., 12th Maine Infantry. Cos. G & I. Enlisted: 11/9/1861 for 3 years. Mustered into service: 11/16/1861 at Cape Elizabeth, ME. Age at enlistment: 30. Description at enlistment: Eyes: blue. Hair: dark. Complexion: sandy. Height: 5'10½". Marital status at enlistment: Married. Occupation at enlistment: Farmer. Residence at enlistment: Dead River, ME. Born: New Portland, ME. Died: 5/6/1862 at Ship Island, MS. Buried: Ship Island, MS, Cemetery; re-interred in 12/1867 at Chalmette, LA, National Cemetery in Section 99, Grave #333.

Perkins, Wilson Pvt., 15th Maine Infantry. Co. H. Enlisted: 11/22/1861 for 3 years. Mustered into service: 12/17/1861 at Augusta, ME. Age at enlistment: 21. Description at enlistment: Eyes: blue. Hair: brown. Complexion: light. Height: 5'5". Marital status at enlistment: Single. Occupation at enlistment: Laborer. Residences at enlistment: Athens and Drexter, ME. Born: Athens, ME. Died: 5/28/1862 at Ship Island, MS, due to disease. Buried: Ship Island, MS, Cemetery; re-interred in 12/1867 at Chalmette, LA, National Cemetery in Section 99, Grave #359.

Pierson, William Cpl., 74th United States Colored Troops. Co. C. Buried: Ship Island, MS, Cemetery; re-interred in 12/1867 at Chalmette, LA, National Cemetery in Section 138, Grave #511.

Pike, George Pvt., 15th Maine Infantry. Co. E. Buried: Ship Island, MS, Cemetery; re-interred in 12/1867 at Chalmette, LA, National Cemetery in Section 29, Grave #309.

Piper, Daniel Pvt., 8th New Hampshire Infantry. Co. E. Enlisted: 10/26/1861; Mustered into service: 12/20/1861. Age at enlistment: 26. Residence at enlistment: Campton, NH. Born: Holderness, NH. Died: 4/29/1862 at Ship Island, MS, due to disease. Buried: Ship Island, MS, Cemetery; re-interred in 12/1867 at Chalmette, LA, National Cemetery in Section 29, Grave #250.

Platt, James S. Seaman, U.S.A. Navy. Buried: Ship Island, MS, Cemetery; re-interred in 12/1867 at Chalmette, LA, National Cemetery in Section 29, Grave #296.

Potter, Charles H. Sgt./1st Lt., 24th United States Colored Troops. Co. H. Enlisted: 3/23/1865 for 3 years. Commissioned: 3/23/1865. Mustered out of service: 10/1/1865. Died: Ship Island, MS. Buried: Ship Island, MS, Cemetery; re-interred in 12/1867 at Chalmette, LA, National Cemetery in Section 99, Grave #368.

Prentiss, Charles (AKA Prentice) Pvt., 13th Maine Infantry. Co. C. Enlisted: 12/2/1861 for 3 years. Mustered into service: 12/4/1861 at Augusta, ME. Age at enlistment: 21. Description at enlistment: Eyes: light. Hair: light. Complexion: light. Height: 5'7½". Marital status at enlistment: Single. Occupation at enlistment: Farmer. Residence at enlistment: Troy, ME. Born: Unity, ME. Died: 6/25/1862 at Ship Island, MS. Buried: Ship Island, MS, Cemetery; re-interred in 12/1867 at Chalmette, LA, National Cemetery in Section 99, Grave #379.

Preston, Charles E. (AKA E.C.) Pvt., 12th Maine Infantry. Co. B. Enlisted: 11/15/1861 for 3 years. Mustered into service: 11/20/1861 at Cape Elizabeth, ME. Age at enlistment: 18. Description at enlistment: Eyes: blue. Hair: auburn. Complexion: light. Height: 5'5¾". Marital status at enlistment: Single. Occupation at enlistment: Fisherman. Residence at enlistment: Eastport, ME. Born: Township 14, ME. Died: 4/5/1862 at Ship Island, MS, due to drowning. Buried: Ship Island, MS, Cemetery; re-interred in 12/1867 at Chalmette, LA, National Cemetery in Section 99, Grave #364. Soldier also enlisted on 10/26/1861 with the 1st Maine Artillery Battery. Co. C.

Pugsley, Ira (AKA Pongsley) Pvt., 13th Maine Infantry. Co. G. Enlisted: 10/12/1861 for 3 years. Mustered into service: 12/12/1861 at Augusta, ME. Age at enlistment: 20. Description at enlistment: Eyes: hazel. Hair: brown. Complexion: dark. Height: 5'9¼". Marital status at enlistment: Single. Occupation at enlistment: Farmer. Residence at enlistment: Hiram, ME. Born: Hiram, ME. Died: 6/10/1862 at Ship Island, MS, due to disease. Buried: Ship Island, MS, Cemetery; re-interred in 12/1867 at Chalmette, LA, National Cemetery in Section 29, Grave #311.

Quimby, Marshall H. (AKA Quinn) Cpl., 13th Maine Infantry. Co. E. Enlisted: 10/22/1861 for 3 years. Mustered into service: 12/10/1861 at Augusta, ME. Age at enlistment: 24. Description at enlistment: Eyes: blue. Hair: light. Complexion: light. Height: 5'8". Marital status at enlistment: Single. Occupation at enlistment: Manufacturer. Residence at enlistment: Westbrook, ME. Born: Sacarappa, ME. Died: 7/18/1862 at Ship Island, MS. Buried: Ship Island, MS, Cemetery; re-interred in 12/1867 at Chalmette, LA, National Cemetery in an unmarked grave.

Reily, F. Pvt., 24th Connecticut Infantry. Co. I. Buried: Ship Island, MS, Cemetery; re-interred in 12/1867 at Chalmette, LA, National Cemetery in Section 19, Grave #492.

Reynolds, Charles Pvt., 14th Maine Infantry. Cos. C & I. Enlisted: 12/26/1861 for 3 years. Mustered into service: 1/2/1862 at Augusta, ME. Age at enlistment: 44. Description at enlistment: Eyes: blue. Hair: brown. Complexion: light. Height: 5'10". Marital status at enlistment: Married. Occupation at enlistment: Farmer. Residence at enlistment: Bingham, ME. Born: Bingham, ME. Died: 4/12/1862 at Ship Island, MS. Buried: Ship Island, MS, Cemetery; re-interred in 12/1867 at Chalmette, LA, National Cemetery in Section 29, Grave #312.

Reynolds, Christopher (AKA Christian) Cpl./Pvt., 14th Maine Infantry. Co. I. Enlisted: 12/26/1861 for 3 years. Mustered into service: 1/2/1862 at Augusta, ME. Age at enlistment: 37 or 44. Description at enlistment: Eyes: blue. Hair: brown. Complexion: dark. Height: 5'10". Marital status at enlistment: Married. Occupation at enlistment: Farmer. Residence at enlistment: Burnham, ME. Born: Burnham, ME. Died: 5/21/1862 at Ship Island, MS. Buried: Ship Island, MS, Cemetery; re-interred in 12/1867 at Chalmette, LA, National Cemetery in Section 99, Grave #342.

Reynolds, William H. Pvt., 13th Connecticut Infantry. Co. C. Enlisted: 11/11/1861 for 3 years. Mustered into service: 11/27/1861 at Durham and Booth Carriage Factory, Chapel St., New Haven, CT. Residence at enlistment: Kent, CT. Died: 5/14/1862 at Ship Island, MS. Buried: Ship Island, MS, Cemetery; re-interred in 12/1867 at Chalmette, LA, National Cemetery in an unmarked grave.

Richardson, Joseph M. Pvt., 4th Massachusetts Light Artillery. Enlisted: 12/17/1861 for 3 years. Mustered into service: 12/23/1861. Age at enlistment: 21. Occupation at enlistment: Teamster. Residence at enlistment: Middleton, MA. Died: 2/14/1862 at Ship Island, MS, due to disease. Buried: Ship Island, MS, Cemetery; re-interred in 12/1867 at Chalmette, LA, National Cemetery in an unmarked grave.

Ring, James W. Pvt., 15th Maine Infantry. Co. K. Enlisted: 12/17/1861 for 3 years. Mustered into service: 12/16/1861 at Augusta, ME. Age at enlistment: 19. Description at enlistment: Eyes: blue. Hair: brown. Complexion: fair. Height: 5'6". Marital status at enlistment: Single. Occupation at enlistment: Fisherman. Residence at enlistment: Lubec, ME. Born: Lubec, ME. Died: 6/17/1862 at Ship Island, MS, due to disease. Buried: Ship Island, MS, Cemetery; re-interred in 12/1867 at Chalmette, LA, National Cemetery in Section 99, Grave #366.

Risley, Wait Pvt., 6th Michigan Infantry. Co. B. Enlisted: 8/8/1861 for 3 years. Mustered into service: 8/20/1861 at Kalamazoo, MI. Age at enlistment: 18. Residence at enlistment: Berrien County, MI. Died: 3/16/1862 at Ship Island, MS, due to disease. Buried: Ship Island, MS, Cemetery; re-interred in 12/1867 at Chalmette, LA, National Cemetery in an unmarked grave.

Roberts, Daniel L. (AKA B.S., D.S., S.D.) Pvt./Cpl., 12th Maine Infantry. Co. K. Enlisted: 10/6/1861 for 3 years. Mustered into service: 11/20/1861 at Cape Elizabeth, ME. Age at enlistment: 24. Description at enlistment: Eyes: blue. Hair: brown. Complexion: light. Height: 5'9". Marital status at enlistment: Single. Occupation at enlistment: Farmer. Residence at enlistment: Gorham, ME. Born: Gorham, ME. Died: 5/15/1862 at Ship Island, MS, due to disease. Buried: Ship Island, MS, Cemetery; re-interred in 12/1867 at Chalmette, LA, National Cemetery in Section 29, Grave #256.

Robinson, Alexander Pvt., 19th United States Colored Troops. Co. E. Enlisted: 1/5/1864 for 3 years. Mustered into service: 1/5/1864. Died: 1/8/1864 at Ship Island, MS. Buried: Ship Island, MS, Cemetery; re-interred in 12/1867 at Chalmette, LA, National Cemetery in an unmarked grave. Soldier also served as a Pvt. with the 2nd Louisiana Native Guards. Co. K.

Rodgeres, Heptken Pvt., 31st Massachusetts. Co. A. Buried: Ship Island, MS, Cemetery; re-interred in 12/1867 at Chalmette, LA, National Cemetery in Section 19, Grave #506.

Ross, William Pvt., 31st Massachusetts Infantry. Co. I. Enlisted: 12/18/1861 for 3 years. Mustered into service: 1/28/1862. Age at enlistment: 20. Occupation at enlistment: Paper Maker. Residence at enlistment: South Lee, MA. Died: 4/20/1862 at Ship Island, MS, due to disease. Buried: Ship Island, MS, Cemetery; re-interred in 12/1867 at Chalmette, LA, National Cemetery in an unmarked grave.

Royal, Moses B. (AKA Morris J.) Pvt., 14th Maine Infantry. Co. E. Enlisted: 11/3/1861 for 3 years. Mustered into service: 12/11/1861 at Augusta, ME. Age at enlistment: 25. Description at enlistment: Eyes: gray. Hair: black. Complexion: dark. Height: 5'9½". Marital status at enlistment: Single. Occupation at enlistment: Farmer. Residence at enlistment: Solon, ME. Born: Cornville, ME. Died: 6/10/1862 at Ship Island, MS, due to disease. Buried: Ship Island, MS, Cemetery; re-interred in 12/1867 at Chalmette, LA, National Cemetery in Section 99, Grave #365.

Ruggles, Stephen Pvt., 31st Massachusetts Infantry. Co. D. (No War Dept. Record)

Russell, George E. Pvt., 14th Maine Infantry. Co. A. Died: 5/24/1862 at Ship Island, MS. Buried: Ship Island, MS, Cemetery; re-interred in 12/1867 at Chalmette, LA, National Cemetery in an unmarked grave.

Sanford, Crowell Cpl., 13th Maine Infantry. Co. D. Residence at enlistment: Smithfield, ME. Died: 9/1/1862 at Ship Island, MS. Buried: Ship Island, MS, Cemetery; re-interred in 12/1867 at Chalmette, LA, National Cemetery in an unmarked grave.

Saunders, James (AKA Sanders) Pvt., 4th Wisconsin Cavalry. Co. B. Enlisted: 7/2/1861 for 3 years. Mustered into service: 7/2/1861 at Racine, WI. Died: 4/6/1862 at Ship Island, MS, due to disease. Ship Island, MS, Cemetery; re-interred in 12/1867 at Chalmette, LA, National Cemetery in Section 29, Grave #275.

Sly, Moses Pvt., 17th Indiana Infantry. Co. B. Buried: Ship Island, MS, Cemetery; re-interred in 12/1867 at Chalmette, LA, National Cemetery in Section 99, Grave #338.

Small, Oscar C. (AKA Mall, O.D.) Pvt., 13th Maine Infantry. Co. I. Enlisted: 11/14/1861 for 3 years. Mustered into service: 12/12/1861 at Augusta, ME. Age at enlistment: 21. Description at enlistment: Eyes: black. Hair: black. Complexion: dark. Height: 6'0". Marital status at enlistment: Single. Occupation at enlistment: Lumberman. Residence at enlistment: Cherryfield, ME. Born: Cherryfield, ME. Died: 6/30/1862 at Ship Island, MS, due to disease. Buried: Ship Island, MS, Cemetery; re-interred in 12/1867 at Chalmette, LA, National Cemetery in an unmarked grave.

Smith, Alfred H. Pvt., 26th Massachusetts Infantry. Co. E. (Military Convict). Enlisted: 9/23/1861 for 3 years. Mustered into service: 10/18/1861. Age at enlistment: 22. Occupation at enlistment: Farmer. Sentenced by General Court-Martial to imprisonment in the Ship Island, MS, stockade on 11/24/1863; Received at Ship Island, MS, on 11/25/1863. Died: 9/13/1864 at Ship Island, MS. Buried: Ship Island, MS, Cemetery; re-interred in 12/1867 at Chalmette, LA, National Cemetery in an unmarked grave.

Snee, John T. Pvt., 13th Maine Infantry. Co. E. (No War Dept. Record)

Stanley, Stillman G. Pvt./Cpl., 14th Maine Infantry. Co. A. Enlisted: 11/1/1861 for 3 years. Mustered into service: 12/14/1861 at Augusta, ME. Age at enlistment: 27. Description at enlistment: Eyes: black. Hair: black. Complexion: dark. Height: 6'0". Marital status at enlistment: Single. Occupation at enlistment: Seaman. Residence at enlistment: Cranberry Isle, ME. Born: Cranberry Isle, ME. Died: 6/16/1862 at Ship Island, MS, due to disease. Buried: Ship Island, MS, Cemetery; re-interred in 12/1867 at Chalmette, LA, National Cemetery in Section 29, Grave #316.

Starkey, Frank A. Pvt., 3rd Massachusetts Cavalry, 1st Co. Enlisted: 12/9/1861 for 3 years. Mustered into service: 12/27/1861. Age at enlistment: 20. Residence at enlistment: Brighton, MA. Occupation at enlistment: Clerk. Died: 4/14/1862 at Ship Island, MS, due to disease. Buried: Ship Island, MS, Cemetery; re-interred in 12/1867 at Chalmette, LA, National Cemetery in an unmarked grave.

Stewart, Chandler Seaman, U.S.A. Navy (USS *New London*). Born: Wellfleet, Cape Cod, MA. Died: 1/2/1862. Buried: Ship Island, MS, Cemetery; re-interred in 12/1867 at Chalmette, LA, National Cemetery in Section 29, Grave #289.

Strong, Edmund (AKA Edward) Pvt., 31st Massachusetts Infantry. Co. A. Buried: Ship Island, MS, Cemetery; re-interred in 12/1867 at Chalmette, LA, National Cemetery in Section 29, Grave #270.

Taylor, Austin Wagoner/Pvt., 8th New Hampshire Infantry. Cos. G & H. Enlisted: 11/19/1861 for 3 years. Mustered into service: 12/20/1861. Age at enlistment: 40. Residence at enlistment: Sugar Hill, Lisbon, NH. Born: Bethlehem, NH. Received a Disability Discharge on 4/10/1862 at Ship Island, MS. Died: 4/20/1862 at Ship Island, MS, due to disability. Buried: Ship Island, MS, Cemetery; re-interred in 12/1867 at Chalmette, LA, National Cemetery in an unmarked grave.

Thompson, Samuel Pvt., 13th Maine Infantry. Co. D. Enlisted: 10/28/1861 for 3 years. Mustered into service: 12/10/1861 at Augusta, ME. Age at enlistment: 21. Description at enlistment: Eyes: dark. Hair: dark. Complexion: light. Height: 5'11". Marital status at enlistment: Married. Occupation at enlistment: Farmer. Residence at enlistment: Madison, ME. Born: Concord, ME. Died: 6/8/1862 at Ship Island, MS, due to disease. Buried: Ship Island, MS, Cemetery; re-interred in 12/1867 at Chalmette, LA, National Cemetery in an unmarked grave.

Townes, Oliver, Jr. (AKA Towns) Pvt., 8th New Hampshire Infantry. Cos. C & E. Enlisted: 10/17/1861; Mustered into service: 12/20/1861. Age at enlistment: 35. Residence at enlistment: Nashua, NH. Transferred from Co. C to Co. E on 12/23/1861. Received a Disability Discharge on 4/10/1862 at Ship Island, MS. Died: 4/21/1862 at Ship Island, MS. Buried: Ship Island, MS, Cemetery; re-interred in 12/1867 at Chalmette, LA, National Cemetery in an unmarked grave.

Tracy, Stephen G. Pvt., 12th Maine Infantry. Co. D. Enlisted: 10/5/1861 for 3 years. Mustered into service: 11/15/1861 at Cape Elizabeth, ME. Age at enlistment: 40. Description at enlistment: Eyes: blue. Hair: light. Complexion: sandy. Height: 5'10½". Marital status at enlistment: Married. Occupation at enlistment: Farmer. Residence at enlistment: Franklin Plantation, ME. Born: Boudoin, ME. Died: 4/6/1862 at Ship Island, MS, due to disease. Buried: Ship Island, MS, Cemetery; re-interred in 12/1867 at Chalmette, LA, National Cemetery in an unmarked grave.

Trafton, Harrison Pvt., 14th Maine Infantry. Co. E. Enlisted: 11/12/1861 for 3 years. Mustered into service: 12/11/1861 at Augusta, ME. Age at enlistment: 20. Description at enlistment: Eyes: blue. Hair: dark. Complexion: light. Height: 5'7¾". Marital status at enlistment: Single. Occupation at enlistment: Farmer. Residence at enlistment: Wellington, ME. Born: Augusta, ME. Died: 6/25/1862 at Ship Island, MS, due to disease. Buried: Ship Island, MS, Cemetery; re-interred in 12/1867 at Chalmette, LA, National Cemetery in Section 105, Grave #8680.

Trask, Oliver (AKA Trasn) Pvt., 14th Maine Infantry. Co. H. Enlisted: 12/14/1861 for 3 years. Mustered into service: 12/14/1861 at Augusta, ME. Age at enlistment: 44. Residence at enlistment: Mount Vernon, ME. Died: 5/9/1862 at Ship Island, MS. Buried: Ship Island, MS, Cemetery; re-interred in 12/1867 at Chalmette, LA, National Cemetery in Section 29, Grave #265.

Triens, F. Pvt., U.S. Regular Army. Co. __. Buried: Ship Island, MS, Cemetery; re-interred in 12/1867 at Chalmette, LA, National Cemetery in Section 99, Grave #335.

Trussell, George E. (AKA Trusseli, Trussely) Pvt., 14th Maine Infantry. Co. A. Enlisted: 12/3/1861 for 3 years. Mustered into service: 12/14/1861 at Augusta, ME. Age at enlistment: 19. Description at enlistment: Eyes: blue. Hair: brown. Complexion: light. Height: 6'1". Marital status at enlistment: Single. Occupation at enlistment: Seaman. Residence at enlistment: Cranberry Isle, ME. Born: Orland, ME. Died: 5/29/1862 at Ship Island, MS, due to disease. Buried: Ship Island, MS, Cemetery; re-interred in 12/1867 at Chalmette, LA, National Cemetery in Section 99, Grave #347.

Turner, Theodore Pvt., 13th Maine Infantry. Co. E. Enlisted: 2/13/1862 for 3 years. Mustered into service: 2/17/1862 at Augusta, ME. Age at enlistment: 20. Description at enlistment: Eyes: gray. Hair: brown. Complexion: fair. Height: 6'0". Marital status at enlistment: Single. Occupation at enlistment: Farmer. Residence at enlistment: #6 Plantation, Frank County, ME. Born: Barnstead Community, ME. Died: 3/29/1862 at Ship Island, MS. Buried: Ship Island, MS, Cemetery; re-interred in 12/1867 at Chalmette, LA, National Cemetery in an unmarked grave.

Tuttle, Alonzo Pvt., 13th Maine Infantry. Co. A. Enlisted: 10/20/1861 for 3 years. Mustered into service: 11/20/1861 at Augusta, ME. Age at enlistment: 18. Description at enlistment: Eyes: brown. Hair: brown. Complexion: dark. Height: 5'9". Marital status at enlistment: Single. Occupation at enlistment: Farmer. Residence at enlistment: Athens, ME. Born: Brighton, ME. Died: 5/20/1862 at Ship Island, MS, due to disease. Buried: Ship Island, MS, Cemetery; re-interred in 12/1867 at Chalmette, LA, National Cemetery in Section 99, Grave #346.

Vanvaulkenburgh, A.B. (AKA Van Alkenter, Van Vaulkenberg) Pvt./Musician, 21st Indiana Infantry. Co. K. Enlisted: 7/24/1861 for 3 years. Mustered into service: 7/24/1861 at Indianapolis, IN. Died: 4/28/1862 at Ship Island, MS, due to disease. Buried: Ship Island, MS, Cemetery; re-interred in 12/1867 at Chalmette, LA, National Cemetery in Section 29, Grave #261.

Vanorden, Norman (AKA Vangarder, Vangorder) Pvt., Ohio Light Artillery. 2nd Battery. Died: 5/15/1865 at Ship Island, MS, due to inflammation of the stomach and intestines. Buried: Ship Island, MS, Cemetery; re-interred in 12/1867 at Chalmette, LA, National Cemetery in Section 29, Grave #328.

Walker, George Cpl., 8th Vermont Infantry. Co. G. Enlisted: 12/14/1861 for 3 years. Mustered into service: 2/18/1862 at Camp Holbrook, Brattleboro, VT. Residence at enlistment: Randolph, VT. Died: 4/27/1862 at Ship Island, MS, due to disease. Buried: Ship Island, MS, Cemetery; re-interred in 12/1867 at Chalmette, LA, National Cemetery in Section 29, Grave #263.

Walsh, Robert (AKA Welsh) Pvt., 9th Connecticut Infantry. Co. E. Enlisted: 10/23/1861 for 3 years. Mustered into service: 10/30/1861. Residence at enlistment: New Haven, CT. Died: 4/14/1862 at Ship Island, MS, due to accidental death. Buried: Ship Island, MS, Cemetery; re-interred in 12/1867 at Chalmette, LA, National Cemetery in Section 29, Grave #318.

Walter, Henry R. Pvt., U.S. Regulars 1st Light Artillery. Battery H. Buried: Ship Island, MS, Cemetery; re-interred in 12/1867 at Chalmette, LA, National Cemetery in Section 29, Grave #307.

Washburn, Watson J. (AKA Washburne) Pvt., 14th Maine Infantry. Cos. G & H. Enlisted: 12/26/1861 for 3 years. Mustered into service: 12/31/1861 at Augusta, ME. Age at enlistment: 21. Description at enlistment: Eyes: blue. Hair: light. Complexion: light. Height: 6'0". Marital status at enlistment: Single. Occupation at enlistment: Farmer. Residence at enlistment: Oxford, ME. Born: Oxford, ME. Died: 6/10/1862 at Ship Island, MS. Buried: Ship Island, MS, Cemetery; re-interred in 12/1867 at Chalmette, LA, National Cemetery in Section 29, Grave #314.

Watson, Charles Pvt., 12th Maine Infantry. Co. K. Enlisted: 10/30/1861 for 3 years. Mustered into service: 11/20/1861 at Cape Elizabeth, ME. Age at enlistment: 26. Description at enlistment: Eyes: blue. Hair: light. Complexion: light. Height: 5'8". Marital status at enlistment: Single. Occupation at enlistment: Lumberman. Residence at enlistment: Calais, ME. Born: Calais, ME. Died: 5/25/1862 at Ship Island, MS, due to disease. Buried: Ship Island, MS, Cemetery; re-interred in 12/1867 at Chalmette, LA, National Cemetery in Section 19, Grave #487.

Weldy, Edward W. (AKA Webby, E. M) Musician, 13th Maine Infantry. Co. I. Buried: Ship Island, MS, Cemetery; re-interred in 12/1867 at Chalmette, LA, National Cemetery in Section 29, Grave #271.

Wentworth, Sewall (AKA Seawall, Sewell) Pvt., 15th Maine Infantry. Co. I. Enlisted: 1/5/1862 for 3 years. Mustered into service: 1/16/1862 at Augusta, ME. Age at enlistment: 19. Description at enlistment: Eyes: blue. Hair: brown. Complexion: dark. Height: 5'11½". Marital status at enlistment: Single. Occupation at enlistment: Farmer. Residence at enlistment: Bristol, ME. Born: Bristol, ME. Died: 6/13/1862 at Ship Island, MS, due to typhoid fever. Buried: Ship Island, MS, Cemetery; re-interred in 12/1867 at Chalmette, LA, National Cemetery in Section 11, Grave #1042.

Wheeler, John D. Pvt., 31st Massachusetts Infantry. Co. K. Enlisted: 2/10/1862 for 3 years. Mustered into service: 2/14/1862. Age at enlistment: 27. Occupation at enlistment: Carriage Maker. Residence at enlistment: Roxbury, MA. Died: 4/12/1862 at Ship Island, MS, due to being struck by lightning. Buried: Ship Island, MS, Cemetery; re-interred in 12/1867 at Chalmette, LA, National Cemetery in Section 99, Grave #374.

White, Woodbury C. Pvt., 8th New Hampshire Infantry. Co. B. Enlisted: 12/2/1861 for 3 years. Mustered into service: 12/20/1861. Age at enlistment: 18. Residence at enlistment: Exeter, NH. Born: Moultonborough, NH. Died: 5/12/1862 at Ship Island, MS, due to disease. Buried: Ship Island, MS, Cemetery; re-interred in 12/1867 at Chalmette, LA, National Cemetery in Section 99, Grave #360.

Wilder, Edward M. (AKA Edwin W.) Musician, 13th Maine Infantry. Co. I. Enlisted: 11/11/1861 for 3 years. Mustered into service: 12/12/1861 at Augusta, ME. Age at enlistment: 17. Description at enlistment: Eyes: black. Hair: brown. Complexion: light. Height: 5'5". Marital status at enlistment: Single. Occupation at enlistment: Painter. Residence at enlistment: Machias, ME. Born: Castine, ME. Died: 6/25/1862 at Ship Island, MS, due to disease. Buried: Ship Island, MS, Cemetery; re-interred in 12/1867 at Chalmette, LA, National Cemetery in an unmarked grave.

Williams, Ansel W. Pvt., 3rd Massachusetts Cavalry. Co. L. Enlisted: 11/23/1861 for 3 years. Mustered into service: 12/27/1861. Age at enlistment: 26. Occupation at enlistment: Farmer. Residence at enlistment: Tewksbury, MA. Died: 2/18/1862 at Ship Island, MS. Buried: Ship Island, MS, Cemetery; re-interred in 12/1867 at Chalmette, LA, National Cemetery in an unmarked grave.

Williams, George H. Pvt., 26th Massachusetts Infantry. Cos. D & F. Enlisted: 3/15/1863 for 3 years. Mustered into service: 3/27/1863. Residence at enlistment: Lawrence, MA. Mustered out of service: 11/7/1864. Buried: Ship Island, MS, Cemetery; re-interred in 12/1867 at Chalmette, LA, National Cemetery in Section 99, Grave #330.

Wilson, Joseph Pvt., 2nd Louisiana Native Guards. Co. K. Age at enlistment: 20. Died: Ship Island, MS. Buried: Ship Island, MS, Cemetery; re-interred in 12/1867 at Chalmette, LA, National Cemetery in an unmarked grave.

Winchester, Orrin (AKA Orson) Pvt., 7th Vermont Infantry. Co. A. Buried: Ship Island, MS, Cemetery; re-interred in 12/1867 at Chalmette, LA, National Cemetery in 99, Grave #349.

Witham, A.H. Seaman, U.S.A. Navy. Buried: Ship Island, MS, Cemetery; re-interred in 12/1867 at Chalmette, LA, National Cemetery in Section 19, Grave #496.

Woodman, Albert H. Pvt., 13th Maine Infantry. Co. G. Enlisted: 1/28/1862 for 3 years. Mustered into service: 1/25/1862 at Augusta, ME. Age at enlistment: 20. Description at enlistment: Eyes: blue. Hair: light. Complexion: light. Height: 5'6". Marital status at enlistment: Single. Occupation at enlistment: Farmer. Residence at enlistment: Hiram, ME. Born: Buxton, ME. Died: 6/29/1862 at Ship Island, MS, due to disease. Buried: Ship Island, MS, Cemetery; re-interred in 12/1867 at Chalmette, LA, National Cemetery in Section 29, Grave #301.

Wright, Charles U. (AKA Wight, C.N.) Pvt., 13th Maine Infantry. Co. H. Enlisted: 10/14/1861 for 3 years. Mustered into service: 12/12/1861 at Augusta, ME. Age at enlistment: 22. Description at enlistment: Eyes: blue. Hair: brown. Complexion: light. Height: 5'9". Marital status at enlistment: Single. Occupation at enlistment: Carpenter. Residence at enlistment: Newry, ME. Born: Newry, ME. Died: 6/27/1862 at Ship Island, MS, due to disease. Buried: Ship Island, MS, Cemetery; re-interred in 12/1867 at Chalmette, LA, National Cemetery in Section 99, Grave #372.

Wright, William Pvt., 12th Connecticut Infantry. Co. E. Buried: Ship Island, MS, Cemetery; re-interred in 12/1867 at Chalmette, LA, National Cemetery in Section 99, Grave #377.

Wyman, Wallace W. Pvt., 13th Maine Infantry. Co. B. Enlisted: 11/18/1861 for 3 years. Mustered into service: 11/28/1861 at Augusta, ME. Age at enlistment: 19. Description at enlistment: Eyes: blue. Hair: light. Complexion: light. Height: 5'9". Marital status at enlistment: Single. Occupation at enlistment: Farmer. Residence at enlistment: Kingsbury, ME. Born: Kingsbury, ME. Died: 6/1/1862 at Ship Island, MS. Buried: Ship Island, MS, Cemetery; re-interred in 12/1867 at Chalmette, LA, National Cemetery Section 29, Grave #293.

Alabama Prisoners of War

Acker, J.N. Pvt., 36th Alabama Infantry. Co. K. Federal Rolls of Prisoners of War: Captured at Spanish Fort, AL, on 4/8/1865; Received at Ship Island, MS, on 4/10/1865. Transferred to Vicksburg, MS, for exchange on 5/1/1865; Exchanged at Camp Townsend, MS, on 5/6/1865.

Acree, Alfred W. (AKA Acre) Pvt., 1st Alabama Artillery Battalion. Co. D. Federal Rolls of Prisoners of War: Captured at Blakely, AL, on 4/9/1865; Received at Ship Island, MS, on 4/15/1865. Transferred to Vicksburg, MS, for exchange on 5/1/1865; Exchanged at Camp Townsend, MS, on 5/6/1865.

Acton, J.G. (AKA Actin) Pvt., 21st Alabama Infantry. Co. F. Federal Rolls of Prisoners of War: Captured at Spanish Fort, AL, on 4/8/1865; Received at Ship Island, MS, on 4/10/1865. Transferred to Vicksburg, MS, for exchange on 5/1/1865; Exchanged at Camp Townsend, MS, on 5/6/1865.

Acton, J.V. (AKA Actin) Pvt., 21st Alabama Infantry. Co. F. Enlisted: 1862 at Talladega, AL. Federal Rolls of Prisoners of War: Captured at Fort Gaines, AL, on 8/8/1864; Transferred to Ship Island, MS, from New Orleans, LA, on 10/25/1864. Forwarded to Fort Columbus, New York Harbor, NY, on 11/5/1864; Exchanged on 1/4/1865. Confederate Pension Application on file at the Alabama Department of Archives and History. Target Name: Acton, J.V. Record Card Number: 3592. County: Jefferson.

Adams, A.B. Pvt., 63rd Alabama Infantry. Co. F. Enlisted: 3/9/1864 at Greenville, AL. Age at enlistment: 17. Description at enlistment: Eyes: dark. Hair: dark. Complexion: dark. Height: 5'8½". Rolls for 9/1864 through 10/1864: Deserted on 10/27/1864. Federal Rolls of Prisoners of War: Captured at Blakely, AL, on 4/9/1865; Received at Ship Island, MS, on 4/15/1865. Transferred to Vicksburg, MS, for exchange on 5/1/1865; Exchanged at Camp Townsend, MS, on 5/6/1865. Rolls of Prisoners of War, C.S.A: Surrendered at Citronelle, AL, on 5/4/1865; Paroled at Meridian, MS, on 5/11/1865. Residence at parole: Butler County, AL.

Adams, Jesse W. (AKA J.R.) Capt., 1st Alabama Artillery Battalion. Cos. D & K. Died: 11/14/1864 at Ship Island, MS, due to chronic diarrhea. Buried: Ship Island, MS, Cemetery in Grave #19.

Adams, M. Pvt., 21st Alabama Infantry. Co. C. Federal Rolls of Prisoners of War: Captured at Fort Gaines, AL, on 8/8/1864; Transferred to Ship Island, MS, from New Orleans, LA, on 10/25/1864. Forwarded to Fort Columbus, New York Harbor, NY, on 11/5/1864; Exchanged on 1/4/1865.

Adams, Newton A. (AKA Nurburson) Pvt., 63rd Alabama Infantry. Co. A. Federal Rolls of Prisoners of War: Captured at Blakely, AL, on 4/9/1865; Received at Ship Island, MS, on 4/15/1865. Transferred to Vicksburg, MS, for exchange on 5/1/1865; Exchanged at Camp Townsend, MS, on 5/6/1865. Rolls of Prisoners of War, C.S.A: Surrendered at Citronelle, AL, on 5/4/1865; Paroled at Meridian, MS, on 5/11/1865. Residence at parole: Chambers County, AL.

Adams, Samuel H. Pvt., 1st Alabama Artillery Battalion. Co. E. Federal Rolls of Prisoners of War: Captured at Fort Gaines, AL, on 8/8/1864; Received at Ship Island, MS, from New Orleans, LA, on 10/25/1864. Exchanged on 1/4/1865.

Adams, Zachariah T. Pvt., 63rd Alabama Infantry. Co. B. Enlisted: 8/15/1864 at Pollard, AL. Rolls for 9/1864 through 10/1864: Absent, on sick furlough since 10/17/1864. Federal Rolls of Prisoners of War: Captured at Blakely, AL, on 4/9/1865; Received at Ship Island, MS, on 4/15/1865. Transferred to Vicksburg, MS, for exchange on 5/1/1865; Exchanged at Camp Townsend, MS, on 5/6/1865. Rolls of Prisoners of War, C.S.A: Surrendered at Citronelle, AL, on 5/4/1865; Paroled at Meridian, MS, on 5/11/1865. Residence at parole: Dale County, AL.

Adcock, John C. Pvt., 21st Alabama Infantry. Co. C. Federal Rolls of Prisoners of War: Captured at Fort Gaines, AL, on 8/8/1864; Received at Ship Island, MS, from New Orleans, LA, on 10/25/1864. Died: 11/6/1864 at Ship Island, MS, due to chronic diarrhea. Buried: Ship Island, MS, Cemetery in Grave #12.

Addesholt, M. (AKA Aderholt) Pvt., 63rd Alabama Infantry. Co. H. Enlisted: 3/16/1864 at Springville,

AL. Age at enlistment: 17. Description at enlistment: Eyes: dark. Hair: dark. Complexion: dark. Rolls for 9/1864 through 10/1864: Present. Federal Rolls of Prisoners of War: Captured at Blakely, AL, on 4/9/1865; Received at Ship Island, MS, on 4/15/1865. Transferred to Vicksburg, MS, for exchange on 5/1/1865; Exchanged at Camp Townsend, MS, on 5/6/1865. Rolls of Prisoners of War, C.S.A: Surrendered at Citronelle, AL, on 5/4/1865; Paroled at Meridian, MS, on 5/11/1865. Residence at parole: St. Clair County, AL.

Addington, W. Pvt., 63rd Alabama Infantry. Co. K. Enlisted: 7/30/1864 at Carrolton, AL. Rolls for 9/1864 through 10/1864: Present. Federal Rolls of Prisoners of War: Captured at Blakely, AL, on 4/9/1865; Received at Ship Island, MS, on 4/15/1865. Transferred to Vicksburg, MS, for exchange on 5/1/1865; Exchanged at Camp Townsend, MS, on 5/6/1865. Rolls of Prisoners of War, C.S.A: Surrendered at Citronelle, AL, on 5/4/1865; Paroled at Meridian, MS, on 5/11/1865.

Adduck, T.F. (AKA T.T.) Pvt., 63rd Alabama Infantry. Co. B. Federal Rolls of Prisoners of War: Captured at Blakely, AL, on 4/9/1865; Received at Ship Island, MS, on 4/15/1865. Transferred to Vicksburg, MS, for exchange on 5/1/1865; Exchanged at Camp Townsend, MS, on 5/6/1865.

Agely, H.K. Pvt., 21st Alabama Infantry. Co. K. Federal Rolls of Prisoners of War: Captured at Spanish Fort, AL, on 4/8/1865; Received at Ship Island, MS, on 4/10/1865. Transferred to Vicksburg, MS, for exchange on 5/1/1865; Exchanged at Camp Townsend, MS, on 5/6/1865.

Aiken, E.T. (AKA A.J.) Pvt., 21st Alabama Infantry. Co. E. Federal Rolls of Prisoners of War: Captured at Fort Gaines, AL, on 8/8/1864; Transferred to Ship Island, MS, from New Orleans, LA, on 10/25/1864. Forwarded to Fort Columbus, New York Harbor, NY, on 11/5/1864; Exchanged on 1/4/1865.

Aldridge, J.K. Pvt., 21st Alabama Infantry. Co. G. Federal Rolls of Prisoners of War: Captured at Fort Gaines, AL, on 8/8/1864; Received at Ship Island, MS, from New Orleans, LA, on 10/25/1864. Forwarded to Fort Columbus, New York Harbor, NY, on 11/5/1864; Exchanged on 1/4/1865. Confederate Widows Pension Application on file at the Alabama Department of Archives and History. Target Name: Aldridge, Mattie. Record Card Number: 36505. County: Lee.

Aldridge, James L. (AKA Aldredge) Pvt./Sgt., 21st Alabama Infantry. Co. C. Federal Rolls of Prisoners of War: Captured at Blakely, AL, on 4/9/1865; Received at Ship Island, MS, on 4/15/1865. Transferred to Vicksburg, MS, for exchange on 5/1/1865; Exchanged at Camp Townsend, MS, on 5/6/1865.

Alexander, E.S. 1st Lt., 63rd Alabama Infantry. Co. C. Enlisted: 9/20/1864 at Baldwin County, AL. Rolls for 9/1864 through 10/1864: Absent, in hospital at Mobile, AL, since 10/28/1864. Federal Rolls of Prisoners of War: Captured at Blakely, AL, on 4/9/1865; Received at Ship Island, MS, on 4/15/1865. Transferred to Vicksburg, MS, for exchange on 4/28/1865; Confined at New Orleans, LA, on 4/30/1865. Exchanged at Camp Townsend, MS, on 5/6/1865. Rolls of Prisoners of War, C.S.A: Surrendered at Citronelle, AL, on 5/4/1865; Paroled at Meridian, MS, on 5/11/1865.

Alexander, William 2nd Sgt./Pvt., 63rd Alabama Infantry. Co. I. Rolls for 9/1864 through 10/1864: Present. Federal Rolls of Prisoners of War: Captured at Blakely, AL, on 4/9/1865; Received at Ship Island, MS, on 4/15/1865. Transferred to Vicksburg, MS, for exchange on 5/1/1865; Exchanged at Camp Townsend, MS, on 5/6/1865. Rolls of Prisoners of War, C.S.A: Surrendered at Citronelle, AL, on 5/4/1865; Paroled at Meridian, MS, on 5/13/1865. Residence at parole: Pickens County, AL.

Allan, A.D. Pvt., 21st Alabama Infantry. Co. C. Died: 11/22/1864 at Ship Island, MS. Buried: Ship Island, MS, Cemetery.

Allen, George W. Pvt., 21st Alabama Infantry. Co. G. Died: 11/23/1864 at Ship Island, MS, due to pneumonia. Buried: Ship Island, MS, Cemetery in Grave #39.

Allen, Green B. Pvt., 63rd Alabama Infantry. Co. B. Enlisted: 3/23/1864 at Montgomery, AL. Age at enlistment: 17. Rolls for 9/1864 through 10/1864: Absent, sick since 9/8/1864. Federal Rolls of Prisoners of War: Captured at Blakely, AL, on 4/9/1865; Received at Ship Island, MS, on 4/15/1865. Transferred to Vicksburg, MS, for exchange on 5/1/1865. On Register of U.S.A. General Hospital #2, Vicksburg, MS: Admitted from steamer on 5/3/1865 due to acute diarrhea. Died: 5/13/1865 while hospitalized. Age at death: 18.

Allen, W.S. (AKA W.H.) Pvt./Sgt., 63rd Alabama Infantry. Co. I. Federal Rolls of Prisoners of War: Captured at Blakely, AL, on 4/9/1865; Received at Ship Island, MS, on 4/15/1865. Transferred to Vicksburg, MS, for exchange on 5/1/1865; Exchanged at Camp Townsend, MS, on 5/6/1865. Rolls of Prisoners of War, C.S.A: Surrendered at Citronelle, AL, on 5/4/1865; Paroled at Meridian, MS, on 5/13/1865. Residence at parole: Pickens County, AL.

Allen, William Pvt., 21st Alabama Infantry. Co. I. Federal Rolls of Prisoners of War: Captured at Fort Gaines, AL, on 8/8/1864; Received at Ship Island, MS, from New Orleans, LA, on 10/25/1864. Forwarded to Fort Columbus, New York Harbor, NY, on 11/5/1864; Exchanged on 1/4/1865.

Allen, Y.M. Pvt., 21st Alabama Infantry. Co. G. Federal Rolls of Prisoners of War: Captured at Fort Gaines, AL, on 8/8/1864; Received at Ship Island, MS, from New Orleans, LA, on 10/25/1864. Died: 11/22/1864 at Ship Island, MS, due to diarrhea. Buried: Ship Island, MS, Cemetery in Grave #36.

Allrest, J. (AKA Allnet) Pvt., 21st Alabama Infantry. Co. C. Federal Rolls of Prisoners of War: Captured at Blakely, AL, on 4/9/1865; Received at Ship Island, MS, on 4/15/1865. Transferred to Vicksburg, MS, for exchange on 5/1/1865; Exchanged at Camp Townsend, MS, on 5/6/1865.

Anderson, C.D. Col., 21st Alabama Infantry. F & S. Federal Rolls of Prisoners of War: Captured at Fort Gaines, AL, on 8/8/1864; Received at Ship Island, MS, from New Orleans, LA, on 11/25/1864. Exchanged on 1/4/1865.

Anderson, C.K. (AKA C.R.) Pvt., 63rd Alabama Infantry. Co. E. Enlisted: 7/27/1864 at Montgomery, AL. Age at enlistment: 17. Description at enlistment: Eyes: blue. Hair: light. Complexion: light. Rolls for 9/1864 through 10/1864: Absent, on 30 day furlough since 10/3/1864. Federal Rolls of Prisoners of War:

Captured at Blakely, AL, on 4/9/1865. Name on list dated Headquarters, 23rd Iowa Infantry. U.S.A. near Spanish Fort, AL, 4/12/1865 of Prisoners of War requiring hospitalization due to pneumonia. Received at Ship Island, MS, on 5/1/1865. Rolls of Prisoners of War, C.S.A: Surrendered at Citronelle, AL, on 5/4/1865; Paroled at Meridian, MS, on 5/13/1865.

Anderson, J. Pvt., 63rd Alabama Infantry. Co. F. Federal Rolls of Prisoners of War: Captured at Blakely, AL, on 4/9/1865; Received at Ship Island, MS, on 4/15/1865. Rolls of Prisoners of War, C.S.A: Surrendered at Citronelle, AL, on 5/4/1865; Paroled at Meridian, MS, on 5/11/1865. Residence: Mountain Creek, AL, Confederate Soldier's Home in 1915.

Anderson, James C. (AKA J.R., J.W.M.) Pvt., 38th Alabama Infantry. Co. D. Enlisted: 4/5/1862 at Clark City, AL. Age at enlistment: 25. On Roll dated Camp Holt, near Mobile, AL, for 6/12/1862: Present. On Montgomery Hospital Examining Board report dated Selma, AL, 3/28/1864: V.L.M.B. across shin bone not healed. Federal Rolls of Prisoners of War: Captured at Blakely, AL, on 4/9/1865; Received at Ship Island, MS, on 4/15/1865. Transferred to Vicksburg, MS, for exchange on 5/1/1865; Exchanged at Camp Townsend, MS, on 5/6/1865. Rolls of Prisoners of War, C.S.A: Surrendered at Citronelle, AL, on 5/4/1865; Paroled at Meridian, MS, on 5/9/1865.

Anderson, John P. Pvt./Sgt., 38th Alabama Infantry. Co. E. Enlisted: 4/17/1862 at Mobile, AL. Age at enlistment: 17. On Register of St. Mary's Hospital, Dalton, GA: Admitted on 6/5/1863 due to febris continua; Released on 6/22/1863. Federal Rolls of Prisoners of War: Captured at Blakely, AL, on 4/9/1865; Received at Ship Island, MS, on 4/15/1865. Transferred to Vicksburg, MS, for exchange on 5/1/1865; Exchanged at Camp Townsend, MS, on 5/6/1865. Confederate Pension Application on file at the Alabama Department of Archives and History. Target Name: Anderson, John P. Record Card Number: 10894. County: Coneuch.

Anderson, R.F.B. (AKA Robert B., R.T.B.) 2nd Lt., 62nd Alabama Infantry. Co. H. Federal Rolls of Prisoners of War: Captured at Fort Gaines, AL, on 8/8/1864; Received at Ship Island, MS, from New Orleans, LA, on 11/25/1864. Exchanged on 1/11/1865. Federal Rolls of Prisoners of War: Captured at Blakely, AL, on 4/9/1865; Received at Ship Island, MS, on 4/15/1865. Transferred to Vicksburg, MS, for exchange on 4/28/1865; Confined at New Orleans, LA, on 4/30/1865. Exchanged at Camp Townsend, MS, on 5/6/1865.

Andrews, Wade L. Pvt., 21st Alabama Infantry. Co. E. Federal Rolls of Prisoners of War: Captured at Fort Gaines, AL, on 8/8/1864; Received at Ship Island, MS, from New Orleans, LA, on 10/25/1864. Forwarded to Fort Columbus, New York Harbor, NY, on 11/5/1864; Exchanged on 1/4/1865.

Anglin, W.H. Pvt., 1st Alabama Cavalry. Co. E. Federal Rolls of Prisoners of War: Captured in Florida on 3/25/1865; Received at Ship Island, MS. Transferred to Vicksburg, MS, for exchange on 5/1/1865; Exchanged at Camp Townsend, MS, on 5/6/1865.

Archer, C.B. Pvt., 63rd Alabama Infantry. Co. F. Enlisted: 8/15/1864 at Georgiana, AL. Rolls for 9/1864 through 10/1864: Present. Federal Rolls of Prisoners of War: Captured at Blakely, AL, on 4/9/1865; Received at Ship Island, MS, on 4/15/1865. Transferred to Vicksburg, MS, for exchange on 5/1/1865. On Register of U.S.A. General Hospital #2, Vicksburg, MS: Admitted from steamer on 5/3/1865 due to remittent fever. Age at admittance: 16.

Archibald, C.H. Pvt., 7th Alabama Cavalry. Co. __. Federal Rolls of Prisoners of War: Captured at Mobile Point, AL, on 7/22/1864; Received at Ship Island, MS, from New Orleans, LA, on 10/7/1864. Forwarded to Fort Columbus, New York Harbor, NY, on 11/5/1864.

Archibald, Edwin M. Pvt., 7th Alabama Cavalry. Co. B. Enlisted: 8/22/1863 for the duration of the war. Federal Rolls of Prisoners of War: Captured at Mobile Bay, AL, in 8/1864; Forwarded to Fort Pickens, FL. Transferred to Steam Levee Press #4, New Orleans, LA, in 9/1864. On Register of St. Louis U.S.A. General Hospital, New Orleans, LA: Admitted on 9/29/1864 due to diarrhea; Returned to duty on 10/5/1864. Received at Ship Island, MS, on 10/6/1864; Forwarded to Fort Columbus, New York Harbor, NY, on 11/5/1864. Received on 11/16/1864. On Register of U.S.A. General Hospital, Fort Columbus, New York Harbor, NY: Admitted on 11/17/1864 due to chronic diarrhea. Died: 12/17/1864 at Fort Columbus, New York Harbor, NY, due to chronic diarrhea. Buried: Cypress Hill Cemetery located at Governor's Island, NY, in Grave #1269.

Armistead, B.B. Pvt., 21st Alabama Infantry. Co. C. Federal Rolls of Prisoners of War: Captured at Fort Gaines, AL, on 8/8/1864; Received at Ship Island, MS, from New Orleans, LA, on 10/25/1864. Exchanged on 1/4/1865. Federal Rolls of Prisoners of War: Captured at Blakely, AL, on 4/9/1865; Received at Ship Island, MS, on 4/15/1865. Transferred to Vicksburg, MS, for exchange on 5/1/1865; Exchanged at Camp Townsend, MS, on 5/6/1865.

Armistead, I.M. (AKA Armistead, J.W.) Pvt., 21st Alabama Infantry. Co. C. Federal Rolls of Prisoners of War: Captured at Fort Gaines, AL, on 8/8/1864; Received at Ship Island, MS, from New Orleans, LA, on 10/25/1864. Forwarded to Fort Columbus, New York Harbor, NY, on 11/5/1864; Exchanged on 1/4/1865.

Armstrong, Elias (AKA E.T.) Pvt./Mechanic, 7th Alabama Cavalry. Federal Rolls of Prisoners of War: Captured at Tensas Parish, LA, on 9/19/1864; Received at Ship Island, MS, from New Orleans, LA, on 10/7/1864. Forwarded to Fort Columbus, New York Harbor, NY, on 11/5/1864.

Armstrong, James 1st Lt./Capt., 63rd Alabama Infantry. Co. A. Rolls for 1/1864 through 2/1864: Present, elected 1st Lt. on 1/1/1864. Rolls for 9/1864 through 10/1864: Present, promoted to Capt. on 8/16/1864. Federal Rolls of Prisoners of War: Captured at Blakely, AL, on 4/9/1865; Received at Ship Island, MS, on 4/15/1865. Transferred to Vicksburg, MS, for exchange on 4/28/1865; Confined at New Orleans, LA, on 4/30/1865. Exchanged at Camp Townsend, MS, on 5/6/1865. Rolls of Prisoners of War, C.S.A: Surrendered at Citronelle, AL, on 5/4/1865; Paroled at Meridian, MS, on 5/12/1865.

Armstrong, Stephen Francis Pvt., 1st Alabama Artillery Battalion. Co. B. Enlisted: 1862 at Greenville, AL. Federal Rolls of Prisoners of War: Captured at Fort Gaines, AL, on 8/8/1864; Received at Ship Island, MS, from New Orleans, LA, on 12/13/1864. Transferred to Vicksburg, MS, for exchange on 5/1/1865; Exchanged at Camp Townsend, MS, on 5/6/1865.

Armstrong, William Pvt., 63rd Alabama Infantry. Co. I. Federal Rolls of Prisoners of War: Captured at Blakely, AL, on 4/9/1865; Received at Ship Island, MS, on 4/15/1865. Transferred to Vicksburg, MS, for exchange on 5/1/1865; Exchanged at Camp Townsend, MS, on 5/6/1865.

Arnold, Henry Pvt., 63rd Alabama Infantry. Co. D. Enlisted: 8/11/1864 at Pollard, AL. Rolls for 9/1864 through 10/1864: Present. On Register of 1st Mississippi C.S.A. Hospital, Jackson, MS: Admitted on 9/25/1864 due to rubeola; Returned to duty on 10/13/1864. Federal Rolls of Prisoners of War: Captured at Blakely, AL, on 4/9/1865; Received at Ship Island, MS, on 4/15/1865. Transferred to Vicksburg, MS, for exchange on 5/1/1865; Exchanged at Camp Townsend, MS, on 5/6/1865. Rolls of Prisoners of War, C.S.A: Surrendered at Citronelle, AL, on 5/4/1865; Paroled at Meridian, MS, on 5/10/1865 while a patient in Quintard Hospital.

Askew, Samuel H. Sgt. Maj./2nd Lt., 62nd Alabama Infantry. Co. I. Federal Rolls of Prisoners of War: Captured at Blakely, AL, on 4/9/1865; Received at Ship Island, MS, on 4/15/1865. Transferred to Vicksburg, MS, for exchange on 4/28/1865; Confined at New Orleans, LA, on 4/30/1865. Exchanged at Camp Townsend, MS, on 5/6/1865.

Atkins, Thomas J. Pvt., 63rd Alabama Infantry. Cos. A & C. Enlisted: 7/1/1864 at Chambers County, AL. Rolls for 9/1864 through 10/1864: Present, detailed as Regimental Teamster. Federal Rolls of Prisoners of War: Captured at Blakely, AL, on 4/9/1865; Received at Ship Island, MS, on 4/15/1865. Transferred to Vicksburg, MS, for exchange on 5/1/1865; Exchanged at Camp Townsend, MS, on 5/6/1865. Rolls of Prisoners of War, C.S.A: Surrendered at Citronelle, AL, on 5/4/1865; Paroled at Meridian, MS, on 5/11/1865.

Atkinson, Samuel A. Pvt., 63rd Alabama Infantry. Co. D. Enlisted: 7/30/1864 at Russell County, AL. Age at enlistment: 17. Description at enlistment: Eyes: blue. Hair: dark. Complexion: fair. Height: 5'8". Rolls for 9/1864 through 10/1864: Present. Federal Rolls of Prisoners of War: Captured at Blakely, AL, on 4/9/1865; Received at Ship Island, MS, on 4/15/1865. Transferred to Vicksburg, MS, for exchange on 5/1/1865; Exchanged at Camp Townsend, MS, on 5/6/1865. Rolls of Prisoners of War, C.S.A: Captured at Citronelle, AL, on 5/4/1865; Paroled at Meridian, MS, on 5/10/1865 while a patient in Quintard Hospital. Residence at parole: Russell County, AL. Soldier also served as a Pvt. with the Alabama Reserves—Capt. Zorn's Company.

Aubert, F.H. Pvt., 21st Alabama Infantry. Co. K. Federal Rolls of Prisoners of War: Captured at Spanish Fort, AL, on 4/8/1865; Received at Ship Island, MS, on 4/10/1865. Transferred to Vicksburg, MS, for exchange on 5/1/1865; Exchanged at Camp Townsend, MS, on 5/6/1865.

Averett, A.M. (AKA Averitt) Pvt., 21st Alabama Infantry. Cos. G & I. Federal Rolls of Prisoners of War: Captured at Fort Gaines, AL, on 8/8/1864; Received at Ship Island, MS, from New Orleans, LA, on 10/25/1864. Forwarded to Fort Columbus, New York Harbor, NY, on 11/5/1864; Exchanged on 1/4/1865.

Averheart, T.M. Pvt., 21st Alabama Infantry. Co. D. Federal Rolls of Prisoners of War: Captured at Blakely, AL, on 4/9/1865; Received at Ship Island, MS, on 4/15/1865. Transferred to Vicksburg, MS, for exchange on 5/1/1865; Exchanged at Camp Townsend, MS, on 5/6/1865.

Avery, William Pvt., 8th Alabama Cavalry. Co. A. Federal Rolls of Prisoners of War: Captured in Alabama on 3/24/1865; Received at Ship Island, MS. Transferred to Vicksburg, MS, for exchange on 5/1/1865; Exchanged at Camp Townsend, MS, on 5/6/1865.

Ayer, B.H. Pvt., 21st Alabama Infantry. Co. __. Federal Rolls of Prisoners of War: Captured at Fort Gaines, AL, on 8/8/1864; Received at Ship Island, MS, from New Orleans, LA, on 10/25/1864. Forwarded to Fort Columbus New York Harbor, NY, on 11/5/1864; Exchanged on 1/4/1865.

Bachelor, J. Pvt., 62nd Alabama Infantry. Co. A. Federal Rolls of Prisoners of War: Captured at Blakely, AL, on 4/9/1865; Received at Ship Island, MS, on 4/15/1865. Transferred to Vicksburg, MS, for exchange on 5/1/1865; Exchanged at Camp Townsend, MS, on 5/6/1865.

Bachelor, T.J. Pvt., 62nd Alabama Infantry. Co. E. Federal Rolls of Prisoners of War: Captured at Blakely, AL, on 4/9/1865; Received at Ship Island, MS, on 4/15/1865. Transferred to Vicksburg, MS, for exchange on 5/1/1865; Exchanged at Camp Townsend, MS, on 5/6/1865. Soldier also served as a Pvt. with the 1st Alabama Reserves.

Badger, William S. 2nd Lt./1st Lt., 21st Alabama Infantry. Co. __. Federal Rolls of Prisoners of War: Captured at Fort Gaines, AL, on 8/8/1864; Received at Ship Island, MS, from New Orleans, LA, on 11/25/1864. Transferred to Vicksburg, MS, for exchange on 4/28/1865; Confined at New Orleans, LA, on 4/30/1865. Exchanged at Camp Townsend, MS, on 5/6/1865.

Baggett, H.P. Pvt., 62nd Alabama Infantry. Co. F. Federal Rolls of Prisoners of War: Captured at Blakely, AL, on 4/9/1865; Received at Ship Island, MS, on 4/15/1865. Transferred to Vicksburg, MS, for exchange on 5/1/1865; Exchanged at Camp Townsend, MS, on 5/6/1865. Soldier also served as a Pvt. with the 1st Alabama Reserves.

Baggett, John D.I. Pvt., 1st Alabama Artillery Battalion. Co. B. Federal Rolls of Prisoners of War: Captured at Blakely, AL, on 4/9/1865; Received at Ship Island, MS, on 4/15/1865. Transferred to Vicksburg, MS, for exchange on 5/1/1865; Exchanged at Camp Townsend, MS, on 5/6/1865.

Baggett, Julius C.A. (AKA J.G.) Pvt., 1st Alabama Artillery Battalion. Cos. B & C. Federal Rolls of Prisoners of War: Captured at Fort Gaines, AL, on 8/8/1864; Received at Ship Island, MS, from New Orleans, LA, on 10/25/1864. Exchanged on 1/4/1865.

Bailey, J.A. Pvt., 21st Alabama Infantry. Co. I. Federal Rolls of Prisoners of War: Captured at Fort Gaines, AL, on 8/8/1864; Received at Ship Island, MS, from New Orleans, LA, on 10/29/1864. Died: 11/24/1864 at Ship Island, MS, due to dysentery. Buried: Ship Island, MS, Cemetery in Grave #41.

Bailey, Jeremiah W. (AKA W.W.) Pvt., 36th Alabama Infantry. Co. A. Enlisted: Sumpter County, AL. Age at enlistment: 21. Federal Rolls of Prisoners of War: Captured at Spanish Fort, AL, on 4/8/1865; Received at Ship Island, MS, on 4/10/1865. Transferred to Vicksburg, MS, for exchange on 5/1/1865; Exchanged at Camp Townsend, MS, on 5/6/1865. Rolls of Prisoners of War, C.S.A: Surrendered at Citronelle, AL, on 5/4/1865; Paroled at Gainesville, AL, on 6/30/1865.

Bailey, J. Taylor Pvt., 62nd Alabama Infantry. Co. G. Federal Rolls of Prisoners of War: Captured at Blakely, AL, on 4/9/1865; Received at Ship Island, MS, on 4/15/1865. Transferred to Vicksburg, MS, for exchange on 5/1/1865; Exchanged at Camp Townsend, MS, on 5/6/1865.

Bailey, W.G. Pvt., 21st Alabama Infantry. Co. G. Died: 11/27/1864 at Ship Island, MS, due to pneumonia. Buried: Ship Island, MS, Cemetery in Grave #46.

Baily, J.F. (AKA G.F.) Pvt., 63rd Alabama Infantry. Co. F. Enlisted: 5/30/1864 at Georgiana, AL. Age at enlistment: 17. Description at enlistment: Eyes: hazel. Hair: dark. Complexion: dark. Height: 5'6". Rolls for 6/1864 through 7/1864: Absent, sick. Rolls for 9/1864 through 10/1864: Present. Federal Rolls of Prisoners of War: Captured at Blakely, AL, on 4/9/1865; Received at Ship Island, MS, on 4/15/1865. Transferred to Vicksburg, MS, for exchange on 5/1/1865; Exchanged at Camp Townsend, MS, on 5/6/1865. Rolls of Prisoners of War, C.S.A: Surrendered at Citronelle, AL, on 5/4/1865; Paroled at Meridian, MS, on 5/10/1865. Residence at parole: Butler County, AL.

Baily, U.J. Pvt., 21st Alabama Infantry. Co. F. Federal Rolls of Prisoners of War: Captured at Fort Gaines, AL, on 8/8/1864; Received at Ship Island, MS, from New Orleans, LA, on 10/25/1864. Exchanged on 1/4/1865.

Bairfield, A.D. Pvt., 62nd Alabama Infantry. Co. A. Federal Rolls of Prisoners of War: Captured at Blakely, AL, on 4/9/1865; Received at Ship Island, MS, on 4/15/1865. Transferred to Vicksburg, MS, for exchange on 5/1/1865; Exchanged at Camp Townsend, MS, on 5/6/1865. Soldier also served as a Pvt. with the 1st Alabama Reserves.

Baker, Allen Pvt., 21st Alabama Infantry. Co. B. Federal Rolls of Prisoners of War: Captured at Fort Gaines, AL, on 8/8/1864; Received at Ship Island, MS, from New Orleans, LA, on 10/25/1864. Died: 12/11/1864 at Ship Island, MS, due to chronic dysentery. Buried: Ship Island, MS, Cemetery in Grave #77.

Baker, George Franklin Pvt./5th Sgt., 63rd Alabama Infantry. Co. I. Enlisted: 7/28/1864 at Columbiana, AL. Rolls for 9/1864 through 10/1864: Absent, sick in Moore Hospital since 10/15/1864. Federal Rolls of Prisoners of War: Captured at Blakely, AL, on 4/9/1865; Received at Ship Island, MS, on 4/15/1865. Transferred to Vicksburg, MS, for exchange on 5/1/1865; Exchanged at Camp Townsend, MS, on 5/6/1865. Rolls of Prisoners of War, C.S.A: Surrendered at Citronelle, AL, on 5/4/1865; Paroled at Meridian, MS, on 5/13/1865. Residence at parole: Shelby County, AL.

Baker, O.H.P. Pvt., 63rd Alabama Infantry. Co. E. Federal Rolls of Prisoners of War: Captured at Blakely, AL, on 4/9/1865; Received at Ship Island, MS, on 4/15/1865. Rolls of Prisoners of War, C.S.A: Surrendered at Citronelle, AL, on 5/4/1865; Paroled at Meridian, MS, on 5/13/1865.

Baldwyn, Ralph P. Cpl./2nd Lt., 21st Alabama Infantry. Co. E. Federal Rolls of Prisoners of War: Captured at Fort Gaines, AL, on 8/8/1864; Received at Ship Island, MS, from New Orleans, LA, on 11/25/1864. Exchanged on 1/4/1865.

Banks, Robert Pvt., 63rd Alabama Infantry. Co. G. Enlisted: 4/19/1864 at Troy, AL. Age at enlistment: 17. Description at enlistment: Eyes: blue. Hair: dark. Complexion: fair. Height: 5'7". Residence at enlistment: Pike County, AL. Rolls for 9/1864 through 10/1864: Absent, in hospital. On Register of Ross Hospital, Mobile, AL: Admitted on 9/20/1864 due to rubeola; Returned to duty on 10/3/1864. Federal Rolls of Prisoners of War: Captured at Blakely, AL, on 4/9/1865; Received at Ship Island, MS, on 4/15/1865. Transferred to Vicksburg, MS, for exchange on 5/1/1865; Exchanged at Camp Townsend, MS, on 5/6/1865. Rolls of Prisoners of War, C.S.A: Surrendered at Citronelle, AL, on 5/4/1865; Paroled at Meridian, MS, on 5/13/1865.

Barkley, F.M. Pvt., 62nd Alabama Infantry. Co. A. Federal Rolls of Prisoners of War: Captured at Blakely, AL, on 4/9/1865; Received at Ship Island, MS, on 4/15/1865. Transferred to Vicksburg, MS, for exchange on 5/1/1865; Exchanged at Camp Townsend, MS, on 5/6/1865.

Barksdale, C.H. (AKA G.H.) Pvt., Tarrant's Artillery Battery. Enlisted: 7/11/1863 at Tuscaloosa, AL. Federal Rolls of Prisoners of War: Captured at Blakely, AL, on 4/9/1865; Received at Ship Island, MS, on 4/15/1865. Transferred to Vicksburg, MS, for exchange on 5/1/1865; Exchanged at Camp Townsend, MS, on 5/6/1865.

Barksdale, W.B. Pvt., Tarrant's Artillery Battery. Federal Rolls of Prisoners of War: Captured at Blakely, AL, on 4/9/1865; Received at Ship Island, MS, on 4/15/1865. Transferred to Vicksburg, MS, for exchange on 5/1/1865; Exchanged at Camp Townsend, MS, on 5/6/1865.

Barley, I. (AKA J.) Pvt., 21st Alabama Infantry. Co. I. Federal Rolls of Prisoners of War: Captured at Fort Gaines, AL, on 8/8/1864; Received at Ship Island, MS, from New Orleans, LA, on 10/25/1864. Died: 11/24/1864 at Ship Island, MS, due to dysentery. Buried: Ship Island, MS, Cemetery in Grave #41.

Barnabus, Gabel (AKA Gilley) Pvt., 36th Alabama Infantry. Co. A. Federal Rolls of Prisoners of War: Captured at Spanish Fort, AL, on 4/8/1865; Received at Ship Island, MS, on 4/10/1865. Transferred to Vicksburg, MS, for exchange on 5/1/1865; Exchanged at Camp Townsend, MS, on 5/6/1865.

Barnes, Thomas J. Musician, 21st Alabama Infantry. Co. C. Federal Rolls of Prisoners of War: Captured at Fort Gaines, AL, on 8/8/1864; Received at Ship Island, MS, from New Orleans, LA, on 10/25/1864. Exchanged on 1/4/1865.

Barnett, James Madison (AKA J.W.) Pvt., 62nd Alabama Infantry. Co. K. Enlisted: 1/3/1864 at Selma, AL. Federal Rolls of Prisoners of War: Captured at Blakely, AL, on 4/9/1865; Received at Ship Island, MS, on 4/15/1865. Transferred to Vicksburg, MS, for exchange on 5/1/1865; Exchanged at Camp Townsend, MS, on

5/6/1865. Born: 9/11/1846 at Perry County, AL. Residence after war: Perry County, AL.

Barnett, James W. (AKA J.M.) Pvt., 62nd Alabama Infantry. Co. K. Federal Rolls of Prisoners of War: Captured at Blakely, AL, on 4/9/1865; Received at Ship Island, MS, on 4/15/1865. Transferred to Vicksburg, MS, for exchange on 5/1/1865; Exchanged at Camp Townsend, MS, on 5/6/1865. Soldier also served as a Pvt. with the 1st Alabama Reserves.

Barnett, S.C. Pvt., 62nd Alabama Infantry. Co. A. Federal Rolls of Prisoners of War: Captured at Blakely, AL, on 4/9/1865; Received at Ship Island, MS, on 4/15/1865. Transferred to Vicksburg, MS, for exchange on 5/1/1865; Exchanged at Camp Townsend, MS, on 5/6/1865. Soldier also served as a Pvt. with the 1st Alabama Reserves.

Barnett, William Franklin Pvt., 62nd Alabama Infantry. Co. A. Enlisted: 1863 at Bibb County, AL. Federal Rolls of Prisoners of War: Captured at Blakely, AL, on 4/9/1865; Received at Ship Island, MS, on 4/15/1865. Transferred to Vicksburg, MS, for exchange on 5/1/1865; Exchanged at Camp Townsend, MS, on 5/6/1865. Born: 3/27/1847 at Bibb County, AL. Died: After 1921. Buried: Bibb County, AL.

Barneycastle, Henry (AKA Bareycastle) Pvt., 18th Alabama Infantry. Co. H. Federal Rolls of Prisoners of War: Captured at Blakely, AL, on 4/9/1865; Received at Ship Island, MS, on 4/15/1865. Transferred to Vicksburg, MS, for exchange on 5/1/1865; Exchanged at Camp Townsend, MS, on 5/6/1865.

Barr, George W. Pvt., 63rd Alabama Infantry. Co. H. Federal Rolls of Prisoners of War: Captured at Blakely, AL, on 4/9/1865; Received at Ship Island, MS, on 4/15/1865. Transferred to Vicksburg, MS, for exchange on 5/1/1865; Exchanged at Camp Townsend, MS, on 5/6/1865.

Barr, James M. Pvt., 21st Alabama Infantry. Co. C. On Register of Selma, AL, Hospital: Admitted on 5/13/1863 due to febris intermittens; Returned to duty on 7/17/1863. Federal Rolls of Prisoners of War: Captured at Fort Gaines, AL, on 8/8/1864; Received at Ship Island, MS, from New Orleans, LA, on 10/25/1864. Exchanged on 1/4/1865.

Barret, John W. Pvt., 21st Alabama Infantry. Co. H. Federal Rolls of Prisoners of War: Captured at Fort Gaines, AL, on 8/8/1864; Received at Ship Island, MS, from New Orleans, LA, on 10/25/1864. Exchanged on 1/4/1865. Confederate Widows Pension Application on file at the Alabama Department of Archives and History. Target Name: Barret, Camilla D. Record Card Number: 38326. County: Mobile.

Barrett, G.D. (AKA Barnett) Pvt., 62nd Alabama Infantry. Co. C. Federal Rolls of Prisoners of War: Captured at Blakely, AL, on 4/9/1865; Received at Ship Island, MS, on 4/15/1865. Transferred to Vicksburg, MS, for exchange on 5/1/1865; Exchanged at Camp Townsend, MS, on 5/6/1865.

Barron, James P. Pvt., 63rd Alabama Infantry. Co. A. Enlisted: 1/1/1864 at Tallapoosa County, AL. Rolls for 1/1864 through 2/1864: Present. Rolls for 9/1864 through 10/1864: Present. Federal Rolls of Prisoners of War: Captured at Blakely, AL, on 4/9/1865; Received at Ship Island, MS, on 4/15/1865. Transferred to Vicksburg, MS, for exchange on 5/1/1865; Exchanged at Camp Townsend, MS, on 5/6/1865. Rolls of Prisoners of War, C.S.A: Surrendered at Citronelle, AL, on 5/4/1865; Paroled at Meridian, MS, on 5/13/1865.

Barron, John W. (AKA J.D.) Pvt., 63rd Alabama Infantry. Co. D. Federal Rolls of Prisoners of War: Captured at Blakely, AL, on 4/9/1865; Received at Ship Island, MS, on 4/15/1865. Transferred to Vicksburg, MS, for exchange on 5/1/1865; Exchanged at Camp Townsend, MS, on 5/6/1865. Rolls of Prisoners of War, C.S.A: Surrendered at Citronelle, AL, on 5/4/1865; Paroled at Meridian, MS, on 5/13/1865.

Baskins, Peter B. (AKA Baskins, T.B.) Pvt., 63rd Alabama Infantry. Co. G. Enlisted: 5/16/1864 at Troy, AL. Age at enlistment: 17. Description at enlistment: Eyes: blue. Hair: dark. Complexion: dark. Height: 5'7". Residence at enlistment: Montgomery County, AL. Rolls for 9/1864 through 10/1864: Absent, in hospital at Lauderdale, MS, since 8/20/1864. Federal Rolls of Prisoners of War: Captured at Blakely, AL, on 4/9/1865; Received at Ship Island, MS, on 4/15/1865. Transferred to Vicksburg, MS, for exchange on 5/1/1865. On Register of U.S.A. General Hospital #2, Vicksburg, MS: Admitted from steamer on 5/3/1865 due to chronic bronchitis; Returned to duty on 5/21/1865.

Bassett, John A. Pvt./Cpl., 63rd Alabama Infantry. Cos. D & I. Enlisted: 4/15/1864 at Columbiana, AL. Rolls for 9/1864 through 10/1864: Absent, on detached service. Federal Rolls of Prisoners of War: Captured at Blakely, AL, on 4/9/1865; Received at Ship Island, MS, on 4/15/1865. Transferred to Vicksburg, MS, for exchange on 5/1/1865; Exchanged at Camp Townsend, MS, on 5/6/1865. Rolls of Prisoners of War, C.S.A: Surrendered at Citronelle, AL, on 5/4/1865; Paroled at Meridian, MS, on 5/13/1865.

Battle, R.R., Jr. 2nd Lt./2nd Alabama Reserves. Co. K. Enlisted: 10/1/1864 at Blakely, AL. Rolls for 9/1864 through 10/1864: Present. Federal Rolls of Prisoners of War: Captured at Blakely, AL, on 4/9/1865; Received at Ship Island, MS, on 4/16/1865. Transferred to Vicksburg, MS, for exchange on 4/28/1865; Confined at New Orleans, LA, on 4/30/1865. Exchanged at Camp Townsend, MS, on 5/6/1865. Rolls of Prisoners of War, C.S.A: Surrendered at Citronelle, AL, on 5/4/1865; Paroled at Meridian, MS, on 5/11/1865.

Baxley, John P. Pvt., 63rd Alabama Infantry. Co. B. Enlisted: 4/14/1864 at Montgomery County, AL. Age at enlistment: 17. Rolls for 9/1864 through 10/1864: Present. Federal Rolls of Prisoners of War: Captured at Blakely, AL, on 4/9/1865; Received at Ship Island, MS, on 4/15/1865. Transferred to Vicksburg, MS, for exchange on 5/1/1865; Exchanged at Camp Townsend, MS, on 5/6/1865. Rolls of Prisoners of War, C.S.A: Surrendered at Citronelle, AL, on 5/4/1865; Paroled at Meridian, MS, on 5/11/1865.

Bean, Bartlett M. Sgt., 63rd Alabama Infantry. Co. G. Enlisted: 4/16/1864 at Troy, AL. Age at enlistment: 17. Description at enlistment: Eyes: dark. Hair: dark. Complexion: fair. Height: 5'10". Rolls for 9/1864 through 10/1864: Present. Federal Rolls of Prisoners of War: Captured at Blakely, AL, on 4/9/1865; Received at Ship Island, MS, on 4/15/1865. Transferred to Vicksburg, MS, for exchange on 5/1/1865; Exchanged at Camp Townsend, MS, on 5/6/1865. Rolls of Prisoners of War, C.S.A: Surrendered at

Citronelle, AL, on 5/4/1865; Paroled at Meridian, MS, on 5/13/1865.

Beard, David J. (AKA D.J.S., D.T.) Pvt., 62nd Alabama Infantry. Co. E. Enlisted: 1/18/1864 at Talladega, AL. Age at enlistment: 17. Federal Rolls of Prisoners of War: Captured at Blakely, AL, on 4/9/1865; Received at Ship Island, MS, on 4/15/1865. Transferred to Vicksburg, MS, for exchange on 5/1/1865; Exchanged at Camp Townsend, MS, on 5/6/1865.

Beard, J.A. Pvt., 63rd Alabama Infantry. Co. K. Enlisted: 8/6/1864 at Russell County, AL. Rolls for 9/1864 through 10/1864: Present. Federal Rolls of Prisoners of War: Captured at Blakely, AL, on 4/9/1865; Received at Ship Island, MS, on 4/15/1865. Transferred to Vicksburg, MS, for exchange on 5/1/1865; Exchanged at Camp Townsend, MS, on 5/6/1865. Rolls of Prisoners of War, C.S.A: Surrendered at Citronelle, AL, on 5/4/1865; Paroled at Meridian, MS, on 5/13/1865.

Beasley, James (AKA Beasly) Pvt., 62nd Alabama Infantry. Co. D. Federal Rolls of Prisoners of War: Captured at Blakely, AL, on 4/9/1865; Received at Ship Island, MS, on 4/15/1865. Transferred to Vicksburg, MS, for exchange on 5/1/1865; Exchanged at Camp Townsend, MS, on 5/6/1865.

Beckham, T.W. Pvt., Tarrant's Artillery Battery. Federal Rolls of Prisoners of War: Captured at Blakely, AL, on 4/9/1865; Received at Ship Island, MS, on 4/15/1865. Transferred to Vicksburg, MS, for exchange on 5/1/1865; Exchanged at Camp Townsend, MS, on 5/6/1865.

Belcher, J.H. Pvt., 21st Alabama Infantry. Co. F. Federal Rolls of Prisoners of War: Captured at Fort Gaines, AL, on 8/8/1864; Received at Ship Island, MS, from New Orleans, LA, on 10/25/1864. Exchanged on 1/4/1865.

Belcher, W.E. Pvt., 63rd Alabama Infantry. Co. K. Enlisted: 8/15/1864 at Choctaw County, AL. Rolls for 9/1864 through 10/1864: Absent, in hospital at Mobile, AL, since 10/25/1864. Federal Rolls of Prisoners of War: Captured at Blakely, AL, on 4/9/1865; Received at Ship Island, MS, on 4/15/1865. Transferred to Vicksburg, MS, for exchange on 5/1/1865; Exchanged at Camp Townsend, MS, on 5/6/1865. Rolls of Prisoners of War, C.S.A: Surrendered at Citronelle, AL, on 5/4/1865; Paroled at Meridian, MS, on 5/13/1865.

Bell, Edward Pvt., 21st Alabama Infantry. Cos. A & B. Federal Rolls of Prisoners of War: Captured at Fort Gaines, AL, on 8/8/1864; Received at Ship Island, MS, from New Orleans, LA, on 10/25/1864. Exchanged on 1/4/1865.

Bell, J.T. Pvt., 63rd Alabama Infantry. Co. F. Enlisted: 7/23/1864 at Greenville, AL. Rolls for 9/1864 through 10/1864: Present. Federal Rolls of Prisoners of War: Captured at Blakely, AL, on 4/9/1865; Received at Ship Island, MS, on 4/15/1865. Transferred to Vicksburg, MS, for exchange on 5/1/1865; Exchanged at Camp Townsend, MS, on 5/6/1865. Rolls of Prisoners of War, C.S.A: Surrendered at Citronelle, AL, on 5/4/1865; Paroled at Meridian, MS, on 5/11/1865.

Bell, John W. Pvt., Pelham Cadets. Co. A. Federal Rolls of Prisoners of War: Captured at Fort Gaines, AL, on 8/8/1864; Received at Ship Island, MS, from New Orleans, LA, on 10/25/1864. Exchanged on 1/4/1865.

Bell, S.W. Pvt., 1st Alabama Artillery Battalion. Co. D. Federal Rolls of Prisoners of War: Captured at Fort Gaines, AL, on 8/8/1864; Received at Ship Island, MS, from New Orleans, LA, on 10/25/1864. Exchanged on 1/4/1865.

Bell, William H. Pvt., 38th Alabama Infantry. Co. E. Enlisted: 4/7/1862 at Mobile, AL. Age at enlistment: 20. On Register of St. Mary's Hospital, Dalton, GA: Admitted on 6/27/1863 due to debilitas; Received at the Convalescent Camp, Dalton, GA, on 7/9/1863. Detailed as Cooper at Tyner's Station, TN, on 8/15/1863. Federal Rolls of Prisoners of War: Captured at Blakely, AL, on 4/9/1865; Received at Ship Island, MS, on 4/15/1865. Transferred to Vicksburg, MS, for exchange on 5/1/1865; Exchanged at Camp Townsend, MS, on 5/6/1865.

Benbow, Richard N. (AKA Bembow, R.M.) Pvt., 63rd Alabama Infantry. Co. F. Enlisted: 5/30/1864 at Montgomery, AL. Age at enlistment: 17. Description at enlistment: Eyes: dark. Hair: dark. Complexion: dark. Height: 5'6". Residence at enlistment: Pike County, AL. Rolls for 9/1864 through 10/1864: Absent, sick since 8/29/1864. Federal Rolls of Prisoners of War: Captured at Blakely, AL, on 4/9/1865; Received at Ship Island, MS, on 4/15/1865. Transferred to Vicksburg, MS, for exchange on 5/1/1865; Exchanged at Camp Townsend, MS, on 5/6/1865. Rolls of Prisoners of War, C.S.A: Surrendered at Citronelle, AL, on 5/4/1865; Paroled at Meridian, MS, on 5/11/1865. Born: 2/4/1846 at Pike County, AL. Soldier is recorded on the 1907 Alabama Census of Confederate Veterans and Widows. Residence: Crenshaw County, AL.

Benefield, James A. (AKA Bennifield) Pvt., 63rd Alabama Infantry. Co. D. Enlisted: 7/30/1864 at Macon County, AL. Age at enlistment: 17. Description at enlistment: Eyes: blue. Hair: light. Complexion: fair. Height: 5'4". Residence at enlistment: Henry County, AL. Rolls for 9/1864 through 10/1864: Absent, sick in hospital at Mobile, AL, since 10/1/1864. Federal Rolls of Prisoners of War: Captured at Blakely, AL, on 4/9/1865; Received at Ship Island, MS, on 4/15/1865. Transferred to Vicksburg, MS, for exchange on 5/1/1865; Exchanged at Camp Townsend, MS, on 5/6/1865. Rolls of Prisoners of War, C.S.A: Surrendered at Citronelle, AL, on 5/4/1865; Paroled at Meridian, MS, on 5/11/1865. Born: 1/19/1847 at Barbour County, AL. Soldier is recorded on the 1907 Alabama Census of Confederate Veterans and Widows. Residence: Geneva County, AL.

Benson, R.P. Pvt., 38th Alabama Infantry. Co. A. On Register of Floyd House and Ocmulgee Hospital, Macon, GA: Admitted on 11/28/1863 due to v. con. hip. Federal Rolls of Prisoners of War: Captured at Spanish Fort, AL, on 4/8/1865; Received at Ship Island, MS, on 4/10/1865. Transferred to Vicksburg, MS, for exchange on 5/1/1865; Exchanged at Camp Townsend, MS, on 5/6/1865.

Berdaux, J.W. (AKA Berdeau) Pvt., 63rd Alabama Infantry. Co. F. Enlisted: 9/19/1864 at Haynesville, AL. Rolls for 9/1864 through 10/1864: Present. Federal Rolls of Prisoners of War: Captured at Blakely, AL, on 4/9/1865; Received at Ship Island, MS, on 4/15/1865. Transferred to Vicksburg, MS, for exchange on 5/1/1865; Exchanged at Camp Townsend, MS, on 5/6/1865. Rolls of Prisoners of War, C.S.A: Surrendered at Citronelle, AL, on 5/4/1865; Paroled at Meridian, MS, on 5/11/1865.

Berry, Harry B. Pvt., 38th Alabama Infantry. Co. F. Enlisted: 5/3/1862 at Fayette County, AL. Age at enlistment: 20. On Register of Ocmulgee Hospital, Macon, GA: Admitted on 9/20/1864; Returned to duty on 11/12/1864. Federal Rolls of Prisoners of War: Captured at Spanish Fort, AL, on 4/8/1865; Received at Ship Island, MS, on 4/10/1865. Transferred to Vicksburg, MS, for exchange on 5/1/1865; Exchanged at Camp Townsend, MS, on 5/6/1865.

Berry, William E. Pvt., 38th Alabama Infantry. Co. E. Enlisted: 4/7/1862 at Mobile, AL. Received sick furlough of 40 days on 12/4/1863 near Dalton, GA. On Register of Watts Hospital, Montgomery, AL: Admitted on 11/15/1864. Federal Rolls of Prisoners of War: Captured at Blakely, AL, on 4/9/1865; Received at Ship Island, MS, on 4/15/1865. Transferred to Vicksburg, MS, for exchange on 5/1/1865; Exchanged at Camp Townsend, MS, on 5/6/1865.

Besley, John Pvt., 1st Alabama Artillery Battalion. Co. D. Federal Rolls of Prisoners of War: Captured at Fort Gaines, AL, on 8/8/1864; Received at Ship Island, MS, from New Orleans, LA, on 10/25/1864. Exchanged on 3/2/1865.

Best, George M. (AKA G.W.) Pvt., 1st Alabama Artillery Battalion. Co. D. Federal Rolls of Prisoners of War: Captured at Fort Gaines, AL, on 8/8/1864; Received at Ship Island, MS, from New Orleans, LA, on 10/25/1864. Exchanged on 1/4/1865.

Betts, William H. Pvt., 63rd Alabama Infantry. Co. C. Enlisted: 7/3/1864 at Macon County, AL. Rolls for 9/1864 through 10/1864: Present. Federal Rolls of Prisoners of War: Captured at Blakely, AL, on 4/9/1865; Received at Ship Island, MS, on 4/15/1865. Transferred to Vicksburg, MS, for exchange on 5/1/1865; Exchanged at Camp Townsend, MS, on 5/6/1865. Rolls of Prisoners of War, C.S.A: Surrendered at Citronelle, AL, on 5/4/1865; Paroled at Meridian, MS, on 5/11/1865. Residence at parole: Chambers County, AL.

Bevill, R.W. Cpl./Pvt., 62nd Alabama Infantry. Co. C. Federal Rolls of Prisoners of War: Captured at Blakely, AL, on 4/9/1865; Received at Ship Island, MS, on 4/15/1865. Transferred to Vicksburg, MS, for exchange on 5/1/1865; Exchanged at Camp Townsend, MS, on 5/6/1865.

Bide, J.H. Pvt., Tarrant's Artillery Battery. Federal Rolls of Prisoners of War: Captured at Blakely, AL, on 4/9/1865; Received at Ship Island, MS, on 4/15/1865. Transferred to Vicksburg, MS, for exchange on 5/1/1865; Exchanged at Camp Townsend, MS, on 5/6/1865.

Binford, John M. (AKA Brufot, Burford) Pvt., Pelham Cadets. Co. A. Federal Rolls of Prisoners of War: Captured at Fort Gaines, AL, on 8/8/1864; Received at Ship Island, MS, from New Orleans, LA, on 10/25/1864. Died: 11/22/1864 at Ship Island, MS, due to pneumonia. Buried: Ship Island, MS, Cemetery in Grave #35.

Binford, Peter Pvt./Asst. Surg., 38th Alabama Infantry. F & S. Enlisted: 5/15/1862; Appointed Assistant Surgeon on 4/25/1863. Federal Rolls of Prisoners of War: Captured at Spanish Fort, AL, on 4/8/1865; Received at Ship Island, MS, on 4/10/1865. Transferred to Vicksburg, MS, for exchange on 4/28/1865; Confined at New Orleans, LA, on 4/30/1865. Exchanged at Camp Townsend, MS, on 5/6/1865.

Bishop, J. Uriah Pvt., 21st Alabama Infantry. Co. C. Federal Rolls of Prisoners of War: Captured at Fort Gaines, AL, on 8/8/1864; Received at Ship Island, MS, from New Orleans, LA, on 10/25/1864. Exchanged on 1/4/1865.

Bishop, John A. Cpl./Pvt., 63rd Alabama Infantry. Co. K. Federal Rolls of Prisoners of War: Captured at Blakely, AL, on 4/9/1865; Received at Ship Island, MS, on 4/15/1865. Transferred to Vicksburg, MS, for exchange on 5/1/1865; Exchanged at Camp Townsend, MS, on 5/6/1865. Rolls of Prisoners of War, C.S.A: Surrendered at Citronelle, AL, on 5/4/1865; Paroled at Meridian, MS, on 5/13/1865. Residence at parole: Bibb County, AL.

Bishop, Reuben Pvt., 62nd Alabama Infantry. Co. D. Federal Rolls of Prisoners of War: Captured at Blakely, AL, on 4/9/1865; Received at Ship Island, MS, on 4/15/1865. Transferred to Vicksburg, MS, for exchange on 5/1/1865; Exchanged at Camp Townsend, MS, on 5/6/1865.

Bishop, Robert A. Pvt./Cpl., 62nd Alabama Infantry. Co. C. Federal Rolls of Prisoners of War: Captured at Blakely, AL, on 4/9/1865; Received at Ship Island, MS, on 4/15/1865. Transferred to Vicksburg, MS, for exchange on 5/1/1865; Exchanged at Camp Townsend, MS, on 5/6/1865.

Bishop, William Pvt., 21st Alabama Infantry. Co. I. Federal Rolls of Prisoners of War: Captured at Fort Gaines, AL, on 8/8/1864; Received at Ship Island, MS, from New Orleans, LA, on 10/25/1864. Exchanged on 1/4/1865.

Blackburn, J.J. Pvt., Tarrant's Artillery Battery. Enlisted: 9/25/1863 at Perry County, AL. Federal Rolls of Prisoners of War: Captured at Blakely, AL, on 4/9/1865; Received at Ship Island, MS, on 4/15/1865. Transferred to Vicksburg, MS, for exchange on 5/1/1865; Exchanged at Camp Townsend, MS, on 5/6/1865. Born: 1821. Married: Sarah Blackburn. Occupation: Farmer.

Blackburn, T.C. Pvt., 21st Alabama Infantry. Co. F. Federal Rolls of Prisoners of War: Captured at Fort Gaines, AL, on 8/8/1864; Received at Ship Island, MS, from New Orleans, LA, on 10/25/1864. Exchanged on 1/4/1865. Born: 1838. Married: Sara Blackburn. Children: 10. Occupation: Farmer.

Blackburn, Thomas J. Pvt., Tarrant's Artillery Battery. Enlisted: 8/1/1864 at Atlanta, GA. Federal Rolls of Prisoners of War: Captured at Blakely, AL, on 4/9/1865; Received at Ship Island, MS, on 4/15/1865. Transferred to Vicksburg, MS, for exchange on 5/1/1865; Exchanged at Camp Townsend, MS, on 5/6/1865. Born: 8/4/1849 at Ironville, Perry County, AL. Residence after war: Perry County, AL.

Blackburn, William Pinkney Pvt., Tarrant's Artillery Battery. Enlisted: 1862 at Pollard, AL. Federal Rolls of Prisoners of War: Captured at Blakely, AL, on 4/9/1865; Received at Ship Island, MS, on 4/15/1865. Transferred to Vicksburg, MS, for exchange on 5/1/1865; Exchanged at Camp Townsend, MS, on 5/6/1865. Married: Mary Blackburn. Residence after war: Perry County, AL.

Blackman, Theophilus B. (AKA Blackmon, Blackmond) Pvt., 63rd Alabama Infantry. Co. G. Enlisted: 7/1/1864 at Troy, AL. Age at enlistment: 17. Description at enlistment: Eyes: dark. Hair: dark. Complexion: fair. Height: 5'5". Rolls for 9/1864 through 10/1864:

Present. Federal Rolls of Prisoners of War: Captured at Blakely, AL, on 4/9/1865; Received at Ship Island, MS, on 4/15/1865. Transferred to Vicksburg, MS, for exchange on 5/1/1865; Exchanged at Camp Townsend, MS, on 5/6/1865. Rolls of Prisoners of War, C.S.A: Surrendered at Citronelle, AL, on 5/4/1865; Paroled at Meridian, MS, on 5/13/1865. Residence at parole: Butler County, AL.

Blackshire, W.A. (AKA Blacksher) Cpl., 38th Alabama Infantry. Co. C. Federal Rolls of Prisoners of War: Captured at Blakely, AL, on 4/9/1865; Received at Ship Island, MS, on 4/15/1865. Transferred to Vicksburg, MS, for exchange on 5/1/1865; Exchanged at Camp Townsend, MS, on 5/6/1865.

Blackwood, Alexander S. Pvt., 62nd Alabama Infantry. Co. B. Federal Rolls of Prisoners of War: Captured at Blakely, AL, on 4/9/1865; Received at Ship Island, MS, on 4/15/1865. Transferred to Vicksburg, MS, for exchange on 5/1/1865; Exchanged at Camp Townsend, MS, on 5/6/1865.

Blair, James Pvt., 1st Alabama Artillery Battalion. Co. B. Federal Rolls of Prisoners of War: Captured at Fort Gaines, AL, on 8/8/1864; Received at Ship Island, MS, from New Orleans, LA, on 10/25/1864. Exchanged on 1/4/1865.

Blakenship, William Pvt., 36th Alabama Infantry. Co. E. Enlisted: 10/25/1861 at Mobile, AL. Federal Rolls of Prisoners of War: Captured at Spanish Fort, AL, on 4/8/1865; Received at Ship Island, MS, on 4/10/1865. Transferred to Vicksburg, MS, for exchange on 5/1/1865; Exchanged at Camp Townsend, MS, on 5/6/1865. Born: 8/19/1842 at Washington County, AL. Residence after war: Mobile County, AL.

Bledsoe, N.S. Pvt., 62nd Alabama Infantry. Co. A. Federal Rolls of Prisoners of War: Captured at Blakely, AL, on 4/9/1865; Received at Ship Island, MS, on 4/15/1865. Transferred to Vicksburg, MS, for exchange on 5/1/1865; Exchanged at Camp Townsend, MS, on 5/6/1865.

Boman, John F. Pvt., 63rd Alabama Infantry. Cos. C & I. Enlisted: 5/31/1864 at Montgomery, AL. Age at enlistment: 17. Description at enlistment: Eyes: grey. Hair: light. Complexion: light. Height: 5'6". Residence at enlistment: Carnes Cross Roads, Dale County, AL. Rolls for 9/1864 through 10/1864: Present. Federal Rolls of Prisoners of War: Captured at Blakely, AL, on 4/9/1865; Received at Ship Island, MS, on 4/15/1865. Transferred to Vicksburg, MS, for exchange on 5/1/1865; Exchanged at Camp Townsend, MS, on 5/6/1865. Rolls of Prisoners of War, C.S.A: Surrendered at Citronelle, AL, on 5/4/1865; Paroled at Meridian, MS, on 5/11/1865. Residence at parole: Dale County, AL.

Bond, J.A. (AKA Bonds) Pvt., 63rd Alabama Infantry. Co. E. Federal Rolls of Prisoners of War: Captured at Blakely, AL, on 4/9/1865; Received at Ship Island, MS, on 4/15/1865. Transferred to Vicksburg, MS, for exchange on 5/1/1865; Exchanged at Camp Townsend, MS, on 5/6/1865.

Bond, John Frank 2nd Lt./1st Lt., 1st Alabama Artillery Battalion. Cos. A, C, D & F. Federal Rolls of Prisoners of War: Captured at Blakely, AL, on 4/9/1865; Received at Ship Island, MS, on 4/15/1865. Transferred to Vicksburg, MS, for exchange on 4/28/1865; Confined at New Orleans, LA, on 4/30/1865. Exchanged at Camp Townsend, MS, on 5/6/1865

Bonds, J.A. Pvt., 63rd Alabama Infantry. Co. E. Federal Rolls of Prisoners of War: Captured at Blakely, AL, on 4/9/1865; Received at Ship Island, MS, on 4/15/1865. Transferred to Vicksburg, MS, for exchange on 5/1/1865. On Register of U.S.A. General Hospital #2, Vicksburg, MS: Admitted from steamer on 5/2/1865 due to acute diarrhea; Returned to duty on 5/8/1865. Age at admittance: 16. Rolls of Prisoners of War, C.S.A: Surrendered at Citronelle, AL, on 5/4/1865; Paroled at Jackson, MS, on 5/11/1865. Residence at parole: Monroe County, AL.

Bonifay, George Pvt./Sgt. Maj./Pvt., 62nd Alabama Infantry. Co. B/F & S. Federal Rolls of Prisoners of War: Captured at Blakely, AL, on 4/9/1865; Received at Ship Island, MS, on 4/15/1865. Transferred to Vicksburg, MS, for exchange on 5/1/1865; Exchanged at Camp Townsend, MS, on 5/6/1865.

Boone, Samuel D. (AKA Boon) Pvt., 21st Alabama Infantry. Co. C. Enlisted: 4/3/1863 at Choctaw Bluff, AL. Federal Rolls of Prisoners of War: Captured at Fort Gaines, AL, on 8/8/1864; Received at Ship Island, MS, from New Orleans, LA, on 10/25/1864. Died: 12/29/1864 at Ship Island, MS, due to chronic dysentery. Buried: Ship Island, MS, Cemetery in Grave #120. Soldier also served as a Pvt. with the 40th Alabama Infantry. Co. A. Enlisted: 3/17/1862 at Gaston, Sumter County, AL. Age at enlistment: 21. Description at enlistment: Eyes: blue. Hair: light. Complexion: fair. Height: 5'4". Occupation at enlistment: Farmer. Medical Discharge on 7/8/1862 by Surgeon George Colgin due to measles, severe bronchitis, and chronic diarrhea.

Booth, William Pvt., 62nd Alabama Infantry. Co. D. Federal Rolls of Prisoners of War: Captured at Blakely, AL, on 4/9/1865; Received at Ship Island, MS, on 4/15/1865. Transferred to Vicksburg, MS, for exchange on 5/1/1865; Exchanged at Camp Townsend, MS, on 5/6/1865.

Bouden, Henry (AKA Burdin) Pvt., 21st Alabama Infantry. Co. I. Federal Rolls of Prisoners of War: Captured at Fort Gaines, AL, on 8/8/1864; Received at Ship Island, MS, from New Orleans, LA, on 10/25/1864. Exchanged on 1/4/1865.

Bowers, James Pvt., Lockhart's Battalion Infantry. Co. H. Federal Rolls of Prisoners of War: Captured at Fort Gaines, AL, on 8/8/1864; Received at Ship Island, MS, from New Orleans, LA, on 10/25/1864. Exchanged on 1/4/1865.

Bowler, J.W. (AKA Bouler) Pvt., 21st Alabama Infantry. Co. B. Federal Rolls of Prisoners of War: Captured at Fort Gaines, AL, on 8/8/1864; Received at Ship Island, MS, from New Orleans, LA, on 10/25/1864. Died: 11/30/1864 at Ship Island, MS, due to dysentery. Buried: Ship Island, MS, Cemetery in Grave #53.

Bowman, Edwin 4th Cpl./Pvt., 63rd Alabama Infantry. Co. B. Enlisted: 3/23/1864 at Montgomery County, AL. Rolls for 9/1864 through 10/1864: Present. Federal Rolls of Prisoners of War: Captured at Blakely, AL, on 4/9/1865; Received at Ship Island, MS, on 4/15/1865. Transferred to Vicksburg, MS, for exchange on 5/1/1865; Exchanged at Camp Townsend, MS, on 5/6/1865. Rolls of Prisoners of War, C.S.A: Surrendered at Citronelle, AL, on 5/4/1865; Paroled at Meridian, MS, on 5/11/1865. Residence at parole: Montgomery County, AL.

Bowman, G.S. (AKA Boman) Pvt., Lockhart's Battalion Infantry. Cos. E & F. Federal Rolls of Prisoners of War: Captured at Fort Gaines, AL, on 8/8/1864; Received at Ship Island, MS, from New Orleans, LA, on 10/25/1864. Exchanged on 3/2/1865.

Box, James R. (AKA Bix) Pvt., 21st Alabama Infantry. Co. G. Federal Rolls of Prisoners of War: Captured at Fort Gaines, AL, on 8/8/1864; Received at Ship Island, MS, from New Orleans, LA, on 10/25/1864. Exchanged on 1/4/1865. Born: 3/31/1832. Died: 2/21/1917. Buried: Mount Pleasant Baptist Church Cemetery located at Grimes, AL.

Boyd, J.C. Pvt., 62nd Alabama Infantry. Co. I. Federal Rolls of Prisoners of War: Captured at Blakely, AL, on 4/9/1865; Received at Ship Island, MS, on 4/15/1865. Transferred to Vicksburg, MS, for exchange on 5/1/1865; Exchanged at Camp Townsend, MS, on 5/6/1865.

Boyles, Jesse Ransom Pvt., Tarrant's Artillery Battery. Enlisted: 7/1864 at Augusta, GA. Federal Rolls of Prisoners of War: Captured at Blakely, AL, on 4/9/1865; Received at Ship Island, MS, on 4/15/1865. Transferred to Vicksburg, MS, for exchange on 5/1/1865; Exchanged at Camp Townsend, MS, on 5/6/1865. Residence after war: Perry County, AL. Died: 3/11/1895. Buried: Mt. Zion Methodist Church Cemetery located at Perry County, AL.

Bradfield, James R. Pvt./4th Cpl., 63rd Alabama Infantry. Co. C. Enlisted: 4/30/1864 at Chambers County, AL. Age at enlistment: 17. Description at enlistment: Eyes: blue. Hair: black. Complexion: fair. Height: 5'8". Residence at enlistment: West Point, GA. Rolls for 9/1864 through 10/1864: Present. Federal Rolls of Prisoners of War: Captured at Gravel Hill, AL, on 3/24/1865; Received at Ship Island, MS, on 4/4/1865. Transferred to Vicksburg, MS, for exchange on 5/1/1865; Exchanged at Camp Townsend, MS, on 5/6/1865. Born: 1847. Died: 1922. Buried: Chambers County, AL.

Bradford, J.A. Pvt., 62nd Alabama Infantry. Co. I. Federal Rolls of Prisoners of War: Captured at Blakely, AL, on 4/9/1865; Received at Ship Island, MS, on 4/15/1865. Transferred to Vicksburg, MS, for exchange on 5/1/1865; Exchanged at Camp Townsend, MS, on 5/6/1865.

Bradley, Irwin P. (AKA T.D.) Pvt., 63rd Alabama Infantry. Co. G. Enlisted: 5/16/1864 at Troy, AL. Age at enlistment: 17. Description at enlistment: Eyes: grey. Hair: red. Complexion: fair. Height: 5'8". Rolls for 9/1864 through 10/1864: Present. Federal Rolls of Prisoners of War: Captured at Blakely, AL, on 4/9/1865; Received at Ship Island, MS, on 4/15/1865. Transferred to Vicksburg, MS, for exchange on 5/1/1865. On Register of U.S.A. General Hospital #2, Vicksburg, MS: Admitted from steamer on 5/2/1865 due to acute diarrhea; Returned to duty on 5/10/1865. Born: 1846. Died: 1926. Buried: Friendship Cemetery located at Coffee County, AL.

Bradshaw, S. Pvt., 15th Alabama Infantry. Cos. A & B. Federal Rolls of Prisoners of War: Captured at Spanish Fort, AL, on 4/8/1865; Received at Ship Island, MS, on 4/10/1865. Transferred to Vicksburg, MS, for exchange on 5/1/1865; Exchanged at Camp Townsend, MS, on 5/6/1865.

Branch, John (AKA Branck) Pvt., 63rd Alabama Infantry. Co. D. Enlisted: 7/30/1864 at Macon County, AL. Age at enlistment: 17. Description at enlistment: Eyes: grey. Hair: light. Complexion: fair. Height: 5'6". Residence at enlistment: Clayton, Barbour County, AL. Rolls for 9/1864 through 10/1864: Present. Federal Rolls of Prisoners of War: Captured at Blakely, AL, on 4/9/1865; Received at Ship Island, MS, on 4/15/1865. Transferred to Vicksburg, MS, for exchange on 5/1/1865; Exchanged at Camp Townsend, MS, on 5/6/1865. Rolls of Prisoners of War, C.S.A: Surrendered at Citronelle, AL, on 5/4/1865; Paroled at Meridian, MS, on 5/13/1865. Residence at parole: Barbour County, AL.

Brannin, Seabron R. Pvt., 63rd Alabama Infantry. Co. B. Enlisted: 8/15/1864 at Pollard, AL. Rolls for 9/1864 through 10/1864: Present. Federal Rolls of Prisoners of War: Captured at Blakely, AL, on 4/9/1865; Received at Ship Island, MS, on 4/15/1865. Transferred to Vicksburg, MS, for exchange on 5/1/1865; Exchanged at Camp Townsend, MS, on 5/6/1865. Rolls of Prisoners of War, C.S.A: Surrendered at Citronelle, AL, on 5/4/1865; Paroled at Meridian, MS, on 5/11/1865. Residence at parole: Dale County, AL.

Braswell, Eli (AKA Brasil, Brassell, Brueil) Pvt., 21st Alabama Infantry. Co. H. Enlisted: 10/18/1862 at Wilcox County, AL. Federal Rolls of Prisoners of War: Captured at Fort Gaines, AL, on 8/8/1864; Received at Ship Island, MS, from New Orleans, LA, on 10/25/1864. Died: 11/27/1864 at Ship Island, MS, due to pneumonia. Buried: Ship Island, MS, Cemetery in Grave #45. Born: 1823. His brother-in-law stated he died from "inhumane treatment by negroes and yankees." Wife learned of his death in 5/1865.

Brazell, John D. (AKA Brazel, J.L.) Pvt., 62nd Alabama Infantry. Co. A. Federal Rolls of Prisoners of War: Captured at Blakely, AL, on 4/9/1865; Received at Ship Island, MS, on 4/15/1865. Transferred to Vicksburg, MS, for exchange on 5/1/1865; Exchanged at Camp Townsend, MS, on 5/6/1865.

Breed, A.N. Pvt., 62nd Alabama Infantry. Co. I. Federal Rolls of Prisoners of War: Captured at Blakely, AL, on 4/9/1865; Received at Ship Island, MS, on 4/15/1865. Transferred to Vicksburg, MS, for exchange on 5/1/1865; Exchanged at Camp Townsend, MS, on 5/6/1865.

Breed, J.W. Pvt., 62nd Alabama Infantry. Co. I. Age at enlistment: 16. Description at enlistment: Eyes: blue. Hair: light. Complexion: light. Height: 5'7". Federal Rolls of Prisoners of War: Captured at Blakely, AL, on 4/9/1865; Received at Ship Island, MS, on 4/15/1865. Transferred to Vicksburg, MS, for exchange on 5/1/1865; Exchanged at Camp Townsend, MS, on 5/6/1865. Born: Randolph County, AL.

Brent, F.C. Pvt./Sgt., 62nd Alabama Infantry. Co. B. Federal Rolls of Prisoners of War: Captured at Blakely, AL, on 4/9/1865; Received at Ship Island, MS, on 4/15/1865. Transferred to Vicksburg, MS, for exchange on 5/1/1865; Exchanged at Camp Townsend, MS, on 5/6/1865.

Brewer, Drew M.E. Pvt., 63rd Alabama Infantry. Co. A. Enlisted: 1/1/1864 at Tallapoosa County, AL. Rolls for 1/1864 through 2/1864: Present. Rolls for 9/1864 through 10/1864: Present, sick in quarters. Federal Rolls of Prisoners of War: Captured at Blakely, AL, on 4/9/1865; Received at Ship Island, MS, on 4/15/1865. Transferred to Vicksburg, MS, for exchange on 5/1/1865; Exchanged at Camp Townsend, MS, on

5/6/1865. Rolls of Prisoners of War, C.S.A: Surrendered at Citronelle, AL, on 5/4/1865; Paroled at Meridian, MS, on 5/13/1865. Residence: Tallapoosa County, AL.

Brewer, Edmond H. Pvt., 63rd Alabama Infantry. Co. B. Enlisted: 8/15/1864 at Pollard, AL. Rolls for 9/1864 through 10/1864: Present. Federal Rolls of Prisoners of War: Captured at Blakely, AL, on 4/9/1865; Received at Ship Island, MS, on 4/15/1865. Transferred to Vicksburg, MS, for exchange on 5/1/1865; Exchanged at Camp Townsend, MS, on 5/6/1865. Rolls of Prisoners of War, C.S.A: Surrendered at Citronelle, AL, on 5/4/1865; Paroled at Meridian, MS, on 5/11/1865. Residence at parole: Dale County, AL.

Brewer, Lucius L. Pvt., 63rd Alabama Infantry. Co. B. Enlisted: 1/1/1864 at Tallapoosa County, AL. Age at enlistment: 17. Rolls for 1/1864 through 2/1864: Present. Rolls for 9/1864 through 10/1864: Absent, on 60 day Medical Examining Board furlough since 10/5/1864. Federal Rolls of Prisoners of War: Captured at Blakely, AL, on 4/9/1865; Received at Ship Island, MS, on 4/15/1865. Transferred to Vicksburg, MS, for exchange on 5/1/1865; Exchanged at Camp Townsend, MS, on 5/6/1865. Rolls of Prisoners of War, C.S.A: Surrendered at Citronelle, AL, on 5/4/1865; Paroled at Meridian, MS, on 5/13/1865. Residence at parole: Tallapoosa County, AL.

Brinson, William C. Pvt., 63rd Alabama Infantry. Co. C. Enlisted: 6/15/1864 at Macon County, AL. Age at enlistment: 17. Description at enlistment: Eyes: hazel. Hair: red. Complexion: dark. Height: 5'7". Residence at enlistment: Society Hill, Macon County, AL. Rolls for 9/1864 through 10/1864: Present. Federal Rolls of Prisoners of War: Captured at Blakely, AL, on 4/9/1865; Received at Ship Island, MS, on 4/15/1865. Transferred to Vicksburg, MS, for exchange on 5/1/1865; Exchanged at Camp Townsend, MS, on 5/6/1865. Rolls of Prisoners of War, C.S.A: Surrendered at Citronelle, AL, on 5/4/1865; Paroled at Meridian, MS, on 5/11/1865. Residence at parole: Macon County, AL.

Broadus, Moses Pvt., 21st Alabama Infantry. Co. I. Enlisted: 10/13/1861 at Hall's Mill, Mobile County, AL. Federal Rolls of Prisoners of War: Captured at Fort Gaines, AL, on 8/8/1864; Received at Ship Island, MS, from New Orleans, LA, on 10/25/1864. Exchanged on 1/5/1865. Born: 12/24/1839 at Biloxi, MS. Residence after war: Mobile County, AL.

Brock, N.P. Pvt., 62nd Alabama Infantry. Co. C. Federal Rolls of Prisoners of War: Captured at Blakely, AL, on 4/9/1865; Received at Ship Island, MS, on 4/15/1865. Transferred to Vicksburg, MS, for exchange on 5/1/1865; Exchanged at Camp Townsend, MS, on 5/6/1865.

Brooks, G.E. Pvt., 63rd Alabama Infantry. Co. F. Enlisted: 8/1/1864 at Georgianna, AL. Rolls for 9/1864 through 10/1864: Absent, in hospital at Mobile, AL. Federal Rolls of Prisoners of War: Captured at Blakely, AL, on 4/9/1865; Received at Ship Island, MS, on 4/15/1865. Transferred to Vicksburg, MS, for exchange on 5/1/1865. On Register of U.S.A. General Hospital #2, Vicksburg, MS: Admitted from steamer on 5/3/1865 due to measles; Returned to duty on 5/22/1865.

Brooks, G.L. Pvt., 63rd Alabama Infantry. Co. F. Enlisted: 3/7/1864 at Greenville, AL. Age at enlistment: 17. Description at enlistment: Eyes: blue. Hair: light. Complexion: fair. Height: 5'6". Residence at enlistment: Butler County, AL. Rolls for 9/1864 through 10/1864: Absent, in hospital at Mobile, AL, since 10/13/1864. Federal Rolls of Prisoners of War: Captured at Blakely, AL, on 4/9/1865; Received at Ship Island, MS, on 4/15/1865. Transferred to Vicksburg, MS, for exchange on 5/1/1865; Exchanged at Camp Townsend, MS, on 5/6/1865. Rolls of Prisoners of War, C.S.A: Surrendered at Citronelle, AL, on 5/4/1865; Paroled at Meridian, MS, on 5/11/1865. Residence at parole: Butler County, AL.

Brooks, William C. Pvt., 63rd Alabama Infantry. Co. A. Enlisted: 1/1/1864 at Tallapoosa County, AL. Rolls for 1/1864 through 2/1864: Present. Rolls for 9/1864 through 10/1864: Present. Federal Rolls of Prisoners of War: Captured at Blakely, AL, on 4/9/1865; Received at Ship Island, MS, on 4/15/1865. Transferred to Vicksburg, MS, for exchange on 5/1/1865; Exchanged at Camp Townsend, MS, on 5/6/1865. Rolls of Prisoners of War, C.S.A: Surrendered at Citronelle, AL, on 5/4/1865; Paroled at Meridian, MS, on 5/13/1865. Residence at parole: Tallapoosa County, AL.

Brown, B. Pvt., Alabama State Guards. Federal Rolls of Prisoners of War: Captured in Alabama on 3/24/1865; Received at Ship Island, MS. Transferred to Vicksburg, MS, for exchange on 5/1/1865; Exchanged at Camp Townsend, MS, on 5/6/1865.

Brown, J.H. Pvt., Tarrant's Artillery Battery. Enlisted: 7/29/1863 at Tuscaloosa, AL. Federal Rolls of Prisoners of War: Captured at Blakely, AL, on 4/9/1865; Received at Ship Island, MS, on 4/15/1865. Transferred to Vicksburg, MS, for exchange on 5/1/1865; Exchanged at Camp Townsend, MS, on 5/6/1865.

Brown, John Mordichai Pvt./Sgt., 63rd Alabama Infantry. Co. K. Enlisted: 8/6/1864 at Russell County, AL. Rolls for 9/1864 through 10/1864: Present. Federal Rolls of Prisoners of War: Captured at Blakely, AL, on 4/9/1865; Received at Ship Island, MS, on 4/15/1865. Transferred to Vicksburg, MS, for exchange on 5/1/1865; Exchanged at Camp Townsend, MS, on 5/6/1865. Rolls of Prisoners of War, C.S.A: Surrendered at Citronelle, AL, on 5/4/1865; Paroled at Meridian, MS, on 5/13/1865. Residence at parole: Macon County, AL. Born: 9/16/1846 at Jackson, Calhoun County, AL. Soldier is recorded on the 1907 Alabama Census of Confederate Veterans and Widows. Residence: Butler County, AL.

Brown, Oakley (AKA O.K.) Pvt./Cpl., 21st Alabama Infantry. Co. D. Federal Rolls of Prisoners of War: Captured at Blakely, AL, on 4/9/1865; Received at Ship Island, MS, on 4/15/1865. Disposition unknown.

Brown, W.J. Pvt., 63rd Alabama Infantry. Co. H. Enlisted: 7/23/1864 at Selma, AL. Age at enlistment: 17. Description at enlistment: Eyes: blue. Hair: light. Complexion: fair. Rolls for 9/1864 through 10/1864: Present. Federal Rolls of Prisoners of War: Captured at Blakely, AL, on 4/9/1865; Received at Ship Island, MS, on 4/15/1865. Transferred to Vicksburg, MS, for exchange on 5/1/1865; Exchanged at Camp Townsend, MS, on 5/6/1865.

Bryan, William F. Pvt., 37th Alabama Infantry. Co. C. Enlisted: 3/24/1862 at Leon, AL. Wounded at Iuka, MS, on 9/19/1862 and received a Disability Discharge.

Re-enlisted: 3/1863 as Enrolling Officer at Andalusia, AL. Federal Rolls of Prisoners of War: Captured at Andalusia, AL; Received at Ship Island, MS. Transferred to Vicksburg, MS, for exchange on 5/1/1865; Exchanged at Camp Townsend, MS, on 5/6/1865. Born: 2/6/1839. Confederate Pension Application on file at the Alabama Department of Archives and History. Target Name: Bryan, William F. Record Card Number: 11340. County: Crenshaw.

Bryant, Frank Pvt., 62nd Alabama Infantry. Co. F. Federal Rolls of Prisoners of War: Captured at Blakely, AL, on 4/9/1865; Received at Ship Island, MS, on 4/15/1865. Died: 5/2/1865 at Ship Island, MS, due to diagnolia and typhoid fever. Buried: Ship Island, MS, Cemetery in Grave #153.

Bryant, J. Cpl., 21st Alabama Infantry. Co. C. Federal Rolls of Prisoners of War: Captured at Blakely, AL, on 4/9/1865; Received at Ship Island, MS, on 4/15/1865. Transferred to Vicksburg, MS, for exchange on 5/1/1865; Exchanged at Camp Townsend, MS, on 5/6/1865.

Bryant, J.W. Pvt., 62nd Alabama Infantry. Co. F. Federal Rolls of Prisoners of War: Captured at Blakely, AL, on 4/9/1865; Received at Ship Island, MS, on 4/15/1865. Transferred to Vicksburg, MS, for exchange on 5/1/1865; Exchanged at Camp Townsend, MS, on 5/6/1865.

Bryant, Samuel Pvt., 1st Alabama Artillery Battalion. Co. E. Federal Rolls of Prisoners of War: Captured at Blakely, AL, on 4/9/1865; Received at Ship Island, MS, on 4/15/1865. Died: 5/2/1865 at Ship Island, MS, due to remitten fever. Buried: Ship Island, MS, Cemetery.

Budershan, Joseph S. Pvt., 63rd Alabama Infantry. Co. B. Enlisted: 8/15/1864 at Pollard, AL. Rolls for 9/1864 through 10/1864: Present. Federal Rolls of Prisoners of War: Captured at Blakely, AL, on 4/9/1865; Received at Ship Island, MS, on 4/15/1865. Transferred to Vicksburg, MS, for exchange on 5/1/1865; Exchanged at Camp Townsend, MS, on 5/6/1865. Rolls of Prisoners of War, C.S.A: Surrendered at Citronelle, AL, on 5/4/1865; Paroled at Meridian, MS, on 5/11/1865. Residence at parole: Dale County, AL.

Bunelon, J.C. Pvt., Lockhart's Battalion Infantry. Co. K. Federal Rolls of Prisoners of War: Captured at Fort Gaines, AL, on 8/8/1864; Received at Ship Island, MS, from New Orleans, LA, on 10/25/1864, Died: 12/15/1864 at Ship Island, MS, due to dysentery. Buried: Ship Island, MS, Cemetery in Grave #91.

Buntyn, George M. Pvt./Sgt., 1st Alabama Artillery Battalion. Co. F. Federal Rolls of Prisoners of War: Captured at Fort Gaines, AL, on 8/8/1864; Received at Ship Island, MS, from New Orleans, LA, on 10/25/1864. Exchanged on 1/4/1865.

Burck, J.W. (AKA Buck) Pvt., 62nd Alabama Infantry. Cos. A & H. Federal Rolls of Prisoners of War: Captured at Blakely, AL, on 4/9/1865; Received at Ship Island, MS, on 4/15/1865. Transferred to Vicksburg, MS, for exchange on 5/1/1865; Exchanged at Camp Townsend, MS, on 5/6/1865.

Burke, A. (AKA H.) Pvt., 62nd Alabama Infantry. Co. C. Federal Rolls of Prisoners of War: Captured at Blakely, AL, on 4/9/1865; Received at Ship Island, MS, on 4/15/1865. Transferred to Vicksburg, MS, for exchange on 5/1/1865; Exchanged at Camp Townsend, MS, on 5/6/1865.

Burkett, Joshua Pvt., 1st Alabama Artillery Battalion. Co. A. Federal Rolls of Prisoners of War: Captured at Blakely, AL, on 4/9/1865; Received at Ship Island, MS, on 4/15/1865. Transferred to Vicksburg, MS, for exchange on 5/1/1865; Exchanged at Camp Townsend, MS, on 5/6/1865.

Burney, Marshall D. (AKA Berney) Pvt., 63rd Alabama Infantry. Co. G. Enlisted: 8/1/1864 at Pollard, AL. Age at enlistment: 17. Description at enlistment: Eyes: grey. Hair: light. Complexion: fair. Height: 5'3". Rolls for 9/1864 through 10/1864: Present. Federal Rolls of Prisoners of War: Captured at Blakely, AL, on 4/9/1865; Received at Ship Island, MS, on 4/15/1865. Transferred to Vicksburg, MS, for exchange on 5/1/1865; Exchanged at Camp Townsend, MS, on 5/6/1865. Rolls of Prisoners of War, C.S.A: Surrendered at Citronelle, AL, on 5/4/1865; Paroled at Meridian, MS, on 5/13/1865. Residence at parole: Pike County, AL.

Burton, John H. (AKA J.A.) Pvt., 62nd Alabama Infantry. Co. B. Federal Rolls of Prisoners of War: Captured at Blakely, AL, on 4/9/1865; Received at Ship Island, MS, on 4/15/1865. Transferred to Vicksburg, MS, for exchange on 5/1/1865; Exchanged at Camp Townsend, MS, on 5/6/1865.

Busby, S.A. (AKA Bunsley) Pvt., 62nd Alabama Infantry. Co. H. Federal Rolls of Prisoners of War: Captured at Blakely, AL, on 4/9/1865; Received at Ship Island, MS, on 4/15/1865. Died: 4/16/1865 at Ship Island, MS, due to diarrhea. Buried: Ship Island, MS, Cemetery in Grave #146.

Bush, Americus B., Jr. 2nd Lt./1st Sgt., 63rd Alabama Infantry. Co. D. Enlisted: 7/30/1864 at Macon County, AL. Age at enlistment: 17. Description at enlistment: Eyes: blue. Hair: dark. Complexion: fair. Height: 6'0". Residence at enlistment: Bushville, Barbour County, AL. Rolls for 9/1864 through 10/1864: Present; Resigned as Jr. 2nd. Lt. on 11/11/1864. Federal Rolls of Prisoners of War: Captured at Blakely, AL, on 4/9/1865; Received at Ship Island, MS, on 4/15/1865. Transferred to Vicksburg, MS, for exchange on 5/1/1865; Exchanged at Camp Townsend, MS, on 5/6/1865. Rolls of Prisoners of War, C.S.A: Surrendered at Citronelle, AL, on 5/4/1865; Paroled at Meridian, MS, on 5/13/1865. Residence at parole: Barbour County, AL.

Bush, Hebert H. Pvt., 63rd Alabama Infantry. Cos. D & F. Enlisted: 7/30/1864 at Macon County, AL. Age at enlistment: 17. Description at enlistment: Eyes: blue. Hair: light. Complexion: fair. Height: 5'6". Residence at enlistment: Eufaula, Barbour County, AL. Rolls for 9/1864 through 10/1864: Present. Federal Rolls of Prisoners of War: Captured at Blakely, AL, on 4/9/1865; Received at Ship Island, MS, on 4/15/1865. Transferred to Vicksburg, MS, for exchange on 5/1/1865; Exchanged at Camp Townsend, MS, on 5/6/1865. Rolls of Prisoners of War, C.S.A: Surrendered at Citronelle, AL, on 5/4/1865; Paroled at Meridian, MS, on 5/13/1865 while a patient in Quintard Hospital. Residence at parole: Barbour County, AL.

Bush, John E. Pvt./Cpl., 63rd Alabama Infantry. Co. C. Enlisted: 5/25/1864 at Russell County, AL. Age at enlistment: 17. Description at enlistment: Eyes:

black. Hair: black. Complexion: dark. Height: 5'10". Residence at enlistment: Sand Fort, AL. Rolls for 9/1864 through 10/1864: Present. Federal Rolls of Prisoners of War: Captured at Blakely, AL, on 4/9/1865; Received at Ship Island, MS, on 4/15/1865. Transferred to Vicksburg, MS, for exchange on 5/1/1865; Exchanged at Camp Townsend, MS, on 5/6/1865. Rolls of Prisoners of War, C.S.A: Surrendered at Citronelle, AL, on 5/4/1865; Paroled at Meridian, MS, on 5/11/1865. Residence at parole: Russell County, AL.

Bush, Ryan O. 1st Sgt., 63rd Alabama Infantry. Co. D. Enlisted: 7/30/1864 at Macon County, AL. Age at enlistment: 17. Description at enlistment: Eyes: dark. Hair: dark. Complexion: dark. Height: 5'6". Residence at enlistment: Bushville, Barbour County, AL. Rolls for 9/1864 through 10/1864: Present. Federal Rolls of Prisoners of War: Captured at Blakely, AL, on 4/9/1865; Received at Ship Island, MS, on 4/15/1865. Transferred to Vicksburg, MS, for exchange on 5/1/1865; Exchanged at Camp Townsend, MS, on 5/6/1865. Rolls of Prisoners of War, C.S.A: Surrendered at Citronelle, AL, on 5/4/1865; Paroled at Meridian, MS, on 5/13/1865. Residence at parole: Barbour County, AL.

Butts, Phillips Adam Pvt., 63rd Alabama Infantry. Co. D. Enlisted: 7/30/1864 at Macon County, AL. Age at enlistment: 17. Description at enlistment: Eyes: dark. Hair: dark. Complexion: dark. Height: 5'5". Residence at enlistment: Texasville, Barbour County, AL. Rolls for 9/1864 through 10/1864: Present. Federal Rolls of Prisoners of War: Captured at Blakely, AL, on 4/9/1865; Received at Ship Island, MS, on 4/15/1865. Transferred to Vicksburg, MS, for exchange on 5/1/1865; Exchanged at Camp Townsend, MS, on 5/6/1865. Rolls of Prisoners of War, C.S.A: Surrendered at Citronelle, AL, on 5/4/1865; Paroled at Meridian, MS, on 5/13/1865. Residence at parole: Barbour County County, AL.

Caffee, J.C. Pvt., Tarrant's Artillery Battery. Enlisted: 7/6/1863 at Tuscaloosa, AL. Federal Rolls of Prisoners of War: Captured at Blakely, AL, on 4/9/1865; Received at Ship Island, MS, on 4/15/1865. Transferred to Vicksburg, MS, for exchange on 5/1/1865; Exchanged at Camp Townsend, MS, on 5/6/1865.

Cain, Jessee T. Pvt., 21st Alabama Infantry. Co. E. Federal Rolls of Prisoners of War: Captured at Fort Gaines, AL, on 8/8/1864; Received at Ship Island, MS, from New Orleans, LA, on 10/25/1864. Exchanged on 1/4/1865.

Caldwell, H.M. (AKA H.W.) Pvt., 21st Alabama Infantry. Co. G. Federal Rolls of Prisoners of War: Captured at Fort Gaines, AL, on 8/8/1864; Received at Ship Island, MS, from New Orleans, LA, on 10/25/1864. Died: 12/22/1864 at Ship Island, MS, due to dysentery. Buried: Ship Island, MS, Cemetery in Grave #107.

Caldwell, M.J. 1st Sgt., 63rd Alabama Infantry. Co. K. Enlisted: 6/8/1864 at Macon County, AL. Rolls for 9/1864 through 10/1864: Present. Federal Rolls of Prisoners of War: Captured at Blakely, AL, on 4/9/1865; Received at Ship Island, MS, on 4/15/1865. Transferred to Vicksburg, MS, for exchange on 5/1/1865; Exchanged at Camp Townsend, MS, on 5/6/1865. Rolls of Prisoners of War, C.S.A: Surrendered at Citronelle, AL, on 5/4/1865; Paroled at Meridian, MS, on 5/13/1865. Residence at parole: Macon County, AL.

Caldwell, W. Pvt., 63rd Alabama Infantry. Co. B. Federal Rolls of Prisoners of War: Captured at Blakely, AL, on 4/9/1865; Received at Ship Island, MS, on 4/15/1865. Transferred to Vicksburg, MS, for exchange on 5/1/1865; Exchanged at Camp Townsend, MS, on 5/6/1865. Rolls of Prisoners of War, C.S.A: Surrendered at Citronelle, AL, on 5/4/1865; Paroled at Meridian, MS, on 5/11/1865.

Calhoun, Evander M. Pvt., 1st Alabama Battalion Infantry. Co. B. Enlisted: 5/1864 at Mobile, AL. Federal Rolls of Prisoners of War: Captured at Fort Gaines, AL, on 8/8/1864; Received at Ship Island, MS, from New Orleans, LA, on 10/25/1864. Disposition unknown. Born: 2/8/1847 at Clark City, AL, to Daniel and Christian (Graham) Calhoun. Married: Miss Mat P. Thompson in Alabama on 8/10/1910. Children: 8. Occupation: Farmer. Religion: Methodist. Died: 1929. Buried: Covington County, AL.

Calhoun, James B. Pvt., 6th Alabama Cavalry. Co. E. Enlisted: 1862 at Franklin, Alabama. Federal Rolls of Prisoners of War: Captured at Blakely, AL, on 4/9/1865; Received at Ship Island, MS, on 4/15/1865. Transferred to Vicksburg, MS, on 5/1/1865; Exchanged at Camp Townsend, MS, on 5/6/1865. Soldier also served as a Pvt. with Winston's Artillery Battery (Tennessee). Born: 1845 at Henry County, AL.

Calhoun, Thomas J. 1st Lt./A.A.Q.M., 63rd Alabama Infantry. Co. B.F. & S. Enlisted: 3/23/1864 at Montgomery, AL. Rolls for 9/1864 through 10/1864: Present, detailed as Regimental Quartermaster since 8/10/1864. Federal Rolls of Prisoners of War: Captured at Blakely, AL, on 4/9/1865; Received at Ship Island, MS, on 4/15/1865. Transferred to Vicksburg, MS, for exchange on 4/28/1865; Confined at New Orleans, LA, on 4/30/1865. Exchanged at Camp Townsend, MS, on 5/6/1865. Rolls of Prisoners of War, C.S.A: Surrendered at Citronelle, AL, on 5/4/1865; Paroled at Meridian, MS, on 5/11/1865. Residence at parole: Tuskegee, AL.

Callahan, J.W. Pvt., 6th Alabama Cavalry. Cos. A & G. Federal Rolls of Prisoners of War: Captured at Flintday, AL, on 3/25/1865; Received at Ship Island, MS. Transferred to Vicksburg, MS, for exchange on 5/1/1865; Exchanged at Camp Townsend, MS, on 5/6/1865.

Callaway, Zachary T. Pvt., 63rd Alabama Infantry. Co. A. Enlisted: 5/1/1864 at Chambers County, AL. Rolls for 9/1864 through 10/1864: Present. Federal Rolls of Prisoners of War: Captured at Blakely, AL, on 4/9/1865; Received at Ship Island, MS, on 4/15/1865. Transferred to Vicksburg, MS, for exchange on 5/1/1865; Exchanged at Camp Townsend, MS, on 5/6/1865. Rolls of Prisoners of War, C.S.A: Surrendered at Citronelle, AL, on 5/4/1865; Paroled at Meridian, MS, on 5/13/1865. Residence at parole: Chambers County, AL.

Calloway, George A. Pvt., 62nd Alabama Infantry. Cos. D & E. Federal Rolls of Prisoners of War: Captured at Blakely, AL, on 4/9/1865; Received at Ship Island, MS, on 4/15/1865. Transferred to Vicksburg, MS, for exchange on 5/1/1865; Exchanged at Camp Townsend, MS, on 5/6/1865.

Campbell, Daniel W. (AKA L.W.) Pvt., 62nd Alabama

Infantry. Co. A. Federal Rolls of Prisoners of War: Captured at Blakely, AL, on 4/9/1865; Received at Ship Island, MS, on 4/15/1865. Transferred to Vicksburg, MS, for exchange on 5/1/1865; Exchanged at Camp Townsend, MS, on 5/6/1865.

Campbell, J.A. Pvt., 21st Alabama Infantry. Co. G. Federal Rolls of Prisoners of War: Captured at Fort Gaines, AL, on 8/8/1864; Received at Ship Island, MS, from New Orleans, LA, on 10/25/1864. Exchanged on 1/4/1865.

Campbell, John A. Sgt., 6th Alabama Cavalry. Co. F. Federal Rolls of Prisoners of War: Captured at Flintday, AL, on 3/25/1865; Received at Ship Island, MS. Transferred to Vicksburg, MS, for exchange on 5/1/1865; Exchanged at Camp Townsend, MS, on 5/6/1865.

Campbell, Thomas B. Pvt., 62nd Alabama Infantry. Co. H. Federal Rolls of Prisoners of War: Captured at Blakely, AL, on 4/9/1865; Received at Ship Island, MS, on 4/15/1865. Transferred to Vicksburg, MS, for exchange on 5/1/1865; Exchanged at Camp Townsend, MS, on 5/6/1865. Born: 1845.

Campbell, W.B. Sgt., 21st Alabama Infantry. Co. A. Federal Rolls of Prisoners of War: Captured at Fort Gaines, AL, on 8/8/1864; Received at Ship Island, MS, from New Orleans, LA, on 10/25/1864. Exchanged on 1/4/1865.

Canarny, James Pvt., 1st Alabama Artillery Battalion. Cos. B & E. Federal Rolls of Prisoners of War: Captured at Fort Gaines, AL, on 8/8/1864; Received at Ship Island, MS, from New Orleans, LA, on 10/25/1864. Exchanged on 1/4/1865.

Cane, S.P. Pvt., 63rd Alabama Infantry. Co. F. Enlisted: 8/4/1864 at Georgiana, AL. Rolls for 9/1864 through 10/1864: Absent, in hospital at Mobile, AL, since 10/21/1864. Federal Rolls of Prisoners of War: Captured at Blakely, AL, on 4/9/1865; Received at Ship Island, MS, on 4/15/1865. Transferred to Vicksburg, MS, for exchange on 5/1/1865. On Register of U.S.A. General Hospital #2, Vicksburg, MS: Admitted from steamer on 5/3/1865 due to acute diarrhea; Returned to duty on 5/8/1865. Age at admittance: 16.

Canerghton, James B. (AKA Courington) Pvt., 62nd Alabama Infantry. Co. I. Federal Rolls of Prisoners of War: Captured at Blakely, AL, on 4/9/1865; Received at Ship Island, MS, on 4/15/1865. Transferred to Vicksburg, MS, for exchange on 5/1/1865; Exchanged at Camp Townsend, MS, on 5/6/1865.

Cannan, Stephen Pvt., 63rd Alabama Infantry. Co. B. Enlisted: 6/25/1864 at Montgomery, AL. Rolls for 9/1864 through 10/1864: Present. Federal Rolls of Prisoners of War: Captured at Blakely, AL, on 4/9/1865; Received at Ship Island, MS, on 4/15/1865. Transferred to Vicksburg, MS, for exchange on 5/1/1865; Exchanged at Camp Townsend, MS, on 5/6/1865. Rolls of Prisoners of War, C.S.A: Surrendered at Citronelle, AL, on 5/4/1865; Paroled at Meridian, MS, on 5/11/1865. Residence at parole: Lowndes County, AL.

Canon, P.J. Sgt., 62nd Alabama Infantry. Co. F. Federal Rolls of Prisoners of War: Captured at Blakely, AL, on 4/9/1865; Received at Ship Island, MS, on 4/15/1865. Transferred to Vicksburg, MS, for exchange on 5/1/1865; Exchanged at Camp Townsend, MS, on 5/6/1865.

Capps, D.C. Pvt., 63rd Alabama Infantry. Co. E. Enlisted: 9/12/1864 at Camp Hood, GA. Rolls for 9/1864 through 10/1864: Absent, sick in hospital since 10/7/1864. Federal Rolls of Prisoners of War: Captured at Blakely, AL, on 4/9/1865; Received at Ship Island, MS, on 4/15/1865. Transferred to Vicksburg, MS, for exchange on 5/1/1865; Exchanged at Camp Townsend, MS, on 5/6/1865. Rolls of Prisoners of War, C.S.A: Surrendered at Citronelle, AL, on 5/4/1865; Paroled at Meridian, MS, on 5/13/1865. Residence at parole: Monroe County, AL.

Carlee, T.E. (AKA Carbe) Cpl., 62nd Alabama Infantry. Co. F. Federal Rolls of Prisoners of War: Captured at Blakely, AL, on 4/9/1865; Received at Ship Island, MS, on 4/15/1865. Transferred to Vicksburg, MS, for exchange on 5/1/1865; Exchanged at Camp Townsend, MS, on 5/6/1865.

Carlen, John G. Pvt./Cpl., 21st Alabama Infantry. Co. E. Federal Rolls of Prisoners of War: Captured at Fort Gaines, AL, on 8/8/1864; Received at Ship Island, MS, from New Orleans, LA, on 10/25/1864. Exchanged on 1/4/1865.

Carleton, J. (AKA A.) Pvt., 21st Alabama Infantry. Co. E. Federal Rolls of Prisoners of War: Captured at Fort Gaines, AL, on 8/8/1864; Received at Ship Island, MS, from New Orleans, LA, on 10/25/1864. Exchanged on 1/4/1865.

Carley, John Pvt., 21st Alabama Infantry. Co. C. Federal Rolls of Prisoners of War: Captured at Fort Gaines, AL, on 8/8/1864; Received at Ship Island, MS, from New Orleans, LA, on 10/25/1864. Exchanged on 1/4/1865.

Carlisle, E.T. (AKA E.F.) Pvt., 21st Alabama Infantry. Co. C. Federal Rolls of Prisoners of War: Captured at Fort Gaines, AL, on 8/8/1864; Received at Ship Island, MS, from New Orleans, LA, on 10/25/1864. Died: 12/3/1864 at Ship Island, MS, due to dysentery. Buried: Ship Island, MS, Cemetery in Grave #61.

Carlisle, S.B. (AKA R.H.) Pvt., 6th Alabama Cavalry. Co. C. Federal Rolls of Prisoners of War: Captured at Flintday, AL, on 3/25/1865; Received at Ship Island, MS. Transferred to Vicksburg, MS, for exchange on 5/1/1865; Exchanged at Camp Townsend, MS, on 5/6/1865.

Carmichael, John Duncan Pvt., 62nd Alabama Infantry. Co. B. Federal Rolls of Prisoners of War: Captured at Blakely, AL, on 4/9/1865; Received at Ship Island, MS, on 4/15/1865. Transferred to Vicksburg, MS, for exchange on 5/1/1865; Exchanged at Camp Townsend, MS, on 5/6/1865. Born: 12/18/1845 at Talladega County, AL. Married: Lucy Williams. Died: 10/28/1924. Buried: Hatchett Creek located at Clay County, AL.

Carpenter, Nathan M. (AKA N.W.) Capt., 36th Alabama Infantry. Co. B. Federal Rolls of Prisoners of War: Captured at Spanish Fort, AL, on 4/8/1865; Received at Ship Island, MS, on 4/10/1865. Transferred to Vicksburg, MS, for exchange on 4/28/1865; Confined at New Orleans, LA, on 4/30/1865. Exchanged at Camp Townsend, MS, on 5/6/1865.

Carr, E.T. Cpl./Pvt., 62nd Alabama Infantry & Lockhart's Battalion Infantry. Cos. E, F & H. Federal Rolls of Prisoners of War: Captured at Blakely, AL, on 4/9/1865; Received at Ship Island, MS, on 4/15/1865. Transferred to Vicksburg, MS, for exchange on 5/1/1865; Exchanged at Camp Townsend, MS, on 5/6/1865.

Carr, W.S. Pvt., 62nd Alabama Infantry. Cos. F & H.

Federal Rolls of Prisoners of War: Captured at Blakely, AL, on 4/9/1865; Received at Ship Island, MS, on 4/15/1865. Transferred to Vicksburg, MS, for exchange on 5/1/1865; Exchanged at Camp Townsend, MS, on 5/6/1865.

Carr, William S. Sgt., 63rd Alabama Infantry. Co. B. Enlisted: 3/23/1864 at Montgomery, AL. Age at enlistment: 17. Rolls for 9/1864 through 10/1864: Present. Federal Rolls of Prisoners of War: Captured at Blakely, AL, on 4/9/1865; Received at Ship Island, MS, on 4/15/1865. Transferred to Vicksburg, MS, for exchange on 5/1/1865; Exchanged at Camp Townsend, MS, on 5/6/1865. Rolls of Prisoners of War, C.S.A: Surrendered at Citronelle, AL, on 5/4/1865; Paroled at Meridian, MS, on 5/11/1865. Residence at parole: Macon County, AL.

Carrington, Algernon S. 1st Lt./Capt., 21st Alabama Infantry. Cos. E & H. Federal Rolls of Prisoners of War: Captured at Fort Gaines, AL, on 8/8/1864; Received at Ship Island, MS, from New Orleans, LA, on 10/25/1864. Exchanged on 1/4/1865.

Carrington, John Pvt., 21st Alabama Infantry. Co. A. Federal Rolls of Prisoners of War: Captured at Fort Gaines, AL, on 8/8/1864; Received at Ship Island, MS, from New Orleans, LA, on 10/25/1864. Exchanged on 1/4/1865.

Carrington, Lester Pvt., Pelham Cadets. Co. A. Federal Rolls of Prisoners of War: Captured at Fort Gaines, AL, on 8/8/1865; Received at Ship Island, MS, from New Orleans, LA, on 10/25/1864. Exchanged on 1/4/1865.

Carroll, Daniel (AKA Carrol) Pvt., 1st Alabama Artillery Battalion. Co. E. Federal Rolls of Prisoners of War: Captured at Fort Gaines, AL, on 8/8/1864; Received at Ship Island, MS, from New Orleans, LA, on 10/25/1864. Died: 12/12/1864 at Ship Island, MS, due to chronic dysentery. Buried: Ship Island, MS, Cemetery in Grave #81. Born: 10/16/1837.

Carroll, John A. (AKA A.J.) Pvt., 63rd Alabama Infantry. Co. G. Federal Rolls of Prisoners of War: Captured at Blakely, AL, on 4/9/1865; Received at Ship Island, MS, on 4/15/1865. Transferred to Vicksburg, MS, for exchange on 5/1/1865; Exchanged at Camp Townsend, MS, on 5/6/1865.

Carroll, John L. Pvt., 62nd Alabama Infantry. Co. E. Federal Rolls of Prisoners of War: Captured at Blakely, AL, on 4/9/1865; Received at Ship Island, MS, on 4/15/1865. Transferred to Vicksburg, MS, for exchange on 5/1/1865; Exchanged at Camp Townsend, MS, on 5/6/1865.

Carroll, R. Thomas Pvt., 21st Alabama Infantry. Co. G. Federal Rolls of Prisoners of War: Captured at Fort Gaines, AL, on 8/8/1864; Received at Ship Island, MS, from New Orleans, LA, on 10/25/1864. Exchanged on 1/4/1865.

Carter, Charles W. Pvt., 63rd Alabama Infantry. Co. C. Federal Rolls of Prisoners of War: Captured at Blakely, AL, on 4/9/1865; Received at Ship Island, MS, on 4/15/1865. Transferred to Vicksburg, MS, for exchange on 5/1/1865; Exchanged at Camp Townsend, MS, on 5/6/1865.

Carter, E.L. Pvt., 21st Alabama Infantry. Co. C. Federal Rolls of Prisoners of War: Captured at Fort Gaines, AL, on 8/8/1865; Received at Ship Island, MS, from New Orleans, LA, on 10/25/1864. Exchanged on 1/4/1865.

Carter, Thomas W. Pvt., 63rd Alabama Infantry. Co. B. Enlisted: 6/25/1864 at Montgomery, AL. Rolls for 9/1864 through 10/1864: Absent, sick since 7/20/1864. Federal Rolls of Prisoners of War: Captured at Blakely, AL, on 4/9/1865; Received at Ship Island, MS, on 4/15/1865. Transferred to Vicksburg, MS, for exchange on 5/1/1865; Exchanged at Camp Townsend, MS, on 5/6/1865. Rolls of Prisoners of War, C.S.A: Surrendered at Citronelle, AL, on 5/4/1865; Paroled at Meridian, MS, on 5/10/1865 while a patient in Quintard Hospital. Residence at parole: Coosa County, AL.

Carter, W.R. Pvt., 21st Alabama Infantry. Co. C. Federal Rolls of Prisoners of War: Captured at Blakely, AL, on 4/9/1865; Received at Ship Island, MS, on 4/15/1865. Transferred to Vicksburg, MS, for exchange on 5/1/1865; Exchanged at Camp Townsend, MS, on 5/6/1865.

Casey, J. Pvt., 63rd Alabama Infantry. Cos. E & I. Federal Rolls of Prisoners of War: Captured at Blakely, AL, on 4/9/1865; Received at Ship Island, MS, on 4/15/1865. Transferred to Vicksburg, MS, for exchange on 5/1/1865; Exchanged at Camp Townsend, MS, on 5/6/1865. Rolls of Prisoners of War, C.S.A: Surrendered at Citronelle, AL, on 5/4/1865; Paroled at Meridian, MS, on 5/13/1865. Residence at parole: Barbour County, AL.

Casey, W.A. Pvt., Tarrant's Artillery Battery. Federal Rolls of Prisoners of War: Captured at Blakely, AL, on 4/9/1865; Received at Ship Island, MS, on 4/15/1865. Transferred to Vicksburg, MS, for exchange on 5/1/1865; Exchanged at Camp Townsend, MS, on 5/6/1865.

Cason, Daniel M. Pvt., 63rd Alabama Infantry. Co. B. Enlisted: 4/23/1864 at Montgomery, AL. Rolls for 9/1864 through 10/1864: Absent, detached by Special Order #35 of Brig. Gen. St. John R. Liddell on 9/25/1864. Federal Rolls of Prisoners of War: Captured at Blakely, AL, on 4/9/1865; Received at Ship Island, MS, on 4/15/1865. Transferred to Vicksburg, MS, for exchange on 5/1/1865; Exchanged at Camp Townsend, MS, on 5/6/1865. Rolls of Prisoners of War, C.S.A: Surrendered at Citronelle, AL, on 5/4/1865; Paroled at Meridian, MS, on 5/11/1865. Residence at parole: Coosa County, AL.

Cast, Robert (AKA Cash, Cost) Pvt., 62nd Alabama Infantry. Co. C. Federal Rolls of Prisoners of War: Captured at Blakely, AL, on 4/9/1865; Received at Ship Island, MS, on 4/15/1865. Transferred to Vicksburg, MS, for exchange on 5/1/1865; Exchanged at Camp Townsend, MS, on 5/6/1865.

Cates, John M. Pvt., 62nd Alabama Infantry. Co. A. Federal Rolls of Prisoners of War: Captured at Blakely, AL, on 4/9/1865; Received at Ship Island, MS, on 4/15/1865. Transferred to Vicksburg, MS, for exchange on 5/1/1865; Exchanged at Camp Townsend, MS, on 5/6/1865. Born: 1846. Died: 1905. Buried: Macedonia Baptist Church Cemetery located at Chilton County, AL.

Cawley, John (AKA Corley) Pvt., 21st Alabama Infantry. Co. C. Federal Rolls of Prisoners of War: Captured at Fort Gaines, AL, on 8/8/1864; Received at Ship Island, MS, from New Orleans, LA, on 10/25/1864. Exchanged on 1/4/1865.

Chaitan, C.B. (AKA Chatain) Pvt., 21st Alabama Infantry. Co. G. Federal Rolls of Prisoners of War:

Captured at Fort Gaines, AL, on 8/8/1864; Received at Ship Island, MS, from New Orleans, LA, on 10/25/1864. Exchanged on 1/4/1865.

Chalker, William D. Pvt., Morrison's Cavalry Regiment. Co. A. Enlisted: 1863 at Blakely, AL. Federal Rolls of Prisoners of War: Received at Ship Island, MS. Transferred to Vicksburg, MS, for exchange on 5/1/1865; Exchanged at Camp Townsend, MS, on 5/6/1865. Born: 1842 at Warren County, GA. Soldier is recorded on the 1907 Alabama Census of Confederate Veterans and Widows. Residence: Dale County, AL.

Chalmers, William E., Jr. 2nd Lt., 63rd Alabama Infantry. Co. C. Federal Rolls of Prisoners of War: Captured at Blakely, AL, on 4/9/1865; Received at Ship Island, MS, on 4/15/1865. Transferred to Vicksburg, MS, for exchange on 4/28/1865; Confined at New Orleans, LA, on 4/30/1865. Exchanged at Camp Townsend, MS, on 5/6/1865.

Chambliss, Phil S. Pvt., 38th Alabama Infantry. Co. F. Enlisted: 5/1/1862 at Fayette County, AL. Federal Rolls of Prisoners of War: Captured at Spanish Fort, AL, on 4/8/1865; Received at Ship Island, MS, on 4/10/1865. Transferred to Vicksburg, MS, for exchange on 5/1/1865; Exchanged at Camp Townsend, MS, on 5/6/1865.

Champion, Lorenzo Richard Pvt., 62nd Alabama Infantry. Co. B. Enlisted: 11/1863 at Talladega, AL. Federal Rolls of Prisoners of War: Captured at Blakely, AL, on 4/9/1865; Received at Ship Island, MS, on 4/15/1865. Transferred to Vicksburg, MS, for exchange on 5/1/1865; Exchanged at Camp Townsend, MS, on 5/6/1865. Born: 10/16/1844 at Gainesville, Hall County, GA. Residence after war: Calhoun County, AL.

Chandler, S.J. Pvt., 6th Alabama Cavalry. Co. E. Federal Rolls of Prisoners of War: Captured at Flintday, AL, on 3/25/1865; Received at Ship Island, MS. Transferred to Vicksburg, MS, for exchange on 5/1/1865; Exchanged at Camp Townsend, MS, on 5/6/1865.

Chandler, T.S. Sgt., 63rd Alabama Infantry. Co. K. Federal Rolls of Prisoners of War: Captured at Blakely, AL, on 4/9/1865; Received at Ship Island, MS, on 4/15/1865. Transferred to Vicksburg, MS, for exchange on 5/1/1865; Exchanged at Camp Townsend, MS, on 5/6/1865.

Chapman, A.J. Pvt., 21st Alabama Infantry. Co. C. Federal Rolls of Prisoners of War: Captured at Fort Gaines, AL, on 8/8/1864; Received at Ship Island, MS, from New Orleans, LA, on 10/25/1864. Died: 11/17/1864 at Ship Island, MS, due to diarrhea. Buried: Ship Island, MS, Cemetery in Grave #24.

Chapman, E. Pvt., 62nd Alabama Infantry. Co. K. Federal Rolls of Prisoners of War: Captured at Blakely, AL, on 4/9/1865; Received at Ship Island, MS, on 4/15/1865. Transferred to Vicksburg, MS, for exchange on 5/1/1865; Exchanged at Camp Townsend, MS, on 5/6/1865.

Chapman, W.A. Pvt., 63rd Alabama Infantry. Co. I. Federal Rolls of Prisoners of War: Captured at Blakely, AL, on 4/9/1865; Received at Ship Island, MS, on 4/15/1865. Transferred to Vicksburg, MS, for exchange on 5/1/1865; Exchanged at Camp Townsend, MS, on 5/6/1865.

Chapman, W.T. (AKA W.P.) Pvt., 21st Alabama Infantry. Co. C. Federal Rolls of Prisoners of War: Captured at Fort Gaines, AL, on 8/8/1864; Received at Ship Island, MS, from New Orleans, LA, on 10/25/1864. Died: 12/27/1864 at Ship Island, MS, due to dysentery. Buried: Ship Island, MS, Cemetery in Grave #113.

Chesser, T.N. (AKA Cheeney, Cheeser), Jr. 2nd Lt., 8th Alabama Cavalry. Co. C. Federal Rolls of Prisoners of War: Captured in Florida on 3/25/1865; Received at Ship Island, MS. Transferred to Vicksburg, MS, for exchange on 4/28/1865; Confined at New Orleans, LA, on 4/30/1865. Exchanged at Camp Townsend, MS, on 5/6/1865.

Chestnut, Samuel (AKA S.M., S.N.) Pvt., Lockhart's Battalion Infantry. Co. I. Federal Rolls of Prisoners of War: Captured at Fort Gaines, AL, on 8/8/1864; Received at Ship Island, MS, from New Orleans, LA, on 10/29/1864. Died: 12/16/1864 at Ship Island, MS, due to consumption. Buried: Ship Island, MS, Cemetery in Grave #93.

Childers, Paul A. Pvt., 63rd Alabama Infantry. Co. A. Enlisted: 5/1/1864 at Tallapoosa County, AL. Federal Rolls of Prisoners of War: Captured at Blakely, AL, on 4/9/1865; Received at Ship Island, MS, on 4/15/1865. Transferred to Vicksburg, MS, for exchange on 5/1/1865; Exchanged at Camp Townsend, MS, on 5/6/1865. Rolls of Prisoners of War, C.S.A: Surrendered at Citronelle, AL, on 5/4/1865; Paroled at Meridian, MS, on 5/13/1865. Residence at parole: Tallapoosa County, AL.

Christian, John M. Cpl., 21st Alabama Infantry. Co. C. Federal Rolls of Prisoners of War: Captured at Fort Gaines, AL, on 8/8/1864; Received at Ship Island, MS, from New Orleans, LA, on 10/25/1864. Exchanged on 1/4/1865.

Clancy, P.D. Pvt., 63rd Alabama Infantry. Co. F. Enlisted: 5/30/1864 at Montgomery, AL. Age at enlistment: 17. Description at enlistment: Eyes: blue. Hair: dark. Complexion: fair. Height: 5'9". Residence at enlistment: Butler County, AL. Rolls for 9/1864 through 10/1864: Absent, in hospital at Mobile, AL, since 10/28/1864. Federal Rolls of Prisoners of War: Captured at Blakely, AL, on 4/9/1865; Received at Ship Island, MS, on 4/15/1865. Transferred to Vicksburg, MS, for exchange on 5/1/1865; Exchanged at Camp Townsend, MS, on 5/6/1865. Rolls of Prisoners of War, C.S.A: Surrendered at Citronelle, AL, on 5/4/1865; Paroled at Meridian, MS, on 5/11/1865. Residence at parole: Butler County, AL. Born: 4/13/1847. Died: 5/13/1935. Buried: Oakwood Cemetery located at Smith County, TX.

Clapton, David (AKA Clopton) Pvt., 1st Alabama Artillery Battalion. Cos. A & D. Federal Rolls of Prisoners of War: Captured at Fort Gaines, AL, on 8/8/1864; Received at Ship Island, MS, from New Orleans, LA, on 10/25/1864. Exchanged on 1/4/1865.

Clark, F.P. Pvt., 62nd Alabama Infantry. Co. A. Federal Rolls of Prisoners of War: Captured at Blakely, AL, on 4/9/1865; Received at Ship Island, MS, on 4/15/1865. Transferred to Vicksburg, MS, for exchange on 5/1/1865; Exchanged at Camp Townsend, MS, on 5/6/1865.

Clark, J. Pvt., 63rd Alabama Infantry. Co. E. Enlisted: 4/8/1864 at Pollard, AL. Age at enlistment: 17. Description at enlistment: Eyes: dark. Hair: dark. Complexion: dark. Rolls for 9/1864 through 10/1864:

Present. Federal Rolls of Prisoners of War: Captured at Blakely, AL, on 4/9/1865; Received at Ship Island, MS, on 4/15/1865. Transferred to Vicksburg, MS, for exchange on 5/1/1865; Exchanged at Camp Townsend, MS, on 5/6/1865. Rolls of Prisoners of War, C.S.A: Surrendered at Citronelle, AL, on 5/4/1865; Paroled at Meridian, MS, on 5/13/1865. Residence at parole: Henry County, AL.

Clark, James Pvt., 63rd Alabama Infantry. Co. E. Federal Rolls of Prisoners of War: Captured at Blakely, AL, on 4/9/1865; Received at Ship Island, MS, on 4/15/1865. Transferred to Vicksburg, MS, for exchange on 5/1/1865; Exchanged at Camp Townsend, MS, on 5/6/1865.

Clark, John Isaac (AKA Clarke, J.T.) Pvt., 62nd Alabama Infantry. Cos. D & H. Enlisted: 1/12/1863 at Selma, AL. Federal Rolls of Prisoners of War: Captured at Blakely, AL, on 4/9/1865; Received at Ship Island, MS, on 4/15/1865. Transferred to Vicksburg, MS, for exchange on 5/1/1865; Exchanged at Camp Townsend, MS, on 5/6/1865. Born: 1/19/1843 at Scottsville, Bibb County, AL. Residence after war: Mobile County, AL.

Clark, J.T. (AKA Clarke) Pvt., Lockhart's Battalion Infantry. Co. H. Federal Rolls of Prisoners of War: Captured at Fort Gaines, AL, on 8/8/1864; Received at Ship Island, MS, from New Orleans, LA, on 10/25/1864. Exchanged on 1/5/1865.

Clarke, J.T. Pvt., 62nd Alabama Infantry. Cos. D & H. Federal Rolls of Prisoners of War: Captured at Blakely, AL, on 4/9/1865; Received at Ship Island, MS, on 4/15/1865. Transferred to Vicksburg, MS, for exchange on 5/1/1865; Exchanged at Camp Townsend, MS, on 5/6/1865.

Clark, R.H. Cpl., 62nd Alabama Infantry. Co. C. Federal Rolls of Prisoners of War: Captured at Blakely, AL, on 4/9/1865; Received at Ship Island, MS, on 4/15/1865. Transferred to Vicksburg, MS, for exchange on 5/1/1865; Exchanged at Camp Townsend, MS, on 5/6/1865.

Clarke, James I. (AKA J.J.) Pvt., 62nd Alabama Infantry. Cos. D & H. Federal Rolls of Prisoners of War: Captured at Blakely, AL, on 4/9/1865; Received at Ship Island, MS, on 4/15/1865. Transferred to Vicksburg, MS, for exchange on 5/1/1865; Exchanged at Camp Townsend, MS, on 5/6/1865.

Clayton, Webster Henry Sgt., 6th Alabama Cavalry. Co. F. Federal Rolls of Prisoners of War: Captured at Flintday, AL, on 3/25/1865; Received at Ship Island, MS. Transferred to Vicksburg, MS, for exchange on 5/1/1865; Exchanged at Camp Townsend, MS, on 5/6/1865.

Clements, A. Pvt., 62nd Alabama Infantry. Co. D. Federal Rolls of Prisoners of War: Captured at Blakely, AL, on 4/9/1865; Received at Ship Island, MS, on 4/15/1865. Transferred to Vicksburg, MS, for exchange on 5/1/1865; Exchanged at Camp Townsend, MS, on 5/6/1865.

Clements, A.R. Ord. Sgt., Tarrant's Artillery Battery. Federal Rolls of Prisoners of War: Captured at Blakely, AL, on 4/9/1865; Received at Ship Island, MS, on 4/15/1865. Transferred to Vicksburg, MS, for exchange on 5/1/1865; Exchanged at Camp Townsend, MS, on 5/6/1865.

Clements, Charles (AKA Clement) Pvt., 21st Alabama Infantry. Co. I. Federal Rolls of Prisoners of War: Captured at Fort Gaines, AL, on 8/8/1864; Received at Ship Island, MS, from New Orleans, LA, on 10/25/1864. Died: 12/12/1864 at Ship Island, MS, due to chronic dysentery. Buried: Ship Island, MS, Cemetery in Grave #84.

Clements, Joshua W. Pvt., 62nd Alabama Infantry. Cos. A & I. Enlisted: 10/13/1861 at Hall's Mill, Mobile County, AL. Federal Rolls of Prisoners of War: Captured at Blakely, AL, on 4/9/1865; Received at Ship Island, MS, on 4/15/1865. Transferred to Vicksburg, MS, for exchange on 5/1/1865; Exchanged at Camp Townsend, MS, on 5/6/1865. Born: 11/25/1832 at Hall's Mill, Mobile County, AL. Residence after war: Mobile County, AL.

Cleveland, J.H. (AKA Clieland) Pvt./Cpl., 21st Alabama Infantry. Co. C. Federal Rolls of Prisoners of War: Captured at Fort Gaines, AL, on 8/8/1864; Received at Ship Island, MS, from New Orleans, LA, on 10/25/1864. Exchanged on 1/4/1865.

Clifford, George T. Pvt., 62nd Alabama Infantry. Co. B. Federal Rolls of Prisoners of War: Captured at Blakely, AL, on 4/9/1865; Received at Ship Island, MS, on 4/15/1865. Transferred to Vicksburg, MS, for exchange on 5/1/1865; Exchanged at Camp Townsend, MS, on 5/6/1865.

Clinton, W. Pvt., 62nd Alabama Infantry. Cos. D & F. Federal Rolls of Prisoners of War: Captured at Blakely, AL, on 4/9/1865; Received at Ship Island, MS, on 4/15/1865. Transferred to Vicksburg, MS, for exchange on 5/1/1865; Exchanged at Camp Townsend, MS, on 5/6/1865.

Cobb, John N. (AKA Cobbs) Cpl., 63rd Alabama Infantry. Co. H. Enlisted: 8/4/1864 at Selma, AL. Age at enlistment: 17. Description at enlistment: Eyes: blue. Hair: dark. Complexion: dark. Rolls for 9/1864 through 10/1864: Present. Federal Rolls of Prisoners of War: Captured at Blakely, AL, on 4/9/1865; Received at Ship Island, MS, on 4/15/1865. Transferred to Vicksburg, MS, for exchange on 5/1/1865. On Register of U.S.A. General Hospital #2, Vicksburg, MS: Admitted from steamer on 5/3/1865 due to acute diarrhea; Returned to duty on 5/23/1865.

Cobb, William Pvt., 36th Alabama Infantry. Co. G. Enlisted: 9/19/1862 at Clarke County, AL. Age at enlistment: 18. Occupation at enlistment: Farmer. Federal Rolls of Prisoners of War: Captured at Spanish Fort, AL, on 4/8/1865; Received at Ship Island, MS, on 4/10/1865. Transferred to Vicksburg, MS, for exchange on 5/1/1865; Exchanged at Camp Townsend, MS, on 5/6/1865. Born: Alabama.

Coburn, Stanley D. Pvt./Sgt., 1st Alabama Artillery Battalion. Co. D. Federal Rolls of Prisoners of War: Captured at Fort Gaines, AL, on 8/8/1864; Received at Ship Island, MS, from New Orleans, LA, on 10/25/1864. Exchanged on 1/4/1865.

Cockrell, L.D. (AKA Cocknells) Pvt., 36th Alabama Infantry. Co. B. Enlisted: Sumpter County, AL. Age at enlistment: 17. Federal Rolls of Prisoners of War: Captured at Spanish Fort, AL, on 4/8/1865; Received at Ship Island, MS, on 4/10/1865. Transferred to Vicksburg, MS, for exchange on 5/1/1865; Exchanged at Camp Townsend, MS, on 5/6/1865.

Cogburn, Samuel H. Pvt., 6th Alabama Cavalry. Co. F. Federal Rolls of Prisoners of War: Captured at Flintday, AL, on 3/25/1865; Received at Ship Island, MS. Transferred to Vicksburg, MS, for exchange on

5/1/1865; Exchanged at Camp Townsend, MS, on 5/6/1865.

Coker, John Pvt., 1st Alabama Artillery Battalion. Co. D. Federal Rolls of Prisoners of War: Captured at Fort Gaines, AL, on 8/8/1864; Received at Ship Island, MS, from New Orleans, LA, on 10/25/1864. Exchanged on 1/4/1865.

Coker, Thomas Pvt., 1st Alabama Artillery Battalion. Co. D. Federal Rolls of Prisoners of War: Captured at Fort Gaines, AL, on 8/8/1864; Received at Ship Island, MS, on 10/29/1864. Exchanged on 1/4/1865.

Colburn, C.C. Cpl., 62nd Alabama Infantry. Co. C. Federal Rolls of Prisoners of War: Captured at Blakely, AL, on 4/9/1865; Received at Ship Island, MS, on 4/15/1865. Transferred to Vicksburg, MS, for exchange on 5/1/1865; Exchanged at Camp Townsend, MS, on 5/6/1865.

Colby, F.M. Pvt., 63rd Alabama Infantry. Cos. A & B. Federal Rolls of Prisoners of War: Captured at Blakely, AL, on 4/9/1865; Received at Ship Island, MS, on 4/15/1865. Transferred to Vicksburg, MS, for exchange on 5/1/1865; Exchanged at Camp Townsend, MS, on 5/6/1865. Rolls of Prisoners of War, C.S.A: Surrendered at Citronelle, AL, on 5/4/1865; Paroled at Meridian, MS, on 5/11/1865. Residence at parole: Coosa County, AL.

Coleman, Abner N. (AKA A.M.) Pvt., 62nd Alabama Infantry. Cos. D & F. Federal Rolls of Prisoners of War: Captured at Blakely, AL, on 4/9/1865; Received at Ship Island, MS, on 4/15/1865. Transferred to Vicksburg, MS, for exchange on 5/1/1865; Exchanged at Camp Townsend, MS, on 5/6/1865.

Coleman, C.F. Pvt., Lockhart's Battalion Infantry. Co. I. Federal Rolls of Prisoners of War: Captured at Fort Gaines, AL, on 8/8/1864; Received at Ship Island, MS, from New Orleans, LA, on 10/25/1864. Died: 12/19/1864 at Ship Island, MS, due to chronic dysentery. Buried: Ship Island, MS, Cemetery in Grave #100.

Coleman, W.S. Pvt./1st Lt., 38th Alabama Infantry. Co. E. Enlisted: 4/7/1862 at Mobile, AL. Age at enlistment: 18. Elected 1st Lt. on 9/23/1864. Federal Rolls of Prisoners of War: Captured at Blakely, AL, on 4/9/1865; Received at Ship Island, MS, on 4/16/1865. Transferred to Vicksburg, MS, for exchange on 4/28/1865; Confined at New Orleans, LA, on 4/30/1865. Exchanged at Camp Townsend, MS, on 5/6/1865. Rolls of Prisoners of War, C.S.A: Surrendered at Citronelle, AL, on 5/4/1865; Paroled at Meridian, MS, on 5/11/1865.

Collins, G.W. Pvt., 18th Alabama Infantry. Co. B. Federal Rolls of Prisoners of War: Captured at Spanish Fort, AL, on 4/8/1865; Received at Ship Island, MS, on 4/10/1865. Transferred to Vicksburg, MS, for exchange on 5/1/1865; Exchanged at Camp Townsend, MS, on 5/6/1865.

Collum, J.M. Pvt., Tarrant's Artillery Battery. Federal Rolls of Prisoners of War: Captured at Blakely, AL, on 4/9/1865; Received at Ship Island, MS, on 4/15/1865. Transferred to Vicksburg, MS, for exchange on 5/1/1865; Exchanged at Camp Townsend, MS, on 5/6/1865.

Connally, John W. (AKA J.M.) Cpl./Pvt., 58th Alabama Infantry. Cos. B & I. Federal Rolls of Prisoners of War: Captured at Spanish Fort, AL, on 4/8/1865; Received at Ship Island, MS, on 4/10/1865. Transferred to Vicksburg, MS, for exchange on 5/1/1865; Exchanged at Camp Townsend, MS, on 5/6/1865.

Coney, W.C. Pvt., 63rd Alabama Infantry. Co. F. Enlisted: 5/30/1864 at Montgomery, AL. Age at enlistment: 17. Description at enlistment: Eyes: light. Hair: light. Complexion: fair. Height: 5'1". Residence at enlistment: Butler County, AL. Rolls for 9/1864 through 10/1864: Present. Federal Rolls of Prisoners of War: Captured at Blakely, AL, on 4/9/1865; Received at Ship Island, MS, on 4/15/1865. Transferred to Vicksburg, MS, for exchange on 5/1/1865; Exchanged at Camp Townsend, MS, on 5/6/1865. Rolls of Prisoners of War, C.S.A: Surrendered at Citronelle, AL, on 5/4/1865; Paroled at Meridian, MS, on 5/11/1865. Residence at parole: Butler County, AL.

Connally, John W (AKA Conley, J.H.) Cpl./Pvt., 58th Alabama Infantry. Co. I. Federal Rolls of Prisoners of War: Captured at Spanish Fort, AL, on 4/8/1865; Received at Ship Island, MS, on 4/10/1865. Transferred to Vicksburg, MS, for exchange on 5/1/1865; Exchanged at Camp Townsend, MS, on 5/6/1865.

Conold, R.O. Pvt., 62nd Alabama Infantry. Co. D. Federal Rolls of Prisoners of War: Captured at Blakely, AL, on 4/9/1865; Received at Ship Island, MS, on 4/15/1865. Transferred to Vicksburg, MS, for exchange on 5/1/1865; Exchanged at Camp Townsend, MS, on 5/6/1865.

Cook, J.R. Pvt., Tarrant's Artillery Battery. Federal Rolls of Prisoners of War: Captured at Blakely, AL, on 4/9/1865; Received at Ship Island, MS, on 4/15/1865. Transferred to Vicksburg, MS, for exchange on 5/1/1865; Exchanged at Camp Townsend, MS, on 5/6/1865.

Cook, William C. Pvt., 1st Alabama Artillery Battalion. Co. D. Federal Rolls of Prisoners of War: Captured at Fort Gaines, AL, on 8/8/1864; Received at Ship Island, MS, from New Orleans, LA, on 10/25/1864. Exchanged on 1/4/1865.

Cooper, Joseph (AKA James) Cpl./Pvt., 21st Alabama Infantry. Co. F. Federal Rolls of Prisoners of War: Captured at Fort Gaines, AL, on 8/8/1864; Received at Ship Island, MS, from New Orleans, LA, on 10/25/1864. Exchanged on 1/4/1865.

Cooper, Wesley A. Pvt., 63rd Alabama Infantry. Co. B. Enlisted: 4/14/1864 at Montgomery County, AL. Rolls for 9/1864 through 10/1864: Absent. Federal Rolls of Prisoners of War: Captured at Blakely, AL, on 3/24/1865; Received at Ship Island, MS, on 4/15/1865. Transferred to Vicksburg, MS, for exchange on 5/1/1865; Exchanged at Camp Townsend, MS, on 5/6/1865.

Copeland, Eugenius W. 4th Cpl., 63rd Alabama Infantry. Co. G. Enlisted: 5/16/1864 at Troy, AL. Age at enlistment: 17. Description at enlistment: Eyes: grey. Hair: dark. Complexion: fair. Height: 4'9". Residence at enlistment: Pike County, AL. Rolls for 9/1864 through 10/1864: Present. Federal Rolls of Prisoners of War: Captured at Blakely, AL, on 4/9/1865; Received at Ship Island, MS, on 4/15/1865. Transferred to Vicksburg, MS, for exchange on 5/1/1865; Exchanged at Camp Townsend, MS, on 5/6/1865. Rolls of Prisoners of War, C.S.A: Surrendered at Citronelle, AL, on 5/4/1865; Paroled at Meridian, MS, on 5/13/1865.

Copeland, Hilliard A. Pvt., 63rd Alabama Infantry.

Co. G. Enlisted: 5/16/1864 at Troy, AL. Age at enlistment: 16. Description at enlistment: Eyes: grey. Hair: dark. Complexion: fair. Height: 5'7". Rolls for 9/1864 through 10/1864: Present. Federal Rolls of Prisoners of War: Captured at Blakely, AL, on 4/9/1865; Received at Ship Island, MS, on 4/15/1865. Transferred to Vicksburg, MS, for exchange on 5/1/1865; Exchanged at Camp Townsend, MS, on 5/6/1865. Rolls of Prisoners of War, C.S.A: Surrendered at Citronelle, AL, on 5/4/1865; Paroled at Meridian, MS, on 5/13/1865. Residence at parole: Pike County, AL.

Copeland, J.D. (AKA Coupland) Sgt., 63rd Alabama Infantry. Co. H. Enlisted: 3/15/1864 at Springville, AL. Age at enlistment: 17. Description at enlistment: Eyes: blue. Hair: light. Complexion: fair. Rolls for 9/1864 through 10/1864: Present. Federal Rolls of Prisoners of War: Captured at Blakely, AL, on 4/9/1865; Received at Ship Island, MS, on 4/15/1865. Transferred to Vicksburg, MS, for exchange on 5/1/1865; Exchanged at Camp Townsend, MS, on 5/6/1865. Rolls of Prisoners of War, C.S.A: Surrendered at Citronelle, AL, on 5/4/1865; Paroled at Meridian, MS, on 5/11/1865. Residence at parole: Jefferson County, AL.

Corley, P.J. Pvt., 58th Alabama Infantry. Co. I. Federal Rolls of Prisoners of War: Captured at Spanish Fort, AL, on 4/8/1865; Received at Ship Island, MS, on 4/10/1865. Transferred to Vicksburg, MS, for exchange on 5/1/1865; Exchanged at Camp Townsend, MS, on 5/6/1865.

Corntings, J.B. (AKA J.D.) Pvt., 63rd Alabama Infantry. Co. G. Federal Rolls of Prisoners of War: Captured at Blakely, AL, on 4/9/1865; Received at Ship Island, MS, on 4/15/1865. Transferred to Vicksburg, MS, for exchange on 5/1/1865; Exchanged at Camp Townsend, MS, on 5/6/1865.

Cort, J.B. (AKA Cost) Pvt., 62nd Alabama Infantry. Co. H. Federal Rolls of Prisoners of War: Captured at Blakely, AL, on 4/9/1865; Received at Ship Island, MS, on 4/15/1865. Transferred to Vicksburg, MS, for exchange on 5/1/1865; Exchanged at Camp Townsend, MS, on 5/6/1865.

Cosby, ? Pvt., 62nd Alabama Infantry. Co. A. Federal Rolls of Prisoners of War: Captured at Blakely, AL, on 4/9/1865; Received at Ship Island, MS, on 4/15/1865. Transferred to Vicksburg, MS, for exchange on 5/1/1865; Exchanged at Camp Townsend, MS, on 5/6/1865.

Cowart, Alford Johnson (AKA Coward, Alfred) 4th Sgt., 63rd Alabama Infantry. Co. G. Enlisted: 5/16/1864 at Troy, AL. Age at enlistment: 17. Description at enlistment: Eyes: dark. Hair: dark. Complexion: dark. Height: 5'11". Residence at enlistment: Pike County, AL. Rolls for 9/1864 through 10/1864: Absent, in hospital at Mobile, AL, since 9/25/1864. Federal Rolls of Prisoners of War: Captured at Blakely, AL, on 4/9/1865; Received at Ship Island, MS, on 4/15/1865. Transferred to Vicksburg, MS, for exchange on 5/1/1865. On Register of U.S.A. General Hospital #2, Vicksburg, MS: Admitted from steamer on 5/3/1865 due to remittent fever; Returned to duty on 5/23/1865. Born: 5/28/1846 at Little Oak, Pike County, AL. Soldier is recorded on the 1907 Census of Alabama Confederate Veterans and Widows. Residence: Pike County, AL.

Cox, James E. Pvt., 63rd Alabama Infantry. Co. D. Enlisted: 7/30/1864 at Macon County, AL. Age at enlistment: 17. Description at enlistment: Eyes: grey. Hair: auburn. Complexion: light. Height: 5'6". Residence at enlistment: Eufaula, Barbour County, AL. Rolls for 9/1864 through 10/1864: Present. Federal Rolls of Prisoners of War: Captured at Blakely, AL, on 4/9/1865; Received at Ship Island, MS, on 4/15/1865. Transferred to Vicksburg, MS, for exchange on 5/1/1865; Exchanged at Camp Townsend, MS, on 5/6/1865. Rolls of Prisoners of War, C.S.A: Surrendered at Citronelle, AL, on 5/4/1865; Paroled at Meridian, MS, on 5/13/1865. Residence at parole: Barbour County, AL.

Cox, Taylor Pvt., 63rd Alabama Infantry. Cos. A & K. Enlisted: 1/1/1864 at Macon County, AL. Age at enlistment: 16. Rolls for 1/1864 through 2/1864: Present. Rolls for 9/1864 through 10/1864: Present. Federal Rolls of Prisoners of War: Captured at Blakely, AL, on 4/9/1865; Received at Ship Island, MS, on 4/15/1865. Transferred to Vicksburg, MS, for exchange on 5/1/1865; Exchanged at Camp Townsend, MS, on 5/6/1865. Rolls of Prisoners of War, C.S.A: Surrendered at Citronelle, AL, on 5/4/1865; Paroled at Meridian, MS, on 5/13/1865. Residence at parole: Chambers County, AL.

Cox, Thomas J. Pvt., 62nd Alabama Infantry. Co. A. Federal Rolls of Prisoners of War: Captured near Spanish Fort, AL, on 3/27/1865; Received at Ship Island, MS, on 4/10/1865. Transferred to Vicksburg, MS, for exchange on 5/1/1865; Exchanged at Camp Townsend, MS, on 5/6/1865.

Coy, James A. (AKA Coe) 2nd Lt., 6th Alabama Cavalry. Co. E. Federal Rolls of Prisoners of War: Captured in Florida on 3/25/1865; Received at Ship Island, MS. Transferred to Vicksburg, MS, for exchange on 4/28/1865; Confined at New Orleans, LA, on 4/30/1865. Exchanged at Camp Townsend, MS, on 5/6/1865.

Cozby, N.W. Pvt., 63rd Alabama Infantry. Cos. A & H. Enlisted: 3/15/1864 at Springville, AL. Age at enlistment: 17. Description at enlistment: Eyes: dark. Hair: dark. Complexion: dark. Rolls for 9/1864 through 10/1864: Present. Federal Rolls of Prisoners of War: Captured at Blakely, AL, on 4/9/1865; Received at Ship Island, MS, on 4/15/1865. Transferred to Vicksburg, MS, for exchange on 5/1/1865; Exchanged at Camp Townsend, MS, on 5/6/1865.

Craddock, Benjamin F. (AKA Caddock) Pvt., 6th Alabama Cavalry. Co. E. Federal Rolls of Prisoners of War: Captured at Flintday, AL, on 3/25/1865; Received at Ship Island, MS. Transferred to Vicksburg, MS, for exchange on 5/1/1865; Exchanged at Camp Townsend, MS, on 5/6/1865.

Craig, Robert D. Pvt., 62nd Alabama Infantry. Co. D. Enlisted: 1863 at Selma, AL. Federal Rolls of Prisoners of War: Captured at Blakely, AL, on 4/9/1865; Received at Ship Island, MS, on 4/15/1865. Transferred to Vicksburg, MS, for exchange on 5/1/1865; Exchanged at Camp Townsend, MS, on 5/6/1865. Born: 9/8/1845 at Marion, Perry County, AL. Residence after war: Dallas County, AL.

Crain, Joseph (AKA Crane) Pvt., 62nd Alabama Infantry. Co. I. Federal Rolls of Prisoners of War: Captured at Blakely, AL, on 4/9/1865; Received at Ship Island, MS, on 4/15/1865. Transferred to Vicksburg, MS, for exchange on 5/1/1865; Exchanged at Camp Townsend, MS, on 5/6/1865.

Craine, John Pvt., 38th Alabama Infantry. Co. C. Enlisted: 4/2/1862 at Choctaw, AL. Federal Rolls of Prisoners of War: Captured at Spanish Fort, AL, on 4/8/1865; Received at Ship Island, MS, on 4/10/1865. Transferred to Vicksburg, MS, for exchange on 5/1/1865; Exchanged at Camp Townsend, MS, on 5/6/1865.

Crane, William J. (AKA Crune) Pvt., 63rd Alabama Infantry. Co. H. Federal Rolls of Prisoners of War: Captured at Blakely, AL, on 4/9/1865; Received at Ship Island, MS, on 4/15/1865. Transferred to Vicksburg, MS, for exchange on 5/1/1865; Exchanged at Camp Townsend, MS, on 5/6/1865.

Cranfield, W.G.S. Pvt., 36th Alabama Infantry. Co. A. Federal Rolls of Prisoners of War: Captured at Spanish Fort, AL, on 4/8/1865; Received at Ship Island, MS, on 4/10/1865. Transferred to Vicksburg, MS, for exchange on 5/1/1865; Exchanged at Camp Townsend, MS, on 5/6/1865.

Craps, P. (AKA D.C.) Pvt., 63rd Alabama Infantry. Co. E. Federal Rolls of Prisoners of War: Captured at Blakely, AL, on 4/9/1865; Received at Ship Island, MS, on 4/15/1865. Transferred to Vicksburg, MS, for exchange on 5/1/1865; Exchanged at Camp Townsend, MS, on 5/6/1865.

Craven, John Pvt., 21st Alabama Infantry. Co. G. Federal Rolls of Prisoners of War: Captured at Fort Gaines, AL, on 8/8/1864; Received at Ship Island, MS, from New Orleans, LA, on 10/25/1864. Exchanged on 1/4/1865.

Crawford, H.A. Pvt., Tarrant's Artillery Battery. Enlisted: 7/6/1863 at Tuscaloosa, AL. Federal Rolls of Prisoners of War: Captured at Blakely, AL, on 4/9/1865; Received at Ship Island, MS, on 4/15/1865. Transferred to Vicksburg, MS, for exchange on 5/1/1865; Exchanged at Camp Townsend, MS, on 5/6/1865.

Crawson, B.C. (AKA Z.C.) Pvt., 63rd Alabama Infantry. Co. I. Federal Rolls of Prisoners of War: Captured at Blakely, AL, on 4/9/1865; Received at Ship Island, MS, on 4/15/1865. Transferred to Vicksburg, MS, for exchange on 5/1/1865; Exchanged at Camp Townsend, MS, on 5/6/1865.

Creel, John W. Pvt., 1st Alabama Artillery Battalion. Co. D. Federal Rolls of Prisoners of War: Captured at Fort Gaines, AL, on 8/8/1864; Received at Ship Island, MS, from New Orleans, LA, on 10/25/1864. Exchanged on 1/4/1865.

Cregg, R. Pvt., 62nd Alabama Infantry. Co. F. Federal Rolls of Prisoners of War: Captured at Blakely, AL, on 4/9/1865; Received at Ship Island, MS, on 4/15/1865. Transferred to Vicksburg, MS, for exchange on 5/1/1865; Exchanged at Camp Townsend, MS, on 5/6/1865.

Crenshaw, James Arnet Pvt., 21st Alabama Infantry. Co. C. Federal Rolls of Prisoners of War: Captured at Fort Gaines, AL, on 8/8/1864; Received at Ship Island, MS, from New Orleans, LA, on 10/25/1864. Died: Ship Island, MS, on 1/3/1865 due to pneumonia. Buried: Ship Island, MS, Cemetery in Grave #129. Born: 11/1/1849 to G.W. Crenshaw.

Crenshaw, M.V. Capt., 21st Alabama Infantry. Co. I. Federal Rolls of Prisoners of War: Captured at Fort Gaines, AL, on 8/8/1864; Received at Ship Island, MS, from New Orleans, LA, on 10/25/1864. Exchanged on 1/4/1865.

Crenshaw, William L. Pvt., 36th Alabama Infantry. Co. A. Federal Rolls of Prisoners of War: Captured at Spanish Fort, AL, on 4/8/1865; Received at Ship Island, MS, on 4/10/1865. Transferred to Vicksburg, MS, for exchange on 5/1/1865; Exchanged at Camp Townsend, MS, on 5/6/1865.

Crews, Frank L. Pvt., 62nd Alabama Infantry. Cos. D & K. Federal Rolls of Prisoners of War: Captured at Blakely, AL, on 4/9/1865; Received at Ship Island, MS, on 4/15/1865. Transferred to Vicksburg, MS, for exchange on 5/1/1865; Exchanged at Camp Townsend, MS, on 5/6/1865.

Crider, Henry (AKA J.H.) Cpl., 62nd Alabama Infantry. Co. B. Federal Rolls of Prisoners of War: Captured at Blakely, AL, on 4/9/1865; Received at Ship Island, MS, on 4/15/1865. Transferred to Vicksburg, MS, for exchange on 5/1/1865; Exchanged at Camp Townsend, MS, on 5/6/1865.

Crocker, W.S. Pvt., Tarrant's Artillery Battery. Federal Rolls of Prisoners of War: Captured at Blakely, AL, on 4/9/1865; Received at Ship Island, MS, on 4/15/1865. Transferred to Vicksburg, MS, for exchange on 5/1/1865; Exchanged at Camp Townsend, MS, on 5/6/1865.

Crole, J.A. Pvt., 62nd Alabama Infantry. Co. E. Federal Rolls of Prisoners of War: Captured at Blakely, AL, on 4/9/1865; Received at Ship Island, MS, on 4/15/1865. Transferred to Vicksburg, MS, for exchange on 5/1/1865; Exchanged at Camp Townsend, MS, on 5/6/1865.

Crooks, L.M. Pvt., 62nd Alabama Infantry. Cos. E & H. Federal Rolls of Prisoners of War: Captured at Blakely, AL, on 4/9/1865; Received at Ship Island, MS, on 4/15/1865. Transferred to Vicksburg, MS, for exchange on 5/1/1865; Exchanged at Camp Townsend, MS, on 5/6/1865.

Crosby, John Pvt., 58th Alabama Infantry. Co. C. Federal Rolls of Prisoners of War: Captured at Spanish Fort, AL, on 4/8/1865; Received at Ship Island, MS, on 4/10/1865. Transferred to Vicksburg, MS, for exchange on 5/1/1865; Exchanged at Camp Townsend, MS, on 5/6/1865.

Crosby, William 1st Sgt., 36th Alabama Infantry. Co. G. Federal Rolls of Prisoners of War: Captured at Spanish Fort, AL, on 4/8/1865; Received at Ship Island, MS, on 4/10/1865. Transferred to Vicksburg, MS, for exchange on 5/1/1865; Exchanged at Camp Townsend, MS, on 5/6/1865.

Cross, J. Wesley Pvt., 62nd Alabama Infantry. Co. F. Federal Rolls of Prisoners of War: Captured at Blakely, AL, on 4/9/1865; Received at Ship Island, MS, on 4/15/1865. Transferred to Vicksburg, MS, for exchange on 5/1/1865; Exchanged at Camp Townsend, MS, on 5/6/1865.

Crow, J.A. Pvt., 62nd Alabama Infantry. Cos. A & H. Federal Rolls of Prisoners of War: Captured at Blakely, AL, on 4/9/1865; Received at Ship Island, MS, on 4/15/1865. Transferred to Vicksburg, MS, for exchange on 5/1/1865; Exchanged at Camp Townsend, MS, on 5/6/1865.

Crowson, Zachariah C. (AKA B.C.) Pvt., 63rd Alabama Infantry. Co. I. Enlisted: Columbiana, AL. Rolls for 9/1864 through 10/1864: Present. Federal Rolls of Prisoners of War: Captured at Blakely, AL, on 4/9/1865; Received at Ship Island, MS, on 4/15/1865. Transferred to Vicksburg, MS, for exchange on

5/1/1865; Exchanged at Camp Townsend, MS, on 5/6/1865. Rolls of Prisoners of War, C.S.A: Surrendered at Citronelle, AL, on 5/4/1865; Paroled at Meridian, MS, on 5/13/1865. Residence at parole: Shelby County, AL.

Crumpton, M.M. Pvt., 1st Alabama Artillery Battalion. Cos. B & D. Federal Rolls of Prisoners of War: Captured at Fort Gaines, AL, on 8/8/1864; Received at Ship Island, MS, from New Orleans, LA, on 10/25/1864. Exchanged on 1/4/1865.

Crune, W.J. Pvt., 63rd Alabama Infantry. Co. H. Enlisted: 3/15/1864 at Montevallo, AL. Age at enlistment: 17. Description at enlistment: Eyes: dark. Hair: dark. Complexion: dark. Rolls for 9/1864 through 10/1864: Absent, in camp of correction since 8/14/1864. Federal Rolls of Prisoners of War: Captured at Blakely, AL, on 4/9/1865; Received at Ship Island, MS, on 4/15/1865. Transferred to Vicksburg, MS, for exchange on 5/1/1865; Exchanged at Camp Townsend, MS, on 5/6/1865. Rolls of Prisoners of War, C.S.A: Surrendered at Citronelle, AL, on 5/4/1865; Paroled at Meridian, MS, on 5/11/1865. Residence at parole: Jefferson County, AL.

Culberson, James Pvt., 62nd Alabama Infantry. Co. F. Federal Rolls of Prisoners of War: Captured at Blakely, AL, on 4/9/1865; Received at Ship Island, MS, on 4/15/1865. Transferred to Vicksburg, MS, for exchange on 5/1/1865; Exchanged at Camp Townsend, MS, on 5/6/1865.

Culpepper, J.B. Pvt., 63rd Alabama Infantry. Co. K. Federal Rolls of Prisoners of War: Captured at Blakely, AL, on 4/9/1865; Received at Ship Island, MS, on 4/15/1865. Transferred to Vicksburg, MS, for exchange on 5/1/1865; Exchanged at Camp Townsend, MS, on 5/6/1865. Rolls of Prisoners of War, C.S.A: Surrendered at Citronelle, AL, on 5/4/1865; Paroled at Meridian, MS, on 5/13/1865. Residence at parole: Choctaw County, AL.

Cummings, Dennis Flynn Pvt., 62nd Alabama Infantry. Co. A. Enlisted: Selma, AL. Federal Rolls of Prisoners of War: Captured at Blakely, AL, on 4/9/1865; Received at Ship Island, MS, on 4/15/1865. Transferred to Vicksburg, MS, for exchange on 5/1/1865; Exchanged at Camp Townsend, MS, on 5/6/1865. Born: 6/1845 at Perryville, Perry County, AL. Residence after war: Perry County, AL.

Cummings, S. Pvt., 62nd Alabama Infantry. Co. H. Federal Rolls of Prisoners of War: Captured at Blakely, AL, on 4/9/1865; Received at Ship Island, MS, on 4/15/1865. Transferred to Vicksburg, MS, for exchange on 5/1/1865; Exchanged at Camp Townsend, MS, on 5/6/1865.

Cummings, Thomas Pvt., Pelham Cadets. Cos. A & B. Federal Rolls of Prisoners of War: Captured at Fort Gaines, AL, on 8/8/1864; Received at Ship Island, MS, from New Orleans, LA, on 10/25/1864. Exchanged on 1/4/1865.

Curtis, John Robert 2nd Cpl./Pvt., 63rd Alabama Infantry. Cos. E & G. Enlisted: 5/16/1864 at Troy, AL. Age at enlistment: 17. Description at enlistment: Eyes: blue. Hair: light. Complexion: fair. Residence at enlistment: Pike County, AL. Rolls for 9/1864 through 10/1864: Present, reduced to Pvt. by Regimental Court Martial on 10/17/1864. Federal Rolls of Prisoners of War: Captured at Blakely, AL, on 4/9/1865; Received at Ship Island, MS, on 4/15/1865. Transferred to Vicksburg, MS, for exchange on 5/1/1865; Exchanged at Camp Townsend, MS, on 5/6/1865. Rolls of Prisoners of War, C.S.A: Surrendered at Citronelle, AL, on 5/4/1865; Paroled at Meridian, MS, on 5/13/1865. Residence at parole: Pike County, AL. Born: 9/14/1846 at Hickory Grove, GA. Soldier is recorded on the 1907 Census of Alabama Confederate Veterans and Widows. Residence: Pike County, AL.

Dailey, William G. (AKA Daily, W.C.) Pvt., 21st Alabama Infantry. Co. G. Federal Rolls of Prisoners of War: Captured at Fort Gaines, AL, on 8/8/1864; Received at Ship Island, MS, from New Orleans, LA, on 10/25/1864. Died: 11/27/1864 at Ship Island, MS, due to pneumonia. Buried: Ship Island, MS, Cemetery in Grave #46.

Daily, W.F. Pvt., 21st Alabama Infantry. Co. E. Federal Rolls of Prisoners of War: Captured at Fort Gaines, AL, on 8/8/1864; Received at Ship Island, MS, from New Orleans, LA, on 10/25/1864. Exchanged on 1/4/1865.

Dalton, Perry W. Pvt., 21st Alabama Infantry. Co. G. Federal Rolls of Prisoners of War: Captured at Fort Gaines, AL, on 8/8/1864; Received at Ship Island, MS, from New Orleans, LA, on 10/25/1864. Exchanged on 1/4/1865.

Danneburg, A.C. (AKA Darandbury) Pvt., Lockhart's Battalion Infantry. Co. H. Federal Rolls of Prisoners of War: Captured at Fort Gaines, AL, on 8/8/1864; Received at Ship Island, MS, from New Orleans, LA, on 10/25/1864. Exchanged on 1/4/1865.

Dansby, A. Pvt., 63rd Alabama Infantry. Co. E. Federal Rolls of Prisoners of War: Captured at Blakely, AL, on 4/9/1865; Received at Ship Island, MS, on 4/15/1865. Transferred to Vicksburg, MS, for exchange on 5/1/1865; Exchanged at Camp Townsend, MS, on 5/6/1865. Rolls of Prisoners of War, C.S.A: Surrendered at Citronelle, AL, on 5/4/1865; Paroled at Meridian, MS, on 5/13/1865. Residence at parole: Barbour County, AL.

Danzey, S.W. (AKA L.R.) Cpl., 21st Alabama Infantry. Co. H. Federal Rolls of Prisoners of War: Captured at Fort Gaines, AL, on 8/8/1864; Received at Ship Island, MS, from New Orleans, LA, on 10/25/1864. Exchanged on 1/4/1865.

Daugherty, A. (AKA Daughety, Daugety) Pvt., 63rd Alabama Infantry. Co. E. Enlisted: 8/8/1864 at Pollard, AL. Age at enlistment: 17. Description at enlistment: Eyes: dark. Hair: dark. Complexion: dark. Rolls for 9/1864 through 10/1864: Absent, in hospital since 10/16/1864. On Register of Ross Hospital, Mobile, AL: Admitted on 10/16/1864 due to jaundice; Sent to General Hospital Hustis on 11/30/1864. Federal Rolls of Prisoners of War: Captured at Blakely, AL, on 4/9/1865; Received at Ship Island, MS, on 4/15/1865. Transferred to Vicksburg, MS, for exchange on 5/1/1865; Exchanged at Camp Townsend, MS, on 5/6/1865. Rolls of Prisoners of War, C.S.A: Surrendered at Citronelle, AL, on 5/4/1865; Paroled at Meridian, MS, on 5/13/1865. Residence at parole: Henry County, AL.

Davidson, Henry Pvt., 21st Alabama Infantry. Co. G. Federal Rolls of Prisoners of War: Captured at Fort Gaines, AL, on 8/8/1864; Received at Ship Island, MS, from New Orleans, LA, on 10/25/1864. Died: 12/30/1864 at Ship Island, MS, due to dysentery. Buried: Ship Island, MS, Cemetery in Grave #121.

Davis, H.C. Cpl., 21st Alabama Infantry. Co. I. Federal Rolls of Prisoners of War: Captured at Fort Gaines, AL, on 8/8/1864; Received at Ship Island, MS, from New Orleans, LA, on 10/25/1864. Exchanged on 1/4/1865.

Davis, J.T. Pvt., 63rd Alabama Infantry. Co. E. Enlisted: 4/1/1864 at Clayton, AL. Age at enlistment: 17. Description at enlistment: Eyes: blue. Hair: light. Complexion: fair. Rolls for 9/1864 through 10/1864: Present. Federal Rolls of Prisoners of War: Captured at Blakely, AL, on 4/9/1865; Received at Ship Island, MS, on 4/15/1865. Transferred to Vicksburg, MS, for exchange on 5/1/1865; Exchanged at Camp Townsend, MS, on 5/6/1865. Rolls of Prisoners of War, C.S.A: Surrendered at Citronelle, AL, on 5/4/1865; Paroled at Meridian, MS, on 5/13/1865. Residence at parole: Coffee County, AL.

Davis, J.W. Pvt., 63rd Alabama Infantry. Co. K. Federal Rolls of Prisoners of War: Captured at Blakely, AL, on 4/9/1865; Received at Ship Island, MS, on 4/15/1865. Transferred to Vicksburg, MS, for exchange on 5/1/1865; Exchanged at Camp Townsend, MS, on 5/6/1865.

Davis, J.W. (AKA J.N.) Pvt., 38th Alabama Infantry. Co. E. Federal Rolls of Prisoners of War: Captured at Blakely, AL, on 4/9/1865; Received at Ship Island, MS, on 4/15/1865. Transferred to Vicksburg, MS, for exchange on 5/1/1865; Exchanged at Camp Townsend, MS, on 5/6/1865.

Davis, Jefferson Pvt., 63rd Alabama Infantry. Co. E. Enlisted: 8/5/1864 at Montgomery, AL. Rolls for 9/1864 through 10/1864: Absent, without leave since 10/23/1864. Federal Rolls of Prisoners of War: Captured at Blakely, AL, on 4/9/1865; Received at Ship Island, MS, on 4/15/1865. Transferred to Vicksburg, MS, for exchange on 5/1/1865; Exchanged at Camp Townsend, MS, on 5/6/1865. Rolls of Prisoners of War, C.S.A: Surrendered at Citronelle, AL, on 5/4/1865; Paroled at New Orleans, LA, on 5/16/1865. On Register of St. Louis U.S.A. General Hospital, New Orleans, LA: Admitted on 5/16/1865 due to chronic diarrhea; Transferred to U.S.A. Marine General Hospital on 5/16/1865.

Davis, John D. Pvt., 21st Alabama Infantry. Co. H. Federal Rolls of Prisoners of War: Captured at Fort Gaines, AL, on 8/8/1864; Received at Ship Island, MS, from New Orleans, LA, on 10/25/1864. Exchanged on 1/4/1865.

Davis, John E. Pvt., 63rd Alabama Infantry. Co. B. Enlisted: 4/16/1864 at Montgomery, AL. Age at enlistment: 16. Rolls for 9/1864 through 10/1864: Present. Federal Rolls of Prisoners of War: Captured at Blakely, AL, on 4/9/1865; Received at Ship Island, MS, on 4/15/1865. Transferred to Vicksburg, MS, for exchange on 5/1/1865; Exchanged at Camp Townsend, MS, on 5/6/1865. Rolls of Prisoners of War, C.S.A: Surrendered at Citronelle, AL, on 5/4/1865; Paroled at Meridian, MS, on 5/11/1865. Residence at parole: Montgomery County, AL.

Davis, John P. (AKA J.R.) Pvt., 1st Alabama Artillery Battalion. Cos. B, C & D. Federal Rolls of Prisoners of War: Captured at Blakely, AL, on 4/9/1865; Received at Ship Island, MS, on 4/15/1865. Transferred to Vicksburg, MS, for exchange on 5/1/1865; Exchanged at Camp Townsend, MS, on 5/6/1865.

Davis, Jospeh C. Cpl., Lockhart's Battalion Infantry. Co. __. Federal Rolls of Prisoners of War: Captured at Fort Gaines, AL, on 8/8/1864; Received at Ship Island, MS, from New Orleans, LA, on 10/25/1864. Died: 11/3/1864 at Ship Island, MS, due to rubeola. Buried: Ship Island, MS, Cemetery in Grave #8.

Davis, W.A., Jr. 2nd Lt., 63rd Alabama Infantry. Co. H. Age at enlistment: 19. Description at enlistment: Eyes: dark. Hair: dark. Complexion: dark. Elected 2nd Lt. on 8/21/1864. Rolls for 9/1864 through 10/1864: Absent, sick in hospital since 10/28/1864. Federal Rolls of Prisoners of War: Captured at Blakely, AL, on 4/9/1865; Received at Ship Island, MS, on 4/15/1865. Transferred to Vicksburg, MS, for exchange on 4/28/1865; Confined at New Orleans, LA, on 4/30/1865. Exchanged at Camp Townsend, MS, on 5/6/1865. Rolls of Prisoners of War, C.S.A: Surrendered at Citronelle, AL, on 5/4/1865; Paroled at Meridian, MS, on 5/10/1865.

Davis, W.B. Pvt., 15th Alabama Infantry. Co. E. Federal Rolls of Prisoners of War: Captured at Spanish Fort, AL, on 4/8/1865; Received at Ship Island, MS, on 4/10/1865. Transferred to Vicksburg, MS, for exchange on 5/1/1865; Exchanged at Camp Townsend, MS, on 5/6/1865.

Dearman, S. Pvt., 63rd Alabama Infantry. Co. K. Enlisted: 8/28/1864 at Sumpter County, AL. Rolls for 9/1864 through 10/1864: Absent, in hospital at Mobile, AL, since 10/4/1864. Federal Rolls of Prisoners of War: Captured at Blakely, AL, on 4/9/1865; Received at Ship Island, MS, on 4/15/1865. Transferred to Vicksburg, MS, for exchange on 5/1/1865; Exchanged at Camp Townsend, MS, on 5/6/1865. Rolls of Prisoners of War, C.S.A: Surrendered at Citronelle, AL, on 5/4/1865; Paroled at Meridian, MS, on 5/13/1865. Residence at parole: Sumpter County, AL.

Deason, John (AKA Deasin, John) Pvt., Tarrant's Artillery Battery. Federal Rolls of Prisoners of War: Captured at Blakely, AL, on 4/9/1865; Received at Ship Island, MS, on 4/15/1865. Transferred to Vicksburg, MS, for exchange on 5/1/1865; Exchanged at Camp Townsend, MS, on 5/6/1865. Died: Texas.

DeBerry, W.S. (AKA DeBery, DeLerry) Pvt., 62nd Alabama Infantry. Cos. B & I. Federal Rolls of Prisoners of War: Captured at Blakely, AL, on 4/9/1865; Received at Ship Island, MS, on 4/15/1865. Transferred to Vicksburg, MS, for exchange on 5/1/1865; Exchanged at Camp Townsend, MS, on 5/6/1865.

Dees, J.A. Pvt., 18th Alabama Infantry. Co. G. Federal Rolls of Prisoners of War: Captured at Spanish Fort, AL, on 4/8/1865; Received at Ship Island, MS, on 4/10/1865. Transferred to Vicksburg, MS, for exchange on 5/1/1865; Exchanged at Camp Townsend, MS, on 5/6/1865.

DeJames, C.R. (AKA DeJarnette) Cpl., 1st Alabama Artillery Battalion. Cos. B & D. Federal Rolls of Prisoners of War: Captured at Blakely, AL, on 4/9/1865; Received at Ship Island, MS, on 4/15/1865. Transferred to Vicksburg, MS, for exchange on 5/1/1865; Exchanged at Camp Townsend, MS, on 5/6/1865.

Delery, W.S. (AKA Delerry, Deleery) Pvt., Lockhart's Battalion Infantry. Cos. B & I. Federal Rolls of Prisoners of War: Captured at Fort Gaines, AL, on 8/8/1864; Received at Ship Island, MS, from New Orleans, LA, on 10/25/1864. Exchanged on 1/4/1865.

DeLoach, S. Wesley Pvt., 21st Alabama Infantry. Co.

H. Federal Rolls of Prisoners of War: Captured at Fort Gaines, AL, on 8/8/1864; Received at Ship Island, MS, from New Orleans, LA, on 10/25/1864. Died: 12/17/1864 at Ship Island, MS, due to dysentery. Buried: Ship Island, MS, Cemetery in Grave #95.

Demony, William Sgt./1st Lt., 21st Alabama Infantry. Co. G. Federal Rolls of Prisoners of War: Captured at Fort Gaines, AL, on 8/8/1864; Received at Ship Island, MS, from New Orleans, LA, on 11/25/1864. Exchanged on 1/4/1865.

Dennis, James Pvt., Lockhart's Battalion Infantry. Co. H. Federal Rolls of Prisoners of War: Captured at Fort Gaines, AL, on 8/8/1864; Received at Ship Island, MS, from New Orleans, LA, on 10/25/1864. Exchanged on 1/4/1865.

Dennis, Patrick C. Pvt., 63rd Alabama Infantry. Co. B. Enlisted: 4/14/1864 at Montgomery, AL. Age at enlistment: 17. Rolls for 9/1864 through 10/1864: Absent, sick since 10/5/1864. Federal Rolls of Prisoners of War: Captured at Blakely, AL, on 4/9/1865; Received at Ship Island, MS, on 4/15/1865. Transferred to Vicksburg, MS, for exchange on 5/1/1865; Exchanged at Camp Townsend, MS, on 5/6/1865. Rolls of Prisoners of War, C.S.A: Surrendered at Citronelle, AL, on 5/4/1865; Paroled at Meridian, MS, on 5/11/1865. Residence at parole: Autauga County, AL.

Dent, Richard H. (AKA R.A.) Pvt., 63rd Alabama Infantry. Co. C. Enlisted: 6/22/1864 at Russell County, AL. Age at enlistment: 17. Description at enlistment: Eyes: grey. Hair: dark. Complexion: dark. Height: 5'4". Residence at enlistment: Russell County, AL. Rolls for 9/1864 through 10/1864: Present. Federal Rolls of Prisoners of War: Captured at Blakely, AL, on 4/9/1865; Received at Ship Island, MS, on 4/15/1865. Transferred to Vicksburg, MS, for exchange on 5/1/1865; Exchanged at Camp Townsend, MS, on 5/6/1865. Rolls of Prisoners of War, C.S.A: Surrendered at Citronelle, AL, on 5/4/1865; Paroled at Meridian, MS, on 5/11/1865. Residence at parole: Russell County, AL.

Denty, J.M. Pvt., 62nd Alabama Infantry. Co. C. Federal Rolls of Prisoners of War: Captured at Blakely, AL, on 4/9/1865; Received at Ship Island, MS, on 4/15/1865. Transferred to Vicksburg, MS, for exchange on 5/1/1865; Exchanged at Camp Townsend, MS, on 5/6/1865.

Denwitt, J.A. (AKA Duett, A.) Pvt., 63rd Alabama Infantry. Co. F. Federal Rolls of Prisoners of War: Captured at Blakely, AL, on 4/9/1865; Received at Ship Island, MS, on 4/15/1865. Transferred to Vicksburg, MS, for exchange on 5/1/1865; Exchanged at Camp Townsend, MS, on 5/6/1865.

Deshazo, T.L. (AKA Deshay) Pvt., 63rd Alabama Infantry. Co. D. Federal Rolls of Prisoners of War: Captured at Blakely, AL, on 4/9/1865 with a gunshot wound in arm. Received at Ship Island, MS, on 4/15/1865. Transferred to Vicksburg, MS, for exchange on 5/1/1865; Exchanged at Camp Townsend, MS, on 5/6/1865. Rolls of Prisoners of War, C.S.A: Surrendered at Citronelle, AL, on 5/4/1865; Paroled at Meridian, MS, on 5/13/1865. Residence at parole: Barbour County, AL.

DeVaughn, John (AKA DeVaun) Pvt., 62nd Alabama Infantry. Cos. G & I. Federal Rolls of Prisoners of War: Captured at Blakely, AL, on 4/9/1865; Received at Ship Island, MS, on 4/15/1865. Transferred to Vicksburg, MS, for exchange on 5/1/1865; Exchanged at Camp Townsend, MS, on 5/6/1865.

Diamond, William A. Pvt., 21st Alabama Infantry. Co. H. Federal Rolls of Prisoners of War: Captured at Fort Gaines, AL, on 8/8/1864; Received at Ship Island, MS, from New Orleans, LA, on 10/25/1864. Died: Ship Island, MS, on 12/1/1864 due to dysentery. Buried: Ship Island, MS, Cemetery in Grave #56.

Dickens, Hampton Pvt., 21st Alabama Infantry. Co. I. Federal Rolls of Prisoners of War: Captured at Fort Gaines, AL, on 8/8/1864; Received at Ship Island, MS, from New Orleans, LA, on 10/25/1864. Exchanged on 1/4/1865. Born: 8/6/1842. Died: 4/8/1928. Buried: Union Cemetery.

Dickins, J.N. Pvt., 36th Alabama Infantry. Co. C. Federal Rolls of Prisoners of War: Captured in Alabama on 3/24/1865; Received at Ship Island, MS. Transferred to Vicksburg, MS, for exchange on 5/1/1865; Exchanged at Camp Townsend, MS, on 5/6/1865.

Dickinson, B.L. (AKA Dickerson, B.S., S.B.) Pvt., 62nd Alabama Infantry & Lockhart's Battalion Infantry. Co. H. Federal Rolls of Prisoners of War: Captured at Blakely, AL, on 4/9/1865; Received at Ship Island, MS, on 4/15/1865. Transferred to Vicksburg, MS, for exchange on 5/1/1865; Exchanged at Camp Townsend, MS, on 5/6/1865.

Dismukes, G.W. Pvt., 21st Alabama Infantry. Co. C. Federal Rolls of Prisoners of War: Captured at Fort Gaines, AL, on 8/8/1864; Received at Ship Island, MS, from New Orleans, LA, on 10/25/1864. Exchanged on 1/4/1865.

Dodds, Charles A. Pvt., 62nd Alabama Infantry. Co. D. Federal Rolls of Prisoners of War: Captured at Blakely, AL, on 4/9/1865; Received at Ship Island, MS, on 4/15/1865. Transferred to Vicksburg, MS, for exchange on 5/1/1865; Exchanged at Camp Townsend, MS, on 5/6/1865.

Dodson, G.W. Pvt., 38th Alabama Infantry. Co. H. Enlisted: 5/13/1862 at Fort Gaines, AL. Age at enlistment: 22. Federal Rolls of Prisoners of War: Captured at Spanish Fort, AL, on 4/8/1865; Received at Ship Island, MS, on 4/10/1865. Transferred to Vicksburg, MS, for exchange on 5/1/1865; Exchanged at Camp Townsend, MS, on 5/6/1865.

Doggett, George W. (AKA J.W.) Pvt., 38th Alabama Infantry. Cos. C & G. Received sick furlough on 7/18/1863 through 8/27/1863. Federal Rolls of Prisoners of War: Captured at Spanish Fort, AL, on 4/8/1865; Received at Ship Island, MS, on 4/10/1865. Transferred to Vicksburg, MS, for exchange on 5/1/1865; Exchanged at Camp Townsend, MS, on 5/6/1865.

Dollar, Elisha Pvt., 63rd Alabama Infantry. Co. A. Enlisted: 7/17/1864 at Macon County, AL. Rolls for 9/1864 through 10/1864: Present. Federal Rolls of Prisoners of War: Captured at Blakely, AL, on 4/9/1865; Received at Ship Island, MS, on 4/15/1865. Transferred to Vicksburg, MS, for exchange on 5/1/1865; Exchanged at Camp Townsend, MS, on 5/6/1865. Rolls of Prisoners of War, C.S.A: Surrendered at Citronelle, AL, on 5/4/1865; Paroled at Meridian, MS, on 5/13/1865. Residence at parole: Macon County, AL.

Dollar, W.H. (AKA W.T., N.T.) Pvt., Lockhart's Battalion Infantry. Co. H. Federal Rolls of Prisoners of War: Captured at Fort Gaines, AL, on 8/8/1864; Received at Ship Island, MS, from New Orleans, LA, on 10/25/1864. Exchanged on 1/4/1865.

Dominick, J.L. Pvt., Tarrant's Artillery Battery. Federal Rolls of Prisoners of War: Captured at Blakely, AL, on 4/9/1865; Received at Ship Island, MS, on 4/15/1865. Transferred to Vicksburg, MS, for exchange on 5/1/1865; Exchanged at Camp Townsend, MS, on 5/6/1865.

Dominick, W.D. Pvt., Tarrant's Artillery Battery. Federal Rolls of Prisoners of War: Captured at Blakely, AL, on 4/9/1865; Received at Ship Island, MS, on 4/15/1865. Transferred to Vicksburg, MS, for exchange on 5/1/1865; Exchanged at Camp Townsend, MS, on 5/6/1865.

Donald, William Pvt./2nd Lt., 63rd Alabama Infantry. Co. F. Enlisted: 5/30/1864; Elected 2nd Lt. on 6/28/1864. Age at enlistment: 17. Description at enlistment: Eyes: blue. Hair: dark. Complexion: fair. Height: 5'8½". Residence at enlistment: Richmond, VA. Rolls for 9/1864 through 10/1864: Present. Federal Rolls of Prisoners of War: Captured at Blakely, AL, on 4/9/1865; Received at Ship Island, MS, on 4/16/1865. Transferred to Vicksburg, MS, for exchange on 4/28/1865; Confined at New Orleans, LA, on 4/30/1865. Exchanged at Camp Townsend, MS, on 5/6/1865.

Doss, F. Pvt., 63rd Alabama Infantry. Co. F. Federal Rolls of Prisoners of War: Captured at Blakely, AL, on 4/9/1865; Received at Ship Island, MS, on 4/15/1865. Transferred to Vicksburg, MS, for exchange on 5/1/1865; Exchanged at Camp Townsend, MS, on 5/6/1865. Rolls of Prisoners of War, C.S.A: Surrendered at Citronelle, AL, on 5/4/1865; Paroled at Meridian, MS, on 5/11/1865. Residence at parole: Dallas County, AL.

Douglas, S.W. Pvt., 8th Alabama Cavalry. Co. F. Federal Rolls of Prisoners of War: Captured in Florida on 3/20/1865; Received at Ship Island, MS. Transferred to Vicksburg, MS, for exchange on 5/1/1865; Exchanged at Camp Townsend, MS, on 5/6/1865.

Douglas, Walton (AKA Walter) Sgt., Lockhart's Battalion Infantry. Co. H. Federal Rolls of Prisoners of War: Captured at Fort Gaines, AL, on 8/8/1864; Received at Ship Island, MS, from New Orleans, LA, on 10/25/1864. Exchanged on 1/4/1865.

Douglas, William E. (AKA Walton) Sgt., 62nd Alabama Infantry. Co. H. Federal Rolls of Prisoners of War: Captured at Blakely, AL, on 4/9/1865; Received at Ship Island, MS, on 4/15/1865. Transferred to Vicksburg, MS, for exchange on 5/1/1865; Exchanged at Camp Townsend, MS, on 5/6/1865.

Dowling, J.C. Pvt., Tarrant's Artillery Battery. Federal Rolls of Prisoners of War: Captured at Blakely, AL, on 4/9/1865; Received at Ship Island, MS, on 4/15/1865. Transferred to Vicksburg, MS, for exchange on 5/1/1865; Exchanged at Camp Townsend, MS, on 5/6/1865.

Dowling, W.T. Pvt., 63rd Alabama Infantry. Co. E. Federal Rolls of Prisoners of War: Captured at Blakely, AL, on 4/9/1865; Received at Ship Island, MS, on 4/15/1865. Transferred to Vicksburg, MS, for exchange on 5/1/1865. On Register of U.S.A. General Hospital #2, Vicksburg, MS: Admitted from steamer on 5/3/1865 due to chronic diarrhea; Returned to duty on 5/12/1865. On Register of U.S.A. Post Hospital, Jackson, MS: Admitted on 5/15/1865 due to chronic diarrhea.

Downey, John (AKA Donnio) Pvt., 21st Alabama Infantry. Co. C. Federal Rolls of Prisoners of War: Captured at Fort Gaines, AL, on 8/8/1864; Received at Ship Island, MS, from New Orleans, LA, on 10/25/1864. Died: 11/17/1864 at Ship Island, MS, due to diarrhea. Buried: Ship Island, MS, Cemetery in Grave #25.

Downey, William J. Pvt., 38th Alabama Infantry. Co. C. Enlisted: 5/13/1862 at Choctaw, AL; Mustered into service: 5/27/1862 near Fort Stoddard, AL. Age at enlistment: 20. On extra duty from 1/1863 through 3/1863 as Teamster at camp near Mobile, AL, and 4/1863 through 5/1863 at Wartrace, TN. On extra duty as Teamster from 8/1863 through 11/1863. Federal Rolls of Prisoners of War: Captured at Blakely, AL, on 4/9/1865; Received at Ship Island, MS, on 4/15/1865. Transferred to Vicksburg, MS, for exchange on 5/1/1865; Exchanged at Camp Townsend, MS, on 5/6/1865.

Downs, Willis A. Pvt., 63rd Alabama Infantry. Co. A. Enlisted: 1/1/1864 at Tallapoosa County, AL. Rolls for 1/1864 through 2/1864: Present. Rolls for 9/1864 through 10/1864: Absent, sick in hospital at Greenville, AL, since 9/5/1864. Federal Rolls of Prisoners of War: Captured at Blakely, AL, on 4/9/1865; Received at Ship Island, MS, on 4/15/1865. Transferred to Vicksburg, MS, for exchange on 5/1/1865; Exchanged at Camp Townsend, MS, on 5/6/1865. Rolls of Prisoners of War, C.S.A: Surrendered at Citronelle, AL, on 5/4/1865; Paroled at Meridian, MS, on 5/13/1865. Residence at parole: Tallapoosa County, AL.

Draper, J. Pvt., 62nd Alabama Infantry. Co. D. Federal Rolls of Prisoners of War: Captured at Blakely, AL, on 4/9/1865; Received at Ship Island, MS, on 4/15/1865. Transferred to Vicksburg, MS, for exchange on 5/1/1865; Exchanged at Camp Townsend, MS, on 5/6/1865.

Draper, P.M. Pvt., 21st Alabama Infantry. Co. D. Federal Rolls of Prisoners of War: Captured at Blakely, AL, on 4/9/1865; Received at Ship Island, MS, on 4/15/1865. Transferred to Vicksburg, MS, for exchange on 5/1/1865; Exchanged at Camp Townsend, MS, on 5/6/1865.

Driver, W.T. Pvt., 63rd Alabama Infantry. Co. F. Enlisted: 3/9/1864 at Greenville, AL. Age at enlistment: 17. Description at enlistment: Eyes: blue. Hair: light. Complexion: sallow. Height: 5'7". Residence at enlistment: Butler County, AL. Rolls for 9/1864 through 10/1864: Absent, in hospital since 8/12/1864. Federal Rolls of Prisoners of War: Captured at Blakely, AL, on 4/9/1865; Received at Ship Island, MS, on 4/15/1865. Transferred to Vicksburg, MS, for exchange on 5/1/1865; Exchanged at Camp Townsend, MS, on 5/6/1865. Rolls of Prisoners of War, C.S.A: Surrendered at Citronelle, AL, on 5/4/1865; Paroled at Meridian, MS, on 5/11/1865. Residence at parole: Butler County, AL.

Drummond, W.H. Ord. Sgt., 36th Alabama Infantry. Co. I. Federal Rolls of Prisoners of War: Captured at Spanish Fort, AL, on 4/8/1865; Received at Ship Island, MS, on 4/10/1865. Transferred to Vicksburg, MS, for exchange on 5/1/1865; Exchanged at Camp Townsend, MS, on 5/6/1865.

Drummonds, Benjamin F. (AKA Drummond) Pvt., 62nd Alabama Infantry. Co. E. Federal Rolls of Prisoners of War: Captured at Blakely, AL, on 4/9/1865; Received at Ship Island, MS, on 4/15/1865. Transferred to Vicksburg, MS, for exchange on 5/1/1865; Exchanged at Camp Townsend, MS, on 5/6/1865.

Duberry, Thomas (AKA W.T.) Pvt., 63rd Alabama Infantry. Co. E. Federal Rolls of Prisoners of War: Captured at Blakely, AL, on 4/9/1865; Received at Ship Island, MS, on 4/15/1865. Transferred to Vicksburg, MS, for exchange on 5/1/1865; Exchanged at Camp Townsend, MS, on 5/6/1865.

DuBose, C.B. (AKA V.B.) Pvt., 21st Alabama Infantry. Co. C. Federal Rolls of Prisoners of War: Captured at Fort Gaines, AL, on 8/8/1864; Received at Ship Island, MS, from New Orleans, LA, on 10/25/1864. Exchanged on 1/4/1865.

Duggan, Patrick Pvt., 21st Alabama Infantry. Co. B. Federal Rolls of Prisoners of War: Captured at Fort Gaines, AL, on 8/8/1864; Received at Ship Island, MS, from New Orleans, LA, on 10/25/1864. Exchanged on 1/4/1865.

Duite, W.G.B. Pvt., 62nd Alabama Infantry. Co. B. Federal Rolls of Prisoners of War: Captured at Blakely, AL, on 4/9/1865; Received at Ship Island, MS, on 4/15/1865. Transferred to Vicksburg, MS, for exchange on 5/1/1865; Exchanged at Camp Townsend, MS, on 5/6/1865.

Duke, J.H. Pvt., 63rd Alabama Infantry. Co. E. Enlisted: 8/25/1864 at Blakely, AL. Age at enlistment: 17. Description at enlistment: Eyes: dark. Hair: dark. Complexion: dark. Rolls for 9/1864 through 10/1864: Absent, in hospital since 9/25/1864. On Register of Ross Hospital, Mobile, AL: Admitted on 9/26/1864 due to acute diarrhea, febris remittens, and rubeola; Received 30 day sick furlough. Federal Rolls of Prisoners of War: Captured at Blakely, AL, on 4/9/1865; Received at Ship Island, MS, on 4/15/1865. Transferred to Vicksburg, MS, for exchange on 5/1/1865; Exchanged at Camp Townsend, MS, on 5/6/1865. Rolls of Prisoners of War, C.S.A: Surrendered at Citronelle, AL, on 5/4/1865; Paroled at Meridian, MS, on 5/13/1865. Residence at parole: Dale County, AL.

Dunaway, Jesse M. Pvt., 21st Alabama Infantry. Co. __. Federal Rolls of Prisoners of War: Captured at Fort Gaines, AL, on 8/8/1864; Received at Ship Island, MS, from New Orleans, LA, on 10/25/1864. Transferred to Vicksburg, MS, for exchange on 5/1/1865; Exchanged at Camp Townsend, MS, on 5/6/1865. Rolls of Prisoners of War, C.S.A: Surrendered at Citronelle, AL, on 5/4/1865; Paroled at Meridian, MS, in 5/1865. He wrote to *Confederate Veteran Magazine* in 1905 regarding his wartime experiences.

Duncan, Rhodes Pvt., 63rd Alabama Infantry. Co. E. Enlisted: Rockford, AL. Rolls for 9/1864 through 10/1864: Present. Federal Rolls of Prisoners of War: Captured at Blakely, AL, on 4/9/1865; Received at Ship Island, MS, on 4/15/1865. Transferred to Vicksburg, MS, for exchange on 5/1/1865; Exchanged at Camp Townsend, MS, on 5/6/1865. Rolls of Prisoners of War, C.S.A: Surrendered at Citronelle, AL, on 5/4/1865; Paroled at Meridian, MS, on 5/11/1865. Residence at parole: Coosa County, AL. Confederate Pension Application dated 1915 on file at the Texas State Library and Archives Commission. Target Name: Duncan, Rhodes. Pension Number: 33568. County: Eastland. Also a Confederate Widows Pension Application on file. Target Name: Duncan, Rhodes Mrs. Pension Number: 43780. County: Eastland.

Dunclin, Joseph C. (AKA Dunklin, Dunclaire) Pvt., Lockhart's Battalion Infantry. Co. K. Federal Rolls of Prisoners of War: Captured at Fort Gaines, AL, on 8/8/1864; Received at Ship Island, MS, from New Orleans, LA, on 10/25/1864. Died: 12/15/1864 at Ship Island, MS, due to gunshot from a sentinel. Buried: Ship Island, MS, Cemetery in Grave #91.

Dunlap, Ezekiel H. (AKA Dulap) Pvt., 62nd Alabama Infantry. Co. A. Federal Rolls of Prisoners of War: Captured at Blakely, AL, on 4/9/1865; Received at Ship Island, MS, on 4/15/1865. Transferred to Vicksburg, MS, for exchange on 5/1/1865; Exchanged at Camp Townsend, MS, on 5/6/1865. Buried: Bibb County, AL.

Dunn, J.A. Pvt., 6th Alabama Cavalry. Co. E. Federal Rolls of Prisoners of War: Captured at Flintday, AL, on 3/25/1865; Received at Ship Island, MS. Transferred to Vicksburg, MS, for exchange on 5/1/1865; Exchanged at Camp Townsend, MS, on 5/6/1865.

Dunn, John B (AKA J.A.). Pvt., 1st Alabama Artillery Battalion. Co. D. Federal Rolls of Prisoners of War: Captured at Fort Gaines, AL, on 8/8/1864; Received at Ship Island, MS, on 10/25/1864. Died: 12/24/1864 at Ship Island, MS, due to dysentery. Buried: Ship Island, MS, Cemetery in Grave #110.

Dunn, William J. Pvt., 21st Alabama Infantry. Co. D. Federal Rolls of Prisoners of War: Captured at Blakely, AL, on 4/9/1865; Received at Ship Island, MS, on 4/15/1865. Transferred to Vicksburg, MS, for exchange on 5/1/1865; Exchanged at Camp Townsend, MS, on 5/6/1865.

Dunnam, E.C. Pvt./Cpl., 62nd Alabama Infantry. Co. I. Federal Rolls of Prisoners of War: Captured at Blakely, AL, on 4/9/1865; Received at Ship Island, MS, on 4/15/1865. Transferred to Vicksburg, MS, for exchange on 5/1/1865; Exchanged at Camp Townsend, MS, on 5/6/1865.

Dunnard, F.M. Pvt., Lockhart's Battalion Infantry. Co. I. Federal Rolls of Prisoners of War: Captured at Fort Gaines, AL, on 8/8/1864; Received at Ship Island, MS, from New Orleans, LA, on 10/25/1864. Exchanged on 3/2/1865.

Dunnaway, Jesse W. Pvt., 21st Alabama Infantry. Co. G. Federal Rolls of Prisoners of War: Captured at Fort Gaines, AL, on 8/8/1864; Received at Ship Island, MS, from New Orleans, LA, on 10/25/1864. Exchanged on 1/4/1865.

Durrett, N.B. Pvt., Tarrant's Artillery Battery. Federal Rolls of Prisoners of War: Captured at Blakely, AL, on 4/9/1865; Received at Ship Island, MS, on 4/15/1865. Transferred to Vicksburg, MS, for exchange on 5/1/1865; Exchanged at Camp Townsend, MS, on 5/6/1865.

Early, William G. 1st Sgt., 21st Alabama Infantry. Co. G. Federal Rolls of Prisoners of War: Captured at Fort Gaines, AL, on 8/8/1864; Received at Ship Island, MS, from New Orleans, LA, on 10/25/1864. Exchanged on 1/4/1865.

East, Benjamin R. Cpl./Pvt., 62nd Alabama Infantry. Co. G. Federal Rolls of Prisoners of War: Captured at Blakely, AL, on 4/9/1865; Received at Ship Island, MS, on 4/15/1865. Transferred to Vicksburg, MS, for exchange on 5/1/1865; Exchanged at Camp Townsend, MS, on 5/6/1865.

Echols, Benson W. Pvt., 63rd Alabama Infantry. Co. B. Enlisted: 8/15/1864 at Pollard, AL. Rolls for 9/1864 through 10/1864: Present. Federal Rolls of Prisoners of War: Captured at Blakely, AL, on 4/9/1865; Received at Ship Island, MS, on 4/15/1865. Transferred to Vicksburg, MS, for exchange on 5/1/1865; Exchanged at Camp Townsend, MS, on 5/6/1865. Rolls of Prisoners of War, C.S.A: Surrendered at Citronelle, AL, on 5/4/1865; Paroled at Meridian, MS, on 5/11/1865. Residence at parole: Dale County, AL.

Echols, John H. Capt./Maj./Lt. Col., 63rd Alabama Infantry. Co. A.F. & S. Elected Capt. on 1/1/1864. Rolls for 1/1864 through 2/1864: Absent, detached on 12/1/1863 as Acting Provost Marshal at Montgomery, AL, per Special Order #262. Rolls for 7/1864 through 8/1864: Present, appointed Major on 8/16/1864 by order of the Secretary of War. Rolls for 9/1864 through 10/1864: Absent, on 12 day furlough since 10/20/1864 by order of Maj. Gen. Dabney H. Maury. Federal Rolls of Prisoners of War: Captured at Blakely, AL, on 4/9/1865; Confined for one day at Spanish Fort, AL. Received at Ship Island, MS, on 4/16/1865; Transferred to Vicksburg, MS, for exchange on 4/28/1865. Confined at New Orleans, LA, on 4/30/1865; Exchanged at Camp Townsend, MS, on 5/6/1865. Rolls of Prisoners of War, C.S.A: Surrendered at Citronelle, AL, on 5/4/1865; Paroled at Meridian, MS, on 5/12/1865.

Edgar, A.A. Pvt./1st Lt., 63rd Alabama Infantry. Co. F. Enlisted: 3/9/1864 at Butler County, AL; Elected 1st Lt. on 6/28/1864. Age at enlistment: 46. Description at enlistment: Eyes: blue. Hair: dark. Height: 5'8". Residence at enlistment: Butler County, AL. Rolls for 9/1864 through 10/1864: Present. Federal Rolls of Prisoners of War: Captured at Blakely, AL, on 4/9/1865; Confined one day at Spanish Fort, AL. Received at Ship Island, MS, on 4/16/1865; Transferred to Vicksburg, MS, for exchange on 4/28/1865. Confined at New Orleans, LA, on 4/30/1865; Exchanged at Camp Townsend, MS, on 5/6/1865. Rolls of Prisoners of War, C.S.A: Surrendered at Citronelle, AL, on 5/4/1865; Paroled at Meridian, MS, on 5/11/1865.

Edgar, H. Cpl., 58th Alabama Infantry. Co. K. Federal Rolls of Prisoners of War: Captured at Spanish Fort, AL, on 4/8/1865; Received at Ship Island, MS, on 4/10/1865. Transferred to Vicksburg, MS, for exchange on 5/1/1865; Exchanged at Camp Townsend, MS, on 5/6/1865.

Edgar, J. Pvt., 58th Alabama Infantry. Co. K. Federal Rolls of Prisoners of War: Captured at Spanish Fort, AL, on 4/8/1865; Received at Ship Island, MS, on 4/10/1865. Transferred to Vicksburg, MS, for exchange on 5/1/1865; Exchanged at Camp Townsend, MS, on 5/6/1865.

Edings, S.A. Pvt., 62nd Alabama Infantry. Co. A. Federal Rolls of Prisoners of War: Captured at Blakely, AL, on 4/9/1865; Received at Ship Island, MS, on 4/15/1865. Transferred to Vicksburg, MS, for exchange on 5/1/1865; Exchanged at Camp Townsend, MS, on 5/6/1865.

Edmonds, R.S. (AKA Edwards) Pvt., 8th Alabama Cavalry. Co. D. Federal Rolls of Prisoners of War: Captured in Alabama on 3/24/1864; Received at Ship Island, MS. Transferred to Vicksburg, MS, for exchange on 5/1/1865; Exchanged at Camp Townsend, MS, on 5/6/1865.

Edmundson, J. (AKA Edmondson) Pvt., 21st Alabama Infantry. Co. C. Federal Rolls of Prisoners of War: Captured at Fort Gaines, AL, on 8/8/1864; Received at Ship Island, MS, from New Orleans, LA, on 10/25/1864. Exchanged on 1/4/1865.

Edwards, Alva C. Pvt., 63rd Alabama Infantry. Co. A. Enlisted: 3/1/1864 at Coosa County, AL. Rolls for 9/1864 through 10/1864: Absent, sick in hospital at Mobile, AL, since 10/15/1864. Federal Rolls of Prisoners of War: Captured at Blakely, AL, on 4/9/1865; Received at Ship Island, MS, on 4/15/1865. Transferred to Vicksburg, MS, for exchange on 5/1/1865; Exchanged at Camp Townsend, MS, on 5/6/1865. Rolls of Prisoners of War, C.S.A: Surrendered at Citronelle, AL, on 5/4/1865; Paroled at Meridian, MS, on 5/13/1865. Residence at parole: Coosa County, AL.

Edwards, Benjamin Pvt., 21st Alabama Infantry. Co. H. Federal Rolls of Prisoners of War: Captured at Fort Gaines, AL, on 8/8/1864; Received at Ship Island, MS, from New Orleans, LA, on 10/25/1864. Died: 12/11/1864 at Ship Island, MS, due to chronic dysentery. Buried: Ship Island, MS, Cemetery in Grave #78.

Edwards, W. Sgt., 62nd Alabama Infantry. Co. I. Federal Rolls of Prisoners of War: Captured at Blakely, AL, on 4/9/1865; Received at Ship Island, MS, on 4/15/1865. Transferred to Vicksburg, MS, for exchange on 5/1/1865; Exchanged at Camp Townsend, MS, on 5/6/1865.

Eisland, George W. (AKA Eland, Erland) Pvt., 63rd Alabama Infantry. Co. H. Enlisted: 9/12/1864 near Blakely, AL. Age at enlistment: 17. Description at enlistment: Eyes: dark. Hair: dark. Complexion: dark. Rolls for 9/1864 through 10/1864: Present. Federal Rolls of Prisoners of War: Captured at Blakely, AL, on 4/9/1865; Received at Ship Island, MS, on 4/15/1865. Transferred to Vicksburg, MS, for exchange on 5/1/1865. On Register of St. Louis U.S.A. General Hospital, New Orleans, LA: Admitted on 5/3/1865 due to chronic diarrhea; Transferred to U.S.A. Marine General Hospital on 5/16/1865. Rolls of Prisoners of War, C.S.A: Surrendered at Citronelle, AL, on 5/4/1865; Paroled at New Orleans, LA, on 5/16/1865.

Elam, J.W. Pvt., 7th Alabama Cavalry. Co. C. Federal Rolls of Prisoners of War: Captured at Baton Rouge, LA, on 4/2/1864; Received at Ship Island, MS, from New Orleans, LA, on 10/7/1864. Transferred to Fort Columbus, New York Harbor, NY, on 11/5/1864.

Elliott, Charles Pvt., 21st Alabama Infantry. Co. F. Federal Rolls of Prisoners of War: Captured at Fort Gaines, AL, on 8/8/1864; Received at Ship Island, MS, from New Orleans, LA, on 10/25/1864. Exchanged on 1/4/1865.

Elliott, J.M. Pvt., 21st Alabama Infantry. Co. D. Federal Rolls of Prisoners of War: Captured at Fort Gaines, AL, on 8/8/1864; Received at Ship Island, MS, from New Orleans, LA, on 10/25/1864. Exchanged on 1/4/1865.

Elliott, Samuel J. (AKA Ellett) Pvt., 1st Alabama Artillery

Battalion. Co. B. Federal Rolls of Prisoners of War: Captured at Fort Gaines, AL, on 8/8/1864; Received at Ship Island, MS, from New Orleans, LA, on 10/25/1864. Exchanged on 1/4/1865.

Ellis, Benjamin Franklin Pvt., 63rd Alabama Infantry. Co. G. Enlisted: 3/16/1864 at Troy, AL. Age at enlistment: 17. Description at enlistment: Eyes: blue. Hair: light. Complexion: fair. Height: 5'5". Residence at enlistment: Coffee County, AL. Rolls for 9/1864 through 10/1864: Present. Federal Rolls of Prisoners of War: Captured at Blakely, AL, on 4/9/1865; Received at Ship Island, MS, on 4/15/1865. Transferred to Vicksburg, MS, for exchange on 5/1/1865; Exchanged at Camp Townsend, MS, on 5/6/1865. Rolls of Prisoners of War, C.S.A: Surrendered at Citronelle, AL, on 5/4/1865; Paroled at Meridian, MS, on 5/13/1865. Residence at parole: Pike County, AL. Born: 2/28/1847 at Taylor County, GA. Soldier is recorded on the 1907 Alabama Census of Confederate Veterans and Widows. Residence: Crenshaw County, AL.

Ellis, E. (Elles) Sgt., Tarrant's Artillery Battery. Federal Rolls of Prisoners of War: Captured at Blakely, AL, on 4/9/1865; Received at Ship Island, MS, on 4/15/1865. Transferred to Vicksburg, MS, for exchange on 5/1/1865; Exchanged at Camp Townsend, MS, on 5/6/1865.

Ellis, J. Hosp. Stew., 38th Alabama Infantry. F & S. Federal Rolls of Prisoners of War: Captured at Spanish Fort, AL, on 4/8/1865; Received at Ship Island, MS, on 4/10/1865. Transferred to Vicksburg, MS, for exchange on 5/1/1865; Exchanged at Camp Townsend, MS, on 5/6/1865.

Ellis, J.F. (AKA F.F.) Cpl., 62nd Alabama Infantry. Co. I. Federal Rolls of Prisoners of War: Captured at Blakely, AL, on 4/9/1865; Received at Ship Island, MS, on 4/15/1865. Transferred to Vicksburg, MS, for exchange on 5/1/1865; Exchanged at Camp Townsend, MS, on 5/6/1865.

Ellis, S.L. Pvt., 62nd Alabama Infantry. Co. F. Federal Rolls of Prisoners of War: Captured at Blakely, AL, on 4/9/1865; Received at Ship Island, MS, on 4/15/1865. Transferred to Vicksburg, MS, for exchange on 5/1/1865; Exchanged at Camp Townsend, MS, on 5/6/1865.

Ellis, Thomas J. 2nd Lt., Lockhart's Battalion Infantry. Co. I. Federal Rolls of Prisoners of War: Captured at Fort Gaines, AL, on 8/8/1864; Received at Ship Island, MS, from New Orleans, LA, on 10/25/1864. Exchanged on 1/4/1865.

Ellison, Samuel Pvt., 63rd Alabama Infantry. Co. I. Federal Rolls of Prisoners of War: Captured at Blakely, AL, on 4/9/1865; Received at Ship Island, MS, on 4/15/1865. Transferred to Vicksburg, MS, for exchange on 5/1/1865; Exchanged at Camp Townsend, MS, on 5/6/1865. Rolls of Prisoners of War, C.S.A: Surrendered at Citronelle, AL, on 5/4/1865; Paroled at Meridian, MS, on 5/13/1865. Residence at parole: Shelby County, AL.

Emmerson, F.H. (AKA Emerson, T.H.) Pvt., 1st Alabama Battalion Cadets. Co. A. Federal Rolls of Prisoners of War: Captured at Fort Gaines, AL, on 8/8/1864; Received at Ship Island, MS, from New Orleans, LA, on 10/29/1864. Exchanged on 1/4/1865.

English, Alfred Pvt., 63rd Alabama Infantry. Co. C. Enlisted: 5/11/1864 at Russell County, AL. Age at enlistment: 17. Description at enlistment: Eyes: hazel. Hair: light. Complexion: sallow. Height: 5'7". Residence at enlistment: Columbus, GA. Rolls for 9/1864 through 10/1864: Present. Federal Rolls of Prisoners of War: Captured at Blakely, AL, on 4/9/1865; Received at Ship Island, MS, on 4/15/1865. Transferred to Vicksburg, MS, for exchange on 5/1/1865; Exchanged at Camp Townsend, MS, on 5/6/1865. Rolls of Prisoners of War, C.S.A: Surrendered at Citronelle, AL, on 5/4/1865; Paroled at Meridian, MS, on 5/10/1865 while a patient in Quintard Hospital. Residence at parole: Russell County, AL.

Enzor, Henry Pvt., 63rd Alabama Infantry. Co. A. Enlisted: 2/1/1864 at Montgomery, AL. Rolls for 9/1864 through 10/1864: Present. Federal Rolls of Prisoners of War: Captured at Blakely, AL, on 4/9/1865; Received at Ship Island, MS, on 4/15/1865. Transferred to Vicksburg, MS, for exchange on 5/1/1865; Exchanged at Camp Townsend, MS, on 5/6/1865. Rolls of Prisoners of War, C.S.A: Surrendered at Citronelle, AL, on 5/4/1865; Paroled at Meridian, MS, on 5/13/1865. Residence at parole: Montgomery County, AL.

Essels, Andus Cpl., 6th Alabama Cavalry. Co. C. Federal Rolls of Prisoners of War: Captured at Flintday, AL, on 3/25/1864; Received at Ship Island, MS. Disposition unknown.

Essman, Charles E. Sgt., 63rd Alabama Infantry. Co. I. Enlisted: 4/15/1864 at Columbiana, AL. Rolls for 9/1864 through 10/1864: Present. Federal Rolls of Prisoners of War: Captured at Blakely, AL, on 4/9/1865; Received at Ship Island, MS, on 4/15/1865. Transferred to Vicksburg, MS, for exchange on 5/1/1865; Exchanged at Camp Townsend, MS, on 5/6/1865. Rolls of Prisoners of War, C.S.A: Surrendered at Citronelle, AL, on 5/4/1865; Paroled at Meridian, MS, on 5/13/1865. Residence at parole: Shelby County, AL.

Etheredge, J.W. (AKA Esturedge) Pvt., 21st Alabama Infantry. Co. C. Federal Rolls of Prisoners of War: Captured at Fort Gaines, AL, on 8/8/1864; Received at Ship Island, MS, from New Orleans, LA, on 10/25/1864. Exchanged on 1/4/1865.

Etheredge, S.E. (AKA Etherage) Pvt., 21st Alabama Infantry. Co. C. Federal Rolls of Prisoners of War: Captured at Fort Gaines, AL, on 8/8/1864; Received at Ship Island, MS, from New Orleans, LA, on 10/25/1864. Exchanged on 1/4/1865.

Etheredge, W.J. Pvt., 21st Alabama Infantry. Co. C. Federal Rolls of Prisoners of War: Captured at Fort Gaines, AL, on 8/8/1864; Received at Ship Island, MS, from New Orleans, LA, on 10/25/1864. Exchanged on 1/4/1865.

Etheridge, E.T. (AKA Esturedge) Pvt., 21st Alabama Infantry. Co. C. Federal Rolls of Prisoners of War: Captured at Fort Gaines, AL, on 8/8/1864; Received at Ship Island, MS, from New Orleans, LA, on 10/25/1864. Exchanged on 1/4/1865.

Eubanks, J.P. Pvt., 62nd Alabama Infantry. Co. E. Federal Rolls of Prisoners of War: Captured at Blakely, AL, on 4/9/1865; Received at Ship Island, MS, on 4/15/1865. Transferred to Vicksburg, MS, for exchange on 5/1/1865; Exchanged at Camp Townsend, MS, on 5/6/1865.

Euzon, A. Pvt., 63rd Alabama Infantry. Co. A. Federal Rolls of Prisoners of War: Captured at Blakely, AL, on 4/9/1865; Received at Ship Island, MS, on 4/15/1865. Transferred to Vicksburg, MS, for exchange on 5/1/1865; Exchanged at Camp Townsend, MS, on 5/6/1865.

Evans, Fielden Pvt., 62nd Alabama Infantry. Co. B. Federal Rolls of Prisoners of War: Captured at Blakely, AL, on 4/9/1865; Received at Ship Island, MS, on 4/15/1865. Transferred to Vicksburg, MS, for exchange on 5/1/1865; Exchanged at Camp Townsend, MS, on 5/6/1865.

Evans, John T. (AKA T.I., T.J.) Cpl./Pvt., 63rd Alabama Infantry. Co. I. Enlisted: 4/15/1864 at Columbiana, AL. Rolls for 9/1864 through 10/1864: Present. On Register of Ross Hospital, Mobile, AL: Admitted on 11/11/1864 due to febris intermittens; Returned to duty on 11/18/1864. Federal Rolls of Prisoners of War: Captured at Blakely, AL, on 4/9/1865; Received at Ship Island, MS, on 4/15/1865. Transferred to Vicksburg, MS, for exchange on 5/1/1865; Exchanged at Camp Townsend, MS, on 5/6/1865. Rolls of Prisoners of War, C.S.A: Surrendered at Citronelle, AL, on 5/4/1865; Paroled at Meridian, MS, on 5/13/1865. Residence at parole: Shelby County, AL.

Evans, Thomas Pvt., 32nd Alabama Infantry. Co. A. Federal Rolls of Prisoners of War: Captured at Spanish Fort, AL, on 4/8/1865; Received at Ship Island, MS, on 4/10/1865. Transferred to Vicksburg, MS, for exchange on 5/1/1865; Exchanged at Camp Townsend, MS, on 5/6/1865.

Ewing, J. Pvt., 1st Alabama Artillery Battalion. Co.__. Federal Rolls of Prisoners of War: Captured at Blakely, AL, on 4/9/1865; Received at Ship Island, MS, on 4/15/1865. Transferred to Vicksburg, MS, for exchange on 5/1/1865; Exchanged at Camp Townsend, MS, on 5/6/1865.

Ezell, G.W. (AKA Ezzell) Pvt., 21st Alabama Infantry. Co. H. Federal Rolls of Prisoners of War: Captured at Fort Gaines, AL, on 8/8/1864; Received at Ship Island, MS, from New Orleans, LA, on 10/25/1864. Exchanged on 1/4/1865.

Faber, Phillip Pvt., 63rd Alabama Infantry. Co. B. Federal Rolls of Prisoners of War: Captured at Blakely, AL, on 4/9/1865; Received at Ship Island, MS, on 4/15/1865. Transferred to Vicksburg, MS, for exchange on 5/1/1865; Exchanged at Camp Townsend, MS, on 5/6/1865.

Fagan, Edward A. Pvt., 62nd Alabama Infantry. Co. A. Enlisted: 3/24/1864 at Selma, AL. Federal Rolls of Prisoners of War: Captured at Blakely, AL, on 4/9/1865; Received at Ship Island, MS, on 4/15/1865. Transferred to Vicksburg, MS, for exchange on 5/1/1865; Exchanged at Camp Townsend, MS, on 5/6/1865. Born: 1/31/1847 at Marion, Perry County, AL. Residence after war: Calhoun County, AL.

Fails, G.B. Pvt., 63rd Alabama Infantry. Co. F. Enlisted: 7/4/1864 at Lowndes County, AL. Age at enlistment: 17. Description at enlistment: Eyes: blue. Hair: dark. Complexion: ruddy. Height: 5'9". Residence at enlistment: Lowndes County, AL. Rolls for 9/1864 through 10/1864: Present. Federal Rolls of Prisoners of War: Captured at Blakely, AL, on 4/9/1865; Received at Ship Island, MS, on 4/15/1865. Transferred to Vicksburg, MS, for exchange on 5/1/1865; Exchanged at Camp Townsend, MS, on 5/6/1865. Rolls of Prisoners of War, C.S.A: Surrendered at Citronelle, AL, on 5/4/1865; Paroled at Meridian, MS, on 5/10/1865 while a patient in Quintard Hospital. Residence at parole: Lowndes County, AL.

Fair, A.J. Pvt., Tarrant's Artillery Battery. Enlisted: 7/8/1863 at Tuscaloosa, AL. Federal Rolls of Prisoners of War: Captured at Blakely, AL, on 4/9/1865; Received at Ship Island, MS, on 4/15/1865. Transferred to Vicksburg, MS, for exchange on 5/1/1865; Exchanged at Camp Townsend, MS, on 5/6/1865.

Fair, G.W. Pvt., Tarrant's Artillery Battery. Enlisted: 7/8/1863 at Tuscaloosa, AL. Federal Rolls of Prisoners of War: Captured at Blakely, AL, on 4/9/1865; Received at Ship Island, MS, on 4/15/1865. Transferred to Vicksburg, MS, for exchange on 5/1/1865; Exchanged at Camp Townsend, MS, on 5/6/1865.

Farber, Phillip Pvt., 63rd Alabama Infantry. Co. B. Enlisted: 4/23/1864 at Montgomery County, AL. Age at enlistment: 16. Rolls for 9/1864 through 10/1864: Present. Federal Rolls of Prisoners of War: Captured at Blakely, AL, on 4/9/1865; Received at Ship Island, MS, on 4/15/1865. Transferred to Vicksburg, MS, for exchange on 5/1/1865; Exchanged at Camp Townsend, MS, on 5/6/1865. Rolls of Prisoners of War, C.S.A: Surrendered at Citronelle, AL, on 5/4/1865; Paroled at Meridian, MS, on 5/11/1865. Residence at parole: Montgomery County, AL.

Farley, P. Pvt., 21st Alabama Infantry. Co. F. Federal Rolls of Prisoners of War: Captured at Blakely, AL, on 4/9/1865; Received at Ship Island, MS, on 4/15/1865. Transferred to Vicksburg, MS, for exchange on 5/1/1865; Exchanged at Camp Townsend, MS, on 5/6/1865.

Farley, Robert J. Pvt., 63rd Alabama Infantry. Co. I. Federal Rolls of Prisoners of War: Captured at Blakely, AL, on 4/9/1865; Received at Ship Island, MS, on 4/15/1865. Transferred to Vicksburg, MS, for exchange on 5/1/1865; Exchanged at Camp Townsend, MS, on 5/6/1865. Rolls of Prisoners of War, C.S.A: Surrendered at Citronelle, AL, on 5/4/1865; Paroled at Meridian, MS, on 5/13/1865. Residence at parole: Shelby County, AL.

Farmer, T.J. Sgt., Tarrant's Artillery Battery. Federal Rolls of Prisoners of War: Captured at Blakely, AL, on 4/9/1865; Received at Ship Island, MS, on 4/15/1865. Transferred to Vicksburg, MS, for exchange on 5/1/1865; Exchanged at Camp Townsend, MS, on 5/6/1865.

Farmer, W.C. Pvt., Tarrant's Artillery Battery. Enlisted: 7/18/1863 at Tuscaloosa, AL. Federal Rolls of Prisoners of War: Captured at Blakely, AL, on 4/9/1865; Received at Ship Island, MS, on 4/15/1865. Transferred to Vicksburg, MS, for exchange on 5/1/1865; Exchanged at Camp Townsend, MS, on 5/6/1865.

Farr, James L. Pvt./Cpl., 63rd Alabama Infantry. Co. B. Enlisted: 4/14/1864 at Montgomery County, AL. Age at enlistment: 17. Rolls for 9/1864 through 10/1864: Present. Federal Rolls of Prisoners of War: Captured at Blakely, AL, on 4/9/1865; Received at Ship Island, MS, on 4/15/1865. Transferred to Vicksburg, MS, for exchange on 5/1/1865; Exchanged at Camp Townsend, MS, on 5/6/1865. Rolls of Prisoners of War, C.S.A: Surrendered at Citronelle, AL, on 5/4/1865; Paroled at Meridian, MS, on 5/11/1865. Residence at parole: Autauga County, AL. Born: 1846. Died 1904. Buried: Verbena Cemetery located at Chilton County, AL.

Farrinas, William Drummer, 62nd Alabama Infantry. Co. B. Federal Rolls of Prisoners of War: Captured at Blakely, AL, on 4/9/1865; Received at Ship Island, MS, on 4/15/1865. Transferred to Vicksburg, MS, for exchange on 5/1/1865; Exchanged at Camp Townsend, MS, on 5/6/1865.

Farrington, J.D. Pvt., 62nd Alabama Infantry. Co. A. Federal Rolls of Prisoners of War: Captured at Blakely, AL, on 4/9/1865; Received at Ship Island, MS, on 4/15/1865. Transferred to Vicksburg, MS, for exchange on 5/1/1865; Exchanged at Camp Townsend, MS, on 5/6/1865.

Farrior, James L. (AKA J.S.) Pvt., 63rd Alabama Infantry. Co. B. Enlisted: 3/23/1864 at Montgomery County, AL. Age at enlistment: 17. Rolls for 9/1864 through 10/1864: Absent, sick since 10/17/1864. Federal Rolls of Prisoners of War: Captured at Blakely, AL, on 4/9/1865; Received at Ship Island, MS, on 4/15/1865. Transferred to Vicksburg, MS, for exchange on 5/1/1865; Exchanged at Camp Townsend, MS, on 5/6/1865. Rolls of Prisoners of War, C.S.A: Surrendered at Citronelle, AL, on 5/4/1865; Paroled at Meridian, MS, on 5/11/1865. Residence at parole: Montgomery County, AL.

Faulk, J.P. Pvt., 63rd Alabama Infantry. Co. E. Enlisted: 3/15/1864 at Clayton, AL. Age at enlistment: 17. Description at enlistment: Eyes: dark. Hair: dark. Complexion: dark. Rolls for 9/1864 through 10/1864: Absent, in hospital since 10/12/1864. Federal Rolls of Prisoners of War: Captured at Blakely, AL, on 4/9/1865; Received at Ship Island, MS, on 4/15/1865. Transferred to Vicksburg, MS, for exchange on 5/1/1865. On Register of U.S.A. General Hospital #2, Vicksburg, MS: Admitted from steamer on 5/3/1865 due to acute diarrhea; Returned to duty on 5/8/1865. Rolls of Prisoners of War, C.S.A: Surrendered at Citronelle, AL, on 5/4/1865; Paroled at Meridian, MS, on 5/11/1865. Residence at parole: Montgomery County, AL.

Faulk, W.W. (AKA W.R.) Pvt., 63rd Alabama Infantry. Co. E. Federal Rolls of Prisoners of War: Captured at Blakely, AL, on 4/9/1865; Received at Ship Island, MS, on 4/15/1865. Transferred to Vicksburg, MS, for exchange on 5/1/1865; Exchanged at Camp Townsend, MS, on 5/6/1865.

Faulkner, Larkin C. Pvt., 63rd Alabama Infantry. Co. I. Federal Rolls of Prisoners of War: Captured at Blakely, AL, on 4/9/1865; Received at Ship Island, MS, on 4/15/1865. Transferred to Vicksburg, MS, for exchange on 5/1/1865; Exchanged at Camp Townsend, MS, on 5/6/1865.

Faulkner, Richard Pvt., 21st Alabama Infantry. Co. G. Federal Rolls of Prisoners of War: Captured at Fort Gaines, AL, on 8/8/1864; Received at Ship Island, MS, from New Orleans, LA, on 10/25/1864. Exchanged on 1/4/1865.

Faur, J.J. (AKA Fauer) Pvt., 6th Alabama Cavalry. Co. B. Federal Rolls of Prisoners of War: Captured in Alabama on 3/24/1865; Received at Ship Island, MS. Transferred to Vicksburg, MS, for exchange on 5/1/1865; Exchanged at Camp Townsend, MS, on 5/6/1865.

Fentrell, William E. Pvt., 62nd Alabama Infantry. Co. G. Federal Rolls of Prisoners of War: Captured at Blakely, AL, on 4/9/1865; Received at Ship Island, MS, on 4/15/1865. Transferred to Vicksburg, MS, for exchange on 5/1/1865; Exchanged at Camp Townsend, MS, on 5/6/1865.

Ferguay, Calvin D. Sgt., 63rd Alabama Infantry. Co. D. Federal Rolls of Prisoners of War: Captured at Blakely, AL, on 4/9/1865; Received at Ship Island, MS, on 4/15/1865. Transferred to Vicksburg, MS, for exchange on 5/1/1865; Exchanged at Camp Townsend, MS, on 5/6/1865.

Ferguson, A.J. Pvt./Cpl., 62nd Alabama Infantry. Co. F. Federal Rolls of Prisoners of War: Captured at Blakely, AL, on 4/9/1865; Received at Ship Island, MS, on 4/15/1865. Transferred to Vicksburg, MS, for exchange on 5/1/1865; Exchanged at Camp Townsend, MS, on 5/6/1865.

Ferguson, J.M. (AKA M.J.) Pvt., 62nd Alabama Infantry. Co. F. Federal Rolls of Prisoners of War: Captured at Blakely, AL, on 4/9/1865; Received at Ship Island, MS, on 4/15/1865. Transferred to Vicksburg, MS, for exchange on 5/1/1865; Exchanged at Camp Townsend, MS, on 5/6/1865.

Fields, John C. Pvt./Sgt., 1st Alabama Artillery Battalion. Cos. F & H. Federal Rolls of Prisoners of War: Captured at Fort Gaines, AL, on 8/8/1864; Received at Ship Island, MS, from New Orleans, LA, on 10/25/1864. Exchanged on 1/4/1865.

Fikes, T. Pvt., 36th Alabama Infantry. Co. H. Federal Rolls of Prisoners of War: Captured at Spanish Fort, AL, on 4/8/1865; Received at Ship Island, MS, on 4/10/1865. Transferred to Vicksburg, MS, for exchange on 5/1/1865; Exchanged at Camp Townsend, MS, on 5/6/1865.

Finch, P.A. Pvt./Cpl., Lockhart's Battalion Infantry. Co. __. Federal Rolls of Prisoners of War: Captured at Fort Gaines, AL, on 8/8/1864; Received at Ship Island, MS, from New Orleans, LA, on 10/29/1864. Exchanged on 1/4/1865.

Fincher, A.M. Pvt., 62nd Alabama Infantry. Co. I. Federal Rolls of Prisoners of War: Captured at Blakely, AL, on 4/9/1865; Received at Ship Island, MS, on 4/15/1865. Transferred to Vicksburg, MS, for exchange on 5/1/1865; Exchanged at Camp Townsend, MS, on 5/6/1865.

Fincher, Elijah Pvt., 62nd Alabama Infantry. Federal Rolls of Prisoners of War: Captured at Blakely, AL, on 4/9/1865; Received at Ship Island, MS, on 4/15/1865. Transferred to Vicksburg, MS, for exchange on 5/1/1865; Exchanged at Camp Townsend, MS, on 5/6/1865. Parents: Hilliard J. and Ruth Elmira Fincher. Married: Septima Abigail Anderson on 5/2/1866 in Sumpter County, AL.

Fincher, J.T. Pvt., 62nd Alabama Infantry. Co. A. Federal Rolls of Prisoners of War: Captured at Blakely, AL, on 4/9/1865; Received at Ship Island, MS, on 4/15/1865. Transferred to Vicksburg, MS, for exchange on 5/1/1865; Exchanged at Camp Townsend, MS, on 5/6/1865.

Fincher, P.H. Pvt., 62nd Alabama Infantry. Co. A. Federal Rolls of Prisoners of War: Captured at Blakely, AL, on 4/9/1865; Received at Ship Island, MS, on 4/15/1865. Transferred to Vicksburg, MS, for exchange on 5/1/1865; Exchanged at Camp Townsend, MS, on 5/6/1865.

Finchols, A. Pvt., 62nd Alabama Infantry. Co. G. Federal Rolls of Prisoners of War: Captured at Blakely, AL, on 4/9/1865; Received at Ship Island, MS, on 4/15/1865. Transferred to Vicksburg, MS, for exchange on

5/1/1865; Exchanged at Camp Townsend, MS, on 5/6/1865.
Finley, James Pvt., 36th Alabama Infantry. Co. I. Enlisted: Wayne County, MS. Age at enlistment: 20. Federal Rolls of Prisoners of War: Captured at Spanish Fort, AL, on 4/8/1865; Received at Ship Island, MS, on 4/10/1865. Transferred to Vicksburg, MS, for exchange on 5/1/1865; Exchanged at Camp Townsend, MS, on 5/6/1865.
Finley, Patrick Pvt./Cpl., 21st Alabama Infantry. Co. B. Federal Rolls of Prisoners of War: Captured at Fort Gaines, AL, on 8/8/1864; Received at Ship Island, MS, from New Orleans, LA, on 10/25/1864. Exchanged on 1/4/1865.
Fitzgerald, A.C. (AKA A.K.) Pvt., 62nd Alabama Infantry. Co. F. Federal Rolls of Prisoners of War: Captured at Blakely, AL, on 4/9/1865; Received at Ship Island, MS, on 4/15/1865. Transferred to Vicksburg, MS, for exchange on 5/1/1865; Exchanged at Camp Townsend, MS, on 5/6/1865.
Flanagan, F.L. Pvt., 21st Alabama Infantry. Co. C. Federal Rolls of Prisoners of War: Captured at Fort Gaines, AL, on 8/8/1864; Received at Ship Island, MS, from New Orleans, LA, on 10/25/1864. Exchanged on 1/4/1865.
Fleming, H.S. Pvt., Tarrant's Artillery Battery. Enlisted: 6/26/1863 at Tuscaloosa, AL. Federal Rolls of Prisoners of War: Captured at Blakely, AL, on 4/9/1865; Received at Ship Island, MS, on 4/15/1865. Transferred to Vicksburg, MS, for exchange on 5/1/1865; Exchanged at Camp Townsend, MS, on 5/6/1865.
Flincher, E. Sgt., 62nd Alabama Infantry. Co. F. Federal Rolls of Prisoners of War: Captured at Blakely, AL, on 4/9/1865; Received at Ship Island, MS, on 4/15/1865. Transferred to Vicksburg, MS, for exchange on 5/1/1865; Exchanged at Camp Townsend, MS, on 5/6/1865.
Floyd, John A. 1st Lt./Capt., 8th Alabama Cavalry. Co. C. Federal Rolls of Prisoners of War: Captured in Alabama on 3/22/1865; Received at Ship Island, MS. Transferred to Vicksburg, MS, for exchange on 4/28/1865; Confined at New Orleans, LA, on 4/30/1865. Exchanged at Camp Townsend, MS, on 5/6/1865.
Fluker, J.S. Pvt., 62nd Alabama Infantry. Co. A. Federal Rolls of Prisoners of War: Captured at Blakely, AL, on 4/9/1865; Received at Ship Island, MS, on 4/15/1865. Transferred to Vicksburg, MS, for exchange on 5/1/1865; Exchanged at Camp Townsend, MS, on 5/6/1865.
Force, Francis M. (AKA Ford) Pvt., 62nd Alabama Infantry. Cos. B & G. Federal Rolls of Prisoners of War: Captured at Blakely, AL, on 4/9/1865; Received at Ship Island, MS, on 4/15/1865. Transferred to Vicksburg, MS, for exchange on 5/1/1865; Exchanged at Camp Townsend, MS, on 5/6/1865.
Forshee, J.N. (AKA I.N.) Pvt., Lockhart's Battalion Infantry. Co. __. Federal Rolls of Prisoners of War: Captured at Fort Gaines, AL, on 8/8/1864; Received at Ship Island, MS, from New Orleans, LA, on 10/25/1864. Exchanged on 1/4/1865.
Fountain, H.T. Pvt., 62nd Alabama Infantry. Cos. A & H. Federal Rolls of Prisoners of War: Captured at Blakely, AL, on 4/9/1865; Received at Ship Island, MS, on 4/15/1865. Transferred to Vicksburg, MS, for exchange on 5/1/1865; Exchanged at Camp Townsend, MS, on 5/6/1865.
Fowler, D.W. Cpl./Sgt., 62nd Alabama Infantry. Co. B. Federal Rolls of Prisoners of War: Captured at Blakely, AL, on 4/9/1865; Received at Ship Island, MS, on 4/15/1865. Transferred to Vicksburg, MS, for exchange on 5/1/1865; Exchanged at Camp Townsend, MS, on 5/6/1865.
Frails, G.B. Pvt., 63rd Alabama Infantry. Co. F. Federal Rolls of Prisoners of War: Captured at Blakely, AL, on 4/9/1865; Received at Ship Island, MS, on 4/15/1865. Transferred to Vicksburg, MS, for exchange on 5/1/1865; Exchanged at Camp Townsend, MS, on 5/6/1865.
Frasier, E.P. Pvt., 63rd Alabama Infantry. Co. F. Federal Rolls of Prisoners of War: Captured at Blakely, AL, on 4/9/1865; Received at Ship Island, MS, on 4/15/1865. Transferred to Vicksburg, MS, for exchange on 5/1/1865; Exchanged at Camp Townsend, MS, on 5/6/1865.
Freeman, John Pvt., 63rd Alabama Infantry. Co. A. Federal Rolls of Prisoners of War: Captured at Blakely, AL, on 4/9/1865; Received at Ship Island, MS, on 4/15/1865. Transferred to Vicksburg, MS, for exchange on 5/1/1865; Exchanged at Camp Townsend, MS, on 5/6/1865.
Freeman, Newton Pvt., 63rd Alabama Infantry. Co. A. Federal Rolls of Prisoners of War: Captured at Blakely, AL, on 4/9/1865; Received at Ship Island, MS, on 4/15/1865. Transferred to Vicksburg, MS, for exchange on 5/1/1865; Exchanged at Camp Townsend, MS, on 5/6/1865.
Fulford, J.B. Sgt., 21st Alabama Infantry. Co. C. Federal Rolls of Prisoners of War: Captured at Fort Gaines, AL, on 8/8/1864; Received at Ship Island, MS, from New Orleans, LA, on 10/25/1864. Died: 12/31/1864 at Ship Island, MS, due to chronic dysentery. Buried: Ship Island, MS, Cemetery in Grave #128.
Fuller, Thomas S. Pvt., 63rd Alabama Infantry. Co. I. Federal Rolls of Prisoners of War: Captured at Blakely, AL, on 4/9/1865; Received at Ship Island, MS, on 4/15/1865. Transferred to Vicksburg, MS, for exchange on 5/1/1865; Exchanged at Camp Townsend, MS, on 5/6/1865. Born: 1/1/1847. Died: 4/10/1929. Buried: Bethel Cemetery located in Alabama.
Fuller, W.D. Pvt., 63rd Alabama Infantry. Co. F. Federal Rolls of Prisoners of War: Captured at Blakely, AL, on 4/9/1865; Received at Ship Island, MS, on 4/15/1865. Transferred to Vicksburg, MS, for exchange on 5/1/1865; Exchanged at Camp Townsend, MS, on 5/6/1865.
Fuller, William C. Pvt./Q.M. Sgt., 63rd Alabama Infantry. Co. A/F & S. Federal Rolls of Prisoners of War: Captured at Blakely, AL, on 4/9/1865; Received at Ship Island, MS, on 4/15/1865. Transferred to Vicksburg, MS, for exchange on 5/1/1865; Exchanged at Camp Townsend, MS, on 5/6/1865.
Fulmer, W.F. Pvt., 62nd Alabama Infantry. Co. A. Federal Rolls of Prisoners of War: Captured at Blakely, AL, on 4/9/1865; Received at Ship Island, MS, on 4/15/1865. Transferred to Vicksburg, MS, for exchange on 5/1/1865; Exchanged at Camp Townsend, MS, on 5/6/1865.
Fulton, William B. Capt., 63rd Alabama Infantry. Co. I. Federal Rolls of Prisoners of War: Captured at Blakely, AL, on 4/9/1865; Received at Ship Island, MS, on 4/15/1865. Transferred to Vicksburg, MS, for

exchange on 5/1/1865; Exchanged at Camp Townsend, MS, on 5/6/1865.

Gallaway, Eli (AKA J.E.) Pvt. 63rd Alabama Infantry. Co. B. Federal Rolls of Prisoners of War: Captured at Blakely, AL, on 4/9/1865; Received at Ship Island, MS, on 4/15/1865. Transferred to Vicksburg, MS, for exchange on 5/1/1865; Exchanged at Camp Townsend, MS, on 5/6/1865.

Gallespie, Wesley Pvt., 63rd Alabama Infantry. Co. A. Enlisted: 1/1/1864 at Montgomery County, AL. Rolls for 1/1864 through 2/1864: Present. Rolls for 9/1864 through 10/1864: Present. Federal Rolls of Prisoners of War: Captured at Blakely, AL, on 4/9/1865; Received at Ship Island, MS, on 4/15/1865. Transferred to Vicksburg, MS, for exchange on 5/1/1865; Exchanged at Camp Townsend, MS, on 5/6/1865. Rolls of Prisoners of War, C.S.A: Surrendered at Citronelle, AL, on 5/4/1865; Paroled at Meridian, MS, on 5/13/1865. Residence at parole: Montgomery, AL.

Galloway, Eli (AKA J.E.) Pvt., 63rd Alabama Infantry. Co. B. Enlisted: 8/15/1864 at Pollard, AL. Rolls for 9/1864 through 10/1864: Present. Federal Rolls of Prisoners of War: Captured at Blakely, AL, on 4/9/1865; Received at Ship Island, MS, on 4/15/1865. Transferred to Vicksburg, MS, for exchange on 5/1/1865; Exchanged at Camp Townsend, MS, on 5/6/1865. Rolls of Prisoners of War, C.S.A: Surrendered at Citronelle, AL, on 5/4/1865; Paroled at Meridian, MS, on 5/13/1865. Residence at parole: Dale County, AL.

Galloway, Francis M. Pvt., 21st Alabama Infantry. Co. G. Federal Rolls of Prisoners of War: Captured at Fort Gaines, AL, on 8/8/1864; Received at Ship Island, MS, from New Orleans, LA, on 10/25/1864. Exchanged on 1/4/1865.

Galloway, R.C. Pvt., 21st Alabama Infantry. Cos. B & I. Federal Rolls of Prisoners of War: Captured at Fort Gaines, AL, on 8/8/1864; Received at Ship Island, MS, from New Orleans, LA, on 10/25/1864. Exchanged on 1/4/1865.

Gamble, W.T. Pvt., 18th Alabama Infantry. Co. B. Federal Rolls of Prisoners of War: Captured at Spanish Fort, AL, on 4/8/1865; Received at Ship Island, MS, on 4/10/1865. Transferred to Vicksburg, MS, for exchange on 5/1/1865; Exchanged at Camp Townsend, MS, on 5/6/1865.

Gammell, John W. Pvt., 63rd Alabama Infantry. Co. C. Enlisted: 5/10/1864 at Tallapoosa County, AL. Age at enlistment: 17. Description at enlistment: Eyes: blue. Hair: light. Complexion: fair. Height: 5'4". Rolls for 9/1864 through 10/1864: Absent, in hospital at Mobile, AL, since 10/28/1864. Federal Rolls of Prisoners of War: Captured at Blakely, AL, on 4/9/1865; Received at Ship Island, MS, on 4/15/1865. Transferred to Vicksburg, MS, for exchange on 5/1/1865; Exchanged at Camp Townsend, MS, on 5/6/1865. Rolls of Prisoners of War, C.S.A: Surrendered at Citronelle, AL, on 5/4/1865; Paroled at Meridian, MS, on 5/11/1865. Residence at parole: Tallapoosa County, AL.

Gantray, Benjamin J. (AKA Guthrie) Pvt., 63rd Alabama Infantry. Cos. A & B. Federal Rolls of Prisoners of War: Captured at Blakely, AL, on 4/9/1865; Received at Ship Island, MS, on 4/15/1865. Transferred to Vicksburg, MS, for exchange on 5/1/1865; Exchanged at Camp Townsend, MS, on 5/6/1865.

Gantray, William T. (AKA Guthrie) Pvt., 63rd Alabama Infantry. Co. B. Federal Rolls of Prisoners of War: Captured at Blakely, AL, on 4/9/1865; Received at Ship Island, MS, on 4/15/1865. Transferred to Vicksburg, MS, for exchange on 5/1/1865; Exchanged at Camp Townsend, MS, on 5/6/1865.

Garner, John Pvt./Sgt., Pelham Cadets. Co. A. Federal Rolls of Prisoners of War: Captured at Fort Gaines, AL, on 8/8/1864; Received at Ship Island, MS, from New Orleans, LA, on 10/25/1864. Exchanged on 1/4/1865.

Garrett, H.H. (AKA H.R.) Pvt., 6th Alabama Cavalry. Co. L. Federal Rolls of Prisoners of War: Captured in Florida on 3/25/1865; Received at Ship Island, MS. Transferred to Vicksburg, MS, for exchange on 5/1/1865; Exchanged at Camp Townsend, MS, on 5/6/1865.

Garrett, J.F. Pvt., 21st Alabama Infantry. Co. F. Federal Rolls of Prisoners of War: Captured at Fort Gaines, AL, on 8/8/1864; Received at Ship Island, MS, from New Orleans, LA, on 10/25/1864. Exchanged on 1/4/1865.

Garrett, J.W. Pvt., 62nd Alabama Infantry. Cos. B & G. Federal Rolls of Prisoners of War: Captured at Blakely, AL, on 4/9/1865; Received at Ship Island, MS, on 4/15/1865. Transferred to Vicksburg, MS, for exchange on 5/1/1865; Exchanged at Camp Townsend, MS, on 5/6/1865.

Garris, William A. (AKA Garriss) Pvt., 1st Alabama Artillery Battalion. Co. B. Federal Rolls of Prisoners of War: Captured at Fort Gaines, AL, on 8/8/1864; Received at Ship Island, MS, from New Orleans, LA, on 10/25/1864. Died: 12/15/1864 at Ship Island, MS, due to chronic dysentery. Buried: Ship Island, MS, Cemetery in Grave #89.

Garrison, Andrew J. Sgt., 62nd Alabama Infantry. Cos. G & I. Federal Rolls of Prisoners of War: Captured at Blakely, AL, on 4/9/1865; Received at Ship Island, MS, on 4/15/1865. Transferred to Vicksburg, MS, for exchange on 5/1/1865; Exchanged at Camp Townsend, MS, on 5/6/1865.

Garrity, Patrick Pvt./Sgt., 21st Alabama Infantry. Co. B. Federal Rolls of Prisoners of War: Captured at Fort Gaines, AL, on 8/8/1864; Received at Ship Island, MS, from New Orleans, LA, on 10/25/1864. Exchanged on 1/4/1865.

Genright, John Pvt., 63rd Alabama Infantry. Co. G. Enlisted: 5/16/1864 at Troy, AL. Rolls for 9/1864 through 10/1864: Present. Federal Rolls of Prisoners of War: Captured at Blakely, AL, on 4/9/1865; Received at Ship Island, MS, on 4/15/1865. Transferred to Vicksburg, MS, for exchange on 5/1/1865; Exchanged at Camp Townsend, MS, on 5/6/1865. Rolls of Prisoners of War, C.S.A: Surrendered at Citronelle, AL, on 5/4/1865; Paroled at Meridian, MS, on 5/13/1865. Residence at parole: Henry County, AL.

Gholston, Thomas Marion Pvt., 1st Alabama Cavalry. Co. B. Enlisted: 11/1861 at Montgomery, AL; Discharged in 6/1862 at Sailer's Creek, MS. Re-enlisted: 2/1863 in the 6th Alabama Cavalry. Co.B. Discharged at the close of the war from Ship Island, MS. Born: 1/27/1840 near Pike Road, Montgomery County, AL.

Gibbs, A.W. Pvt., 63rd Alabama Infantry. Co. H. Enlisted: 3/15/1864 at Montevallo, AL. Age at enlistment: 17. Description at enlistment: Eyes: dark.

Hair: light. Complexion: fair. Rolls for 9/1864 through 10/1864: Present. Federal Rolls of Prisoners of War: Captured at Blakely, AL, on 4/9/1865; Received at Ship Island, MS, on 4/15/1865. Transferred to Vicksburg, MS, for exchange on 5/1/1865. On Register of U.S.A. General Hospital #2, Vicksburg, MS: Admitted from steamer on 5/3/1865 due to acute bronchitis; Returned to duty on 5/12/1865.

Gibson, C. Pvt., 62nd Alabama Infantry. Cos. A & H. Federal Rolls of Prisoners of War: Captured at Blakely, AL, on 4/9/1865; Received at Ship Island, MS, on 4/15/1865. Transferred to Vicksburg, MS, for exchange on 5/1/1865; Exchanged at Camp Townsend, MS, on 5/6/1865.

Giddons, P. Pvt., 21st Alabama Infantry. Co. C. Federal Rolls of Prisoners of War: Captured at Blakely, AL, on 4/9/1865; Received at Ship Island, MS, on 4/15/1865. Transferred to Vicksburg, MS, for exchange on 5/1/1865; Exchanged at Camp Townsend, MS, on 5/6/1865.

Giddons, W.C. (AKA Gilden) Pvt., 63rd Alabama Infantry. Cos. A & B. Federal Rolls of Prisoners of War: Captured at Blakely, AL, on 4/9/1865; Received at Ship Island, MS, on 4/15/1865. Transferred to Vicksburg, MS, for exchange on 5/1/1865; Exchanged at Camp Townsend, MS, on 5/6/1865. Rolls of Prisoners of War, C.S.A: Surrendered at Citronelle, AL, on 5/4/1865; Paroled at Meridian, MS, on 5/13/1865. Residence at parole: Lowndes County, AL.

Gilbert, John Pvt., 1st Alabama Artillery. Co. D. Federal Rolls of Prisoners of War: Captured at Fort Gaines, AL, on 8/8/1864; Received at Ship Island, MS, from New Orleans, LA, on 10/25/1864. Exchanged on 1/4/1865.

Gilder, Joseph (AKA Gilden) Pvt., 63rd Alabama Infantry. Cos. A & B. Enlisted: 5/10/1864 at Chambers County, AL. Rolls for 9/1864 through 10/1864: Present. Federal Rolls of Prisoners of War: Captured at Blakely, AL, on 4/9/1865; Received at Ship Island, MS, on 4/15/1865. Transferred to Vicksburg, MS, for exchange on 5/1/1865; Exchanged at Camp Townsend, MS, on 5/6/1865. Rolls of Prisoners of War, C.S.A: Surrendered at Citronelle, AL, on 5/4/1865; Paroled at Meridian, MS, on 5/10/1865 while a patient in Quintard Hospital. Residence at parole: Lafayette, AL.

Gill, Charles Pvt., 21st Alabama Infantry. Co. E. Federal Rolls of Prisoners of War: Captured at Fort Gaines, AL, on 8/8/1864; Received at Ship Island, MS, from New Orleans, LA, on 10/25/1864. Exchanged on 3/2/1865.

Gilland, James P. (AKA J.T.) Pvt., 6th Alabama Cavalry. Co. L. Federal Rolls of Prisoners of War: Captured in Florida on 3/25/1865; Received at Ship Island, MS. Transferred to Vicksburg, MS, for exchange on 5/1/1865; Exchanged at Camp Townsend, MS, on 5/6/1865.

Gilliland, A.J. Pvt., 8th Alabama Cavalry. Cos. A & E. Federal Rolls of Prisoners of War: Captured in Florida on 3/25/1865; Received at Ship Island, MS. Transferred to Vicksburg, MS, for exchange on 5/1/1865; Exchanged at Camp Townsend, MS, on 5/6/1865.

Gilmore, A.A. (Gillmore) Pvt./Sgt., 21st Alabama Infantry. Co. A. Federal Rolls of Prisoners of War: Captured at Fort Gaines, AL, on 8/8/1864; Received at Ship Island, MS, from New Orleans, LA, on 10/25/1864. Died: 12/8/1864 at Ship Island, MS, due to pneumonia. Buried: Ship Island, MS, Cemetery in Grave #74.

Gilmore, J.M. Pvt., 63rd Alabama Infantry. Co. E. Enlisted: 8/8/1864 at Pollard, AL. Age at enlistment: 17. Description at enlistment: Eyes: blue. Hair: light. Complexion: fair. Rolls for 9/1864 through 10/1864: Absent, in hospital since 10/19/1864. Federal Rolls of Prisoners of War: Captured at Blakely, AL, on 4/9/1865; Received at Ship Island, MS, on 4/15/1865. Transferred to Vicksburg, MS, for exchange on 5/1/1865; Exchanged at Camp Townsend, MS, on 5/6/1865. Rolls of Prisoners of War, C.S.A: Surrendered at Citronelle, AL, on 5/4/1865; Paroled at Meridian, MS, on 5/13/1865 and Montgomery, AL, on 5/24/1865. Residence at parole: Henry County, AL.

Gilmore, J.W. (AKA Gillmore, I.W.) Pvt., 63rd Alabama Infantry. Co. E. Federal Rolls of Prisoners of War: Captured at Blakely, AL, on 4/9/1865; Received at Ship Island, MS, on 4/15/1865. Transferred to Vicksburg, MS, for exchange on 5/1/1865; Exchanged at Camp Townsend, MS, on 5/6/1865.

Glass, M. Pvt., 21st Alabama Infantry. Co. C. Federal Rolls of Prisoners of War: Captured at Fort Gaines, AL, on 8/8/1864; Received at Ship Island, MS, from New Orleans, LA, on 10/25/1864. Exchanged on 1/4/1865.

Glass, W.R. Pvt., 21st Alabama Infantry. Co. C. Federal Rolls of Prisoners of War: Captured at Fort Gaines, AL, on 8/8/1864; Received at Ship Island, MS, from New Orleans, LA, on 10/25/1864. Exchanged on 1/4/1865.

Glaze, J.M. Pvt., 62nd Alabama Infantry. Cos. B & C. Federal Rolls of Prisoners of War: Captured at Blakely, AL, on 4/9/1865; Received at Ship Island, MS, on 4/15/1865. Transferred to Vicksburg, MS, for exchange on 5/1/1865; Exchanged at Camp Townsend, MS, on 5/6/1865.

Glenn, Adolphus (AKA Glen) Pvt., 62nd Alabama Infantry. Cos. G & H. Federal Rolls of Prisoners of War: Captured at Blakely, AL, on 4/9/1865; Received at Ship Island, MS, on 4/15/1865. Transferred to Vicksburg, MS, for exchange on 5/1/1865; Exchanged at Camp Townsend, MS, on 5/6/1865.

Glosson, James M. Pvt., 63rd Alabama Infantry. Co. G. Enlisted: 4/16/1864 at Troy, AL. Age at enlistment: 17. Description at enlistment: Eyes: grey. Hair: dark. Complexion: florid. Height: 5'9". Residence at enlistment: Pike County, AL. Rolls for 9/1864 through 10/1864: Present. Federal Rolls of Prisoners of War: Captured at Blakely, AL, on 4/9/1865; Received at Ship Island, MS, on 4/15/1865. Transferred to Vicksburg, MS, for exchange on 5/1/1865; Exchanged at Camp Townsend, MS, on 5/6/1865. Rolls of Prisoners of War, C.S.A.: Surrendered at Citronelle, AL, on 5/4/1865; Paroled at Meridian, MS, on 5/13/1865. Residence at parole: Pike County, AL.

Godsey, Madison M. Pvt., 21st Alabama Infantry. Co. G. Federal Rolls of Prisoners of War: Captured at Fort Gaines, AL, on 8/8/1864; Received at Ship Island, MS, from New Orleans, LA, on 10/25/1864. Exchanged on 1/4/1865.

Godwin, David Pvt., 63rd Alabama Infantry. Co. F. Enlisted: 7/14/1864 at Lowndes County, AL. Age at enlistment: 17. Description at enlistment: Eyes:

hazel. Hair: light. Complexion: fair. Height: 5'6". Residence: Lowndes County, AL. Rolls for 9/1864 through 10/1864: Present. Federal Rolls of Prisoners of War: Captured at Blakely, AL, on 4/9/1865; Received at Ship Island, MS, on 4/15/1865. Transferred to Vicksburg, MS, for exchange on 5/1/1865; Exchanged at Camp Townsend, MS, on 5/6/1865. Rolls of Prisoners of War, C.S.A: Surrendered at Citronelle, AL, on 5/4/1865; Paroled at Meridian, MS, on 5/11/1865. Residence at parole: Lowndes County, AL. Born: 1846. Died: 1926. Buried: Bragg Cemetery located at Lowndes County, AL.

Godwin, Henry J. (AKA Goodwin) Pvt., 63rd Alabama Infantry. Co. F. Enlisted: 5/30/1864 at Montgomery, AL. Age at enlistment: 17. Description at enlistment: Eyes: dark. Hair: dark. Complexion: dark. Height: 5'6". Residence at enlistment: Lowndes County, AL. Rolls for 9/1864 through 10/1864: Absent, sick in hospital at Mobile, AL, since 10/15/1864. Federal Rolls of Prisoners of War: Captured at Blakely, AL, on 4/9/1865; Received at Ship Island, MS, on 4/15/1865. Transferred to Vicksburg, MS, for exchange on 5/1/1865; Exchanged at Camp Townsend, MS, on 5/6/1865. Rolls of Prisoners of War, C.S.A: Surrendered at Citronelle, AL, on 5/4/1865; Paroled at Meridian, MS, on 5/11/1865. Residence at parole: Lowndes County, AL. Born: 9/15/1845 at Lowndes County, AL. Soldier is recorded on the 1907 Alabama Census of Confederate Veterans and Widows. Residence: Lowndes County, AL.

Godwin, J.K. Pvt., 63rd Alabama Infantry. Co. E. Enlisted: 7/27/1864 at Montgomery, AL. Age at enlistment: 17. Description at enlistment: Eyes: blue. Hair: light. Complexion: fair. Rolls for 9/1864 through 10/1864: Present. Federal Rolls of Prisoners of War: Captured at Blakely, AL, on 4/9/1865; Received at Ship Island, MS, on 4/15/1865. Transferred to Vicksburg, MS, for exchange on 5/1/1865; Exchanged at Camp Townsend, MS, on 5/6/1865. Rolls of Prisoners of War, C.S.A: Surrendered at Citronelle, AL, on 5/4/1865; Paroled at Meridian, MS, on 5/13/1865. Residence at parole: Wilcox County, AL.

Golson, John N. (AKA Golsan, J.L.) Lt., 8th Alabama Cavalry. Co. A. Federal Rolls of Prisoners of War: Captured in Alabama on 3/17/1865; Received at Ship Island, MS. Transferred to Vicksburg, MS, for exchange on 4/28/1865; Confined at New Orleans, LA, on 4/30/1865. Exchanged at Camp Townsend, MS, on 5/6/1865.

Gonzalez, John B. Pvt., 62nd Alabama Infantry. Co. B. Federal Rolls of Prisoners of War: Captured at Blakely, AL, on 4/9/1865; Received at Ship Island, MS, on 4/15/1865. Transferred to Vicksburg, MS, for exchange on 5/1/1865; Exchanged at Camp Townsend, MS, on 5/6/1865.

Goodall, William S. Pvt./Sgt., 21st Alabama Infantry. Co. E. Federal Rolls of Prisoners of War: Captured at Fort Gaines, AL, on 8/8/1864; Received at Ship Island, MS, from New Orleans, LA, on 10/25/1864. Exchanged on 1/4/1865.

Goode, D.W. Pvt., 21st Alabama Infantry. Co. F. Federal Rolls of Prisoners of War: Captured at Fort Gaines, AL, on 8/8/1864; Received at Ship Island, MS, from New Orleans, LA, on 10/25/1864. Died: 11/23/1864 at Ship Island, MS, due to unknown causes. Buried: Ship Island, MS, Cemetery in Grave #39.

Goode, Robert Pvt., 21st Alabama Infantry. Co. F. Federal Rolls of Prisoners of War: Captured at Fort Gaines, AL, on 8/8/1864; Received at Ship Island, MS, from New Orleans, LA, on 10/25/1864. Exchanged on 1/4/1865.

Gooding, D.W. Pvt., 62nd Alabama Infantry. Co. B. Federal Rolls of Prisoners of War: Captured at Blakely, AL, on 4/9/1865; Received at Ship Island, MS, on 4/15/1865. Transferred to Vicksburg, MS, for exchange on 5/1/1865; Exchanged at Camp Townsend, MS, on 5/6/1865.

Goodloe, Charles H. (AKA Goddloe, Godlor, C.M.) 1st Sgt., Lockhart's Battalion Infantry. Co. H. Federal Rolls of Prisoners of War: Captured at Fort Gaines, AL, on 8/8/1864; Received at Ship Island, MS, from New Orleans, LA, on 10/25/1864. Died: 11/10/1864 at Ship Island, MS, due to chronic diarrhea. Buried: Ship Island, MS, Cemetery in Grave #15.

Goodwin, Elijah Pvt., 62nd Alabama Infantry. Co. E. Federal Rolls of Prisoners of War: Captured in Alabama on 3/24/1865; Received at Ship Island, MS. Transferred to Vicksburg, MS, for exchange on 5/1/1865; Exchanged at Camp Townsend, MS, on 5/6/1865.

Goodwin, J. Pvt., 1st Alabama Artillery Battalion. Co. __. Federal Rolls of Prisoners of War: Captured at Blakely, AL, on 4/9/1865; Received at Ship Island, MS, on 4/15/1865. Transferred to Vicksburg, MS, for exchange on 5/1/1865; Exchanged at Camp Townsend, MS, on 5/6/1865.

Goodwin, James Pvt./4th Cpl./2nd Cpl., 63rd Alabama Infantry. Co. A. Enlisted: Montgomery County, AL. Rolls for 9/1864 through 10/1864: Present. Federal Rolls of Prisoners of War: Captured at Blakely, AL, on 4/9/1865; Received at Ship Island, MS, on 4/15/1865. Transferred to Vicksburg, MS, for exchange on 5/1/1865; Exchanged at Camp Townsend, MS, on 5/6/1865. Rolls of Prisoners of War, C.S.A: Surrendered at Citronelle, AL, on 5/4/1865; Paroled at Meridian, MS, on 5/11/1865. Residence at parole: Montgomery County, AL.

Goodwin, William W. Pvt., 1st Alabama Artillery Battalion. Co. D. Federal Rolls of Prisoners of War: Captured at Fort Gaines, AL, on 8/8/1864; Received at Ship Island, MS, from New Orleans, LA, on 10/25/1864. Died: 12/25/1864 at Ship Island, MS, due to chronic dysentery. Buried: Ship Island, MS, Cemetery in Grave #111.

Goodwyn, D. (AKA Godwin) Pvt., 63rd Alabama Infantry. Co. F. Federal Rolls of Prisoners of War: Captured at Blakely, AL, on 4/9/1865; Received at Ship Island, MS, on 4/15/1865. Transferred to Vicksburg, MS, for exchange on 5/1/1865; Exchanged at Camp Townsend, MS, on 5/6/1865.

Goodwyn, J.F. (AKA H.J.) Pvt., 63rd Alabama Infantry. Co. F. Federal Rolls of Prisoners of War: Captured at Blakely, AL, on 4/9/1865; Received at Ship Island, MS, on 4/15/1865. Transferred to Vicksburg, MS, for exchange on 5/1/1865; Exchanged at Camp Townsend, MS, on 5/6/1865.

Gordy, W.F. Pvt., 62nd Alabama Infantry. Cos. E & G. Federal Rolls of Prisoners of War: Captured at Blakely, AL, on 4/9/1865; Received at Ship Island, MS, on 4/15/1865. Transferred to Vicksburg, MS, for

exchange on 5/1/1865; Exchanged at Camp Townsend, MS, on 5/6/1865.

Grace, Baylis E. Pvt., 62nd Alabama Infantry. Cos. A & H. Federal Rolls of Prisoners of War: Captured at Blakely, AL, on 4/9/1865; Received at Ship Island, MS, on 4/15/1865. Transferred to Vicksburg, MS, for exchange on 5/1/1865; Exchanged at Camp Townsend, MS, on 5/6/1865.

Grace, George T. (AKA G.M.) Pvt., 21st Alabama Infantry. Co. G. Federal Rolls of Prisoners of War: Captured at Fort Gaines, AL, on 8/8/1864; Received at Ship Island, MS, from New Orleans, LA, on 10/25/1864. Died: 12/28/1864 at Ship Island, MS, due to smallpox. Buried: Ship Island, MS, Cemetery in Grave #117.

Gracey, William C. (AKA Grody) Pvt., 62nd Alabama Infantry. Co. G. Federal Rolls of Prisoners of War: Captured at Blakely, AL, on 4/9/1865; Received at Ship Island, MS, on 4/15/1865. Transferred to Vicksburg, MS, for exchange on 5/1/1865; Exchanged at Camp Townsend, MS, on 5/6/1865.

Grady, J. Pvt., 62nd Alabama Infantry. Cos. D & H. Federal Rolls of Prisoners of War: Captured at Blakely, AL, on 4/9/1865; Received at Ship Island, MS, on 4/15/1865. Transferred to Vicksburg, MS, for exchange on 5/1/1865; Exchanged at Camp Townsend, MS, on 5/6/1865.

Grady, N.A. Pvt., 62nd Alabama Infantry. Cos. H & K. Federal Rolls of Prisoners of War: Captured at Blakely, AL, on 4/9/1865; Received at Ship Island, MS, on 4/15/1865. Transferred to Vicksburg, MS, for exchange on 5/1/1865; Exchanged at Camp Townsend, MS, on 5/6/1865.

Graham, Daniel (AKA David) Pvt., 21st Alabama Infantry. Co. F. Federal Rolls of Prisoners of War: Captured at Fort Gaines, AL, on 8/8/1864; Received at Ship Island, MS, from New Orleans, LA, on 10/25/1864. Exchanged on 1/4/1865.

Graham, H. (AKA Walter) Pvt., 21st Alabama Infantry. Cos. B & F. Federal Rolls of Prisoners of War: Captured at Fort Gaines, AL, on 8/8/1864; Received at Ship Island, MS, on 10/25/1864. Died: 11/23/1864 at Ship Island, MS, due to pneumonia. Buried: Ship Island, MS, Cemetery in Grave #38.

Graham, J.P. (AKA J.D.) Pvt., 21st Alabama Infantry. Co. B. Federal Rolls of Prisoners of War: Captured at Fort Gaines, AL, on 8/8/1864; Received at Ship Island, MS, from New Orleans, LA, on 10/25/1864. Died: 12/29/1864 at Ship Island, MS, due to dysentery. Buried: Ship Island, MS, Cemetery in Grave #119.

Graham, Walter (AKA William) Pvt., 21st Alabama Infantry. Cos. B & F. Federal Rolls of Prisoners of War: Captured at Fort Gaines, AL, on 8/8/1864; Received at Ship Island, MS, from New Orleans, LA, on 10/25/1864. Exchanged on 1/4/1865.

Grant, John C. Pvt., 63rd Alabama Infantry. Co. G. Enlisted: Troy, AL. Age at enlistment: 17. Description at enlistment: Eyes: grey. Hair: light. Complexion: dark. Height: 5'7". Residence at enlistment: Coffee County, AL. Rolls for 9/1864 through 10/1864: Present. Federal Rolls of Prisoners of War: Captured at Blakely, AL, on 4/9/1865; Received at Ship Island, MS, on 4/15/1865. Transferred to Vicksburg, MS, for exchange on 5/1/1865; Exchanged at Camp Townsend, MS, on 5/6/1865. Rolls of Prisoners of War, C.S.A: Surrendered at Citronelle, AL, on 5/4/1865; Paroled at Meridian, MS, on 5/13/1865. Residence at parole: Coffee County, AL. Born: 1841. Died: 1915. Buried: Mount Pleasant Cemetery located at Grimes, AL.

Grant, P.F. Pvt., 6th Alabama Cavalry. Cos. C & D. Federal Rolls of Prisoners of War: Captured in Florida on 3/25/1865; Received at Ship Island, MS. Transferred to Vicksburg, MS, for exchange on 5/1/1865; Exchanged at Camp Townsend, MS, on 5/6/1865.

Grantham, A.A. Pvt., 63rd Alabama Infantry. Co. G. Enlisted: 5/16/1864 at Troy, AL. Age at enlistment: 17. Description at enlistment: Eyes: grey. Hair: light. Complexion: dark. Height: 5'7". Rolls for 9/1864 through 10/1864: Absent, on 60 day furlough from hospital at Lauderdale, MS, since 10/20/1864. Federal Rolls of Prisoners of War: Captured at Blakely, AL, on 4/9/1865; Received at Ship Island, MS, on 4/15/1865. Transferred to Vicksburg, MS, for exchange on 5/1/1865; Exchanged at Camp Townsend, MS, on 5/6/1865. Rolls of Prisoners of War, C.S.A: Surrendered at Citronelle, AL, on 5/4/1865; Paroled at Meridian, MS, on 5/13/1865. Residence at parole: Pike County, AL.

Granthan, T.W. Pvt., 21st Alabama Infantry. Co. H. Federal Rolls of Prisoners of War: Captured at Fort Gaines, AL, on 8/8/1864; Received at Ship Island, MS, from New Orleans, LA, on 10/25/1864. Exchanged on 1/4/1865.

Gratrix, Robert Pvt./Sgt., 21st Alabama Infantry. Co. D. Federal Rolls of Prisoners of War: Captured at Blakely, AL, on 4/9/1865; Received at Ship Island, MS, on 4/15/1865. Transferred to Vicksburg, MS, for exchange on 5/1/1865; Exchanged at Camp Townsend, MS, on 5/6/1865.

Graves, J.T.J. Pvt./Cpl., 63rd Alabama Infantry. Co. F. Enlisted: 7/14/1864 at Lowndes County, AL. Age at enlistment: 17. Description at enlistment: Eyes: blue. Hair: light. Complexion: fair. Height: 5'0". Residence at enlistment: Lowndes County, AL. Rolls for 9/1864 through 10/1864: Present, promoted to Cpl. on 10/15/1864. Federal Rolls of Prisoners of War: Captured at Blakely, AL, on 4/9/1865; Received at Ship Island, MS, on 4/15/1865. Transferred to Vicksburg, MS, for exchange on 5/1/1865; Exchanged at Camp Townsend, MS, on 5/6/1865. Rolls of Prisoners of War, C.S.A: Surrendered at Citronelle, AL, on 5/4/1865; Paroled at Meridian, MS, on 5/11/1865. Residence at parole: Lowndes County, AL.

Gray, Charles B. Pvt., 21st Alabama Infantry. Co. E. Federal Rolls of Prisoners of War: Captured at Fort Gaines, AL, on 8/8/1864; Received at Ship Island, MS, from New Orleans, LA, on 10/25/1864. Exchanged on 1/4/1865.

Gray, John Pvt./Cpl., 21st Alabama Infantry. Co. D. Federal Rolls of Prisoners of War: Captured at Blakely, AL, on 4/9/1865; Received at Ship Island, MS, on 4/15/1865. Transferred to Vicksburg, MS, for exchange on 5/1/1865; Exchanged at Camp Townsend, MS, on 5/6/1865.

Gray, John Pvt., 62nd Alabama Infantry. Co. F. Federal Rolls of Prisoners of War: Captured at Blakely, AL, on 4/9/1865; Received at Ship Island, MS, on 4/15/1865. Transferred to Vicksburg, MS, for exchange on 5/1/1865; Exchanged at Camp Townsend, MS, on 5/6/1865.

Gray, John J. Sgt., Tarrant's Artillery Battery. Federal Rolls of Prisoners of War: Captured at Blakely, AL, on 4/9/1865; Received at Ship Island, MS, on 4/15/1865. Transferred to Vicksburg, MS, for exchange on 5/1/1865; Exchanged at Camp Townsend, MS, on 5/6/1865.

Gray, Samuel Sgt./Pvt., 63rd Alabama Infantry. Cos. A & B. Federal Rolls of Prisoners of War: Captured at Blakely, AL, on 4/9/1865; Received at Ship Island, MS, on 4/15/1865. Transferred to Vicksburg, MS, for exchange on 5/1/1865; Exchanged at Camp Townsend, MS, on 5/6/1865.

Gray, T.J. Pvt., 21st Alabama Infantry. Co. C. Federal Rolls of Prisoners of War: Captured at Blakely, AL, on 4/9/1865; Received at Ship Island, MS, on 4/15/1865. Transferred to Vicksburg, MS, for exchange on 5/1/1865; Exchanged at Camp Townsend, MS, on 5/6/1865.

Grayson, Y.W. Pvt., 21st Alabama Infantry. Co. I. Federal Rolls of Prisoners of War: Captured at Fort Gaines, AL, on 8/8/1864; Received at Ship Island, MS, from New Orleans, LA, on 10/25/1864. Exchanged on 1/4/1865.

Green, A.T. (AKA A.F.) Pvt., 62nd Alabama Infantry. Cos. G & H. Federal Rolls of Prisoners of War: Captured at Blakely, AL, on 4/9/1865; Received at Ship Island, MS, on 4/15/1865. Transferred to Vicksburg, MS, for exchange on 5/1/1865; Exchanged at Camp Townsend, MS, on 5/6/1865.

Green, Charles Pvt., 63rd Alabama Infantry. Cos. A & B. Enlisted: 8/1/1864 at Chambers County, AL. Rolls for 9/1864 through 10/1864: Present. Federal Rolls of Prisoners of War: Captured at Blakely, AL, on 4/9/1865; Received at Ship Island, MS, on 4/15/1865. Transferred to Vicksburg, MS, for exchange on 5/1/1865; Exchanged at Camp Townsend, MS, on 5/6/1865. Rolls of Prisoners of War, C.S.A: Surrendered at Citronelle, AL, on 5/4/1865; Paroled at Meridian, MS, on 5/13/1865. Residence at parole: Chambers County, AL.

Green, James T. Pvt., Lockhart's Battalion Infantry. Co. H. Federal Rolls of Prisoners of War: Captured at Fort Gaines, AL, on 8/8/1864; Received at Ship Island, MS, from New Orleans, LA, on 10/25/1864. Died: 11/19/1864 at Ship Island, MS, due to pneumonia. Buried: Ship Island, MS, Cemetery in Grave #27.

Green, Thomas R. Pvt., 21st Alabama Infantry. Co. H. Federal Rolls of Prisoners of War: Captured at Fort Gaines, AL, on 8/8/1864; Received at Ship Island, MS, from New Orleans, LA, on 10/25/1864. Died: 11/19/1864 at Ship Island, MS. Buried: Ship Island, MS, Cemetery.

Green, W.J. Pvt., 63rd Alabama Infantry. Co. F. Enlisted: 3/9/1864 at Greenville, AL. Age at enlistment: 17. Description at enlistment: Eyes: dark. Hair: dark. Complexion: dark. Height: 5'6". Residence at enlistment: Butler County, AL. Rolls for 9/1864 through 10/1864: Present. Federal Rolls of Prisoners of War: Captured at Blakely, AL, on 4/9/1865; Received at Ship Island, MS, on 4/15/1865. Transferred to Vicksburg, MS, for exchange on 5/1/1865; Exchanged at Camp Townsend, MS, on 5/6/1865. Rolls of Prisoners of War, C.S.A: Surrendered at Citronelle, AL, on 5/4/1865; Paroled at Meridian, MS, on 5/11/1865. Residence at parole: Butler County, AL.

Greer, Daniel C. (AKA Grear) Pvt., 63rd Alabama Infantry. Co. H. Federal Rolls of Prisoners of War: Captured at Blakely, AL, on 4/9/1865; Received at Ship Island, MS, on 4/15/1865. Transferred to Vicksburg, MS, for exchange on 5/1/1865; Exchanged at Camp Townsend, MS, on 5/6/1865.

Gregory, W.H. Pvt., 63rd Alabama Infantry. Co. F. Federal Rolls of Prisoners of War: Captured at Blakely, AL, on 4/9/1865; Received at Ship Island, MS, on 4/15/1865. Transferred to Vicksburg, MS, for exchange on 5/1/1865; Exchanged at Camp Townsend, MS, on 5/6/1865.

Grenshaw, James Pvt., 21st Alabama Infantry. Co. C. Federal Rolls of Prisoners of War: Captured at Fort Gaines, AL, on 8/8/1864; Received at Ship Island, MS, from New Orleans, LA, on 10/25/1864. Died: 1/3/1865 at Ship Island, MS, due to pneumonia. Buried: Ship Island, MS, Cemetery in Grave #129.

Griffin, R.C. Pvt., 8th Alabama Cavalry. Co. H. Federal Rolls of Prisoners of War: Captured at Blakely, AL, on 4/9/1865; Received at Ship Island, MS, on 4/15/1865. Transferred to Vicksburg, MS, for exchange on 5/1/1865; Exchanged at Camp Townsend, MS, on 5/6/1865.

Griffin, T.R. (AKA Guffin) Pvt., 36th Alabama Infantry. Co. G. Federal Rolls of Prisoners of War: Captured at Spanish Fort, AL, on 4/8/1865; Received at Ship Island, MS, on 4/10/1865. Transferred to Vicksburg, MS, for exchange on 5/1/1865; Exchanged at Camp Townsend, MS, on 5/6/1865.

Griffin, W.A. Pvt., 62nd Alabama Infantry. Cos. F & H. Federal Rolls of Prisoners of War: Captured at Blakely, AL, on 4/9/1865; Received at Ship Island, MS, on 4/15/1865. Transferred to Vicksburg, MS, for exchange on 5/1/1865; Exchanged at Camp Townsend, MS, on 5/6/1865.

Griffin, William A. Sgt., 6th Alabama Cavalry. Cos. B & C. Federal Rolls of Prisoners of War: Captured in Florida on 3/25/1865; Received at Ship Island, MS. Transferred to Vicksburg, MS, for exchange on 5/1/1865; Exchanged at Camp Townsend, MS, on 5/6/1865.

Griffing, Stephen Henry (AKA L.) Pvt./Sgt., 21st Alabama Infantry. Co. E. Federal Rolls of Prisoners of War: Captured at Fort Gaines, AL, on 8/8/1864; Received at Ship Island, MS, from New Orleans, LA, on 10/25/1864. Exchanged on 1/4/1865.

Grimes, J.E. Pvt., 62nd Alabama Infantry. Co. I. Federal Rolls of Prisoners of War: Captured at Blakely, AL, on 4/9/1865; Received at Ship Island, MS, on 4/15/1865. Transferred to Vicksburg, MS, for exchange on 5/1/1865; Exchanged at Camp Townsend, MS, on 5/6/1865.

Groce, David (AKA Grop, Gross) Pvt., 21st Alabama Infantry. Co. I. Federal Rolls of Prisoners of War: Captured at Fort Gaines, AL, on 8/8/1864; Received at Ship Island, MS, from New Orleans, LA, on 10/25/1864. Died: 11/27/1864 at Ship Island, MS, due to dysentery. Buried: Ship Island, MS, Cemetery in Grave #47.

Grogan, Patrick T. (AKA P.J.) Pvt., 58th Alabama Infantry. Co. F. Federal Rolls of Prisoners of War: Captured at Spanish Fort, AL, on 4/8/1865; Received at Ship Island, MS, on 4/10/1865. Transferred to Vicksburg, MS, for exchange on 5/1/1865; Exchanged at Camp Townsend, MS, on 5/6/1865.

Groom, William E. Pvt., 21st Alabama Infantry. Co. H. Federal Rolls of Prisoners of War: Captured at Fort Gaines, AL, on 8/8/1864; Received at Ship Island, MS, from New Orleans, LA, on 10/25/1864. Died: 11/21/1864 at Ship Island, MS, due to pneumonia. Buried: Ship Island, MS, Cemetery in Grave #32.

Grose, G.S. Pvt., 21st Alabama Infantry. Co. G. Federal Rolls of Prisoners of War: Captured at Fort Gaines, AL, on 8/8/1864; Received at Ship Island, MS, from New Orleans, LA, on 10/25/1864. Died: 12/28/1864 at Ship Island, MS, due to smallpox. Buried: Ship Island, MS, Cemetery in Grave #117.

Gunn, George W. 4th Cpl., 63rd Alabama Infantry. Cos. A & B. Enlisted: 1/1/1864 at Macon County, AL. Rolls for 1/1864 through 2/1864: Present. Rolls for 9/1864 through 10/1864: Present, sick in quarters. Federal Rolls of Prisoners of War: Captured at Blakely, AL, on 4/9/1865; Received at Ship Island, MS, on 4/15/1865. Transferred to Vicksburg, MS, for exchange on 5/1/1865; Exchanged at Camp Townsend, MS, on 5/6/1865. Rolls of Prisoners of War, C.S.A: Surrendered at Citronelle, AL, on 5/4/1865; Paroled at Meridian, MS, on 5/13/1865. Residence at parole: Macon County, AL.

Gunn, James H. Cpl./Pvt., 62nd Alabama Infantry. Cos. E & H. Federal Rolls of Prisoners of War: Captured at Blakely, AL, on 4/9/1865; Received at Ship Island, MS, on 4/15/1865. Transferred to Vicksburg, MS, for exchange on 5/1/1865; Exchanged at Camp Townsend, MS, on 5/6/1865.

Guthrie, Benjamin J. Pvt., 63rd Alabama Infantry. Cos. A & B. Enlisted: 1/1/1864 at Tallapoosa County, AL. Age at enlistment: 17. Rolls for 1/1864 through 2/1864: Present. Rolls for 9/1864 through 10/1864: Present. Federal Rolls of Prisoners of War: Captured at Blakely, AL, on 4/9/1865; Received at Ship Island, MS, on 4/15/1865. Transferred to Vicksburg, MS, for exchange on 5/1/1865; Exchanged at Camp Townsend, MS, on 5/6/1865. Rolls of Prisoners of War, C.S.A: Surrendered at Citronelle, AL, on 5/4/1865; Paroled at Meridian, MS, on 5/13/1865. Residence at parole: Tallapoosa County, AL.

Guthrie, William T. Pvt., 63rd Alabama Infantry. Cos. A & B. Enlisted: 1/1/1864 at Tallapoosa County, AL. Age at enlistment: 15. Rolls for 1/1864 through 2/1864: Present. Rolls for 9/1864 through 10/1864: Present. Federal Rolls of Prisoners of War: Captured at Blakely, AL, on 4/9/1865; Received at Ship Island, MS, on 4/15/1865. Transferred to Vicksburg, MS, for exchange on 5/1/1865; Exchanged at Camp Townsend, MS, on 5/6/1865. Rolls of Prisoners of War, C.S.A: Surrendered at Citronelle, AL, on 5/4/1865; Paroled at Meridian, MS, on 5/13/1865. Residence at parole: Tallapoosa County, AL.

Guy, James M. Pvt., 32nd Alabama Infantry. Co. D. Federal Rolls of Prisoners of War: Captured at Spanish Fort, AL, on 4/8/1865; Received at Ship Island, MS, on 4/10/1865. Transferred to Vicksburg, MS, for exchange on 5/1/1865; Exchanged at Camp Townsend, MS, on 5/6/1865.

Guymor, James O. Pvt., Lockhart's Battalion Infantry. Co. I. Federal Rolls of Prisoners of War: Captured at Fort Gaines, AL, on 8/8/1864; Received at Ship Island, MS, on 10/25/1864. Died: 12/12/1864 at Ship Island, MS, due to dysentery. Buried: Ship Island, MS, Cemetery in Grave #83.

Hadden, John T. Pvt., 63rd Alabama Infantry. Co. B. Enlisted: 8/15/1864 at Pollard, AL. Rolls for 9/1864 through 10/1864: Present. Federal Rolls of Prisoners of War: Captured at Blakely, AL, on 4/9/1865; Received at Ship Island, MS, on 4/15/1865. Transferred to Vicksburg, MS, for exchange on 5/1/1865; Exchanged at Camp Townsend, MS, on 5/6/1865. Rolls of Prisoners of War, C.S.A: Surrendered at Citronelle, AL, on 5/4/1865; Paroled at Meridian, MS, on 5/11/1865. Residence at parole: Dale County, AL.

Hadley, Thomas (AKA F.) Pvt., 63rd Alabama Infantry. Co. B. Federal Rolls of Prisoners of War: Captured at Blakely, AL, on 4/9/1865; Received at Ship Island, MS, on 4/15/1865. Transferred to Vicksburg, MS, for exchange on 5/1/1865; Exchanged at Camp Townsend, MS, on 5/6/1865.

Hagaman, Tappen Pvt./Cpl., 1st Alabama Artillery Battalion. Co. B. Federal Rolls of Prisoners of War: Captured at Blakely, AL, on 4/9/1865; Received at Ship Island, MS, on 4/15/1865. Transferred to Vicksburg, MS, for exchange on 5/1/1865; Exchanged at Camp Townsend, MS, on 5/6/1865.

Haisley, A.J. Pvt., 8th Alabama Cavalry. Co. A. Federal Rolls of Prisoners of War: Captured in Florida on 3/25/1865; Received at Ship Island, MS. Transferred to Vicksburg, MS, for exchange on 5/1/1865; Exchanged at Camp Townsend, MS, on 5/6/1865.

Hale, James Pvt., 1st Alabama Artillery Battalion. Co. B. Federal Rolls of Prisoners of War: Captured at Fort Gaines, AL, on 8/8/1864; Received at Ship Island, MS, from New Orleans, LA, on 10/25/1864. Exchanged on 1/4/1865.

Hall, E. (AKA Hail) Pvt., 38th Alabama Infantry. Co. __. Federal Rolls of Prisoners of War: Captured at Blakely, AL, on 4/9/1865; Received at Ship Island, MS, from New Orleans, LA, on 4/15/1865. Transferred to Vicksburg, MS, for exchange on 5/1/1865; Exchanged at Camp Townsend, MS, on 5/6/1865.

Hall, H.F. (AKA Hale) Pvt., 38th Alabama Infantry. Co. __. Federal Rolls of Prisoners of War: Captured at Blakely, AL, on 4/9/1865; Received at Ship Island, MS, on 4/15/1865. Transferred to Vicksburg, MS, for exchange on 5/1/1865; Exchanged at Camp Townsend, MS, on 5/6/1865.

Hall, J.P. Sgt., 62nd Alabama Infantry. Cos. D & E. Federal Rolls of Prisoners of War: Captured at Blakely, AL, on 4/9/1865; Received at Ship Island, MS, on 4/15/1865. Transferred to Vicksburg, MS, for exchange on 5/1/1865; Exchanged at Camp Townsend, MS, on 5/6/1865.

Hall, John Pvt., 21st Alabama Infantry. Co. B. Federal Rolls of Prisoners of War: Captured at Fort Gaines, AL, on 8/8/1864; Received at Ship Island, MS, from New Orleans, LA, on 10/25/1864. Died: 12/12/1864 at Ship Island, MS, due to chronic dysentery. Buried: Ship Island, MS, Cemetery in Grave #79.

Hall, Lafayette Pvt., 7th Alabama Cavalry. Co. __. Federal Rolls of Prisoners of War: Captured at Swan's Plantation, AL, on 7/25/1864; Received at Ship Island, MS, from New Orleans, LA, on 10/25/1864. Died: 10/22/1864 at Ship Island, MS, due to consumption. Buried: Ship Island, MS, Cemetery in Grave #3.

Hall, M.W. Sgt., 63rd Alabama Infantry. Co. E. Federal Rolls of Prisoners of War: Captured at Blakely, AL, on 4/9/1865; Received at Ship Island, MS, on

4/15/1865. Transferred to Vicksburg, MS, for exchange on 5/1/1865; Exchanged at Camp Townsend, MS, on 5/6/1865.

Hallmark, Claborn W. Pvt., 21st Alabama Infantry. Co. G. Federal Rolls of Prisoners of War: Captured at Fort Gaines, AL, on 8/8/1864; Received at Ship Island, MS, from New Orleans, LA, on 10/25/1864. Exchanged on 1/4/1865.

Hambright, Hugh Sgt., 62nd Alabama Infantry. Cos. G & H. Federal Rolls of Prisoners of War: Captured at Blakely, AL, on 4/9/1865; Received at Ship Island, MS, on 4/15/1865. Transferred to Vicksburg, MS, for exchange on 5/1/1865; Exchanged at Camp Townsend, MS, on 5/6/1865.

Hamer, John Smith Cpl., Tarrant's Artillery Battery. Enlisted: 7/1863. Federal Rolls of Prisoners of War: Captured at Blakely, AL, on 4/9/1865. Received at Ship Island, MS, on 4/15/1865. Transferred to Vicksburg, MS, for exchange on 5/1/1865; Exchanged at Camp Townsend, MS, on 5/6/1865. Paroled at Meridian, MS, on 5/11/1865. Born: 8/30/1820. Died: 9/4/1907. Buried: Hamner Family Cemetery located near Taylorville, Tuscaloosa, Alabama.

Hamilton, E.J. Pvt., 62nd Alabama Infantry. Cos. E & H. Federal Rolls of Prisoners of War: Captured at Blakely, AL, on 4/9/1865; Received at Ship Island, MS, on 4/15/1865. Transferred to Vicksburg, MS, for exchange on 5/1/1865; Exchanged at Camp Townsend, MS, on 5/6/1865.

Hamilton, F.J. Cpl., 21st Alabama Infantry. Co. D. Federal Rolls of Prisoners of War: Captured at Fort Gaines, AL, on 8/8/1864; Received at Ship Island, MS, from New Orleans, LA, on 10/25/1864. Exchanged on 1/4/1865.

Hamilton, Henry Clay Pvt., 63rd Alabama Infantry. Co. I. Enlisted: 4/15/1864 at Columbiana, AL. Rolls for 9/1864 through 10/1864: Present. Federal Rolls of Prisoners of War: Captured at Blakely, AL, on 4/9/1865; Received at Ship Island, MS, on 4/15/1865. Transferred to Vicksburg, MS, for exchange on 5/1/1865; Exchanged at Camp Townsend, MS, on 5/6/1865. Rolls of Prisoners of War, C.S.A: Surrendered at Citronelle, AL, on 5/4/1865; Paroled at Meridian, MS, on 5/13/1865. Residence at parole: Shelby County, AL.

Hamilton, J.C. (AKA Hambleton, C.J.) Pvt., 63rd Alabama Infantry. Co. I. Enlisted: 4/15/1864 at Wedowee, AL. Rolls for 9/1864 through 10/1864: Absent, on 30 day furlough since 9/27/1864. Federal Rolls of Prisoners of War: Captured at Blakely, AL, on 4/9/1865; Received at Ship Island, MS, on 4/15/1865. Transferred to Vicksburg, MS, for exchange on 5/1/1865; Exchanged at Camp Townsend, MS, on 5/6/1865.

Hamilton, Robert Cpl., 21st Alabama Infantry. Co. I. Federal Rolls of Prisoners of War: Captured at Fort Gaines, AL, on 8/8/1864; Received at Ship Island, MS, from New Orleans, LA, on 10/25/1864. Exchanged on 1/4/1865.

Hamlet, A.B. Pvt., 6th Alabama Cavalry. Co. A. Federal Rolls of Prisoners of War: Captured in Alabama on 4/1/1865; Received at Ship Island, MS. Transferred to Vicksburg, MS, for exchange on 5/1/1865; Exchanged at Camp Townsend, MS, on 5/6/1865.

Hammett, G. Pvt., 62nd Alabama Infantry. Co. C. Federal Rolls of Prisoners of War: Captured near Spanish Fort, AL, on 3/30/1865; Received at Ship Island, MS. Transferred to Vicksburg, MS, for exchange on 5/1/1865; Exchanged at Camp Townsend, MS, on 5/6/1865.

Hammonds, H.K.P. Sgt., Tarrant's Artillery Battery. Federal Rolls of Prisoners of War: Captured at Blakely, AL, on 4/9/1865; Received at Ship Island, MS, on 4/15/1865. Transferred to Vicksburg, MS, for exchange on 5/1/1865; Exchanged at Camp Townsend, MS, on 5/6/1865.

Hamner, W.J. (AKA Hammer) 1st Lt., 63rd Alabama Infantry. Co. K. Enlisted: 10/1/1864 at Blakely, AL. Federal Rolls of Prisoners of War: Captured at Blakely, AL, on 4/9/1865; Received at Ship Island, MS, on 4/16/1865. Transferred to Vicksburg, MS, for exchange on 4/28/1865; Confined at New Orleans, LA, on 4/30/1865. Exchanged at Camp Townsend, MS, on 5/6/1865. Rolls of Prisoners of War, C.S.A: Surrendered at Citronelle, AL, on 5/4/1865; Paroled at Meridian, MS, on 5/12/1865.

Hand, Neil Pvt., 21st Alabama Infantry. Co. F. Federal Rolls of Prisoners of War: Captured at Fort Gaines, AL, on 8/8/1864; Received at Ship Island, MS, from New Orleans, LA, on 10/28/1864. Died: 12/8/1864 at Ship Island, MS. Buried: Ship Island, MS, Cemetery.

Hand, Robert M. Pvt., 36th Alabama Infantry. Co. A. Federal Rolls of Prisoners of War: Captured at Spanish Fort, AL, on 4/8/1865; Received at Ship Island, MS, on 4/10/1865. Transferred to Vicksburg, MS, for exchange on 5/1/1865; Exchanged at Camp Townsend, MS, on 5/6/1865.

Hand, W.W. (AKA W.D., W.N.) Pvt., 21st Alabama Infantry. Cos. A & F. Federal Rolls of Prisoners of War: Captured at Fort Gaines, AL, on 8/8/1864; Received at Ship Island, MS, from New Orleans, LA, on 10/25/1864. Died: 12/8/1864 at Ship Island, MS, due to chronic dysentery. Buried: Ship Island, MS, Cemetery in Grave #73.

Hanes, B.F. Pvt., 36th Alabama Infantry. Co. I. Federal Rolls of Prisoners of War: Captured at Spanish Fort, AL, on 4/8/1865; Received at Ship Island, MS, on 4/10/1865. Transferred to Vicksburg, MS, for exchange on 5/1/1865; Exchanged at Camp Townsend, MS, on 5/6/1865.

Hanley, Francis H. Pvt., 21st Alabama Infantry. Cos. B & C. Enlisted: 11/1861. Detailed to the Co. C, 2nd Regiment Engineer Troops, in 9/1863. Federal Rolls of Prisoners of War: Captured at Blakely, AL, on 4/9/1865; Received at Ship Island, MS, on 4/15/1865. Transferred to Vicksburg, MS, for exchange on 5/1/1865; Exchanged at Camp Townsend, MS, on 5/6/1865. Born: 1/15/1841 at Mount Mellick County, Queens, Ireland.

Hannelly, A.O. (AKA Honnelly) Pvt./Sgt., 6th Alabama Cavalry. Co. E. Federal Rolls of Prisoners of War: Captured in Florida on 3/25/1865; Received at Ship Island, MS. Transferred to Vicksburg, MS, for exchange on 5/1/1865; Exchanged at Camp Townsend, MS, on 5/6/1865.

Hannelly, John (AKA Honnelly) Pvt., 6th Alabama Cavalry. Co. E. Federal Rolls of Prisoners of War: Captured in Florida on 3/25/1865; Received at Ship Island, MS. Transferred to Vicksburg, MS, for exchange on 5/1/1865; Exchanged at Camp Townsend, MS, on 5/6/1865.

Hanson, D.C. Pvt., 6th Alabama Cavalry. Co. C. Federal Rolls of Prisoners of War: Captured at Spanish

Fort, AL, on 4/8/1865; Received at Ship Island, MS, on 4/10/1865. Transferred to Vicksburg, MS, for exchange on 5/1/1865; Exchanged at Camp Townsend, MS, on 5/6/1865.

Hanson, William Rodford Pvt./Cpl., 62nd Alabama Infantry. Co. A. Enlisted: 1863 at Selma, AL. Federal Rolls of Prisoners of War: Captured at Blakely, AL, on 4/9/1865; Received at Ship Island, MS, on 4/15/1865. Transferred to Vicksburg, MS, for exchange on 5/1/1865; Exchanged at Camp Townsend, MS, on 5/6/1865. Born: 1/16/1847 at Perryville, Perry County, AL. Residence after war: Perry County, AL.

Hanwell, Robert R. (AKA Hannerly) 2nd Lt./1st Lt., 38th Alabama Infantry. Co. A. Federal Rolls of Prisoners of War: Captured at Spanish Fort, AL, on 4/8/1865; Received at Ship Island, MS, on 4/10/1865. Transferred to Vicksburg, MS, for exchange on 4/28/1865; Confined at New Orleans, LA, on 4/30/1865. Exchanged at Camp Townsend, MS, on 5/6/1865.

Happell, Thomas J. Sgt./Pvt., Lockhart's Battalion Infantry. Co. K. Federal Rolls of Prisoners of War: Captured at Fort Gaines, AL, on 8/8/1864; Received at Ship Island, MS, from New Orleans, LA, on 10/25/1864. Exchanged on 1/4/1865.

Hardeman, W.J. (AKA Hardman) 2nd Lt., 6th Alabama Cavalry. Co. B. Federal Rolls of Prisoners of War: Captured in Florida on 3/25/1865; Received at Ship Island, MS. Transferred to Vicksburg, MS, for exchange on 4/28/1865; Confined at New Orleans, LA, on 4/30/1865. Exchanged at Camp Townsend, MS, on 5/6/1865.

Harden, John G. Pvt., 63rd Alabama Infantry. Co. B. Enlisted: 3/23/1864 at Montgomery, AL. Age at enlistment: 17. Rolls for 9/1864 through 10/1864: Present. Federal Rolls of Prisoners of War: Captured at Gravel Hill, AL, on 3/24/1865; Received at Ship Island, MS, on 4/4/1865. Transferred to Vicksburg, MS, for exchange on 5/1/1865; Exchanged at Camp Townsend, MS, on 5/6/1865. Rolls of Prisoners of War, C.S.A: Surrendered at Citronelle, AL, on 5/4/1865; Paroled at Meridian, MS, on 5/11/1865. Residence at parole: Coosa County, AL.

Hardwick, John G. Sgt., Tarrant's Artillery Battery. Enlisted: 7/20/1863 at Tuscaloosa, AL. Federal Rolls of Prisoners of War: Captured at Blakely, AL, on 4/9/1865; Received at Ship Island, MS, on 4/15/1865. Transferred to Vicksburg, MS, for exchange on 5/1/1865; Exchanged at Camp Townsend, MS, on 5/6/1865.

Hargis, R.W. Pvt., 62nd Alabama Infantry. Co. B. Federal Rolls of Prisoners of War: Captured at Blakely, AL, on 4/9/1865; Received at Ship Island, MS, on 4/15/1865. Transferred to Vicksburg, MS, for exchange on 5/1/1865; Exchanged at Camp Townsend, MS, on 5/6/1865.

Hargrove, W.F. (AKA Hargroves, W.S.) Pvt., 21st Alabama Infantry. Co. H. Federal Rolls of Prisoners of War: Captured at Fort Gaines, AL, on 8/8/1864; Received at Ship Island, MS, from New Orleans, LA, on 10/25/1864. Exchanged on 1/4/1865.

Harper, A.T. (AKA A.Y.) Pvt., 62nd Alabama Infantry. Cos. E & F. Federal Rolls of Prisoners of War: Captured at Blakely, AL, on 4/9/1865; Received at Ship Island, MS, on 4/15/1865. Transferred to Vicksburg, MS, for exchange on 5/1/1865; Exchanged at Camp Townsend, MS, on 5/6/1865.

Harris, B.F. Pvt., 36th Alabama Infantry. Co. I. Enlisted: Wayne County, MS. Age at enlistment: 19. Federal Rolls of Prisoners of War: Captured at Spanish Fort, AL, on 4/8/1865; Received at Ship Island, MS, on 4/10/1865. Transferred to Vicksburg, MS, for exchange on 5/1/1865; Exchanged at Camp Townsend, MS, on 5/6/1865.

Harris, Eli Pvt., 62nd Alabama Infantry. Cos. F & H. Federal Rolls of Prisoners of War: Captured at Blakely, AL, on 4/9/1865; Received at Ship Island, MS, on 4/15/1865. Transferred to Vicksburg, MS, for exchange on 5/1/1865; Exchanged at Camp Townsend, MS, on 5/6/1865.

Harris, George W. (AKA William G.) Pvt., 63rd Alabama Infantry. Co. B. Federal Rolls of Prisoners of War: Captured at Blakely, AL, on 4/9/1865; Received at Ship Island, MS, on 4/15/1865. Transferred to Vicksburg, MS, for exchange on 5/1/1865; Exchanged at Camp Townsend, MS, on 5/6/1865.

Harris, J. Pvt., 62nd Alabama Infantry. Cos. F & H. Federal Rolls of Prisoners of War: Captured at Blakely, AL, on 4/9/1865; Received at Ship Island, MS, on 4/15/1865. Transferred to Vicksburg, MS, for exchange on 5/1/1865; Exchanged at Camp Townsend, MS, on 5/6/1865.

Harris, J.T. Pvt., 63rd Alabama Infantry. Cos. C & F. Federal Rolls of Prisoners of War: Captured at Blakely, AL, on 4/9/1865; Received at Ship Island, MS, from New Orleans, LA, on 4/15/1865. Transferred to Vicksburg, MS, for exchange on 5/1/1865; Exchanged at Camp Townsend, MS, on 5/6/1865.

Harris, James T. (1) Pvt., 63rd Alabama Infantry. Co. C. Enlisted: 5/11/1864 at Russell County, AL. Age at enlistment: 17. Description at enlistment: Eyes: hazel. Hair: dark. Complexion: dark. Height: 5'8½". Residence at enlistment: Salem, Russell County, AL. Rolls for 9/1864 through 10/1864: Present. Federal Rolls of Prisoners of War: Captured at Blakely, AL, on 4/9/1865; Received at Ship Island, MS, on 4/15/1865. Transferred to Vicksburg, MS, for exchange on 5/1/1865; Exchanged at Camp Townsend, MS, on 5/6/1865. Rolls of Prisoners of War, C.S.A: Surrendered at Citronelle, AL, on 5/4/1865; Paroled at Meridian, MS, on 5/11/1865. Residence at parole: Russell County, AL.

Harris, James T. (2) Pvt., 63rd Alabama Infantry. Co. I. Enlisted: 5/9/1864 at Macon County, AL. Age at enlistment: 17. Description at enlistment: Eyes: hazel. Hair: dark. Complexion: florid. Height: 5'6". Residence at enlistment: Guerryton, Macon County, AL. Rolls for 9/1864 through 10/1864: Absent, in hospital at Mobile, AL, since 9/11/1864. Federal Rolls of Prisoners of War: Captured at Blakely, AL, on 4/9/1865; Received at Ship Island, MS, on 4/15/1865. Transferred to Vicksburg, MS, for exchange on 5/1/1865; Exchanged at Camp Townsend, MS, on 5/6/1865. Rolls of Prisoners of War, C.S.A: Surrendered at Citronelle, AL, on 5/4/1865; Paroled at Meridian, MS, on 5/11/1865. Residence at parole: Russell County, AL.

Harris, James T. Cpl./Sgt., 1st Alabama Artillery Battalion. Cos. B, D & G. Federal Rolls of Prisoners of War: Captured at Spanish Fort, AL, on 4/8/1865; Received at Ship Island, MS, on 4/10/1865. Transferred to Vicksburg, MS, for exchange on 5/1/1865; Exchanged at Camp Townsend, MS, on 5/6/1865.

Harris, John Pvt., 36th Alabama Infantry. Co. E. Age at enlistment: 25. Federal Rolls of Prisoners of War: Captured at Spanish Fort, AL, on 4/8/1865; Received at Ship Island, MS, on 4/10/1865. Transferred to Vicksburg, MS, for exchange on 5/1/1865; Exchanged at Camp Townsend, MS, on 5/6/1865. Buried: Insley Cemetery located in Alabama.

Harris, Simeon B. Pvt., 63rd Alabama Infantry. Co. A. Enlisted: 1/1/1864 at Tallapoosa County, AL. Age at enlistment: 17. Rolls for 9/1864 through 10/1864: Absent, on 60 day Medical Examining Board furlough since 10/21/1864. Federal Rolls of Prisoners of War: Captured at Blakely, AL, on 4/9/1865; Received at Ship Island, MS, on 4/15/1865. Transferred to Vicksburg, MS, for exchange on 5/1/1865; Exchanged at Camp Townsend, MS, on 5/6/1865. Rolls of Prisoners of War, C.S.A: Surrendered at Citronelle, AL, on 5/4/1865; Paroled at Meridian, MS, on 5/13/1865. Residence at parole: Tallapoosa County, AL.

Harris, T.H. Sgt., Lockhart's Battalion Infantry. Co. I. Federal Rolls of Prisoners of War: Captured at Fort Gaines, AL, on 8/8/1864; Received at Ship Island, MS, from New Orleans, LA, on 10/25/1864. Exchanged on 1/4/1865.

Harris, W. Pvt., 63rd Alabama Infantry. Co. B. Federal Rolls of Prisoners of War: Captured at Blakely, AL, on 4/9/1865; Received at Ship Island, MS, on 4/15/1865. Transferred to Vicksburg, MS, for exchange on 5/1/1865; Exchanged at Camp Townsend, MS, on 5/6/1865.

Harris, W.J. Pvt., 63rd Alabama Infantry. Co. F. Enlisted: 5/30/1864 at Montgomery, AL. Age at enlistment: 17. Description at enlistment: Eyes: blue. Hair: dark. Complexion: dark. Height: 5'8". Residence at enlistment: Autauga County, AL. Rolls for 9/1864 through 10/1864: Present, sick. Federal Rolls of Prisoners of War: Captured at Blakely, AL, on 4/9/1865; Received at Ship Island, MS, on 4/15/1865. Transferred to Vicksburg, MS, for exchange on 5/1/1865. On Register of U.S.A. General Hospital #2, Vicksburg, MS: Admitted from steamer on 5/3/1865 due to lung inflammation; Returned to duty on 5/23/1865. Age at admittance: 18.

Harris, William G. Pvt., 63rd Alabama Infantry. Co. B. Enlisted: 3/23/1864 at Montgomery County, AL. Age at enlistment: 17. Rolls for 9/1864 through 10/1864: Absent, sick since 10/13/1864. On Register of Ross Hospital, Mobile, AL: Admitted on 12/31/1864 due to anasarca; Returned to duty on 1/23/1865. Federal Rolls of Prisoners of War: Captured at Blakely, AL, on 4/9/1865; Received at Ship Island, MS, on 4/15/1865. Transferred to Vicksburg, MS, for exchange on 5/1/1865; Exchanged at Camp Townsend, MS, on 5/6/1865. Rolls of Prisoners of War, C.S.A: Surrendered at Citronelle, AL, on 5/4/1865; Paroled at Meridian, MS, on 5/11/1865. Residence at parole: Russell County, AL.

Harrison, Edward Pvt., 1st Alabama Artillery Battalion. Co. __. Federal Rolls of Prisoners of War: Captured at Spanish Fort, AL, on 4/8/1865; Received at Ship Island, MS, on 4/10/1865. Transferred to Vicksburg, MS, for exchange on 5/1/1865; Exchanged at Camp Townsend, MS, on 5/6/1865.

Harrison, G.W. Pvt., 38th Alabama Infantry. Co. I. Federal Rolls of Prisoners of War: Captured at Spanish Fort, AL, on 4/8/1865; Received at Ship Island, MS, on 4/10/1865. Transferred to Vicksburg, MS, for exchange on 5/1/1865; Exchanged at Camp Townsend, MS, on 5/6/1865.

Harrison, J. Pvt., 63rd Alabama Infantry. Co. F. Enlisted: 5/30/1864 at Montgomery, AL. Age at enlistment: 17. Description at enlistment: Eyes: dark. Hair: dark. Complexion: dark. Height: 5'8". Residence at enlistment: Butler County, AL. Rolls for 9/1864 through 10/1864: Present. Federal Rolls of Prisoners of War: Captured at Blakely, AL, on 4/9/1865; Received at Ship Island, MS, on 4/15/1865. Transferred to Vicksburg, MS, for exchange on 5/1/1865; Exchanged at Camp Townsend, MS, on 5/6/1865. Rolls of Prisoners of War, C.S.A: Surrendered at Citronelle, AL, on 5/4/1865; Paroled at Meridian, MS, on 5/11/1865. Residence at parole: Butler County, AL.

Harrison, J.A. Pvt., 63rd Alabama Infantry. Co. F. Federal Rolls of Prisoners of War: Captured at Blakely, AL, on 4/9/1865; Received at Ship Island, MS, on 4/15/1865. Transferred to Vicksburg, MS, for exchange on 5/1/1865; Exchanged at Camp Townsend, MS, on 5/6/1865.

Harrison, Morris Pvt., 63rd Alabama Infantry. Cos. A & G. Enlisted: 10/1/1864 at Blakely, AL. Age at enlistment: 17. Rolls for 9/1864 through 10/1864: Present. Federal Rolls of Prisoners of War: Captured at Blakely, AL, on 4/9/1865; Received at Ship Island, MS, on 4/15/1865. Transferred to Vicksburg, MS, for exchange on 5/1/1865; Exchanged at Camp Townsend, MS, on 5/6/1865. Rolls of Prisoners of War, C.S.A: Surrendered at Citronelle, AL, on 5/4/1865; Paroled at Meridian, MS, on 5/13/1865. Residence at parole: Coffee County, AL.

Harrison, Samuel Pvt., 1st Alabama Artillery Battalion. Cos. A, B & D. Federal Rolls of Prisoners of War: Captured at Fort Gaines, AL, on 8/8/1864; Transferred to Ship Island, MS, from New Orleans, LA, on 10/25/1864. Exchanged on 1/4/1865.

Harrold, Burrel W. Pvt., 63rd Alabama Infantry. Co. B. Federal Rolls of Prisoners of War: Captured at Blakely, AL, on 4/9/1865; Received at Ship Island, MS, on 4/15/1865. Transferred to Vicksburg, MS, for exchange on 5/1/1865; Exchanged at Camp Townsend, MS, on 5/6/1865.

Harrolson, James M. Pvt., 63rd Alabama Infantry. Co. C. Enlisted: 5/17/1864 at Tallapoosa County, AL. Age at enlistment: 17. Description at enlistment: Eyes: hazel. Hair: dark. Complexion: dark. Height: 5'2½". Residence at enlistment: Dadeville, Tallapoosa County, AL. On Register of Ross Hospital, Mobile, AL: Admitted on 9/3/1864 due to acute diarrhea; Sent to Greenville, AL, General Hospital on 9/13/1864. Rolls for 9/1864 through 10/1864: Absent, at hospital in Montgomery, AL, since 10/28/1864. Federal Rolls of Prisoners of War: Captured at Blakely, AL, on 4/9/1865; Received at Ship Island, MS, on 4/15/1865. Transferred to Vicksburg, MS, for exchange on 5/1/1865; Exchanged at Camp Townsend, MS, on 5/6/1865. Rolls of Prisoners of War, C.S.A: Surrendered at Citronelle, AL, on 5/4/1865; Paroled at Meridian, MS, on 5/11/1865. Residence at parole: Tallapoosa County, AL.

Hart, Allen Thomas Pvt./Sgt., 25th Alabama Infantry. Co. A. Federal Rolls of Prisoners of War: Captured in Alabama on 3/22/1865; Received at Ship Island,

MS. Transferred to Vicksburg, MS, for exchange on 5/1/1865; Exchanged at Camp Townsend, MS, on 5/6/1865. Born 12/7/1840. Died: 8/19/1874. Buried: Magnolia Cemetery located at Andalusia, Covington County, AL.

Hart, Elisha Pvt., 38th Alabama Infantry. Co. E. Federal Rolls of Prisoners of War: Captured at Blakely, AL, on 4/9/1865; Received at Ship Island, MS, on 4/15/1865. Transferred to Vicksburg, MS, for exchange on 5/1/1865; Exchanged at Camp Townsend, MS, on 5/6/1865.

Hart, H.F. Pvt., 38th Alabama Infantry. Co. E. Federal Rolls of Prisoners of War: Captured at Blakely, AL, on 4/9/1865; Received at Ship Island, MS, on 4/15/1865. Transferred to Vicksburg, MS, for exchange on 5/1/1865; Exchanged at Camp Townsend, MS, on 5/6/1865.

Hartley, J.K. 2nd Lt., 63rd Alabama Infantry. Co. I. Elected 2nd Lt. on 11/24/1864. Federal Rolls of Prisoners of War: Captured at Blakely, AL, on 4/9/1865; Received at Ship Island, MS, on 4/16/1865. Transferred to Vicksburg, MS, for exchange on 4/28/1865; Confined at New Orleans, LA, on 4/30/1865. Exchanged at Camp Townsend, MS, on 5/6/1865. Rolls of Prisoners of War, C.S.A: Surrendered at Citronelle, AL, on 5/4/1865; Paroled at Meridian, MS, on 5/11/1865.

Hartley, William E. (AKA W.A.) Pvt., 62nd Alabama Infantry. Cos. A & K. Federal Rolls of Prisoners of War: Captured at Blakely, AL, on 4/9/1865; Received at Ship Island, MS, on 4/15/1865. Transferred to Vicksburg, MS, for exchange on 5/1/1865; Exchanged at Camp Townsend, MS, on 5/6/1865.

Harvey, E.W. (AKA Hobby) Pvt., 63rd Alabama Infantry. Co. F. Federal Rolls of Prisoners of War: Captured at Blakely, AL, on 4/9/1865; Received at Ship Island, MS, on 4/15/1865. Transferred to Vicksburg, MS, for exchange on 5/1/1865; Exchanged at Camp Townsend, MS, on 5/6/1865.

Harwell, E.W. (AKA Harnell) Pvt., 21st Alabama Infantry. Cos. C & K. Federal Rolls of Prisoners of War: Captured at Fort Gaines, AL, on 8/8/1864; Received at Ship Island, MS, from New Orleans, LA, on 10/25/1864. Exchanged on 1/4/1865.

Harwell, Robert R. (AKA Harivelle) 2nd Lt./1st Lt., 38th Alabama Infantry. Co. A. Enlisted: 5/15/1862. Elected 2nd Lt. on 3/22/1863; Promoted to 1st Lt. on 9/20/1863. Federal Rolls of Prisoners of War: Captured at Spanish Fort, AL, on 4/8/1865; Received at Ship Island, MS, on 4/10/1865. Transferred to Vicksburg, MS, for exchange on 4/28/1865; Confined at New Orleans, LA, on 4/30/1865. Exchanged at Camp Townsend, MS, on 5/6/1865.

Hatton, T.J. 2nd Lt., 21st Alabama Infantry. Co. B. Federal Rolls of Prisoners of War: Captured at Fort Gaines, AL, on 8/8/1864; Received at Ship Island, MS, from New Orleans, LA, on 11/25/1864. Exchanged on 1/4/1865.

Haupt, James E. (AKA J.P.) Pvt., 21st Alabama Infantry. Co. E. Federal Rolls of Prisoners of War: Captured at Fort Gaines, AL, on 8/8/1864; Received at Ship Island, MS, from New Orleans, LA, on 10/25/1864. Exchanged on 1/4/1865.

Hawkins, W.A. Cpl., 21st Alabama Infantry. Co. H. Federal Rolls of Prisoners of War: Captured at Fort Gaines, AL, on 8/8/1864; Received at Ship Island, MS, from New Orleans, LA, on 10/25/1864. Exchanged on 1/4/1865.

Hay, A.J. (AKA J.A.) Pvt., Lockhart's Battalion Infantry. Co. H. Federal Rolls of Prisoners of War: Captured at Fort Gaines, AL, on 8/8/1864; Received at Ship Island, MS, from New Orleans, LA, on 10/25/1864. Died: 12/8/1864 at Ship Island, MS, due to dysentery. Buried: Ship Island, MS, Cemetery in Grave #71.

Hayes, M.V.B. Pvt., Tarrant's Artillery Battery. Federal Rolls of Prisoners of War: Captured at Blakely, AL, on 4/9/1865; Received at Ship Island, MS, on 4/15/1865. Transferred to Vicksburg, MS, for exchange on 5/1/1865; Exchanged at Camp Townsend, MS, on 5/6/1865.

Hayes, William Pvt., 62nd Alabama Infantry. Cos. A & D. Federal Rolls of Prisoners of War: Captured at Blakely, AL, on 4/9/1865; Received at Ship Island, MS, on 4/15/1865. Transferred to Vicksburg, MS, for exchange on 5/1/1865; Exchanged at Camp Townsend, MS, on 5/6/1865.

Haynes, J.M. (AKA J.D.) Pvt., 21st Alabama Infantry. Co.G. Federal Rolls of Prisoners of War: Captured at Fort Gaines, AL, on 8/8/1864; Received at Ship Island, MS, from New Orleans, LA, on 10/25/1864. Exchanged on 1/4/1865.

Hays, Andrew W. Pvt., 62nd Alabama Infantry. Co. A. Federal Rolls of Prisoners of War: Captured at Blakely, AL, on 4/9/1865; Received at Ship Island, MS, on 4/15/1865. Transferred to Vicksburg, MS, for exchange on 5/1/1865; Exchanged at Camp Townsend, MS, on 5/6/1865.

Hays, Jesse Pvt., Lockhart's Battalion Infantry. Co. I. Federal Rolls of Prisoners of War: Captured at Fort Gaines, AL, on 8/8/1864; Received at Ship Island, MS, from New Orleans, LA, on 10/25/1864. Died: 12/12/1864 at Ship Island, MS, due to chronic dysentery. Buried: Ship Island, MS, Cemetery in Grave #80.

Hays, John N. Pvt., 62nd Alabama Infantry. Co. A. Federal Rolls of Prisoners of War: Captured at Blakely, AL, on 4/9/1865; Received at Ship Island, MS, on 4/15/1865. Transferred to Vicksburg, MS, for exchange on 5/1/1865; Exchanged at Camp Townsend, MS, on 5/6/1865.

Hays, L.F. Pvt., 36th Alabama Infantry. Co. D. Federal Rolls of Prisoners of War: Captured at Spanish Fort, AL, on 4/8/1865; Received at Ship Island, MS, on 4/10/1865. Transferred to Vicksburg, MS, for exchange on 5/1/1865; Exchanged at Camp Townsend, MS, on 5/6/1865.

Hays, N.H. Pvt., 62nd Alabama Infantry. Cos. A & D. Federal Rolls of Prisoners of War: Captured at Blakely, AL, on 4/9/1865; Received at Ship Island, MS, on 4/15/1865. Transferred to Vicksburg, MS, for exchange on 5/1/1865; Exchanged at Camp Townsend, MS, on 5/6/1865.

Hays, R.D. (AKA R.A.) Pvt., 62nd Alabama Infantry. Co. I. Federal Rolls of Prisoners of War: Captured at Blakely, AL, on 4/9/1865; Received at Ship Island, MS, on 4/15/1865. Transferred to Vicksburg, MS, for exchange on 5/1/1865; Exchanged at Camp Townsend, MS, on 5/6/1865.

Hays, William Pvt., 36th Alabama Infantry. Co. I. Enlisted: Wayne County, MS. Age at enlistment: 31. Federal Rolls of Prisoners of War: Captured at Spanish Fort, AL, on 4/8/1865; Received at Ship Island,

MS, on 4/10/1865. Transferred to Vicksburg, MS, for exchange on 5/1/1865; Exchanged at Camp Townsend, MS, on 5/6/1865.

Hazes, J.F. Pvt., Tarrant's Artillery Battery. Federal Rolls of Prisoners of War: Captured at Blakely, AL, on 4/9/1865; Received at Ship Island, MS, on 4/15/1865. Transferred to Vicksburg, MS, for exchange on 5/1/1865; Exchanged at Camp Townsend, MS, on 5/6/1865.

Head, R.A. 2nd Lt., 6th Alabama Cavalry. Co. D. Federal Rolls of Prisoners of War: Captured in Florida on 3/25/1865; Received at Ship Island, MS. Transferred to Vicksburg, MS, for exchange on 5/1/1865; Exchanged at Camp Townsend, MS, on 5/6/1865.

Head, William R. Capt., 6th Alabama Infantry. Cos. D & H. Federal Rolls of Prisoners of War: Captured at Bluff Springs, AL, on 3/25/1865; Received at Ship Island, MS. Transferred to Vicksburg, MS, for exchange on 4/28/1865; Confined at New Orleans, LA, on 4/30/1865. Exchanged at Camp Townsend, MS, on 5/6/1865.

Healey, P.B. Pvt., Tarrant's Artillery Battery. Enlisted: 7/20/1863 at Tuscaloosa, AL. Federal Rolls of Prisoners of War: Captured at Blakely, AL, on 4/9/1865; Received at Ship Island, MS, on 4/15/1865. Transferred to Vicksburg, MS, for exchange on 5/1/1865; Exchanged at Camp Townsend, MS, on 5/6/1865.

Heard, John F.M. Pvt., 21st Alabama Infantry. Co. G. Federal Rolls of Prisoners of War: Captured at Fort Gaines, AL, on 8/8/1864; Received at Ship Island, MS, from New Orleans, LA, on 10/25/1864. Died: 11/30/1864 at Ship Island, MS, due to dysentery. Buried: Ship Island, MS, Cemetery in Grave #54.

Hearn, C.C. (AKA Hern, Heron) Pvt., Lockhart's Battalion Infantry. Co. C. Federal Rolls of Prisoners of War: Captured at Fort Gaines, AL, on 8/8/1864; Received at Ship Island, MS, from New Orleans, LA, on 10/25/1864. Exchanged on 1/4/1865.

Hearn, N.G. Pvt., 62nd Alabama Infantry. Co. G. Federal Rolls of Prisoners of War: Captured at Blakely, AL, on 4/9/1865; Received at Ship Island, MS, on 4/15/1865. Transferred to Vicksburg, MS, for exchange on 5/1/1865; Exchanged at Camp Townsend, MS, on 5/6/1865.

Heath, M.T. Pvt., 62nd Alabama Infantry. Co. C. Federal Rolls of Prisoners of War: Captured at Blakely, AL, on 4/9/1865; Received at Ship Island, MS, on 4/15/1865. Transferred to Vicksburg, MS, for exchange on 5/1/1865; Exchanged at Camp Townsend, MS, on 5/6/1865.

Heath, W.H. Pvt., 63rd Alabama Infantry. Co. F. Federal Rolls of Prisoners of War: Captured at Blakely, AL, on 4/9/1865; Received at Ship Island, MS, on 4/15/1865. Transferred to Vicksburg, MS, for exchange on 5/1/1865; Exchanged at Camp Townsend, MS, on 5/6/1865.

Heatherton, E. Pvt., 63rd Alabama Infantry. Co. H. Federal Rolls of Prisoners of War: Captured at Blakely, AL, on 4/9/1865; Received at Ship Island, MS, on 4/15/1865. Transferred to Vicksburg, MS, for exchange on 5/1/1865; Exchanged at Camp Townsend, MS, on 5/6/1865.

Height, H. (AKA Hight) Pvt., 63rd Alabama Infantry. Co. E. Federal Rolls of Prisoners of War: Captured at Blakely, AL, on 4/9/1865; Received at Ship Island, MS, on 4/15/1865. Transferred to Vicksburg, MS, for exchange on 5/1/1865; Exchanged at Camp Townsend, MS, on 5/6/1865.

Heite, H.U. Pvt., 21st Alabama Infantry. Co. D. Federal Rolls of Prisoners of War: Captured at Blakely, AL, on 4/9/1865; Received at Ship Island, MS, on 4/15/1865. Transferred to Vicksburg, MS, for exchange on 5/1/1865; Exchanged at Camp Townsend, MS, on 5/6/1865.

Hellington, F.K. (AKA Hethington) Pvt., 62nd Alabama Infantry. Cos. H & K. Federal Rolls of Prisoners of War: Captured at Blakely, AL, on 4/9/1865; Received at Ship Island, MS, on 4/15/1865. Transferred to Vicksburg, MS, for exchange on 5/1/1865; Exchanged at Camp Townsend, MS, on 5/6/1865.

Henderson, B.S. Pvt., 63rd Alabama Infantry. Co. K. Enlisted: 8/31/1864 at Greene County, AL. Rolls for 9/1864 through 10/1864: Present. Federal Rolls of Prisoners of War: Captured at Blakely, AL, on 4/9/1865; Received at Ship Island, MS, on 4/15/1865. Transferred to Vicksburg, MS, for exchange on 5/1/1865; Exchanged at Camp Townsend, MS, on 5/6/1865. Rolls of Prisoners of War, C.S.A: Surrendered at Citronelle, AL, on 5/4/1865; Paroled at Meridian, MS, on 5/13/1865. Residence at parole: Greene County, AL.

Henderson, Charles Pvt., Tarrant's Artillery Battery. Federal Rolls of Prisoners of War: Captured at Blakely, AL, on 4/9/1865; Received at Ship Island, MS, on 4/15/1865. Transferred to Vicksburg, MS, for exchange on 5/1/1865; Exchanged at Camp Townsend, MS, on 5/6/1865.

Henderson, S.M. (AKA S.N.) Pvt., 63rd Alabama Infantry. Co. K. Enlisted: 8/31/1864 at Greene County, AL. Rolls for 9/1864 through 10/1864: Absent, in hospital at Mobile, AL, since 10/14/1864. Federal Rolls of Prisoners of War: Captured at Blakely, AL, on 4/9/1865; Received at Ship Island, MS, on 4/15/1865. Transferred to Vicksburg, MS, for exchange on 5/1/1865; Exchanged at Camp Townsend, MS, on 5/6/1865. Rolls of Prisoners of War, C.S.A: Surrendered at Citronelle, AL, on 5/4/1865; Paroled at Meridian, MS, on 5/13/1865. Residence at parole: Greene County, AL.

Hendly, J.W. Pvt., 63rd Alabama Infantry. Co. H. Enlisted: 3/15/1864 at Randolph County, AL. Age at enlistment: 17. Description at enlistment: Eyes: blue. Hair: light. Complexion: fair. Rolls for 9/1864 through 10/1864: Present. Federal Rolls of Prisoners of War: Captured at Blakely, AL, on 4/9/1865; Received at Ship Island, MS, on 4/15/1865. Transferred to Vicksburg, MS, for exchange on 5/1/1865; Exchanged at Camp Townsend, MS, on 5/6/1865. Rolls of Prisoners of War, C.S.A: Surrendered at Citronelle, AL, on 5/4/1865; Paroled at Meridian, MS, on 5/11/1865. Residence at parole: Bibb County, AL.

Hendricks, W.J. Pvt., Tarrant's Artillery Battery. Federal Rolls of Prisoners of War: Captured at Blakely, AL, on 4/9/1865; Received at Ship Island, MS, on 4/15/1865. Transferred to Vicksburg, MS, for exchange on 5/1/1865; Exchanged at Camp Townsend, MS, on 5/6/1865.

Hendriks, David (AKA Hendricks, Hendrix) Pvt., 8th Alabama Cavalry. Co. C. Federal Rolls of Prisoners of War: Captured in Alabama on 3/24/1865; Received at Ship Island, MS. Died: 4/15/1865 at Ship Island, MS, due to diarrhea. Buried: Ship Island, MS, Cemetery in Grave #147.

Henford, ? Pvt., 63rd Alabama Infantry. Co. __.

Federal Rolls of Prisoners of War: Captured at Blakely, AL, on 4/9/1865; Received at Ship Island, MS, on 4/15/1865. Transferred to Vicksburg, MS, for exchange on 5/1/1865; Exchanged at Camp Townsend, MS, on 5/6/1865.

Henley, Hezekiah Pvt., 63rd Alabama Infantry. Cos. D & I. Enlisted: 6/30/1864 at Macon County, AL. Age at enlistment: 17. Description at enlistment: Eyes: blue. Hair: light. Complexion: fair. Height: 5'6". Residence at enlistment: Buford, Barbour County, AL. Rolls for 9/1864 through 10/1864: Present. Federal Rolls of Prisoners of War: Captured at Blakely, AL, on 4/9/1865; Received at Ship Island, MS, on 4/15/1865. Transferred to Vicksburg, MS, for exchange on 5/1/1865; Exchanged at Camp Townsend, MS, on 5/6/1865. Rolls of Prisoners of War, C.S.A: Surrendered at Citronelle, AL, on 5/4/1865; Paroled at Meridian, MS, on 5/13/1865. Residence at parole: Barbour County, AL.

Henley, J.P. Pvt., 21st Alabama Infantry. Co. __. Federal Rolls of Prisoners of War: Captured at Fort Gaines, AL, on 8/8/1864; Received at Ship Island, MS, from New Orleans, LA, on 10/25/1864. Exchanged on 1/4/1865.

Henning, Elisha (AKA Hennig, Hening) Pvt., 36th Alabama Infantry. Co. K. Federal Rolls of Prisoners of War: Captured at Spanish Fort, AL, on 4/8/1865; Received at Ship Island, MS, on 4/10/1865. Transferred to Vicksburg, MS, for exchange on 5/1/1865; Exchanged at Camp Townsend, MS, on 5/6/1865.

Henson, James M. (AKA Hinson, Joseph) Pvt., 21st Alabama Infantry. Co. C. Federal Rolls of Prisoners of War: Captured at Blakely, AL, on 4/9/1865; Received at Ship Island, MS, on 4/15/1865. Transferred to Vicksburg, MS, for exchange on 5/1/1865; Exchanged at Camp Townsend, MS, on 5/6/1865.

Henson, John Cpl., 21st Alabama Infantry. Cos. C & D. Federal Rolls of Prisoners of War: Captured at Blakely, AL, on 4/9/1865; Received at Ship Island, MS, on 4/15/1865. Transferred to Vicksburg, MS, for exchange on 5/1/1865; Exchanged at Camp Townsend, MS, on 5/6/1865.

Henson, William R. (AKA Hinson) Pvt., 21st Alabama Infantry. Co. C. Federal Rolls of Prisoners of War: Captured at Blakely, AL, on 4/9/1865; Received at Ship Island, MS, on 4/15/1865. Transferred to Vicksburg, MS, for exchange on 5/1/1865; Exchanged at Camp Townsend, MS, on 5/6/1865.

Hercomb, James (AKA Hercum) Pvt., 1st Alabama Artillery. Co. D. Federal Rolls of Prisoners of War: Captured at Blakely, AL, on 4/9/1865; Received at Ship Island, MS, on 4/15/1865. Transferred to Vicksburg, MS, for exchange on 5/1/1865; Exchanged at Camp Townsend, MS, on 5/6/1865.

Herring, Elisha Sgt., 36th Alabama Infantry. Co. K. Enlisted: Tuscaloosa, AL. Age at enlistment: 28. Federal Rolls of Prisoners of War: Captured at Spanish Fort, AL, on 4/8/1865; Received at Ship Island, MS, on 4/10/1865. Transferred to Vicksburg, MS, for exchange on 5/1/1865; Exchanged at Camp Townsend, MS, on 5/6/1865.

Herring, Emanuel Sgt., 21st Alabama Infantry. Co. G. Federal Rolls of Prisoners of War: Captured at Fort Gaines, AL, on 8/8/1864; Received at Ship Island, MS, from New Orleans, LA, on 10/25/1864. Died: 12/21/1864 at Ship Island, MS. Buried: Ship Island, MS, Cemetery.

Herron, Stephen W. Pvt., 63rd Alabama Infantry. Co. A. Federal Rolls of Prisoners of War: Captured at Blakely, AL, on 4/9/1865; Received at Ship Island, MS, on 4/15/1865. Transferred to Vicksburg, MS, for exchange on 5/1/1865; Exchanged at Camp Townsend, MS, on 5/6/1865.

Herzey, P. Pvt., 21st Alabama Infantry. Co. D. Federal Rolls of Prisoners of War: Captured at Blakely, AL, on 4/9/1865; Received at Ship Island, MS, on 4/15/1865. Transferred to Vicksburg, MS, for exchange on 5/1/1865; Exchanged at Camp Townsend, MS, on 5/6/1865.

Heustis, H.M. Pvt., 1st Alabama Infantry. Co. K. Federal Rolls of Prisoners of War: Captured at Spanish Fort, AL, on 4/8/1865; Received at Ship Island, MS, on 4/10/1865. Transferred to Vicksburg, MS, for exchange on 5/1/1865; Exchanged at Camp Townsend, MS, on 5/6/1865.

Hicks, F.N. (AKA F.M.) Pvt., 1st Alabama Artillery Battalion. Cos. A, B & D. Federal Rolls of Prisoners of War: Captured at Fort Gaines, AL, on 8/8/1864; Transferred to Ship Island, MS, from New Orleans, LA, on 10/25/1864. Exchanged on 1/4/1865.

Hicks, John T. Pvt., 21st Alabama Infantry. Cos. B & K. Federal Rolls of Prisoners of War: Captured at Fort Gaines, AL, on 8/8/1864; Received at Ship Island, MS, from New Orleans, LA, on 10/25/1864. Exchanged on 1/4/1865.

Hicks, Walter W. (AKA W.V.) Pvt., 1st Alabama Artillery Battalion. Cos. B & D. Federal Rolls of Prisoners of War: Captured at Blakely, AL, on 4/9/1865; Received at Ship Island, MS, on 4/15/1865. Transferred to Vicksburg, MS, for exchange on 5/1/1865; Exchanged at Camp Townsend, MS, on 5/6/1865.

Hightower, A.W. Cpl./Sgt., 8th Alabama Cavalry. Co. C. Federal Rolls of Prisoners of War: Captured in Florida on 3/25/1865; Received at Ship Island, MS. Transferred to Vicksburg, MS, for exchange on 5/1/1865; Exchanged at Camp Townsend, MS, on 5/6/1865.

Hill, G.B. Pvt., 21st Alabama Infantry. Co. C. Federal Rolls of Prisoners of War: Captured at Fort Gaines, AL, on 8/8/1864; Received at Ship Island, MS, from New Orleans, LA, on 10/25/1864. Exchanged on 1/4/1865.

Hill, George W. Pvt., 1st Alabama Artillery. Co. D. Federal Rolls of Prisoners of War: Captured at Fort Gaines, AL, on 8/8/1864; Transferred to Ship Island, MS, from New Orleans, LA, on 10/25/1864. Died: 12/13/1864 at Ship Island, MS, due to chronic dysentery. Buried: Ship Island, MS, Cemetery in Grave #87.

Hill, Henry J. Pvt., 21st Alabama Infantry. Co. H. Federal Rolls of Prisoners of War: Captured at Fort Gaines, AL, on 8/8/1864; Received at Ship Island, MS, from New Orleans, LA, on 10/25/1864. Exchanged on 1/4/1865.

Hill, J.T. (AKA I.T.) Pvt., 62nd Alabama Infantry. Co. B. Federal Rolls of Prisoners of War: Captured at Blakely, AL, on 4/9/1865; Received at Ship Island, MS, on 4/15/1865. Transferred to Vicksburg, MS, for exchange on 5/1/1865; Exchanged at Camp Townsend, MS, on 5/6/1865.

Hill Robert D. Sgt./2nd Lt., 62nd Alabama Infantry. Co. A. Federal Rolls of Prisoners of War: Captured at Blakely, AL, on 4/9/1865; Received at Ship Island,

MS, on 4/15/1865. Transferred to Vicksburg, MS, for exchange on 4/28/1865; Confined at New Orleans, LA, on 4/30/1865. Exchanged at Camp Townsend, MS, on 5/6/1865.

Hill, William M. (AKA W.H.) Pvt., 63rd Alabama Infantry. Cos. B & K. Federal Rolls of Prisoners of War: Captured at Blakely, AL, on 4/9/1865; Received at Ship Island, MS, on 4/15/1865. Transferred to Vicksburg, MS, for exchange on 5/1/1865; Exchanged at Camp Townsend, MS, on 5/6/1865.

Hilton, Thomas (AKA Hylton, Thomas S.) Drummer, 21st Alabama Infantry. Co. C. Federal Rolls of Prisoners of War: Captured at Fort Gaines, AL, on 8/8/1864; Received at Ship Island, MS, from New Orleans, LA, on 10/25/1864. Exchanged on 1/4/1865.

Hilton, V.A. (AKA Hylton) Q.M. Sgt., 21st Alabama Infantry. Co. I. Federal Rolls of Prisoners of War: Captured at Blakely, AL, on 4/9/1865; Received at Ship Island, MS, from New Orleans, LA, on 4/15/1865. Transferred to Vicksburg, MS, for exchange on 5/1/1865; Exchanged at Camp Townsend, MS, on 5/6/1865.

Hinckell, John (AKA Hinkle) Pvt., 62nd Alabama Infantry. Co. A. Federal Rolls of Prisoners of War: Captured at Blakely, AL, on 4/9/1865; Received at Ship Island, MS, on 4/15/1865. Transferred to Vicksburg, MS, for exchange on 5/1/1865; Exchanged at Camp Townsend, MS, on 5/6/1865.

Hinson, Edward Pvt., 1st Alabama Artillery Battalion. Federal Rolls of Prisoners of War: Captured at Fort Gaines, AL, on 8/8/1864; Received at Ship Island, MS, from New Orleans, LA, on 10/25/1864. Died: 11/9/1864 at Ship Island, MS, due to pneumonia. Buried: Ship Island, MS, Cemetery in Grave #14.

Hinton, John S. Pvt., 6th Alabama Cavalry. Cos. C & D. Federal Rolls of Prisoners of War: Captured in Florida on 3/25/1865; Received at Ship Island, MS. Transferred to Vicksburg, MS, for exchange on 5/1/1865; Exchanged at Camp Townsend, MS, on 5/6/1865.

Hinton, W.H. Pvt., Tarrant's Artillery Battery. Enlisted: 7/25/1863 at Tuscaloosa, AL. Federal Rolls of Prisoners of War: Captured at Blakely, AL, on 4/9/1865; Received at Ship Island, MS, on 4/15/1865. Transferred to Vicksburg, MS, for exchange on 5/1/1865; Exchanged at Camp Townsend, MS, on 5/6/1865.

Hirrick, T. (AKA Hinnick, S.) Pvt., 62nd Alabama Infantry. Cos. A & K. Federal Rolls of Prisoners of War: Captured at Blakely, AL, on 4/9/1865; Received at Ship Island, MS, on 4/15/1865. Transferred to Vicksburg, MS, for exchange on 5/1/1865; Exchanged at Camp Townsend, MS, on 5/6/1865.

Hitt, J.A. (AKA Hite) Pvt., 62nd Alabama Infantry. Co. C. Federal Rolls of Prisoners of War: Captured at Blakely, AL, on 4/9/1865; Received at Ship Island, MS, on 4/15/1865. Transferred to Vicksburg, MS, for exchange on 5/1/1865; Exchanged at Camp Townsend, MS, on 5/6/1865.

Hixon, Daniel A. Sgt., 63rd Alabama Infantry. Cos. D & G. Federal Rolls of Prisoners of War: Captured at Blakely, AL, on 4/9/1865; Received at Ship Island, MS, on 4/15/1865. Transferred to Vicksburg, MS, for exchange on 5/1/1865; Exchanged at Camp Townsend, MS, on 5/6/1865.

Hode, James A. Pvt., 62nd Alabama Infantry. Co. E. Federal Rolls of Prisoners of War: Captured at Blakely, AL, on 4/9/1865; Received at Ship Island, MS, on 4/15/1865. Transferred to Vicksburg, MS, for exchange on 5/1/1865; Exchanged at Camp Townsend, MS, on 5/6/1865.

Hogan, W.R. Pvt., 62nd Alabama Infantry. Co. B. Federal Rolls of Prisoners of War: Captured at Blakely, AL, on 4/9/1865; Received at Ship Island, MS, on 4/15/1865. Transferred to Vicksburg, MS, for exchange on 5/1/1865; Exchanged at Camp Townsend, MS, on 5/6/1865.

Holdsworth, William Pvt., 21st Alabama Infantry. Cos. B & K. Federal Rolls of Prisoners of War: Captured at Fort Gaines, AL, on 8/8/1864; Received at Ship Island, MS, from New Orleans, LA, on 10/25/1864. Exchanged on 1/4/1865.

Holifield, Joel Pvt., Tarrant's Artillery Battery. Federal Rolls of Prisoners of War: Captured at Blakely, AL, on 4/9/1865; Received at Ship Island, MS, on 4/15/1865. Transferred to Vicksburg, MS, for exchange on 5/1/1865; Exchanged at Camp Townsend, MS, on 5/6/1865.

Hollace, J.E. Pvt., 62nd Alabama Infantry. Cos. A & E. Federal Rolls of Prisoners of War: Captured at Blakely, AL, on 4/9/1865; Received at Ship Island, MS, on 4/15/1865. Transferred to Vicksburg, MS, for exchange on 5/1/1865; Exchanged at Camp Townsend, MS, on 5/6/1865.

Holland, Brit Pvt., 4th Alabama Cavalry. Co. __. Federal Rolls of Prisoners of War: Captured in Florida on 3/25/1865; Received at Ship Island, MS. Transferred to Vicksburg, MS, for exchange on 5/1/1865; Exchanged at Camp Townsend, MS, on 5/6/1865.

Holley, A. Pvt., Lockhart's Artillery Battery. Co. H. Federal Rolls of Prisoners of War: Captured at Fort Gaines, AL, on 8/8/1864; Received at Ship Island, MS, from New Orleans, LA, on 10/25/1864. Died: 11/4/1864 at Ship Island, MS, due to rubeola. Buried: Ship Island, MS, Cemetery in Grave #10.

Holley, Milton (AKA Halley, Millon) Pvt., 1st Alabama Artillery Battalion. Co. D. Federal Rolls of Prisoners of War: Captured at Fort Gaines, AL, on 8/8/1864; Received at Ship Island, MS, from New Orleans, LA, on 10/25/1864. Exchanged on 1/4/1865.

Holley, William J. (AKA Holly) Pvt., 6th Alabama Cavalry. Co. C. Federal Rolls of Prisoners of War: Captured in Alabama on 3/24/1865; Received at Ship Island, MS. Transferred to Vicksburg, MS, for exchange on 5/1/1865; Exchanged at Camp Townsend, MS, on 5/6/1865.

Hollingshead, J.W. Pvt., Tarrant's Artillery Battery. Federal Rolls of Prisoners of War: Captured at Blakely, AL, on 4/9/1865; Received at Ship Island, MS, on 4/15/1865. Transferred to Vicksburg, MS, for exchange on 5/1/1865; Exchanged at Camp Townsend, MS, on 5/6/1865.

Hollingsworth, George W. Pvt., 63rd Alabama Infantry. Co. A. Federal Rolls of Prisoners of War: Captured at Blakely, AL, on 4/9/1865; Received at Ship Island, MS, on 4/15/1865. Transferred to Vicksburg, MS, for exchange on 5/1/1865; Exchanged at Camp Townsend, MS, on 5/6/1865.

Holly, Amond D. Sgt., 62nd Alabama Infantry. Co. G. Federal Rolls of Prisoners of War: Captured at Blakely, AL, on 4/9/1865; Received at Ship Island, MS, on 4/15/1865. Transferred to Vicksburg, MS, for

exchange on 5/1/1865; Exchanged at Camp Townsend, MS, on 5/6/1865.

Holly, Thomas R. Pvt., 62nd Alabama Infantry. Co. G. Federal Rolls of Prisoners of War: Captured at Blakely, AL, on 4/9/1865; Received at Ship Island, MS, on 4/15/1865. Transferred to Vicksburg, MS, for exchange on 5/1/1865; Exchanged at Camp Townsend, MS, on 5/6/1865.

Holmes, B.R. Sgt., 21st Alabama Infantry. Co. H. Federal Rolls of Prisoners of War: Captured at Fort Gaines, AL, on 8/8/1864; Received at Ship Island, MS, from New Orleans, LA, on 10/25/1864. Exchanged on 1/4/1865.

Holt, A.D. (AKA H.D.) Pvt., 21st Alabama Infantry. Co. E. Federal Rolls of Prisoners of War: Captured at Fort Gaines, AL, on 8/8/1864; Received at Ship Island, MS, from New Orleans, LA, on 10/25/1864. Exchanged on 1/4/1865.

Honeycutt, William L. Pvt., 62nd Alabama Infantry. Co. A. Federal Rolls of Prisoners of War: Captured at Blakely, AL, on 4/9/1865; Received at Ship Island, MS, on 4/15/1865. Transferred to Vicksburg, MS, for exchange on 5/1/1865; Exchanged at Camp Townsend, MS, on 5/6/1865.

Honnelly, John Pvt., 6th Alabama Cavalry. Co. E. Federal Rolls of Prisoners of War: Captured in Florida on 3/25/1865; Received at Ship Island, MS. Transferred to Vicksburg, MS, for exchange on 5/1/1865; Exchanged at Camp Townsend, MS, on 5/6/1865.

Horne, William H. (AKA Horn) Pvt., 21st Alabama Infantry. Co. D. Federal Rolls of Prisoners of War: Captured at Blakely, AL, on 4/9/1865; Received at Ship Island, MS, on 4/15/1865. Transferred to Vicksburg, MS, for exchange on 5/1/1865; Exchanged at Camp Townsend, MS, on 5/6/1865.

Houston, W.T. Pvt., 21st Alabama Infantry. Co. G. Federal Rolls of Prisoners of War: Captured at Fort Gaines, AL, on 8/8/1864; Transferred to Ship Island, MS, from New Orleans, LA, on 10/25/1864. Exchanged on 1/4/1865.

Howard, G.W. Pvt., Tarrant's Artillery Battery. Federal Rolls of Prisoners of War: Captured at Blakely, AL, on 4/9/1865; Received at Ship Island, MS, on 4/15/1865. Transferred to Vicksburg, MS, for exchange on 5/1/1865.

Howard, Harris Pvt., 18th Alabama Infantry. Co. H. Federal Rolls of Prisoners of War: Captured at Blakely, AL, on 4/9/1865; Received at Ship Island, MS, on 4/15/1865. Transferred to Vicksburg, MS, for exchange on 5/1/1865; Exchanged at Camp Townsend, MS, on 5/6/1865.

Howard, J.M. Pvt., Tarrant's Artillery Battery. Federal Rolls of Prisoners of War: Captured at Blakely, AL, on 4/9/1865; Received at Ship Island, MS, on 4/15/1865. Transferred to Vicksburg, MS, for exchange on 5/1/1865; Exchanged at Camp Townsend, MS, on 5/6/1865.

Howard, J.M. Pvt., 18th Alabama Infantry. Co. B. Federal Rolls of Prisoners of War: Captured at Spanish Fort, AL, on 4/8/1865; Received at Ship Island, MS, on 4/10/1865. Transferred to Vicksburg, MS, for exchange on 5/1/1865; Exchanged at Camp Townsend, MS, on 5/6/1865.

Howard, James Pvt., 63rd Alabama Infantry. Co. B. Federal Rolls of Prisoners of War: Captured in Alabama on 3/24/1865; Received at Ship Island, MS. Transferred to Vicksburg, MS, for exchange on 5/1/1865; Exchanged at Camp Townsend, MS, on 5/6/1865.

Howard, John Pvt., Tarrant's Artillery Battery. Federal Rolls of Prisoners of War: Captured at Blakely, AL, on 4/9/1865; Received at Ship Island, MS, on 4/15/1865. Transferred to Vicksburg, MS, for exchange on 5/1/1865; Exchanged at Camp Townsend, MS, on 5/6/1865.

Howard, L.A. (AKA S.A.) Pvt., 18th Alabama Infantry. Co. B. Federal Rolls of Prisoners of War: Captured at Spanish Fort, AL, on 4/8/1865; Received at Ship Island, MS, on 4/10/1865. Transferred to Vicksburg, MS, for exchange on 5/1/1865; Exchanged at Camp Townsend, MS, on 5/6/1865.

Howell, James Pvt./Cpl., 21st Alabama Infantry. Co. I. Federal Rolls of Prisoners of War: Captured at Fort Gaines, AL, on 8/8/1864; Received at Ship Island, MS, from New Orleans, LA, on 10/25/1864. Exchanged on 1/4/1865.

Howell, Phil M. Pvt., 21st Alabama Infantry. Co. I. Federal Rolls of Prisoners of War: Captured at Fort Gaines, AL, on 8/8/1864; Received at Ship Island, MS, from New Orleans, LA, on 10/25/1864. Died: 12/15/1864 at Ship Island, MS, due to chronic dysentery. Buried: Ship Island, MS, Cemetery in Grave #90.

Hubbard, M.A. (AKA M.O.) Pvt., 21st Alabama Infantry. Co. G. Federal Rolls of Prisoners of War: Captured at Fort Gaines, AL, on 8/8/1864; Received at Ship Island, MS, from New Orleans, LA, on 10/25/1864. Exchanged on 1/4/1865; Released at New Orleans, LA, by order of Maj. Gen.E.R.S. Canby on 4/10/1865. Residence at release: Mobile, AL. Description at release: Eyes: brown. Hair: brown. Complexion: ruddy. Height: 5'7".

Hubbard, W.L. (AKA Hybbard, N.L.) Pvt., 36th Alabama Infantry. Co. G. Federal Rolls of Prisoners of war: Captured at Spanish Fort, AL, on 4/8/1865; Received at Ship Island, MS, on 4/10/1865. Transferred to Vicksburg, MS, for exchange on 5/1/1865; Exchanged at Camp Townsend, MS, on 5/6/1865.

Huckaby, G.J. (AKA Huckabee) Pvt., 21st Alabama Infantry. Co. C. Federal Rolls of Prisoners of War: Captured at Fort Gaines, AL, on 8/8/1864; Received at Ship Island, MS, from New Orleans, LA, on 10/25/1864. Exchanged on 1/4/1865.

Huckaby, R.P. Pvt., 21st Alabama Infantry. Cos. C & H. Federal Rolls of Prisoners of War: Captured at Fort Gaines, AL, on 8/8/1864; Received at Ship Island, MS, from New Orleans, LA, on 10/25/1864. Exchanged on 1/4/1865.

Huckaby, Robert Pvt., 21st Alabama Infantry. Cos. C & H. Federal Rolls of Prisoners of War: Captured at Fort Gaines, AL, on 8/8/1864; Received at Ship Island, MS, from New Orleans, LA, on 10/25/1864. Exchanged on 1/4/1865.

Huckaby, W.B. (AKA Huckabee) Pvt., 21st Alabama Infantry. Cos. C & H. Federal Rolls of Prisoners of War: Captured at Fort Gaines, AL, on 8/8/1864; Received at Ship Island, MS, from New Orleans, LA, on 10/25/1864. Exchanged on 1/4/1865.

Hudson, Burrell Pvt., 21st Alabama Infantry. Co. C. Federal Rolls of Prisoners of War: Captured at Fort Gaines, AL, on 8/8/1864; Received at Ship Island, MS, from New Orleans, LA, on 10/25/1864. Died:

12/21/1864 at Ship Island, MS, due to pneumonia. Buried: Ship Island, MS, Cemetery in Grave #21.

Hudson, J.W. Pvt., 62nd Alabama Infantry. Cos. E & H. Federal Rolls of Prisoners of War: Captured at Blakely, AL, on 4/9/1865; Received at Ship Island, MS, on 4/15/1865. Transferred to Vicksburg, MS, for exchange on 5/1/1865; Exchanged at Camp Townsend, MS, on 5/6/1865.

Hudson, Thomas A. Pvt., Lockhart's Artillery Battery. Co. E. Federal Rolls of Prisoners of War: Captured at Fort Gaines, AL, on 8/8/1864; Received at Ship Island, MS, from New Orleans, LA, on 10/25/1864. Died: 12/5/1864 at Ship Island, MS, due to typhoid fever. Buried: Ship Island, MS, Cemetery in Grave #66.

Huey, S.H. Pvt., 18th Alabama Infantry. Co. G. Federal Rolls of Prisoners of War: Captured at Spanish Fort, AL, on 4/8/1865; Received at Ship Island, MS, on 4/10/1865. Transferred to Vicksburg, MS, for exchange on 5/1/1865; Exchanged at Camp Townsend, MS, on 5/6/1865.

Huey, Samuel B. (AKA Henry, T.B.) Pvt., 63rd Alabama Infantry. Co. C. Federal Rolls of Prisoners of War: Captured at Blakely, AL, on 4/9/1865; Received at Ship Island, MS, on 4/15/1865. Transferred to Vicksburg, MS, for exchange on 5/1/1865; Exchanged at Camp Townsend, MS, on 5/6/1865.

Huff, John M. (AKA J.N.) Musician/Pvt., 62nd Alabama Infantry. Co. A. Federal Rolls of Prisoners of War: Captured at Blakely, AL, on 4/9/1865; Received at Ship Island, MS, on 4/15/1865. Transferred to Vicksburg, MS, for exchange on 5/1/1865; Exchanged at Camp Townsend, MS, on 5/6/1865.

Huffman, J.R. (AKA I.) Pvt., 63rd Alabama Infantry. Co. F. Federal Rolls of Prisoners of War: Captured at Blakely, AL, on 4/9/1865; Received at Ship Island, MS, on 4/15/1865. Transferred to Vicksburg, MS, for exchange on 5/1/1865; Exchanged at Camp Townsend, MS, on 5/6/1865.

Hunt, J.H. Pvt., 62nd Alabama Infantry. Co. K. Federal Rolls of Prisoners of War: Captured at Blakely, AL, on 4/9/1865; Received at Ship Island, MS, on 4/15/1865. Transferred to Vicksburg, MS, for exchange on 5/1/1865; Exchanged at Camp Townsend, MS, on 5/6/1865.

Hunt, William Pvt., 21st Alabama Infantry. Co. B. Federal Rolls of Prisoners of War: Captured at Fort Gaines, AL, on 8/8/1864; Received at Ship Island, MS, from New Orleans, LA, on 10/25/1864. Exchanged on 1/4/1865.

Hutchings, George T. (AKA Hutchins) Pvt., 1st Alabama Artillery Battalion. Co. E. Federal Rolls of Prisoners of War: Captured at Blakely, AL, on 4/9/1865; Received at Ship Island, MS, on 4/15/1865. Transferred to Vicksburg, MS, for exchange on 5/1/1865; Exchanged at Camp Townsend, MS, on 5/6/1865.

Hutchins, H.C. (AKA Hutchens) Pvt., 36th Alabama Cavalry. Co. H. Federal Rolls of Prisoners of War: Captured in Alabama on 3/24/1865; Received at Ship Island, MS. Transferred to Vicksburg, MS, for exchange on 5/1/1865; Exchanged at Camp Townsend, MS, on 5/6/1865.

Ingraham, T.E.R. Pvt., 21st Alabama Infantry. Co. I. Federal Rolls of Prisoners of War: Captured at Fort Gaines, AL, on 8/8/1864; Received at Ship Island, MS, from New Orleans, LA, on 10/25/1864. Exchanged on 1/4/1865.

Jackson, Daniel S. Pvt., 8th Alabama Cavalry. Co. C. Federal Rolls of Prisoners of War: Captured in Florida on 3/25/1865; Received at Ship Island, MS. Transferred to Vicksburg, MS, for exchange on 5/1/1865; Exchanged at Camp Townsend, MS, on 5/6/1865.

Jackson, J.F. Pvt., 21st Alabama Infantry. Co. H. Federal Rolls of Prisoners of War: Captured at Fort Gaines, AL, on 8/8/1864; Received at Ship Island, MS, from New Orleans, LA, on 10/25/1864. Exchanged on 1/4/1865.

Jackson, J.W. Pvt., 21st Alabama Infantry. Cos. C & H. Federal Rolls of Prisoners of War: Captured at Fort Gaines, AL, on 8/8/1864; Received at Ship Island, MS, from New Orleans, LA, on 10/25/1864. Exchanged on 1/4/1865.

Jackson, Joseph A.T. Pvt., 63rd Alabama Infantry. Co. C. Federal Rolls of Prisoners of War: Captured at Blakely, AL, on 4/9/1865; Received at Ship Island, MS, on 4/15/1865. Transferred to Vicksburg, MS, for exchange on 5/1/1865; Exchanged at Camp Townsend, MS, on 5/6/1865.

Jackson, M.H. Pvt., 21st Alabama Infantry. Co. C. Federal Rolls of Prisoners of War: Captured at Fort Gaines, AL, on 8/8/1864; Received at Ship Island, MS, from New Orleans on 10/25/1864. Exchanged on 1/4/1865.

Jackson, Shields Pvt., 21st Alabama Infantry. Cos. C & H. Federal Rolls of Prisoners of War: Captured at Fort Gaines, AL, on 8/8/1864; Received at Ship Island, MS, from New Orleans, LA, on 10/25/1864. Exchanged on 1/4/1865.

James, C.A. Pvt., 63rd Alabama Infantry. Co. E. Federal Rolls of Prisoners of War: Captured at Blakely, AL, on 4/9/1865; Received at Ship Island, MS, on 4/15/1865. Transferred to Vicksburg, MS, for exchange on 5/1/1865; Exchanged at Camp Townsend, MS, on 5/6/1865.

Janvasett, A. (AKA Jerneah) Pvt., 6th Alabama Cavalry. Co. H. Federal Rolls of Prisoners of War: Captured in Florida on 3/25/1865; Received at Ship Island, MS. Transferred to Vicksburg, MS, for exchange on 5/1/1865; Exchanged at Camp Townsend, MS, on 5/6/1865.

Jaramey, E. Pvt., 6th Alabama Cavalry. Co. D. Federal Rolls of Prisoners of War: Captured in Florida on 3/25/1865; Received at Ship Island, MS. Transferred to Vicksburg, MS, for exchange on 5/1/1865; Exchanged at Camp Townsend, MS, on 5/6/1865.

Jarman, John L. Pvt., 62nd Alabama Infantry. Co. A. Federal Rolls of Prisoners of War: Captured at Blakely, AL, on 4/9/1865; Received at Ship Island, MS, on 4/15/1865. Transferred to Vicksburg, MS, for exchange on 5/1/1865; Exchanged at Camp Townsend, MS, on 5/6/1865.

Jarome, E. (AKA Jerome) Pvt., 6th Alabama Cavalry. Co. D. Federal Rolls of Prisoners of War: Captured in Florida on 3/25/1865; Received at Ship Island, MS. Transferred to Vicksburg, MS, for exchange on 5/1/1865; Exchanged at Camp Townsend, MS, on 5/6/1865.

Jarrard, J.T. 1st Sgt., Lockhart's Battalion Infantry. Cos. E & F. Federal Rolls of Prisoners of War: Captured at Fort Gaines, AL, on 8/8/1864; Received at

Ship Island, MS, from New Orleans, LA, on 10/25/1864. Exchanged on 1/4/1865.

Jennery, J.H. (AKA Jennesy) Pvt., 36th Alabama Infantry. Co. D. Federal Rolls of Prisoners of War: Captured in Alabama on 3/24/1865; Received at Ship Island, MS. Transferred to Vicksburg, MS, for exchange on 5/1/1865; Exchanged at Camp Townsend, MS, on 5/6/1865.

Jennings, H. Pvt., 63rd Alabama Infantry. Co. C. Federal Rolls of Prisoners of War: Captured at Blakely, AL, on 4/9/1865; Received at Ship Island, MS, on 4/15/1865. Transferred to Vicksburg, MS, for exchange on 5/1/1865; Exchanged at Camp Townsend, MS, on 5/6/1865.

Jennings, J.W. (AKA J.W.J.) Pvt., 62nd Alabama Infantry. Co. A. Federal Rolls of Prisoners of War: Captured at Blakely, AL, on 4/9/1865; Received at Ship Island, MS, on 4/15/1865. Transferred to Vicksburg, MS, for exchange on 5/1/1865; Exchanged at Camp Townsend, MS, on 5/6/1865.

Joey, N. Pvt., 62nd Alabama Infantry. Co. G. Federal Rolls of Prisoners of War: Captured at Blakely, AL, on 4/9/1865; Received at Ship Island, MS, on 4/15/1865. Transferred to Vicksburg, MS, for exchange on 5/1/1865; Exchanged at Camp Townsend, MS, on 5/6/1865.

Johns, E.N. Pvt., 63rd Alabama Infantry. Co. G. Federal Rolls of Prisoners of War: Captured at Blakely, AL, on 4/9/1865; Received at Ship Island, MS, on 4/15/1865. Transferred to Vicksburg, MS, for exchange on 5/1/1865; Exchanged at Camp Townsend, MS, on 5/6/1865.

Johnson, Charles Moore (AKA C.W.) Cpl., 62nd Alabama Infantry. Co. I. Enlisted: 4/1864. Federal Rolls of Prisoners of War: Captured at Blakely, AL, on 4/9/1865; Received at Ship Island, MS, on 4/15/1865. Transferred to Vicksburg, MS, for exchange on 5/1/1865; Exchanged at Camp Townsend, MS, on 5/6/1865. Residence after war: Dallas County, AL. Born: 8/6/1846 at Selma, AL.

Johnson, F.C. Pvt., Lockhart's Battalion Infantry. Co. H. Federal Rolls of Prisoners of War: Captured at Fort Gaines, AL, on 8/8/1864; Received at Ship Island, MS, from New Orleans, LA, on 10/25/1864. Exchanged on 1/4/1865.

Johnson, Herbert P. 2nd Lt., 63rd Alabama Infantry. Co. D. Federal Rolls of Prisoners of War: Captured at Blakely, AL, on 4/9/1865; Received at Ship Island, MS, on 4/15/1865. Transferred to Vicksburg, MS, for exchange on 4/28/1865; Confined at New Orleans, LA, on 4/30/1865. Exchanged at Camp Townsend, MS, on 5/6/1865.

Johnson, J.H. Pvt., Lockhart's Battalion Infantry. Co. __. Federal Rolls of Prisoners of War: Captured at Fort Gaines, AL, on 8/8/1864; Received at Ship Island, MS, from New Orleans, LA, on 10/25/1864. Exchanged on 1/4/1865.

Johnson, M.A. (AKA M.W.) Pvt., 62nd Alabama Infantry. Co. F. Federal Rolls of Prisoners of War: Captured at Blakely, AL, on 4/9/1865; Received at Ship Island, MS, on 4/15/1865. Transferred to Vicksburg, MS, for exchange on 5/1/1865; Exchanged at Camp Townsend, MS, on 5/6/1865.

Johnson, R.W. Pvt., Lockhart's Battalion Infantry. Co. I. Federal Rolls of Prisoners of War: Captured at Fort Gaines, AL, on 8/8/1864; Received at Ship Island, MS, from New Orleans, LA, on 10/25/1864. Died: 11/16/1864 at Ship Island, MS, due to chronic diarrhea. Buried: Ship Island, MS, Cemetery in Grave #22.

Johnson, Robert Pvt., 1st Alabama Cavalry. Co. H. Federal Rolls of Prisoners of War: Captured at Mobile Point, AL, on 7/22/1864; Received at Ship Island, MS, from New Orleans, LA, on 10/7/1864. Transferred to Fort Columbus, New York Harbor, NY, on 11/5/1864.

Johnson, T. (AKA Johnston) Pvt., 62nd Alabama Infantry. Co. I. Federal Rolls of Prisoners of War: Captured at Blakely, AL, on 4/9/1865; Received at Ship Island, MS, on 4/15/1865. Transferred to Vicksburg, MS, for exchange on 5/1/1865; Exchanged at Camp Townsend, MS, on 5/6/1865.

Johnson, Thomas J. (AKA T.I.) Pvt., Lockhart's Battalion Infantry. Co. H. Federal Rolls of Prisoners of War: Captured at Fort Gaines, AL, on 8/8/1864; Received at Ship Island, MS, from New Orleans, LA, on 10/25/1864. Died: 10/31/1864 at Ship Island, MS, due to chronic diarrhea. Buried: Ship Island, MS, Cemetery in Grave #6.

Johnson, William Cpl./Sgt., 63rd Alabama Infantry. Co. A. Federal Rolls of Prisoners of War: Captured at Blakely, AL, on 4/9/1865; Received at Ship Island, MS, on 4/15/1865. Transferred to Vicksburg, MS, for exchange on 5/1/1865; Exchanged at Camp Townsend, MS, on 5/6/1865.

Johnston, Charles B. Capt./Maj., 21st Alabama Infantry. F & S. Federal Rolls of Prisoners of War: Captured at Fort Gaines, AL, on 8/8/1864; Received at Ship Island, MS, from New Orleans, LA, on 11/25/1864. Transferred to Vicksburg, MS, for exchange on 4/28/1865; Confined at New Orleans, LA, on 4/30/1865. Exchanged at Camp Townsend, MS, on 5/6/1865.

Johnston, David (AKA E.) Sgt./Sgt. Maj., 63rd Alabama Infantry. Co. A. Federal Rolls of Prisoners of War: Captured at Blakely, AL, on 4/9/1865; Received at Ship Island, MS, on 4/15/1865. Transferred to Vicksburg, MS, for exchange on 5/1/1865; Exchanged at Camp Townsend, MS, on 5/6/1865.

Johnston, James P. Pvt./Cpl., 63rd Alabama Infantry. Co. A. Federal Rolls of Prisoners of War: Captured at Blakely, AL, on 4/9/1865; Received at Ship Island, MS, on 4/15/1865. Transferred to Vicksburg, MS, for exchange on 5/1/1865; Exchanged at Camp Townsend, MS, on 5/6/1865.

Johnston, John W. Pvt., 63rd Alabama Infantry. Co. C. Federal Rolls of Prisoners of War: Captured at Blakely, AL, on 4/9/1865; Received at Ship Island, MS, on 4/15/1865. Transferred to Vicksburg, MS, for exchange on 5/1/1865; Exchanged at Camp Townsend, MS, on 5/6/1865.

Jones, A.J. Pvt., 62nd Alabama Infantry. Co. B. Federal Rolls of Prisoners of War: Captured at Blakely, AL, on 4/9/1865; Received at Ship Island, MS, on 4/15/1865. Transferred to Vicksburg, MS, for exchange on 5/1/1865; Exchanged at Camp Townsend, MS, on 5/6/1865.

Jones, C.C. Pvt., 62nd Alabama Infantry. Co. C. Federal Rolls of Prisoners of War: Captured at Blakely, AL, on 4/9/1865; Received at Ship Island, MS, on 4/15/1865. Transferred to Vicksburg, MS, for exchange on 5/1/1865; Exchanged at Camp Townsend, MS, on 5/6/1865.

Jones, C.M. (AKA C.W.) Cpl., 62nd Alabama Infantry. Co. I. Federal Rolls of Prisoners of War: Captured at Blakely, AL, on 4/9/1865; Received at Ship Island, MS, on 4/15/1865. Transferred to Vicksburg, MS, for exchange on 5/1/1865; Exchanged at Camp Townsend, MS, on 5/6/1865.

Jones, D. Pvt., 8th Alabama Cavalry. Cos. A & E. Federal Rolls of Prisoners of War: Captured in Alabama on 3/27/1865; Received at Ship Island, MS. Transferred to Vicksburg, MS, for exchange on 5/1/1865; Exchanged at Camp Townsend, MS, on 5/6/1865.

Jones, F.J. Pvt., 21st Alabama Infantry. Co. E. Federal Rolls of Prisoners of War: Captured at Fort Gaines, AL, on 8/8/1864; Received at Ship Island, MS, from New Orleans, LA, on 10/25/1864. Exchanged on 1/4/1865.

Jones, Henry M. Pvt., 21st Alabama Infantry. Co. D. Federal Rolls of Prisoners of War: Captured at Fort Gaines, AL, on 8/8/1864; Received at Ship Island, MS, from New Orleans, LA, on 10/25/1864. Exchanged on 1/4/1865.

Jones, J.K. Pvt., Lockhart's Battalion Infantry. Co. E. Federal Rolls of Prisoners of War: Captured at Fort Gaines, AL, on 8/8/1864; Received at Ship Island, MS, from New Orleans, LA, on 10/25/1864. Died: 12/4/1864 at Ship Island, MS, due to dysentery. Buried: Ship Island, MS, Cemetery in Grave #63.

Jones, James Pvt., 62nd Alabama Infantry. Co. G. Federal Rolls of Prisoners of War: Captured at Blakely, AL, on 4/9/1865; Received at Ship Island, MS, on 4/15/1865. Transferred to Vicksburg, MS, for exchange on 5/1/1865; Exchanged at Camp Townsend, MS, on 5/6/1865.

Jones, James K. Pvt., Lockhart's Artillery Battery. Co. E. Federal Rolls of Prisoners of War: Captured at Fort Gaines, AL, on 8/8/1864; Received at Ship Island, MS, on 10/25/1864. Died: 12/3/1864 at Ship Island, MS, due to typhoid fever. Buried: Ship Island, MS, Cemetery in Grave #63.

Jones, James L. Pvt., 38th Alabama Infantry. Co. E. Enlisted: 4/7/1862 at Mobile, AL. Age at enlistment: 21. On Register of Hospital, Tunnel Hill, GA: Admitted on 6/27/1863 due to acute diarrhea; Furloughed on 8/7/1863. Paid $19.80 for commutation of rations while on sick leave from 8/8/1863 through 10/26/1863. Federal Rolls of Prisoners of War: Captured at Blakely, AL, on 4/9/1865; Received at Ship Island, MS, on 4/15/1865. Transferred to Vicksburg, MS, for exchange on 5/1/1865; Exchanged at Camp Townsend, MS, on 5/6/1865.

Jones, John A. Pvt., 63rd Alabama Infantry. Co. C. Federal Rolls of Prisoners of War: Captured at Blakely, AL, on 4/9/1865; Received at Ship Island, MS, on 4/15/1865. Transferred to Vicksburg, MS, for exchange on 5/1/1865; Exchanged at Camp Townsend, MS, on 5/6/1865.

Jones, O.H. (AKA H.) Pvt., 62nd Alabama Infantry. Co. I. Federal Rolls of Prisoners of War: Captured at Blakely, AL, on 4/9/1865; Received at Ship Island, MS, on 4/15/1865. Transferred to Vicksburg, MS, for exchange on 5/1/1865; Exchanged at Camp Townsend, MS, on 5/6/1865.

Jones, W.E. 1st Sgt./2nd Lt., 63rd Alabama Infantry. Co. E. Federal Rolls of Prisoners of War: Captured at Blakely, AL, on 4/9/1865; Received at Ship Island, MS, on 4/15/1865. Transferred to Vicksburg, MS, for exchange on 4/28/1865; Confined at New Orleans, LA, on 4/30/1865. Exchanged at Camp Townsend, MS, on 5/6/1865.

Jones, W.J. Pvt./Cpl., 63rd Alabama Infantry. Co. F. Federal Rolls of Prisoners of War: Captured at Blakely, AL, on 4/9/1865; Received at Ship Island, MS, on 4/15/1865. Transferred to Vicksburg, MS, for exchange on 5/1/1865; Exchanged at Camp Townsend, MS, on 5/6/1865.

Jones, W.P. Sgt., 62nd Alabama Infantry. Cos. D & K. Federal Rolls of Prisoners of War: Captured at Blakely, AL, on 4/9/1865; Received at Ship Island, MS, on 4/15/1865. Transferred to Vicksburg, MS, for exchange on 5/1/1865; Exchanged at Camp Townsend, MS, on 5/6/1865.

Jones, W.R. (AKA W.B.) Pvt., 1st Alabama Cavalry. Co. __. Federal Rolls of Prisoners of War: Captured at Tensas Parish, LA, on 7/22/1864; Received at Ship Island, MS, from New Orleans, LA, on 10/7/1864. Transferred to Fort Columbus, New York Harbor, NY, on 11/5/1864.

Jordan, G.M. Sgt., 63rd Alabama Infantry. Co. E. Federal Rolls of Prisoners of War: Captured at Blakely, AL, on 4/9/1865; Received at Ship Island, MS, on 4/15/1865. Transferred to Vicksburg, MS, for exchange on 5/1/1865; Exchanged at Camp Townsend, MS, on 5/6/1865.

Kain, G.W. Sgt., 21st Alabama Infantry. Co. F. Federal Rolls of Prisoners of War: Captured at Fort Gaines, AL, on 8/8/1864; Received at Ship Island, MS, from New Orleans, LA, on 10/25/1864. Exchanged on 1/4/1865.

Kaplan, H.C. Pvt., 1st Alabama Artillery. Co. B. Federal Rolls of Prisoners of War: Captured at Fort Gaines, AL, on 8/8/1864; Received at Ship Island, MS, from New Orleans, LA, on 10/25/1864. Exchanged on 1/4/1865.

Kates, H. Pvt., 36th Alabama Infantry. Co. G. Federal Rolls of Prisoners of War: Captured at Spanish Fort, AL, on 4/8/1865; Received at Ship Island, MS, on 4/10/1865. Transferred to Vicksburg, MS, for exchange on 5/1/1865; Exchanged at Camp Townsend, MS, on 5/6/1865.

Keath, Jospeh (AKA Keith) Pvt./Sgt., 62nd Alabama Infantry. Cos. C & E. Federal Rolls of Prisoners of War: Captured at Blakely, AL, on 4/9/1865; Received at Ship Island, MS, on 4/15/1865. Transferred to Vicksburg, MS, for exchange on 5/1/1865; Exchanged at Camp Townsend, MS, on 5/6/1865.

Keel, James F. (AKA Kiel) Cpl./Pvt., 18th Alabama Infantry. Co. B. Federal Rolls of Prisoners of War: Captured at Spanish Fort, AL, on 4/8/1865; Received at Ship Island, MS, on 4/10/1865. Transferred to Vicksburg, MS, for exchange on 5/1/1865; Exchanged at Camp Townsend, MS, on 5/6/1865.

Keely, John T. Pvt., 18th Alabama Infantry. Co. B. Federal Rolls of Prisoners of War: Captured at Spanish Fort, AL, on 4/8/1865; Received at Ship Island, MS, on 4/10/1865. Transferred to Vicksburg, MS, for exchange on 5/1/1865; Exchanged at Camp Townsend, MS, on 5/6/1865.

Keifer, J.M. Pvt., 18th Alabama Infantry. Co. B. Federal Rolls of Prisoners of War: Captured at Spanish Fort, AL, on 4/8/1865; Received at Ship Island, MS, on 4/10/1865. Transferred to Vicksburg, MS, for exchange

on 5/1/1865; Exchanged at Camp Townsend, MS, on 5/6/1865.

Kellum, William Allen Pvt., 62nd Alabama Infantry. Co. A. Enlisted: 9/15/1863 at Selma, AL. Federal Rolls of Prisoners of War: Captured at Blakely, AL, on 4/9/1865; Received at Ship Island, MS, on 4/15/1865. Transferred to Vicksburg, MS, for exchange on 5/1/1865; Exchanged at Camp Townsend, MS, on 5/6/1865. Born: 5/28/1847 at Blockton, Bibb County, AL.

Kelly, Berry (AKA Kelley) Pvt., 63rd Alabama Infantry. Co. B. Enlisted: 7/15/1864 at Pollard, AL. Rolls for 9/1864 through 10/1864: Present. Federal Rolls of Prisoners of War: Captured at Blakely, AL, on 4/9/1865; Received at Ship Island, MS, on 4/15/1865. Transferred to Vicksburg, MS, for exchange on 5/1/1865; Exchanged at Camp Townsend, MS, on 5/6/1865. Rolls of Prisoners of War, C.S.A: Surrendered at Citronelle, AL, on 5/4/1865; Paroled at Meridian, MS, on 5/11/1865. Residence at parole: Coosa County, AL.

Kelly, E.D. Pvt., 21st Alabama Infantry. Co. C. Federal Rolls of Prisoners of War: Captured at Blakely, AL, on 4/9/1865; Received at Ship Island, MS, on 4/15/1865. Transferred to Vicksburg, MS, for exchange on 5/1/1865; Exchanged at Camp Townsend, MS, on 5/6/1865.

Kelly, G.P. Pvt., 21st Alabama Infantry. Cos. C & D. Federal Rolls of Prisoners of War: Captured at Blakely, AL, on 4/9/1865; Received at Ship Island, MS, on 4/15/1865. Transferred to Vicksburg, MS, for exchange on 5/1/1865; Exchanged at Camp Townsend, MS, on 5/6/1865.

Kelly, Henry (AKA Kelley) Pvt., 63rd Alabama Infantry. Co. B. Enlisted: 8/2/1864 at Montgomery, AL. Rolls for 9/1864 through 10/1864: Present. Federal Rolls of Prisoners of War: Captured at Blakely, AL, on 4/9/1865; Received at Ship Island, MS, on 4/15/1865. Transferred to Vicksburg, MS, for exchange on 5/1/1865; Exchanged at Camp Townsend, MS, on 5/6/1865. Rolls of Prisoners of War, C.S.A: Surrendered at Citronelle, AL, on 5/4/1865; Paroled at Meridian, MS, on 5/11/1865. Residence at parole: Coosa County, AL.

Kelly, W.R. Pvt., 63rd Alabama Infantry. Co. D. Enlisted: 8/5/1864 at Elba, AL. Rolls for 8/30/1864 through 10/30/1864: Present. Federal Rolls of Prisoners of War: Captured at Blakely, AL, on 4/9/1865; Received at Ship Island, MS, on 4/15/1865. Transferred to Vicksburg, MS, for exchange on 5/1/1865; Exchanged at Camp Townsend, MS, on 5/6/1865. Rolls of Prisoners of War, C.S.A: Surrendered at Citronelle, AL, on 5/4/1865; Paroled at Meridian, MS, on 5/13/1865. Residence at parole: Coffee County, AL.

Kemp, James Pvt./Cpl., 1st Alabama Artillery. Co. D. Federal Rolls of Prisoners of War: Captured at Fort Gaines, AL, on 8/8/1864; Received at Ship Island, MS, from New Orleans, LA, on 10/25/1864. Exchanged on 1/4/1865.

Kennedy, Daniel Pvt./Cpl., 21st Alabama Infantry. Co. B. Federal Rolls of Prisoners of War: Captured at Fort Gaines, AL, on 8/8/1864; Received at Ship Island, MS, from New Orleans, LA, on 10/25/1864. Exchanged on 1/4/1865.

Kennedy, Edward Pvt., 21st Alabama Infantry. Co. B. Federal Rolls of Prisoners of War: Captured at Fort Gaines, AL, on 8/8/1864; Received at Ship Island, MS, from New Orleans, LA, on 10/25/1864. Exchanged on 1/4/1865.

Kennedy, Edward M. Pvt., 62nd Alabama Infantry. Co. E. Federal Rolls of Prisoners of War: Captured at Blakely, AL, on 4/9/1865; Received at Ship Island, MS, on 4/15/1865. Transferred to Vicksburg, MS, for exchange on 5/1/1865; Exchanged at Camp Townsend, MS, on 5/6/1865.

Kennedy, Edward W. (AKA Canaday) Pvt., 21st Alabama Infantry. Co. F. Federal Rolls of Prisoners of War: Captured at Fort Gaines, AL, on 8/8/1864; Received at Ship Island, MS, from New Orleans, LA, on 10/25/1864. Died: 12/13/1864 at Ship Island, MS, due to dysentery. Buried: Ship Island, MS, Cemetery in Grave #85.

Kennedy, S.R. Pvt., 21st Alabama Infantry. Co. F. Federal Rolls of Prisoners of War: Captured at Fort Gaines, AL, on 8/8/1864; Received at Ship Island, MS, from New Orleans, LA, on 10/25/1864. Died: 12/20/1864 at Ship Island, MS, due to dysentery. Buried: Ship Island, MS, Cemetery in Grave #104.

Kennedy, Walton E. (AKA Walter, Warren, William) Pvt., Lockhart's Battalion Infantry. Co. H. Federal Rolls of Prisoners of War: Captured at Fort Gaines, AL, on 8/8/1864; Received at Ship Island, MS, from New Orleans, LA, on 10/25/1864. Died: 12/17/1864 at Ship Island, MS, due to dysentery. Buried: Ship Island, MS, Cemetery in Grave #96.

Kennedy, W.L. Pvt., 8th Alabama Cavalry. Co. B. Federal Rolls of Prisoners of War: Captured in Florida on 3/25/1865; Received at Ship Island, MS. Transferred to Vicksburg, MS, for exchange on 5/1/1865; Exchanged at Camp Townsend, MS, on 5/6/1865.

Kennedy, William W. Pvt., 63rd Alabama Infantry. Cos. D & E. Enlisted: 7/30/1864 at Macon County, AL. Age at enlistment: 17. Description at enlistment: Eyes: gray. Hair: dark. Complexion: fair. Height: 5'10". Residence at enlistment: Clayton, Barbour County, AL. Rolls for 9/1864 through 10/1864: Present. Federal Rolls of Prisoners of War: Captured at Blakely, AL, on 4/9/1865; Received at Ship Island, MS, on 4/15/1865. Transferred to Vicksburg, MS, for exchange on 5/1/1865; Exchanged at Camp Townsend, MS, on 5/6/1865. Rolls of Prisoners of War, C.S.A: Surrendered at Citronelle, AL, on 5/4/1865; Paroled at Meridian, MS, on 5/13/1865. Residence at parole: Barbour County, AL.

Kenney, W.J. (AKA Kinney) Pvt., 62nd Alabama Infantry. Co. C. Federal Rolls of Prisoners of War: Captured at Blakely, AL, on 4/9/1865; Received at Ship Island, MS, on 4/15/1865. Transferred to Vicksburg, MS, for exchange on 5/1/1865; Exchanged at Camp Townsend, MS, on 5/6/1865.

Kent, W.P. (AKA W.R.) Pvt., 63rd Alabama Infantry. Cos. D & K. Enlisted: 8/25/1864 at Blakely, AL. Rolls for 9/1864 through 10/1864: Present, transferred to Co. K on 9/28/1864. Federal Rolls of Prisoners of War: Captured at Blakely, AL, on 4/9/1865; Received at Ship Island, MS, on 4/15/1865. Transferred to Vicksburg, MS, for exchange on 5/1/1865; Exchanged at Camp Townsend, MS, on 5/6/1865. Rolls of prisoners of War, C.S.A: Surrendered at Citronelle, AL, on 5/4/1865; Paroled at Meridian, MS, on 5/13/1865. Residence at parole: Chambers County, AL.

Kentland, W. Pvt., 36th Alabama Infantry. Co. E.

Federal Rolls of Prisoners of War: Captured at Spanish Fort, AL, on 4/8/1865; Received at Ship Island, MS, on 4/10/1865. Transferred to Vicksburg, MS, for exchange on 5/1/1865; Exchanged at Camp Townsend, MS, on 5/6/1865.

Ketchum, D. Pvt., 23rd Alabama Infantry. Co. I. Federal Rolls of Prisoners of War: Captured in Alabama on 3/24/1865; Received at Ship Island, MS. Transferred to Vicksburg, MS, for exchange on 5/1/1865; Exchanged at Camp Townsend, MS, on 5/6/1865.

Kiffer, James M. (AKA Kifer) Pvt., 18th Alabama Infantry. Co. D. Federal Rolls of Prisoners of War: Captured at Blakely, AL, on 4/9/1865; Received at Ship Island, MS, on 4/15/1865. Transferred to Vicksburg, MS, for exchange on 5/1/1865; Exchanged at Camp Townsend, MS, on 5/6/1865.

Killaugh, Martin 3rd Sgt./1st Sgt., 63rd Alabama Infantry. Co. B. Enlisted: 3/23/1864 at Montgomery County, AL. Age at enlistment: 17. Rolls for 9/1864 through 10/1864: Present. Federal Rolls of Prisoners of War: Captured at Blakely, AL, on 4/9/1865; Received at Ship Island, MS, on 4/15/1865. Transferred to Vicksburg, MS, for exchange on 5/1/1865; Exchanged at Camp Townsend, MS, on 5/6/1865. Rolls of Prisoners of War, C.S.A: Surrendered at Citronelle, AL, on 5/4/1865; Paroled at Meridian, MS, on 5/11/1865. Residence at parole: Montgomery County, AL.

Killingsworth, J.J. Pvt., 6th Alabama Cavalry. Co. E. Federal Rolls of Prisoners of War: Captured in Florida on 3/25/1865; Received at Ship Island, MS. Transferred to Vicksburg, MS, for exchange on 5/1/1865; Exchanged at Camp Townsend, MS, on 5/6/1865.

Kilpatrick, Alick H (AKA A.A.) Pvt., 63rd Alabama Infantry. Co. E. Federal Rolls of Prisoners of War: Captured at Blakely, AL, on 4/9/1865; Received at Ship Island, MS, on 4/15/1865. Transferred to Vicksburg, MS, for exchange on 5/1/1865. On Register of U.S.A. General Hospital #2, Vicksburg, MS: Admitted from steamer on 5/3/1865 due to measles; Returned to duty on 5/10/1865. Age at admittance: 18. Confederate Pension Application dated 1919 on file at the Oklahoma State Archives. Target Name: Kilpatrick, Alick H. Application Number: 3837. Microfilm Reel Number: 10.

Kilpatrick, James E. Pvt., 63rd Alabama Infantry. Co. A. Enlisted: 1/1/1864 at Tallapoosa County, AL. Age at enlistment: 16. Rolls for 1/1864 through 2/1864: Present. Rolls for 9/1864 through 10/1864: Present. Federal Rolls of Prisoners of War: Captured at Blakely, AL, on 4/9/1865; Received at Ship Island, MS, on 4/15/1865. Transferred to Vicksburg, MS, for exchange on 5/1/1865. On Register of U.S.A. General Hospital #2, Vicksburg, MS: Admitted on 5/3/1865 from steamer due to tertium intermittens fever; Returned to duty on 5/12/1865. Age at admittance: 19. Rolls of Prisoners of War, C.S.A: Surrendered at Citronelle, AL, on 5/4/1865; Paroled at Meridian, MS, on 5/14/1865. Residence at parole: Tallapoosa County, AL.

King, George D. Pvt., 21st Alabama Infantry. Co. G. Federal Rolls of Prisoners of War: Captured at Fort Gaines, AL, on 8/8/1864; Received at Ship Island, MS, from New Orleans, LA, on 10/25/1864. Exchanged on 1/4/1865.

King, Thomas Pvt., 63rd Alabama Infantry. Cos. A & H. Enlisted: 3/15/1864 at Springville, AL. Age at enlistment: 17. Description at enlistment: Eyes: hazel. Hair: auburn. Complexion: fair. Rolls for 9/1864 through 10/1864: Absent, sick in hospital at Mobile, AL, since 9/10/1864. On Register of Ross Hospital, Mobile, AL: Admitted on 9/16/1864 due to febris intermittens quot.; Received 30 day sick furlough on 10/15/1864. Federal Rolls of Prisoners of War: Captured at Blakely, AL, on 4/9/1865; Received at Ship Island, MS, on 4/15/1865. Transferred to Vicksburg, MS, for exchange on 5/1/1865; Exchanged at Camp Townsend, MS, on 5/6/1865. Rolls of Prisoners of War, C.S.A: Surrendered at Citronelle, AL, on 5/4/1865; Paroled at Meridian, MS, on 5/11/1865. Residence at parole: St. Clair County, AL.

Kintland, W. (AKA Kirtland) Pvt., 36th Alabama Infantry. Co. A. Federal Rolls of Prisoners of War: Captured at Spanish Fort, AL, on 4/8/1865; Received at Ship Island, MS, on 4/10/1865. Transferred to Vicksburg, MS, for exchange on 5/1/1865; Exchanged at Camp Townsend, MS, on 5/6/1865.

Kirby, James W. Pvt., 58th Alabama Infantry. Cos. E & F. Federal Rolls of Prisoners of War: Captured at Spanish Fort, AL, on 4/8/1865; Received at Ship Island, MS, on 4/10/1865. Transferred to Vicksburg, MS, for exchange on 5/1/1865; Exchanged at Camp Townsend, MS, on 5/6/1865.

Kirkham, H.H. Pvt., 58th Alabama Infantry. Cos. F & K. Federal Rolls of Prisoners of War: Captured at Spanish Fort, AL, on 4/8/1865; Received at Ship Island, MS, on 4/10/1865. Transferred to Vicksburg, MS, for exchange on 5/1/1865; Exchanged at Camp Townsend, MS, on 5/6/1865.

Kirkland, William J. Pvt., 63rd Alabama Infantry. Co. E. Enlisted: 8/8/1864 at Pollard, AL. Age at enlistment: 17. Description at enlistment: Eyes: dark. Hair: dark. Complexion: dark. Rolls for 9/1864 through 10/1864: Present. On Register of Ross Hospital, Mobile, AL: Admitted on 9/18/1864 due to rubeola; Returned to duty on 9/26/1864. Federal Rolls of Prisoners of War: Captured at Blakely, AL, on 4/9/1865; Received at Ship Island, MS, on 4/15/1865. Transferred to Vicksburg, MS, for exchange on 5/1/1865; Exchanged at Camp Townsend, MS, on 5/6/1865. Rolls of Prisoners of War, C.S.A: Surrendered at Citronelle, AL, on 5/4/1865; Paroled at Meridian, MS, on 5/13/1865. Residence at parole: Henry County, AL. Born: 1847 at Henry County, AL. Soldier is recorded on the 1907 Alabama Census of Confederate Veterans and Widows. Residence: Henry County, AL.

Kline, George A. (AKA Klie) Sgt./Pvt., 21st Alabama Infantry. Co. C. Federal Rolls of Prisoners of War: Captured at Blakely, AL, on 4/9/1865; Received at Ship Island, MS, on 4/15/1865. Transferred to Vicksburg, MS, for exchange on 5/1/1865; Exchanged at Camp Townsend, MS, on 5/6/1865.

Klinet, Crawford W. Pvt., 62nd Alabama Infantry. Co. A. Federal Rolls of Prisoners of War: Captured at Blakely, AL, on 4/9/1865; Received at Ship Island, MS, on 4/15/1865. Transferred to Vicksburg, MS, for exchange on 5/1/1865; Exchanged at Camp Townsend, MS, on 5/6/1865.

Knight, James M. Pvt., 63rd Alabama Infantry. Co. G. Enlisted: 5/16/1864 at Troy, AL. Age at enlistment:

17. Description at enlistment: Eyes: black. Hair: dark. Complexion: dark. Height: 5'8". Residence at enlistment: Coffee County, AL. Rolls for 5/16/1864 through 9/7/1864: Present. Rolls for 9/1864 through 10/1864: Absent, in hospital at Mobile, AL, since 10/15/1864. Federal Rolls of Prisoners of War: Captured at Blakely, AL, on 4/9/1865; Received at Ship Island, MS, on 4/15/1865. Transferred to Vicksburg, MS, for exchange on 5/1/1865; Exchanged at Camp Townsend, MS, on 5/6/1865. Rolls of Prisoners of War, C.S.A: Surrendered at Citronelle, AL, on 5/4/1865; Paroled at Meridian, MS, on 5/13/1865. Residence at parole: Coffee County, AL. Born: 1844. Died: 1896. Buried: Herbron Cemetery located at Coffee County, AL.

Knight, John J. Pvt., 21st Alabama Infantry. Cos. G & I. Federal Rolls of Prisoners of War: Captured at Fort Gaines, AL, on 8/8/1864; Received at Ship Island, MS, from New Orleans, LA, on 10/25/1864. Exchanged on 1/4/1865.

Knotts, J.D. (AKA Notts) Sgt., 6th Alabama Cavalry. Co. D. Federal Rolls of Prisoners of War: Captured at Blakely, AL, on 4/9/1865; Received at Ship Island, MS, on 4/15/1865. Transferred to Vicksburg, MS, for exchange on 5/1/1865; Exchanged at Camp Townsend, MS, on 5/6/1865.

Knowland, John (AKA Nowland) Pvt., 18th Alabama Infantry. Co. A. Federal Rolls of Prisoners of War: Captured at Spanish Fort, AL, on 4/8/1865; Received at Ship Island, MS, on 4/10/1865. Disposition unknown.

Knowles, Raymond Sgt., 62nd Alabama Infantry. Cos. B & C. Federal Rolls of Prisoners of War: Captured at Blakely, AL, on 4/9/1865; Received at Ship Island, MS, on 4/15/1865. Transferred to Vicksburg, MS, for exchange on 5/1/1865; Exchanged at Camp Townsend, MS, on 5/6/1865.

Knox, J.H. Pvt., 36th Alabama Infantry. Co. A. Federal Rolls of Prisoners of War: Captured at Spanish Fort, AL, on 4/8/1865; Received at Ship Island, MS, on 4/10/1865. Transferred to Vicksburg, MS, for exchange on 5/1/1865; Exchanged at Camp Townsend, MS, on 5/6/1865.

Kolb, Andrew Pvt., 1st Alabama Artillery. Co. B. Federal Rolls of Prisoners of War: Captured at Fort Gaines, AL, on 8/8/1864; Received at Ship Island, MS, from New Orleans, LA, on 10/25/1864. Exchanged on 1/4/1865.

Kyle, Willie D. 2nd Lt., 63rd Alabama Infantry. Co. A. Rolls for 1/1864 through 2/1864: Present, promoted to Lt. on 3/23/1864. Rolls for 9/1864 through 10/1864: Absent, furloughed for 10 days on 10/26/1864 by Maj. Gen. Dabney H. Maury. Federal Rolls of Prisoners of War: Captured at Blakely, AL, on 4/9/1865; Received at Ship Island, MS, on 4/15/1865. Transferred to Vicksburg, MS, for exchange on 4/28/1865; Confined at New Orleans, LA, on 4/30/1865. Exchanged at Camp Townsend, MS, on 5/6 1865. Rolls of Prisoners of War, C.S.A: Surrendered at Citronelle, AL, on 5/4/1865; Paroled at Meridian, MS, on 5/11/1865.

Kyles, J.B. Sgt., 36th Alabama Infantry. Co. D. Federal Rolls of Prisoners of War: Captured at Spanish Fort, AL, on 4/8/1865; Received at Ship Island, MS, on 4/10/1865. Transferred to Vicksburg, MS, for exchange on 5/1/1865; Exchanged at Camp Townsend, MS, on 5/6/1865.

Kyles, W.H. (AKA W.D.) Lt., 63rd Alabama Infantry. Co. __. Federal Rolls of Prisoners of War: Captured at Blakely, AL, on 4/9/1865; Received at Ship Island, MS, on 4/15/1865. Transferred to Vicksburg, MS, for exchange on 4/28/1865; Confined at New Orleans, LA, on 4/30/1865. Exchanged at Camp Townsend, MS, on 5/6/1865.

Kyzer, E. Pvt., 62nd Alabama Infantry. Co. K. Federal Rolls of Prisoners of War: Captured at Blakely, AL, on 4/9/1865; Received at Ship Island, MS, on 4/15/1865. Transferred to Vicksburg, MS, for exchange on 5/1/1865; Exchanged at Camp Townsend, MS, on 5/6/1865.

Lacey, Thomas A. Cpl., 63rd Alabama Infantry. Co. H. Enlisted: 3/15/1864 at Elyton, AL. Age at enlistment: 17. Description at enlistment: Eyes: grey. Hair: light. Complexion: fair. Rolls for 9/1864 through 10/1864: Absent, sick in hospital at Selma, AL, since 9/21/1864. Federal Rolls of Prisoners of War: Captured at Blakely, AL, on 4/9/1865; Received at Ship Island, MS, on 4/15/1865. Transferred to Vicksburg, MS, for exchange on 5/1/1865. On Register of U.S.A. General Hospital #2, Vicksburg, MS: Admitted from steamer on 5/3/1865 due to acute diarrhea; Returned to duty on 5/8/1865. Age at admittance: 18.

Lacey, William E. Pvt., 63rd Alabama Infantry. Co. H. Enlisted: 3/15/1864 at Elyton, AL. Age at enlistment: 16. Description at enlistment: Eyes: gray. Hair: dark. Complexion: dark. Rolls for 9/1864 through 10/1864: Present. On Register of Ross Hospital, Mobile, AL: Admitted on 10/10/1864 due to acute dysentery; Returned to duty on 10/26/1864. Federal Rolls of Prisoners of War: Captured at Blakely, AL, on 4/9/1865; Received at Ship Island, MS, on 4/15/1865. Transferred to Vicksburg, MS, for exchange on 5/1/1865; Exchanged at Camp Townsend, MS, on 5/6/1865. Rolls of Prisoners of War, C.S.A: Surrendered at Citronelle, AL, on 5/4/1865; Paroled at Meridian, MS, on 5/11/1865. Residence at parole: Jefferson County, AL.

Lagrone, William S. (AKA W.L.) Pvt., Lockhart's Battalion Infantry. Co. K. Federal Rolls of Prisoners of War: Captured at Fort Gaines, AL, on 8/8/1864; Received at Ship Island, MS, on 10/25/1864. Exchanged on 1/4/1865.

Lagrove, J.G. (AKA Lagrone, J.H.) Pvt., 21st Alabama Infantry. Co. I. Federal Rolls of Prisoners of War: Captured at Fort Gaines, AL, on 8/8/1864; Received at Ship Island, MS, on 10/25/1864. Exchanged on 1/4/1865.

Lambert, Frank Pvt., 21st Alabama Infantry. Co. H. Federal Rolls of Prisoners of War: Captured at Fort Gaines, AL, on 8/8/1864; Received at Ship Island, MS, from New Orleans, LA, on 10/25/1864. Exchanged on 1/4/1865.

Lambert, William Pvt., 21st Alabama Infantry. Co. H. Federal Rolls of Prisoners of War: Captured at Fort Gaines, AL, on 8/8/1864; Received at Ship Island, MS, from New Orleans, LA, on 10/25/1864. Exchanged on 1/4/1865.

Lambreth, Z.T. Pvt., 63rd Alabama Infantry. Co. E. Enlisted: 7/28/1864 at Montgomery, AL. Age at enlistment: 17. Description at enlistment: Eyes: blue. Hair: light. Complexion: fair. On Register of Ross Hospital, Mobile, AL: Admitted on 9/29/1864 due to febris intermittens tert.; Returned to duty on 10/18/

1864. Rolls for 9/1864 through 10/1864: Present. Federal Rolls of Prisoners of War: Captured at Blakely, AL, on 4/9/1865; Received at Ship Island, MS, on 4/15/1865. Transferred to Vicksburg, MS, for exchange on 5/1/1865; Exchanged at Camp Townsend, MS, on 5/6/1865. Rolls of Prisoners of War, C.S.A: Surrendered at Citronelle, AL, on 5/4/1865; Paroled at Meridian, MS, on 5/13/1865. Residence at parole: Coosa County, AL.

Lancaster, John M. 2nd Lt., 63rd Alabama Infantry. Co. C. Enlisted: 5/4/1864 at Chambers County, AL; Elected 2nd Lt. on 6/20/1864. Age at enlistment: 17. Description at enlistment: Eyes: blue. Hair: light. Complexion: fair. Height: 5'8". Residence at enlistment: Cusseta, Chambers County, AL. Rolls for 9/1864 through 10/1864: Absent, sick in hospital at Mobile, AL, since 10/19/1864. Federal Rolls of Prisoners of War: Captured at Blakely, AL, on 4/9/1865; Received at Ship Island, MS, on 4/16/1865. Transferred to Vicksburg, MS, for exchange on 4/28/1865; Confined at New Orleans, LA, on 4/30/1865. Exchanged at Camp Townsend, MS, on 5/6/1865. Rolls of Prisoners of War, C.S.A: Surrendered at Citronelle, AL, on 5/4/1865; Paroled at Meridian, MS, on 5/11/1865.

Landreth, John (AKA Landerth) Pvt., 6th Alabama Cavalry. Co. C. Federal Rolls of Prisoners of War: Captured in Florida on 3/25/1865; Received at Ship Island, MS. Transferred to Vicksburg, MS, for exchange on 5/1/1865; Exchanged at Camp Townsend, MS, on 5/6/1865.

Landrum, Samuel W. 2nd Lt./Capt., 38th Alabama Infantry. Co. E. Enlisted: 4/7/1863 at Mobile, AL, and elected 2nd Lt. same day; Promoted to Capt. on 11/24/1863. On Register of St. Mary's Hospital, LaGrange, GA: Admitted on 6/21/1864; Returned to duty on 7/3/1864. On Register of Ocmulgee Hospital, Macon, GA: Admitted on 7/24/1864 due to gunshot wound in left leg; Furloughed for 30 days ending on 9/15/1864. On Register of Ocmulgee Hospital, Macon, GA: Admitted on 9/15/1864 due to gunshot wound in left leg still open; Simple dressing applied and transferred on 9/27/1864. Residence at admittance: Augusta, Conecuh County, AL. Federal Rolls of Prisoners of War: Captured at Blakely, AL, on 4/9/1865; Received at Ship Island, MS, on 4/16/1865. Transferred to Vicksburg, MS, for exchange on 4/28/1865; Confined at New Orleans, LA, on 4/30/1865. Exchanged at Camp Townsend, MS, on 5/6/1865.

Landsden, J.A. Pvt., 63rd Alabama Infantry. Co. F. Federal Rolls of Prisoners of War: Captured at Blakely, AL, on 4/9/1865; Received at Ship Island, MS, on 4/15/1865. Transferred to Vicksburg, MS, for exchange on 5/1/1865; Exchanged at Camp Townsend, MS, on 5/6/1865.

Landsdon, J.A. Pvt., 63rd Alabama Infantry. Co. F. Enlisted: 8/24/1864 at Greenville, AL. Rolls for 9/1864 through 10/1864: Present. Federal Rolls of Prisoners of War: Captured at Blakely, AL, on 4/9/1865; Received at Ship Island, MS, on 4/15/1865. Transferred to Vicksburg, MS, for exchange on 5/1/1865; Exchanged at Camp Townsend, MS, on 5/6/1865. Rolls of Prisoners of War, C.S.A: Surrendered at Citronelle, AL, on 5/4/1865; Paroled at Meridian, MS, on 5/11/1865. Residence at parole: Butler County, AL.

Landsford, J.P. Pvt., 1st Alabama Artillery. Co. D. Federal Rolls of Prisoners of War: Captured in Alabama on 3/24/1865; Received at Ship Island, MS. Transferred to Vicksburg, MS, for exchange on 5/1/1865; Exchanged at Camp Townsend, MS, on 5/6/1865.

Lane, Alexander (AKA Laine) Pvt., 21st Alabama Infantry. Co. I. Federal Rolls of Prisoners of War: Captured at Fort Gaines, AL, on 8/8/1864; Received at Ship Island, MS, from New Orleans, LA, on 10/25/1864. Exchanged on 1/4/1865.

Lane, J.H. Pvt., 38th Alabama Infantry. Co. B. Federal Rolls of Prisoners of War: Captured at Spanish Fort, AL, on 4/8/1865; Received at Ship Island, MS, on 4/10/1865. Transferred to Vicksburg, MS, on 5/1/1865; Exchanged at Camp Townsend, MS, on 5/6/1865.

Lane, J.M. 3rd Lt./2nd Lt., 63rd Alabama Infantry. Co. D. Enlisted: 8/30/1864 at Blakely, AL. Rolls for 9/1864 through 10/1864: Present. Federal Rolls of Prisoners of War: Captured at Blakely, AL, on 4/9/1865; Confined at Spanish Fort, AL, for one day. Received at Ship Island, MS, on 4/16/1865; Transferred to Vicksburg, MS, for exchange on 4/28/1865. Confined at New Orleans, LA, on 4/30/1865; Exchanged at Camp Townsend, MS, on 5/6/1865. Rolls of Prisoners of War, C.S.A: Surrendered at Citronelle, AL, on 5/4/1865; Paroled at Meridian, MS, on 5/11/1865.

Lane, John J. Pvt./Sgt., 63rd Alabama Infantry. Co. A. Enlisted: 1/1/1864 at Lowndes County, AL. Age at enlistment: 16. Rolls for 1/1864 through 2/1864: Present. Rolls for 9/1864 through 10/1864: Present. Federal Rolls of Prisoners of War: Captured at Blakely, AL, on 4/9/1865; Received at Ship Island, MS, on 4/15/1865. Transferred to Vicksburg, MS, for exchange on 5/1/1865; Exchanged at Camp Townsend, MS, on 5/6/1865. Rolls of Prisoners of War, C.S.A: Surrendered at Citronelle, AL, on 5/4/1865; Paroled at Meridian, MS, on 5/13/1865. Residence at parole: Lowndes County, AL.

Lannery, J.R. Pvt., 36th Alabama Infantry. Co. C. Federal Rolls of Prisoners of War: Captured at Spanish Fort, AL, on 4/8/1865; Received at Ship Island, MS, on 4/10/1865. Transferred to Vicksburg, MS, on 5/1/1865; Exchanged at Camp Townsend, MS, on 5/6/1865.

Lassiter, James Pvt., 63rd Alabama Infantry. Co. G. Federal Rolls of Prisoners of War: Captured at Blakely, AL, on 4/9/1865; Received at Ship Island, MS, on 4/15/1865. Transferred to Vicksburg, MS, for exchange on 5/1/1865; Exchanged at Camp Townsend, MS, on 5/6/1865. Rolls of Prisoners of War, C.S.A: Surrendered at Citronelle, AL, on 5/4/1865; Paroled at Meridian, MS, on 5/13/1865. Residence at parole: Coffee County, AL.

Latimer, M. Pvt./Sgt., 62nd Alabama Infantry. Co. F. Federal Rolls of Prisoners of War: Captured at Blakely, AL, on 4/9/1865; Received at Ship Island, MS, on 4/15/1865. Transferred to Vicksburg, MS, for exchange on 5/1/1865; Exchanged at Camp Townsend, MS, on 5/6/1865.

Lavener, J.R. Pvt., 38th Alabama Infantry. Co. E. Federal Rolls of Prisoners of War: Captured at Blakely, AL, on 4/9/1865; Received at Ship Island, MS, on 4/15/1865. Transferred to Vicksburg, MS, for exchange

on 5/1/1865; Exchanged at Camp Townsend, MS, on 5/6/1865.

Law, J.A. Lt. Col., 63rd Alabama Infantry. F & S. Rolls for 7/1864 through 8/1864: Present, appointed Lt. Col. on 8/16/1864 by order of the Secretary of War. Rolls for 9/1864 through 10/1864: Absent, on 30 day sick furlough since 9/28/1864 by order of Maj. Gen. Dabney H. Maury. Federal Rolls of Prisoners of War: Captured at Blakely, AL, on 4/9/1865; Confined one day at Spanish Fort, AL. Received at Ship Island, MS, on 4/15/1865; Transferred to Vicksburg, MS, for exchange on 4/28/1865. Confined at New Orleans, LA, on 4/30/1865. On Register of U.S.A. General Hospital #2, Vicksburg, MS: Admitted from steamer with remittent fever; Returned to duty on 5/8/1865. Rolls of Prisoners of War, C.S.A: Surrendered at Citronelle, AL, on 5/4/1865; Paroled at Meridian, MS, on 5/11/1865.

Lawless, Caleb R. Pvt., Lockhart's Battalion Infantry. Co. K. Federal Rolls of Prisoners of War: Captured at Fort Gaines, AL, on 8/8/1864; Received at Ship Island, MS, on 10/25/1864. Exchanged on 1/4/1865.

Lawless, E. (AKA Lovelace) Pvt., 6th Alabama Cavalry. Co. H. Federal Rolls of Prisoners of War: Captured in Florida on 3/25/1865; Received at Ship Island, MS. Transferred to Vicksburg, MS, for exchange on 5/1/1865; Exchanged at Camp Townsend, MS, on 5/6/1865.

Lawrence, A.J. Pvt., 36th Alabama Infantry. Co. C. Federal Rolls of Prisoners of War: Captured at Spanish Fort, AL, on 4/8/1865; Received at Ship Island, MS, on 4/10/1865. Transferred to Vicksburg, MS, for exchange on 5/1/1865; Exchanged at Camp Townsend, MS, on 5/6/1865.

Lawson, Aaron Sgt., Lockhart's Battalion Infantry. Co. K. Federal Rolls of Prisoners of War: Captured at Fort Gaines, AL, on 8/8/1864; Received at Ship Island, MS, from New Orleans, LA, on 10/25/1864. Exchanged on 1/4/1865.

Lawson, J.M. 4th Cpl., 63rd Alabama Infantry. Co. H. Enlisted: 3/16/1864 at Montevallo, AL. Age at enlistment: 17. Description at enlistment: Eyes: gray. Hair: dark. Complexion: dark. Rolls for 9/1864 through 10/1864: Present. Federal Rolls of Prisoners of War: Captured at Blakely, AL, on 4/9/1865; Received at Ship Island, MS, on 4/15/1865. Transferred to Vicksburg, MS, for exchange on 5/1/1865; Exchanged at Camp Townsend, MS, on 5/6/1865. Rolls of Prisoners of War, C.S.A: Surrendered at Citronelle, AL, on 5/4/1865; Paroled at Meridian, MS, on 5/11/1865. Residence at parole: Jefferson County, AL.

Lay, E.C. Pvt./Cpl., 21st Alabama Infantry. Cos. F & I. Federal Rolls of Prisoners of War: Captured at Fort Gaines, AL, on 8/8/1864; Received at Ship Island, MS, from New Orleans, LA, on 10/25/1864. Exchanged on 1/4/1865.

Lay, J.S. (AKA J.P.) Pvt., 36th Alabama Infantry. Co. I. Federal Rolls of Prisoners of War: Captured at Spanish Fort, AL, on 4/8/1865; Received at Ship Island, MS, on 4/10/1865. Transferred to Vicksburg, MS, for exchange on 5/1/1865; Exchanged at Camp Townsend, MS, on 5/6/1865.

Layet, Adolphe Cpl./Q.M. Sgt., 21st Alabama Infantry. F & S. Federal Rolls of Prisoners of War: Captured at Fort Gaines, AL, on 8/8/1864; Received at Ship Island, MS, from New Orleans, LA, on 10/25/1864. Exchanged on 1/4/1865.

Leach, Hugh A. Pvt., 62nd Alabama Infantry. Co. I. Federal Rolls of Prisoners of War: Captured at Blakely, AL, on 4/9/1865; Received at Ship Island, MS, on 4/15/1865. Transferred to Vicksburg, MS, for exchange on 5/1/1865; Exchanged at Camp Townsend, MS, on 5/6/1865.

League, R.M. Pvt./Sgt., 62nd Alabama Infantry. Co. B. Federal Rolls of Prisoners of War: Captured at Blakely, AL, on 4/9/1865; Received at Ship Island, MS, on 4/15/1865. Transferred to Vicksburg, MS, for exchange on 5/1/1865; Exchanged at Camp Townsend, MS, on 5/6/1865.

Leap, William E. Cpl./Sgt., 21st Alabama Infantry. Co. B. Federal Rolls of Prisoners of War: Captured at Fort Gaines, AL, on 8/8/1864; Received at Ship Island, MS, from New Orleans, LA, on 10/25/1864. Exchanged on 1/4/1865.

Leavens, E.B. Pvt., 21st Alabama Infantry. Cos. F & I. Federal Rolls of Prisoners of War: Captured at Fort Gaines, AL, on 8/8/1864; Received at Ship Island, MS, from New Orleans, LA, on 10/25/1864. Exchanged on 1/4/1865.

Leavens, I.F. Pvt., 21st Alabama Infantry. Cos. F & I. Federal Rolls of Prisoners of War: Captured at Fort Gaines, AL, on 8/8/1864; Received at Ship Island, MS, from New Orleans, LA, on 10/25/1864. Exchanged on 1/4/1865.

Ledlow, J.W. Pvt., 63rd Alabama Infantry. Co. K. Enlisted: 9/20/1864 at Rockford, AL. Rolls for 9/1864 through 10/1864: Present. Federal Rolls of Prisoners of War: Captured at Blakely, AL, on 4/9/1865; Received at Ship Island, MS, on 4/15/1865. Transferred to Vicksburg, MS, for exchange on 5/1/1865; Exchanged at Camp Townsend, MS, on 5/6/1865. Rolls of Prisoners of War, C.S.A: Surrendered at Citronelle, AL, on 5/4/1865; Paroled at Meridian, MS, on 5/13/1865. Residence at parole: Coosa County, AL.

Lee, A.V. Capt., 63rd Alabama Infantry. Co. E. Enlisted: 3/20/1864 at Clayton, AL; Elected Capt. on 3/25/1864. Age at enlistment: 20. Description at enlistment: Eyes: dark. Hair: dark. Rolls for 9/1864 through 10/1864: Present. Federal Rolls of Prisoners of War: Captured at Blakely, AL, on 4/9/1865; Confined one day at Spanish Fort, AL. Received at Ship Island, MS, on 4/16/1865; Transferred to Vicksburg, MS, for exchange on 4/28/1865. Confined at New Orleans, LA, on 4/30/1865; Exchanged at Camp Townsend, MS, on 5/6/1865. Rolls of Prisoners of War, C.S.A: Surrendered at Citronelle, AL, on 5/4/1865; Paroled at Meridian, MS, on 5/11/1865. Residence at parole: Columbus, GA.

Lee, C.S. Capt., 6th Alabama Cavalry. Co. __. Federal Rolls of Prisoners of War: Captured in Florida on 3/25/1865; Received at Ship Island, MS. Transferred to Vicksburg, MS, for exchange on 4/28/1865; Confined at New Orleans, LA, on 4/30/1865. Exchanged at Camp Townsend, MS, on 5/6/1865.

Lee, Columbus P. Pvt., 62nd Alabama Infantry. Co. A. Federal Rolls of Prisoners of War: Captured at Blakely, AL, on 4/9/1865; Received at Ship Island, MS, on 4/15/1865. Transferred to Vicksburg, MS, for exchange on 5/1/1865; Exchanged at Camp Townsend, MS, on 5/6/1865.

Lee, General T. Pvt., 63rd Alabama Infantry. Cos. B & D. Enlisted: 7/30/1864 at Macon County, AL. Age at enlistment: 17. Description at enlistment: Eyes: grey. Hair: light. Complexion: fair. Residence at enlistment: Clayton, Barbour County, AL. Rolls for 9/1864 through 10/1864: Absent, on 30 day sick furlough by the Medical Examining Board since 10/24/1864. Federal Rolls of Prisoners of War: Captured at Blakely, AL, on 4/9/1865; Received at Ship Island, MS, on 4/15/1865. Transferred to Vicksburg, MS, for exchange on 5/1/1865; Exchanged at Camp Townsend, MS, on 5/6/1865. Rolls of Prisoners of War, C.S.A: Surrendered at Citronelle, AL, on 5/4/1865; Paroled at Meridian, MS, on 5/13/1865. Residence at parole: Barbour County, AL.

Lee, J. Cpl., 62nd Alabama Infantry. Co. E. Federal Rolls of Prisoners of War: Captured at Blakely, AL, on 4/9/1865; Received at Ship Island, MS, on 4/15/1865. Transferred to Vicksburg, MS, for exchange on 5/1/1865; Exchanged at Camp Townsend, MS, on 5/6/1865.

Lee, T.N. Pvt./Sgt., 62nd Alabama Infantry. Co. G. Federal Rolls of Prisoners of War: Captured at Blakely, AL, on 4/9/1865; Received at Ship Island, MS, on 4/15/1865. Transferred to Vicksburg, MS, for exchange on 5/1/1865; Exchanged at Camp Townsend, MS, on 5/6/1865.

Lee, William Pvt., 1st Alabama Artillery. Co. D. Federal Rolls of Prisoners of War: Captured at Fort Gaines, AL, on 8/8/1864; Received at Ship Island, MS, from New Orleans, LA, on 10/25/1864. Died: 12/20/1864 at Ship Island, MS, due to erysepilas. Buried: Ship Island, MS, Cemetery in Grave #103.

Lees, Thomas Pvt., 21st Alabama Infantry. Co. B. Federal Rolls of Prisoners of War: Captured at Fort Gaines, AL, on 8/8/1864; Received at Ship Island, MS, from New Orleans, LA, on 10/25/1864. Exchanged on 1/4/1865.

Leister, E.F. (AKA Lester, F.E.) Pvt., 62nd Alabama Infantry. Co. F. Federal Rolls of Prisoners of War: Captured at Blakely, AL, on 4/9/1865; Received at Ship Island, MS, on 4/15/1865. Transferred to Vicksburg, MS, for exchange on 5/1/1865; Exchanged at Camp Townsend, MS, on 5/6/1865.

Lenville, W.W. (AKA Linville) Pvt., Lockhart's Battalion Infantry. Cos. E & F. Federal Rolls of Prisoners of War: Captured at Fort Gaines, AL, on 8/8/1864; Received at Ship Island, MS, from New Orleans, LA, on 10/28/1864. Died: 11/18/1864 at Ship Island, MS, due to chronic diarrhea. Buried: Ship Island, MS, cemetery in Grave #18.

Leonard, Thomas Pvt., 21st Alabama Infantry. Co. B. Federal Rolls of Prisoners of War: Captured at Fort Gaines, AL, on 8/8/1864; Received at Ship Island, MS, from New Orleans, LA, on 10/25/1864. Exchanged on 1/4/1865.

Lester, William A. Pvt., 62nd Alabama Infantry. Co. E. Federal Rolls of Prisoners of War: Captured in Alabama on 3/24/1865; Received at Ship Island, MS. Transferred to Vicksburg, MS, for exchange on 5/1/1865; Exchanged at Camp Townsend, MS, on 5/6/1865.

Leverett, John D. (AKA Levvett) Pvt., 63rd Alabama Infantry. Co. A. Enlisted: 2/1/1864 at Chambers County, AL. Rolls for 1/1864 through 2/1864: Present. Rolls for 9/1864 through 10/1864: Present, sick in quarters. Federal Rolls of Prisoners of War: Captured at Blakely, AL, on 4/9/1865; Received at Ship Island, MS, on 4/15/1865. Transferred to Vicksburg, MS, for exchange on 5/1/1865; Exchanged at Camp Townsend, MS, on 5/6/1865. Rolls of Prisoners of War, C.S.A: Surrendered at Citronelle, AL, on 5/4/1865; Paroled at Meridian, MS, on 5/13/1865. Residence at parole: Chambers County, AL. Born: 9/26/1864. Died: 4/27/1909. Buried: Bowling Family Cemetery located at Chambers County, AL.

Lewis, F.M. Pvt., 63rd Alabama Infantry. Co. E. Enlisted: 4/5/1864 at Clayton, AL. Age at enlistment: 17. Description at enlistment: Eyes: blue. Hair: light. Complexion: fair. Rolls for 9/1864 through 10/1864: Absent, sick in hospital since 9/15/1864. Federal Rolls of Prisoners of War: Captured at Blakely, AL, on 4/9/1865; Received at Ship Island, MS, on 4/15/1865. Transferred to Vicksburg, MS, for exchange on 5/1/1865; Exchanged at Camp Townsend, MS, on 5/6/1865. Rolls of Prisoners of War, C.S.A: Surrendered at Citronelle, AL, on 5/4/1865; Paroled at Meridian, MS, on 5/13/1865 while a patient in Quintard Hospital. Residence at parole: Barbour County, AL.

Lewis, J.J. (AKA Louis) Pvt., 63rd Alabama Infantry. Co. H. Federal Rolls of Prisoners of War: Captured at Blakely, AL, on 4/9/1865; Received at Ship Island, MS, on 4/15/1865. Transferred to Vicksburg, MS, for exchange on 5/1/1865; Exchanged at Camp Townsend, MS, on 5/6/1865.

Liddell, Robert F. Pvt., 21st Alabama Infantry. Cos. C & H. Federal Rolls of Prisoners of War: Captured at Fort Gaines, AL, on 8/8/1864; Received at Ship Island, MS, from New Orleans, LA, on 10/25/1864. Exchanged on 1/4/1865.

Liddell, William Pvt., 21st Alabama Infantry. Co. H. Federal Rolls of Prisoners of War: Captured at Fort Gaines, AL, on 8/8/1864; Received at Ship Island, MS, from New Orleans, LA, on 10/25/1864. Exchanged on 1/4/1865.

Lightfoot, Allen Pvt., 63rd Alabama Infantry. Co. G. Enlisted: 5/18/1864 at Troy, AL. Age at enlistment: 17. Description at enlistment: Eyes: blue. Hair: dark. Complexion: fair. Height: 5'11". Residence at enlistment: Pike County, AL. Rolls for 9/1864 through 10/1864: Absent, sick in hospital at Greenville, AL, since 9/1/1864. Federal Rolls of Prisoners of War: Captured at Blakely, AL, on 4/9/1865; Received at Ship Island, MS, on 4/15/1865. Transferred to Vicksburg, MS, for exchange on 5/1/1865; Exchanged at Camp Townsend, MS, on 5/6/1865. Rolls of Prisoners of War, C.S.A: Surrendered at Citronelle, AL, on 5/4/1865; Paroled at Meridian, MS, on 5/13/1865. Residence at parole: Pike County, AL.

Lightfoot, James Henry Pvt., 63rd Alabama Infantry. Co. G. Enlisted: 5/18/1864 at Troy, AL. Age at enlistment: 16. Description at enlistment: Eyes: grey. Hair: dark. Complexion: fair. Height: 5'8". Residence at enlistment: Pike County, AL. Rolls for 9/1864 through 10/1864: Present. Federal Rolls of Prisoners of War: Captured at Blakely, AL, on 4/9/1865; Received at Ship Island, MS, on 4/15/1865. Transferred to Vicksburg, MS, for exchange on 5/1/1865; Exchanged at Camp Townsend, MS, on 5/6/1865. Rolls of Prisoners of War, C.S.A: Surrendered at Citronelle, AL, on 5/4/1865; Paroled at Meridian, MS, on 5/13/1865. Residence at parole: Pike County, AL. Born: 8/25/1843 at Victoria, Coffee County, AL.

Soldier is recorded on the 1907 Alabama Census of Confederate Veterans and Widows. Residence: Pike County, AL.

Lingo, B. Pvt., 21st Alabama Infantry. Co. I. Federal Rolls of Prisoners of War: Captured at Fort Gaines, AL, on 8/8/1864; Received at Ship Island, MS, from New Orleans, LA, on 10/25/1864. Exchanged on 1/4/1865.

Linville, W.W. Pvt., Lockhart's Battalion Infantry. Co. E. Federal Rolls of Prisoners of War: Captured at Fort Gaines, AL, on 8/8/1864; Received at Ship Island, MS, from New Orleans, LA, on 10/25/1864. Died: 11/14/1864 at Ship Island, MS, due to chronic diarrhea. Buried: Ship Island, MS, Cemetery in Grave #18.

Lisenby, Anthony L. Pvt., 63rd Alabama Infantry. Co. C. Enlisted: 6/1/1864 at Russell County, AL. Age at enlistment: 17. Description at enlistment: Eyes: grey. Hair: light. Complexion: fair. Height: 5'9¼". Residence at enlistment: Columbus, GA. Rolls for 9/1864 through 10/1864: Deserted on 9/20/1864 at Blakely, AL. Federal Rolls of Prisoners of War: Captured at Blakely, AL, on 4/9/1865; Received at Ship Island, MS, on 4/15/1865. Transferred to Vicksburg, MS, for exchange on 5/1/1865; Exchanged at Camp Townsend, MS, on 5/6/1865. Rolls of Prisoners of War, C.S.A: Surrendered at Citronelle, AL, on 5/4/1865; Paroled at Meridian, MS, on 5/11/1865. Residence at parole: Russell County, AL.

Little, H.B. Pvt., 6th Alabama Cavalry. Co. C. Federal Rolls of Prisoners of War: Captured in Florida on 3/25/1865; Received at Ship Island, MS. Transferred to Vicksburg, MS, for exchange on 5/1/1865; Exchanged at Camp Townsend, MS, on 5/6/1865.

Little, James M.K. Pvt., 57th Alabama Infantry. Co. G. Federal Rolls of Prisoners of War: Captured in Alabama on 3/24/1865; Received at Ship Island, MS. Transferred to Vicksburg, MS, for exchange on 5/1/1865; Exchanged at Camp Townsend, MS, on 5/6/1865.

Little, Jefferson J. Pvt., 36th Alabama Infantry. Co. G. Federal Rolls of Prisoners of War: Captured at Spanish Fort, AL, on 4/8/1865; Received at Ship Island, MS, on 4/10/1865. Transferred to Vicksburg, MS, on 5/1/1865; Exchanged at Camp Townsend, MS, on 5/6/1865.

Littlejohn, William Pvt., 21st Alabama Infantry. Co. D. Federal Rolls of Prisoners of War: Captured at Blakely, AL, on 4/9/1865; Received at Ship Island, MS, on 4/15/1865. Transferred to Vicksburg, MS, for exchange on 5/1/1865; Exchanged at Camp Townsend, MS, on 5/6/1865.

Lloyd, Jesse C. Pvt., 62nd Alabama Infantry. Co. B. Federal Rolls of Prisoners of War: Captured at Blakely on 4/9/1865; Received at Ship Island, MS, on 4/15/1865. Transferred to Vicksburg, MS, for exchange on 5/1/1865; Exchanged at Camp Townsend, MS, on 5/6/1865.

Loftin, Thomas Green Pvt., 63rd Alabama Infantry. Co. B. Enlisted: 8/15/1864 at Pollard, AL. On Register of Ross Hospital, Mobile, AL: Admitted on 9/20/1864 due to pneumonia; Furloughed for 30 days on 10/6/1864. Rolls for 9/1864 through 10/1864: Absent, sick furlough since 10/6/1864. Federal Rolls of Prisoners of War: Captured at Blakely, AL, on 4/9/1865; Received at Ship Island, MS, on 4/15/1865. Transferred to Vicksburg, MS, for exchange on 5/1/1865; Exchanged at Camp Townsend, MS, on 5/6/1865. Rolls of Prisoners of War, C.S.A: Surrendered at Citronelle, AL, on 5/4/1865; Paroled at Meridian, MS, on 5/11/1865. Residence at parole: Dale County, AL. Born: 11/3/1846 at Dale County, AL.

Loftis, Samuel (AKA L.) Pvt., 62nd Alabama Infantry. Co. A. Federal Rolls of Prisoners of War: Captured at Blakely, AL, on 4/9/1865; Received at Ship Island, MS, on 4/15/1865. Transferred to Vicksburg, MS, for exchange on 5/1/1865; Exchanged at Camp Townsend, MS, on 5/6/1865.

Logan, N.H. Pvt., 21st Alabama Infantry. Co. C. Federal Rolls of Prisoners of War: Captured at Fort Gaines, AL, on 8/8/1864; Received at Ship Island, MS, from New Orleans, LA, on 10/25/1864. Exchanged on 1/4/1865.

Logan, Samuel H. Pvt., 63rd Alabama Infantry. Co. H. Enlisted: 3/15/1864 at Montevallo, AL. Age at enlistment: 17. Description at enlistment: Eyes: blue. Hair: light. Complexion: fair. Rolls for 9/1864 through 10/1864: Present. Federal Rolls of Prisoners of War: Captured at Blakely, AL, on 4/9/1865. Name on List dated Headquarters, 23rd Iowa Infantry. 4/12/1864: Prisoner requires medical treatment for dysentery. Received at Ship Island, MS, on 4/15/1865; Transferred to Vicksburg, MS, for exchange on 5/1/1865. Exchanged at Camp Townsend, MS, on 5/6/1865. Rolls of Prisoners of War, C.S.A: Surrendered at Citronelle, AL, on 5/4/1865; Paroled at Meridian, MS, on 5/11/1865. Residence at parole: Bibb County, AL.

Long, N.L. (AKA Lang) Pvt., Pelham Cadets. Co. A. Federal Rolls of Prisoners of War: Captured at Fort Gaines, AL, on 8/8/1864; Received at Ship Island, MS, from New Orleans, LA, on 10/25/1864. Exchanged on 1/4/1865.

Long, Thomas A. Cpl./Sgt., 21st Alabama Infantry. Co. I. Federal Rolls of Prisoners of War: Captured at Fort Gaines, AL, on 8/8/1864; Received at Ship Island, MS, from New Orleans, LA, on 10/25/1864. Exchanged on 1/4/1865.

Lorieum, J.N. (AKA Lovieurn) Pvt./Sgt., 62nd Alabama Infantry. Co. B. Federal Rolls of Prisoners of War: Captured at Blakely, AL, on 4/9/1865; Received at Ship Island, MS, on 4/15/1865. Transferred to Vicksburg, MS, for exchange on 5/1/1865; Exchanged at Camp Townsend, MS, on 5/6/1865.

Lott, Heuston Alexander Pvt., 36th Alabama Infantry. Co. G. Enlisted: 1861 at Mobile, AL. Federal Rolls of Prisoners of War: Captured at Spanish Fort, AL, on 4/8/1865; Received at Ship Island, MS, on 4/10/1865. Transferred to Vicksburg, MS, for exchange on 5/1/1865; Exchanged at Camp Townsend, MS, on 5/6/1865. Born: 12/22/1844 at Georgetown, Mobile County, AL.

Louis, John J. Pvt., 63rd Alabama Infantry. Co. H. Enlisted: 8/9/1864 at Mobile, AL. Age at enlistment: 17. Description at enlistment: Eyes: dark. Hair: dark. Complexion: fair. Rolls for 9/1864 through 10/1864: Absent, sick in hospital at Mobile, AL, since 10/30/1864. Federal Rolls of Prisoners of War: Captured at Blakely, AL, on 4/9/1865; Received at Ship Island, MS, on 4/15/1865. Transferred to Vicksburg, MS, for exchange on 5/1/1865; Exchanged at Camp Townsend, MS, on 5/6/1865. Rolls of Prisoners of War, C.S.A: Surrendered at Citronelle, AL, on

5/4/1865; Paroled at Meridian, MS, on 5/11/1865. Residence at parole: Clarke County, AL.

Lounan, G.F. (AKA Lonnan) Pvt./Sgt., 62nd Alabama Infantry. Co. C. Federal Rolls of Prisoners of War: Captured at Blakely, AL, on 4/9/1865; Received at Ship Island, MS, on 4/15/1865. Transferred to Vicksburg, MS, for exchange on 5/1/1865; Exchanged at Camp Townsend, MS, on 5/6/1865.

Lowary, H. Pvt., 21st Alabama Infantry. Co. E. Federal Rolls of Prisoners of War: Captured at Fort Gaines, AL, on 8/8/1864; Received at Ship Island, MS, from New Orleans, LA, on 10/25/1864. Transferred to New Orleans, LA, on 2/15/1865; Refused to be exchanged.

Lowe, J.D. Pvt., 38th Alabama Infantry. Co. D. Federal Rolls of Prisoners of War: Captured at Spanish Fort, AL, on 4/8/1865; Received at Ship Island, MS, on 4/10/1865. Transferred to Vicksburg, MS, for exchange on 5/1/1865; Exchanged at Camp Townsend, MS, on 5/6/1865.

Loyal, James Pvt., Lockhart's Battalion Infantry. Co. __. Federal Rolls of Prisoners of War: Captured at Fort Gaines, AL, on 8/8/1864; Received at Ship Island, MS, from New Orleans, LA, on 1/25/1865. Exchanged on 3/2/1865.

Lucas, J.N. Pvt., 21st Alabama Infantry. Co. F. Federal Rolls of Prisoners of War: Captured at Spanish Fort, AL, on 4/8/1865; Received at Ship Island, MS, on 4/10/1865. Transferred to Vicksburg, MS, for exchange on 5/1/1865; Exchanged at Camp Townsend, MS, on 5/6/1865.

Lunsford, W.N. Pvt., 18th Alabama Infantry. Co. A. Federal Rolls of Prisoners of War: Captured at Spanish Fort, AL, on 4/8/1865; Received at Ship Island, MS, on 4/10/1865. Transferred to Vicksburg, MS, for exchange on 5/1/1865; Exchanged at Camp Townsend, MS, on 5/6/1865.

Luten, Lewis (AKA Luton) Pvt., 62nd Alabama Infantry. Co. A. Federal Rolls of Prisoners of War: Captured at Blakely, AL, on 4/9/1865; Received at Ship Island, MS, on 4/15/1865. Transferred to Vicksburg, MS, for exchange on 5/1/1865; Exchanged at Camp Townsend, MS, on 5/6/1865.

Lyens, J.M. (AKA Lynn) Pvt., 38th Alabama Infantry. Co. E. Federal Rolls of Prisoners of War: Captured at Blakely, AL, on 4/9/1865; Received at Ship Island, MS, on 4/15/1865. Transferred to Vicksburg, MS, for exchange on 5/1/1865; Exchanged at Camp Townsend, MS, on 5/6/1865.

Lyles, John Pvt., 21st Alabama Infantry. Cos. C & H. Federal Rolls of Prisoners of War: Captured at Fort Gaines, AL, on 8/8/1864; Received at Ship Island, MS, from New Orleans, LA, on 10/25/1864. Exchanged on 1/4/1865.

Lynch, Patrick Pvt., 38th Alabama Infantry. Co. K. Enlisted: 9/12/1862 at Mobile, AL. On Register of Stonewall Hospital, Montgomery, AL: Admitted on 10/1/1863. Federal Rolls of Prisoners of War: Captured at Spanish Fort, AL, on 4/8/1865; Received at Ship Island, MS, on 4/10/1865. Transferred to Vicksburg, MS, for exchange on 5/1/1865; Exchanged at Camp Townsend, MS, on 5/6/1865.

Lynn, J.M. Pvt. 38th Alabama Infantry. Co. E. Issued clothing in Hospital, Atlanta, GA, on 7/30/1863. Federal Rolls of Prisoners of War: Captured at Blakely, AL, on 4/9/1865; Received at Ship Island, MS, on 4/15/1865. Transferred to Vicksburg, MS, for exchange on 5/1/1865; Exchanged at Camp Townsend, MS, on 5/6/1865.

Lynn, W.B. Pvt., 38th Alabama Infantry. Co. E. Issued clothing at Marshall Hospital, Columbus, GA, on 6/2/1864. Federal Rolls of Prisoners of War: Captured at Blakely, AL, on 4/9/1865; Received at Ship Island, MS, on 4/15/1865. Transferred to Vicksburg, MS, for exchange on 5/1/1865; Exchanged at Camp Townsend, MS, on 5/6/1865.

McAffee, Henry (AKA McAfee) Pvt., 62nd Alabama Infantry. Co. E. Federal Rolls of Prisoners of War: Captured at Blakely, AL, on 4/9/1865; Received at Ship Island, MS, on 4/15/1865. Transferred to Vicksburg, MS, for exchange on 5/1/1865; Exchanged at Camp Townsend, MS, on 5/6/1865.

McAllister, T.H. Pvt., 6th Alabama Cavalry. Cos. C & D. Federal Rolls of Prisoners of War: Captured in Florida on 3/25/1865; Received at Ship Island, MS. Transferred to Vicksburg, MS, for exchange on 5/1/1865; Exchanged at Camp Townsend, MS, on 5/6/1865.

McBride, Patrick Pvt., 21st Alabama Infantry. Co. B. Federal Rolls of Prisoners of War: Captured at Fort Gaines, AL, on 8/8/1864; Received at Ship Island, MS, from New Orleans, LA, on 10/25/1864. Exchanged on 1/4/1865.

McCain, George H. (AKA McCane) 2nd Lt., 36th Alabama Infantry. Co. A. Federal Rolls of Prisoners of War: Captured at Spanish Fort, AL, on 4/8/1865; Received at Ship Island, MS, on 4/10/1865. Transferred to Vicksburg, MS, for exchange on 4/28/1865; Confined at New Orleans, LA, on 4/30/1865. Exchanged at Camp Townsend, MS, on 5/6/1865.

McCall, James (AKA McCaw) Pvt., 1st Alabama Artillery Battalion. Co. A. Federal Rolls of Prisoners of War: Captured at Fort Gaines, AL, on 8/8/1864; Received at Ship Island, MS, from New Orleans, LA, on 10/25/1864. Exchanged on 3/2/1865.

McCall, John W. Pvt., 62nd Alabama Infantry. Co. G. Federal Rolls of Prisoners of War: Captured at Blakely, AL, on 4/9/1865; Received at Ship Island, MS, on 4/15/1865. Transferred to Vicksburg, MS, for exchange on 5/1/1865; Exchanged at Camp Townsend, MS, on 5/6/1865.

McCall, R.L. (AKA R.S.) Pvt., 36th Alabama Infantry. Co. C. Federal Rolls of Prisoners of War: Captured at Spanish Fort, AL, on 4/8/1865; Received at Ship Island, MS, on 4/10/1865. Transferred to Vicksburg, MS, for exchange on 5/1/1865; Exchanged at Camp Townsend, MS, on 5/6/1865.

McCane, George 3rd Cpl./4th Sgt., 63rd Alabama Infantry. Co. B. Enlisted: 3/23/1864 at Montgomery, AL. Age at enlistment: 17. Rolls for 9/1864 through 10/1864: Present. Federal Rolls of Prisoners of War: Captured at Blakely, AL, on 4/9/1865; Received at Ship Island, MS, on 4/15/1865. Transferred to Vicksburg, MS, for exchange on 5/1/1865; Exchanged at Camp Townsend, MS, on 5/6/1865. Rolls of Prisoners of War, C.S.A: Surrendered at Citronelle, AL, on 5/4/1865; Paroled at Meridian, MS, on 5/11/1865. Residence at parole: Coosa County, AL.

McCardley, Calvin M. (AKA McCarley) Pvt., 63rd Alabama Infantry. Cos. A & C. Enlisted: 1/1/1864 at Coosa County, AL. Age at enlistment: 16. Rolls for 1/1864 through 2/1864: Present. Rolls for 9/1864 through 10/1864: Present. Federal Rolls of Prisoners of War: Captured at Blakely, AL, on 4/9/1865; Received at Ship Island, MS, on 4/15/1865. Transferred to Vicksburg, MS, for exchange on 5/1/1865; Exchanged at Camp Townsend, MS, on 5/6/1865. Rolls of Prisoners of War, C.S.A: Surrendered at Citronelle, AL, on 5/4/1865; Paroled at Meridian, MS, on 5/13/1865. Residence at parole: Coosa County, AL.

McCarey, B.S. (AKA McCary, S.B.) Pvt., 63rd Alabama Infantry. Co. H. Federal Rolls of Prisoners of War: Captured at Blakely, AL, on 4/9/1865; Received at Ship Island, MS, on 4/15/1865. Transferred to Vicksburg, MS, for exchange on 5/1/1865; Exchanged at Camp Townsend, MS, on 5/6/1865.

McCarley, S.A. Pvt., 63rd Alabama Infantry. Co. A. Federal Rolls of Prisoners of War: Captured at Blakely, AL, on 4/9/1865; Received at Ship Island, MS, on 4/15/1865. Transferred to Vicksburg, MS, for exchange on 5/1/1865. Rolls of Prisoners of War, C.S.A: Surrendered at Citronelle, AL, on 5/4/1865; Paroled at Meridian, MS, on 5/13/1865. Residence at parole: Coosa County, AL.

McCarthy, D.A. Pvt., 63rd Alabama Infantry. Cos. A & I. Federal Rolls of Prisoners of War: Captured at Blakely, AL, on 4/9/1865; Received at Ship Island, MS, on 4/15/1865. Transferred to Vicksburg, MS, for exchange on 5/1/1865; Exchanged at Camp Townsend, MS, on 5/6/1865. Rolls of Prisoners of War, C.S.A: Surrendered at Citronelle, AL, on 5/4/1865; Paroled at Meridian, MS, on 5/13/1865. Residence at parole: Coosa County, AL.

McCartney, M.E. (AKA N.E.) Pvt./2nd Lt., 21st Alabama Infantry. Cos. F & K. Federal Rolls of Prisoners of War: Captured at Fort Gaines, AL, on 8/8/1864; Received at Ship Island, MS, from New Orleans, LA, on 10/25/1864. Exchanged on 1/4/1865.

McCartney, Thomas N. 2nd Lt., 21st Alabama Infantry. Co. F. Federal Rolls of Prisoners of War: Captured at Fort Gaines, AL, on 8/8/1864; Received at Ship Island, MS, from New Orleans, LA, on 10/25/1864. Exchanged on 1/4/1865.

McCarty, J.D. Pvt., 63rd Alabama Infantry. Co. F. Enlisted: 7/12/1864 at Lowndes County, AL. Age at enlistment: 17. Description at enlistment: Eyes: hazel. Hair: dark. Complexion: sallow. Height: 5'5". Residence at enlistment: Lowndes County, AL. Rolls for 9/1864 through 10/1864: Present. Federal Rolls of Prisoners of War: Captured at Blakely, AL, on 4/9/1865; Received at Ship Island, MS, on 4/15/1865. Transferred to Vicksburg, MS, for exchange on 5/1/1865. On Register of U.S.A. General Hospital #2, Vicksburg, MS: Admitted from steamer on 5/3/1865 due to acute diarrhea; Returned to duty on 5/8/1865.

McCarty, S.B. Pvt., 63rd Alabama Infantry. Co. H. Enlisted: 3/15/1864 at Randolph County, AL. Age at enlistment: 17. Description at enlistment: Eyes: hazel. Hair: light. Complexion: dark. Rolls for 9/1864 through 10/1864: Absent, sick in hospital since 10/10/1864. On Register of Ross Hospital, Mobile, AL: Admitted on 10/10/1864 due to febris intermittens; Transferred to Greenville, AL, General Hospital on 10/25/1864. Federal Rolls of Prisoners of War: Captured at Blakely, AL, on 4/9/1865; Received at Ship Island, MS, on 4/15/1865. Transferred to Vicksburg, MS, for exchange on 5/1/1865; Exchanged at Camp Townsend, MS, on 5/6/1865. Rolls of Prisoners of War, C.S.A: Surrendered at Citronelle, AL, on 5/4/1865; Paroled at Meridian, MS, on 5/11/1865. Residence at parole: Bibb County, AL.

McCauley, Felix M. (AKA McCawley) Pvt., Lockhart's Battalion Infantry. Co. K. Federal Rolls of Prisoners of War: Captured at Fort Gaines, AL, on 8/8/1864; Received at Ship Island, MS, from New Orleans, LA, on 10/25/1864. Exchanged on 3/2/1865.

McClain, J.S. Pvt., 26th Alabama Infantry. Co. H. Federal Rolls of Prisoners of War: Captured at Spanish Fort, AL, on 4/8/1865; Received at Ship Island, MS, on 4/10/1865. Transferred to Vicksburg, MS, for exchange on 5/1/1865; Exchanged at Camp Townsend, MS, on 5/6/1865.

McClain, William F. (AKA McCain) Cpl./Pvt., 62nd Alabama Infantry. Co. G. Federal Rolls of Prisoners of War: Captured at Blakely, AL, on 4/9/1865; Received at Ship Island, MS, on 4/15/1865. Transferred to Vicksburg, MS, for exchange on 5/1/1865; Exchanged at Camp Townsend, MS, on 5/6/1865.

McClan, J.M. Cpl., 38th Alabama Infantry. Co. B. Federal Rolls of Prisoners of War: Captured at Spanish Fort, AL, on 4/8/1865; Received at Ship Island, MS, on 4/10/1865. Transferred to Vicksburg, MS, for exchange on 5/1/1865; Exchanged at Camp Townsend, MS, on 5/6/1865.

McClusky, James H. (AKA J.A.) Pvt., 1st Alabama Artillery Battalion. Cos. B & E. Federal Rolls of Prisoners of War: Captured at Blakely, AL, on 4/9/1865; Received at Ship Island, MS, on 4/15/1865. Transferred to Vicksburg, MS, for exchange on 5/1/1865; Exchanged at Camp Townsend, MS, on 5/6/1865.

McCollars, Benjamin B. (AKA McCollen) Pvt., 63rd Alabama Infantry. Cos. B & F. Enlisted: 5/30/1864 at Montgomery, AL. Age at enlistment: 17. Description at enlistment: Eyes: grey. Hair: dark. Complexion: fair. Height: 5'7". Residence at enlistment: Coosa County, AL. Rolls for 9/1864 through 10/1864: Present. Federal Rolls of Prisoners of War: Captured at Blakely, AL, on 4/9/1865; Received at Ship Island, MS, on 4/15/1865. Transferred to Vicksburg, MS, for exchange on 5/1/1865; Exchanged at Camp Townsend, MS, on 5/6/1865. Rolls of Prisoners of War, C.S.A: Surrendered at Citronelle, AL, on 5/4/1865; Paroled at Meridian, MS, on 5/11/1865. Residence at parole: Coosa County, AL.

McConnelly, J.C. Cpl., 38th Alabama Infantry. Co. B. Federal Rolls of Prisoners of War: Captured at Spanish Fort, AL, on 4/8/1865; Received at Ship Island, MS, on 4/10/1865. Transferred to Vicksburg, MS, for exchange on 5/1/1865; Exchanged at Camp Townsend, MS, on 5/6/1865.

McCormick, W.J. (AKA J.) Pvt., 63rd Alabama Infantry. Co. F. Enlisted: 10/10/1864 at Greenville, AL. Rolls for 9/1864 through 10/1864: Present. Federal Rolls of Prisoners of War: Captured at Blakely, AL, on 4/9/1865; Received at Ship Island, MS, on 4/15/1865. Transferred to Vicksburg, MS, for exchange on 5/1/1865; Exchanged at Camp Townsend, MS, on 5/6/1865. Rolls of Prisoners of War, C.S.A: Surrendered at Citronelle, AL, on 5/4/1865; Paroled at Meridian, MS, on 5/11/1865. Residence at parole: Butler County, AL.

McCowan, James Pvt., 63rd Alabama Infantry. Co. K. Enlisted: 8/25/1864 at Tallapoosa County, AL. Rolls for 9/1864 through 10/1864: Present. Federal Rolls of

Prisoners of War: Captured at Blakely, AL, on 4/9/1865; Received at Ship Island, MS, on 4/15/1865. Transferred to Vicksburg, MS, for exchange on 5/1/1865; Exchanged at Camp Townsend, MS, on 5/6/1865. Rolls of Prisoners of War, C.S.A: Surrendered at Citronelle, AL, on 5/4/1865; Paroled at Meridian, MS, on 5/13/1865. Residence at parole: Tallapoosa County, AL.

McCoy, John Pvt., 8th Alabama Cavalry. Co. K. Federal Rolls of Prisoners of War: Captured in Alabama on 3/24/1865; Received at Ship Island, MS. Transferred to Vicksburg, MS, for exchange on 5/1/1865; Exchanged at Camp Townsend, MS, on 5/6/1865.

McCrory, R. (AKA McRory, William) Pvt., 21st Alabama Infantry. Cos. H & I. Federal Rolls of Prisoners of War: Captured at Fort Gaines, AL, on 8/8/1864; Received at Ship Island, MS, from New Orleans, LA, on 10/25/1864. Exchanged on 1/4/1865.

McCrory, T.M. Pvt., 6th Alabama Cavalry. Co. E. Federal Rolls of Prisoners of War: Captured in Florida on 3/25/1865; Received at Ship Island, MS. Transferred to Vicksburg, MS, for exchange on 5/1/1865; Exchanged at Camp Townsend, MS, on 5/6/1865.

McCullough, David S. (AKA D.M.) Sgt./2nd Lt., 21st Alabama Infantry. Cos. A & B. Federal Rolls of Prisoners of War: Captured at Fort Gaines, AL, on 8/8/1864; Received at Ship Island, MS, from New Orleans, LA, on 10/25/1864. Exchanged on 1/4/1865.

McCurdy, A.J. Pvt./Cpl., 62nd Alabama Infantry. Co. F. Federal Rolls of Prisoners of War: Captured at Blakely, AL, on 4/9/1865; Received at Ship Island, MS, on 4/15/1865. Transferred to Vicksburg, MS, for exchange on 5/1/1865; Exchanged at Camp Townsend, MS, on 5/6/1865.

McDaniel, David Pvt., Lockhart's Battalion Infantry. Co. K. Federal Rolls of Prisoners of War: Captured at Fort Gaines, AL, on 8/8/1864; Received at Ship Island, MS, from New Orleans, LA, on 10/24/1864. Died: 11/16/1864 at Ship Island, MS, due to typhoid fever. Buried: Ship Island, MS, Cemetery in Grave #23.

McDaniel, John G. (AKA J.S.) Pvt., 62nd Alabama Infantry. Co. K. Federal Rolls of Prisoners of War: Captured at Blakely, AL, on 4/9/1865; Received at Ship Island, MS, on 4/15/1865. Transferred to Vicksburg, MS, for exchange on 5/1/1865; Exchanged at Camp Townsend, MS, on 5/6/1865.

McDaniel, W.A. Pvt., 18th Alabama Infantry. Co. E. Federal Rolls of Prisoners of War: Captured at Spanish Fort, AL, on 4/8/1865; Received at Ship Island, MS, on 4/10/1865. Transferred to Vicksburg, MS, for exchange on 5/1/1865; Exchanged at Camp Townsend, MS, on 5/6/1865.

McDonald, B.H. (AKA R.H.) Pvt., 63rd Alabama Infantry. Co. I. Enlisted: 4/25/1864 at Talladega, AL. Rolls for 9/1864 through 10/1864: Absent, on 30 day furlough since 9/27/1864. Federal Rolls of Prisoners of War: Captured at Blakely, AL, on 4/9/1865; Received at Ship Island, MS, on 4/15/1865. Died: 4/30/1865 at Ship Island, MS, due to dysentery. Buried: Ship Island, MS, Cemetery in Grave #151.

McDonald, Thomas Pvt., 1st Alabama Artillery Battalion. Co. K. Federal Rolls of Prisoners of War: Captured at Fort Gaines, AL, on 8/8/1864; Received at Ship Island, MS, from New Orleans, LA, on 10/25/1864. Exchanged on 1/4/1865.

McDonald, William Pvt., 36th Alabama Infantry. Co. K. Federal Rolls of Prisoners of War: Captured at Spanish Fort, AL, on 4/8/1865; Received at Ship Island, MS, on 4/10/1865. Transferred to Vicksburg, MS, for exchange on 5/1/1865; Exchanged at Camp Townsend, MS, on 5/6/1865.

McDonald, William A. Pvt., 62nd Alabama Infantry. Co. H. Federal Rolls of Prisoners of War: Captured at Blakely, AL, on 4/9/1865; Received at Ship Island, MS, on 4/15/1865. Transferred to Vicksburg, MS, for exchange on 5/1/1865; Exchanged at Camp Townsend, MS, on 5/6/1865.

McDonnica, William (AKA McDermia) Pvt., 1st Alabama Artillery. Co. B. Federal Rolls of Prisoners of War: Captured at Blakely, AL, on 4/9/1865; Received at Ship Island, MS, on 4/15/1865. Transferred to Vicksburg, MS, for exchange on 5/1/1865; Exchanged at Camp Townsend, MS, on 5/6/1865.

McDuffie, W.K. Pvt./Sgt., 21st Alabama Infantry. Co. C. Federal Rolls of Prisoners of War: Captured at Fort Gaines, AL, on 8/8/1864; Received at Ship Island, MS, from New Orleans, LA, on 10/25/1864. Exchanged on 1/4/1865.

McElhaney, W.T. Pvt., 21st Alabama Infantry. Co. F. Federal Rolls of Prisoners of War: Captured at Fort Gaines, AL, on 8/8/1864; Received at Ship Island, MS, from New Orleans, LA, on 10/24/1864. Exchanged on 1/4/1865.

McElrath, S.B. Pvt., Lockhart's Battalion Infantry. Co. H. Federal Rolls of Prisoners of War: Captured at Fort Gaines, AL, on 8/8/1864; Received at Ship Island, MS, from New Orleans, LA, on 10/24/1864. Died: 12/17/1864 at Ship Island, MS, due to pneumonia. Buried: Ship Island, MS, Cemetery in Grave #97.

McGinnis, Thomas Pvt., 18th Alabama Infantry. Co. I. Federal Rolls of Prisoners of War: Captured at Spanish Fort, AL, on 4/8/1865; Received at Ship Island, MS, on 4/10/1865. Transferred to Vicksburg, MS, for exchange on 5/1/1865; Exchanged at Camp Townsend, MS, on 5/6/1865.

McGriff, R. Pvt., 6th Alabama Cavalry. Co. E. Federal Rolls of Prisoners of War: Captured in Florida on 3/25/1865; Received at Ship Island, MS. Transferred to Vicksburg, MS, for exchange on 5/1/1865; Exchanged at Camp Townsend, MS, on 5/6/1865.

McGriff, Richard Patrick Pvt., 6th Alabama Cavalry. Co. E. Enlisted: 1863 at Abbeville, AL. Federal Rolls of Prisoners of War: Captured near Blakely, AL, in 3/1865; Received at Ship Island, MS. Transferred to Vicksburg, MS, for exchange on 5/1/1865; Exchanged at Camp Townsend, MS, on 5/6/1865. Born: 3/16/1847 at Columbia, Henry County, AL. Soldier is recorded on the 1907 Alabama Census of Confederate Veterans and Widows. Residence: Houston County, AL.

McGuinty, James A. (AKA McGinty) 4th Sgt., 63rd Alabama Infantry. Co. C. Enlisted: 5/11/1864 at Chambers County, AL. Age at enlistment: 17. Description at enlistment: Eyes: blue. Hair: light. Complexion: fair. Height: 5'9". Residence at enlistment: Cusseta, Chambers County, AL. Rolls for 9/1864 through 10/1864: Absent, in hospital at Mobile, AL, since 10/18/1864. Federal Rolls of Prisoners of War: Captured at Blakely, AL, on 4/9/1865; Received at Ship Island, MS, on 4/15/1865.

Transferred to Vicksburg, MS, for exchange on 5/1/1865; Exchanged at Camp Townsend, MS, on 5/6/1865. Rolls of Prisoners of War, C.S.A: Surrendered at Citronelle, AL, on 5/4/1865; Paroled at Meridian, MS, on 5/11/1865. Residence at parole: Chambers County, AL.

McInnis, M. 1st Lt., 21st Alabama Infantry. Co. I. Federal Rolls of Prisoners of War: Captured at Fort Gaines, AL, on 8/8/1864; Received at Ship Island, MS, from New Orleans, LA, on 10/25/1864. Exchanged on 1/4/1865.

McKeithern, J.S. (AKA S.J.) Pvt., 38th Alabama Infantry. Co. C. Federal Rolls of Prisoners of War: Captured at Spanish Fort, AL, on 4/8/1865; Received at Ship Island, MS, on 4/10/1865. Transferred to Vicksburg, MS, for exchange on 5/1/1865; Exchanged at Camp Townsend, MS, on 5/6/1865.

McKenin, J.P. Sgt., 36th Alabama Infantry. Co. A. Federal Rolls of Prisoners of War: Captured at Spanish Fort, AL, on 4/8/1865; Received at Ship Island, MS, on 4/10/1865. Transferred to Vicksburg, MS, for exchange on 5/1/1865; Exchanged at Camp Townsend, MS, on 5/6/1865.

McKenny, S.J. Pvt., 38th Alabama Infantry. Co. C. Federal Rolls of Prisoners of War: Captured at Spanish Fort, AL, on 4/8/1865; Received at Ship Island, MS, on 4/10/1865. Transferred to Vicksburg, MS, for exchange on 5/1/1865; Exchanged at Camp Townsend, MS, on 5/6/1865.

McKenzie, Aaron (AKA McKinsey) Pvt., 36th Alabama Infantry. Co. F. Federal Rolls of Prisoners of War: Captured at Spanish Fort, AL, on 4/8/1865; Received at Ship Island, MS, on 4/10/1865. Transferred to Vicksburg, MS, for exchange on 5/1/1865; Exchanged at Camp Townsend, MS, on 5/6/1865.

McKinney, James M. Pvt., 6th Alabama Cavalry. Co. C. Enlisted: 9/10/1863 at Blue Mountain, AL. Captured on 3/15/1865; Received at Ship Island, MS. Transferred to Vicksburg, MS, for exchange on 5/1/1865; Exchanged at Camp Townsend, MS, on 5/6/1865. Born: 12/25/1841 at McDonald, Carroll County, GA. Residence after war: Perry County, AL.

McKissick, William Pvt., 63rd Alabama Infantry. Co. B. Enlisted: 3/23/1864 at Montgomery County, AL. Age at enlistment: 16. Rolls for 9/1864 through 10/1864: Present. Federal Rolls of Prisoners of War: Captured at Blakely, AL, on 4/9/1865; Received at Ship Island, MS, on 4/15/1865. Transferred to Vicksburg, MS, for exchange on 5/1/1865; Exchanged at Camp Townsend, MS, on 5/6/1865. Rolls of Prisoners of War, C.S.A: Surrendered at Citronelle, AL, on 5/4/1865; Paroled at Meridian, MS, on 5/11/1865. Residence at parole: Coosa County, AL.

McLarney, Frank H. Pvt./Sgt., 21st Alabama Infantry. Co. E. Federal Rolls of Prisoners of War: Captured at Fort Gaines, AL, on 8/8/1864; Received at Ship Island, MS, from New Orleans, LA, on 10/25/1864. Exchanged on 1/4/1865.

McLaughlin, William D. 1st Sgt./Lt., 2nd Alabama Infantry. Co. __. Federal Rolls of Prisoners of War: Captured at Blakely, AL, on 4/9/1865; Received at Ship Island, MS, on 4/15/1865. Transferred to Vicksburg, MS, for exchange on 4/28/1865; Confined at New Orleans, LA, on 4/30/1865. Exchanged at Camp Townsend, MS, on 5/6/1865.

McLean, S.S. Pvt., 21st Alabama Infantry. Co. G. Federal Rolls of Prisoners of War: Captured at Fort Gaines, AL, on 8/8/1864; Received at Ship Island, MS, on 10/24/1864. Died: 11/25/1864 at Ship Island, MS, due to dysentery. Buried: Ship Island, MS, Cemetery in Grave #42.

McMath, W. 5th Sgt., 63rd Alabama Infantry. Co. H. Enlisted: 8/7/1864 at Selma, AL. Age at enlistment: 17. Description at enlistment: Eyes: blue. Hair: dark. Complexion: fair. Rolls for 9/1864 through 10/1864: Absent, sick in hospital at Greenville, AL, since 9/6/1864. Federal Rolls of Prisoners of War: Captured at Blakely, AL, on 4/9/1865; Received at Ship Island, MS, on 4/15/1865. Transferred to Vicksburg, MS, for exchange on 5/1/1865; Exchanged at Camp Townsend, MS, on 5/6/1865. Rolls of Prisoners of War, C.S.A: Surrendered at Citronelle, AL, on 5/4/1865; Paroled at Meridian, MS, on 5/11/1865. Residence at parole: Jefferson County, AL.

McMillan, J.A. Pvt., 21st Alabama Infantry. Co. C. Federal Rolls of Prisoners of War: Captured at Fort Gaines, AL, on 8/8/1864; Received at Ship Island, MS, from New Orleans, LA, on 10/25/1864. Exchanged on 1/4/1865.

McNair, Charles T. (AKA Z.T.) Pvt., 63rd Alabama Infantry. Co. D. Federal Rolls of Prisoners of War: Captured at Blakely, AL, on 4/9/1865; Received at Ship Island, MS, on 4/15/1865. Transferred to Vicksburg, MS, for exchange on 5/1/1865; Exchanged at Camp Townsend, MS, on 5/6/1865.

McNair, J.F. Pvt., 63rd Alabama Infantry. Co. K. Enlisted: 8/5/1864 at Perry County, AL. Rolls for 9/1864 through 10/1864: Present. Federal Rolls of Prisoners of War: Captured at Blakely, AL, on 4/9/1865; Received at Ship Island, MS, on 4/15/1865. Transferred to Vicksburg, MS, for exchange on 5/1/1865; Exchanged at Camp Townsend, MS, on 5/6/1865. Rolls of Prisoners of War, C.S.A: Surrendered at Citronelle, AL, on 5/4/1865; Paroled at Meridian, MS, on 5/13/1865. Residence at parole: Shelby County, AL.

McQuote, Lillie (AKA McQuoto, S.) Sgt., 8th Alabama Cavalry. Cos. D & E. Federal Rolls of Prisoners of War: Captured in Florida on 3/25/1865; Received at Ship Island, MS. Transferred to Vicksburg, MS, for exchange on 5/1/1865; Exchanged at Camp Townsend, MS, on 5/6/1865.

McRae, Alex Pvt., 62nd Alabama Infantry. Co. B. Federal Rolls of Prisoners of War: Captured at Blakely, AL, on 4/9/1865; Received at Ship Island, MS, on 4/15/1865. Transferred to Vicksburg, MS, for exchange on 5/1/1865; Exchanged at Camp Townsend, MS, on 5/6/1865.

McRae, Christopher C. Pvt., 63rd Alabama Infantry. Co. D. Enlisted: 7/30/1864 at Macon County, AL. Age at enlistment: 17. Description at enlistment: Eyes: blue. Hair: light. Complexion: fair. Height: 5'5". Residence at enlistment: Clayton, Barbour County, AL. Rolls for 9/1864 through 10/1864: Present. Federal Rolls of Prisoners of War: Captured at Blakely, AL, on 4/9/1865; Received at Ship Island, MS, on 4/15/1865. Transferred to Vicksburg, MS, for exchange on 5/1/1865; Exchanged at Camp Townsend, MS, on 5/6/1865. Rolls of Prisoners of War, C.S.A: Surrendered at Citronelle, AL, on 5/4/1865; Paroled at Meridian, MS, on 5/13/1865. Residence at parole: Barbour County, AL.

McRae, Daniel A. (AKA McKees) Pvt., 63rd Alabama Infantry. Co. A. Enlisted: 1/1/1864 at Pollard, AL. Age at enlistment: 17. Rolls for 1/1864 through 2/1864: Present. Rolls for 9/1864 through 10/1864: Present. Federal Rolls of Prisoners of War: Captured at Blakely, AL, on 4/9/1865; Received at Ship Island, MS, on 4/15/1865. Transferred to Vicksburg, MS, for exchange on 5/1/1865; Exchanged at Camp Townsend, MS, on 5/6/1865. Rolls of Prisoners of War, C.S.A: Surrendered at Citronelle, AL, on 5/4/1865; Paroled at Meridian, MS, on 5/13/1865. Residence at parole: Tallapoosa County, AL. Confederate Widows Pension Application dated 1915 on file at the Oklahoma State Archives. Target Name: McRae, Mary E. Application Number: 1985. Microfilm Reel: 6.

McRae, James Capt., 6th Alabama Infantry. Cos. D & E. Federal Rolls of Prisoners of War: Captured in Florida on 3/25/1865; Received at Ship Island, MS. Transferred to Vicksburg, MS, for exchange on 4/28/1865; Confined at New Orleans, LA, on 4/30/1865. Exchanged at Camp Townsend, MS, on 5/6/1865.

McRae, P. Pvt., 36th Alabama Infantry. Co. I. Federal Rolls of Prisoners of War: Captured at Spanish Fort, AL, on 4/8/1865; Received at Ship Island, MS, on 4/10/1865. Transferred to Vicksburg, MS, for exchange on 5/1/1865; Exchanged at Camp Townsend, MS, on 5/6/1865.

McRae, William Pvt., 63rd Alabama Infantry. Co. B. Enlisted: 4/14/1864 at Montgomery County, AL. Age at enlistment: 16. Rolls for 9/1864 through 10/1864: Present. On Register of Ross Hospital, Mobile, AL: Admitted on 11/17/1864 due to febris intermittens tert.; Returned to duty on 11/29/1864. Federal Rolls of Prisoners of War: Captured at Blakely, AL, on 4/9/1865; Received at Ship Island, MS, on 4/15/1865. Transferred to Vicksburg, MS, for exchange on 5/1/1865; Exchanged at Camp Townsend, MS, on 5/6/1865. Rolls of Prisoners of War, C.S.A: Surrendered at Citronelle, AL, on 5/4/1865; Paroled at Meridian, MS, on 5/11/1865. Residence at parole: Montgomery County, AL.

McRae, William N. Pvt., 63rd Alabama Infantry. Co. D. Enlisted: 7/30/1864 at Macon County, AL. Age at enlistment: 17. Description at enlistment: Eyes: grey. Hair: light. Complexion: florid. Height: 5'7". Residence at enlistment: Clayton, Barbour County, AL. Rolls for 9/1864 through 10/1864: Present. On Register of Ross Hospital, Mobile, AL: Admitted on 11/5/1864 due to febris intermittens tert.; Furloughed for 30 days on 11/24/1864. Federal Rolls of Prisoners of War: Captured at Blakely, AL, on 4/9/1865; Received at Ship Island, MS, on 4/15/1865. Transferred to Vicksburg, MS, for exchange on 5/1/1865; Exchanged at Camp Townsend, MS, on 5/6/1865. Rolls of Prisoners of War, C.S.A: Surrendered at Citronelle, AL, on 5/4/1865; Paroled at Meridian, MS, on 5/13/1865. Residence at parole: Barbour County, AL.

McRee, Mark C. (AKA McRae) Pvt., 63rd Alabama Infantry. Co. A. Enlisted: 7/20/1864 at Lowndes County, AL. Rolls for 9/1864 through 10/1864: Absent, sick in hospital at West Point, GA, since 8/5/1864. Federal Rolls of Prisoners of War: Captured at Blakely, AL, on 4/9/1865; Received at Ship Island, MS, on 4/15/1865. Transferred to Vicksburg, MS, for exchange on 5/1/1865; Exchanged at Camp Townsend, MS, on 5/6/1865. Rolls of Prisoners of War, C.S.A: Surrendered at Citronelle, AL, on 5/4/1865; Paroled at Meridian, MS, on 5/13/1865. Residence at parole: Lowndes County, AL.

McRessick, W.F. Pvt., 63rd Alabama Infantry. Co. B. Federal Rolls of Prisoners of War: Captured at Blakely, AL, on 4/9/1865; Received at Ship Island, MS, on 4/15/1865. Transferred to Vicksburg, MS, for exchange on 5/1/1865; Exchanged at Camp Townsend, MS, on 5/6/1865.

McVey, H. Pvt., Pelham Cadets. Co. A. Federal Rolls of Prisoners of War: Captured at Fort Gaines, AL, on 8/8/1864; Received at Ship Island, MS, from New Orleans, LA, on 10/24/1864. Exchanged on 1/4/1865.

McVoy, M.W. Pvt., 21st Alabama Infantry. Co. E. Federal Rolls of Prisoners of War: Captured at Fort Gaines, AL, on 8/8/1864; Received at Ship Island, MS, from New Orleans, LA, on 10/24/1864. Exchanged on 1/4/1865.

McWhorter, Eliphalet A. Maj., 6th Alabama Cavalry. F & S. Federal Rolls of Prisoners of War: Captured in Florida on 3/25/1865; Received at Ship Island, MS. Transferred to Vicksburg, MS, for exchange on 4/28/1865; Confined at New Orleans, LA, on 4/30/1865. Exchanged at Camp Townsend, MS, on 5/6/1865.

Maddox, W. (AKA Madox) Pvt., 1st Alabama Artillery. Co. B. Federal Rolls of Prisoners of War: Captured at Fort Gaines, AL, on 8/8/1864; Received at Ship Island, MS, from New Orleans, LA, on 10/24/1864. Exchanged on 1/4/1865.

Madison, A. Pvt., 1st Alabama Artillery. Co. D. Federal Rolls of Prisoners of War: Captured at Fort Gaines, AL, on 8/8/1864; Received at Ship Island, MS, from New Orleans, LA, on 10/24/1864. Exchanged on 1/4/1865.

Madison, Alexander Pvt./Sgt., 21st Alabama Infantry. Cos. H & I. Federal Rolls of Prisoners of War: Captured at Fort Gaines, AL, on 8/8/1864; Received at Ship Island, MS, from New Orleans, LA, on 10/25/1864. Exchanged on 1/4/1865.

Madison, James (AKA J.S.) Pvt., 21st Alabama Infantry. Cos. H & I. Federal Rolls of Prisoners of War: Captured at Fort Gaines, AL, on 8/8/1864; Received at Ship Island, MS, from New Orleans, LA, on 10/25/1864. Exchanged on 1/4/1865.

Maguire, John P. (AKA McGuire) Pvt., 21st Alabama Infantry. Co. E. Federal Rolls of Prisoners of War: Captured at Fort Gaines, AL, on 8/8/1864; Received at Ship Island, MS, from New Orleans, LA, on 10/25/1864. Exchanged on 1/4/1865.

Mahearn, J.A. Pvt., 38th Alabama Infantry. Co. C. Federal Rolls of Prisoners of War: Captured at Spanish Fort, AL, on 4/8/1865; Received at Ship Island, MS, on 4/10/1865. Transferred to Vicksburg, MS, for exchange on 5/1/1865; Exchanged at Camp Townsend, MS, on 5/6/1865.

Mahoney, John Pvt., 21st Alabama Infantry. Co. B. Federal Rolls of Prisoners of War: Captured at Fort Gaines, AL, on 8/8/1864; Received at Ship Island, MS, from New Orleans, LA, on 10/25/1864. Exchanged on 1/4/1865.

Majors, Edward (AKA Nafors) Pvt., 21st Alabama Infantry. Co. F. Federal Rolls of Prisoners of War: Captured at Fort Gaines, AL, on 8/8/1864; Received at Ship Island, MS, from New Orleans, LA, on 10/29/

1864. Died: 12/10/1864 at Ship Island, MS, due to chronic dysentery. Buried: Ship Island, MS, Cemetery in Grave #75.

Malloy, E.J. (AKA Mallory) Pvt., 63rd Alabama Infantry. Co. E. Enlisted: 6/1/1864 at Clayton, AL. Age at enlistment: 17. Description at enlistment: Eyes: dark. Hair: dark. Complexion: dark. Rolls for 9/1864 through 10/1864: Present. On Register of Ross Hospital, Mobile, AL: Admitted on 11/5/1864 due to acute diarrhea; Transferred to General Hospital on 11/30/1864. Federal Rolls of Prisoners of War: Captured at Blakely, AL, on 4/9/1865; Received at Ship Island, MS, on 4/15/1865. Transferred to Vicksburg, MS, for exchange on 5/1/1865; Exchanged at Camp Townsend, MS, on 5/6/1865. Rolls of Prisoners of War, C.S.A: Surrendered at Citronelle, AL, on 5/4/1865; Paroled at Meridian, MS, on 5/13/1865. Residence at parole: Coffee County, AL.

Manchew, J. Pvt., 63rd Alabama Infantry. Co. E. Federal Rolls of Prisoners of War: Captured at Blakely, AL, on 4/9/1865; Received at Ship Island, MS, on 4/15/1865. Transferred to Vicksburg, MS, for exchange on 5/1/1865; Exchanged at Camp Townsend, MS, on 5/6/1865. Rolls of Prisoners of War, C.S.A: Surrendered at Citronelle, AL, on 5/4/1865; Paroled at Meridian, MS, on 5/13/1865. Residence at parole: Barbour County, AL.

Mann, J.W. Sgt., 6th Alabama Cavalry. Cos. B & C. Federal Rolls of Prisoners of War: Captured in Florida on 3/25/1865; Received at Ship Island, MS. Transferred to Vicksburg, MS, for exchange on 5/1/1865; Exchanged at Camp Townsend, MS, on 5/6/1865.

Manning, Thomas Pvt., 1st Alabama Artillery. Cos. A, B & D. Federal Rolls of Prisoners of War: Captured at Fort Gaines, AL, on 8/8/1864; Received at Ship Island, MS, from New Orleans, LA, on 10/24/1864. Exchanged on 1/4/1865.

Manor, J.D. (Manner) Pvt., 63rd Alabama Infantry. Co. E. Enlisted: 8/8/1864 at Pollard, AL. Age at enlistment: 17. Description at enlistment: Eyes: blue. Hair: light. Complexion: fair. Rolls for 9/1864 through 10/1864: Present. Federal Rolls of Prisoners of War: Captured at Blakely, AL, on 4/9/1865; Received at Ship Island, MS, on 4/15/1865. Transferred to Vicksburg, MS, for exchange on 5/1/1865; Exchanged at Camp Townsend, MS, on 5/6/1865. Rolls of Prisoners of War, C.S.A: Surrendered at Citronelle, AL, on 5/4/1865; Paroled at Meridian, MS, on 5/13/1865. Residence at parole: Henry County, AL.

Maples, Simeon (AKA Simon) Pvt., 21st Alabama Infantry. Co. I. Federal Rolls of Prisoners of War: Captured at Fort Gaines, AL, on 8/8/1864; Received at Ship Island, MS, from New Orleans, LA, on 10/25/1864. Died: 12/26/1864 at Ship Island, MS, due to dysentery. Buried: Ship Island, MS, Cemetery in Grave #102.

Marion, Jerome Pvt., 21st Alabama Infantry. Co. C. Federal Rolls of Prisoners of War: Captured at Fort Gaines, AL, on 8/8/1864; Received at Ship Island, MS, from New Orleans, LA, on 10/25/1864. Exchanged on 1/4/1865.

Marshal, S.J. Pvt., 38th Alabama Infantry. Co. A. Federal Rolls of Prisoners of War: Captured at Spanish Fort, AL, on 4/8/1865; Received at Ship Island, MS, on 4/10/1865. Disposition unknown.

Marshall, J.S. Pvt., 38th Alabama Infantry. Co. A. Federal Rolls of Prisoners of War: Captured at Spanish Fort, AL, on 4/8/1865; Received at Ship Island, MS, on 4/10/1865. Transferred to Vicksburg, MS, for exchange on 5/1/1865; Exchanged at Camp Townsend, MS, on 5/6/1865.

Martin, A. Pvt., 62nd Alabama Infantry. Co. C. Federal Rolls of Prisoners of War: Captured at Blakely, AL, on 4/9/1865; Received at Ship Island, MS, on 4/15/1865. Transferred to Vicksburg, MS, for exchange on 5/1/1865; Exchanged at Camp Townsend, MS, on 5/6/1865.

Martin, C.L. Pvt./Cpl., 60th Alabama Infantry. Co. H. Federal Rolls of Prisoners of War: Captured in Alabama on 3/22/1865; Received at Ship Island, MS. Transferred to Vicksburg, MS, for exchange on 5/1/1865; Exchanged at Camp Townsend, MS, on 5/6/1865.

Martin, Charles W. 1st Lt./Capt. 63rd Alabama Infantry. Co. C. Enlisted: 6/22/1864 at Macon County, AL. Age at enlistment: 17. Description at enlistment: Eyes: hazel. Hair: dark. Complexion: fair. Height: 5'8½". Residence at enlistment: Tuskegee, AL. Rolls for 9/1864 through 10/1864: Present. Federal Rolls of Prisoners of War: Captured at Blakely, AL, on 4/9/1865; Confined one day at Spanish Fort, AL. Received at Ship Island, MS, on 4/16/1865; Transferred to Vicksburg, MS, for exchange on 4/28/1865. Confined at New Orleans, LA, on 4/30/1865; Exchanged at Camp Townsend, MS, on 5/6/1865. Rolls of Prisoners of War, C.S.A: Surrendered at Citronelle, AL, on 5/4/1865; Paroled at Meridian, MS, on 5/11/1865.

Martin, Edward Drummer, 21st Alabama Infantry. Co. E. Federal Rolls of Prisoners of War: Captured at Fort Gaines, AL, on 8/8/1864; Received at Ship Island, MS, from New Orleans, LA, on 10/25/1864. Exchanged on 1/4/1865.

Martin, M.M. Pvt., 63rd Alabama Infantry. Co. D. Enlisted: 8/8/1864 at Newton, AL. Rolls for 9/1864 through 10/1864: Absent, sick in hospital at Mobile, AL, since 10/28/1864. Federal Rolls of Prisoners of War: Captured at Blakely, AL, on 4/9/1865; Received at Ship Island, MS, on 4/15/1865. Transferred to Vicksburg, MS, for exchange on 5/1/1865; Exchanged at Camp Townsend, MS, on 5/6/1865. Rolls of Prisoners of War, C.S.A: Surrendered at Citronelle, AL, on 5/4/1865; Paroled at Meridian, MS, on 5/13/1865. Residence at parole: Dale County, AL.

Martin, Ransom H. Sgt./2nd Lt., 21st Alabama Infantry. Co. G. Federal Rolls of Prisoners of War: Captured at Fort Gaines, AL, on 8/8/1864; Received at Ship Island, MS, from New Orleans, LA, on 10/25/1864. Exchanged on 1/4/1865.

Martin, Sanders Pvt., 62nd Alabama Infantry. Co. G. Federal Rolls of Prisoners of War: Captured at Blakely, AL, on 4/9/1865; Received at Ship Island, MS, on 4/15/1865. Transferred to Vicksburg, MS, for exchange on 5/1/1865; Exchanged at Camp Townsend, MS, on 5/6/1865.

Martin, W. (AKA H.) Pvt., Lockhart's Battalion Infantry. Co. K. Federal Rolls of Prisoners of War: Captured at Fort Gaines, AL, on 8/8/1864; Received at Ship Island, MS, from New Orleans, LA, on 10/25/1864. Died: 12/18/1864 at Ship Island, MS. Buried: Ship Island, MS, Cemetery.

Martin, W.F. Pvt./2nd Lt., 18th Alabama Infantry. Co.

B. Federal Rolls of Prisoners of War: Captured at Spanish Fort, AL, on 4/8/1865; Received at Ship Island, MS, on 4/10/1865. Transferred to Vicksburg, MS, for exchange on 4/28/1865; Confined at New Orleans, LA, on 4/30/1865. Exchanged at Camp Townsend, MS, on 5/6/1865.

Martin, W.H. Pvt., 36th Alabama Infantry. Co. A. Federal Rolls of Prisoners of War: Captured at Spanish Fort, AL, on 4/8/1865; Received at Ship Island, MS, on 4/10/1865. Transferred to Vicksburg, MS, for exchange on 5/1/1865; Exchanged at Camp Townsend, MS, on 5/6/1865.

Martin, William M. Cpl./Sgt., 21st Alabama Infantry. Co. E. Federal Rolls of Prisoners of War: Captured at Fort Gaines, AL, on 8/8/1864; Received at Ship Island, MS, from New Orleans, LA, on 10/24/1864. Exchanged on 1/4/1865.

Martins, T.P. Pvt., 63rd Alabama Infantry. Co. C. Federal Rolls of Prisoners of War: Captured at Blakely, AL, on 4/9/1865; Received at Ship Island, MS, on 4/15/1865. Transferred to Vicksburg, MS, for exchange on 5/1/1865; Exchanged at Camp Townsend, MS, on 5/6/1865.

Mask, Dudley Pvt., 21st Alabama Infantry. Co. C. Federal Rolls of Prisoners of War: Captured at Fort Gaines, AL, on 8/8/1864; Received at Ship Island, MS, from New Orleans, LA, on 10/25/1864. Exchanged on 1/4/1865.

Mask, Phil Pvt., 21st Alabama Infantry. Co. C. Federal Rolls of Prisoners of War: Captured at Fort Gaines, AL, on 8/8/1864; Received at Ship Island, MS, from New Orleans, LA, on 10/25/1864. Exchanged on 1/4/1865.

Mason, J.C. Pvt./Cpl., 63rd Alabama Infantry. Co. F. Enlisted: 3/9/1864 at Greenville, AL. Age at enlistment: 17. Description at enlistment: Eyes: blue. Hair: dark. Complexion: dark. Height: 5'8". Residence at enlistment: Butler County, AL. Rolls for 9/1864 through 10/1864: Present, promoted to Cpl. on 10/25/1864. Federal Rolls of Prisoners of War: Captured at Blakely, AL, on 4/9/1865; Received at Ship Island, MS, on 4/15/1865. Transferred to Vicksburg, MS, for exchange on 5/1/1865; Exchanged at Camp Townsend, MS, on 5/6/1865. Rolls of Prisoners of War, C.S.A: Surrendered at Citronelle, AL, on 5/4/1865; Paroled at Meridian, MS, on 5/11/1865. Residence at parole: Butler County, AL.

Mason, Robert Pvt., 21st Alabama Infantry. Co. F. Federal Rolls of Prisoners of War: Captured at Spanish Fort, AL, on 4/8/1865; Received at Ship Island, MS, on 4/10/1865. Transferred to Vicksburg, MS, for exchange on 5/1/1865; Exchanged at Camp Townsend, MS, on 5/6/1865.

Mathews, G.W. Pvt., Lockhart's Battalion Infantry. Co. I. Federal Rolls of Prisoners of War: Captured at Fort Gaines, AL, on 8/8/1864; Received at Ship Island, MS, from New Orleans, LA, on 10/24/1864. Died: 12/18/1864 at Ship Island, MS, due to dysentery. Buried: Ship Island, MS, Cemetery in Grave #98.

Matkins, R. Pvt., 21st Alabama Infantry. Co. I. Federal Rolls of Prisoners of War: Captured at Fort Gaines, AL, on 8/8/1864; Received at Ship Island, MS, from New Orleans, LA, on 10/25/1864. Exchanged on 1/4/1865.

Maton, Robert (AKA Mayton) Pvt., 21st Alabama Infantry. Co. C. Federal Rolls of Prisoners of War: Captured at Blakely, AL, on 4/9/1865; Received at Ship Island, MS, on 4/15/1865. Transferred to Vicksburg, MS, for exchange on 5/1/1865; Exchanged at Camp Townsend, MS, on 5/6/1865.

Mattison, B.S. Sgt./Pvt., 62nd Alabama Infantry. Co. B. Federal Rolls of Prisoners of War: Captured at Blakely, AL, on 4/9/1865; Received at Ship Island, MS, on 4/15/1865. Transferred to Vicksburg, MS, for exchange on 5/1/1865; Exchanged at Camp Townsend, MS, on 5/6/1865.

May, Benjamin H. Pvt., 21st Alabama Infantry. Co. D. Federal Rolls of Prisoners of War: Captured at Blakely, AL, on 4/9/1865; Received at Ship Island, MS, on 4/15/1865. Transferred to Vicksburg, MS, for exchange on 5/1/1865; Exchanged at Camp Townsend, MS, on 5/6/1865.

May, F.T. Pvt., 63rd Alabama Infantry. Co. K. Enlisted: 8/31/1864 at Greene County, AL. Rolls for 9/1864 through 10/1864: Absent, sick in hospital at Mobile, AL, since 10/26/1864. Federal Rolls of Prisoners of War: Captured at Blakely, AL, on 4/9/1865; Received at Ship Island, MS, on 4/15/1865. Transferred to Vicksburg, MS, for exchange on 5/1/1865; Exchanged at Camp Townsend, MS, on 5/6/1865. Rolls of Prisoners of War, C.S.A: Surrendered at Citronelle, AL, on 5/4/1865; Paroled at Meridian, MS, on 5/13/1865. Residence at parole: Greene County, AL.

May, John D. Cpl., 21st Alabama Infantry. Co. H. Federal Rolls of Prisoners of War: Captured at Fort Gaines, AL, on 8/8/1864; Received at Ship Island, MS, from New Orleans, LA, on 10/25/1864. Exchanged on 1/4/1865.

May, M.M. Sgt., 8th Alabama Cavalry. Co. D. Federal Rolls of Prisoners of War: Captured at Blakely, AL, on 4/9/1865; Received at Ship Island, MS, on 4/15/1865. Transferred to Vicksburg, MS, for exchange on 5/1/1865; Exchanged at Camp Townsend, MS, on 5/6/1865.

May, Peter D. Pvt./1st Sgt., 21st Alabama Infantry. Cos. C & E. Federal Rolls of Prisoners of War: Captured at Fort Gaines, AL, on 8/8/1864; Received at Ship Island, MS, from New Orleans, LA, on 10/25/1864. Exchanged on 1/4/1865.

Maynor, J.T. (AKA Mayner) Pvt., 6th Alabama Cavalry. Co. G. Federal Rolls of Prisoners of War: Captured in Alabama on 3/29/1865; Received at Ship Island, MS. Transferred to Vicksburg, MS, for exchange on 5/1/1865; Exchanged at Camp Townsend, MS, on 5/6/1865.

Meadows, Daniel P. Pvt., 63rd Alabama Infantry. Co. C. Enlisted: 6/20/1864 at Macon County, AL. Age at enlistment: 17. Description at enlistment: Eyes: grey. Hair: light. Complexion: dark. Height: 5'7½". Residence at enlistment: Salem, Russell County, AL. Rolls for 9/1864 through 10/1864: Present. Federal Rolls of Prisoners of War: Captured at Blakely, AL, on 4/9/1865; Received at Ship Island, MS, on 4/15/1865. Transferred to Vicksburg, MS, for exchange on 5/1/1865; Exchanged at Camp Townsend, MS, on 5/6/1865. Rolls of Prisoners of War, C.S.A: Surrendered at Citronelle, AL, on 5/4/1865; Paroled at Meridian, MS, on 5/11/1865 while a patient in Quintard Hospital.

Meadows, William S. Pvt., 63rd Alabama Infantry. Co. C. Federal Rolls of Prisoners of War: Captured at Blakely, AL, on 4/9/1865; Received at Ship Island, MS, on 4/15/1865. Transferred to Vicksburg, MS, for exchange on 5/1/1865; Exchanged at Camp Townsend, MS, on 5/6/1865. Born: 1847. Died: 1920 at Houston County, AL.

Meggingon, D.A. (AKA Megginson) Pvt., 21st Alabama Infantry. Cos. A & C. Federal Rolls of Prisoners of War: Captured at Fort Gaines, AL, on 8/8/1864; Received at Ship Island, MS, from New Orleans, LA, on 10/24/1864. Exchanged on 1/4/1865.

Melton, Albert L. Pvt., 62nd Alabama Infantry. Co. A. Federal Rolls of Prisoners of War: Captured at Blakely, AL, on 4/9/1865; Received at Ship Island, MS, on 4/15/1865. Transferred to Vicksburg, MS, for exchange on 5/1/1865; Exchanged at Camp Townsend, MS, on 5/6/1865.

Melton, James H. Pvt., 63rd Alabama Infantry. Co. A. Enlisted: 1/1/1864 at Lowndes County, AL. Age at enlistment: 16. Rolls for 1/1864 through 2/1864: Present. Rolls for 9/1864 through 10/1864: Present. Federal Rolls of Prisoners of War: Captured at Blakely, AL, on 4/9/1865; Received at Ship Island, MS, on 4/15/1865. Transferred to Vicksburg, MS, for exchange on 5/1/1865; Exchanged at Camp Townsend, MS, on 5/6/1865. Rolls of Prisoners of War, C.S.A: Surrendered at Citronelle, AL, on 5/4/1865; Paroled at Meridian, MS, on 5/13/1865. Residence at parole: Lowndes County, AL.

Meredith, E.C. Pvt./Cpl., 62nd Alabama Infantry. Co. F. Federal Rolls of Prisoners of War: Captured at Blakely, AL, on 4/9/1865; Received at Ship Island, MS, on 4/15/1865. Transferred to Vicksburg, MS, for exchange on 5/1/1865; Exchanged at Camp Townsend, MS, on 5/6/1865.

Meredith, P. (AKA F.) Pvt., Lockhart's Battalion Infantry. Co. K. Federal Rolls of Prisoners of War: Captured at Fort Gaines, AL, on 8/8/1864; Received at Ship Island, MS, from New Orleans, LA, on 10/25/1864. Exchanged on 1/4/1865.

Meredith, Samuel Pvt., 36th Alabama Infantry. Co. A. Federal Rolls of Prisoners of War: Captured at Spanish Fort, AL, on 4/8/1865; Received at Ship Island, MS, on 4/10/1865. Transferred to Vicksburg, MS, for exchange on 5/1/1865; Exchanged at Camp Townsend, MS, on 5/6/1865.

Merrill, Benjamin (AKA R.B.) Pvt., Lockhart's Battalion Infantry. Co. K. Federal Rolls of Prisoners of War: Captured at Fort Gaines, AL, on 8/8/1864; Received at Ship Island, MS, from New Orleans, LA, on 10/24/1864. Died: 11/1/1864 at Ship Island, MS, due to diarrhea. Buried: Ship Island, MS, Cemetery in Grave #7.

Merrill, G. (AKA Merritt) Pvt., 62nd Alabama Infantry. Co. C. Federal Rolls of Prisoners of War: Captured near Spanish Fort, AL, on 3/30/1865; Received at Ship Island, MS. Transferred to Vicksburg, MS, on 5/1/1865; Exchanged at Camp Townsend, MS, on 5/6/1865.

Merritt, J.F. Pvt., 6th Alabama Cavalry. Cos. C & I. Federal Rolls of Prisoners of War: Captured in Florida on 3/25/1865; Received at Ship Island, MS. Transferred to Vicksburg, MS, for exchange on 5/1/1865; Exchanged at Camp Townsend, MS, on 5/6/1865.

Merritt, Marion Pvt., 18th Alabama Infantry. Co. B. Federal Rolls of Prisoners of War: Captured at Spanish Fort, AL, on 4/8/1865; Received at Ship Island, MS, on 4/10/1865. Transferred to Vicksburg, MS, for exchange on 5/1/1865; Exchanged at Camp Townsend, MS, on 5/6/1865.

Messer, Alex Pvt., 63rd Alabama Infantry. Co. E. Federal Rolls of Prisoners of War: Captured at Blakely, AL, on 4/9/1865; Received at Ship Island, MS, on 4/15/1865. Transferred to Vicksburg, MS, for exchange on 5/1/1865; Exchanged at Camp Townsend, MS, on 5/6/1865. Rolls of Prisoners of War, C.S.A: Surrendered at Citronelle, AL, on 5/4/1865; Paroled at Meridian, MS, on 5/13/1865. Residence at parole: Barbour County, AL.

Messer, Peter Pvt., 6th Alabama Cavalry. Cos. D & E. Federal Rolls of Prisoners of War: Captured in Florida on 3/25/1865; Received at Ship Island, MS. Transferred to Vicksburg, MS, for exchange on 5/1/1865; Exchanged at Camp Townsend, MS, on 5/6/1865.

Michael, D.L. (AKA Michel) Pvt., 6th Alabama Cavalry. Co. A. Federal Rolls of Prisoners of War: Captured in Florida on 3/25/1865; Received at Ship Island, MS. Transferred to Vicksburg, MS, for exchange on 5/1/1865; Exchanged at Camp Townsend, MS, on 5/6/1865.

Middleton, W.E. Pvt., 63rd Alabama Infantry. Co. E. Enlisted: 7/25/1864 at Montgomery, AL. Age at enlistment: 17. Description at enlistment: Eyes: dark. Hair: dark. Complexion: dark. Rolls for 9/1864 through 10/1864: Absent, in hospital since 8/17/1864. Federal Rolls of Prisoners of War: Captured at Blakely, AL, on 4/9/1865; Received at Ship Island, MS, on 4/15/1865. Transferred to Vicksburg, MS, for exchange on 5/1/1865; Exchanged at Camp Townsend, MS, on 5/6/1865. Rolls of Prisoners of War, C.S.A: Surrendered at Citronelle, AL, on 5/4/1865; Paroled at Meridian, MS, on 5/13/1865. Residence at parole: Monroe County, AL.

Miller, A.J. Pvt., 18th Alabama Infantry. Co. A. Federal Rolls of Prisoners of War: Captured at Spanish Fort, AL, on 4/8/1865; Received at Ship Island, MS, on 4/10/1865. Transferred to Vicksburg, MS, for exchange on 5/1/1865; Exchanged at Camp Townsend, MS, on 5/6/1865.

Miller, J.R. Pvt., 6th Alabama Cavalry. Co. A. Federal Rolls of Prisoners of War: Captured at Spanish Fort, AL, on 4/8/1865; Received at Ship Island, MS, on 4/10/1865. Transferred to Vicksburg, MS, for exchange on 5/1/1865; Exchanged at Camp Townsend, MS, on 5/6/1865.

Miller, Julius A. (AKA A.J.) Pvt., Lockhart's Battalion Infantry. Co. K. Federal Rolls of Prisoners of War: Captured at Fort Gaines, AL, on 8/8/1864; Received at Ship Island, MS, from New Orleans, LA, on 10/25/1864. Exchanged on 1/4/1865.

Miller, M.D.L. Pvt., 63rd Alabama Infantry. Co. K. Enlisted: 10/5/1864 at Rockford, AL. Rolls for 9/1864 through 10/1864: Present. Federal Rolls of Prisoners of War: Captured at Blakely, AL, on 4/9/1865; Received at Ship Island, MS, on 4/15/1865. Transferred to Vicksburg, MS, for exchange on 5/1/1865; Exchanged at Camp Townsend, MS, on 5/6/1865. Rolls of Prisoners of War, C.S.A: Surrendered at Citronelle, AL, on 5/4/1865; Paroled at Meridian, MS, on 5/13/1865. Residence at parole: Coosa County, AL. Born: 1846. Died: 1928. Buried: Chestnut Creek Baptist Church located at Chilton County, AL.

Miller, R.B. Pvt., 21st Alabama Infantry. Co. F. Federal Rolls of Prisoners of War: Captured at Fort Gaines, AL, on 8/8/1864; Received at Ship Island, MS, from New Orleans, LA, on 10/28/1864. Exchanged on 1/4/1865.

Miller, T. Pvt., 62nd Alabama Infantry. Co. C. Federal Rolls of Prisoners of War: Captured at Blakely, AL, on 4/9/1865; Received at Ship Island, MS, on 4/15/1865. Transferred to Vicksburg, MS, for exchange on 5/1/1865; Exchanged at Camp Townsend, MS, on 5/6/1865.

Miller, W.D.L. (AKA Millner) Pvt., 63rd Alabama Infantry. Co. K. Federal Rolls of Prisoners of War: Captured at Blakely, AL, on 4/9/1865; Received at Ship Island, MS, on 4/15/1865. Transferred to Vicksburg, MS, for exchange on 5/1/1865; Exchanged at Camp Townsend, MS, on 5/6/1865.

Miller, Warren P. (AKA Millner) Pvt., 63rd Alabama Infantry. Co. A. Enlisted: 1/1/1864 at Tallapoosa County, AL. Rolls for 1/1864 through 2/1864: Present. Rolls for 9/1864 through 10/1864: Present, sick in quarters. Federal Rolls of Prisoners of War: Captured at Blakely, AL, on 4/9/1865; Received at Ship Island, MS, on 4/15/1865. Transferred to Vicksburg, MS, for exchange on 5/1/1865. On Register of U.S.A. General Hospital #2, Vicksburg, MS: Admitted on 5/3/1865 due to acute diarrhea; Returned to duty on 5/12/1865. Age at admittance: 18. Rolls of Prisoners of War, C.S.A: Surrendered at Citronelle, AL, on 5/4/1865; Paroled at Meridian, MS, on 5/14/1865. Residence at parole: Tallapoosa County, AL.

Milley, N.H. Pvt., 62nd Alabama Infantry. Co. B. Federal Rolls of Prisoners of War: Captured at Blakely, AL, on 4/9/1865; Received at Ship Island, MS, on 4/15/1865. Transferred to Vicksburg, MS, for exchange on 5/1/1865; Exchanged at Camp Townsend, MS, on 5/6/1865.

Millner, W.A. (AKA W.S.) Pvt., 63rd Alabama Infantry. Co. A. Federal Rolls of Prisoners of War: Captured at Blakely, AL, on 4/9/1865; Received at Ship Island, MS, on 4/15/1865. Transferred to Vicksburg, MS, for exchange on 5/1/1865; Exchanged at Camp Townsend, MS, on 5/6/1865.

Millsap, T.E. (AKA Z.E.) Sgt., Alabama Reserves. Co. __. Federal Rolls of Prisoners of War: Captured near Milton, FL, on 12/24/1864; Received at Ship Island, MS, on 1/25/1865. Transferred to Vicksburg, MS, for exchange on 5/1/1865; Exchanged at Camp Townsend, MS, on 5/6/1865.

Milstead, W.H.C. Pvt., 63rd Alabama Infantry. Co. H. Enlisted: 3/15/1864 at Randolph County, AL. Age at enlistment: 17. Description at enlistment: Eyes: dark. Hair: dark. Complexion: fair. Rolls for 9/1864 through 10/1864: Absent, sick in hospital at Mobile, AL. Federal Rolls of Prisoners of War: Captured at Blakely, AL, on 4/9/1865; Received at Ship Island, MS, on 4/15/1865. Transferred to Vicksburg, MS, for exchange on 5/1/1865; Exchanged at Camp Townsend, MS, on 5/6/1865. Rolls of Prisoners of War, C.S.A: Surrendered at Citronelle, AL, on 5/4/1865; Paroled at Meridian, MS, on 5/11/1865. Residence at parole: Bibb County, AL.

Milton, John L. Pvt., 8th Alabama Cavalry. Co. E. Federal Rolls of Prisoners of War: Captured in Florida on 3/25/1865; Received at Ship Island, MS. Transferred to Vicksburg, MS, for exchange on 5/1/1865; Exchanged at Camp Townsend, MS, on 5/6/1865.

Mims, Hames M. Sgt./2nd Lt/Adjt., 21st Alabama Infantry. Cos. D & H.F. & S. Federal Rolls of Prisoners of War: Captured at Fort Gaines, AL, on 8/8/1864; Received at Ship Island, MS, from New Orleans, LA, on 10/25/1864. Exchanged on 1/4/1865.

Minor, Pickens Pvt., 62nd Alabama Infantry. Co. C. Federal Rolls of Prisoners of War: Captured at Blakely, AL, on 4/9/1865; Received at Ship Island, MS, on 4/15/1865. Transferred to Vicksburg, MS, for exchange on 5/1/1865; Exchanged at Camp Townsend, MS, on 5/6/1865. Born: 6/12/1847 at Edgefield County, SC.

Mitchel, A. Landers Pvt., 18th Alabama Infantry. Co. H. Federal Rolls of Prisoners of War: Captured at Blakely, AL, on 4/9/1865; Received at Ship Island, MS, on 4/15/1865. Transferred to Vicksburg, MS, for exchange on 5/1/1865; Exchanged at Camp Townsend, MS, on 5/6/1865.

Mitchell, Benjamin Pvt., 6th Alabama Cavalry. Co. I. Federal Rolls of Prisoners of War: Captured in Alabama on 3/23/1865; Received at Ship Island, MS. Transferred to Vicksburg, MS, for exchange on 5/1/1865; Exchanged at Camp Townsend, MS, on 5/6/1865.

Mitchell, H. (AKA A.) Pvt., 63rd Alabama Infantry. Co. K. Enlisted: 9/2/1864 at Bibb County, AL. Rolls for 9/1864 through 10/1864: Present. Federal Rolls of Prisoners of War: Captured at Blakely, AL, on 4/9/1865; Received at Ship Island, MS, on 4/15/1865. Transferred to Vicksburg, MS, for exchange on 5/1/1865; Exchanged at Camp Townsend, MS, on 5/6/1865. Rolls of Prisoners of War, C.S.A: Surrendered at Citronelle, AL, on 5/4/1865; Paroled at Meridian, MS, on 5/13/1865. Residence at parole: Bibb County, AL.

Mitchell, Hiram Pvt., 63rd Alabama Infantry. Co. D. Enlisted: 7/30/1864 at Macon County, AL. Age at enlistment: 17. Description at enlistment: Eyes: blue. Hair: light. Complexion: fair. Height: 5'5". Residence at enlistment: Clayton, Barbour County, AL. Rolls for 9/1864 through 10/1864: Present. Federal Rolls of Prisoners of War: Captured at Blakely, AL, on 4/9/1865; Received at Ship Island, MS, on 4/15/1865. Transferred to Vicksburg, MS, for exchange on 5/1/1865; Exchanged at Camp Townsend, MS, on 5/6/1865. Rolls of Prisoners of War, C.S.A: Surrendered at Citronelle, AL, on 5/4/1865; Paroled at Meridian, MS, on 5/13/1865. Residence at parole: Barbour County, AL.

Mitchell, J. Pvt., 6th Alabama Cavalry. Co. E. Federal Rolls of Prisoners of War: Captured in Alabama on 3/23/1865; Received at Ship Island, MS. Transferred to Vicksburg, MS, for exchange on 5/1/1865; Exchanged at Camp Townsend, MS, on 5/6/1865.

Mitchell, Joseph A. Ord. Sgt./Pvt., 6th Alabama Cavalry. Co. H. Federal Rolls of Prisoners of War: Captured in Florida on 3/25/1865; Received at Ship Island, MS. Transferred to Vicksburg, MS, for exchange on 5/1/1865; Exchanged at Camp Townsend, MS, on 5/6/1865.

Mitchell, Reuben H. (AKA Mitchel) Pvt., 62nd Alabama Infantry. Co. G. Federal Rolls of Prisoners of War: Captured at Blakely, AL, on 4/9/1865; Received at Ship Island, MS, on 4/15/1865. Transferred to Vicksburg,

MS, for exchange on 5/1/1865; Exchanged at Camp Townsend, MS, on 5/6/1865.

Mitchell, T.H. Pvt., 8th Alabama Cavalry. Co. F. Federal Rolls of Prisoners of War: Captured in Florida on 3/25/1865; Received at Ship Island, MS. Transferred to Vicksburg, MS, for exchange on 5/1/1865; Exchanged at Camp Townsend, MS, on 5/6/1865.

Mon, Edmond (AKA Edward) Pvt., 21st Alabama Infantry. Cos. H & I. Federal Rolls of Prisoners of War: Captured at Fort Gaines, AL, on 8/8/1864; Received at Ship Island, MS, from New Orleans, LA, on 10/24/1864. Exchanged on 1/4/1865. Born: 3/25/1843. Died: 8/23/1920. Buried: Bellande Cemetery located in Mississippi.

Moody, Thomas J. (AKA J.T.) 5th Sgt./Pvt., 38th Alabama Infantry. Co. B. Federal Rolls of Prisoners of War: Captured at Spanish Fort, AL, on 4/8/1865; Received at Ship Island, MS, on 4/10/1865. Transferred to Vicksburg, MS, for exchange on 5/1/1865; Exchanged at Camp Townsend, MS, on 5/6/1865.

Mooney, J.D. Sgt., 36th Alabama Infantry. Co. C. Federal Rolls of Prisoners of War: Captured at Spanish Fort, AL, on 4/8/1865; Received at Ship Island, MS, on 4/10/1865. Transferred to Vicksburg, MS, for exchange on 5/1/1865; Exchanged at Camp Townsend, MS, on 5/6/1865.

Mooney, James W. Pvt., 26th Alabama Infantry. Co. H. Federal Rolls of Prisoners of War: Captured at Spanish Fort, AL, on 4/8/1865; Received at Ship Island, MS, on 4/10/1865. Transferred to Vicksburg, MS, for exchange on 5/1/1865; Exchanged at Camp Townsend, MS, on 5/6/1865.

Moor, James (AKA Moon) Pvt., 63rd Alabama Infantry. Co. A. Federal Rolls of Prisoners of War: Captured at Blakely, AL, on 4/9/1865; Received at Ship Island, MS, on 4/15/1865. Transferred to Vicksburg, MS, for exchange on 5/1/1865; Exchanged at Camp Townsend, MS, on 5/6/1865. Rolls of Prisoners of War, C.S.A: Surrendered at Citronelle, AL, on 5/4/1865; Paroled at Meridian, MS, on 5/13/1865. Residence at parole: Macon County, AL.

Moore, B.G. Asst. Surg., 1st Alabama Infantry. F & S. Federal Rolls of Prisoners of War: Captured at Blakely, AL, on 4/9/1865; Received at Ship Island, MS, on 4/15/1865. Transferred to Vicksburg, MS, for exchange on 4/28/1865; Confined at New Orleans, LA, on 4/30/1865. Exchanged at Camp Townsend, MS, on 5/6/1865.

Moore, W.D. (AKA Moor) Pvt., 36th Alabama Infantry. Co. C. Federal Rolls of Prisoners of War: Captured at Spanish Fort, AL, on 4/8/1865; Received at Ship Island, MS, on 4/10/1865. Transferred to Vicksburg, MS, for exchange on 5/1/1865; Exchanged at Camp Townsend, MS, on 5/6/1865.

Moore, W.W. Pvt., 62nd Alabama Infantry. Co. I. Federal Rolls of Prisoners of War: Captured at Blakely, AL, on 4/9/1865; Received at Ship Island, MS, on 4/15/1865. Transferred to Vicksburg, MS, for exchange on 5/1/1865; Exchanged at Camp Townsend, MS, on 5/6/1865.

Moose, A.J. Pvt., 8th Alabama Cavalry. Co. E. Federal Rolls of Prisoners of War: Captured in Florida on 3/25/1865; Received at Ship Island, MS. Transferred to Vicksburg, MS, for exchange on 5/1/1865; Exchanged at Camp Townsend, MS, on 5/6/1865.

Morefield, Thomas W. Pvt./Sgt., 63rd Alabama Infantry. Co. B. Enlisted: 3/23/1864 at Montgomery, AL. Age at enlistment: 17. Rolls for 9/1864 through 10/1864: Absent, without leave since 9/26/1864. Federal Rolls of Prisoners of War: Captured at Blakely, AL, on 4/9/1865; Received at Ship Island, MS, on 4/15/1865. Transferred to Vicksburg, MS, for exchange on 5/1/1865; Exchanged at Camp Townsend, MS, on 5/6/1865. Rolls of Prisoners of War, C.S.A: Surrendered at Citronelle, AL, on 5/4/1865; Paroled at Meridian, MS, on 5/11/1865. Residence at parole: Montgomery County, AL.

Morgan, Giles D. Pvt., 62nd Alabama Infantry. Co. G. Federal Rolls of Prisoners of War: Captured at Blakely, AL, on 4/9/1865; Received at Ship Island, MS, on 4/15/1865. Transferred to Vicksburg, MS, for exchange on 5/1/1865; Exchanged at Camp Townsend, MS, on 5/6/1865.

Morris, E.J. Pvt., 63rd Alabama Infantry. Co. F. Enlisted: 7/12/1864 at Lowndes County, AL. Age at enlistment: 17. Description at enlistment: Eyes: dark. Hair: dark. Complexion: dark. Height: 5'6½". Residence at enlistment: Lowndes County, AL. Rolls for 9/1864 through 10/1864: Absent, in hospital at Mobile, AL, on 9/14/1864. Federal Rolls of Prisoners of War: Captured at Blakely, AL, on 4/9/1865; Received at Ship Island, MS, on 4/15/1865. Transferred to Vicksburg, MS, for exchange on 5/1/1865; Exchanged at Camp Townsend, MS, on 5/6/1865. Rolls of Prisoners of War, C.S.A: Surrendered at Citronelle, AL, on 5/4/1865; Paroled at Meridian, MS, on 5/11/1865. Residence at parole: Lowndes County, AL.

Morris, J.W. 3rd Lt./2nd Lt., 62nd Alabama Infantry. Co. C. Federal Rolls of Prisoners of War: Captured at Blakely, AL, on 4/9/1865; Received at Ship Island, MS, on 4/15/1865. Transferred to Vicksburg, MS, for exchange on 4/28/1865; Confined at New Orleans, LA, on 4/30/1865. Exchanged at Camp Townsend, MS, on 5/6/1865.

Morris, John Pvt., 21st Alabama Infantry. Cos. H & I. Federal Rolls of Prisoners of War: Captured at Fort Gaines, AL, on 8/8/1864; Received at Ship Island, MS, from New Orleans, LA, on 10/25/1864. Exchanged on 1/4/1865.

Morris, John E. Pvt., 21st Alabama Infantry. Co. G. Federal Rolls of Prisoners of War: Captured at Fort Gaines, AL, on 8/8/1864; Received at Ship Island, MS, from New Orleans, LA, on 10/25/1864. Exchanged on 1/4/1865.

Morris, W.H. Lt., 6th Alabama Cavalry. Co. __. Federal Rolls of Prisoners of War: Captured in Alabama on 3/24/1865; Received at Ship Island, MS. Transferred to Vicksburg, MS, for exchange on 4/28/1865; Confined at New Orleans, LA, on 4/30/1865. Exchanged at Camp Townsend, MS, on 5/6/1865.

Morrison, Daniel A. Pvt., 63rd Alabama Infantry. Co. D. Enlisted: 7/30/1864 at Macon County, AL. Age at enlistment: 17. Description at enlistment: Eyes: dark. Hair: dark. Complexion: dark. Height: 5'6". Residence at enlistment: White Oak Springs, Barbour County, AL. Rolls for 9/1864 through 10/1864: Present. Federal Rolls of Prisoners of War: Captured at Blakely, AL, on 4/9/1865; Received at Ship Island, MS, on 4/15/1865. Transferred to Vicksburg, MS, for exchange on 5/1/1865; Exchanged at Camp Townsend, MS, on 5/6/1865. Rolls of Prisoners of War, C.S.A:

Surrendered at Citronelle, AL, on 5/4/1865; Paroled at Meridian, MS, on 5/13/1865. Residence at parole: Barbour County, AL. Born: 10/15/1810. Died: 10/28/1880. Buried: Hatchett Creek located at Clay County, AL.

Morrison, Edward Pvt., 1st Alabama Artillery. Co. D. Federal Rolls of Prisoners of War: Captured at Fort Gaines, AL, on 8/8/1864; Received at Ship Island, MS, from New Orleans, LA, on 10/25/1864. Died: 11/9/1864 at Ship Island, MS, due to chronic diarrhea. Buried: Ship Island, MS, Cemetery in Grave #14.

Morton, Dallas M. (AKA Morten) Pvt., 63rd Alabama Infantry. Co. H. Enlisted: 8/7/1864 at Selma, AL. Age at enlistment: 17. Description at enlistment: Eyes: blue. Hair: dark. Complexion: dark. Rolls for 9/1864 through 10/1864: Absent, sick in hospital at Mobile, AL, since 10/8/1864. Federal Rolls of Prisoners of War: Captured at Blakely, AL, on 4/9/1865; Received at Ship Island, MS, on 4/15/1865. Transferred to Vicksburg, MS, for exchange on 5/1/1865; Exchanged at Camp Townsend, MS, on 5/6/1865. Rolls of Prisoners of War, C.S.A: Surrendered at Citronelle, AL, on 5/4/1865; Paroled at Meridian, MS, on 5/11/1865. Residence at parole: Blount County, AL.

Morton, William T. (AKA W.P.) Pvt., 63rd Alabama Infantry. Co. A. Enlisted: 3/29/1864 at Chambers County, AL. Rolls for 9/1864 through 10/1864: Present. Federal Rolls of Prisoners of War: Captured at Blakely, AL, on 4/9/1865; Received at Ship Island, MS, on 4/15/1865. Transferred to Vicksburg, MS, for exchange on 5/1/1865; Exchanged at Camp Townsend, MS, on 5/6/1865. Rolls of Prisoners of War, C.S.A: Surrendered at Citronelle, AL, on 5/4/1865; Paroled at Meridian, MS, on 5/13/1865. Residence at parole: Chambers County, AL.

Moseley, A.A. Sgt., 6th Alabama Cavalry. Co. E. Federal Rolls of Prisoners of War: Captured in Florida on 3/25/1865; Received at Ship Island, MS. Transferred to Vicksburg, MS, for exchange on 5/1/1865; Exchanged at Camp Townsend, MS, on 5/6/1865.

Motley, Edwin (AKA Moltey, Maley, Mealey) Pvt., 21st Alabama Infantry. Co. G. Federal Rolls of Prisoners of War: Captured at Fort Gaines, AL, on 8/8/1864; Received at Ship Island, MS, from New Orleans, LA, on 10/25/1864. Died: 12/20/1864 at Ship Island, MS, due to dysentery. Buried: Ship Island, MS, Cemetery in Grave #101. Born: Milton, Autauga County, AL, to Goin and Nancy Motley. Marital status at death: Single. Soldier also served as a Pvt. with the 1st Alabama Militia Regiment. Co. B and the 1st Alabama Conscripts Regiment. Co.K.

Moyes, John Pvt., 1st Alabama Artillery. Co. B. Federal Rolls of Prisoners of War: Captured at Fort Gaines, AL, on 8/8/1864; Received at Ship Island, MS, from New Orleans, LA, on 10/24/1864. Exchanged on 1/4/1865.

Mullins, William S. (AKA Mullings) Pvt., 63rd Alabama Infantry. Co. H. Enlisted: 8/16/1864 at Blakely, AL. Age at enlistment: 17. Description at enlistment: Eyes: dark. Hair: dark. Complexion: dark. Rolls for 9/1864 through 10/1864: Present. On Register of Ross Hospital, Mobile, AL: Admitted on 9/26/1864 due to rubeola; Returned to duty on 10/27/1864. Federal Rolls of Prisoners of War: Captured at Blakely, AL, on 4/9/1865; Received at Ship Island, MS, on 4/15/1865. Transferred to Vicksburg, MS, for exchange on 5/1/1865; Exchanged at Camp Townsend, MS, on 5/6/1865. Rolls of Prisoners of War, C.S.A: Surrendered at Citronelle, AL, on 5/4/1865; Paroled at Meridian, MS, on 5/11/1865. Residence at parole: Bibb County, AL.

Murphey, B.J. (AKA Murfey) Pvt., 8th Alabama Cavalry. Co. A. Federal Rolls of Prisoners of War: Captured in Alabama on 3/24/1865; Received at Ship Island, MS. Transferred to Vicksburg, MS, for exchange on 5/1/1865; Exchanged at Camp Townsend, MS, on 5/6/1865.

Murphy, E.G. Sgt., 6th Alabama Cavalry. Co. B. Federal Rolls of Prisoners of War: Captured in Florida on 3/25/1865; Received at Ship Island, MS. Transferred to Vicksburg, MS, for exchange on 5/1/1865; Exchanged at Camp Townsend, MS, on 5/6/1865.

Murphy, Emanuel M. Pvt., 63rd Alabama Infantry. Co. B. Enlisted: 7/11/1864 at Montgomery, AL. Rolls for 9/1864 through 10/1864: Present. Federal Rolls of Prisoners of War: Captured at Blakely, AL, on 4/9/1865; Received at Ship Island, MS, on 4/15/1865. Transferred to Vicksburg, MS, for exchange on 5/1/1865; Exchanged at Camp Townsend, MS, on 5/6/1865. Rolls of Prisoners of War, C.S.A: Surrendered at Citronelle, AL, on 5/4/1865; Paroled at Meridian, MS, on 5/11/1865. Residence at parole: Coosa County, AL.

Myrick, F. Pvt., 62nd Alabama Infantry. Co. H. Federal Rolls of Prisoners of War: Captured at Blakely, AL, on 4/9/1865; Received at Ship Island, MS, on 4/15/1865. Transferred to Vicksburg, MS, for exchange on 5/1/1865; Exchanged at Camp Townsend, MS, on 5/6/1865.

Naler, J. Pvt., 8th Alabama Cavalry. Co. F. Federal Rolls of Prisoners of War: Captured in Florida on 3/25/1865; Received at Ship Island, MS. Transferred to Vicksburg, MS, for exchange on 5/1/1865; Exchanged at Camp Townsend, MS, on 5/6/1865.

Nash, Abner D. Pvt., 63rd Alabama Infantry. Co. G. Enlisted: 5/1/1864 at Troy, AL. Age at enlistment: 17. Description at enlistment: Eyes: grey. Hair: dark. Complexion: fair. Height: 5'6". Residence at enlistment: Pike County, AL. Rolls for 9/1864 through 10/1864: Present. Federal Rolls of Prisoners of War: Captured at Blakely, AL, on 4/9/1865; Received at Ship Island, MS, on 4/15/1865. Transferred to Vicksburg, MS, for exchange on 5/1/1865; Exchanged at Camp Townsend, MS, on 5/6/1865. Rolls of Prisoners of War, C.S.A: Surrendered at Citronelle, AL, on 5/4/1865; Paroled at Meridian, MS, on 5/13/1865. Residence at parole: Pike County, AL.

Nelms, Charles D. Pvt., 63rd Alabama Infantry. Co. A. Enlisted: 5/18/1864 at Russell County, AL. Rolls for 9/1864 through 10/1864: Present. Federal Rolls of Prisoners of War: Captured at Blakely, AL, on 4/9/1865; Received at Ship Island, MS, on 4/15/1865. Transferred to Vicksburg, MS, for exchange on 5/1/1865; Exchanged at Camp Townsend, MS, on 5/6/1865. Rolls of Prisoners of War, C.S.A: Surrendered at Citronelle, AL, on 5/4/1865; Paroled at Meridian, MS, on 5/13/1865. Residence at parole: Russell County, AL.

Nelson, J.H. Pvt., 6th Alabama Cavalry. Co. H. Federal Rolls of Prisoners of War: Captured at Blakely, AL, on 4/9/1865; Received at Ship Island, MS, on 4/15/1865. Transferred to Vicksburg, MS, for exchange

on 5/1/1865; Exchanged at Camp Townsend, MS, on 5/6/1865.

Nelson, J.L. Pvt., 6th Alabama Cavalry. Co. C. Federal Rolls of Prisoners of War: Captured in Florida on 3/25/1865; Received at Ship Island, MS. Transferred to Vicksburg, MS, for exchange on 5/1/1865; Exchanged at Camp Townsend, MS, on 5/6/1865.

Nelson, John H. Pvt., Lockhart's Battalion Infantry. Co. H. Federal Rolls of Prisoners of War: Captured at Fort Gaines, AL, on 8/8/1864; Received at Ship Island, MS, from New Orleans, LA, on 10/25/1864. Exchanged on 1/4/1865.

Nelson, T.J. Pvt., 8th Alabama Cavalry. Co. C. Federal Rolls of Prisoners of War: Captured in Florida on 3/25/1865; Received at Ship Island, MS. Transferred to Vicksburg, MS, for exchange on 5/1/1865; Exchanged at Camp Townsend, MS, on 5/6/1865.

Newman, William D. (AKA B.) Pvt., Lockhart's Battalion Infantry. Co. H. Federal Rolls of Prisoners of War: Captured at Fort Gaines, AL, on 8/8/1864; Received at New Orleans, LA, on 10/25/1864. Exchanged on 1/4/1865.

Newson, Thomas P. Pvt., 63rd Alabama Infantry. Co. B. Enlisted: 8/15/1864 at Pollard, AL. Rolls for 9/1864 through 10/1864: Present. Federal Rolls of Prisoners of War: Captured at Blakely, AL, on 4/9/1865; Received at Ship Island, MS, on 4/15/1865. Transferred to Vicksburg, MS, for exchange on 5/1/1865; Exchanged at Camp Townsend, MS, on 5/6/1865. Rolls of Prisoners of War, C.S.A: Surrendered at Citronelle, AL, on 5/4/1865; Paroled at Meridian, MS, on 5/11/1865. Residence at parole: Dale County, AL.

Newton, A. Pvt., 6th Alabama Cavalry. Co. B. Federal Rolls of Prisoners of War: Captured at Blakely, AL, on 4/9/1865; Received at Ship Island, MS, on 4/15/1865. Transferred to Vicksburg, MS, for exchange on 5/1/1865; Exchanged at Camp Townsend, MS, on 5/6/1865.

Newton, C.L. (AKA C.S.) Pvt., 63rd Alabama Infantry. Co. A. Federal Rolls of Prisoners of War: Captured at Blakely, AL, on 4/9/1865; Received at Ship Island, MS, on 4/15/1865. Transferred to Vicksburg, MS, for exchange on 5/1/1865; Exchanged at Camp Townsend, MS, on 5/6/1865.

Newton, S.T. Pvt., 38th Alabama Infantry. Co. I. Federal Rolls of Prisoners of War: Captured at Spanish Fort, AL, on 4/8/1865; Received at Ship Island, MS, on 4/10/1865. Transferred to Vicksburg, MS, for exchange on 5/1/1865; Exchanged at Camp Townsend, MS, on 5/6/1865.

Nichols, J.J. Pvt., 6th Alabama Cavalry. Co. E. Federal Rolls of Prisoners of War: Captured at Spanish Fort, AL, on 4/8/1865; Received at Ship Island, MS, on 4/10/1865. Transferred to Vicksburg, MS, for exchange on 5/1/1865; Exchanged at Camp Townsend, MS, on 5/6/1865.

Nichols, John Pvt., 1st Alabama Artillery. Cos. D & G. Federal Rolls of Prisoners of War: Captured at Fort Gaines, AL, on 8/8/1864; Received at Ship Island, MS, from New Orleans, LA, on 10/25/1864. Exchanged on 1/4/1865.

Nichols, W.N. (AKA W.H.) Pvt., 21st Alabama Infantry. Cos. C & D. Federal Rolls of Prisoners of War: Captured at Fort Gaines, AL, on 8/8/1864; Received at Ship Island, MS, from New Orleans, LA, on 10/25/1864. Exchanged on 1/4/1865.

Nixon, William Pvt., 21st Alabama Infantry. Co. B. Federal Rolls of Prisoners of War: Captured at Fort Gaines, AL, on 8/8/1864; Received at Ship Island, MS, from New Orleans, LA, on 10/25/1864. Exchanged on 1/4/1865.

Noble, W.A. Pvt., 63rd Alabama Infantry. Co. B. Federal Rolls of Prisoners of War: Captured at Gravel Hill, AL, on 3/24/1865; Received at Ship Island, MS. Transferred to Vicksburg, MS, for exchange on 5/1/1865; Exchanged at Camp Townsend, MS, on 5/6/1865. Rolls of Prisoners of War, C.S.A: Surrendered at Citronelle, AL, on 5/4/1865; Paroled at Meridian, MS, on 5/11/1865. Residence at parole: Montgomery County, AL.

Nobles, William B. Pvt., 21st Alabama Infantry. Co. G. Federal Rolls of Prisoners of War: Captured at Fort Gaines, AL, on 8/8/1864; Received at Ship Island, MS, from New Orleans, LA, on 10/25/1864. Exchanged on 1/4/1865.

Noel, J.R. (AKA Newell) Pvt., 21st Alabama Infantry. Cos. A & I. Federal Rolls of Prisoners of War: Captured at Fort Gaines, AL, on 8/8/1864; Received at Ship Island, MS, from New Orleans, LA, on 10/25/1864. Exchanged on 1/4/1865.

Nolan, P. Pvt., 18th Alabama Infantry. Co. G. Federal Rolls of Prisoners of War: Captured at Spanish Fort, AL, on 4/8/1865; Received at Ship Island, MS, on 4/10/1865. Transferred to Vicksburg, MS, for exchange on 5/1/1865; Exchanged at Camp Townsend, MS, on 5/6/1865.

Nolan, William Pvt., 21st Alabama Infantry. Co. H. Federal Rolls of Prisoners of War: Captured at Fort Gaines, AL, on 8/8/1864; Received at Ship Island, MS, from New Orleans, LA, on 10/25/1864. Exchanged on 1/4/1865.

Norris, C. Pvt., 6th Alabama Cavalry. Co. H. Federal Rolls of Prisoners of War: Captured at Blakely, AL, on 4/9/1865; Received at Ship Island, MS, on 4/15/1865. Transferred to Vicksburg, MS, for exchange on 5/1/1865; Exchanged at Camp Townsend, MS, on 5/6/1865.

Norris, Frank Cpl., 62nd Alabama Infantry. Co. B. Federal Rolls of Prisoners of War: Captured at Blakely, AL, on 4/9/1865; Received at Ship Island, MS, on 4/15/1865. Transferred to Vicksburg, MS, for exchange on 5/1/1865; Exchanged at Camp Townsend, MS, on 5/6/1865.

Norris, J.B. Pvt., 3rd Alabama Reserves. Co. A. Federal Rolls of Prisoners of War: Captured in Alabama on 3/24/1865; Received at Ship Island, MS. Transferred to Vicksburg, MS, for exchange on 5/1/1865; Exchanged at Camp Townsend, MS, on 5/6/1865.

Northrup, Albert 1st Sgt/1st Lt., 21st Alabama Infantry. Federal Rolls of Prisoners of War: Captured at Fort Gaines, AL, on 8/8/1864; Received at Ship Island, MS, from New Orleans, LA, on 11/25/1864. Exchanged on 1/4/1865.

Northrup, F. Pvt., 1st Alabama Artillery. Co. C. Federal Rolls of Prisoners of War: Captured at Fort Gaines, AL, on 8/8/1864; Received at Ship Island, MS, from New Orleans, LA, on 10/28/1864. Exchanged on 1/4/1865.

Norton, Thomas C. Pvt., 63rd Alabama Infantry. Co. D. Enlisted: 7/30/1864 at Macon County, AL. Age at enlistment: 17. Description at enlistment: Eyes: dark. Hair: light. Complexion: fair. Height: 5'3".

Residence at enlistment: Clayton, Barbour County, AL. Rolls for 9/1864 through 10/1864: Present. Federal Rolls of Prisoners of War: Captured at Blakely, AL, on 4/9/1865; Received at Ship Island, MS, on 4/15/1865. Transferred to Vicksburg, MS, for exchange on 5/1/1865; Exchanged at Camp Townsend, MS, on 5/6/1865. Rolls of Prisoners of War, C.S.A: Surrendered at Citronelle, AL, on 5/4/1865; Paroled at Meridian, MS, on 5/13/1865. Residence at parole: Barbour County, AL.

Norwood, F. Pvt., 63rd Alabama Infantry. Co. H. Enlisted: 3/15/1864 at Montevallo, AL. Age at enlistment: 17. Description at enlistment: Eyes: dark. Hair: dark. Complexion: dark. Rolls for 9/1864 through 10/1864: Absent, in camp of correction since 8/14/1864. Federal Rolls of Prisoners of War: Captured at Blakely, AL, on 4/9/1865; Received at Ship Island, MS, on 4/15/1865. Transferred to Vicksburg, MS, for exchange on 5/1/1865; Exchanged at Camp Townsend, MS, on 5/6/1865. Rolls of Prisoners of War, C.S.A: Surrendered at Citronelle, AL, on 5/4/1865; Paroled at Meridian, MS, on 5/11/1865. Residence at parole: Jefferson County, AL.

Norwood, T.D. Pvt., 62nd Alabama Infantry. Co. F. Federal Rolls of Prisoners of War: Captured at Blakely, AL, on 4/9/1865; Received at Ship Island, MS, on 4/15/1865. Transferred to Vicksburg, MS, for exchange on 5/1/1865; Exchanged at Camp Townsend, MS, on 5/6/1865.

Nunn, Thomas Pvt., 62nd Alabama Infantry. Co. F. Federal Rolls of Prisoners of War: Captured at Blakely, AL, on 4/9/1865; Received at Ship Island, MS, on 4/15/1865. Transferred to Vicksburg, MS, for exchange on 5/1/1865; Exchanged at Camp Townsend, MS, on 5/6/1865.

O'Connor, John F. 1st Lt./Capt., 21st Alabama Infantry. Co. B. Federal Rolls of Prisoners of War: Captured at Fort Gaines, AL, on 8/8/1864; Received at Ship Island, MS, from New Orleans, LA, on 12/18/1864. Exchanged on 1/4/1865.

O'Farrell, Patrick Drummer, 21st Alabama Infantry. Co. B. Federal Rolls of Prisoners of War: Captured at Fort Gaines, AL, on 8/8/1864; Received at Ship Island, MS, from New Orleans, LA, on 10/25/1864. Exchanged on 1/4/1865.

O'Guyon, James W. (AKA O'Gwinn, O'Guynn) Cpl., Lockhart's Battalion Infantry. Co. I. Federal Rolls of Prisoners of War: Captured at Fort Gaines, AL, on 8/8/1864; Received at Ship Island, MS, from New Orleans, LA, on 10/25/1864. Died: 12/12/1864 at Ship Island, MS, due to pneumonia. Buried: Ship Island, MS, Cemetery in Grave #83.

O'Neill, John H. Cpl./1st Sgt., 21st Alabama Infantry. Co. B. Federal Rolls of Prisoners of War: Captured at Fort Gaines, AL, on 8/8/1864; Received at Ship Island, MS, from New Orleans, LA, on 10/25/1864. Exchanged on 1/4/1865.

O'Neill, W. Pvt., 21st Alabama Infantry. Co. F. Federal Rolls of Prisoners of War: Captured at Fort Gaines, AL, on 8/8/1864; Received at Ship Island, MS, from New Orleans, LA, on 10/25/1864. Exchanged on 1/4/1865.

O'Quinn, John Pvt., 18th Alabama Infantry. Co. E. Federal Rolls of Prisoners of War: Captured at Spanish Fort, AL, on 4/8/1865; Received at Ship Island, MS, on 4/10/1865. Transferred to Vicksburg, MS, for exchange on 5/1/1865; Exchanged at Camp Townsend, MS, on 5/6/1865.

O'Reilly, J. Pvt., 21st Alabama Infantry. Co. H. Federal Rolls of Prisoners of War: Captured at Fort Gaines, AL, on 8/8/1864; Received at Ship Island, MS, from New Orleans, LA, on 10/25/1864. Exchanged on 1/4/1865.

Oakley, A.P. (AKA Oakly, G.P.) Pvt., 21st Alabama Infantry. Co. C. Federal Rolls of Prisoners of War: Captured at Fort Gaines, AL, on 8/8/1864; Received at Ship Island, MS, from New Orleans, LA, on 10/25/1864. Died: 12/10/1864 at Ship Island, MS, due to chronic dysentery. Buried: Ship Island, MS, Cemetery in Grave #76.

Oaks, J.D. (AKA Oakes) Pvt., 62nd Alabama Infantry. Co. D. Federal Rolls of Prisoners of War: Captured at Blakely, AL, on 4/9/1865; Received at Ship Island, MS, on 4/15/1865. Transferred to Vicksburg, MS, for exchange on 5/1/1865; Exchanged at Camp Townsend, MS, on 5/6/1865.

Odel, Marcus L. Pvt., 62nd Alabama Infantry. Co. F. Federal Rolls of Prisoners of War: Captured at Blakely, AL, on 4/9/1865; Received at Ship Island, MS, on 4/15/1865. Transferred to Vicksburg, MS, for exchange on 5/1/1865; Exchanged at Camp Townsend, MS, on 5/6/1865.

Oden, Thomas (AKA T.E.) Pvt., 62nd Alabama Infantry. Co. C. Federal Rolls of Prisoners of War: Captured near Spanish Fort, AL, on 3/30/1865; Received at Ship Island, MS. Transferred to Vicksburg, MS, for exchange on 5/1/1865; Exchanged at Camp Townsend, MS, on 5/6/1865.

Odom, J.J.I. Pvt., 63rd Alabama Infantry. Co. F. Enlisted: 5/30/1864 at Montgomery, AL. Age at enlistment: 17. Description at enlistment: Eyes: grey. Hair: light. Complexion: fair. Height: 5'7". Residence at enlistment: Butler County, AL. Federal Rolls of Prisoners of War: Captured at Blakely, AL, on 4/9/1865; Received at Ship Island, MS, on 4/15/1865. Transferred to Vicksburg, MS, for exchange on 5/1/1865; Exchanged at Camp Townsend, MS, on 5/6/1865. Rolls of Prisoners of War, C.S.A: Surrendered at Citronelle, AL, on 5/4/1865; Paroled at Meridian, MS, on 5/11/1865. Residence at parole: Butler County, AL.

Ogley, Elbert Pvt., 62nd Alabama Infantry. Co. C. Federal Rolls of Prisoners of War: Captured at Blakely, AL, on 4/9/1865; Received at Ship Island, MS, on 4/15/1865. Transferred to Vicksburg, MS, for exchange on 5/1/1865; Exchanged at Camp Townsend, MS, on 5/6/1865.

Oldfield, George L. Pvt., 6th Alabama Cavalry. Cos. F & H. Federal Rolls of Prisoners of War: Captured in Florida on 3/25/1865; Received at Ship Island, MS. Transferred to Vicksburg, MS, for exchange on 5/1/1865; Exchanged at Camp Townsend, MS, on 5/6/1865.

Olive, George W. Pvt., 63rd Alabama Infantry. Co. G. Enlisted: 4/27/1864 at Troy, AL. Age at enlistment: 17. Description at enlistment: Eyes: hazel. Hair: light. Complexion: florid. Height: 5'7". Residence at enlistment: Covington County, AL. Rolls for 9/1864 through 10/1864: Present. Federal Rolls of Prisoners of War: Captured at Blakely, AL, on 4/9/1865; Received at Ship Island, MS, on 4/15/1865. Transferred to Vicksburg, MS, for exchange on

5/1/1865. On Register of U.S.A. General Hospital #2, Vicksburg, MS: Admitted from steamer on 5/3/1865 due to remittal fever. Age at admittance: 18.

Oliver, Charlton C. Sgt. Maj./2nd Lt., 63rd Alabama Infantry. Co. I/F & S. Enlisted: 8/28/1864 at Blakely, AL. Rolls for 9/1864 through 10/1864: Present, elected 2nd Lt. on 9/26/1864. Federal Rolls of Prisoners of War: Captured at Blakely, AL, on 4/9/1865; Confined one day at Spanish Fort, AL. Received at Ship Island, MS, on 4/16/1865; Transferred to Vicksburg, MS, for exchange on 4/28/1865. Confined at New Orleans, LA, on 4/30/1865; Exchanged at Camp Townsend, MS, on 5/6/1865. Rolls of Prisoners of War, C.S.A: Surrendered at Citronelle, AL, on 5/4/1865; Paroled at Meridian, MS, on 5/11/1865.

Oliver, John Pvt./Sgt., 63rd Alabama Infantry. Co. B. Enlisted: 3/23/1864 at Montgomery County, AL. Age at enlistment: 17. Rolls for 9/1864 through 10/1864: Present. Federal Rolls of Prisoners of War: Captured at Blakely, AL, on 4/9/1865; Received at Ship Island, MS, on 4/15/1865. Transferred to Vicksburg, MS, for exchange on 5/1/1865; Exchanged at Camp Townsend, MS, on 5/6/1865. Rolls of Prisoners of War, C.S.A: Surrendered at Citronelle, AL, on 5/4/1865; Paroled at Meridian, MS, on 5/11/1865. Residence at parole: Tallapoosa County, AL.

Overstreet, B. Pvt., 36th Alabama Infantry. Co. I. Federal Rolls of Prisoners of War: Captured at Spanish Fort, AL, on 4/8/1865; Received at Ship Island, MS, on 4/10/1865. Transferred to Vicksburg, MS, for exchange on 5/1/1865; Exchanged at Camp Townsend, MS, on 5/6/1865.

Owen, Edward H. 1st Sgt., 63rd Alabama Infantry. Co. G. Enlisted: 9/5/1864 at Blakely, AL. Age at enlistment: 17. Description at enlistment: Eyes: black. Hair: black. Complexion: dark. Height: 5'4". Residence at enlistment: Tuscaloosa County, AL. Rolls for 9/1864 through 10/1864: Present, appointed 1st Sgt. from the Cadet Corps on 9/5/1864. Federal Rolls of Prisoners of War: Captured at Blakely, AL, on 4/9/1865; Received at Ship Island, MS, on 4/15/1865. Transferred to Vicksburg, MS, for exchange on 5/1/1865; Exchanged at Camp Townsend, MS, on 5/6/1865. Rolls of Prisoners of War, C.S.A: Surrendered at Citronelle, AL, on 5/4/1865; Paroled at Meridian, MS, on 5/13/1865. Residence at parole: Tuscaloosa County, AL.

Owens, A.C. (AKA Owen) Pvt., 6th Alabama Cavalry. Co. C. Federal Rolls of Prisoners of War: Captured in Florida on 3/25/1865; Received at Ship Island, MS. Transferred to Vicksburg, MS, for exchange on 5/1/1865; Exchanged at Camp Townsend, MS, on 5/6/1865.

Owens, Elijah E. Pvt., 62nd Alabama Infantry. Co. E. Federal Rolls of Prisoners of War: Captured at Blakely, AL, on 4/9/1865; Received at Ship Island, MS, on 4/15/1865. Transferred to Vicksburg, MS, for exchange on 5/1/1865; Exchanged at Camp Townsend, MS, on 5/6/1865.

Owens, W.H. (AKA Owings) Pvt., 36th Alabama Infantry. Co. H. Federal Rolls of Prisoners of War: Captured at Spanish Fort, AL, on 4/8/1865; Received at Ship Island, MS, on 4/10/1865. Transferred to Vicksburg, MS, for exchange on 5/1/1865; Exchanged at Camp Townsend, MS, on 5/6/1865.

Owens, William Pvt., 62nd Alabama Infantry. Co. B. Federal Rolls of Prisoners of War: Captured at Blakely, AL, on 4/9/1865; Received at Ship Island, MS, on 4/15/1865. Transferred to Vicksburg, MS, for exchange on 5/1/1865; Exchanged at Camp Townsend, MS, on 5/6/1865.

Pace, W.H. Cpl., 38th Alabama Infantry. Co. I. Enlisted: 3/1/1862 at Mobile, AL. On Register of Madison House Hospital, Montgomery, AL: Admitted on 10/9/1864. Federal Rolls of Prisoners of War: Captured at Spanish Fort, AL, on 4/8/1865; Received at Ship Island, MS, on 4/10/1865. Transferred to Vicksburg, MS, for exchange on 5/1/1865; Exchanged at Camp Townsend, MS, on 5/6/1865.

Pack, John A. Pvt., 62nd Alabama Infantry. Cos. A & D. Federal Rolls of Prisoners of War: Captured at Blakely, AL, on 4/9/1865; Received at Ship Island, MS, on 4/15/1865. Transferred to Vicksburg, MS, for exchange on 5/1/1865; Exchanged at Camp Townsend, MS, on 5/6/1865.

Palmer, J.D. Pvt., 58th Alabama Infantry. Co. E. Federal Rolls of Prisoners of War: Captured at Spanish Fort, AL, on 4/8/1865; Received at Ship Island, MS, on 4/10/1865. Transferred to Vicksburg, MS, for exchange on 5/1/1865; Exchanged at Camp Townsend, MS, on 5/6/1865.

Palmer, L. Cpl., 36th Alabama Infantry. Co. A. Federal Rolls of Prisoners of War: Captured at Spanish Fort, AL, on 4/8/1865; Received at Ship Island, MS, on 4/10/1865. Transferred to Vicksburg, MS, for exchange on 5/1/1865; Exchanged at Camp Townsend, MS, on 5/6/1865.

Parker, Alvis J. Bvt. 2nd Lt., 8th Alabama Cavalry. Co. E. Federal Rolls of Prisoners of War: Captured at Blakely, AL, on 4/9/1865; Received at Ship Island, MS, on 4/15/1865. Transferred to Vicksburg, MS, for exchange on 4/28/1865; Confined at New Orleans, LA, on 4/30/1865. Exchanged at Camp Townsend, MS, on 5/6/1865.

Parker, Creach H. Pvt., 5th Alabama Battalion Cavalry (Chisom's). Enlisted: 1/9/1864 at Henry County, AL. Federal Rolls of Prisoners of War: Captured at Euchee Anna, AL, on 9/23/1864; Received at Ship Island, MS. Transferred to Fort Columbus, New York Harbor, NY; Forwarded to Elmira, NY. Sent to James River, VA, for exchange on 2/20/1865. On Register of Howard's Grove Hospital, Richmond, VA: Admitted on 2/25/1865; Furloughed on 3/8/1865. Married: Penelope Page on 4/5/1863. Died: 6/10/1865 at Butler County, GA. Confederate Widows Pension Application dated 1925 on file at the Florida State Library and Archives. Target Name: Penelope Page Jones. County: Jackson. 10 pages.

Parker, E.J. (AKA Packer) Pvt., 62nd Alabama Infantry. Co. H. Federal Rolls of Prisoners of War: Captured at Blakely, AL, on 4/9/1865; Received at Ship Island, MS, on 4/15/1865. Transferred to Vicksburg, MS, for exchange on 5/1/1865; Exchanged at Camp Townsend, MS, on 5/6/1865.

Parker, Edward Cpl., 6th Alabama Cavalry. Co. A. Federal Rolls of Prisoners of War: Captured in Florida on 3/25/1865; Received at Ship Island, MS.

Transferred to Vicksburg, MS, for exchange on 5/1/1865; Exchanged at Camp Townsend, MS, on 5/6/1865.

Parker, H.W. Pvt., 62nd Alabama Infantry. Cos. C & K. Federal Rolls of Prisoners of War: Captured at Blakely, AL, on 4/9/1865; Received at Ship Island, MS, on 4/15/1865. Transferred to Vicksburg, MS, for exchange on 5/1/1865; Exchanged at Camp Townsend, MS, on 5/6/1865.

Parker, Martin V.B. Cpl./Pvt., 1st Alabama Artillery. Cos. B & D. Federal Rolls of Prisoners of War: Captured at Fort Gaines, AL, on 8/8/1864; Received at Ship Island, MS, from New Orleans, LA, on 10/25/1864. Died: 11/29/1864 at Ship Island, MS, due to dysentery. Buried: Ship Island, MS, Cemetery in Grave #52.

Parker, R.B. (AKA R.D.) Pvt., Lockhart's Battalion Infantry. Co. I. Federal Rolls of Prisoners of War: Captured at Blakely, AL, on 4/9/1865; Received at Ship Island, MS, on 4/15/1865. Transferred to Vicksburg, MS, for exchange on 5/1/1865; Exchanged at Camp Townsend, MS, on 5/6/1865.

Parker, S.J. Pvt., 62nd Alabama Infantry. Co. H. Federal Rolls of Prisoners of War: Captured at Blakely, AL, on 4/9/1865; Received at Ship Island, MS, on 4/15/1865. Transferred to Vicksburg, MS, for exchange on 5/1/1865; Exchanged at Camp Townsend, MS, on 5/6/1865.

Parker, W.H. Pvt., 63rd Alabama Infantry. Co. H. Enlisted: 3/15/1864 at Centerville, AL. Age at enlistment: 17. Description at enlistment: Eyes: blue. Hair: dark. Complexion: dark. Rolls for 9/1864 through 10/1864: Present. Federal Rolls of Prisoners of War: Captured at Blakely, AL, on 4/9/1865; Received at Ship Island, MS, on 4/15/1865. Transferred to Vicksburg, MS, for exchange on 5/1/1865; Exchanged at Camp Townsend, MS, on 5/6/1865. Rolls of Prisoners of War, C.S.A: Surrendered at Citronelle, AL, on 5/4/1865; Paroled at Meridian, MS, on 5/11/1865. Residence at parole: Bibb County, AL.

Parker, W.P.L.Q. Pvt., 63rd Alabama Infantry. Co. E. Federal Rolls of Prisoners of War: Captured at Blakely, AL, on 4/9/1865; Received at Ship Island, MS, on 4/15/1865. Transferred to Vicksburg, MS, for exchange on 5/1/1865; Exchanged at Camp Townsend, MS, on 5/6/1865. Rolls of Prisoners of War, C.S.A: Surrendered at Citronelle, AL, on 5/4/1865; Paroled at Meridian, MS, on 5/13/1865. Residence at parole: Sumpter County, AL.

Parrish, J.P. (AKA Parish, J.T.) Pvt., 63rd Alabama Infantry. Co. F. Enlisted: 5/30/1864 at Montgomery, AL. Age at enlistment: 17. Description at enlistment: Eyes: grey. Hair: light. Complexion: fair. Height: 5'7". Residence at enlistment: Butler County, AL. Rolls for 9/1864 through 10/1864: Absent, in camp of correction since 8/14/1864. Federal Rolls of Prisoners of War: Captured at Blakely, AL, on 4/9/1865; Received at Ship Island, MS, on 4/15/1865. Transferred to Vicksburg, MS, for exchange on 5/1/1865; Exchanged at Camp Townsend, MS, on 5/6/1865. Rolls of Prisoners of War, C.S.A: Surrendered at Citronelle, AL, on 5/4/1865; Paroled at Meridian, MS, on 5/11/1865. Residence at parole: Autauga County, AL.

Parrish, Jacob Pvt., 21st Alabama Infantry. Co. E. Federal Rolls of Prisoners of War: Captured at Fort Gaines, AL, on 8/8/1864; Received at Ship Island, MS, from New Orleans, LA, on 10/29/1864. Exchanged on 1/4/1865.

Parsons, G.B. Pvt., 38th Alabama Infantry. Co. B. Issued clothing on 7/28/1863 at Dalton, GA, Hospital. Federal Rolls of Prisoners of War: Captured at Spanish Fort, AL, on 4/8/1865; Received at Ship Island, MS, on 4/10/1865. Transferred to Vicksburg, MS, for exchange on 5/1/1865; Exchanged at Camp Townsend, MS, on 5/6/1865.

Parsons, J. Pvt., 36th Alabama Infantry. Co. G. Federal Rolls of Prisoners of War: Captured at Spanish Fort, AL, on 4/8/1865; Received at Ship Island, MS, on 4/10/1865. Transferred to Vicksburg, MS, for exchange on 5/1/1865; Exchanged at Camp Townsend, MS, on 5/6/1865.

Parsons, R.S. Pvt., 18th Alabama Infantry. Co. G. Federal Rolls of Prisoners of War: Captured at Spanish Fort, AL, on 4/8/1865; Received at Ship Island, MS, on 4/10/1865. Transferred to Vicksburg, MS, for exchange on 5/1/1865; Exchanged at Camp Townsend, MS, on 5/6/1865.

Parsons, W. Pvt., 18th Alabama Infantry. Co. G. Federal Rolls of Prisoners of War: Captured at Spanish Fort, AL, on 4/8/1865; Received at Ship Island, MS, on 4/10/1865. Transferred to Vicksburg, MS, for exchange on 5/1/1865; Exchanged at Camp Townsend, MS, on 5/6/1865.

Parsons, Young Pvt., 18th Alabama Infantry. Co. G. Federal Rolls of Prisoners of War: Captured at Spanish Fort, AL, on 4/8/1865; Received at Ship Island, MS, on 4/10/1865. Transferred to Vicksburg, MS, for exchange on 5/1/1865; Exchanged at Camp Townsend, MS, on 5/6/1865.

Parten, A.J. Pvt., 21st Alabama Infantry. Cos. C & F. Federal Rolls of Prisoners of War: Captured at Fort Gaines, AL, on 8/8/1864; Received at Ship Island, MS, from New Orleans, LA, on 10/25/1864. Died: 12/31/1864 at Ship Island, MS, due to dropsy from hepatic disease. Buried: Ship Island, MS, Cemetery in Grave #122.

Passeuary, George Pvt., 18th Alabama Infantry. Co. B. Federal Rolls of Prisoners of War: Captured at Spanish Fort, AL, on 4/8/1865; Received at Ship Island, MS, on 4/10/1865. Disposition unaccounted for.

Pate, John Pvt., 21st Alabama Infantry. Co. B. Federal Rolls of Prisoners of War: Captured at Fort Gaines, AL, on 8/8/1864; Received at Ship Island, MS, from New Orleans, LA, on 10/25/1864. Exchanged on 1/4/1865.

Paterson, J.P. Pvt., 62nd Alabama Infantry. Co. K. Federal Rolls of Prisoners of War: Captured at Blakely, AL, on 4/9/1865; Received at Ship Island, MS, on 4/15/1865. Transferred to Vicksburg, MS, for exchange on 5/1/1865; Exchanged at Camp Townsend, MS, on 5/6/1865.

Patterson, Ezekiel (AKA Patterison) Pvt., 63rd Alabama Infantry. Co. G. Enlisted: 5/16/1864 at Troy, AL. Age at enlistment: 17. Description at enlistment: Eyes: grey. Hair: light. Complexion: fair. Height: 5'7". Residence at enlistment: Covington County, AL. Rolls for 9/1864 through 10/1864: Absent on furlough; Furlough extended for 30 days on 10/19/1864 by the Greenville, AL, Medical Examining Board. Federal Rolls of Prisoners of War: Captured at

Blakely, AL, on 4/9/1865; Received at Ship Island, MS, on 4/15/1865. Transferred to Vicksburg, MS, for exchange on 5/1/1865; Exchanged at Camp Townsend, MS, on 5/6/1865. Rolls of Prisoners of War, C.S.A: Surrendered at Citronelle, AL, on 5/4/1865; Paroled at Meridian, MS, on 5/13/1865. Residence at parole: Covington County, AL.

Paul, W.D. Pvt., 38th Alabama Infantry. Co. D. Federal Rolls of Prisoners of War: Captured at Blakely, AL, on 4/9/1865; Received at Ship Island, MS, on 4/15/1865. Transferred to Vicksburg, MS, for exchange on 5/1/1865; Exchanged at Camp Townsend, MS, on 5/6/1865.

Peacock, James B. Pvt., 63rd Alabama Infantry. Co. D. Enlisted: 9/5/1864 at Blakely, AL. Rolls for 9/1864 through 10/1864: Present. On Register of Ross Hospital, Mobile, AL: Admitted on 9/18/1864 due to rubeola; Returned to duty on 10/6/1864. Federal Rolls of Prisoners of War: Captured at Blakely, AL, on 4/9/1865; Received at Ship Island, MS, on 4/15/1865. Transferred to Vicksburg, MS, for exchange on 5/1/1865; Exchanged at Camp Townsend, MS, on 5/6/1865. Rolls of Prisoners of War, C.S.A: Surrendered at Citronelle, AL, on 5/4/1865; Paroled at Meridian, MS, on 5/11/1865. Residence at parole: Coffee County, AL.

Pearce, A.C. Pvt., 62nd Alabama Infantry. Co. K. Federal Rolls of Prisoners of War: Captured at Blakely, AL, on 4/9/1865; Received at Ship Island, MS, on 4/15/1865. Transferred to Vicksburg, MS, for exchange on 5/1/1865; Exchanged at Camp Townsend, MS, on 5/6/1865.

Pearce, James A. (AKA A.J.) Pvt., Lockhart's Battalion Infantry. Co. K. Federal Rolls of Prisoners of War: Captured at Fort Gaines, AL, on 8/8/1864; Received at Ship Island, MS, from New Orleans, LA, on 10/25/1864. Exchanged on 1/4/1865.

Pearce, John T. 2nd Lt./1st Lt., 62nd Alabama Infantry. Co. F. Federal Rolls of Prisoners of War: Captured at Blakely, AL, on 4/9/1865; Received at Ship Island, MS, on 4/15/1865. Transferred to Vicksburg, MS, for exchange on 4/28/1865; Confined at New Orleans, LA, on 4/30/1865. Exchanged at Camp Townsend, MS, on 5/6/1865.

Pearson, Robert H. Pvt./1st Lt./Capt., 63rd Alabama Infantry. Co. D. Enlisted: 3/2/1864 at Blakely, AL; Elected 1st Lt. on 7/30/1864. Age at enlistment: 17. Description at enlistment: Eyes: grey. Hair: dark. Complexion: fair. Height: 5'8". Residence at enlistment: Clayton, Barbour County, AL. Rolls for 9/1864 through 10/1864: Present. Federal Rolls of Prisoners of War: Captured at Blakely, AL, on 4/9/1865; Confined one day at Spanish Fort, AL. Received at Ship Island, MS, on 4/16/1865; Transferred to Vicksburg, MS, for exchange on 4/28/1865. Confined at New Orleans, LA, on 4/30/1865; Exchanged at Camp Townsend, MS, on 5/6/1865. Rolls of Prisoners of War, C.S.A: Surrendered at Citronelle, AL, on 5/4/1865; Paroled at Meridian, MS, on 5/11/1865.

Pearson, W.B. Pvt., 63rd Alabama Infantry. Co. F. Enlisted: 3/9/1864 at Greenville, AL. Age at enlistment: 17. Description at enlistment: Eyes: hazel. Hair: dark. Complexion: fair. Height: 5'7". Residence at enlistment: Butler County, AL. Rolls for 9/1864 through 10/1864: Present. On Register of Ross Hospital, Mobile, AL: Admitted on 9/18/1864 due to rubeola; Returned to duty on 10/6/1864. Federal Rolls of Prisoners of War: Captured at Blakely, AL, on 4/9/1865; Received at Ship Island, MS, on 4/15/1865. Transferred to Vicksburg, MS, for exchange on 5/1/1865; Exchanged at Camp Townsend, MS, on 5/6/1865. Rolls of Prisoners of War, C.S.A: Surrendered at Citronelle, AL, on 5/4/1865; Paroled at Meridian, MS, on 5/11/1865. Residence at parole: Butler County, AL.

Perdue, J.N. Pvt., Lockhart's Battalion Infantry. Co. I. Federal Rolls of Prisoners of War: Captured at Fort Gaines, AL, on 8/8/1864; Received at Ship Island, MS, from New Orleans, LA, on 10/25/1864. Exchanged on 1/4/1865.

Perdue, John L. (AKA Perden) Pvt., 38th Alabama Infantry. Co. E. On Register of St. Mary's Hospital, Dalton, GA: Admitted on 9/6/1863 due to febris remittens. Federal Rolls of Prisoners of War: Captured at Blakely, AL, on 4/9/1865; Received at Ship Island, MS, on 4/15/1865. Transferred to Vicksburg, MS, for exchange on 5/1/1865; Exchanged at Camp Townsend, MS, on 5/6/1865.

Perkins, P.H. Pvt., 6th Alabama Cavalry. Cos. B & C. Federal Rolls of Prisoners of War: Captured in Florida on 3/25/1865; Received at Ship Island, MS. Transferred to Vicksburg, MS, for exchange on 5/1/1865; Exchanged at Camp Townsend, MS, on 5/6/1865.

Perkins, Robert D. Cpl., 63rd Alabama Infantry. Co. G. Enlisted: 4/27/1864 at Troy, AL. Age at enlistment: 17. Description at enlistment: Eyes: blue. Hair: dark. Complexion: dark. Height: 5'9". Rolls for 9/1864 through 10/1864: Absent, in hospital at Mobile, AL, since 10/20/1864. Federal Rolls of Prisoners of War: Captured at Blakely, AL, on 4/9/1865; Received at Ship Island, MS, on 4/15/1865. Transferred to Vicksburg, MS, for exchange on 5/1/1865; Exchanged at Camp Townsend, MS, on 5/6/1865. Rolls of Prisoners of War, C.S.A: Surrendered at Citronelle, AL, on 5/4/1865; Paroled at Meridian, MS, on 5/13/1865. Residence at parole: Pike County, AL.

Perry, David D. Pvt., 62nd Alabama Infantry. Co. K. Federal Rolls of Prisoners of War: Captured at Blakely, AL, on 4/9/1865; Received at Ship Island, MS, on 4/15/1865. Transferred to Vicksburg, MS, for exchange on 5/1/1865; Exchanged at Camp Townsend, MS, on 5/6/1865.

Perry, John D. Pvt., 62nd Alabama Infantry. Co. I. Federal Rolls of Prisoners of War: Captured at Blakely, AL, on 4/9/1865; Received at Ship Island, MS, on 4/15/1865. Transferred to Vicksburg, MS, for exchange on 5/1/1865; Exchanged at Camp Townsend, MS, on 5/6/1865.

Persky, John Sgt., 8th Alabama Cavalry. Co. E. Federal Rolls of Prisoners of War: Captured in Florida on 3/25/1865; Received at Ship Island, MS. Transferred to Vicksburg, MS, for exchange on 5/1/1865; Exchanged at Camp Townsend, MS, on 5/6/1865.

Pery, W.N. Pvt., 62nd Alabama Infantry. Co. G. Federal Rolls of Prisoners of War: Captured at Blakely, AL, on 4/9/1865; Received at Ship Island, MS, on 4/15/1865. Transferred to Vicksburg, MS, for exchange on 5/1/1865; Exchanged at Camp Townsend, MS, on 5/6/1865.

Peterson, Freeman F. Pvt., 63rd Alabama Infantry. Co. F. Enlisted: 7/12/1864 at Greenville, AL. Rolls for

9/1864 through 10/1864: Present. Federal Rolls of Prisoners of War: Captured at Blakely, AL, on 4/9/1865; Received at Ship Island, MS, on 4/15/1865. Transferred to Vicksburg, MS, for exchange on 5/1/1865; Exchanged at Camp Townsend, MS, on 5/6/1865. Rolls of Prisoners of War, C.S.A: Surrendered at Citronelle, AL, on 5/4/1865; Paroled at Meridian, MS, on 5/11/1865. Residence at parole: Butler County, AL. Born: 7/13/1847 at Butler County, AL. Soldier is recorded on the 1907 Alabama Census of Confederate Veterans and Widows. Residence: Crenshaw County, AL.

Peterson, M. (AKA W.) Pvt., 63rd Alabama Infantry. Co. D. Enlisted: 9/5/1864 at Blakely, AL. Rolls for 9/1864 through 10/1864: Present. Federal Rolls of Prisoners of War: Captured at Blakely, AL, on 4/9/1865; Received at Ship Island, MS, on 4/15/1865. Transferred to Vicksburg, MS, for exchange on 5/1/1865; Exchanged at Camp Townsend, MS, on 5/6/1865. Rolls of Prisoners of War, C.S.A: Surrendered at Citronelle, AL, on 5/4/1865; Paroled at Meridian, MS, on 5/13/1865. Residence at parole: Barbour County, AL.

Peterson, Robert I. (AKA R.S.) Pvt., 63rd Alabama Infantry. Cos. D & F. Enlisted: 8/1/1864 at Abbeville, AL. Rolls for 9/1864 through 10/1864: Present. Federal Rolls of Prisoners of War: Captured at Blakely, AL, on 4/9/1865; Received at Ship Island, MS, on 4/15/1865. Transferred to Vicksburg, MS, for exchange on 5/1/1865; Exchanged at Camp Townsend, MS, on 5/6/1865. Rolls of Prisoners of War, C.S.A: Surrendered at Citronelle, AL, on 5/4/1865; Paroled at Meridian, MS, on 5/11/1865. Residence at parole: Henry County, AL. Born: 3/28/1848 at Butler County, AL. Soldier is recorded on the 1907 Alabama Census of Confederate Veterans and Widows. Residence: Crenshaw County, AL.

Phelan, C. Pvt., 1st Alabama Artillery Battalion. Co. B. Federal Rolls of Prisoners of War: Captured at Fort Gaines, AL, on 8/8/1864; Received at Ship Island, MS, from New Orleans, LA, on 10/25/1864. Exchanged on 1/4/1865.

Phelan, M. (AKA Phelin, Philen) Pvt., 62nd Alabama Infantry. Co. F. Federal Rolls of Prisoners of War: Captured at Blakely, AL, on 4/9/1865; Received at Ship Island, MS, on 4/15/1865. Transferred to Vicksburg, MS, for exchange on 5/1/1865; Exchanged at Camp Townsend, MS, on 5/6/1865.

Philan, W. Sidney (AKA Phelen, Philen) Pvt., 38th Alabama Infantry. Co. B. Enlisted: 3/29/1862 at Bethel Beat, Wilcox County, AL. Age at enlistment: 34. Discharged on 6/21/1862 at Camp Holt near Mobile, AL, due to disability. Paid $30.43 for 2 months and 23 days of service. Age at enlistment: 34. Description at enlistment: Eyes: blue. Complexion: dark. Height: 5'8". Occupation at enlistment: Farmer. Soldier later enlisted in the 21st Alabama Infantry. Co.G. Federal Rolls of Prisoners of War: Captured at Fort Gaines, AL, on 8/8/1864; Received at Ship Island, MS, from New Orleans, LA, on 10/25/1864. Died: 12/23/1864 at Ship Island, MS, due to pneumonia. Buried: Ship Island, MS, Cemetery in Grave #108. Born: Wilcox County, AL.

Phillips, George A Pvt., 37th Alabama Infantry. Co. H. Age at enlistment: 16. Federal Rolls of Prisoner of War: Captured near Pollard, AL, on 12/15/1864; Received at Ship Island, MS, on 1/22/1865. Federal Rolls of Prisoners of War: Captured at Blakely, AL, on 4/9/1865; Received at Ship Island, MS, on 4/15/1865. Transferred to New Orleans, LA. Died: 5/21/1865 in St. Louis U.S.A. General Hospital, New Orleans, LA, due to chronic diarrhea. Buried: Monument Cemetery in Square 19, Grave #775. Father: Thomas Phillips of Atkins Mills, Barbour County, AL.

Phillips, J.J. Pvt., 58th Alabama Infantry. Cos. C & E. Federal Rolls of Prisoners of War: Captured at Spanish Fort, AL, on 4/8/1865; Received at Ship Island, MS, on 4/10/1865. Transferred to Vicksburg, MS, for exchange on 5/1/1865; Exchanged at Camp Townsend, MS, on 5/6/1865.

Phillips, James Irwin Pvt., 33rd Alabama Infantry. Co. A. Enlisted: 3/11/1861 at Elba, AL. Federal Rolls of Prisoners of War: Captured at Spanish Fort, AL, on 4/8/1865; Received at Ship Island, MS, on 4/10/1865. Disposition unknown. Born: 2/2/1843 at Elba, Coffee County, AL. Soldier is recorded on the 1907 Alabama Census of Confederate Veterans and Widows. Residence: Geneva County, AL.

Phipps, John G. Pvt., Lockhart's Battalion Infantry. Cos. H & K. Federal Rolls of Prisoners of War: Captured at Blakely, AL, on 4/9/1865; Received at Ship Island, MS, on 4/15/1865. Transferred to Vicksburg, MS, for exchange on 5/1/1865; Exchanged at Camp Townsend, MS, on 5/6/1865.

Pickett, Abner Pvt., 63rd Alabama Infantry. Co. D. Enlisted: 7/30/1864 at Macon County, AL. Age at enlistment: 17. Description at enlistment: Eyes: blue. Hair: light. Complexion: florid. Height: 5'8". Residence at enlistment: Clayton, Barbour County, AL. Rolls for 9/1864 through 10/1864: Present. Federal Rolls of Prisoners of War: Captured at Blakely, AL, on 4/9/1865; Received at Ship Island, MS, on 4/15/1865. Transferred to Vicksburg, MS, for exchange on 5/1/1865; Exchanged at Camp Townsend, MS, on 5/6/1865. Rolls of Prisoners of War, C.S.A: Surrendered at Citronelle, AL, on 5/4/1865; Paroled at Meridian, MS, on 5/13/1865. Residence at parole: Barbour County, AL.

Pickett, Andrew J. Pvt., 6th Alabama Cavalry. Co. __. Wounded through the torso at the Battle of Perryville, KY. Federal Rolls of Prisoners of War: Captured at Pine Barren, FL, on 3/25/1865; Received at Ship Island, MS. Transferred to Vicksburg, MS, for exchange on 5/1/1865; Exchanged at Camp Townsend, MS, on 5/6/1865. Born: 3/15/1838 at Pike County, AL. Married: Torbut Sloan on 12/15/1858 at Lowndes County, AL; Augusta Siler in 12/1867 at Orion, AL; Alice McLaurine of Virginia on 4/29/1875, producing 6 children. Occupations: Church Clerk and Deacon. Died: 8/25/1911 due to paralysis. Soldier also served as a Pvt. with the 1st Alabama Cavalry. A synopsis of his life appeared in *Confederate Veteran Magazine* in 1898 and 1912.

Pickett, J.R.W. (AKA J.R.A.) Pvt., 6th Alabama Cavalry. Co. B. Federal Rolls of Prisoners of War: Captured in Florida on 3/25/1865; Received at Ship Island, MS. Transferred to Vicksburg, MS, for exchange on 5/1/1865; Exchanged at Camp Townsend, MS, on 5/6/1865.

Pierce, A.C. Pvt., 63rd Alabama Infantry. Co. F. Federal Rolls of Prisoners of War: Captured at Blakely,

AL, on 4/9/1865; Received at Ship Island, MS, on 4/15/1865. Transferred to Vicksburg, MS, for exchange on 5/1/1865; Exchanged at Camp Townsend, MS, on 5/6/1865. Rolls of Prisoners of War, C.S.A: Surrendered at Citronelle, AL, on 5/4/1865; Paroled at Meridian, MS, on 5/11/1865. Residence at parole: Butler County, AL.

Pierce, Labrazan Mitchell (AKA Pearce, M.L.) Pvt., 63rd Alabama Infantry. Co. F. Enlisted: 3/9/1864 at Greenville, AL. Age at enlistment: 17. Description at enlistment: Eyes: grey. Hair: light. Complexion: sallow. Height: 5'9". Residence at enlistment: Butler County, AL. Rolls for 9/1864 through 10/1864: Present. Federal Rolls of Prisoners of War: Captured at Blakely, AL, on 4/9/1865; Received at Ship Island, MS, on 4/15/1865. Transferred to Vicksburg, MS, for exchange on 5/1/1865; Exchanged at Camp Townsend, MS, on 5/6/1865. Rolls of Prisoners of War, C.S.A: Surrendered at Citronelle, AL, on 5/4/1865; Paroled at Meridian, MS, on 5/11/1865. Residence at parole: Butler County, AL. Born: 12/29/1846 at Macon County, AL. Soldier is recorded on the 1907 Alabama Census of Confederate Veterans and Widows. Residence: Pike County, AL.

Pierce, S.H. (AKA Perce) Pvt./Sgt., 8th Alabama Cavalry. Co. A. Federal Rolls of Prisoners of War: Captured in Florida on 3/25/1865; Received at Ship Island, MS. Transferred to Vicksburg, MS, for exchange on 5/1/1865; Exchanged at Camp Townsend, MS, on 5/6/1865.

Piper, A.W. (AKA A.M.W.) Pvt., 62nd Alabama Infantry. Cos. C & K. Federal Rolls of Prisoners of War: Captured at Blakely, AL, on 4/9/1865; Received at Ship Island, MS, on 4/15/1865. Transferred to Vicksburg, MS, for exchange on 5/1/1865; Exchanged at Camp Townsend, MS, on 5/6/1865.

Pipes, Asa C. Pvt., 62nd Alabama Infantry. Co. C. Enlisted: 11/3/1863 at Wilsonville, AL. Federal Rolls of Prisoners of War: Captured at Blakely, AL, on 4/9/1865; Received at Ship Island, MS, on 4/15/1865. Transferred to Vicksburg, MS, for exchange on 5/1/1865; Exchanged at Camp Townsend, MS, on 5/6/1865.

Pistol, C.W. (AKA Pistole, Pistoll) Cpl./Pvt., 63rd Alabama Infantry. Co. I. Enlisted: 4/15/1864 at Talladega, AL. Rolls for 9/1864 through 10/1864: Absent, sick in Moore Hospital since 10/15/1864. Federal Rolls of Prisoners of War: Captured at Blakely, AL, on 4/9/1865; Received at Ship Island, MS, on 4/15/1865. Transferred to Vicksburg, MS, for exchange on 5/1/1865; Exchanged at Camp Townsend, MS, on 5/6/1865. Rolls of Prisoners of War, C.S.A: Surrendered at Citronelle, AL, on 5/4/1865; Paroled at Meridian, MS, on 5/13/1865 while a patient in Quintard Hospital. Residence at parole: Randolph County, AL.

Pittman, H.R. Pvt., Alabama Cavalry (Chisolm's). Enlisted: 1/9/1864 at Henry County, AL. Federal Rolls of Prisoners of War: Captured at Marianna, FL, on 9/27/1864; Forwarded to New Orleans, LA, on 10/8/1864. Received at Ship Island, MS, on 10/24/1864; Transferred to Fort Columbus, New York Harbor, NY, on 11/5/1864. Sent to Elmira, NY, on 11/20/1864; Released from Elmira, NY, on 5/29/1865.

Pitts, John Pvt., 21st Alabama Infantry. Co. G. Federal Rolls of Prisoners of War: Captured at Fort Gaines, AL, on 8/8/1864; Received at Ship Island, MS, from New Orleans, LA, on 10/25/1864. Died: 12/15/1864 at Ship Island, MS, due to pneumonia. Buried: Ship Island, MS, Cemetery in Grave #88.

Pitts, John M. Wesley Pvt., 62nd Alabama Infantry. Co. H. Federal Rolls of Prisoners of War: Captured at Blakely, AL, on 4/9/1865; Received at Ship Island, MS, on 4/15/1865. Transferred to Vicksburg, MS, for exchange on 5/1/1865; Exchanged at Camp Townsend, MS, on 5/6/1865. Born: 8/5/1836 at Dallas County, AL.

Poellnitz, Edwin A. 2nd Lt., 21st Alabama Infantry. Co. C. Federal Rolls of Prisoners of War: Captured at Fort Gaines, AL, on 8/8/1864; Received at Ship Island, MS, from New Orleans, LA, on 10/25/1864. Exchanged on 1/4/1865.

Poellnitz, James A. Pvt./2nd Lt., 21st Alabama Infantry. Co. C. Federal Rolls of Prisoners of War: Captured at Fort Gaines, AL, on 8/8/1864; Received at Ship Island, MS, from New Orleans, LA, on 10/25/1864. Exchanged on 1/4/1865.

Poittat, John T. Pvt., 21st Alabama Infantry. Co. G. Federal Rolls of Prisoners of War: Captured at Fort Gaines, AL, on 8/8/1864; Received at Ship Island, MS, on 10/25/1864. Died: 12/15/1864 at Ship Island, MS, due to dysentery. Buried: Ship Island, MS, Cemetery in Grave #88.

Pollard, James M. (AKA Pollerd) Pvt., 63rd Alabama Infantry. Co. C. Enlisted: 5/10/1864 at Russell County, AL. Age at enlistment: 17. Description at enlistment: Eyes: blue. Hair: dark. Complexion: fair. Height: 5'4". Residence at enlistment: Hartsville, Russell County, AL. Rolls for 9/1864 through 10/1864: Present. Federal Rolls of Prisoners of War: Captured at Blakely, AL, on 4/9/1865; Received at Ship Island, MS, on 4/15/1865. Transferred to Vicksburg, MS, for exchange on 5/1/1865; Exchanged at Camp Townsend, MS, on 5/6/1865. Rolls of Prisoners of War, C.S.A: Surrendered at Citronelle, AL, on 5/4/1865; Paroled at Meridian, MS, on 5/11/1865. Residence at parole: Russell County, AL.

Ponder, Finus W. (AKA T.W.) Pvt., Lockhart's Battalion Infantry. Co. K. Federal Rolls of Prisoners of War: Captured at Fort Gaines, AL, on 8/8/1864; Received at Ship Island, MS, from New Orleans, LA, on 10/25/1864. Exchanged on 3/2/1865.

Ponder, William L. Pvt., Lockhart's Battalion Infantry. Co. K. Federal Rolls of Prisoners of War: Captured at Fort Gaines, AL, on 8/8/1864; Received at Ship Island, MS, from New Orleans, LA, on 10/29/1864. Exchanged on 1/4/1865.

Pool, J. (AKA C.F.) Sgt., 63rd Alabama Infantry. Co. K. Federal Rolls of Prisoners of War: Captured at Blakely, AL, on 4/9/1865; Received at Ship Island, MS, on 4/15/1865. Transferred to Vicksburg, MS, for exchange on 5/1/1865; Exchanged at Camp Townsend, MS, on 5/6/1865.

Poole, C.F. 4th Sgt., 63rd Alabama Infantry. Co. K. Enlisted: 9/3/1864 at Macon County, AL. Rolls for 9/1864 through 10/1864: Present. Federal Rolls of Prisoners of War: Captured at Blakely, AL, on 4/9/1865; Received at Ship Island, MS, on 4/15/1865. Transferred to Vicksburg, MS, for exchange on 5/1/1865; Exchanged at Camp Townsend, MS, on 5/6/1865. Rolls of Prisoners of War, C.S.A: Surrendered at Citronelle, AL, on 5/4/1865; Paroled at Meridian,

MS, on 5/10/1865 while a patient in Quintard Hospital. Residence at parole: Butler County, AL.

Poole, E.H. (AKA Pool) Pvt., 63rd Alabama Infantry. Co. K. Enlisted: 9/16/1864 at Bibb County, AL. Rolls for 9/1864 through 10/1864: Present. Federal Rolls of Prisoners of War: Captured at Blakely, AL, on 4/9/1865; Received at Ship Island, MS, on 4/15/1865. Transferred to Vicksburg, MS, for exchange on 5/1/1865; Exchanged at Camp Townsend, MS, on 5/6/1865. Rolls of Prisoners of War, C.S.A: Surrendered at Citronelle, AL, on 5/4/1865; Paroled at Meridian, MS, on 5/13/1865. Residence at parole: Bibb County, AL.

Poole, T.M. Pvt., 63rd Alabama Infantry. Co. F. Enlisted: 5/30/1864 at Montgomery, AL. Age at enlistment: 17. Description at enlistment: Eyes: blue. Hair: light. Complexion: fair. Height: 5'8". Residence at enlistment: Autauga County, AL. Rolls for 9/1864 through 10/1864: Absent, in hospital at Greenville, AL, since 7/31/1864. Federal Rolls of Prisoners of War: Captured at Blakely, AL, on 4/9/1865; Received at Ship Island, MS, on 4/15/1865. Transferred to Vicksburg, MS, for exchange on 5/1/1865; Exchanged at Camp Townsend, MS, on 5/6/1865. Rolls of Prisoners of War, C.S.A: Surrendered at Citronelle, AL, on 5/4/1865; Paroled at Meridian, MS, on 5/11/1865. Residence at parole: Autauga County, AL.

Pope, W.C. Pvt., 63rd Alabama Infantry. Co. K. Enlisted: 8/17/1864 at Talladega, AL. Rolls for 9/1864 through 10/1864: Present. Federal Rolls of Prisoners of War: Captured at Blakely, AL, on 4/9/1865; Received at Ship Island, MS, on 4/15/1865. Transferred to Vicksburg, MS, for exchange on 5/1/1865; Exchanged at Camp Townsend, MS, on 5/6/1865. Rolls of Prisoners of War, C.S.A: Surrendered at Citronelle, AL, on 5/4/1865; Paroled at Meridian, MS, on 5/13/1865. Residence at parole: Talladega County, AL.

Porter, G.W. Pvt., 62nd Alabama Infantry. Cos. C & K. Federal Rolls of Prisoners of War: Captured at Blakely, AL, on 4/9/1865; Received at Ship Island, MS, on 4/15/1865. Transferred to Vicksburg, MS, for exchange on 5/1/1865; Exchanged at Camp Townsend, MS, on 5/6/1865.

Powell, J.W. (AKA Privett) Pvt., 21st Alabama Infantry. Co. C. Federal Rolls of Prisoners of War: Captured at Fort Gaines, AL, on 8/8/1864; Received at Ship Island, MS, from New Orleans, LA, on 10/25/1864. Exchanged on 1/4/1865.

Powell, N. Pvt., 62nd Alabama Infantry. Co. H. Federal Rolls of Prisoners of War: Captured at Blakely, AL, on 4/9/1865; Received at Ship Island, MS, on 4/15/1865. Transferred to Vicksburg, MS, for exchange on 5/1/1865; Exchanged at Camp Townsend, MS, on 5/6/1865.

Powell, W.C. Cpl., 63rd Alabama Infantry. Co. H. Enlisted: 3/15/1864 at Centerville, AL. Age at enlistment: 17. Description at enlistment: Eyes: grey. Hair: dark. Complexion: fair. Rolls for 9/1864 through 10/1864: Present. Federal Rolls of Prisoners of War: Captured at Blakely, AL, on 4/9/1865; Received at Ship Island, MS, on 4/15/1865. Transferred to Vicksburg, MS, for exchange on 5/1/1865; Exchanged at Camp Townsend, MS, on 5/6/1865. Rolls of Prisoners of War, C.S.A: Surrendered at Citronelle, AL, on 5/4/1865; Paroled at Meridian, MS, on 5/11/1865. Residence at parole: Bibb County, AL.

Powers, Edward A. Cpl., Lockhart's Battalion Infantry. Co. K. Federal Rolls of Prisoners of War: Captured at Fort Gaines, AL, on 8/8/1864; Received at Ship Island, MS, from New Orleans, LA, on 10/25/1864. Exchanged on 1/4/1865.

Powers, Felix F. Pvt., 1st Alabama Artillery. Cos. D & E. Federal Rolls of Prisoners of War: Captured at Fort Gaines, AL, on 8/8/1864; Received at Ship Island, MS, from New Orleans, LA, on 10/25/1864. Exchanged on 1/4/1865.

Powers, James M. Pvt., 63rd Alabama Infantry. Co. A. Enlisted: 1/1/1864 at Tallapoosa County, AL. Age at enlistment: 17. Rolls for 1/1864 through 2/1864: Present. Rolls for 9/1864 through 10/1864: Present. Federal Rolls of Prisoners of War: Captured at Blakely, AL, on 4/9/1865; Received at Ship Island, MS, on 4/15/1865. Transferred to Vicksburg, MS, for exchange on 5/1/1865; Exchanged at Camp Townsend, MS, on 5/6/1865. Rolls of Prisoners of War, C.S.A: Surrendered at Citronelle, AL, on 5/4/1865; Paroled at Meridian, MS, on 5/13/1865. Residence at parole: Tallapoosa County, AL.

Powers, W.L. (AKA M.L.) Pvt., 63rd Alabama Infantry. Co. F. Enlisted: 7/12/1864 at Lowndes County, AL. Age at enlistment: 17. Description at enlistment: Eyes: grey. Hair: dark. Complexion: fair. Height: 5'5". Residence at enlistment: Lowndes County, AL. Rolls for 9/1864 through 10/1864: Present. On Register of Ross Hospital, Mobile, AL: Admitted on 11/24/1864 due to febris remittens; Sent to General Hospital Nidelet on 11/30/1864. Federal Rolls of Prisoners of War: Captured at Blakely, AL, on 4/9/1865; Received at Ship Island, MS, on 4/15/1865. Transferred to Vicksburg, MS, for exchange on 5/1/1865; Exchanged at Camp Townsend, MS, on 5/6/1865. Rolls of Prisoners of War, C.S.A: Surrendered at Citronelle, AL, on 5/4/1865; Paroled at Meridian, MS, on 5/11/1865. Residence at parole: Lowndes County, AL.

Prestridge, B.F. Pvt., 62nd Alabama Infantry. Cos. C & K. Federal Rolls of Prisoners of War: Captured at Blakely, AL, on 4/9/1865; Received at Ship Island, MS, on 4/15/1865. Transferred to Vicksburg, MS, for exchange on 5/1/1865; Exchanged at Camp Townsend, MS, on 5/6/1865.

Prewitt, N.C. Pvt., 38th Alabama Infantry. Co. H. Enlisted: 5/13/1862 at Fort Gaines, AL. Age at enlistment: 20. Federal Rolls of Prisoners of War: Captured at Spanish Fort, AL, on 4/8/1865; Received at Ship Island, MS, on 4/10/1865. Transferred to Vicksburg, MS, for exchange on 5/1/1865; Exchanged at Camp Townsend, MS, on 5/6/1865.

Price, B.F. Pvt., 36th Alabama Infantry. Co. K. Federal Rolls of Prisoners of War: Captured at Spanish Fort, AL, on 4/8/1865; Received at Ship Island, MS, on 4/10/1865. Transferred to Vicksburg, MS, for exchange on 5/1/1865; Exchanged at Camp Townsend, MS, on 5/6/1865.

Price, Lewis Pvt./Cpl., 36th Alabama Infantry. Cos. D & G. Federal Rolls of Prisoners of War: Captured at Spanish Fort, AL, on 4/8/1865; Received at Ship Island, MS, on 4/10/1865. Transferred to Vicksburg, MS, for exchange on 5/1/1865; Exchanged at Camp Townsend, MS, on 5/6/1865.

Price, M.L. (AKA W.L.) Pvt., 8th Alabama Cavalry. Cos. B & C. Federal Rolls of Prisoners of War: Captured in Florida on 3/25/1865; Received at Ship Island, MS. Transferred to Vicksburg, MS, for exchange on 5/1/1865; Exchanged at Camp Townsend, MS, on 5/6/1865.

Pritchard, Hezekiah Pvt., 62nd Alabama Infantry. Co. H. Federal Rolls of Prisoners of War: Captured at Blakely, AL, on 4/9/1865; Received at Ship Island, MS, on 4/15/1865. Transferred to Vicksburg, MS, for exchange on 5/1/1865; Exchanged at Camp Townsend, MS, on 5/6/1865.

Pritchett, W.H. Pvt., 38th Alabama Infantry. Co. E. Enlisted: 1/18/1864 at Dalton, GA. On Register of Blackie Hospital, Madison, GA: Admitted in 1/1864; Discharged in 2/1864. Federal Rolls of Prisoners of War: Captured at Blakely, AL, on 4/9/1865; Received at Ship Island, MS, on 4/15/1865. Transferred to Vicksburg, MS, for exchange on 5/1/1865; Exchanged at Camp Townsend, MS, on 5/6/1865.

Pruett, Darling H. (AKA Pruitt) Pvt., 63rd Alabama Infantry. Co. G. Enlisted: 5/16/1864 at Troy, AL. Age at enlistment: 17. Description at enlistment: Eyes: grey. Hair: light. Complexion: fair. Height: 5'8". Residence at enlistment: Coffee County, AL. Rolls for 9/1864 through 10/1864: Present. Federal Rolls of Prisoners of War: Captured at Blakely, AL, on 4/9/1865; Received at Ship Island, MS, on 4/15/1865. Transferred to Vicksburg, MS, for exchange on 5/1/1865; Exchanged at Camp Townsend, MS, on 5/6/1865. Rolls of Prisoners of War, C.S.A: Surrendered at Citronelle, AL, on 5/4/1865; Paroled at Meridian, MS, on 5/13/1865. Residence at parole: Pike County, AL.

Puckett, Pinkney S. Pvt., 62nd Alabama Infantry. Co. G. Federal Rolls of Prisoners of War: Captured at Blakely, AL, on 4/9/1865; Received at Ship Island, MS, on 4/15/1865. Transferred to Vicksburg, MS, for exchange on 5/1/1865; Exchanged at Camp Townsend, MS, on 5/6/1865.

Purmer, J.R. Pvt., 18th Alabama Infantry. Co __. Federal Rolls of Prisoners of War: Captured at Blakely, AL, on 4/9/1865; Received at Ship Island, MS, on 4/15/1865. Transferred to Vicksburg, MS, for exchange on 5/1/1865; Exchanged at Camp Townsend, MS, on 5/6/1865.

Purnell, N.B. (AKA Purnail) Pvt., 38th Alabama Infantry. Co. E. Federal Rolls of Prisoners of War: Captured at Blakely, AL, on 4/9/1865; Received at Ship Island, MS, on 4/15/1865. Transferred to Vicksburg, MS, for exchange on 5/1/1865; Exchanged at Camp Townsend, MS, on 5/6/1865.

Pylant, William M. Pvt., 63rd Alabama Infantry. Co. B. Enlisted: 7/17/1864 at Montgomery, AL. Rolls for 9/1864 through 10/1864: Present. Federal Rolls of Prisoners of War: Captured at Blakely, AL, on 4/9/1865; Received at Ship Island, MS, on 4/15/1865. Transferred to Vicksburg, MS, for exchange on 5/1/1865; Exchanged at Camp Townsend, MS, on 5/6/1865. Rolls of Prisoners of War, C.S.A: Surrendered at Citronelle, AL, on 5/4/1865; Paroled at Meridian, MS, on 5/11/1865. Residence at parole: Coosa County, AL.

Pyne, Columbus C. Sgt., 63rd Alabama Infantry. Co. D. Enlisted: 7/20/1864 at Macon County, AL. Age at enlistment: 17. Description at enlistment: Eyes: dark. Hair: dark. Complexion: dark. Height: 5'6". Residence at enlistment: Clayton, Barbour County, AL. Rolls for 9/1864 through 10/1864: Present. Federal Rolls of Prisoners of War: Captured at Blakely, AL, on 4/9/1865; Received at Ship Island, MS, on 4/15/1865. Transferred to Vicksburg, MS, for exchange on 5/1/1865; Exchanged at Camp Townsend, MS, on 5/6/1865. Rolls of Prisoners of War, C.S.A: Surrendered at Citronelle, AL, on 5/4/1865; Paroled at Meridian, MS, on 5/13/1865. Residence at parole: Barbour County, AL.

Quarles, F.W. Pvt./Cpl., 38th Alabama Infantry. Co. __. Federal Rolls of Prisoners of War: Captured at Blakely, AL, on 4/9/1865; Received at Ship Island, MS, on 4/15/1865. Transferred to Vicksburg, MS, for exchange on 5/1/1865; Exchanged at Camp Townsend, MS, on 5/6/1865.

Quarles, Thomas W. Pvt., 38th Alabama Infantry. Co. K. Enlisted: 5/14/1862 at Benton, AL. Age at enlistment: 21. Federal Rolls of Prisoners of War: Captured at Blakely, AL, on 4/9/1865; Received at Ship Island, MS, on 4/15/1865. Transferred to Vicksburg, MS, for exchange on 5/1/1865; Exchanged at Camp Townsend, MS, on 5/6/1865.

Quartermus, W.H. Pvt., 62nd Alabama Infantry. Co. I. Federal Rolls of Prisoners of War: Captured at Blakely, AL, on 4/9/1865; Received at Ship Island, MS, on 4/15/1865. Transferred to Vicksburg, MS, for exchange on 5/1/1865; Exchanged at Camp Townsend, MS, on 5/6/1865.

Quinn, R.L. Pvt., Tarrant's Artillery Battery. Federal Rolls of Prisoners of War: Captured at Blakely, AL, on 4/9/1865; Received at Ship Island, MS, on 4/15/1865. Transferred to Vicksburg, MS, for exchange on 5/1/1865; Exchanged at Camp Townsend, MS, on 5/6/1865.

Railey, Green Pvt., 21st Alabama Infantry. Co. C. Federal Rolls of Prisoners of War: Captured at Fort Gaines, AL, on 8/8/1864; Received at Ship Island, MS, from New Orleans, LA, on 10/25/1864. Exchanged on 1/4/1865.

Randall, B.F. (AKA Randle) Pvt., 62nd Alabama Infantry. Co. C. Enlisted: 3/8/1864. Federal Rolls of Prisoners of War: Captured at Blakely, AL, on 4/9/1865; Received at Ship Island, MS, on 4/15/1865. Transferred to Vicksburg, MS, for exchange on 5/1/1865; Exchanged at Camp Townsend, MS, on 5/6/1865.

Rasberry, R.H. Pvt., 42nd Alabama Infantry. Cos. G & I. Enlisted: 5/12/1862 at Mobile County, AL. Federal Rolls of Prisoners of War: Captured at Blakely, AL, on 4/9/1865; Received at Ship Island, MS, on 4/15/1865. Transferred to Vicksburg, MS, for exchange on 5/1/1865; Exchanged at Camp Townsend, MS, on 5/6/1865. Confederate Widows Pension Application dated 1908 on file at the Alabama Department of Archives and History. Target Name: Rasberry, M.C. County: Mobile.

Rawls, William S. (AKA Rawes) Pvt./Cpl., 38th Alabama Infantry. Co. I. Enlisted: 3/17/1862 at Fort Pillow, TN. Age at enlistment: 18. Federal Rolls of Prisoners of War: Captured at Spanish Fort, AL, on 4/8/1865; Received at Ship Island, MS, on 4/10/1865. Transferred to Vicksburg, MS, for exchange on 5/1/1865; Exchanged at Camp Townsend, MS, on 5/6/1865.

Ray, Christopher C. Pvt., 62nd Alabama Infantry. Co. D. Age at enlistment: 18. Federal Rolls of Prisoners of War: Captured at Blakely, AL, on 4/9/1865; Received at Ship Island, MS, on 4/15/1865. Transferred to Vicksburg, MS, for exchange on 5/1/1865; Exchanged at Camp Townsend, MS, on 5/6/1865.

Ray, Marion A. Pvt., 63rd Alabama Infantry. Co. A. Enlisted: 7/17/1864 at Butler County, AL. Rolls for 9/1864 through 10/1864: Present. Federal Rolls of Prisoners of War: Captured at Blakely, AL, on 4/9/1865; Received at Ship Island, MS, on 4/15/1865. Transferred to Vicksburg, MS, for exchange on 5/1/1865; Exchanged at Camp Townsend, MS, on 5/6/1865. Rolls of Prisoners of War, C.S.A: Surrendered at Citronelle, AL, on 5/4/1865; Paroled at Meridian, MS, on 5/13/1865. Residence at parole: Butler County, AL. Confederate Widows Pension Application dated 1915 on file at the Alabama Department of Archives and History. Target Name: Ray, Eliza C. County: Butler.

Rayburn, R. Pvt., 63rd Alabama Infantry. Co. F. Federal Rolls of Prisoners of War: Captured at Blakely, AL, on 4/9/1865; Received at Ship Island, MS, on 4/15/1865. Transferred to Vicksburg, MS, for exchange on 5/1/1865; Exchanged at Camp Townsend, MS, on 5/6/1865. Rolls of Prisoners of War, C.S.A: Surrendered at Citronelle, AL, on 5/4/1865; Paroled at Meridian, MS, on 5/11/1865. Residence at parole: Lowndes County, AL.

Rayfield, L.H. Pvt., 62nd Alabama Infantry. Co. D. Federal Rolls of Prisoners of War: Captured at Blakely, AL, on 4/9/1865; Received at Ship Island, MS, on 4/15/1865. Transferred to Vicksburg, MS, for exchange on 5/1/1865; Exchanged at Camp Townsend, MS, on 5/6/1865.

Rayford, John Pvt., 62nd Alabama Infantry. Co. B. Federal Rolls of Prisoners of War: Captured at Blakely, AL, on 4/9/1865; Received at Ship Island, MS, on 4/15/1865. Transferred to Vicksburg, MS, for exchange on 5/1/1865; Exchanged at Camp Townsend, MS, on 5/6/1865.

Reader, A.J. (AKA Reider) Pvt., 18th Alabama Infantry. Co. B. Enlisted: 12/1861 at Mobile, AL. Federal Rolls of Prisoners of War: Captured at Spanish Fort, AL, on 4/8/1865; Received at Ship Island, MS, on 4/10/1865. Transferred to Vicksburg, MS, for exchange on 5/1/1865; Exchanged at Camp Townsend, MS, on 5/6/1865.

Reaves, James (AKA Reeves, J.H.) Pvt., 62nd Alabama Infantry. Cos. C & K. Enlisted: 12/1863 at Coosa Bridge in AL. Federal Rolls of Prisoners of War: Captured at Blakely, AL, on 4/9/1865; Received at Ship Island, MS, on 4/15/1865. Transferred to Vicksburg, MS, for exchange on 5/1/1865; Exchanged at Camp Townsend, MS, on 5/6/1865.

Reddock, William M. (AKA Reddick) Pvt., 63rd Alabama Infantry. Cos. B & G. Enlisted: 5/16/1864 at Troy, AL. Age at enlistment: 17. Description at enlistment: Eyes: black. Hair: dark. Complexion: florid. Height: 5'2". Federal Rolls of Prisoners of War: Captured at Blakely, AL, on 4/9/1865; Received at Ship Island, MS, on 4/15/1865. Transferred to Vicksburg, MS, for exchange on 5/1/1865; Exchanged at Camp Townsend, MS, on 5/6/1865. Rolls of Prisoners of War, C.S.A: Surrendered at Citronelle, AL, on 5/4/1865; Paroled at Meridian, MS, on 5/13/1865. Residence at parole: Pike County, AL. Confederate Widows Pension Application on file at the Alabama Department of Archives and History: Target Name: Reddock, Mary. Application #33336. County: Geneva.

Reeves, J.M. Pvt., 38th Alabama Infantry. Co. G. Federal Rolls of Prisoners of War: Captured at Spanish Fort, AL, on 4/8/1865; Received at Ship Island, MS, on 4/10/1865. Transferred to Vicksburg, MS, for exchange on 5/1/1865; Exchanged at Camp Townsend, MS, on 5/6/1865.

Reeves, M.D. (AKA Reaves, McD.) Pvt., 21st Alabama Infantry. Cos. F & I. Federal Rolls of Prisoners of War: Captured at Fort Gaines, AL, on 8/8/1864; Received at Ship Island, MS, from New Orleans, LA, on 10/25/1864. Exchanged on 1/4/1865.

Reeves, William M. Pvt., 63rd Alabama Infantry. Cos. B & G. Enlisted: 5/16/1864 at Troy, AL. Age at enlistment: 17. Description at enlistment: Eyes: grey. Hair: light. Complexion: dark. Height: 5'3". Residence at enlistment: Pike County, AL. Rolls for 9/1864 through 10/1864: Absent, on Medical Examining Board furlough through 10/30/1864. Federal Rolls of Prisoners of War: Captured at Blakely, AL, on 4/9/1865; Received at Ship Island, MS, on 4/15/1865. Transferred to Vicksburg, MS, for exchange on 5/1/1865; Exchanged at Camp Townsend, MS, on 5/6/1865. Rolls of Prisoners of War, C.S.A: Surrendered at Citronelle, AL, on 5/4/1865; Paroled at Meridian, MS, on 5/13/1865. Residence at parole: Pike County, AL.

Reil, J.R. Pvt., 62nd Alabama Infantry. Co. D. Federal Rolls of Prisoners of War: Captured at Blakely, AL, on 4/9/1865; Received at Ship Island, MS, on 4/15/1865. Transferred to Vicksburg, MS, for exchange on 5/1/1865; Exchanged at Camp Townsend, MS, on 5/6/1865.

Reilly, J.C. (AKA Riley) Pvt./Nurse, 18th Alabama Infantry. Co. G. Enlisted: 7/1861. Federal Rolls of Prisoners of War: Captured at Spanish Fort, AL, on 4/8/1865; Received at Ship Island, MS, on 4/10/1865. Transferred to Vicksburg, MS, for exchange on 5/1/1865; Exchanged at Camp Townsend, MS, on 5/6/1865.

Renfroe, W.H. Pvt., 63rd Alabama Infantry. Co. F. Federal Rolls of Prisoners of War: Captured at Blakely, AL, on 4/9/1865; Received at Ship Island, MS, on 4/15/1865. Transferred to Vicksburg, MS, for exchange on 5/1/1865; Exchanged at Camp Townsend, MS, on 5/6/1865. Rolls of Prisoners of War, C.S.A: Surrendered at Citronelle, AL, on 5/4/1865; Paroled at Meridian, MS, on 5/11/1865. Description at parole: Eyes: blue. Hair: dark. Complexion: fair. Height: 5'4". Residence at parole: Butler County, AL.

Rentz, J. Pvt., 21st Alabama Infantry. Co. C. Enlisted: 2/1863 at Marengo County, AL. Federal Rolls of Prisoners of War: Captured at Fort Gaines, AL, on 8/8/1864; Received at Ship Island, MS, from New Orleans, LA, on 10/25/1864. Exchanged on 1/4/1865. Federal Rolls of Prisoners of War: Captured at Blakely, AL, on 4/9/1865; Received at Ship Island, MS, on 4/15/1865. Transferred to Vicksburg, MS, for exchange on 5/1/1865; Exchanged at Camp Townsend, MS, on 5/6/1865.

Reyburn, George W. (AKA Rayburn) Pvt., 38th Alabama Infantry. Co. B. Enlisted: Dalton, GA, for the duration of the war. Federal Rolls of Prisoners of War: Captured at Spanish Fort, AL, on 4/8/1865;

Received at Ship Island, MS, on 4/10/1865. Transferred to Vicksburg, MS, for exchange on 5/1/1865; Exchanged at Camp Townsend, MS, on 5/6/1865. Born: 1/4/1848 at Wilcox County, AL.

Rhode, G. (AKA Rhodes, Rode) Pvt./3rd Cpl., 63rd Alabama Infantry. Cos. G & K. Enlisted: 9/4/1864 at Walker County, AL. Rolls for 9/1864 through 10/1864: Present. Federal Rolls of Prisoners of War: Captured at Blakely, AL, on 4/9/1865; Received at Ship Island, MS, on 4/15/1865. Transferred to Vicksburg, MS, for exchange on 5/1/1865; Exchanged at Camp Townsend, MS, on 5/6/1865. Rolls of Prisoners of War, C.S.A: Surrendered at Citronelle, AL, on 5/4/1865; Paroled at Meridian, MS, on 5/13/1865. Residence at parole: Walker County, AL.

Rhodes, E. Pvt., 1st Alabama Artillery. Co. B. Federal Rolls of Prisoners of War: Captured at Fort Gaines, AL, on 8/8/1864; Received at Ship Island, MS, from New Orleans, LA, on 10/25/1864. Exchanged on 1/4/1865.

Rhodes, I.C. Cpl., 1st Alabama Artillery. Co. B. Federal Rolls of Prisoners of War: Captured at Fort Gaines, AL, on 8/8/1864; Received at Ship Island, MS, from New Orleans, LA, on 10/25/1864. Exchanged on 1/4/1865.

Richards, Thomas S. Capt., 6th Alabama Cavalry, F & S. Federal Rolls of Prisoners of War: Captured in Alabama on 3/25/1865; Received at Ship Island, MS. Transferred to Vicksburg, MS, for exchange on 4/28/1865; Confined at New Orleans, LA, on 4/30/1865. Exchanged at Camp Townsend, MS, on 5/6/1865.

Richardson, Samuel Pvt., 63rd Alabama Infantry. Co. A. Enlisted: 1/1/1864 at Tallapoosa County, AL. Age at enlistment: 16. Rolls for 1/1864 through 2/1864: Present. Rolls for 9/1864 through 10/1864: Present. Federal Rolls of Prisoners of War: Captured at Blakely, AL, on 4/9/1865; Received at Ship Island, MS, on 4/15/1865. Transferred to Vicksburg, MS, for exchange on 5/1/1865; Exchanged at Camp Townsend, MS, on 5/6/1865. Rolls of Prisoners of War, C.S.A: Surrendered at Citronelle, AL, on 5/4/1865; Paroled at Meridian, MS, on 5/13/1865. Residence at parole: Tallapoosa County, AL.

Richey, B.L. Pvt., Tarrant's Artillery Battery. Enlisted: 7/1863. Federal Rolls of Prisoners of War: Captured at Blakely, AL, on 4/9/1865; Received at Ship Island, MS, on 4/15/1865. Transferred to Vicksburg, MS, for exchange on 5/1/1865; Exchanged at Camp Townsend, MS, on 5/6/1865.

Riggs, Calvin Pvt., 8th Alabama Cavalry. Co. A. Federal Rolls of Prisoners of War: Captured at Blakely, AL, on 4/9/1865; Received at Ship Island, MS, on 4/15/1865. Transferred to Vicksburg, MS, for exchange on 5/1/1865; Exchanged at Camp Townsend, MS, on 5/6/1865.

Rikard, William Pvt., 62nd Alabama Infantry. Cos. E & H. Federal Rolls of Prisoners of War: Captured at Blakely, AL, on 4/9/1865; Received at Ship Island, MS, on 4/15/1865. Transferred to Vicksburg, MS, for exchange on 5/1/1865; Exchanged at Camp Townsend, MS, on 5/6/1865.

Riley, George Pvt., 62nd Alabama Infantry. Cos. B, I & K. Federal Rolls of Prisoners of War: Captured at Blakely, AL, on 4/9/1865; Received at Ship Island, MS, on 4/15/1865. Transferred to Vicksburg, MS, for exchange on 5/1/1865; Exchanged at Camp Townsend, MS, on 5/6/1865.

Riley, George W. Pvt., Lockhart's Battalion Infantry. Cos. B & I. Federal Rolls of Prisoners of War: Captured at Fort Gaines, AL, on 8/8/1864; Received at Ship Island, MS, from New Orleans, LA, on 10/29/1864. Exchanged on 1/4/1865.

Riley, J.A. Pvt., 63rd Alabama Infantry. Co. C. Enlisted: 8/1864 at Montgomery, AL. Rolls for 9/1864 through 10/1864: Present. Federal Rolls of Prisoners of War: Captured at Blakely, AL, on 4/9/1865, where he was wounded; Received at Ship Island, MS, on 4/15/1865. Transferred to Vicksburg, MS, for exchange on 5/1/1865; Exchanged at Camp Townsend, MS, on 5/6/1865. Rolls of Prisoners of War, C.S.A: Surrendered at Citronelle, AL, on 5/4/1865; Paroled at Meridian, MS, on 5/11/1865. Residence at parole: Russell County, AL. Confederate Pension Application on file at the Alabama Department of Archives and History. Target Name: Riley, J.A. Application #36707. County: Lee.

Riley, Martin (AKA W.) Cpl./Pvt., 63rd Alabama Infantry. Cos. G & K. Enlisted: 11/1863 at Centreville, AL. Federal Rolls of Prisoners of War: Captured at Blakely, AL, on 4/9/1865; Received at Ship Island, MS, on 4/15/1865. Transferred to Vicksburg, MS, for exchange on 5/1/1865; Exchanged at Camp Townsend, MS, on 5/6/1865. Confederate Pension Application dated 1907 on file at the Alabama Department of Archives and History. Target Name: Riley, Martin. County: Bibb.

Riley, Thomas J. Pvt., 63rd Alabama Infantry. Co. H. Federal Rolls of Prisoners of War: Captured at Blakely, AL, on 4/9/1865; Received at Ship Island, MS, on 4/15/1865. Transferred to Vicksburg, MS, for exchange on 5/1/1865; Exchanged at Camp Townsend, MS, on 5/6/1865. Rolls of Prisoners of War, C.S.A: Surrendered at Citronelle, AL, on 5/4/1865; Paroled at Meridian, MS, on 5/11/1865. Residence at parole: Jefferson County, AL. Confederate Widows Pension Application dated 1899 on file at the Alabama Department of Archives and History. Target Name: Riley, Sarah D. County: Jefferson.

Riley, W. 3rd Cpl./Pvt., 63rd Alabama Infantry. Cos. G & K. Enlisted: 5/11/1864 at Bibb County, AL. Rolls for 9/1864 through 10/1864: Present. Federal Rolls of Prisoners of War: Captured at Blakely, AL, on 4/9/1865; Received at Ship Island, MS, on 4/15/1865. Transferred to Vicksburg, MS, for exchange on 5/1/1865; Exchanged at Camp Townsend, MS, on 5/6/1865. Rolls of Prisoners of War, C.S.A: Surrendered at Citronelle, AL, on 5/4/1865; Paroled at Meridian, MS, on 5/13/1865. Residence at parole: Bibb County, AL.

Roberson, Raymond Pvt., 63rd Alabama Infantry. Co. B. Enlisted: 3/23/1864 at Montgomery, AL. Age at enlistment: 16. Rolls for 9/1864 through 10/1864: Present. Federal Rolls of Prisoners of War: Captured at Blakely, AL, on 4/9/1865; Received at Ship Island, MS, on 4/15/1865. Transferred to Vicksburg, MS, for exchange on 5/1/1865; Exchanged at Camp Townsend, MS, on 5/6/1865. On Register of U.S.A. General Hospital #2, Vicksburg, MS: Admitted from steamer on 5/3/1865 due to acute diarrhea; Returned to duty on 5/8/1865. Rolls of Prisoners of War, C.S.A: Surrendered at Citronelle, AL, on 5/4/1865; Paroled at 16th U.S. Army Corps Headquarters, Montgomery, AL, on 6/23/1865. Description at parole: Eyes: blue. Hair: light. Complexion: fair. Height: 5'0".

Roberts, George T. Pvt./Sgt., 6th Alabama Cavalry. Cos. A, B & E. Enlisted: 1861 at Abbeville, AL. Absent, with leave in Henry County, AL; Returned to duty 1/13/1862. Federal Rolls of Prisoners of War: Captured in Florida on 3/25/1865; Received at Ship Island, MS. Transferred to Vicksburg, MS, for exchange on 5/1/1865; Exchanged at Camp Townsend, MS, on 5/6/1865. Confederate Pension Application on file at the Alabama Department of Archives and History. Target Name: Roberts, George T. Application #13435. County: Henry. Also a Confederate Widows Pension Application on file dated 1920 at the Alabama Department of Archives and History. Target Name: Roberts, Sarah. County: Henry. Soldier also served with the 15th Alabama Infantry. Co.G.

Roberts, I.W. (AKA J.W.) Pvt./Sgt., 63rd Alabama Infantry. Co. E. Enlisted: 8/1/1864 at Montgomery, AL. Age at enlistment: 17. Description at enlistment: Eyes: blue. Hair: light. Complexion: fair. Rolls for 9/1864 through 10/1864: Absent, on 30 day furlough since 10/20/1864. Federal Rolls of Prisoners of War: Captured at Blakely, AL, on 4/9/1865; Received at Ship Island, MS, on 4/15/1865. Transferred to Vicksburg, MS, for exchange on 5/1/1865; Exchanged at Camp Townsend, MS, on 5/6/1865. Rolls of Prisoners of War, C.S.A: Surrendered at Citronelle, AL, on 5/4/1865; Paroled at Meridian, MS, on 5/13/1865. Residence at parole: Montgomery, AL.

Roberts, Richard Pvt., 21st Alabama Infantry. Cos. B & C. Federal Rolls of Prisoners of War: Captured at Fort Gaines, AL, on 8/8/1864; Received at Ship Island, MS, from New Orleans, LA, on 10/25/1864. Exchanged on 1/4/1865.

Robertson, D.G. Pvt., 21st Alabama Infantry. Co. B. Federal Rolls of Prisoners of War: Captured at Fort Gaines, AL, on 8/8/1864; Received at Ship Island, MS, from New Orleans, LA, on 10/25/1864. Exchanged on 1/4/1865.

Robertson, Daniel S. 4th Sgt./Pvt., 63rd Alabama Infantry. Co. B. Enlisted: 4/8/1864 at Montgomery County, AL. Age at enlistment: 17. Rolls for 9/1864 through 10/1864: Present. Federal Rolls of Prisoners of War: Captured at Blakely, AL, on 4/9/1865; Received at Ship Island, MS, on 4/15/1865. Transferred to Vicksburg, MS, for exchange on 5/1/1865; Exchanged at Camp Townsend, MS, on 5/6/1865. Rolls of Prisoners of War, C.S.A: Surrendered at Citronelle, AL, on 5/4/1865; Paroled at Meridian, MS, on 5/11/1865. Residence at parole: Chambers County, AL.

Robertson, John Thomas 1st Sgt., 6th Alabama Cavalry. Cos. F & H. Enlisted: 11/1862 at Montgomery, AL. Federal Rolls of Prisoners of War: Captured in Florida on 3/25/1865; Received at Ship Island, MS. Transferred to Vicksburg, MS, for exchange on 5/1/1865; Exchanged at Camp Townsend, MS, on 5/6/1865.

Robertson, Leonard J. (AKA L.B.) Pvt., 63rd Alabama Infantry. Co. A. Enlisted: 1/1/1864 at Macon County, AL. Age at enlistment: 16. Rolls for 1/1864 through 2/1864: Present. Rolls for 9/1864 through 10/1864: Present. Federal Rolls of Prisoners of War: Captured at Blakely, AL, on 4/9/1865; Received at Ship Island, MS, on 4/15/1865. Transferred to Vicksburg, MS, for exchange on 5/1/1865; Exchanged at Camp Townsend, MS, on 5/6/1865. Rolls of Prisoners of War, C.S.A: Surrendered at Citronelle, AL, on 5/4/1865; Paroled at Meridian, MS, on 5/13/1865. Residence at parole: Macon County, AL.

Robertson, T.L. (AKA T.D.) Pvt., Tarrant's Artillery Battery. Federal Rolls of Prisoners of War: Captured at Blakely, AL, on 4/9/1865; Received at Ship Island, MS, on 4/15/1865. Transferred to Vicksburg, MS, for exchange on 5/1/1865; Exchanged at Camp Townsend, MS, on 5/6/1865.

Robinson, A.K. (AKA Robison) Pvt./Cpl., 21st Alabama Infantry. Co. C. Enlisted: 1861. Federal Rolls of Prisoners of War: Captured at Fort Gaines, AL, on 8/8/1864; Received at Ship Island, MS, from New Orleans, LA, on 10/25/1864. Exchanged on 1/4/1865. Confederate Pension Application on file at the Alabama Department of Archives and History. Target Name: Robinson, A.K. Application #15814. County: Marengo.

Robinson, Daniel S. Sgt./Pvt., 63rd Albama Infantry. Co.B. Federal Rolls of Prisoners of War: Captured at Blakely, AL, on 4/9/1865; Received at Ship Island, MS, on 4/15/1865. Transferred to Vicksburg, MS, for exchange on 5/1/1865; Exchanged at Camp Townsend, MS, on 5/6/1865.

Robinson, M.E. (AKA W.E.) Pvt., Pelham Cadets. Cos. A & B. Federal Rolls of Prisoners of War: Captured at Blakely, AL, on 4/9/1865; Received at Ship Island, MS, on 4/15/1865. Died: 11/15/1864 at Ship Island, MS, due to typhoid fever. Buried: Ship Island, MS, Cemetery in Grave #21.

Robinson, W.A. (AKA U.A.) Pvt., 62nd Alabama Infantry. Co. D. Federal Rolls of Prisoners of War: Captured at Blakely, AL, on 4/9/1865; Received at Ship Island, MS, on 4/15/1865. Transferred to Vicksburg, MS, for exchange on 5/1/1865; Exchanged at Camp Townsend, MS, on 5/6/1865.

Robinson, Z.D. Pvt., 63rd Alabama Infantry. Co. I. Federal Rolls of Prisoners of War: Captured at Blakely, AL, on 4/9/1865; Received at Ship Island, MS, on 4/15/1865. Transferred to Vicksburg, MS, for exchange on 5/1/1865; Exchanged at Camp Townsend, MS, on 5/6/1865. Rolls of Prisoners of War, C.S.A: Surrendered at Citronelle, AL, on 5/4/1865; Paroled at Meridian, MS, on 5/13/1865. Residence at parole: Shelby County, AL.

Rodgers, Baine M. Pvt., 63rd Alabama Infantry. Cos. A & G. Federal Rolls of Prisoners of War: Captured at Blakely, AL, on 4/9/1865; Received at Ship Island, MS, on 4/15/1865. Transferred to Vicksburg, MS, for exchange on 5/1/1865; Exchanged at Camp Townsend, MS, on 5/6/1865.

Rodgers, Thomas (AKA Rogers) Pvt., 21st Alabama Infantry. Co. E. Federal Rolls of Prisoners of War: Captured at Fort Gaines, AL, on 8/8/1864; Received at Ship Island, MS, from New Orleans, LA, on 10/25/1864. Died: 11/29/1864 at Ship Island, MS, due to dysentery. Buried: Ship Island, MS, cemetery in Grave #50.

Roebuck, T.W. (AKA G.W.) Sgt., Lockhart's Battalion Infantry. Co. I. Federal Rolls of Prisoners of War: Captured at Fort Gaines, AL, on 8/8/1864; Received at Ship Island, MS, from New Orleans, LA, on 10/25/1864. Exchanged on 1/4/1865.

Rogers, Beasley Manly (AKA Baize) Pvt., 63rd Alabama Infantry. Co. G. Enlisted: 5/16/1864 at Troy, AL. Age at enlistment: 17. Description at enlistment: Eyes: grey. Hair: light. Complexion: fair. Height: 5'2". Residence at enlistment: Montgomery, AL. Rolls for 9/1864 through 10/1864: Present. Federal Rolls of Prisoners of War: Captured at Blakely, AL, on 4/9/1865; Received at Ship Island, MS, on 4/15/1865. Transferred to Vicksburg, MS, for exchange on 5/1/1865; Exchanged at Camp Townsend, MS, on 5/6/1865. Rolls of Prisoners of War, C.S.A: Surrendered at Citronelle, AL, on 5/4/1865; Paroled at Meridian, MS, on 5/13/1865. Residence at parole: Montgomery County, AL. Born: 4/3/1847 at High Log, Montgomery County, AL. Soldier is recorded on the 1907 Alabama Census of Confederate Veterans and Widows. Residence: Pike County, AL.

Rogers, M.W. Pvt., 63rd Alabama Infantry. Cos. B & G. Enlisted: 8/1/1864 at Pollard, AL. Age at enlistment: 17. Description at enlistment: Eyes: grey. Hair: light. Complexion: fair. Height: 5'5". Residence at enlistment: Covington County, AL. Rolls for 9/1864 through 10/1864: Absent, in hospital at Greenville, AL, since 9/29/1864. Federal Rolls of Prisoners of War: Captured at Blakely, AL, on 4/9/1865; Received at Ship Island, MS, on 4/15/1865. Transferred to Vicksburg, MS, for exchange on 5/1/1865; Exchanged at Camp Townsend, MS, on 5/6/1865. Rolls of Prisoners of War, C.S.A: Surrendered at Citronelle, AL, on 5/4/1865; Paroled at Meridian, MS, on 5/13/1865. Residence at parole: Pike County, AL.

Rogers, Robert L. Cpl./5th Sgt., 63rd Alabama Infantry. Co. G. Enlisted: 7/1/1864 at Troy, AL. Age at enlistment: 17. Description at enlistment: Eyes: grey. Hair: dark. Complexion: fair. Height: 5'6". Residence at enlistment: Pike County, AL. Rolls for 9/1864 through 10/1864: Present, appointed 5th Sgt. on 10/19/1864. Federal Rolls of Prisoners of War: Captured at Blakely, AL, on 4/9/1865; Received at Ship Island, MS, on 4/15/1865. Transferred to Vicksburg, MS, for exchange on 5/1/1865; Exchanged at Camp Townsend, MS, on 5/6/1865. Rolls of Prisoners of War, C.S.A: Surrendered at Citronelle, AL, on 5/4/1865; Paroled at Meridian, MS, on 5/13/1865. Residence at parole: Pike County, AL.

Rogers, T.J. Pvt., 62nd Alabama Infantry. Cos. E & K. Federal Rolls of Prisoners of War: Captured at Blakely, AL, on 4/9/1865; Received at Ship Island, MS, on 4/15/1865. Transferred to Vicksburg, MS, for exchange on 5/1/1865; Exchanged at Camp Townsend, MS, on 5/6/1865.

Rogers, W.J. Sgt./Pvt., 6th Alabama Cavalry. Cos. I. Federal Rolls of Prisoners of War: Captured in Alabama on 3/23/1865; Received at Ship Island, MS. Transferred to Vicksburg, MS, for exchange on 5/1/1865; Exchanged at Camp Townsend, MS, on 5/6/1865.

Rogers, William A. Pvt., 62nd Alabama Infantry. Cos. A & D. Federal Rolls of Prisoners of War: Captured at Blakely, AL, on 4/9/1865; Received at Ship Island, MS, on 4/15/1865. Transferred to Vicksburg, MS, for exchange on 5/1/1865; Exchanged at Camp Townsend, MS, on 5/6/1865.

Rolan, W.N. (AKA Rolen) Pvt., 62nd Alabama Infantry. Co. E. Federal Rolls of Prisoners of War: Captured at Blakely, AL, on 4/9/1865; Received at Ship Island, MS, on 4/15/1865. Transferred to Vicksburg, MS, for exchange on 5/1/1865; Exchanged at Camp Townsend, MS, on 5/6/1865.

Roland, A.U.B. (AKA A.W.B.) Pvt., Tarrant's Artillery Battery. Federal Rolls of Prisoners of War: Captured at Blakely, AL, on 4/9/1865; Received at Ship Island, MS, on 4/15/1865. Transferred to Vicksburg, MS, for exchange on 5/1/1865; Exchanged at Camp Townsend, MS, on 5/6/1865.

Rolins, J. Pvt., 62nd Alabama Infantry. Co. A. Federal Rolls of Prisoners of War: Captured at Blakely, AL, on 4/9/1865; Received at Ship Island, MS, on 4/15/1865. Transferred to Vicksburg, MS, for exchange on 5/1/1865; Exchanged at Camp Townsend, MS, on 5/6/1865.

Roper, Dick 2nd Lt./1st Lt., Pelham Cadets. Co. A. Federal Rolls of Prisoners of War: Captured at Fort Gaines, AL, on 8/8/1864; Received at Ship Island, MS, from New Orleans, LA, on 10/25/1864. Exchanged on 1/4/1865.

Ross, T.M. Pvt., 21st Alabama Infantry. Co. C. Federal Rolls of Prisoners of War: Captured at Fort Gaines, AL, on 8/8/1864; Received at Ship Island, MS, from New Orleans, LA, on 10/25/1864. Exchanged on 1/4/1865.

Rouse, Alonzo D. Pvt., 63rd Alabama Infantry. Co. B. Enlisted: 4/11/1864 at Montgomery, AL. Rolls for 9/1864 through 10/1864: Present. Federal Rolls of Prisoners of War: Captured at Blakely, AL, on 4/9/1865; Received at Ship Island, MS, on 4/15/1865. Transferred to Vicksburg, MS, for exchange on 5/1/1865; Exchanged at Camp Townsend, MS, on 5/6/1865. Rolls of Prisoners of War, C.S.A: Surrendered at Citronelle, AL, on 5/4/1865; Paroled at Meridian, MS, on 5/11/1865. Residence at parole: Montgomery County, AL.

Rowell, Andrew J. Pvt., 62nd Alabama Infantry. Co. D. Federal Rolls of Prisoners of War: Captured at Blakely, AL, on 4/9/1865; Received at Ship Island, MS, on 4/15/1865. Transferred to Vicksburg, MS, for exchange on 5/1/1865; Exchanged at Camp Townsend, MS, on 5/6/1865.

Rowell, Robert William Pvt./Sgt., 63rd Alabama Infantry. Co. A. Enlisted: 1/1/1864 at Macon County, AL. Age at enlistment: 16. Rolls for 1/1864 through 2/1864: Present. Rolls for 9/1864 through 10/1864: Present, sick in quarters. Federal Rolls of Prisoners of War: Captured at Blakely, AL, on 4/9/1865; Received at Ship Island, MS, on 4/15/1865. Transferred to Vicksburg, MS, for exchange on 5/1/1865; Exchanged at Camp Townsend, MS, on 5/6/1865. Rolls of Prisoners of War, C.S.A: Surrendered at Citronelle, AL, on 5/4/1865; Paroled at Meridian, MS, on 5/13/1865. Residence at parole: Macon County, AL. Buried: Notasulga, Macon County, AL.

Rowland, T.J. (AKA Rowlin) Cpl., 6th Alabama Cavalry. Cos. F & H. Federal Rolls of Prisoners of War: Captured in Florida on 3/25/1865; Received at Ship Island, MS. Transferred to Vicksburg, MS, for exchange on 5/1/1865; Exchanged at Camp Townsend, MS, on 5/6/1865.

Royal, F.A. Pvt., 8th Alabama Cavalry. Cos. B & C. Federal Rolls of Prisoners of War: Captured in Florida on 3/25/1865; Received at Ship Island, MS. Transferred to Vicksburg, MS, for exchange on 5/1/1865; Exchanged at Camp Townsend, MS, on 5/6/1865.

Rugeby, H.R. (AKA Rugely) Pvt., Rebel Home Guards. Federal Rolls of Prisoners of War: Captured in

Alabama on 3/24/1865; Received at Ship Island, MS. Transferred to Vicksburg, MS, for exchange on 5/1/1865; Exchanged at Camp Townsend, MS, on 5/6/1865.

Russell, Benjamin Pvt., 62nd Alabama Infantry. Co. D. Federal Rolls of Prisoners of War: Captured at Blakely, AL, on 4/9/1865; Received at Ship Island, MS, on 4/15/1865. Transferred to Vicksburg, MS, for exchange on 5/1/1865; Exchanged at Camp Townsend, MS, on 5/6/1865.

Russell, J.P. Pvt., 62nd Alabama Infantry. Co. K. Federal Rolls of Prisoners of War: Captured at Blakely, AL, on 4/9/1865; Received at Ship Island, MS, from New Orleans, LA, on 4/15/1865. Transferred to Vicksburg, MS, for exchange on 5/1/1865; Exchanged at Camp Townsend, MS, on 5/6/1865.

Russell, J.W. Pvt., 62nd Alabama Infantry. Co. C. Federal Rolls of Prisoners of War: Captured at Blakely, AL, on 4/9/1865; Received at Ship Island, MS, on 4/15/1865. Transferred to Vicksburg, MS, for exchange on 5/1/1865; Exchanged at Camp Townsend, MS, on 5/6/1865.

Russell W. Pvt./Sgt., 6th Alabama Cavalry. Cos. A & I. Federal Rolls of Prisoners of War: Captured in Florida on 3/25/1865; Received at Ship Island, MS. Transferred to Vicksburg, MS, for exchange on 5/1/1865; Exchanged at Camp Townsend, MS, on 5/6/1865.

Russoe, George (AKA Russo) Pvt., 18th Alabama Infantry. Co. __. Federal Rolls of Prisoners of War: Captured at Spanish Fort, AL, on 4/8/1865; Received at Ship Island, MS, on 4/10/1865. Disposition unknown.

Rutherford, Eli S. 1st Sgt./Pvt., 63rd Alabama Infantry. Co. C. Enlisted: 6/4/1864 at Russell County, AL. Age at enlistment: 17. Description at enlistment: Eyes: grey. Hair: light. Complexion: fair. Height: 5'5½". Residence at enlistment: Dover, Russell County, AL. Rolls for 9/1864 through 10/1864: Present. Federal Rolls of Prisoners of War: Captured at Blakely, AL, on 4/9/1865; Received at Ship Island, MS, on 4/15/1865. Transferred to Vicksburg, MS, for exchange on 5/1/1865; Exchanged at Camp Townsend, MS, on 5/6/1865. Rolls of Prisoners of War, C.S.A: Surrendered at Citronelle, AL, on 5/4/1865; Paroled at Meridian, MS, on 5/11/1865. Residence at parole: Russell County, AL.

Rutland, Z.T. Pvt., 63rd Alabama Infantry. Co. D. Enlisted: 8/28/1864 at Pollard, AL. Rolls for 9/1864 through 10/1864: Present. Federal Rolls of Prisoners of War: Captured at Blakely, AL, on 4/9/1865; Received at Ship Island, MS, on 4/15/1865. Transferred to Vicksburg, MS, for exchange on 5/1/1865; Exchanged at Camp Townsend, MS, on 5/6/1865. Rolls of Prisoners of War, C.S.A: Surrendered at Citronelle, AL, on 5/4/1865; Paroled at Meridian, MS, on 5/13/1865. Residence at parole: Barbour County, AL.

Rutledge, A.B. Pvt./Cpl., 62nd Alabama Infantry. Co. A. Federal Rolls of Prisoners of War: Captured at Blakely, AL, on 4/9/1865; Received at Ship Island, MS, on 4/15/1865. Transferred to Vicksburg, MS, for exchange on 5/1/1865; Exchanged at Camp Townsend, MS, on 5/6/1865.

Ryals, H. Pvt., 63rd Alabama Infantry. Co. F. Enlisted: 7/12/1864 at Lowndes County, AL. Age at enlistment: 17. Description at enlistment: Eyes: grey. Hair: light. Complexion: sallow. Height: 5'7". Residence at enlistment: Lowndes County, AL. Rolls for 9/1864 through 10/1864: Present. Federal Rolls of Prisoners of War: Captured at Blakely, AL, on 4/9/1865; Received at Ship Island, MS, on 4/15/1865. Transferred to Vicksburg, MS, for exchange on 5/1/1865; Exchanged at Camp Townsend, MS, on 5/6/1865. Rolls of Prisoners of War, C.S.A: Surrendered at Citronelle, AL, on 5/4/1865; Paroled at Meridian, MS, on 5/11/1865. Residence at parole: Lowndes County, AL.

Ryan, Joseph Henry Pvt., Tarrant's Artillery Battery. Enlisted: 12/1863. Federal Rolls of Prisoners of War: Captured at Blakely, AL, on 4/9/1865; Received at Ship Island, MS, on 4/15/1865. Transferred to Vicksburg, MS, for exchange on 5/1/1865; Exchanged at Camp Townsend, MS, on 5/6/1865. Wounded by being ran over by gun carriage and cannon in the march from Atlanta, GA, to Tennessee and injured his leg and chest near Gadsden, AL, east of Coosa river at age 17. Died: 7/26/1920 at his home in Alabama. Buried: Little Sandy Baptist Church located in Alabama. Married: Elnora Hinton on 1/10/1871. Wife born: 2/13/1851. Wife died: 11/8/1903. Number of children: 11. Post-war occupations: Merchant and Tax Collector at Tuscaloosa, AL.

Saddler, Thomas A. 3rd Sgt., 63rd Alabama Infantry. Co. H. Enlisted: 3/15/1864 at Elyton, AL. Age at enlistment: 17. Description at enlistment: Eyes: blue. Hair: dark. Complexion: dark. Rolls for 9/1864 through 10/1864: Absent, sick in hospital at Mobile, AL, since 10/8/1864. Federal Rolls of Prisoners of War: Captured at Blakely, AL, on 4/9/1865; Received at Ship Island, MS, on 4/15/1865. Transferred to Vicksburg, MS, for exchange on 5/1/1865; Exchanged at Camp Townsend, MS, on 5/6/1865. Rolls of Prisoners of War, C.S.A: Surrendered at Citronelle, AL, on 5/4/1865; Paroled at Meridian, MS, on 5/11/1865. Residence at parole: Jefferson County, AL.

Sale, R.A. (AKA Sales, N.A.) Pvt., 21st Alabama Infantry. Co. G. Federal Rolls of Prisoners of War: Captured at Fort Gaines, AL, on 8/8/1864; Received at Ship Island, MS, from New Orleans, LA, on 10/25/1864. Died: 11/22/1864 at Ship Island, MS, due to diarrhea. Buried: Ship Island, MS, Cemetery in Grave #24.

Sally, John Cpl., 21st Alabama Infantry. Co. C. Federal Rolls of Prisoners of War: Captured at Blakely, AL, on 4/9/1865; Received at Ship Island, MS, on 4/15/1865. Transferred to Vicksburg, MS, for exchange on 5/1/1865; Exchanged at Camp Townsend, MS, on 5/6/1865.

Salter, J.W. Pvt., 63rd Alabama Infantry. Co. F. Enlisted: 5/30/1864 at Montgomery, AL. Age at enlistment: 17. Description at enlistment: Eyes: dark. Hair: dark. Complexion: dark. Height: 5'9". Residence at enlistment: Coosa County, AL. Rolls for 9/1864 through 10/1864: Present, sick in quarters. Federal Rolls of Prisoners of War: Captured at Blakely, AL, on 4/9/1865; Received at Ship Island, MS, on 4/15/1865. Transferred to Vicksburg, MS, for exchange on 5/1/1865; Exchanged at Camp Townsend, MS, on 5/6/1865. Rolls of Prisoners of War, C.S.A: Surrendered at Citronelle, AL, on 5/4/1865; Paroled at Meridian, MS, on 5/11/1865. Residence at parole: Coosa County, AL.

Samples, William P. Cpl., 62nd Alabama Infantry. Co. E. Federal Rolls of Prisoners of War: Captured at Blakely, AL, on 4/9/1865; Received at Ship Island, MS, on 4/15/1865. Transferred to Vicksburg, MS, for exchange on 5/1/1865; Exchanged at Camp Townsend, MS, on 5/6/1865.

Sanders, Charles Pvt., 63rd Alabama Infantry. Co. G. Enlisted: 5/16/1864 at Troy, AL. Age at enlistment: 16. Description at enlistment: Eyes: blue. Hair: light. Complexion: fair. Height: 5'8". Residence at enlistment: Pike County, AL. Rolls for 9/1864 through 10/1864: Absent, on 10 day furlough since 9/10/1864. Federal Rolls of Prisoners of War: Captured at Blakely, AL, on 4/9/1865; Received at Ship Island, MS, on 4/15/1865. Transferred to Vicksburg, MS, for exchange on 5/1/1865; Exchanged at Camp Townsend, MS, on 5/6/1865. Rolls of Prisoners of War, C.S.A: Surrendered at Citronelle, AL, on 5/4/1865; Paroled at Meridian, MS, on 5/13/1865. Residence at parole: Pike County, AL.

Sanders, S. Pvt., Tarrant's Artillery Battery. Federal Rolls of Prisoners of War: Captured at Blakely, AL, on 4/9/1865; Received at Ship Island, MS, on 4/15/1865. Transferred to Vicksburg, MS, for exchange on 5/1/1865; Exchanged at Camp Townsend, MS, on 5/6/1865.

Sanders, William H. Pvt., 62nd Alabama Infantry. Co. D. Federal Rolls of Prisoners of War: Captured at Blakely, AL, on 4/9/1865; Received at Ship Island, MS, on 4/15/1865. Transferred to Vicksburg, MS, for exchange on 5/1/1865; Exchanged at Camp Townsend, MS, on 5/6/1865.

Sanderson, Blaney Pvt., 6th Alabama Cavalry. Co. E. Federal Rolls of Prisoners of War: Captured in Florida on 3/25/1865; Received at Ship Island, MS. Transferred to Vicksburg, MS, for exchange on 5/1/1865; Exchanged at Camp Townsend, MS, on 5/6/1865.

Sanford, Samuel G. Pvt., 63rd Alabama Infantry. Co. B. Enlisted: 7/20/1864 at Montgomery, AL. Rolls for 9/1864 through 10/1864: Present. Federal Rolls of Prisoners of War: Captured at Blakely, AL, on 4/9/1865; Received at Ship Island, MS, on 4/15/1865. Transferred to Vicksburg, MS, for exchange on 5/1/1865; Exchanged at Camp Townsend, MS, on 5/6/1865. Rolls of Prisoners of War, C.S.A: Surrendered at Citronelle, AL, on 5/4/1865; Paroled at Meridian, MS, on 5/11/1865. Residence at parole: Coosa County, AL.

Sangsing, J.D. Pvt., Tarrant's Artillery Battery. Federal Rolls of Prisoners of War: Captured at Blakely, AL, on 4/9/1865; Received at Ship Island, MS, on 4/15/1865. Transferred to Vicksburg, MS, for exchange on 5/1/1865; Exchanged at Camp Townsend, MS, on 5/6/1865.

Saunders, J.M. (AKA Sanders) Sgt., 21st Alabama Infantry. Co. H. Federal Rolls of Prisoners of War: Captured at Fort Gaines, AL, on 8/8/1864; Received at Ship Island, MS, from New Orleans, LA, on 10/25/1864. Exchanged on 1/4/1865.

Sawyer, Barney Pvt., Lockhart's Battalion Infantry. Co. H. Federal Rolls of Prisoners of War: Captured at Blakely, AL, on 4/9/1865; Received at Ship Island, MS, on 4/15/1865. Transferred to Vicksburg, MS, for exchange on 5/1/1865; Exchanged at Camp Townsend, MS, on 5/6/1865.

Sawyer, Thomas Johnston Pvt./Sgt., 63rd Alabama Infantry. Co. A. Enlisted: 7/10/1864 at Lowndes County, AL. Rolls for 9/1864 through 10/1864: Present. Federal Rolls of Prisoners of War: Captured at Blakely, AL, on 4/9/1865; Received at Ship Island, MS, on 4/15/1865. Transferred to Vicksburg, MS, for exchange on 5/1/1865; Exchanged at Camp Townsend, MS, on 5/6/1865. Rolls of Prisoners of War, C.S.A: Surrendered at Citronelle, AL, on 5/4/1865; Paroled at Meridian, MS, on 5/13/1865. Residence at parole: Lowndes County, AL. Confederate Pension Application dated 1915 on file at the Texas State Library and Archives. Target Name: Sawyer, Mrs.M.L. County: Brazos.

Scarborough, E. Pvt., 21st Alabama Infantry. Co. K. Federal Rolls of Prisoners of War: Captured at Fort Gaines, AL, on 8/8/1864; Received at Ship Island, MS, from New Orleans, LA, on 10/25/1864. Exchanged on 1/4/1865.

Scarborough, G.G. (AKA Scarbough) Pvt., 62nd Alabama Infantry. Co. C. Federal Rolls of Prisoners of War: Captured at Blakely, AL, on 4/9/1865; Received at Ship Island, MS, on 4/15/1865. Transferred to Vicksburg, MS, for exchange on 5/1/1865; Exchanged at Camp Townsend, MS, on 5/6/1865.

Scarborough, J. (AKA M.) Pvt., 21st Alabama Infantry. Cos. I & K. Federal Rolls of Prisoners of War: Captured at Fort Gaines, AL, on 8/8/1864; Received at Ship Island, MS, from New Orleans, LA, on 10/25/1864. Exchanged on 1/4/1865.

Scarborough, Jepp P. (AKA Scarbough) Pvt., 62nd Alabama Infantry. Co. K. Federal Rolls of Prisoners of War: Captured at Blakely, AL, on 4/9/1865; Received at Ship Island, MS, on 4/15/1865. Transferred to Vicksburg, MS, for exchange on 5/1/1865; Exchanged at Camp Townsend, MS, on 5/6/1865.

Schwin, W.E. (AKA Schrium) Pvt., 62nd Alabama Infantry. Co. G. Federal Rolls of Prisoners of War: Captured at Blakely, AL, on 4/9/1865; Received at Ship Island, MS, on 4/15/1865. Transferred to Vicksburg, MS, for exchange on 5/1/1865; Exchanged at Camp Townsend, MS, on 5/6/1865.

Scott, David M. Sgt./Pvt., 62nd Alabama Infantry. Cos. A & K. Federal Rolls of Prisoners of War: Captured at Blakely, AL, on 4/9/1865; Received at Ship Island, MS, on 4/15/1865. Transferred to Vicksburg, MS, for exchange on 5/1/1865; Exchanged at Camp Townsend, MS, on 5/6/1865.

Scott, Jeremiah Pvt., 21st Alabama Infantry. Co. B. Federal Rolls of Prisoners of War: Captured at Fort Gaines, AL, on 8/8/1864; Received at Ship Island, MS, from New Orleans, LA, on 10/25/1864. Exchanged on 1/4/1865.

Scott, W.T. Pvt., 63rd Alabama Infantry. Co. E. Enlisted: 8/8/1864 at Pollard, AL. Age at enlistment: 17. Description at enlistment: Eyes: blue. Hair: light. Complexion: fair. Rolls for 9/1864 through 10/1864: Absent, in hospital since 9/17/1864. Federal Rolls of Prisoners of War: Captured at Blakely, AL, on 4/9/1865; Received at Ship Island, MS, on 4/15/1865. Transferred to Vicksburg, MS, for exchange on 5/1/1865; Exchanged at Camp Townsend, MS, on 5/6/1865. Rolls of Prisoners of War, C.S.A: Surrendered at Citronelle, AL, on 5/4/1865; Paroled at Meridian, MS, on 5/13/1865. Residence at parole: Henry County, AL.

Scott, W.W. 2nd Sgt., 63rd Alabama Infantry. Co. D. Enlisted: 9/15/1864 at Blakely, AL. Rolls for 9/1864 through 10/1864: Absent, on 60 day Medical Examining Board furlough since 10/2/1864. Federal Rolls of Prisoners of War: Captured at Blakely, AL, on 4/9/1865; Received at Ship Island, MS, on 4/15/1865. Transferred to Vicksburg, MS, for exchange on 5/1/1865; Exchanged at Camp Townsend, MS, on 5/6/1865. Rolls of Prisoners of War, C.S.A: Surrendered at Citronelle, AL, on 5/4/1865; Paroled at Meridian, MS, on 5/13/1865. Residence at parole: Barbour County, AL.

Scott, Winfield Pvt., Tarrant's Artillery Battery. Enlisted: 7/22/1863 at Tuscaloosa, AL. Federal Rolls of Prisoners of War: Captured at Blakely, AL, on 4/9/1865; Received at Ship Island, MS, on 4/15/1865. Transferred to Vicksburg, MS, for exchange on 5/1/1865; Exchanged at Camp Townsend, MS, on 5/6/1865.

Seabrook, D.O. Pvt., 21st Alabama Infantry. Cos. C & D. Federal Rolls of Prisoners of War: Captured at Blakely, AL, on 4/9/1865; Received at Ship Island, MS, on 4/15/1865. Transferred to Vicksburg, MS, for exchange on 5/1/1865; Exchanged at Camp Townsend, MS, on 5/6/1865.

Seabrook, John P. (AKA J.R.) 1st Lt./2nd Lt., 38th Alabama Infantry. Co. I. Elected 2nd Lt. on 10/1/1863. Federal Rolls of Prisoners of War: Captured while wounded at Missionary Ridge, TN, on 11/25/1863; Admitted to U.S. 1st Division, 15th Army Corps Hospital, Chattanooga, TN, on 11/25/1863 due to comp. comm. fracture of right humerus that was amputated up to third humerus by Dr. Carhart. On G.F. Hospital Register, Army of Chattanooga, Chattanooga, TN: Admitted to Ward E on 2/1/1864 due to amputation of right arm; Sent to Chattanooga, TN, General Hospital on 2/15/1864. On Register of U.S.A. General Hospital, Nashville, TN: Admitted on 2/16/1864 due to amputation of right arm; Transferred to the U.S. Provost Marshal, Nashville, TN, on 2/19/1864. Received at the U.S.A. Military Prison, Louisville, KY, on 2/20/1864; Forwarded to Camp Chase, OH, on 3/2/1864. Received at Fort Delaware, DE, on 3/27/1864; Paroled at Fort Delaware, DE, on 9/14/1864. Transferred to Aiken's Landing, VA, for exchange on 9/18/1864; Received at Varina, VA, on 9/22/1864. On Register of C.S.A. General Hospital #4, Richmond, VA: Admitted on 9/21/1864 due to amputation of right arm; Returned to duty on 9/27/1864. Federal Rolls of Prisoners of War: Captured at Blakely, AL, on 4/9/1865; Received at Ship Island, MS, on 4/16/1865. Transferred to Vicksburg, MS, for exchange on 4/28/1865; Confined at New Orleans, LA, on 4/30/1865. Exchanged at Camp Townsend, MS, on 5/6/1865. Rolls of Prisoners of War, C.S.A: Surrendered at Citronelle, AL, on 5/4/1865; Paroled at Meridian, MS, on 5/11/1865.

Seale, H.T. Pvt., 62nd Alabama Infantry. Cos. C & G. Federal Rolls of Prisoners of War: Captured at Blakely, AL, on 4/9/1865; Received at Ship Island, MS, on 4/15/1865. Transferred to Vicksburg, MS, for exchange on 5/1/1865; Exchanged at Camp Townsend, MS, on 5/6/1865.

Seale, Littlepage B. Pvt., 21st Alabama Infantry. Co. C. Enlisted: 5/1861 at Rembert Hills, Marengo County, AL. Federal Rolls of Prisoners of War: Captured at Fort Gaines, AL, on 8/8/1864; Received at Ship Island, MS, from New Orleans, LA, on 10/25/1864. Exchanged on 1/4/1865.

Seals, A.T. Pvt., Tarrant's Artillery Battery. Federal Rolls of Prisoners of War: Captured at Blakely, AL, on 4/9/1865; Received at Ship Island, MS, on 4/15/1865. Transferred to Vicksburg, MS, for exchange on 5/1/1865; Exchanged at Camp Townsend, MS, on 5/6/1865.

Seals, James (AKA Seales) Pvt., 62nd Alabama Infantry. Co. E. Federal Rolls of Prisoners of War: Captured at Blakely, AL, on 4/9/1865; Received at Ship Island, MS, on 4/15/1865. Transferred to Vicksburg, MS, for exchange on 5/1/1865; Exchanged at Camp Townsend, MS, on 5/6/1865.

Seawell, Charles (AKA Seawall) Pvt., Lockhart's Battalion Infantry. Co. I. Federal Rolls of Prisoners of War: Captured at Fort Gaines, AL, on 8/8/1864; Received at Ship Island, MS, from New Orleans, LA, on 10/25/1864. Died: 11/10/1864 at Ship Island, MS, due to diarrhea. Buried: Ship Island, MS, Cemetery in Grave #16.

Seay, Thomas J. 1st Sgt./Sgt., Lockhart's Battalion Infantry. Co. K. Federal Rolls of Prisoners of War: Captured at Fort Gaines, AL, on 8/8/1864; Received at Ship Island, MS, from New Orleans, LA, on 10/25/1864. Exchanged on 1/4/1865.

Segars, James (AKA Segres) Pvt., 1st Alabama Artillery Battalion. Co. B. Federal Rolls of Prisoners of War: Captured at Fort Gaines, AL, on 8/8/1864; Received at Ship Island, MS, from New Orleans, LA, on 10/24/1864. Exchanged on 1/4/1865.

Seitz, W.J. Pvt., Tarrant's Artillery Battery. Federal Rolls of Prisoners of War: Captured at Blakely, AL, on 4/9/1865; Received at Ship Island, MS, on 4/15/1865. Transferred to Vicksburg, MS, for exchange on 5/1/1865; Exchanged at Camp Townsend, MS, on 5/6/1865.

Self, Elijah Pvt., 21st Alabama Infantry. Co. F. Federal Rolls of Prisoners of War: Captured at Fort Gaines, AL, on 8/8/1864; Received at Ship Island, MS, from New Orleans, LA, on 10/25/1864. Died: 11/23/1864 at Ship Island, MS, due to diarrhea. Buried: Ship Island, MS, Cemetery in Grave #38.

Self, William W. Pvt., 21st Alabama Infantry. Cos. E & F. Federal Rolls of Prisoners of War: Captured at Fort Gaines, AL, on 8/8/1864; Received at Ship Island, MS, from New Orleans, LA, on 10/25/1864. Exchanged on 1/4/1865.

Sells, James H. (AKA Sills) Pvt., 62nd Alabama Infantry. Cos. A & D. Federal Rolls of Prisoners of War: Captured at Blakely, AL, on 4/9/1865; Received at Ship Island, MS, on 4/15/1865. Transferred to Vicksburg, MS, for exchange on 5/1/1865; Exchanged at Camp Townsend, MS, on 5/6/1865.

Sewall, Charles Pvt., Lockhart's Battalion Infantry. Co. I. Federal Rolls of Prisoners of War: Captured at Fort Gaines, AL, on 8/8/1864; Received at Ship Island, MS, from New Orleans, LA, on 10/25/1864. Died: 11/10/1864 at Ship Island, MS, due to typhoid fever. Buried: Ship Island, MS, Cemetery in Grave #16.

Sewell, Alfred (AKA Sowell) Pvt., 38th Alabama Infantry. Co. E. Enlisted: 4/7/1862 at Mobile, AL. On List of Quartermaster Dept. Employees detailed by order of General Braxton Bragg: Transferred by

A.Q.M.J.M. Denison to Jonesboro, GA, A.Q.M. Donald McKenzie on 3/12/1864; Paid .75 cents per day. On extra duty as Teamster at Graysville, GA, from 6/18/1863 through 7/31/1863; Teamster from 8/1863 through 9/5/1863 at Calhoun, GA. Teamster from 12/1863 through 3/8/1864 at unknown location; Teamster at Abingdon, VA, from 3/9/1864 through 4/12/1864. Teamster at Bristol, TN, from 4/13/1864 through 4/30/1864. Federal Rolls of Prisoners of War: Captured at Blakely, AL, on 4/9/1865; Received at Ship Island, MS, on 4/15/1865. Transferred to Vicksburg, MS, for exchange on 5/1/1865; Exchanged at Camp Townsend, MS, on 5/6/1865.

Sexton, G.W. Pvt., 21st Alabama Infantry. Co. D. Federal Rolls of Prisoners of War: Captured at Blakely, AL, on 4/9/1865; Received at Ship Island, MS, on 4/15/1865. Transferred to Vicksburg, MS, for exchange on 5/1/1865; Exchanged at Camp Townsend, MS, on 5/6/1865.

Shadix, D. Pvt., 62nd Alabama Infantry. Co. F. Federal Rolls of Prisoners of War: Captured at Blakely, AL, on 4/9/1865; Received at Ship Island, MS, on 4/15/1865. Transferred to Vicksburg, MS, for exchange on 5/1/1865; Exchanged at Camp Townsend, MS, on 5/6/1865.

Sharp, J.J. Pvt., 62nd Alabama Infantry. Co. F. Federal Rolls of Prisoners of War: Captured at Blakely, AL, on 4/9/1865; Received at Ship Island, MS, on 4/15/1865. Transferred to Vicksburg, MS, for exchange on 5/1/1865; Exchanged at Camp Townsend, MS, on 5/6/1865.

Shearer, E.W. (AKA Sherrer) Sgt., 21st Alabama Infantry. Co. H. Federal Rolls of Prisoners of War: Captured at Fort Gaines, AL, on 8/8/1864; Received at Ship Island, MS, from New Orleans, LA, on 10/25/1864. Exchanged on 1/4/1865.

Sheffield, James Pvt., 38th Alabama Infantry. Co. B. Federal Rolls of Prisoners of War: Captured at Blakely, AL, on 4/9/1865; Received at Ship Island, MS, on 4/15/1865. Transferred to Vicksburg, MS, for exchange on 5/1/1865; Exchanged at Camp Townsend, MS, on 5/6/1865.

Sheffield, William H. Pvt., 38th Alabama Infantry. Co. B. Issued clothing on 11/2/1863 and 12/24/1863 while a patient at Atlanta, GA, Hospital. Federal Rolls of Prisoners of War: Captured at Blakely, AL, on 4/9/1865; Received at Ship Island, MS, on 4/15/1865. Transferred to Vicksburg, MS, for exchange on 5/1/1865; Exchanged at Camp Townsend, MS, on 5/6/1865.

Shelby, Thomas M. Pvt., 63rd Alabama Infantry. Co. A. Enlisted: 4/25/1864 at Montgomery, AL. Rolls for 9/1864 through 10/1864: Present, sick in quarters. On Register of Ross Hospital, Mobile, AL: Admitted on 9/2/1864 due to febris remittens; Returned to duty on 9/7/1864. Federal Rolls of Prisoners of War: Captured at Blakely, AL, on 4/9/1865; Received at Ship Island, MS, on 4/15/1865. Transferred to Vicksburg, MS, for exchange on 5/1/1865; Exchanged at Camp Townsend, MS, on 5/6/1865. Rolls of Prisoners of War, C.S.A: Surrendered at Citronelle, AL, on 5/4/1865; Paroled at Meridian, MS, on 5/13/1865. Residence at parole: Montgomery County, AL.

Shell, C.D. 5th Sgt./2nd Sgt., 63rd Alabama Infantry. Co. F. Enlisted: 3/9/1864 at Greenville, AL. Age at enlistment: 17. Description at enlistment: Eyes: grey. Hair: dark. Complexion: sallow. Height: 5'7". Residence at enlistment: Butler County, AL. Rolls for 9/1864 through 10/1864: Present. Federal Rolls of Prisoners of War: Captured at Blakely, AL, on 4/9/1865; Received at Ship Island, MS, on 4/15/1865. Transferred to Vicksburg, MS, for exchange on 5/1/1865; Exchanged at Camp Townsend, MS, on 5/6/1865. Rolls of Prisoners of War, C.S.A: Surrendered at Citronelle, AL, on 5/4/1865; Paroled at Meridian, MS, on 5/11/1865. Residence at parole: Butler County, AL.

Shepard, Joseph Cpl./Pvt., 62nd Alabama Infantry. Co. D. Federal Rolls of Prisoners of War: Captured at Blakely, AL, on 4/9/1865; Received at Ship Island, MS, on 4/15/1865. Transferred to Vicksburg, MS, for exchange on 5/1/1865; Exchanged at Camp Townsend, MS, on 5/6/1865.

Shepherd, J.A. Pvt., 63rd Alabama Infantry. Co. F. Enlisted: 3/9/1864 at Greenville, AL. Age at enlistment: 17. Description at enlistment: Eyes: blue. Hair: light. Complexion: fair. Height: 5'8". Residence at enlistment: Butler County, AL. Rolls for 9/1864 through 10/1864: Present. Federal Rolls of Prisoners of War: Captured at Blakely, AL, on 4/9/1865; Received at Ship Island, MS, on 4/15/1865. Transferred to Vicksburg, MS, for exchange on 5/1/1865; Exchanged at Camp Townsend, MS, on 5/6/1865. Rolls of Prisoners of War, C.S.A: Surrendered at Citronelle, AL, on 5/4/1865; Paroled at Meridian, MS, on 5/11/1865. Residence at parole: Butler County, AL.

Shepherd, John J. (AKA Shepped) Sgt./Pvt., 21st Alabama Infantry. Co. E. Federal Rolls of Prisoners of War: Captured at Fort Gaines, AL, on 8/8/1864; Received at Ship Island, MS, from New Orleans, LA, on 10/25/1864. Exchanged on 1/4/1865.

Sherbert, Samuel D. Pvt., 62nd Alabama Infantry. Cos. A & D. Federal Rolls of Prisoners of War: Captured at Blakely, AL, on 4/9/1865; Received at Ship Island, MS, on 4/15/1865. Transferred to Vicksburg, MS, for exchange on 5/1/1865; Exchanged at Camp Townsend, MS, on 5/6/1865.

Sherman, Charles K. Capt., Lockhart's Battalion Infantry. Co. __. Federal Rolls of Prisoners of War: Captured at Fort Gaines, AL, on 8/8/1864; Received at Ship Island, MS, from New Orleans, LA, on 10/25/1864. Transferred to Fort Columbus, New York Harbor, NY, in 11/1864.

Shins, D. (AKA Shehan) Pvt., 62nd Alabama Infantry. Co. H. Federal Rolls of Prisoners of War: Captured at Blakely, AL, on 4/9/1865; Received at Ship Island, MS, on 4/15/1865. Transferred to Vicksburg, MS, for exchange on 5/1/1865; Exchanged at Camp Townsend, MS, on 5/6/1865.

Shirley, C. Pvt., 62nd Alabama Infantry. Co. I. Federal Rolls of Prisoners of War: Captured at Blakely, AL, on 4/9/1865; Received at Ship Island, MS, on 4/15/1865. Transferred to Vicksburg, MS, for exchange on 5/1/1865; Exchanged at Camp Townsend, MS, on 5/6/1865.

Shirley, W.B. Pvt., Tarrant's Artillery Battery. Enlisted: 7/27/1863 at Tuscaloosa, AL. Federal Rolls of Prisoners of War: Captured at Blakely, AL, on 4/9/1865; Received at Ship Island, MS, on 4/15/1865. Transferred to Vicksburg, MS, for exchange on 5/1/1865; Exchanged at Camp Townsend, MS, on 5/6/1865.

Shoemaker, James H. Pvt., 21st Alabama Infantry. Co. E. Federal Rolls of Prisoners of War: Captured at Fort Gaines, AL, on 8/8/1864; Received at Ship Island, MS, from New Orleans, LA, on 10/25/1864. Exchanged on 1/4/1865.

Shorter, R.C. Pvt./Sgt., 1st Alabama Artillery Battalion. Co. B. Federal Rolls of Prisoners of War: Federal Rolls of Prisoners of War: Captured at Fort Gaines, AL, on 8/8/1864; Received at Ship Island, MS, from New Orleans, LA, on 10/24/1864. Exchanged on 1/4/1865.

Shortridge, George O. (AKA G.D.) Capt., 62nd Alabama Infantry. Co. I. Federal Rolls of Prisoners of War: Captured at Blakely, AL, on 4/9/1865; Received at Ship Island, MS, on 4/15/1865. Transferred to Vicksburg, MS, for exchange on 5/1/1865; Exchanged at Camp Townsend, MS, on 5/6/1865.

Showers, James B. (AKA Shows) Pvt., 62nd Alabama Infantry. Cos. A & D. Federal Rolls of Prisoners of War: Captured at Blakely, AL, on 4/9/1865; Received at Ship Island, MS, on 4/15/1865. Transferred to Vicksburg, MS, for exchange on 5/1/1865; Exchanged at Camp Townsend, MS, on 5/6/1865.

Shropshier, Robert Pvt., 62nd Alabama Infantry. Cos. A & D. Federal Rolls of Prisoners of War: Captured at Blakely, AL, on 4/9/1865; Received at Ship Island, MS, on 4/15/1865. Transferred to Vicksburg, MS, for exchange on 5/1/1865; Exchanged at Camp Townsend, MS, on 5/6/1865.

Shurer, J.G. Pvt., 62nd Alabama Infantry. Co. E. Federal Rolls of Prisoners of War: Captured at Blakely, AL, on 4/9/1865; Received at Ship Island, MS, on 4/15/1865. Transferred to Vicksburg, MS, for exchange on 5/1/1865; Exchanged at Camp Townsend, MS, on 5/6/1865.

Sidebottom, James H. Pvt., 62nd Alabama Infantry. Co. H. Federal Rolls of Prisoners of War: Captured at Blakely, AL, on 4/9/1865; Received at Ship Island, MS, on 4/15/1865. Transferred to Vicksburg, MS, for exchange on 5/1/1865; Exchanged at Camp Townsend, MS, on 5/6/1865.

Sigler, C.P. (AKA C.J.) Pvt., 62nd Alabama Infantry. Co. H. Federal Rolls of Prisoners of War: Captured at Blakely, AL, on 4/9/1865; Received at Ship Island, MS, on 4/15/1865. Transferred to Vicksburg, MS, for exchange on 5/1/1865; Exchanged at Camp Townsend, MS, on 5/6/1865.

Silliman, R.M.E. (AKA R. McF.) Pvt./Asst. Surg., 36th Alabama Infantry. F & S. Federal Rolls of Prisoners of War: Captured at Spanish Fort, AL, on 4/8/1865; Received at Ship Island, MS, on 4/10/1865. Transferred to Vicksburg, MS, for exchange on 4/28/1865; Confined at New Orleans, LA, on 4/30/1865. Exchanged at Camp Townsend, MS, on 5/6/1865.

Simmerly, T.D. Pvt., 63rd Alabama Infantry. Co. F. Enlisted: 5/30/1864 at Montgomery, AL. Age at enlistment: 17. Description at enlistment: Eyes: grey. Hair: dark. Complexion: ruddy. Height: 5'6". Residence at enlistment: Butler County, AL. Rolls for 9/1864 through 10/1864: Present. Federal Rolls of Prisoners of War: Captured at Blakely, AL, on 4/9/1865; Received at Ship Island, MS, on 4/15/1865. Transferred to Vicksburg, MS, for exchange on 5/1/1865; Exchanged at Camp Townsend, MS, on 5/6/1865. Rolls of Prisoners of War, C.S.A: Surrendered at Citronelle, AL, on 5/4/1865; Paroled at Meridian, MS, on 5/10/1865 while a patient in Quintard Hospital. Residence at parole: Butler County, AL.

Simmons, Andrew J. Pvt., 63rd Alabama Infantry. Co. A. Enlisted: 1/1/1864 at Tallapoosa County, AL. Age at enlistment: 16. Rolls for 1/1864 through 2/1864: Present. Rolls for 9/1864 through 10/1864: Present. Federal Rolls of Prisoners of War: Captured at Blakely, AL, on 4/9/1865; Received at Ship Island, MS, on 4/15/1865. Transferred to Vicksburg, MS, for exchange on 5/1/1865; Exchanged at Camp Townsend, MS, on 5/6/1865. Rolls of Prisoners of War, C.S.A: Surrendered at Citronelle, AL, on 5/4/1865; Paroled at Meridian, MS, on 5/13/1865. Residence at parole: Tallapoosa County, AL.

Simmons, H.W. Pvt., 62nd Alabama Infantry. Co. F. Federal Rolls of Prisoners of War: Captured at Blakely, AL, on 4/9/1865; Received at Ship Island, MS, on 4/15/1865. Transferred to Vicksburg, MS, for exchange on 5/1/1865; Exchanged at Camp Townsend, MS, on 5/6/1865.

Simmons, J.A. (AKA Simonds) Pvt., 6th Alabama Cavalry. Co. A. Federal Rolls of Prisoners of War: Captured in Florida on 3/25/1865; Received at Ship Island, MS. Transferred to Vicksburg, MS, for exchange on 5/1/1865; Exchanged at Camp Townsend, MS, on 5/6/1865.

Simmons, James R. Pvt., 62nd Alabama Infantry. Co. E. Federal Rolls of Prisoners of War: Captured at Blakely, AL, on 4/9/1865; Received at Ship Island, MS, on 4/15/1865. Transferred to Vicksburg, MS, for exchange on 5/1/1865; Exchanged at Camp Townsend, MS, on 5/6/1865.

Simmons, James R. Pvt., 63rd Alabama Infantry. Co. A. Enlisted: 3/1/1864 at Macon County, AL. Rolls for 9/1864 through 10/1864: Present. Federal Rolls of Prisoners of War: Captured at Blakely, AL, on 4/9/1865; Received at Ship Island, MS, on 4/15/1865. Transferred to Vicksburg, MS, for exchange on 5/1/1865; Exchanged at Camp Townsend, MS, on 5/6/1865. Rolls of Prisoners of War, C.S.A: Surrendered at Citronelle, AL, on 5/4/1865; Paroled at Meridian, MS, on 5/13/1865. Description at parole: Eyes: blue. Hair: light. Complexion: fair. Height: 5'8". Residence at parole: Macon County, AL.

Simms, Charles W. (AKA Sims, C.H.) 2nd Lt., Lockhart's Battalion Infantry. Co. H. Federal Rolls of Prisoners of War: Captured at Fort Gaines, AL, on 8/8/1864; Received at Ship Island, MS, from New Orleans, LA, on 10/25/1864. Exchanged on 1/4/1865.

Simon, H.H. Pvt., Lockhart's Battalion Infantry. Co. H. Federal Rolls of Prisoners of War: Captured at Fort Gaines, AL, on 8/8/1864; Received at Ship Island, MS, from New Orleans, LA, on 10/25/1864. Exchanged on 1/4/1865.

Simonton, J.H. (AKA Simonston) Cpl., 6th Alabama Cavalry. Co. E. Federal Rolls of Prisoners of War: Captured in Florida on 3/25/1865; Received at Ship Island, MS. Transferred to Vicksburg, MS, for exchange on 5/1/1865; Exchanged at Camp Townsend, MS, on 5/6/1865.

Simpson, John J. Pvt., 62nd Alabama Infantry. Co. E. Federal Rolls of Prisoners of War: Captured at Blakely, AL, on 4/9/1865; Received at Ship Island, MS, on 4/15/1865. Transferred to Vicksburg, MS, for exchange on 5/1/1865; Exchanged at Camp Townsend, MS, on 5/6/1865.

Simpson, Louis Pvt./Sgt., 21st Alabama Infantry. Cos. E & H. Federal Rolls of Prisoners of War: Captured at Fort Gaines, AL, on 8/8/1864; Received at Ship Island, MS, from New Orleans, LA, on 10/25/1864. Exchanged on 1/4/1865.

Simpson, R.T. Capt., 63rd Alabama Infantry. Co. F. Elected Capt. on 11/28/1864. Federal Rolls of Prisoners of War: Captured at Blakely, AL, on 4/9/1865; Confined one day at Spanish Fort, AL. Received at Ship Island, MS, on 4/16/1865; Transferred to Vicksburg, MS, for exchange on 4/28/1865. Confined at New Orleans, LA, on 4/30/1865; Exchanged at Camp Townsend, MS, on 5/6/1865. Rolls of Prisoners of War, C.S.A: Surrendered at Citronelle, AL, on 5/4/1865; Paroled at Meridian, MS, on 5/10/1865.

Sims, John M. 2nd Lt., 62nd Alabama Infantry. Co. E. Federal Rolls of Prisoners of War: Captured at Blakely, AL, on 4/9/1865; Received at Ship Island, MS, on 4/15/1865. Transferred to Vicksburg, MS, for exchange on 4/28/1865; Confined at New Orleans, LA, on 4/30/1865. Exchanged at Camp Townsend, MS, on 5/6/1865.

Sims, Reuben (AKA Simms) Pvt., 21st Alabama Infantry. Cos. I & K. Federal Rolls of Prisoners of War: Captured at Fort Gaines, AL, on 8/8/1864; Received at Ship Island, MS, from New Orleans, LA, on 10/25/1864. Exchanged on 1/4/1865.

Singleton, J.F. Pvt., 62nd Alabama Infantry. Cos. F & K. Federal Rolls of Prisoners of War: Captured at Blakely, AL, on 4/9/1865; Received at Ship Island, MS, on 4/15/1865. Transferred to Vicksburg, MS, for exchange on 5/1/1865; Exchanged at Camp Townsend, MS, on 5/6/1865.

Singleton, R. Pvt., 38th Alabama Infantry. Co. K. Federal Rolls of Prisoners of War: Captured at Spanish Fort, AL, on 4/8/1865; Received at Ship Island, MS, on 4/10/1865. Transferred to Vicksburg, MS, for exchange on 5/1/1865; Exchanged at Camp Townsend, MS, on 5/6/1865.

Skeen, J.M. Pvt., 63rd Alabama Infantry. Co. E. Enlisted: 8/9/1864 at Pollard, AL. Rolls for 9/1864 through 10/1864: Absent, in hospital since 9/25/1864. Federal Rolls of Prisoners of War: Captured at Blakely, AL, on 4/9/1865; Received at Ship Island, MS, on 4/15/1865. Transferred to Vicksburg, MS, for exchange on 5/1/1865. On Register of U.S.A. General Hospital #2, Vicksburg, MS: Admitted from steamer on 5/3/1865 due to acute diarrhea; Returned to duty on 5/10/1865. Age at admittance: 17.

Skinner, B.P. Pvt., 21st Alabama Infantry. Co. H. Federal Rolls of Prisoners of War: Captured at Fort Gaines, AL, on 8/8/1864; Received at Ship Island, MS, from New Orleans, LA, on 10/25/1864. Exchanged on 1/4/1865.

Skinner, N.B. Pvt., 62nd Alabama Infantry. Co. G. Federal Rolls of Prisoners of War: Captured at Blakely, AL, on 4/9/1865; Received at Ship Island, MS, on 4/15/1865. Transferred to Vicksburg, MS, for exchange on 5/1/1865; Exchanged at Camp Townsend, MS, on 5/6/1865.

Skinner, W.A. 2nd Lt., 63rd Alabama Infantry. Co. K. Enlisted: 10/1/1864 at Blakely, AL. Rolls for 9/1864 through 10/1864: Absent, on sick furlough through 11/12/1864; Elected 2nd Lt. on 10/1/1864. Federal Rolls of Prisoners of War: Captured at Blakely, AL, on 4/9/1865; Received at Ship Island, MS, on 4/16/1865; Transferred to Vicksburg, MS, for exchange on 4/28/1865. Confined at New Orleans, LA, on 4/30/1865; Exchanged at Camp Townsend, MS, on 5/6/1865. Rolls of Prisoners of War, C.S.A: Surrendered at Citronelle, AL, on 5/4/1865; Paroled at Meridian, MS, on 5/11/1865.

Skipper, J.A. Pvt., 21st Alabama Infantry. Cos. C & H. Federal Rolls of Prisoners of War: Captured at Fort Gaines, AL, on 8/8/1864; Received at Ship Island, MS, from New Orleans, LA, on 10/25/1864. Exchanged on 1/4/1865.

Skipper, J.B. Pvt., 21st Alabama Infantry. Cos. C & H. Federal Rolls of Prisoners of War: Captured at Fort Gaines, AL, on 8/8/1864; Received at Ship Island, MS, from New Orleans, LA, on 10/25/1864. Exchanged on 1/4/1865.

Skirlock, Daniel N. Pvt., 63rd Alabama Infantry. Co. A. Enlisted: 1/1/1864 at Tallapoosa County, AL. Age at enlistment: 17. Rolls for 1/1864 through 2/1864: Present. Rolls for 9/1864 through 10/1864: Present, sick in quarters. Federal Rolls of Prisoners of War: Captured at Blakely, AL, on 4/9/1865; Received at Ship Island, MS, on 4/15/1865. Transferred to Vicksburg, MS, for exchange on 5/1/1865; Exchanged at Camp Townsend, MS, on 5/6/1865. Rolls of Prisoners of War, C.S.A: Surrendered at Citronelle, AL, on 5/4/1865; Paroled at Meridian, MS, on 5/15/1865. Residence at parole: Tallapoosa County, AL.

Slaton, William (AKA Slayton) Cpl., 21st Alabama Infantry. Co. H. Federal Rolls of Prisoners of War: Captured at Fort Gaines, AL, on 8/8/1864; Received at Ship Island, MS, from New Orleans, LA, on 10/25/1864. Exchanged on 1/4/1865.

Slaughter, J.I. (AKA J.T.) Pvt., Lockhart's Battalion Infantry. Co. H. Federal Rolls of Prisoners of War: Captured at Fort Gaines, AL, on 8/8/1864; Received at Ship Island, MS, from New Orleans, LA, on 10/25/1864. Died: 11/3/1864 at Ship Island, MS, due to diarrhea. Buried: Ship Island, MS, Cemetery in Grave #9.

Slaughter, John B. Pvt., 6th Alabama Cavalry. Cos. C & D. Federal Rolls of Prisoners of War: Captured in Florida on 3/25/1865; Received at Ship Island, MS. Transferred to Vicksburg, MS, for exchange on 5/1/1865; Exchanged at Camp Townsend, MS, on 5/6/1865.

Smeller, J.L.H. Pvt., 62nd Alabama Infantry. Co. C. Federal Rolls of Prisoners of War: Captured at Blakely, AL, on 4/9/1865; Received at Ship Island, MS, on 4/15/1865. Transferred to Vicksburg, MS, for exchange on 5/1/1865; Exchanged at Camp Townsend, MS, on 5/6/1865.

Smith, A.T. Pvt., 62nd Alabama Infantry. Co. G. Federal Rolls of Prisoners of War: Captured at Blakely, AL, on 4/9/1865; Received at Ship Island, MS, on 4/15/1865. Transferred to Vicksburg, MS, for exchange on 5/1/1865; Exchanged at Camp Townsend, MS, on 5/6/1865.

Smith, A.W. (AKA Abb.) Pvt. 21st Alabama Infantry. Co. E. Federal Rolls of Prisoners of War: Captured at Fort Gaines, AL, on 8/8/1864; Received at Ship Island, MS, from New Orleans, LA, on 10/25/1864. Died: 12/13/1864 at Ship Island, MS, due to chronic dysentery. Buried: Ship Island, MS, Cemetery in Grave #86.

Smith, D. Pvt., 6th Alabama Cavalry. Cos. D & F.

Federal Rolls of Prisoners of War: Captured in Alabama on 3/24/1865; Received at Ship Island, MS. Transferred to Vicksburg, MS, for exchange on 5/1/1865; Exchanged at Camp Townsend, MS, on 5/6/1865.

Smith, George Pvt., 21st Alabama Infantry. Co. D. Federal Rolls of Prisoners of War: Captured at Blakely, AL, on 4/9/1865; Received at Ship Island, MS, on 4/15/1865. Transferred to Vicksburg, MS, for exchange on 5/1/1865; Exchanged at Camp Townsend, MS, on 5/6/1865.

Smith, H.(AKA J.H.) Pvt., Lockhart's Battalion Infantry. Co. K. Federal Rolls of Prisoners of War: Captured at Fort Gaines, AL, on 8/8/1864; Received at Ship Island, MS, from New Orleans, LA, on 10/25/1864. Died: 12/3/1864 at Ship Island, MS, due to dysentery. Buried: Ship Island, MS, Cemetery in Grave #59.

Smith, J. Pvt., 62nd Alabama Infantry. Co. D. Federal Rolls of Prisoners of War: Captured at Blakely, AL, on 4/9/1865; Received at Ship Island, MS, on 4/15/1865. Transferred to Vicksburg, MS, for exchange on 5/1/1865; Exchanged at Camp Townsend, MS, on 5/6/1865.

Smith, J.D. Pvt., 63rd Alabama Infantry. Co. A. Federal Rolls of Prisoners of War: Captured at Blakely, AL, on 4/9/1865; Received at Ship Island, MS, on 4/15/1865. Transferred to Vicksburg, MS, for exchange on 5/1/1865; Exchanged at Camp Townsend, MS, on 5/6/1865. Rolls of Prisoners of War, C.S.A: Surrendered at Citronelle, AL, on 5/4/1865; Paroled at Meridian, MS, on 5/13/1865. Residence at parole: Macon County, AL.

Smith, J.R. Pvt., Tarrant's Artillery Battery. Federal Rolls of Prisoners of War: Captured at Blakely, AL, on 4/9/1865; Received at Ship Island, MS, on 4/15/1865. Transferred to Vicksburg, MS, for exchange on 5/1/1865; Exchanged at Camp Townsend, MS, on 5/6/1865.

Smith, J.T. Pvt., 38th Alabama Infantry. Co. E. Federal Rolls of Prisoners of War: Captured at Blakely, AL, on 4/9/1865; Received at Ship Island, MS, on 4/15/1865. Transferred to Vicksburg, MS, for exchange on 5/1/1865; Exchanged at Camp Townsend, MS, on 5/6/1865.

Smith, J.T. Pvt., Tarrant's Artillery Battery. Federal Rolls of Prisoners of War: Captured at Blakely, AL, on 4/9/1865; Received at Ship Island, MS, on 4/15/1865. Transferred to Vicksburg, MS, for exchange on 5/1/1865; Exchanged at Camp Townsend, MS, on 5/6/1865.

Smith, James J. Pvt., 21st Alabama Infantry. Co. H. Federal Rolls of Prisoners of War: Captured at Fort Gaines, AL, on 8/8/1864; Received at Ship Island, MS, from New Orleans, LA, on 10/25/1864. Exchanged on 1/4/1865.

Smith, John C. Cpl., 62nd Alabama Infantry. Cos. A & D. Federal Rolls of Prisoners of War: Captured at Blakely, AL, on 4/9/1865; Received at Ship Island, MS, on 4/15/1865. Transferred to Vicksburg, MS, for exchange on 5/1/1865; Exchanged at Camp Townsend, MS, on

Smith, John H. Pvt./Cpl., 38th Alabama Infantry. Cos. E & K. Federal Rolls of Prisoners of War: Captured at Blakely, AL, on 4/9/1865; Received at Ship Island, MS, on 4/15/1865. Transferred to Vicksburg, MS, for exchange on 5/1/1865; Exchanged at Camp Townsend, MS, on 5/6/1865.

Smith, John H. Pvt., 1st Alabama Artillery Battalion. Co. G. Federal Rolls of Prisoners of War: Captured at Fort Gaines, AL, on 8/8/1864; Received at Ship Island, MS, from New Orleans, LA, on 10/24/1864. Exchanged on 1/4/1865.

Smith, Joseph W. Cpl., 21st Alabama Infantry. Co. G. Federal Rolls of Prisoners of War: Captured at Fort Gaines, AL, on 8/8/1864; Received at Ship Island, MS, from New Orleans, LA, on 10/25/1864. Exchanged on 1/4/1865.

Smith, Neil Pvt., 63rd Alabama Infantry. Co. G. Enlisted: 5/16/1864 at Troy, AL. Age at enlistment: 17. Description at enlistment: Eyes: blue. Hair: dark. Complexion: dark. Height: 5'10". Residence at enlistment: Pike County, AL. Rolls for 9/1864 through 10/1864: Present. Federal Rolls of Prisoners of War: Captured at Blakely, AL, on 4/9/1865; Received at Ship Island, MS, on 4/15/1865. Transferred to Vicksburg, MS, for exchange on 5/1/1865; Exchanged at Camp Townsend, MS, on 5/6/1865. Rolls of Prisoners of War, C.S.A: Surrendered at Citronelle, AL, on 5/4/1865; Paroled at Meridian, MS, on 5/13/1865. Residence at parole: Pike County, AL.

Smith, R.A. Pvt., 21st Alabama Infantry. Co. H. Federal Rolls of Prisoners of War: Captured at Fort Gaines, AL, on 8/8/1864; Received at Ship Island, MS, from New Orleans, LA, on 10/25/1864. Died: 12/2/1864 at Ship Island, MS, due to typhoid fever. Buried: Ship Island, MS, Cemetery in Grave #58.

Smith, S.T. Pvt., 6th Alabama Cavalry. Co. C. Federal Rolls of Prisoners of War: Captured in Florida on 3/25/1865; Received at Ship Island, MS. Transferred to Vicksburg, MS, for exchange on 5/1/1865; Exchanged at Camp Townsend, MS, on 5/6/1865.

Smith, Seaborn Pvt./2nd Cpl., 63rd Alabama Infantry. Co. G. Enlisted: 5/16/1864 at Troy, AL. Age at enlistment: 17. Description at enlistment: Eyes: blue. Hair: light. Complexion: fair. Height: 5'10". Residence at enlistment: Montgomery County, AL. Rolls for 9/1864 through 10/1864: Present, reduced to Pvt. by Regimental Court Martial on 10/19/1864. Federal Rolls of Prisoners of War: Captured at Blakely, AL, on 4/9/1865; Received at Ship Island, MS, on 4/15/1865. Transferred to Vicksburg, MS, for exchange on 5/1/1865. Rolls of Prisoners of War, C.S.A: Surrendered at Citronelle, AL, on 5/4/1865; Paroled at Meridian, MS, on 5/13/1865. Residence at parole: Montgomery County, AL.

Smith, W.F. (AKA W.T.) Pvt., Lockhart's Battalion Infantry. Co. F. Federal Rolls of Prisoners of War: Captured at Fort Gaines, AL, on 8/8/1864; Received at Ship Island, MS, from New Orleans, LA, on 12/13/1864. Exchanged on 1/4/1865.

Smith, William H. Pvt., 38th Alabama Infantry. Co. E. Enlisted: 4/7/1862 at Mobile, AL. Age at enlistment: 39. Federal Rolls of Prisoners of War: Captured at Blakely, AL, on 4/9/1865; Received at Ship Island, MS, on 4/15/1865. Disposition unknown.

Smith, Z.T. Pvt., 63rd Alabama Infantry. Co. I. Enlisted: 4/16/1864 at Talladega, AL. Rolls for 9/1864 through 10/1864: Absent, on 30 day furlough since 9/29/1864. Federal Rolls of Prisoners of War: Captured at Blakely, AL, on 4/9/1865; Received at Ship Island, MS, on 4/15/1865. Transferred to Vicksburg,

MS, for exchange on 5/1/1865; Exchanged at Camp Townsend, MS, on 5/6/1865. Rolls of Prisoners of War, C.S.A: Surrendered at Citronelle, AL, on 5/4/1865; Paroled at Meridian, MS, on 5/13/1865. Residence at parole: Randolph County, AL.

Smitherman, William J. (AKA J.W.) Pvt., 62nd Alabama Infantry. Co. D. Federal Rolls of Prisoners of War: Captured at Blakely, AL, on 4/9/1865; Received at Ship Island, MS, on 4/15/1865. Transferred to Vicksburg, MS, for exchange on 5/1/1865; Exchanged at Camp Townsend, MS, on 5/6/1865.

Smithey, Robert Pvt., 21st Alabama Infantry. Cos. C & E. Federal Rolls of Prisoners of War: Captured at Fort Gaines, AL, on 8/8/1864; Received at Ship Island, MS, from New Orleans, LA, on 10/25/1864. Exchanged on 1/4/1864.

Smoke, Robert (AKA Smoky) Pvt., 8th Alabama Cavalry. Co. B. Federal Rolls of Prisoners of War: Captured in Florida on 3/25/1865; Received at Ship Island, MS. Transferred to Vicksburg, MS, for exchange on 5/1/1865; Exchanged at Camp Townsend, MS, on 5/6/1865.

Snider, Francis M. Pvt., 63rd Alabama Infantry. Co. G. Enlisted: 5/18/1864 at Troy, AL. Age at enlistment: 17. Description at enlistment: Eyes: grey. Hair: dark. Complexion: florid. Height: 5'0". Residence at enlistment: Pike County, AL. Rolls for 9/1864 through 10/1864: Present. Federal Rolls of Prisoners of War: Captured at Blakely, AL, on 4/9/1865; Received at Ship Island, MS, on 4/15/1865. Transferred to Vicksburg, MS, for exchange on 5/1/1865; Exchanged at Camp Townsend, MS, on 5/6/1865. Rolls of Prisoners of War, C.S.A: Surrendered at Citronelle, AL, on 5/4/1865; Paroled at Meridian, MS, on 5/13/1865. Residence at parole: Pike County, AL.

Snow, William A. Pvt., 21st Alabama Infantry. Co. E. Federal Rolls of Prisoners of War: Captured at Fort Gaines, AL, on 8/8/1864; Received at Ship Island, MS, from New Orleans, LA, on 10/25/1864. Exchanged on 1/4/1865.

Soloman, James A. Pvt., 21st Alabama Infantry. Co. E. Federal Rolls of Prisoners of War: Captured at Fort Gaines, AL, on 8/8/1864; Received at Ship Island, MS, from New Orleans, LA, on 10/25/1864. Exchanged on 1/4/1865.

Sorrel, Green B.W. Pvt., 63rd Alabama Infantry. Co. A. Enlisted: 4/8/1864 at Chambers County, AL. Rolls for 9/1864 through 10/1864: Present, sick in quarters. On Register of Ross Hospital, Mobile, AL: Admitted on 9/2/1864 due to febris remittens; Returned to duty on 9/8/1864. Federal Rolls of Prisoners of War: Captured at Blakely, AL, on 4/9/1865; Received at Ship Island, MS, on 4/15/1865. Transferred to Vicksburg, MS, for exchange on 5/1/1865; Exchanged at Camp Townsend, MS, on 5/6/1865. Rolls of Prisoners of War, C.S.A: Surrendered at Citronelle, AL, on 5/4/1865; Paroled at Meridian, MS, on 5/13/1865. Residence at parole: Chambers County, AL.

Sowell, Alfred Pvt., 38th Alabama Infantry. Co. E. Detailed as a Teamster. Age at enlistment: 29. Federal Rolls of Prisoners of War: Captured at Blakely, AL, on 4/9/1865; Recevied at Ship Island, MS, on 4/15/1865. Transferred for Vicksburg, MS, for exchange on 5/1/1865; Exchanged at Camp Townsend, MS, on 5/6/1865.

Speigner, M. (AKA Spigner) Pvt., 21st Alabama Infantry. Co. D. Federal Rolls of Prisoners of War: Captured at Blakely, AL, on 4/9/1865; Received at Ship Island, MS, on 4/15/1865. Transferred to Vicksburg, MS, for exchange on 5/1/1865; Exchanged at Camp Townsend, MS, on 5/6/1865.

Spencer, Julius P. Pvt., 63rd Alabama Infantry. Co. D. Enlisted: 7/30/1864 at Macon County, AL. Age at enlistment: 17. Description at enlistment: Eyes: grey. Hair: light. Complexion: fair. Height: 4'6". Residence at enlistment: Clayton, AL. Rolls for 9/1864 through 10/1864: Absent, on 60 day Medical Examining Board furlough since 9/20/1864. Federal Rolls of Prisoners of War: Captured at Blakely, AL, on 4/9/1865; Received at Ship Island, MS, on 4/15/1865. Transferred to Vicksburg, MS, for exchange on 5/1/1865; Exchanged at Camp Townsend, MS, on 5/6/1865. Rolls of Prisoners of War, C.S.A: Surrendered at Citronelle, AL, on 5/4/1865; Paroled at Meridian, MS, on 5/13/1865. Residence at parole: Barbour County, AL.

Spencer, William O. Asst. Surg., Tarrant's Artillery Battery. F & S. Federal Rolls of Prisoners of War: Captured at Blakely, AL, on 4/9/1865; Received at Ship Island, MS, on 4/15/1865. Transferred to Vicksburg, MS, for exchange on 4/28/1865; Confined at New Orleans, LA, on 4/30/1865. Exchanged at Camp Townsend, MS, on 5/6/1865.

Spigner, Samuel Pvt., Tarrant's Artillery Battery. Federal Rolls of Prisoners of War: Captured at Blakely, AL, on 4/9/1865; Received at Ship Island, MS, on 4/15/1865. Transferred to Vicksburg, MS, for exchange on 5/1/1865; Exchanged at Camp Townsend, MS, on 5/6/1865.

Spiller, J.W. Pvt., 62nd Alabama Infantry. Co. F. Federal Rolls of Prisoners of War: Captured at Blakely, AL, on 4/9/1865; Received at Ship Island, MS, on 4/15/1865. Transferred to Vicksburg, MS, for exchange on 5/1/1865; Exchanged at Camp Townsend, MS, on 5/6/1865.

Spinks, W.H. Sgt., Lockhart's Battalion Infantry. Co. __. Federal Rolls of Prisoners of War: Captured at Fort Gaines, AL, on 8/8/1864; Received at Ship Island, MS, from New Orleans, LA, on 10/25/1864. Exchanged on 1/4/1865.

Spivey, William Pvt., Tarrant's Artillery Battery. Federal Rolls of Prisoners of War: Captured at Blakely, AL, on 4/9/1865; Received at Ship Island, MS, on 4/15/1865. Transferred to Vicksburg, MS, for exchange on 5/1/1865; Exchanged at Camp Townsend, MS, on 5/6/1865.

Sprayberry, Jerry P. (AKA Sprabury) Pvt., 62nd Alabama Infantry. Co. G. Federal Rolls of Prisoners of War: Captured at Blakely, AL, on 4/9/1865; Received at Ship Island, MS, on 4/15/1865. Transferred to Vicksburg, MS, for exchange on 5/1/1865; Exchanged at Camp Townsend, MS, on 5/6/1865.

Springer, J. Pvt., Tarrant's Artillery Battery. Federal Rolls of Prisoners of War: Captured at Blakely, AL, on 4/9/1865; Received at Ship Island, MS, on 4/15/1865. Transferred to Vicksburg, MS, for exchange on 5/1/1865; Exchanged at Camp Townsend, MS, on 5/6/1865.

Stabler, Malachi Pvt., 38th Alabama Infantry. Co. A. Federal Rolls of Prisoners of War: Captured at Spanish Fort, AL, on 4/8/1865; Received at Ship Island,

MS, on 4/10/1865. Transferred to Vicksburg, MS, for exchange on 5/1/1865; Exchanged at Camp Townsend, MS, on 5/6/1865.

Staggers, D.J. Pvt., 6th Alabama Cavalry. Co. A. Federal Rolls of Prisoners of War: Captured in Florida on 3/25/1865; Received at Ship Island, MS. Transferred to Vicksburg, MS, for exchange on 5/1/1865; Exchanged at Camp Townsend, MS, on 5/6/1865.

Staller, M.H. Pvt., 21st Alabama Infantry. Co. G. Federal Rolls of Prisoners of War: Captured at Fort Gaines, AL, on 8/8/1864; Received at Ship Island, MS, from New Orleans, LA, on 10/25/1864. Exchanged on 1/4/1865.

Stallworth, William M., Jr. Pvt., 38th Alabama Infantry. Co. E. Enlisted: 4/7/1862 at Mobile, AL. Age at enlistment: 22. Federal Rolls of Prisoners of War: Captured at Blakely, AL, on 4/9/1865; Received at Ship Island, MS, on 4/15/1865. Transferred to Vicksburg, MS, for exchange on 5/1/1865; Exchanged at Camp Townsend, MS, on 5/6/1865.

Stanfield, James Pvt., Hundon's Bat.. Co. __. Died: 3/15/1865 at Ship Island, MS, due to phthisis pulmonary. Buried: Ship Island, MS, Cemetery in Grave #140.

Stanfield, William H. Cpl./Pvt., 62nd Alabama Infantry. Co. G. Federal Rolls of Prisoners of War: Captured at Blakely, AL, on 4/9/1865; Received at Ship Island, MS, on 4/15/1865. Transferred to Vicksburg, MS, for exchange on 5/1/1865; Exchanged at Camp Townsend, MS, on 5/6/1865.

Stanley, A.T. (AKA Stanly) Pvt., 63rd Alabama Infantry. Co. F. Enlisted: 5/30/1864 at Montgomery, AL. Age at enlistment: 17. Description at enlistment: Eyes: blue. Hair: light. Complexion: fair. Height: 5'7". Residence at enlistment: Coosa County, AL. Rolls for 9/1864 through 10/1864: Present, sick. Federal Rolls of Prisoners of War: Captured at Blakely, AL, on 4/9/1865; Received at Ship Island, MS, on 4/15/1865. Transferred to Vicksburg, MS, for exchange on 5/1/1865; Exchanged at Camp Townsend, MS, on 5/6/1865. Rolls of Prisoners of War, C.S.A: Surrendered at Citronelle, AL, on 5/4/1865; Paroled at Meridian, MS, on 5/11/1865. Residence at parole: Coosa County, AL.

Stanley, J.A. Pvt., 63rd Alabama Infantry. Co. G. Federal Rolls of Prisoners of War: Captured at Blakely, AL, on 4/9/1865; Received at Ship Island, MS, on 4/15/1865. Transferred to Vicksburg, MS, for exchange on 5/1/1865; Exchanged at Camp Townsend, MS, on 5/6/1865. Rolls of Prisoners of War, C.S.A: Surrendered at Citronelle, AL, on 5/4/1865; Paroled at Meridian, MS, on 5/13/1865. Residence at parole: Pike County, AL.

Stansel, Jesse P. (AKA Stancel) Pvt., 62nd Alabama Infantry. Co. G. Federal Rolls of Prisoners of War: Captured at Blakely, AL, on 4/9/1865; Received at Ship Island, MS, on 4/15/1865. Transferred to Vicksburg, MS, for exchange on 5/1/1865; Exchanged at Camp Townsend, MS, on 5/6/1865.

Stansel, T.J. Pvt., 62nd Alabama Infantry. Co. G. Federal Rolls of Prisoners of War: Captured at Blakely, AL, on 4/9/1865; Received at Ship Island, MS, on 4/15/1865. Transferred to Vicksburg, MS, for exchange on 5/1/1865; Exchanged at Camp Townsend, MS, on 5/6/1865.

Staples, T.A. Pvt., 62nd Alabama Infantry. Co. D. Federal Rolls of Prisoners of War: Captured at Blakely, AL, on 4/9/1865; Received at Ship Island, MS, on 4/15/1865. Transferred to Vicksburg, MS, for exchange on 5/1/1865; Exchanged at Camp Townsend, MS, on 5/6/1865.

Stark, T.J. Pvt., 62nd Alabama Infantry. Co. C. Federal Rolls of Prisoners of War: Captured at Blakely, AL, on 4/9/1865; Received at Ship Island, MS, on 4/15/1865. Transferred to Vicksburg, MS, for exchange on 5/1/1865; Exchanged at Camp Townsend, MS, on 5/6/1865.

Starr, William Cpl., 21st Alabama Infantry. Cos. B & K. Federal Rolls of Prisoners of War: Captured at Fort Gaines, AL, on 8/8/1864; Received at Ship Island, MS, from New Orleans, LA, on 10/25/1864. Exchanged on 1/4/1865.

Steele, W.B. Pvt., 21st Alabama Infantry. Co. H. Federal Rolls of Prisoners of War: Captured at Fort Gaines, AL, on 8/8/1864; Received at Ship Island, MS, from New Orleans, LA, on 10/25/1864. Exchanged on 1/4/1865.

Stegall, Ralph Pvt., 21st Alabama Infantry. Co. C. Federal Rolls of Prisoners of War: Captured at Fort Gaines, AL, on 8/8/1864; Received at Ship Island, MS, from New Orleans, LA, on 10/25/1864. Exchanged on 1/4/1865.

Stephens, J.S. Pvt., 6th Alabama Cavalry. Cos. D & L. Federal Rolls of Prisoners of War: Captured in Alabama on 3/24/1865; Received at Ship Island, MS. Transferred to Vicksburg, MS, for exchange on 5/1/1865; Exchanged at Camp Townsend, MS, on 5/6/1865.

Stephens, John L. Pvt., 8th Alabama Infantry. Co. __. Federal Rolls of Prisoners of War: Captured at Blakely, AL, on 4/9/1865; Received at Ship Island, MS, on 4/15/1865. Transferred to Vicksburg, MS, for exchange on 5/1/1865; Exchanged at Camp Townsend, MS, on 5/6/1865.

Stephens, L. Pvt., 63rd Alabama Infantry. Co. E. Enlisted: 3/8/1864 at Clayton, AL. Age at enlistment: 17. Description at enlistment: Eyes: dark. Hair: dark. Complexion: dark. Rolls for 9/1864 through 10/1864: Present. Federal Rolls of Prisoners of War: Captured at Blakely, AL, on 4/9/1865; Received at Ship Island, MS, on 4/15/1865. Transferred to Vicksburg, MS, for exchange on 5/1/1865; Exchanged at Camp Townsend, MS, on 5/6/1865. Rolls of Prisoners of War, C.S.A: Surrendered at Citronelle, AL, on 5/4/1865; Paroled at Meridian, MS, on 5/13/1865. Residence at parole: Barbour County, AL.

Stephens, R.W. Pvt., 63rd Alabama Infantry. Co. A. Federal Rolls of Prisoners of War: Captured at Blakely, AL, on 4/9/1865; Received at Ship Island, MS, on 4/15/1865. Transferred to Vicksburg, MS, for exchange on 5/1/1865; Exchanged at Camp Townsend, MS, on 5/6/1865. Rolls of Prisoners of War, C.S.A: Surrendered at Citronelle, AL, on 5/4/1865; Paroled at Meridian, MS, on 5/13/1865. Residence at parole: Macon County, AL.

Stephens, William (AKA Stevens) Pvt., 1st Alabama Artillery Battalion. Co. B. Federal Rolls of Prisoners of War: Captured at Fort Gaines, AL, on 8/8/1864; Received at Ship Island, MS, from New Orleans, LA, on 10/24/1864. Exchanged on 1/4/1865.

Stern, Kiley (AKA Hiley) Pvt., Lockhart's Battalion Infantry. Co. __. Federal Rolls of Prisoners of War:

Captured at Fort Gaines, AL, on 8/8/1864; Received at Ship Island, MS, from New Orleans, LA, on 10/25/1864. Exchanged on 1/4/1865.

Stevens, H. Pvt., 63rd Alabama Infantry. Co. K. Enlisted: 9/10/1864 at Perry County, AL. Rolls for 9/1864 through 10/1864: Present. Federal Rolls of Prisoners of War: Captured at Blakely, AL, on 4/9/1865; Received at Ship Island, MS, on 4/15/1865. Transferred to Vicksburg, MS, for exchange on 5/1/1865; Exchanged at Camp Townsend, MS, on 5/6/1865. Rolls of Prisoners of War, C.S.A: Surrendered at Citronelle, AL, on 5/4/1865; Paroled at Meridian, MS, on 5/13/1865. Residence at parole: Pickens County, AL.

Stevens, J.N. (AKA Stephens) Pvt., Lockhart's Battalion Infantry. Co. K. Federal Rolls of Prisoners of War: Captured at Fort Gaines, AL, on 8/8/1864; Received at Ship Island, MS, from New Orleans, LA, on 10/25/1864. Died: 11/20/1864 at Ship Island, MS, due to diarrhea. Buried: Ship Island, MS, Cemetery in Grave #31.

Stevens, James B. Lockhart's Battalion Infantry. Co. B. Federal Rolls of Prisoners of War: Captured at Fort Gaines, AL, on 8/8/1864; Received at Ship Island, MS, from New Orleans, LA, on 10/29/1864. Exchanged on 1/4/1865.

Stevens, John (AKA Stephens) Pvt., 21st Alabama Infantry. Co. K. Federal Rolls of Prisoners of War: Captured at Fort Gaines, AL, on 8/8/1864; Received at Ship Island, MS, from New Orleans, LA, on 10/25/1864. Exchanged on 1/4/1865.

Stevenson, J.M. Pvt., Tarrant's Artillery Battery. Federal Rolls of Prisoners of War: Captured at Blakely, AL, on 4/9/1865; Received at Ship Island, MS, on 4/15/1865. Transferred to Vicksburg, MS, for exchange on 5/1/1865; Exchanged at Camp Townsend, MS, on 5/6/1865.

Stewart, John A. Pvt., 6th Alabama Cavalry. Cos. B & C. Federal Rolls of Prisoners of War: Captured in Florida on 3/25/1865; Received at Ship Island, MS. Transferred to Vicksburg, MS, for exchange on 5/1/1865; Exchanged at Camp Townsend, MS, on 5/6/1865.

Stick, Leander F. Pvt., 62nd Alabama Infantry. Co. E. Federal Rolls of Prisoners of War: Captured at Blakely, AL, on 4/9/1865; Received at Ship Island, MS, on 4/15/1865. Transferred to Vicksburg, MS, for exchange on 5/1/1865; Exchanged at Camp Townsend, MS, on 5/6/1865.

Stillwell, G.W. Pvt., 63rd Alabama Infantry. Co. K. Enlisted: 8/12/1864 at Columbus, GA. Rolls for 9/1864 through 10/1864: Present. Federal Rolls of Prisoners of War: Captured at Blakely, AL, on 4/9/1865; Received at Ship Island, MS, on 4/15/1865. Transferred to Vicksburg, MS, for exchange on 5/1/1865; Exchanged at Camp Townsend, MS, on 5/6/1865. Rolls of Prisoners of War, C.S.A: Surrendered at Citronelle, AL, on 5/4/1865; Paroled at Meridian, MS, on 5/13/1865. Residence at parole: Russell County, AL.

Stinson, Samuel N. (AKA S.T.) Pvt., 21st Alabama Infantry. Co. H. Federal Rolls of Prisoners of War: Captured at Fort Gaines, AL, on 8/8/1864; Received at Ship Island, MS, from New Orleans, LA, on 10/25/1864. Died: 1/1/1865 at Ship Island, MS, due to dysentery. Buried: Ship Island, MS, Cemetery in Grave #127.

Stockey, W.A. Pvt., 38th Alabama Infantry. Co. E. Federal Rolls of Prisoners of War: Captured at Blakely, AL, on 4/9/1865; Received at Ship Island, MS, on 4/15/1865. Transferred to Vicksburg, MS, for exchange on 5/1/1865; Exchanged at Camp Townsend, MS, on 5/6/1865.

Stockman, F. (AKA T.) Pvt., 21st Alabama Infantry. Co. F. Federal Rolls of Prisoners of War: Captured at Fort Gaines, AL, on 8/8/1864; Received at Ship Island, MS, from New Orleans, LA, on 10/25/1864. Died: 11/27/1864 at Ship Island, MS, due to dysentery. Buried: Ship Island, MS, Cemetery in Grave #49.

Stokes, W.W. Pvt., 63rd Alabama Infantry. Co. E. Enlisted: 8/8/1864 at Pollard, AL. Age at enlistment: 17. Description at enlistment: Eyes: dark. Hair: dark. Complexion: dark. Rolls for 9/1864 through 10/1864: Absent, in hospital since 10/7/1864. Federal Rolls of Prisoners of War: Captured at Blakely, AL, on 4/9/1865; Received at Ship Island, MS, on 4/15/1865. Transferred to Vicksburg, MS, for exchange on 5/1/1865; Exchanged at Camp Townsend, MS, on 5/6/1865. Rolls of Prisoners of War, C.S.A.: Surrendered at Citronelle, AL, on 5/4/1865; Paroled at Meridian, MS, on 5/13/1865. Residence at parole: Henry County, AL.

Stone, J.D. Pvt., 1st Alabama Artillery Battalion. Co. B. Federal Rolls of Prisoners of War: Captured at Fort Gaines, AL, on 8/8/1864; Received at Ship Island, MS, from New Orleans, LA, on 10/24/1864. Exchanged on 1/4/1865.

Stone, J.F. (AKA J.T.) Pvt., Lockhart's Battalion Infantry. Co. H. Federal Rolls of Prisoners of War: Captured at Fort Gaines, AL, on 8/8/1864; Received at Ship Island, MS, from New Orleans, LA, on 10/29/1864. Exchanged on 1/4/1865.

Stone, John Bestor 2nd Lt., 62nd Alabama Infantry. Co. I. Federal Rolls of Prisoners of War: Captured at Blakely, AL, on 4/9/1865; Received at Ship Island, MS, on 4/15/1865. Transferred to Vicksburg, MS, for exchange on 4/28/1865; Confined at New Orleans, LA, on 4/30/1865. Exchanged at Camp Townsend, MS, on 5/6/1865. Rolls of Prisoners of War, C.S.A: Surrendered at Citronelle, AL, on 5/4/1865; Paroled at Meridian, MS, on 5/11/1865. Soldier also served as a 5th Cpl. with the 4th Alabama Infantry. Co.A. Enlisted: 4/26/1861 at Selma, AL. Wounded at Second Mannassas, VA, Chickamauga, GA, and Cold Harbor, VA. Received the United Daughters of the Confederacy Cross of Honor for his wartime service. Born: 12/5/1842 to John M. Stone and Permelia Caroline Roberts at Marion, Perry County, AL.

Stone, John M. Pvt./1st Sgt., 1st Alabama Artillery Battalion. Co. B. Federal Rolls of Prisoners of War: Captured at Fort Gaines, AL, on 8/8/1864; Received at Ship Island, MS, from New Orleans, LA, on 10/25/1864. Exchanged on 1/4/1865.

Stone, W.H. Pvt., Lockhart's Battalion Infantry. Co. H. Federal Rolls of Prisoners of War: Captured at Fort Gaines, AL, on 8/8/1864; Received at Ship Island, MS, from New Orleans, LA, on 10/25/1864. Died: 12/12/1864 at Ship Island, MS, due to pneumonia. Buried: Ship Island, MS, Cemetery in Grave #82.

Stowe, Leroy Pvt., 63rd Alabama Infantry. Co. A. Enlisted: 1/1/1864 at Montgomery County, AL. Age at enlistment: 16. Rolls for 1/1864 through 2/1864:

Present. Rolls for 9/1864 through 10/1864: Present. Federal Rolls of Prisoners of War: Captured at Blakely, AL, on 4/9/1865; Received at Ship Island, MS, on 4/15/1865. Transferred to Vicksburg, MS, for exchange on 5/1/1865; Exchanged at Camp Townsend, MS, on 5/6/1865. Rolls of Prisoners of War, C.S.A: Surrendered at Citronelle, AL, on 5/4/1865; Paroled at Meridian, MS, on 5/13/1865. Residence at parole: Montgomery County, AL.

Strather, John M. (AKA Strother) Pvt., 63rd Alabama Infantry. Co. A. Enlisted: 4/8/1864 at Chambers County, AL. Rolls for 9/1864 through 10/1864: Present. On Register of Ross Hospital, Mobile, AL: Admitted on 11/11/1864 due to febris intermittens; Sent to Nidelet General Hospital on 11/20/1864. Federal Rolls of Prisoners of War: Captured at Blakely, AL, on 4/9/1865; Received at Ship Island, MS, on 4/15/1865. Transferred to Vicksburg, MS, for exchange on 5/1/1865; Exchanged at Camp Townsend, MS, on 5/6/1865. Rolls of Prisoners of War, C.S.A: Surrendered at Citronelle, AL, on 5/4/1865; Paroled at Meridian, MS, on 5/13/1865. Residence at parole: Chambers County, AL. Confederate Pension Application dated 1911 on file at the Louisiana State Archives. Microfilm Reel: CP1.134. Microdex 1. Sequence 22. Target Card: Strother, J.M. Parish: Lincoln. 8 pages.

Strickland, H. Pvt., 63rd Alabama Infantry. Co. E. Enlisted: 8/8/1864 at Pollard, AL. Age at enlistment: 17. Description at enlistment: Eyes: dark. Hair: dark. Complexion: dark. Rolls for 9/1864 through 10/1864: Present. Federal Rolls of Prisoners of War: Captured at Blakely, AL, on 4/9/1865; Received at Ship Island, MS, on 4/15/1865. Transferred to Vicksburg, MS, for exchange on 5/1/1865; Exchanged at Camp Townsend, MS, on 5/6/1865. Rolls of Prisoners of War, C.S.A: Surrendered at Citronelle, AL, on 5/4/1865; Paroled at Meridian, MS, on 5/13/1865. Residence at parole: Henry County, AL.

Stringfellow, D. Pvt., 63rd Alabama Infantry. Cos. D & K. Enlisted: 8/25/1864 at Greene County, AL. Rolls for 9/1864 through 10/1864: Present. Federal Rolls of Prisoners of War: Captured at Blakely, AL, on 4/9/1865; Received at Ship Island, MS, on 4/15/1865. Transferred to Vicksburg, MS, for exchange on 5/1/1865; Exchanged at Camp Townsend, MS, on 5/6/1865. Rolls of Prisoners of War, C.S.A: Surrendered at Citronelle, AL, on 5/4/1865; Paroled at Meridian, MS, on 5/13/1865. Residence at parole: Greene County, AL.

Stringfellow, James R. Pvt., 62nd Alabama Infantry. Co. B. Federal Rolls of Prisoners of War: Captured at Blakely, AL, on 4/9/1865; Received at Ship Island, MS, on 4/15/1865. Transferred to Vicksburg, MS, for exchange on 5/1/1865; Exchanged at Camp Townsend, MS, on 5/6/1865.

Stringfellow, P.W.K. Pvt., Tarrant's Artillery Battery. Federal Rolls of Prisoners of War: Captured at Blakely, AL, on 4/9/1865; Received at Ship Island, MS, on 4/15/1865. Transferred to Vicksburg, MS, for exchange on 5/1/1865; Exchanged at Camp Townsend, MS, on 5/6/1865.

Strong, R.R. Pvt., 62nd Alabama Infantry. Co. I. Federal Rolls of Prisoners of War: Captured at Blakely, AL, on 4/9/1865; Received at Ship Island, MS, on 4/15/1865. Transferred to Vicksburg, MS, for exchange on 5/1/1865; Exchanged at Camp Townsend, MS, on 5/6/1865.

Suggs, John Pvt., 62nd Alabama Infantry. Co. F. Federal Rolls of Prisoners of War: Captured at Blakely, AL, on 4/9/1865; Received at Ship Island, MS, on 4/15/1865. Transferred to Vicksburg, MS, for exchange on 5/1/1865; Exchanged at Camp Townsend, MS, on 5/6/1865.

Summerlin, Columbus Pvt., 63rd Alabama Infantry. Co. D. Enlisted: 7/30/1864 at Macon County, AL. Age at enlistment: 17. Description at enlistment: Eyes: dark. Hair: light. Complexion: florid. Height: 5'9". Residence at enlistment: Eufaula, Barbour County, AL. Rolls for 9/1864 through 10/1864: Absent; in hospital at Greenville, AL, since 9/10/1864. Federal Rolls of Prisoners of War: Captured at Blakely, AL, on 4/9/1865; Received at Ship Island, MS, on 4/15/1865. Transferred to Vicksburg, MS, for exchange on 5/1/1865; Exchanged at Camp Townsend, MS, on 5/6/1865. Rolls of Prisoners of War, C.S.A: Surrendered at Citronelle, AL, on 5/4/1865; Paroled at Meridian, MS, on 5/13/1865. Residence at parole: Barbour County, AL.

Summerlin, Thomas S. Pvt., 63rd Alabama Infantry. Co. F. Enlisted: 5/30/1864 at Montgomery, AL. Age at enlistment: 17. Description at enlistment: Eyes: dark. Hair: dark. Complexion: dark. Height: 5'7". Residence at enlistment: Butler County, AL. Rolls for 9/1864 through 10/1864: Present. Federal Rolls of Prisoners of War: Captured at Blakely, AL, on 4/9/1865; Received at Ship Island, MS, on 4/15/1865. Transferred to Vicksburg, MS, for exchange on 5/1/1865; Exchanged at Camp Townsend, MS, on 5/6/1865. Rolls of Prisoners of War, C.S.A: Surrendered at Citronelle, AL, on 5/4/1865; Paroled at Meridian, MS, on 5/11/1865. Residence at parole: Butler County, AL. Born: 5/7/1846 at Lowndes County, AL. Soldier is recorded on the 1907 Alabama Census of Confederate Veterans and Widows. Residence: Crenshaw County, AL.

Summers, L.F. Pvt., 62nd Alabama Infantry. Co. D. Federal Rolls of Prisoners of War: Captured in Alabama on 3/23/1865; Received at Ship Island, MS. Transferred to Vicksburg, MS, for exchange on 5/1/1865; Exchanged at Camp Townsend, MS, on 5/6/1865.

Summers, Zimri Franklin Pvt., 62nd Alabama Infantry. Co. __. Enlisted: 1864 at Mobile, AL. Federal Rolls of Prisoners of War: Captured at Blakely, AL, on 4/9/1865; Received at Ship Island, MS, 4/15/1865. Transferred to Vicksburg, MS, for exchange on 5/1/1865; Exchanged at Camp Townsend, MS, on 5/6/1865. Born: 8/13/1847 at Augustine, Perry County, AL.

Sumner, J. Pvt., 18th Alabama Infantry. Co. B. Federal Rolls of Prisoners of War: Captured at Blakely, AL, on 4/9/1865; Received at Ship Island, MS, on 4/15/1865. Transferred to Vicksburg, MS, for exchange on 5/1/1865; Exchanged at Camp Townsend, MS, on 5/6/1865.

Sumner, Truman L. Pvt., 62nd Alabama Infantry. Co. A. Federal Rolls of Prisoners of War: Captured at Blakely, AL, on 4/9/1865; Received at Ship Island, MS, on 4/15/1865. Transferred to Vicksburg, MS, for exchange on 5/1/1865; Exchanged at Camp Townsend, MS, on 5/6/1865.

Sumons, A. Pvt., 62nd Alabama Infantry. Co. K. Federal Rolls of Prisoners of War: Captured at Blakely, AL, on 4/9/1865; Received at Ship Island, MS, on 4/15/1865. Transferred to Vicksburg, MS, for exchange on 5/1/1865; Exchanged at Camp Townsend, MS, on 5/6/1865.

Swearingen, J.W. (AKA Swearinger) Sgt., 21st Alabama Infantry. Co. G. Federal Rolls of Prisoners of War: Captured at Fort Gaines, AL, on 8/8/1864; Received at Ship Island, MS, from New Orleans, LA, on 10/25/1864. Died: 12/21/1864 at Ship Island, MS, due to chronic dysentery. Buried: Ship Island, MS, Cemetery in Grave #106.

Swope, W. Pvt., 63rd Alabama Infantry. Co. K. Enlisted: 10/5/1864 at Talladega, AL. Rolls for 9/1864 through 10/1864: Present. On Register of Ross Hospital, Mobile, AL: Admitted on 11/5/1864 due to rubeola; Returned to duty on 11/14/1864. Federal Rolls of Prisoners of War: Captured at Blakely, AL, on 4/9/1865; Received at Ship Island, MS, on 4/15/1865. Transferred to Vicksburg, MS, for exchange on 5/1/1865; Exchanged at Camp Townsend, MS, on 5/6/1865. Rolls of Prisoners of War, C.S.A: Surrendered at Citronelle, AL, on 5/4/1865; Paroled at Meridian, MS, on 5/13/1865. Residence at parole: Talladega County, AL.

Sylvester, William Oscar Cpl./Sgt., 63rd Alabama Infantry. Co. E. Enlisted: 3/18/1864 at Clayton, AL. Age at enlistment: 17. Description at enlistment: Eyes: dark. Hair: dark. Complexion: dark. On Register of Ross Hospital, Mobile, AL: Admitted on 9/18/1864 due to febris intermittens; Returned to duty on 9/26/1864. Rolls for 9/1864 through 10/1864: Present. Federal Rolls of Prisoners of War: Captured at Blakely, AL, on 4/9/1865; Received at Ship island, MS, on 4/15/1865. Transferred to Vicksburg, MS, for exchange on 5/1/1865; Exchanged at Camp Townsend, MS, on 5/6/1865. Rolls of Prisoners of War, C.S.A: Surrendered at Citronelle, AL, on 5/4/1865; Paroled at Meridian, MS, on 5/13/1865. Residence at parole: Eufaula, Barbour County, AL. Born: 12/3/1846 at Eufaula, AL. Soldier is recorded on the 1907 Alabama Census of Confederate Veterans and Widows.

Tabor, Beverly K. (AKA Taber) Pvt., 18th Alabama Infantry. Cos. B & G. Federal Rolls of Prisoners of War: Captured at Spanish Fort, AL, on 4/8/1865; Received at Ship Island, MS, on 4/10/1865. Transferred to Vicksburg, MS, for exchange on 5/1/1865; Exchanged at Camp Townsend, MS, on 5/6/1865.

Talbert, J. Pvt., 21st Alabama Infantry. Co. C. Federal Rolls of Prisoners of War: Captured at Fort Gaines, AL, on 8/8/1864; Received at Ship Island, MS, from New Orleans, LA, on 10/25/1864. Exchanged on 1/4/1865.

Talbert, James B. (AKA J.W.) Pvt., 21st Alabama Infantry. Co. C. Federal Rolls of Prisoners of War: Captured at Fort Gaines, AL, on 8/8/1864; Received at Ship Island, MS, from New Orleans, LA, on 10/25/1864. Died: 11/15/1864 at Ship Island, MS, due to chronic dysentery. Buried: Ship Island, MS, Cemetery in Grave #20.

Tanner, G.L. Pvt., 36th Alabama Infantry. Co. D. Federal Rolls of Prisoners of War: Captured in Alabama on 3/24/1865; Received at Ship Island, MS. Transferred to Vicksburg, MS, for exchange on 5/1/1865; Exchanged at Camp Townsend, MS, on 5/6/1865.

Tansey, John Pvt., 21st Alabama Infantry. Co. B. Federal Rolls of Prisoners of War: Captured at Fort Gaines, AL, on 8/8/1864; Received at Ship Island, MS, from New Orleans, LA, on 10/25/1864. Exchanged on 1/4/1865.

Tarrant, Edward Christopher Columbus Capt., Tarrant's Artillery Battery. Occupation at enlistment: Educator from 1849 through 1862 as President of the Columbian Institute at Taylorsville, AL. Federal Rolls of Prisoners of War: Captured at Blakely, AL, on 4/9/1865; Received at Ship Island, MS, on 4/15/1865. Transferred to Vicksburg, MS, for exchange on 4/28/1865; Confined at New Orleans, LA, on 4/30/1865. Exchanged at Camp Townsend, MS, on 5/6/1865. Born: 7/5/1819 at Jefferson County, AL. Died: 6/19/1878 at Taylorsville, Tuscaloosa County, AL. Married: 1837 to Permelia Ann VanZandt in 1837. Children: 5. Buried: Tarrant Family Cemetery located at Taylorsville, AL.

Tarrant, Edward William 2nd Lt., Tarrant's Artillery Battery. Enlisted: 4/1861. Federal Rolls of Prisoners of War: Captured at Blakely, AL, on 4/9/1865; Received at Ship Island, MS, on 4/15/1865. Transferred to Vicksburg, MS, for exchange on 4/28/1865; Confined at New Orleans, LA, on 4/30/1865. Exchanged at Camp Townsend, MS, on 5/6/1865. Born: 9/14/1842 at Jefferson County, AL. Married: Annie E. Spencer in 12/1869 at Tuscaloosa, AL, and Emma Fisher. Children: 8. First wife died: 1896 at Brenham, TX. Second wife died: 1912. Post-war occupation: Teacher, Methodist Preacher, and Superintendent of the State Orphan Home at Navarro County, TX.

Tarrant, John B. Pvt., Tarrant's Artillery Battery. Federal Rolls of Prisoners of War: Captured at Blakely, AL, on 4/9/1865; Received at Ship Island, MS, on 4/15/1865. Transferred to Vicksburg, MS, for exchange on 5/1/1865; Exchanged at Camp Townsend, MS, on 5/6/1865.

Tarver, Stephen T. Pvt., 36th Alabama Infantry. Co. G. Federal Rolls of Prisoners of War: Captured at Spanish Fort, AL, on 4/8/1865; Received at Ship Island, MS, on 4/10/1865. Transferred to Vicksburg, MS, for exchange on 5/1/1865; Exchanged at Camp Townsend, MS, on 5/6/1865.

Tate, George W. (AKA G.H.) Pvt., 21st Alabama Infantry. Co. H. Federal Rolls of Prisoners of War: Captured at Fort Gaines, AL, on 8/8/1864; Received at Ship Island, MS, from New Orleans, LA, on 10/25/1864. Died: 11/12/1864 at Ship Island, MS, due to typhoid fever. Buried: Ship Island, MS, Cemetery in Grave #17.

Tate, J.R. Pvt., 21st Alabama Infantry. Co. C. Federal Rolls of Prisoners of War: Captured at Fort Gaines, AL, on 8/8/1864; Received at Ship Island, MS, from New Orleans, LA, on 10/25/1864. Exchanged on 1/4/1865.

Tatum, Henry Pvt., 21st Alabama Infantry. Co. I. Federal Rolls of Prisoners of War: Captured at Fort Gaines, AL, on 8/8/1864; Received at Ship Island, MS, from New Orleans, LA, on 10/25/1864. Died: 12/4/1864 at Ship Island, MS, due to typhoid fever. Buried: Ship Island, MS, Cemetery in Grave #64.

Taul, A.T. Pvt., Lockhart's Battalion Infantry. Co. E. Federal Rolls of Prisoners of War: Captured at Fort Gaines, AL, on 8/8/1864; Received at Ship Island,

MS, from New Orleans, LA, on 10/25/1864. Died: 12/31/1864 at Ship Island, MS, due to chronic dysentery. Buried: Ship Island, MS, Cemetery in Grave #124.

Taylor, A.J. Pvt., 62nd Alabama Infantry. Co. C. Federal Rolls of Prisoners of War: Captured at Blakely, AL, on 4/9/1865; Received at Ship Island, MS, on 4/15/1865. Transferred to Vicksburg, MS, for exchange on 5/1/1865; Exchanged at Camp Townsend, MS, on 5/6/1865.

Taylor, Abner R. (AKA A.K.) Pvt., 1st Alabama Artillery Battalion. Co. D. Federal Rolls of Prisoners of War: Captured at Fort Gaines, AL, on 8/8/1864; Received at Ship Island, MS, from New Orleans, LA, on 10/25/1864. Died: 12/27/1864 at Ship Island, MS, due to chronic dysentery. Buried: Ship Island, MS, Cemetery in Grave #115.

Taylor, B.H. Pvt., 38th Alabama Infantry. Co. E. Age at enlistment: 20. Federal Rolls of Prisoners of War: Captured at Spanish Fort, AL, on 4/8/1865; Received at Ship Island, MS, on 4/10/1865. Transferred to Vicksburg, MS, for exchange on 5/1/1865; Exchanged at Camp Townsend, MS, on 5/6/1865.

Taylor, Benjamin F. Pvt./Cpl., 1st Alabama Artillery Battalion. Co. D. Federal Rolls of Prisoners of War: Captured at Blakely, AL, on 4/9/1865; Received at Ship Island, MS, on 4/15/1865. Transferred to Vicksburg, MS, for exchange on 5/1/1865; Exchanged at Camp Townsend, MS, on 5/6/1865.

Taylor, E.D. Pvt., 62nd Alabama Infantry. Cos. F & H. Federal Rolls of Prisoners of War: Captured at Blakely, AL, on 4/9/1865; Received at Ship Island, MS, on 4/15/1865. Transferred to Vicksburg, MS, for exchange on 5/1/1865; Exchanged at Camp Townsend, MS, on 5/6/1865.

Taylor, H.H. Pvt., 63rd Alabama Infantry. Co. F. Federal Rolls of Prisoners of War: Captured at Blakely, AL, on 4/9/1865; Received at Ship Island, MS, on 4/15/1865. Transferred to Vicksburg, MS, for exchange on 5/1/1865; Exchanged at Camp Townsend, MS, on 5/6/1865. Rolls of Prisoners of War, C.S.A: Surrendered at Citronelle, AL, on 5/4/1865; Paroled at Meridian, MS, on 5/11/1865. Residence at parole: Butler County, AL.

Taylor, J.A. Pvt., 63rd Alabama Infantry. Co. D. Federal Rolls of Prisoners of War: Captured at Spanish Fort, AL, on 4/8/1865; Received at Ship Island, MS, on 4/10/1865. Transferred to Vicksburg, MS, for exchange on 5/1/1865; Exchanged at Camp Townsend, MS, on 5/6/1865.

Taylor, James M. Pvt., 63rd Alabama Infantry. Co. B. Enlisted: 8/15/1864 at Pollard, AL. Rolls for 9/1864 through 10/1864: Present. Federal Rolls of Prisoners of War: Captured at Blakely, AL, on 4/9/1865; Received at Ship Island, MS, on 4/15/1865. Transferred to Vicksburg, MS, for exchange on 5/1/1865; Exchanged at Camp Townsend, MS, on 5/6/1865. Rolls of Prisoners of War, C.S.A: Surrendered at Citronelle, AL, on 5/4/1865; Paroled at Meridian, MS, on 5/11/1865. Residence at parole: Dale County, AL.

Taylor, John Pvt., 18th Alabama Infantry. Co. B. Federal Rolls of Prisoners of War: Captured at Spanish Fort, AL, on 4/8/1865; Received at Ship Island, MS, on 4/10/1865. Transferred to Vicksburg, MS, for exchange on 5/1/1865; Exchanged at Camp Townsend, MS, on 5/6/1865.

Taylor, R.F. (AKA W.J.) Cpl., 1st Alabama Artillery Battalion. Co. __. Federal Rolls of Prisoners of War: Captured at Fort Gaines, AL, on 8/8/1864; Received at Ship Island, MS, from New Orleans, LA, on 10/25/1864. Exchanged on 1/4/1865.

Taylor, W.W. Pvt., 18th Alabama Infantry. Co. B. Federal Rolls of Prisoners of War: Captured at Spanish Fort, AL, on 4/8/1865; Received at Ship Island, MS, on 4/10/1865. Transferred to Vicksburg, MS, for exchange on 5/1/1865; Exchanged at Camp Townsend, MS, on 5/6/1865.

Teadue, F.M. (AKA Teadway, Teager) Pvt., 6th Alabama Cavalry. Co. E. Federal Rolls of Prisoners of War: Captured in Florida on 3/25/1865; Received at Ship Island, MS. Transferred to Vicksburg, MS, for exchange on 5/1/1865; Exchanged at Camp Townsend, MS, on 5/6/1865.

Teat, Wade Hampton (AKA M.H.) Pvt., 38th Alabama Infantry. Co. F. Federal Rolls of Prisoners of War: Captured at Spanish Fort, AL, on 4/8/1865; Received at Ship Island, MS, on 4/10/1865. Transferred to Vicksburg, MS, for exchange on 5/1/1865; Exchanged at Camp Townsend, MS, on 5/6/1865. Buried: Confederate Memorial Park Cemetery #1 located at Mountain Creek, AL. Born: 1/15/1829 at Jasper County, GA. Married: Susan Taylor. Wife Buried: Millerville City Cemetery located at Millerville, AL.

Templeton, W.T. Pvt., 62nd Alabama Infantry. Co. B. Federal Rolls of Prisoners of War: Captured at Blakely, AL, on 4/9/1865; Received at Ship Island, MS, on 4/15/1865. Transferred to Vicksburg, MS, for exchange on 5/1/1865; Exchanged at Camp Townsend, MS, on 5/6/1865.

Thigpen, J.E. Pvt., 63rd Alabama Infantry. Co. F. Enlisted: 5/30/1864 at Montgomery, AL. Age at enlistment: 17. Description at enlistment: Eyes: dark. Hair: dark. Complexion: dark. Height: 5'7". Residence at enlistment: Butler County, AL. Rolls for 9/1864 through 10/1864: Present. Federal Rolls of Prisoners of War: Captured at Blakely, AL, on 4/9/1865; Received at Ship Island, MS, on 4/15/1865. Transferred to Vicksburg, MS, for exchange on 5/1/1865; Exchanged at Camp Townsend, MS, on 5/6/1865. Rolls of Prisoners of War, C.S.A: Surrendered at Citronelle, AL, on 5/4/1865; Paroled at Meridian, MS, on 5/11/1865. Residence at parole: Butler County, AL.

Thigpen, L.G. Pvt., 21st Alabama Infantry. Co. E. Federal Rolls of Prisoners of War: Captured at Fort Gaines, AL, on 8/8/1864; Received at Ship Island, MS, from New Orleans, LA, on 10/25/1864. Exchanged on 1/4/1865.

Thigpen, L. Gray Pvt., 1st Alabama Artillery Battalion. Co. B. Federal Rolls of Prisoners of War: Captured at Fort Gaines, AL, on 8/8/1864; Received at Ship Island, MS, from New Orleans, LA, on 10/25/1864. Died: 11/20/1864 at Ship Island, MS, due to diarrhea. Buried: Ship Island, MS, Cemetery in Grave #30.

Thigpen, S.W. (AKA G.W.) Pvt., 21st Alabama Infantry. Co. E. Federal Rolls of Prisoners of War: Captured at Fort Gaines, AL, on 8/8/1864; Received at Ship Island, MS, from New Orleans, LA, on 10/25/1864. Exchanged on 1/4/1865.

Thomas, ? Pvt., 62nd Alabama Infantry. Co. I. Federal Rolls of Prisoners of War: Captured at Blakely, AL, on 4/9/1865; Received at Ship Island, MS, on 4/15/1865. Transferred to Vicksburg, MS, for exchange on 5/1/1865; Exchanged at Camp Townsend, MS, on 5/6/1865.

Thomas, B.F. Pvt., 62nd Alabama Infantry. Co. K. Federal Rolls of Prisoners of War: Captured at Blakely, AL, on 4/9/1865; Received at Ship Island, MS, on 4/15/1865. Transferred to Vicksburg, MS, for exchange on 5/1/1865; Exchanged at Camp Townsend, MS, on 5/6/1865.

Thomas, B.H. Pvt., 38th Alabama Infantry. Co. E. Federal Rolls of Prisoners of War: Captured at Blakely, AL, on 4/9/1865; Received at Ship Island, MS, on 4/15/1865. Transferred to Vicksburg, MS, for exchange on 5/1/1865; Exchanged at Camp Townsend, MS, on 5/6/1865.

Thomas, J.H. Pvt., 6th Alabama Cavalry. Co. B. Federal Rolls of Prisoners of War: Captured in Florida on 3/25/1865; Received at Ship Island, MS. Transferred to Vicksburg, MS, for exchange on 5/1/1865; Exchanged at Camp Townsend, MS, on 5/6/1865.

Thomas, H. Pvt., 36th Alabama Infantry. Co. F. Federal Rolls of Prisoners of War: Captured at Spanish Fort, AL, on 4/8/1865; Received at Ship Island, MS, on 4/10/1865. Transferred to Vicksburg, MS, for exchange on 5/1/1865; Exchanged at Camp Townsend, MS, on 5/6/1865.

Thomas, James C. Pvt., Alabama Cavalry (Chisolm's). Enlisted: 2/10/1864 at Marianna, FL. Federal Rolls of Prisoners of War: Captured at Euchee Anna, FL, on 9/23/1864; Received at Ship Island, MS. Forwarded to Fort Columbus, New York Harbor, NY; Transferred to Elmira, NY. Died: 12/7/1864 at Elmira, NY, due to diarrhea. Buried: Woodlawn National Cemetery, Chemung County, NY. Married: Sarah A. _. Wife is recorded on the List of Indigent Families of Levy County, FL.

Thomas, John L. Pvt., 63rd Alabama Infantry. Co. A. Enlisted: 4/13/1864 at Butler County, AL. Rolls for 9/1864 through 10/1864: Present, sick in quarters. Federal Rolls of Prisoners of War: Captured at Blakely, AL, on 4/9/1865; Received at Ship Island, MS, on 4/15/1865. Transferred to Vicksburg, MS, for exchange on 5/1/1865; Exchanged at Camp Townsend, MS, on 5/6/1865. Rolls of Prisoners of War, C.S.A: Surrendered at Citronelle, AL, on 5/4/1865; Paroled at Meridian, MS, on 5/13/1865. Residence at parole: Butler County, AL.

Thomas, M. Pvt., 63rd Alabama Infantry. Co. E. Enlisted: 8/8/1864 at Pollard, AL. Age at enlistment: 17. Description at enlistment: Eyes: dark. Hair: dark. Complexion: dark. Rolls for 9/1864 through 10/1864: Absent, in hospital since 9/24/1864. Federal Rolls of Prisoners of War: Captured at Blakely, AL, on 4/9/1865; Received at Ship Island, MS, on 4/15/1865. Transferred to Vicksburg, MS, for exchange on 5/1/1865; Exchanged at Camp Townsend, MS, on 5/6/1865. Rolls of Prisoners of War, C.S.A: Surrendered at Citronelle, AL, on 5/4/1865; Paroled at Meridian, MS, on 5/13/1865. Residence at parole: Henry County, AL.

Thompson, Andrew J. Pvt., 63rd Alabama Infantry. Co. C. Enlisted: 5/12/1864 at Macon County, AL. Age at enlistment: 17. Description at enlistment: Eyes: black. Hair: dark. Complexion: dark. Height: 5'6". Residence at enlistment: Society Hill, Macon County, AL. Rolls for 9/1864 through 10/1864: Present. Federal Rolls of Prisoners of War: Captured at Blakely, AL, on 4/9/1865; Received at Ship Island, MS, on 4/15/1865. Transferred to Vicksburg, MS, for exchange on 5/1/1865; Exchanged at Camp Townsend, MS, on 5/6/1865. Rolls of Prisoners of War, C.S.A: Surrendered at Citronelle, AL, on 5/4/1865; Paroled at Meridian, MS, on 5/11/1865. Residence at parole: Macon County, AL.

Thompson, B. Pvt., 63rd Alabama Infantry. Co. B. Federal Rolls of Prisoners of War: Captured at Blakely, AL, on 4/9/1865; Received at Ship Island, MS, on 4/15/1865. Transferred to Vicksburg, MS, for exchange on 5/1/1865; Exchanged at Camp Townsend, MS, on 5/6/1865.

Thompson, B.F. Pvt., Tarrant's Artillery Battery. Federal Rolls of Prisoners of War: Captured at Blakely, AL, on 4/9/1865; Received at Ship Island, MS, on 4/15/1865. Transferred to Vicksburg, MS, for exchange on 5/1/1865; Exchanged at Camp Townsend, MS, on 5/6/1865.

Thompson, J.H. Pvt., 1st Alabama Artillery Battalion. Co. _. Federal Rolls of Prisoners of War: Captured at Fort Gaines, AL, on 8/8/1864; Received at Ship Island, MS, from New Orleans, LA, on 10/25/1864. Exchanged on 1/4/1865.

Thompson, J.H. Pvt./Sgt., 63rd Alabama Infantry. Co. B. Federal Rolls of Prisoners of War: Captured at Blakely, AL, on 4/9/1865; Received at Ship Island, MS, on 4/15/1865. Transferred to Vicksburg, MS, for exchange on 5/1/1865. On Register of U.S.A. General Hospital #2, Vicksburg, MS: Admitted from steamer on 5/4/1865 due to acute diarrhea; Returned to duty on 5/8/1865.

Thompson, L.J. Pvt., Tarrant's Artillery Battery. Federal Rolls of Prisoners of War: Captured at Blakely, AL, on 4/9/1865; Received at Ship Island, MS, on 4/15/1865. Transferred to Vicksburg, MS, for exchange on 5/1/1865; Exchanged at Camp Townsend, MS, on 5/6/1865.

Thompson, P.M. Pvt., 63rd Alabama Infantry. Co. F. Enlisted: 3/9/1864 at Greenville, AL. Age at enlistment: 17. Description at enlistment: Eyes: dark. Hair: dark. Complexion: dark. Height: 5'6". Residence at enlistment: Butler County, AL. Rolls for 9/1864 through 10/1864: Present. Federal Rolls of Prisoners of War: Captured at Blakely, AL, on 4/9/1865; Received at Ship Island, MS, on 4/15/1865. Transferred to Vicksburg, MS, for exchange on 5/1/1865; Exchanged at Camp Townsend, MS, on 5/6/1865. Rolls of Prisoners of War, CSA: Surrendered at Citronelle, AL, on 5/4/1865; Paroled at Meridian, MS, on 5/11/1865. Residence at parole: Butler County, AL.

Thompson, Robert F. Pvt., 36th Alabama Infantry. Cos. D & F. Federal Rolls of Prisoners of War: Captured at Spanish Fort, AL, on 4/8/1865; Received at Ship Island, MS, on 4/10/1865. Transferred to Vicksburg, MS, for exchange on 5/1/1865; Exchanged at Camp Townsend, MS, on 5/6/1865.

Thompson, S. Sgt., 21st Alabama Infantry. Co. I. Federal Rolls of Prisoners of War: Captured at Fort Gaines, AL, on 8/8/1864; Received at Ship Island, MS, from New Orleans, LA, on 10/25/1864. Died: 1/1/1865 at Ship Island, MS, due to dysentery. Buried: Ship Island, MS, Cemetery in Grave #125.

Thompson, W.W. Pvt., 1st Alabama Artillery Battalion. Co. B. Federal Rolls of Prisoners of War: Captured at Fort Gaines, AL, on 8/8/1864; Received at Ship Island, MS, from New Orleans, LA, on 10/25/1864. Exchanged on 1/4/1865.

Thornton, James T. Pvt., 63rd Alabama Infantry. Co. G. Enlisted: 10/11/1864 at Blakely, AL. Rolls for 9/1864 through 10/1864: Present. Federal Rolls of Prisoners of War: Captured at Blakely, AL, on 4/9/1865; Received at Ship Island, MS, on 4/15/1865. Transferred to Vicksburg, MS, for exchange on 5/1/1865; Exchanged at Camp Townsend, MS, on 5/6/1865. Rolls of Prisoners of War, C.S.A: Surrendered at Citronelle, AL, on 5/4/1865; Paroled at Meridian, MS, on 5/13/1865. Residence at parole: Pike County, AL. Confederate Pension Application dated 1915 on file at the Georgia State Archives.

Thornton, S.S. (AKA J.S.) Cpl., 63rd Alabama Infantry. Co. K. Enlisted: 5/23/1864 at Greene County, AL. Rolls for 9/1864 through 10/1864: Present. Federal Rolls of Prisoners of War: Captured at Blakely, AL, on 4/9/1865; Received at Ship Island, MS, on 4/15/1865. Transferred to Vicksburg, MS, for exchange on 5/1/1865; Exchanged at Camp Townsend, MS, on 5/6/1865. Rolls of Prisoners of War, C.S.A: Surrendered at Citronelle, AL, on 5/4/1865; Paroled at Meridian, MS, on 5/13/1865. Residence at parole: Greene County, AL. Confederate Pension Application dated 1920 on file at the Alabama State Archives.

Thrower, Peter J. (AKA T.J.) Pvt., 63rd Alabama Infantry. Co. F. Enlisted: 7/12/1864 at Lowndes County, AL. Age at enlistment: 17. Description at enlistment: Eyes: dark. Hair: dark. Complexion: fair. Height: 5'9". Residence at enlistment: Lowndes County, AL. Rolls for 9/1864 through 10/1864: Present. Federal Rolls of Prisoners of War: Captured at Blakely, AL, on 4/9/1865; Received at Ship Island, MS, on 4/15/1865. Transferred to Vicksburg, MS, for exchange on 5/1/1865; Exchanged at Camp Townsend, MS, on 5/6/1865. Rolls of Prisoners of War, C.S.A: Surrendered at Citronelle, AL, on 5/4/1865; Paroled at Meridian, MS, on 5/11/1865. Residence at parole: Lowndes County, AL. Born: 4/20/1848 at Helicon, Lowndes County, AL. Soldier is recorded on the 1907 Alabama Census of Confederate Veterans and Widows. Residence: Crenshaw County, AL.

Thurmond, D. Pvt./1st Cpl., 63rd Alabama Infantry. Cos. D & E. Enlisted: 8/8/1864 at Pollard, AL. Age at enlistment: 17. Description at enlistment: Eyes: blue. Hair: light. Complexion: fair. Rolls for 9/1864 through 10/1864: Present. Federal Rolls of Prisoners of War: Captured at Blakely, AL, on 4/9/1865; Received at Ship Island, MS, on 4/15/1865. Transferred to Vicksburg, MS, for exchange on 5/1/1865; Exchanged at Camp Townsend, MS, on 5/6/1865. Rolls of Prisoners of War, C.S.A: Surrendered at Citronelle, AL, on 5/4/1865; Paroled at Meridian, MS, on 5/13/1865. Residence at parole: Dale County, AL.

Tidmore, ? Pvt., 62nd Alabama Infantry. Co. F. Federal Rolls of Prisoners of War: Captured at Blakely, AL, on 4/9/1865; Received at Ship Island, MS, on 4/15/1865. Transferred to Vicksburg, MS, for exchange on 5/1/1865; Exchanged at Camp Townsend, MS, on 5/6/1865.

Tidmore, William T. Pvt., 62nd Alabama Infantry. Co. K. Federal Rolls of Prisoners of War: Captured at Blakely, AL, on 4/9/1865; Received at Ship Island, MS, on 4/15/1865. Transferred to Vicksburg, MS, for exchange on 5/1/1865; Exchanged at Camp Townsend, MS, on 5/6/1865.

Tidwell, J.F. Pvt., 62nd Alabama Infantry. Co. D. Federal Rolls of Prisoners of War: Captured at Blakely, AL, on 4/9/1865; Received at Ship Island, MS, on 4/15/1865. Transferred to Vicksburg, MS, for exchange on 5/1/1865; Exchanged at Camp Townsend, MS, on 5/6/1865.

Tillman, James P. (AKA J.C., J.K.P.) Pvt., 21st Alabama Infantry. Co. I. Federal Rolls of Prisoners of War: Captured at Fort Gaines, AL, on 8/8/1864; Received at Ship Island, MS, from New Orleans, LA, on 10/25/1864. Died: 11/23/1864 at Ship Island, MS, due to dysentery. Buried: Ship Island, MS, Cemetery in Grave #40.

Tingle, William P. Pvt., Lockhart's Battalion Infantry. Co. K. Federal Rolls of Prisoners of War: Captured at Fort Gaines, AL, on 8/8/1864; Received at Ship Island, MS, from New Orleans, LA, on 10/25/1864. Exchanged on 1/4/1865.

Tipton, William R. (AKA McCrory, Thomas M.) Pvt., 1st Alabama Artillery Battalion. Co. E. Federal Rolls of Prisoners of War: Captured at Blakely, AL, on 4/9/1865; Received at Ship Island, MS, on 4/15/1865. Transferred to Vicksburg, MS, for exchange on 5/1/1865; Exchanged at Camp Townsend, MS, on 5/6/1865.

Todd, M. Pvt., 62nd Alabama Infantry. Co. C. Federal Rolls of Prisoners of War: Captured at Blakely, AL, on 4/9/1865; Received at Ship Island, MS, on 4/15/1865. Transferred to Vicksburg, MS, for exchange on 5/1/1865; Exchanged at Camp Townsend, MS, on 5/6/1865.

Tool, J.R. (AKA Teel) Pvt., Tarrant's Artillery Battery. Federal Rolls of Prisoners of War: Captured at Spanish Fort, AL, on 4/8/1865; Received at Ship Island, MS, on 4/10/1865. Transferred to Vicksburg, MS, for exchange on 5/1/1865; Exchanged at Camp Townsend, MS, on 5/6/1865.

Torrant, S. (AKA Tonant) Pvt., 62nd Alabama Infantry. Co. B. Federal Rolls of Prisoners of War: Captured at Blakely, AL, on 4/9/1865; Received at Ship Island, MS, on 4/15/1865. Transferred to Vicksburg, MS, for exchange on 5/1/1865; Exchanged at Camp Townsend, MS, on 5/6/1865.

Toulmin, John F. Sgt./1st Lt., 21st Alabama Infantry. Cos. D & K. Federal Rolls of Prisoners of War: Captured at Fort Gaines, AL, on 8/8/1864; Received at Ship Island, MS, on 10/25/1864. Exchanged on 1/4/1865.

Townsend, Phillip A. 2nd Lt., 63rd Alabama Infantry. Co. B. Elected 2nd Lt. on 3/23/1864. Rolls for 9/1864 through 10/1864: Present. Federal Rolls of Prisoners of War: Captured at Blakely, AL, on 4/9/1865; Confined one day near Spanish Fort, AL. Received at Ship Island, MS, on 4/16/1865; Transferred to Vicksburg, MS, for exchange on 4/28/1865. Confined at New Orleans, LA, on 4/30/1865; Exchanged at Camp Townsend, MS, on 5/6/1865. Rolls of Prisoners of War, C.S.A: Surrendered at Citronelle, AL, on 5/4/1865; Paroled at Meridian, MS, on 5/11/1865. Residence at parole: Montgomery County, AL.

Trammell, David (AKA Trimmold, B.D.) Pvt., 63rd Alabama Infantry. Co. A. Enlisted: 1/1/1864 at

Tallapoosa County, AL. Age at enlistment: 16. Rolls for 1/1864 through 2/1864: Present. Rolls for 9/1864 through 10/1864: Present. Federal Rolls of Prisoners of War: Captured at Blakely, AL, on 4/9/1865; Received at Ship Island, MS, on 4/15/1865. Transferred to Vicksburg, MS, for exchange on 5/1/1865; Exchanged at Camp Townsend, MS, on 5/6/1865. Rolls of Prisoners of War, C.S.A: Surrendered at Citronelle, AL, on 5/4/1865; Paroled at Meridian, MS, on 5/13/1865. Residence at parole: Tallapoosa County, AL.

Traywick, Harrison Pvt., 63rd Alabama Infantry. Co. A. Enlisted: 1/1/1864 at Macon County, AL. Age at enlistment: 16. Rolls for 1/1864 through 2/1864: Present. Rolls for 9/1864 through 10/1864: Present, sick in quarters. Federal Rolls of Prisoners of War: Captured at Blakely, AL, on 4/9/1865; Received at Ship Island, MS, on 4/15/1865. Transferred to Vicksburg, MS, for exchange on 5/1/1865; Exchanged at Camp Townsend, MS, on 5/6/1865. Rolls of Prisoners of War, C.S.A: Surrendered at Citronelle, AL, on 5/4/1865; Paroled at Meridian, MS, on 5/13/1865. Residence at parole: Macon County, AL.

Trennelly, C.D. Pvt., 21st Alabama Infantry. Co. C. Federal Rolls of Prisoners of War: Captured at Fort Gaines, AL, on 8/8/1864; Received at Ship Island, MS, from New Orleans, LA, on 10/25/1864. Exchanged on 1/4/1865.

Triplit, C.T. (AKA Telplit) Pvt., Tarrant's Artillery Battery. Federal Rolls of Prisoners of War: Captured at Spanish Fort, AL, on 4/8/1865; Received at Ship Island, MS, on 4/10/1865. Transferred to Vicksburg, MS, for exchange on 5/1/1865; Exchanged at Camp Townsend, MS, on 5/6/1865.

Trott, Wiley R. Pvt., 62nd Alabama Infantry. Cos. A & D. Federal Rolls of Prisoners of War: Captured at Blakely, AL, on 4/9/1865; Received at Ship Island, MS, on 4/15/1865. Transferred to Vicksburg, MS, for exchange on 5/1/1865; Exchanged at Camp Townsend, MS, on 5/6/1865.

Troy, R. Pvt., 62nd Alabama Infantry. Co. I. Federal Rolls of Prisoners of War: Captured at Blakely, AL, on 4/9/1865; Received at Ship Island, MS, on 4/15/1865. Transferred to Vicksburg, MS, for exchange on 5/1/1865; Exchanged at Camp Townsend, MS, on 5/6/1865.

Truffey, James A. Pvt., 62nd Alabama Infantry. Co. B. Federal Rolls of Prisoners of War: Captured at Blakely, AL, on 4/9/1865; Received at Ship Island, MS, on 4/15/1865. Transferred to Vicksburg, MS, for exchange on 5/1/1865; Exchanged at Camp Townsend, MS, on 5/6/1865.

Tubb, Job (AKA Joseph) Pvt., 62nd Alabama Infantry. Co. B. Federal Rolls of Prisoners of War: Captured at Blakely, AL, on 4/9/1865; Received at Ship Island, MS, on 4/15/1865. Transferred to Vicksburg, MS, for exchange on 5/1/1865; Exchanged at Camp Townsend, MS, on 5/6/1865.

Tubb, Reuben (AKA Trubb) Pvt., 62nd Alabama Infantry. Co. D. Federal Rolls of Prisoners of War: Captured at Blakely, AL, on 4/9/1865; Received at Ship Island, MS, on 4/15/1865. Transferred to Vicksburg, MS, for exchange on 5/1/1865; Exchanged at Camp Townsend, MS, on 5/6/1865.

Tuck, W.T. Pvt., Tarrant's Artillery Battery. Federal Rolls of Prisoners of War: Captured at Spanish Fort, AL, on 4/8/1865; Received at Ship Island, MS, on 4/10/1865. Transferred to Vicksburg, MS, for exchange on 5/1/1865; Exchanged at Camp Townsend, MS, on 5/6/1865.

Tucker, E. Pvt., 62nd Alabama Infantry. Co. F. Federal Rolls of Prisoners of War: Captured at Blakely, AL, on 4/9/1865; Received at Ship Island, MS, on 4/15/1865. Transferred to Vicksburg, MS, for exchange on 5/1/1865; Exchanged at Camp Townsend, MS, on 5/6/1865.

Tucker, George W. 4th Cpl., 63rd Alabama Infantry. Co. C. Enlisted: 5/27/1864 at Russell County, AL. Age at enlistment: 17. Description at enlistment: Eyes: grey. Hair: dark. Complexion: fair. Height: 5'6½". Residence at enlistment: Opelika, Russell County, AL. Rolls for 9/1864 through 10/1864: Present. Federal Rolls of Prisoners of War: Captured at Blakely, AL, on 4/9/1865; Received at Ship Island, MS, on 4/15/1865. Transferred to Vicksburg, MS, for exchange on 5/1/1865; Exchanged at Camp Townsend, MS, on 5/6/1865. Rolls of Prisoners of War, C.S.A: Surrendered at Citronelle, AL, on 5/4/1865; Paroled at Meridian, MS, on 5/10/1865 while a patient in Quintard Hospital. Residence at parole: Russell County, AL.

Tucker, George W. Pvt., 1st Alabama Artillery Battalion. Co. F. Federal Rolls of Prisoners of War: Captured at Fort Morgan, AL, on 8/23/1864; Received at Ship Island, MS, from New Orleans, LA, on 10/7/1864. Transferred to Fort Columbus, New York Harbor, NY, on 11/5/1864.

Tucker, J.E. Pvt., 6th Alabama Cavalry. Cos. F & H. Federal Rolls of Prisoners of War: Captured in Florida on 3/25/1865; Received at Ship Island, MS. Transferred to Vicksburg, MS, for exchange on 5/1/1865; Exchanged at Camp Townsend, MS, on 5/6/1865.

Tucker, James Pvt., 21st Alabama Infantry. Cos. B & H. Federal Rolls of Prisoners of War: Captured at Fort Gaines, AL, on 8/8/1864; Received at Ship Island, MS, from New Orleans, LA, on 10/25/1864. Exchanged on 1/4/1865.

Tucker, W.S. Pvt., 38th Alabama Infantry. Co. B. On Register of Madison Hospital, Montgomery, AL: Admitted in 5/1864. Federal Rolls of Prisoners of War: Captured at Spanish Fort, AL, on 4/8/1865; Received at Ship Island, MS, on 4/10/1865. Transferred to Vicksburg, MS, for exchange on 5/1/1865; Exchanged at Camp Townsend, MS, on 5/6/1865.

Tucker, William Pvt., 63rd Alabama Infantry. Co. C. Enlisted: 5/3/1864 at Russell County, AL. Age at enlistment: 17. Description at enlistment: Eyes: grey. Hair: light. Complexion: fair. Height: 5'7½". Residence at enlistment: Osichee, Russell County, AL. Rolls for 9/1864 through 10/1864: Present. Federal Rolls of Prisoners of War: Captured at Blakely, AL, on 4/9/1865; Received at Ship Island, MS, on 4/15/1865. Transferred to Vicksburg, MS, for exchange on 5/1/1865; Exchanged at Camp Townsend, MS, on 5/6/1865. Rolls of Prisoners of War, C.S.A: Surrendered at Citronelle, AL, on 5/4/1865; Paroled at Meridian, MS, on 5/11/1865. Residence at parole: Russell County, AL.

Turbenville, J. (AKA Turnbenville) Pvt., 21st Alabama Infantry. Co. D. Federal Rolls of Prisoners of War: Captured at Blakely, AL, on 4/9/1865; Received at

Ship Island, MS, on 4/15/1865. Transferred to Vicksburg, MS, for exchange on 5/1/1865; Exchanged at Camp Townsend, MS, on 5/6/1865.

Turner, Austin H. Pvt., 21st Alabama Infantry. Co. H. Federal Rolls of Prisoners of War: Captured at Fort Gaines, AL, on 8/8/1864; Received at Ship Island, MS, from New Orleans, LA, on 10/25/1864. Exchanged on 1/4/1865.

Turner, E.L. Pvt., 63rd Alabama Infantry. Co. K. Enlisted: 9/12/1864 at Talladega, AL. Rolls for 9/1864 through 10/1864: Present. Federal Rolls of Prisoners of War: Captured at Blakely, AL, on 4/9/1865; Received at Ship Island, MS, on 4/15/1865. Transferred to Vicksburg, MS, for exchange on 5/1/1865; Exchanged at Camp Townsend, MS, on 5/6/1865. Rolls of Prisoners of War, C.S.A: Surrendered at Citronelle, AL, on 5/4/1865; Paroled at Meridian, MS, on 5/13/1865. Residence at parole: Tuscaloosa County, AL.

Turner, James Pvt., Tarrant's Artillery Battery. Federal Rolls of Prisoners of War: Captured at Spanish Fort, AL, on 4/8/1865; Received at Ship Island, MS, on 4/10/1865. Transferred to Vicksburg, MS, for exchange on 5/1/1865; Exchanged at Camp Townsend, MS, on 5/6/1865.

Turner, John W. Pvt., 63rd Alabama Infantry. Co. D. Enlisted: 7/10/1864 at Tallapoosa County, AL. Age at enlistment: 17. Description at enlistment: Eyes: grey. Hair: dark. Complexion: florid. Height: 5'3". Residence at enlistment: Barnesville, AL. Rolls for 9/1864 through 10/1864: Present. Federal Rolls of Prisoners of War: Captured at Blakely, AL, on 4/9/1865; Received at Ship Island, MS, on 4/15/1865. Transferred to Vicksburg, MS, for exchange on 5/1/1865; Exchanged at Camp Townsend, MS, on 5/6/1865. Rolls of Prisoners of War, C.S.A: Surrendered at Citronelle, AL, on 5/4/1865; Paroled at Meridian, MS, on 5/13/1865. Residence at parole: Tallapoosa County, AL.

Turner, Mark A. Pvt., 63rd Alabama Infantry. Co. D. Enlisted: 7/10/1864 at Tallapoosa County, AL. Age at enlistment: 17. Description at enlistment: Eyes: grey. Hair: dark. Complexion: florid. Height: 5'2". Residence at enlistment: Barnesville, AL. Rolls for 9/1864 through 10/1864: Absent, sick in hospital at Mobile, AL, since 10/27/1864. Federal Rolls of Prisoners of War: Captured at Blakely, AL, on 4/9/1865; Received at Ship Island, MS, on 4/15/1865. Transferred to Vicksburg, MS, for exchange on 5/1/1865; Exchanged at Camp Townsend, MS, on 5/6/1865. Rolls of Prisoners of War, C.S.A: Surrendered at Citronelle, AL, on 5/4/1865; Paroled at Meridian, MS, on 5/13/1865. Residence at parole: Tallapoosa County, AL.

Turner, O.N. (AKA O.W.) Pvt., 21st Alabama Infantry. Co. E. Federal Rolls of Prisoners of War: Captured at Fort Gaines, AL, on 8/8/1864; Received at Ship Island, MS, from New Orleans, LA, on 10/25/1864. Died: 1/2/1865 at Ship Island, MS, due to dysentery. Buried: Ship Island, MS, Cemetery in Grave #128.

Turner, Thomas Pvt., 1st Alabama Artillery Battalion. Co. __. Federal Rolls of Prisoners of War: Captured at Fort Gaines, AL, on 8/8/1864; Received at Ship Island, MS, from New Orleans, LA, on 12/13/1864. Exchanged on 1/4/1865.

Turner, William Pvt., 1st Alabama Artillery Battalion. Co. D. Federal Rolls of Prisoners of War: Captured at Fort Gaines, AL, on 8/8/1864; Received at Ship Island, MS, from New Orleans, LA, on 12/13/1864. Exchanged on 1/4/1865.

Turnham, Joseph C. Pvt., 21st Alabama Infantry. Co. G. Federal Rolls of Prisoners of War: Captured at Fort Gaines, AL, on 8/8/1864; Received at Ship Island, MS, from New Orleans, LA, on 10/25/1864. Exchanged on 1/4/1865.

Twiford, D. 2nd Cpl./Pvt., 63rd Alabama Infantry. Co. K. Enlisted: 9/14/1864 at Bibb County, AL. Rolls for 9/1864 through 10/1864: Absent, sick in hospital at Mobile, AL, since 10/20/1864. Federal Rolls of Prisoners of War: Captured at Blakely, AL, on 4/9/1865; Received at Ship Island, MS, on 4/15/1865. Transferred to Vicksburg, MS, for exchange on 5/1/1865; Exchanged at Camp Townsend, MS, on 5/6/1865. Rolls of Prisoners of War, C.S.A: Surrendered at Citronelle, AL, on 5/4/1865; Paroled at Meridian, MS, on 5/13/1865. Residence at parole: Bibb County, AL.

Tyler, John Pvt., 63rd Alabama Infantry. Co. D. Federal Rolls of Prisoners of War: Captured at Blakely, AL, on 4/9/1865; Received at Ship Island, MS, on 4/15/1865. Transferred to Vicksburg, MS, for exchange on 5/1/1865; Exchanged at Camp Townsend, MS, on 5/6/1865. Rolls of Prisoners of War, C.S.A: Surrendered at Citronelle, AL, on 5/4/1865; Paroled at Meridian, MS, on 5/13/1865. Residence at parole: Henry County, AL.

Tyler, R. Pvt., 38th Alabama Infantry. Co. B. Federal Rolls of Prisoners of War: Captured at Spanish Fort, AL, on 4/8/1865; Received at Ship Island, MS, on 4/10/1865. Transferred to Vicksburg, MS, for exchange on 5/1/1865. On Register of U.S.A. General Hospital #2, Vicksburg, MS: Admitted from steamer on 5/6/1865 due to measles; Returned to duty on 5/12/1865.

Tyus, F.J. Pvt., 1st Alabama Artillery Battalion. Co. B. Federal Rolls of Prisoners of War: Captured at Fort Gaines, AL, on 8/8/1864; Received at Ship Island, MS, from New Orleans, LA, on 10/25/1864. Died: 12/5/1864 at Ship Island, MS, due to chronic dysentery. Buried: Ship Island, MS, Cemetery in Grave #67.

Underwood, John Pvt., 1st Alabama Infantry. Co. B. Federal Rolls of Prisoners of War: Captured at Fort Gaines, AL, on 8/8/1864; Received at Ship Island, MS, from New Orleans, LA, on 10/25/1864. Died: 11/22/1864 at Ship Island, MS, due to pneumonia. Buried: Ship Island, MS, Cemetery in Grave #36.

Upton, James Pvt, 8th Alabama Cavalry. Cos. B & F. Federal Rolls of Prisoners of War: Captured in Florida on 3/25/1865; Received at Ship Island, MS. Transferred to Vicksburg, MS, for exchange on 5/1/1865; Exchanged at Camp Townsend, MS, on 5/6/1865.

Vann, William C.H. Pvt., 6th Alabama Cavalry. Co. __. Federal Rolls of Prisoners of War: Captured at Bluff Springs, AL, on 3/25/1865; Received at Ship Island, MS. Transferred to Vicksburg, MS, for exchange on 5/1/1865; Exchanged at Camp Townsend, MS, on 5/6/1865. Rolls of Prisoners of War, C.S.A: Surrendered at Citronelle, AL, on 5/4/1865; Paroled at Meridian, MS, on 5/13/1865. Born: 5/4/1845 at Washington, Washington County, GA. Soldier is recorded on the 1907 Alabama Census of Confederate Veterans and Widows. Residence: Henry County, AL.

Varnon, McB. Pvt., 62nd Alabama Infantry. Cos. B & E. Federal Rolls of Prisoners of War: Captured at Blakely, AL, on 4/9/1865; Received at Ship Island, MS, on 4/15/1865. Transferred to Vicksburg, MS, for exchange on 5/1/1865; Exchanged at Camp Townsend, MS, on 5/6/1865.

Vaughan, Frederick A. Pvt., 6th Alabama Cavalry. Cos. C & E. Federal Rolls of Prisoners of War: Captured in Florida on 3/25/1865; Received at Ship Island, MS. Transferred to Vicksburg, MS, for exchange on 5/1/1865; Exchanged at Camp Townsend, MS, on 5/6/1865.

Vaughn, J.H. Cpl., 6th Alabama Cavalry. Cos. C & D. Federal Rolls of Prisoners of War: Captured in Florida on 3/25/1865; Received at Ship Island, MS. Transferred to Vicksburg, MS, for exchange on 5/1/1865; Exchanged at Camp Townsend, MS, on 5/6/1865.

Vaughn, R.E. (AKA Van Horn) Pvt., 21st Alabama Infantry. Cos. G & I. Federal Rolls of Prisoners of War: Captured at Fort Gaines, AL, on 8/8/1864; Received at Ship Island, MS, from New Orleans, LA, on 10/25/1864. Exchanged on 1/4/1865.

Vaun, W.C.H. Pvt., 6th Alabama Cavalry. Co. E. Federal Rolls of Prisoners of War: Captured in Florida on 3/25/1865; Received at Ship Island, MS. Transferred to Vicksburg, MS, for exchange on 5/1/1865; Exchanged at Camp Townsend, MS, on 5/6/1865.

Veasey, Simon C. (AKA Lyman C.) Pvt., 63rd Alabama Infantry. Co. A. Enlisted: 1/1/1864 at Tallapoosa County, AL. Age at enlistment: 16. Rolls for 1/1864 through 2/1864: Present. Rolls for 9/1864 through 10/1864: Present. Federal Rolls of Prisoners of War: Captured at Blakely, AL, on 4/9/1865; Received at Ship Island, MS, on 4/15/1865. Transferred to Vicksburg, MS, for exchange on 5/1/1865; Exchanged at Camp Townsend, MS, on 5/6/1865. Rolls of Prisoners of War, C.S.A: Surrendered at Citronelle, AL, on 5/4/1865; Paroled at Meridian, MS, on 5/13/1865. Residence at parole: Tallapoosa County, AL.

Vernon, E.W. Pvt., 63rd Alabama Infantry. Co. C. Federal Rolls of Prisoners of War: Captured at Blakely, AL, on 4/9/1865; Received at Ship Island, MS, on 4/15/1865. Transferred to Vicksburg, MS, for exchange on 5/1/1865; Exchanged at Camp Townsend, MS, on 5/6/1865. Rolls of Prisoners of War, C.S.A: Surrendered at Citronelle, AL, on 5/4/1865; Paroled at Meridian, MS, on 5/11/1865. Residence at parole: Chambers County, AL.

Vernon, W.J. Pvt., 8th Alabama Cavalry. Co. B. Federal Rolls of Prisoners of War: Captured in Florida on 3/24/1865; Received at Ship Island, MS. Died: 4/30/1865 at Ship Island, MS, due to congestive fever. Buried: Ship Island, MS, Cemetery in Grave #152.

Vessels, Andrew J. Pvt., 6th Alabama Cavalry. Cos. C & E. Federal Rolls of Prisoners of War: Captured in Florida on 3/25/1865; Received at Ship Island, MS. Transferred to Vicksburg, MS, for exchange on 5/1/1865; Exchanged at Camp Townsend, MS, on 5/6/1865.

Vick, J.A. Pvt., 62nd Alabama Infantry. Cos. B & C. Federal Rolls of Prisoners of War: Captured at Blakely, AL, on 4/9/1865; Received at Ship Island, MS, on 4/15/1865. Transferred to Vicksburg, MS, for exchange on 5/1/1865; Exchanged at Camp Townsend, MS, on 5/6/1865.

Vick, R.R. Pvt., 62nd Alabama Infantry. Co. C. Federal Rolls of Prisoners of War: Captured at Blakely, AL, on 4/9/1865; Received at Ship Island, MS, on 4/15/1865. Transferred to Vicksburg, MS, for exchange on 5/1/1865; Exchanged at Camp Townsend, MS, on 5/6/1865.

Vickers, A. (AKA Vickerz) Pvt., 6th Alabama Cavalry. Cos. C & D. Federal Rolls of Prisoners of War: Captured in Florida on 3/25/1865; Received at Ship Island, MS. Transferred to Vicksburg, MS, for exchange on 5/1/1865; Exchanged at Camp Townsend, MS, on 5/6/1865.

Vickers, Jesse Pvt., 6th Alabama Cavalry. Co. E. Federal Rolls of Prisoners of War: Captured in Florida on 3/25/1865; Received at Ship Island, MS. Transferred to Vicksburg, MS, for exchange on 5/1/1865; Exchanged at Camp Townsend, MS, on 5/6/1865.

Vines, George W. Pvt., 6th Alabama Cavalry. Co. C. Federal Rolls of Prisoners of War: Captured in Florida on 3/25/1865; Received at Ship Island, MS. Transferred to Vicksburg, MS, for exchange on 5/1/1865; Exchanged at Camp Townsend, MS, on 5/6/1865.

Vines, J. Pvt., 63rd Alabama Infantry. Co. H. Enlisted: 7/29/1864 at Selma, AL. Age at enlistment: 17. Description at enlistment: Eyes: dark. Hair: dark. Complexion: dark. Rolls for 9/1864 through 10/1864: Absent, in camp of correction since 8/14/1864. Federal Rolls of Prisoners of War: Captured at Blakely, AL, on 4/9/1865; Received at Ship Island, MS, on 4/15/1865. Transferred to Vicksburg, MS, for exchange on 5/1/1865; Exchanged at Camp Townsend, MS, on 5/6/1865. Rolls of Prisoners of War, C.S.A: Surrendered at Citronelle, AL, on 5/4/1865; Paroled at Meridian, MS, on 5/11/1865. Residence at parole: Jefferson County, AL.

Vines, William Pvt., 63rd Alabama Infantry. Co. G. Federal Rolls of Prisoners of War: Captured at Spanish Fort, AL, on 4/8/1865; Received at Ship Island, MS, on 4/10/1865. Transferred to Vicksburg, MS, for exchange on 5/1/1865; Exchanged at Camp Townsend, MS, on 5/6/1865.

Vinson, Robert (AKA Vincent) Pvt., 63rd Alabama Infantry. Co. B. Enlisted: 3/23/1864 at Montgomery, AL. Age at enlistment: 16. Rolls for 9/1864 through 10/1864: Present. Federal Rolls of Prisoners of War: Captured at Blakely, AL, on 4/9/1865; Received at Ship Island, MS, on 4/15/1865. Transferred to Vicksburg, MS, for exchange on 5/1/1865; Exchanged at Camp Townsend, MS, on 5/6/1865. Rolls of Prisoners of War, C.S.A: Surrendered at Citronelle, AL, on 5/4/1865; Paroled at Meridian, MS, on 5/11/1865. Residence at parole: Coosa County, AL.

Voeglin, Phillip C. Pvt., Tarrant's Artillery Battery. Federal Rolls of Prisoners of War: Captured at Blakely, AL, on 4/9/1865; Received at Ship Island, MS, on 4/15/1865. Transferred to Vicksburg, MS, for exchange on 5/1/1865; Exchanged at Camp Townsend, MS, on 5/6/1865.

Waddill, W. (AKA Waddle) Pvt., 62nd Alabama Infantry. Co. C. Federal Rolls of Prisoners of War: Captured at Blakely, AL, on 4/9/1865; Received at Ship Island, MS, on 4/15/1865. Transferred to Vicksburg, MS, for exchange on 5/1/1865; Exchanged at Camp Townsend, MS, on 5/6/1865.

Wade, Charles B. Pvt., 63rd Alabama Infantry. Co. C.

Enlisted: 4/24/1864 at Russell County, AL. Age at enlistment: 17. Description at enlistment: Eyes: grey. Hair: dark. Complexion: dark. Height: 5'7¼". Residence at enlistment: Russell County, AL. Rolls for 9/1864 through 10/1864: Present. Federal Rolls of Prisoners of War: Captured at Blakely, AL, on 4/9/1865; Received at Ship Island, MS, on 4/15/1865. Transferred to Vicksburg, MS, for exchange on 5/1/1865; Exchanged at Camp Townsend, MS, on 5/6/1865.

Wade, William A. Pvt., 38th Alabama Infantry. Co. E. Enlisted: 4/7/1862 at Mobile, AL. Age at enlistment: 24. Federal Rolls of Prisoners of War: Captured at Blakely, AL, on 4/9/1865; Received at Ship Island, MS, on 4/15/1865. Transferred to Vicksburg, MS, for exchange on 5/1/1865; Forwarded to Camp Townsend, MS, on parole on 5/6/1865.

Wadsworth, J.P. (AKA J.M.) Pvt., 63rd Alabama Infantry. Cos. F & H. Enlisted: 5/30/1864 at Montgomery, AL. Age at enlistment: 17. Description at enlistment: Eyes: grey. Hair: light. Complexion: fair. Height: 5'4". Residence at enlistment: Autauga County, AL. Rolls for 9/1864 through 10/1864: Present, sick. Federal Rolls of Prisoners of War: Captured at Blakely, AL, on 4/9/1865; Received at Ship Island, MS, on 4/15/1865. Transferred to Vicksburg, MS, for exchange on 5/1/1865. On Register of U.S.A. General Hospital #2, Vicksburg, MS: Admitted from steamer on 5/3/1865 due to acute diarrhea; Returned to duty on 5/8/1865.

Wages, J.E. Pvt., 18th Alabama Infantry. Cos. B & E. Federal Rolls of Prisoners of War: Captured at Spanish Fort, AL, on 4/8/1865; Received at Ship Island, MS, on 4/10/1865. Transferred to Vicksburg, MS, for exchange on 5/1/1865; Exchanged at Camp Townsend, MS, on 5/6/1865.

Walden, N. Pvt., 6th Alabama Cavalry. Co. A. Federal Rolls of Prisoners of War: Captured in Florida on 3/25/1865; Received at Ship Island, MS. Transferred to Vicksburg, MS, for exchange on 5/1/1865; Exchanged at Camp Townsend, MS, on 5/6/1865.

Wales, M. Pvt., 62nd Alabama Infantry. Co. A. Federal Rolls of Prisoners of War: Captured at Blakely, AL, on 4/9/1865; Received at Ship Island, MS, on 4/15/1865. Transferred to Vicksburg, MS, for exchange on 5/1/1865; Exchanged at Camp Townsend, MS, on 5/6/1865.

Walker, A.C. Pvt., 8th Alabama Cavalry. Co. E. Federal Rolls of Prisoners of War: Captured at Blakely, AL, on 4/9/1865; Received at Ship Island, MS, on 4/15/1865. Transferred to Vicksburg, MS, for exchange on 5/1/1865; Exchanged at Camp Townsend, MS, on 5/6/1865.

Walker, Bryant S. Cpl./Pvt., 63rd Alabama Infantry. Co. B. Federal Rolls of Prisoners of War: Captured at Blakely, AL, on 4/9/1865; Received at Ship Island, MS, on 4/15/1865. Transferred to Vicksburg, MS, for exchange on 5/1/1865; Exchanged at Camp Townsend, MS, on 5/6/1865.

Walker, David L. Pvt., 63rd Alabama Infantry. Co. D. Enlisted: 7/30/1864 at Macon County, AL. Age at enlistment: 17. Description at enlistment: Eyes: dark. Hair: dark. Complexion: dark. Height: 6'3". Residence at enlistment: Buford, Barbour County, AL. Rolls for 8/1864 through 10/1864: Present. Federal Rolls of Prisoners of War: Captured at Blakely, AL, on 4/9/1865; Received at Ship Island, MS, on 4/15/1865. Transferred to Vicksburg, MS, for exchange on 5/1/1865; Exchanged at Camp Townsend, MS, on 5/6/1865. Rolls of Prisoners of War, C.S.A: Surrendered at Citronelle, AL, on 5/4/1865; Paroled at Meridian, MS, on 5/13/1865. Residence at parole: Barbour County, AL.

Walker, J.F. Pvt., 63rd Alabama Infantry. Cos. F & H. Enlisted: 5/30/1864 at Montgomery, AL. Age at enlistment: 17. Description at enlistment: Eyes: blue. Hair: light. Complexion: fair. Height: 5'8". Residence at enlistment: Butler County, AL. Rolls for 6/1864 through 7/1864: Present. Rolls for 9/1864 through 10/1864: Present. Federal Rolls of Prisoners of War: Captured at Blakely, AL, on 4/9/1865; Received at Ship Island, MS, on 4/15/1865. Transferred to Vicksburg, MS, for exchange on 5/1/1865; Exchanged at Camp Townsend, MS, on 5/6/1865. Rolls of Prisoners of War, C.S.A: Surrendered at Citronelle, AL, on 5/4/1865; Paroled at Meridian, MS, on 5/11/1865. Residence at parole: Butler County, AL.

Walker, J.W. Pvt., 62nd Alabama Infantry. Co. I. Federal Rolls of Prisoners of War: Captured at Blakely, AL, on 4/9/1865; Received at Ship Island, MS, on 4/15/1865. Transferred to Vicksburg, MS, for exchange on 5/1/1865; Exchanged at Camp Townsend, MS, on 5/6/1865.

Walker, James J. Pvt., 63rd Alabama Infantry. Co. G. Enlisted: 5/16/1864 at Troy, AL. Age at enlistment: 17. Description at enlistment: Eyes: grey. Hair: light. Complexion: florid. Height: 5'8". Residence at enlistment: Pike County, AL. Rolls for 9/1864 through 10/1864: Present. Rolls of Prisoners of War, C.S.A: Surrendered at Citronelle, AL, on 5/4/1865; Paroled at Meridian, MS, on 5/11/1865. Residence at parole: Pike County, AL. Born: 7/16/1847 at Columbus, Muscogee County, GA. Soldier is recorded on the 1907 Census of Alabama Confederate Veterans and Widows. Residence: Crenshaw County, AL.

Walker, John M. (AKA J.W.) Pvt., 63rd Alabama Infantry. Co. F & H. Enlisted: 7/12/1864 at Lowndes County, AL. Age at enlistment: 17. Description at enlistment: Eyes: blue. Hair: dark. Complexion: dark. Height: 5'8". Residence at enlistment: Lowndes County, AL. Rolls for 7/12/1864 through 7/25/1864: Present. Rolls for 9/1864 through 10/1864: Present, sick. Federal Rolls of Prisoners of War: Captured at Blakely, AL, on 4/9/1865; Received at Ship Island, MS, on 4/15/1865. Transferred to Vicksburg, MS, for exchange on 5/1/1865; Exchanged at Camp Townsend, MS, on 5/6/1865. Rolls of Prisoners of War, C.S.A: Surrendered at Citronelle, AL, on 5/4/1865; Paroled at Meridian, MS, on 5/11/1865. Residence at parole: Lowndes County, AL. Born: 12/1/1846 at Lowndes County, AL. Soldier is recorded on the 1907 Alabama Census of Confederate Veterans and Widows. Residence: Crenshaw County, AL.

Walkley, Bryant S. 2nd Cpl./Pvt., 63rd Alabama Infantry. Co. B. Enlisted: 3/23/1864 at Montgomery, AL. Age at enlistment: 17. Rolls for 9/1864 through 10/1864: Absent, on sick furlough since 10/28/1864. Federal Rolls of Prisoners of War: Captured at Blakely, AL, on 4/9/1865; Received at Ship Island, MS, on 4/15/1865. Transferred to Vicksburg, MS, for exchange on 5/1/1865; Exchanged at Camp Townsend, MS, on 5/6/1865. Rolls of Prisoners of War, CSA: Surrendered at Citronelle, AL, on 5/4/1865; Paroled at Meridian, MS, on 5/13/1865. Residence at parole: Coosa County, AL.

Wallace, Julius Monroe Cpl., Lockhart's Battalion Infantry. Cos. E & F. Enlisted: 11/17/1863 at Talladega, AL. Federal Rolls of Prisoners of War: Captured at Fort Gaines, AL, on 8/8/1864; Received at Ship Island, MS, from New Orleans, LA, on 10/25/1864. Exchanged on 1/4/1865. Born: 10/6/1846 at Bibb County, AL. Residence after war: Bibb County, AL.

Walls, Robert (AKA B.) Pvt., Lockhart's Battalion Infantry. Cos. E & F. Federal Rolls of Prisoners of War: Captured at Fort Gaines, AL, on 8/8/1864; Received at Ship Island, MS, from New Orleans, LA, on 10/25/1864. Exchanged on 1/4/1865.

Walls, T. Pvt., Lockhart's Battalion Infantry. Co. H. Federal Rolls of Prisoners of War: Captured at Fort Gaines, AL, on 8/8/1864; Received at Ship Island, MS, from New Orleans, LA, on 10/25/1864. Exchanged on 1/4/1865.

Walsh, Rufus F. Pvt., 36th Alabama Infantry. Co. A. Federal Rolls of Prisoners of War: Captured at Spanish Fort, AL, on 4/8/1865; Received at Ship Island, MS, on 4/10/1865. Transferred to Vicksburg, MS, for exchange on 5/1/1865; Exchanged at Camp Townsend, MS, on 5/6/1865.

Walter, J. Pvt., 21st Alabama Infantry. Co. I. Federal Rolls of Prisoners of War: Captured at Fort Gaines, AL, on 8/8/1864; Received at Ship Island, MS, from New Orleans, LA, on 10/25/1864. Exchanged on 1/4/1865.

Ward, A.T. Pvt., 6th Alabama Cavalry. Co. E. Federal Rolls of Prisoners of War: Captured in Florida on 3/25/1865; Received at Ship Island, MS. Transferred to Vicksburg, MS, for exchange on 5/1/1865; Exchanged at Camp Townsend, MS, on 5/6/1865.

Ward, Charles Cpl., 21st Alabama Infantry. Co. G. Federal Rolls of Prisoners of War: Captured at Fort Gaines, AL, on 8/8/1864; Received at Ship Island, MS, from New Orleans, LA, on 10/25/1864. Died: 12/27/1864 at Ship Island, MS, due to smallpox. Buried: Ship Island, MS, Cemetery in Grave #114.

Ward, James Pvt., 6th Alabama Cavalry. Co. F. Federal Rolls of Prisoners of War: Captured in Florida on 3/25/1865; Received at Ship Island, MS. Transferred to Vicksburg, MS, for exchange on 5/1/1865; Exchanged at Camp Townsend, MS, on 5/6/1865.

Ward, John Pvt., 62nd Alabama Infantry. Co. B. Federal Rolls of Prisoners of War: Captured at Blakely, AL, on 4/9/1865; Received at Ship Island, MS, on 4/15/1865. Transferred to Vicksburg, MS, for exchange on 5/1/1865; Exchanged at Camp Townsend, MS, on 5/6/1865.

Ward, John Pvt., 36th Alabama Infantry. Co. G. Federal Rolls of Prisoners of War: Captured at Spanish Fort, AL, on 4/8/1865; Received at Ship Island, MS, on 4/10/1865. Transferred to Vicksburg, MS, for exchange on 5/1/1865; Exchanged at Camp Townsend, MS, on 5/6/1865.

Ward, M. Hosp. Steward, 1st Alabama Infantry. F & S. Federal Rolls of Prisoners of War: Captured at Blakely, AL, on 4/9/1865; Received at Ship Island, MS, on 4/15/1865. Transferred to Vicksburg, MS, on 5/1/1865; Exchanged at Camp Townsend, MS, on 5/6/1865.

Ward, Thomas R. Pvt., 62nd Alabama Infantry. Co. B. Federal Rolls of Prisoners of War: Captured at Blakely, AL, on 4/9/1865; Received at Ship Island, MS, on 4/15/1865. Transferred to Vicksburg, MS, for exchange on 5/1/1865; Exchanged at Camp Townsend, MS, on 5/6/1865.

Warren, J.B. Pvt., 62nd Alabama Infantry. Co. B. Federal Rolls of Prisoners of War: Captured at Blakely, AL, on 4/9/1865; Received at Ship Island, MS, on 4/15/1865. Transferred to Vicksburg, MS, for exchange on 5/1/1865; Exchanged at Camp Townsend, MS, on 5/6/1865.

Warren, Johnson Cpl./Pvt., 62nd Alabama Infantry. Co. B. Federal Rolls of Prisoners of War: Captured at Blakely, AL, on 4/9/1865; Received at Ship Island, MS, on 4/15/1865. Transferred to Vicksburg, MS, for exchange on 5/1/1865; Exchanged at Camp Townsend, MS, on 5/6/1865.

Watkins, Micajah L. Pvt., 63rd Alabama Infantry. Co. D. Enlisted: 7/30/1864 at Macon County, AL. Age at enlistment: 17. Description at enlistment: Eyes: grey. Hair: auburn. Complexion: fair. Height: 5'7". Residence at enlistment: Barbour County, AL. Rolls for 8/1864 through 10/1864: Present. Federal Rolls of Prisoners of War: Captured at Blakely, AL, on 4/9/1865; Received at Ship Island, MS, on 4/15/1865. Transferred to Vicksburg, MS, for exchange on 5/1/1865; Exchanged at Camp Townsend, MS, on 5/6/1865. Rolls of Prisoners of War, C.S.A: Surrendered at Citronelle, AL, on 5/4/1865; Paroled at Meridian, MS, on 5/13/1865. Residence at parole: Barbour County, AL. Born: 2/9/1847 at Andalusia, Covington County, AL. Soldier is recorded on the 1907 Alabama Census of Confederate Veterans and Widows. Residence: Pike County, AL.

Watson, A.M. Pvt., 63rd Alabama Infantry. Cos. F & H. Enlisted: 3/9/1864 at Greenville, AL. Age at enlistment: 17. Description at enlistment: Eyes: grey. Hair: brown. Complexion: fair. Height: 5'4". Residence at enlistment: Butler County, AL. Rolls for 3/1864 through 7/25/1864: Present, at Georgiana, AL. Rolls for 9/1864 through 10/1864: Present. Federal Rolls of Prisoners of War: Captured at Blakely, AL, on 4/9/1865; Received at Ship Island, MS, on 4/15/1865. Transferred to Vicksburg, MS, for exchange on 5/1/1865; Exchanged at Camp Townsend, MS, on 5/6/1865. Rolls of Prisoners of War, C.S.A: Surrendered at Citronelle, AL, on 5/4/1865; Paroled at Meridian, MS, on 5/11/1865. Residence at parole: Butler County, AL.

Watson, John H. Pvt., 38th Alabama Infantry-Co. C. On Register of Tunnel Hill, GA, Hospital: Admitted on 6/27/1863 due to febris remittens; Returned to duty on 8/28/1863. Remarks: No disability noted at Chattanooga, TN. Federal Rolls of Prisoners of War: Captured at Spanish Fort, AL, on 4/8/1865; Received at Ship Island, MS, on 4/10/1865; Transferred to Vicksburg, MS, for exchange on 5/1/1865; Exchanged at Camp Townsend, MS, on 5/6/1865.

Weatherly, L.F. Cpl./Pvt., 21st Alabama Infantry. Cos. C & D. Federal Rolls of Prisoners of War: Captured at Blakely, AL, on 4/9/1865; Received at Ship Island, MS, on 4/15/1865. Transferred to Vicksburg, MS, for exchange on 5/1/1865; Exchanged at Camp Townsend, MS, on 5/6/1865.

Weathers, F.M. Pvt., 36th Alabama Infantry. Co. K.

Federal Rolls of Prisoners of War: Captured at Spanish Fort, AL, on 4/8/1865; Received at Ship Island, MS, on 4/10/1865. Transferred to Vicksburg, MS, for exchange on 5/1/1865; Exchanged at Camp Townsend, MS, on 5/6/1865.

Webb, A.T. Pvt./Cpl., 21st Alabama Infantry. Co. C. Federal Rolls of Prisoners of War: Captured at Fort Gaines, AL, on 8/8/1864; Received at Ship Island, MS, from New Orleans, LA, on 10/25/1864. Exchanged on 1/4/1865.

Webb, James G. Pvt., 38th Alabama Infantry. Co. A. Age at enlistment: 25. Paid .25 cents per day for extra duty as Teamster at Chattanooga, TN, for 7/1863; Detailed as Teamster for 8/1863 through 9/1863 and 10/5/1863 through 12/31/1863. Federal Rolls of Prisoners of War: Captured at Spanish Fort, AL, on 4/8/1865; Received at Ship Island, MS, on 4/10/1865. Transferred to Vicksburg, MS, for exchange on 5/1/1865; Exchanged at Camp Townsend, MS, on 5/6/1865.

Webb, James T. Pvt., 38th Alabama Infantry. Co. A. Age at enlistment: 32. Federal Rolls of Prisoners of War: Captured at Spanish Fort, AL, on 4/8/1865; Received at Ship Island, MS, on 4/10/1865. Transferred to Vicksburg, MS, for exchange on 5/1/1865; Exchanged at Camp Townsend, MS, on 5/6/1865.

Webb, William T. Pvt., 63rd Alabama Infantry. Co. A. Enlisted: 1/1/1864 at Macon County, AL. Age at enlistment: 16. Rolls for 1/1864 through 2/1864: Present. Rolls for 9/1864 through 10/1864: Sick, in quarters. Federal Rolls of Prisoners of War: Captured at Blakely, AL, on 4/9/1865; Received at Ship Island, MS, on 4/15/1865. Transferred to Vicksburg, MS, for exchange on 5/1/1865; Exchanged at Camp Townsend, MS, on 5/6/1865. Rolls of Prisoners of War, C.S.A: Surrendered at Citronelle, AL, on 5/4/1865; Paroled at Meridian, MS, on 5/13/1865. Residence at parole: Macon County, AL.

Wells, James M. Pvt., 63rd Alabama Infantry. Co. A. Enlisted: 1/1/1864 at Coosa County, AL. Age at enlistment: 16. Rolls for 1/1864 through 2/1864: Absent, sick at Stonewall Hospital. Rolls for 9/1864 through 10/1864: Present, sick in quarters. Federal Rolls of Prisoners of War: Captured at Blakely, AL, on 4/9/1865; Received at Ship Island, MS, on 4/15/1865. Transferred to Vicksburg, MS, for exchange on 5/1/1865; Exchanged at Camp Townsend, MS, on 5/6/1865. Rolls of Prisoners of War, C.S.A: Surrendered at Citronelle, AL, on 5/4/1865; Paroled at Meridian, MS, on 5/11/1865. Residence at parole: Bibb County, AL.

West, Amos W. Pvt., 63rd Alabama Infantry. Co. D. Enlisted: 7/30/1864 at Macon County, AL. Age at enlistment: 17. Description at enlistment: Eyes: blue. Hair: dark. Complexion: fair. Height: 5'6". Residence at enlistment: Barbour County, AL. Rolls for 8/1864 through 10/1864: Present. Federal Rolls of Prisoners of War: Captured at Blakely, AL, on 4/9/1865; Received at Ship Island, MS, on 4/15/1865. Transferred to Vicksburg, MS, for exchange on 5/1/1865; Exchanged at Camp Townsend, MS, on 5/6/1865. Rolls of Prisoners of War, C.S.A: Surrendered at Citronelle, AL, on 5/4/1865; Paroled at Meridian, MS, on 5/13/1865. Residence at parole: Barbour County, AL.

West, Henry F. 1st Cpl./5th Sgt., 63rd Alabama Infantry. Co. I. Enlisted: 4/15/1864 at Columbiana, AL. Rolls for 9/1864 through 10/1864: Absent since 10/28/1864. Federal Rolls of Prisoners of War: Captured at Blakely, AL, on 4/9/1865; Received at Ship Island, MS, on 4/15/1865. Transferred to Vicksburg, MS, for exchange on 5/1/1865; Exchanged at Camp Townsend, MS, on 5/6/1865. Rolls of Prisoners of War, C.S.A: Surrendered at Citronelle, AL, on 5/4/1865; Paroled at Meridian, MS, on 5/13/1865. Residence at parole: Shelby County, AL.

Whatley, David A.J. (AKA L.J.) Pvt./Cpl., 62nd Alabama Infantry. Co. A. Federal Rolls of Prisoners of War: Captured at Blakely, AL, on 4/9/1865; Received at Ship Island, MS, on 4/15/1865. Transferred to Vicksburg, MS, for exchange on 5/1/1865; Exchanged at Camp Townsend, MS, on 5/6/1865.

Whatley, S.J. Pvt., 63rd Alabama Infantry. Co. K. Enlisted: 8/8/1864 at Montgomery County, AL. Rolls for 9/1864 through 10/1864: Absent, in hospital at Mobile, AL, since 10/26/1864. Federal Rolls of Prisoners of War: Captured at Blakely, AL, on 4/9/1865; Received at Ship Island, MS, on 4/15/1865. Transferred to Vicksburg, MS, for exchange on 5/1/1865; Exchanged at Camp Townsend, MS, on 5/6/1865. Rolls of Prisoners of War, C.S.A: Surrendered at Citronelle, AL, on 5/4/1865; Paroled at Meridian, MS, on 5/13/1865. Residence at parole: Montgomery County, AL.

Whatley, W.H. 2nd Sgt., 63rd Alabama Infantry. Cos. D & H. Enlisted: 3/15/1864 at Centerville, AL. Age at enlistment: 17. Description at enlistment: Eyes: blue. Hair: dark. Complexion: fair. Rolls for 9/1864 through 10/1864: Present. Federal Rolls of Prisoners of War: Captured at Blakely, AL, on 4/9/1865; Received at Ship Island, MS, on 4/15/1865. Transferred to Vicksburg, MS, for exchange on 5/1/1865; Exchanged at Camp Townsend, MS, on 5/6/1865.

Wheat, William L. Pvt., 63rd Alabama Infantry. Co. A. Enlisted: 1/1/1864 at Macon County, AL. Age at enlistment: 15. Rolls for 1/1864 through 2/1864: Present. Rolls for 9/1864 through 10/1864: Present. Federal Rolls of Prisoners of War: Captured at Blakely, AL, on 4/9/1865; Received at Ship Island, MS, on 4/15/1865. Transferred to Vicksburg, MS, for exchange on 5/1/1865; Exchanged at Camp Townsend, MS, on 5/6/1865. Rolls of Prisoners of War, C.S.A: Surrendered at Citronelle, AL, on 5/4/1865; Paroled at Meridian, MS, on 5/13/1865. Residence at parole: Macon County, AL.

Wheatley, William Pvt., 21st Alabama Infantry. Co. F. Federal Rolls of Prisoners of War: Captured at Spanish Fort, AL, on 4/8/1865; Received at Ship Island, MS, on 4/10/1865. Transferred to Vicksburg, MS, for exchange on 5/1/1865; Exchanged at Camp Townsend, MS, on 5/6/1865.

Wheeles, Edward J. Pvt., 63rd Alabama Infantry. Co. A. Enlisted: 1/1/1864 at Macon County, AL. Age at enlistment: 17. Rolls for 1/1864 through 2/1864: Present. Rolls for 9/1864 through 10/1864: Present. Federal Rolls of Prisoners of War: Captured at Blakely, AL, on 4/9/1865; Received at Ship Island, MS, on 4/15/1865. Transferred to Vicksburg, MS, for exchange on 5/1/1865; Exchanged at Camp Townsend, MS, on 5/6/1865. Rolls of Prisoners of War, C.S.A: Surrendered at Citronelle, AL, on 5/4/1865; Paroled at Meridian, MS, on 5/13/1865. Residence at parole: Macon County, AL.

Whidby, Thomas Pvt., 63rd Alabama Infantry. Co. H. Enlisted: 3/15/1864 at Randolph County, AL. Age at enlistment: 17. Description at enlistment: Eyes: blue. Hair: dark. Complexion: dark. Rolls for 9/1864 through 10/1864: Present. Federal Rolls of Prisoners of War: Captured at Blakely, AL, on 4/9/1865; Received at Ship Island, MS, on 4/15/1865. Transferred to Vicksburg, MS, for exchange on 5/1/1865; Exchanged at Camp Townsend, MS, on 5/6/1865. Rolls of Prisoners of War, C.S.A: Surrendered at Citronelle, AL, on 5/4/1865; Paroled at Meridian, MS, on 5/11/1865. Residence at parole: Bibb County, AL.

Whissenhunt, John F. Pvt., 38th Alabama Infantry. Cos. A & G. Age at enlistment: 24. Federal Rolls of Prisoners of War: Captured at Spanish Fort, AL, on 4/8/1865; Received at Ship Island, MS, on 4/10/1865. Transferred to Vicksburg, MS, for exchange on 5/1/1865; Exchanged at Camp Townsend, MS, on 5/6/1865.

White, H.E. Pvt., 38th Alabama Infantry. Co. H. Federal Rolls of Prisoners of War: Captured at Spanish Fort, AL, on 4/8/1865; Received at Ship Island, MS, on 4/10/1865. Transferred to Vicksburg, MS, for exchange on 5/1/1865; Exchanged at Camp Townsend, MS, on 5/6/1865.

White, James Andrew Pvt., Tarrant's Artillery Battery. Enlisted: 2/2/1862 at Tuscaloosa, AL. Federal Rolls of Prisoners of War: Captured at Blakely, AL, on 4/9/1865; Received at Ship Island, MS, on 4/15/1865. Transferred to Vicksburg, MS, for exchange on 5/1/1865; Exchanged at Camp Townsend, MS, on 5/6/1865. Born: 11/10/1846 at Scottsville, Bibb County, AL. Died: 5/5/1921. Buried: Bibb County, AL.

White, W.T. Pvt., 36th Alabama Infantry. Co. D. Federal Rolls of Prisoners of War: Captured in Alabama on 3/24/1865; Received at Ship Island, MS. Transferred to Vicksburg, MS, for exchange on 5/1/1865; Exchanged at Camp Townsend, MS, on 5/6/1865.

Whitman, James Pvt., 63rd Alabama Infantry. Co. E. Federal Rolls of Prisoners of War: Captured at Blakely, AL, on 4/9/1865; Received at Ship Island, MS, on 4/15/1865. Transferred to Vicksburg, MS, for exchange on 5/1/1865; Exchanged at Camp Townsend, MS, on 5/6/1865. Rolls of Prisoners of War, C.S.A: Surrendered at Citronelle, AL, on 5/4/1865; Paroled at Meridian, MS, on 5/13/1865. Residence at parole: Russell County, AL.

Whittle, Elisha Pvt., 63rd Alabama Infantry. Co. G. Enlisted: 5/16/1864 at Troy, AL. Age at enlistment: 17. Description at enlistment: Eyes: black. Hair: black. Complexion: fair. Height: 5'7". Residence at enlistment: Pike County, AL. Rolls for 9/1864 through 10/1864: Present. Federal Rolls of Prisoners of War: Captured at Blakely, AL, on 4/9/1865; Received at Ship Island, MS, on 4/15/1865. Transferred to Vicksburg, MS, for exchange on 5/1/1865; Exchanged at Camp Townsend, MS, on 5/6/1865. Rolls of Prisoners of War, C.S.A: Surrendered at Citronelle, AL, on 5/4/1865; Paroled at Meridian, MS, on 5/13/1865. Residence at parole: Pike County, AL.

Wicks, H. Pvt., Pelham Cadets. Co. A. Federal Rolls of Prisoners of War: Captured at Fort Gaines, AL, on 8/8/1864; Received at Ship Island, MS, from New Orleans, LA, on 10/25/1864. Exchanged on 1/4/1865.

Wiggins, Jasper W. (AKA W.J.) Pvt., 63rd Alabama Infantry. Co. B. Enlisted: 8/15/1864 at Pollard, AL. Rolls for 9/1864 through 10/1864: Present. Federal Rolls of Prisoners of War: Captured at Blakely, AL, on 4/9/1865; Received at Ship Island, MS, on 4/15/1865. Transferred to Vicksburg, MS, for exchange on 5/1/1865; Exchanged at Camp Townsend, MS, on 5/6/1865. Rolls of Prisoners of War, C.S.A: Surrendered at Citronelle, AL, on 5/4/1865; Paroled at Meridian, MS, on 5/11/1865. Residence at parole: Dale County, AL.

Wigham, R.N. Pvt., 58th Alabama Infantry. Co. K. Federal Rolls of Prisoners of War: Captured at Spanish Fort, AL, on 4/8/1865; Received at Ship Island, MS, on 4/10/1865. Transferred to Vicksburg, MS, for exchange on 5/1/1865.

Wilburn, J.D. (AKA Wilborn) Pvt., Tarrant's Artillery Battery. Federal Rolls of Prisoners of War: Captured at Blakely, AL, on 4/9/1865; Received at Ship Island, MS, on 4/15/1865. Transferred to Vicksburg, MS, for exchange on 5/1/1865; Exchanged at Camp Townsend, MS, on 5/6/1865.

Wilder, J.M. Pvt., Tarrant's Artillery Battery. Federal Rolls of Prisoners of War: Captured at Blakely, AL, on 4/9/1865; Received at Ship Island, MS, on 4/15/1865. Transferred to Vicksburg, MS, for exchange on 5/1/1865; Exchanged at Camp Townsend, MS, on 5/6/1865.

Wilkerson, D.P. Pvt., 63rd Alabama Infantry. Cos. F & H. Enlisted: 3/9/1864 at Greenville, AL. Age at enlistment: 17. Description at enlistment: Eyes: grey. Hair: brown. Complexion: fair. Height: 5'8". Residence at enlistment: Butler County, AL. Rolls for 3/1864 through 10/1864: Present. Federal Rolls of Prisoners of War: Captured at Blakely, AL, on 4/9/1865; Received at Ship Island, MS, on 4/15/1865. Transferred to Vicksburg, MS, for exchange on 5/1/1865; Exchanged at Camp Townsend, MS, on 5/6/1865. On Register of U.S.A. General Hospital #2, Vicksburg, MS: Admitted from steamer on 5/3/1865 with intermittent fever; Returned to duty on 5/10/1865. Age at admittance: 17. Rolls of Prisoners of War, C.S.A: Surrendered at Citronelle, AL, on 5/4/1865; Paroled at Selma, AL, on 5/25/1865. Residence at parole: Russell County, AL.

Williams, Daniel J. Pvt., 40th Alabama Infantry. Co. I. Enlisted: 1861 at Mobile, AL. Federal Rolls of Prisoners of War: Captured at Andalusia, AL, on 4/15/1865; Received at Ship Island, MS. Transferred to Vicksburg, MS, for exchange on 5/1/1865; Exchanged at Camp Townsend, MS, on 5/6/1865. Born: 8/16/1837 at Houston County, GA. Soldier is recorded on the 1907 Alabama Census of Confederate Veterans and Widows. Residence: Geneva County, AL.

Williams, David Pvt., 29th Alabama Infantry. Co. G. Enlisted: 1861 at Eufaula, AL. Transferred to the C.S. Navy in 1863 for duty on the CSS *Tennessee*. Federal Rolls of Prisoners of War: Captured at Mobile Bay, AL, on 8/5/1864; Received at Ship Island, MS. Federal Rolls of Prisoners of War: Captured at Blakely, AL, on 4/9/1865; Received at Ship Island, MS, on 4/15/1865. Transferred to Vicksburg, MS, for exchange on 5/1/1865; Exchanged at Camp Townsend, MS, on 5/6/1865. Description at exchange: Eyes: blue. Hair: dark. Complexion: light. Height: 5'11½". Residence at exchange: Lafourche Parish, LA. Born: 6/18/1826 at Mount Andrews, Barbour County, AL.

Soldier is recorded on the 1907 Alabama Census of Confederate Veterans and Widows. Residence: Bullock County, AL.

Williams, H.H. Pvt., 63rd Alabama Infantry. Co. F. Enlisted: 3/9/1864 at Greenville, AL. Age at enlistment: 17. Description at enlistment: Eyes: blue. Hair: light. Complexion: fair. Height: 5'5". Residence at enlistment: Butler County, AL. Rolls for 3/1864 through 10/1864: Present. Federal Rolls of Prisoners of War: Captured at Blakely, AL, on 4/9/1865; Received at Ship Island, MS, on 4/15/1865. Transferred to Vicksburg, MS, for exchange on 5/1/1865; Exchanged at Camp Townsend, MS, on 5/6/1865. Rolls of Prisoners of War, C.S.A: Surrendered at Citronelle, AL, on 5/4/1865; Paroled at Meridian, MS, on 5/11/1865. Residence at parole: Butler County, AL.

Williams, Henry Pvt., 36th Alabama Infantry. Co. __. Federal Rolls of Prisoners of War: Captured in Alabama on 3/23/1865; Received at Ship Island, MS. Transferred to Vicksburg, MS, on 5/1/1865; Exchanged at Camp Townsend, MS, on 5/6/1865.

Williams, James P. (AKA P.) Pvt., 62nd Alabama Infantry. Co. A. Federal Rolls of Prisoners of War: Captured at Blakely, AL, on 4/9/1865; Received at Ship Island, MS, on 4/15/1865. Transferred to Vicksburg, MS, for exchange on 5/1/1865; Exchanged at Camp Townsend, MS, on 5/6/1865.

Williams, John W. Pvt., 18th Alabama Infantry. Co. B. Federal Rolls of Prisoners of War: Captured at Spanish Fort, AL, on 4/8/1865; Received at Ship Island, MS, on 4/10/1865. Transferred to Vicksburg, MS, for exchange on 5/1/1865; Exchanged at Camp Townsend, MS, on 5/6/1865.

Williams, Thomas Pvt., 18th Alabama Infantry. Co. B. Federal Rolls of Prisoners of War: Captured at Spanish Fort, AL, on 4/8/1865; Received at Ship Island, MS, on 4/10/1865. Transferred to Vicksburg, MS, for exchange on 5/1/1865; Exchanged at Camp Townsend, MS, on 5/6/1865.

Williams, W.N.L. Pvt., 63rd Alabama Infantry. Co. G. Enlisted: 5/16/1864 at Troy, AL. Age at enlistment: 17. Description at enlistment: Eyes: grey. Hair: dark. Complexion: florid. Height: 5'8". Residence at enlistment: Pike County, AL. Rolls for 9/1864 through 10/1864: Present. Federal Rolls of Prisoners of War: Captured at Blakely, AL, on 4/9/1865; Received at Ship Island, MS, on 4/15/1865. Transferred to Vicksburg, MS, for exchange on 5/1/1865; Exchanged at Camp Townsend, MS, on 5/6/1865. Rolls of Prisoners of War, C.S.A: Surrendered at Citronelle, AL, on 5/4/1865; Paroled at Meridian, MS, on 5/13/1865. Residence at parole: Pike County, AL.

Williams, Z. Pvt., 3rd Alabama Cavalry. Co. __. Federal Rolls of Prisoners of War: Captured near Mobile, AL, on 12/17/1864; Received at Ship Island, MS, from New Orleans, LA, on 1/25/1865. Transferred to Vicksburg, MS, for exchange on 5/1/1865; Exchanged at Camp Townsend, MS, on 5/6/1865.

Williamson, J.T.F. (AKA Williams) Pvt., 21st Alabama Infantry. Co. D. Federal Rolls of Prisoners of War: Captured at Blakely, AL, on 4/9/1865; Received at Ship Island, MS, on 4/15/1865. Transferred to Vicksburg, MS, for exchange on 5/1/1865; Exchanged at Camp Townsend, MS, on 5/6/1865.

Williamson, Monroe Pvt., 63rd Alabama Infantry. Co. G. Enlisted: 8/1/1864 at Pollard, AL. Age at enlistment: 17. Description at enlistment: Eyes: grey. Hair: light. Complexion: florid. Height: 5'8". Rolls for 9/1864 through 10/1864: Present. Federal Rolls of Prisoners of War: Captured at Blakely, AL, on 4/9/1865; Received at Ship Island, MS, on 4/15/1865. Transferred to Vicksburg, MS, for exchange on 5/1/1865. On Register of U.S.A. General Hospital #2, Vicksburg, MS: Admitted from steamer on 5/3/1865 with acute diarrhea; Returned to duty on 5/8/1865. Age at admittance: 17.

Williamson, S.D. Pvt., 38th Alabama Infantry. Co. E. Federal Rolls of Prisoners of War: Captured at Blakely, AL, on 4/9/1865; Received at Ship Island, MS, on 4/15/1865. Transferred to Vicksburg, MS, for exchange on 5/1/1865; Exchanged at Camp Townsend, MS, on 5/6/1865.

Willis, Francis M. 3rd Cpl./4th Cpl., 63rd Alabama Infantry. Co. I. Enlisted: 7/20/1864 at Selma, AL. Rolls for 9/1864 through 10/1864: Present. Federal Rolls of Prisoners of War: Captured at Blakely, AL, on 4/9/1865; Received at Ship Island, MS, on 4/15/1865. Transferred to Vicksburg, MS, for exchange on 5/1/1865; Exchanged at Camp Townsend, MS, on 5/6/1865. Rolls of Prisoners of War, C.S.A: Surrendered at Citronelle, AL, on 5/4/1865; Paroled at Meridian, MS, on 5/13/1865. Residence at parole: Shelby County, AL.

Wilson, Augustus Pvt., 62nd Alabama Infantry. Co. A. Federal Rolls of Prisoners of War: Captured at Blakely, AL, on 4/9/1865; Received at Ship Island, MS, on 4/15/1865. Transferred to Vicksburg, MS, for exchange on 5/1/1865; Exchanged at Camp Townsend, MS, on 5/6/1865.

Wilson, H. Pvt., Pelham Cadets. Co. A. Federal Rolls of Prisoners of War: Captured at Fort Gaines, AL, on 8/8/1864; Received at Ship Island, MS, from New Orleans, LA, on 10/25/1864. Exchanged on 1/4/1865.

Wilson, James Pvt., Lockhart's Battalion Infantry. Cos. I & K. Federal Rolls of Prisoners of War: Captured at Fort Gaines, AL, on 8/8/1864; Received at Ship Island, MS, from New Orleans, LA, on 10/25/1864. Exchanged on 1/4/1865.

Wilson, James B. Pvt., Lockhart's Battalion Infantry. Co. I. Federal Rolls of Prisoners of War: Captured at Fort Gaines, AL, on 8/8/1864; Received at Ship Island, MS, from New Orleans, LA, on 10/25/1864. Exchanged on 1/4/1865.

Wilson, Jerry (AKA J.C.) Pvt., Lockhart's Battalion Infantry. Co. H. Federal Rolls of Prisoners of War: Captured at Fort Gaines, AL, on 8/8/1864; Received at Ship Island, MS, from New Orleans, LA, on 10/25/1864. Exchanged on 1/4/1865.

Wilson, John T. Pvt., 63rd Alabama Infantry. Co. G. Enlisted: 5/16/1864 at Troy, AL. Age at enlistment: 17. Description at enlistment: Eyes: dark. Hair: dark. Complexion: dark. Height: 5'6". Residence at enlistment: Pike County, AL. Rolls for 9/1864 through 10/1864: Present. Federal Rolls of Prisoners of War: Captured at Blakely, AL, on 4/9/1865; Received at Ship Island, MS, on 4/15/1865. Transferred to Vicksburg, MS, for exchange on 5/1/1865; Exchanged at Camp Townsend, MS, on 5/6/1865. Rolls of Prisoners of War, C.S.A: Surrendered at Citronelle, AL, on 5/4/1865; Paroled at Meridian, MS, on 5/13/1865. Residence at parole: Pike County, AL.

Wilson, Joseph H. Pvt., 63rd Alabama Infantry. Co.

I. Enlisted: 8/1/1864 at Selma, AL. Rolls for 9/1864 through 10/1864: Present. Federal Rolls of Prisoners of War: Captured at Blakely, AL, on 4/9/1865; Received at Ship Island, MS, on 4/15/1865. Transferred to Vicksburg, MS, for exchange on 5/1/1865; Exchanged at Camp Townsend, MS, on 5/6/1865. Rolls of Prisoners of War, C.S.A: Surrendered at Citronelle, AL, on 5/4/1865; Paroled at Meridian, MS, on 5/13/1865. Residence at parole: Sumpter County, AL.

Wilson, S.S. Pvt., 62nd Alabama Infantry. Cos. B & D. Federal Rolls of Prisoners of War: Captured at Blakely, AL, on 4/9/1865; Received at Ship Island, MS, on 4/15/1865. Transferred to Vicksburg, MS, for exchange on 5/1/1865; Exchanged at Camp Townsend, MS, on 5/6/1865.

Wilson, V.A. Pvt., 63rd Alabama Infantry. Co. H. Enlisted: 3/15/1864 at Elyton, AL. Age at enlistment: 16. Description at enlistment: Eyes: dark. Hair: dark. Complexion: dark. Rolls for 9/1864 through 10/1864: Present. Federal Rolls of Prisoners of War: Captured at Blakely, AL, on 4/9/1865; Received at Ship Island, MS, on 4/15/1865. Transferred to Vicksburg, MS, for exchange on 5/1/1865; Exchanged at Camp Townsend, MS, on 5/6/1865. Rolls of Prisoners of War, C.S.A: Surrendered at Citronelle, AL, on 5/4/1865; Paroled at Meridian, MS, on 5/11/1865. Residence at parole: Jefferson County, AL.

Wims, T.J. Pvt., 63rd Alabama Infantry. Co. E. Enlisted: 8/8/1864 at Pollard, AL. Age at enlistment: 17. Description at enlistment: Eyes: dark. Hair: dark. Complexion: florid. Rolls for 9/1864 through 10/1864: Present. Federal Rolls of Prisoners of War: Captured at Blakely, AL, on 4/9/1865; Received at Ship Island, MS, on 4/15/1865. Transferred to Vicksburg, MS, for exchange on 5/1/1865. On Register of U.S.A. General Hospital #2, Vicksburg, MS: Admitted from steamer on 5/3/1865 due to remittent fever; Returned to duty on 5/10/1865. Age at admittance: 18.

Winn, Moses C. (AKA W.) Cpl., 62nd Alabama Infantry. Cos. A & D. Federal Rolls of Prisoners of War: Captured at Blakely, AL, on 4/9/1865; Received at Ship Island, MS, on 4/15/1865. Transferred to Vicksburg, MS, for exchange on 5/1/1865; Exchanged at Camp Townsend, MS, on 5/6/1865.

Winslet, A.W. 5th Sgt./Pvt., 63rd Alabama Infantry. Co. G. Enlisted: 5/16/1864 at Troy, AL. Age at enlistment: 16. Description at enlistment: Eyes: blue. Hair: light. Complexion: fair. Height: 5'10". Residence at enlistment: Covington County, AL. Rolls for 9/1864 through 10/1864: Present. Federal Rolls of Prisoners of War: Captured at Blakely, AL, on 4/9/1865; Received at Ship Island, MS, on 4/15/1865. Transferred to Vicksburg, MS, for exchange on 5/1/1865; Exchanged at Camp Townsend, MS, on 5/6/1865. Rolls of Prisoners of War, C.S.A: Surrendered at Citronelle, AL, on 5/4/1865; Paroled at Meridian, MS, on 5/13/1865. Residence at parole: Pike County, AL.

Winston, W.E. Lt., 36th Alabama Infantry. Co. A. Federal Rolls of Prisoners of War: Captured at Spanish Fort, AL, on 4/8/1865; Received at Ship Island, MS, on 4/10/1865. Transferred to Vicksburg, MS, for exchange on 4/28/1865; Confined at New Orleans, LA, on 4/30/1865. Exchanged at Camp Townsend, MS, on 5/6/1865. Residence after war: Roswell, NM. He wrote to *Confederate Veteran Magazine* in 1905 regarding his wartime experiences.

Wisengur, W. (AKA Wisinger) Pvt./Cpl., 62nd Alabama Infantry. Co. H. Federal Rolls of Prisoners of War: Captured at Blakely, AL, on 4/9/1865; Received at Ship Island, MS, on 4/15/1865. Transferred to Vicksburg, MS, for exchange on 5/1/1865; Exchanged at Camp Townsend, MS, on 5/6/1865.

Womack, William (AKA Wommack) Pvt., 62nd Alabama Infantry. Co. A. Federal Rolls of Prisoners of War: Captured at Blakely, AL, on 4/9/1865; Received at Ship Island, MS, on 4/15/1865. Transferred to Vicksburg, MS, for exchange on 5/1/1865; Exchanged at Camp Townsend, MS, on 5/6/1865.

Wood, George M. Cpl., Tarrant's Artillery Battery. Federal Rolls of Prisoners of War: Captured at Blakely, AL, on 4/9/1865; Received at Ship Island, MS, on 4/15/1865. Transferred to Vicksburg, MS, for exchange on 5/1/1865; Exchanged at Camp Townsend, MS, on 5/6/1865.

Wood, Joseph F. (AKA F.) Pvt., 62nd Alabama Infantry. Co. A. Federal Rolls of Prisoners of War: Captured at Blakely, AL, on 4/9/1865; Received at Ship Island, MS, on 4/15/1865. Transferred to Vicksburg, MS, for exchange on 5/1/1865; Exchanged at Camp Townsend, MS, on 5/6/1865.

Woods, A. Pvt., 6th Alabama Cavalry. Co. D. Federal Rolls of Prisoners of War: Captured in Florida on 3/25/1865; Received at Ship Island, MS. Transferred to Vicksburg, MS, for exchange on 5/1/1865; Exchanged at Camp Townsend, MS, on 5/6/1865.

Woods, James Pvt., 1st Alabama Artillery Battalion. Cos. B & D. Federal Rolls of Prisoners of War: Captured at Fort Gaines, AL, on 8/8/1864; Received at Ship Island, MS, from New Orleans, LA, on 10/25/1864. Exchanged on 1/4/1865.

Woods, John W. (AKA J.M.) Sgt./Pvt., 6th Alabama Cavalry. Co. __. Federal Rolls of Prisoners of War: Captured in Florida on 3/25/1865; Received at Ship Island, MS. Transferred to Vicksburg, MS, for exchange on 5/1/1865; Exchanged at Camp Townsend, MS, on 5/6/1865.

Woods, R.Y. Sgt., Tarrant's Artillery Battery. Enlisted: 7/25/1863 at Tuscaloosa, AL. Federal Rolls of Prisoners of War: Captured at Blakely, AL, on 4/9/1865; Received at Ship Island, MS, on 4/15/1865. Transferred to Vicksburg, MS, for exchange on 5/1/1865; Exchanged at Camp Townsend, MS, on 5/6/1865.

Woodward, F.A. Pvt., Tarrant's Artillery Battery. Enlisted: 7/8/1863 at Tuscaloosa, AL. Federal Rolls of Prisoners of War: Captured at Blakely, AL, on 4/9/1865; Received at Ship Island, MS, on 4/15/1865. Transferred to Vicksburg, MS, for exchange on 5/1/1865; Exchanged at Camp Townsend, MS, on 5/6/1865.

Woolley, Wyman Adair (AKA Wooley) Pvt., Tarrant's Artillery Battery. Federal Rolls of Prisoners of War: Captured at Blakely, AL, on 4/9/1865; Received at Ship Island, MS, on 4/15/1865. Transferred to Vicksburg, MS, for exchange on 5/1/1865; Exchanged at Camp Townsend, MS, on 5/6/1865.

Wright, J.H. (AKA T.H.) Pvt., 63rd Alabama Infantry. Cos. G & K. Enlisted: 10/13/1864 at Sumpter County, AL. Rolls for 9/1864 through 10/1864: Present. Federal Rolls of Prisoners of War: Captured at Blakely, AL, on 4/9/1865; Received at Ship Island, MS, on

4/15/1865. Transferred to Vicksburg, MS, for exchange on 5/1/1865; Exchanged at Camp Townsend, MS, on 5/6/1865. Rolls of Prisoners of War, C.S.A: Surrendered at Citronelle, AL, on 5/4/1865; Paroled at Meridian, MS, on 5/13/1865. Residence at parole: Shelby County, AL.

Wright, James Pvt., 6th Alabama Cavalry. Co. F. Federal Rolls of Prisoners of War: Captured in Alabama on 3/22/1865; Received at Ship Island, MS. Transferred to Vicksburg, MS, for exchange on 5/1/1865; Exchanged at Camp Townsend, MS, on 5/6/1865.

Wright, Thomas Harrison Pvt., 62nd Alabama Infantry. Co. K. Enlisted: 10/1/1864 at Mobile, AL. Federal Rolls of Prisoners of War: Captured at Blakely, AL, on 4/9/1865; Received at Ship Island, MS, on 4/15/1865. Transferred to Vicksburg, MS, for exchange on 5/1/1865; Exchanged at Camp Townsend, MS, on 5/6/1865. Residence after war: Perry County, AL.

Wyatt, H.G. Pvt., 36th Alabama Infantry. Co. H. Federal Rolls of Prisoners of War: Captured at Spanish Fort, AL, on 4/8/1865; Received at Ship Island, MS, on 4/10/1865. Transferred to Vicksburg, MS, for exchange on 5/1/1865; Exchanged at Camp Townsend, MS, on 5/6/1865.

Wyatte, Silas M. Pvt., 63rd Alabama Infantry. Co. C. Enlisted: 5/1/1864 at Macon County, AL. Age at enlistment: 17. Description at enlistment: Eyes: blue. Hair: dark. Complexion: fair. Height: 5'1". Residence at enlistment: Lafayette, Chambers County, AL. Rolls for 5/1864 through 6/1864: Present. Rolls for 9/1864 through 10/1864: Present. Federal Rolls of Prisoners of War: Captured at Blakely, AL, on 4/9/1865; Received at Ship Island, MS, on 4/15/1865. Transferred to Vicksburg, MS, for exchange on 5/1/1865; Exchanged at Camp Townsend, MS, on 5/6/1865. Rolls of Prisoners of War, C.S.A: Surrendered at Citronelle, AL, on 5/4/1865; Paroled at Meridian, MS, on 5/10/1865 while a patient in Quintard Hospital. Residence at parole: Fayette, AL.

Young, John Francis Pvt., 62nd Alabama Infantry. Co. A. Enlisted: 5/1864 at Selma, AL. Federal Rolls of Prisoners of War: Captured at Blakely, AL, on 4/9/1865; Received at Ship Island, MS, on 4/15/1865. Transferred to Vicksburg, MS, for exchange on 5/1/1865; Exchanged at Camp Townsend, MS, on 5/6/1865. Residence after war: Perry County, AL.

Young, Levy Pvt., 38th Alabama Infantry. Co. E. Deserted on 10/24/1864. Federal Rolls of Prisoners of War: Captured at Blakely, AL, on 4/9/1865; Received at Ship Island, MS, on 4/15/1865. Transferred to Vicksburg, MS, for exchange on 5/1/1865; Exchanged at Camp Townsend, MS, on 5/6/1865.

Zimmerman, Eugene Pvt./Ensign, 63rd Alabama Infantry. Co. A.F. & S. Enlisted: 1/1/1864 at Montgomery County, AL. Age at enlistment: 17. Rolls for 1/1864 through 2/1864: Present. Rolls for 9/1864 through 10/1864: Transferred to the 2nd Alabama Reserves. Co. B per special order. Rolls for 9/1864 through 10/1864: Present; Appointed Ensign by Colonel Rice on 9/21/1864 near Mobile, AL. Federal Rolls of Prisoners of War: Captured at Spanish Fort, AL, on 4/9/1865; Received at Ship Island, MS, on 4/16/1865. Transferred to Vicksburg, MS, for exchange on 4/28/1865; Confined at New Orleans, LA, on 4/30/1865. Exchanged at Camp Townsend, MS, on 5/1/1865. Rolls of Prisoners of War, C.S.A: Surrendered at Citronelle, AL, on 5/4/1865; Paroled at Meridian, MS, on 5/11/1865. Residence at parole: Montgomery County, AL.

Zuber, C.W.F. Pvt., 63rd Alabama Infantry. Cos. C & H. Enlisted: 7/25/1864 at Macon County, AL. Rolls for 9/1864 through 10/1864: Present. Federal Rolls of Prisoners of War: Captured at Blakely, AL, on 4/9/1865; Received at Ship Island, MS, on 4/15/1865. Transferred to Vicksburg, MS, for exchange on 5/1/1865; Exchanged at Camp Townsend, MS, on 5/6/1865. Rolls of Prisoners of War, C.S.A: Surrendered at Citronelle, AL, on 5/4/1865; Paroled at Meridian, MS, on 5/11/1865. Residence at parole: Macon County, AL.

Arkansas Prisoners of War

Epler, Rufus (AKA Eppler, H.K., H.R.) Cpl./1st Sgt., 11th & 17th Arkansas Infantry (Consolidated). Co. I. Enlisted: 11/13/1861 at Fort Smith, AR. Federal Rolls of Prisoners of War: Captured at Port Hudson, LA, on 6/20/1863; Received at Ship Island, MS, from New Orleans, LA, on 10/28/1864. Transferred to Fort Columbus, New York Harbor, NY, on 11/5/1864; Paroled at New York on 2/13/1865 and sent to James River, VA, for exchange. Rolls of Prisoners of War, C.S.A: Surrendered at Citronelle, AL, on 5/4/1865; Paroled at Jackson, MS, on 5/13/1865.

Fenner, James W. (AKA J.K.) Pvt., 4th Field Artillery Battery (West's). Federal Rolls of Prisoners of War: Captured at Morganza, LA, on 8/17/1864; Received at Ship Island, MS. Died: 10/17/1864 at Ship Island, MS, due to consumption. Buried: Ship Island, MS, Cemetery in Grave #1.

Gibson, Emanual Mercer Pvt./2nd Lt., 17th Arkansas Infantry (Griffith's). Co. I. Federal Rolls of Prisoners of War: Captured at Tensas Parish, LA, on 11/22/1864; Received at Ship Island, MS, from New Orleans, LA, on 1/25/1865. Transferred to New Orleans, LA, for exchange on 3/31/1865. Married: Elizabeth Berry. He lived his last years at the Beauvoir Confederate Soldier's Home at Biloxi, MS. Born: Natchez, MS. Died: 4/20/1933 at the age of 88. Buried: Beauvoir Cemetery, Biloxi, Harrison County, MS.

Gray, Oliver Crosby (AKA Grey) 1st Sgt./Capt., 3rd Arkansas Cavalry. Co. A. Federal Rolls of Prisoners of War: Captured at Choctaw Bend, MS, on 11/16/1864; Transferred to New Orleans, LA, from Natchez, MS, on 11/21/1864. Received at Ship Island, MS, from New Orleans, LA, on 12/15/1864; Exchanged on 3/2/1865. Born: 12/30/1862 to Dr. Peter Tufts Gray and Elizabeth Kennedy at Jefferson, Lincoln County, ME. Married: Virginia Lafayette Davis on 5/28/1858 at Cushing, Lincoln County, ME, and Mary Beattie on 6/17/1889 at Little Rock, AR. Children: 3. Died: 12/9/1905 in Arkansas. Buried: Evergreen Cemetery at Fayetteville, Arkansas.

Hallbertson, J.H. Pvt., 8th Arkansas Infantry. Co. __. Federal Rolls of Prisoners of War: Captured in Arkansas on 11/20/1864; Received at Ship Island, MS, from New Orleans, LA, on 12/13/1864. Transferred to New Orleans, LA, for exchange on 3/21/1865.

Petty, J.B. (AKA T.B.) Pvt., 17th Arkansas Cavalry. Co. K. Federal Rolls of Prisoners of War: Captured at Jackson, LA, on 11/15/1864; Received at Ship Island, MS, from New Orleans, LA, on 12/13/1864. Transferred to Vicksburg, MS, for exchange on 5/1/1865; Exchanged at Camp Townsend, MS, on 5/6/1865. Rolls of Prisoners of War, C.S.A: Surrendered at Citronelle, AL, on 5/4/1865; Paroled at Jackson, MS, on 5/13/1865.

Pike, M.F. Pvt., 47th Arkansas Cavalry. Co. H. Federal Rolls of Prisoners of War: Captured at Arkansas County, AR, on 9/14/1864; Received at Ship Island, MS, from New Orleans, LA, on 12/13/1864. Transferred to New Orleans, LA, for exchange on 3/31/1865. Confederate Pension Application dated 1901 on file at the Arkansas Department of Archives and History. Target Name: Pike, M.F. Veteran Number: 33.

Toffier, William A. (AKA A.W.) Pvt., 4th Field Artillery Battery (West's). Federal Rolls of Prisoners of War: Captured at Bayou Sara, LA, on 9/6/1864; Received at Ship Island, MS, from New Orleans, LA, on 10/7/1864. Transferred to Fort Columbus, New York Harbor, NY, on 11/5/1864. Died: 6/13/1920 at Garland County, AR. Buried: Hollywood Cemetery, Hot Springs, Garland County, AR. Confederate Widow's Pension Application dated 8/18/1921 on file at the Arkansas Department of Archives and History. Target Name: Toffier, Georgia. Application Number: 21940. Soldier also served as a Pvt. with the 2nd Louisiana Cavalry. Co. I and as a Pvt. with the Iberville Squadron Militia Cavalry—Independent Rangers.

Florida Prisoners of War

Abercrombie, Peter F. (AKA P.T.) Pvt., 1st Florida Reserves (Poe's). Co. C. Federal Rolls of Prisoners of War: Captured at Marianna, FL, on 9/27/1864; Sent to Fort Pickens, FL. Forwarded to New Orleans, LA, on 10/8/1864; Received at Ship Island, MS, on 10/24/1864. Died: 1/13/1865 at Ship Island, MS, due to chronic dysentery. Buried: Ship Island, MS, Cemetery in Grave #130.

Abercrombie, William A. (AKA J.A.) Pvt., Campbellton Cavalry Company (Godwin's). Federal Rolls of Prisoners of War: Captured at Marianna, FL, on 9/27/1864 with his son, Peter F. Abercrombie; Sent to Fort Pickens, FL. Forwarded to New Orleans, LA, on 10/8/1864; Received at Ship Island, MS, on 10/24/1864. Died: 11/4/1864 at Ship Island, MS, due to chronic diarrhea. Buried: Ship Island, MS, Cemetery in Grave #11. Age at capture: 64.

Alley, John Pvt., 1st Florida Reserves (Poe's). Co. C. Enlisted: 8/12/1864 at Marianna, FL. Federal Rolls of Prisoners of War: Captured at Marianna, FL, on 9/27/1864; Sent to Fort Pickens, FL. Forwarded to New Orleans, LA, on 10/8/1864; Received at Ship Island, MS, on 10/24/1864. Transferred to Fort Columbus, New York Harbor, NY, on 11/5/1864; Forwarded to Elmira, NY, on 11/20/1864. Died: 2/25/1865 at Elmira, NY, due to diarrhea. Buried: Woodlawn National Cemetery, Chemung County, NY, in Grave #2376.

Alstead, John Pvt., Florida Home Guards (Norwood's). Federal Rolls of Prisoners of War: Captured at Marianna, FL, on 9/27/1864; Sent to Fort Pickens, FL. Forwarded to New Orleans, LA, on 10/8/1864; Received at Ship Island, MS, on 10/24/1864. Disposition unknown.

Anderson, John C. Cpl., 1st Florida Reserves (Poe's). Co. C. Federal Rolls of Prisoners of War: Captured at Marianna, FL, on 9/27/1864; Sent to Fort Pickens, FL. Forwarded to New Orleans, LA, on 10/8/1864; Received at Ship Island, MS, on 10/24/1864. Transferred to Fort Columbus, New York Harbor, NY, on 11/5/1864; Forwarded to Elmira, NY, on 11/20/1864.

Austin, John Pvt., Florida Home Guards (Norwood's). Federal Rolls of Prisoners of War: Captured at Marianna, FL, on 9/27/1864; Sent to Fort Pickens, FL. Forwarded to New Orleans, LA, on 10/8/1864; Received at Ship Island, MS, on 10/24/1864. Died: 1/1/1865 at Ship Island, MS, due to chronic dysentery. Buried: Ship Island, MS, Cemetery in Grave #126.

Balson, F.W. Pvt., Florida Home Guards (Norwood's). Federal Rolls of Prisoners of War: Captured at Marianna, FL, on 9/27/1864; Sent to Fort Pickens, FL. Forwarded to New Orleans, LA, on 10/8/1864; Received at Ship Island, MS, on 10/24/1864. Transferred to Vicksburg, MS, for exchange on 5/1/1865; Exchanged at Camp Townsend, MS, on 5/6/1865.

Baltzell, Thomas W. Pvt., Florida Home Guards (Norwood's). Federal Rolls of Prisoners of War: Captured at Marianna, FL, on 9/27/1864 while wounded in finger; Sent to Fort Pickens, FL. Forwarded to New Orleans, LA, on 10/8/1864; Received at Ship Island, MS, on 10/24/1864. Unable to be forwarded to Fort Columbus, New York Harbor, NY, on 11/5/1864 due to illness. Transferred to Vicksburg, MS, for exchange on 5/1/1865; Exchanged at Camp Townsend, MS, on 5/6/1865. Age at capture: 15.

Blaney, John J. (AKA Barney, Blarney) Pvt., Florida Home Guards (Norwood's). Federal Rolls of Prisoners of War: Captured at Marianna, FL, on 9/27/1864; Sent to Fort Pickens, FL. Forwarded to New Orleans, LA, on 10/8/1864; Received at Ship Island, MS, on 10/24/1864. Transferred to Fort Columbus, New York Harbor, NY, on 11/5/1864; Forwarded to Elmira, NY, on 11/20/1864. Died: 12/25/1864 at Elmira, NY, due to pneumonia. Buried: Woodlawn National Cemetery, Chemung County, NY, in Grave #1216.8. Age at capture: 50. Occupation at capture: Member of the Florida State Legislature.

Bowlin, William (AKA Bolin) Cpl./Pvt., 5th Florida Battalion Cavalry. Co. E. Federal Rolls of Prisoners of War: Captured at Saint Andrews Bay, FL, on 11/30/1864; Received at Ship Island, MS, from New Orleans, LA, on 1/25/1865. Transferred to Vicksburg, MS, for exchange on 5/1/1865; Exchanged at Camp Townsend, MS, on 5/6/1865.

Brown, Joel M. Pvt., 1st Florida Reserves (Poe's). Co. C. Federal Rolls of Prisoners of War: Captured at Marianna, FL, on 9/27/1864; Sent to Fort Pickens, FL. Forwarded to New Orleans, LA, on 10/8/1864; Received at Ship Island, MS, on 10/24/1864. Transferred to Fort Columbus, New York Harbor, NY, on 11/5/1864; Sent to Elmira, NY, on 11/20/1864. Died: 3/9/1865 at Elmira, NY, due to chronic diarrhea. Buried: Woodlawn National Cemetery, Chemung County, NY.

Burnett, E.M. Sgt., 5th Florida Battalion Cavalry. Co. __. Federal Rolls of Prisoners of War: Captured at East Baton Rouge Parish, LA, on 1/9/1865; Received at Ship Island, MS, from New Orleans, LA, on 1/25/1865. Transferred to Vicksburg, MS, for exchange on 5/1/1865; Exchanged at Camp Townsend, MS, on 5/6/1865.

Bush, Albert G. Pvt., Florida Home Guards (Jackson's). Enlisted: 9/26/1861. Federal Rolls of Prisoners of War: Captured at Marianna, FL, on 9/27/1864; Sent to Fort Pickens, FL. Forwarded to New Orleans, LA, on 10/8/1864; Received at Ship Island, MS, on 10/24/1864. Transferred to Fort Columbus, New York Harbor, NY, on 11/5/1864; Forwarded to Elmira, NY, on 11/20/1864. Paroled at Elmira, NY, in 1865. Age at capture: 49. Occupation at capture: Farmer.

Bush, Allen Henry Pvt., Florida Home Guards (Norwood's). Federal Rolls of Prisoners of War: Captured at Marianna, FL, on 9/27/1864; Sent to Fort Pickens, FL. Forwarded to New Orleans, LA, on 10/8/1864; Received at Ship Island, MS, on 10/24/1864. Transferred to Fort Columbus, New York Harbor, NY, on 11/5/1864; Forwarded to Elmira, NY, on 11/20/1864. Paroled at Elmira, NY, in 1865. Age at capture: 55. Description at capture: Eyes: gray. Hair: dark. Complexion: dark. Height: 5'4". Occupation at capture: Attorney and Circuit Judge. Was a delegate to the Florida Constitutional Convention on 10/25/1865 and regarded as being friendly to the carpetbaggers.

Carlton, William C. Pvt., 1st Florida Special Cavalry Battalion. Co. __. Federal Rolls of Prisoners of War: Captured at Saint Andrews Bay, FL, on 10/12/1864; Received at Ship Island, MS, on 1/27/1865. Transferred to Vicksburg, MS, for exchange on 5/1/1865; Exchanged at Camp Townsend, MS, on 5/6/1865.

Carraway, Lelan (AKA Caraway, Laban) Pvt., 2nd Florida Cavalry. Co. E. Federal Rolls of Prisoners of War: Captured at Wakulla County, FL, on 10/19/1864; Received at Ship Island, MS, from New Orleans, LA, on 12/13/1864. Transferred to Vicksburg, MS, for exchange on 5/1/1865; Exchanged at Camp Townsend, MS, on 5/6/1865.

Chapman, B.D. Sgt., Florida Home Guards. Co. B. Federal Rolls of Prisoners of War: Captured in Florida on 3/24/1865; Received at Ship Island, MS. Transferred to Vicksburg, MS, for exchange on 5/1/1865; Exchanged at Camp Townsend, MS, on 5/6/1865.

Chason, John Pvt., Florida Home Guards (Norwood's). Federal Rolls of Prisoners of War: Captured while wounded at Marianna, FL, on 9/27/1864; Sent to Fort Pickens, FL. Forwarded to New Orleans, LA, on 10/8/1864; Received at Ship Island, MS, on 10/24/1864. Died: 12/19/1864 at Ship Island, MS, due to chronic dysentery. Buried: Ship Island, MS, Cemetery in Grave #99. Age at capture: 57. Occupation at capture: Farmer.

Clarke, Edward A. Pvt., 1st Florida Special Cavalry Battalion. Co. A. Federal Rolls of Prisoners of War: Captured at Hernando County, FL, on 7/8/1864; Received at Ship Island, MS, on 12/8/1864. Occupation: Merchant, owned the Blue Store in Tampa, FL.

Clayton, William T. Pvt., Campbellton Cavalry Company (Godwin's). Federal Rolls of Prisoners of War: Captured at Marianna, FL, on 9/27/1864; Sent to Fort Pickens, FL. Forwarded to New Orleans, LA, on 10/8/1864; Received at Ship Island, MS, on 10/24/1864. Transferred to Fort Columbus, New York Harbor, NY, on 11/5/1864; Forwarded to Elmira, NY, on 11/20/1864. Died: 1/13/1865 at Elmira, NY, due to bronchitis. Buried: Woodlawn National Cemetery, Chemung County, NY, in Grave #1468.

Council, John Cecil (AKA Counsel, Councill) Pvt., 2nd Florida Cavalry. Cos. E & G. Enlisted: 8/7/1862 at Tallahassee. Federal Rolls of Prisoners of War: Captured at Wakulla County, FL, on 10/19/1864; Received at Ship Island, MS, from New Orleans, LA, on 12/13/1864. Transferred to Vicksburg, MS, for exchange on 5/1/1865; Exchanged at Camp Townsend, MS, on 5/6/1865. Born: 1833 in Alabama. Married 1: Delaura Feraby Posey. Married 2: Missouri Redd Smith. Died: 2/3/1910. Buried: Council Cemetery, Crawfordville, FL. Confederate Widows Pension Application dated 1907 on file at the Florida State Library and Archives. Target Name: Missouri Redd Council. Application Number: A11555. County: Wakulla. Soldier also served in the 5th Florida Cavalry. Co.G.

Curl, Cullin (AKA Cullen) Pvt., Campbellton Cavalry Company (Godwin's). Enlisted: 3/23/1863 at Marianna, FL; Resigned at Camp Stonewall, FL, on 2/11/1864 due to illness. Federal Rolls of Prisoners of War: Captured at Marianna, FL, on 9/27/1864; Sent to Fort Pickens, FL. Forwarded to New Orleans, LA, on 10/8/1864; Received at Ship Island, MS, on 10/24/1864. Transferred to Fort Columbus, New York Harbor, NY, on 11/5/1864; Forwarded to Elmira, NY, on 11/20/1864. Paroled at Elmira, NY, on 2/9/1865; Listed as too ill to be exchanged from Elmira, on 2/13/1865. Released on the U.S. Oath of Allegiance from Fort McHenry, MD, on 6/9/1865. Description at oath: Eyes: blue. Hair: light. Complexion: light. Height: 6'1". Age at capture: 31. In 1866, he won a court case against a former slave. In 1877, he was involved in a running gun battle from north Jackson County, FL, to Holmes County, FL, when he discovered four former slaves stealing cotton from his homestead.

Daniel, William (AKA Daniels) Pvt., Campbellton Cavalry Company (Godwin's). Federal Rolls of Prisoners of War: Captured at Marianna, FL, on 9/27/1864; Sent to Fort Pickens, FL. Forwarded to New Orleans, LA, on 10/8/1864; Received at Ship Island, MS, on 10/24/1864. Transferred to Fort Columbus, New York Harbor, NY, on 11/5/1864; Sent to Elmira, NY, on 11/20/1864. Died: 12/25/1864 at Elmira, NY, due to chronic diarrhea. Buried: Woodlawn National Cemetery, Chemung County, NY. Age at capture: 59. Occupation at capture: Farmer.

Darby, Thomas J. Pvt., 1st Florida Cavalry. Co. K. Federal Rolls of Prisoners of War: Captured at Florida on 7/8/1864; Received at Ship Island, MS, from New Orleans, LA, on 12/13/1864. Transferred to Vicksburg,

MS, for exchange on 5/1/1865; Exchanged at Camp Townsend, MS, on 5/6/1865.

Davis, Ellis Fairbanks Pvt., Florida Home Guards (Norwood's). Federal Rolls of Prisoners of War: Captured at Marianna, FL, on 9/26/1864; Sent to Fort Pickens, FL. Forwarded to New Orleans, LA, on 10/8/1864; Received at Ship Island, MS, on 10/24/1864. Transferred to Fort Columbus, New York Harbor, NY, on 11/5/1864; Sent to Elmira, NY, on 11/20/1864. Paroled at Elmira, NY, on 2/13/1865. Soldier also served with the 11th Florida Infantry. Co.A. Born: 1814 in Mississippi. Married: Elizabeth Brickhouse on 2/2/1854. Residence at capture: Jackson County, FL. Occupations at capture: Farmer and member of the Florida State Legislature. Children: 9 — His son, Walter B. Davis, served in Smith's Florida Cavalry Company and died on 6/28/1862 due to disease.

Dickson, John J. Pvt., Greenwood Club Cavalry Company (Robinson's). Federal Rolls of Prisoners of War: Captured at Marianna, FL, on 9/27/1864 while wounded by a blow to the head; Sent to Fort Pickens, FL. Forwarded to New Orleans, LA, on 10/8/1864; Received at Ship Island, MS, on 10/24/1864. Transferred to Fort Columbus, New York Harbor, NY, on 11/5/1864. Died: 12/19/1864 at Fort Columbus, New York Harbor, NY, due to chronic diarrhea. Buried: Cypress Hills National Cemetery, Brooklyn, NY. Age at capture: 59. Occupation at capture: Wheelwright. Residence at capture: Greenwood, FL.

Duggans, Thomas (AKA Duggan, Duggar) Pvt., 2nd Florida Cavalry. Co. D. Enlisted: 3/5/1862 at Tallahassee, FL. Federal Rolls of Prisoners of War: Captured at Wakulla County, FL, on 10/19/1864; Received at Ship Island, MS, from New Orleans, LA, on 12/13/1864. Transferred to Vicksburg, MS, for exchange on 5/1/1865; Exchanged at Camp Townsend, MS, on 5/6/1865.

Duggar, Francis James (AKA James Francis) Pvt., 2nd Florida Cavalry. Co. E. Federal Rolls of Prisoners of War: Captured at Wakulla County, FL, on 10/19/1864; Received at Ship Island, MS, from New Orleans, LA, on 12/13/1864. Transferred to Vicksburg, MS, for exchange on 5/1/1865; Exchanged at Camp Townsend, MS, on 5/6/1865. Wounded: Skull fracture. Born: 7/28/1840 in Georgia. Died: 5/14/1920. Married: Almira J. __ in Wakulla County, FL. Confederate Widow's Pension Application dated 1902 on file at the Florida State Library and Archives. Target Name: Roberts, Almira J. Application Number: A02256. County: Liberty.

Duggar, Jonathan Wesley (AKA Dugger) Pvt., 2nd Florida Cavalry. Co. D. Enlisted: 6/9/1863 at Newport, FL. Federal Rolls of Prisoners of War: Captured at Marsh Island, FL, on 10/19/1864; Received at Ship Island, MS, from New Orleans, LA, on 12/13/1864. Transferred to Vicksburg, MS, for exchange on 5/1/1865; Exchanged at Camp Townsend, MS, on 5/6/1865. Born: 12/22/1845 at Thomas County, GA. Buried: Dugger Cemetery located at Ivan, Wakulla County, FL. Confederate Pension application dated 1903 on file at the Florida State Library and Archives. Target Name: Duggar, John Wesley. Application Number: A05836. County: Wakulla.

Dugger, Thomas O. Pvt., 2nd Florida Cavalry. Co. D. Enlisted: 3/5/1862 at Tallahassee, FL. Federal Rolls of Prisoners of War: Captured at Marsh Island, FL, on 10/19/1864; Received at Ship Island, MS, from New Orleans, LA, on 12/13/1864. Transferred to Vicksburg, MS, for exchange on 5/1/1865; Exchanged at Camp Townsend, MS, on 5/6/1865. Confederate Pension Application dated 1910 on file at the Georgia State Archives. Target Name: Dugger, Thomas O. County: Grady.

Elmore, Mark Pvt., Campbellton Cavalry Company (Godwin's). Federal Rolls of Prisoners of War: Captured at Marianna, FL, on 9/27/1864; Sent to Fort Pickens, FL. Forwarded to New Orleans, LA, on 10/8/1864; Received at Ship Island, MS, on 10/24/1864. Transferred to Fort Columbus, New York Harbor, NY, on 11/5/1864; Forwarded to Elmira, NY, on 11/20/1864. Died: 12/12/1864 at Elmira, NY due to pneumonia. Buried: Woodlawn National Cemetery, Chemung County, NY. Age at capture: 70.

Everett, Miles (AKA Everitt) Pvt., Florida Home Guards (Norwood's). Federal Rolls of Prisoners of War: Captured at Marianna, FL, on 9/27/1864; Sent to Fort Pickens, FL. Forwarded to New Orleans, LA, on 10/8/1864; Received at Ship Island, MS, on 10/24/1864. Transferred to Fort Columbus, New York Harbor, NY, on 11/5/1864; Sent to Elmira, NY, on 11/20/1864. Paroled at Elmira, NY, on 3/2/1865. Hospitalized at Richmond, VA, until 5/14/1865. Soldier also served with the 1st Florida Infantry. Co.A.

Evers, David K. (AKA Evans, Daniel, J.K.) Pvt./Musician, 2nd Florida Infantry. Cos. C & L. Enlisted: 7/13/1861. Wounded at Seven Pines, VA, on 5/31/1862. Federal Rolls of Prisoners of War: Captured at Taylor County, FL, on 3/21/1864; Received at Ship Island, MS, from New Orleans, LA, on 12/10/1864. Died: 12/20/1864 at Ship Island, MS, due to chronic dysentery. Buried: Ship Island, MS, Cemetery in Grave #102.

Gammons, Samuel B. Pvt., Florida Home Guards (Norwood's). Federal Rolls of Prisoners of War: Captured at Marianna, FL, on 9/27/1864; Sent to Fort Pickens, FL. Forwarded to New Orleans, LA, on 10/8/1864; Received at Ship Island, MS, on 10/24/1864. Died: 12/8/1864 at Ship Island, MS, due to typhoid fever. Buried: Ship Island, MS, Cemetery in Grave #72. Age at capture: 56. Occupation at capture: Farmer.

Grice, Hansel (AKA Greise, Amstead) Pvt., Greenwood Club Cavalry Company (Scarborough's). Federal Rolls of Prisoners of War: Captured at Marianna, FL, on 9/27/1864; Sent to Fort Pickens, FL. Forwarded to New Orleans, LA, on 10/8/1864; Received at Ship Island, MS, on 10/24/1864. Transferred to Fort Columbus, New York Harbor, NY, on 11/5/1864; Forwarded to Elmira, NY, on 11/20/1864. Paroled at Elmira, NY, on 2/25/1865.

Hartsfield, John W. Pvt., Florida Home Guards (Norwood's). Federal Rolls of Prisoners of War: Captured at Marianna, FL, on 9/27/1864; Sent to Fort Pickens, FL. Forwarded to New Orleans, LA, on 10/8/1864; Received at Ship Island, MS, on 10/24/1864. Transferred to Fort Columbus, New York Harbor, NY, on 11/5/1864. Died: 2/15/1865 at Fort Columbus, New York Harbor, NY, due to diarrhea. Buried: Cypress Hills National Cemetery, Brooklyn, NY.

Hatton, William L. Sgt., 5th Florida Cavalry. Co. I. Federal Rolls of Prisoners of War: Captured at

Marianna, FL, on 9/27/1864; Sent to Fort Pickens, FL. Forwarded to New Orleans, LA, on 10/8/1864; Received at Ship Island, MS, on 10/24/1864. Transferred to Fort Columbus, New York Harbor, NY, on 11/5/1864; Forwarded to Elmira, NY, on 11/20/1864. Died: 12/24/1864 at Elmira, NY, due to diarrhea. Buried: Woodlawn National Cemetery, Chemung County, NY.

Haywood, T.B. (AKA F.B., F.P.) Pvt., Campbellton Cavalry Company (Godwin's). Federal Rolls of Prisoners of War: Captured at Marianna, FL, on 9/27/1864; Sent to Fort Pickens, FL. Forwarded to New Orleans, LA, on 10/8/1864; Received at Ship Island, MS, on 10/24/1864. Transferred to Fort Columbus, New York Harbor, NY, on 11/5/1864; Forwarded to Elmira, NY, on 11/20/1864. Released by U.S. Presidential Pardon on 12/12/1864. Description at release: Eyes: blue. Hair: dark. Complexion: dark. Height: 5'11½".

Hentz, Thaddeus H., Dr. (AKA T.W.) Pvt., Florida Home Guards (Norwood's). Federal Rolls of Prisoners of War: Captured at Marianna, FL, on 9/27/1864 after losing a finger in the battle; Sent to Fort Pickens, FL. Forwarded to New Orleans, LA, on 10/8/1864; Received at Ship Island, MS, on 10/24/1864. Transferred to Fort Columbus, New York Harbor, NY, on 11/5/1864; Sent to Elmira, NY, on 11/20/1864. Paroled at Elmira, NY, on 3/2/1865. Admitted to hospital at Richmond, VA; Discharged on 3/14/1865. Age at capture: 30. Occupation at capture: Dentist. Soldier also served with the Florida Reserve Artillery (Gamble's). Enlisted: 5/27/1863 at Tallahassee, FL; Dropped from Rolls in 10/1863 due to sickness. Born: 1/20/1830 at Chapel Hill, NC. Married: Hattie Godfrey on 1/29/1857. Died: 6/13/1878 at Marianna, FL. Buried: Episcopal Cemetery, Marianna, Jackson County, FL. Confederate Widows Pension Application dated 1907 on file at the Florida State Library and Archives. Target Name: Godfrey, Hattie. Application Number: A00640. County: Jackson.

Irwin, Freeman B. Pvt., Florida Home Guards (Jones'). Federal Rolls of Prisoners of War: Captured at Marianna, FL, on 9/27/1864; Sent to Fort Pickens, FL. Forwarded to New Orleans, LA, on 10/8/1864; Received at Ship Island, MS, on 10/24/1864. Transferred to Fort Columbus, New York Harbor, NY, on 11/5/1864; Forwarded to Elmira, NY, on 11/20/1864. Died: 2/7/1865 at Elmira, NY, due to general debility. Buried: Woodlawn National Cemetery, Chemung County, NY, in Grave #1924. Residence at capture: Washington County, FL. Represented Washington County, FL, at the Florida Secession Convention. Born: Georgia. Married: Rachel Irwin. Children: 8.

Johns, Shadrick Pvt., Florida Home Guards (Jones'). Federal Rolls of Prisoners of War: Captured at Marianna, FL, on 9/27/1864; Sent to Fort Pickens, FL. Forwarded to New Orleans, LA, on 10/8/1864; Received at Ship Island, MS, on 10/24/1864. Transferred to Fort Columbus, New York Harbor, NY, on 11/5/1864; Sent to Elmira, NY, on 11/20/1864. Applied to take the U.S. Oath of Allegiance on 12/16/1864. Remarks: Stated he was over 60 years old and a Union supporter, desires to return to Pensacola, FL. Released on the U.S. Oath of Allegiance on 5/29/1865. Description at release: Eyes: blue. Hair: gray. Complexion: fair. Height: 5'8½".

Jones, Enoch Pvt., Florida Home Guards (Jones'). Enlisted: 11/20/1863 near Vernon, FL. Federal Rolls of Prisoners of War: Captured at Marianna, FL, on 9/27/1864; Sent to Fort Pickens, FL. Forwarded to New Orleans, LA, on 10/8/1864; Received at Ship Island, MS, on 10/24/1864. Transferred to Fort Columbus, New York Harbor, NY, on 11/5/1864; Sent to Elmira, NY, on 11/20/1864. Applied to take the U.S. Oath of Allegiance on 12/16/1864. Remarks: Stated that he was a Union man. Died: 12/27/1864 at Elmira, NY, due to variola. Buried: Woodlawn National Cemetery, Chemung County, NY.

Jones, William Blunt 2nd Lt., Florida Home Guards (Jones'). Enlisted: 3/8/1862 at Vernon County, FL; Resigned on 6/25/1863 after being elected Senator to the Florida State Legislature. Federal Rolls of Prisoners of War: Captured near Geneva, FL, in 1864 by a Union raiding party; Sent to Ship Island, MS. Received at Fort Lafayette, New York Harbor, NY, on 10/20/1864; Forwarded to Elmira, NY. Born: 1825. Married: Leah Godwin on 9/15/1847. Died: 11/1894 at Washington County, FL. Buried: Washington County, FL.

Justiss, J.B. (AKA Captain, Justus) Pvt., Florida Home Guards (Norwood's). Federal Rolls of Prisoners of War: Captured at Marianna, FL, on 9/27/1864; Sent to Fort Pickens, FL. Forwarded to New Orleans, LA, on 10/8/1864; Received at Ship Island, MS, on 10/24/1864. Transferred to Fort Columbus, New York Harbor, NY, on 11/5/1864; Sent to Elmira, NY, on 11/20/1864. Paroled at Elmira, NY, in 3/1865. On Register of Howard's Grove Hospital, Richmond, VA: Admitted in 3/1865; Returned to duty on 3/15/1865.

Kersey, David Emanuel Pvt. 2nd Florida Cavalry. Co. E. Enlisted: 5/15/1861 at Camp Gladden, FL. Federal Rolls of Prisoners of War: Captured at Marsh Island, Wakulla County, FL, on 10/19/1864; Received at Ship Island, MS, on 12/13/1864. Transferred to Vicksburg, MS, on 5/1/1865; Exchanged at Camp Townsend, MS, on 5/6/1864. Born: 1846. Married: Mary Nashville Mackery on 10/20/1878. Died: 8/28/1901 at Franklin County, FL. Buried: Carabelle Cemetery located at Franklin County, FL. Confederate Widows Pension Application dated 1903 on file at the Florida State Library and Archives. Target Name: Mackery, Mary. Application Number: A00235. County: Franklin.

Kiel, Mathney (AKA Keill) Pvt., 1st Florida Reserves (Poe's). Co. C. Federal Rolls of Prisoners of War: Captured at Marianna, FL, on 9/27/1864; Sent to Fort Pickens, AL. Forwarded to New Orleans, LA, on 10/8/1864; Received at Ship Island, MS, on 10/24/1864. Transferred to Vicksburg, MS, for exchange on 5/1/1865; Exchanged at Camp Townsend, MS, on 5/6/1865.

Kimball, W.H. Pvt., Greenwood Club Cavalry Company (Robinson's). Federal Rolls of Prisoners of War: Captured at Marianna, FL, on 9/27/1864; Sent to Fort Pickens, FL. Forwarded to New Orleans, LA, on 10/8/1864; Received at Ship Island, MS, on 10/24/1864. Transferred to Fort Columbus, New York Harbor, NY, on 11/5/1864; Forwarded to Elmira, NY, on 11/20/1864. Paroled at Elmira, NY, on 5/29/1865. Age at capture: 34. Occupation at capture: Sheriff of Jackson County, FL, through 1867. Requested that the 1866 Fourth of July celebration not be observed in Jackson County, FL, for fear that Lincoln's portrait might incite violence. Elected to the Florida

State Legislature in 1877. Co-founder of Bascom, FL, Methodist Church.

Lanier, A.J. Pvt., Florida Home Guards. Federal Rolls of Prisoners of War: Captured at Lafayette County, FL, on 8/18/1864; Received at Ship Island, MS, from New Orleans, LA, on 12/13/1864. Transferred to Vicksburg, MS, for exchange on 5/1/1865; Exchanged at Camp Townsend, MS, on 5/6/1865.

Long, Felix H.G. Pvt., Florida Home Guards (Norwood's). Federal Rolls of Prisoners of War: Captured at Marianna, FL, on 9/27/1864; Sent to Fort Pickens, FL. Forwarded to New Orleans, LA, on 10/8/1864; Transferred to Ship Island, MS, on 10/24/1864. Forwarded to Fort Lafayette, NY; Released from Fort Lafayette, NY, on 12/14/1864 due to a stroke. Age at capture: 47. Occupation at capture: Planter. Soldier also served as a Pvt. with the 11th Florida Infantry.

Long, Nicholas A. Pvt., Florida Home Guards (Norwood's). Federal Rolls of Prisoners of War: Captured at Marianna, FL, on 9/27/1864; Sent to Fort Pickens, FL. Forwarded to New Orleans, LA, on 10/8/1864; Transferred to Ship Island, MS, on 10/24/1864. Forwarded to Fort Lafayette, NY; Released from Fort Lafayette, NY, on 12/14/1864. Age at capture: 49. Occupations at capture: Planter and Doctor. Served in the Florida State Legislature in 1849 and was a delegate to the 1848 National Whig Convention. Soldier also served as a Pvt. with the 11th Florida Infantry.

McBright, Israel (AKA Isreal) Pvt., Florida Home Guards (Norwood's). Federal Rolls of Prisoners of War: Captured at Marianna, FL, on 9/27/1864; Sent to Fort Pickens, FL. Forwarded to New Orleans, LA, on 10/8/1864; Transferred to Ship Island, MS, on 10/24/1864. Forwarded to Fort Columbus, New York Harbor, NY, on 11/5/1864; Sent to Elmira, NY, on 11/20/1864. Released from Elmira, NY, on the U.S. Oath of Allegiance on 5/29/1865. Description at release: Eyes: blue. Hair: dark. Complexion: fair. Height: 5'7".

Mathews, William (AKA Matthews) Pvt. Campbellton Cavalry Company (Godwin's). Federal Rolls of Prisoners of War: Captured at Marianna, FL, on 9/27/1864; Sent to Fort Pickens, FL. Forwarded to New Orleans, LA, on 10/8/1864; Received at Ship Island, MS, on 10/24/1864. Transferred to Fort Columbus, New York Harbor, NY, on 11/5/1864; Forwarded to Elmira, NY, on 11/20/1864. Died: 12/24/1864 at Elmira, NY. Buried: Woodlawn National Cemetery, Chemung County, NY, in Grave #1201.

Meeks, William S. (AKA Micks) Pvt., 5th Florida Rangers. Co. A. Federal Rolls of Prisoners of War: Captured at Sewanee River, FL, on 9/10/1864; Received at Ship Island, MS. Died: 2/3/1865 at Ship Island, MS, due to dysentery. Buried: Ship Island, MS, Cemetery in Grave #133. Confederate Widows Pension Application dated 1903 on file at the Florida State Library and Archives. Application Number: A01446. Target Name: Moore, Laura. County: Hillsborough. 17 pages.

Merritt, Alexander S. Pvt., Florida Home Guards (Norwood's). Federal Rolls of Prisoners of War: Captured at Marianna, FL, on 9/27/1864; Sent to Fort Pickens, FL. Forwarded to New Orleans, LA, on 10/8/1864; Received at Ship Island, MS, on 10/24/1864. Transferred to Fort Columbus, New York Harbor, NY, on 11/5/1864; Sent to Elmira, NY, on 11/20/1864. Paroled at Elmira, NY, on 12/12/1864. Age at capture: 32. Occupation at capture: Merchant. Description at release: Eyes: dark. Hair: black. Complexion: fair. Height: 5'9". Born: 1831. Died: 1906. Buried: Episcopal Cemetery, Marianna, Jackson County, Florida.

Miller, Nathaniel Pvt., Florida Home Guards (Jones'). Federal Rolls of Prisoners of War: Captured at Marianna, FL, on 9/27/1864; Sent to Fort Pickens, FL. Forwarded to New Orleans, LA, on 10/8/1864; Received at Ship Island, MS, on 10/24/1864. Transferred to Fort Columbus, New York Harbor, NY, on 11/5/1864; Sent to Elmira, NY, on 11/20/1864. Died: 3/13/1865 at Elmira, NY, due to diarrhea. Buried: Woodlawn National Cemetery, Chemung County, NY, in Grave #1949.

Mooring, Edwin W. (AKA Morning, Edward) Pvt./Adjt., Florida Home Guards (Norwood's). Federal Rolls of Prisoners of War: Captured at Marianna, FL, on 9/27/1864; Sent to Fort Pickens, FL. Forwarded to New Orleans, LA, on 10/8/1864; Received at Ship Island, MS, on 10/24/1864. Transferred to Fort Columbus, New York Harbor, NY, on 11/5/1864; Sent to Elmira, NY, on 11/20/1864. Released from Elmira, NY, in 1865. Age at capture: 36. Occupations at capture: Merchant, Distiller, and member of the Florida State Legislature.

Myrick, John T., Jr. (AKA Jack) Pvt., Florida Home Guards (Norwood's). Federal Rolls of Prisoners of War: Captured at Marianna, FL, on 9/27/1864; Sent to Fort Pickens, FL. Forwarded to New Orleans, LA, on 10/8/1864; Transferred to Ship Island, MS, on 10/24/1864. Forwarded to Fort Columbus, New York Harbor, NY, on 11/5/1864; Sent to Elmira, NY, on 11/20/1864. Paroled at Elmira, NY, on 5/29/1865. Age at capture: 16. Convicted in 10/1869 of killing local Marianna, FL, black leader Matt Nichols, his wife, and son. He was also charged with assault and battery in connection with another crime, and accused of ambushing a party of freed slaves near Blue Spring, FL. He fled from Florida to avoid punishment and eventually surfaced in Texas.

Nelson, John Pvt., Florida Home Guards (Jones'). Federal Rolls of Prisoners of War: Captured at Marianna, FL, on 9/27/1864; Sent to Fort Pickens, FL. Forwarded to New Orleans, LA, on 10/8/1864; Received at Ship Island, MS, on 10/24/1864. Transferred to Fort Columbus, New York Harbor, NY, on 11/5/1864; Sent to Elmira, NY, on 11/20/1864. Released on the U.S. Oath of Allegiance on 5/29/1865. Description at release: Eyes: blue. Hair: dark. Complexion: dark. Height: 5'6". Residence at release: Pensacola, FL. Born: 4/22/1812 at Hadersley, Denmark. Occupation: Farmer. Died: 4/14/1865. Buried: Orange Hill, Florida.

O'Neal, James Daniel (AKA John) Pvt., Florida Home Guards (Norwood's). Age at enlistment: 54. Federal Rolls of Prisoners of War: Captured at Marianna, FL, on 9/27/1864; Sent to Fort Pickens, FL. Forwarded to New Orleans, LA, on 10/8/1864; Received at Ship Island, MS, on 10/24/1864. Transferred to Fort Columbus, New York Harbor, NY, on 11/5/1864; Sent to Elmira, NY, on 11/20/1864. Listed as too ill to be paroled from Elmira, NY, on 2/13/1865. Died: 3/5/1865 at Elmira, NY, due to pneumonia. Buried:

Woodlawn National Cemetery, Chemung County, NY, in Grave #2387. Age at capture: 51.

Parker, Creach H. Pvt., 5th Florida Battalion Cavalry. Federal Rolls of Prisoners of War: Captured at Marianna, FL, 9/27/1864; Received at Ship Island, MS, from New Orleans, LA, on 10/21/1864. Transferred to Fort Columbus, New York Harbor, NY, on 11/5/1864. Confederate Widows Pension Application dated 1925 on file at the Florida State Library and Archives. Target Name: Jones, Penelope Page. Application Number: A02576. County: Jackson.

Perry, J. Pvt., 7th Florida Cavalry. Co. __. Federal Rolls of Prisoners of War: Captured at St. Marks, FL, on 10/19/1864; Received at Ship Island, MS, from New Orleans, LA, on 1/25/1865. Transferred to Vicksburg, MS, for exchange on 5/1/1865; Exchanged at Camp Townsend, MS, on 5/6/1865.

Pittman, Frederick R. (AKA H.R.) Pvt., Florida Home Guards (Norwood's). Enlisted: 9/26/1861. Federal Rolls of Prisoners of War: Captured at Marianna, FL, on 9/27/1864; Sent to Fort Pickens, FL. Forwarded to New Orleans, LA, on 10/8/1864; Received at Ship Island, MS, on 10/24/1864. Forwarded to Fort Columbus, New York Harbor, NY, on 11/5/1864; Sent to Elmira, NY, on 11/20/1864. Paroled at Elmira, NY, on 12/12/1864. Age at capture: 51. Occupation at capture: Member of Florida State Legislature. Soldier also served as a Pvt. with the 11th Florida Infantry.

Posey, Noah, Jr. Pvt., 2nd Florida Cavalry. Co. D. Enlisted: 3/5/1862 at Tallahassee, FL. Federal Rolls of Prisoners of War: Captured at Marsh Island, FL, on 10/19/1864; Received at Ship Island, MS, from New Orleans, LA, on 12/13/1864. Transferred to Vicksburg, MS, for exchange on 5/1/1865; Exchanged at Camp Townsend, MS, on 5/6/1865. Married: Penelope J. __ on 4/26/1855. Buried: Council Cemetery located at Crawfordville, Wakulla County, FL. Confederate Widows Pension Application dated 1899 on file at the Florida State Library and Archives. Target Name: Posey, Penelope J. Application Number: A11714. County: Wakulla.

Rhodes, B.H. (AKA E.) Pvt., 5th Florida Battalion Cavalry. Co. C. Federal Rolls of Prisoners of War: Captured at Wakulla County, FL, on 10/19/1864; Received at Ship Island, MS, from New Orleans, LA, on 12/13/1864. Transferred to Vicksburg, MS, for exchange on 5/1/1865; Exchanged at Camp Townsend, MS, on 5/6/1865.

Rodack, J.B. (AKA Rolack) Pvt., Florida Home Guard (Norwood's). Federal Rolls of Prisoners of War: Captured at Marianna, FL, on 9/27/1864; Received at Ship Island, MS, from New Orleans, LA, on 10/27/1864. Transferred to Fort Columbus, New York Harbor, NY, on 11/5/1864.

Sheffield, George Washington Pvt., Florida Home Guards (Jones'). Federal Rolls of Prisoners of War: Captured at Marianna, FL, on 9/27/1864; Sent to Fort Pickens, FL. Forwarded to New Orleans, LA, on 10/8/1864; Received at Ship Island, MS, on 10/24/1864. Applied to take the U.S. Oath of Allegiance and join the U.S. Army on 12/25/1864. Buried: New Hope Cemetery, Vernon, FL. Confederate Widows Pension Application dated 1908 on file at the Florida State Library and Archives. Target Name: Taylor, Martha. Application Number: A01459. County: Washington.

Sheffield, John Pvt., Florida Home Guards (Norwood's). Federal Rolls of Prisoners of War: Captured at Marianna, FL, on 9/27/1864; Sent to Fort Pickens, AL. Forwarded to New Orleans, LA, on 10/8/1864; Received at Ship Island, MS, on 10/24/1864. Transferred to Vicksburg, MS, for exchange on 5/1/1865; Exchanged at Camp Townsend, MS, on 5/6/1865.

Shipman, James Pvt., 6th Florida Cavalry. Co. C. Federal Rolls of Prisoners of War: Captured at Juniper, FL, on 5/6/1864; Received at Ship Island, MS, on 12/13/1864. Died: 3/31/1865 at Ship Island, MS, due to chronic dysentery. Buried: Ship Island, MS, Cemetery in Grave #145.

Shiver, W.N.W. Pvt., 1st Florida Reserves (Poe's). Co. C. Federal Rolls of Prisoners of War: Captured at Marianna, FL, on 9/27/1864 while wounded; Sent to Fort Pickens, FL. Forwarded to New Orleans, LA, on 10/8/1864; Received at Ship Island, MS, on 10/24/1864. Transferred to Fort Columbus, New York Harbor, NY, on 11/5/1864; Forwarded to Elmira, NY, on 11/20/1864. Died: 12/1/1864 at Elmira, NY, due to pneumonia. Buried: Woodlawn National Cemetery, Chemung County, NY.

Sims, Miles (AKA Syms, Myles) Pvt., 1st Florida Reserves (Poe's). Co. C. Federal Rolls of Prisoners of War: Captured at Marianna, FL, on 9/27/1864; Sent to Fort Pickens, FL. Forwarded to New Orleans, LA, on 10/8/1864; Received at Ship Island, MS, on 10/24/1864. Transferred to Fort Columbus, New York Harbor, NY, on 11/5/1864; Sent to Elmira, NY, on 11/20/1864. Died: 3/19/1865 at Elmira, NY, due to chronic diarrhea. Buried: Woodlawn National Cemetery, Chemung County, NY.

Stanfield, James M. Pvt., 1st Florida Special Battalion Cavalry. Co. A. Federal Rolls of Prisoners of War: Captured at Hernando County, FL, on 7/8/1864; Received at Ship Island, MS, from New Orleans, LA, on 12/13/1864. Died: 3/15/1865 at Ship Island, MS, due to pneumonia. Buried: Ship Island, MS, Cemetery in Grave #140.

Stones, B.F. (AKA Stokes) Sgt., 1st Florida Special Battalion Cavalry. Co. A. Federal Rolls of Prisoners of War: Captured at Sewanee River, FL, on 8/18/1864; Received at Ship Island, MS, from New Orleans, LA, on 12/13/1864. Transferred to Vicksburg, MS, for exchange on 5/1/1865; Exchanged at Camp Townsend, MS, on 5/6/1865.

Strickland, Alsamore M. Pvt./Sgt., 2nd Florida Cavalry. Co. G. Federal Rolls of Prisoners of War: Captured at Wakulla County, FL, on 10/19/1864; Received at Ship Island, MS, on 12/13/1864. Transferred to Vicksburg, MS, for exchange on 5/1/1865; Exchanged at Camp Townsend, MS, on 5/6/1865. Died: 12/19/1901 at Gadsden County, FL. Confederate Widows Pension Application dated 1901 on file at the Florida State Library and Archives. Target Name: Strickland, Flora A. Application Number: A12848. County: Gadsden.

Strickland, William Pvt., 6th Florida Battalion Infantry. Co. C. Federal Rolls of Prisoners of War: Captured at Juniper, FL, on 5/6/1864; Received at Ship Island, MS, on 12/13/1864. Transferred to Vicksburg, MS, for exchange on 5/1/1865; Exchanged at Camp Townsend, MS, on 5/6/1865.

Syms, M. (AKA Sims) Pvt., Florida Home Guards. Federal Rolls of Prisoners of War: Captured at

Marianna, FL, on 9/27/1864; Received at Ship Island, MS, from New Orleans, LA, on 10/21/1864. Transferred to Fort Columbus, New York Harbor, NY, on 11/5/1864.

Taylor, Cary Pvt., Florida Home Guards (Jones'). Federal Rolls of Prisoners of War: Captured at Marianna, FL, on 9/27/1864; Sent to Fort Pickens, FL. Forwarded to New Orleans, LA, on 10/8/1864; Received at Ship Island, MS, on 10/24/1864. Transferred to Fort Columbus, New York Harbor, NY, on 11/5/1864; Sent to Elmira, NY, on 11/20/1864. Died: 12/27/1864 at Elmira, NY, due to pneumonia. Buried: Woodlawn National Cemetery, Chemung County, NY, in Grave #1281.

Thomas, J.C. Pvt., Florida Home Guards (Chisholm's). Federal Rolls of Prisoners of War: Captured at Marianna, FL, on 9/27/1864; Sent to Fort Pickens, FL. Forwarded to New Orleans, LA, on 10/8/1864; Received at Ship Island, MS, on 10/24/1864. Transferred to Fort Columbus, New York Harbor, NY, on 11/5/1864; Sent to Elmira, NY, on 11/20/1864. Died: 12/11/1864 at Elmira, NY, due to chronic diarrhea. Buried: Woodlawn National Cemetery, Chemung County, NY.

Tippins, D.W. (AKA G.L.) Pvt./2nd Lt., 1st Florida Infantry. Co. H. Federal Rolls of Prisoners of War: Captured in Alabama on 3/26/1865; Received at Ship Island, MS. Transferred to Vicksburg, MS, for exchange on 4/28/1865; Confined at New Orleans, LA, on 4/30/1865. Exchanged at Camp Townsend, MS, on 5/6/1865.

Tippins, P.H.M. Pvt./1st Sgt., 1st Florida Infantry. Co. H. Federal Rolls of Prisoners of War: Captured in Alabama on 3/26/1865; Received at Ship Island, MS. Transferred to Vicksburg, MS, for exchange on 5/1/1865; Exchanged at Camp Townsend, MS, on 5/6/1865.

Tipton, Charles G. Sgt./Pvt., 11th Florida Infantry. Co. F. Federal Rolls of Prisoners of War: Captured at Marianna, FL, on 9/27/1864; Sent to Fort Pickens, FL. Forwarded to New Orleans, LA, on 10/8/1864; Received at Ship Island, MS, on 10/21/1864. Transferred to Fort Columbus, New York Harbor, NY, on 11/5/1864.

Tucker, Charles Pvt., Florida Home Guards (Norwood's). Federal Rolls of Prisoners of War: Captured at Marianna, FL, on 9/27/1864; Sent to Fort Pickens, FL. Forwarded to New Orleans, LA, on 10/8/1864; Received at Ship Island, MS, on 10/24/1864. Transferred to Fort Columbus, New York Harbor, NY, on 11/5/1864; Sent to Elmira, NY, on 11/20/1864. Died: 12/11/1864 at Elmira, NY, due to diarrhea. Buried: Woodlawn National Cemetery, Chemung County, NY, in Grave #1107.18. Residence at capture: Quincy, FL. Occupation at capture: Member of the Florida State Legislature.

Tyer, Benjamin (AKA Tyre) Pvt., 2nd Florida Cavalry. Co. H. Enlisted: 8/29/1862 at Gainesville, FL. Federal Rolls of Prisoners of War: Captured at Hillboro County, FL, on 5/6/1864; Received at Ship Island, MS, on 12/13/1864. Transferred to Vicksburg, MS, for exchange on 5/1/1865; Exchanged at Camp Townsend, MS, on 5/6/1865. Born: 1830. Married: Celia Harris on 12/26/1858. Died: 11/3/1882 at Polk County, FL. Buried: Green Pond Cemetery, Polk County, FL. Confederate Pension Application dated 1900 on file at the Florida State Library and Archives. Target Name: Harris, Celia. Application Number: A00784. County: Polk.

Vickers, J.M. Pvt., Florida Home Guards. Federal Rolls of Prisoners of War: Captured in Alabama on 3/24/1865; Received at Ship Island, MS. Transferred to Vicksburg, MS, for exchange on 5/1/1865; Exchanged at Camp Townsend, MS, on 5/6/1865.

Walker, Berry A. Pvt., 1st Florida Infantry. Co. E. Federal Rolls of Prisoners of War: Captured at Vernon, FL, on 9/27/1864; Received at Ship Island, MS, from New Orleans, LA, on 10/21/1864. Transferred to Fort Columbus, New York Harbor, NY, on 11/5/1864. Confederate Widows Pension Application dated 1902 on file at the Florida State Library and Archives. Target Name: Ackridge, Margaret. Application Number: A00221. County: Liberty.

Watson, Cornelius Thomas Pvt., Florida Home Guards. Enlisted: 9/9/1862 at Wakulla County, FL. Detached to Major White's commissary on 6/14/1864. Federal Rolls of Prisoners of War: Captured at Milton, FL, on 10/19/1864; Received at Ship Island, MS. Transferred to Vicksburg, MS, for exchange on 5/1/1865; Exchanged at Camp Townsend, MS, on 5/6/1865. Born: 9/22/1827 at Leon County, FL. Married: Mary Ann Coleman on 1/24/1850. Died: 10/13/1869 due to pneumonia.

Watson, James J. Pvt., 2nd Florida Cavalry. Co. D. Enlisted: 4/19/1862 at Camp Johnston, FL. Transferred to the 5th Florida Cavalry. Co. C on 8/23/1863. Federal Rolls of Prisoners of War: Captured at Marsh Island, FL, on 10/19/1864; Received at Ship Island, MS, on 12/13/1864. Transferred to Vicksburg, MS, for exchange on 5/1/1865; Exchanged at Camp Townsend, MS, on 5/6/1865. Soldier served in the 2nd Florida Cavalry with his father, Jonathan Watson.

Watson, Jonathan Henry Pvt., 2nd Florida Cavalry. Co. D. Enlisted 3/5/1862 at Tallahassee. Transferred to the 5th Florida Cavalry. Co. C on 8/23/1863. Federal Rolls of Prisoners of War: Captured at Marsh Island, FL, on 10/19/1864; Received at Ship Island, MS, on 12/13/1864. Transferred to Vicksburg, MS, for exchange on 5/1/1865; Exchanged at Camp Townsend, MS, on 5/6/1865. Born: 1/17/1845 at Wakulla County, FL. Married: Catherine Whaley on 2/1/1866. Died: 5/7/1907 at Carrabelle, FL. Buried: Carrabelle Cemetery located at Franklin County, FL.

White, William B. Pvt., 7th Florida Infantry. Co. B. Federal Rolls of Prisoners of War: Captured in south Florida on 5/6/1864; Received at Ship Island, MS, from New Orleans, LA, on 12/13/1864. Transferred to Vicksburg, MS, for exchange on 5/1/1865; Exchanged at Camp Townsend, MS, on 5/6/1865.

Whitehurst, John B. Pvt., Florida Home Guards (Norwood's). Federal Rolls of Prisoners of War: Captured at Marianna, FL, on 9/27/1864; Sent to Fort Pickens, FL. Forwarded to New Orleans, LA, on 10/8/1864; Received at Ship Island, MS, on 10/24/1864. Died: 10/25/1864 at Ship Island, MS, due to typhoid fever. Buried: Ship Island, MS, Cemetery in Grave #4. Age at capture: 40. Occupation at capture: Justice of the Peace.

Williams, J.J. Pvt., Florida Home Guards. Federal Rolls of Prisoners of War: Captured at Marianna, FL, on 9/27/1864; Sent to Fort Pickens, FL. Forwarded to New

Orleans, LA, on 10/8/1864; Received at Ship Island, MS, on 10/24/1864. Forwarded to Fort Columbus, New York Harbor, NY, on 11/5/1864; Sent to Elmira, NY, on 11/20/1864.

Williams, John R. Pvt., 1st Florida Reserves (Poe's). Co. C. Enlisted: 5/2/1864 at Marianna, FL. Federal Rolls of Prisoners of War: Captured at Marianna, FL, on 9/27/1864; Sent to Fort Pickens, FL. Forwarded to New Orleans, LA, on 10/8/1864; Received at Ship Island, MS, on 10/24/1864. Transferred to Fort Columbus, New York Harbor, NY, on 11/5/1864; Forwarded to Elmira, NY, on 11/20/1864. Died: 3/13/1865 at Elmira, NY due to smallpox. Buried: Woodlawn National Cemetery, Chemung County, NY, in Grave #1939.

Williamson, A. Pvt., Florida Reserves. Co. E. Federal Rolls of Prisoners of War: Captured at Pine Barren, FL, on 11/17/1864; Received at Ship Island, MS, from New Orleans, LA, on 12/13/1864. Transferred to Vicksburg, MS, for exchange on 5/1/1865; Exchanged at Camp Townsend, MS, on 5/6/1865.

Wynn, William B. Pvt., Florida Home Guards (Norwood's). Federal Rolls of Prisoners of War: Captured at Marianna, FL, on 9/27/1864; Sent to Fort Pickens, FL. Forwarded to New Orleans, LA, on 10/8/1864; Received at Ship Island, MS, on 10/24/1864. Transferred to Fort Columbus, New York Harbor, NY, on 11/5/1864. Died: 12/21/1864 at Fort Columbus, New York Harbor, NY. Buried: Cypress Hill National Cemetery, Brooklyn, NY, in Grave #2194.

Georgia Prisoners of War

Alford, Y.N. Pvt., 1st Georgia Infantry. Co. F. Federal Rolls of Prisoners of War: Captured at Fort Gaines, AL, on 8/8/1864; Received at Ship Island, MS, from New Orleans, LA, on 10/25/1864. Exchanged on 1/4/1865.

Laynard, E. W. (AKA Leonard) Pvt., 1st Georgia Infantry. Co. E. Federal Rolls of Prisoners of War: Captured at Fort Gaines, AL, on 8/8/1864; Received at Ship Island, MS, from New Orleans, LA, on 10/25/1864. Exchanged on 1/4/1865.

Peas, George A. Pvt., 1st Georgia Artillery Battery. Federal Rolls of Prisoners of War. Captured at Spanish Fort, AL, on 4/8/1865; Received at Ship Island, MS, on 4/10/1865. Disposition unknown.

Louisiana Prisoners of War

Abvitton, A.I. Pvt., 3rd Louisiana Cavalry. Co. H. Federal Rolls of Prisoners of War: Captured at Liberty, MS, on 11/18/1864; Received at Ship Island, MS, from New Orleans, LA, on 12/13/1864. Transferred to Vicksburg, MS, for exchange on 5/1/1865; Exchanged at Camp Townsend, MS, on 5/6/1865.

Achord, J.C. (AKA Ancord, Anchord, I.C.) Pvt., 3rd Louisiana Cavalry (Wingfield's). Co. D. Enlisted: 8/3/1862 at Livingston, LA. Rolls for 8/3/1862 through 9/1862: Present. Federal Rolls of Prisoners of War: Captured and paroled at Port Hudson, LA, on 7/4/1863. Federal Rolls of Prisoners of War: Captured near Jackson, LA, on 11/20/1864; Sent to New Orleans, LA, on 11/23/1864. Received at Ship Island, MS, on 12/13/1864; Transferred to Vicksburg, MS, for exchange on 5/1/1865. Exchanged at Camp Townsend, MS, on 5/6/1865.

Ackley, John Pvt., 14th Louisiana Battalion Sharpshooters. Co. A. Enlisted: 8/18/1861 at Camp Moore, LA. Rolls for 7/1862 through 4/1863: Present. Federal Rolls of Prisoners at War: Captured at Missionary Ridge, TN, on 11/25/1863; Forwarded to the U.S. Military Prison, Louisville, KY, from Nashville, TN, on 12/7/1863. Sent to Rock Island Barracks, IL, on 12/11/1863; Transferred to Boulware Wharf, VA, for exchange on 2/25/1865. Exchanged on 3/6/1865. Federal Rolls of Prisoners of War: Captured at Gravel Hill, AL, on 3/24/1865; Received at Ship Island, MS, on 4/4/1865. Transferred to Vicksburg, MS, for exchange on 5/1/1865; Exchanged at Camp Townsend, MS, on 5/6/1865.

Adams, Samuel Pvt., 18th Louisiana Battalion Cavalry. Co. A. Federal Rolls of Prisoners of War: Captured at East Baton Rouge Parish, LA, on 9/21/1864; Received at New Orleans, LA, on 10/10/1864. Transferred to Ship Island, MS, by order of Maj. Gen.E.R.S. Canby on 10/20/1864; Sent to Fort Columbus, New York Harbor, NY, on 11/10/1864. Forwarded to Elmira, NY. Died: 2/28/1865 at Elmira, NY. Buried: Woodlawn National Cemetery, Chemung County, NY.

Adams, W.H. Pvt., 14th Louisiana Infantry. Co. G. Federal Rolls of Prisoners of War: Captured at Baker's Farm, LA, on 4/10/1864; Received at New Orleans, LA, on 4/20/1864. Escaped on passage from New Orleans, LA, to Red River Landing, LA, on 7/21–22/1864; Received at New Orleans on 9/5/1864. Transferred to Ship Island, MS, by order of General E.R.S. Canby on 10/5/1864; Forwarded to Fort Columbus, New York Harbor, NY, on 11/16/1864. Received at Elmira, NY, on 11/19/1864; Paroled at Elmira, NY, on 3/10/1865. Sent to James River, VA, for exchange on 3/15/1865.

Addison, D.H. (AKA D.R.) Pvt., 17th Louisiana Infantry. Co. B. Federal Rolls of Prisoners of War: Captured at Bruinsburg, LA, on 11/2/1864; Received at New Orleans, LA, from Natchez, MS, on 12/21/1864. Forwarded to Ship Island, MS, on 1/25/1865; Transferred to Vicksburg, MS, for exchange on 5/1/1865. Exchanged at Camp Townsend, MS, on 5/6/1865.

Albritton, A.J. (AKA Allbreton, A.I.) Pvt., 3rd Louisiana Cavalry. Co. H. Enlisted 6/12/1862 at Camp Moore, LA. Federal Rolls of Prisoners of War: Captured at Brookhaven, MS, or Liberty, MS, on 11/18/1864; Received at Ship Island, MS, from New Orleans, LA, on 12/13/1864. Transferred to Vicksburg, MS, for exchange on 5/1/1865; Exchanged at Camp Townsend, MS, on 5/6/1865. Confederate Widows Pension Application on file at the Louisiana State Archives. Microfilm Reel: CP1.1. Microdex 4. Sequence 52. Target Card: Albritton, Margarette Adella (Kelly). Parish: East Feliciana. 7 pages.

Alexander, G. Pvt., 1st Louisiana Heavy Artillery. Co. G. Regimental Return for 6/1862: On detached service on the CSS *Arkansas* in accordance with orders from Brigade Heaquarters on 6/25/1862. Federal Rolls of Prisoners of War: Captured at Blakely, AL, on 4/9/1865; Received at Ship Island, MS, on 4/15/1865. Transferred to Vicksburg, MS, for exchange on 5/1/1865; Exchanged at Camp Townsend, MS, on 5/6/1865.

Alford, William B. (AKA W.M.) Pvt., Miles Legion. Co. C. Enlisted: 11/10/1862 at Covington, LA. Federal Rolls of Prisoners of War: Captured at Greensburg, LA, on 11/10/1864; Sent to New Orleans, LA, on 11/23/1864. Received at Ship Island, MS, on 12/13/1864; Transferred to Vicksburg, MS, for exchange on 5/1/1865. Exchanged at Camp Townsend, MS, on 5/6/1865.

Confederate Widows Pension Application on file at the Louisiana State Archives. Microfilm Reel: CP1.2. Microdex 1. Sequence 25. Target Card: Alford, Harriett (Cooper). Parish: Tangipahoa. 22 pages.

Allain, David J. (AKA E.J.) Pvt., 9th Louisiana Infantry. Cos. B & D. Federal Rolls of Prisoners of War: Captured near Morganza, LA, on 8/20/1864; Forwarded from New Orleans, LA, to Ship Island, MS, on 10/7/1864.

Allain, E.J. Pvt., Ogden's Cavalry Battalion. Co. B. Federal Rolls of Prisoners of War: Transferred from New Orleans, LA, to Ship Island, MS, by order of Maj. Gen.E.R.S. Canby on 10/5/1864.

Allen, Columbus H. 2nd Lt., Ogden's Cavalry Battalion. Co. __. Federal Rolls of Prisoners of War: Captured at Dutch Stores, LA, on 10/14/1864; Received at New Orleans, LA, on 10/20/1864. Transferred to Ship Island, MS, on 11/5/1864; Forwarded to Fort Lafayette, New York Harbor, NY, on 11/20/1864. Received at Fort Warren, MA, on 12/21/1864; Released on the U.S. Oath of Allegiance. Residence at oath: Memphis, TN. Description at oath: Eyes: blue. Hair: light. Complexion: light. Height: 5'6". Confederate Widows Pension Application on file at the Louisiana State Archives. Microfilm Reel: CP1.2. Microdex 3. Sequence: 2. Target Card: Allen, Beulah Emma (James) Posthlewaite. Parish: Orleans. 27 pages.

Allen, D.J. (AKA Allain, D.J.) Pvt., 14th Louisiana Cavalry. Co. __. Federal Rolls of Prisoners of War: Captured at Morganza, LA, on 8/20/1861; Forwarded to Ship Island, MS, from New Orleans, LA, on 10/7/1864. Transferred to Fort Columbus, New York Harbor, NY, on 11/5/1864.

Allen, David J. (AKA Allain, D.J.) Pvt., Ogden's Cavalry Battalion. Co. B. Federal Rolls of Prisoners of War: Captured near Morganza, LA, on 8/20/1864; Sent to New Orleans, LA, on 8/25/1864. On Register of St. Louis U.S.A. General Hospital, New Orleans, LA: Admitted on 9/10/1864; Returned to duty on 9/16/1864. Forwarded to Ship Island, MS, on 11/7/1864; Transferred to Fort Columbus, New York Harbor, NY, on 11/16/1864. Received at Elmira, NY, on 11/19/1864; Died: 12/22/1864 at Elmira, NY. Buried: Woodlawn National Cemetery, Chemung County, NY.

Allen, W.F. Pvt., 5th Louisiana Cavalry. Co. A. Federal Rolls of Prisoners of War: Captured at Natchez, MS, on 9/19/1864. On Register of U.S.A. General Hospital, New Orleans, LA: Admitted in 9/1864. Transferred to Ship Island, MS, on 10/5/1864.

Ambrose, W. Pvt., 5th Louisiana Cavalry. Co. E. Federal Rolls of Prisoners of War: Captured at Baton Rouge, LA, on 12/24/1864; Received at Ship Island, MS, from New Orleans, LA, on 1/25/1865. Transferred to Vicksburg, MS, for exchange on 5/1/1865; Exchanged at Camp Townsend, MS, on 5/6/1865.

Ambrose, William Pvt., 7th Louisiana Infantry. Co. B. Enlisted: 3/24/1862 at Baton Rouge, LA. Rolls for 3/24/1862 through 12/1863: Present. Rolls for 1/864 through 2/1864: Absent without leave. Rolls for 4/30/1864 through 8/31/1864: Deserted. Federal Rolls of Prisoners of War: Captured at East Baton Rouge Parish, LA, on 12/21/1864; Received at New Orleans, LA, on 12/28/1864. Forwarded to Ship Island, MS, on 1/25/1865; Transferred to Vicksburg, MS, for exchange on 5/1/1865. Exchanged at Camp Townsend, MS, on 5/6/1865.

Ames, Oliver (AKA Aymes, O.) Pvt., Ogden's Cavalry Battalion. Co. A. Federal Rolls of Prisoners of War: Captured at East Baton Rouge Parish, LA, on 9/17/1864; Transferred to Ship Island, MS, from New Orleans, LA, on 10/27/1864. Exchanged on 3/2/1865.

Anderson, A.A. Pvt., 26th Louisiana Infantry. Co. __. Federal Rolls of Prisoners of War: Captured at Morganza, LA, on 8/8/1864; Received at Fort Columbus, New York Harbor, NY, from Ship Island, MS, on 11/16/1864. Sent to Elmira, NY. Transferred from Elmira, NY, to James River, VA, for exchange on 11/18/1864.

Anderson, I.C. Pvt., 5th Louisiana Cavalry. Co. B. Federal Rolls of Prisoners of War: Captured at Liberty, MS, on 11/16/1864; Sent to Ship Island, MS, from New Orleans, LA, on 11/13/1864. Exchanged on 3/2/1865.

Anderson, J.C. Pvt., 5th Louisiana Cavalry. Co. B. Federal Rolls of Prisoners of War: Captured near Liberty, MS, on 11/6/1864; Received at New Orleans, LA, on 11/23/1864. Transferred to Ship Island, MS, on 12/10/1864; Exchanged on 3/2/1865. Endorsement shows: Flag of Truce Steamer Nashua, Mobile Bay, AL, 3/4/1865: Received the Prisoners of War borne on above roll.

Andrews, Rapson K. Pvt., 16th Louisiana Infantry. Co. C. Enlisted: 9/29/1861 at Camp Moore, LA. Rolls for 9/29/1861 through 7/1862: Present. Rolls for 8/1862 through 10/30/1862: Absent, detached as Teamster since 8/27/1862. Rolls for 1/1863 through 6/1863: Present. Rolls for 7/863 through 8/1863: Absent, sent to hospital at Montgomery, AL, on 7/25/1863. Rolls for 9/1863 through 10/1863: Present. Rolls for 1/1864 through 2/1864: Absent, sick in hospital at Marietta, GA. Rolls for 5/1864 through 8/1864: Absent, sent to hospital at Gainesville, AL. Rolls for 9/1864 through 2/1865: Present. Federal Rolls of Prisoners of War: Captured at Spanish Fort, AL, on 4/8/1865; Received at Ship Island, MS, on 4/10/1865. Transferred to Vicksburg, MS, for exchange on 5/1/1865; Exchanged at Camp Townsend, MS, on 5/6/1865.

Andrews, T.L. Pvt., 3rd Louisiana Cavalry. Co. I. Federal Rolls of Prisoners of War: Captured at Liberty, MS, on 11/18/1864; Sent to New Orleans, LA, on 11/23/1864. Transferred to Ship Island, MS, on 12/10/1864; Exchanged on 3/2/1865 at Mobile Bay, AL. Rolls of Prisoners of War, C.S.A: Surrendered at Citronelle, AL, on 5/4/1865; Paroled at Gainesville, AL, on 5/12/1865. Residence at parole: Wilkinson County, MS. Confederate Widows Pension Application on file at the Louisiana State Archives. Microfilm Reel: CP1.3. Microdex 3. Sequence 23. Target Card: Andrews, Malvina A. (Davis). Parish: East Feliciana. 9 pages.

Anselm, Benoit B. (AKA Berrit, P.B.) Pvt., 2nd Louisiana Cavalry. Co. I. Federal Rolls of Prisoners of War: Captured at Stone's Plantation, LA, on 9/16/1864; Received at Ship Island, MS, from New Orleans, LA, on 10/7/1864. Sent to Fort Columbus, New York Harbor, NY, on 11/16/1864; Forwarded to Elmira, NY, on 11/25/1864. Paroled at Elmira, NY, on 2/25/1865; Sent to James River, VA, for exchange. Born: 1/6/1828. Died: 1/22/1900. Buried: St. John the Evangelist Cemetery at Plaquemine, Iberville Parish, LA. Confederate Widows Pension Application on file at the Louisiana State Archives. Microfilm Reel:

CP1.3. Microdex 4. Sequence 16. Target Card: Anselm, Emma (Buck). Parish: Iberville. 2 pages.

Aroine, J. Mechanic, 2nd Louisiana Cavalry. Co. __. Federal Rolls of Prisoners of War: Captured at Tensas Parish, LA, on 9/19/1864; Received at Fort Columbus, New York Harbor, NY, from Ship Island, MS, on 11/16/1864. Transferred to Elmira, NY, on 11/18/1864, Released on the U.S. Oath of Allegiance on 1/28/1865.

Atkinson, James W. (AKA J.N.) Pvt., 26th Louisiana Infantry. Co. I. Federal Rolls of Prisoners of War: Captured near Lavinia, LA, on 9/22/1864; Admitted to St. Louis U.S.A. General Hospital, New Orleans, LA, on 9/30/1864. Transferred to Ship Island, MS, on 10/5/1864; Exchanged on 3/2/1865.

Atteburg, Charles (AKA Attleburg) Pvt., 2nd Louisiana Cavalry. Co. C. Federal Rolls of Prisoners of War: Captured at Alexandria, LA; Forwarded to Ship Island, MS, from New Orleans, LA, on 10/21/1864.

Aucoin, Franklin Pvt., 18th Louisiana Infantry. Co. G. Enlisted: 10/5/1861 at Camp Moore, LA. Rolls for 10/5/1861 through 2/1862: Present. Rolls for 5/1862 through 6/1862: Absent, wounded at the Battle of Shiloh, TN, on 4/6/1862; Furloughed for 30 days on 4/15/1862. Rolls for 7/1862 through 8/1862: Absent, wounded at the Battle of Shiloh, TN, on 4/6/1862 and furloughed for 60 days on 4/15/1862. Remarks: Heard from him, unwell. Federal Rolls of Prisoners of War: Captured at Lafourche, LA, on 11/21/1862; Exchanged from steamer *Frolic*, near Baton Rouge, LA, on 2/23/1863. Rolls for 1/1863 through 2/1863: Absent, without leave since 10/27/1862; Remained behind in the retreat after the Battle of Texana Road. Federal Rolls of Prisoners of War: Captured at Lafourche Parish, LA, on 9/26/1864; Received at New Orleans, LA, on 10/31/1864. Sent to Ship Island, MS, on 11/2/1864; Forwarded to Fort Columbus, New York Harbor, NY, on 11/16/1864. Transferred to Elmira, NY, on 11/19/1864; Paroled at Elmira, NY, on 2/9/1865. Sent to James River, VA, for exchange on 2/20–21/1865; Entry Cancelled with remarks: Not able to travel. Took the U.S. Oath of Allegiance at Elmira, NY, on 6/19/1865. Description at oath: Eyes: blue. Hair: auburn. Complexion: florid. Height: 5'11". Residence at oath: New Orleans, LA. Born: 3/27/1843. Died: 8/16/1920. Buried: St. Joseph Catholic Cemetery, Thibodeaux, Lafourche Parish, LA, with a Confederate 2nd National Flag inscribed on his tomb. Confederate Pension Application on file at the Louisiana State Archives. Microfilm Reel: CP1.5. Microdex 1. Sequence 6. Target Card: Aucoin, Franklin. Parish: LaFourche. 9 pages.

Aycock, R.W. Pvt., 25th Louisiana Infantry. Co. G. Enlisted: 3/15/1862 at Lisbon, LA. Rolls for 4/1862 through 2/1863: Absent, sick at Murfreesboro, TN. Rolls for 7/1863 through 2/1865: Present. Federal Rolls of Prisoners of War: Captured at Spanish Fort, AL, on 4/8/1865; Sent to Ship Island, MS, on 4/9/1865. Transferred to Vicksburg, MS, for exchange on 5/1/1865; Exchanged at Camp Townsend, MS, on 5/6/1865.

Aymes, O. Pvt., Ogden's Cavalry Battalion. Co. A. Federal Rolls of Prisoners of War: Captured at East Baton Rouge Parish, LA, on 9/17/1864; Sent to New Orleans, LA, on 9/21/1864. Received at Ship Island, MS, on 10/24/1864; Transferred to Elmira, NY, from Fort Columbus, New York Harbor, NY, on 11/20/1864. Paroled at Elmira, NY, on 2/13/1865; Sent to James River, VA, for exchange. Exchanged at Point Lookout, MD, on 2/20–21/1865.

Baar, J.M. Pvt., 13th Louisiana Infantry. Co. __. Federal Rolls of Prisoners of War: Captured at Spanish Fort, AL, on 4/8/1865; Received at Ship Island, MS, on 4/10/1865. Transferred to Vicksburg, MS, for exchange on 5/1/1865; Exchanged at Camp Townsend, MS, on 5/6/1865.

Bailey, William B. Pvt., 19th Louisiana Infantry. Co. F. Enlisted: 12/11/1861 at Camp Moore, LA. Rolls for 12/11/1861 through 2/1865: Present. Federal Rolls of Prisoners of War: Captured at Spanish Fort, AL, on 4/8/1865; Received at Ship Island, MS, on 4/10/1865. Transferred to Vicksburg, MS, for exchange on 5/1/1865; Exchanged at Camp Townsend, MS, on 5/6/1865.

Baker, George Pvt., 1st Louisiana Cavalry. Co. G. Enlisted: 10/4/1861 at Baton Rouge, LA. Rolls for 10/4/1861 through 8/1862: Present. Rolls for 9/1862 through 2/1863: Absent. Rolls for 2/28/1863 through 6/30/1863: Present. Rolls for 11/1863 through 12/1863: Absent, on furlough through 12/10/1863. Rolls for 1/1864 through 2/1864: Absent, without leave since 1/20/1864. Federal Rolls of Prisoners of War: Captured at Liberty, MS, on 11/18/1864; Sent to New Orleans, LA, on 11/23/1864. Forwarded to Ship Island, MS, on 12/10/1864; Transferred to Vicksburg, MS, for exchange on 5/1/1865. Exchanged at Camp Townsend, MS, on 5/6/1865.

Baldwin, John Pvt., 25th Louisiana Infantry. Co. C. Federal Rolls of Prisoners of War: Captured at Spanish Fort, AL, on 4/8/1865; Received at Ship Island, MS, on 4/10/1865. Transferred to Vicksburg, MS, for exchange on 5/1/1865; Exchanged at Camp Townsend, MS, on 5/6/1865.

Barrett, A.C. (AKA J.C.) Cpl., 3rd Louisiana Cavalry. Co. H. Enlisted: 6/12/1862 at Camp Moore, LA. On undated Roll: Present. Federal Rolls of Prisoners of War: Captured and paroled at Port Hudson, LA, in 7/1863. Federal Rolls of Prisoners of War: Captured at Clinton, LA, on 11/16/1864; Sent to New Orleans, LA, on 11/23/1864; Received at Ship Island, MS, on 12/10/1864. Returned to New Orleans, LA, on 3/9/1865; Released on the U.S. Oath of Allegiance on 3/9/1865 by order of Maj. Gen.E.R.S. Canby. Remarks: Deserter. Residence at oath: Fanada, Somerset County, MO. Description at oath: Eyes: hazel. Hair: brown. Complexion: light. Height: 6'0".

Barrett, Charles C. Pvt., 30th Louisiana Infantry. Co. D. Enlisted: 3/1/1862 at New Orleans, LA. Rolls for 3/1862 through 6/1863: Present. Federal Rolls of Prisoners of War: Captured and paroled at Port Hudson, LA, in 7/1863. Rolls for 10/1863 through 2/1865: Present. Federal Rolls of Prisoners of War: Captured at Spanish Fort, AL, on 4/8/1865; Received at Ship Island, MS, on 4/10/1865. Transferred to Vicksburg, MS, for exchange on 5/1/1865; Exchanged at Camp Townsend, MS, on 5/6/1865. Born: 5/22/1839. Died: 11/1/1895. Buried: Georgetown City Cemetery, Georgetown, Grant Parish, LA.

Barrett, V. (AKA Berthelotte, N., J.) Pvt., 30th Louisiana Infantry. Co. F. Federal Rolls of Prisoners of War: Captured at Spanish Fort, AL, on 4/8/1865; Received at Ship Island, MS, on 4/10/1865. Transferred to

Vicksburg, MS, for exchange on 5/1/1865; Exchanged at Camp Townsend, MS, on 5/6/1865.

Baunett, J.C. Pvt., 3rd Louisiana Cavalry. Co. H. Federal Rolls of Prisoners of War: Captured at Clinton, LA, on 11/16/1864; Sent to New Orleans, LA, on 12/13/1864. Received at Ship Island, MS. Transferred to New Orleans, LA, for exchange on 1/8/1865.

Bazer, Jerry E. (AKA J.E., I.E., Z.E.) Pvt., 19th Louisiana Infantry. Co. F. Enlisted: 12/11/1861 at Camp Moore, LA. Rolls for 12/11/1861 through 12/1863: Present. Rolls for 1/1864 through 4/1864: Reenlisted at Dalton, GA, on 1/20/1864; Absent, in hospital at Marietta, GA. Rolls for 5/1864 through 2/1865: Present. Federal Rolls of Prisoners of War: Captured at Spanish Fort, AL, on 4/8/1865; Received at Ship Island, MS, on 4/10/1865. Transferred to Vicksburg, MS, for exchange on 5/1/1865; Exchanged at Camp Townsend, MS, on 5/6/1865. Confederate Pension Application on file at the Louisiana State Archives. Microfilm Reel: CP1.8. Microdex 4. Sequence 13. Target Card: Bazer, Z.E. Parish: Caddo. 8 pages.

Beauchamp, James T. (AKA Beauchampe, J.S.) Pvt., 6th Louisiana Cavalry. Co. E. Federal Rolls of Prisoners of War: Captured at Bullet's Bay, LA, on 9/26/1864; Forwarded to New Orleans, LA, from Natchez, MS, on 10/15/1864. Received at Ship Island, MS, on 10/20/1864; Transferred to Fort Columbus, New York Harbor, NY, on 11/16/1864. Sent to Elmira, NY, on 11/20/1864. Died: 2/10/1865 at Elmira, NY. Buried: Woodlawn National Cemetery, Chemung County, NY.

Beaupeurt, J.C.C. (AKA Beaupert, J.A., C.E.) Pvt., 2nd Louisiana Cavalry. Co. I. Federal Rolls of Prisoners of War: Captured near Morganza, LA, on 8/20/1864; Received at New Orleans, LA, on 8/25/1864. Forwarded to Ship Island, MS, on 10/5/1864; Sent to Fort Columbus, New York Harbor, NY, on 11/5/1864. Received at Fort Columbus, New York Harbor, NY, on 11/16/1864; Forwarded to Elmira, NY, on 11/19/1864. Took the U.S. Oath of Allegiance on 6/19/1865. Residence at oath: Bayou Goula, LA. Description at oath: Eyes: dark. Hair: dark. Complexion: dark. Height: 5'3".

Becnel, F. (AKA Becnel, T.) Cpl., Consolidated Crescent Regiment. Co. E. Federal Rolls of Prisoners of War: Captured at Assumption Parish, LA, on 7/28/1864; Received at New Orleans, LA, on 8/7/1864. Forwarded to Ship Island, MS, on 10/5/1864; Sent to Fort Columbus, New York Harbor, NY, on 11/16/1864. Forwarded to Elmira, NY, on 11/19/1864. Paroled at Elmira, NY, on 2/9/1865. Sent to St. James River, VA, for exchange.

Beftin, Gustav Pvt., Cage's Cavalry Battalion. Co. A. Federal Rolls of Prisoners of War: Captured at Clinton, LA, on 11/16/1864; Transferred to Ship Island, MS, from New Orleans, LA, on 12/13/1864.

Bell, C.W. Sgt., 19th Louisiana Infantry. Co. K. Enlisted: 12/15/1861 at New Orleans, LA. Rolls for 12/15/1861 through 2/28/1865: Present. Rolls for 3/1865 through 4/1865: Absent, prisoner of war. Federal Rolls of Prisoners of War: Captured at Spanish Fort, AL, on 4/8/1865; Received at Ship Island, MS, on 4/10/1865. Transferred to Vicksburg, MS, for exchange on 5/1/1865; Exchanged at Camp Townsend, MS, on 5/6/1865. Residence at exchange: Homer, LA.

Belsom, Phil Pvt./4th Cpl., 30th Louisiana Infantry. Co. C. Enlisted: 4/15/1862 at Camp Lewis, LA. Rolls for 4/15/1862 through 6/30/1862: Present. Rolls for 7/1862 through 8/1862: Present, promoted to 4th Cpl. on 8/29/1862. Rolls for 9/1862 through 2/1865: Present. Federal Rolls of Prisoners of War: Captured at Spanish Fort, AL, on 4/8/1865; Received at Ship Island, MS, on 4/10/1865. Transferred to Vicksburg, MS, for exchange on 5/1/1865; Exchanged at Camp Townsend, MS, on 5/6/1865.

Benton, Thomas (AKA Theodore) Pvt., 1st Louisiana Cavalry. Co. B. Federal Rolls of Prisoners of War: Captured at West Baton Rouge Parish, LA, on 10/24/1864; Sent to New Orleans, LA, on 10/25/1864. Transferred to Ship Island, MS, on 10/27/1864; Received at Ship Island, MS, on 10/28/1864. Sent to New York on 11/5/1864; Received at Fort Columbus, New York Harbor, NY, on 11/16/1864. Forwarded to Elmira, NY, on 11/20/1864. Died: 12/10/1864 at Elmira, New York. Buried: Woodlawn National Cemetery, Chemung County, NY.

Bergeron, Omer Pvt., 26th Louisiana Infantry. Co. C. Enlisted: 3/27/1862 at Assumption Parish, LA. Rolls for 3/27/1862 through 10/1862: Present. Federal Rolls of Prisoners of War: Captured and paroled at Vicksburg, MS, on 7/4/1863. Federal Rolls of Prisoners of War: Captured at Grand Lake, LA, on 7/29/1864; Sent to New Orleans, LA, on 7/5/1864. Transferred to Ship Island, MS, on 10/5/1864; Forwarded to Fort Columbus, New York Harbor, NY, on 11/16/1864. Received at Elmira, NY, on 11/19/1864; Paroled at Elmira, NY, on 2/25/1865. Transferred to James River, VA, for exchange. Confederate Pension Application on file at the Louisiana State Archives. Microfilm Reel: CP1.10. Microdex 2. Sequence 31. Target Card: Bergeron, Omer. Parish: Assumption. 6 pages.

Bernard, E. (AKA C.) Pvt., 30th Louisiana Infantry. Cos. A & D. Enlisted: 2/23/1862 at Algiers, LA. Rolls for 2/23/1862 through 8/1863: Present. Rolls for 9/1863 through 10/1863: Absent, sick. Rolls for 3/1864 through 2/1865: Present. Federal Rolls of Prisoners of War: Captured at Spanish Fort, AL, on 4/8/1865; Forwarded to Ship Island, MS, on 4/10/1865. Transferred to Vicksburg, MS, for exchange on 5/1/1865; Exchanged at Camp Townsend, MS, on 5/6/1865.

Bertin, Gustave Pvt./Sgt., Ogden's Cavalry Battalion. Co. E. Federal Rolls of Prisoners of War: Captured at Clinton, LA, on 11/16/1864; Forwarded to New Orleans, LA, on 11/23/1864. Received at Ship Island, MS, on 12/13/1864; Transferred to Vicksburg, MS, for exchange on 5/1/1865. Exchanged at Camp Townsend, MS, on 5/6/1865.

Berton, A. Pvt., Ogden's Cavalry Battalion. Co. A. Federal Rolls of Prisoners of War: Captured near Jackson, LA, on 11/15/1864; Sent to New Orleans, LA, on 11/23/1864. Received at Ship Island, MS, on 12/13/1864; Transferred to Vicksburg, MS, for exchange on 5/1/1865. Exchanged at Camp Townsend, MS, on 5/6/1865.

Betat, Charles Pvt., 30th Louisiana Infantry. Co. F. Enlisted: 6/3/1863 at Mobile, AL. Rolls for 6/1863 through 4/1864: Present. Rolls for 7/1864 through 8/1864: Absent, in hospital due to wounds received on 7/28/1864. Federal Rolls of Prisoners of War: Captured at East Baton Rouge Parish, LA, on 3/24/1865; Received at Ship Island, MS, on 4/4/1865. On

Register of U.S.A. General Hospital, New Orleans, LA: Admitted on 4/26/1865. Rolls of Prisoners of War, C.S.A: Surrendered at Citronelle, AL, on 5/4/1865; Paroled at New Orleans, LA, on 5/6/1865. Soldier also served as a Pvt. with the Orleans Guard Louisiana Militia. Born: 1843. Died: 7/18/1877. Buried: St. Louis Cemtery # 1, located between St. Louis Street and Conti Street at New Orleans, Orleans Parish, LA.

Blache, C. (AKA Blackey) Pvt., 30th Louisiana Infantry. Co. F. Enlisted: 11/13/1862 at Port Hudson, LA. Rolls for 11/13/1862 through 2/28/1865: Present. Federal Rolls of Prisoners of War: Captured at Spanish Fort, AL, on 4/8/1865; Received at Ship Island, MS, on 4/10/1865. Transferred to Vicksburg, MS, for exchange on 5/1/1865; Exchanged at Camp Townsend, MS, on 5/6/1865. Soldier also served as a Pvt. with the Orleans Guard Louisiana State Militia. Cos. C & D. Confederate Widows Pension Application on file at the Louisiana State Archives. Microfilm Reel: CP1.12. Microdex 1. Sequence 9. Target Card: Blanche, Georgianna (Durel, Duval). Parish: Orleans. 5 pages.

Blackstone, John H. Pvt., 25th Louisiana Infantry. Co. H. Enlisted: 3/19/1862 at New Orleans, LA. Rolls for 3/19/1862 through 6/30/1862: Absent, in hospital. Rolls for 11/1862 through 6/1863: Present. Rolls for 7/1863 through 8/1863: Absent, on 30 day furlough since 8/15/1863. Rolls for 10/1863 through 2/1864: Absent, sick by order of Dr. Ware. Rolls for 3/1864 through 2/1865: Present. Federal Rolls of Prisoners of War: Captured at Spanish Fort, AL, on 4/8/1865; Received at Ship Island, MS, on 4/10/1865. Transferred to Vicksburg, MS, for exchange on 5/1/1865; Exchanged at Camp Townsend, MS, on 5/6/1865. Rolls of Prisoners of War, C.S.A: Surrendered at Citronelle, AL, on 5/4/1865; Paroled at Meridian, MS, on 5/10/1865. Residence at parole: Jefferson, TX.

Bland, Thomas G. (AKA J.Y.) 1st Lt., 10th Louisiana Infantry. Co. C. Federal Rolls of Prisoners of War: Captured at Highlands, LA, on 9/15/1864; Sent to Baton Rouge, LA, on 9/19/1864. Received at Ship Island, MS, on 11/5/1864; Transferred to Fort Lafayette, New York Harbor, NY, on 11/20/1864. Forwarded to Fort Delaware, DE, on 3/14/1865; Released on the U.S. Oath of Allegiance on 5/11/1865. Description at oath: Eyes: hazel. Hair: brown. Complexion: fair. Height: 5'8". Residence at oath: New Orleans, LA.

Booth, William S. (AKA W.F.) Pvt., 1st Louisiana Cavalry. Co. B. Enlisted: 9/5/1861 at Baton Rouge, LA. Rolls for 9/5/1861 through 12/1863: Present. Federal Rolls of Prisoners of War: Captured at East Baton Rouge Parish, LA, on 10/24/1864; Sent to New Orleans, LA, on 10/25/1864. Transferred to Ship Island, MS, on 10/27/1864; Received at Fort Columbus, New York Harbor, NY, on 11/5/1864. Forwarded to Elmira, NY, on 11/19/1864; Escaped en route. Rolls of Prisoners of War, C.S.A: Surrendered at Citronelle, AL, on 5/4/1865; Paroled at Gainesville, AL, on 5/12/1865. The following is a statement from A.B. Booth, Commissioner of Louisiana Miltary Records: "I state this soldier was my brother. We know that he escaped from a railroad train of prisoners en route from New York City to Elmira Prison, worked his way to New York City, to Chicago, to St. Louis, thence down the Mississippi River on Steamer Magenta, back to his command via Natchez, MS. This fact is also reported on page 164 of the history of his regiment, known as 'A Cavalryman's Reminiscences of the Civil War,' by Howell Carter."

Boudreaux, Jules Pvt., 1st Louisiana Heavy Artillery. Co. C. Enlisted: Conscripted on 10/20/1862 per Order # 9, Louisiana Heavy Artillery Headquarters. Rolls for 10/20/1862 through 2/1863: Present. Rolls for 3/1863 through 4/1863: Absent, sick in city hospital. Rolls for 9/1863 through 10/1863: In hospital at Enterprise, MS. Rolls for 11/1863 through 10/1864: Present. Federal Rolls of Prisoners of War: Captured at Blakely, AL, on 4/9/1865; Received at Ship Island, MS, on 4/15/1865. Transferred to Vicksburg, MS, for exchange on 5/1/1865; Exchanged at Camp Townsend, MS, on 5/6/1865. Buried: St. Alphonsus Catholic Church Cemetery on Hwy. 167 in Maurice, Vermillion Parish, LA. Confederate Widows Pension Application on file at the Louisiana State Archives. Microfilm Reel: CP1.14. Microdex 4. Sequence 28. Target Card: Boudreaux, Marie Azelema Monte. Parish: Arcadia. 26 pages.

Bourg, T.V. Pvt., 2nd Louisiana Cavalry. Co. I. Federal Rolls of Prisoners of War: Captured at Bayou Sara, LA, on 9/22/1864; Received at New Orleans, LA, on 9/25/1864. Transferred to Ship Island, MS, on 10/5/1864; Sent to Fort Columbus, New York Harbor, NY, on 11/16/1864. Forwarded to Elmira, NY, on 11/19/1864; Paroled at Elmira, NY. Sent to James River, VA, for exchange on 2/13/1865. Federal Rolls of Prisoners of War: Captured at the mouth of Red River, LA, on 4/5/1865; Sent to New Orleans, LA, on 4/7/1865. Transferred from New Orleans, LA, to the mouth of Red River, LA, on 5/2/1865 by order of Maj. Gen.E.R.S. Canby.

Bourgeois, Adam Pvt., 26th Louisiana Infantry. Co. H. Enlisted: 3/21/1861 at Terrebonne Parish, LA. Rolls for 3/21/1861 through 10/1862: Present. Federal Rolls of Prisoners of War: Captured and paroled at Vicksburg, MS, on 7/4/1863. Federal Rolls of Prisoners of War: Captured on 10/6/1864; Received at New Orleans, LA, on 10/15/1864. Transferred to Ship Island, MS, on 10/20/1864; Forwarded to Fort Columbus, New York Harbor, NY, on 11/5/1864. Sent to Elmira, NY, on 11/19/1864; Paroled at Elmira, NY, on 2/25/1865. Exchanged at James River, VA. Residence at exchange: St. James Parish, LA. Description at exchange: Eyes: black. Hair: dark. Complexion: dark. Height: 5'9". Died: 4/10/1910 at age 65. Buried: Greenwood Cemetery on City Park Ave., New Orleans, Orleans Parish, LA.

Bourgeois, Theogene (AKA T.) Pvt., Ogden's Cavalry Battalion. Co. E. Federal Rolls of Prisoners of War: Captured at Jackson, LA, on 11/16/1864; Received at New Orleans, LA, on 11/23/1864. Forwarded to Ship Island, MS, on 12/13/1864. Federal Rolls of Prisoners of War: Captured near Whitehall Mills, LA, on 12/14/1864; Sent to U.S. Military Division of West Mississippi on 12/21/1864. Forwarded to New Orleans, LA, on 12/24/1864; Received at Ship Island, MS, on 1/2/1865. Transferred to Vicksburg, MS, for exchange on 5/1/1865; Exchanged at Camp Townsend, MS, on 5/6/1865. On Register of U.S.A. General Hospital # 2, Vicksburg, MS: Admitted on 5/14/1865; Returned to duty on 5/21/1865.

Bourguin, Gustave Adolphe Pvt., 9th Louisiana

Infantry. Co. I. Federal Rolls of Prisoners of War: Captured at Morganza, LA, on 8/2/1864. Sent to U.S.A. Saint Louis General Hospital, New Orleans, LA, on 8/15/1864; Returned to duty on 9/8/1864. On Register of U.S.A. General Hospital, New Orleans, LA: Admitted on 9/16/1864; Returned to duty on 10/6/1864. Transferred to Ship Island, MS, on 10/5/1864; Sent to New York on 11/5/1864. Received at Fort Columbus, New York Harbor, NY, on 11/16/1864; Forwarded to Elmira, NY, on 11/19/1864. Released on the U.S. Oath of Allegiance on 5/13/1865; Transferred to James River, VA, for exchange. Description at exchange: Eyes: blue. Hair: brown. Complexion: fair. Height: 5'7½". Residence at exchange: Norfolk, VA. Born: 1/15/1844. Died: 1/3/1889. Buried: Forest Park Cemetery, Shreveport, Caddo Parish, LA.

Bovard, William (AKA W.T.) Pvt., 1st Louisiana Cavalry. Co. B. Enlisted: 2/21/1863 at Baton Rouge, LA. Rolls for 2/21/1862 through 12/1862: Present. Rolls for 1/1863 through 2/1863: Absent, without leave since 2/8/1863. Rolls for 3/1863 through 12/1863: Present. Federal Rolls of Prisoners of War: Captured near Clinton, LA, on 8/20/1864. On Register of St. Louis U.S.A. General Hospital, New Orleans, LA: Admitted on 10/1/1864; Returned to duty on 10/10/1864. Received at Ship Island, MS, from New Orleans, LA, on 10/20/1864. Died: 11/25/1864 at Ship Island, MS, due to dysentery. Buried: Ship Island, MS, Cemetery in Grave #43.

Bowden, Andrew Jackson Pvt., 4th Louisiana Battalion Infantry. Co. C. Enlisted: 4/14/1862 at Winnsboro, LA. Rolls for 4/14/1862 through 2/1865: Present. Federal Rolls of Prisoners of War: Captured at Spanish Fort, AL, on 4/8/1865; Received at Ship Island, MS, on 4/10/1865. Transferred to Vicksburg, MS, for exchange on 5/1/1865; Exchanged at Camp Townsend, MS, on 5/6/1865. Born: 1846. Died: 8/6/1904. Buried: Bowden Family Cemetery off Hwy. 562 between Fort Necesssity and Extension in Franklin Parish, LA.

Bowen, L.M. Pvt., 3rd Louisiana Cavalry. Co. E. Federal Rolls of Prisoners of War: Captured near Clinton, LA, on 8/25/1864; Received at Ship Island, MS, from New Orleans, LA.

Bowman, F.W. Pvt., 3rd Louisiana Cavalry. Co. E. Federal Rolls of Prisoners of War: Captured near Clinton, LA, on 8/25/1864; Received at New Orleans, LA, on 8/31/1864. Sent to Ship Island, MS, on 10/7/1864; Transferred to Fort Columbus, New York Harbor, NY, on 11/5/1864. Received at Fort Columbus, New York Harbor, NY, on 11/16/1864; Forwarded to Elmira, NY, on 11/19/1864. Paroled at Elmira, NY, on 3/10/1865; Sent to James River, VA, for exchange on 3/15/1865.

Bowman, William M. 1st Lt./Capt., 15th Louisiana Infantry. Co. C. Enlisted: 7/2/1861 at New Orleans, LA; Appointed 1st Lt. same day. Marital status at enlistment: Single. Occupation at enlistment: Carpenter. Rolls for 7/2/1861 through 2/1862: Present. Rolls for 3/1862 through 4/1862: Absent, on sick leave at Richmond, VA. Rolls for 5/1862 through 6/1862: Present, promoted to Capt. on 6/26/1862. Rolls for 10/1862 through 2/1864: Present. Rolls for 5/1864 through 9/1864: Absent, ordered to report to Brig. Gen. Harry T. Hays in Louisiana on 9/1/1864. Federal Rolls of Prisoners of War: Captured at Pointe Coupée Parish, LA, on 10/8/1864; Received at New Orleans, LA, on 10/15/1864. Forwarded to Ship Island, MS, on 11/2/1864; Sent to Fort Lafayette, New York Harbor, NY, on 11/20/1864. Transferred to Fort Warren, MA, on 12/21/1864; Released on the U.S. Oath of Allegiance on 6/12/1865. Description at oath: Eyes: grey. Hair: dark. Complexion: dark. Height: 5'7". Residence at oath: Iberville Parish, LA.

Bowry, F.B. Pvt., 2nd Louisiana Cavalry. Co. __. Federal Rolls of Prisoners of War: Captured at Alabama Bay, AL, on 9/22/1864; Received at Fort Columbus, New York Harbor, NY, from Ship Island, MS, on 11/16/1861. Transferred to Elmira, NY, on 11/18/1864.

Boyd, Henry Pvt., 1st Louisiana Cavalry. Co. D. Federal Rolls of Prisoners of War: Captured at Clinton, LA, on 11/16/1864; Sent to New Orleans, LA, on 11/23/1864. Received at Ship Island, MS, on 12/13/1864; Transferred to Vicksburg, MS, for exchange on 5/1/1865. Exchanged at Camp Townsend, MS, on 5/6/1865.

Bracken, Thomas O. Pvt., 2nd Louisiana Cavalry. Co. I. Federal Rolls of Prisoners of War: Captured at Bayou Alabama, LA, on 9/22/1864; Received at New Orleans, LA, on 9/25/1864. Transferred to Ship Island, MS, on 10/5/1864; Received at New York, NY, on 11/5/1864. Forwarded to Fort Columbus, New York Harbor, NY, on 11/16/1864; Transferred to Elmira, NY, on 11/19/1864. Sent to James River, VA, for exchange on 2/20/1865.

Brashears, W.F. Pvt., 3rd Louisiana Cavalry (Harrison's). Co. H. Federal Rolls of Prisoners of War: Captured near Brookhaven, MS, on 11/18/1864; Sent to New Orleans, LA, on 11/23/1864. Received at Ship Island, MS, on 12/13/1864; Transferred to Vicksburg, MS, for exchange on 5/1/1865. Exchanged at Camp Townsend, MS, on 5/6/1865. Born: 7/27/1847. Died: 8/15/1922. Buried: Concord Cemetery, McFall, Franklin County, MS.

Briggs, George Pvt., 3rd Louisiana Cavalry (Wingfield's). Co. I. Federal Rolls of Prisoners of War: Captured and paroled at Port Hudson, LA, in 7/1863. Federal Rolls of Prisoners of War: Captured at Bayou Sara, LA, on 10/3/1864; Transferred to New Orleans, LA, on 10/10/1864. Received at Ship Island, MS, on 10/20/1864. Died: 11/19/1864 at Ship Island, MS, due to pneumonia. Buried: Ship Island, MS, Cemetery in Grave #28.

Brill, Charles (AKA A.C.) Pvt./3rd Cpl./4th Sgt., 18th Louisiana Infantry. Co. I. Enlisted: 6/19/1861. Rolls for 6/19/1861 through 6/1862: Present, promoted to 3rd Cpl. on 6/25/1862. Rolls for 7/1862 through 8/1862: Present, promoted to 4th Sgt. on 8/9/1862. Federal Rolls of Prisoners of War: Captured and paroled at Labadieville, LA, on 10/27/1862. Rolls for 1/1863 through 2/1863: Absent, supposed to have been taken prisoner on 10/27/1862; Reported absent without leave. Federal Rolls of Prisoners of War: Captured at Bayou Teche, LA, on 4/14/1863; Sent to New Orleans, LA, for exchange. Exchanged at Prophet's Island, below Port Hudson, LA, on 5/5/1863. Rolls for 5/1863 through 6/1863: Absent, prisoner of war on parole. Rolls for 7/1863 through 8/1863: Absent, prisoner of war. Soldier also served as a Sgt. with Holmes' Louisiana Light Artillery Battery. Enlisted: New Orleans, LA. Federal Rolls of

Prisoners of War: Captured at Brookhaven, MS, on 11/17/1864; Sent to New Orleans, LA, on 11/23/1864. Received at Ship Island, MS, on 12/13/1864; Paroled at New Orleans, LA, on 1/1/1865. Transferred to Vicksburg, MS, for exchange on 5/1/1865; Exchange at Camp Townsend, MS, on 5/6/1865. Residence at parole: Pass Christian, MS. Confederate Widows Pension Application on file at the Louisiana State Archives. Microfilm Reel: CP1.17. Microdex 3. Sequence 7. Target Card: Brill, Wilhemina. Parish: Orleans. 4 pages.

Brinberry, John F. (AKA Brinsberry, F.F., J.T.) Pvt., Miles' Legion. Co. C. Enlisted: 3/24/1862 at Covington, LA. Rolls for 3/24/1862 through 6/1862: Present. Federal Rolls of Prisoners of War: Captured and paroled at Port Hudson, LA, in 7/1863. Federal Rolls of Prisoners of War: Captured at Clinton, LA, on 11/16/1864; Sent to New Orleans, LA, on 11/23/1864. Transferred to Ship Island, MS, on 12/10/1864; Forwarded to Vicksburg, MS, for exchange on 5/1/1865. Exchanged at Camp Townsend, MS, on 5/6/1865.

Brinsbergm, F.F. Pvt., Miles' Legion. Co. C. Federal Rolls of Prisoners of War: Captured at Clinton, LA, on 11/16/1864; Received at Ship Island. MS from New Orleans, LA, on 11/13/1864. Transferred to Vicksburg. MS for exchange on 5/1/1865; Exchanged at Camp Townsend, MS, on 5/6/1865.

Broder, John Pvt., 13th Louisiana Infantry. Co. B. Enlisted: 9/11/1861 at Camp Moore, LA. Rolls for 3/1862 through 4/1862: Absent, wounded at the Battle of Shiloh, TN, in 4/1862. Rolls for 10/1862 through 12/1862: Present. Rolls for 1/1863 through 4/1863: Absent, detailed as Nurse at Ringgold, GA, by order of Gen. Braxton Bragg. Rolls for 6/1863 through 2/1865: Present. Federal Rolls of Prisoners of War: Captured at Spanish Fort, AL, on 4/8/1865; Received at Ship Island, MS, on 4/10/1865. Transferred to Vicksburg, MS, for exchange on 5/1/1865; Exchanged at Camp Townsend, MS, on 5/6/1865.

Brogden, Joseph Pvt., 4th Louisiana Cavalry. Co. C. Federal Rolls of Prisoners of War: Captured at Bay Pigeon, LA, on 9/11/1864; Received at New Orleans, LA, on 9/20/1864. Sent to Ship Island, MS, on 10/7/1864; Transferred to Fort Columbus, New York Harbor, NY, on 11/16/1864. Received at Elmira, NY, on 11/19/1864; Paroled at Elmira, NY, on 2/25/1865. Exchanged at James River, VA, in early 1865.

Brother, John Pvt., 13th Louisiana Infantry. Co. B. Federal Rolls of Prisoners of War: Captured at Spanish Fort, AL, on 4/6/1865; Received at Ship Island, MS, on 4/10/1865. Transferred to Vicksburg, MS, for exchange on 5/1/1865; Exchanged at Camp Townsend, MS, on 5/6/1865.

Broughton, A. Benjamin 2nd Lt./Adjt., 19th Louisiana Infantry. Co. A/F & S. Enlisted: 12/11/1861 at Camp Moore, LA; Elected 2nd Lt. on 8/22/1861. Rolls for 12/11/1861 through 5/1862: Present, appointed Adjutant on 5/8/1862. Rolls for 6/1862 through 4/1864: Present. Rolls for 7/1864 through 8/1864: Absent, sent to hospital wounded on 7/28/1864. Rolls for 9/1864 through 2/28/1865: Absent, on detached service on the steamer *Jeff Davis*. Federal Rolls of Prisoners of War: Captured at New River, AL, on the gunboat CSS *Morganza* on 4/19/1865; Received at Ship Island, MS, from Mobile, AL, on 5/13/1865. Transferred to New Orleans, LA, on 6/8/1865.

Brown, W.E. Pvt., 1st Louisiana Cavalry. Co. B. Enlisted: 9/5/1861 at Baton Rouge, LA. Rolls for 9/5/1861 through 6/1863: Present. Rolls for 11/1863 through 12/1863: Absent, without leave since 10/1863. Federal Rolls of Prisoners of War: Captured at Clinton, LA, on 10/6/1864; Sent to Baton Rouge, LA, on 10/10/1864. Received at New Orleans, LA, on 10/14/1864; Transferred to Ship Island, MS, on 10/20/1864. Forwarded to New York on 11/5/1864; Received at Fort Columbus, New York Harbor, NY, on 11/16/1864. Transferred to Elmira, NY, on 11/20/1864; Paroled at Elmira, NY, on 2/13/1865. Sent to James River, VA, for exchange on 2/20–21/1865.

Brown, William Pvt., 4th Louisiana Infantry. Co. D. Enlisted: 3/1/1863 at Port Hudson, LA. Rolls for 3/1863 through 6/1863: Present. Rolls for 7/1863 through 8/1863: Deserted from Enterprise, MS, on 8/12/1863. Rolls for 9/1863 through 2/1865: Present. Federal Rolls of Prisoners of War: Captured at Spanish Fort, AL, on 4/8/1865; Received at Ship Island, MS, on 4/10/1865. Transferred to Vicksburg, MS, for exchange on 5/1/1865; Exchanged at Camp Townsend, MS, on 5/6/1865.

Bruce, A.B. Pvt., Ogden's Cavalry Battalion. Co. A. Federal Rolls of Prisoners of War: Captured at East Baton Rouge Parish, LA, on 1/9/1865; Sent to New Orleans, LA, on 1/17/1865. Forwarded to Ship Island, MS, on 1/25/1865; Transferred to Vicksburg, MS, for exchange on 5/1/1865. Exchanged at Camp Townsend, MS, on 5/6/1865.

Bullock, C.M. Pvt., 4th Louisiana Battalion Infantry. Co. B. Enlisted: 6/4/1861 at Monroe, LA. Rolls for 6/4/1861 through 2/1865: Present. Federal Rolls of Prisoners of War: Captured at Spanish Fort, AL, on 4/8/1865; Received at Ship Island. MS on 4/10/1865. Transferred to Vicksburg, MS, for exchange on 5/1/1865; Exchanged at Camp Townsend, MS, on 5/6/1865.

Burch, John W. 2nd Lt., 18th Louisiana Battalion Infantry. Co. B. Federal Rolls of Prisoners of War: Captured at Davidson's Ford, MS, on 11/15/1864; Transferred to Ship Island, MS, from New Orleans, LA, on 12/18/1864. Paroled and exchanged at Ship Island, MS, on 3/2/1865; Endorsement shows: Received on board the Flag of Trust Steamer *Nashua* at Mobile Bay, AL, on 3/4/1865 and exchanged. Elected 2nd Lt. on 1/25/1865.

Burnes, Samuel (AKA Burns) Pvt., Miles Legion. Co. A. Enlisted: 1/1/1863 at Baton Rouge, LA. Rolls for 1/1863 through 3/1863: Present. Federal Rolls of Prisoners of War: Captured and paroled at Port Hudson, LA, in 7/1863. Rolls for 7/1863 through 12/1863: Present. Federal Rolls of Prisoners of War: Captured at Amite River, LA, on 10/2/1864; Received at New Orleans, LA, on 10/10/1864. Transferred to Ship Island, MS, on 10/20/1864; Received at Fort Columbus, New York Harbor, NY, on 11/16/1864. Transferred to Elmira, NY, on 11/19/1864; Released on the U.S. Oath of Allegiance on 5/17/1865. Remarks: Volunteered on 4/27/1862; Desires to go to New York City, where he has relatives living. At the time of his capture he was absent from his command on furlough and was on his way to New Orleans, LA, to give himself up to the Federal authorities.

Byrd, J.F. Pvt., 2nd Louisiana Cavalry. Co. __. Federal Rolls of Prisoners of War: Captured at Pascagoula,

LA, on 1/14/1865; Sent to New Orleans, LA, on 1/18/1865. Forwarded to Ship Island, MS, on 1/22/1865; Transferred to Vicksburg, MS, for exchange on 5/1/1865. Exchanged at Camp Townsend, MS, on 5/6/1865.

Cailey, William Pvt., Louisiana Supporting Forces. Co. __. Federal Rolls of Prisoners of War: Captured in Mississippi on 12/5/1864; Transferred to Ship Island, MS, from New Orleans, LA, on 1/25/1865.

Caistis, George Pvt., 13th Louisiana Infantry. Co. D. Enlisted: 8/18/1861 at Camp Moore, LA. Rolls for 8/18/1861 through 11/1863: Present. Rolls for 12/1863 through 4/1864: Present, on extra duty as Brigade Ambulance Driver. Rolls for 5/1864 through 8/1864: Present, on medical duty by order of Dr. Holt. Rolls for 11/1864 through 2/25/1865: Present. Federal Rolls of Prisoners of War: Captured at Spanish Fort, AL, on 4/8/1865; Received at Ship Island, MS, on 4/10/1865. Transferred to Vicksburg, MS, for exchange on 5/1/1865; Exchanged at Camp Townsend, MS, on 5/6/1865.

Campbell, Eugene Pvt., 1st Louisiana Cavalry. Co. F. Enlisted: 10/3/1861 at Vidalia, LA. Rolls for 10/1861 through 2/1864: Present. Federal Rolls of Prisoners of War: Captured at Tunica, LA, on 9/14/1864; Received at Baton Rouge, LA, on 10/6/1864. Sent to New Orleans, LA, on 10/10/1864; Transferred to Ship Island, MS, on 10/20/1864. Forwarded to Fort Columbus, New York Harbor, NY, on 11/16/1864; Received at Elmira, NY, on 11/19/1864. Died: 1/10/1865 at Elmira, NY, due to variola. Buried: Woodlawn National Cemetery, Chemung County, NY.

Campbell, John B. Pvt., Louisiana Supporting Forces. Co. A. Federal Rolls of Prisoners of War: Captured at Clinton, LA, on 11/16/1864; Received at New Orleans, LA, on 11/23/1864. Transferred to Ship Island, MS, on 12/10/1864; Forwarded to Vicksburg, MS, for exchange on 5/1/1865. Exchanged at Camp Townsend, MS, on 5/6/1865.

Canney, William E. (AKA Canoy) Pvt., 3rd Louisiana Cavalry (Wingfield's). Co. H. Enlisted: 6/12/1862 at Camp Moore, LA. Federal Rolls of Prisoners of War: Captured and paroled at Port Hudson, LA, in 7/1863. Federal Rolls of Prisoners of War: Captured near Brookhaven, MS, on 11/18/1864; Received at New Orleans, LA, on 11/23/1865. Sent to Ship Island, MS, on 12/13/1864; Transferred to Vicksburg, MS, for exchange on 5/1/1865. Exchanged at Camp Townsend, MS, on 5/6/1865.

Careter, George (AKA Carter) Pvt., 13th Louisiana Infantry. Co. D. Federal Roll of Prisoners of War: Captured at Spanish Fort, AL, on 4/8/1865; Received at Ship Island, MS, on 4/10/1865. Transferred to Vicksburg, MS, for exchange on 5/1/1865; Exchanged at Camp Townsend, MS, on 5/6/1865.

Carey, F.S. Pvt., Fenner's Light Artillery Battery (Louisiana). Enlisted: 5/10/1863 at Mobile, AL. Rolls for 5/10/1863 through 8/1863: Present. Rolls for 10/1863 through 12/1863: Absent, sick in hospital at Mobile, AL. Federal Rolls of Prisoners of War: Captured at Gravel Hill, AL, on 3/24/1864; Sent to Ship Island, MS, on 4/4/1865. Transferred to Vicksburg, MS, for exchange on 5/1/1865; Exchanged at Camp Townsend, MS, on 5/6/1865.

Carley, William Pvt., Louisiana Supporting Forces. Co. __. Federal Rolls of Prisoners of War: Captured at Ena, MS, on 12/5/1864; Sent to New Orleans, LA, on 12/19/1864. Received at Ship Island, MS, on 1/25/1865; Transferred to Vicksburg, MS, for exchange on 5/1/1865. Exchanged at Camp Townsend, MS, on 5/6/1865.

Carmena, Leroy Pvt., 2nd Louisiana Cavalry. Co. K. Federal Rolls of Prisoners of War: Captured near Alexandria, LA, on 4/1/1864; Received at New Orleans, LA, on 8/5/1864. Escaped from the U.S. Military Prison, New Orleans, LA, on 8/14/1864. Federal Rolls of Prisoners of War: Captured near Houma, LA, on 9/9/1864; Received at New Orleans, LA, on 9/20/1864. Transferred to Ship Island, MS, on 10/5/1864; Forwarded to Fort Columbus, New York Harbor, NY, on 11/16/1864. Sent to Elmira, NY, on 11/19/1864; Paroled at Elmira, NY, on 2/9/1865. Sent to James River, VA, for exchange.

Carmonche, Avelaid Pvt., 2nd Louisiana Cavalry. Co. K. Enlisted: 9/1/1862 at New Roads, LA. Rolls for 1/1863 through 2/1863: Absent, without leave. Rolls for 5/1863 through 8/1863: Present. Federal Rolls of Prisoners of War: Captured near Natchitoches, LA, on 3/21/1864; Received at New Orleans, LA, on 3/26/1864. Transferred from New Orleans, LA, and exchanged at Red River Landing, LA, on 7/22/1864. Federal Rolls of Prisoners of War: Captured at False River, LA, on 10/19/1864; Transferred from New Orleans, LA, to Ship Island, MS, on 10/27/1864. Sent to Fort Columbus, New York Harbor, NY, on 11/16/1864; Forwarded to Elmira, NY, on 11/20/1864. Paroled at Elmira, NY, on 2/28/1865; Exchanged at James River, VA.

Carmouche, Alcide (AKA Carmonche) Pvt., 2nd Louisiana Cavalry. Co. K. Enlisted: 9/1/1862 at New Roads, LA. Rolls for 1/1863 through 2/1863: Absent, with leave. Rolls for 5/1863 through 8/1863: Present. Federal Rolls of Prisoners of War: Captured near Natchitoches, LA, on 3/21/1864; Received at New Orleans, LA, on 3/26/1864. Transferred to Ship Island, MS, on 10/5/1864; Forwarded to Fort Columbus, New York Harbor, NY, on 11/16/1864. Sent to Elmira, NY, on 11/19/1864; Died: 12/12/1864 at Elmira, NY, due to variola. Buried: Woodlawn National Cemetery, Chemung County, NY. Memorial marker at Cottonwood Cemetery, Lottie, Pointe Coupée Parish, LA. Confederate Pension Application on file at the Louisiana State Archives. Microfilm Reel: CP1.24. Microdex 2. Sequence 24. Target Card: Carmouche, Alcide. Parish: Pointe Coupée. 4 pages.

Carter, M.D. (AKA Cater) Pvt., 19th Louisiana Infantry. Co. I. Federal Rolls of Prisoners of War: Captured at Spanish Fort, AL, on 4/8/1865; Received at Ship Island, MS, on 4/10/1865. Tansferred to Vicksburg, MS, for exchange on 5/1/1865; Exchanged at Camp Townsend, MS, on 5/6/1865.

Carty, Thomas Pvt./1st Sgt./2nd Lt., 7th Louisiana Infantry. Co. F. Enlisted: 6/7/1861 at Camp Moore, LA. Age at enlistment: 28. Marital Status at enlistment: Single. Occupation at enlistment: Stone Cutter. Rolls for 6/1861 through 8/1861: Present. Rolls for 9/1861 through 10/1861: Present or absent not stated. Rolls for 11/1861 through 12/1861: Elected 2nd Lt. on 11/25/1861 from 1st Sgt. Rolls for 1/1862 through 2/1862: Present or absent not stated. Federal Rolls of Prisoners of War: Captured at Richmond, VA, on 6/28/1862; Sent to Fort Columbus, New York Harbor,

NY, on 7/3/1862. Forwarded to Fort Warren, MA, on 7/9/1862; Transferred to Fort Monroe, VA, on 7/31/1862. Exchanged at Aiken's Landing, VA, on 8/5/1862. Rolls for 1/1863 through 4/1863: Present. Rolls for 5/1863 through 6/1863: Absent, wounded and sent to rear at Winchester, VA, on 6/14/1863. Rolls for 9/1863 through 10/1863: Absent, sick. Rolls for 11/1863 through 2/1864: Absent, wounded while acting under orders from the Secretary of War. Rolls for 5/1864 through 8/1864: Absent, wounded on detached service. Federal Rolls of Prisoners of War: Captured at Liberty, MS, on 11/16/1864; Received at New Orleans, LA, on 11/23/1864. Sent to Ship Island, MS, on 12/15/1864; Transferred to Vicksburg, MS, for exchange on 4/28/1865. Confined at New Orleans, LA, on 4/30/1865; Exchanged at Camp Townsend, MS, on 5/6/1865. Rolls of Prisoners of War, C.S.A: Surrendered at Appomattox, VA, on 4/9/1865; Paroled at Jackson, MS, on 5/15/1865. Residence at parole: New Orleans, LA. Born: Ireland.

Carver, Hiram H. Pvt., 2nd Louisiana Cavalry. Co. H. Enlisted: 9/1/1862 at Napoleonville, LA. Federal Rolls of Prisoners of War: Captured near Bayou Godell, LA, on 4/7/1865; Sent to New Orleans, LA, on 4/11/1865. Forwarded to Ship Island, MS, on 4/28/1865; Transferred from Ship Island, MS, to the mouth of Red River, LA, for exchange on 5/2/1865. Name on List dated Office of the Provost Marshal, Napoleonville, LA, of Surrendered and Paroled Prisoners of War who have reported and registered by 11/1/1865. Residence at registry: Assumption Parish, LA. Died: 9/9/1903. Buried: Ascension Catholic Church Cemetery on Opelousas St. at Donaldsonville, Ascension Parish, LA. Confederate Pension Application on file at the Louisiana State Archives. Microfilm Reel: CP1.25. Microdex 3. Sequence 7. Target Card: Carver, Hiram H. Parish: Ascension. 4 pages.

Cason, Benton W. Pvt./2nd Cpl./3rd Sgt., 18th Louisiana Infantry. Co. I. Enlisted: 9/20/1861 at State Powder House, Baton Rouge, LA. Rolls for 9/20/1861 through 6/1862: Present, promoted to 2nd Cpl. on 6/25/1862. Rolls for 7/1862 through 8/1862: Present, promoted to 3rd Sgt. on 8/9/1862. Rolls for 1/1863 through 2/1863: Present. Federal Rolls of Prisoners of War: Captured at Bayou Teche, LA, on 4/14/1863; Sent to New Orleans, LA, for exchange. Exchanged at Prophet's Island, below Port Hudson, LA, on 5/5/1863. Rolls for 5/1863 through 6/1863: Absent, prisoner of war on parole. Rolls for 7/1863 through 8/1863: Absent, prisoner of war. Soldier also served as a Pvt. with Ogden's Cavalry Battalion (Louisiana). Co. __. Federal Rolls of Prisoners of War: Captured near Greensburg, LA, on 10/7/1864; Received at Ship Island, MS, from New Orleans, LA, on 11/25/1864. Sent to Fort Lafayette, New York Harbor, NY, on 1/1/1865; Transferred to Fort Delaware, DE, on 3/14/1865. Released from Fort Delaware, DE, on the U.S. Oath of Allegiance on 6/17/1865. Description at oath: Eyes: blue. Hair: light. Complexion: light. Height: 5'10". Residence at oath: Orleans Parish, LA.

Chaddock, Isaac (AKA Chaddick, Caddick) Pvt., 19th Louisiana Infantry. Co. K. Enlisted: 5/14/1862 at Sabine Parish, LA. Rolls for 7/1862 through 10/1863: Wounded and absent since the Battle of Chickamauga, GA, on 9/20/1863. Rolls for 1/1864 through 4/1864: Present. Federal Rolls of Prisoners of War: Captured at Spanish Fort, AL, on 4/8/1865; Received at Ship Island, MS, on 4/10/1865. Transferred to Vicksburg, MS, for exchange on 5/1/1865; Exchanged at Camp Townsend, MS, on 5/1/1865. Confederate Widows Pension Application on file at the Louisiana State Archives. Microfilm Reel: CP1.26. Microdex 1. Sequence 23. Target Card: Chaddick, M.J. (Crowell). Parish: Vernon. 7 pages.

Chancey, R.L. (AKA B.L., L.R.) Pvt., 4th Louisiana Infantry. Co. A. Federal Rolls of Prisoners of War: Captured at Clinton, LA, on 10/6/1864; Received at Ship Island, MS, from New Orleans, LA, on 10/21/1864. Transferred to Fort Columbus, New York Harbor, NY, on 11/16/1864; Forwarded to Elmira, NY, on 11/19/1864. Transferred to Point Lookout, MD, for exchange on 2/13/1865.

Chandler, D. Pvt., 30th Louisiana Infantry. Co. D. Federal Rolls of Prisoners of War: Captured at Spanish Fort, AL, on 4/8/1865; Received at Ship Island, MS, on 4/10/1865. Transferred to Vicksburg, MS, for exchange on 5/1/1865; Exchanged at Camp Townsend, MS, on 5/6/1865.

Chandler, James Samuel (AKA S.J.) Pvt., 9th Louisiana Infantry. Co. G. Enlisted: 5/15/1862 at Amite Springs, LA. Rolls for 5/1862 through 6/1862: Absent, sick. Rolls for 7/1862 through 4/1863: Present. Rolls for 5/1863 through 10/1863: Absent with leave. Rolls for 11/1863 through 12/1863: Absent, without leave, furloughed in 9/1863 for 30 days. Rolls for 1/1864 through 2/1864: Absent without leave since 9/28/1863. Deserted on 5/1/1864. Born: 6/18/1840 in Louisiana. Occupation at enlistment: Farmer. Age at enlistment: 22. Residence at enlistment: Livingston Parish, LA. Marital Status at enlistment: Single. Soldier also served as a Pvt. with the 1st Louisiana Cavalry. Co.B. Federal Rolls of Prisoners of War: Captured at Greenville Springs, LA, on 11/22/1863; Sent to the U.S. Provost Guard, New Orleans, LA, on 12/3/1863. Paroled for exchange at New Orleans, LA, on 8/21/1864; Received at place of exchange near Red Wood Creek on the Plank Road, between Baton Rouge, LA, and Clinton, LA, on 8/22/1864. Age at capture: 23. Description at capture: Eyes: dark. Hair: dark. Complexion: dark. Height: 6'0". Soldier also served as a Pvt. with the 30th Louisiana Infantry. Co. I and the 1st Louisiana Infantry. Co.B. Federal Rolls of Prisoners of War: Captured at Spanish Fort, AL, on 4/8/1865; Received at Ship Island, MS, on 4/10/1865. Transferred to Vicksburg, MS, for exchange on 5/1/1865; Exchanged at Camp Townsend, MS, on 5/6/1865. Born: 6/18/1840. Died: 2/1/1925. Buried: Live Oak Methodist Church Cemetery on Hwy. 1019 at Watson, Livingston Parish, LA. Confederate Pension Application on file at the Louisiana State Archives. Microfilm Reel: CP1.26. Microdex 3. Sequence 12. Target Card: Chandler, Samuel J. Parish: Livingston. 12 pages. Soldier also served with the 1st Louisiana Cavalry. Co. B and the 30th Louisiana Infantry. Co.I.

Chaney, Levy R. (AKA Chansey, R.L.) Pvt., 4th Louisiana Infantry. Co. A. Enlisted: 5/25/1861 at Camp Moore, LA. Rolls for 5/25/1861 through 2/1862: Present. Rolls for 11/1862 through 8/1864: Absent, due to wounds received at Baton Rouge, LA, on 8/9/1862. Federal Rolls of Prisoners of War:

Captured at Clinton, LA, on 10/6/1864; Received at Baton Rouge, LA, on 10/10/1864. Forwarded to New Orleans, LA, on 10/14/1864; Received at Ship Island, MS, on 10/21/1864. Transferred to Fort Columbus, New York Harbor, NY, on 11/16/1864; Sent to Elmira, NY, on 11/20/1864. Paroled at Elmira, NY, on 2/9/1865; Sent to James River, VA, for exchange. Exchanged at James River, VA, on 2/20–21/1865. Born: 4/18/1838. Died: 3/28/1904. Buried: Magnolia Cemetery on 19th St. and Florida Blvd. at Baton Rouge, East Baton Rouge Parish, LA. Confederate Pension Application on file at the Louisiana State Archives. Microfilm Reel: CP1.26. Microdex 3. Sequence 19. Target Card: Chaney, Levy R. Parish: East Baton Rouge. 9 pages. Also a Confederate Widows Pension Application on file. Microfilm Reel: CP1.26. Microdex 3. Sequence 22. Target Card: Chaney, Mary M. (Smith). Parish: Tangipahoa. 21 pages.

Christin, Ernest F. (AKA F. Ernest) Pvt., 1st Louisiana Cavalry. Co. A. Enlisted: 8/26/1861 at Camp Schlatre, LA. Rolls for 8/26/1861 through 2/1863: Present. Rolls for 3/1863 through 6/1863: Absent, 30 day furlough on 3/10/1863 due to sickness; Reported by Surgeon's Certificate on 5/16/1863. Rolls for 11/1863 through 2/1864: Present. Federal Rolls of Prisoners of War: Captured at East Baton Rouge, LA, on 11/9/1864; Sent to New Orleans, LA, on 11/16/1864. Received at Ship Island, MS, on 12/13/1864; Forwarded to New Orleans, LA, for exchange on 5/1/1865. Paroled on 5/13/1865. Age: 25. Buried: St. Joseph Catholic Church Cemetery, East Baton Rouge Parish, LA

Clampett, William Pvt., 3rd Louisiana Cavalry (Wingfield's). Co. G. Federal Rolls of Prisoners of War: Captured at Clinton, LA, on 10/6/1864; Sent to Baton Rouge, LA, on 10/10/1864. Received at New Orleans, LA, on 10/15/1864; Forwarded to Ship Island, MS, on 10/20/1864. Transferred to Vicksburg, MS, for exchange on 5/1/1865; Exchanged at Camp Townsend, MS, on 5/6/1865.

Clark, L. Pvt., 5th Louisiana Cavalry. Co. __. Federal Rolls of Prisoners of War: Captured near Liberty, MS, on 11/18/1864; Sent to New Orleans, LA, on 11/22/1864. Received at Ship Island, MS, on 12/13/1864; Transferred to Vicksburg, MS, for exchange on 5/1/1865. Exchanged at Camp Townsend, MS, on 5/6/1865.

Clark, W.H. Pvt., Washington Artillery. Co. A. Federal Rolls of Prisoners of War: Captured at West Baton Rouge Parish, LA, on 11/12/1864; Received at Ship Island, MS, from New Orleans, LA, on 12/13/1864. Returned to New Orleans, LA, on 3/31/1865.

Clarke, William L. Pvt., Washington Artillery. 1st Company Battalion. Enlisted: 4/28/1863 at Port Hudson, LA. Age at enlistment: 17. Occupation at enlistment: Student. Marital Status at enlistment: Single. Residence at enlistment: Lobdell's Store, West Baton Rouge Parish, LA. Rolls for 5/1863 through 2/1864: Present. Rolls for 3/1864 through 10/1864: Absent, sick. Federal Rolls of Prisoners of War: Captured at West Baton Rouge Parish, LA, on 11/20/1864; Received at New Orleans, LA, on 11/24/1864. Transferred to Ship Island, MS, on 12/13/1864; Returned to New Orleans, LA, on 4/1/1865. Exchanged on 4/9/1865. Rolls of Prisoners of War, C.S.A: Surrendered at New Orleans, LA, on 5/26/1865; Paroled at Natchitoches, LA, on 6/6/1865. Residence at parole: West Baton Rouge Parish, LA. Born: Louisiana.

Cockrell, T.J. (AKA Cocknell, F.J.) Pvt., 4th Louisiana Battalion Infantry. Co. E. Enlisted: 10/12/1864 at Brookhaven, MS. Rolls for 10/12/1864 through 2/1865: Present. Federal Rolls of Prisoners of War: Captured at Spanish Fort, AL, on 4/8/1865; Received at Ship Island, MS, on 4/10/1865. Transferred to Vicksburg, MS, for exchange on 5/1/1865; Exchanged at Camp Townsend, MS, on 5/6/1865. Buried: Confederate Cemetery, Higginsville, Lafayette County, MO.

Cody, William A. Pvt., 19th Louisiana Infantry. Co. __. Federal Rolls of Prisoners of War: Captured at Spanish Fort, AL, on 4/8/1865; Received at Ship Island, MS, on 4/10/1865. Transferred to Vicksburg, MS, for exchange on 5/1/1865; Exchanged at Camp Townsend, MS, on 5/6/1865.

Coff, W. Pvt., 25th Louisiana Infantry. Co. C. Federal Rolls of Prisoners of War: Captured at Spanish Fort, AL, on 4/8/1865; Received at Ship Island, MS, on 4/10/1865. Transferred to Vicksburg, MS, for exchange on 5/1/1865; Exchanged at Camp Townsend, MS, on 5/6/1865.

Coleson D.R. Pvt., 25th Louisiana Infantry. Co. E. Enlisted: 4/9/1863 at Union Parish, LA. Rolls for 9/1/1864 through 2/28/1865: Present. Federal Rolls of Prisoners of War: Captured at Spanish Fort, AL, on 4/8/1865; Received at Ship Island, MS, on 4/10/1865. Transferred to Vicksburg, MS, for exchange on 5/1/1865; Exchanged at Camp Townsend, MS, on 5/6/1865. Rolls of Prisoners of War, C.S.A: Surrendered at Citronelle, AL, on 5/4/1865; Paroled at Meridian, MS, on 5/10/1865. Residence at parole: Union Parish, LA.

Collins, Paul William (AKA Collens) Pvt., 12th Louisiana Battalion Heavy Artillery. Co. B. Federal Rolls of Prisoners of War: Captured and paroled at Port Hudson, LA, on 7/8/1863. Federal Rolls of Prisoners of War: Captured at Liberty, MS, on 11/14/1864; Forwarded to New Orleans, LA, on 11/23/1864. Received at Ship Island, MS, on 12/13/1864; Exchanged on 3/4/1865. Rolls of Prisoners of War, C.S.A: Surrendered at Citronelle, AL, on 5/4/1865; Paroled at Meridian, MS, on 5/11/1865. Residence at parole: New Orleans, LA. Soldier also served as a Pvt. with the 3rd Louisiana Cavalry (Wingfield's). Born: 1834. Died: 9/16/1878. Buried: St. Louis Cemetery # 1 between St. Louis St. and Conti St. at New Orleans, Orleans Parish, LA.

Comeau, Louis O. (AKA Commeaux) Pvt., Jefferson Mounted Guards Cavalry. Co. A. Enlisted: 5/5/1862 at Camp Moore, LA. Rolls for 5/1862 through 6/1864: Present. Federal Rolls of Prisoners of War: Captured near Bayou Manchac, LA, on 10/11/1864; Received at New Orleans, LA, on 10/15/1864. Transferred to Ship Island, MS, on 10/20/1864; Received at Elmira, NY, on 11/20/1864. Paroled at Elmira, NY, on 2/25/1865; Sent to James River, VA, for exchange.

Comfort, Charles L. (AKA Canford, C.S.) 1st Sgt./Lt., 11th Louisiana Infantry. Cos. E & I. Enlisted: 8/18/1861 at Camp Moore, LA. Rolls from 8/18/1861 through 10/1861: Present. Federal Rolls of Prisoners of War: Captured at Liberty, MS, on 11/16/1864; Received at Ship Island, MS, on 12/15/1864. Exchanged on 3/2/1865.

Cook, William Pvt., 3rd Louisiana Infantry. Co. A. Federal Rolls of Prisoners of War: Captured near Wilson's Ferry, LA, on 10/9/1864; Received at Fort Columbus, New York Harbor, NY, from Ship Island, MS, on 11/5/1864. Forwarded to Elmira, NY, on 11/20/1864; Released on the U.S. Oath of Allegiance on 5/17/1864.

Cook, William C. (AKA W.M.) Pvt., 9th Louisiana Battalion Infantry. Co. A. Enlisted: 5/15/1862 at Camp Moore, LA. Rolls for 9/1862 through 10/1862: Present. Federal Rolls of Prisoners of War: Captured near Wilson's Ferry, LA, on 10/9/1864; Sent to Baton Rouge, LA, on 10/10/1864. Forwarded to New Orleans, LA, on 10/15/1864; Transferred to Ship Island, MS, on 10/20/1864. Received at Fort Columbus, New York Harbor, NY, on 11/16/1864; Forwarded to Elmira, NY, on 11/19/1864. Released on the U.S. Oath of Allegiance on 5/17/1865. Description at release: Eyes: blue. Complexion: dark. Height: 5'9". Residence at release: East Baton Rouge Parish, LA. Born: 9/10/1841 in England. Died: 10/24/1924. Buried: Bethel Church Cemetery on Hwy. 64 near Indian Mound, East Baton Rouge Parish, LA. Confederate Pension Application on file at the Louisiana State Archives. Microfilm Reel: CP1.31. Microdex 1. Sequence 21. Target Card: Cook, William M. Parish: East Baton Rouge. 6 pages. Also a Confederate Widows Pension Application on file. Microfilm Reel: CP1.31. Microdex 1. Sequence 1. Target Card: Cook, Delidia. Parish: Orleans. 112 pages. (This pension file contains information on a lawsuit filed by William Cook against Delidia Cook)

Cooper, J.B. Pvt., 5th Louisiana Cavalry. Co. F. Federal Rolls of Prisoners of War: Captured at East Baton Rouge Parish, LA, on 12/24/1864; Sent to New Orleans, LA, on 12/28/1864. Forwarded to Ship Island, MS, on 1/25/1865; Transferred to Vicksburg, MS, for exchange on 5/1/1865. Exchanged at Camp Townsend, MS, on 5/6/1865.

Cooty, Thomas 1st Lt., 7th Louisiana Infantry. Co. F. Federal Rolls of Prisoners of War: Captured at Brookhaven, MS, on 11/23/1864; Transferred from New Orleans, LA, to Ship Island, MS, on 12/18/1865.

Corcom, John Pvt., 3rd Louisiana Cavalry. Co. __. Federal Rolls of Prisoners of War: Captured near Liberty, MS, on 11/17/1864; Forwarded to Ship Island, MS, from New Orleans, LA, on 12/13/1864.

Corkern, John (AKA Cookern) Pvt., 3rd Louisiana Cavalry (Wingfield's). Cos. A & H. Enlisted: 12/22/1862 at Covington, LA. Federal Rolls of Prisoners of War: Captured and paroled at Port Hudson, LA, on 7/8/1863. Federal Rolls of Prisoners of War: Captured near Liberty, MS, on 11/17/1864; Sent to New Orleans, LA, on 11/23/1864. Received at Ship Island, MS, on 12/13/1864; Transferred to Vicksburg, MS, for exchange on 5/1/1865. Exchanged at Camp Townsend, MS, on 5/6/1865.

Cortiss, George Pvt., 31st Louisiana Infantry. Co. D. Federal Rolls of Prisoners of War: Captured at Spanish Fort, AL, on 4/8/1865; Received at Ship Island, MS, on 4/10/1865. Transferred to Vicksburg, MS, for exchange on 5/1/1865; Exchanged at Camp Townsend, MS, on 5/6/1865.

Costello, John C. Pvt., Miles Legion. Co. A. Enlisted: 3/19/1862 at New Orleans, LA. Rolls for 5/1862 through 6/1862: Present. Federal Rolls of Prisoners of War: Captured and paroled at Port Hudson, LA, on 7/8/1863. Federal Rolls of Prisoners of War: Captured at Amite River, LA, on 10/2/1864; Received at New Orleans, LA, on 10/10/1864. Transferred to Ship Island, MS, on 10/20/1864; Drowned at sea enroute to Fort Columbus, New York Harbor, NY, on 11/8/1864.

Couisinard, Charles Pvt., Ogden's Cavalry Battalion. Co. D. Federal Rolls of Prisoners of War: Captured at Clinton, LA, on 11/18/1864; Sent to New Orleans, LA, on 11/23/1864. Received at Ship Island, MS, on 12/13/1864; Transferred to Vicksburg, MS, for exchange on 5/1/1865. Exchanged at Camp Townsend, MS, on 5/6/1865.

Courcey, J.W. Pvt., 1st Louisiana Battalion Infantry. Co. C. Federal Rolls of Prisoners of War: Captured on 10/10/1864; Received at Ship Island, MS. Forwarded to Fort Columbus, New York Harbor, NY, from Ship Island, MS, on 11/16/1864. Transferred to Elmira, NY, on 11/19/1864.

Courtney, Henry S. Q.M. Sgt., 3rd Louisiana Cavalry (Harrison's). Co. D. Federal Rolls of Prisoners of War: Captured near Liberty, MS, on 11/16/1864; Sent to New Orleans, LA, on 11/23/1864. Transferred to Ship Island, MS, on 12/10/1864; Received at Vicksburg, MS, for exchange on 5/1/1865; Exchanged at Camp Townsend, MS, on 5/6/1865. Born: 1/25/1844. Died: 7/19/1908. Buried: Metairie Cemetery on Pontchartrain Blvd., New Orleans, Orleans Parish, LA.

Cousins, Richard M. (AKA Couzens) Pvt., Miles Legion. Co. A. Federal Rolls of Prisoners of War: Captured and paroled at Port Hudson, LA, on 7/8/1864. Federal Rolls of Prisoners of War: Captured at Amite River, LA, on 10/2/1864; Received at New Orleans, LA, on 10/10/1864. Transferred to Ship Island, MS, on 10/20/1864; Forwarded to Fort Columbus, New York Harbor, NY, on 11/16/1864. Received at Elmira, NY, on 11/20/1864; Released on the U.S. Oath of Allegiance on 5/17/1865. Description at oath: Eyes: blue. Hair: dark. Complexion: fair. Height: 5'7⅛". Residence at oath: New Orleans, LA.

Cox, J.L. (AKA J.S.) Cpl., 30th Louisiana Infantry. Co.I. Federal Rolls of Prisoners of War: Captured at Spanish Fort, AL, on 4/8/1865; Received at Ship Island, MS, on 4/10/1865. Transferred to Vicksburg, MS, for exchange on 5/1/1865; Exchanged at Camp Townsend, MS, on 5/6/1865.

Cox, John J. Pvt./Cpl., 19th Louisiana Infantry. Co. F. Enlisted: 12/11/1861 at Camp Moore, LA. Rolls for 12/11/1861 through 12/1863: Present; Re-enlisted for the duration of the war on 1/20/1864 at Dalton, GA. Rolls for 1/1864 through 2/1865: Present. Federal Rolls of Prisoners of War: Captured at Spanish Fort, AL, on 4/8/1865; Received at Ship Island, MS, on 4/10/1865. Transferred to Vicksburg, MS, for exchange on 5/1/1865; Exchanged at Camp Townsend, MS, on 5/6/1865. Died: 6/16/1910. Buried: Old Friendship Cemetery located south of Grand Cane, DeSoto Parish, LA. Confederate Pension Application on file at the Louisiana State Archives. Microfilm Reel: CP1.32. Microdex 4. Sequence 16. Target Card: Cox, John J. Parish: DeSoto. 15 pages. Also a Confederate Widows Pension Application on file. Microfilm Reel: CP1.32. Microdex 4. Sequence

20. Target Card: Cox, Lizzie (Richardson). Parish: DeSoto. 4 pages.

Coyle, W.H. (AKA H.W.) Pvt., Grosse Tête Flying Artillery. Federal Rolls of Prisoners of War: Captured at Williamsport, LA, on 8/8/1864; Received at New Orleans, LA, on 8/15/1864. Transferred to Ship Island, MS, on 10/5/1864; Sent to Fort Columbus, New York Harbor, NY, on 11/16/1864. Forwarded to Elmira, NY, on 11/19/1865; Paroled at Elmira, NY, on 2/25/1865. Sent to James River, VA, for exchange. Born: 1844. Died: 1878. Buried: St. Stephen's Episcopal Church Cemetery, Innis, Pointe Coupée Parish, LA. Confederate Widows Pension Application on file at the Louisiana State Archives. Microfilm Reel: CP1.112. Microdex 4. Sequence 5. Target Card: Pratt, Mrs. M.E. Coyle (Seaman). Parish: Pointe Coupée. 5 pages. Wife later remarried Doctor J.W. Pratt.

Cozzens, Richard M. (AKA R.M. Cojjens) Pvt., Miles Legion. Co. A. Federal Rolls of Prisoners of War: Captured at Amite River, LA, on 10/2/1864; Received at Ship Island, MS, from New Orleans, LA, on 10/21/1864. Transferred to Fort Columbus, New York Harbor, NY, on 11/6/1864.

Crawford, John Pvt., Miles Legion. Co. C. Federal Rolls of Prisoners of War: Captured at Osyka, MS, on 10/7/1864; Received at Ship Island, MS, from New Orleans, LA, on 10/21/1864. Transferred to Fort Columbus, New York Harbor, NY, on 11/5/1864.

Crayon, William Cpl., Pointe Coupée Artillery. Federal Rolls of Prisoners of War: Captured at East Pascagoula, MS, on 12/18/1864; Received at Ship Island, MS, from New Orleans, LA, on 1/25/1865.

Crickenones, H.C. (AKA Creckmore) Sgt., 4th Louisiana Infantry. Co. __. Federal Rolls of Prisoners of War: Captured at Spanish Fort, AL, on 4/8/1865; Received at Ship Island, MS, on 4/10/1865. Transferred to Vicksburg, MS, for exchange on 5/1/1865; Exchanged at Camp Townsend, MS, on 5/6/1865.

Crockett, B.F. Pvt., 4th Louisiana Infantry. Cos. B & C. Enlisted: 5/25/1861 at Camp Moore, LA. Rolls for 5/25/1861 through 12/1862: Present. Federal Rolls of Prisoners of War: Captured and paroled at Port Hudson, LA, on 7/8/1863. Rolls for 11/1863 through 12/1863: Present, temporarily attached to Co.B. Rolls for 5/1864 through 8/1864: Absent, temporarily attached to Co. C and sick in hospital. Rolls for 9/1864 through 2/28/1865: Present. Federal Rolls of Prisoners of War: Captured at Spanish Fort, AL, on 4/3/1865; Received at Ship Island, MS, on 4/10/1865. Transferred to Vicksburg, MS, for exchange on 5/1/1865; Exchanged at Camp Townsend, MS, on 5/6/1865.

Crump, Robert W. (AKA W.R.) Pvt., 25th Louisiana Infantry. Co. H. Enlisted: 3/19/1862 at New Orleans, LA. Rolls for 3/19/1862 through 6/1862: Absent, in hospital. Rolls for 11/1862 through 12/1862: Present. Rolls for 1/1863 through 2/1863: Absent, on detached service as a Pioneer since 2/6/1862. Rolls for 5/1863 through 2/1864: Absent, sent to hospital at Dallas, GA, by order of Dr. Wilkerson. Rolls for 3/1864 through 4/1864: Absent, on 60 day medical furlough from hospital at Madison, GA, since 4/5/1864. Rolls for 5/1864 through 8/1864: Absent, sick by order of Dr. Ware since 4/6/1864. Rolls for 9/1864 through 2/28/1865: Present. Federal Rolls of Prisoners of War: Captured at Spanish Fort, AL, on 4/8/1865; Received at Ship Island, MS, on 4/10/1865. Transferred to Vicksburg, MS, for exchange on 5/1/1865; Exchanged at Camp Townsend, MS, on 5/6/1865. Rolls of Prisoners of War, C.S.A: Surrendered at Citronelle, AL, on 5/4/1865; Paroled at Meridian, MS, on 5/10/1865. Residence at parole: Shreveport, LA.

Culbertson, C.W. 2nd Lt., 22nd Louisiana Infantry (Consolidated). Co. E. Enlisted: 6/7/1863 at Mobile, AL. Rolls for 3/1864 through 4/1864: Present, elected 2nd Lt. on 2/16/1864; Assigned to duty per Special Order # 13 of Col. A. Fuller and detached for duty to Maj. R.A. Harris. Rolls for 7/1864 through 8/1864: Absent, in hospital at Mobile, AL, since 8/25/1864. Rolls for 9/1864 through 10/1864: Absent, on sick furlough. Federal Rolls of Prisoners of War: Captured at East Pascagoula, MS, on 12/16/1864; Received at Ship Island, MS. Paroled on 5/12/1865 at Ship Island, MS, by order of Maj. Gen. E.R.S. Canby. Age at parole: 29. Description at parole: Eyes: gray. Hair: dark. Complexion: fair. Height: 5'11¾". Residence at parole: New Orleans, LA.

Currey, I.M. Pvt., 1st Louisiana Battalion Cavalry. Co. __. Federal Rolls of Prisoners of War: Captured at Osyka, MS, on 10/10/1864; Received at Ship Island, MS, from New Orleans, LA, on 10/21/1864. Transferred to Fort Columbus, New York Harbor, New York on 11/5/1864.

Curry, John M. (AKA Courey, Correy, Currey, J.W.) Pvt., 1st Louisiana Battalion Cavalry. Co. C. Federal Rolls of Prisoners of War: Captured at Osyka, MS, on 10/10/1864; Received at New Orleans, LA, on 10/15/1864. Transferred to Ship Island, MS, on 10/20/1864; Sent to New York on 11/5/1864. Forwarded to Fort Columbus, New York Harbor, NY, on 11/16/1864; Transferred to Elmira, NY, on 11/20/1864. Paroled at Elmira, NY, on 2/25/1865; Sent to James River, VA, for exchange. Confederate Pension Application on file at the Louisiana State Archives. Microfilm Reel: CP1.34. Microdex 2. Sequence 17. Target Card: Curry, John M. Parish: St. Landry. 6 pages.

Dahm, Michael Pvt./2nd Cpl./Musician, 20th Louisiana Infantry. Co. C/F & S. Enlisted: 12/21/1861 at Camp Lewis, LA. Rolls for 12/21/1861 through 4/1862: Present. Rolls for 5/1862 through 6/1862: Present, appointed 2nd Cpl. on 5/5/1862. Rolls for 7/1862 through 10/1862: Dropped from rolls by order of Lt. Col. Von Zinken. Rolls for 11/1862 through 4/1863: Present. Rolls for 7/1863 through 10/1863: Transferred to the regimental band on 8/31/1863 by order of Col. Randall Lee Gibson. Rolls for 7/1864 through 2/28/1865: Present. Federal Rolls of Prisoners of War: Captured at Spanish Fort, AL, on 4/8/1865; Received at Ship Island, MS, on 4/10/1865. Transferred to Vicksburg, MS, for exchange on 5/1/1865; Exchanged at Camp Townsend, MS, on 5/6/1865.

Daigle, Aristide (AKA Daigne) Pvt., 28th Louisiana Infantry (Thomas'). Co. H. Federal Rolls of Prisoners of War: Captured at Bayou Goula, LA, on 8/29/1864; Sent to Ship Island, MS. Received at Fort Columbus, New York Harbor, NY, on 11/16/1864; Transferred to Elmira, NY, on 11/18/1864. Confederate Widows Pension Application on file at the Louisiana State Archives. Microfilm Reel: CP1.34. Microdex 3. Sequence 29. Target Card: Daigle, Armentine (Simoneaux). Parish: Assumption. 6 pages.

Daigre, Aristide (AKA Daigle) Pvt., 20th Louisiana Infantry. Co. H. Federal Rolls of Prisoners of War: Captured at Bayou Goula, LA, on 8/20/1864; Received at Ship Island, MS, on 10/28/1864. Forwarded to Fort Columbus, New York Harbor, NY, on 11/5/1864 by order of Capt. Marston.

Daigree, Aristide (AKA Daigle) Pvt., 28th Louisiana Infantry (Thomas'). Co. H. Federal Rolls of Prisoners of War: Captured near Bayou Goula, LA, on 8/20/1864; Transferred from New Orleans, LA, to Ship Island, MS, on 10/27/1864. Received at Fort Columbus, New York Harbor, NY, on 11/16/1864; Forwarded to Elmira, NY, on 11/20/1864. Paroled at Elmira, NY, on 2/25/1865; Sent to James River, VA, and exchanged.

Daimand, F. Pvt., 4th Louisiana Infantry. Co. __. Federal Rolls of Prisoners of War: Captured at Clinton, LA, on 11/15/1864; Transferred to Ship Island, MS, from New Orleans, LA, on 12/13/1864.

Daprie, O.P. Pvt., 2nd Louisiana Cavalry. Co. __. Federal Rolls of Prisoners of War: Captured at Bayou Grosse Tête, LA, on 8/10/1864; Received at Fort Columbus, New York Harbor, NY, from Ship Island, MS, on 11/16/1864. Transferred to Elmira, NY, on 11/18/1864.

D'Armond, Frank Kenneth (AKA Dearmond, T. Frank) Pvt., 4th Louisiana Infantry. Co. G. Enlisted: 10/1/1861 at Camp Moore, LA. Rolls for 10/1861 through 4/20/1862: Present. Rolls for 11/1862 through 6/1863: Absent, on detached duty in Commissary at Clinton, LA. Rolls for 7/1863 through 8/1863: Absent, on detached duty as a Clerk in Commissary near Enterprise, MS. Rolls for 9/1863 through 10/1863: Absent, without leave at Clinton, LA. Rolls for 11/1863 through 12/1863: Present or absent not stated. Rolls for 5/1864 through 8/1864: Absent, wounded on 7/28/1864 near Atlanta, GA. Federal Rolls of Prisoners of War: Captured at Clinton, LA, on 11/16/1864; Confined in the U.S. Military Prison, New Orleans, LA, on 11/23/1864. Transferred to Ship Island, MS, on 12/10/1864. Soldier also served as a Pvt. with the 3rd Louisiana Cavalry. Co.I. Confederate Widows Pension Application on file at the Louisiana State Archives. Microfilm Reel: CP1.35. Microdex 3. Sequence 17. Target Card: D'Armond, Florence (Rhea). Parish: East Feliciana. 28 pages.

David, Charles King Pvt., 5th Louisiana Cavalry. Cos. A & F. Federal Rolls of Prisoners of War: Captured at East Baton Rouge Parish, LA, on 1/9/1865; Received at New Orleans, LA, on 1/19/1865. Transferred to Ship Island, MS, on 1/22/1865. Died: 7/22/1928. Buried: Magnolia Cemetery at the corner of 19th St. and Florida Blvd. at Baton Rouge, East Baton Rouge Parish, LA.

David, Isaac Johnson (AKA J.J.) Pvt., 5th Louisiana Cavalry. Co. F. Federal Rolls of Prisoners of War: Captured at East Baton Rouge Parish, LA, on 1/9/1865; Received at New Orleans, LA, on 1/17/1865. Forwarded to Ship Island, MS, on 1/22/1865; Transferred to Vicksburg, MS, for exchange on 5/1/1865. Exchanged at Camp Townsend, MS, on 5/6/1865. Born: 1/21/1846. Died: 4/17/1927. Buried: Magnolia Cemetery at the corner of 19th St. and Florida Blvd. at Baton Rouge, East Baton Rouge Parish, LA. Confederate Pension Application on file at the Louisiana State Archives. Microfilm Reel: CP1.36. Microdex 1. Sequence 12. Target Card: David, I. Johnson. Parish: East Baton Rouge. 8 pages. Also a Confederate Widows Pension Application on file. Microfilm Reel: CP1.36. Microdex 1. Sequence 25. Target Card: David, Rosa (Heroman). Parish: East Baton Rouge. 8 pages.

Davis, Hugh H., Sr. Sgt., Ogden's Cavalry Battalion. Co. C. Federal Rolls of Prisoners of War: Captured at Clinton, LA, on 11/16/1864; Forwarded to New Orleans, LA, on 11/23/1864. Received at Ship Island, MS, on 12/10/1864; Exchanged on 3/4/1865. Confederate Pension Application on file at the Louisiana State Archives. Microfilm Reel: CP1.36. Microdex 2. Sequence 26. Target Card: Davis, Hugh H. Parish: East Baton Rouge. 5 pages.

Davis, John Chappel Pvt., 19th Louisiana Infantry. Co. D. Enlisted: 12/27/1861 at Camp Roman, LA. Age at enlistment: 23. Rolls for 1/1862 through 12/1863: Present. Rolls for 1/1864 through 4/1864: Absent, sent to hospital at Marietta, GA, on 3/3/1864 and furloughed for 60 days by the Medical Examining Board. Rolls for 5/1864 through 2/1865: Present. Rolls for 3/1865 through 4/1865: Absent, captured at Spanish Fort, AL, on 4/8/1865. Federal Rolls of Prisoners of War: Captured at Spanish Fort, AL, on 4/8/1865; Received at Ship Island, MS, on 4/10/1865. Transferred to Vicksburg, MS, for exchange on 5/1/1865; Exchanged at Camp Townsend, MS, on 5/6/1865. Confederate Pension Application on file at the Louisiana State Archives. Microfilm Reel: CP1.36. Microdex 3. Sequence 3. Target Card: Davis, J.C. Parish: Natchitoches. 7 pages. Also a Confederate Widows Pension Application on file. Microfilm Reel: CP1.36. Microdex 2. Sequence 12. Target Card: Davis, Dama Adams. Parish: Natchitoches. 8 pages.

Davis, O. Pvt., 4th Louisiana Infantry. Co. __. Federal Rolls of Prisoners of War: Captured near Plaquemine, LA, on 9/11/1864; Received at Ship Island, MS. Died: 9/11/1864 at Ship Island, MS, due to rubeola. Buried: Ship Island, MS, Cemetery in Grave #13.

Davis, William Sgt., Gober's Regiment Mounted Infantry. Co. C. Federal Rolls of Prisoners of War: Captured in Louisiana on 10/17/1864; Sent to Baton Rouge, LA, on 10/19/1864. Received at New Orleans, LA, on 10/21/1864; Transferred to Ship Island, MS, on 10/28/1864. Forwarded to Fort Columbus, New York Harbor, NY, on 11/16/1864; Received at Elmira, NY, on 11/20/1864. Remarks: Desires to take the U.S. Oath of Allegiance at Elmira, NY. Volunteered on 4/15/1862. Deserted his regiment at Liberty, MS, on 10/10/1864 and came into the Union picket line 3 miles from Baton Rouge, LA. Gave himself up voluntarily on 10/13/1864 and was sent to New Orleans, LA, and treated as a Prisoner of War, he thinks by mistake. Desires to go to New York City. Released on the U.S. Oath of Allegiance on 5/19/1865. Description at oath: Hair: light. Complexion: light. Height: 5'11". Residence at oath: New Orleans, LA.

Day, B.M. (AKA B.N.) Pvt., Gober's Mounted Infantry Regiment. Co. H. Federal Rolls of Prisoners of War: Captured at Morganza, LA, on 8/25/1864; Transferred to Ship Island, MS, from New Orleans, LA, on 10/5/1864. Sent to Fort Columbus, New York Harbor, NY, on 11/16/1864; Forwarded to Elmira, NY, on 11/19/1864. Released on the U.S. Oath of Allegiance on 7/1/1865.

Day, John H. Pvt., 6th Louisiana Cavalry. Co. C. Federal Rolls of Prisoners of War: Captured at Jackson, LA, on 11/16/1864; Forwarded to New Orleans, LA, on 11/23/1864. Received at Ship Island, MS, on 12/10/1864; Transferred to Vicksburg, MS, for exchange on 5/1/1864. Exchanged at Camp Townsend, MS, on 5/6/1865.

Delery, I.D. Pvt., 3rd Louisiana Battalion Cavalry. Co. I. Federal Rolls of Prisoners of War: Captured near Jackson, LA, on 11/15/1864; Received at Ship Island, MS, from New Orleans, LA, on 12/13/1864.

Demoulin, Augustin (AKA Demilin) Pvt., 2nd Louisiana Cavalry. Co. K. Federal Rolls of Prisoners of War: Captured near False River, LA, on 10/20/1864; Received at Ship Island, MS, from New Orleans, LA, on 10/28/1864. Transferred to Fort Columbus, New York Harbor, NY, on 11/5/1864. Confederate Pension Application on file at the Louisiana State Archives. Microfilm Reel: CP1.38. Microdex 2. Sequence 19. Target Card: Demoulin, Augustin. Parish: Pointe Coupée. 3 pages.

Dewart, J.D. (AKA Dutart) Pvt., 3rd Louisiana Cavalry. Co. I. Federal Rolls of Prisoners of War: Captured at Clinton, LA, on 11/16/1864; Received at Ship Island, MS, from New Orleans, LA, on 12/13/1864.

Dicheny, Francis (AKA Dicherry) Pvt., Ogden's Cavalry Battalion. Co. F. Federal Rolls of Prisoners of War: Captured near East Baton Rouge Parish, LA, on 1/5/1865; Received at New Orleans, LA, on 1/14/1865. Transferred to Ship Island, MS, on 1/22/1865.

Dicheny, H. (AKA Dicherry) Pvt., Ogden's Cavalry Battalion. Co. F. Federal Rolls of Prisoners of War: Captured at Bayou Conway, LA, on 1/5/1865; Received at Ship Island, MS. Transferred to Vicksburg, MS, for exchange on 5/1/1865; Exchanged at Camp Townsend, MS, on 5/6/1865.

Dickson, John B. Pvt., 19th Louisiana Infantry. Co. F. Enlisted: 12/11/1861 at Camp Moore, LA. Rolls from 12/11/1862 through 8/1862: Present. Rolls from 10/31/1862 through 12/1862: Absent, in hospital at Greenville, AL. Rolls for 1/1863 through 2/1863: Present. Rolls for 7/1863 through 8/1863: Absent, in hospital at Greenville, AL, since 8/17/1863. Rolls for 9/1863 through 10/1863: Absent, in hospital by order of Asst. Surgeon Philson. Rolls for 11/1863 through 4/1864: Present. Rolls for 4/1864 through 5/30/1864: Admitted to Floyd House Hospital, Macon, GA, on 5/30/1864. Rolls for 6/1864 through 2/1865: Present. Rolls for 3/1865 through 4/1865: Absent. Federal Rolls of Prisoners of War: Captured at Spanish Fort, AL, on 4/8/1865; Received at Ship Island, MS, on 4/10/1865. Transferred to Vicksburg, MS, for exchange on 5/1/1865; Exchanged at Camp Townsend, MS, on 5/6/1865.

Dieherman, Joseph Pvt., 30th Louisiana Infantry. Co. D. Enlisted: 10/15/1862 at Mobile, AL. Rolls for 10/15/1862 through 4/1864: Present. Rolls for 11/1864 through 2/28/1865: Present, captured while detached to Co. C with its officers. Federal Rolls of Prisoners of War: Captured at Spanish Fort, AL, on 4/8/1865; Received at Ship Island, MS, on 4/10/1865. Transferred to Vicksburg, MS, for exchange on 5/1/1865; Exchanged at Camp Townsend, MS, on 5/6/1865.

Dieman, J. Pvt., 20th Louisiana Infantry. Co. B. Federal Rolls of Prisoners of War: Captured at Spanish Fort, AL, on 4/8/1865; Received at Ship Island, MS, on 4/10/1865. Transferred to Vicksburg, MS, for exchange on 5/1/1865; Exchanged at Camp Townsend, MS, on 5/6/1865.

Dimitry, Theodore J. (AKA Dimity) Pvt., Louisiana Guard Artillery Battery. Enlisted: 4/26/1861 at New Orleans, LA. Rolls for 4/26/1861 through 2/1863: Present. Rolls for 3/1863 through 4/1863: Absent, on 30 day furlough since 3/13/1863; Furlough extended for 30 days. Rolls for 5/1863 through 6/1863: Present, returned to duty on 6/4/1863 with a Certificate of Detention due to Union raids. Rolls for 7/1863 through 8/1863: Present. Rolls for 9/1863 through 10/1863: Absent, sent to the rear sick on 10/19/1863. Rolls for 11/1863 through 10/1864: Absent, detailed for Provost duty at Covington, LA, by special order # 278 of the Secretary of War dated 11/23/1863. Rolls for 11/1864 through 12/1864: Absent, taken as a prisoner of war at Osyka, MS, on 10/6/1864 while detailed on Provost duty. Rolls for 1/1865 through 2/1865: Absent, on parole furlough awaiting exchange. Federal Rolls of Prisoners of War: Captured at Osyka, MS, on 10/7/1864; Sent to Ship Island, MS. Transferred to New York on 11/5/1864; Received at Fort Columbus, New York Harbor, NY, on 11/16/1864. Forwarded to Elmira, NY, on 11/19/1864; Paroled at Elmira, NY, on 2/9/1865 and sent to James River, VA, for exchange. Received at Boulware and Cox Wharf, James River, VA, on 2/20/1865 and exchanged. Confederate Widows Pension Application on file at the Louisiana State Archives. Microfilm Reel: CP1.39. Microdex 4. Sequence 23. Target Card: Dimitry, Irene May (Scott). Parish: Orleans. 4 pages.

Dixon, William P. Pvt., Ogden's Cavalry Battalion. Co. A. Federal Rolls of Prisoners of War: Captured near New River, LA, on 11/17/1864; Sent to New Orleans, LA, on 12/24/1864. Transferred to Ship Island, MS, on 1/22/1865; Forwarded to Vicksburg, MS, for exchange on 5/1/1865. Exchanged at Camp Townsend, MS, on 5/6/1865. Soldier also served as a Pvt. with the 7th Louisiana Infantry. Co.B. Born: 9/6/1841. Died: 1/23/1924. Buried: Oak Grove City Cemetery located at the intersection of Hwy. 73 and Hwy. 42 at Oak Grove, Ascension Parish, LA. Confederate Pension Application on file at the Louisiana State Archives. Microfilm Reel: CP1.40. Microdex 1. Sequence 3. Target Card: Dixon, William P. Parish: Ascension. 8 pages. Also a Confederate Widows Pension Application on file. Microfilm Reel: CP1.39. Microdex 4. Sequence 36. Target Card: Dixon, Kate (Brown). Parish: Ascension. 5 pages.

Doherty, Peter (AKA Dougherty) Pvt., 2nd Louisiana Cavalry. Co. I. Enlisted: 9/1/1862 at New Roads, LA. Rolls for 1/1863 through 2/1863: Present. Federal Rolls of Prisoners of War: Captured at Tunica, LA, on 9/14/1864; Sent to Baton Rouge, LA, on 10/6/1864. Received at New Orleans, LA, on 10/10/1864; Transferred to Ship Island, MS, on 10/20/1864. Forwarded to Fort Columbus, New York Harbor, NY, on 11/16/1864; Sent to Elmira, NY, on 11/19/1864. Released from Elmira, NY, on 5/29/1865.

Doherty, Stephen C. (AKA J.C.) Pvt., 3rd Louisiana Cavalry (Harrison's). Cos. D & I. Federal Rolls of Prisoners of War: Captured at Tunica Bend, LA, on 11/7/1864; Sent from Morganza, LA, to the U.S. Commissary of Prisoners on 11/11/1864. Received at Ship Island, MS, from New Orleans, LA, on 12/10/

1864; Returned to New Orleans, LA, on 4/1/1865. Transferred to the mouth of Red River, LA, for exchange on 4/7/1865.

Dougherty, A.R. (AKA Doherty) Sgt., 3rd Louisiana Cavalry. Co. I. Federal Rolls of Prisoners of War: Captured and paroled at Port Hudson, LA, on 7/8/1863. Federal Rolls of Prisoners of War: Captured at Bayou Sara, LA, on 10/3/1864; Forwarded to New Orleans, LA, on 10/10/1864. Received at Ship Island, MS, on 10/21/1864; Forwarded to Fort Columbus, New York Harbor, NY, on 11/5/1864.

Dunn, W.L. Sgt., 2nd Louisiana Cavalry. Co. A. Federal Rolls of Prisoners of War: Captured near Clinton, LA, on 8/25/1864; Transferred to Ship Island, MS, from New Orleans, LA, on 10/5/1864. Forwarded to Fort Columbus, New York Harbor, NY, on 11/16/1864; Received at Elmira, NY, on 11/19/1864. Paroled at Elmira, NY, on 2/25/1865; Sent to James River, VA, for exchange.

Dunn, William L. (AKA W.A.) Pvt./Sgt., 27th Louisiana Infantry. Co. A. Enlisted: 3/29/1862 at Camp Moore, LA. Age at enlistment: 18. Occupation at enlistment: Student. Description at enlistment. Eyes: gray. Hair: light. Complexion: light. Height: 5'7". Rolls for 4/1862 through 12/1862: Present. Federal Rolls of Prisoners of War: Captured at Vicksburg, MS, on 7/4/1863; Paroled on 7/14/1863. Soldier also served with the 2nd La. Cavalry. Co. A. Federal Rolls of Prisoners of War: Captured near Clinton, LA, on 8/25/1864; Transferred to Ship Island, MS, from New Orleans, LA, on 10/5/1864. Forwarded to Fort Columbus, New York Harbor, NY, on 11/16/1864; Received at Elmira, NY, on 11/19/1864. Paroled at Elmira, NY, on 2/25/1865; Sent to James River, VA, for exchange. Born: East Feliciana Parish, LA.

Dupuy, Paul Adonis (AKA Duprey, O.P., P.O.) Pvt., 2nd Louisiana Cavalry. Co. I. Enlisted: 9/1/1862 at New Roads, LA. Rolls for 1/1863 through 2/1863: Present. Federal Rolls of Prisoners of War: Captured at Bayou Gross Tête, LA, on 8/10/1864; Received at New Orleans, LA, on 8/15/1864. Transferred to Ship Island, MS, on 10/5/1864; Sent to Fort Columbus, New York Harbor, NY, on 11/16/1864. Transferred to Elmira, NY, on 11/19/1864; Released from Elmira, NY, on 5/17/1865. Confederate Pension Application on file at the Louisiana State Archives. Microfilm Reel: CP1.44. Microdex 1. Sequence 19. Target Card: Dupuy, P.A. Parish: Iberia. 15 pages.

Duvio, Octave Pvt., 4th Louisiana Infantry. Co. C. Federal Rolls of Prisoners of War: Captured at White Pigeon, AL, on 9/9/1864; Received at Ship Island, MS, on 10/7/1864. Died: 11/8/1864 at Ship Island, MS, due to chronic diarrhea. Buried: Ship Island, MS, Cemetery in Grave #13.

Edwards, J. Pvt., 5th Louisiana Infantry. Co. __. Federal Rolls of Prisoners of War: Captured at Vernon, FL, on 9/29/1864; Forwarded to New Orleans, LA. Transferred to Ship Island, MS, on 10/21/1864.

Edwards, T.B. Pvt., 2nd Louisiana Cavalry. Co. I. Federal Rolls of Prisoners of War: Captured at Bayou Grosse Tête, LA, on 10/27/1864; Received at New Orleans, LA, from Morganza, LA, on 10/31/1864. Transferred to Ship Island, MS, on 11/2/1864; Forwarded to New York on 11/5/1864. Received at Fort Columbus, New York Harbor, NY, on 11/16/1864; Sent to Elmira, NY, on 11/19/1864. Paroled at Elmira NY on 2/25/1865; Sent to James River, VA, for exchange.

Elam, John F. Pvt., Grosse Tête Flying Artillery. Federal Rolls of Prisoners of War: Captured at Bayou Lafourche, LA, on 10/4/1864; Forwarded from Morganza, LA, to the U.S. Commissary of Prisoners on 10/7/1864. Received at New Orleans, LA, on 10/10/1864; Transferred to Ship Island, MS, on 10/21/1864. Sent to New York on 11/5/1864; Received at Fort Columbus, New York Harbor, NY, on 11/16/1864. Transferred to Elmira, NY, on 11/19/1864; Sent from Elmira, NY, to James River, VA, for exchange on 2/20/1865. Died: 6/16/1865. Buried: Hollywood Cemetery, Richmond, Henrico County, VA.

Elfair, Eugene (AKA Elfer) Pvt., Miles Legion. Co. A. Enlisted: 9/1/1862 at Baton Rouge, LA. Rolls for 11/1862 through 12/1863: Present. Federal Rolls of Prisoners of War: Captured near Baton Rouge, LA, on 4/29/1864; Received at New Orleans, LA, on 5/5/1864. Transferred to Ship Island, MS, on 10/5/1864; Forwarded to Fort Columbus, New York Harbor, NY, on 11/16/1864. Sent to Elmira, NY, on 11/19/1864; Died: 12/22/1864 at Elmira, NY, due to pneumonia. Buried: Woodlawn National Cemetery, Chemung County, NY.

Erskins, William (AKA Erskin, Esgue, Erekin) Pvt., 5th Louisiana Cavalry. Co. B. Federal Rolls of Prisoners of War: Captured at Bayou Grosse Tête, on 11/16/1864; Sent to New Orleans, LA, from Morganza, LA, on 11/22/1864. Forwarded to Ship Island, MS, on 12/10/1864. Name on a Return dated Military and Political Prisoners in Confinement at Ship Island, MS, on 4/1865, commanded by Col. Ernest W. Holmstedt. Remarks: Captured at Point Coupée Parish, LA, on 11/20/1864; Transferred to New Orleans, LA, per orders from Headquarters, Military Division of West MS. Rolls of Prisoners of War, C.S.A: Surrendered at New Orleans, LA, on 5/26/1865; Paroled at New Orleans, LA, on 6/17/1865. Born: 1809 in Scotland. Died: 1865. Buried: Willis/Rolen Cemetery located at Sikes, Winn Parish, LA.

Essan, W.J. (AKA Eisau, Eisare, G.W., I.W.) Pvt., 4th Louisiana Infantry. Co. __. Federal Rolls of Prisoners of War: Captured near Port Hudson, LA, on 2/4/1864 or Baton Rouge, LA, on 4/15/1864. Appears on Roll of Prisoners of War at New Orleans, LA, who are desirous of taking the U.S. Oath of Allegiance. Remarks: Says he is a Deserter, wants to take the Oath. Transferred to Ship Island, MS, on 10/5/1864; Left sick at Ship Island, MS, on 11/5/1864. Died: 11/27/1864 at Ship Island, MS, due to dysentery. Buried: Ship Island, MS, Cemetery.

Fairchild, J.F. (AKA Fairchilds, Firchilds, S.F., J.S.) Pvt., 3rd Louisiana Cavalry (Harrison's). Co. F. Federal Rolls of Prisoners of War: Captured at East Baton Rouge Parish, LA, on 9/15/1864; Confined in the U.S. Provost Jail, Baton Rouge, LA, on 9/19/1864. Forwarded to New Orleans, LA; Transferred to Ship Island, MS, on 10/27/1864. Sent to New York on 11/5/1864; Received at Fort Columbus, New York Harbor, NY, on 11/16/1864. Transferred to Elmira, NY, on 11/19/1864; Paroled at Elmira, NY, on 2/9/1865. Sent to James River, VA, for exchange; Received at Boulware and Cox Wharf, James River, VA, on 2/20–21/1865 and exchanged.

Fanchee, U. Pvt., 30th Louisiana Infantry. Co. F. Federal Rolls of Prisoners of War: Captured at Spanish Fort, AL, on 4/8/1865; Received at Ship Island, MS, on 4/10/1865. Transferred to Vicksburg, MS, for exchange on 5/1/1865; Exchanged at Camp Townsend, MS, on 5/6/1865.

Farnott, S. Cpl., 4th Louisiana Infantry. Co. F. Federal Rolls of Prisoners of War: Captured at Spanish Fort, AL, on 4/8/1865; Received at Ship Island, MS, on 4/10/1865. Transferred to Vicksburg, MS, for exchange on 5/1/1865; Exchanged at Camp Townsend, MS, on 5/6/1865.

Farrell, John (AKA O'Farrell) Pvt., Ogden's Cavalry Battalion. Co. __. Federal Rolls of Prisoners of War: Captured near Natchez, MS, on 9/29/1864; Received at New Orleans, LA, on 10/20/1864. Transferred to Ship Island, MS, on 10/21/1864; Forwarded to New York on 11/5/1864. Received at Fort Columbus, New York Harbor, NY, on 11/16/1864; Sent to Elmira, NY, on 11/20/1864. Paroled at Elmira, NY, on 2/9/1865; Sent to James River, VA, for exchange. Received at Boulware and Cox Wharf, James River, VA, on 2/20–21/1865 and exchanged.

Faucher, J. Pvt., 30th Louisiana Infantry. Co. F. Federal Rolls of Prisoners of War : Captured at Spanish Fort, AL, on 4/8/1865; Received at Ship Island, MS, on 4/10/1865. Transferred to Vicksburg, MS, for exchange on 5/1/1865; Exchanged at Camp Townsend, MS, on 5/6/1865.

Favrot, St. Clair (AKA Farrot, S.) Pvt./Cpl., 4th Louisiana Infantry. Co. F. Enlisted: 5/25/1861 at Tangipahoa, LA. Rolls for 5/25/1861 through 2/28/1865: Present. Federal Rolls of Prisoners of War: Captured at Spanish Fort, AL, on 4/8/1865; Received at Ship Island, MS, on 4/10/1865. Transferred to Vicksburg, MS, for exchange on 5/1/1865; Exchanged at Camp Townsend, MS, on 5/6/1865. On Register of U.S.A. Post Hospital, Jackson, MS: Admitted on 5/8/1865; Returned to duty on 5/25/1865. Rolls of Prisoners of War, C.S.A: Surrendered at Citronelle, AL, on 5/4/1865; Paroled at Jackson, MS, on 5/12/1865. Residence at parole: Baton Rouge, LA.

Fazende, Numa Pvt., 30th Louisiana Infantry. Co. F. Enlisted: 10/12/1862 at Port Hudson, LA. Rolls for 10/12/1862 through 2/28/1865: Present. Federal Rolls of Prisoners of War: Captured at Spanish Fort, AL, on 4/8/1865; Received at Ship Island, MS, on 4/10/1865. Transferred to Vicksburg, MS, for exchange on 5/1/1865; Exchanged at Camp Townsend, MS, on 5/6/1865. Confederate Widows Pension Application on file at the Louisiana State Archives. Microfilm Reel: CP1.48. Microdex 1. Sequence 3. Target Card: Fazende, Eamelie. Parish: Orleans. 2 pages.

Fecel, Jules N. Pvt., 30th Louisiana Infantry. Co. F. Enlisted: 3/11/1862 at New Orleans, LA. Rolls for 5/1862 through 6/1862: Present. Rolls for 7/1863 through 10/1863: Absent, sick at Pascagoula, MS. Rolls for 3/1864 through 2/28/1865: Present. Federal Rolls of Prisoners of War: Captured at Spanish Fort, AL, on 4/8/1865; Received at Ship Island, MS, on 4/10/1865. Transferred to Vicksburg, MS, for exchange on 5/1/1865; Exchanged at Camp Townsend, MS, on 5/6/1865. Soldier also served as a Pvt. with the Orleans Guard Louisiana Militia. Co. 4. Confederate Pension Application on file at the Louisiana State Archives. Microfilm Reel: CP1.48. Microdex 1. Sequence 14. Target Card: Fecel, J. Parish: Iberville. 14 pages. Also a Confederate Widows Pension Application on file. Microfilm Reel: CP1.48. Microdex 1. Sequence 13. Target Card: Fecel, Delia (Devillier). Parish: Orleans. 16 pages.

Feldue, A.G. (AKA Felder) Cpl., 3rd Louisiana Cavalry (Wingfield's). Co. __. Federal Rolls of Prisoners of War: Captured near Liberty, MS, on 11/5/1864; Forwarded to New Orleans, LA, on 11/17/1864. Received at Ship Island, MS, on 12/10/1864; Transferred to Vicksburg, MS, for exchange on 5/1/1865. Exchanged at Camp Townsend, MS, on 5/6/1865.

Fellows, Samuel (AKA Fellers) Sgt., 1st Louisiana Cavalry. Co. D. Enlisted: 9/12/1861 at Baton Rouge, LA. Rolls for 5/1862 through 12/1863: Present. Federal Rolls of Prisoners of War: Captured at Somerset, KY, on 3/30/1863; Received at the U.S. Military Prison, Louisville, KY, on 4/4/1863. Sent from the U.S. Military Prison, Louisville, KY, to Baltimore, MD, enroute to City Point, VA, for exchange on 4/13/1863; Received at City Point, VA, on 4/22/1863 and paroled for exchange. Federal Rolls of Prisoners of War: Captured near Liberty, MS, on 11/16/1864; Forwarded to New Orleans, LA, on 11/23/1864. Received at Ship Island, MS, on 12/10/1864; Transferred to Vicksburg, MS, for exchange on 5/1/1865. Exchanged at Camp Townsend, MS, on 5/6/1865. Born: 1836. Died: 2/19/1906. Buried: Mt. Olivet Cemetery, Pineville, Rapides Parish, LA.

Ferriott, H. (AKA Fernot) Pvt., Orleans Guards Louisiana Militia. Co. C. Federal Rolls of Prisoners of War: Captured at East Pascagoula, MS, on 4/17/1865; Received at Ship Island, MS. Transferred to Vicksburg, MS, for exchange on 5/1/1865; Exchanged at Camp Townsend, MS, on 5/6/1865.

Flavin, James Pvt., 25th Louisiana Infantry. Cos. A & K. Enlisted: 3/20/1862 at Providence, LA. Rolls for 6/1862 through 4/1864: Absent, detached as Carpenter per order of General Braxton Bragg since 6/1862. Rolls for 5/1864 through 8/1864: Present or absent not stated. Rolls for 9/1864 through 2/28/1865: Present. Federal Rolls of Prisoners of War: Captured at Spanish Fort, AL, on 4/8/1865; Received at Ship Island, MS, on 4/10/1865. Transferred to Vicksburg, MS, for exchange on 5/1/1865; Exchanged at Camp Townsend, MS, on 5/6/1865.

Flemens, F.A. Pvt., 25th Louisiana Infantry. Co. A. Federal Rolls of Prisoners of War: Captured near Spanish Fort, AL, on 4/8/1865; Received at Ship Island, MS, on 4/10/1865. Transferred to Vicksburg, MS, for exchange on 5/1/1865; Exchanged at Camp Townsend, MS, on 5/6/1865.

Forbes, Alexander Ambrose Pvt., 30th Louisiana Infantry. Co. E. Enlisted: 3/3/1862 at New Orleans, LA. Rolls for 3/3/1862 through 6/1863: Present. Rolls for 7/1863 through 4/1864: Absent, detailed as a Baker at Mobile, AL, General Hospital by order of Brig. Gen. James Cantey. Rolls for 11/1864 through 2/28/1865: Present. Federal Rolls of Prisoners of War: Captured at Spanish Fort, AL, on 4/8/1865; Received at Ship Island, MS, on 4/10/1865. Transferred to Vicksburg, MS, for exchange on 5/1/1865; Exchanged at Camp Townsend, MS, on 5/6/1865.

Ford, Ben Pvt., Louisiana Cavalry. Co. I. Enlisted: 5/1/1863 at Bloomfield, KY. Rolls for 11/1863 through 2/1864: Present. Federal Rolls of Prisoners of War:

Captured near Liberty, MS, on 11/17/1864; Forwarded to New Orleans, LA, on 11/23/1864. Received at Ship Island, MS, on 12/10/1864; Transferred to Vicksburg, MS, for exchange on 5/1/1865; Exchanged at Camp Townsend, MS, on 5/6/1865.

Forestier, Urbin (AKA Forrister) Pvt., Orleans Guards Louisiana Militia. Co. A. On Roll dated 2/24/1862: Ordered into the service of the State of Louisiana. Federal Rolls of Prisoners of War: Captured at New Orleans, LA, on 12/13/1864; Transferred to Ship Island, MS, on 1/22/1865. Remarks: Was committed to prison on 12/13/1864 and held as a prisoner of war; Paroled under Maj. Gen. Benjamin F. Butler, but has since never reported to the U.S. Provost Marshall. Transferred to Vicksburg, MS, for exchange on 5/1/1865; Exchanged at Camp Townsend, MS, on 5/6/1865.

Fortlouis, Leopold (AKA Forthewis, Lewis, Louis) Pvt./Driver, Pointe Coupée Artillery. Enlisted: 6/29/1861 at New Orleans, LA. Rolls for 6/29/1861 through 12/1861: Present, appointed Driver on 8/7/1861. Federal Rolls of Prisoners of War: Captured and paroled at Vicksburg, MS, on 7/4/1863. Rolls for 3/1864 through 8/1864: Absent, captured and paroled at Vicksburg, MS, on 7/4/1863 and now in the Trans-Mississippi Army. Federal Rolls of Prisoners of War: Captured at Morganza, LA, on 6/18/1864; Received at Ship Island, MS, on 10/7/1864. Sent to New York Harbor, NY, on 11/16/1864; Transferred to Elmira, NY, on 11/19/1864. Died: 11/29/1864 at Elmira, NY, due to pneumonia. Buried: Woodlawn National Cemetery, Chemung County, NY.

Fortlouis, Michel Louis Pvt./Cpl., Pointe Coupée Artillery. Enlisted: 6/20/1861 at New Orleans, LA. Rolls for 6/20/1861 through 10/1861: Present, elected Cpl. on 8/7/1861. Rolls for 11/1861 through 12/1861: Present. Rolls for 3/1864 through 4/1864: Present. On Roll dated 8/31/1864: Absent without leave since 4/1864 at West Feliciana Parish, LA. Federal Rolls of Prisoners of War: Captured at Clinton, LA, on 8/20/1864; Received at New Orleans, LA, on 9/10/1864. Transferred to Ship Island, MS, by order of Maj. Gen.E.R.S. Canby on 10/5/1864; Sent to New York. Died: 11/29/1864 at Elmira, NY, Hospital Barracks #3 due to pneumonia. Buried: Woodlawn National Cemetery, Chemung County, NY. Age at death: 27.

Foster, Jesse M. Pvt., Gober's Mounted Infantry Regiment. Co. D. Federal Rolls of Prisoners of War: Captured at Clinton, LA, on 8/25/1864; Received at New Orleans, LA, on 8/31/1864. Transferred to Ship Island, MS, on 10/5/1864; Sent to Fort Columbus, New York Harbor, NY. Forwarded to Elmira, NY, on 11/19/1864; Sent to James River, VA, for exchange on 2/20/1865. Soldier also served as a Pvt. with the Pointee Coupée Artillery (Louisiana). Co. B. Buried: Day Cemetery located on Hwy. 43 at Easleyville, St. Helena Parish, LA. Confederate Widows Pension Application on file at the Louisiana State Archives. Microfilm Reel: CP1.50. Microdex 4. Sequence 7. Target Card: Foster, Emily E. Parish: St. Helena. 13 pages.

Foster, N.H. Pvt., 2nd Louisiana Cavalry. Co. __. Federal Rolls of Prisoners of War: Captured at Tensas Parish, LA, on 9/30/1864; Received at Ship Island, MS, on 10/21/1864. Sent to Fort Columbus, New York Harbor, NY, on 11/5/1864.

Foster, N.H. Pvt., 3rd Louisiana Cavalry (Harrison's). Co. A. Federal Rolls of Prisoners of War: Captured at Tensas Parish, LA, on 9/30/1864; Received at New Orleans, LA, on 10/20/1864. Transferred to Ship Island, MS, on 10/21/1864; Sent to New York on 11/5/1864. Forwarded to Fort Columbus, New York Harbor, NY, on 11/16/1864; Transferred to Elmira, NY, on 11/20/1864. Paroled at Elmira, NY, on 2/9/1865; Sent to James River, VA, for exchange. Received at Boulware and Cox Wharf, James River, VA, on 2/20–21/1865 and exchanged.

Foster, William H. Pvt., Pointe Coupée Artillery. Federal Rolls of Prisoners of War: Captured and paroled at Vicksburg, MS, on 7/4/1863. Federal Rolls of Prisoners of War: Captured near Liberty, MS, on 11/17/1864; Received at New Orleans, LA, on 11/23/1864. Transferred to Ship Island, MS, on 12/10/1864; Forwarded to Vicksburg, MS, for exchange on 5/1/1865. Exchanged at Camp Townsend, MS, on 5/6/1865.

French, Robert Pvt., Ogden's Cavalry Battalion. Co. B. Federal Rolls of Prisoners of War: Captured at Clinton, LA, on 11/16/1864; Forwarded to New Orleans, LA, on 11/23/1864. Received at Ship Island, MS, on 12/10/1864. Died: Ship Island, MS, on 4/23/1865 due to cancer. Buried: Ship Island, MS, Cemetery in Grave #148.

Fridge, John D. Pvt., 27th Louisiana Infantry. Co. A. Enlisted: 3/29/1862 at Camp Moore, LA. Rolls for 4/1862 through 5/1/1862: Present. Rolls for 5/1862 through 6/1862: Absent, on detached service with Col. Henry W. Allen. Rolls for 7/1862 through 11/1/1862: Absent, at home recovering from wound received at the Battle of Baton Rouge, LA. Rolls for 11/1862 through 12/1862: Present. Federal Rolls of Prisoners of War: Captured at East Baton Rouge Parish, LA, on 12/24/1864; Received at Ship Island, MS, from New Orleans, LA, on 1/25/1865 and applied to take the U.S. Oath of Allegiance. Transferred to Vicksburg, MS, for exchange on 5/1/1865; Exchanged at Camp Townsend, MS, on 5/6/1865. Wounded: Yes, in left shoulder at the Battle of Baton Rouge, LA, while on detached duty with the 4th Louisiana Infantry. Born: 3/5/1830 at East Baton Rouge Parish, LA. Married: Elizabeth Wren on 2/15/1859 at Baton Rouge, LA. Children: 7 — 3 Sons and 4 Daughters. Occupation: Farmer. Residences: East Feliciana Parish, LA, and East Baton Rouge Parish, LA. Died: 1/29/1908 at Baton Rouge, LA. Buried: Magnolia Cemetery, located at 19th St. and Florida Blvd., Baton Rouge, LA. Confederate Pension Application dated 6/8/1907 on file at the Louisiana State Archives. Microfilm Reel: CP1.51. Microdex 3. Sequence 30. Target Card: Fridge, John D. 6 pages. Also a Confederate Widows Pension Application dated 2/26/1908 on file. Microfilm Reel: CP1.51. Microdex 3. Sequence 29. Target Card: Fridge, Elizabeth. Parish: East Baton Rouge. 2 pages. Also a Confederate Proof and Land Warrant Application on file. Name: Fridge, J.D. Microfilm Reel: 1. Frame Number: 0215. Act: 116. 2 pages. Parish: East Feliciana.

Gabble, J. Pvt., 6th Louisiana Infantry. Co. F. Federal Rolls of Prisoners of War: Captured at Vernon, FL, on 9/29/1864; Transferred to Ship Island, MS, from New Orleans, LA, on 10/21/1864 from New Orleans, LA.

Gaines, D. (AKA Gause, Gauze, Gauce) Pvt., 16th Louisiana Infantry. Co. B. Federal Rolls of Prisoners of War: Captured near Greensburg, LA, on 10/7/1864; Confined in the U.S. Provost Jail, Baton Rouge, LA, on 10/10/1864. Sent to Steam Levee Press # 4, New Orleans, LA, on 10/14/1864; Received at Ship Island, MS, on 10/21/1864. Transferred to Elmira, NY, on 11/20/1864. Died: 2/13/1865 at Elmira, NY, due to general debility. Buried: Woodlawn National Cemetery, Chemung County, NY.

Gallaway, George W. Pvt., 15th Louisiana Infantry. Co. B. Federal Rolls of Prisoners of War: Captured at Tunica Bend, LA, on 11/23/1864; Forwarded to New Orleans, LA, on 12/7/1864. Received at Ship Island, MS, on 12/13/1864; Made application to take the U.S. Oath of Allegiance. Transferred to Vicksburg, MS, for exchange on 5/1/1865; Exchanged at Camp Townsend, MS, on 5/6/1865.

Ganett, J.S. Pvt., 4th Louisiana Cavalry. Co. B. Federal Rolls of Prisoners of War: Captured at Spanish Fort, AL, on 4/8/1865; Received at Ship Island, MS, on 4/10/1865. Transferred to Vicksburg, MS, for exchange on 5/1/1865; Exchanged at Camp Townsend, MS, on 5/6/1865.

Gardner, Richard H. (AKA Gardiner) Pvt., 1st Louisiana Heavy Artillery (Regulars). Co. C. Enlisted: 10/1/1862 at St. Landry Parish, LA. Rolls for 1/1864 through 2/1864: Present, temporarily attached. Rolls for 3/1864 through 6/1864: Present. Rolls for 9/1864 through 10/1864: Transferred to the 1st Louisiana Heavy Artillery. Co. C by Special Order # 300, Headquarters, Dept. of the Gulf, on 10/26/1864. Rolls for 7/1864 through 8/1864: Present, temporarily attached per Special Order from Headquarters, Higgins Brigade, on 8/16/1864. Rolls for 3/1865 through 4/1865: Absent, taken prisoner of war at Blakely, AL, on 4/10/1865. Federal Rolls of Prisoners of War: Captured at Blakely, AL, on 4/9/1865; Received at Ship Island, MS, on 4/15/1865. Transferred to Vicksburg, MS, for exchange on 5/1/1865; Exchanged at Camp Townsend, MS, on 5/6/1865.

Garrett, Isaiah (AKA Garrett, J.L.) Pvt., 4th Louisiana Battalion Infantry. Co. B. Enlisted: 9/23/1862 at Monroe, LA. Rolls for 1/1864 through 2/1865: Present. Rolls for 3/1865 through 4/1865: Absent. Federal Rolls of Prisoners of War: Captured at Spanish Fort, AL, on 4/8/1865; Sent to Ship Island, MS, on 4/10/1865. Transferred to Vicksburg, MS, for exchange on 5/1/1865; Exchanged at Camp Townsend, MS, on 5/6/1865. Born: 1/1/1845. Died: 11/16/1897. Buried: Old Monroe City Cemetery, Monroe, Ouachita Parish, LA.

Gasque, Wilson H. (AKA Gasquett) Pvt./Sgt., 2nd Louisiana Cavalry. Co. I. Enlisted: 9/1/1862 at New Roads, LA. Rolls for 1/1863 through 2/1863: Present. Federal Rolls of Prisoners of War: Captured near Lampton's Ferry, LA, on 10/10/1864; Forwarded from Morganza, LA, to New Orleans, LA, on 10/15/1864. Received at Ship Island, MS, on 10/21/1864; Sent to Fort Columbus, New York Harbor, NY, on 11/20/1864. Died: 1/19/1865 due to typhoid fever.

Gately, Thomas (AKA Gaiteley) Pvt., 4th Louisiana Infantry. Co. D. Enlisted: 5/25/1861 at Tangipahoa, LA. Rolls for 5/25/1861 through 12/1862: Present. Rolls for 1/1863 through 4/1863: Absent, on detached duty at Port Hudson, LA. Rolls for 5/1863 through 8/1863: Absent, detailed at Bayou Sara, LA. Rolls for 9/1863 through 10/1863: Absent, without leave. Rolls for 11/1863 through 12/1863: Deserted in 8/1863. Federal Rolls of Prisoners of War: Captured at Morganza, LA, on 9/30/1863. On Register of St. Louis U.S.A. General Hospital, New Orleans, LA: Admitted on 6/7/1864; Returned to duty on 6/16/1864. Federal Rolls of Prisoners of War: Escaped from the U.S. Military Prison, New Orleans, LA, on 8/14/1864; Recaptured at Bayou Sara, LA, on 9/21/1864. Sent to the U.S. Commissary of Prisoners on 10/2/1864; Received at Steam Levee Press # 4 Prison, New Orleans, LA, on 10/4/1864. Transferred to Ship Island, MS, on 10/20/1864; Forwarded to Elmira, NY. Took the U.S. Oath of Allegiance at Elmira, NY, on 5/17/1865. Description at oath: Eyes: blue. Hair: black. Complexion: fair. Height: 5'7½". Residence at oath: Baltimore, MD.

Gaudin, C.A. Sgt., Ogden's Cavalry Battalion. Co. E. Federal Rolls of Prisoners of War: Captured at Jackson, LA, on 11/16/1864; Forwarded to New Orleans, LA, on 11/27/1864. Received at Ship Island, MS, on 12/13/1864; Transferred to Vicksburg, MS, for exchange on 5/1/1865. Exchanged at Camp Townsend, MS, on 5/6/1865.

Gautreau, Richard (AKA Gautreaux, Gautrau) Pvt., Ogden's Cavalry Battalion. Co. A. Federal Rolls of Prisoners of War: Captured at Jackson, LA, on 11/16/1864; Forwarded to New Orleans, LA, on 11/23/1864. Received at Ship Island, MS, on 12/13/1864; Transferred to Vicksburg, MS, for exchange on 5/1/1865. Exchanged at Camp Townsend, MS, on 5/6/1865. Born: 1/11/1844. Died: 5/7/1921. Buried: Holy Rosary Cemetery located on Hwy. 429 at St. Amant, Ascension Parish, LA. Confederate Pension Application on file at the Louisiana State Archives. Microfilm Reel: CP1.53. Microdex 4. Sequence 31. Target Card: Gautreau, Richard. Parish: Ascension. 6 pages. Also a Confederate Widows Pension Application on file. Microfilm Reel: CP1.53. Microdex 4. Sequence 17. Target Card: Gautreau, Emelie (Dille). Parish: Ascension. 4 pages.

Gay, Andrew Hynes Pvt., 1st Louisiana Cavalry. Co. A. Enlisted: 8/26/1861 at Camp Schlatre, LA. Rolls for 5/1862 through 12/1862: Present. Rolls for 1/1863 through 2/1863: Absent, on 30 day furlough since 1/24/1863. Rolls for 3/1863 through 6/1863: Present, reported for duty from furlough 16 days late on 3/12/1863. Rolls for 11/1863 through 2/1864: Present. Federal Rolls of Prisoners of War: Captured at Pointe Coupée Parish, LA, on 11/20/1864; Forwarded from Morganza, LA, to New Orleans, LA, on 11/22/1864. Received at Ship Island, MS, on 12/13/1864; Returned to New Orleans, LA, on 4/1/1865. Exchanged at the mouth of Red River, LA, on 4/7/1865. Born: 9/25/1841. Died: 11/29/1914. Buried: Bellefontaine Cemetery, St. Louis, St. Louis County, MO.

Geary, James (AKA Gerry, Grey) Pvt., 21st Louisiana Infantry (Patton's). Co. A. Enlisted: 6/19/1861 at New

Orleans, LA. Rolls for 6/19/1861 through 4/1862: Present. Rolls for 7/1862 through 12/1862: Present, slightly wounded in left leg by fuse plug. Rolls for 1/1863 through 2/1863: Present. Rolls for 6/1863 through 12/1863: Absent, left wounded at Vicksburg, MS. Federal Rolls of Prisoners of War: Captured at Vicksburg, MS, on 7/4/1863; Paroled at Vicksburg, MS, on 7/16/1863. Federal Rolls of Prisoners of War: Captured at Joseph, LA, on 10/8/1864; Forwarded to New Orleans, LA, on 10/10/1864. Received at Ship Island, MS, on 10/20/1864; Transferred to Fort Columbus, New York Harbor, NY, on 11/10/1864. Forwarded to Elmira, NY, on 11/20/1864; Paroled at Elmira, NY, on 2/25/1865. Exchanged at Point Lookout, MD. Rolls of Prisoners of War, C.S.A: Surrendered at Citronelle, AL, on 5/4/1865; Paroled at Meridian, MS, on 5/10/1865. Residence at parole: New Orleans, LA.

Gerard, Joseph W. Pvt., Crescent Artillery. Co. A. Federal Rolls of Prisoners of War: Captured at Fort DeRussy, LA, on 3/14/1864; Received at Baton Rouge, LA, on 3/17/1864. Sent to New Orleans, LA, on 3/20/1864. Remarks: Applied to take the U.S. Oath of Allegiance on 5/31/1864. Transferred to Ship Island, MS, on 10/5/1864; Forwarded to New York on 11/5/1864. Received at Fort Columbus, New York Harbor, NY, on 11/16/1864; Transferred to Elmira, NY, on 11/19/1864. Released from Elmira, NY, on the U.S. Oath of Allegiance on 5/15/1865. Description at release: Eyes: blue. Hair: black. Complexion: dark. Height: 5'6". Residence at release: New Orleans, LA. Died: 4/22/1871. Buried: Girod St. Cemetery, New Orleans, Orleans Parish, LA. (This cemetery was disinterred in the 1970's and the Louisiana Superdome built on top of the location).

Gilpin, Thomas B. Pvt., 25th Louisiana Infantry. Co. A. Enlisted: 3/14/1862 at New Orleans, LA. Rolls for 3/14/1862 through 2/1865: Present. Federal Rolls of Prisoners of War: Captured at Spanish Fort, AL, on 4/8/1865; Received at Ship Island, MS, on 4/10/1865. Transferred to Vicksburg, MS, for exchange on 5/1/1865; Exchanged at Camp Townsend, MS, on 5/6/1865.

Girard, J. Pvt., Crescent Artillery. Co. A. Federal Rolls of Prisoners of War: Captured at Fort DeRussy, LA, on 3/14/1864; Transferred to Ship Island, MS, from New Orleans, LA, on 10/7/1864.

Glasscock, James P. (AKA Joseph) Cpl., 5th Louisiana Cavalry. Co. K. Federal Rolls of Prisoners of War: Captured near Liberty, MS, on 11/18/1864; Forwarded to New Orleans, LA, on 11/23/1864. Received at Ship Island, MS, on 12/13/1864; Transferred to Vicksburg, MS, for exchange on 5/1/1865. Exchanged at Camp Townsend, MS, on 5/6/1865. Soldier also served as a Pvt. with the 16th Louisiana Infantry. Co.D. Confederate Pension Application on file at the Louisiana State Archives. Microfilm Reel: CP1.55. Microdex 3. Sequence 8. Target Card: Glasscock, J.P. Parish: Livingston. 7 pages.

Goodman, D. Pvt., 4th Louisiana Infantry. Co. I. Enlisted: 3/15/1864 at Mobile, AL. Rolls for 3/1864 through 8/1864: Absent, sick in hospital at Griffin, AL. Rolls for 8/1864 through 2/1865: Absent without leave. Federal Rolls of Prisoners of War: Captured at Spanish Fort, AL, on 4/8/1865; Received at Ship Island, MS, on 4/10/1865. Transferred to Vicksburg, MS, for exchange on 5/1/1865; Exchanged at Camp Townsend, MS, on 5/6/1865.

Graham, J.H. Sgt., Louisiana Supporting Forces. Co. A. Federal Rolls of Prisoners of War: Captured at Clinton, LA, on 11/16/1864; Sent to Ship Island, MS, from New Orleans, LA, on 12/13/1864. Transferred to Vicksburg, MS, for exchange on 5/1/1865; Exchanged at Camp Townsend, MS, on 5/6/1865.

Grandchampt, E. Pvt., 26th Louisiana Infantry. Co. G. Enlisted: 4/7/1862 at New Orleans, LA. Rolls for 4/7/1862 through 10/1862: Present. Federal Rolls of Prisoners of War: Captured and paroled at Vicksburg, MS, on 7/4/1863. On List dated Headquarters, Allen's Brigade, Shreveport, LA, 3/29/1864: Reported for exchange at Alexandria, LA, before 4/1/1864. Federal Rolls of Prisoners of War: Captured at Bruinsburg, LA, on 11/22/1864; Received at Ship Island, MS, on 1/22/1865. Transferred to Vicksburg, MS, for exchange on 5/1/1865; Exchanged at Camp Townsend, MS, on 5/6/1865.

Graves, William (AKA Gray) Pvt., 25th Louisiana Infantry. Co. A. Federal Rolls of Prisoners of War: Captured at Spanish Fort, AL, on 4/8/1865; Forwarded to Ship Island, MS, on 4/10/1865. Transferred to Vicksburg, MS, on 5/1/1865; Exchanged at Camp Townsend, MS, on 5/6/1865.

Green, John Pvt., 3rd Louisiana Cavalry (Wingfield's). Co. D. Federal Rolls of Prisoners of War: Captured at Brookhaven, MS, on 11/18/1864; Received at Ship Island, MS, from New Orleans, LA, on 12/13/1864.

Green, John Herbert Pvt./3rd Cpl./Pvt., 4th Louisiana Infantry. Co. K. Enlisted: 5/29/1862 at Clinton, LA. On Regimental Return dated 12/1861: Blockading bay and stopping mouth of river. Rolls for 11/1862 through 12/1862: Present, promoted to 3rd Cpl. on 11/20/1862. Rolls for 12/1862 through 6/1863: Present. Rolls for 7/1863 through 8/1863: Deserted on 7/17/1863 on the retreat from Jackson, MS. Rolls for 9/1863 through 10/1863: Present, but absent without leave from 8/8/1863 through 10/25/1863. Rolls for 11/1863 through 12/1863: Present. Rolls for 5/1864 through 7/1864: Absent, on sick furlough at Clinton, LA. Rolls for 8/1864 through 2/1865: Absent, taken prisoner of war. Federal Rolls of Prisoners of War: Captured at Clinton, LA, on 10/6/1864; Sent to the U.S. Provost Jail, Baton Rouge, LA, on 10/10/1864. Forwarded to New Orleans, LA, on 10/14/1864; Received at Ship Island, MS, on 10/21/1864. Transferred to Fort Columbus, New York Harbor, NY, on 11/5/1864; Received at Elmira, NY, on 11/19/1864. Confederate Widows Pension Application on file at the Louisiana State Archives. Microfilm Reel: CP1.57. Microdex 4. Sequence 3. Target Card: Green, Lethia A. (Deville). Parish: Rapides. 17 pages. Wife remarried S.A. Parker.

Green, John M. (AKA Greer) Pvt., 7th Louisiana Cavalry. Co. __. Federal Rolls of Prisoners of War: Captured at Fifteen Mile Station, LA, on 7/22/1864; Received at Ship Island, MS. Transferred to Vicksburg, MS, for exchange on 5/1/1865; Exchanged at Camp Townsend, MS, on 5/6/1865. Soldier also served with the 7th Alabama Cavalry. Co. I.

Griffin, John Pvt., 25th Louisiana Infantry. Co. A. Federal Rolls of Prisoners of War: Captured at Spanish Fort, AL, on 4/8/1865; Received at Ship Island, MS, on 4/10/1865. Transferred to Vicksburg, MS, for

exchange on 5/1/1865; Exchanged at Camp Townsend, MS, on 5/6/1865.

Grimes, Joseph E. Pvt., 30th Louisiana Infantry. Co. B. Enlisted: 3/1/1862 at New Orleans, LA. Rolls for 9/1862 and 10/1862: Present, returned prisoner temporarily attached. Rolls from 11/1862 through 8/1863: Present. Rolls for 9/1863 and 10/1863: Absent, sick. Rolls from 3/1864 through 2/1865: Present. Federal Rolls of Prisoners of War: Captured at Spanish Fort, AL, on 4/8/1865; Received at Ship Island, MS, on 4/10/1865. Transferred to Vicksburg, MS, for exchange on 5/1/1865; Exchanged at Camp Townsend, MS, on 5/6/1865.

Grount, William Pvt., Stewart's Legion. Co. __. (No War Dept. Record) Sentenced to imprisonment at Ship Island, MS, by Maj. Gen. Benjamin F. Butler due to transporting contraband through the Union lines; Received at Ship Island, MS, on 10/28/1862. Released by order of Maj. General Nathaniel P. Banks on 8/15/1863.

Guedry, Jules (AKA Guidry) Pvt., Donaldsonville Artillery. Enlisted: 3/21/1862 at New Orleans, LA. Rolls for 3/21/1862 through 6/1862: Present. Rolls for 7/1862 through 2/1863: Present, sick in hospital at Richmond, VA. Rolls for 3/1863 through 8/1864: Present. Rolls for 9/1864 through 10/1864: Absent, without leave. Federal Rolls of Prisoners of War: Captured at Osyka, MS, on 10/7/1864; Forwarded to Baton Rouge, LA, on 10/10/1864. Received at New Orleans, LA, on 10/14/1864; Transferred to Ship Island, MS, on 10/20/1864. Received at Fort Columbus, New York Harbor, NY, on 11/16/1864; Sent to Elmira, NY, on 11/20/1864. Paroled at Elmira, NY, on 2/9/1865; Exchanged at Boulware and Cox Wharf, James River, VA, on 2/20–21/1865.

Gum, John Pvt., 3rd Louisiana Cavalry. Co. __. Federal Rolls of Prisoners of War: Captured near Brookhaven, MS, on 11/18/1864; Forwarded to New Orleans, LA, on 11/23/1864. Received at Ship Island, MS, on 12/10/1864; Transferred to Vicksburg, MS, for exchange on 5/1/1865. Exchanged at Camp Townsend, MS, on 5/6/1865.

Hall, Hopewell Pvt., 3rd Louisiana Cavalry. Co. H. Federal Rolls of Prisoners of War: Captured at Liberty, MS, on 11/17/1864; Received at Ship Island, MS, from New Orleans, LA, on 12/13/1864. Transferred to New Orleans, LA, for exchange on 1/25/1865.

Hamilton, Henry Pvt., 3rd Louisiana Cavalry. Co. I. Federal Rolls of Prisoners of War: Captured near Liberty, MS, on 11/18/1864; Forwarded to New Orleans, LA, on 11/23/1864. Received at Ship Island, MS, on 12/13/1864; Transferred to Vicksburg, MS, for exchange on 5/1/1865. Exchanged at Camp Townsend, MS, on 5/6/1865. Rolls of Prisoners of War, C.S.A: Surrendered at Citronelle, AL, on 5/4/1865; Paroled at Jackson, MS, on 5/19/1865. Residence at parole: Copiah County, MS.

Hamilton, J.S. (AKA Hamelton, J.T.) Pvt., 30th Louisiana Infantry. Co. __. Federal Rolls of Prisoners of War: Captured at East Baton Rouge Parish, LA, on 12/21/1864; Received at Ship Island, MS, from New Orleans, LA, on 1/25/1865.

Hammond, Thomas Pvt., 18th Louisiana Battalion Cavalry. Co. F. Federal Rolls of Prisoners of War: Captured at Clinton, LA, on 10/6/1864; Sent to New Orleans, LA, on 10/14/1864. Received at Ship Island, MS, on 10/21/1864; Transferred to Fort Columbus, New York Harbor, NY, on 11/16/1864. Forwarded to Elmira, NY, on 11/20/1864; Paroled at Elmira, NY, on 2/25/1865. Exchanged at James River, VA, in 1865.

Hamplin, J.J. Pvt., 4th Louisiana Battalion Infantry. Co. __. Federal Rolls of Prisoners of War: Captured at Spanish Fort, AL, on 4/8/1865; Received at Ship Island, MS, on 4/10/1865. Transferred to Vicksburg, MS, for exchange on 5/1/1865; Exchanged at Camp Townsend, MS, on 5/6/1865.

Haney, L. Pvt., 30th Louisiana Infantry. Co. __. Federal Rolls of Prisoners of War: Captured at Spanish Fort, AL, on 4/8/1865; Received at Ship Island, MS, on 4/10/1865. Transferred to Vicksburg, MS, for exchange on 5/1/1865; Exchanged at Camp Townsend, MS, on 5/6/1865.

Harley, David (AKA Hurley, Daniel) Pvt., Miles Legion. Co. G. Enlisted: 4/15/1862 at New Orleans, LA. Rolls for 4/1862 through 6/1862: Present. Federal Rolls of Prisoners of War: Captured and paroled at Port Hudson, LA, on 7/8/1863. Federal Rolls of Prisoners of War: Captured at Atchafalaya, LA, on 9/25/1864; Transferred to New Orleans, LA, on 9/25/1864. Received at Ship Island, MS, on 10/5/1864; Forwarded to Fort Columbus, New York Harbor, NY, on 11/16/1864. Sent to Elmira, NY, on 11/19/1864. Died: 12/15/1864 at Elmira, NY. Buried: Woodlawn National Cemetery, Chemung County, NY.

Harrelson, J. Samuel (AKA Hardson) Pvt., 3rd Louisiana Cavalry (Wingfield's). Co. G. Enlisted: 6/5/1862 at Denham Springs, LA. Rolls for 6/5/1862 through 9/19/1862: Present or absent not stated. Federal Rolls of Prisoners of War: Captured and paroled at Port Hudson, LA, on 7/8/1863. Federal Rolls of Prisoners of War: Captured at East Baton Rouge Parish, LA, on 1/9/1865; Sent to New Orleans, LA, on 1/17/1865. Received at Ship Island, MS, on 1/22/1865; Transferred to Vicksburg, MS, for exchange on 5/1/1865. Exchanged at Camp Townsend, MS, on 5/6/1865.

Harrick, E.G. Pvt., 3rd Louisiana Cavalry (Harrison's). Co. __. Federal Rolls of Prisoners of War: Captured at Escambia County, FL, on 12/15/1864; Sent to Ship Island, MS, from New Orleans, LA, on 1/25/1865.

Harries, George P. (AKA Harriss), Jr. 2nd Lt./Pvt., Fenner's Artillery Battery. Enlisted: 5/16/1862 at Jackson, MS. Rolls for 5/1862 through 8/1863: Present. Rolls for 9/1863 through 10/1863: Resigned on 10/20/1863. Federal Rolls of Prisoners of War: Captured at Clinton, LA, on 10/6/1864; Sent to New Orleans, LA, on 10/14/1864. Received at Ship Island, MS, on 10/20/1864; Transferred to Fort Columbus, New York Harbor, NY, on 11/16/1864. Forwarded to Elmira, NY, on 11/20/1864; Paroled and transferred to James River, VA, for exchange on 2/25/1865.

Harris, Charles Pvt., 2nd Louisiana Cavalry. Co. __. Federal Rolls of Prisoners of War: Captured near St. Martinville, LA, on 12/21/1864 or 1/11/1865; Received at New Orleans, LA, on 1/20/1865. Forwarded to Ship Island, MS, on 1/25/1865; Returned to New Orleans, LA, for exchange on 4/1/1865. Exchanged on 4/9/1865.

Harris, Charles Pvt., Groves' Artillery Battery. Co. __. Federal Rolls of Prisoners of War: Captured near St. Martinville, LA, on 1/11/1865; Received at Ship Island, MS. Transferred to New Orleans, LA, for exchange on 1/20/1865. Exchanged at New Orleans, LA, on 4/9/1865.

Harris, John Pvt., 10th Louisiana Infantry. Co. E. Federal Rolls of Prisoners of War: Captured near Port Hudson, LA, on 7/13/1864; Received at Ship Island, MS, from New Orleans, LA, on 10/28/1864. Transferred to Fort Columbus, New York Harbor, NY, on 11/16/1864; Forwarded to Elmira, NY, on 11/20/1864. Released on the U.S. Oath of Allegiance on 5/17/1865. Description at release: Eyes: blue. Hair: light. Complexion: fair. Height: 6'½". Residence at release: Franklin, TN.

Harris, Joseph Pvt./Sgt., Miles Legion. Co. A. Enlisted: 2/10/1862 at Iberville, LA. Rolls for 5/1862 through 6/1862: Present, promoted to Sgt. on 5/13/1862. Federal Rolls of Prisoners of War: Captured and paroled at Port Hudson, LA, on 7/8/1863. Federal Rolls of Prisoners of War: Captured at Plaquemine, LA, on 12/21/1864; Sent to New Orleans, LA, on 1/9/1865. Received at Ship Island, MS, on 1/25/1865; Returned to New Orleans, LA, in 1865. Transferred to the mouth of Red River Landing, LA, for exchange on 4/7/1865; Exchanged on 4/9/1865.

Harrod, Walter (AKA Harard) Pvt., Ogden's Cavalry Battalion. Co. __. Federal Rolls of Prisoners of War: Captured near Lake Pontchartrain, LA, on 9/4/1864; Sent to New Orleans, LA, on 9/5/1864. Received at Ship Island, MS, on 10/7/1864; Transferred to Fort Columbus, New York Harbor, NY, on 11/16/1864.

Hart, R.T. Pvt., 9th Battalion Partisan Rangers. Co. __. Federal Rolls of Prisoners of War: Captured at Natchez, MS, on 9/29/1864; Received at Ship Island, MS. Transferred to Fort Columbus, New York Harbor, NY, on 11/5/1864; Received at Elmira, NY, on 11/19/1864.

Hart, Thomas Pvt., Ogden's Cavalry Battalion. Co. __. Federal Rolls of Prisoners of War: Captured at Natchez, MS, on 9/29/1864; Sent to New Orleans, LA, in 10/1864. Transferred to Ship Island, MS, on 10/20/1864; Received at Fort Columbus, New York Harbor, NY, on 11/5/1864. Forwarded to Elmira, NY, on 11/20/1864; Paroled at Elmira, NY, and transferred for exchange on 2/9/1865. Received at Boulware and Cox Wharf, James River, VA, on 2/20–21/1865 and exchanged.

Harvard, W. Pvt., 2nd Louisiana Cavalry. Cos. D & I. Federal Rolls of Prisoners of War: Captured near Lake Pontchartrain, LA, on 9/4/1864; Transferred from New Orleans, LA, to Ship Island, MS, in 10/1864. Received at Fort Columbus, New York Harbor, NY, on 11/5/1864; Transferred to Elmira, NY, on 11/19/1864. Released from Elmira, NY, on 7/11/1865.

Harvell, William Castle Pvt., Ogden's Cavalry Battalion. Co. __. Federal Rolls of Prisoners of War: Captured at Greensburg, LA, on 10/7/1864; Sent to Steam Levee Press, New Orleans, LA, from Baton Rouge, LA, on 10/14/1864. Received at Ship Island, MS, on 10/21/1864; Transferred to Fort Columbus, New York Harbor, NY, on 11/16/1864. Forwarded to Elmira, NY, on 11/20/1864; Paroled at Elmira, NY, and transferred for exchange on 3/10/1865. Received at Boulware Wharf, James River, VA, on 3/15/1865 and exchanged. Born: 5/14/1835. Died: 12/6/1912. Buried: Greensburg City Cemetery located on Hwy. 1042 at Greensburg, St. Helena Parish, LA.

Heatherington, William H. (AKA W.G.) Pvt., 4th Louisiana Infantry. Co. A. Enlisted: 5/25/1861 at Camp Moore, LA. Rolls for 5/25/1861 through 12/1863: Present. Rolls for 5/1864 through 8/1864: Absent, wounded in a skirmish at Vinnings Station, GA, on 7/4/1864. Rolls for 10/1864 through 2/28/1865: Absent, take prisoner of war in 10/1864. Federal Rolls of Prisoners of War: Captured at Clinton, LA, on 10/6/1864; Sent to New Orleans, LA, on 10/14/1864. Received at Ship Island, MS, on 10/21/1864; Transferred to Fort Columbus, New York Harbor, NY, on 11/16/1864. Sent to Elmira, NY, on 11/20/1864; Paroled at Elmira, NY, on 2/25/1865. Exchanged at James River, VA, in 1865. Died: 4/6/1911. Buried: Greenwood Cemetery, located on City Park Ave. at New Orleans, Orleans Parish, LA. Confederate Pension Application on file at the Louisiana State Archives. Microfilm Reel: CP1.64. Microdex 2. Sequence 27. Target Card: Heatherington, William H. Parish: East Feliciana. 4 pages.

Hebert, A.J. Pvt., 4th Louisiana Cavalry. Co. C. Federal Rolls of Prisoners of War: Captured near Plaquemine, LA, on 9/11/1864; Sent from Napoleonville, LA, to Capt.B.B. Campbell, Assistant Adjutant General of the U.S. Lafourche District on 9/12/1864. Received at New Orleans, LA, on 9/20/1864; Transferred to Ship Island, MS, on 10/5/1864. Forwarded to Fort Columbus, New York Harbor, NY, on 11/16/1864; Received at Elmira, NY, on 11/19/1864. Paroled at Elmira, NY, in 1864; Transferred to James River, VA, for exchange. Exchanged at Boulware and Cox Wharf, James River, VA, on 3/15/1865.

Hebert, Adrien (AKA Adrian) Pvt., 1st Louisiana Heavy Artillery (Regulars). Co. C. Enlisted: 10/20/1862 as a conscript per General Order # 9, 1st Louisiana Heavy Artillery Headquarters. Rolls for 10/1862 through 2/1863: Present. Federal Rolls of Prisoners of War: Captured at Vicksburg, MS, on 7/4/1863; Refused to sign parole. Rolls through 12/1863: Absent, sick in hospital. Rolls for 1/1864 through 10/1864: Present. Rolls for 3/1865 through 4/1865: Absent, taken prisoner of war. Federal Rolls of Prisoners of War: Captured at Blakely, AL, on 4/9/1865; Received at Ship Island, MS, on 4/15/1865. Transferred to Vicksburg, MS, for exchange on 5/1/1865; Exchanged at Camp Townsend, MS, on 5/6/1865. Buried: St. John the Evangelist Church Cemetery, located on St. Nicholas Sreet at Jeanerette, Iberia Parish, LA. Confederate Pension Application on file at the Louisiana State Archives. Microfilm Reel: CP1.64. Microdex 2. Sequence 37. Target Card: Hebert, Adrien. Parish: Assumption. 4 pages.

Hebert, J. Grey Pvt., 2nd Louisiana Cavalry. Co. I. Enlisted: 9/1/1862 at New Roads, LA. Rolls for 1/1863 through 2/1863: Present. Federal Rolls of Prisoners of War: Captured at Plaquemine, LA, on 10/25/1863; Sent to New Orleans, LA. Escaped on 2/24/1864. Federal Rolls of Prisoners of War: Captured in 12/1864 as an escapee; Received at Ship Island, MS, from New Orleans, LA, on 1/22/1865. Returned to New Orleans, LA, on 4/1/1865; Exchanged at the mouth of Red River, LA, on 4/7/1865.

Hebert, Jules A., Sr. (AKA Herbert) Pvt., 30th Louisiana Infantry. Cos. E & H. Enlisted: 3/12/1862 at Plaquemine, LA. Rolls for 3/1862 through 8/1862: Deserted at New Orleans, LA, on 4/25/1862. Rolls for 9/1862 through 10/1862: Present. Rolls for 11/1862 through 6/1863: Present. Rolls for 7/1863 through 4/1864: Deserted while on furlough ending 8/24/1863. Federal Rolls of Prisoners of War: Captured at Plaquemine, LA, on 11/21/1864 or 12/21/1864; Received at Ship Island, MS, from New Orleans, LA, on 1/25/1865. Born: 7/18/1839. Died: 2/16/1878. Buried: St. John the Evangelist Church Cemetery on Main St. at Plaquemine, Iberville Parish, LA. Confederate Pension Application on file at the Louisiana State Archives. Microfilm Reel: CP1.65. Microdex 1. Sequence 19. Target Card: Hebert, Jules A. (Sr.). Parish: Iberville. 11 pages.

Helm, L.R. (AKA Helon) Pvt., 4th Louisiana Battalion Infantry. Co. D. Enlisted: 4/12/1862 at Carroll Parish, LA. Rolls for 12/1863 through 2/1865: Present. Rolls for 3/1865 through 4/1865: Absent, captured at Spanish Fort, AL, on 4/8/1865. Federal Rolls of Prisoners of War: Captured at Spanish Fort, AL, on 4/8/1865; Received at Ship Island, MS, on 4/10/1865. Transferred to Vicksburg, MS, for exchange on 5/1/1865; Exchanged at Camp Townsend, MS, on 5/6/1865.

Henderson, B.F. Pvt., 3rd Louisiana Cavalry. Co. I. Federal Rolls of Prisoners of War: Captured near Clinton, LA, on 8/25/1864; Received at Ship Island, MS, from New Orleans, LA, on 10/7/1864.

Henderson, James D. Pvt., 4th Louisiana Cavalry. Co. A. Federal Rolls of Prisoners of War: Captured at Ascension Parish, LA, on 12/13/1864; Sent to New Orleans, LA, on 12/14/1864. Received at Ship Island, MS, on 1/25/1865; Returned to New Orleans, LA, on 4/1/1865. Exchanged at Red River Landing, LA, on 4/9/1865.

Hendrick, A.J. Pvt., 19th Louisiana Infantry. Co. I. Enlisted: 4/15/1863 at Pollard, AL. Rolls for 7/1863 through 12/1863: Absent, sick at Macon, MS, since 7/20/1863 by order of Dr. LeGare. Rolls for 1/1864 through 4/1864: Absent in hospital at Kingston, GA, by order of Dr. Philson. Rolls for 6/1864 through 8/1864: Absent, sick at Augusta, GA, since 6/1/1864 by order of Dr. Thornton. Rolls for 9/1864 through 2/1865: Present. Rolls for 3/1865 through 4/1865: Absent, taken prisoner of war on 4/8/1865. Federal Rolls of Prisoners of War: Captured at Spanish Fort, AL, on 4/8/1865; Received at Ship Island, MS, on 4/10/1865. Transferred to Vicksburg, MS, for exchange on 5/1/1865; Exchanged at Camp Townsend, MS, on 5/6/1865.

Henry, August J. Pvt., 2nd Louisiana Cavalry. Co. C. Federal Rolls of Prisoners of War: Captured at Morganza, LA, on 8/20/1864; Received at Ship Island, MS, from New Orleans, LA, on 10/7/1864. Transferred to Fort Columbus, New York Harbor, NY, on 11/5/1864. Soldier also served as a Pvt. with the 7th Louisiana Cavalry. Co. A. Confederate Pension Application on file at the Louisiana State Archives. Microfilm Reel: CP1.65. Microdex 4. Sequence 35. Target Card: Henry, Augustus. Parish: Calcasieu. 5 pages.

Henry, Joseph Oscar Pvt., 2nd Louisiana Cavalry. Co. I. Federal Rolls of Prisoners of War: Captured at Morganza, LA, on 8/20/1864; Sent to New Orleans, LA. On Register of St. Louis U.S.A. General Hospital, New Orleans, LA: Admitted on 8/29/1864. Received at Ship Island, MS, on 10/7/1864; Forwarded to Fort Columbus, New York Harbor, NY, on 11/16/1864. On Register of U.S.A. General Hospital, Fort Columbus, NY: Admitted on 11/17/1864; Discharged on 12/4/1864. Sent to Elmira, NY, on 12/5/1864; Paroled at Elmira NY on 2/25/1865. Exchanged at James River, VA. Confederate Pension Application on file at the Louisiana State Archives. Microfilm Reel: CP1.66. Microdex 1. Sequence 8. Target Card: Henry, J. Oscar. Parish: Iberville. 4 pages.

Henson, J.B. (AKA Henston, Hinston) Pvt., 5th Louisiana Cavalry. Co. K. Federal Rolls of Prisoners of War: Captured near Liberty, MS, on 11/17/1864; Sent to New Orleans, LA, on 11/23/1864. Received at Ship Island, MS, on 12/10/1864; Transferred to Vicksburg, MS, for exchange on 5/1/1865. Exchanged at Camp Townsend, MS, on 5/6/1865. Confederate Pension Application on file at the Louisiana State Archives. Microfilm Reel: CP1.66. Microdex 1. Sequence 7. Target Card: Henson, J.B. Parish:

Herard, W. Pvt., 9th Battalion Partisan Rangers. Co. ___. Federal Rolls of Prisoners of War: Captured near Lake Pontchartrain, LA, on 7/22/1864; Received at Ship Island, MS. Forwarded to Fort Columbus, New York Harbor, NY, on 11/16/1864; Transferred to Elmira, NY, on 11/18/1864.

Hickman, Josiah A. Pvt., 19th Louisiana Infantry. Co. A. Enlisted: 12/11/1861 at Camp Moore, LA. Rolls for 12/11/1861 through 10/1863: Present. Rolls for 11/1863 through 12/1863: Absent, on 16 day furlough since 12/28/1863 by order of Lt. Gen. William J. Hardee. Rolls for 1/1864 through 4/1864: Present. Rolls for 5/1864 through 8/1864: Absent, at Griffin, GA, since 7/28/1864 due to wounds by order of Dr. Philson. Rolls for 3/1865 through 4/1865: Absent, taken prisoner of war. Federal Rolls of Prisoners of War: Captured at Spanish Fort, AL, on 4/8/1865; Received at Ship Island, MS, on 4/10/1865. Transferred to Vicksburg, MS, for exchange on 5/1/1865; Exchanged at Camp Townsend, MS, on 5/6/1865. Rolls of Prisoners of War, C.S.A: Surrendered at Citronelle, AL, on 5/4/1865; Paroled at Meridian, MS, on 5/10/1865. Residence at parole: Bossier Parish, LA.

Hide, Jesse Pvt., 13th Louisiana Infantry. Co. B. Federal Rolls of Prisoners of War: Captured at Spanish Fort, AL, on 4/8/1865; Received at Ship Island, MS, on 4/10/1865. Transferred to Vicksburg, MS, for exchange on 5/1/1865; Exchanged at Camp Townsend, MS, on 5/6/1865.

Hogan, Michael Pvt., 1st Louisiana Heavy Artillery (Regulars). Co. B. Federal Rolls of Prisoners of War: Captured at Blakely, AL, on 4/9/1865; Received at Ship Island, MS, on 4/15/1865. Transferred to Vicksburg, MS, for exchange on 5/1/1865; Exchanged at Camp Townsend, MS, on 5/6/1865.

Holland, Ebinezer H. (AKA Ebenezer) Pvt., 3rd Louisiana Cavalry (Wingfield's). Co. H. Enlisted: 6/12/1862 at Camp Moore, LA. Rolls for 6/12/1862 through 9/1862: Present or absent not stated. Federal Rolls of Prisoners of War: Captured near Liberty, MS, on 11/16/1864; Received at Ship Island, MS, from New Orleans, LA, on 12/13/1864. Transferred to Vicksburg, MS, for exchange on 5/1/1865; Exchanged at Camp Townsend, MS, on 5/6/1865. Confederate Pension Application on file at the Louisiana State Archives. Microfilm Reel: CP1.68. Microdex 2. Sequence 15. Target Card: Hlland, Ebinezer H. Parish: Grant. 7 pages.

Holly, W.J. Pvt., 6th Louisiana Cavalry. Co. C. Enlisted: 2/17/1863 at Okolona, MS. Federal Rolls of Prisoners of War: Captured at Gravel Hill, AL, on 3/24/1865; Received at Ship Island, MS, on 4/4/1865. Transferred to Vicksburg, MS, for exchange on 5/1/1865; Exchanged at Camp Townsend, MS, on 5/6/1865.

Holmes, Edward (AKA Howe) Pvt., 14th Battalion Louisiana Sharp Shooters (Austin's). Co. A. Federal Rolls of Prisoners of War: Captured at Spanish Fort, AL, on 4/8/1865; Received at Ship Island, MS, on 4/10/1865. Transferred to Vicksburg, MS, for exchange on 5/1/1865; Exchanged at Camp Townsend, MS, on 5/6/1865.

Holmes, William McC. Pvt., Washington Artillery. Co. 4. Enlisted: 5/1/1864 at Petersburg, VA. Occupation at enlistment: Clerk. Rolls for 5/1864 through 6/1864: Present; Wounded in head on 5/16/1864 at Drewry's Bluff, VA. Rolls for 7/1864 through 10/1864: Absent, sick since 8/1864. Rolls for 1/1865 through 2/1865: Absent, taken prisoner of war in 11/1864. Federal Rolls of Prisoners of War: Captured at Clinton, LA, on 10/6/1864; Sent to Steam Levee Press # 4, New Orleans, LA, on 10/14/1864. Received at Ship Island, MS, on 10/21/1864; Transferred to Fort Columbus, New York Harbor, NY, on 11/16/1864. Forwarded to Elmira, NY, on 11/20/1864; Paroled at Elmira, NY, on 2/9/1865 and transferred for exchange. Age at parole: 17. Residence at parole: New Orleans, LA. Born: Louisiana.

Holstein, D.C. (AKA Holsteine, D.O.) Pvt., 15th Battalion Louisiana Cavalry (Harrison's). Co. A. Federal Rolls of Prisoners of War: Captured at Sicily Island, LA, on 9/30/1864; Sent to Natchez, MS, on 10/15/1864. Received at New Orleans, LA, on 10/20/1864; Transferred to Ship Island, MS, on 10/21/1864. Forwarded to Fort Columbus, New York Harbor, NY, on 11/16/1864; Sent to Elmira, NY, on 11/20/1864. Paroled at Elmira, NY, on 2/9/1865; Sent to James River, VA, for exchange on 2/25/1865. Received at Boulware and Cox Wharf, James River, VA, on 2/20–21/1865 and exchanged.

Holtree, Richard J. (AKA Haldtree) Pvt./Sgt., 1st Battalion Louisiana State Guards Cavalry. Co. B. Federal Rolls of Prisoners of War: Captured at Harrisonburg, LA, on 10/14/1864; Sent to the U.S. Military Prison, Natchez, MS, on 10/15/1864. Received at New Orleans, LA, on 10/20/1864; Forwarded to Ship Island, MS, on 10/21/1864. Transferred to Fort Columbus, New York Harbor, NY, on 11/16/1864; Sent to Elmira, NY, on 12/5/1864. Died: 2/19/1865 at Elmira, NY, due to pneumonia. Buried: Woodlawn National Cemetery, Chemung County, NY.

Homburger, J. Pvt., 3rd Louisiana Cavalry. Co. A. Federal Rolls of Prisoners of War: Captured at Tensas Parish, LA, on 9/30/1864; Sent to Natchez, MS, on 10/15/1864. Forwarded to New Orleans, LA, on 10/16/1864; Transferred to Ship Island, MS, on 10/20/1864. Received at Fort Columbus, New York Harbor, NY, on 11/16/1864; Forwarded to Elmira, NY, on 11/20/1864. Paroled at Elmira, NY, on 2/9/1865; Exchanged at Boulware and Cox Wharf, James River, VA, on 2/20–21/1865.

Homstedt, D.O. Pvt., 19th Battalion Louisiana Cavalry. Co. __. Federal Rolls of Prisoners of War: Captured at Sicily Island, LA, on 9/30/1864; Received at Ship Island, MS, from New Orleans, LA, on 10/21/1864. Transferred to Fort Columbus, New York Harbor, NY, on 11/5/1864.

Hooker, James Pvt., 19th Louisiana Infantry. Co. C. Enlisted: 3/4/1863 at Homer, LA. Rolls for 2/1863 through 10/1863: Present. Rolls for 11/1863 through 12/1863: Absent, wounded in hospital at Montgomery, AL, since 11/25/1863. Rolls for 1/1864 through 2/1865: Present. Rolls for 3/1865 through 4/1865: Absent, taken prisoner of war. Federal Rolls of Prisoners of War: Captured at Spanish Fort, AL, on 4/8/1865; Received at Ship Island, MS, on 4/10/1865. Transferred to Vicksburg, MS, for exchange on 5/1/1865; Exchanged at Camp Townsend, MS, on 5/6/1865. Born: 2/4/1829. Died: 6/18/1875. Buried: Nashville Cemetery, Howard County, AR.

Horgan, Michael (also Hougan) Pvt., 1st Louisiana Heavy Artillery. Co. C. Enlisted: 5/7/1864 at Dallas, AL. Rolls for 3/1865 through 4/1865: Absent, taken prisoner of war. Federal Rolls of Prisoners of War: Captured at Blakely, AL, on 4/9/1865; Received at Ship Island, MS, on 4/15/1865. Transferred to Vicksburg, MS, for exchange on 5/1/1865; Exchanged at Camp Townsend, MS, on 5/6/1865.

Hornberger, I. Pvt., 10th Battalion Louisiana Cavalry. Co. __. Federal Rolls of Prisoners of War: Captured at Tensas Parish, LA, on 9/30/1864; Received at Ship Island, MS, from New Orleans, LA, on 10/21/1864. Transferred to Fort Columbus, New York Harbor, NY, on 11/5/1864.

Horr, John Pvt., Stewart's Legion. Co. __. (No War Dept. Record) Sentenced to imprisonment at Ship Island, MS, by Maj. Gen. Benjamin F. Butler for an unknown offense; Received at Ship Island, MS, on 10/28/1862. Released by order of Maj. Gen. Nathaniel P. Banks on 8/15/1863.

Howe, Edward Pvt., 14th Battalion Louisiana Sharpshooters (Austin's). Co. A. Enlisted: 8/13/1861 at Camp Moore, LA. Rolls for 7/1862 through 2/1865: Present. Rolls for 3/1865 through 4/1865: Absent, taken prisoner of war. Federal Rolls of Prisoners of War: Captured at Spanish Fort, AL, on 4/8/1865; Received at Ship Island, MS, on 4/10/1865.

Howze, Morris (AKA Honzo) Pvt., Ogden's Cavalry Battalion. Co. C. Federal Rolls of Prisoners of War: Captured at Liberty, MS, on 11/16/1864; Received at Ship Island, MS, on 12/13/1864. Transferred to Vicksburg, MS, for exchange on 5/1/1865; Exchanged at Camp Townsend, MS, on 5/6/1865.

Hucker, J.S. Pvt., 19th Louisiana Infantry. Federal Rolls of Prisoners of War: Captured at Spanish Fort, AL, on 4/8/1865; Received at Ship Island, MS, on 4/10/1865. Transferred to Vicksburg, MS, for exchange on 5/1/1865; Exchanged at Camp Townsend, MS, on 5/6/1865.

Hull, Hopewell Pvt., 3rd Louisiana Cavalry (Wingfield's). Co. H. Enlisted: 6/12/1862 at Camp Moore, LA. Rolls for 6/12/1862 through 9/1862: Present or absent not stated. Federal Rolls of Prisoners of War: Captured near Liberty, MS, on 11/17/1864; Received at Ship Island, MS, from New Orleans, LA, on 12/13/1864. Returned to New Orleans, LA, on 2/15/1865; Exchanged at New Orleans, LA, on 5/16/1865.

Humphries, H.M. Pvt., 3rd Louisiana Cavalry. Co. F. Federal Rolls of Prisoners of War: Captured at Clinton, LA, on 10/6/1864; Forwarded to New Orleans,

LA, on 10/14/1864. Received at Ship Island, MS, on 10/21/1864; Transferred to Vicksburg, MS, for exchange on 5/1/1865. Exchanged at Camp Townsend, MS, on 5/6/1865.

Hunt, Thomas Pvt., Louisiana Supporting Forces. Co. A. Federal Rolls of Prisoners of War: Captured at Clinton, LA, on 11/16/1864; Sent to New Orleans, LA, on 11/23/1864. Received at Ship Island, MS, on 12/13/1864; Transferred to Vicksburg, MS, for exchange on 5/1/1865. Exchanged at Camp Townsend, MS, on 5/6/1865.

Hurley, Daniel (AKA Hurly) Pvt., Miles Legion. Co. G. Federal Rolls of Prisoners of War: Captured at Atchafalaya, LA, on 9/19/1864; Received at Ship Island, MS. Forwarded to Fort Columbus, New York Harbor, NY, on 11/16/1864; Transferred to Elmira, NY, on 11/18/1864. Died: 12/15/1864 at Elmira, NY. Buried: Woodlawn National Cemetery, Chemung County, NY.

Hutches, James Pvt., 2nd Louisiana Cavalry. Co. I. Federal Rolls of Prisoners of War: Captured at Bayou Grosse Tête, LA, on 10/27/1864; Sent from Morganza, LA, to New Orleans, LA, on 10/27/1864. Forwarded to New Orleans, LA, on 10/31/1864; Transferred to Ship Island, MS, on 11/2/1864. Received at Fort Columbus, New York Harbor, NY, on 11/16/1864; Forwarded to Elmira, NY, on 11/19/1864. Paroled at Elmira, NY, on 2/25/1865; Sent to James River, VA, for exchange. Buried: St. Charles Cemetery, Grand Coteau, St. Landry Parish, LA. Confederate Pension Application on file at the Louisiana State Archives. Microfilm Reel: CP1.71. Microdex 1. Sequence 17. Target Card: Hutches, James. Parish: Iberville. 5 pages. Also a Confederate Widows pension Application on file. Microfilm Reel: CP1.71. Microdex 1. Sequence 15. Target Card: Hutches, Clarisse (Lastrapes). Parish: St. Landry. 9 pages.

Hutchinson, J.P. Sgt., 3rd Louisiana Cavalry (Wingfield's). Co. F. Enlisted: 7/2/1862 at Camp Moore, LA. Rolls for 7/2/1862 through 9/1862: Present. Federal Rolls of Prisoners of War: Captured and paroled at Port Hudson, LA, in 7/1863. Federal Rolls of Prisoners of War; Captured at East Baton Rouge Parish, LA, on 11/22/1863; Sent to New Orleans, LA, on 12/15/1863. On Register of U.S.A. Barracks Hospital, New Orleans, LA: Escaped on 5/30/1864. On Register of U.S. Commissary of Prisoners, New Orleans, LA: Recaptured on 7/7/1864. Transferred to Ship Island, MS, on 10/27/1864; Forwarded to New York on 11/5/1864. Sent to Fort Columbus, New York harbor, NY, on 11/16/1864; Received at Elmira, NY, on 11/20/1864. Paroled at Elmira, NY, on 2/25/1865; Transferred to James River, VA, for exchange. Federal Rolls of Prisoners of War: Captured at East Baton Rouge Parish, LA, on 4/1/1865; Sent from Baton Rouge, LA, to New Orleans, LA, on 4/7/1865. Exchanged on 5/11/1865.

Hutchinson, Joseph (AKA Hutchingson) Pvt., Richardson's Cavalry Regiment. Co. __. Federal Rolls of Prisoners of War: Captured at Clinton, LA, on 11/16/1864; Sent to New Orleans, LA, on 11/23/1864. Received at Ship Island, MS, on 12/13/1864; Transferred to Vicksburg, MS, for exchange on 5/1/1865. Exchanged at Camp Townsend, MS, on 5/6/1865.

Hyce, James Pvt., 14th Louisiana Cavalry. Co. F. Federal Rolls of Prisoners of War: Captured at Port Hudson, LA, on 9/24/1864; Sent to New Orleans, LA, on 10/10/1864. Transferred to Ship Island, MS, on 10/21/1864; Received at New York on 11/5/1864. Forwarded to Fort Columbus, New York Harbor, NY, on 11/16/1864; Received at Elmira, NY on 11/20/1864. Transferred for exchange on 2/13/1865.

Irvin, John Jay (AKA Irving) Pvt., 3rd Louisiana Infantry. Co. I. Enlisted: 5/17/1861 at New Orleans, LA. Rolls for 5/17/1861 through 10/1862: Present. Rolls for 11/1862 through 12/1862: Absent, detailed to take charge of baggage at Watersford, MS. Rolls for 1/1863 through 2/1863: Absent, sick at Canton, MS. Federal Rolls of Prisoners of War: Captured near Williams Ferry, LA, on 10/9/1864; Sent to Baton Rouge, LA, on 10/10/1864. Received at New Orleans, LA, on 10/15/1864; Transferred to Ship Island, MS, on 10/20/1864. Forwarded to Fort Columbus, New York Harbor, NY, on 11/16/1864; Sent to Elmira, NY, on 11/20/1864. Paroled at Elmira, NY, on 2/9/1865; Sent to James River, VA, for exchange. Received at Boulware and Cox Wharf, James River, VA, on 2/20–21/1865 and exchanged. Born: 1830. Died: 1926 in West Virginia. Buried: Texas State Cemetery located at 909 Navasota St., Austin, Travis County, TX.

Irving, W. (AKA Irwin, Irwina) Pvt., 3rd Louisiana Cavalry (Harrison's). Co. I. Federal Rolls of Prisoners of War: Captured at Tunica, LA, on 9/14/1864; Sent to Baton Rouge, LA, on 10/6/1864. Received at New Orleans, LA, on 10/10/1864; Forwarded to Ship Island, MS, on 10/20/1864. Transferred to Fort Columbus, New York Harbor, NY, on 11/16/1864; Forwarded to Elmira, NY, on 11/19/1864. Paroled at Elmira, NY, on 2/9/1865; Sent to James River, VA, for exchange. Received at Boulware and Cox Wharf, James River, VA, on 2/20–21/1865 and exchanged.

Irwin, J.J. Pvt., 3rd Louisiana Cavalry. Co. __. Federal Rolls of Prisoners of War: Captured near Wilson's Ferry, LA, on 10/9/1864; Received at Ship Island, MS. Forwarded to Fort Columbus, New York Harbor, NY, on 11/16/1864; Transferred to Elmira, NY, on 11/19/1864.

Israel, Clement B. Sgt. Maj./Sgt., Donaldsonville Artillery. Enlisted: 9/13/1861 at Donaldsonville, LA. Rolls for 9/13/1861 through 8/1864: Present. Rolls for 9/1864 through 10/1864: Absent, without leave. Federal Rolls of Prisoners of War: Captured at Osyka, MS, on 10/7/1864; Sent to Baton Rouge, LA, on 10/10/1864. Received at New Orleans, LA, on 10/14/1864; Transferred to Ship Island, MS, on 10/20/1864. Forwarded to Fort Columbus, New York Harbor, NY, on 11/16/1864; Sent to Elmira, NY, on 11/20/1864. Paroled at Elmira, NY, on 2/9/1865; Sent to James River, VA, for exchange. Received at Boulware and Cox Wharf, James River, VA, on 2/20–21/1865 and exchanged. Confederate Widows Pension Application on file at the Louisiana State Archives. Microfilm Reel: CP1.71. Microdex 3. Sequence 32. Target Card: Israel, Sidonia (Vives). Parish: Ascension. 4 pages.

Jackson, A.E. Pvt., 16th Louisiana Infantry. Co. A. Enlisted: 9/29/1861 at Camp Moore, LA. Rolls for 10/1861 through 6/1863: Present. Rolls for 7/1863 through 8/1863: Absent, without leave since 8/5/1863. Rolls for 9/1863 through 2/28/1865: Present. Federal Rolls of Prisoners of War: Captured at Spanish Fort,

AL, on 4/8/1865; Received at Ship Island, MS, on 4/10/1865.

Jackson, William P. Pvt., Gober's Mounted Infantry Regiment. Cos. B & D. Federal Rolls of Prisoners of War: Captured at Dutch Stores, LA, on 10/14/1864; Received at New Orleans, LA, on 10/20/1864. Sent to Ship Island, MS, on 10/21/1864; Forwarded to Fort Columbus, New York Harbor, NY, on 11/16/1864. Transferred to Elmira, NY, on 11/19/1864; Paroled at Elmira, NY, on 2/25/1865. Sent to James River, VA, for exchange.

Joel, Moses Pvt., 22nd Louisiana Infantry (Consolidated). Co. A. Enlisted: 5/11/1864 at Mobile, AL. Rolls for 5/1864 through 8/1864: Present. Rolls for 9/1864 through 10/1864: Absent, without leave. Federal Rolls of Prisoners of War: Captured at Spanish Fort, AL, on 4/8/1865; Received at Ship Island, MS, on 4/10/1865. Transferred to Vicksburg, MS, for exchange on 5/1/1865; Exchanged at Camp Townsend, MS, on 5/6/1865.

Joffrion, Ernest J. (AKA Jeffien, Jeffion, J.J.) Pvt., Grosse Tête Flying Artillery. Federal Rolls of Prisoners of War: Captured at Bayou Grosse Tête, LA, on 8/21/1864 or 9/6/1864; Received at New Orleans, LA, on 9/15/1864. Transferred to Ship Island, MS, on 10/5/1864; Sent to Fort Columbus, New York Harbor, NY, on 11/16/1864. Forwarded to Elmira, NY, on 11/19/1864; Paroled at Elmira NY on 2/9/1865. Sent to James River, VA, for exchange; Exchanged at Boulware and Cox Wharf, James River, VA, on 2/20–21/1865. Soldier also served as a Pvt. with West Artillery Battery (Louisiana). Confederate Pension Application on file at the Louisiana State Archives. Microfilm Reel: CP1.73. Microdex 1. Sequence 12. Target Card: Joffrion, Ernest J. Parish: East Baton Rouge. 10 pages.

Johnson, S.L. (AKA S.T., J.L.) Pvt., 11th Battalion Louisiana Infantry. Co. G. Federal Rolls of Prisoners of War: Captured at Denham Springs, LA, on 9/17/1864; Transferred to Ship Island, MS, from New Orleans, LA, on 10/27/1864. Received at Fort Columbus, New York Harbor, NY, on 11/16/1864; Forwarded to Elmira, NY, on 11/19/1864. Died: 12/14/1864 at Elmira, NY, due to pneumonia. Buried: Woodlawn National Cemetery, Chemung County, NY.

Kasson, Leverett Pvt./3rd Cpl., 18th Louisiana Infantry. Co. I. Enlisted: 6/19/1861 at New Orleans, LA. Rolls for 6/19/1861 through 4/1862: Present; promoted from Pvt. to 3rd Cpl. on 8/9/1862. Rolls for 1/1863 through 2/1863: Present. Rolls for 5/1863 through 6/1863: Present, Clerk at regimental headquarters. Rolls for 7/1863 through 8/1863: Absent, sick in hospital. Soldier also served with the 18th Louisiana Infantry and Yellow Jacket Battalion Infantry (Consolidated). Co. H. Federal Rolls of Prisoners of War: Captured at Vermillionville, LA, on 10/9/1864; Received at New Orleans, LA, on 10/27/1864. Sent to Ship Island, MS, on 10/28/1864; Forwarded to Fort Columbus, New York Harbor, NY, on 11/5/1864. Transferred to Elmira, NY, on 11/20/1864; Released on the U.S. Oath of Allegiance on 3/24/1865. Age at release: 24. Description at release: Eyes: blue. Hair: brown. Complexion: ruddy. Height: 5'10½". Residence at release: New Orleans, LA. Confederate Widows Pension Application on file at the Louisiana State Archives. Microfilm Reel: CP1.75. Microdex 3. Sequence 17. Target Card: Kasson, Maria (Thomas). Parish: Orleans. 8 pages.

Kelly, Thomas Pvt., 1st Louisiana Infantry (Strawbridge's). Cos. E & G. Enlisted: 4/17/1861 at New Orleans, LA. Rolls for 4/17/1861 through 2/28/1865: Present. Federal Rolls of Prisoners of War: Captured at Spanish Fort, AL, on 4/8/1865; Received at Ship Island, MS, on 4/10/1865. Transferred to Vicksburg, MS, for exchange on 5/1/1865; Exchanged at Camp Townsend, MS, on 5/6/1865.

Kemp, Joy (AKA Iby, Jug) Pvt., Edwards' Battalion Cavalry. Co. B. Federal Rolls of Prisoners of War: Captured at Greensburg, LA, on 11/16/1864; Forwarded to New Orleans, LA, on 11/23/1864. Received at Ship Island, MS, on 12/13/1864; Applied to take the U.S. Oath of Allegiance and join the Ohio Light Artillery on 2/7/1865. Transferred to Vicksburg, MS, for exchange on 5/1/1865; Exchanged at Camp Townsend, MS, on 5/6/1865.

Kennerly, J.C. Pvt., Grosse Tête Flying Artillery. Federal Rolls of Prisoners of War: Captured at Atchafalaya, LA, on 10/3/1864; Sent to Morganza, LA, on 10/10/1864. Forwarded to New Orleans, LA, on 10/10/1864; Transferred to Ship Island, MS, on 10/21/1864. Received at Fort Columbus, New York Harbor, NY, on 11/16/1864; Forwarded to Elmira, NY, on 11/20/1864. Paroled at Elmira, NY, on 2/9/1865; Sent to James River, VA, for exchange. Received at Boulware and Cox Wharf, James River, VA, on 2/20–21/1865 and exchanged.

Key, Cornelius N. Pvt., 19th Louisiana Infantry. Co. C. Enlisted: 4/27/1862 at Corinth, MS. Rolls for 4/27/1862 through 2/1863: Present. Rolls for 7/1863 through 10/1863: Absent, sick in hospital at Greenville, AL. Rolls for 11/1863 through 4/1864: Present. Rolls for 5/1864 through 8/1864: Absent, in hospital wounded since 7/28/1864. Rolls for 9/1864 through 2/1865: Present. Federal Rolls of Prisoners of War: Captured at Spanish Fort, AL, on 4/8/1865; Received at Ship Island, MS, on 4/10/1865. Transferred to Vicksburg, MS, for exchange on 5/1/1865; Exchanged at Camp Townsend, MS, on 5/6/1865. Buried: Mount Patrick Cemetery located 3 miles northeast of Shiloh, Union Parish, LA. Confederate Pension Application on file at the Louisiana State Archives. Microfilm Reel: CP1.76. Microdex 4. Sequence 20. Target Card: Key, Cornelius. Parish: Winn. 4 pages.

Killian, John D. (AKA Kilian) Pvt./3rd Lt./2nd Lt., 4th Louisiana Infantry. Co. I. Enlisted: 4/20/1861 at New Orleans, LA. Rolls for 4/20/1861 through 12/1863: Present. Rolls for 3/1864 through 8/1864: Present, promoted to 3rd Lt. on 7/9/1864. Rolls for 8/1864 through 2/1865: Present. Federal Rolls of Prisoners of War: Captured at Spanish Fort, AL, on 4/8/1865; Received at Ship Island, MS, on 4/10/1865. Confined at New Orleans, LA, on 4/30/1865; Transferred to Vicksburg, MS, for exchange on 5/1/1865. Exchanged at camp Townsend, MS, on 5/6/1865. Rolls of Prisoners of War, C.S.A: Surrendered at Citronelle, LA, on 5/4/1865; Paroled at Jackson, MS, on 5/15/1865. Residence at parole: St. Helena Parish, LA. Born: 8/12/1840. Died: 11/5/1898. Buried: Kilian Chapel Cemetery located at the intersection of Hwy. 16 and Hwy. 441 in St. Helena Parish, LA. Confederate Pension Application on file at the Louisiana State

Archives. Microfilm Reel: CP1.77. Microdex 1. Sequence 26. Target Card: Killian, John D. Parish: Tangipahoa. 4 pages. Also a Confederate Widows Pension Application on file. Microfilm Reel: CP1.77. Microdex 1. Sequence 27. Target Card: Killian, Lizzie (Dellehay). Parish: Tangipahoa. 10 pages.

Kinchen, H. Pvt., 2nd Louisiana Cavalry. Co. H. Federal Rolls of Prisoners of War: Captured at Brookline, MS, on 11/18/1864; Received at Ship Island, MS. Transferred to New Orleans, LA, on 12/13/1864.

Kinchen, John W. Pvt., 3rd Louisiana Cavalry (Wingfield's). Co. H. Enlisted: 8/10/1862 at Camp Moore, LA. Rolls for 8/10/1862 through 9/1862: Present or absent not stated. Federal Rolls of Prisoners of War: Captured near Brookhaven, MS, on 11/17/1864; Forwarded to New Orleans, LA, on 11/23/1864. Received at Ship Island, MS, on 12/10/1864; Transferred to Vicksburg, MS, for exchange on 5/1/1865. Exchanged at Camp Townsend, MS, on 5/6/1865. Born: 10/28/1844. Died: 5/6/1930.

Kinchen, N. Pvt., 3rd Louisiana Cavalry (Harrison's). Co. H. Federal Rolls of Prisoners of War: Captured at Brookhaven, MS, on 11/18/1864; Received at Ship Island, MS, from New Orleans, LA, on 12/13/1864.

Kirby, William Pvt., 1st Louisiana Cavalry. Cos. B & D. Enlisted: 9/5/1861 at Baton Rouge, LA. Rolls for 5/1862 through 12/1863: Present. Federal Rolls of Prisoners of War: Captured at Clinton, LA, on 11/16/1864; Forwarded to New Orleans, LA, on 11/23/1864. Received at Ship Island, MS, on 12/13/1864; Transferred to Vicksburg, MS, for exchange on 5/1/1865. Exchanged at Camp Townsend, MS, on 5/6/1865. Buried: St. Joseph Catholic Cemetery located on Main St. at Baton Rouge, East Baton Rouge Parish, LA.

Kittrell, G. (AKA Keptnell) Pvt., 4th Louisiana Battalion Infantry. Co. E. Enlisted: 5/10/1862 at Washington County, GA. Rolls for 8/31/1864 through 2/28/1865: Present. Federal Rolls of Prisoners of War: Captured at Spanish Fort, AL, on 4/8/1865; Received at Ship Island, MS, on 4/10/1865. Transferred to Vicksburg, MS, for exchange on 5/1/1865; Exchanged at Camp Townsend, MS, on 5/6/1865. On Rolls of Federal Headquarters for Exchange of Prisoners, Camp Townsend, MS: Received on 5/6/1865. Rolls of Prisoners of War, C.S.A: Surrendered at Citronelle, AL, on 5/4/1865; Paroled at Meridian, MS, on 5/10/1865. Residence at parole: Washington County, GA.

Kling, Bernard L. Pvt., 28th Louisiana Infantry (Thomas's). Co. E. Enlisted: 5/5/1862 at Camp Moore, LA. Rolls for 5/5/1862 through 2/1863: Present. Federal Rolls of Prisoners of War: Captured and paroled at Vicksburg, MS, on 7/4/1863. Federal Rolls of Prisoners of War: Received at New Orleans, LA, on 10/15/1864; Transferred to Ship Island, MS, on 10/20/1864. Forwarded to Fort Columbus, New York Harbor, NY, on 11/16/1864; Received at Elmira, NY, on 11/20/1864. Paroled at Elmira, NY, on 2/9/1865; Sent to James River, VA, for exchange. Received at Boulware and Cox Wharf, James River, VA, on 2/20–21/1865 and exchanged. Federal Rolls of Prisoners of War: Captured in hospital at Richmond, VA, on 4/3/1865; Escaped from hospital on 4/24/1865. Born: 5/22/1833. Died: 1/4/1904. Buried: Prairieville City Cemetery located off Hwy. 73 on Tiggy Duplesis Rd. at Prairieville, Ascension Parish, LA.

Kling, Cyrille Pvt., 28th Louisiana Infantry (Thomas's). Co. E. Enlisted: 4/3/1862 at Ascension Parish, LA. Rolls for 4/1862 through 2/1863: Present. Federal Rolls of Prisoners of War: Captured and paroled at Vicksburg, MS, on 7/4/1863. Federal Rolls of Prisoners of War: Captured at Hampton's Ferry, LA, on 10/12/1864; Received at New Orleans, LA, on 10/15/1864. Transferred to Ship Island, MS, on 10/20/1864; Forwarded to Fort Columbus, New York Harbor, NY, on 11/19/1864. Sent to Elmira, NY, on 11/20/1864; Paroled at Elmira, NY, on 2/25/1865. Sent to James River, VA, for exchange.

LaBlanc, Dosite Pvt., 4th Louisiana Cavalry. Cos. C & K. Federal Rolls of Prisoners of War: Captured near Plaquemine, LA, on 9/12/1864; Received at New Orleans, LA, on 9/20/1864. Transferred to Ship Island, MS, on 10/5/1864; Received at Fort Columbus, New York Harbor, NY, on 11/16/1864. Forwarded to Elmira, NY, on 11/19/1864; Died: 1/20/1865 at Elmira, NY, due to pneumonia. Buried: Woodlawn National Cemetery, Chemung County, NY.

LaBlanc, E. Pvt., Ogden's Cavalry Battalion. Co. __. Federal Rolls of Prisoners of War: Captured at Liberty, MS, on 11/16/1864; Received at Ship Island, MS, from New Orleans, LA, on 12/13/1864.

LaBlanc, Jackson (AKA LeBlanc) Pvt., Ogden's Cavalry Battalion. Co. F. Federal Rolls of Prisoners of War: Captured at Jackson, LA, on 11/16/1864; Transferred to New Orleans, LA, on 11/23/1864. Received at Ship Island, MS, on 12/13/1864; Transferred to Vicksburg, MS, for exchange on 5/1/1865. Exchanged at Camp Townsend, MS, on 5/6/1865.

Lacock, H. Pvt., 2nd Louisiana Cavalry. Co. I. Federal Rolls of Prisoners of War: Captured at Pointe Coupée Parish, LA, on 9/29/1864; Sent to New Orleans, LA, on 10/4/1864. Transferred to Ship Island, MS; Forwarded to Fort Columbus, New York Harbor, NY, on 11/5/1864. Received at Elmira, NY, on 11/20/1864; Paroled at Elmira, NY, on 2/9/1865. Sent to James River, VA, for exchange; Received at Boulware and Cox Wharf, James River, VA, on 2/20–21/1865 and exchanged.

Lambert, J. Edgar (AKA Ed) 2nd Lt./1st Lt./Capt., 22nd Louisiana Infantry (Consolidated). Cos. A & E. Enlisted: 9/11/1861 at New Orleans, LA. Rolls for 4/1863 through 12/1863: Absent, detached in 1862 by order of Maj. Gen. Martin L. Smith as recruiting officer at Brookhaven, MS; Appointed 2nd Lt. on 5/25/1862 and 1st Lt. on 3/1/1863. Rolls for 1/1864 through 2/1864: Present, transferred to Co. A by election and General Order # 16 consolidating the 22nd and 23rd Louisiana Infantries. Rolls for 3/1864 through 6/1864: Present, commanding company. Rolls for 7/1864 through 8/1864: Absent, detached on 8/17/1864 by Special Order # 120 from Brig. Gen. Edward Higgins. Rolls for 9/1864 through 10/1864: Present, commanding company. Federal Rolls of Prisoners of War: Captured at Spanish Fort, AL, on 4/8/1865; Received at Ship Island, MS, on 4/10/1865. Confined at New Orleans, LA, on 4/28/1865; Transferred to Vicksburg, MS, for exchange on 4/29/1865. Exchanged at Camp Townsend, MS, on 5/6/1865. Rolls of Prisoners of War, C.S.A: Surrendered at Citronelle, AL, on 5/4/1865; Paroled at Jackson, MS, on

5/15/1865. Residence at parole: New Orleans, LA. Confederate Widows Pension Application on file at the Louisiana State Archives. Microfilm Reel: CP1.79. Microdex 4. Sequence 27. Target Card: Lambert, Emma Engervan. Parish: Lafourche. 6 pages.

Lambert, John C. Pvt., 2nd Louisiana Cavalry. Co. __. Federal Rolls of Prisoners of War: Captured at Pointe Coupée Parish, LA, on 9/29/1864; Received at New Orleans, LA, on 10/5/1864. Transferred to Ship Island, MS, on 10/20/1864 by order of Maj. Gen.E.R.S. Canby.

Lane, Kingsbury Cpl., 3rd Louisiana Infantry. Co. G. Federal Rolls of Prisoners of War: Captured near Natchitoches, LA, on 4/11/1864. Name on list dated Office of Agent of Exchange, of Prisoners of War for whom special application for release is to be made. Received at Exchange Office on 8/13/1864; Forwarded to New Orleans, LA, on 10/15/1864. Transferred to Ship Island, MS, on 10/20/1864; Received at the mouth of Red River, LA, for exchange on 10/22/1864. Rolls of Prisoners of War, C.S.A: Surrendered at New Orleans, LA, on 5/26/1865; Paroled at Natchitoches, LA, on 6/7/1865. Residence at parole: Natchitoches, LA.

Lanehart, Jacob E. Pvt., 25th Louisiana Infantry. Co. C. Enlisted: 3/18/1862 at Monterey, LA. Rolls for 3/18/1862 through 2/1863: Present. Rolls for 5/1863 through 6/1863: Absent, on detached service as Teamster by Special Order # 63 from Brig. Gen. Daniel W. Adams. Rolls for 7/1863 through 8/1863: Deserted on 7/29/1863 near Morton, MS. Federal Rolls of Prisoners of War: Captured at Adams County, MS, on 11/2/1864; Received at New Orleans, LA, from Natchez, MS, on 11/21/1864. Transferred to Ship Island, MS, on 12/13/1864. Name on List of Prisoners of War confined at Ship Island, MS, who have applied to take the U.S. Oath of Allegiance on 2/7/1865. Transferred to Vicksburg, MS, for exchange on 5/1/1865; Exchanged at Camp Townsend, MS, on 5/6/1865. Born: 12/24/1832. Died: 3/21/1909. Buried: Hebert Family Cemetery located on Hwy. 1112, approximately 2.1 miles from Hwy. 1111, in Acadia Parish, LA.

Langlett, Charles Pvt., 22nd Louisiana Infantry (Consolidated). Co. G. Enlisted: 3/21/1862 at New Orleans, LA. On Roll dated 4/30/1864: Present, paroled prisoner absent with leave from parole camp. Rolls for 5/1864 through 6/1864: Absent, with leave from parole camp since 1/24/1864. Rolls for 7/1864 through 8/1864: Present. Rolls for 9/1864 through 10/1864: Present, detailed as Orderly to the Col. since 9/1/1864. Federal Rolls of Prisoners of War: Captured at Spanish Fort, AL, on 4/8/1865; Received at Ship Island, MS, on 4/10/1865. Transferred to Vicksburg, MS, for exchange on 5/1/1865; Exchanged at Camp Townsend, MS, on 5/6/1865.

Langlois, J.V. Pvt., 2nd Louisiana Cavalry. Co. I. Enlisted: 9/1/1862 at New Roads, LA. Rolls for 11/1862 through 12/1862: Left sick at Camp Vincent, LA, on 10/25/1862. Rolls for 1/1863 through 2/1863: Left sick at Rosedale, LA, on 2/8/1863. Federal Rolls of Prisoners of War: Captured at Bayou Teche, LA, on 4/14/1863; Sent to New Orleans, LA, for exchange. Federal Rolls of Prisoners of War: Captured at Big Cane, LA, on 3/30/1864; Received at New Orleans, LA, on 4/20/1864. On Register of St. Louis U.S.A. General Hospital, New Orleans, LA: Admitted on 5/11/11864; Transferred to Barracks U.S.A. General Hospital, New Orleans, LA. Sent to Prison on 8/8/1864; Forwarded to Ship Island, MS, on 10/5/1864. Sent to New York on 11/5/1864; Received at Fort Columbus, New York Harbor, NY, on 11/16/1864. Transferred to Elmira, NY, on 11/19/1864; Paroled at Elmira, NY, on 2/9/1865. Sent to James River, VA, for exchange; Received at Boulware and Cox Wharf, James River, VA, on 2/20–21/1865 and exchanged.

Lanie, A.R. (AKA Lowne, A.R.) Capt., 5th Louisiana Cavalry. Co. G. Federal Rolls of Prisoners of War: Captured at Indigo Bayou, LA, on 12/8/1864; Received at Ship Island, MS, from New Orleans, LA, on 12/15/1864. Sent from Ship Island, MS, to New Orleans, LA, on 3/27/1865; Transferred to mouth of Red River, LA, for exchange on 4/7/1865. Exchanged on 5/13/1865. Remarks: Delivered on parole, but equivalents promised next exchange.

Lanie, C.A. Lt., 5th Louisiana Cavalry. Co. G. Federal Rolls of Prisoners of War: Captured at Indigo Bayou, LA, on 12/8/1864; Received at Ship Island, MS, from New Orleans, LA, on 12/15/1864. Forwarded from Ship Island, MS, to New Orleans, LA, on 3/27/1865; Transferred to mouth of Red River, LA, for exchange on 4/7/1865. Exchanged on 5/13/1865. Remarks: Delivered on parole, but equivalent promised next exchange.

Lanier, R.J. Pvt., 4th Louisiana Battalion Infantry. Co. E. Enlisted: 8/15/1861 at Natchez, MS. Rolls for 8/15/1861 through 6/1862: Present. Rolls for 11/1862 through 12/1862: Absent, sick in camp at Savannah, GA. Rolls for 1/1863 through 2/1863: Present. Rolls for 1/1864 through 2/1864: Absent, sick in hospital since 9/5/1863. Rolls for 8/31/1864 through 2/28/1865: Absent, assumed to be a Prisoner of War. Rolls for 3/1865 through 4/1865: Absent, Prisoner of War since 7/1/1864. Federal Rolls of Prisoners of War: Captured near Rodney, MS, on 7/19/1864; Confined in the U.S. Military Prison, Natchez, MS, on 8/6/1864. Received at New Orleans, LA, on 9/10/1864; Transferred to Ship Island, MS, on 10/5/1864. Forwarded to Fort Columbus, New York Harbor, NY, on 11/16/1864; Sent to Elmira, NY, on 11/19/1864. Paroled at Elmira, NY, on 2/9/1865; Sent to James River, VA, for Exchange. Received at Boulware and Cox Wharf, James River, VA, on 2/20–21/1865 and exchanged.

LaSalle, Bertrand (AKA Lassale) Pvt., Ogden's Cavalry Battalion. Co. A. Federal Rolls of Prisoners of War: Captured at East Baton Rouge Parish, LA, on 9/15/1864; Sent to New Orleans, LA, from Baton Rouge, LA, on 9/19/1864. Received at Ship Island, MS, on 10/28/1864; Transferred to Fort Columbus, New York Harbor, NY, on 11/16/1864. Forwarded to Elmira, NY, on 11/20/1864; Paroled at Elmira, NY, on 2/25/1865 and sent to James River, VA, for exchange.

Lashly, William Pvt., Miles Legion. Co. A. Federal Rolls of Prisoners of War: Captured at New River, LA, on 12/17/1864; Forwarded New Orleans, LA, on 12/24/1864. Received at Ship Island, MS, on 1/22/1865; Transferred to Vicksburg, MS, for exchange on 5/1/1865. Exchanged at Camp Townsend, MS, on 5/6/1865.

Laterriere, Charles (AKA Latternine) Pvt., 30th Louisiana Infantry. Co. F. Enlisted: 3/11/1862 at New Orleans, LA. Rolls for 3/11/1862 through 8/1862: Absent, sick. Rolls for 9/1862 through 6/1863: Present.

Rolls for 7/1863 through 8/1863: Absent, sick. Rolls for 9/1863 through 10/1863: Absent, sick at Mobile, AL. Rolls for 3/1864 through 2/1865: Present. Federal Rolls of Prisoners of War: Captured at Spanish Fort, AL, on 4/8/1865; Received at Ship Island, MS, on 4/10/1865. Transferred to Vicksburg, MS, for exchange on 5/1/1865; Exchanged at Camp Townsend, MS, on 5/6/1865. Confederate Widows Pension Application on file at the Louisiana State Archives. Microfilm Reel: CP1.81. Microdex 4. Sequence 26. Target Card: Laterriere, Mrs. Cora (North). Parish: Orleans. 4 pages.

Laurent, A. Pvt./1st Cpl./5th Sgt./4th Sgt., 4th Louisiana Infantry. Co. B. Enlisted: 2/9/1863 at Port Hudson, LA. Rolls for 2/9/1863 through 4/1863: Present. Rolls for 5/1863 through 6/1863: Absent, sick in hospital at Jackson, MS. Rolls for 7/1863 through 8/1863: Absent, sick in hospital at Lauderdale Springs, MS. Rolls for 9/1863 through 10/1863: Present, appointed 1st Cpl. on 10/1/1863. Rolls for 11/1863 through 8/1864: Absent, sick at Lauderdale Springs, MS; Promoted to 5th Sgt. on 11/1/1863 and 4th Sgt. on 7/1/1864. Federal Rolls of Prisoners of War: Captured near West Baton Rouge Parish, LA, on 10/3/1864; Forwarded from Morganza, LA, to the U.S. Commissary of Prisoners on 10/7/1864. Received at Ship Island, MS, from New Orleans, LA, on 10/20/1864; Sent to Fort Columbus, New York Harbor, NY, on 11/16/1864. Transferred to Elmira, NY, on 11/19/1864; Paroled at Elmira, NY, on 2/25/1865 and sent to James River, VA, for exchange.

Lavergne, Seymour L. (AKA Seymore) Pvt., 4th Louisiana Infantry. Co. D. Enlisted: 5/25/1861 at Tangipahoa, LA. Rolls for 5/25/1861 through 2/1862: Present. Rolls for 9/1862 through 12/1862: Absent, sick. Rolls for 1/1863 through 8/1864: Present. Rolls for 9/1864 through 2/1865: Absent without leave. Federal Rolls of Prisoners of War: Captured near Spanish Fort, AL, on 4/8/1865; Received at Ship Island, MS, on 4/10/1865. Transferred to Vicksburg, MS, for exchange on 5/1/1865; Exchanged at Camp Townsend, MS, on 5/6/1865. Born: 1841. Died: 1924. Buried: Grace Episcopal Church Cemetery located on Hwy. 10 at St. Francisville, West Feliciana Parish, LA. Confederate Pension Application on file at the Louisiana State Archives. Microfilm Reel: CP1.82. Microdex 1. Sequence 26. Target Name: Lavergne, Seymore L. Parish: West Feliciana. 6 pages.

Lawrence, Joseph F. (AKA Laurence) Pvt., Consolidated Crescent Regiment. Co. H. Enlisted: 7/1/1862 at Pointe Coupée Parish, LA. Rolls for 1/1864 through 2/1864: Present. Federal Rolls of Prisoners of War: Captured at Fort DeRussy, LA, on 3/14/1864; Received at Baton Rouge, LA, on 3/17/1864. Forwarded to New Orleans, LA, on 3/20/1864; Received at Ship Island, MS, on 10/5/1864. Transferred to Fort Columbus, New York Harbor, NY, on 11/16/1864; Sent to Elmira, NY, on 11/19/1864. Paroled at Elmira, NY, on 2/25/1865; Sent to James River, VA, for exchange. Soldier also served as a Pvt. with the 12th Louisiana Battalion Infantry. Co.A. Confederate Pension Application on file at the Louisiana State Archives. Microfilm Reel: CP1.82. Microdex 2. Sequence 14. Target Card: Lawrence, Joseph. Parish: Rapides. 4 pages.

Leach, M. (AKA Leaehy, W. Leech) Sgt., Ogden's Cavalry Battalion. Co. B. Federal Rolls of Prisoners of War: Captured at Ascension Parish, LA, on 6/24/1864. On Register of St. Louis U.S.A. General Hospital, New Orleans, LA: Admitted on 8/27/1864; Discharged on 9/5/1864. Sent to Ship Island, MS, on 10/7/1864; Transferred to Fort Columbus, New York Harbor, NY, on 11/16/1864. Forwarded to Elmira, NY, on 11/19/1864; Released on the U.S. Oath of Allegiance on 6/14/1865. Description at oath: Eyes: blue. Hair: auburn. Complexion: florid. Height: 5'5". Residence at oath: New Orleans, LA.

LeBlance, E. Pvt., Ogden's Cavalry Battalion. Co. A. Federal Rolls of Prisoners of War: Captured at Liberty, MS, on 11/16/1864; Forwarded to New Orleans, LA, on 11/23/1864. Received at Ship Island, MS, on 12/10/1864; Transferred to Vicksburg, MS, for exchange on 5/1/1865. Exchanged at Camp Townsend, MS, on 5/6/1865.

LeClercq, A. Pvt., 4th Louisiana Infantry. Co. F. Enlisted: 4/27/1862 at Port Hudson, LA. Rolls for 5/1862 through 12/1863: Present. Rolls for 5/1864 through 8/1864: Absent, wounded at the Battle of the Poor House, GA, on 7/28/1864. Rolls for 9/1864 through 2/1865: Present. Federal Rolls of Prisoners of War: Captured at Spanish Fort, AL, on 4/5/1865; Received at Ship Island, MS, on 4/10/1865. Transferred to Vicksburg, MS, for exchange on 5/1/1865; Exchanged at Camp Townsend, MS, on 5/6/1865.

Lee, E.G. Pvt., 7th Louisiana Cavalry. Co. G. Federal Rolls of Prisoners of War: Captured near Natchez, MS, on 11/17/1864; Forwarded to New Orleans, LA, on 11/21/1864. Received at Ship Island, MS on 12/13/1864; Transferred to Vicksburg, MS, for exchange on 5/1/1865. Exchanged at Camp Townsend, MS, on 5/6/1865.

Lee, J.W. Pvt., 1st Louisiana Cavalry. Co. E. Enlisted: 5/5/1862 at Alabama. Rolls for 5/5/1862 through 12/1862: Present. Rolls for 1/1863 through 2/1863: In Louisiana on furlough from 1/22/1863 through 2/22/1863. Rolls for 3/1863 through 12/1863: Present. Federal Rolls of Prisoners of War: Captured at Clinton, LA, on 10/6/1864; Sent to Baton Rouge, LA, on 10/10/1864. Received at New Orleans, LA, on 10/15/1864; Transferred to Ship Island, MS, on 10/20/1864. Forwarded to Fort Columbus, New York Harbor, NY, on 11/16/1864; Sent to Elmira, NY, on 11/19/1864. Rolls of Prisoners of War, C.S.A: Surrendered at Citronelle, AL, on 5/4/1865; Paroled at Gainesville, AL, on 5/12/1865. Residence at parole: West Feliciana Parish, LA.

Lee, Lawrence Pvt., Groves' Artillery Battery. Federal Rolls of Prisoners of War: Captured at Grand River, LA, on 1/11/1865; Received at New Orleans, LA, on 1/20/1865. Forwarded to Ship Island, MS, on 1/25/1865; Returned to New Orleans, LA, on 4/1/1865. Exchanged on 4/9/1865.

Leicank, Joseph (AKA Leisence) Pvt., 30th Louisiana Infantry. Co. B. Enlisted: 10/10/1862 at Port Hudson, LA. Rolls for 9/1862 through 10/1862: Present, returned prisoner temporarily attached. Rolls for 11/1862 through 12/1862: Present. Rolls for 5/1863 through 10/1863: Absent, detached as Hospital Nurse at Jackson, MS, on 5/25/1863. Rolls for 3/1864 through 4/1864: Present. Rolls for 11/1864 through 2/1865: Absent, left sick at Port Hudson, LA, on 5/6/1863. Federal Rolls of Prisoners of War: Captured at Fort Gaines, AL, on 8/8/1864; Received at Ship Island, MS, from New Orleans, LA, on 10/25/1864. Name on List of Prisoners of War at Ship Island, MS, who refused exchange and applied to take the U.S. Oath of Allegiance on 4/16/1865.

Lejeune, Theodule Pvt., 30th Louisiana Infantry. Co. A. Enlisted: 3/11/1863 at New Orleans, LA. Rolls for 5/1863 through 6/1863: Absent, in hospital at Clinton, LA. Rolls for 7/1863 through 2/1865: Present. Federal Rolls of Prisoners of War: Captured at Spanish Fort, AL, on 4/8/1865; Received at Ship Island, MS, on 4/10/1865. Transferred to Vicksburg, MS, for exchange on 5/1/1865; Exchanged at Camp Townsend, MS, on 5/6/1865. Born: 11/1825. Died: 10/25/1912. Buried: Chenal Cemetery, Rougon, Pointe Coupée Parish, LA. Confederate Pension Application on file at the Louisiana State Archives. Microfilm Reel: CP1.84. Microdex 3. Sequence 22. Target Card: Lejeune, Theodule. Parish: Pointe Coupée. 7 pages. Also a Confederate Widows Pension Application on file. Microfilm Reel: CP1.84. Microdex 3. Sequence 18. Target Card: Lejeune, Julia (Bizett). Parish: West Baton Rouge. 3 pages.

Lemoine, Cesaire (AKA Caesar) Pvt./3rd Cpl., 1st Louisiana Cavalry. Co. G. Enlisted: 10/4/1861 at Baton Rouge, LA. Rolls for 5/1862 through 2/1863: Present. Rolls for 3/1863 through 6/1863: Present, elected 3rd Cpl. on 3/1/1863. Rolls for 11/1863 through 2/1864: Present. Federal Rolls of Prisoners of War: Captured at Moody's Ferry, LA, on 12/5/1864; Forwarded to New Orleans, LA, on 12/19/1864. Received at Ship Island, MS, on 1/25/1865; Transferred to Vicksburg, MS, for exchange on 5/1/1865. Exchanged at Camp Townsend, MS, on 5/6/1865. Buried: St. Mary's Assumption Catholic Church Cemetery on Main St. at Cottonport, Avoyelles Parish, LA.

Lemp, John Pvt., Ogden's Cavalry Battalion. Co. __. Federal Rolls of Prisoners of War: Captured at East Baton Rouge Parish, LA, on 1/4/1865; Forwarded New Orleans, LA, on 1/12/1865. Received at Ship Island, MS, on 1/25/1865; Transferred to Vicksburg, MS, for exchange on 5/1/1865. Exchanged at Camp Townsend, MS, on 5/6/1865.

Leopold, Wiliam Pvt., 22nd Louisiana Infantry (Consolidated). Co. A. Enlisted: 12/5/1861 at Camp Lewis, LA. Rolls for 12/5/1861 through 12/1862: Present. Federal Rolls of Prisoners of War: Captured and paroled at Vicksburg, MS, on 7/4/1863. On List dated Parole Camp, Enterprise, MS, 10/13/1863: Present. On List not dated: Furnished from 22nd Louisiana Infantry to Heavy Artillery Brigade Headquarters for exchange on 10/19/1863. Rolls for 1/1864 through 6/1864: Present. Rolls for 7/1864 through 8/1864: Absent, sick in hospital. Rolls for 9/1864 through 10/1864: Present. Federal Rolls of Prisoners of War: Captured at Spanish Fort, AL, on 4/8/1865; Received at Ship Island, MS, on 4/10/1865. Transferred to Vicksburg, MS, for exchange on 5/1/1865; Exchanged at Camp Townsend, MS, on 5/6/1865.

Letain, Edward (AKA Lebain) Pvt., 4th Louisiana Cavalry. Co. __. Federal Rolls of Prisoners of War: Captured at Ascension Parish, LA, on 12/13/1864; Forwarded to New Orleans, LA, on 12/14/1864. Received at Ship Island, MS, from New Orleans, LA, on 1/25/1865; Transferred to New Orleans, LA, from Ship Island, MS, on 3/27/1865. Forwarded to the mouth of Red River, LA, for exchange on 4/7/1865; Exchanged on 4/9/1865.

Lewis, Daniel (AKA Leri) Lt., 5th Louisiana Cavalry. Co. A. Federal Rolls of Prisoners of War: Captured at Pointe Coupée Parish, LA, on 11/20/1864. Sent from Morganza, LA, to New Orleans, LA, on 11/22/1864. Received at Ship Island, MS, on 12/15/1864. Transferred from Ship Island, MS, to New Orleans, LA, on 3/27/1865. Forwarded to mouth of the Red River for exchange on 5/2/1865 by order of Maj. Gen.E.R.S. Canby. Rolls of Prisoners of War, C.S.A: Captured at New Orleans, LA, on 5/26/1865; Paroled at the Provost Marshal's Office, Baton Rouge, LA, on 6/19/1865.

Lewis, Henry H. (AKA H.C.) Pvt., 16th Louisiana Infantry. Cos. F & H. Enlisted: 9/29/1861 at Camp Moore, LA. Rolls through 10/1861: Absent, on sick furlough. Rolls for 11/1861 through 6/1862: Present. Rolls for 7/1862 through 10/1862: Absent, on sick furlough. Rolls for 1/1863 through 2/1863: Absent, without leave since 10/1/1862. Rolls for 5/1863 through 6/1863: Present. Rolls for 7/1863 through 10/1863: Deserted on 7/25/1863 from Jackson, MS. Federal Rolls of Prisoners of War: Captured at Livingston Parish, LA, on 12/27/1864; Forwarded to New Orleans, LA, from Baton Rouge, LA, on 1/12/1865. Received at Ship Island, MS, on 1/25/1865; Transferred to Vicksburg, MS, for exchange on 5/1/1865. Exchanged at Camp Townsend, MS, on 5/6/1865. Confederate Widows Pension Application on file at the Louisiana State Archives. Microfilm Reel: CP1.85. Microdex 4. Sequence 17. Target Card: Lewis, Frances Jane (Harvard). Parish: Livingston. 11 pages.

Lewis, T. Pvt., Louisiana Infantry (Grant's). Co. __. Federal Rolls of Prisoners of War: Captured near Brookhaven, MS, on 11/17/1864; Forwarded to New Orleans, LA, on 11/23/1864. Received at Ship Island, MS, on 12/10/1864; Transferred to Vicksburg, MS, for exchange on 5/1/1865. Exchanged at Camp Townsend, MS, on 5/6/1865.

Lilly, A.K. (AKA Libbey, A.R.) Pvt., 3rd Louisiana Cavalry (Harrison's). Co. H. Federal Rolls of Prisoners of War: Captured at Adams County, MS, on 11/2/1864; Forwarded to New Orleans, LA, on 11/21/1864. Received at Ship Island, MS, on 12/10/1864. Died: 2/25/1865 at Ship Island, MS, due to hepatitis. Buried: Ship Island, MS, Cemetery in Grave #136.

Links, R. (AKA Richard Loucks) Pvt., Ogden's Cavalry Battalion. Co. __. Federal Rolls of Prisoners of War: Captured near Mobile, AL, on 12/22/1864; Received at Ship Island, MS. Transferred to Vicksburg, MS, for exchange on 5/1/1865; Exchanged at Camp Townsend, MS, on 5/6/1865.

Lisbony, Auguste R. Pvt., 30th Louisiana Infantry. Co. F. Enlisted: 7/21/1863 at Greenville, AL. Rolls for 3/1864 through 4/1864: Present. On Register of 1st Mississippi C.S.A. Hospital: Admitted on 12/1/1864. Rolls for 1/1865 through 2/1865: Present. Federal Rolls of Prisoners of War: Captured at Spanish Fort, AL, on 4/8/1865; Received at Ship Island, MS, on 4/10/1865. Transferred to Vicksburg, MS, for exchange on 5/1/1865; Exchanged at Camp Townsend, MS, on 5/6/1865. Buried: St. John's Cathedral Cemetery located on West University Ave. at Lafayette, Lafayette Parish, LA. Confederate Widows Pension

Application on file at the Louisiana State Archives. Microfilm Reel: CP1.86. Microdex 2. Sequence 32. Target Card: Lisbony, Anna Marie (Stentwhite). Parish: Saint Landry. 14 pages.

Lobell, L. Pvt., Cage's Cavalry Battalion. Co. __. Federal Rolls of Prisoners of War: Captured at Clinton, LA, on 11/17/1864; Received at Ship Island, MS, from New Orleans, LA, on 12/13/1864.

Lobell, S. Pvt., Ogden's Cavalry Battalion. Co. F. Federal Rolls of Prisoners of War: Captured at Clinton, LA, on 11/17/1864; Forwarded to New Orleans, LA, on 11/23/1864. Received at Ship Island, MS, on 12/13/1864; Transferred to Vicksburg, MS, for exchange on 5/1/1865. Exchanged at Camp Townsend, MS, on 5/6/1865.

Loflin, James (AKA Lofland) Pvt., 25th Louisiana Infantry. Co. K. Enlisted: 3/20/1862 at Providence, LA. Rolls for 7/1862 through 12/1862: Absent, sick since 5/28/1862. Rolls for 1/1863 through 2/1863: Discharged on 11/19/1862. Federal Rolls of Prisoners of War: Captured at Spanish Fort, AL, on 4/8/1865; Received at Ship Island, MS, on 4/10/1865. Transferred to Vicksburg, MS, for exchange on 5/1/1865; Exchanged at Camp Townsend, MS, on 5/6/1865.

Lombard, Edward Homer Ord. Sgt./2nd Lt./1st Lt., Pointe Coupée Artillery. Co. A. Enlisted: 6/29/1861 at New Orleans, LA. Rolls for 7/1861 through 12/1861: Present. Rolls for 3/1864 through 8/1864: Present. Federal Rolls of Prisoners of War: Captured at Liberty, MS, on 11/17/1864; Transferred from New Orleans, LA, to Ship Island, MS, on 12/15/1864. Exchanged on 3/2/1865. Rolls of Prisoners of War, C.S.A: Surrendered at Citronelle, AL, on 5/4/1865; Paroled at Meridian, MS, on 5/10/1865. Born: 1841. Died: 5/5/1903. Buried: Metairie Cemetery located on Pontchartrain Blvd. at New Orleans, Orleans Parish, LA. Confederate Widows Pension Application on file at the Louisiana State Archives. Microfilm Reel: CP1.86. Microdex 4. Sequence 39. Target Card: Lombard, Laura Virginia (Levy). Parish: Orleans. 2 pages.

Lorio, Leonce Pvt., 30th Louisiana Infantry. Co. G. Enlisted: 4/10/1862 at New Orleans, LA. Rolls for 11/1862 through 4/1864: Present. Roll for 11/1864 through 2/1865: Absent, sick in hospital at Montgomery, AL, since 11/1/1864. Federal Rolls of Prisoners of War: Captured at Spanish Fort, AL, on 4/8/1865; Received at Ship Island, MS, on 4/10/1865. Transferred to Vicksburg, MS, for exchange on 5/1/1865; Exchanged at Camp Townsend, MS, on 5/6/1865. Confederate Widows Pension Application on file at the Louisiana State Archives. Microfilm Reel: CP1.87. Microdex 1. Sequence 27. Target Card: Lorio, Mary Blushera (Hotard). Parish: Orleans. 5 pages.

Lott, F.M. Pvt., 25th Louisiana Infantry. Co. D. Enlisted: 3/6/1862 at Morehouse Parish, LA. Rolls for 3/6/1862 through 2/1865: Present. Rolls for 3/1865 through 4/1865: Absent, taken Prisoner of War. Federal Rolls of Prisoners of War: Captured at Spanish Fort, AL, on 4/8/1865; Received at Ship Island, MS, on 4/10/1865. Transferred to Vicksburg, MS, for exchange on 5/1/1865; Exchanged at Camp Townsend, MS, on 5/6/1865

Lovett, John B. Pvt., Holmes' Light Artillery Battery. Federal Rolls of Prisoners of War: Captured at Brookhaven, MS, on 11/18/1864; Forwarded to New Orleans, LA, on 11/23/1864. Received at Ship Island, MS, on 12/10/1864; Transferred to Vicksburg, MS, for exchange on 5/1/1865. Exchanged at Camp Townsend, MS, on 5/6/1865.

Lugenbuhl, Peter Pvt., Crescent Artillery. Co. A. Federal Rolls of Prisoners of War: Captured at Fort DeRussy, LA, on 3/14/1864; Received at Baton Rouge, LA, on 3/17/1864. Sent to New Orleans, LA, on 3/20/1864. Name on List dated Office of Commissary of Prisoners, Dept. of the Gulf, New Orleans, LA, 7/7/1864. Transferred to Ship Island, MS, on 10/5/1864; Forwarded to Fort Columbus, New York Harbor, NY, on 11/16/1864. Sent to Elmira, NY, on 11/19/1864. Name on List of Prisoners of War who desire to take the U.S. Oath of Allegiance at Elmira, NY, on 11/30/1864; Remarks: Was conscripted on 3/14/1863. His mother and other relatives live at New Orleans, LA, where he desires to go. Took the U.S. Oath of Allegiance at Elmira, NY, on 5/17/1865. Description at oath: Eyes: blue. Hair: light. Complexion: dark. Height: 5'10". Residence at oath: New Orleans, LA.

Lyden, P.O. Pvt., 7th Louisiana Cavalry. Co. G. Federal Rolls of Prisoners of War: Captured near Natchez, MS, on 11/15/1864; Forwarded to New Orleans, LA, on 11/21/1864. Received at Ship Island, MS, on 12/30/1864; Transferred to Vicksburg, MS, for exchange on 5/1/1865. Exchanged at Camp Townsend, MS, on 5/6/1865.

Lynch, S.P. (AKA Linch, Synch, S.S.) Pvt., 1st Louisiana Cavalry. Co. G. Enlisted: 12/4/1863 at Dalton, GA. Rolls for 12/4/1863 through 2/1864: Present. Federal Rolls of Prisoners of War: Captured at Clinton, LA, on 10/6/1864; Sent to Baton Rouge, LA, on 10/10/1864. Forwarded to New Orleans, LA, on 10/15/1864; Received at Ship Island, MS, on 10/20/1864. Died: 3/29/1865 at Ship Island, MS, due to chronic dysentery. Buried: Ship Island, MS, Cemetery in Grave #144.

Lyrio, Leonce Pvt., 30th Louisiana Infantry. Co. G. Enlisted: 2/23/1862 at New Orleans, LA. Rolls for 11/1862 through 4/1864: Present. Rolls for 11/1864 through 2/1865: Absent, sick in hospital at Montgomery, AL, since 11/1/1864. Federal Rolls of Prisoners of War: Captured at Spanish Fort, AL, on 4/8/1865; Received at Ship Island, MS, on 4/10/1865. Transferred to Vicksburg, MS, for exchange on 5/1/1865; Exchanged at Camp Townsend, MS, on 5/6/1865.

McCant, G.C. (AKA McCoats) Pvt., 3rd Louisiana Cavalry. Co. I. Federal Rolls of Prisoners of War: Captured at East Baton Rouge Parish, LA, on 9/20/1864; Sent to New Orleans, LA, on 10/10/1864. Received at Ship Island, MS, on 10/21/1864; Transferred to Fort Columbus, New York Harbor, NY, on 11/5/1864. Forwarded to Elmira, NY, on 11/20/1864; Paroled at Elmira, NY, for exchange on 3/2/1865. Exchanged at James River, VA.

McChein, R. (AKA McChin) Pvt., 2nd Louisiana Cavalry. Co. I. Federal Rolls of Prisoners of War: Captured at Pointe Coupée Parish, LA, on 9/29/1864; Forwarded to New Orleans, LA, on 10/5/1864. Received at Ship Island, MS, on 10/21/1864; Forwarded to Fort Columbus, New York Harbor, NY, on 11/16/1864. Sent to Elmira, NY, on 11/20/1864; Paroled at Elmira, NY, for exchange on 2/25/1865. Exchanged at James River, VA.

McCormick, B.B. Pvt., 19th Louisiana Infantry. Co. E. Enlisted: 9/6/1862 at Pollard, AL. Rolls for 9/6/1862 through 12/1862: Present. Rolls for 1/1863 through 2/1863: Absent, in hospital at Greenville, AL. Rolls for 7/1863 through 10/1863: Present. Rolls for 11/1863 through 12/1863: Absent, wounded at Missionary Ridge, TN, on 11/25/1863. Rolls for 1/1864 through 2/1865: Present. Rolls for 3/1865 through 4/1865: Absent, taken Prisoner of War. Federal Rolls of Prisoners of War: Captured at Spanish Fort, AL, on 4/8/1865; Received at Ship Island, MS, on 4/10/1865. Transferred to Vicksburg, MS, for exchange on 5/1/1865; Exchanged at Camp Townsend, MS, on 5/6/1865. Rolls of Prisoners of War, C.S.A: Surrendered at Citronelle, AL, on 5/4/1865; Paroled at Meridian, MS, on 5/10/1865. Residence at parole: Bossier Parish, LA. Soldier also served as a Pvt. with the Pelican Infantry Regiment (Louisiana). Co.A.

McCrory, Robert P. Pvt., 9th Louisiana Battalion Infantry. Co. B. Enlisted: 5/15/1862 at Camp Moore, LA. Rolls for 9/1862 through 10/1862: Present. Federal Rolls of Prisoners of War: Captured at Ascension Parish, LA, on 6/24/1864; Forwarded to New Orleans, LA, for exchange on 7/10/1864. Exchanged on 8/22/1864 on Plank Road, near Redwood Creek, LA, between Baton Rouge, LA, and Clinton, LA. Federal Rolls of Prisoners of War: Captured at Bayou Manchac, LA, on 1/14/1865; Received at Ship Island, MS, on 1/25/1865. Transferred to Vicksburg, MS, for exchange on 5/1/1865; Exchanged at Camp Townsend, MS, on 5/6/1865.

McDonald, J.B. Pvt., 18th Louisiana Battalion Cavalry. Co. E. Federal Rolls of Prisoners of War: Captured at Liberty, MS, on 11/23/1864; Received at Ship Island, MS, from New Orleans, LA, on 12/13/1864. Transferred to Vicksburg, MS, for exchange on 5/1/1865; Exchanged at Camp Townsend, MS, on 5/6/1865.

McDonald, J.H. Pvt., 1st Louisiana Battalion Cavalry (State Guard). Co. D. Federal Rolls of Prisoners of War: Captured at Daniels Ferry, LA, on 11/24/1864; Forwarded to New Orleans, LA, from Natchez, MS, on 12/10/1864. Received at Ship Island, MS, on 12/10/1864; Returned to New Orleans, LA, on 4/1/1865. Exchanged at the mouth of Red River, LA, on 4/9/1865.

McGowan, James Sgt., 13th Louisiana Infantry. Co. K. Federal Rolls of Prisoners of War: Captured at Spanish Fort, AL, on 4/8/1865; Received at Ship Island, MS, on 4/10/1865. Transferred to Vicksburg, MS, for exchange on 5/1/1865; Exchanged at Camp Townsend, MS, on 5/6/1865.

McGowans, I. (AKA James McGowen) Pvt., 18th Louisiana Infantry. Co. __. Federal Rolls of Prisoners of War: Captured at Spanish Fort, AL, on 4/8/1865; Received at Ship Island, MS, on 4/10/1865. Transferred to Vicksburg, MS, for exchange on 5/1/1865; Exchanged at Camp Townsend, MS, on 5/6/1865. Soldier also served as a Pvt. with the 18th Louisiana Infantry and Yellow Jacket Louisiana Battalion Infantry (Consolidated).

McHatton, Robert E. Pvt., Pointe Coupeé Artillery. Co. B. Enlisted: 8/8/1861 at Baton Rouge, LA. Rolls for 8/8/1861 through 12/1861: Present. Federal Rolls of Prisoners of War: Captured at Vicksburg, MS, on 7/4/1863; Paroled on 7/16/1863. Federal Rolls of Prisoners of War: Captured at Osyka, MS, on 10/7/1864; Forwarded to New Orleans, LA, on 10/14/1864. Received at Ship Island, MS, on 10/21/1864; Transferred to Fort Columbus, New York Harbor, NY, on 11/16/1864. Sent to Elmira, NY, on 11/19/1864; Paroled at Elmira, NY, on 2/9/1865. Forwarded to Point Lookout, MD, for exchange on 2/13/1865; Exchanged at James River, VA, on 2/20–21/1865. Rolls of Prisoners of War, C.S.A: Surrendered at New Orleans, LA, on 5/26/1865; Paroled at Jackson, MS, on 5/19/1865. Residence at parole: St. Helena Parish, LA.

McHethey, R. Pvt., Gober's Mounted Infantry Regiment. Co. E. Federal Rolls of Prisoners of War: Captured at Clinton, LA, on 10/6/1864; Sent to Baton Rouge, LA, on 10/10/1864. Received at New Orleans, LA, on 10/14/1864; Transferred to Ship Island, MS, on 10/20/1864. Forwarded to Fort Columbus, New York Harbor, NY, on 11/16/1864; Received at Elmira, NY, on 11/20/1864. Paroled at Elmira, NY, on 2/25/1865; Transferred to James River, VA, for exchange in 1865.

McLane, W. (AKA McLean) Pvt., 10th Louisiana Battalion Infantry. Co. __. Federal Rolls of Prisoners of War: Captured near Port Hudson, LA, on 5/15/1864; Forwarded to Ship Island, MS, from New Orleans, LA, on 10/28/1864. Sent to Fort Columbus, New York Harbor, NY, on 11/16/1864; Forwarded to Elmira, NY, on 11/20/1864. Paroled at Elmira, NY, for exchange on 2/9/1865; Exchanged at Boulware and Cox Wharf, James River, VA, on 2/20–21/1865.

McLane, William Capt., 30th Louisiana Infantry. Co. __. (No War Dept. Record.) Sentenced to imprisonment at Ship Island, MS, by Maj. Gen. Benjamin F. Butler for violation of parole; Received at Ship Island, MS, on 9/4/1862. Released by order of Maj. Gen. Nathaniel P. Banks on 9/4/1863.

McLean, J.M. Pvt., 10th Louisiana Battalion Cavalry. Co. __. Federal Rolls of Prisoners of War: Captured in 1864; Transferred to Ship Island, MS, from New Orleans, LA, on 10/28/1864.

McLinn, H. (AKA McLynn) Pvt., 5th Louisiana Cavalry. Co. __. Federal Rolls of Prisoners of War: Captured at Brookhaven, MS, on 11/17/1864; Received at Ship Island, MS, from New Orleans, LA, on 12/13/1864. Transferred to Vicksburg, MS, on 5/1/1865; Exchanged at Camp Townsend, MS, on 5/6/1865.

McLinn, H. Pvt., 10th Louisiana Battalion Cavalry. Co. I. Federal Rolls of Prisoners of War: Captured at Liberty, MS, on 11/17/1864; Received at Ship Island, MS, from New Orleans, LA, on 12/13/1864. Transferred to Vicksburg, MS, for exchange on 5/1/1865; Exchanged at Camp Townsend, MS, on 5/6/1865.

McNeely, M.A. Pvt., 3rd Louisiana Cavalry. Co. D. Federal Rolls of Prisoners of War: Captured at Adams County, MS, on 11/2/1864; Forwarded to New Orleans, LA, from Natchez, MS, on 11/21/1864. Received at Ship Island, MS, on 12/13/1864; Transferred to Vicksburg, MS, for exchange on 5/1/1865. Exchanged at Camp Townsend, MS, on 5/6/1865.

McToohey, M. Sgt., Crescent Infantry Regiment. Co. I. Enlisted: 3/8/1862 at New Orleans, LA. Rolls for 5/1862 through 6/1862: Absent, detailed as a Guard at Gen. P.G.T. Beauregard's Headquarters. Rolls for 12/1862 through 2/1863: Absent, detailed as Clerk to the commander of Gen. Braxton Bragg's Wagon

Train. Rolls for 5/1863 through 6/1863: Dropped from the Rolls by order of Col.A.W. Bosworth. Federal Rolls of Prisoners of War: Captured at Clinton, LA, on 11/16/1864; Received at Ship Island, MS, on 12/10/1864. Transferred to Vicksburg, MS, for exchange on 5/1/1865; Exchanged at Camp Townsend, MS, on 5/6/1865.

McVay, F.S. Pvt., 3rd Louisiana Cavalry. Co. __. Federal Rolls of Prisoners of War: Captured at Clinton, LA, on 8/25/1864; Received at Ship Island, MS, from New Orleans, LA, on 10/7/1864. Transferred to Fort Columbus, New York Harbor, NY, on 11/5/1864.

McVea, Thomas Scott (AKA McVeel) Pvt., 3rd Louisiana Cavalry. Co. I. Federal Rolls of Prisoners of War: Captured at Clinton, LA, on 8/25/1864; Forwarded to New Orleans, LA, on 8/31/1864. Received at Ship Island, MS, from hospital on 10/7/1864; Sent to Fort Columbus, New York Harbor, NY; on 11/5/1864. Transferred to Elmira, NY, on 11/19/1864; Paroled at Elmira, NY, for exchange on 2/9/1865. Exchanged at Boulware and Cox Wharf, James River, VA, on 2/20/1865. Born: 11/28/1845. Died: 11/7/1885. Buried: Young Cemetery located on Hwy. 964 off the Plains/Port Hudson Rd. at East Baton Rouge Parish, LA. Confederate Widows Pension Application on file at the Louisiana State Archives. Microfilm Reel: CP1.96. Microdex 1. Sequence 43. Target Card: McVea, Arminia Neville. Parish: East Baton Rouge. 7 pages.

Mack, Peter Pvt., Louisiana Supporting Forces. Co. A. Federal Rolls of Prisoners of War: Captured at Clinton, LA, on 11/16/1864; Forwarded to New Orleans, LA, on 11/23/1864. Received at Ship Island, MS, on 12/10/1864; Transferred to Vicksburg, MS, for exchange on 5/1/1865. Exchanged at Camp Townsend, MS, on 5/6/1865.

Magoran, James Pvt./Sgt., 13th Louisiana Infantry. Co. K. Enlisted: 9/26/1861 at New Orleans, LA. Rolls for 6/1862 through 4/1863: Absent, wounded and taken Prisoner of War at Perryville, KY, on 10/8/1862. Federal Rolls of Prisoners of War: Captured at Harrodsburg, KY, on 10/11/1862; Forwarded from the U.S. Military Prison, Louisville, KY, to Camp Butler, IL, on 3/14/1863. Rolls for 6/1863 through 12/1863: Absent, detached in the General Hospital as unfit for field service due to wounds received at Perryville, KY, on 10/8/1862. Rolls for 1/1864 through 2/1865: Absent, detached at Selma, AL, as unfit for field service in 10/1863. Federal Rolls of Prisoners of War: Captured at Spanish Fort, AL, on 4/8/1865; Received at Ship Island, MS, on 4/10/1865. Transferred to Vicksburg, MS, for exchange on 5/1/1865; Exchanged at Camp Townsend, MS, on 5/6/1865.

Manberet, A. Pvt., Holmes' Light Artillery Battery. Enlisted: 3/5/1862 at New Orleans, LA. Federal Rolls of Prisoners of War: Captured at Clinton, LA, on 8/25/1864. On Register of St. Louis U.S.A. General Hospital, New Orleans, LA: Admitted on 9/14/1864. Received at Ship Island, MS, on 10/7/1864; Transferred to Fort Columbus, New York Harbor, NY, on 11/16/1864. Forwarded to Elmira, NY, on 10/7/1864 or 11/19/1864; Paroled at Elmira, NY, for exchange on 3/14/1865. Exchanged at Boulware and Cox Wharf, James River, VA, on 3/18/1865.

Marie, Jean Pvt., 13th Louisiana Infantry. Co. __. Federal Rolls of Prisoners of War: Captured at Spanish Fort, AL, on 4/8/1865; Received at Ship Island, MS, on 4/10/1865. Transferred to Vicksburg, MS, for exchange on 5/1/1865; Exchanged at Camp Townsend, MS, on 5/6/1865.

Marrs, J.L. Sgt., 3rd Louisiana Cavalry. Co. __. Federal Rolls of Prisoners of War: Captured at Clinton, LA, on 11/16/1864; Received at Ship Island, MS, from New Orleans, LA, on 12/13/1864.

Marten, Davis (AKA Maitin, Martin, David) Pvt., 2nd Louisiana Cavalry. Co. I. Federal Rolls of Prisoners of War: Captured at Morganza, LA, on 9/15/1864; Received at Ship Island, MS, from New Orleans, LA, on 10/28/1864. Forwarded to Fort Columbus, New York Harbor, NY, on 11/16/1864; Transferred to Elmira, NY, on 11/20/1864. Died: 3/21/1865 at Elmira, NY. Buried: Woodlawn National Cemetery, Chemung County, NY.

Martin, Adam A. Pvt., Miles Legion. Cos. A & H. Enlisted: 3/20/1862 at New Orleans, LA. Federal Rolls of Prisoners of War: Captured and paroled at Port Hudson, LA, on 7/10/1863. Federal Rolls of Prisoners of War: Captured at his home on Springfield Road, LA, on 10/22/1864; Received at Ship Island, MS, on 10/27/1864. Transferred to New Orleans, LA, on 10/31/1864.

Martin, G.M. Pvt., 5th Louisiana Cavalry. Co. I. Federal Rolls of Prisoners of War: Captured near Liberty, MS, on 11/18/1864; Received at Ship Island, MS, from New Orleans, LA, on 12/13/1864. Name on Escape Return for 4/5/1865: Escaped from Ship Island, MS, on the night of 4/4/1865 with four other prisoners by securing a small boat; Disposition unaccounted for.

Martin, G.W. (AKA Martins) Pvt., 5th Louisiana Cavalry. Co. I. Federal Rolls of Prisoners of War: Captured at Liberty, MS, on 11/18/1864; Received at Ship Island, MS, from New Orleans, LA, on 12/13/1864. Transferred to Vicksburg, MS, for exchange on 5/1/1865; Exchanged at Camp Townsend, MS, on 5/6/1865.

Martin, George M. Pvt., 5th Louisiana Cavalry. Co. I. Federal Rolls of Prisoners of War: Captured at Liberty, MS, on 11/18/1864; Forwarded to New Orleans, LA, on 11/23/1864. Received at Ship Island, MS, on 12/10/1864. Name on Petition dated: Camp, near Verona, MS, 1/17/1865, of W.W. Guthrie, Q.M. Sgt. of the 12th Louisiana Infantry asking to be transferred to the 5th Louisiana Cavalry. Co. I, because of his having been elected Jr. 2nd Lt. of that Company. Rolls of Prisoners of War, C.S.A: Surrendered at New Orleans, LA, on 5/26/1865; Paroled at Monroe, LA, on 6/12/1865. Residence at parole: Union Parish, LA.

Martin, I.W. Pvt., 5th Louisiana Cavalry. Co. I. Federal Rolls of Prisoners of War: Captured near Liberty, MS, on 11/18/1864; Received at Ship Island, MS, from New Orleans, LA, on 12/13/1864. Transferred to Vicksburg, MS, for exchange on 5/1/1865; Exchanged at Camp Townsend, MS, on 5/6/1865.

Martin, J.A. Pvt., 19th Louisiana Infantry. Co. A. Federal Rolls Prisoners of War: Captured at Spanish Fort, AL, on 4/8/1865; Received at Ship Island, MS, on 4/10/1865. Transferred to Vicksburg, MS, for exchange on 5/1/1865; Exchanged at Camp Townsend, MS, on 5/6/1865.

Martin, J.W. (AKA J.M.) Pvt., 5th Louisiana Cavalry. Co. I. Federal Rolls of Prisoners of War: Captured near Liberty, MS, on 11/18/1864; Received at Ship Island, MS, from New Orleans, LA, on 11/25/1864. Name on Escape Return for 4/5/1865: Escaped on the night of 4/4/1865 with four other prisoners by securing a small boat; Disposition unaccounted for.

Martin, John E.A. Pvt., 5th Louisiana Cavalry. Co. I. Federal Rolls of Prisoners of War: Captured at Liberty, MS, on 11/18/1864; Forwarded to New Orleans, LA, on 11/23/1864. Received at Ship Island, MS, on 12/10/1864; Transferred to Vicksburg, MS, for exchange on 5/1/1865. Exchanged at Camp Townsend, MS, on 5/6/1865. Born: 2/24/1848 in Mississippi. Died: 1924. Buried: Butler Cemetery, located 6 miles northwest of Mississippi City, Smith County, MS.

Martin, Julius A. Pvt., 19th Louisiana Infantry. Co. A. Enlisted: 12/11/1861 at Camp Moore, LA. Rolls through 12/1861: Present. On Register of 1st Mississippi C.S.A. Hospital, Jackson, MS: Admitted on 3/17/1862. Rolls for 5/1862 through 6/1862: Absent, on detached service. Rolls for 7/1862 through 8/1863: Present. Rolls for 9/1863 through 12/1863: Absent, sick at Rome, GA, since 9/8/1863 by order of Dr. Denson. Rolls for 1/1864 through 2/1865: Present. Rolls for 3/1865 through 4/1865: Absent, taken Prisoner of War. Federal Rolls of Prisoners of War: Captured at Spanish Fort, AL, on 4/8/1865; Received at Ship Island, MS, on 4/10/1865. Transferred to Vicksburg, MS, for exchange on 5/1/1865; Exchanged at Camp Townsend, MS, on 5/6/1865. Rolls of Prisoners of War, C.S.A: Surrendered at Citronelle, AL, on 5/4/1865; Paroled at Meridian, MS, on 5/10/1865. Residence at parole: Bossier Parish, LA. Born: 8/8/1833. Died: 10/27/1906. Buried: Boggs Cemetery located northeast of Plain Dealing, Bossier Parish, LA. Confederate Pension Application on file at the Louisiana State Archives. Microfilm Reel: CP1.91. Microdex 1. Sequence 17. Target Card: Martin, Julius A. Parish: Bossier. 10 pages.

Mather, James Pvt., Ogden's Cavalry Battalion. Co. __. Federal Rolls of Prisoners of War: Captured at East Baton Rouge Parish, LA, on 1/15/1865; Forwarded to New Orleans, LA, on 1/17/1865. Received at Ship Island, MS, on 1/22/1865.

Mathews, J. Pvt., Ogden's Cavalry Battalion. Co. __. Federal Rolls of Prisoners of War: Captured at East Baton Rouge Parish, LA, on 1/15/1865; Received at Ship Island, MS, from New Orleans, LA, on 1/25/1865.

Mathews, Thomas Pvt., Pelican Light Artillery. Federal Rolls of Prisoners of War: Received at Fort Columbus, New York Harbor, NY, from Ship Island, MS, on 11/16/1864; Transferred to Elmira, NY, on 11/19/1864.

Mathews, Thomas Pvt., 5th Louisiana Cavalry. Co. __. Federal Rolls of Prisoners of War: Received at Fort Columbus, New York Harbor, NY, from Ship Island, MS, on 11/5/1864; Transferred to Elmira, NY, on 11/20/1864.

Mathews, Thompson B. (AKA Matthews) Pvt., 4th Louisiana Battalion Infantry. Co. A. Enlisted: 5/25/1861 at Richmond, LA. Rolls for 5/25/1861 through 6/1862: Present. Regimental Return for 8/1862: Under arrest at Savannah, GA. Regimental Return for 9/1862: In barracks at Savannah, GA. Rolls for 11/1862 through 2/1865: Present. Rolls for 3/1865 through 4/1865: Absent, taken Prisoner of War. Federal Rolls of Prisoners of War: Captured at Spanish Fort, AL, on 4/8/1865; Received at Ship Island, MS, on 4/10/1865. Transferred to Vicksburg, MS, for exchange on 5/1/1865; Exchanged at Camp Townsend, MS, on 5/6/1865.

Merle, Ernest Pvt., 2nd Louisiana Cavalry. Co. I. Federal Rolls of Prisoners of War: Captured at Stone's Plantation, LA, on 9/16/1864; Forwarded to New Orleans, LA, on 9/20/1864. Received at Ship Island, MS; Transferred to Fort Columbus, New York Harbor, NY, on 11/16/1864. Forwarded to Elmira, NY, on 11/19/1864; Paroled at Elmira, NY, on 11/19/1864 for exchange. Exchanged at James River, VA, in late 1864.

Merrett, Marion Pvt., 18th Louisiana Infantry. Co. __. Federal Rolls of Prisoners of War: Captured at Spanish Fort, AL, on 4/8/1865; Received at Ship Island, MS, on 5/10/1865. Transferred to Vicksburg, MS, for exchange on 5/1/1865; Exchanged at Camp Townsend, MS, on 5/6/1865. Soldier also served with the Consolidated 18th Louisiana Infantry and the Yellow Jacket Battalion Infantry (Louisiana).

Michaux, Frank W. (AKA Michaus) Pvt., 17th Louisiana Infantry. Co. B. On List dated Parole Camp, Enterprise, MS, 11/8/1863: Detailed as Clerk to Capt. Pennington. Federal Rolls of Prisoners of War: Captured at Liberty, MS, on 11/16/1864; Forwarded to New Orleans, LA, on 11/23/1864. Received at Ship Island, MS, on 12/13/1864; Transferred to Vicksburg, MS, for exchange on 5/1/1865. Exchanged at Camp Townsend, MS, on 5/6/1865. Rolls of Prisoners of War, C.S.A: Surrendered at Citronelle, AL, on 5/4/1865; Paroled at Meridian, MS, on 5/15/1865. Residence at parole: New Orleans, LA. Died: 1878. Buried: St. Louis Cemetery # 1 located between St. Louis St. and Conti St. at New Orleans, Orleans Parish, LA.

Millener, Jeff Pvt., 18th Louisiana Infantry. Co. __. Federal Rolls of Prisoners of War: Captured at Spanish Fort, AL, on 4/8/1865; Received at Ship Island, MS, on 4/10/1865. Transferred to Vicksburg, MS, for exchange on 5/1/1865; Exchanged at Camp Townsend, MS, on 5/6/1865. Soldier also served with the Consolidated 18th Louisiana Infantry and Yellow Jacket Battalion Infantry (Louisiana). Co.C.

Miller, J.R. Pvt., 6th Louisiana Cavalry. Co. A. Enlisted: 9/9/1862 at Shreveport, LA. Rolls for 9/9/1862 through 10/1862: Detailed in pursuit of deserters. Federal Rolls of Prisoners of War: Captured at Gaines Landing, AR, on 2/12/1865; Forwarded to Memphis, TN. Transferred to Vicksburg, MS, for exchange on 3/12/1865. Federal Rolls of Prisoners of War: Captured at Spanish Fort, AL, on 4/8/1865; Received at Ship Island, MS, on 4/10/1865. Transferred to Vicksburg, MS, for exchange on 5/1/1865; Exchanged at Camp Townsend, MS, on 5/6/1865. Rolls of Prisoners of War, C.S.A: Surrendered at New Orleans, LA, on 5/26/1865; Paroled at Shreveport, LA, on 6/8/1865. Residence at parole: Caddo Parish, LA.

Miller, James R. Pvt., 4th Louisiana Infantry. Cos. D & K. Enlisted: 8/1/1862 at Port Hudson, LA. Rolls for 11/1862 through 12/1862: Absent without leave. Rolls for 1/1863 through 2/1865: Present. Federal Rolls of Prisoners of War: Captured at Spanish Fort, AL, on 4/8/1865; Received at Ship Island, MS, on

4/10/1865. Transferred to Vicksburg, MS, for exchange on 5/1/1865; Exchanged at Camp Townsend, MS, on 5/6/1865. Born: 1843. Died: 4/30/1924. Buried: Concord Methodist Church Cemetery located on Hwy. 421 at Jackson, West Feliciana Parish, LA. Confederate Pension Application on file at the Louisiana State Archives. Microfilm Reel: CP1.98. Microdex 1. Sequence 15. Target Card: Miller, James R. Parish: West Feliciana. 4 pages. Also a Confederate Widows Pension Application on file. Microfilm Reel: CP1.97. Microdex 3. Sequence 37. Target Card: Miller, Alice A. (Thomas). Parish: West Feliciana. 4 pages.

Miller, Perkins Poole (AKA Perk) Pvt., 4th Louisiana Battalion Infantry. Co. D. Enlisted: 8/9/1861 at Carroll Parish, LA. Rolls for 8/9/1861 through 2/28/1865: Present. Rolls for 3/1865 through 4/1865: Absent, taken Prisoner of War. Federal Rolls of Prisoners of War: Captured at Spanish Fort, AL, on 4/8/1865; Received at Ship Island, MS, on 4/10/1865. Transferred to Vicksburg, MS, for exchange on 5/1/1865; Exchanged at Camp Townsend, MS, on 5/6/1865. Rolls of Prisoners of War, C.S.A: Surrendered at Citronelle, AL, on 5/4/1865; Paroled at Meridian, MS, on 5/10/1865. Residence at parole: Monroe, Ouachita Parish, LA. Description at enlistment. Eyes: blue with heavy eyebrows. Hair: sandy red and short. Goatee: red. Complexion: red. Weight: 160. Height: 5'10". Speech: slow. Disposition: genial with "fire" about him. Born: 1835 in Alabama. Occupation: Farmer. Residences: Mississippi and Union Parish, LA; Elm Mott, McLennan County, TX, beginning in 1884. Died: 10/2/1911. Buried: Travis State Cemetery located at 909 Navasota St., Austin, Travis County, TX. Confederate Pension Application dated 11/27/1899 on file at the Texas State Library and Archives Commission. Name: Miller, Perkins. Pension Number: 05805. County: McLennan.

Miller, R. Pvt., 4th Louisiana Infantry. Co. D. Federal Rolls of Prisoners of War: Captured at Spanish Fort, AL, on 4/8/1865; Received at Ship Island, MS, on 4/10/1865. Transferred to Vicksburg, MS, for exchange on 5/1/1865; Exchanged at Camp Townsend, MS, on 5/6/1865.

Mitchel, H. Pvt., 15th Louisiana Infantry. Co. E. (Confederate Military Convict.) Confederate Rolls of Court Martialed Soldiers: Arrested due to stealing by order of Capt. Killborn and committed to the Police Jail on 8/27/1861; Transferred to Ship Island, MS, on 9/7/1861.

Mitchel, James Pvt., 28th Louisiana Infantry (Thomas'). Co. E. Enlisted: 4/30/1862 at Ascension Parish, LA. Rolls for 5/1862 through 8/1862: Absent, in hospital at Mississippi Springs, MS, since 6/14/1862. Rolls for 10/1862 through 2/1863: Present. Federal Rolls of Prisoners of War: Captured and paroled at Vicksburg, MS, on 7/4/1863. Federal Rolls of Prisoners of War: Captured near Hampton Ferry, LA, on 10/12/1864; Received at New Orleans, LA, on 10/15/1864. Forwarded to Fort Columbus, New York Harbor, NY, from Ship Island, MS, on 11/5/1864; Transferred to Elmira, NY, on 11/20/1864. Paroled at Elmira, NY, on 3/10/1865; Sent to James River, VA, for exchange. Exchanged at Boulware Wharf, James River, VA, on 3/15/1865. Federal Rolls of Prisoners of War: Captured at Richmond, VA, on 4/3/1865. Remarks: Escaped from the hospital on 4/24/1865. Paroled at Richmond, VA, on 4/18/1865. Rolls of Prisoners of War, C.S.A: Surrendered at New Orleans, LA, on 5/26/1865; Paroled in 6/1865. Residence at parole: Winn Parish, LA.

Mitchell, J.M. Pvt., 3rd Louisiana Cavalry. Co. C. Federal Rolls of Prisoners of War: Captured near Hampton Ferry, LA, on 10/12/1864; Received at Ship Island, MS, from New Orleans, LA, on 10/21/1864. Transferred to Fort Columbus, New York Harbor, NY, on 11/16/1864. Forwarded to Elmira, NY, on 11/19/1864.

Mitchell, James M. Pvt., 28th Louisiana Infantry. Co. E. Federal Rolls of Prisoners of War: Captured at Hampton Ferry, LA, on 10/12/1864; Received at Ship Island, MS, from New Orleans, LA, on 10/21/1864.

Mixon, Harvey Pvt., 9th Louisiana Infantry. Co. F. Enlisted: 3/8/1862 at Mansfield, LA. Age at enlistment: 35. Marital status at enlistment: Married. Occupation at enlistment: Farmer. Residence at enlistment: Mansfield, LA. Rolls for 3/8/1862 through 7/1862: Present or absent not stated. Rolls for 11/1862 through 4/1863: Present. Federal Rolls of Prisoners of War: Captured at Fredericksburg, VA, on 5/3/1863; Forwarded from the Old Capitol Prison, Washington, DC, to Fort Delaware, DE, on 5/7/1863. Paroled from Fort Delaware, DE, for exchange in 5/1863; Exchanged at City Point, VA, on 5/23/1863. Rolls for 7/1863 through 8/1863: Present. Rolls for 9/1863 through 10/1863: Absent with leave. Rolls for 11/1863 through 12/1863: Absent, sick in hospital at Lynchburg, VA, since 11/1/1863. Rolls for 1/1864 through 2/1864: Present. Federal Rolls of Prisoners of War: Captured at Rodney, MS, on 7/19/1864; Forwarded to New Orleans, LA, from the U.S. Military Prison, Natchez, MS, on 9/10/1864. Received at Ship Island, MS, on 10/7/1864; Transferred to Fort Columbus, New York Harbor, NY, on 11/16/1864. Received at Elmira, NY, on 11/18/1864. Died: 11/30/1864 at Elmira, NY, due to pneumonia. Buried: Woodlawn National Cemetery, Chemung County, NY. Born: Alabama.

Monteith, A. Pvt., 2nd Louisiana Cavalry. Co. K. Federal Rolls of Prisoners of War: Captured near Morganza, LA, on 7/31/1864; Forwarded to New Orleans, LA, from Morganza, LA, on the Steamer *Chouteau* on 8/1/1864. Received at Ship Island, MS, on 10/7/1864; Sent to Fort Columbus, New York Harbor, NY, on 11/16/1864. Transferred to Elmira, NY, on 11/19/1864; Paroled at Elmira, NY, for exchange on 2/25/1865. Exchanged at James River, VA.

Mooney, J.H. Pvt., 19th Louisiana Infantry. Co. C. Federal Rolls of Prisoners of War: Captured at Spanish Fort, AL, on 4/8/1865; Received at Ship Island, MS, on 4/10/1865. Transferred to Vicksburg, MS, for exchange on 5/1/1865; Exchanged at Camp Townsend, MS, on 5/6/1865.

Mooney, James L. Pvt., 2nd Louisiana Cavalry. Co. I. Enlisted: 9/8/1862 at Camp Thompson, LA. Rolls for 1/1863 through 2/1863: Present. Federal Rolls of Prisoners of War: Captured at Bayou Teche, LA, on 5/11/1863; Paroled for exchange at Port Hudson, LA, in 5/1863. Exchanged at New Orleans, LA. Federal Rolls of Prisoners of War: Captured at Pascagoula, MS, on 1/14/1865; Forwarded to New Orleans, LA, on 1/18/1865. Received at Ship Island, MS, on 1/25/1865; Transferred to Vicksburg, MS, for exchange on 5/1/1865. Exchanged at Camp Townsend, MS, on 5/6/1865. Rolls of Prisoners of War, C.S.A: Surrendered at New Orleans, LA, on 5/26/1865; Paroled at Alexandria, LA, on 6/4/1865. Residence at parole: Pointe Coupée Parish, LA.

Moore, J.H. Pvt., 19th Louisiana Infantry. Co. C. Enlisted: 4/25/1863 at Homer, LA. Rolls for 4/25/1863 through 2/1865: Present. Rolls for 3/1865 through 4/1865: Absent, taken prisoner of war on 4/8/1865. Federal Rolls of Prisoners of War: Captured at Spanish Fort, AL, on 4/8/1865; Received at Ship Island, MS, on 4/10/1865. Transferred to Vicksburg, MS, for exchange on 5/1/1865; Exchanged at Camp Townsend, MS, on 5/6/1865. Rolls of Prisoners of War, C.S.A: Surrendered at Citronelle, AL, on 5/4/1865; Paroled at Meridian, MS, on 5/13/1865. Residence at parole: Homer, LA.

Moore, W.R. Pvt., 20th Louisiana Infantry. Co. A. Federal Rolls of Prisoners of War: Captured at Yellow Bayou, LA, on 5/15/1864; Received at Ship Island, MS, from New Orleans, LA, on 10/7/1864. Forwarded to Fort Columbus, New York Harbor, NY, on 10/7/1864; Transferred to Elmira, NY, on 11/16/1864. Released from Elmira, NY, on 5/19/1865.

Moore, William R. Pvt., 28th Louisiana Infantry (Gray's). Co. A. Enlisted: 5/8/1862 at Monroe, LA. Federal Rolls of Prisoners of War: Captured at Bayou Teche, LA, on 4/14/1863; Paroled below Port Hudson, LA, on 5/11/1863 and sent to New Orleans, LA, for exchange. Federal Rolls of Prisoners of War: Captured at Yellow Bayou, LA, on 5/18/1864; Forwarded to New Orleans, LA, on 5/21/1864. Received at Ship Island, MS, on 10/5/1864. Name on Rolls of Prisoners of War at Ship Island, MS, who applied to take the U.S. Oath of Allegiance. Sent to Fort Columbus, New York Harbor, NY, from Ship Island, MS, on 11/16/1864; Forwarded to Elmira, NY, on 11/19/1864. Name on Rolls of Prisoners of War at Elmira, NY, who desire to take the U.S. Oath of Allegiance on 11/30/1864; Released on the U.S. Oath of Allegiance on 5/19/1865. Description at release: Eyes: blue. Hair: auburn. Complexion: florid. Height: 6'0". Residence at release: St. Louis, MO. Confederate Widows Pension Application on file at the Louisiana State Archives. CP1.100. Microdex 1. Sequence 10. Target Card: Moore, Alice (Riborn). Parish: Natchitoches. 4 pages.

Moran, Charles E. Sgt./Pvt., 6th Louisiana Infantry. Co. E. Enlisted: 6/4/1861 at Camp Moore, LA. Age at enlistment: 19. Occupation at enlistment: Clerk. Marital status at enlistment: Single. Residence at enlistment: New Orleans, LA. Rolls for 7/1861 through 8/1863: Present, on extra duty in Brigade Commissary Dept. Rolls for 10/1863 through 12/1863: Absent, sick since 10/27/1863. Rolls for 1/1864 through 4/1864: Absent, detailed as a Clerk at the Provost Marshall Office, Lake Shore District, LA, by order of the Secretary of War. Rolls for 9/1864 through 10/1864: Absent, taken Prisoner of War. Federal Rolls of Prisoners of War: Captured at Osyka, MS, on 10/7/1864; Forwarded to New Orleans, LA, from Baton Rouge, LA, on 10/14/1864. Received at Ship Island, MS, on 10/21/1864; Forwarded to Fort Columbus, New York Harbor, NY, on 11/16/1864. Transferred to Elmira, NY, on 11/20/1864; Paroled at Elmira, NY, in 2/1865 for exchange. Exchanged at Boulware and Cox Wharf, James River, VA, on 2/20–21/1865. Rolls of Prisoners of War, C.S.A: Surrendered at Appomattox Court House, VA, on 4/9/1865; Paroled at Appomattox Court House, VA, on 4/10/1865. Born: New Orleans, LA.

Moreau, F. (AKA Mareau) Pvt., 1st Louisiana Cavalry. Co. G. Federal Rolls of Prisoners of War: Captured near Liberty, MS, on 11/18/1864; Forwarded to New Orleans, LA, on 11/23/1864. Received at Ship Island, MS, on 12/13/1864; Transferred to Vicksburg, MS, for exchange on 5/1/1865. Exchanged at Camp Townsend, MS, on 5/6/1865.

Morgan, J.H. (AKA I.H.) Pvt., 4th Louisiana Infantry. Co. K. Enlisted: 5/28/1862 at Clinton, LA. Rolls for 11/1862 through 12/1862: Absent, in hospital at Clinton, LA. Rolls for 1/1863 through 4/1863: Present or absent not stated. Rolls for 5/1863 through 6/1863: Deserted on the march from Port Hudson, LA. Rolls for 7/1863 through 12/1863: Deserted at Williams Bridge, LA, on 5/7/1863. Federal Rolls of Prisoners of War: Captured at Clinton, LA, on 10/6/1864 or Williams Bridge, LA, on 10/9/1864; Sent to Baton Rouge, LA, on 10/10/1864. Forwarded to New Orleans, LA, on 10/14/1864; Received at Ship Island, MS, on 10/21/1864. Sent to Fort Columbus, New York Harbor, NY, on 11/16/1864; Transferred to Elmira, NY, on 11/20/1864. Released from Elmira, NY, on the U.S. Oath of Allegiance on 5/29/1865. Description at release: Eyes: hazel. Hair: dark. Complexion: fair. Height: 5'6". Residence at release: Baton Rouge, LA.

Morgan, John Pvt., Gober's Mounted Infantry Regiment. Co. C. Federal Rolls of Prisoners of War: Captured at Clinton, LA, on 8/25/1864; Forwarded to New Orleans, LA, on 10/5/1864. Received at Ship Island, MS, on 11/5/1864; Forwarded to Fort Columbus, New York Harbor, NY, on 11/16/1864. Received at Elmira, NY, on 11/19/1864; Paroled at Elmira, NY, on 2/9/1865. Transferred to James River, VA, for exchange; Exchanged at Boulware and Cox Wharf, VA, on 2/20–21/1865.

Morris, I.L. Sgt., 3rd Louisiana Cavalry. Co. K. Federal Rolls of Prisoners of War: Captured at Clinton, LA, on 11/16/1864; Received at Ship Island, MS, from New Orleans, LA, on 12/13/1864. Transferred to Vicksburg, MS, for exchange on 5/1/1865; Exchanged at Camp Townsend, MS, on 5/6/1865.

Morris, J.L. Pvt., 3rd Louisiana Cavalry (Wingfield's). Cos. A & K. Enlisted: 5/13/1862 at Camp Moore, LA. Federal Rolls of Prisoners of War: Captured and paroled at Port Hudson, LA, on 7/8/1863. Federal Rolls of Prisoners of War: Captured at Clinton, LA, on 11/16/1864; Received at Ship Island, MS, from New Orleans, LA, on 12/13/1864. Transferred to Vicksburg, MS, for exchange on 5/1/1865; Exchanged at Camp Townsend, MS, on 5/6/1865.

Mullen, Thomas Pvt., Pelican Light Artillery. Federal Rolls of Prisoners of War: Captured at East Baton Rouge Parish, LA, on 10/29/1864; Received at Ship Island, MS, from New Orleans, LA, in 11/1864. Forwarded to Fort Columbus, New York Harbor, NY, on 11/16/1864; Transferred to Elmira, NY, on 11/19/1864.

Mullens, Thomas Pvt., 5th Louisiana Cavalry. Co. F. Federal Rolls of Prisoners of War: Captured at East Baton Rouge Parish, LA, on 10/29/1864; Forwarded to New Orleans, LA, on 11/2/1864. Received at Ship Island, MS, on 11/5/1864.

Muse, Eli Pvt., 27th Louisiana Infantry. Co. H. Enlisted: 4/10/1862 at Camp Moore, LA. Rolls for 4/10/1862 through 12/1862: Present. Rolls for 1/1863 through 5/1863: Absent, detached as Teamster from 12/27/1862 through 5/13/1863 by order of Colonel Leon D. Marks. Federal Rolls of Prisoners of War: Captured at Vicksburg, MS, on 7/4/1863; Paroled on 7/7/1863. Federal Rolls of Prisoners of War: Captured at Livingston Parish, LA, on 12/27/1864; Confined at the U.S. Provost Jail, Baton Rouge, LA. Forwarded to New Orleans, LA, from Baton Rouge, LA, on 1/12/1865; Transferred to Ship Island, MS, on 1/22/1865. Received on 1/25/1865; Escaped on the night of 4/4/1865 with four other prisoners by securing a small boat. Wounded: No. Born: 10/13/1836 at Eferham County, IL. Married: Mary Ann Belew on 12/12/1878 at St. Helena Parish, LA. Children: 7 — 3 Sons and 4 Daughters. Occupation: Farmer. Residences: Livingston Parish and St. Helena Parish, LA, since 1855. Died: 7/18/1916 at Hall, Livingston Parish, LA, due to old age. Buried: Salem Baptist Church Cemetery located at Livingston Parish, LA. Wife died: 11/27/1923. Soldier is listed on the 1911 LA Census of Confederate Veterans and their Widows. Residence: Ward 1, Livingston Parish. Age: 75. Property Owned/Assessed: Real Estate. Amount of assessment: $200. Occupation: Farmer. Confederate Pension Application dated 6/20/1909 on file at the Louisiana State Archives. Microfilm Reel: CP1.102. Microdex 3. Sequence 22. Target Card: Muse, Eli. Parish: Livingston. 8 pages. Also a Confederate Widows Pension Application dated 9/8/1916 on file. Microfilm Reel: CP1.102. Microdex 3. Sequence 26. Target Card: Muse, Mary A. (Belew). Parish: East Baton Rouge. 5 pages.

Nash, James E. Pvt./Cpl./Sgt., 22nd Louisiana Infantry (Consolidated). Co. F. Enlisted: 5/25/1861 at Camp Moore, LA. Rolls for 3/1864 through 4/1864: Absent, transferred from the 4th Louisiana Infantry on 3/1/1864 by order of Maj. Gen. Dabney H. Maury. Rolls for 5/1864 through 6/1864: Present. Rolls for 7/1864 through 8/1864: Absent, sick at Pollard, AL; Promoted to Cpl. on 7/1/1864. Rolls for 9/1864 through 10/1864: Present. Federal Rolls of Prisoners of War: Captured at Spanish Fort, AL, on 4/8/1865; Received at Ship Island, MS, on 4/10/1865. Transferred to Vicksburg, MS, for exchange on 5/1/1865; Exchanged at Camp Townsend, MS, on 5/6/1865. Soldier also served as a Pvt. with the 4th Louisiana Infantry. Cos. B & G. Confederate Pension Application on file at the Louisiana State Archives. CP1.103. Microdex 1. Sequence 21. Target Card: Nash, James E. Parish: East Feliciana. 7 pages. Also a Confederate Widows Pension Application on file. Microfilm Reel: CP1.103. Microdex 1. Sequence 26. Target Card: Nash, Mary A. (Patrick). Parish: East Feliciana. 7 pages.

Nickens, Seborn (AKA Seaborn, Sebron) Pvt., 9th Louisiana Battalion Infantry. Co. B. Enlisted: 5/15/1862 at Camp Moore, LA. Rolls for 9/1862 through 10/1862: Absent, sick. Federal Rolls of Prisoners of War: Captured and paroled at Port Hudson, LA, on 7/8/1863. Federal Rolls of Prisoners of War: Captured at New River, LA, on 10/14/1864; Forwarded to New Orleans, LA, on 10/20/1864. Received at Ship Island, MS, on 10/21/1864; Forwarded to Fort Columbus, New York Harbor, NY, on 11/19/1864. Transferred to Elmira, NY, on 11/20/1864; Name on List of Prisoners of War at Elmira, NY, who wish to take the U.S. Oath of Allegiance on 11/30/1864. Remarks: Volunteered on 5/15/1862, was captured and paroled at Port Hudson, LA, and has never been in the Rebel Army since, but has kept at home at Donaldsonville, Ascension Parish, LA, within the Federal lines. Desires to go back there. Took the U.S. Oath of Allegiance at Elmira, NY, on 5/29/1865. Description at oath: Eyes: hazel. Hair: dark. Complexion: light. Height: 6'0". Residence at oath: Donaldsonville, LA. Born: 6/4/1838. Died: 8/23/1922. Buried: Mt. Zion Cemetery located on Hwy. 933 at Galvez, Ascension Parish, LA. Confederate Pension Application on file at the Louisiana State Archives. CP1.104. Microdex 1. Sequence 25. Target Card: Nickens, Seborn. Parish: Ascension. 12 pages.

Nowell, Charles C. Cpl./5th Sgt./Pvt., 19th Louisiana Infantry. Co. A. Enlisted: 12/11/1861 at Camp Moore, LA. Rolls for 5/1862 through 6/1862: Present. Rolls for 7/1862 through 10/1862: Present, reduced to ranks from 5th Sgt. on 7/31/1862. Rolls for 11/1862 through 12/1862: Absent, on detached service since 11/10/1862. Rolls for 1/1863 through 2/1863: Present. Rolls for 7/1863 through 8/1863: Absent, on detached service to bring up extra baggage since 8/26/1863 by order of Capt. Kennedy. Rolls for 9/1862 through 12/1862: Present. Rolls for 1/1864 through 4/1864: Present, re-enlisted on 1/20/1864 at Dalton, GA. Rolls for 5/1864 through 2/1865: Present. Rolls for 3/1865 through 4/1865: Absent, taken prisoner of war. Federal Rolls of Prisoners of War: Captured at Spanish Fort, AL, on 4/8/1865; Received at Ship Island, MS, on 4/10/1865. Transferred to Vicksburg, MS, for exchange on 5/1/1865; Exchanged at Camp Townsend, MS, on 5/6/1865. Rolls of Prisoners of War, C.S.A: Surrendered at Citronelle, AL, on 5/4/1865; Paroled at Meridian, MS, on 5/10/1865. Residence at parole: Bossier Parish, LA. Buried: Fillmore Cemetery located on Fillmore Cemetery Rd. at Bossier Parish, LA.

Noyes, Richard E. Pvt., 25th Louisiana Infantry. Co. C. Enlisted: 3/18/1862 at Monterey, LA. Rolls for 3/18/1862 through 4/1862: Present. Rolls for 5/1862 through 6/1862: Absent, sick. Rolls for 11/1862 through 2/1863: Absent, sick in hospital at Dalton, GA, since 9/1/1862 by order of the regimental surgeon. Rolls for 5/1863 through 8/1863: Present. Rolls for 10/1863 through 4/1864: Absent, sick by order of Dr. Wilkerson since 10/12/1863. Rolls for 5/1864 through 2/1865: Present. Rolls for 3/1865 through 4/1865: Absent, taken prisoner of war. Federal Rolls of Prisoners of War: Captured at Spanish Fort, AL, on 4/8/1865; Received at Ship Island, MS, on 4/10/1865. Transferred to Vicksburg, MS, for exchange on 5/1/1865; Exchanged at Camp Townsend, MS, on 5/6/1865.

O'Banion, W.H. Pvt., 19th Louisiana Infantry. Co. C. Enlisted: 12/11/1861 at Camp Moore, LA. Rolls for 12/11/1861 through 2/1863: Present. Rolls for 7/1863 through 12/1863: Absent, wounded and in hospital at Macon, GA, since 9/20/1863. Rolls for 1/1864 through 4/1864: Present. Rolls for 5/1864 through 8/1864: Absent, on sixty day wounded furlough from 8/17/1864 through 10/16/1864. Rolls for 11/1864 through

2/1865: Present. Rolls for 3/1865 through 4/1865: Absent, taken prisoner of war. Federal Rolls of Prisoners of War: Captured at Spanish Fort, AL, on 4/8/1865; Received at Ship Island, MS, on 4/10/1865. Transferred to Vicksburg, MS, for exchange on 5/1/1865; Exchanged at Camp Townsend, MS, on 5/6/1865.

O'Daniel, William H. Pvt., 19th Louisiana Infantry. Co. A. Enlisted: 12/11/1861 at Camp Moore, LA. Rolls for 12/11/1861 through 10/1863: Present. Rolls for 11/1863 through 8/1864: Absent, on extra duty with the Division Pioneer Corps since 11/15/1863 by order of Maj. Gen. Alexander P. Stewart. Rolls for 9/1864 through 2/1865: Present. Rolls for 3/1865 through 4/1865: Absent, taken prisoner of war. Federal Rolls of Prisoners of War: Captured at Spanish Fort, AL, on 4/8/1865; Received at Ship Island, MS, on 4/10/1865. Transferred to Vicksburg, MS, for exchange on 5/1/1865; Exchanged at Camp Towsend, MS, on 5/6/1865. Rolls of Prisoners of War, C.S.A: Surrendered at Citronelle, AL, on 5/4/1865; Paroled at Meridian, MS, on 5/10/1865. Residence at parole: Bossier Parish, LA. Born: 1/23/1835. Died: 10/26/1867. Buried: Salem Cemetery, located 5 miles northeast of Plain Dealing, Bossier Parish, LA; From La. Hwy. 3 travel east on Hwy. 2 and turn left on Hwy. 157 North (Springhill Hwy.), past the Plain Dealing City Cemetery.

O'Farrell, John Pvt., Ogden's Cavalry Battalion. Co. G. Federal Rolls of Prisoners of War: Captured at Natchez, MS, on 9/29/1864; Forwarded to New Orleans, LA, on 10/20/1864. Received at Ship Island, MS, on 10/21/1864; Sent to Fort Columbus, New York Harbor, NY, on 11/16/1864. Forwarded to Elmira, NY, on 11/20/1864; Paroled at Elmira, NY, on 2/9/1865. Transferred to James River, VA, for exchange; Received at Boulware and Cox Wharf, James River, VA, on 2/20–21/1865 and exchanged.

Oliver, Pierre D. (AKA Olivia, Olivierre) Pvt., 4th Louisiana Cavalry. Co. A. Federal Rolls of Prisoners of War: Captured at Lavinia, LA, on 10/13/1864; Received at New Orleans, LA, on 10/31/1864. Forwarded to Fort Columbus, New York Harbor, NY, from Ship Island, MS, on 11/16/1864. On Register of U.S.A. General Hospital, Fort Columbus, New York Harbor, NY: Admitted on 11/17/1864; Died on 12/11/1864. Age at death: 30. Buried: Cypress Hills National Cemetery, Brooklyn, NY, in Grave #2164.

Ollie, Charles Pvt., 30th Louisiana Infantry. Co. D. Enlisted: 5/11/1862 at New Orleans, LA. Rolls for 5/11/1862 through 10/1863: Present. Rolls for 3/1864 through 4/1864: Present. Rolls for 11/1864 through 2/1865: Absent, taken prisoner of war. Federal Rolls of Prisoners of War: Captured at East Pascagoula, MS, on 12/22/1864; Forwarded to New Orleans, LA, from Morganza, LA, on 12/27/1864. Received at Ship Island, MS, on 1/25/1865; Transferred to Vicksburg, MS, for exchange on 5/1/1865. Exchanged at Camp Townsend, MS, on 5/6/1865.

Ory, James Pvt., Pelican Light Artillery. Federal Rolls of Prisoners of War: Captured near Donaldsonville, LA, on 11/29/1864; Forwarded to New Orleans, LA, from Thibodaux, LA, on 12/11/1864. Received at Ship Island, MS, from New Orleans, LA, on 1/25/1865. Remarks: Applied to take the U.S. Oath of Allegiance. Transferred to New Orleans, LA, from Ship Island, MS, on 3/27/1865. Remarks: Applied to take the U.S. Oath of Allegiance. Rolls of Prisoners of War, C.S.A: Surrendered at New Orleans, LA, on 5/26/1865; Paroled at New Orleans, LA, in 5/1865.

Parham, William H. Pvt., 3rd Louisiana Cavalry (Wingfield's). Co. __. Enlisted: 6/12/1862 at Camp Moore, LA. Rolls for 6/12/1862 through 9/1862: Present or absent not stated. Federal Rolls of Prisoners of War: Captured and paroled at Port Hudson, LA, on 7/9/1863. Federal Rolls of Prisoners of War: Captured near Liberty, MS, on 11/18/1864; Received at Ship Island, MS, from New Orleans, LA, on 12/13/1864. Transferred to Vicksburg, MS, for exchange on 5/1/1865; Exchanged at Camp Townsend, MS, on 5/6/1865.

Parker, A.E. Pvt., 19th Louisiana Infantry. Co. C. Enlisted: 12/11/1861 at Camp Moore, LA. Rolls for 12/11/1861 through 12/1863: Present. Rolls for 1/1864 through 4/1864: Present, re-enlisted at Dalton, GA on 1/20/1864. Rolls for 5/1864 through 8/1864: Absent, wounded and in hospital at Auburn, GA, since 7/28/1864. Rolls for 9/1864 through 2/1865: Absent, wounded and in hospital at Columbus, GA, since 7/28/1864. Rolls for 3/1865 through 4/1865: Absent, taken prisoner of war. Federal Rolls of Prisoners of War: Captured at Spanish Fort, AL, on 4/8/1865; Received at Ship Island, MS, on 4/10/1865. Transferred to Vicksburg, MS, for exchange on 5/1/1865; Exchanged at Camp Townsend, MS, on 5/6/1865. Rolls of Prisoners of War, C.S.A: Surrendered at Citronelle, AL, on 5/4/1865; Paroled at Meridian, MS, on 5/13/1865. Residence at parole: Argis, LA.

Parker, Gray W. Pvt., Ogden's Cavalry Battalion. Co. A. Federal Rolls of Prisoners of War: Captured at New River, LA, on 12/17/1864; Forwarded to New Orleans, LA, on 12/24/1864. Received at Ship Island, MS; Transferred to Vicksburg, MS, for exchange on 5/1/1865. Exchanged at Camp Townsend, MS, on 5/6/1865. Confederate Pension Application on file at the Louisiana State Archives. CP1.107. Microdex 1. Sequence 19. Target Card: Parker, Gray W. Parish: Ascension. 12 pages.

Parker, H.B. Pvt., 2nd Louisiana Cavalry. Co. G. Enlisted: 6/21/1862 at Alexandria, LA. Rolls for 7/1863 through 8/1863: Absent, taken prisoner of war on 5/15/1863. Federal Rolls of Prisoners of War: Captured near New River, LA, on 12/17/1864; Received at Ship Island, MS, from New Orleans, LA, on 1/25/1865.

Parker, Henry B. Pvt., 5th Louisiana Cavalry. Co. D. Federal Rolls of Prisoners of War: Captured near New River, LA, on 12/14/1864; Received at Ship Island, MS, on 1/25/1865. Transferred to Vicksburg, MS, for exchange on 5/1/1865; Exchanged at Camp Townsend, MS, on 5/6/1865.

Parker, Robert L. Pvt., 25th Louisiana Infantry. Co. H. Enlisted: 3/19/1862 at New Orleans, LA. Rolls for 3/19/1862 through 6/1862: Absent, in hospital. Rolls for 3/1864 through 4/1864: Present, taken up and returned to Company after having been dropped from Rolls. Rolls for 5/1864 through 2/1865: Present. Rolls for 3/1865 through 4/1865: Absent, wounded and supposed captured at Spanish Fort, AL, on 4/8/1865. Federal Rolls of Prisoners of War: Captured at Spanish Fort, AL, on 4/8/1865; Received at Ship Island, MS, on 4/10/1865. Transferred to Vicksburg,

MS, for exchange on 5/1/1865; Exchanged at Camp Townsend, MS, on 5/6/1865.

Parsons, J.P. 1st Lt., 22nd Louisiana Infantry (Consolidated). Co. H. Elected 1st Lt. on 1/16/1864. Rolls for 1/1864 through 2/1864: Absent, with leave. Rolls for 3/1864 through 6/1864: Present. Rolls for 7/1864 through 8/1864: Absent, sick in hospital. Rolls for 9/1864 through 10/1864: Present. Rolls for 3/1865 through 4/1865: Absent, taken prisoner of war. Federal Rolls of Prisoners of War: Captured at Spanish Fort, AL, on 4/8/1865; Received at Ship Island, MS, on 4/10/1865. Transferred to Vicksburg, MS, for exchange on 4/28/1865; Confined at New Orleans, LA, on 4/28/1865. Exchanged at Camp Townsend, MS, on 5/6/1865. Soldier also served as a Pvt./1st Lt. with the 17th Louisiana Infantry. Co.I. Elected 1st Lt. on 4/16/1862; Promoted on 5/23/1862. Official Rolls of Paroled Officers, C.S.A: Surrendered at Citronelle, AL, on 5/4/1865; Paroled at Meridian, MS, on 5/12/1865.

Parvin, Jackson L. Pvt., 1st Louisiana Cavalry. Co. K. Enlisted: 6/1/1862 at Courtland, LA. Rolls for 5/1862 through 2/1863: Present. Federal Rolls of Prisoners of War: Captured at Somerset, KY, on 3/30/1863; Received at the U.S. Military Prison, Louisville, KY, on 4/4/1863. Sent to Baltimore, MD, enroute to City Point, VA, for exchange on 4/13/1863; Exchanged at City Point, VA, on 4/22/1863. Rolls for 6/1863 through 12/1863: Present. Federal Rolls of Prisoners of War: Captured near Bayou Sara, LA, on 11/1/1864; Forwarded to New Orleans, LA, on 12/7/1864. Received at Ship Island, MS, on 12/13/1865; Transferred to Vicksburg, MS, for exchange on 5/1/1865. Exchanged at Camp Townsend, MS, on 5/6/1865.

Patterson, W.J. Pvt., 16th Louisiana Infantry. Co. A. Enlisted: 2/3/1862 at New Orleans, LA. Rolls for 2/3/1862 through 10/1862: Absent, in hospital at Chattanooga, TN. Rolls for 1/1863 through 6/1863: Present. Rolls for 7/1863 through 8/1863: Absent, without leave since 8/29/1863. Rolls for 9/1863 through 2/1864: Absent, on parole furlough from Chickamauga, GA, since 9/20/1863. Rolls for 3/1864 through 4/1864: Present, paroled prisoner in camp. Rolls for 5/1864 through 8/1864: Absent, wounded in front of Atlanta, GA, on 7/28/1864. Rolls for 9/1864 through 2/1865: Present. Roll for 4/1865: Absent, sent to Spanish Fort, AL, Hospital on 4/5/1865 by order of Dr. Kelder. Federal Rolls of Prisoners of War: Captured at Spanish Fort, AL, on 4/8/1865; Received at Ship Island, MS, on 4/10/1865. Transferred to Vicksburg, MS, for exchange on 5/1/1865; Exchanged at Camp Townsend, MS, on 5/6/1865.

Patterson, W.J. Pvt., 18th Louisiana Infantry. Co. __. Federal Rolls of Prisoners of War: Transferred from Ship Island, MS, to Vicksburg, MS, for exchange on 5/1/1865; Paroled at Camp Townsend, MS, on 5/6/1865. Soldier also served as a Pvt. with the 18th Louisiana Infantry and Yellow Jacket Battalion Infantry (Consolidated).

Patton, J.F. Pvt., 22nd & 23rd Louisiana Infantry (Consolidated). Co. F. Federal Rolls of Prisoners of War: Captured at Spanish Fort, AL, on 4/8/1865; Received at Ship Island, MS, on 4/10/1865. Transferred to Vicksburg, MS, for exchange on 5/1/1865; Exchanged at Camp Townsend, MS, on 5/6/1865.

Pegger, A. Pvt., 20th Louisiana Infantry. Co. F. Federal Rolls of Prisoners of War: Captured at Spanish Fort, AL, on 4/8/1865; Received at Ship Island, MS, on 4/10/1865. Disposition unknown.

Perry, S.K. Pvt., Ogden's Cavalry Battalion. Co. __. Federal Rolls of Prisoners of War: Captured near Natchitoches, LA, on 12/22/1864; Received at Ship Island, MS, from New Orleans, LA, on 1/25/1865. Transferred to Vicksburg, MS, for exchange on 5/1/1865; Exchanged at Camp Townsend, MS, on 5/6/1865.

Perryman, I.L. Pvt., 5th Louisiana Cavalry. Co. __. Federal Rolls of Prisoners of War: Captured at Clinton, LA, on 10/6/1864; Received at Ship Island, MS, from New Orleans, LA, on 10/21/1864. Transferred to Fort Columbus, New York Harbor, NY, on 11/5/1864.

Perryman, J.L. Pvt., 3rd Louisiana Cavalry (Harrison's). Co. E. Enlisted: 5/25/1861 at Camp Moore, LA. Rolls for 6/1861 through 5/1862: Present. Federal Rolls of Prisoners of War: Captured at Clinton, LA, on 10/6/1864; Forwarded to Baton Rouge, LA, on 10/10/1864. Sent to New Orleans, LA, on 10/15/1864; Received at Ship Island, MS, on 10/20/1864. Transferred to Fort Columbus, New York Harbor, NY, on 11/16/1864; Received at Elmira, NY, on 11/20/1864. Paroled at Elmira, NY, on 2/9/1865; Sent to James River, VA, for exchange. Received at Boulware and Cox Wharf, James River, VA, on 2/20–21/1865.

Pescary, Charles W. (AKA Pescay) Pvt., Consolidated Crescent Infantry Regiment. Co. G. Federal Rolls of Prisoners of War: Captured on 10/13/1864; Forwarded to Morganza, LA, from New Orleans, LA, on 10/15/1864. Received at Ship Island, MS, on 10/20/1864; Transferred to Fort Columbus, New York Harbor, NY, on 11/16/1864. Sent to Elmira, NY, on 11/19/1864. Died: 8/26/1887. Buried: Lafayette Cemetery #1 located at the intersection of Washington Ave. and Prytania St. at New Orleans, Orleans Parish, LA.

Petty, T.R. Pvt., 5th Louisiana Cavalry. Co. __. Federal Rolls of Prisoners of War: Captured at Jackson, LA, on 11/17/1864; Received at Ship Island, MS. Transferred to Vicksburg, MS, for exchange on 5/1/1865; Exchanged at Camp Townsend, MS, on 5/6/1865.

Peyton, George W. Sgt., 1st Louisiana Battalion Cavalry (State Guard). Co. B. Federal Rolls of Prisoners of War: Captured at Daniels Ferry, LA, on 11/24/1864; Forwarded to New Orleans, LA, from Natchez, MS, on 12/12/1864. Received at Ship Island, MS, on 1/25/1865; Returned to New Orleans, LA, on 3/27/1865. Transferred to the mouth of Red River Landing, LA, for exchange on 4/7/1865; Exchanged on 4/9/1865. Soldier also served as a Pvt. with the 8th Louisiana Cavalry (Dismounted). Co. D. Confederate Pension Application on file at the Louisiana State Archives. Microfilm Reel: CP1.109. Microdex 4. Sequence 33. Target Card: Peyton, George W. Parish: DeSoto. 17 pages.

Philips, Alfred Pvt., 13th Louisiana Infantry. Co. D. Enlisted: 8/28/1861 at New Orleans, LA. Rolls for 7/1862 through 10/1862: Absent, left at Glasgow, KY. Rolls for 1/1863 through 4/1863: Present. Rolls for 7/1863 through 10/1863: Absent, wounded at the Battle of Chickamauga, GA. Rolls for 12/1863 through 2/1865: Present. Federal Rolls of Prisoners of War:

Captured at Spanish Fort, AL, on 4/8/1865; Received at Ship Island, MS, on 4/10/1865. Transferred to Vicksburg, MS, for exchange on 5/1/1865; Exchanged at Camp Townsend, MS, on 5/6/1865.

Phillip, William Pvt., 1st Louisiana Cavalry. Co. __. Federal Rolls of Prisoners of War: Captured at Liberty, MS, on 11/17/1864; Received at Ship Island, MS. Transferred to Vicksburg, MS, for exchange on 5/1/1865; Exchanged at Camp Townsend, MS, on 5/6/1865.

Phillips, W.A. Cpl./Sgt., King's Artillery Battery. Federal Rolls of Prisoners of War: Captured at Simmesport, LA, on 8/8/1864; Received at Ship Island, MS, from New Orleans, LA, on 10/21/1864.

Phillips, William A. Pvt./Sgt., Consolidated Crescent Infantry Regiment. Co. B. Enlisted: 7/1/1862 at Pointee Coupée Parish, LA. Rolls for 1/1864 through 2/1864: Present. Federal Rolls of Prisoners of War: Captured at Fort DeRussy, LA, on 3/14/1864; Received at Baton Rouge, LA, on 3/17/1864. Forwarded to New Orleans, LA, on 3/20/1864; Exchanged at Red River Landing, LA, on 7/22/1864. Federal Rolls of Prisoners of War: Captured at Bayou Alabama, LA, on 9/22/1864. On Register of St. Louis U.S.A. General Hospital, New Orleans, LA: Admitted on 8/12/1864; Returned to duty on 8/18/1864. Admitted on 9/20/1864; Returned to duty on 9/22/1864. Admitted on 10/1/1864; Returned to duty on 10/5/1864. Admitted on 10/6/1864; Returned to duty on 10/15/1864. Received at Fort Columbus, New York Harbor, NY, on 11/5/1864 from Ship Island, MS; Transferred to Elmira, NY, on 11/20/1864. Paroled at Elmira, NY, on 2/9/1865; Sent to James River, VA, for exchange. Exchanged at Boulware and Cox Wharf, James River, VA, on 2/20–21/1865. Federal Rolls of Prisoners of War: Captured near the mouth of Red River, LA, on 4/5/1865; Received at New Orleans, LA, on 4/7/1865. Exchanged on 5/2/1865 by order of Maj. Gen. Edward R.S. Canby.

Phillips, William Pvt., 5th Louisiana Cavalry. Co. E. Federal Rolls of Prisoners of War: Captured at Liberty, MS, on 5/17/1864; Forwarded to New Orleans, LA, on 11/23/1864. Received at Ship Island, MS, on 12/10/1864. Born: 10/13/1844. Died: 1/27/1914. Buried: Mora Baptist Church Cemetery, located 2 miles from the Rapides Parish, LA, boundary at Mora, Natchitoches Parish, LA.

Pichard, L. Pvt., 30th Louisiana Infantry. Co. B. Federal Rolls of Prisoners of War: Captured at Spanish Fort, AL, on 4/8/1865; Received at Ship Island, MS, on 4/10/1865. Disposition unknown.

Pick, W.A. Pvt., Washington Artillery. Co. A. Federal Rolls of Prisoners of War: Captured at Summit, MS, on 11/17/1864; Forwarded to New Orleans, LA, on 11/23/1864. Received at Ship Island, MS, on 12/13/1864; Transferred to Vicksburg, MS, for exchange on 5/1/1865. Exchanged at Camp Townsend, MS, on 5/6/1865.

Pideau, L. Pvt., 30th Louisiana Infantry. Co. F. Federal Rolls of Prisoners of War: Captured at Spanish Fort, AL, on 4/8/1865; Received at Ship Island, MS, on 4/10/1865. Disposition unknown.

Pillet, Archibald H. Pvt., 4th Louisiana Infantry. Co. D. Enlisted: 5/25/1861 at Camp Moore, LA. Rolls for 5/25/1861 through 12/1863: Present. Rolls for 5/1864 through 8/1864: Absent, sick in hospital. Rolls for 9/1864 through 2/1865: Present. Federal Rolls of Prisoners of War: Captured at Spanish Fort, AL, on 4/8/1865; Received at Ship Island, MS, on 4/10/1865. Transferred to Vicksburg, MS, for exchange on 5/1/1865; Exchanged at Camp Townsend, MS, on 5/6/1865. Born: 1838. Died: 1893. Buried: Grace Episcopal Church Cemetery located on Hwy. 10 at St. Francisville, West Feliciana Parish, LA. Confederate Widows Pension Application on file at the Louisiana State Archives. CP1.110. Microdex 4. Sequence 21. Target Card: Pillet, Rosalie (Fischer). Parish: West Feliciana. 10 pages.

Pinkard, John M. Pvt., 8th Louisiana Infantry. Co. G. On undated List of Minden Blues who came down from Adkins Landing, Red River, LA, to New Orleans, LA, on the Steamer *Eleanor*, arriving on 6/14/1861. Enlisted: 6/23/1861 at Camp Moore, LA. Marital status at enlistment: Single. Occupation at enlistment: Overseer. Residence at enlistment: Minden, LA. Rolls for 7/1861 through 8/1861: Absent, sick at Culpepper, VA, since 7/10/1861. Rolls for 9/1861 through 10/1861: Present. Rolls for 11/1861 through 12/1861: Present, detached on Signal Duty on 11/7/1861; Returned on 11/30/1861. Rolls for 1/1862 through 4/1862: Present. Rolls for 5/1862 through 6/1862: Absent, sick since 3/5/1862. Rolls for 7/1862 through 10/1863: Present. Rolls for 11/1863 through 8/1864: Absent, wounded on 11/7/1863 and in hospital. Federal Rolls of Prisoners of War: Captured at Simmesport, LA, on 8/8/1864; Received at Fort Columbus, New York Harbor, NY, from Ship Island, MS, on 11/16/1864. Forwarded to Elmira, NY, on 11/20/1864; Died: 12/13/1864 at Elmira, NY, due to pneumonia. Buried: Woodlawn National Cemetery, Chemung County, NY.

Pinkham, J. Pvt., 8th Louisiana Infantry. Co. __. Federal Rolls of Prisoners of War: Captured at Simmesport, LA, on 8/8/1864; Received at Ship Island, MS. Transferred to Fort Columbus, New York Harbor, NY, on 11/16/1864. Escaped while being forwarded to Elmira, NY.

Pinkney, William Elder 2nd Lt./1st Lt., 1st Louisiana Heavy Artillery. Co. E. Enlisted: 3/24/1861 at Fort Jackson, LA. Rolls for 3/24/1861 through 4/30/1861: Absent with leave; Promoted to 1st Lt. and attached to Co. E by order of Headquarters, Military District of Louisiana. Rolls for 5/1861 through 8/1861: Present. Rolls for 9/1861 through 2/1862: Absent, on detached service. Regimental Return for 3/1862: Resignation accepted on 3/1/1862 per Special Order # 60, Adjutant and Inspector General's Office, Richmond, VA. On Roster dated 2/19/1864: Elected Lt. Col. of the 8th Louisiana Battalion Infantry. Federal Rolls of Prisoners of War: Captured at Clinton, LA, on 10/6/1864; Received at Baton Rouge, LA, on 10/10/1864. Forwarded to New Orleans, LA, on 10/15/1864. On Register of U.S.A. General Hospital, New Orleans, LA: Admitted on 10/27/1864; Released on 11/21/1864. Age at admittance: 25. Escaped in transit to Ship Island, MS, on 12/15/1864. Rolls of Prisoners of War, C.S.A: Surrendered at Citronelle, AL, on 5/4/1865; Paroled at Meridian, MS, on 5/6/1865 by order of Maj. Gen.E.R.S. Canby. Age at parole: 25. Description at parole: Eyes: blue. Hair: light. Complexion: fair. Height: 5'11". Residence at parole: New Orleans, LA.

Pinson, William Pvt., 15th Louisiana Battalion Cavalry (Harrison's). Co. A. Federal Rolls of Prisoners of War: Captured at Tensas Parish, LA, on 9/19/1864; Forwarded to New Orleans, LA, on 9/25/1864. Received at Ship Island, MS, on 10/7/1864; Transferred to Elmira, NY, on 11/17/1864. Died: 12/17/1864 at Elmira, NY, due to pneumonia.

Pitre, C.C. Pvt., Crescent Infantry Regiment. Cos. B & C. Enlisted: 3/5/1862 at New Orleans, LA. Rolls for 11/1862 through 2/1863: Present. Rolls for 5/1863 through 6/1863: Present, on extra daily duty with the wagons. Rolls for 7/1863 through 8/1863: Absent, sick in hospital at New Iberia, LA. Soldier also served as a Pvt. with the Consolidated Crescent Infantry Regiment (Louisiana). Cos. B & C. Rolls for 1/1864 through 2/1864: Present. Federal Rolls of Prisoners of War: Captured at Tensas Parish, LA, on 9/19/1864; Forwarded to New Orleans, LA, on 9/25/1864. Received at Ship Island, MS, on 10/7/1864; Transferred to Fort Columbus, New York Harbor, NY, on 11/6/1864. Sent to Elmira, NY, on 11/19/1864; Paroled at Elmira, NY, on 2/25/1865. Sent to James River, VA, for exchange. Federal Rolls of Prisoners of War: Captured near the mouth of Red River, LA, on 4/5/1865; Received at New Orleans, LA, on 4/7/1865. Transferred to Vicksburg, MS, for exchange on 5/2/1865 by order of Maj. Gen.E.R.S. Canby. Rolls of Prisoners of War of Detachments of Diverse Regiments, C.S.A: Surrendered at New Orleans, LA, on 5/26/1865; Paroled at Washington, LA, on 6/18/1865. Residence at parole: St. Landry Parish, LA. Buried: City Corporation Cemetery, Lake Charles, Calcasieu Parish, LA.

Pitre, Leander D. (AKA Leandre) Pvt., 4th Louisiana Infantry. Co. E. Enlisted: 5/25/1861 at Camp Moore, LA. Rolls for 5/25/1861 through 2/1862: Present. Rolls for 11/1862 through 12/1862: Absent, sick. Rolls for 1/1863 through 8/1864: Present. Rolls for 9/1864 through 2/1865: Absent, taken prisoner of war. Federal Rolls of Prisoners of War: Captured near Franklin, TN, on 12/17/1864; Received at the U.S. Military Prison, Louisville, KY, from Nashville, TN, on 1/2/1865. Transferred to Camp Chase, OH, on 1/4/1865; Paroled at Camp Chase, OH, and forwarded to Point Lookout, MD, for exchange on 2/17/1865. Rolls for 3/1865 through 4/1865: Absent, taken prisoner of war. Federal Rolls of Prisoners of War: Captured at Spanish Fort, AL, on 4/8/1865; Received at Ship Island, MS, on 4/10/1865. Transferred to Vicksburg, MS, for exchange on 5/1/1865; Exchanged at Camp Townsend, MS, on 5/6/1865. Confederate Pension Application on file at the Louisiana State Archives. CP1.111. Microdex 1. Sequence 22. Target Card: Pitre, Leandre D. Parish: Lafourche. 10 pages.

Platner, Albert Pvt./Hosp. Stew., 13th Louisiana Infantry. F & S. Enlisted: 9/11/1861 at Camp Moore, LA. Rolls for 7/1862 through 8/1862: Present. Rolls for 9/1862 through 10/1862: Absent, detailed to Medical Staff. Federal Rolls of Prisoners of War: Captured at Murfreesboro, TN, on 12/21/1862; Received at Camp Douglas, IL, on 3/31/1862. Exchanged at City Point, VA, on 4/4/1863. Rolls for 1/1863 through 2/1863: Absent, missing since 12/31/1862 while detailed as Hospital Steward. Rolls # 1 for 3/1863 through 4/1863: Absent, taken prisoner of war. Rolls # 2 for 3/1863 through 4/1863: Appointed Hospital Steward. Rolls for 7/1863 through 10/1863: Present, on extra duty as Hospital Steward by order of the Secretary of War. Rolls for 11/1863 through 12/1863: Absent, sick in hospital. Rolls for 1/1864 through 2/1865: Present. Rolls for 3/1865 through 4/1865: Absent, taken prisoner of war. Federal Rolls of Prisoners of War: Captured at Spanish Fort, AL, on 4/8/1865; Received at Ship Island, MS, on 4/10/1865. Transferred to Vicksburg, MS, for exchange on 5/1/1865; Exchanged at Camp Townsend, MS, on 5/6/1865.

Poche, A. Pvt., 4th Louisiana Infantry. Co. __. Federal Rolls of Prisoners of War: Captured at Spanish Fort, AL, on 4/8/1865; Received at Ship Island, MS, on 4/10/1865. Transferred to Vicksburg, MS, for exchange on 5/1/1865. Exchanged at Camp Townsend, MS, on 5/6/1865.

Pogue, Isaac H. Pvt., 1st Louisiana Cavalry. Co. B. Enlisted: 9/5/1861 at Baton Rouge, LA. Rolls for 5/1862 through 12/1862: Present. Rolls for 1/1863 through 2/1863: Absent, on furlough. Federal Rolls of Prisoners of War: Captured at Somerset, KY, on 3/30/1863; Received at the U.S. Military Prison, Louisville, KY, on 4/6/1863. Sent to Baltimore, MD, enroute to City Point, VA, for exchange on 4/13/1863; Exchanged at City Point, VA, on 4/22/1863. Rolls for 5/1863 through 6/1863: Absent, on regimental detail. Rolls for 11/1863 through 12/1863: Present, acting Q.M. Sgt. Federal Rolls of Prisoners of War: Captured at Liberty, MS, or Brookhaven, MS, on 11/18/1864; Forwarded to New Orleans, LA, on 11/23/1864. Received at Ship Island, MS, on 12/10/1864.

Powell, J.C. Pvt., 12th Louisiana Infantry. Co. __. Federal Rolls of Prisoners of War: Captured at Tensas Parish, LA, on 9/19/1864; Received at Ship Island, MS, from New Orleans, LA, on 10/7/1864.

Powell, J.E. Pvt., 12th Louisiana Infantry. Co. __. Federal Rolls of Prisoners of War: Captured at Tensas Parish, LA, on 9/19/1864; Received at Fort Columbus, New York Harbor, NY, from Ship Island, MS, on 11/16/1864. Transferred to Elmira, NY, on 11/18/1864.

Powell, James E. Pvt., 3rd Louisiana Cavalry (Harrison's). Co. A. Federal Rolls of Prisoners of War: Captured at Tensas Parish, LA, on 9/19/1864; Sent from Natchez, MS, to New Orleans, LA, on 9/24/1864. Forwarded to Fort Columbus, New York Harbor, NY, from Ship Island, MS, on 11/16/1864; Received at Elmira, NY, on 11/19/1864. Died: 1/11/1865 at Elmira, NY, due to pneumonia. Buried: Woodlawn National Cemetery, Chemung County, NY.

Powell, John A. Pvt., 12th Louisiana Infantry. 2nd Co. M. Enlisted: 1/12/1862 at Camp Carondelet, VA. Federal Rolls of Prisoners of War: Captured at Huntsville, AL, on 4/11/1862; Received at Camp Chase, OH, from Johnson's Island, OH, on 5/16/1862. Transferred to Vicksburg, MS, for exchange on 8/25/1862. Rolls for 9/1862 through 12/1862: Present. Rolls for 3/1863 through 4/1863: Present. Rolls for 5/1863 through 6/1863: Absent, missing since the Battle of Baker's Creek, MS. Rolls for 7/1863 through 12/1863: Present. Rolls for 5/1864 through 6/1864: Absent, sent to the hospital on 5/10/1864. Rolls for 7/1864 through 8/1864: Present. Federal Rolls of Prisoners of War: Captured at Tensas Parish, LA, on 9/19/1864;

Received at Ship Island, MS, from New Orleans, LA, on 10/7/1864. Transferred to Fort Columbus, New York Harbor, NY, on 11/5/1864 by order of Capt.M.R. Marston.

Powell, William Pvt., 12th Louisiana Battalion Heavy Artillery. Co. C. Federal Rolls of Prisoners of War: Captured in Alabama on 3/24/1865; Received at Ship Island, MS, on 4/4/1865. Forwarded to Vicksburg, MS, for exchange on 5/1/1865; Exchanged at Camp Townsend, MS, on 5/6/1865.

Pray, Rufus L. (AKA H.L.) Pvt., 3rd Louisiana Cavalry (Wingfield's). Co. E. Enlisted: 5/25/1861 at Camp Moore, LA. Roll for 6/1862 through 7/1862: Present or absent not stated. Federal Rolls of Prisoners of War: Captured near Hampton Ferry, LA, on 10/12/1864; Forwarded to New Orleans, LA, on 10/15/1864. Received at Ship Island, MS, on 10/21/1864; Returned to New Orleans, LA, on 10/28/1864 by order of Capt.M.R. Marston. Took the U.S. Oath of Allegiance at New Orleans, LA, on 10/30/1864. Description at oath: Eyes: dark. Hair: dark. Complexion: dark. Height: 5'10". Residence at oath: New Orleans, LA. Confederate Widows Pension Application on file at the Louisiana State Archives. Microfilm Reel: CP1.112. Microdex 4. Sequence 11. Target Card: Pray, Catherine L. (Draughon). County: Jefferson (Texas). 12 pages.

Quick, James C. Pvt., 5th Louisiana Cavalry. Co. I. Federal Rolls of Prisoners of War: Captured at Brookhaven, MS, on 11/18/1864; Forwarded to New Orleans, LA, on 11/23/1864. Received at Ship Island, MS, on 12/10/1864. Transferred to Vicksburg, MS, for exchange on 5/1/1865; Exchanged at Camp Townsend, MS, on 5/6/1865.

Rainer, G.C. Pvt., 1st Louisiana Cavalry. Co. ___. Federal Rolls of Prisoners of War: Captured at Clinton, LA, on 10/6/1864; Received at Ship Island, MS. Forwarded to Fort Columbus, New York Harbor, NY, on 11/16/1864. Transferred to Elmira, NY, on 11/18/1864.

Rainey, William P. Pvt., 1st Louisiana Cavalry. Co. H. Enlisted: 10/5/1861 at Baton Rouge, LA. Rolls for 9/1862 through 2/1863: Present. Rolls for 3/1863 through 6/1863: Dismounted. Rolls for 11/1863 through 12/1863: Present. Federal Rolls of Prisoners of War: Captured at Livingston Parish, LA, on 12/27/1864; Forwarded to New Orleans, LA, from Baton Rouge, LA, on 1/12/1865. Received at Ship Island, MS, on 1/22/1865.

Raney, John B. (AKA Rainy) Pvt., 1st Louisiana Cavalry. Co. H. Federal Rolls of Prisoners of War: Captured at Ascension Parish, LA, on 12/27/1864; Received at Ship Island, MS, from New Orleans, LA, on 1/25/1865. Transferred to Vicksburg, MS, for exchange on 5/1/1865; Exchanged at Camp Townsend, MS, on 5/6/1865.

Ratlips, J.R. Pvt., Gober's Mounted Infantry Regiment. Co. ___. Federal Rolls of Prisoners of War: Captured near East Baton Rouge Parish, LA, on 9/17/1864; Received at Fort Columbus, New York Harbor, NY, from Ship Island, MS, on 11/5/1864.

Raymond, G.C. (AKA Rainer) Pvt., 3rd Louisiana Cavalry (Harrison's). Co. E. Enlisted: 5/25/1861 at Camp Moore, LA. Rolls for 6/1862 through 7/1862: Present. Federal Rolls of Prisoners of War: Captured at Clinton, LA, on 10/6/1864; Forwarded to New Orleans, LA, from Baton Rouge, LA, on 10/15/1864. Received at Ship Island, MS, on 10/20/1864; Sent to Fort Columbus, New York Harbor, NY, on 11/16/1864. Transferred to Elmira, NY, on 11/20/1864; Paroled at Elmira, NY, on 2/25/1865. Exchanged at James River, VA, in 1865.

Read, John Joseph (AKA Joseph John) Pvt., 25th Louisiana Infantry. Co. D. Enlisted: 3/6/1862 at Morehouse Parish, LA. Name on List of Prisoners leaving Cairo, IL, on 10/25/1862 enroute to Vicksburg, MS, for exchange; Exchanged from the Steamer *Emerald* near Vicksburg, MS, on 11/1/1862. Name on undated List of Confederate Prisoners of War who were paroled by the Federal forces and reported to Confederate Maj.N.G. Watts. Exchanged near Vicksburg, MS, on 12/2/1862. Rolls for 12/1862 through 2/1865: Present. Rolls for 3/1865 through 4/1865: Absent, taken prisoner of war. Federal Rolls of Prisoners of War: Captured at Spanish Fort, AL, on 4/8/1865; Received at Ship Island, MS, on 4/10/1865. Transferred to Vicksburg, MS, for exchange on 5/1/1865; Exchanged at Camp Townsend, MS, on 5/6/1865. Died: 12/13/1872. Buried: Oak Ridge Baptist Church Cemetery located on Hwy. 134 at Oak Ridge, Morehouse Parish, LA.

Redman, Thomas Pvt., 4th Louisiana Infantry. Co. B. Federal Rolls of Prisoners of War: Captured at Spanish Fort, AL, on 4/8/1865; Received at Ship Island, MS, on 4/10/1865.

Reed, William F. (AKA W.T.) Cpl., 2nd Louisiana Infantry. Co. ___. Federal Rolls of Prisoners of War: Captured and paroled at Vicksburg, MS, on 7/4/1863. Federal Rolls of Prisoners of War: Received at Ship Island, MS, from New Orleans, LA, on 10/21/1864; Transferred to Fort Columbus, New York Harbor, NY, on 11/5/1864 by order of Capt.M.R. Marston.

Reed, William F. Pvt./Cpl., 21st Louisiana Infantry (Patton's). Co. B. Enlisted: 6/18/1861 at New Orleans, LA. Rolls for 11/1861 through 2/1863: Present. Rolls for 11/1863 through 12/1863: Absent, without leave; Failed to report to parole camp. Federal Rolls of Prisoners of War: Captured and paroled at Vicksburg, MS, on 7/4/1863. Forwarded to New Orleans, LA, on 10/20/1864; Received at Ship Island, MS, on 10/21/1864. Transferred to Fort Columbus, New York Harbor, NY, on 11/16/1864; Forwarded to Elmira, NY, on 11/20/1864. Name on list of Prisoners of War at Elmira, NY, who desire to take the U.S. Oath of Allegiance on 11/30/1864; Remarks: Volunteered on 6/13/1861 due to over-persuasion and desires to return to New Orleans, LA. Took the U.S. Oath of Allegiance at Elmira, NY, on 5/15/1865; Remarks: Released by order of the Office of the Commissary General of Prisoners, Washington, D.C. on 5/8/1865. Description at oath: Eyes: blue. Hair: black. Complexion: dark. Height: 5'9". Residence at oath: New Orleans, LA.

Reeks, John Pvt., Louisiana Supporting Forces. Co. A. Federal Rolls of Prisoners of War: Captured at Clinton, LA, on 11/16/1864; Received at Ship Island, MS, on 12/13/1864. Transferred to Vicksburg, MS, for exchange on 5/1/1865; Exchanged at Camp Townsend, MS, on 5/6/65.

Reggio, Gus A. Pvt., 30th Louisiana Infantry. Co. F. Enlisted: 6/1/1863 at Mobile, AL. Rolls for 6/1863 through 2/1865: Present. Federal Rolls of Prisoners of War: Captured at Spanish Fort, AL, on 4/8/1865;

Received at Ship Island, MS, on 4/10/1865. Transferred to Vicksburg, MS, for exchange on 5/1/1865; Exchanged at Camp Townsend, MS, on 5/6/1865.

Rhodes, J. William Pvt., 1st Louisiana Cavalry. Co. G. Enlisted: 5/26/1862 at Richmond, VA. Rolls for 3/1863 through 6/1863: Present; Transferred to the 1st Louisiana Cavalry. Co. G on 6/11/1863 by Lt. Coffen of the 6th Louisiana Cavalry. Rolls for 11/1863 through 2/1864: Present. Federal Rolls of Prisoners of War: Captured near Clinton, MS, on 8/25/1864; Forwarded to New Orleans, LA, on 8/31/1864. Received at Ship Island, MS, on 10/5/1864; Transferred to Fort Columbus, New York Harbor, NY, on 11/16/1864. Sent to Elmira, NY, on 11/19/1864; Paroled at Elmira, NY. Forwarded to James River, VA, for exchange on 2/25/1865. Rolls of Prisoners of War, C.S.A: Surrendered at New Orleans, LA, on 5/26/1865; Paroled at Alexandria, LA, on 6/10/1865. Residence at parole: New Orleans, LA.

Richard, Cheri Sgt./Pvt., 30th Louisiana Infantry. Cos. B, G & H. Enlisted: 3/19/1862 at Thibodaux, LA. Rolls for 4/24/1862 through 9/4/1862: Present, resigned as Sgt. on 5/21/1862. Rolls for 10/1862 through 2/1865: Present. Federal Rolls of Prisoners of War: Captured at Spanish Fort, AL, on 4/8/1865; Received at Ship Island, MS, on 4/10/1865. Transferred to Vicksburg, MS, for exchange on 5/1/1865; Exchanged at Camp Townsend, MS, on 5/6/1865.

Richards, A. Pvt., 1st Louisiana Cavalry. Co. A. Federal Rolls of Prisoners of War: Captured at Clinton, LA, on 11/9/1864; Forwarded to New Orleans, LA, on 11/21/1864. Received at Ship Island, MS, on 12/10/1864; Transferred to Vicksburg, MS, for exchange on 5/1/1865. Exchanged at Camp Townsend, MS, on 5/6/1865.

Richards, A. Pvt./Sgt., 3rd Louisiana Cavalry (Harrison's). Co. I. Federal Rolls of Prisoners of War: Captured at East Baton Rouge Parish, LA, on 11/9/1864; Received at Ship Island, MS, from New Orleans, LA, on 12/13/1864.

Richardson, G.P. Pvt., 3rd Louisiana Cavalry. Co. __. Federal Rolls of Prisoners of War: Captured on 10/6/1864; Received at Ship Island, MS, from New Orleans, LA, on 10/21/1864.

Richardson, George P. Pvt., 27th Louisiana Infantry. Co. A. Enlisted: 3/14/1862 at Clinton, LA. Rolls for 3/14/1862 through 5/1/1862: Present. Rolls for 5/1862 through 6/1862: Present or absent not stated. Rolls for 7/1862 through 12/1862: Present. Federal Rolls of Prisoners of War: Captured at Vicksburg, MS, on 7/4/1863; Paroled on 7/8/1863. Federal Rolls of Prisoners of War: Captured at Clinton, LA, on 10/6/1864; Forwarded to New Orleans, LA, from Baton Rouge, LA, on 10/14/1864. Received at Ship Island, MS, on 10/21/1864; Transferred to Fort Columbus, New York Harbor, NY, on 11/16/1864. Sent to Elmira, NY, on 11/20/1864. Died: 1/11/1865 at Elmira, NY, due to typhoid pneumonia. Buried: Woodlawn National Cemetery, Chemung County, NY, in Grave #1396.

Richardson, J.Y.D. Pvt., 4th Louisiana Infantry. Co. A. Enlisted: 9/1/1861 at Camp Moore, LA. Rolls for 9/1861 through 12/1861: Present. Rolls for 1/1862 through 2/1862: Present. Slightly wounded at the Battle of Shiloh, TN, on 4/6/1862. Rolls for 11/1862 through 2/1865: Present. Federal Rolls of Prisoners of War: Captured at Spanish Fort, AL, on 4/8/1865; Received at Ship Island, MS, on 4/10/1865. Transferred to Vicksburg, MS, for exchange on 5/1/1865; Exchanged at Camp Townsend, MS, on 5/6/1865. Soldier also served as a Pvt. with the 13th Louisiana Infantry. Co.A. Confederate Pension Application on file at the Louisiana State Archives. Microfilm Reel: CP1.118. Microdex 1. Sequence 11. Target Card: Richardson, J.Y. Parish: Franklin. 8 pages.

Richardson, S.D. Capt., 5th Louisiana Cavalry. Federal Rolls of Prisoners of War: Captured at Liberty, MS, on 11/16/1864; Forwarded to New Orleans, LA, on 11/23/1864. Received at Ship Island, MS, on 11/25/1864; Transferred to Vicksburg, MS, for exchange on 4/28/1865. Exchanged at Camp Townsend, MS, on 5/6/1865. Rolls of Prisoners of War, C.S.A: Surrendered at New Orleans, LA, on 5/26/1865; Paroled at Jackson, MS, on 5/19/1865. Residence at parole: St. Helena Parish, LA.

Rickart, Henry (AKA Rickert) Pvt./Cpl., 22nd & 23rd Louisiana Infantry (Consolidated). Co. A. Enlisted: 12/5/1861 at Camp Lewis, LA. Rolls for 1/1862 through 12/1862: Present. Federal Rolls of Prisoners of War: Captured and paroled at Vicksburg, MS, on 7/4/1863. On List dated Parole Camp, Enterprise, MS, 10/13/1863: Present in camp; Forwarded for exchange on 10/19/1863. Rolls for 10/1863 through 12/1863: Present. Soldier also served as a Cpl. with the 22nd Louisiana Infantry (Consolidated). Co. A. Rolls for 1/1864 through 4/1864: Present. Rolls for 5/1864 through 6/1864: Absent, sick in hospital at Mobile, AL, on 5/22/1864. Rolls for 7/1864 through 10/1864: Present. Federal Rolls of Prisoners of War: Captured at Spanish Fort, AL, on 4/8/1865; Received at Ship Island, MS, on 4/10/1865. Transferred to Vicksburg, MS, for exchange on 5/1/1865; Paroled at Camp Townsend, MS, on 5/6/1865.

Rideau, L. Pvt., 30th Louisiana Infantry. Co. F. Enlisted: 4/1/1863 at Port Hudson, LA. Rolls for 6/1863 through 4/1864: Present. On Register of 1st Mississippi C.S.A. Hospital, Jackson, MS: Returned to duty on 1/13/1865. Rolls through 2/1865: Present. Federal Rolls of Prisoners of War: Captured at Spanish Fort, AL, on 4/8/1865; Received at Ship Island, MS, on 4/10/1865. Transferred to Vicksburg, MS, for exchange on 5/1/1865; Exchanged at Camp Townsend, MS, on 5/6/1865.

Rills, Edward H. Pvt./Cpl., 2nd Louisiana Cavalry. Co. I. Enlisted: 9/1/1862 at New Roads, LA. Rolls for 11/1862 through 12/1862: Present, $50.00 bounty due. Rolls for 1/1863 through 2/1863: Present. Federal Rolls of Prisoners of War: Captured at Iberville, LA, on 2/4/1864; Forwarded to New Orleans, LA, on 3/21/1864. Transferred to Red River Landing, LA, for exchange on 7/22/1864. Federal Rolls of Prisoners of War: Captured at Bayou Grosse Tête, LA, on 10/27/1864; Forwarded to New Orleans, LA, from Morganza, LA, on 10/31/1864. Received at Ship Island, MS, on 11/2/1864; Transferred to Fort Columbus, New York Harbor, NY, on 11/16/1864. Forwarded to Elmira, NY, on 11/19/1864; Paroled at Elmira, NY, on 3/10/1865. Sent to James River, VA, for exchange; Exchanged at Boulware and Cox Wharf, James River, VA, on 3/15/1865. Confederate Pension Application on file at the Louisiana State Archives. Microfilm Reel: CP1.118. Microdex 4. Sequence 1. Target Card: Rills, E.H. Parish: Ouachita. 3 pages.

Also a Confederate Widows Pension Application on file. Microfilm Reel: CP1.118. Microdex 4. Sequence 2. Target Card: Rills, Emma (Davis). Parish: Ouachita. 9 pages.

Ripley, William P. 1st Lt., 15th Louisiana Battalion Cavalry (Harrison's). Co. __. Federal Rolls of Prisoners of War: Captured at Dutch Stores, LA, on 9/27/1864; Forwarded to Natchez, MS, on 9/30/1864. Sent to New Orleans, LA, on 10/20/1864; Received at Ship Island, MS, on 11/5/1864. Transferred to Fort Lafayette, New York Harbor, NY, on 11/20/1864; Sent to Fort Warren, MA, on 12/21/1864. Released from Fort Warren, MA, on the U.S. Oath of Allegiance on 6/12/1865. Description at oath: Eyes: hazel. Hair: light. Complexion: light. Height: 5'9½". Residence at oath: New Orleans, LA. Died: 11/4/1900. Buried: Greenwood Cemetery, located on City Park Ave. at New Orleans, Orleans Parish, LA.

Roberts, A.E. Pvt., 2nd Louisiana Cavalry. Cos. E & K. Enlisted: 7/15/1862 at Bethel, Natchitoches Parish, LA. Rolls for 1/1863 through 2/1863: Absent, without leave since 2/20/1863. Federal Rolls of Prisoners of War: Captured at Pointe Coupée Parish, LA, on 10/22/1864; Received at Ship Island, MS, on 10/27/1864. Sent to New Orleans, LA, on 10/31/1864; Forwarded to Elmira, NY, on 11/20/1864 from Fort Columbus, New York Harbor, NY. Paroled at Elmira, NY, on 2/25/1865; Sent to James River, VA, for exchange. Born: 1842. Died: 1906. Buried: St. Bernard Catholic Church Cemetery located at the intersection of Main St. and St. Bernard Dr. at Breaux Bridge, St. Martin Parish, LA.

Roberts, C. Pvt., 1st Louisiana Cavalry. Co. K. Federal Rolls of Prisoners of War: Captured at Pointe Coupée Parish, LA, on 10/21/1864; Received at Ship Island, MS, from New Orleans, LA, on 10/28/1864. Transferred to Fort Columbus, New York Harbor, NY, on 11/5/1864.

Roberts, Charles A. Pvt./Cpl., 4th Louisiana Infantry. Cos. A & F. Enlisted: 5/25/1861 at Camp Moore, LA. Rolls for 5/25/1861 through 12/1861: Present. Name on List dated Headquarters, 2nd Brigade, Baton Rouge, LA, 8/8/1862 of Prisoners captured at the Battle of Baton Rouge, LA, on 8/5/1862, together with other Prisoners now on board the Steamer *Diana*. Name on List dated Provost Marshal's Office, New Orleans, LA, 10/5/1862 of Prisoners on board the U.S. Prison Ship *Algerine*; Remarks: Taken prisoner of war at Baton Rouge, LA, on 8/5/1862. Rolls for 9/1862 through 12/1862: Present. Rolls for 1/1863 through 4/1863: Absent, sick at hospital. Rolls for 5/1863 through 8/1863: Present. Rolls for 9/1863 through 10/1863: Present, promoted to Cpl. on 10/11/1863. Rolls for 11/1863 through 12/1863: Present. Soldier also served as a Pvt. with the 2nd Louisiana Cavalry. Federal Rolls of Prisoners of War: Captured at Lavina, LA, on 10/22/1864; Received at Ship Island, MS, from New Orleans, LA, on 10/28/1864. Confederate Pension Application on file at the Louisiana State Archives. Microfilm Reel: CP1.119. Microdex 2. Sequence 8. Target Card: Roberts, Charles A. Parish: Orleans. 10 pages.

Roberts, E.A. Pvt., 1st Louisiana Cavalry. Co. K. Federal Rolls of Prisoners of War: Captured at Pointe Coupée Parish, LA, on 10/21/1864; Received at Ship Island, MS, on 10/28/1864. Transferred to Fort Columbus, New York Harbor, NY, on 11/16/1864; Forwarded to Elmira, NY, on 11/19/1864.

Robertson, J. Sgt., Hunt's Battalion Infantry. Co. __. Federal Rolls of Prisoners of War: Captured at Liberty, MS, on 3/16/1864; Received at Ship Island, MS. Applied to take the U.S. Oath of Allegiance at Ship Island, MS, to join the U.S. Navy; Application received at the U.S. Office of Commissary General of Prisoners on 2/7/1865.

Robertson, Simeon C. Pvt., 3rd Louisiana Cavalry (Harrison's). Co. B. Federal Rolls of Prisoners of War: Captured at Clinton, LA, on 10/6/1864; Forwarded to New Orleans, LA, from Baton Rouge, LA, on 10/20/1864. Received at Ship Island, MS, on 10/21/1864; Transferred to Fort Columbus, New York Harbor, NY, on 11/19/1864. Sent to Elmira, NY, on 11/20/1864. Name on List of Prisoners of War at Elmira, NY, who desire to take the U.S. Oath of Allegiance; Remarks: Volunteered on 7/4/1862. Desires to go to New Orleans, LA, where he has relatives residing. Released on the U.S. Oath of Allegiance from Elmira, NY, on 5/29/1865. Description at oath: Eyes: blue. Hair: autumn. Complexion: florid. Height: 5'7". Residence at oath: New Orleans, LA. Buried: Amite City Cemetery located on Hwy. 16 at Amite, Tangipahoa Parish, LA. Confederate Pension Application on file at the Louisiana State Archives. Microfilm Reel: CP1.119. Microdex 2. Sequence 8. Target Card: Robertson, Simeon C. Parish: Tangipahoa. 14 pages.

Robinson, N.T.N. Capt./A.C.S., 1st Louisiana Cavalry. Artillery Co. F & S. Rolls for 9/1862 through 12/1862: Present or absent not stated. Rolls for 3/1863 through 6/1863: Present. On Roster dated Clinton, LA, 6/21/1864: Transferred to Artillery; Successor: William Hurd. Federal Rolls of Prisoners of War: Captured at Liberty, MS, on 11/16/1864; Received at Ship Island, MS, on 12/15/1864. Paroled at Ship Island, MS, in 1865; Indorsement shows: Exchanged on board the Flag of Truce Steamer *Nashua* at Mobile Bay, AL, on 3/5/1865. Rolls of Prisoners of War of Officers, C.S.A: Surrendered at Citronelle, AL, on 5/4/1865; Paroled at Grenada, MS, on 5/19/1865. Residence at parole: New Orleans, LA.

Robinson, William L. Pvt./Sgt., Holmes' Artillery Battery. Enlisted: 3/5/1862 at New Orleans, LA. Federal Rolls of Prisoners of War: Captured at Liberty, MS, on 11/16/1864; Forwarded to New Orleans, LA, on 11/23/1864. Received at Ship Island, MS, on 12/10/1864. Died: 3/16/1865 at Ship Island, MS, due to dysentery. Buried: Ship Island, MS, Cemetery in Grave #141.

Rochester, Samuel N. (AKA Richester, S.M.) Pvt./Cpl., Crescent Infantry Regiment. Co. A. Enlisted: 3/5/1862 at New Orleans, LA. Rolls for 5/1862 through 6/1862: Present. Rolls for 7/1862 through 8/1862: Absent, transferred from the Crescent Infantry Regiment to the 18th Louisiana Infantry. Co. K at Tupelo, MS, on 7/28/1862 while sick at Enterprise, MS. Rolls for 12/1862 through 8/1863: Present. Rolls for 1/1864 through 2/1864: Absent, detailed with the Signal Corps at Shreveport, LA, per Order # 26 of Maj. Gen. Richard Taylor on 1/26/1864. Federal Rolls of Prisoners of War: Captured at Adams County, MS, on 10/27/1864; Forwarded to New Orleans, LA, from Natchez, MS, on 11/21/1864. Received at Ship Island, MS, on 12/10/1864; Returned to New Orleans,

LA, and took the U.S. Oath of Allegiance on 3/9/1865. Released from New Orleans, LA, on 3/9/1865 by order of Maj. Gen.E.R.S. Canby. Description at oath: Eyes: hazel. Hair: brown. Complexion: light. Height: 5'10". Residence at parole: New Orleans, LA.

Rodgers, Robert Pvt., 5th Louisiana Cavalry. Co. I. Federal Rolls of Prisoners of War: Captured near Liberty, MS, on 11/17/1864; Forwarded to New Orleans, LA, on 11/23/1864. Received at Ship Island, MS, on 12/13/1864; Transferred to Vicksburg, MS, for exchange on 5/1/1865. Exchanged at Camp Townsend, MS, on 5/6/1865.

Roe, E. Pvt., 3rd Louisiana Cavalry. Co. I. Federal Rolls Prisoners of War: Captured at Clinton, LA, on 8/25/1864; Received at Ship Island, MS, from New Orleans, LA, on 10/7/1864.

Roe, Jacob A. (AKA Row) Pvt., 3rd Louisiana Cavalry. Co. I. Federal Rolls of Prisoners of War: Captured near Clinton, LA, on 8/25/1864; Received at Ship Island, MS, from New Orleans, LA, on 10/7/1864. Confederate Widows Pension Application on file at the Louisiana State Archives. Microfilm Reel: CP1.120. Microdex 4. Sequence 2. Target Card: Roe, Mary (Thibodeaux). Parish: East Feliciana. 17 pages.

Rogers, James Pvt., 19th Louisiana Infantry. Co. K. Federal Rolls of Prisoners of War: Captured at Spanish Fort, AL, on 4/8/1865; Received at Ship Island, MS, on 4/10/1865. Died: 4/29/1865 at Ship Island, MS, due to diarrhea. Buried: Ship Island, MS, Cemetery in Grave #150.

Rondes, J.W. Pvt., 12th Louisiana Infantry. Co. __. Federal Rolls of Prisoners of War: Captured near Clinton, LA, on 8/25/1864; Received at Fort Columbus, New York Harbor, NY, from Ship Island, MS, on 11/16/1864. Transferred to Elmira, NY, on 11/18/1864.

Roper, John T. Pvt., 22nd Louisiana Infantry (Consolidated). Co. D. Enlisted: 12/18/1861 at Fort Powell, LA. Rolls for 5/1864 through 6/1864: Present, joined by transfer at Mobile, AL, on 5/24/1864. Rolls for 7/1864 through 8/1864: Present. Rolls for 9/1864 through 10/1864: Absent, sick. Rolls for 3/1865 through 4/1865: Absent, taken prisoner of war. Federal Rolls of Prisoners of War: Captured at Spanish Fort, AL, on 4/8/1865; Received at Ship Island, MS, on 4/10/1865. Transferred to Vicksburg, MS, for exchange on 5/1/1865; Exchanged at Camp Townsend, MS, on 5/6/1865. On Register of U.S.A. General Hospital # 2, Vicksburg, MS: Admitted on 5/6/1865; Released on 5/8/1865. Age at admittance: 26.

Ross, John (AKA J.M.) Pvt./Hosp. Stew., 22nd Louisiana Infantry (Consolidated). Co. G. F & S. Enlisted: 12/28/1862 at Vicksburg, MS. Rolls for 1/1864 through 2/1864: Present, assigned as regimental Hospital Steward. Rolls for 3/1864 through 8/1864: Present. Rolls for 9/1864 through 10/1864: Present, at regimental hospital at Spanish Fort, AL. Federal Rolls of Prisoners of War: Captured at Spanish Fort, AL, on 4/3/1865; Received at Ship Island, MS, on 4/10/1865. Transferred to Vicksburg, MS, for exchange on 5/1/1865; Exchanged at Camp Townsend, MS, on 5/6/1865.

Rousseau, Adolphus Sgt., 9th Louisiana Battalion Infantry. Co. C. Enlisted: 3/18/1862 at Baton Rouge, LA. Rolls for 9/1862 through 10/1862: Present. Federal Rolls of Prisoners of War: Captured at Amite River, LA, on 9/20/1864; Received at Ship Island, MS, from New Orleans, LA, on 10/27/1864. Transferred to Fort Columbus, New York Harbor, NY, on 11/5/1864; Forwarded to Elmira, NY, on 11/20/1864. Name on List of Prisoners of War at Elmira, NY, who desire to take the U.S. Oath of Allegiance on 11/30/1864; Remarks: Volunteered on 5/8/1862. Deserted his command at Clinton, LA, on 8/15/1864 and returned home, near his place of capture. Desires to go to New Orleans, LA. Released from Elmira, NY, on the U.S. Oath of Allegiance on 5/19/1865. Description at oath: Eyes: gray. Hair: dark. Complexion: dark. Height: 5'5½". Residence at oath: New Orleans, LA.

Rousell, James (AKA Russell) Pvt., Ogden's Cavalry Battalion. Co. E. Federal Rolls of Prisoners of War: Captured at Clinton, LA, on 11/16/1864 or Liberty, MS, on 11/17/1864; Forwarded to New Orleans, LA, on 11/23/1864. Received at Ship Island, MS, on 12/10/1864. Name on undated List of Prisoners at Ship Island, MS, who applied to take the U.S. Oath of Allegiance; Received at the U.S. Office of Commissary General of Prisoners on 2/7/1865. Returned to New Orleans, LA, on 4/14/1865; Released on the U.S. Oath of Allegiance on 4/14/1865 by order of Maj. Gen.E.R.S. Canby. Description at oath: Eyes: brown. Hair: brown. Complexion: light. Height: 5'0". Residence at oath: St. John the Baptist Parish, LA.

Roussell, Thomas Pvt., 4th Louisiana Infantry. Co. E. Enlisted: 5/25/1861 at Camp Moore, LA. Rolls for 5/25/1861 through 12/1861: Present. Rolls for 1/1862 through 2/1862: Present or absent not stated. Federal Rolls of Prisoners of War: Captured at Pittsburg Landing, TN, on 4/3/1862; Received at Camp Douglas, IL, on 8/1/1862. Sent to Vicksburg, MS, for exchange in 1862; Remarks: Already gone and accounted for. Rolls for 11/1862 through 12/1862: Present. Federal Rolls of Prisoners of War: Captured at Pointe Coupée Parish, LA, on 5/18/1863; Paroled at Grant's Island, off Mobile, AL, on 5/30/1863. Rolls for 6/1863 through 8/1863: Absent, on detached service at Port Hudson, LA. Rolls for 9/1863 through 8/1864: Present. Rolls for 9/1864 through 2/1865: Absent, taken prisoner of war. Federal Rolls of Prisoners of War: Captured at Nashville, TN, on 12/16/1864; Received at the U.S. Military Prison, Louisville, KY, on 1/3/1865. Transferred to Camp Chase, OH, on 1/4/1865; Paroled at Camp Chase, OH, in 1865. Transferred to Point Lookout, MD, for exchange on 2/17/1865. Roll for 4/1865: Absent, taken prisoner of war. Federal Rolls of Prisoners of War: Captured at Spanish Fort, AL, on 4/8/1865; Received at Ship Island, MS, on 4/10/1865. Transferred to Vicksburg, MS, for exchange on 5/1/1865; Exchanged at Camp Townsend, MS, on 5/6/1865.

Row, E.L. (AKA Roe, E.L.) Pvt., 3rd Louisiana Cavalry (Harrison's). Co. I. Federal Rolls of Prisoners of War: Captured and paroled at Port Hudson, LA, on 7/9/1863. Federal Rolls of Prisoners of War: Captured at Clinton, LA, on 8/25/1864; Forwarded to New Orleans, LA, on 8/31/1864. Received at Ship Island, MS, on 10/5/1864; Transferred to Fort Columbus, New York Harbor, NY, on 11/16/1864. Received at Elmira, NY, on 11/19/1864; Paroled at Elmira, NY, on 2/25/1865. Sent to James River, VA, for exchange.

Row, I.A. Pvt., 3rd Louisiana Cavalry. Co. I. Federal

Rolls of Prisoners of War: Captured at Clinton, LA, on 8/25/1864; Received at Ship Island, MS, from New Orleans, LA, on 10/7/1864. Transferred to Fort Columbus, New York Harbor, NY, on 11/5/1864.

Row, Jacob A. Pvt., 3rd Louisiana Cavalry (Harrison's). Co. I. Federal Rolls of Prisoners of War: Captured and paroled at Port Hudson, LA, on 7/9/1863. Federal Rolls of Prisoners of War: Captured at Clinton, LA, on 8/25/1864; Forwarded to New Orleans, LA, on 8/31/1864. Received at Ship Island, MS, on 10/5/1864; Transferred to Fort Columbus, New York Harbor, NY, on 11/16/1864. Received at Elmira, NY, on 11/19/1864; Paroled at Elmira, NY, on 2/25/1865. Transferred to James River, VA, for exchange.

St. Amant, Ven, Jr. (AKA St. Aman, Anant, Stama, Stamaund, Stuma) 1st Cpl./4th Sgt., 27th Louisiana Infantry. Co. D. Enlisted: 3/8/1862 at Iberville Parish, LA. Rolls for 4/1862 through 12/1862: Present, promoted from 1st Cpl. to 4th Sgt. on 9/25/1862. Federal Rolls of Prisoners of War: Captured at Vicksburg, MS, on 7/4/1863; Paroled on 7/8/1863. Federal Rolls of Prisoners of War: Captured near Pass Manchac, LA, on 9/11/1864; Forwarded to New Orleans, LA, on 9/15/1864. Received at Ship Island, MS, on 10/5/1864; Transferred to Fort Columbus, New York Harbor, NY, on 11/16/1864. Forwarded to Elmira, NY, on 11/19/1864; Paroled at Elmira, NY, and sent to James River, VA, for exchange on 2/25/1865. Transferred to Point Lookout, MD, on 2/29/1865.

St. John, William Cpl./Sgt., 1st Louisiana Cavalry, Co. D. Enlisted: 9/12/1861 at Baton Rouge, LA. Rolls for 4/1862 through 2/1863: Present. Federal Rolls of Prisoners of War: Captured at Somerset, KY, on 3/30/1863; Sent to Baltimore, MD, enroute to City Point, VA, for exchange on 4/13/1863. Exchanged at City Point, VA, on 4/22/1863. Rolls for 6/1863 through 12/1863: Present. Federal Rolls of Prisoners of War: Captured at Liberty, MS, on 11/10/1864; Forwarded to New Orleans, LA, on 11/23/1864. Received at Ship Island, MS, on 11/23/1864; Transferred to Vicksburg, MS, for exchange on 5/1/1865. Exchanged at Camp Townsend, MS, on 5/6/1865.

Sadler, B.F. Pvt., 3rd Louisiana Cavalry (Wingfield's). Co. B. Enlisted: 8/20/1862 at Camp Moore, LA. Rolls for 8/20/1862 through 9/1862: Present. Rolls for 10/1862 through 1/1863: Present. Federal Rolls of Prisoners of War: Captured near Clinton, MS, on 5/25/1864; Forwarded to New Orleans, LA, on 8/31/1864. Received at Ship Island, MS, on 10/5/1864; Transferred to Fort Columbus, New York Harbor, NY, on 11/16/1864. Forwarded to Elmira, NY, on 11/19/1864; Paroled at Elmira, NY, on 2/25/1865. Sent to James River, VA, for exchange. Paroled on 5/22/1865 by order of Maj. Gen. E.R.S. Canby. Age at parole: 30. Description at parole: Eyes: hazel. Hair: dark. Complexion: dark. Height: 5'6". Residence at parole: St. Tammany Parish, LA. Born: 7/6/1834. Died: 6/19/1919. Buried: Beauvoir Cemetery located on Hwy. 98 at Biloxi, Harrison County, MS.

Sadler, John Pvt., Ogden's Cavalry Battalion. Co. B. Federal Rolls of Prisoners of War: Captured at Pearl River, MS, on 3/29/1864; Forwarded to New Orleans, LA, on 9/5/1864. Received at Ship Island, MS, on 10/5/1864; Transferred to Fort Columbus, New York Harbor, NY, on 11/16/1864. Sent to Elmira, NY, on 11/19/1864; Paroled at Elmira, NY, on 2/25/1865. Exchanged at James River, VA.

Sanchez, Joseph Pvt., 4th Louisiana Infantry. Co. E. Enlisted: 5/25/1861 at Camp Moore, LA. Rolls for 5/25/1861 through 12/1863: Present. Rolls for 9/1864 through 2/1865: Absent, wounded at the Battle of the Poor House, GA, on 7/28/1864. Federal Rolls of Prisoners of War: Captured at St. Francisville, LA, on 9/5/1864; Received at Ship Island, MS, from New Orleans, LA, on 11/2/1864. Transferred to Fort Columbus, New York Harbor, NY, on 11/10/1864; Forwarded to Elmira, NY, on 11/19/1864. Name on List dated Prison Camp Headquarters, Elmira, NY, of Prisoners who desire to take the U.S. Oath of Allegiance on 1/16/1865; Remarks: Volunteered on 5/4/1861 for 12 months and re-enlisted for the war in 5/1862. The Prisoner has lost his arm in battle and for this reason desires to return to his family at New Orleans, LA. Paroled at Elmira, NY, on 2/9/1865; Sent to James River, VA, for exchange. Exchanged at Boulware and Cox Wharf, James River, VA, on 2/20–21/1865.

Santana, Charles Pvt., Miles Legion. Co. A. Enlisted: 5/22/1863 at Baton Rouge, LA. Rolls for 5/22/1863 through 8/1863: Present. Rolls for 9/1863 through 12/1863: Present or absent not stated. Federal Rolls of Prisoners of War: Captured at Liberty, MS, on 11/15/1864; Forwarded to New Orleans, LA, on 11/23/1864. Received at Ship Island, MS, on 12/13/1864; Transferred to Vicksburg, MS, for exchange on 5/1/1865. Exchanged at Camp Townsend, MS, on 5/6/1865. Soldier also served as a Pvt. with Ogden's Battalion Cavalry (Louisiana). Died: 9/29/1914. Buried: Metairie Cemetery located on Pontchartrain Blvd. at New Orleans, Orleans Parish, LA.

Saul, Charles (AKA Sauls, Saules) Pvt., 4th Louisiana Battalion Infantry. Co. E. Enlisted: 8/15/1861 at Camp Moore, LA. Rolls for 8/15/1861 through 9/1/1861: Absent, sick in camp with measles. Rolls for 9/1861 through 10/1861: Present. Rolls for 11/1861 through 2/1862: Absent, sick at Richmond, VA. Rolls for 3/1862 through 2/28/1865: Present. Rolls for 3/1865 through 4/1865: Absent, taken prisoner of war at Spanish Fort, AL, on 4/7/1865. Federal Rolls of Prisoners of War: Captured at Spanish Fort, AL, on 4/8/1865; Received at Ship Island, MS, on 4/10/1865. Transferred to Vicksburg, MS, on 5/1/1865; Exchanged at Camp Townsend, MS, on 5/6/1865.

Scarborough, A. Pvt., Grosse Tête Flying Artillery. Federal Rolls of Prisoners of War: Captured at Bayou Grosse Tête, LA, on 10/22/1864; Received at Ship Island, MS, from New Orleans, LA, on 10/31/1864. Transferred to Fort Columbus, New York Harbor, NY, on 11/16/1864; Forwarded to Elmira, NY, on 11/19/1864. Paroled at Elmira, NY, on 2/25/1865; Sent to James River, VA, for exchange.

Schexnaider, Tonsere (AKA Schenxider) Pvt., Ogden's Cavalry Battalion. Co. E. Federal Rolls of Prisoners of War: Captured at Clinton, LA, on 11/16/1864; Forwarded to New Orleans, LA, on 11/23/1864. Received at Ship Island, MS; Transferred to Vicksburg, MS, for exchange on 5/1/1865. Exchanged at Camp Townsend, MS, on 5/6/1865. Buried: Cossinade Cemetery located on Cossinade Rd. at Vermillion Parish, LA. Soldier also served as a Pvt. with the 1st Louisiana Infantry. Co.A. Confederate Widows

Pension Application on file at the Louisiana State Archives. Microfilm Reel: CP1.124. Microdex 3. Sequence 24. Target Card: Schexnaider, Annie Trahan. Parish: Acadia. 6 pages.

Schexnaider, Jacob Pvt., Ogden's Cavalry Battalion. Co. E. Federal Rolls of Prisoners of War: Captured at Clinton, LA, on 11/16/1864; Forwarded to New Orleans, LA, on 11/23/1864. Received at Ship Island, MS; Transferred to Vicksburg, MS, for exchange on 5/1/1865. Exchanged at Camp Townsend, MS, on 5/6/1865.

Schexnaydre, Ozeme Pvt., 30th Louisiana Infantry. Co. G. Enlisted: 11/15/1862 at Port Hudson, LA. Rolls for 1/1863 through 2/1865: Present. Federal Rolls of Prisoners of War: Captured at Spanish Fort, AL, on 4/8/1865; Received at Ship Island, MS, on 4/10/1865. Transferred to Vicksburg, MS, for exchange on 5/1/1865; Exchanged at Camp Townsend, MS, on 5/6/1865. Rolls of Prisoners of War, C.S.A: Surrendered at Citronelle, AL, on 5/4/1865; Paroled at Bonnet Carre, LA, on 5/16/1865.

Schwing, George B. Pvt., 2nd Louisiana Cavalry. Co. I. Enlisted: 9/1/1862 at New Roads, LA. Federal Rolls of Prisoners of War: Captured at Stone's Plantation, LA, on 9/16/1864; Forwarded to New Orleans, LA, on 9/20/1864. Received at Ship Island, MS, on 10/7/1864; Transferred to Fort Columbus, New York Harbor, NY, on 11/16/1864. On Register of U.S.A. General Hospital, Fort Columbus, New York Harbor, NY: Admitted on 11/17/1864; Released on 12/4/1864. Transferred to Elmira, NY, on 11/19/1864; Sent to James River, VA, and exchanged on 2/20/1865.

Schwing, John T. Pvt., 2nd Louisiana Cavalry. Co. I. Enlisted: 9/1/1862 at New Roads, LA. Roll for 9/1862: Absent, sick at home. Rolls for 1/1863 through 2/1863: Present. Federal Rolls of Prisoners of War: Captured near Hampton Ferry, LA, on 10/10/1864; Forwarded to New Orleans, LA, from Morganza, LA, on 10/12/1864. Received at Ship Island, MS, on 10/21/1864; Sent to Fort Columbus, New York Harbor, NY, on 11/16/1864. Transferred to Elmira, NY, on 11/20/1864; Paroled at Elmira, NY, on 2/25/1865. Sent to James River, VA, for exchange. Confederate Pension Application on file at the Louisiana State Archives. Microfilm Reel: CP1.125. Microdex 1. Sequence 17. Target Card: Schwing, John T. Parish: St. Mary. 6 pages.

Scott, Edwin Allen Capt./Maj., 3rd Louisiana Cavalry (Wingfield's). Co. I/F & S. Federal Rolls of Prisoners of War: Captured at Tickfaw Bridge, LA, on 5/1/1863. Federal Rolls of Prisoners of War: Captured in East Louisiana on 11/19/1864; Forwarded to New Orleans, LA, on 11/24/1864. Received at Ship Island, MS, on 12/15/1864; Exchanged on 3/4/1865. Born: 1824. Died: 1903. Buried: Scott Family Cemetery located on the Berger homestead at East Feliciana Parish, LA.

Scott, Em.T. Pvt., 3rd Louisiana Cavalry. Co. __. Federal Rolls Prisoners of War: Captured at Clinton, LA, on 11/16/1864; Received at Ship Island, MS, from New Orleans, LA, on 12/13/1864.

Scott, W.T. Pvt., Louisiana Supporting Forces. Co. A. Federal Rolls Prisoners of War: Captured at Clinton, LA, on 11/16/1864; Forwarded to New Orleans, LA, on 11/23/1864. Received at Ship Island, MS, on 12/13/1864; Transferred to Vicksburg, MS, for exchange on 5/1/1865. Exchanged at Camp Townsend, MS, on 5/6/1865.

Scott, William T. Pvt., 3rd Louisiana Cavalry. Co. __. Federal Rolls of Prisoners of War: Captured at Clinton, LA, on 11/16/1864; Received at Ship Island, MS, on 12/13/1864.

Searcy, Bennett Sgt./Pvt., 3rd Louisiana Cavalry (Harrison's). Co. I. Federal Rolls of Prisoners of War: Captured at Tunica, LA, on 9/14/1864; Forwarded to New Orleans, LA, from Baton Rouge, LA, on 10/10/1864. Received at Ship Island, MS, on 10/21/1864; Forwarded to Fort Columbus, New York Harbor, NY, on 11/16/1864. Transferred to Elmira, NY, on 11/20/1864; Paroled at Elmira, NY, on 2/25/1865. Sent to James River, VA, for exchange. Died: 5/16/1900. Buried: Greenwood Cemetery located on City Park Ave. at New Orleans, Orleans Parish, LA.

Seeders, John Pvt., 4th Louisiana Infantry. Co. B. Enlisted: 5/16/1862 at Edwards Depot, MS. Rolls for 9/1862 through 12/1862: Present. Rolls for 1/1863 through 6/1863: Absent, detailed as Teamster in Louisiana. Rolls for 7/1863 through 8/1864: Present. Federal Rolls of Prisoners of War: Captured at Jonesboro, GA, on 8/31/1864; Exchanged by order of Maj. Gen. William T. Sherman, Commanding the Military Division of the Mississippi at Rough and Ready, GA, on 9/19–22/1864. Rolls for 10/1864 through 2/1865: Present. Federal Rolls of Prisoners of War: Captured at Spanish Fort, AL, on 4/8/1865; Received at Ship Island, MS, on 4/10/1865. Transferred to Vicksburg, MS, for exchange on 5/1/1865; Exchanged at Camp Townsend, MS, on 5/6/1865.

Seeders, Robert Pvt., 4th Louisiana Infantry. Co. D. Enlisted: 5/25/1861 at Camp Moore, LA. Rolls for 5/25/1861 through 10/1862: Present. Rolls for 11/1862 through 12/1862: Absent, sick. Rolls for 1/1863 through 2/1865: Present. Federal Rolls of Prisoners of War: Captured at Spanish Fort, AL, on 4/8/1865; Received at Ship Island, MS, on 4/10/1865. Transferred to Vicksburg, MS, for exchange on 5/1/1865; Exchanged at Camp Townsend, MS, on 5/6/1865.

Sermon, W.H. Pvt., 3rd Louisiana Cavalry (Harrison's). Co. __. Federal Rolls of Prisoners of War: Captured on 10/10/1864; Received at New Orleans, LA, on 10/15/1864. Federal Rolls of Prisoners of War: Captured at Brookhaven, MS, on 11/16/1864; Received at Ship Island, MS. Transferred to Vicksburg, MS, for exchange on 5/1/1865; Exchanged at Camp Townsend, MS, on 5/6/1865.

Setton, Henry Pvt., 1st Louisiana Cavalry. Co. H. Enlisted: 10/5/1861 at Baton Rouge, LA. Rolls for 5/1862 through 8/1862: Absent, on sick furlough by Surgeon's Certificate. Rolls for 9/1862 through 12/1863: Present. Federal Rolls of Prisoners of War: Captured at Ascension Parish, LA, on 12/13/1864; Received at Ship Island, MS, from New Orleans, LA, on 1/22/1865. Transferred to Vicksburg, MS, for exchange on 5/1/1865; Exchanged at Camp Townsend, MS, on 5/6/1865.

Settoon, Archai (AKA Archa) Pvt., Ogden's Cavalry Battalion. Co. E. Federal Rolls of Prisoners of War: Captured near Liberty, MS, on 11/16/1864; Forwarded to New Orleans, LA, on 11/23/1864. Received at Ship Island, MS, on 12/10/1864; Transferred to Vicksburg, MS, for exchange on 5/1/1865. Exchanged at Camp Townsend, MS, on 5/6/1865. Soldier also served as a Pvt. with the 9th Louisiana Battalion Cavalry. Co. A. Confederate Pension Application on file at the Louisiana State Archives. Microfilm Reel: CP1.125. Microdex 4. Sequence 22. Target Card: Settoon, Archai. Parish: Ascension. 6 pages.

Sevinon, W.H. Pvt., 3rd Louisiana Cavalry. Co. __. Federal Rolls of Prisoners of War: Captured at Brookhaven, MS, on 5/1/1865; Received at Ship Island, MS. Transferred to Vicksburg, MS, for exchange on 5/1/1865; Exchanged at Camp Townsend, MS, on 5/6/1865.

Sicard, F.C. Pvt., Grosse Tête Flying Artillery. Federal Rolls of Prisoners of War: Captured at Bayou Grosse Tête, LA, on 10/22/1864; Received at Ship Island, MS, from New Orleans, LA, on 10/31/1864. Forwarded to Fort Columbus, New York Harbor, NY, on 11/5/1864; Transferred to Elmira, NY, on 11/19/1864. Paroled at Elmira, NY, on 2/9/1865; Sent to James River, VA, for exchange. Exchanged at Boulware and Cox Wharf, James River, VA, on 2/20–21/1865.

Simpson, George B. Pvt., Cage's Cavalry Battalion. Co. A. Federal Rolls of Prisoners of War: Captured near Clinton, LA, on 8/25/1864; Forwarded to New Orleans, LA, on 8/31/1864. Received at Ship Island, MS, on 10/7/1864; Transferred to Fort Columbus, New York Harbor, NY, on 11/16/1864. Forwarded to Elmira, NY, on 11/19/1864; Paroled at Elmira, NY, on 2/25/1865. Sent to James River, VA, for exchange.

Skinner, C.A. Pvt., 2nd Louisiana Cavalry. Co. I. Federal Rolls of Prisoners of War: Captured at Bayou Fordoche, LA, on 10/20/1864; Forwarded to New Orleans, LA, on 10/31/1864. Received at Ship Island, MS, on 11/1/1864; Forwarded to Fort Columbus, New York Harbor, NY, on 11/5/1864. Transferred to Elmira, NY, on 11/19/1864; Paroled at Elmira, NY, on 2/9/1865. Sent to James River, VA, for exchange; Exchanged at Boulware and Cox Wharf, James River, VA, on 2/20–21/1865.

Skofield, James P. Lt./1st Lt., 5th Louisiana Cavalry. Co. __. Federal Rolls of Prisoners of War: Captured at Brookhaven, MS, on 11/18/1864; Received at Ship Island, MS, from New Orleans, LA, on 12/15/1864. Exchanged on 3/2/1865. Name on Endorsement Roll of Flag of Truce, Steamer *Nashua*, Mobile Bay, AL: Received Prisoner of War James P. Skofield.

Slaughter, William Shewen Pvt., 3rd Louisiana Cavalry (Harrison's). Co. I. Federal Rolls of Prisoners of War: Captured at East Baton Rouge Parish, LA, on 12/24/1864; Forwarded to New Orleans, LA, on 1/12/1865. Received at Ship Island, MS, on 1/25/1865; Transferred to Vicksburg, MS, for exchange on 5/1/1865. Exchanged at Camp Townsend, MS, on 5/6/1865. Confederate Pension Application on file at the Louisiana State Archives. Microfilm Reel: CP1.128. Microdex 4. Sequence 8. Target Card: Slaughter, William S. Parish: East Baton Rouge. 11 pages.

Slone, Dudley Pvt., Ogden's Cavalry Battalion. Co. A. Federal Rolls of Prisoners of War: Captured at Tensas Parish, LA, on 9/14/1864; Forwarded to New Orleans, LA, from Baton Rouge, LA, on 10/10/1864. Received at Ship Island, MS, on 10/20/1864; Transferred to Fort Columbus, New York Harbor, NY, on 11/16/1864. Forwarded to Elmira, NY, on 11/20/1864; Paroled at Elmira, NY, on 2/25/1865. Sent to James River, VA, for exchange. Name on List dated Office of the Provost Marshall, Donaldsonville, LA, 1/18/1865 of Confederate soldiers who have deserted their commands, come within U.S. lines, and reported at the Provost Marshall's Office at Donaldsonville, LA. Forwarded to Capt.B.B. Campbell, Assistant Adjutant, General Headquarters, Lafourche, LA, District. Remarks: Deserted on 11/17/1864 at Jackson, LA; Reported at this Office on 1/14/1865. Served in Louisiana.

Smith, Felix H. Pvt., Grosse Tête Flying Artillery (Louisiana). Federal Rolls of Prisoners of War: Captured at Morganza, LA, on 8/30/1864; Received at Ship Island, MS, from New Orleans, LA, on 10/27/1864. Forwarded to Fort Columbus, New York Harbor, NY, on 11/16/1864; Transferred to Elmira, NY, on 11/19/1864. Paroled at Elmira, NY, on 2/9/1865; Sent to James River, VA, for exchange. Exchanged at Boulware and Cox Wharf, James River, VA, on 2/20–21/1865; Received at Fort McHenry, MD, on 5/10/1865. Released from Fort McHenry, MD, on 5/12/1865 in accordance with instructions from the U.S. Commissary General of Prisoners, Washington, D.C. on 5/8/1865. Residence at release: New Orleans, LA. Buried: Cottonwood Cemetery, Lottie, Pointe Coupée Parish, LA.

Smith, J.W. Pvt., 4th Louisiana Infantry. Old Co. G. Enlisted: 5/25/1861 at Tangipahoa, LA. Rolls for 5/25/1861 through 2/1862: Present. Federal Rolls of Prisoners of War: Captured at Spanish Fort, AL, on 4/8/1865; Received at Ship Island, MS, on 4/10/1865. Transferred to Vicksburg, MS, for exchange on 5/1/1865; Exchanged at Camp Townsend, MS, on 5/6/1865.

Smith, James Pvt., Ogden's Cavalry Battalion. Co. A. Federal Rolls of Prisoners of War: Captured at East Baton Rouge Parish, LA, on 10/22/1864; Received at Ship Island, MS, on 10/29/1864. Forwarded to Fort Columbus, New York Harbor, NY, on 11/16/1864; Transferred to Elmira, NY, on 11/20/1864. Died: 12/27/1864 at Elmira, NY, on due to pneumonia.

Smith, John Pvt., 25th Louisiana Infantry. Co. C. Enlisted: 3/18/1862 at Monterey, LA. Rolls for 3/18/1862 through 4/1862: Present. Rolls for 5/1862 through 6/1862: Returned to duty on 7/1/1862. Rolls for 12/1862 through 2/1863: Absent, wounded in action before Murfreesboro, TN, on 12/31/1862. Federal Rolls of Prisoners of War: Captured at Murfreesboro, TN, on 1/5/1863; Sent to Camp Morton, in on 3/1/1863. Forwarded to City Point, VA, for exchange; Exchanged on 4/12/1863. Rolls for 4/1864 through 2/1865: Absent, on sick furlough by order of Dr. Bass since 4/13/1864. Rolls for 3/1865 through 4/1865: Absent, taken prisoner of war. Federal Rolls of Prisoners of War: Captured at Blakely, AL, on 4/9/1865; Received at Ship Island, MS, on 4/15/1865. Transferred to Vicksburg, MS, for exchange on 5/1/1865; Exchanged at Camp Townsend, MS, on 5/6/1865. Rolls of Prisoners of War, C.S.A: Surrendered at Citronelle, AL, on 5/4/1865; Paroled at Meridian, MS, on 5/13/1865. Residence at parole: Chambers County, AL.

Smith, Merrick M. Pvt., 4th Louisiana Infantry. Co. K. Enlisted: 3/1/1864 at Mobile, AL. Rolls for 3/1864 through 2/1865: Present. Federal Rolls of Prisoners of War: Captured at Spanish Fort, AL, on 4/8/1865; Received at Ship Island, MS, on 4/10/1865. Transferred to Vicksburg, MS, for exchange on 5/1/1865; Exchanged at Camp Townsend, MS.

Smith, William Pvt., 3rd Louisiana Cavalry (Wingfield's). Co. H. Enlisted: 6/12/1862 at Camp Moore, LA. Rolls for 6/12/1862 through 10/1862: Present or absent not stated. Federal Rolls of Prisoners of War: Captured at Brookhaven, MS, on 11/15/1864 or Liberty, MS, on 11/18/1864; Forwarded to New Orleans, LA, on 11/23/1864. Received at Ship Island, MS, on 12/13/1864; Transferred to Vicksburg, MS, for exchange on 5/1/1865. Exchanged at Camp Townsend, MS, on 5/6/1865.

Smith, William Pvt., Louisiana Supporting Forces. Co. __. Federal Rolls of Prisoners of War: Captured at Brookhaven, MS, on 11/15/1864; Received at Ship Island, MS, from New Orleans, LA, on 12/13/1864.

Smith, William T. (AKA W.J.) Pvt., 5th Louisiana Cavalry. Cos. A & B. Federal Rolls of Prisoners of War: Captured at Summit, MS, on 11/18/1864; Received at Ship Island, MS, on 12/13/1864. On Register of C.S.A. General Hospital, Shreveport, LA: Admitted on 2/21/1865; Returned to duty on 2/25/1865. Rolls of Prisoners of War, C.S.A: Surrendered at New Orleans, LA, on 5/26/1865; Paroled at Monroe, LA, on 6/14/1865. Residence at parole: Floyd, LA. Died: 8/26/1912. Buried: Greenwood Cemetery located on City Park Ave. at New Orleans, Orleans Parish, LA.

Sparks, A.G. Pvt., 2nd Louisiana Cavalry. Co. I. Federal Rolls of Prisoners of War: Captured at Bayou Grosse Tête, LA, on 10/27/1864; Forwarded to New Orleans, LA, from Morganza, LA, on 10/31/1864. Received at Ship Island, MS, on 11/2/1864; Transferred to Fort Columbus, New York Harbor, NY, on 11/16/1864. Sent to Elmira, NY, on 11/19/1864; Paroled at Elmira, NY, on 2/25/1865. Exchanged at James River, VA, in 1865.

Sparks, Charles B. Pvt., 2nd Louisiana Cavalry. Co. I. Federal Rolls of Prisoners of War: Captured at Bayou Grosse Tête, LA, on 10/27/1864; Forwarded to New Orleans, LA, from Morganza, LA, on 10/31/1864. Received at Ship Island, MS, on 11/5/1864; Sent to Fort Columbus, New York Harbor, NY, on 11/16/1864. Transferred to Elmira, NY, on 11/19/1864; Died: 1/1/1865 at Elmira, NY, due to pneumonia.

Spears, W.M. Pvt., 19th Louisiana Infantry. Co. C. Enlisted: 3/31/1862 at Corinth, MS. Rolls for 4/1862 through 5/1862: Present. Rolls for 9/1862 through 10/1862: Discharged due to being overage for service and final statement given on 10/9/1862. Rolls for 3/1865 through 4/1865: Absent, taken prisoner of war. Federal Rolls of Prisoners of War: Captured at Spanish Fort, AL, on 4/8/1865; Received at Ship Island, MS, on 4/10/1865. Transferred to Vicksburg, MS, for exchange on 5/1/1865; Exchanged at Camp Townsend, MS, on 5/6/1865. Rolls of Prisoners of War, C.S.A: Surrendered at Citronelle, AL, on 5/4/1865; Paroled at Meridian, MS, on 5/13/1865. Residence at parole: Argis, LA.

Spellman, M. Pvt., Ogden's Cavalry Battalion. Co. __. Federal Rolls of Prisoners of War: Captured at East Baton Rouge Parish, LA, on 1/11/1865; Forwarded to New Orleans, LA, on 1/11/1865. Received at Ship Island, MS; Transferred to Vicksburg, MS, for exchange on 5/1/1865. Exchanged at Camp Townsend, MS, on 5/6/1865.

Spillers, James R. (AKA Spillars) Pvt., 25th Louisiana Infantry. Co. C. Enlisted: 5/17/1863 at Monroe, LA. Rolls for 1/1864 through 4/1864: Present. Rolls for 7/1864 through 8/1864: Absent, on sick furlough by order of Dr. Bass since 7/28/1864. Rolls for 9/1864 through 2/1865: Present. Rolls for 3/1865 through 4/1865: Absent, taken prisoner of war. Federal Rolls of Prisoners of War: Captured at Spanish Fort, AL, on 4/8/1865; Received at Ship Island, MS, on 4/10/1865. Transferred to Vicksburg, MS, for exchange on 5/1/1865; Exchanged at Camp Townsend, MS, on 5/6/1865. Rolls of Prisoners of War, C.S.A: Surrendered at Citronelle, AL, on 5/4/1865; Paroled at Meridian, MS, on 5/10/1865. Residence at parole: Monroe, LA. Confederate Pension Application on file at the Louisiana State Archives. Microfilm Reel: CP1.131. Microdex 3. Sequence 9. Target Card: Spillers, James R. Parish: Winn. 12 pages.

Spillman, M. Pvt., Miles Legion. Co. A. Enlisted: 5/1/1863 at Baton Rouge, LA, or Redwood, LA. Rolls for 5/1863 through 12/1863: Present. Federal Rolls of Prisoners of War: Captured at Lavinia, LA, on 10/20/1864; Received at Ship Island, MS, on 10/27/1864. Forwarded to New Orleans, LA, on 10/31/1864; Transferred to Fort Columbus, New York Harbor, NY, on 11/16/1864. Sent to Elmira, NY, on 11/19/1864.

Starns, James Purnell Pvt., 3rd Louisiana Cavalry (Wingfield's). Co. B. Enlisted: 5/13/1862 at Camp Moore, LA. Roll dated 1/9/1863: Sick. Federal Rolls of Prisoners of War: Captured and paroled at Port Hudson, LA, on 7/9/1863. Federal Rolls of Prisoners of War: Captured at Clinton, LA, on 11/16/1864; Forwarded to New Orleans, LA, on 11/23/1864. Received at Ship Island, MS, on 12/10/1864; Transferred to Vicksburg, MS, for exchange on 5/1/1865. Exchanged at Camp Townsend, MS, on 5/6/1865. Born: 1/1/1849. Died: 12/11/1929. Buried: Amite City Cemetery located on Hwy. 16 at Amite, Tangipahoa Parish, LA. Soldier also served as a Pvt. with the 9th Louisiana Battalion Cavalry. Co. B. Confederate Pension Application on file at the Louisiana State Archives. Microfilm Reel: CP1.132. Microdex 2. Sequence 21. Target Card: Starns, James P. Parish: Tangipahoa. 7 pages.

Steibelt, Albert Pvt., Louisiana Home Guards. Co. __. Federal Rolls of Prisoners of War: Captured near Greensburg, LA, on 10/7/1864; Forwarded to New Orleans, LA, on 10/15/1864. Transferred to Ship Island, MS, on 10/20/1864; Received at Ship Island, MS, on 10/21/1864. Forwarded to New York on 11/5/1864. Name on List of Prisoners of War at Elmira, NY, who desire to take the U.S. Oath of Allegiance on 11/30/1864; Remarks: Was conscripted on 8/6/1864 at the age of 49. Wishes to go to New Orleans, LA.

Steinberger, Louis (AKA Sternberger, Lewis) Pvt., 3rd Louisiana Cavalry (Wingfield's). Co. H. Enlisted: 6/12/1862 at Camp Moore, LA. Description at enlistment: Eyes: blue. Hair: Sandy. Complexion: light. Height: 5'5". Rolls for 6/12/1862 through 9/1862: Present or absent not stated. Federal Rolls of Prisoners of War: Captured and paroled at Port Hudson, LA, on 7/9/1863. Federal Rolls of Prisoners of War: Captured near Clinton, LA, on 11/16/1864; Forwarded to New Orleans, LA, on 11/23/1864. Received at Ship Island, MS, on 12/13/1864; Returned to New Orleans, LA, on 3/9/1865 and released the same date by order of Maj. Gen.E.R.S. Canby upon taking the U.S. Oath of Allegiance. Remarks: Considered a Deserter.

Description at oath: Eyes: blue. Hair: sandy. Complexion: light. Height: 5'5". Residence at oath: Monroe County, AL. Soldier also served as a Pvt. with the 9th Louisiana Battalion Cavalry. Co. B. Confederate Widows Pension Application on file at the Louisiana State Archives. Microfilm Reel: CP1.132. Microdex 4. Sequence 2. Target Card: Sternberger, Elizabeth Ann (McMichael). Parish: Tangipahoa. 18 pages.

Stephens, F.B. (AKA T.B.) Pvt., 3rd Louisiana Cavalry (Harrison's). Co. B. Federal Rolls Prisoners of War: Captured at Camp Moore, LA, on 10/7/1864; Forwarded to New Orleans, LA, on 10/15/1864. Received at Ship Island, MS, on 10/21/1864. Died: 12/6/1864 at Ship Island, MS, due to chronic diarrhea. Buried: Ship Island, MS, Cemetery in Grave #69. Born: Mississippi. Occupation at enlistment: Planter near Waterproof, Tensas Parish, LA. Age at death: 26.

Stephens, Philip Pvt., 4th Louisiana Infantry. Co. A. Federal Rolls of Prisoners of War: Captured at East Baton Rouge Parish, LA, on 1/11/1865; Received at Ship Island, MS, from New Orleans, LA, on 1/25/1865. Transferred to Vicksburg, MS, for exchange on 5/1/1865; Exchanged at Camp Townsend, MS, on 5/6/1865.

Stewart, Samuel A. Pvt., 1st Louisiana Cavalry. Co. D. Enlisted: 9/12/1861 at Baton Rouge, LA. Rolls for 1/1863 through 2/1863: Present. Rolls for 3/1863 through 6/1863: Present, detailed as Assistant Forage Master. Rolls for 11/1863 through 12/1863: Absent, without leave. Federal Rolls of Prisoners of War: Captured at Liberty, MS, on 11/16/1864; Forwarded to New Orleans, LA, on 11/23/1864. Received at Ship Island, MS, on 12/10/1864; Transferred to Vicksburg, MS, for exchange on 5/1/1865. Exchanged at Camp Townsend, MS, on 5/6/1865.

Stinson, C.H. Pvt., 25th Louisiana Infantry. Co. C. Enlisted: 5/9/1863 at Shreveport, LA. Rolls for 9/1/1864 through 2/1865: Present. Rolls for 3/1865 through 5/1865: Absent. Federal Rolls of Prisoners of War: Captured at Spanish Fort, AL, on 4/8/1865; Received at Ship Island, MS, on 4/10/1865. Transferred to Vicksburg, MS, for exchange on 5/1/1865; Exchanged at Camp Townsend, MS, on 5/6/1865. Rolls of Prisoners of War, C.S.A.: Surrendered at Citronelle, AL, on 5/4/1865; Paroled at Meridian, MS, on 5/10/1865. Residence at parole: Shreveport, LA.

Stockwell, F. Pvt., 9th Louisiana Battalion Cavalry. Co. __. Federal Rolls of Prisoners of War: Captured near Wilson's Ferry, LA, on 10/9/1864; Received at Fort Columbus, New York Harbor, NY, from Ship Island, MS, on 11/16/1864. Transferred to Elmira, NY, on 11/18/1864.

Stockwell, Thomas Pvt., 3rd Louisiana Cavalry (Wingfield's). Co. F. Enlisted: 5/13/1862 at Camp Moore, LA. On Roll not dated: Absent, without leave. Federal Rolls of Prisoners of War: Captured near Wilson's Ferry, LA, on 10/9/1864; Forwarded to New Orleans, LA, from Baton Rouge, LA, on 10/14/1864. Received at Ship Island, MS, on 10/20/1864; Transferred to Fort Columbus, New York Harbor, NY, on 11/16/1864. Forwarded to Elmira, NY, on 11/20/1864. Name on List of Prisoners of War at Elmira, NY, who desire to take the U.S. Oath of Allegiance on 11/30/1864. Remarks: Was conscripted on 7/30/1864 and was captured at his home, where he had been for several weeks due to deserting his command. Prisoner has relatives residing in Illinois, where he desires to go. Released from Elmira, NY, on 5/29/1865 upon taking the U.S. Oath of Allegiance. Description at oath: Eyes: blue. Hair: red. Complexion: florid. Height: 5'6½". Residence at oath: Baton Rouge, LA. Born: 12/15/1832. Died: 9/1/1886. Buried: Buhler Plains Cemetery located on Hwy. 964 at Zachary, East Baton Rouge Parish, LA. Soldier also served as a Pvt. with the 9th Louisiana Battalion Cavalry. Co. F. Confederate Widows Pension Application on file at the Louisiana State Archives. Microfilm Reel: CP1.133. Microdex 2. Sequence 9. Target Card: Stockwell, Nancy Jane (Keown). Parish: East Baton Rouge. 4 pages.

Stokes, C. Lester Cpl., 4th Louisiana Battalion Infantry. Co. C. Enlisted: 8/8/1861 at Winnsboro, LA. Rolls for 8/8/1861 through 2/28/1865: Present. Rolls for 3/1865 through 4/1865: Absent, taken prisoner of war on 4/8/1865. Federal Rolls of Prisoners of War: Captured at Spanish Fort, AL, on 4/8/1865; Received at Ship Island, MS, on 4/10/1865. Transferred to Vicksburg, MS, for exchange on 5/1/1865; Exchanged at Camp Townsend, MS, on 5/6/1865. Rolls of Prisoners of War, C.S.A: Surrendered at Citronelle, AL, on 5/4/1865; Paroled at Meridian, MS, on 5/10/1865. Residence: Winnsboro, Franklin Parish, LA.

Stokes, C.S. Cpl., 25th Louisiana Infantry. Co. C. Federal Rolls of Prisoners of War: Captured at Spanish Fort, AL, on 4/8/1865; Received at Ship Island, MS, on 4/10/1865. Transferred to Vicksburg, MS, for exchange on 5/1/1865; Exchanged at Camp Townsend, MS, on 5/6/1865.

Stone, W.H. Q.M. Sgt., Gober's Mounted Infantry Regiment. Cos. A & E. Federal Rolls of Prisoners of War: Captured at Clinton, LA, on 10/6/1864; Forwarded to New Orleans, LA, on 10/14/1864. Transferred to Ship Island, MS, on 10/20/1864; Received at Ship Island, MS, on 10/21/1864; Forwarded to Fort Columbus, New York Harbor, NY, on 11/16/1864. Sent to Elmira, NY, on 11/20/1864; Paroled at Elmira, NY, on 2/25/1865. Transferred to Point Lookout, MD, for exchange.

Stone, W.H. Q.M. Sgt., 5th Louisiana Cavalry. F & S. Federal Rolls of Prisoners of War: Captured at Clinton, LA, on 10/6/1864; Received at Ship Island, MS. Transferred to Elmira, NY, from Fort Columbus, New York Harbor, NY, on 11/25/1864; Forwarded to Point Lookout, MD, for exchange on 2/25/1865.

Story, William L. Pvt., 1st Louisiana Infantry. Co. G. Federal Rolls of Prisoners of War: Captured at Spanish Fort, AL, on 4/8/1865; Received at Ship Island, MS, on 4/10/1865. Transferred to Vicksburg, MS, for exchange on 5/1/1865; Exchanged at Camp Townsend, MS, on 5/6/1865. On Register of U.S.A. Post Hospital, Jackson, MS: Admitted on 5/16/1865; Discharged on 5/30/1865 on parole. Soldier also served as a Pvt. with the 4th Louisiana Infantry. Cos. F & I, and the 9th Louisiana Battalion Cavalry. Co. E. Confederate Widows Pension Application on file at the Louisiana State Archives. Microfilm Reel: CP1.133. Microdex 3. Sequence 14. Target Card: Story, Mary E. (Leonard). Parish: St. Helena. 4 pages.

Stowers, Louis Edward (AKA Stoners, Stowen, Stevens, Lewis) 1st Lt./Capt., 4th Louisiana Battalion Infantry. Co. D. Enlisted: 8/9/1861 at Carroll Parish, LA. Rolls for 8/9/1861 through 12/1861: Present. Rolls for 1/1862 through 2/1862: Present or absent not stated. Rolls for 3/1862 through 2/1863: Present. Federal Rolls of Prisoners of War: Captured at the Battle of Missionary Ridge, TN, on 11/25/1863; Transferred to Nashville, TN, from the General Field Hospital, Bridgeport, AL, on 12/11/1863. Received at the U.S. Military Prison, Louisville, KY, from Nashville, TN, on 12/20/1863; Transferred to Fort Delaware, DE, on 1/15/1864; Paroled at Fort Delaware, DE, on 10/6/1864. Forwarded to Point Lookout, MD, on 10/11/1864; Exchanged at Boulware and Cox Wharf, James River, VA, on 10/15/1864. Rolls for 10/15/1864 through 2/28/1865: Present. Rolls for 3/1865 through 4/1865: Absent, taken prisoner of war on 4/8/1865. Federal Rolls of Prisoners of War: Captured at Spanish Fort, AL, on 4/8/1865; Received at Ship Island, MS, on 4/10/1865. Transferred to New Orleans, LA, on 4/28/1865; Confined at New Orleans, LA, on 4/30/1865; Exchanged at Camp Townsend, MS, on 5/6/1865. Official Rolls of Paroled Officers, C.S.A: Surrendered at Citronelle, AL, on 5/4/1865; Paroled at Jackson, MS, on 5/11/1865. Residence: Lake Providence, East Carroll Parish, LA. Born: 8/31/1836. Died: 12/19/1872. Buried: Wintergreen Cemetery located at Port Gibson, Claiborne County, MS.

Strahan, Asa Pvt., 3rd Louisiana Cavalry (Wingfield's). Co. A. Enlisted: 5/13/1862 at Camp Moore, LA. Rolls for 5/13/1862 through 9/1862: Present or absent not stated. Federal Rolls of Prisoners of War: Captured and paroled at Port Hudson, LA, on 7/9/1863. Federal Rolls of Prisoners of War: Captured at Clinton, LA, on 11/16/1864; Forwarded to New Orleans, LA, on 11/23/1864. Received at Ship Island, MS, on 12/10/1864; Transferred to Vicksburg, MS, for exchange on 5/1/1865. Exchanged at Camp Townsend, MS, on 5/6/1865. Born: 2/16/1842. Died: 8/20/1892. Buried: Blackwell Cemetery located on Blackwell Cemetery Rd. near Folsom, St. Tammany Parish, LA.

Street, James Pvt., 1st Louisiana Cavalry. Co. B. Enlisted: 2/21/1862 at Baton Rouge, LA. Rolls for 5/1862 through 6/1863: Present. Federal Rolls of Prisoners of War: Captured at East Baton Rouge Parish, LA, on 10/3/1864; Forwarded to New Orleans, LA, from Baton Rouge, LA, on 10/10/1864. Received at Ship Island, MS, on 10/20/1864; Transferred to Fort Columbus, New York Harbor, NY, on 11/5/1864. Forwarded to Elmira, NY, on 11/20/1864; Transferred to James River, VA, on 2/20/1865 and exchanged.

Stroud, J.L. Pvt., 3rd Louisiana Cavalry. Co. __. Federal Rolls Prisoners of War: Captured at Liberty, MS, on 11/17/1864; Received at Ship Island, MS, from New Orleans, LA, on 12/13/1864.

Sturn, Quinn Pvt., Consolidated Crescent Regiment. Co. D. Federal Rolls of Prisoners of War: Captured at Pleasant Hill, LA, on 3/30/1864; Forwarded to New Orleans, LA, on 4/20/1864. Name on List of Prisoners of War at New Orleans, LA, who wish to take the U.S. Oath of Allegiance on 5/31/1864. On Register of St. Louis U.S.A. General Hospital, New Orleans, LA: Admitted on 9/17/1864; Released on 10/3/1864. Age at admittance: 41. Received at Ship Island, MS, on 10/5/1864; Transferred to Fort Columbus, New York Harbor, NY, on 11/16/1864. Name on List of Prisoners of War at Elmira, NY, who wish to take the U.S. Oath of Allegiance on 11/30/1864; Remarks: Was conscripted on 6/6/1863. Claims to be a Union man and would never have been found in arms but was compelled to enter the Rebel ranks. Has lived in Chicago, where he has many friends, and desires to go there. Took the U.S. Oath of Allegiance at Elmira, NY, on 5/29/1865. Description at oath: Eyes: blue. Hair: auburn. Complexion: fair. Height: 5'8". Residence at oath: New York City, NY.

Sucard, F.C. Pvt., West's Artillery Battery. Federal Rolls Prisoners of War: Captured at Bayou Gross Tête, LA. Forwarded to Fort Columbus, New York Harbor, NY, from Ship Island, MS, on 11/16/1864. Transferred to Elmira, NY, on 11/19/1864.

Sullivan, O. Pvt., 3rd Louisiana Cavalry. Co. __. Federal Rolls Prisoners of War: Captured on 12/24/1864; Received at Ship Island, MS, from New Orleans, LA, on 1/25/1865. Transferred to Vicksburg, MS, for exchange on 5/1/1865; Exchanged at Camp Townsend, MS, on 5/6/1865.

Sullivan, Thomas Pvt., 3rd Louisiana Cavalry (Wingfield's). Co. F. Enlisted: 5/13/1862 at Camp. Rolls for 5/13/1862 through 9/1862: Present. Federal Rolls of Prisoners of War: Captured at Greenwell Springs, LA, on 5/2/1863; Paroled at Grant's Island, off Mobile, AL, on 5/30/1863. Federal Rolls of Prisoners of War: Captured at East Baton Rouge Parish, LA, on 12/24/1864; Forwarded to New Orleans, LA, from East Baton Rouge Parish, LA, on 12/27/1864. Received at Ship Island, MS, on 6/22/1864; Transferred to Vicksburg, MS, for exchange on 5/1/1865. Exchanged at Camp Townsend, MS, on 5/6/1865.

Sullivan, William P. Pvt., 3rd Louisiana Cavalry (Wingfield's). Co. G. Enlisted: 6/5/1862 at Denham Springs, LA. Rolls for 6/5/1862 through 9/1862: Present. Federal Rolls of Prisoners of War: Captured at Greenwell Springs, LA, on 5/2/1863; Paroled at Grant's Island, off Mobile, AL, on 5/30/1863. Federal Rolls of Prisoners of War: Captured on 12/29/1864; Received at Ship Island, MS, from New Orleans, LA, on 1/25/1865. Soldier also served as a Pvt. with the 9th Louisiana Battalion Cavalry. Co. G. Confederate Widows Pension Application on file at the Louisiana State Archives. Microfilm Reel: CP1.134. Microdex 2. Sequence 28. Target Card: Sullivan, Agnes (Cunningham). Parish: East Baton Rouge. 8 pages.

Swayze, Thomas Pvt., 25th Louisiana Infantry. Co. D. Enlisted: 3/6/1862 at Morehouse Parish, LA. Rolls for 11/1862 through 10/1863: Present. Rolls for 1/1864 through 8/1864: Absent, sick in hospital by order of Dr. Wilkerson since 12/18/1863. Rolls for 9/1864 through 2/1865: Present. Rolls for 3/1865 through 4/1865: Absent, taken prisoner of war. Federal Rolls of Prisoners of War: Captured at Spanish Fort, AL, on 4/8/1865; Received at Ship Island, MS, on 4/10/1865. Transferred to Vicksburg, MS, for exchange on 5/1/1865; Exchanged at Camp Townsend, MS, on 5/6/1865.

Taber, B.K. Pvt., 18th Louisiana Infantry. Co. G. Federal Rolls of Prisoners of War: Captured at Spanish Fort, AL, on 4/8/1865; Received at Ship Island, MS, on 4/10/1865. Transferred to Vicksburg, MS, for exchange on 5/1/1865. Exchanged at Camp Townsend, MS, on 5/6/1865.

Tacneau, A. Pvt., 4th Louisiana Infantry. Co. F. Enlisted:

9/26/1862 at Port Hudson, LA. Rolls for 10/1862 through 12/1863: Present. Rolls for 5/1864 through 8/1864: Absent, wounded at the Battle of the Poor House, GA, on 7/28/1864. Rolls for 9/1864 through 2/1865: Present. Federal Rolls of Prisoners of War: Captured at Spanish Fort, AL, on 4/8/1865; Received at Ship Island, MS, on 4/10/1865. Transferred to Vicksburg, MS, for exchange on 5/1/1865; Exchanged at Camp Townsend, MS, on 5/6/1865.

Tarver, Isaac Pvt., Ogden's Cavalry Battalion. Co. D. Federal Rolls of Prisoners of War: Captured at Jackson, LA, on 11/15/1864; Forwarded to New Orleans, LA, on 11/23/1864. Received at Ship Island, MS, on 12/13/1864; Transferred to Vicksburg, MS, for exchange on 5/1/1865. Exchanged at Camp Townsend, MS, on 5/6/1865.

Tatier, Beverly K. Pvt., 18th & Yellow Jacket Battalion Louisiana Infantry (Consolidated) Co. __. Federal Rolls of Prisoners of War: Captured at Spanish Fort, AL, on 4/8/1865; Received at Ship Island, MS, on 4/10/1865. Transferred to Vicksburg, MS, for exchange on 5/1/1865; Exchanged at Camp Townsend, MS, on 5/6/1865.

Taylor, Eugene Pvt., 1st Louisiana Cavalry. Co. H. Federal Rolls of Prisoners of War: Captured near Liberty, MS, on 11/19/1864; Forwarded to New Orleans, LA, on 11/23/1864. Received at Ship Island, MS, on 12/13/1864 and desires to take the U.S. Oath of Allegiance; Transferred to Vicksburg, MS, for exchange on 5/1/1865. Exchanged at Camp Townsend, MS, on 5/6/1865.

Taylor, Fred Capt., 30th Louisiana Infantry. Co. __. (No War Dept. Record.) Sentenced to imprisonment at Ship Island, MS, by Maj. Gen. Benjamin F. Butler for an unknown offense; Received at Ship Island, MS, on 10/5/1862. Released on 8/15/1863.

Tearney, Barney (AKA Tanney) Pvt., 19th Louisiana Infantry. Co. B. Enlisted: 12/11/1861 at Camp Moore, LA. Rolls for 12/11/1861 through 8/1863: Present. Rolls for 9/1863 through 10/1863: Absent, on sick furlough by order of Dr. Denson since 9/15/1863. Rolls for 11/1863 through 8/1864: Present. Rolls for 9/1864 through 2/1865: Absent, sick at Macon, MS, by order of Dr. Philson since 1/12/1865. Rolls for 3/1865 through 4/1865: Absent, taken prisoner of war. Federal Rolls of Prisoners of War: Captured at Spanish Fort, AL, on 4/8/1865; Received at Ship Island, MS, on 4/10/1865. Transferred to Vicksburg, MS, for exchange on 5/1/1865; Exchanged at Camp Townsend, MS, on 5/6/1865.

Tellott, Charles L. (AKA Tellett, C.S.) Pvt., Ogden's Cavalry Battalion. Co. A. Federal Rolls of Prisoners of War: Captured near Clinton, LA, on 11/16/1864; Forwarded to New Orleans, LA, on 11/23/1864. Received at Ship Island, MS, on 12/13/1864; Transferred to Vicksburg, MS, for exchange on 5/1/1865. Exchanged at Camp Townsend, MS, on 5/6/1865. Soldier also served as a Pvt. with the 11th Louisiana Infantry. Co.I. Confederate Pension Application on file at the Louisiana State Archives. Microfilm Reel: CP1.136. Microdex 1. Sequence 22. Target Card: Tellott, Charles L. Parish: Ascension. 6 pages.

Templet, Albert Pvt., Ogdens Cavalry Battalion. Co. A. Federal Rolls of Prisoners of War: Captured at Greenwell Springs, LA, on 9/17/1864; Forwarded to New Orleans, LA, from Baton Rouge, LA, on 9/25/1864. Received at Ship Island, MS; Transferred to Fort Columbus, New York Harbor, NY, on 11/16/1864. Sent to Elmira, NY, on 11/19/1864; Paroled at Elmira, NY, on 1/19/1865. Confederate Widows Pension Application on file at the Louisiana State Archives. Microfilm Reel: CP1.136. Microdex 2. Sequence 3. Target Card: Templet, Azelia (Hebert). Parish: East Baton Rouge. 6 pages.

Tenny, William Henry (AKA Tenney, Toney) Pvt., 1st Louisiana Cavalry. Co. A. Federal Rolls of Prisoners of War: Captured at Bayou Sara, LA, on 11/17/1864; Received at Ship Island, MS, from New Orleans, LA, on 12/13/1864. Transferred to Vicksburg, MS, for exchange on 5/1/1865; Exchanged at Camp Townsend, MS, on 5/6/1865. Born: 4/21/1847. Died: 3/4/1910. Buried: Grace Episcopal Church Cemetery located on Hwy. 10 at St. Francisville, West Feliciana Parish, LA. Soldier also served as a Pvt. with the 3rd Louisiana Cavalry and the 9th Louisiana Battalion Cavalry. Co. A. Confederate Widows Pension Application on file at the Louisiana State Archives. Microfilm Reel: CP1.136. Microdex 2. Sequence 11. Target Card: Tenney, Lucy (Powell). Parish: Orleans. 6 pages.

Thibodeaux, Cleber Pvt., 1st Louisiana Heavy Artillery (Regulars). Co. C. Enlisted: 5/24/1862 at Camp Pratt, LA. Rolls for 1/1864 through 10/1864: Present. Rolls for 3/1865 through 4/1865: Absent, taken prisoner of war. Federal Rolls of Prisoners of War: Captured at Blakely, AL, on 4/9/1865; Received at Ship Island, MS, on 4/15/1865. Transferred to Vicksburg, MS, for exchange on 5/1/1865; Exchanged at Camp Townsend, MS, on 5/6/1865.

Thibodeaux, Joseph Pvt., 1st Louisiana Heavy Artillery (Regulars). Co. C. Enlisted: 9/12/1862 at Camp Pratt, LA. Rolls for 1/1864 through 10/1864: Present. Rolls for 3/1865 through 4/1865: Absent, taken prisoner of war. Federal Rolls of Prisoners of War: Captured at Blakely, AL, on 4/9/1865; Received at Ship Island, MS, on 4/15/1865. Transferred to Vicksburg, MS, for exchange on 5/1/1865; Exchanged at Camp Townsend, MS, on 5/6/1865.

Thiroux, Victor Pvt., 22nd and 23rd Louisiana Infantry (Consolidated). Co. E. Enlisted: 3/1/1863 at Vicksburg, MS. Federal Rolls of Prisoners of War: Captured and paroled at Vicksburg, MS, on 7/4/1863. On List dated Parole Camp, Enterprise, MS, 10/13/1863: Present in camp. On undated List: Reported for exchange on 10/19/1863. Rolls for 11/1863 through 12/1863: Present. Soldier also served as a Pvt. with the 22nd Louisiana Infantry (Consolidated). Cos. D & E. Rolls for 1/1864 through 2/1864: Absent without leave. Rolls for 3/1864 through 10/1864: Present. Rolls for 3/1865 through 4/1865: Absent with leave. Federal Rolls of Prisoners of War: Captured at East Pascagoula, MS, on 4/17/1865; Received at Ship Island, MS. Transferred to Vicksburg, MS, for exchange on 5/1/1865; Exchanged at Camp Townsend, MS, on 5/6/1865. Soldier also served as a Pvt. with the 1st Zouave Battalion Infantry (Louisiana). Co. D. Born: 1830. Died: 7/30/1912. Buried: Metairie Cemetery located on Pontchartrain Blvd. at New Orleans, Orleans Parish, LA.

Thompson, Frank H. 2nd Lt./1st Lt., Consolidated Crescent Regiment. Co. E. Enlisted: 10/1/1862. Rolls for 1/1864 through 2/1864: Absent, on detached service as

Provost Guard at Alexandria, LA, since 1/4/1864. Federal Rolls of Prisoners of War: Captured at St. Mary Parish, LA, on 12/8/1864; Received at Ship Island, MS, on 12/15/1864. Transferred to New Orleans, LA, for exchange; Forwarded from New Orleans, LA, on 12/18/1864. Transferred to the mouth of Red River, LA, for exchange on 4/7/1865. Official Rolls of Paroled Officers, C.S.A: Surrendered at New Orleans, LA, on 5/26/1865; Paroled at Natchitoches, LA, on 6/6/1865.

Thompson, James Pvt., 1st Louisiana Heavy Artillery (Regulars). Co. C. Enlisted: 3/16/1862 at Lake Charles, LA. Rolls for 1/1864 through 10/1864: Present. Rolls for 3/1865 through 4/1865: Absent, taken prisoner of war. Federal Rolls of Prisoners of War: Captured at Blakely, AL, on 4/9/1865; Received at Ship Island, MS, on 4/15/1865. Transferred to Vicksburg, MS, for exchange on 5/1/1865; Exchanged at Camp Townsend, MS, on 5/6/1865. Rolls of Prisoners of War, C.S.A: Surrendered at Citronelle, AL, on 5/4/1865; Paroled at Alexandria, LA, on 7/10/1865. Residence at parole: Calcasieu Parish, LA.

Tibbets, Charles Pvt., Ogden's Cavalry Battalion. Co. A. Federal Rolls of Prisoners of War: Captured at Comite River, LA, on 9/16/1864; Forwarded to New Orleans, LA, from Baton Rouge, LA, on 9/10/1864. Received at Ship Island, MS, on 10/27/1864; Transferred to Elmira, NY, from Fort Columbus, New York Harbor, NY, on 11/20/1864. Paroled at Elmira, NY, on 2/9/1865; Sent to James River, VA, for exchange. Exchanged at Boulware and Cox Wharf, James River, VA, on 2/20/-21/1865. Buried: St. Joseph Catholic Cemetery located on Main St. at Baton Rouge, East Baton Rouge Parish, LA.

Tiffith, C. Pvt., Ogden's Cavalry Battalion. Co. A. Federal Rolls of Prisoners of War: Captured at East Baton Rouge Parish, LA, on 10/6/1864; Received at Fort Columbus, New York Harbor, NY, from Ship Island, MS, on 11/16/1864. Transferred to Elmira, NY, on 11/19/1864.

Todd, John P. Pvt., 3rd Louisiana Cavalry. Co. C. Federal Rolls of Prisoners of War: Captured at Casache Bayou, LA, on 3/31/1864; Forwarded to New Orleans, LA, on 4/20/1864 and applied to take the U.S. Oath of Allegiance. Received at Ship Island. MS on 10/5/1864; Forwdarded to New York on 11/5/1864. Transferred to New Orleans, LA, on 11/8/1864; Took the U.S. Oath of Allegiance at New Orleans, LA, on 11/10/1864. Description at oath: Eyes: dark. Hair: dark. Complexion: light. Height: 5'9". Residence at oath: St. Landry Parish, LA.

Toffier, William A. (AKA Taffier, A.W.) Cpl./Pvt., 2nd Louisiana Cavalry. Co. I. Enlisted: 9/1/1862 at New Roads, LA. Rolls for 11/1862 through 12/1862: Present and $50.00 bounty due. Rolls for 1/1863 through 2/1863: Present. Federal Rolls of Prisoners of War: Captured at home near Iberville Parish, LA, on 5/12/1863. Federal Rolls of Prisoners of War: Captured at Natchitoches, LA, on 3/21/1864; Forwarded to New Orleans, LA, on 3/26/1864. On Register of St. Louis U.S.A. General Hospital, New Orleans, LA: Admitted on 5/9/1864 due to diptheria; Paroled on 5/30/1864 for 10 days. Age at admittance: 19. Name on List dated U.S. Office of Commissary of Prisoners, Dept. of the Gulf, New Orleans, LA: Transferred from New Orleans, LA, and exchanged at Red River Landing, LA, on 7/22/1864. Federal Rolls of Prisoners of War: Captured at Bayou Grosse Tête, LA, on 8/10/1864; Forwarded to New Orleans, LA, on 8/15/1864. Name on List dated Office of Agent of Exchange, M.D.W.M., of Prisoners of War for whom special application for release is made on 8/13/1864. On Register of St. Louis U.S.A. General Hospital, New Orleans, LA: Admitted on 8/25/1864 due to intermittent fever; Released on 10/5/1864. Age at admittance: 20. Transferred to Ship Island, MS, on 10/7/1864 by order of Maj. Gen.E.R.S. Canby; Sent to New York on 11/5/1864. Forwarded to Fort Columbus, New York Harbor, NY, on 11/16/1864; Received at Elmira, NY, on 11/19/1864. Paroled at Elmira, NY, on 2/9/1865; Sent to James River, VA, for exchange. Received at Boulware and Cox Wharf, James River, VA, on 2/20-21/1865 and exchanged. Federal Rolls of Prisoners of War: Captured near the mouth of Red River, LA, on 4/1/1865; Received at New Orleans, LA, on 4/7/1865. Transferred from New Orleans, LA, to the mouth of Red River, LA, for exchange on 5/2/1865 by order of Maj. Gen.E.R.S. Canby. Buried: Hollywood Cemetery, Hot Springs, Garland County, AR. Confederate Widow's Pension Application dated 8/18/1921 on file at the Arkansas Department of Archives and History. Target Name: Toffier, Georgia. Application Number: 21940.

Tolef, J.S. Pvt., Miles Legion. Co. E. Federal Rolls of Prisoners of War: Captured at Livingston Parish, LA, on 12/24/1864; Forwarded to New Orleans, LA, from Baton Rouge, LA, on 12/27/1864. Received at Ship Island, MS, on 1/25/1865; Transferred to Vicksburg, MS, for exchange on 5/1/1865. Exchanged at Camp Townsend, MS, on 5/6/1865.

Tomlinson, James W. Pvt., 2nd Louisiana Cavalry. Co. I. On Register of University U.S.A. General Hospital, New Orleans, LA: Admitted on 4/14/1863; Released on 5/29/1863. Federal Rolls of Prisoners of War: Captured at Bayou Grosse Tête, LA, on 10/27/1864; Forwarded to New Orleans, LA. Received at Ship Island, MS, in 10/1864; Transferred to Fort Columbus, New York Harbor, NY, on 11/5/1864. Received at Elmira, NY, on 11/19/1864; Paroled at Elmira, NY, on 2/25/1865. Sent to James River, VA, for exchange.

Tomlinson, Jesse W. Pvt., 30th Louisiana Infantry. Cos. C & I. Enlisted: 9/27/1862 at Port Hudson, LA, or Plaquemine, LA. Rolls for 10/1862 through 8/1863: Present. Rolls for 9/1863 through 10/1863: Present, acting Teamster for regiment. Rolls for 3/1864 through 4/1864: Absent, without leave since 4/10/1864. Federal Rolls of Prisoners of War: Captured at Bayou Grosse Tête, LA, on 10/27/1864; Forwarded to New Orleans, LA, from Morganza, LA, on 10/27/1864. Received at Ship Island, MS, on 11/2/1864; Forwarded to Fort Columbus, New York Harbor, NY, on 11/16/1864. Transferred to Elmira, NY, on 11/19/1864; Paroled at Elmira, NY, on 2/25/1865. Sent to James River, VA, for exchange. Buried: St. Joseph Catholic Cemetery located on Main St. at Baton Rouge, East Baton Rouge Parish, LA. Confederate Widows Pension Application on file at the Louisiana State Archives. Microfilm Reel: CP1.138. Microdex 3. Sequence 17. Target Card: Tomlinson, Mary F. (Einger). Parish: East Baton Rouge. 3 pages.

Tompley, Victorine Pvt., Ogden's Cavalry Battalion.

Co. A. Federal Rolls of Prisoners of War: Captured near New River, LA, on 12/19/1864; Forwarded to New Orleans, LA, on 12/24/1864. Received at Ship Island, MS, on 1/25/1865; Transferred to Vicksburg, MS, for exchange on 5/1/1865. Exchanged at Camp Townsend, MS, on 5/6/1865.

Toney, William Pvt., 3rd Louisiana Cavalry (Wingfield's). Co. A. Enlisted: 12/20/1861 at Covington, LA. Rolls for 12/20/1861 through 9/1862: Present. Federal Rolls of Prisoners of War: Captured at Bayou Sara, LA, on 11/1/1864; Confined in the U.S. Provost Jail, Baton Rouge, LA. Sent to New Orleans, LA, on 11/16/1864; Received at New Orleans, LA, on 11/21/1864. Received at Ship Island, MS, on 12/13/1864; Transferred to Vicksburg, MS, for exchange on 5/1/1865. Exchanged at Camp Townsend, MS, on 5/6/1865.

Towle, S.C. Pvt., 1st Louisiana Cavalry. Co. __. Federal Rolls of Prisoners of War: Captured at Brookhaven, MS, on 11/18/1864; Received at Ship Island, MS, from New Orleans, LA, on 12/13/1864.

Train, H. Pvt., 3rd Louisiana Cavalry. Co. D. Federal Rolls of Prisoners of War: Captured at Ponchatoula, LA, on 11/10/1864; Received at Ship Island, MS, from New Orleans, LA, on 12/13/1864. Transferred to Vicksburg, MS, for exchange on 5/1/1865; Exchanged at Camp Townsend, MS, on 5/6/1865.

Trains, Henry Pvt., 1st Louisiana Cavalry. Co. D. Enlisted: 5/30/1863 at Mobile, AL. Rolls for 6/1863 through 12/1863: Present. Federal Rolls of Prisoners of War: Captured near Pass Manchac, LA, on 11/10/1864; Forwarded to New Orleans, LA, on 11/10/1864. Received at Ship Island, MS, on 12/13/1864; Transferred to Vicksburg, MS, for exchange on 5/1/1865. Exchanged at Camp Townsend, MS, on 5/6/1865.

Troth, Robert S. 2nd Lt., Ogden's Cavalry Battalion. Co. C. Federal Rolls of Prisoners of War: Captured at Dutch Stores, LA, on 10/14/1864; Forwarded to New Orleans, LA, on 10/20/1864. On Register of St. Louis U.S.A. General Hospital, New Orleans, LA: Admitted on 10/30/1864; Released on 11/2/1864. Received at Ship Island, MS, on 11/6/1864; Forwarded to Fort Lafayette, New York Harbor, NY, on 11/30/1864. Transferred to Fort Warren, MA, on 12/21/1864; Released from Fort Warren, MA, on the U.S. Oath of Allegiance on 6/12/1865. Description at oath: Eyes: gray. Hair: brown. Complexion: light. Height: 5'6½". Residence at oath: Dorchester County, MD. Soldier also served as a Pvt. with the 14th Confederate Cavalry. Co. G. Confederate Pension Application on file at the Louisiana State Archives. Microfilm Reel: CP1.139. Microdex 4. Sequence 30. Target Card: Troth, Robert S. Parish: East Baton Rouge. 7 pages. Also a Confederate Widows Pension Application on file. Microfilm Reel: CP1.139. Microdex 4. Sequence 29. Target Card: Troth, May Margaret (Ligon). Parish: East Baton Rouge. 6 pages.

Trotter, William John Pvt., 3rd Louisiana Cavalry (Wingfield's). Co. E. Enlisted: 5/25/1861 at Camp Moore, LA. Rolls for 5/25/1861 through 6/1862: Present. Federal Rolls of Prisoners of War: Captured and paroled at Port Hudson, LA, on 7/9/1863. Federal Rolls of Prisoners of War: Captured at Clinton, LA, on 10/6/1864; Confined in the U.S. Provost Jail, Baton Rouge, LA. Forwarded to New Orleans, LA, from Baton Rouge, LA, on 10/10/1864; Received at Ship Island, MS, on 10/20/1864. Sent to Fort Columbus, New York Harbor, NY, on 11/5/1864; Transferred to Elmira, NY, on 11/20/1864. Paroled at Elmira, NY, on 2/25/1865 for exchange. Exchanged at James River, VA. Died: 9/5/1914. Buried: Greenwood Cemetery located on City Park Ave. at New Orleans, Orleans Parish, LA. Confederate Pension Application on file at the Louisiana State Archives. Microfilm Reel: CP1.139. Microdex 4. Sequence 34. Target Card: Trotter, William J. Parish: St. Helena. 14 pages.

Tullier, J.B. Pvt., 30th Louisiana Infantry. Cos. B & I. Enlisted: 3/12/1862 at Plaquemine, LA. Rolls for 9/1862 through 2/1865: Present. Federal Rolls of Prisoners of War: Captured at Spanish Fort, AL, on 4/8/1865; Received at Ship Island, MS, on 4/10/1865. Transferred to Vicksburg, MS, for exchange on 5/1/1865; Exchanged at Camp Townsend, MS, on 5/6/1865.

Turberville, A.H. Pvt., Jeff Davis Militia Regiment. Norwood's Co. Federal Rolls of Prisoners of War: Captured at Clinton, LA, on 10/6/1864; Confined in the U.S. Provost Jail, Baton Rouge, LA. Forwarded to New Orleans, LA, from Baton Rouge, LA, on 10/21/1864. Received at Ship Island, MS, on 10/27/1864; Transferred to Fort Columbus, New York Harbor, NY, on 11/5/1864. Received at Elmira, NY, on 11/20/1864; Paroled at Elmira, NY, on 2/25/1865. Sent to James River, VA, for exchange.

Turner, Sumpter Pvt./Cpl., Washington Artillery. 1st Co. Enlisted: 4/5/1862 at New Orleans, LA. Age at enlistment: 18. Marital status at enlistment: Single. Occupation at enlistment: Student. Rolls for 4/5/1862 through 8/1862: Present. Rolls for 9/1862 through 12/1862: Absent, accidentally wounded on 9/13/1862. Rolls for 1/1863 through 4/1863: Present. Federal Rolls of Prisoners of War: Captured near Fredericksburg, VA, on 5/3/1863; Forwarded from the Old Capitol Prison, Washington, D.C. to Fort Delaware, DE, on 5/7/1863. Paroled at Fort Delaware, DE, in 1863; Exchanged at City Point, VA, on 5/23/1863. Rolls for 6/1863 through 4/1864: Present. Rolls for 5/1864 through 10/1864: Absent, wounded at Drewry's Bluff, VA, on 5/16/1864. Rolls for 1/1865 through 2/1865: Absent, taken prisoner of war. Federal Rolls of Prisoners of War: Captured at Liberty, MS, on 11/16/1864; Forwarded to New Orleans, LA, on 11/23/1864. Received at Ship Island, MS, on 12/10/1864; Exchanged on 3/2/1865. Rolls for 3/1865 through 4/1865: Present. Rolls of Prisoners of War, C.S.A: Surrendered at Appomattox Court House, VA, on 4/9/1865; Paroled at Meridian, MS, on 5/10/1865. Residence at parole: New Orleans, LA. Born: 1843 in Louisiana. Died: 10/27/1867. Buried: St. Louis Cemetery # 1 located at the intersection of St. Louis St. and Conti St. at New Orleans, Orleans Parish, LA. Confederate Pension Application on file at the Louisiana State Archives. Microfilm Reel: CP1.140. Microdex 3. Sequence 2. Target Card: Turner, Sumpter. Parish: Orleans. 7 pages.

Tussell, William L. Pvt./Cpl., 3rd Louisiana Cavalry (Wingfield's). Co. E. Enlisted: 5/25/1861 at Camp Moore, LA. Rolls for 5/25/1861 through 5/1862: Present, promoted to Cpl. on 5/19/1862. Rolls for 6/1862 through 7/1863: Present. Federal Rolls of Prisoners of War: Captured and paroled at Port Hudson, LA, on 7/9/1863. Federal Rolls of Prisoners of War: Captured at Clinton, LA, on 10/6/1864; Forwarded to New Orleans, LA, on 10/15/1864. Received at Ship Island, MS, on 10/20/1864; Transferred to New Orleans, LA, on 10/28/1864 by order of Capt.M.R. Marston. Took the U.S. Oath of Allegiance at New Orleans, LA, on 10/30/1864. Remarks: Came into U.S. lines at Hampton Ferry, LA. Description at oath: Eyes: dark. Hair: brown. Complexion: light. Height: 5'7". Residence at oath: Amite Station, LA.

Unsell, Alfred Pvt., 5th Louisiana Cavalry. Co. D. Federal Rolls of Prisoners of War: Captured at Liberty, MS, on 11/17/1864; Forwarded to New Orleans, LA, on 11/23/1864. Received at Ship Island, MS, on 12/13/1864 and applied to take the U.S. Oath of Allegiance; Transferred to Vicksburg, MS, for exchange on 5/1/1865. Exchanged at Camp Townsend, MS, on 5/6/1865.

Vernon, J.J. Pvt., 3rd Louisiana Cavalry (Wingfield's). Co. E. Enlisted: 5/25/1861 at Camp Moore, LA. Federal Rolls of Prisoners of War: Captured at Summit, MS, on 11/18/1864; Forwarded to New Orleans, LA, on 11/23/1864. Received at Ship Island, MS, on 12/13/1864; Transferred to Vicksburg, MS, for exchange on 5/1/1865. Exchanged at Camp Townsend, MS, on 5/6/1865.

Vigo, Paul Joseph Pvt., Fenner's Artillery Battery. Enlisted: 6/15/1862 at Jackson, LA. Rolls for 9/1862 through 12/1863: Present. Federal Rolls of Prisoners of War: Captured at Gravel Hill, AL, on 3/24/1865; Received at Ship Island, MS, on 4/4/1865. Transferred to Vicksburg, MS, for exchange on 5/1/1865; Exchanged at Camp Townsend, MS, on 5/6/1865. Soldier also served as a Pvt. with the 1st Louisiana Battalion Infantry (Rightor's). Co. F. Born: 1841. Died: 8/23/1892. Buried: Metairie Cemetery located on Pontchartrain Blvd. at New Orleans, Orleans Parish, LA.

Villa, J. Pvt., 22nd & 23rd Louisiana Infantry (Consolidated). Co. E. Enlisted: 2/15/1862 at New Orleans, LA. Federal Rolls of Prisoners of War: Captured at New Orleans, LA, on 10/17/1862; Exchanged from the Steamer *Frolic*, near Baton Rouge, LA, on 2/23/1863. Rolls for 11/1863 through 12/1863: Absent, left at Vicksburg, MS. Soldier also served as a Pvt. with the 22nd Louisiana Infantry (Consolidated). Co. E. Rolls for 1/1864 through 10/1864: Absent, left at Vicksburg, MS, on 7/4/1863 due to refusing parole. Federal Rolls of Prisoners of War: Captured at Vicksburg, MS, on 7/4/1863; Sent to Memphis, TN, on 7/18/1863. Received at Gratiot Street Military Prison, St. Louis, MO, on 8/13/1863; Forwarded to Camp Morton, in on 8/14/1863. Took the U.S. Oath of Allegiance at Camp Morton, IN on 1/3/1865. Description at oath: Eyes: hazel. Hair: brown. Complexion: dark. Height: 5'7". Residence at oath: New Orleans, LA. Federal Rolls of Prisoners of War: Captured at Spanish Fort, AL, on 4/8/1865; Received at Ship Island, MS, on 4/10/1865. Transferred to Vicksburg, MS, for exchange on 5/1/1865; Exchanged at Camp Townsend, MS, on 5/6/1865.

Waddill, J.J. (AKA Waddille) Pvt./Sgt., 3rd Louisiana Cavalry (Wingfield's). Co. G. Enlisted: 7/10/1862 at Camp Turner, LA. Rolls for 7/10/1862 through 9/19/1862: Absent, sick at home by permission of the Company Capt. Federal Rolls of Prisoners of War: Captured and paroled at Port Hudson, LA, on 7/9/1863. Federal Rolls of Prisoners of War: Captured at East Baton Rouge Parish, LA, on 1/11/1865; Confined in the U.S. Provost Jail, Baton Rouge, LA, on 1/12/1865. Forwarded to New Orleans, LA, on 1/17/1865; Received at Ship Island, MS, on 1/25/1865. Transferred to Vicksburg, MS, for exchange on 5/1/1865; Exchanged at Camp Townsend, MS, on 5/6/1865. Born: 10/7/1847. Died: 4/3/1921. Buried: Greenwood Cemetery located on City Park Ave. at New Orleans, Orleans Parish, LA.

Wade, F.S. Pvt./Sgt., McNelly's Scouts. Co. __. Federal Rolls of Prisoners of War: Captured at Morganza, LA, on 7/21/1864; Name on List of Prisoners of War and Deserters from the Confederate service received at New Orleans, LA, off the Steamer *Chouteau* from Morganza, LA, on 8/5/1864. Received at Ship Island, MS, on 10/5/1864; Transferred to Fort Columbus, New York Harbor, NY, on 11/16/1864. Forwarded to Elmira, NY, on 11/19/1864; Paroled at Elmira, NY, on 2/25/1865. Sent to James River, VA, for exchange.

Wade, James Pvt., 1st Louisiana Cavalry. Co. A. Federal Rolls of Prisoners of War: Captured near Hampton's Ferry, LA, on 10/13/1864; Forwarded to New Orleans, LA, on 10/15/1864. Received at Ship Island, MS, on 10/20/1864; Transferred to Fort Columbus, New York Harbor, NY, on 11/16/1864. Sent to Elmira, NY, on 11/20/1864; Paroled at Elmira, NY, on 2/20/1865. Sent to James River, VA, for exchange.

Wainwright, Nicholas P. (AKA W.P.) Pvt., 3rd Louisiana Cavalry (Wingfield's). Co. H. Enlisted: 6/12/1862 at Camp Moore, LA. Rolls for 6/12/1862 through 9/1862: Present or absent not stated. Federal Rolls of Prisoners of War: Captured at Camp Moore, LA, on 10/7/1864; Confined in the U.S. Provost Jail, Baton Rouge, LA. Forwarded to New Orleans, LA, from Baton Rouge, LA, on 10/14/1864; Received at Ship Island, MS, on 10/20/1864. Transferred to Fort Columbus, New York Harbor, NY, on 11/5/1864; Sent to Elmira, NY, on 11/20/1864. Paroled at Elmira, NY, on 2/25/1865 for exchange; Exchanged at James River, VA. Confederate Widows Pension Application on file at the Louisiana State Archives. Microfilm Reel: CP1.142. Microdex 4. Sequence 6. Target Card: Wainwright, Frances A. (Nurnadt). Parish: LaSalle. 4 pages.

Walker, B.A. Pvt., 1st Louisiana Infantry. Co. E. Federal Rolls of Prisoners of War: Captured near Vernon, FL, on 9/29/1864; Received at Ship Island, MS, from New Orleans, LA, on 10/7/1864.

Wallace, A.J. Pvt., 4th Louisiana Cavalry. Co. __. Federal Rolls of Prisoners of War: Captured at Whitehall Landing, LA, on 1/1/1865; Forwarded to New Orleans, LA, on 1/14/1865. Received at Ship Island, MS, on 1/25/1865; Returned to New Orleans, LA, on 3/27/1865. Transferred to the mouth of Red River, LA, for exchange on 4/7/1865.

Wallace, J.D. (AKA Wallice, D.J.) Pvt., 19th Louisiana Infantry. Co. I. Enlisted: 3/8/1862 at Keatchie, LA; Mustered into service: 3/20/1862 at New Orleans, LA. Rolls for 3/20/1862 through 4/1862: Present. Rolls for 5/1862 through 6/1862: Transferred on 8/17/1862 and furnished with requisite papers to collect dues to that time. Rolls for 7/1862 through 10/1862: Transferred on 9/13/1862 in exchange for A.F.

Tucker by order of the Secretary of War. Rolls for 9/1862 through 10/1862: Present, transferred from the 27th La. Infantry. Co. G by order of the Secretary of War on 9/24/1862. Rolls for 11/1862 through 2/1863: Present. Rolls for 7/1862 through 8/1863: Absent, sick by order of the Surgeon at Chattanooga, TN. Rolls for 9/1863 through 12/1863: Absent, sick at Chattanooga, TN, hospital since 4/20/1863 by order of Dr. Wall. Re-enlisted at Dalton, GA, on 1/20/1864. Rolls for 4/30/1864 through 2/28/1865: Present. Rolls for 3/1865 through 4/1865: Absent, taken prisoner of war on 4/8/1865. Federal Rolls of Prisoners of War: Captured at Spanish Fort, AL, on 4/8/1865; Received at Ship Island, MS, on 4/10/1865. Transferred to Vicksburg, MS, for exchange on 5/1/1865; Exchanged at Camp Townsend, MS, on 5/8/1865. Soldier also served with the 27th Louisiana Infantry. Co.G.

Watson, Asa C. Pvt., 3rd Louisiana Cavalry (Wingfield's). Co. F. Federal Rolls of Prisoners of War: Captured at Clinton, LA, on 10/6/1864; Confined in the Provost Jail, Baton Rouge, LA. Forwarded to New Orleans, LA, on 10/14/1864; Received at Ship Island, MS, on 10/21/1864. Transferred to Fort Columbus, New York Harbor, NY, on 11/16/1864; Sent to Elmira, NY, on 11/20/1864. On undated Roll of Prisoners of War at Elmira, NY: Desires to take the U.S. Oath of Allegiance. Remarks: Volunteered on 3/8/1862 to avoid conscription; Desires to go to Vicksburg, MS, where all his relatives reside. Paroled at Elmira, NY, on 2/25/1865; Sent to James River, VA, for exchange. Rolls of Prisoners of War, C.S.A: Surrendered at Citronelle, AL, on 5/4/1865; Paroled at Jackson, MS, on 5/19/1865. Residence at parole: Copiah County, MS.

Watson, G. Pvt., 1st Louisiana Heavy Artillery (Regulars). Co. __. Federal Rolls of Prisoners of War: Captured at Blakely, AL, on 4/9/1865; Received at Ship Island, MS, on 4/15/1865. Transferred to Vicksburg, MS, for exchange on 5/1/1865; Exchanged at Camp Townsend, MS, on 5/6/1865.

Wattingham, Ulysses (AKA V.) Lt., 30th Louisiana Infantry. Co. __ (No War Dept. Record.) Sentenced to imprisonment at Ship Island, MS, by Maj. Gen. Benjamin F. Butler due to attacking John Williams for taking the U.S. Oath of Allegiance; Received at Ship Island, MS, on 9/18/1862. Released by order of Maj. Gen. Nathaniel P. Banks on 8/15/1863.

Wells, Levy B. (AKA Levi) Pvt., Ogden's Cavalry Battalion. Co. C. Federal Rolls of Prisoners of War: Captured on 11/15/1864 near Jackson, LA, or 11/16/1864 at Liberty, MS; Forwarded to New Orleans, LA, on 11/23/1864. Received at Ship Island, MS, on 12/13/1864; Transferred to Vicksburg, MS, for exchange on 5/1/1865. Exchanged at Camp Townsend, MS, on 5/6/1865. Confederate Pension Application on file at the Louisiana State Archives. Microfilm Reel: CP1.145. Microdex 3. Sequence 20. Target Card: Wells, Levy B. Parish: Tangipahoa. 7 pages.

Wells, T.C. Pvt., 1st Louisiana Heavy Artillery (Regulars). Co. __. Federal Rolls of Prisoners of War: Captured at Blakely, AL, on 4/9/1865; Received at Ship Island, MS, on 4/15/1865. Transferred to Vicksburg, MS, for exchange on 5/1/1865; Exchanged at Camp Townsend, MS, on 5/6/1865.

Westbrood, S.J. Pvt., Ogden's Cavalry Battalion. Co. E. Federal Rolls of Prisoners of War: Captured near Livingston Parish, LA, on 11/12/1864; Received at Ship Island, MS, from New Orleans, LA, on 12/13/1864.

Westbrook, S.J. Pvt., Gober's Regiment Mounted Infantry. Co. H. Federal Rolls of Prisoners of War: Captured at East Baton Rouge, LA, on 11/14/1864; Forwarded to New Orleans, LA, on 11/16/1864. Received at Ship Island, MS, on 12/13/1864; Transferred to Vicksburg, MS, for exchange on 5/1/1865. Exchanged at Camp Townsend, MS, on 5/6/1865.

Westbrook, William M. Pvt., 3rd Louisiana Cavalry. Co. F. Federal Rolls of Prisoners of War: Captured near Clinton, LA, on 8/25/1864; Forwarded to New Orleans, LA, on 8/31/1864. Received at Ship Island, MS, on 10/5/1864; Sent to Fort Columbus, New York Harbor, NY, on 11/16/1864. Transferred to Elmira, NY, on 11/19/1864. Died: 3/10/1865 at Elmira, NY. Buried: Woodlawn National Cemetery, Elmira, Chemung County, NY.

Westmoreland, James Pvt., 3rd Louisiana Cavalry (Wingfield's). Co. E. Enlisted: 5/1/1862 at Camp Moore, LA. Federal Rolls of Prisoners of War: Captured and paroled at Port Hudson, LA, on 7/9/1863. Federal Rolls of Prisoners of War: Captured near Liberty, MS, on 11/17/1864; Forwarded to New Orleans, LA, on 11/23/1864. Received at Ship Island, MS, on 12/13/1864; Transferred to Vicksburg, MS, for exchange on 5/1/1865. Exchanged at Camp Townsend, MS, on 5/6/1865.

Wheat, Hesekiah J. (AKA Kesekiah) 2nd Lt., 16th Louisiana Infantry. Co. E. Enlisted: 9/3/1861 in state service and 9/29/1861 in Confederate service at Camp Moore, LA. Rolls for 9/29/1861 through 6/1862: Present, elected 2nd Lt. on 10/6/1861. Resigned: 8/20/1862; 2nd Lt. Successor: James McArthur. Federal Rolls of Prisoners of War: Captured near Greensburg, LA, on 10/7/1864; Forwarded to New Orleans, LA, from Baton Rouge, LA, on 10/15/1864. Received at Ship Island, MS, on 11/2/1864; Sent to Fort Lafayette, New York Harbor, NY, on 11/30/1864. Transferred to Fort Warren, MA, on 12/17/1864. Born: 3/27/1810. Died: 12/15/1887. Buried: Kilian Chapel Cemetery located at the intersection of Hwy. 16 and Hwy. 441 at St. Helena Parish, LA.

White, Aaron J. Pvt., 3rd Louisiana Cavalry (Wingfield's). Co. D. Enlisted: 6/16/1862 at Livingston Parish, LA. Rolls for 6/16/1862 through 9/19/1862: Present. Federal Rolls of Prisoners of War: Captured and paroled at Port Hudson on 7/9/1863. Federal Rolls of Prisoners of War: Captured near Manchac, LA, on 9/14/1864; Confined in the U.S. Provost Jail at Baton Rouge, LA. Forwarded to New Orleans, LA, from Baton Rouge, LA; Received at Ship Island, MS, on 10/27/1864. Transferred to Fort Columbus, New York Harbor, NY, on 11/16/1864; Sent to Elmira, NY, on 11/20/1864. Born: 9/7/1829. Died: 10/30/1909. Buried: Greenlawn Cemetery located at the intersection of Pecan Street and Western Ave. at Hammond, Tangipahoa Parish, LA.

White, Evans Pvt., Pointe Coupée Artillery. Federal Rolls of Prisoners of War: Captured at Clinton, LA, on 8/26/1864; Received at Ship Island, MS, from New Orleans, LA, on 10/7/1864. Forwarded to Fort Columbus, New York Harbor, NY, on 11/16/1864.

White, M.A. Pvt., Gober's Regiment Mounted Infantry. Co. A. Federal Rolls of Prisoners of War: Captured at Clinton, LA, on 8/25/1864; Forwarded to New Orleans, LA, on 8/31/1864. Received at Ship Island, MS, on 10/5/1864; Transferred to Fort Columbus, New York Harbor, NY, on 11/16/1864. Sent to Elmira, NY, on 11/19/1864; Paroled at Elmira, NY, on 2/25/1865. Forwarded to James River, VA, for exchange.

Whittle, H. Pvt., 22nd Louisiana Heavy Artillery. Co. C. Federal Rolls of Prisoners of War: Captured in AL or FL on 3/24/1865; Received at Ship Island, MS, on 4/4/1865. Transferred to Vicksburg, MS, for exchange on 5/1/1865; Exchanged at Camp Townsend, MS, on 5/6/1865.

Williams, Frank M. 2nd Lt./1st Lt., 1st Louisiana Heavy Artillery (Regulars). Co. C. Commisioned 2nd Lt. on 1/31/1863. Federal Rolls of Prisoners of War: Captured and paroled at Vicksburg, MS, on 7/4/1863. On List dated Parole Camp, Enterprise, MS, 10/13/1863: Present. Rolls for 11/1863 through 10/1864: Present. On Roster dated Mobile, AL, 1/6/1865: Now entitled to promotion by seniority and is serving as 1st Lt. Roll 3/1865 through 4/1865: Absent, taken prisoner of war. Federal Rolls of Prisoners of War: Captured at Blakely, AL, on 4/9/1865; Received at Ship Island, MS, on 4/16/1865. Transferred to Vicksburg, MS, for exchange on 4/28/1865; Confined at New Orleans, LA, on 4/30/1865. Exchanged at Camp Townsend, MS, on 5/1/1865. Rolls of Prisoners of War, C.S.A: Surrendered at Citronelle, AL, on 5/4/1865; Paroled at Meridian, MS, on 5/10/1865 by order of Maj. Gen.E.R.S. Canby.

Williams, G.W. Pvt., 3rd Louisiana Cavalry (Wingfield's). Co. __. Federal Rolls of Prisoners of War: Captured near Mobile, AL, on 12/17/1864; Received at Ship Island, MS. Transferred to Vicksburg, MS, for exchange on 5/1/1865; Paroled at Camp Townsend, MS, on 5/6/1865.

Williams, J.J. Pvt., 22nd Consolidated Louisiana Infantry. Co. D. Rolls for 3/1865 through 4/1865: Absent, missing from Spanish Fort, AL, on 4/8/1865. Federal Rolls of Prisoners of War: Captured at Spanish Fort, AL, on 4/8/1865; Received at Ship Island, MS, on 4/10/1865. Transferred to Vicksburg, MS, on 5/1/1865; Exchanged at Camp Townsend, MS, on 5/6/1865.

Williams, William A. Pvt., 1st Louisiana Cavalry. Cos. A & C. Enlisted: 9/12/1861 at Baton Rouge, LA. Rolls for 5/1862 through 6/1863: Present. Federal Rolls of Prisoners of War: Captured at Irvine, KY, on 7/31/1863; Received at the U.S. Military Prison, Louisville, KY, on 8/3/1863. Forwarded to Camp Chase, OH, on 8/6/1863; Sent to Fort Delaware, DE, on 2/29/1864. Federal Rolls of Prisoners of War: Captured at Bayou Sara, LA, on 9/6/1864; Forwarded to New Orleans, LA, on 9/19/1864. Received at Ship Island, MS, in 10/1864; Sent to Fort Columbus, New York Harbor, NY, on 11/16/1864. Transferred to Elmira, NY, on 11/19/1864. Rolls of Prisoners of War, C.S.A.: Surrendered at Citronelle, AL, on 5/4/1865; Paroled at Gainesville, AL, on 5/12/1865. Residence at parole: West Feliciana Parish, LA. Born: 11/1843. Died: 3/27/1925. Buried: Greenwood Cemetery located on City Park Ave. at New Orleans, Orleans Parish, LA. Confederate Pension Application on file at the Louisiana State Archives. Microfilm Reel: CP1.148. Microdex 3. Sequence 26. Target Card: Williams, W.A. Parish: Pointe Coupée. 8 pages. Also a Confederate Widows Pension Application on file. Microfilm Reel: CP1.148. Microdex 3. Sequence 25. Target Card: Williams, Virginia (Howell). Parish: Ouachita. 4 pages.

Wilmers, A. Pvt., 3rd Louisiana Cavalry (Wingfield's). Co. E. Enlisted: 10/1/1861. Rolls for 10/1/1861 through 6/1/1862: Present. Federal Rolls of Prisoners of War: Captured and paroled at Port Hudson, LA, on 7/9/1863. Federal Rolls of Prisoners of War: Captured near Brookhaven, MS, on 11/16/1864; Forwarded to New Orleans, LA, on 11/23/1864. Received at Ship Island, MS, on 12/13/1864; Transferred to Vicksburg, MS, for exchange on 5/1/1865. Exchanged at Camp Townsend, MS, on 5/6/1865.

Wilson, D.C. (AKA D.L., L.D.) Pvt., 3rd Louisiana Cavalry. Co. F. Federal Rolls of Prisoners of War: Captured near Clinton, LA, on 8/25/1864; Forwarded to New Orleans, LA, on 8/31/1864. Received at Ship Island, MS; Sent to Fort Columbus, New York Harbor, NY, on 11/16/1864. Transferred to Elmira, NY, on 11/19/1864; Paroled at Elmira, NY, on 2/9/1865 for exchange. Exchanged at James River, VA, in 2/1865. Confederate Widows Pension Application on file at the Louisiana State Archives. Microfilm Reel: CP1.149. Microdex 1. Sequence 28. Target Card: Wilson, Senorey (Sody). Parish: Caldwell. 10 pages.

Wilson, Robert Pvt., Louisiana Supporting Forces. Co. __. Federal Rolls of Prisoners of War: Captured at St. Martin, LA, on 1/11/1865; Received at Ship Island, MS, from New Orleans, LA, on 1/20/1865. Returned to New Orleans, LA, on 4/1/1865; Forwarded from New Orleans, LA, to Red River Landing, LA, for exchange on 7/22/1864.

Winston, James H. Pvt., 20th Louisiana Infantry. Co. B. Federal Rolls of Prisoners of War: Captured near Natchez, MS, on 9/2/1864; Forwarded to New Orleans, LA, on 9/25/1864. Received at Ship Island, MS, on 10/5/1864; Transferred to Fort Columbus, New York Harbor, NY, on 11/16/1864. Forwarded to Elmira, NY, on 11/19/1864; Died: 12/17/1864 at Elmira, NY, due to pneumonia.

Wolf, Gustave (AKA Gustav) Pvt., 4th Louisiana Infantry. Co. D. Enlisted: 5/25/1861 at Tangipahoa, LA. Rolls for 5/25/1861 through 6/1863: Present. Rolls for 7/1863 through 10/1863: Absent, sent sick from Brandon, MS, to hospital in 7/1863. Rolls for 9/1863 through 2/1865: Present. Federal Rolls of Prisoners of War: Captured at Spanish Fort, AL. on 4/8/1865; Received at Ship Island, MS, on 4/10/1865. Transferred to Vicksburg, MS, for exchange on 5/1/1865; Exchanged at Camp Townsend, MS, on 5/6/1865. Confederate Pension Application on file at the Louisiana State Archives. Microfilm Reel: CP1.149. Microdex 4. Sequence 3. Target Card: Wolf, Gustav. Parish: Pointe Coupée. 13 pages.

Woodard, Henry Stucky (AKA Woodard, H.S.) Pvt., 19th Louisiana Infantry. Co. D. Enlisted: 12/11/1861 at Camp Moore, LA. Age at enlistment: 27. Rolls for 1/1862 through 2/1865: Present. Rolls for 3/1865 through 4/1865: Absent. Federal Rolls of Prisoners of War: Captured at Spanish Fort, AL, on 4/8/1865; Received at Ship Island, MS, on 4/10/1865. Transferred to Vicksburg, MS, for exchange on 5/1/1865; Exchanged at Camp Townsend, MS, on 5/6/1865. Rolls of Prisoners of War, C.S.A: Surrendered at

Citronelle, AL, on 5/4/1865; Paroled at Meridian, MS, on 5/13/1865. Residence at parole: Sumpter District, SC.

Woods, Lewis E. (AKA Louis S.) 1st Lt., Miles Legion. Co. A. Enlisted: 2/1862. Rolls for 5/1862 through 6/1862: Present or absent not stated. Federal Rolls of Prisoners of War: Captured at Port Hudson, LA, on 7/9/1863; Sent from Port Hudson, LA, to New Orleans, LA, via the Steamer *Zephyr* on 7/13/1863. Escaped on 8/8/1863. Federal Rolls of Prisoners of War: Captured near Plaquemine, LA, on 3/25/1864; Received at New Orleans, LA, on 4/5/1864. Paroled at New Orleans, LA; Exchanged at Red River Landing, LA, on 7/22/1864. Federal Rolls of Prisoners of War: Captured at Liberty, MS, on 11/17/1864; Forwarded to New Orleans, LA, on 11/23/1864. Received at Ship Island, MS, on 12/18/1864; Transferred to Vicksburg, MS, for exchange on 4/28/1865. Exchanged at Camp Townsend, MS, on 5/6/1865. Official Rolls of Paroled Officers, C.S.A: Surrendered at Citronelle, ALon 5/4/1865; Paroled at Jackson, MS, on 5/19/1865. Residence at parole: Iberville Parish, LA. Confederate Widows Pension Application on file at the Louisiana State Archives. Microfilm Reel: CP1.150. Microdex 1. Sequence 25. Target Card: Woods, Medora. Parish: Iberville. 6 pages.

Worsham, Alex Pvt., 1st Louisiana Cavalry. Cos. D & G. Federal Rolls of Prisoners of War: Captured near Clinton, LA, on 8/25/1864; Forwarded to New Orleans, LA, on 8/31/1864. Received at Ship Island, MS, on 10/5/1864; Sent to Fort Columbus, New York Harbor, NY, on 11/16/1864. Transferred to Elmira, NY, on 11/19/1864; Paroled at Elmira, NY. Sent to James River, VA, for exchange; Exchanged at Boulware and Cox Wharf, James River, VA, on 2/20–21/1865.

Yarborough, H. Pvt., 11th Louisiana Battalion Infantry. Co. B. Federal Rolls of Prisoners of War: Captured at Denham Springs, LA, on 9/18/1864; Forwarded to New Orleans, LA, from Baton Rouge, LA, on 9/19/1864. Received at Ship Island, MS, on 10/27/1864; Transferred to Fort Columbus, New York Harbor, NY, on 11/16/1864. Received at Elmira, NY, on 11/19/1864. Died: 3/10/1865 at Elmira, NY. Buried: Woodlawn National Cemetery, Chemung County, NY.

Zachary, Bennett (AKA Zackry, Benett) Pvt., Miles Legion. Co. E. Enlisted: 4/30/1862 at Covington, LA. Rolls for 5/1862 through 6/1862: Absent, sick in hospital at Port Gibson, MS. Federal Rolls of Prisoners of War: Captured at Greensburg, LA, on 11/16/1864; Forwarded to New Orleans, LA, on 11/23/1864. Received at Ship Island, MS, on 12/13/1864; Transferred to Vicksburg, MS, for exchange on 5/1/1865. Exchanged at Camp Townsend, MS, on 5/6/1865. Born: 9/24/1830. Died: 2/5/1916. Buried: Union Baptist Church Cemetery located on Union Church Rd. at Tangipahoa Parish, LA. Confederate Pension Application on file at the Louisiana State Archives. Microfilm Reel: CP1.151. Microdex 4. Sequence 1. Target Card: Zachary, Bennett. Parish: Tangipahoa. 11 pages.

Mississippi Prisoners of War

Abbay, George F. (AKA Abbey) Capt., 1st Mississippi Light Artillery. Co. K. Federal Rolls of Prisoners of War: Captured at Blakely, AL, on 4/9/1865; Received at Ship Island, MS, on 4/15/1865. Transferred to Vicksburg, MS, for exchange on 4/28/1865; Confined at New Orleans, LA, on 4/30/1865. Exchanged at Camp Townsend, MS, on 5/6/1865.

Abbay, Sidney M. (AKA Abbey) Pvt./2nd Lt., 1st Mississippi Light Artillery. Co. K. Federal Rolls of Prisoners of War: Captured at Blakely, AL, on 4/9/1865; Received at Ship Island, MS, on 4/15/1865. Transferred to Vicksburg, MS, for exchange on 4/28/1865; Confined at New Orleans, LA, on 4/30/1865. Exchanged at Camp Townsend, MS, on 5/6/1865.

Adair, F.M. Capt./A.Q.M., 4th Mississippi Infantry. F & S. Federal Rolls of Prisoners of War: Captured at Blakely, AL, on 4/9/1865; Received at Ship Island, MS, on 4/15/1865. Transferred to Vicksburg, MS, for exchange on 4/28/1865; Confined at New Orleans, LA, on 4/30/1865. Exchanged at Camp Townsend, MS, on 5/6/1865.

Adams, Charles F. Pvt./Sgt., 4th Mississippi Infantry. Co. A. Federal Rolls of Prisoners of War: Captured at Blakely, AL, on 4/9/1865; Received at Ship Island, MS, on 4/15/1865. Transferred to Vicksburg, MS, for exchange on 5/1/1865; Exchanged at Camp Townsend, MS, on 5/6/1865.

Adams, Fletcher C. Pvt./Cpl., 1st Mississippi Light Artillery. Cos. D & I. Federal Rolls of Prisoners of War: Captured at Blakely, AL, on 4/9/1865; Received at Ship Island, MS, on 4/15/1865. Transferred to Vicksburg, MS, for exchange on 5/1/1865; Exchanged at Camp Townsend, MS, on 5/6/1865.

Adams, Monroe C. Pvt./Sgt., 35th Mississippi Infantry. Co. B. Federal Rolls of Prisoners of War: Captured at Blakely, AL, on 4/9/1865; Received at Ship Island, MS, on 4/15/1865. Transferred to Vicksburg, MS, for exchange on 5/1/1865; Exchanged at Camp Townsend, MS, on 5/6/1865. Born: Kemp County, MS. Died: Kemp County, MS.

Adams, Spencer Pvt., 1st Mississippi Light Artillery. Co. __. Federal Rolls of Prisoners of War: Captured at Blakely, AL, on 4/9/1865; Received at Ship Island, MS, on 4/15/1865. Transferred to Vicksburg, MS, for exchange on 5/1/1865; Exchanged at Camp Townsend, MS, on 5/6/1865. Soldier also served as a Pvt. with the 6th Alabama Cavalry. Enlisted: 8/5/1864 at Demopolis, AL. Lost horse and attached to the 1st Mississippi Light Artillery on 2/11/1865. Born: 9/11/1847 at New Shiloh, Marengo County, AL. Residence after war: Mobile County, AL.

Adcock, J.P. Pvt., 4th Mississippi Infantry. Co. B. Federal Rolls of Prisoners of War: Captured at Blakely, AL, on 4/9/1865; Received at Ship Island, MS, on 4/15/1865. Transferred to Vicksburg, MS, for exchange on 5/1/1865; Exchanged at Camp Townsend, MS, on 5/6/1865.

Agnew, J.W. Pvt., 1st Mississippi Light Artillery. Co. K. Federal Rolls of Prisoners of War: Captured at Blakely, AL, on 4/9/1865; Received at Ship Island, MS, on 4/15/1865. Transferred to Vicksburg, MS, for exchange on 5/1/1865; Exchanged at Camp Townsend, MS, on 5/6/1865.

Ajaley, John (AKA Ullday, Alday) Pvt., 46th Mississippi Infantry. Co. K. Federal Rolls of Prisoners of War: Captured in Alabama on 4/1/1865; Received at Ship Island, MS. Transferred to Vicksburg, MS, for exchange on 5/1/1865; Exchanged at Camp Townsend, MS, on 5/6/1865.

Aldridge, John H. Sgt., 4th Mississippi Infantry. Co. E. Federal Rolls of Prisoners of War: Captured at Blakely, AL, on 4/9/1865; Received at Ship Island, MS, on 4/15/1865. Transferred to Vicksburg, MS, for exchange on 5/1/1865; Exchanged at Camp Townsend, MS, on 5/6/1865.

Alexander, A.J. Pvt., 39th Mississippi Infantry. Co. G. Federal Rolls of Prisoners of War: Captured at Blakely, AL, on 4/9/1865; Received at Ship Island, MS, on 4/15/1865. Transferred to Vicksburg, MS, for exchange on 5/1/1865; Exchanged at Camp Townsend, MS, on 5/6/1865.

Alexander, J.J. Pvt., 39th Mississippi Infantry. Co. G. Federal Rolls of Prisoners of War: Captured at Blakely, AL, on 4/9/1865; Received at Ship Island, MS, on 4/15/1865. Transferred to Vicksburg, MS, for exchange on 5/1/1865; Exchanged at Camp Townsend, MS, on 5/6/1865.

Alexander, Thaddeus L. Pvt., 4th Mississippi Infantry.

Co. G. Federal Rolls of Prisoners of War: Captured at Blakely, AL, on 4/9/1865; Received at Ship Island, MS, on 4/15/1865. Transferred to Vicksburg, MS, for exchange on 5/1/1865; Exchanged at Camp Townsend, MS, on 5/6/1865.

Alford, Alexander Sgt./2nd Lt., 36th Mississippi Infantry. Co. E. Federal Rolls of Prisoners of War: Captured at Blakely, AL, on 4/9/1865; Received at Ship Island, MS, on 4/15/1865. Transferred to Vicksburg, MS, for exchange on 4/28/1865; Confined at New Orleans, LA, on 4/30/1865. Exchanged at Camp Townsend, MS, on 5/6/1865.

Allen, Clement S. Pvt., 46th Mississippi Infantry. Co. F. Federal Rolls of Prisoners of War: Captured in Alabama on 4/1/1865; Received at Ship Island, MS. Transferred to Vicksburg, MS, for exchange on 5/1/1865; Exchanged at Camp Townsend, MS, on 5/6/1865. Born: 1837 in Mississippi. Died: 1893 at Kemp County, MS.

Allgood, Wyatt Pvt., 1st Mississippi Light Artillery. Co. I. Federal Rolls of Prisoners of War: Captured at Brookhaven, MS, on 11/18/1864; Received at Ship Island, MS, from New Orleans, LA, on 12/13/1864. Transferred to Vicksburg, MS, for exchange on 5/1/1865; Exchanged at Camp Townsend, MS, on 5/6/1865.

Allison, Adam Lafayette Pvt., 1st Mississippi Light Artillery. Cos. A &F. Enlisted: 5/13/1862 at Jackson, MS, for 3 years or the duration of the war. Age at enlistment: 31. Description at enlistment: Eyes: hazel. Hair: dark. Complexion: fair. Height: 5'7¼". Residence at enlistment: Hazelhurst, Copiah County, MS. Rolls for 6/1862 through 2/1863: Present. Slightly wounded in arm and knee at Vicksburg, MS, on 6/25/1863. Federal Rolls of Prisoners of War: Captured at Blakely, AL, on 4/9/1865; Received at Ship Island, MS, on 4/15/1865. Transferred to Vicksburg, MS, for exchange on 5/1/1865; Exchanged at Camp Townsend, MS, on 5/6/1865. Born: North Carolina. Occupation: Printer.

Allison, John Davis Pvt., 1st Mississippi Light Artillery. Co. __. Federal Rolls of Prisoners of War: Captured at Blakely, AL, on 4/9/1865; Received at Ship Island, MS, on 4/15/1865. Transferred to Vicksburg, MS, for exchange on 5/1/1865; Exchanged at Camp Townsend, MS, on 5/6/1865. Confederate Widows Pension Application dated 1924 on file at the Mississippi Department of Archives and History. Target Name: Allison, Margrett. County: Monroe.

Anderson, A.W. (AKA A.M.) Cpl., 46th Mississippi Infantry. Co. G. Federal Rolls of Prisoners of War: Captured in Florida on 3/25/1865; Received at Ship Island, MS. Transferred to Vicksburg, MS, for exchange on 5/1/1865; Exchanged at Camp Townsend, MS, on 5/6/1865.

Anderson, Frank M. Pvt., 39th Mississippi Infantry. Co. B. Federal Rolls of Prisoners of War: Captured at Blakely, AL, on 4/9/1865; Received at Ship Island, MS, on 4/15/1865. Transferred to Vicksburg, MS, for exchange on 5/1/1865; Exchanged at Camp Townsend, MS, on 5/6/1865.

Anderson, H.H. Pvt., 39th Mississippi Infantry. Co. B. Federal Rolls of Prisoners of War: Captured at Blakely, AL, on 4/9/1865; Received at Ship Island, MS, on 4/15/1865. Transferred to Vicksburg, MS, for exchange on 5/1/1865; Exchanged at Camp Townsend, MS, on 5/6/1865.

Anderson, Henry J. Pvt., 39th Mississippi Infantry. Co. I. Federal Rolls of Prisoners of War: Captured at Blakely, AL, on 4/9/1865; Received at Ship Island, MS, on 4/15/1865. Transferred to Vicksburg, MS, for exchange on 5/1/1865; Exchanged at Camp Townsend, MS, on 5/6/1865.

Anderson, W.C. Pvt./2nd Lt., 4th Mississippi Infantry. Co. G. Federal Rolls of Prisoners of War: Captured at Blakely, AL, on 4/9/1865; Received at Ship Island, MS, on 4/15/1865. Transferred to Vicksburg, MS, for exchange on 4/28/1865; Confined at New Orleans, LA, on 4/30/1865. Exchanged at Camp Townsend, MS, on 5/6/1865

Anderson, William Pvt., 46th Mississippi Infantry. Co. G. Federal Rolls of Prisoners of War: Captured in Alabama on 4/1/1865; Received at Ship Island, MS. Transferred to Vicksburg, MS, for exchange on 5/1/1865; Exchanged at Camp Townsend, MS, on 5/6/1865. Confederate Widows Pension Application dated 1916 on file at the Mississippi Department of Archives and History. Target Name: Anderson, Permelia J. County: Rankin.

Anderson, William D. Pvt., 1st Mississippi Light Artillery. Co. G. Federal Rolls of Prisoners of War: Captured at Blakely, MS, on 4/9/1865; Received at Ship Island, MS, on 4/15/1865. Transferred to Vicksburg, MS, for exchange on 5/1/1865; Exchanged at Camp Townsend, MS, on 5/6/1865.

Angle, William J. (AKA Aingell) Pvt., 36th Mississippi Infantry. Cos E & H. Federal Rolls of Prisoners of War: Captured at Blakely, AL, on 4/9/1865; Received at Ship Island, MS, on 4/15/1865. Transferred to Vicksburg, MS, for exchange on 5/1/1865; Exchanged at Camp Townsend, MS, on 5/6/1865.

Ansley, Henry G. Pvt., 36th Mississippi Infantry. Co. I. Federal Rolls of Prisoners of War: Captured at Blakely, AL, on 4/9/1865; Received at Ship Island, MS, on 4/15/1865. Transferred to Vicksburg, MS, for exchange on 5/1/1865; Exchanged at Camp Townsend, MS, on 5/6/1865.

Archer, John H. Cpl., 36th Mississippi Infantry. Co. F. Federal Rolls of Prisoners of War: Captured at Blakely, AL, on 4/9/1865; Received at Ship Island, MS, on 4/15/1865. Transferred to Vicksburg, MS, for exchange on 5/1/1865; Exchanged at Camp Townsend, MS, on 5/6/1865. Born: 1830 at Henry County, GA. Married: Twice — Miss Lemmons and Mrs. Sarah L. Crist Chaffin Anglin. Children: 5. Memberships: Member of the Joe Johnston Camp of the United Confederate Veterans at Mexia, TX. Residences: Georgia, Mississippi, and Texas. Died: 11/13/1914 at his home near Mount Calm, Limestone County, TX. Wife Sarah L. Archer was born 1838 at Houston, TX, and died on 12/7/1838 at home in Limestone, TX. Confederate Widows Pension Application dated 1916 on file at the Mississippi Department of Archives and History. Target Name: Archer, Elizabeth. County: Lowndes.

Archer, Joseph F. (AKA Joseph E.) Pvt., 35th Mississippi Infantry. Co. F. Federal Rolls of Prisoners of War: Captured at Blakely, AL, on 4/9/1865; Received at Ship Island, MS, on 4/15/1865. Transferred to Vicksburg, MS, for exchange on 5/1/1865; Exchanged at Camp Townsend, MS, on 5/6/1865. Confederate Widows Pension Application dated 1906 on file at the Mississippi Department of Archives and History. Target Name: Archer, Fannie. County: Oktibbeha.

Arnold, Felix B. Pvt./Cpl., 35th Mississippi Infantry. Co. F. Federal Rolls of Prisoners of War: Captured at Blakely, AL, on 4/9/1865; Received at Ship Island, MS, on 4/15/1865. Transferred to Vicksburg, MS, for exchange on 5/1/1865; Exchanged at Camp Townsend, MS, on 5/6/1865. Confederate Widows Pension Application dated 1924 on file at the Mississippi Department of Archives and History. Target Name: Arnold, Linda. County: Lee.

Arnold, Felix M. Pvt., 35th Mississippi Infantry. Co. C. Federal Rolls of Prisoners of War: Captured at Blakely, AL, on 4/9/1865; Received at Ship Island, MS, on 4/15/1865. Transferred to Vicksburg, MS, for exchange on 5/1/1865; Exchanged at Camp Townsend, MS, on 5/6/1865. Confederate Pension Application dated 1916 on file at the Mississippi Department of Archives and History. Target Name: Arnold, Felix M. County: Oktibbeha. Also a Confederate Widows Pension Application dated 1924 on file. Target Name: Arnold, Sallie. County: Oktibbeha.

Arnold, Fletcher P. Pvt., 1st Mississippi Light Artillery. Co. D. Federal Rolls of Prisoners of War: Captured at Blakely, AL, on 4/9/1865; Received at Ship Island, MS, on 4/15/1865. Transferred to Vicksburg, MS, for exchange on 5/1/1865; Exchanged at Camp Townsend, MS, on 5/6/1865.

Arnold, W.H. Pvt., 35th Mississippi Infantry. Co. __. Federal Rolls of Prisoners of War: Captured at Blakely, AL, on 4/9/1865; Received at Ship Island, MS, on 4/15/1865. Transferred to Vicksburg, MS, for exchange on 5/1/1865; Exchanged at Camp Townsend, MS, on 5/6/1865.

Arnold, Wiley F. Pvt., 35th Mississippi Infantry. Co. H. Federal Rolls of Prisoners of War: Captured at Blakely, AL, on 4/9/1865; Received at Ship Island, MS, on 4/15/1865. Transferred to Vicksburg, MS, for exchange on 5/1/1865; Exchanged at Camp Townsend, MS, on 5/6/1865.

Ash, Matt P. Hosp. Stew., 1st Mississippi Light Artillery. F & S. Federal Rolls of Prisoners of War: Captured at Blakely, AL, on 4/9/1865; Received at Ship Island, MS, on 4/15/1865. Transferred to Vicksburg, MS, for exchange on 5/1/1865; Exchanged at Camp Townsend, MS, on 5/6/1865.

Ashley, J.H. Cpl., 36th Mississippi Infantry. Co. __. Federal Rolls of Prisoners of War: Captured at Blakely, AL, on 4/9/1865; Received at Ship Island, MS, on 4/15/1865. Transferred to Vicksburg, MS, for exchange on 5/1/1865; Exchanged at Camp Townsend, MS, on 5/6/1865.

Askew, Duke (AKA Askeu) Pvt., 1st Mississippi Light Artillery. Co. G. Federal Rolls of Prisoners of War: Captured at Blakely, AL, on 4/9/1865; Received at Ship Island, MS, on 4/15/1865. Transferred to Vicksburg, MS, for exchange on 5/1/1865; Exchanged at Camp Townsend, MS, on 5/6/1865. Born: 1826. Died: 1902. Buried: Hinds County, MS.

Auter, Albert F. Pvt., 1st Mississippi Light Artillery. Co. G. Federal Rolls of Prisoners of War: Captured at Blakely, AL, on 4/9/1865; Received at Ship Island, MS, on 4/15/1865. Transferred to Vicksburg, MS, for exchange on 5/1/1865; Exchanged at Camp Townsend, MS, on 5/6/1865. Born: 1831. Died: 1903. Buried: Warren County, MS.

Auter, Solomon B. Pvt., 1st Mississippi Light Artillery. Co. G. Federal Rolls of Prisoners of War: Captured at Blakely, AL, on 4/9/1865; Received at Ship Island, MS, on 4/15/1865. Transferred to Vicksburg, MS, for exchange on 5/1/1865; Exchanged at Camp Townsend, MS, on 5/6/1865. Born: 1831. Buried: Warren County, MS.

Babb, John M. Pvt., 36th Mississippi Infantry. Co. __. Federal Rolls of Prisoners of War: Captured at Blakely, AL, on 4/9/1865; Received at Ship Island, MS, on 4/15/1865. Transferred to Vicksburg, MS, for exchange on 5/1/1865; Exchanged at Camp Townsend, MS, on 5/6/1865.

Babers, A.J. Pvt., 36th Mississippi Infantry. Co. C. Federal Rolls of Prisoners of War: Captured at Blakely, AL, on 4/9/1865; Received at Ship Island, MS, on 4/15/1865. Transferred to Vicksburg, MS, for exchange on 5/1/1865; Exchanged at Camp Townsend, MS, on 5/6/1865.

Bailey, Jeremiah W. (AKA W.W.) Pvt., 36th Mississippi Infantry. Co. __. Federal Rolls of Prisoners of War: Captured at Spanish Fort, AL, on 4/8/1865; Received at Ship Island, MS, on 4/10/1865. Transferred to Vicksburg, MS, for exchange on 5/1/1865; Exchanged at Camp Townsend, MS, on 5/6/1865. Rolls of Prisoners of War, C.S.A: Surrendered at Citronelle, AL, on 5/4/1865; Paroled at Gainesville, AL, on 6/30/1865. Born: 1824 at Copiah County, MS. Died: 1906 at Copiah County, MS.

Baird, H. Pvt., 1st Mississippi Light Artillery. Co. B. Federal Rolls of Prisoners of War: Captured at Blakely, AL, on 4/9/1865; Received at Ship Island, MS, on 4/15/1865. Transferred to Vicksburg, MS, for exchange on 5/1/1865; Exchanged at Camp Townsend, MS, on 5/6/1865.

Baldridge, John S. Pvt., 1st Mississippi Light Artillery. Co. K. Federal Rolls of Prisoners of War: Captured at Blakely, AL, on 4/9/1865; Received at Ship Island, MS, on 4/15/1865. Transferred to Vicksburg, MS, for exchange on 5/1/1865; Exchanged at Camp Townsend, MS, on 5/6/1865. Born: 1847. Died: 1932. Buried: Washington County, MS. Confederate Pension Application dated 1916 on file at the Mississippi Department of Archives and History. Target Name: Baldridge, J.S. County: Warren.

Ball, C. Pvt., 4th Mississippi Infantry. Co. __. Federal Rolls of Prisoners of War: Captured at Blakely, AL, on 4/9/1865; Received at Ship Island, MS, on 4/15/1865. Transferred to Vicksburg, MS, for exchange on 5/1/1865; Exchanged at Camp Townsend, MS, on 5/6/1865.

Barksdale, John C. Pvt., 35th Mississippi Infantry. Co. B. Federal Rolls of Prisoners of War: Captured at Blakely, AL, on 4/9/1865; Received at Ship Island, MS, on 4/15/1865. Transferred to Vicksburg, MS, for exchange on 5/1/1865; Exchanged at Camp Townsend, MS, on 5/6/1865.

Barnes, J. Pvt., 4th Mississippi Infantry. Co. E. Federal Rolls of Prisoners of War: Captured at Blakely, AL, on 4/9/1865; Received at Ship Island, MS, on 4/15/1865. Transferred to Vicksburg, MS, for exchange on 5/1/1865; Exchanged at Camp Townsend, MS, on 5/6/1865.

Barry, William S. (AKA Berry) Col., 35th Mississippi Infantry. F & S. Federal Rolls of Prisoners of War: Captured at Blakely, AL, on 4/9/1865; Received at Ship Island, MS, on 4/15/1865. Transferred to Vicksburg, MS, for exchange on 4/28/1865; Confined at

New Orleans, LA, on 4/30/1865. Exchanged at Camp Townsend, MS, on 5/6/1865. Born: 1821 at Lowndes County, MS. Died: 1868 at Lowndes County, MS.

Basye, Smith (AKA Basey) Pvt., 1st Mississippi Light Artillery. Co. F. Federal Rolls of Prisoners of War: Captured at Blakely, AL, on 4/9/1865; Received at Ship Island, MS, on 4/15/1865. Transferred to Vicksburg, MS, for exchange on 5/1/1865; Exchanged at Camp Townsend, MS, on 5/6/1865. Born: 1838 in Virginia. Died: 1922 at Hinds County, MS. Confederate Pension Application dated 1916 on file at the Mississippi Department of Archives and History. Target Name: Basye, Smith W. County: Hinds. Also a Confederate Widows Pension Application dated 1924 on file. Target Name: Basye, Kate. County: Hinds.

Batchelder, Charles H. Pvt., 1st Mississippi Light Artillery. Co. I. Federal Rolls of Prisoners of War: Captured at Blakely, AL, on 4/9/1865; Received at Ship Island, MS, on 4/15/1865. Transferred to Vicksburg, MS, for exchange on 5/1/1865; Exchanged at Camp Townsend, MS, on 5/6/1865.

Beal, F.M. Pvt., 1st Mississippi Light Artillery. Co. _. Federal Rolls of Prisoners of War: Captured at Blakely, AL, on 4/9/1865; Received at Ship Island, MS, on 4/15/1865. Transferred to Vicksburg, MS, for exchange on 5/1/1865; Exchanged at Camp Townsend, MS, on 5/6/1865.

Beall, James R. (AKA Bell) Pvt., 1st Mississippi Light Artillery. Co. I. Federal Rolls of Prisoners of War: Captured at Blakely, AL, on 4/9/1865; Received at Ship Island, MS, on 4/15/1865. Transferred to Vicksburg, MS, for exchange on 5/1/1865; Exchanged at Camp Townsend, MS, on 5/6/1865. Buried: Yazoo County, MS. Confederate Widows Pension Application dated 1904 on file at the Mississippi Department of Archives and History. Target Name: Beall, Charlotte E. County: Yazoo.

Belk, Simeon T. Pvt., 35th Mississippi Infantry. Co. G. Federal Rolls of Prisoners of War: Captured at Blakely, AL, on 4/9/1865; Received at Ship Island, MS, on 4/15/1865. Transferred to Vicksburg, MS, for exchange on 5/1/1865; Exchanged at Camp Townsend, MS, on 5/6/1865.

Bell, B.C. Pvt., 1st Mississippi Light Artillery. Co. B. Federal Rolls of Prisoners of War: Captured at Blakely, AL, on 4/9/1865; Received at Ship Island, MS, on 4/15/1865. Transferred to Vicksburg, MS, for exchange on 5/1/1865; Exchanged at Camp Townsend, MS, on 5/6/1865.

Bell, J.R. Pvt., 1st Mississippi Light Artillery. Co. B. Federal Rolls of Prisoners of War: Captured at Blakely, AL, on 4/9/1865; Received at Ship Island, MS, on 4/15/1865. Transferred to Vicksburg, MS, for exchange on 5/1/1865; Exchanged at Camp Townsend, MS, on 5/6/1865.

Bell, William J. Sgt., 36th Mississippi Infantry. Co. I. Federal Rolls of Prisoners of War: Captured at Blakely, AL, on 4/9/1865; Received at Ship Island, MS, on 4/15/1865. Transferred to Vicksburg, MS, for exchange on 5/1/1865; Exchanged at Camp Townsend, MS, on 5/6/1865.

Bennett, Alexander (AKA Burnett, D.) Pvt., 1st Mississippi Light Artillery. Co. F. Federal Rolls of Prisoners of War: Captured at Brookhaven, MS, on 11/18/1864; Received at Ship Island, MS, from New Orleans, LA, on 12/13/1864. Transferred to Vicksburg, MS, for exchange on 5/1/1865; Exchanged at Camp Townsend, MS, on 5/6/1865.

Bennett, Joshua S. (AKA Benett) Pvt./2nd Lt., 35th Mississippi Infantry. Co. G. Federal Rolls of Prisoners of War: Captured at Blakely, AL, on 4/9/1865; Received at Ship Island, MS, on 4/15/1865. Transferred to Vicksburg, MS, for exchange on 4/28/1865; Confined at New Orleans, LA, on 4/30/1865. Exchanged at Camp Townsend, MS, on 5/6/1865.

Bennett, William R. Pvt., 35th Mississippi Infantry. Co. I. Federal Rolls of Prisoners of War: Captured at Blakely, AL, on 4/9/1865; Received at Ship Island, MS, on 4/15/1865. Transferred to Vicksburg, MS, for exchange on 5/1/1865; Exchanged at Camp Townsend, MS, on 5/6/1865.

Benson, A. Pvt., 1st Mississippi Light Artillery. Co. K. Federal Rolls of Prisoners of War: Captured at Blakely, AL, on 4/9/1865; Received at Ship Island, MS, on 4/15/1865. Transferred to Vicksburg, MS, for exchange on 5/1/1865; Exchanged at Camp Townsend, MS, on 5/6/1865.

Benton, Thomas H. Pvt., 36th Mississippi Infantry. Co. _. Federal Rolls of Prisoners of War: Captured at Blakely, AL, on 4/9/1865; Received at Ship Island, MS, on 4/15/1865. Transferred to Vicksburg, MS, for exchange on 5/1/1865; Exchanged at Camp Townsend, MS, on 5/6/1865. Born: 1831. Died: 1904 at Scott County, MS. Confederate Widows Pension Application dated 1909 on file at the Mississippi Department of Archives and History. Target Name: Benton, Mary. County: Scott.

Berden, William T. (AKA Bearden) Pvt., 35th Mississippi Infantry. Co. F. Federal Rolls of Prisoners of War: Captured at Blakely, AL, on 4/9/1865; Received at Ship Island, MS, on 4/15/1865. Transferred to Vicksburg, MS, for exchange on 5/1/1865; Exchanged at Camp Townsend, MS, on 5/6/1865.

Berry, Charles Pvt., 36th Mississippi Infantry. Co. _. Federal Rolls of Prisoners of War: Captured at Blakely, AL, on 4/9/1865; Received at Ship Island, MS, on 4/15/1865. Transferred to Vicksburg, MS, for exchange on 5/1/1865; Exchanged at Camp Townsend, MS, on 5/6/1865.

Berry, Seth Pvt., 7th Mississippi Battalion Infantry. Co. D. Federal Rolls of Prisoners of War: Captured at Blakely, AL, on 4/9/1865; Received at Ship Island, MS, on 4/15/1865. Transferred to Vicksburg, MS, for exchange on 5/1/1865; Exchanged at Camp Townsend, MS, on 5/6/1865.

Berry, William M. Cpl./Pvt., 1st Mississippi Light Artillery. Co. K. Federal Rolls of Prisoners of War: Captured at Blakely, AL, on 4/9/1865; Received at Ship Island, MS, on 4/15/1865. Transferred to Vicksburg, MS, for exchange on 5/1/1865; Exchanged at Camp Townsend, MS, on 5/6/1865.

Biggs, Eleazer Pvt., 36th Mississippi Infantry. Co. I. Federal Rolls of Prisoners of War: Captured at Blakely, AL, on 4/9/1865; Received at Ship Island, MS, on 4/15/1865. Transferred to Vicksburg, MS, for exchange on 5/1/1865; Exchanged at Camp Townsend, MS, on 5/6/1865.

Billingslea, D.F.C. Pvt., 1st Mississippi Light Artillery. Co. B. Federal Rolls of Prisoners of War: Captured at Blakely, AL, on 4/9/1865; Received at Ship Island, MS, on 4/15/1865. Transferred to Vicksburg, MS, for

exchange on 5/1/1865; Exchanged at Camp Townsend, MS, on 5/6/1865.

Billington, John Webster Pvt., 1st Mississippi Light Artillery. Co. B. Federal Rolls of Prisoners of War: Captured at Blakely, AL, on 4/9/1865; Received at Ship Island, MS, on 4/15/1865. Transferred to Vicksburg, MS, for exchange on 5/1/1865; Exchanged at Camp Townsend, MS, on 5/6/1865. Born: 1844 at Warren County, MS. Died: 1933 at Yazoo County, MS. Buried: Yazoo County, MS. Confederate Pension Application dated 1918 on file at the Mississippi Department of Archives and History. Target Name: Billington, John Webster. County: Calhoun.

Bird, John C. Pvt., 35th Mississippi Infantry. Co. F. Federal Rolls of Prisoners of War: Captured at Blakely, AL, on 4/9/1865; Received at Ship Island, MS, on 4/15/1865. Transferred to Vicksburg, MS, for exchange on 5/1/1865; Exchanged at Camp Townsend, MS, on 5/6/1865.

Bird, Joseph Pvt., 35th Mississippi Infantry. Co. F. Federal Rolls of Prisoners of War: Captured at Blakely, AL, on 4/9/1865; Received at Ship Island, MS, on 4/15/1865. Transferred to Vicksburg, MS, for exchange on 5/1/1865; Exchanged at Camp Townsend, MS, on 5/6/1865.

Bishop, John F. Pvt., 4th Mississippi Infantry. Co. A. Enlisted: 1861 at Handsboro, MS. Age at enlistment: 18. Battles: Baton Rouge and Hammond Station, LA, Port Gibson and Baker's Creek, MS. Wounded: Baker's Creek, MS. While at home recuperating from the wound during the summer of 1863, he joined the Strong River Baptist Church. Federal Rolls of Prisoners of War: Captured at Blakely, AL, on 4/9/1865; Received at Ship Island, MS, on 4/15/1865. Transferred to Vicksburg, MS, for exchange on 5/1/1865; Exchanged at Camp Townsend, MS, on 5/6/1865. Rolls of Prisoners of War, C.S.A: Surrendered at Citronelle, AL, on 5/4/1865; Paroled at Meridian, MS, on 5/13/1865. Born: 6/23/1843 on a farm near Westville, Simpson County, MS, to Elijah and Winnie Bishop. Married: Mary Ann Whitworth of Rockport, MS, on 4/13/1871 by Rev. Middleton. Children: 7. Wife Died: 1893. Remarried: Mrs. Sally Tucker. Second Wife Died: 1903. Residences: During his declining years, he lived with his children, suffering greatly at times from an incurable disease. Confederate Pension Application dated 1916 on file at the Misssissippi Department of Archives and History. Target Name: Bishop, John F. County: Simpson.

Bithune, W.L. (AKA Bethune) Pvt., 1st Mississippi Light Artillery. Co. F. Federal Rolls of Prisoners of War: Captured at Blakely, AL, on 4/9/1865; Received at Ship Island, MS, on 4/15/1865. Transferred to Vicksburg, MS, for exchange on 5/1/1865; Exchanged at Camp Townsend, MS, on 5/6/1865.

Blair, D.S. Pvt./1st Lt., 35th Mississippi Infantry. Cos. F & I. Federal Rolls of Prisoners of War: Captured at Blakely, AL, on 4/9/1865; Received at Ship Island, MS, on 4/15/1865. Transferred to Vicksburg, MS, for exchange on 4/28/1865; Confined at New Orleans, LA, on 4/30/1865. Exchanged at Camp Townsend, MS, on 5/6/1865.

Black, David Pvt., 46th Mississippi Infantry. Co. __. Federal Rolls of Prisoners of War: Captured on 4/1/1865; Received at Ship Island. Transferred to Vicksburg, MS, for exchange on 5/1/1865; Exchanged at Camp Townsend, MS, on 5/6/1865.

Blanchard, Robert Pvt., 7th Mississippi Battalion Infantry. Co. A. Federal Rolls of Prisoners of War: Captured at Blakely, AL, on 4/9/1865; Received at Ship Island, MS, on 4/15/1865. Transferred to Vicksburg, MS, for exchange on 5/1/1865; Exchanged at Camp Townsend, MS, on 5/6/1865.

Blundell, J.R. (AKA J.P.) Pvt., 1st Mississippi Light Artillery. Co. __. Federal Rolls of Prisoners of War: Captured at Blakely, AL, on 4/9/1865; Received at Ship Island, MS, on 4/15/1865. Transferred to Vicksburg, MS, for exchange on 5/1/1865; Exchanged at Camp Townsend, MS, on 5/6/1865.

Bobbits, James J. (AKA Bobbitt) Pvt., 35th Mississippi Infantry. Co. A. Federal Rolls of Prisoners of War: Captured at Blakely, AL, on 4/9/1865; Received at Ship Island, MS, on 4/15/1865. Transferred to Vicksburg, MS, for exchange on 5/1/1865; Exchanged at Camp Townsend, MS, on 5/6/1865.

Bonds, S.A. Pvt., 36th Mississippi Infantry. Co. D. Federal Rolls of Prisoners of War: Captured at Blakely, AL, on 4/9/1865; Received at Ship Island, MS, on 4/15/1865. Transferred to Vicksburg, MS, for exchange on 5/1/1865; Exchanged at Camp Townsend, MS, on 5/6/1865.

Bonduler, Champ D. Pvt., 35th Mississippi Infantry. Co. D. Federal Rolls of Prisoners of War: Captured at Blakely, AL, on 4/9/1865; Received at Ship Island, MS, on 4/15/1865. Transferred to Vicksburg, MS, for exchange on 5/1/1865; Exchanged at Camp Townsend, MS, on 5/6/1865.

Boney, Green L. Pvt., 1st Mississippi Light Artillery. Co. K. Federal Rolls of Prisoners of War: Captured at Blakely, AL, on 4/9/1865; Received at Ship Island, MS, on 4/15/1865. Transferred to Vicksburg, MS, for exchange on 5/1/1865; Exchanged at Camp Townsend, MS, on 5/6/1865.

Bonner, William Pvt., 1st Mississippi Light Artillery. Co. F. Federal Rolls of Prisoners of War: Captured at Blakely, AL, on 4/9/1865; Received at Ship Island, MS, on 4/15/1865. Transferred to Vicksburg, MS, for exchange on 5/1/1865; Exchanged at Camp Townsend, MS, on 5/6/1865. Born: 1837. Died: 1896. Buried: Copiah County, MS.

Boozman, H. Pvt., 1st Mississippi Light Artillery. Co. F. Federal Rolls of Prisoners of War: Captured at Blakely, AL, on 4/9/1865; Received at Ship Island, MS, on 4/15/1865. Transferred to Vicksburg, MS, for exchange on 5/1/1865; Exchanged at Camp Townsend, MS, on 5/6/1865.

Borkin, Thomas (AKA Borkton) Pvt., 46th Mississippi Infantry. Co. G. Federal Rolls of Prisoners of War: Captured at Blakely, AL, on 4/9/1865; Received at Ship Island, MS, on 4/15/1865. Transferred to Vicksburg, MS, for exchange on 5/1/1865; Exchanged at Camp Townsend, MS, on 5/6/1865.

Bosman, Jeff R. (AKA Boman) Pvt., 35th Mississippi Infantry. Co. I. Federal Rolls of Prisoners of War: Captured at Blakely, AL, on 4/9/1865; Received at Ship Island, MS, on 4/15/1865. Transferred to Vicksburg, MS, for exchange on 5/1/1865; Exchanged at Camp Townsend, MS, on 5/6/1865.

Bostick, J.W. Pvt., 35th Mississippi Infantry. Co. K. Federal Rolls of Prisoners of War: Captured at Blakely, AL, on 4/9/1865; Received at Ship Island,

MS, on 4/15/1865. Transferred to Vicksburg, MS, for exchange on 5/1/1865; Exchanged at Camp Townsend, MS, on 5/6/1865.

Bowden, Littlebery B. Pvt., 7th Mississippi Battalion Infantry. Co. E. Federal Rolls of Prisoners of War: Captured at Blakely, AL, on 4/9/1865; Received at Ship Island, MS, on 4/15/1865. Transferred to Vicksburg, MS, for exchange on 5/1/1865; Exchanged at Camp Townsend, MS, on 5/6/1865.

Bower, Edward L. 1st Lt./Capt., 1st Mississippi Light Artillery. Co. I. Federal Rolls of Prisoners of War: Captured at Blakely, AL, on 4/9/1865; Received at Ship Island, MS, on 4/15/1865. Transferred to Vicksburg, MS, for exchange on 4/28/1865; Confined at New Orleans, LA, on 4/30/1865. Exchanged at Camp Townsend, MS, on 5/6/1865.

Bowie, John H. Pvt., 1st Mississippi Light Artillery. Co. K. Federal Rolls of Prisoners of War: Captured at Blakely, AL, on 4/9/1865; Received at Ship Island, MS, on 4/15/1865. Transferred to Vicksburg, MS, for exchange on 5/1/1865; Exchanged at Camp Townsend, MS, on 5/6/1865.

Bowman, John W. Pvt., 1st Mississippi Light Artillery. Co. I. Federal Rolls of Prisoners of War: Captured at Blakely, AL, on 4/9/1865; Received at Ship Island, MS, on 4/15/1865. Transferred to Vicksburg, MS, for exchange on 5/1/1865; Exchanged at Camp Townsend, MS, on 5/6/1865.

Boydston, Benjamin L. Pvt., 35th Mississippi Infantry. Co. A. Federal Rolls of Prisoners of War: Captured at Blakely, AL, on 4/9/1865; Received at Ship Island, MS, on 4/15/1865. Transferred to Vicksburg, MS, for exchange on 5/1/1865; Exchanged at Camp Townsend, MS, on 5/6/1865. Confederate Widows Pension Application dated 1924 on file at the Mississippi Department of Archives and History. Target Name: Boydston, Lucy A. County: Neshoba.

Boykin, W.C. (AKA Borkin) Pvt., 46th Mississippi Infantry. Cos. F & G. Federal Rolls of Prisoners of War: Captured at Blakely, AL, on 4/9/1865; Received at Ship Island, MS, on 4/15/1865. Transferred to Vicksburg, MS, for exchange on 5/1/1865; Exchanged at Camp Townsend, MS, on 5/6/1865.

Bozeman, Alex C. Pvt., 35th Mississippi Infantry. Co. I. Federal Rolls of Prisoners of War: Captured at Blakely, AL, on 4/9/1865; Received at Ship Island, MS, on 4/15/1865. Transferred to Vicksburg, MS, for exchange on 5/1/1865; Exchanged at Camp Townsend, MS, on 5/6/1865. Born: 1844 in Mississippi. Died: 1929. Buried: State Cemetery, Austin, Texas.

Bragg, J.R. Sgt., 36th Mississippi Infantry. Co. __. Federal Rolls of Prisoners of War: Captured at Blakely, AL, on 4/9/1865; Received at Ship Island, MS, on 4/15/1865. Transferred to Vicksburg, MS, for exchange on 5/1/1865; Exchanged at Camp Townsend, MS, on 5/6/1865.

Bramer, Eli (AKA Brannon) Pvt./Sgt., 8th Mississippi Cavalry. Cos. C & I. Federal Rolls of Prisoners of War: Captured near Mobile, AL, on 12/22/1864; Received at Ship Island, MS, from New Orleans, LA, on 1/25/1865. Transferred to Vicksburg, MS, for exchange on 5/1/1865; Exchanged at Camp Townsend, MS, on 5/6/1865.

Brandon, C.C. Pvt., 4th Mississippi Infantry. Cos. A & H. Federal Rolls of Prisoners of War: Captured at Blakely, AL, on 4/9/1865; Received at Ship Island, MS, on 4/15/1865. Transferred to Vicksburg, MS, for exchange on 5/1/1865; Exchanged at Camp Townsend, MS, on 5/6/1865.

Brassfield, Levi Pvt., 35th Mississippi Infantry. Co. G. Federal Rolls of Prisoners of War: Captured at Blakely, AL, on 4/9/1865; Received at Ship Island, MS, on 4/15/1865. Transferred to Vicksburg, MS, for exchange on 5/1/1865; Exchanged at Camp Townsend, MS, on 5/6/1865. Born: 1841 at Chickasaw County, MS. Died: 1916 at Union County, MS. Buried: Union County, MS.

Braswell, S.S. Pvt., 36th Mississippi Infantry. Co. F. Federal Rolls of Prisoners of War: Captured at Blakely, AL, on 4/9/1865; Received at Ship Island, MS, on 4/15/1865. Transferred to Vicksburg, MS, for exchange on 5/1/1865; Exchanged at Camp Townsend, MS, on 5/6/1865.

Brazier, Wyatt (AKA Brasher) Pvt./Sgt., 4th Mississippi Infantry. Cos. D & G. Federal Rolls of Prisoners of War: Captured at Blakely, AL, on 4/9/1865; Received at Ship Island, MS, on 4/15/1865. Transferred to Vicksburg, MS, for exchange on 5/1/1865; Exchanged at Camp Townsend, MS, on 5/6/1865.

Brewer, G.W. Pvt., 35th Mississippi Infantry. Co. K. Federal Rolls of Prisoners of War: Captured at Blakely, AL, on 4/9/1865; Received at Ship Island, MS, on 4/15/1865. Transferred to Vicksburg, MS, for exchange on 5/1/1865; Exchanged at Camp Townsend, MS, on 5/6/1865.

Bridgeforth, William M. Pvt., 1st Mississippi Light Artillery. Co. I. Federal Rolls of Prisoners of War: Captured at Blakely, AL, on 4/9/1865; Received at Ship Island, MS, on 4/15/1865. Transferred to Vicksburg, MS, for exchange on 5/1/1865; Exchanged at Camp Townsend, MS, on 5/6/1865.

Bridges, Parham Plummer 1st Sgt., 39th Mississippi Infantry. Co. F. Federal Rolls of Prisoners of War: Captured and paroled at Port Hudson, LA, on 7/9/1863. Federal Rolls of Prisoners of War: Captured at Blakely, AL, on 4/9/1865; Received at Ship Island, MS, on 4/15/1865. Transferred to Vicksburg, MS, for exchange on 5/1/1865; Exchanged at Camp Townsend, MS, on 5/6/1865. Buried: Spring Hill Cemetery located at Spring Hill, LA. Soldier also served as a Pvt. with the 1st Mississippi Infantry (Percy's). Co.A.

Briggs, J.P. Pvt., 1st Mississippi Light Artillery. Co. B. Federal Rolls of Prisoners of War: Captured at Blakely, AL, on 4/9/1865; Received at Ship Island, MS, on 4/15/1865. Transferred to Vicksburg, MS, for exchange on 5/1/1865; Exchanged at Camp Townsend, MS, on 5/6/1865.

Briggs, James H. Pvt., 7th Mississippi Battalion Infantry. Co. E. Federal Rolls of Prisoners of War: Captured at Blakely, AL, on 4/9/1865; Received at Ship Island, MS, on 4/15/1865. Transferred to Vicksburg, MS, for exchange on 5/1/1865; Exchanged at Camp Townsend, MS, on 5/6/1865. Confederate Widows Pension Application dated 1916 on file at the Mississippi Department of Archives and History. Target Name: Briggs, Clarion. County: Clarke.

Britton, William M. Pvt., 35th Mississippi Infantry. Co. A. Federal Rolls of Prisoners of War: Captured at Blakely, AL, on 4/9/1865; Received at Ship Island, MS, on 4/15/1865. Transferred to Vicksburg, MS, for exchange on 5/1/1865; Exchanged at Camp Townsend, MS, on 5/6/1865.

Britton, William S. (AKA Bruton) Pvt., 35th Mississippi Infantry. Co. A. Federal Rolls of Prisoners of War: Captured at Blakely, AL, on 4/9/1865; Received at Ship Island, MS, on 4/15/1865. Transferred to Vicksburg, MS, for exchange on 5/1/1865; Exchanged at Camp Townsend, MS, on 5/6/1865.

Broadway, Jesse W. (AKA Broadaway) Pvt., 1st Mississippi Light Artillery. Co. D. Federal Rolls of Prisoners of War: Captured at Blakely, AL, on 4/9/1865; Received at Ship Island, MS, on 4/15/1865. Transferred to Vicksburg, MS, for exchange on 5/1/1865; Exchanged at Camp Townsend, MS, on 5/6/1865.

Brown, Jeff Pvt., 1st Mississippi Light Artillery. Co. B. Federal Rolls of Prisoners of War: Captured at Blakely, AL, on 4/9/1865; Received at Ship Island, MS, on 4/15/1865. Transferred to Vicksburg, MS, for exchange on 5/1/1865; Exchanged at Camp Townsend, MS, on 5/6/1865. Confederate Pension Application dated 1926 on file at the Mississippi Department of Archives and History. Target Name: Brown, Jeff. County: Attala.

Brown, Robert Pvt., 7th Mississippi Battalion Infantry. Co. C. Federal Rolls of Prisoners of War: Captured at Blakely, AL, on 4/9/1865; Received at Ship Island, MS, on 4/15/1865. Transferred to Vicksburg, MS, for exchange on 5/1/1865; Exchanged at Camp Townsend, MS, on 5/6/1865.

Brown, T. Pvt., 46th Mississippi Infantry. Co. __. Federal Rolls of Prisoners of War: Captured at Matron County, MS, on 11/6/1864; Received at Ship Island, MS, from New Orleans, LA, on 1/25/1865. Transferred to Vicksburg, MS, for exchange on 5/1/1865; Exchanged at Camp Townsend, MS, on 5/6/1865.

Brown, William R. Pvt., 1st Mississippi Light Artillery. Co. C. Federal Rolls of Prisoners of War: Captured at Blakely, AL, on 4/9/1865; Received at Ship Island, MS, on 4/15/1865. Transferred to Vicksburg, MS, for exchange on 5/1/1865; Exchanged at Camp Townsend, MS, on 5/6/1865.

Brown, William S. Pvt., 7th Mississippi Battalion Infantry. Co. E. Federal Rolls of Prisoners of War: Captured at Blakely, AL, on 4/9/1865; Received at Ship Island, MS, on 4/15/1865. Transferred to Vicksburg, MS, for exchange on 5/1/1865; Exchanged at Camp Townsend, MS, on 5/6/1865.

Brunson, William R. (AKA Bruson) Pvt., 1st Mississippi Light Artillery. Co. I. Federal Rolls of Prisoners of War: Captured at Blakely, AL, on 4/9/1865; Received at Ship Island, MS, on 4/15/1865. Transferred to Vicksburg, MS, for exchange on 5/1/1865; Exchanged at Camp Townsend, MS, on 5/6/1865.

Buckley, J.E. Pvt., 36th Mississippi Infantry. Co. C. Federal Rolls of Prisoners of War: Captured at Blakely, AL, on 4/9/1865; Received at Ship Island, MS, on 4/15/1865. Transferred to Vicksburg, MS, for exchange on 5/1/1865; Exchanged at Camp Townsend, MS, on 5/6/1865.

Bullen, Randal G. Pvt./Cpl., 1st Mississippi Light Artillery. Co. K. Federal Rolls of Prisoners of War: Captured at Blakely, AL, on 4/9/1865; Received at Ship Island, MS, on 4/15/1865. Transferred to Vicksburg, MS, for exchange on 5/1/1865; Exchanged at Camp Townsend, MS, on 5/6/1865.

Bunch, S. Pvt., 1st Mississippi Light Artillery. Co. I. Federal Rolls of Prisoners of War: Captured at Blakely, AL, on 4/9/1865; Received at Ship Island, MS, on 4/15/1865. Transferred to Vicksburg, MS, for exchange on 5/1/1865; Exchanged at Camp Townsend, MS, on 5/6/1865.

Burnett, J.A. (AKA Burnet, A.) Pvt., 1st Mississippi Light Artillery. Co. F. Federal Rolls of Prisoners of War: Captured at Blakely, AL, on 4/9/1865; Received at Ship Island, MS, on 4/15/1865. Transferred to Vicksburg, MS, for exchange on 5/1/1865; Exchanged at Camp Townsend, MS, on 5/6/1865.

Burns, James J. (AKA Barnes) Sgt., 46th Mississippi Infantry. Cos. B & G. Enlisted: 3/17/1862 at Trenton, Smith County, MS. Participated in the battles of Port Gibson, Grand Gulf, Big Black River, and the Siege of Vicksburg. Federal Rolls of Prisoners of War: Captured and paroled at Vicksburg, MS, on 7/4/1863. Federal Rolls of Prisoners of War: Captured at Blakely, AL, on 4/9/1865; Received at Ship Island, MS, on 4/15/1865. Transferred to Vicksburg, MS, for exchange on 5/1/1865; Exchanged at Camp Townsend, MS, on 5/6/1865. Rolls of Prisoners of War, C.S.A: Surrendered at Citronelle, AL, 5/4/1865; Paroled at Meridian, MS, on 5/17/1865. Born: 6/21/1841 at Trenton, MS, to Matthew and Elizabeth Parker Burns. Occupation: Farmer. Died: 3/27/1910 at Trenton, MS. Buried: Burns, Smith County, MS.

Butler, George W. Pvt., 35th Mississippi Infantry. Co. F. Federal Rolls of Prisoners of War: Captured at Blakely, AL, on 4/9/1865; Received at Ship Island, MS, on 4/15/1865. Transferred to Vicksburg, MS, for exchange on 5/1/1865; Exchanged at Camp Townsend, MS, on 5/6/1865.

Byrnes, William Pvt./Cpl., 1st Mississippi Light Artillery. Co. I. Federal Rolls of Prisoners of War: Captured at Blakely, AL, on 4/9/1865; Received at Ship Island, MS, on 4/15/1865. Transferred to Vicksburg, MS, for exchange on 5/1/1865; Exchanged at Camp Townsend, MS, on 5/6/1865.

Cabbrett, G.M. Pvt., 1st Mississippi Light Artillery. Co. __. Federal Rolls of Prisoners of War: Captured at Blakely, AL, on 4/9/1865; Received at Ship Island, MS, on 4/15/1865. Transferred to Vicksburg, MS, for exchange on 5/1/1865; Exchanged at Camp Townsend, MS, on 5/6/1865.

Cabbrett, W.N. Pvt., 1st Mississippi Light Artillery. Co. __. Federal Rolls of Prisoners of War: Captured at Blakely, AL, on 4/9/1865; Received at Ship Island, MS, on 4/15/1865. Transferred to Vicksburg, MS, for exchange on 5/1/1865; Exchanged at Camp Townsend, MS, on 5/6/1865.

Cain, F.M. Pvt., 8th Mississippi Cavalry. Co. G. Federal Rolls of Prisoners of War: Captured in Florida on 11/25/1864; Received at Ship Island, MS, from New Orleans, LA, on 12/13/1864. Transferred to Vicksburg, MS, for exchange on 5/1/1865; Exchanged at Camp Townsend, MS, on 5/6/1865.

Caldwell, H.D. Pvt., 46th Mississippi Infantry. Co. __. Federal Rolls of Prisoners of War: Captured at Blakely, AL, on 4/9/1865; Received at Ship Island, MS, on 4/15/1865. Transferred to Vicksburg, MS, for exchange on 5/1/1865; Exchanged at Camp Townsend, MS, on 5/6/1865.

Campbell, A.D. Pvt., 39th Mississippi Infantry. Co. D. Federal Rolls of Prisoners of War: Captured at Blakely, AL, on 4/9/1865; Received at Ship Island, MS, on 4/15/1865. Transferred to Vicksburg, MS, for exchange on 5/1/1865; Exchanged at Camp Townsend, MS, on 5/6/1865.

Campeen, W.S. (AKA Compere) Pvt./Sgt., 36th Mississippi Infantry. Co. K. Federal Rolls of Prisoners of War: Captured at Blakely, AL, on 4/9/1865; Received at Ship Island, MS, on 4/15/1865. Transferred to Vicksburg, MS, for exchange on 5/1/1865; Exchanged at Camp Townsend, MS, on 5/6/1865.

Canfield, A.R. Pvt./Surgeon, 35th Mississippi Infantry. F & S. Federal Rolls of Prisoners of War: Captured at Blakely, AL, on 4/9/1865; Received at Ship Island, MS, on 4/15/1865. Transferred to Vicksburg, MS, for exchange on 4/28/1865; Confined at New Orleans, LA, on 4/30/1865. Exchanged at Camp Townsend, MS, on 5/6/1865.

Canfield, J.O. Pvt., 35th Mississippi Infantry. Co. C. Federal Rolls of Prisoners of War: Captured at Blakely, AL, on 4/9/1865; Received at Ship Island, MS, on 4/15/1865. Transferred to Vicksburg, MS, for exchange on 5/1/1865; Exchanged at Camp Townsend, MS, on 5/6/1865. Born: 1843 at Lowndes County, MS. Died: 1921 at Lowndes County, MS.

Caraway, R.A. Pvt., Powers Cavalry Regiment. Co. __. Federal Rolls of Prisoners of War: Captured near Liberty, MS, on 11/18/1864; Received at Ship Island, MS, from New Orleans, LA, on 12/13/1864. Disposition unknown.

Carleton, Eugene Cpl./Sgt./Lt., 39th Mississippi Infantry. Co. D. Enlisted: 4/1862 at Decatur, MS. In addition to several skirmishes, he participated in the battles of Corinth, Port Hudson, Kennesaw Mountain, Murfreesboro, Franklin, Atlanta Campaign, and Blakely, AL. Federal Rolls of Prisoners of War: Captured at Blakely, AL, on 4/9/1865; Received at Ship Island, MS, on 4/15/1865. Transferred to Vicksburg, MS, for exchange on 5/1/1865; Exchanged at Camp Townsend, MS, on 5/6/1865. Rolls of Prisoners of War, C.S.A: Surrendered at Citronelle, AL, on 5/4/1865; Paroled at Meridian, MS, on 5/8/1865. Residence at parole: Decatur, MS. Born: 1/31/1840 at Gainesville, AL. Parents: Prudence Isabel Carleton, Sr. and Montgomery Carleton. Occupations: Plantation owner and Chancery Court Clerk. Memberships: Secretary of Evergreen Masonic Lodge for 62 years. Died: 2/22/1933 at Decatur, MS. Confederate Pension Application dated 1924 on file at the Mississippi Department of Archives and History. Name: Carleton, Eugene. County: Newton.

Carmichael, Daniel (AKA Carmicahal) Pvt., 7th Mississippi Battalion Infantry. Co. D. Federal Rolls of Prisoners of War: Captured at Blakely, AL, on 4/9/1865; Received at Ship Island, MS, on 4/15/1865. Transferred to Vicksburg, MS, for exchange on 5/1/1865; Exchanged at Camp Townsend, MS, on 5/6/1865.

Carmichael, John (AKA Carmicahal) Pvt., 7th Mississippi Battalion Infantry. Co. D. Federal Rolls of Prisoners of War: Captured at Blakely, AL, on 4/9/1865; Received at Ship Island, MS, on 4/15/1865. Transferred to Vicksburg, MS, for exchange on 5/1/1865; Exchanged at Camp Townsend, MS, on 5/6/1865.

Carmichael, John B. Pvt., 1st Mississippi Light Artillery. Co. K. Federal Rolls of Prisoners of War: Captured at Blakely, AL, on 4/9/1865; Received at Ship Island, MS, on 4/15/1865. Transferred to Vicksburg, MS, for exchange on 5/1/1865; Exchanged at Camp Townsend, MS, on 5/6/1865.

Carmichael, M.M.C. Pvt., 7th Mississippi Battalion Infantry. Co. D. Federal Rolls of Prisoners of War: Captured at Blakely, AL, on 4/9/1865; Received at Ship Island, MS, on 4/15/1865. Transferred to Vicksburg, MS, for exchange on 5/1/1865; Exchanged at Camp Townsend, MS, on 5/6/1865. Confederate Widows Pension Application dated 1911 on file at the Mississippi Department of Archives and History. Target Name: Carmichael, S.J. County: Clarke.

Carmichael, Michael Pvt., 7th Mississippi Battalion Infantry. Co. D. Federal Rolls of Prisoners of War: Captured at Blakely, AL, on 4/9/1865; Received at Ship Island, MS, on 4/15/1865. Transferred to Vicksburg, MS, for exchange on 5/1/1865; Exchanged at Camp Townsend, MS, on 5/6/1865. Confederate Widows Pension Application dated 1911 on file at the Mississippi Department of Archives and History. Target Name: Carmichael, Martha A.A. County: Clarke.

Carothers, Richard S. (AKA Caruthers, R.J.) Pvt., 1st Mississippi Light Artillery. Co. K. Federal Rolls of Prisoners of War: Captured at Blakely, AL, on 4/9/1865; Received at Ship Island, MS, on 4/15/1865. Transferred to Vicksburg, MS, for exchange on 5/1/1865; Exchanged at Camp Townsend, MS, on 5/6/1865. Confederate Widows Pension Application dated 1922 on file at the Mississippi Department of Archives and History. Target Name: Carothers, Mrs.R.S. County: Jefferson.

Carr, Cicero A. Pvt., 7th Mississippi Battalion Infantry. Co. E. Federal Rolls of Prisoners of War: Captured at Blakely, AL, on 4/9/1865; Received at Ship Island, MS, on 4/15/1865. Transferred to Vicksburg, MS, for exchange on 5/1/1865; Exchanged at Camp Townsend, MS, on 5/6/1865.

Carr, James D. (AKA Kerr) Pvt./Sgt., 35th Mississippi Infantry. Co. B. Federal Rolls of Prisoners of War: Captured at Blakely, AL, on 4/9/1865; Received at Ship Island, MS, on 4/15/1865. Transferred to Vicksburg, MS, for exchange on 5/1/1865; Exchanged at Camp Townsend, MS, on 5/6/1865.

Carr, John N. (AKA J.W.) Pvt./Sgt., 7th Mississippi Battalion Infantry. Co. E. Federal Rolls of Prisoners of War: Captured at Blakely, AL, on 4/9/1865; Received at Ship Island, MS, on 4/15/1865. Transferred to Vicksburg, MS, for exchange on 5/1/1865; Exchanged at Camp Townsend, MS, on 5/6/1865.

Carraway, Richard Thomas Adam Pvt., 7th Mississippi Battalion Infantry. Co. K. Federal Rolls of Prisoners of War: Captured at Blakely, AL, on 4/9/1865; Received at Ship Island, MS, on 4/15/1865. Transferred to Vicksburg, MS, for exchange on 5/1/1865; Exchanged at Camp Townsend, MS, on 5/6/1865. Born: 4/28/1836 at Copiah County, MS. Occupation: Carpenter. Died: 6/2/1904 at Dentville, Copiah County, MS. Buried: Pine Bluff Cemetery located at Dentville, MS. Soldier also served as a Pvt. with Power's Mississippi Cavalry. Co. C.

Carroll, John (AKA Jehu) Pvt., 35th Mississippi Infantry. Co. K. Federal Rolls of Prisoners of War: Captured at Blakely, AL, on 4/9/1865; Received at Ship Island, MS, on 4/15/1865. Transferred to Vicksburg, MS, for exchange on 5/1/1865; Exchanged at Camp Townsend, MS, on 5/6/1865.

Carter, Andrew D. Pvt./Sgt., 7th Mississippi Battalion Infantry. Co. F. Federal Rolls of Prisoners of War: Captured at Blakely, AL, on 4/9/1865; Received at

Ship Island, MS, on 4/15/1865. Transferred to Vicksburg, MS, for exchange on 5/1/1865; Exchanged at Camp Townsend, MS, on 5/6/1865. Confederate Widows Pension Application dated 1916 on file at the Mississippi Department of Archives and History. Target Name: Carter, M.M. County: Forrest.

Carter, James M. Pvt./Sgt., 1st Mississippi Light Artillery. Co. D. Federal Rolls of Prisoners of War: Captured at Blakely, AL, on 4/9/1865; Received at Ship Island, MS, on 4/15/1865. Transferred to Vicksburg, MS, for exchange on 5/1/1865; Exchanged at Camp Townsend, MS, on 5/6/1865. Confederate Widows Pension Application dated 192_ on file at the Mississippi Department of Archives and History. Target Name: Carter, J.E. County: Holmes. Born: 1837. Died: 1873. Buried: Holmes County, MS.

Case, T.J. Pvt., 1st Mississippi Light Artillery. Co. F. Federal Rolls of Prisoners of War: Captured at Blakely, AL, on 4/9/1865; Received at Ship Island, MS, on 4/15/1865. Transferred to Vicksburg, MS, for exchange on 5/1/1865; Exchanged at Camp Townsend, MS, on 5/6/1865. Confederate Widows Pension Application dated 1916 on file at the Mississippi Department of Archives and History. Target Name: Case, Mary A. County: Copiah.

Cater, N.S. Pvt., 1st Mississippi Light Artillery. Co. __. Federal Rolls of Prisoners of War: Captured at Blakely, AL, on 4/15/1865. Transferred to Vicksburg, MS, for exchange on 5/1/1865; Exchanged at Camp Townsend, MS, on 5/6/1865.

Causey, William H. Pvt./Cpl., 46th Mississippi Infantry. Co. E. Federal Rolls of Prisoners of War: Captured at Blakely, AL, on 4/9/1865; Received at Ship Island, MS, on 4/15/1865. Transferred to Vicksburg, MS, for exchange on 5/1/1865; Exchanged at Camp Townsend, MS, on 5/6/1865. Confederate Pension Application dated 1922 on file at the Mississippi Department of Archives and History. Target Name: Causey, William H. County: Amite.

Chamber, D. Pvt., 4th Mississippi Infantry. Co. G. Federal Rolls of Prisoners of War: Captured in Alabama on 4/1/1865; Received at Ship Island, MS. Transferred to Vicksburg, MS, for exchange on 5/1/1865; Exchanged at Camp Townsend, MS, on 5/6/1865.

Chambers, James Pvt., 39th Mississippi Infantry. Co. C. Federal Rolls of Prisoners of War: Captured at Blakely, AL, on 4/9/1865; Received at Ship Island, MS, on 4/15/1865. Transferred to Vicksburg, MS, for exchange on 5/1/1865; Exchanged at Camp Townsend, MS, on 5/6/1865. Confederate Pension Application on file at the Mississippi Department of Archives and History. Target Name: Chambers, James. County: Scott.

Champion, C.C. Pvt., 39th Mississippi Infantry. Co. C. Federal Rolls of Prisoners of War: Captured at Blakely, AL, on 4/9/1865; Received at Ship Island, MS, on 4/15/1865. Transferred to Vicksburg, MS, for exchange on 5/1/1865; Exchanged at Camp Townsend, MS, on 5/6/1865.

Champion, James A. Pvt./Sgt., 7th Mississippi Battalion Infantry. Co. D. Federal Rolls of Prisoners of War: Captured at Blakely, AL, on 4/9/1865; Received at Ship Island, MS, on 4/15/1865. Transferred to Vicksburg, MS, for exchange on 5/1/1865; Exchanged at Camp Townsend, MS, on 5/6/1865.

Chamsen, D. Pvt., 35th Mississippi Infantry. Co. __. Federal Rolls of Prisoners of War: Captured at Blakely, AL, on 4/9/1865; Received at Ship Island, MS, on 4/15/1865. Transferred to Vicksburg, MS, for exchange on 5/1/1865; Exchanged at Camp Townsend, MS, on 5/6/1865.

Chappell, Robert W. Pvt., 1st Mississippi Light Artillery. Co. K. Federal Rolls of Prisoners of War: Captured at Blakely, AL, on 4/9/1865; Received at Ship Island, MS, on 4/15/1865. Transferred to Vicksburg, MS, for exchange on 5/1/1865; Exchanged at Camp Townsend, MS, on 5/6/1865. Born: 1840 at Simpson County, MS. Died: 1901. Confederate Widows Pension Application dated 1916 on file at the Mississippi Department of Archives and History. Target Name: Chappell, Martha J. County: Simpson.

Cherry, Algernon H. Pvt./Sgt., 35th Mississippi Infantry. Co. B. Federal Rolls of Prisoners of War: Captured at Blakely, AL, on 4/9/1865; Received at Ship Island, MS, on 4/15/1865. Transferred to Vicksburg, MS, for exchange on 5/1/1865; Exchanged at Camp Townsend, MS, on 5/6/1865.

Cherry, John H. Pvt., 35th Mississippi Infantry. Co. B. Federal Rolls of Prisoners of War: Captured at Blakely, AL, on 4/9/1865; Received at Ship Island, MS, on 4/15/1865. Transferred to Vicksburg, MS, for exchange on 5/1/1865; Exchanged at Camp Townsend, MS, on 5/6/1865.

Cherry, Joshua Pvt., 39th Mississippi Infantry. Co. C. Federal Rolls of Prisoners of War: Captured at Blakely, AL, on 4/9/1865; Received at Ship Island, MS, on 4/15/1865. Transferred to Vicksburg, MS, for exchange on 5/1/1865; Exchanged at Camp Townsend, MS, on 5/6/1865.

Cherry, Thomas J. Pvt., 35th Mississippi Infantry. Co. B. Federal Rolls of Prisoners of War: Captured at Blakely, AL, on 4/9/1865; Received at Ship Island, MS, on 4/15/1865. Transferred to Vicksburg, MS, for exchange on 5/1/1865; Exchanged at Camp Townsend, MS, on 5/6/1865. Born: 1834 in Alabama. Died: 1911 at Kemp County, MS.

Chevalier, James L. Cpl./Pvt., 36th Mississippi Infantry. Co. H. Federal Rolls of Prisoners of War: Captured at Blakely, AL, on 4/9/1865; Received at Ship Island, MS, on 4/15/1865. Transferred to Vicksburg, MS, for exchange on 5/1/1865; Exchanged at Camp Townsend, MS, on 5/6/1865.

Chisholm, R.G. Pvt., 46th Mississippi Infantry. Co. G. Federal Rolls of Prisoners of War: Captured at Blakely, AL, on 4/9/1865; Received at Ship Island, MS, on 4/15/1865. Transferred to Vicksburg, MS, for exchange on 5/1/1865; Exchanged at Camp Townsend, MS, on 5/6/1865. Confederate Widows Pension Application dated 1916 on file at the Mississippi Department of Archives and History. Target Name: Chisholm, Caroline. County: Smith.

Clark, A.O. Pvt., 1st Mississippi Light Artillery. Co. I. Federal Rolls of Prisoners of War: Captured at Blakely, AL, on 4/9/1865; Received at Ship Island, MS, on 4/15/1865. Transferred to Vicksburg, MS, for exchange on 5/1/1865; Exchanged at Camp Townsend, MS, on 5/6/1865.

Clark, Daniel Pvt., 39th Mississippi Infantry. Co. F. Federal Rolls of Prisoners of War: Captured at Blakely, AL, on 4/9/1865; Received at Ship Island,

MS, on 4/15/1865. Transferred to Vicksburg, MS, for exchange on 5/1/1865; Exchanged at Camp Townsend, MS, on 5/6/1865.

Clark, Elijah Thomas (AKA Eliza) Pvt./Cpl., 1st Mississippi Light Artillery. Co. I. Federal Rolls of Prisoners of War: Captured at Blakely, AL, on 4/9/1865; Received at Ship Island, MS, on 4/15/1865. Transferred to Vicksburg, MS, for exchange on 5/1/1865; Exchanged at Camp Townsend, MS, on 5/6/1865. Born: 1834 at Yazoo County, MS. Died: 1910. Confederate Pension Application dated 1914 on file at the Mississippi Department of Archives and History. Target Name: Clark, E.T. County: Scott. Additional Confederate Pension Application dated 1925 on file. Target Name: Clark, E.T. County: Newton. Also a Confederate Widows Pension Application dated 1924 on file. Target Name: Clark, Mrs.E.T. County: Yazoo. Additional Confederate Widows Pension Application dated 1931 on file. Target Name: Clark, Mrs.E.T. County: Newton.

Clark, James M. Pvt., 1st Mississippi Light Artillery. Co. K. Federal Rolls of Prisoners of War: Captured at Blakely, AL, on 4/9/1865; Received at Ship Island, MS, on 4/15/1865. Transferred to Vicksburg, MS, for exchange on 5/1/1865; Exchanged at Camp Townsend, MS, on 5/6/1865.

Clark, T.M. (AKA T.J.) Pvt., 1st Mississippi Light Artillery. Co. F. Federal Rolls of Prisoners of War: Captured at Blakely, AL, on 4/9/1865; Received at Ship Island, MS, on 4/15/1865. Transferred to Vicksburg, MS, for exchange on 5/1/1865; Exchanged at Camp Townsend, MS, on 5/6/1865.

Clark, William A. Pvt., 36th Mississippi Infantry. Co. I. Federal Rolls of Prisoners of War: Captured at Blakely, AL, on 4/9/1865; Received at Ship Island, MS, on 4/15/1865. Transferred to Vicksburg, MS, for exchange on 5/1/1865; Exchanged at Camp Townsend, MS, on 5/6/1865. Confederate Pension Application dated 1916 on file at the Mississippi Department of Archives and History. Target Name: Clark, William A. County: Newton.

Clawson, William M. (AKA Clauson) Pvt., 1st Mississippi Light Artillery. Co. K. Federal Rolls of Prisoners of War: Captured at Blakely, AL, on 4/9/1865; Received at Ship Island, MS, on 4/15/1865. Transferred to Vicksburg, MS, for exchange on 5/1/1865; Exchanged at Camp Townsend, MS, on 5/6/1865.

Clifford, Charles F. Pvt., 35th Mississippi Infantry. Co. H. Federal Rolls of Prisoners of War: Captured at Blakely, AL, on 4/9/1865; Received at Ship Island, MS, on 4/15/1865. Transferred to Vicksburg, MS, for exchange on 5/1/1865; Exchanged at Camp Townsend, MS, on 5/6/1865.

Clifton, William Pvt., 35th Mississippi Infantry. Co. K. Federal Rolls of Prisoners of War: Captured at Blakely, AL, on 4/9/1865; Received at Ship Island, MS, on 4/15/1865. Transferred to Vicksburg, MS, for exchange on 5/1/1865; Exchanged at Camp Townsend, MS, on 5/6/1865.

Coats, William P. (AKA Wilson) Pvt., 36th Mississippi Infantry. Cos. C & H. Federal Rolls of Prisoners of War: Captured at Blakely, AL, on 4/9/1865; Received at Ship Island, MS, on 4/15/1865. Transferred to Vicksburg, MS, for exchange on 5/1/1865; Exchanged at Camp Townsend, MS, on 5/6/1865.

Cockerel, J.M. Pvt./Sgt., 46th Mississippi Infantry. Co. I. Federal Rolls of Prisoners of War: Captured at Blakely, AL, on 4/9/1865; Received at Ship Island, MS, on 4/15/1865. Transferred to Vicksburg, MS, for exchange on 5/1/1865; Exchanged at Camp Townsend, MS, on 5/6/1865.

Coggins, V.S. Pvt., 35th Mississippi Infantry. Co. __. Federal Rolls of Prisoners of War: Captured at Blakely, AL, on 4/9/1865; Received at Ship Island, MS, on 4/15/1865. Transferred to Vicksburg, MS, for exchange on 5/1/1865; Exchanged at Camp Townsend, MS, on 5/6/1865.

Coker, J.L.F. Pvt., 39th Mississippi Infantry. Co. D. Federal Rolls of Prisoners of War: Captured at Blakely, AL, on 4/9/1865; Received at Ship Island, MS, on 4/15/1865. Transferred to Vicksburg, MS, for exchange on 5/1/1865; Exchanged at Camp Townsend, MS, on 5/6/1865.

Colburn, W.J. (AKA Collum) Pvt., 39th Mississippi Infantry. Co. C. Federal Rolls of Prisoners of War: Captured at Blakely, AL, on 4/9/1865; Received at Ship Island, MS, on 4/15/1865. Transferred to Vicksburg, MS, for exchange on 5/1/1865; Exchanged at Camp Townsend, MS, on 5/6/1865.

Cole, J.S. Pvt., 1st Mississippi Light Artillery. Co. __. Federal Rolls of Prisoners of War: Captured at Blakely, AL, on 4/9/1865; Received at Ship Island, MS, on 4/15/1865. Transferred to Vicksburg, MS, for exchange on 5/1/1865; Exchanged at Camp Townsend, MS, on 5/6/1865.

Cole, Marquis L., Jr. 2nd Lt./Capt., 1st Mississippi Light Artillery. Co. D. Federal Rolls of Prisoners of War: Captured at Blakely, AL, on 4/9/1865; Received at Ship Island, MS, on 4/15/1865. Transferred to Vicksburg, MS, for exchange on 4/28/1865; Confined at New Orleans, LA, on 4/30/1865. Exchanged at Camp Townsend, MS, on 5/6/1865.

Collins, James R. Pvt., 1st Mississippi Light Artillery. Co. B. Federal Rolls of Prisoners of War: Captured at Blakely, AL, on 4/9/1865; Received at Ship Island, MS, on 4/15/1865. Transferred to Vicksburg, MS, for exchange on 5/1/1865; Exchanged at Camp Townsend, MS, on 5/6/1865.

Conklin, James W. Ord. Sgt., 1st Mississippi Light Artillery. Co. G. Federal Rolls of Prisoners of War: Captured at Blakely, AL, on 4/9/1865; Received at Ship Island, MS, on 4/15/1865. Transferred to Vicksburg, MS, for exchange on 5/1/1865; Exchanged at Camp Townsend, MS, on 5/6/1865. Born: 1838 at Warren County, MS. Died: 1908.

Conner, John M. Pvt., 4th Mississippi Infantry. Co. D. Federal Rolls of Prisoners of War: Captured in Alabama on 4/1/1865; Received at Ship Island, MS. Transferred to Vicksburg, MS, for exchange on 5/1/1865; Exchanged at Camp Townsend, MS, on 5/6/1865.

Cook, Marion Pvt., 46th Mississippi Infantry. Co. B. Enlisted: 1862. Residence at enlistment: Marion County, MS. Federal Rolls of Prisoners of War: Captured at Blakely, AL, on 4/9/1865; Received at Ship Island, MS, on 4/15/1865. Transferred to Vicksburg, MS, for exchange on 5/1/1865; Exchanged at Camp Townsend, MS, on 5/6/1865. Parents: William James Cook, Sr. and Sara Temples Cook.

Cook, William Brown Pvt., 36th Mississippi Infantry. Co. B. Federal Rolls of Prisoners of War: Captured at Blakely, AL, on 4/9/1865; Received at Ship Island,

MS, on 4/15/1865. Transferred to Vicksburg, MS, for exchange on 5/1/1865; Exchanged at Camp Townsend, MS, on 5/6/1865. Confederate Pension Application dated 1916 on file at the Mississippi Department of Archives and History. Target Name: Cook, William Brown. County: Copiah.

Cooper, L.L. Pvt., 35th Mississippi Infantry. Co. C. Federal Rolls of Prisoners of War: Captured at Blakely, AL, on 4/9/1865; Received at Ship Island, MS, on 4/15/1865. Transferred to Vicksburg, MS, for exchange on 5/1/1865; Exchanged at Camp Townsend, MS, on 5/6/1865.

Cooper, R.L. Pvt., 35th Mississippi Infantry. Co. C. Federal Rolls of Prisoners of War: Captured at Blakely, AL, on 4/9/1865; Received at Ship Island, MS, on 4/15/1865. Transferred to Vicksburg, MS, for exchange on 5/1/1865; Exchanged at Camp Townsend, MS, on 5/6/1865.

Corn, James Pvt., 36th Mississippi Infantry. Co. G. Federal Rolls of Prisoners of War: Captured at Blakely, AL, on 4/9/1865; Received at Ship Island, MS, on 4/15/1865. Transferred to Vicksburg, MS, for exchange on 5/1/1865; Exchanged at Camp Townsend, MS, on 5/6/1865.

Coulter, E.D. Pvt., 35th Mississippi Infantry. Co. I. Federal Rolls of Prisoners of War: Captured at Blakely, AL, on 4/9/1865; Received at Ship Island, MS, on 4/15/1865. Transferred to Vicksburg, MS, for exchange on 5/1/1865; Exchanged at Camp Townsend, MS, on 5/6/1865.

Coulton, N.J. Pvt., 1st Mississippi Light Artillery. Co. B. Federal Rolls of Prisoners of War: Captured at Blakely, AL, on 4/9/1865; Received at Ship Island, MS, on 4/15/1865. Transferred to Vicksburg, MS, for exchange on 5/1/1865; Exchanged at Camp Townsend, MS, on 5/6/1865.

Cowan, James J. Capt., 1st Mississippi Light Artillery. Co. G. Federal Rolls of Prisoners of War: Captured at Blakely, AL, on 4/9/1865; Received at Ship Island, MS, on 4/15/1865. Transferred to Vicksburg, MS, for exchange on 4/281865; Confined at New Orleans, LA, on 4/30/1865. Exchanged at Camp Townsend, MS, on 5/6/1865.

Cowan, Ludwell B., Jr. 2nd Lt., 1st Mississippi Light Artillery. Co. G. Federal Rolls of Prisoners of War: Captured at Blakely, AL, on 4/9/1865; Received at Ship Island, MS, on 4/15/1865. Transferred to Vicksburg, MS, for exchange on 4/28/1865; Confined at New Orleans, LA, on 4/30/1865. Exchanged at Camp Townsend, MS, on 5/6/1865.

Cowan, Warren Pvt., 1st Mississippi Light Artillery. Co. G. Federal Rolls of Prisoners of War: Captured at Blakely, AL, on 4/9/1865; Received at Ship Island, MS, on 4/15/1865. Transferred to Vicksburg, MS, for exchange on 5/1/1865; Exchanged at Camp Townsend, MS, on 5/6/1865.

Cox, Austin Pvt./Sgt., 36th Mississippi Infantry. Co. B. Federal Rolls of Prisoners of War: Captured at Blakely, AL, on 4/9/1865; Received at Ship Island, MS, on 4/15/1865. Transferred to Vicksburg, MS, for exchange on 5/1/1865; Exchanged at Camp Townsend, MS, on 5/6/1865. Confederate Widows Pension Application dated 1916 on file at the Mississippi Department of Archives and History. Target Name: Cox, Francena. County: Copiah.

Cox, Daniel C. Sgt./Pvt., 36th Mississippi Infantry. Co. I. Federal Rolls of Prisoners of War: Captured at Blakely, AL, on 4/9/1865; Received at Ship Island, MS, on 4/15/1865. Transferred to Vicksburg, MS, for exchange on 5/1/1865; Exchanged at Camp Townsend, MS, on 5/6/1865.

Cox, F.N. Pvt., 35th Mississippi Infantry. Co. K. Federal Rolls of Prisoners of War: Captured at Blakely, AL, on 4/9/1865; Received at Ship Island, MS, on 4/15/1865. Transferred to Vicksburg, MS, for exchange on 5/1/1865; Exchanged at Camp Townsend, MS, on 5/6/1865.

Cox, Willie H. Pvt., 4th Mississippi Cavalry. Co. I. Federal Rolls of Prisoners of War: Captured at Liberty, MS, on 11/16/1864; Received at Ship Island, MS, from New Orleans, LA, on 12/13/1864. Transferred to Vicksburg, MS, for exchange on 5/1/1865; Exchanged at Camp Townsend, MS, on 5/6/1865.

Crawford, J.N. Pvt., 36th Mississippi Infantry. Co. E. Federal Rolls of Prisoners of War: Captured at Spanish Fort, AL, on 4/8/1865; Received at Ship Island, MS, on 4/10/1865. Transferred to Vicksburg, MS, for exchange on 5/1/1865; Exchanged at Camp Townsend, MS, on 5/6/1865.

Creed, Cornelius Pvt., 35th Mississippi Infantry. Co. A. Federal Rolls of Prisoners of War: Captured at Blakely, AL, on 4/9/1865; Received at Ship Island, MS, on 4/15/1865. Transferred to Vicksburg, MS, for exchange on 5/1/1865; Exchanged at Camp Townsend, MS, on 5/6/1865.

Creel, B. Pvt., 4th Mississippi Infantry. Co. I. Federal Rolls of Prisoners of War: Captured in Alabama on 4/1/1865; Received at Ship Island, MS. Transferred to Vicksburg, MS, for exchange on 5/1/1865; Exchanged at Camp Townsend, MS, on 5/6/1865.

Crenshaw, A.D. Pvt., 36th Mississippi Infantry. Co. D. Federal Rolls of Prisoners of War: Captured at Blakely, AL, on 4/9/1865; Received at Ship Island, MS, on 4/15/1865. Transferred to Vicksburg, MS, for exchange on 5/1/1865; Exchanged at Camp Townsend, MS, on 5/6/1865. Confederate Widows Pension Application dated 1920 on file at the Mississippi Department of Archives and History. Target Name: Crenshaw, M.V. County: Neshoba.

Cresswell, R.W. Pvt., 39th Mississippi Infantry. Co. I. Federal Rolls of Prisoners of War: Captured at Blakely, AL, on 4/9/1865; Received at Ship Island, MS, on 4/15/1865. Transferred to Vicksburg, MS, for exchange on 5/1/1865; Exchanged at Camp Townsend, MS, on 5/6/1865.

Crews, Henry C. (AKA Crewis, H.H.) Pvt., 36th Mississippi Infantry. Co. G. Federal Rolls of Prisoners of War: Captured at Blakely, AL, on 4/9/1865; Received at Ship Island, MS, on 4/15/1865. Transferred to Vicksburg, MS, for exchange on 5/1/1865; Exchanged at Camp Townsend, MS, on 5/6/1865. Confederate Pension Application dated 1916 on file at the Mississippi Department of Archives and History. Target Name: Crews, H.H. County: Copiah.

Crow, G.L. Cpl./Pvt., 35th Mississippi Infantry. Co. I. Federal Rolls of Prisoners of War: Captured at Blakely, AL, on 4/9/1865; Received at Ship Island, MS, on 4/15/1865. Transferred to Vicksburg, MS, for exchange on 5/1/1865; Exchanged at Camp Townsend, MS, on 5/6/1865.

Culbertson, John T. Pvt./Cpl., 35th Mississippi Infantry. Co. I. Federal Rolls of Prisoners of War: Captured at Blakely, AL, on 4/9/1865; Received at Ship Island, MS, on 4/15/1865. Transferred to Vicksburg, MS, for exchange on 5/1/1865; Exchanged at Camp Townsend, MS, on 5/6/1865.

Cupps, R.W. (AKA Culls, K.U.) Pvt., 8th Mississippi Cavalry. Co. __. Federal Rolls of Prisoners of War: Captured in Florida on 11/25/1864; Received at Ship Island, MS, from New Orleans, LA, on 12/13/1864. Transferred to Vicksburg, MS, for exchange on 5/1/1865; Exchanged at Camp Townsend, MS, on 5/6/1865.

Curtis, J.A. Pvt., 35th Mississippi Infantry. Co. I. Federal Rolls of Prisoners of War: Captured at Blakely, AL, on 4/9/1865; Received at Ship Island, MS, on 4/15/1865. Transferred to Vicksburg, MS, for exchange on 5/1/1865; Exchanged at Camp Townsend, MS, on 5/6/1865.

Curtis, J.W. Pvt., 35th Mississippi Infantry. Co. __. Federal Rolls of Prisoners of War: Captured at Blakely, AL, on 4/9/1865; Received at Ship Island, MS, on 4/15/1865. Transferred to Vicksburg, MS, for exchange on 5/1/1865; Exchanged at Camp Townsend, MS, on 5/6/1865.

Curtis, S.N. Cpl./Sgt., 35th Mississippi Infantry. Co. D. Federal Rolls of Prisoners of War: Captured at Blakely, AL, on 4/9/1865; Received at Ship Island, MS, on 4/15/1865. Transferred to Vicksburg, MS, for exchange on 5/1/1865; Exchanged at Camp Townsend, MS, on 5/6/1865.

Curtis, S.N. Sgt., 1st Mississippi Light Artillery. Co. __. Federal Rolls of Prisoners of War: Captured at Blakely, AL, on 4/9/1865; Received at Ship Island, MS, on 4/15/1865. Transferred to Vicksburg, MS, for exchange on 5/1/1865; Exchanged at Camp Townsend, MS, on 5/6/1865.

Curtiss, W.H. Ord. Sgt., 7th Mississippi Battalion Infantry. F & S. Federal Rolls of Prisoners of War: Captured at Blakely, AL, on 4/9/1865; Received at Ship Island, MS, on 4/15/1865. Transferred to Vicksburg, MS, for exchange on 5/1/1865; Exchanged at Camp Townsend, MS, on 5/6/1865.

Cutts, R.W. Pvt., 8th Mississippi Cavalry. Co. H. Federal Rolls of Prisoners of War: Captured at Milton, FL, on 11/25/1864; Received at Ship Island, MS, on 12/13/1864. Transferred to Vicksburg, MS, for exchange on 5/1/1865; Exchanged at Camp Townsend, MS, on 5/6/1865.

Dabney, T.G. Cpl./Sgt., 1st Mississippi Light Artillery. Co. I. Federal Rolls of Prisoners of War: Captured at Blakely, AL, on 4/9/1865; Received at Ship Island, MS, on 4/15/1865. Transferred to Vicksburg, MS, for exchange on 5/1/1865; Exchanged at Camp Townsend, MS, on 5/6/1865.

Dabney, William Presley T. Pvt., 1st Mississippi Light Artillery. Co. K. Federal Rolls of Prisoners of War: Captured at Blakely, AL, on 4/9/1865; Received at Ship Island, MS, on 4/15/1865. Transferred to Vicksburg, MS, for exchange on 5/1/1865; Exchanged at Camp Townsend, MS, on 5/6/1865. Born: 1806 at DeSoto County, MS. Died: 1884.

Daniel, Christopher Columbus Pvt., 8th Mississippi Infantry. Co. E. Enlisted: 4/1/1861 near Rolla, MS. Rolls for 4/1861 through 3/1865: Present. Federal Rolls of Prisoners of War: Captured at Blakely, AL, on 4/9/1865; Received at Ship Island, MS, on 4/15/1865. Transferred to Vicksburg, MS, for exchange on 5/1/1865; Exchanged at Camp Townsend, MS, on 5/6/1865. Born: 8/18/1843 near Troy, Pike County, AL. Soldier is recorded on the 1907 Census of Alabama Confederate Veterans and their Widows. Residence: Crenshaw County, AL.

Daniels, C.C. Pvt./Cpl., 7th Mississippi Battalion Infantry. Co. A. Federal Rolls of Prisoners of War: Captured at Blakely, AL, on 4/9/1865; Received at Ship Island, MS, on 4/15/1865. Transferred to Vicksburg, MS, for exchange on 5/1/1865; Exchanged at Camp Townsend, MS, on 5/6/1865.

Datin, William S. (AKA Dulin) Pvt., 4th Mississippi Infantry. Co. K. Federal Rolls of Prisoners of War: Captured at Blakely, AL, on 4/9/1865; Received at Ship Island, MS, on 4/15/1865. Transferred to Vicksburg, MS, for exchange on 5/1/1865; Exchanged at Camp Townsend, MS, on 5/6/1865.

Daudrille, John E. (AKA Daughdrille) Pvt., 46th Mississippi Infantry. Co. G. Federal Rolls of Prisoners of War: Captured at Blakely, AL, on 4/9/1865; Received at Ship Island, MS, on 4/15/1865. Transferred to Vicksburg, MS, for exchange on 5/1/1865; Exchanged at Camp Townsend, MS, on 5/6/1865. Confederate Pension Application dated 1920 on file at the Mississippi Department of Archives and History. Target Name: Daughdrill, J.E. County: Lincoln. Also a Confederate Widows Pension Application dated 1924 on file. Target Name: Daudrille, Amanda E. County: Lincoln.

Daughdrille, William J. Pvt., 46th Mississippi Infantry. Co. G. Federal Rolls of Prisoners of War: Captured at Blakely, AL, on 4/9/1865; Received at Ship Island, MS, on 4/15/1865. Transferred to Vicksburg, MS, for exchange on 5/1/1865; Exchanged at Camp Townsend, MS, on 5/6/1865. Confederate Pension Application dated 1916 on file at the Mississippi Department of Archives and History. Target Name: Daughdrill, William J. County: Lawrence. Also a Confederate Widows Pension Application dated 1924 on file. Target Name: Daughdrill, Jane. County: Lawrence.

Davis, C.J. Sgt., 36th Mississippi Infantry. Co. __. Federal Rolls of Prisoners of War: Captured at Blakely, AL, on 4/9/1865; Received at Ship Island, MS, on 4/15/1865. Transferred to Vicksburg, MS, for exchange on 5/1/1865; Exchanged at Camp Townsend, MS, on 5/6/1865. Confederate Pension Application dated 1916 on file at the Mississippi Department of Archives and History. Target Name: Davis, C.J. County: Copiah. Also a Confederate Widows Pension Application dated 1917 on file. Target Name: Davis, Eliza. County: Copiah.

Davis, Capers L. Pvt., 7th Mississippi Battalion Infantry. Co. D. Federal Rolls of Prisoners of War: Captured at Blakely, AL, on 4/9/1865; Received at Ship Island, MS, on 4/15/1865. Transferred to Vicksburg, MS, for exchange on 5/1/1865; Exchanged at Camp Townsend, MS, on 5/6/1865.

Davis, Edward L.H. Pvt., 1st Mississippi Light Artillery. Co. D. Federal Rolls of Prisoners of War: Captured at Blakely, AL, on 4/9/1865; Received at Ship Island, MS, on 4/15/1865. Transferred to Vicksburg, MS, for exchange on 5/1/1865; Exchanged at Camp Townsend, MS, on 5/6/1865.

Davis, Gales A. Pvt., 7th Mississippi Battalion Infantry. Co. D. Federal Rolls of Prisoners of War: Captured at Blakely, AL, on 4/9/1865; Received at Ship Island,

MS, on 4/15/1865. Transferred to Vicksburg, MS, for exchange on 5/1/1865; Exchanged at Camp Townsend, MS, on 5/6/1865.

Davis, George Pvt., 7th Mississippi Battalion Infantry. Co. K. Federal Rolls of Prisoners of War: Captured at Blakely, AL, on 4/9/1865; Received at Ship Island, MS, on 4/15/1865. Transferred to Vicksburg, MS, for exchange on 5/1/1865; Exchanged at Camp Townsend, MS, on 5/6/1865.

Davis, Green H. Pvt., 39th Mississippi Infantry. Cos. A & F. Federal Rolls of Prisoners of War: Captured at Blakely, AL, on 4/9/1865; Received at Ship Island, MS, on 4/15/1865. Transferred to Vicksburg, MS, for exchange on 5/1/1865; Exchanged at Camp Townsend, MS, on 5/6/1865.

Davis, Henry M. Pvt., 7th Mississippi Battalion Infantry. Co. D. Federal Rolls of Prisoners of War: Captured at Blakely, AL, on 4/9/1865; Received at Ship Island, MS, on 4/15/1865. Transferred to Vicksburg, MS, for exchange on 5/1/1865; Exchanged at Camp Townsend, MS, on 5/6/1865.

Davis, J.P. Pvt., 7th Mississippi Battalion Infantry. Co. E. Federal Rolls of Prisoners of War: Captured at Blakely, AL, on 4/9/1865; Received at Ship Island, MS, on 4/15/1865. Transferred to Vicksburg, MS, for exchange on 5/1/1865; Exchanged at Camp Townsend, MS, on 5/6/1865.

Davis, James J. Pvt., 39th Mississippi Infantry. Co. B. Federal Rolls of Prisoners of War: Captured at Blakely, AL, on 4/9/1865; Received at Ship Island, MS, on 4/15/1865. Transferred to Vicksburg, MS, for exchange on 5/1/1865; Exchanged at Camp Townsend, MS, on 5/6/1865.

Davis, John W. Pvt., 4th Mississippi Infantry. Co. I. Federal Rolls of Prisoners of War: Captured in Alabama on 4/1/1865; Received at Ship Island, MS. Transferred to Vicksburg, MS, for exchange on 5/1/1865; Exchanged at Camp Townsend, MS, on 5/6/1865.

Davis, Joshua D. Pvt., 1st Mississippi Light Artillery. Co. D. Federal Rolls of Prisoners of War: Captured at Blakely, AL, on 4/9/1865; Received at Ship Island, MS, on 4/15/1865. Transferred to Vicksburg, MS, for exchange on 5/1/1865; Exchanged at Camp Townsend, MS, on 5/6/1865.

Davis, Luther Pvt., 1st Mississippi Light Artillery. Co. D. Federal Rolls of Prisoners of War: Captured at Blakely, AL, on 4/9/1865; Received at Ship Island, MS, on 4/15/1865. Transferred to Vicksburg, MS, for exchange on 5/1/1865; Exchanged at Camp Townsend, MS, on 5/6/1865.

Davis, Thomas J. Pvt., 1st Mississippi Light Artillery. Co. D. Federal Rolls of Prisoners of War: Captured at Blakely, AL, on 4/9/1865; Received at Ship Island, MS, on 4/15/1865. Transferred to Vicksburg, MS, for exchange on 5/1/1865; Exchanged at Camp Townsend, MS, on 5/6/1865.

Dawson, William T. Pvt., 4th Mississippi Infantry. Co. A. Federal Rolls of Prisoners of War: Captured at Blakely, AL, on 4/9/1865; Received at Ship Island, MS, on 4/15/1865. Transferred to Vicksburg, MS, for exchange on 5/1/1865; Exchanged at Camp Townsend, MS, on 5/6/1865.

Day, William O. Bugler, 1st Mississippi Light Artillery. Co. K. Federal Rolls of Prisoners of War: Captured at Blakely, AL, on 4/9/1865; Received at Ship Island, MS, on 4/15/1865. Transferred to Vicksburg, MS, for exchange on 5/1/1865; Exchanged at Camp Townsend, MS, on 5/6/1865.

Dear, Hardy C. Pvt., 36th Mississippi Infantry. Co. I. Federal Rolls of Prisoners of War: Captured at Blakely, AL, on 4/9/1865; Received at Ship Island, MS, on 4/15/1865. Transferred to Vicksburg, MS, for exchange on 5/1/1865; Exchanged at Camp Townsend, MS, on 5/6/1865.

Deas, Francis H. Pvt., 1st Mississippi Light Artillery. Co. D. Federal Rolls of Prisoners of War: Captured at Blakely, AL, on 4/9/1865; Received at Ship Island, MS, on 4/15/1865. Transferred to Vicksburg, MS, for exchange on 5/1/1865; Exchanged at Camp Townsend, MS, on 5/6/1865. Confederate Pension Application dated 1926 on file at the Mississippi Department of Archives and History. Target Name: Deas, F.H. County: Clarke.

Deas, Slater Allen Pvt., 1st Mississippi Light Artillery. Co. D. Federal Rolls of Prisoners of War: Captured at Blakely, AL, on 4/9/1865; Received at Ship Island, MS, on 4/15/1865. Transferred to Vicksburg, MS, for exchange on 5/1/1865; Exchanged at Camp Townsend, MS, on 5/6/1865.

Dedlake, James William (AKA Delake, Didlake) Sgt./2nd Lt., 1st Mississippi Light Artillery. Co. F. Federal Rolls of Prisoners of War: Captured at Blakely, AL, on 4/9/1865; Received at Ship Island, MS, on 4/15/1865. Transferred to Vicksburg, MS, for exchange on 4/28/1865; Confined at New Orleans, LA, on 4/30/1865. Exchanged at Camp Townsend, MS, on 5/6/1865. Born: 1836 at Copiah County, MS. Died: 1913.

Denley, John Pvt./Sgt., 4th Mississippi Infantry. Co. F. Federal Rolls of Prisoners of War: Captured at Blakely, AL, on 4/9/1865; Received at Ship Island, MS, on 4/15/1865. Transferred to Vicksburg, MS, for exchange on 5/1/1865; Exchanged at Camp Townsend, MS, on 5/6/1865.

Dennison, J.W. (AKA Denson, Denison) Pvt., 36th Mississippi Infantry. Co. F. Federal Rolls of Prisoners of War: Captured at Blakely, AL, on 4/9/1865; Received at Ship Island, MS, on 4/15/1865. Transferred to Vicksburg, MS, for exchange on 5/1/1865; Exchanged at Camp Townsend, MS, on 5/6/1865.

Denson, James N. Sgt., 36th Mississippi Infantry. Co. F. Federal Rolls of Prisoners of War: Captured at Blakely, AL, on 4/9/1865; Received at Ship Island, MS, on 4/15/1865. Transferred to Vicksburg, MS, for exchange on 5/1/1865; Exchanged at Camp Townsend, MS, on 5/6/1865.

Denton, William M. Pvt., 7th Mississippi Battalion Infantry. Co. B. Federal Rolls of Prisoners of War: Captured at Blakely, AL, on 4/9/1865; Received at Ship Island, MS, on 4/15/1865. Transferred to Vicksburg, MS, for exchange on 5/1/1865; Exchanged at Camp Townsend, MS, on 5/6/1865.

Dickens, R.D. Pvt., 1st Mississippi Light Artillery. Co. __. Federal Rolls of Prisoners of War: Captured at Blakely, AL, on 4/9/1865; Received at Ship Island, MS, on 4/15/1865. Transferred to Vicksburg, MS, for exchange on 5/1/1865; Exchanged at Camp Townsend, MS, on 5/6/1865.

Dillard, Allan (AKA W.A.) Pvt., 7th Mississippi Battalion Infantry. Co. C. Federal Rolls of Prisoners of War: Captured at Blakely, AL, on 4/9/1865; Received at Ship Island, MS, on 4/15/1865. Transferred to

Vicksburg, MS, for exchange on 5/1/1865; Exchanged at Camp Townsend, MS, on 5/6/1865.

Donald, Henry Pvt., 7th Mississippi Battalion Infantry. Co. E. Federal Rolls of Prisoners of War: Captured at Blakely, AL, on 4/9/1865; Received at Ship Island, MS, on 4/15/1865. Transferred to Vicksburg, MS, for exchange on 5/1/1865; Exchanged at Camp Townsend, MS, on 5/6/1865. Confederate Pension Application dated 1910 on file at the Mississippi Department of Archives and History. Target Name: Donald, Henry. County: Clarke. Also a Confederate Widows Pension Application dated 1910 on file. Target Name: Donald, Julia A. County—Clarke.

Donehue, Barney A. Pvt., 7th Mississippi Battalion Infantry. Co. B. Federal Rolls of Prisoners of War: Captured at Blakely, AL, on 4/9/1865; Received at Ship Island, MS, on 4/15/1865. Transferred to Vicksburg, MS, for exchange on 5/1/1865; Exchanged at Camp Townsend, MS, on 5/6/1865.

Donnell, W.P. (AKA Darnell) Pvt., 7th Mississippi Battalion Infantry. Co. G. Federal Rolls of Prisoners of War: Captured at Blakely, AL, on 4/9/1865; Received at Ship Island, MS, on 4/15/1865. Transferred to Vicksburg, MS, for exchange on 5/1/1865; Exchanged at Camp Townsend, MS, on 5/6/1865.

Donovan, David S. (AKA Donavan, D.J.) Pvt., 1st Mississippi Light Artillery. Co. G. Federal Rolls of Prisoners of War: Captured at Blakely, AL, on 4/9/1865; Received at Ship Island, MS, on 4/15/1865. Transferred to Vicksburg, MS, for exchange on 5/1/1865; Exchanged at Camp Townsend, MS, on 5/6/1865. Born: Hinds County, MS.

Dorsey, George H. Pvt., 1st Mississippi Light Artillery. Co. K. Federal Rolls of Prisoners of War: Captured at Blakely, AL, on 4/9/1865; Received at Ship Island, MS, on 4/15/1865. Transferred to Vicksburg, MS, for exchange on 5/1/1865; Exchanged at Camp Townsend, MS, on 5/6/1865. Born: 1844 at Hinds County, MS. Died: 1923. Confederate Pension Application dated 1920 on file at the Mississippi Department of Archives and History. Target Name: Dorsey, George H. County: Hinds.

Dorsey, George W. Pvt., 1st Mississippi Light Artillery. Co. I. Federal Rolls of Prisoners of War: Captured at Blakely, AL, on 4/9/1865; Received at Ship Island, MS, on 4/15/1865. Transferred to Vicksburg, MS, for exchange on 5/1/1865; Exchanged at Camp Townsend, MS, on 5/6/1865.

Dotson, James L. Pvt., 1st Mississippi Light Artillery. Co. B. Federal Rolls of Prisoners of War: Captured at Blakely, AL, on 4/9/1865; Received at Ship Island, MS, on 4/15/1865. Transferred to Vicksburg, MS, for exchange on 5/1/1865; Exchanged at Camp Townsend, MS, on 5/6/1865.

Dotson, John H. Pvt., 1st Mississippi Light Artillery. Co. B. Federal Rolls of Prisoners of War: Captured at Blakely, AL, on 4/9/1865; Received at Ship Island, MS, on 4/15/1865. Transferred to Vicksburg, MS, for exchange on 5/1/1865; Exchanged at Camp Townsend, MS, on 5/6/1865.

Dougherty, J.M. Pvt., 1st Mississippi Light Artillery. Co. __. Federal Rolls of Prisoners of War: Captured at Blakely, AL, on 4/9/1865; Received at Ship Island, MS, on 4/15/1865. Transferred to Vicksburg, MS, for exchange on 5/1/1865; Exchanged at Camp Townsend, MS, on 5/6/1865.

Douglas, Albert B. Pvt., 36th Mississippi Infantry. Cos. A & K. Federal Rolls of Prisoners of War: Captured at Blakely, AL, on 4/9/1865; Received at Ship Island, MS, on 4/15/1865. Transferred to Vicksburg, MS, for exchange on 5/1/1865; Exchanged at Camp Townsend, MS, on 5/6/1865.

Downing, Daniel Whitaker Pvt., 1st Mississippi Light Artillery. Co. B. Federal Rolls of Prisoners of War: Captured at Blakely, AL, on 4/9/1865; Received at Ship Island, MS, on 4/15/1865. Transferred to Vicksburg, MS, for exchange on 5/1/1865; Exchanged at Camp Townsend, MS, on 5/6/1865. Born: 6/12/1844 at Hinds County, MS. Died: 12/28/1916 at Jackson, MS. Confederate Pension Application dated 1916 on file at the Mississippi Department of Archives and History. Target Name: Downing, D.W. County: Hinds. Also a Confederate Widows Pension Application dated 1917 on file. Target Name: Downing, Anna. County: Hinds.

Downing, W.B. Pvt., 1st Mississippi Light Artillery. Co. B. Federal Rolls of Prisoners of War: Captured at Blakely, AL, on 4/9/1865; Received at Ship Island, MS, on 4/15/1865. Transferred to Vicksburg, MS, for exchange on 5/1/1865; Exchanged at Camp Townsend, MS, on 5/6/1865.

DuBose, L.L. (AKA Duboise, S.L.) 1st Sgt./1st Lt., 35th Mississippi Infantry. Co. K. Federal Rolls of Prisoners of War: Captured at Blakely, AL, on 4/9/1865; Received at Ship Island, MS, on 4/15/1865. Transferred to Vicksburg, MS, for exchange on 4/28/1865; Confined at New Orleans, LA, on 4/30/1865. Exchanged at Camp Townsend, MS, on 5/6/1865

Duffie, E.W. (AKA Diffee, Diffey, Diffie) Pvt., 35th Mississippi Infantry. Co. B. Federal Rolls of Prisoners of War: Captured at Blakely, AL, on 4/9/1865; Received at Ship Island, MS, on 4/15/1865. Transferred to Vicksburg, MS, for exchange on 5/1/1865; Exchanged at Camp Townsend, MS, on 5/6/1865.

Dunn, J.A. Pvt./Q.M. Sgt., 1st Mississippi Light Artillery. Co. F. Federal Rolls of Prisoners of War: Captured at Blakely, AL, on 4/9/1865; Received at Ship Island, MS, on 4/15/1865. Transferred to Vicksburg, MS, for exchange on 5/1/1865; Exchanged at Camp Townsend, MS, on 5/6/1865.

Durham, Dewitt Clinton 2nd Lt./1st Lt./Capt., 46th Mississippi Infantry. Co. K. Enlisted: Kemper County, MS, in the Kemper Guards as a 2nd Lt; Assigned to the 59th Virginia Infantry. Wise's Legion and later made Capt. of the 46th Mississippi Infantry. Co.K. Federal Rolls of Prisoners of War: Captured and paroled at Vicksburg, MS, on 7/4/1863. Federal Rolls of Prisoners of War: Captured at Blakely, AL, on 4/9/1865; Received at Ship Island, MS, on 4/15/1865. Transferred to Vicksburg, MS, for exchange on 4/28/1865; Confined at New Orleans, LA, on 4/30/1865. Exchanged at Camp Townsend, MS, on 5/6/1865. Rolls of Prisoners of War, C.S.A: Surrendered at Citronelle, AL, on 5/6/1865; Paroled at Meridian, MS, in 5/1865. Battles: Baker's Creek, MS, Vicksburg Campaign, Atlanta Campaign, and Blakely, AL. Wounded in the head by a spent minié ball at Kennesaw Mountain, GA, and through both thighs by a minié ball in front of Atlanta, GA. Born: 1839 at Cleveland County, NC, to Benjamin Franklin Durham and Elizabeth Evans Durham. Education: Irving College, TN, in 1858 and Judge Pearson's Law School in

North Carolina. Married: Harriet C. Chatfield, the daughter of Rev.G.W. Chatfield, in 1868. Children: 4 — 2 Sons, W.L. Durham and D.C. Durham, and 2 Daughters, Mrs.C.H. Steele and Miss Eloise Durham. Memberships: Walthall Camp, United Confederate Veterans # 25, Meridian, MS. Died: 2/25/1921 at the home of his son at Hattiesburg, MS.

Dykes, James C. Pvt./Cpl., 46th Mississippi Infantry. Co. B. Enlisted: 1862. Age at enlistment: 26. Residence at enlistment: Covington, MS. Federal Rolls of Prisoners of War: Captured at Blakely, AL, on 4/9/1865; Received at Ship Island, MS, on 4/15/1865. Transferred to Vicksburg, MS, for exchange on 5/1/1865; Exchanged at Camp Townsend, MS, on 5/6/1865. Parents: Jacob H. and Sarah E. Dykes.

Eaken, Moses R. Pvt./2nd Lt., 1st Mississippi Light Artillery. Co. D. Federal Rolls of Prisoners of War: Captured at Blakely, AL, on 4/9/1865; Received at Ship Island, MS, on 4/15/1865. Transferred to Vicksburg, MS, for exchange on 4/28/1865; Confined at New Orleans, LA, on 4/30/1865. Exchanged at Camp Townsend, MS, on 5/6/1865.

Earl, Silas (AKA Earles) Pvt., 1st Mississippi Light Artillery. Co. B. Federal Rolls of Prisoners of War: Captured at Blakely, AL, on 4/9/1865; Received at Ship Island, MS, on 4/15/1865. Transferred to Vicksburg, MS, for exchange on 5/1/1865; Exchanged at Camp Townsend, MS, on 5/6/1865.

Eaves, S.G. Pvt., 1st Mississippi Light Artillery. Co. __. Federal Rolls of Prisoners of War: Captured at Blakely, AL, on 4/9/1865; Received at Ship Island, MS, on 4/15/1865. Transferred to Vicksburg, MS, for exchange on 5/1/1865; Exchanged at Camp Townsend, MS, on 5/6/1865.

Eaves, William Pvt., 35th Mississippi Infantry. Co. D. Federal Rolls of Prisoners of War: Captured at Blakely, AL, on 4/9/1865; Received at Ship Island, MS, on 4/15/1865. Transferred to Vicksburg, MS, for exchange on 5/1/1865; Exchanged at Camp Townsend, MS, on 5/6/1865.

Edwards, Benjamin C. (AKA R.C.), Sr. 2nd Lt., 1st Mississippi Light Artillery. Co. G. Federal Rolls of Prisoners of War: Captured at Blakely, AL, on 4/9/1865; Received at Ship Island, MS, on 4/15/1865. Transferred to Vicksburg, MS, for exchange on 4/28/1865; Confined at New Orleans, LA, on 4/30/1865. Exchanged at Camp Townsend, MS, on 5/6/1865.

Edwards, J.F. Pvt., 39th Mississippi Infantry. Co. C. Federal Rolls of Prisoners of War: Captured at Blakely, AL, on 4/9/1865; Received at Ship Island, MS, on 4/15/1865. Transferred to Vicksburg, MS, for exchange on 5/1/1865; Exchanged at Camp Townsend, MS, on 5/6/1865.

Edwards, John J. Pvt., 36th Mississippi Infantry. Co. B. Federal Rolls of Prisoners of War: Captured at Blakely, AL, on 4/9/1865; Received at Ship Island, MS, on 4/15/1865. Transferred to Vicksburg, MS, for exchange on 5/1/1865; Exchanged at Camp Townsend, MS, on 5/6/1865.

Edwins, A.W. Cpl., 1st Mississippi Light Artillery. Co. __. Federal Rolls of Prisoners of War: Captured at Blakely, AL, on 4/9/1865; Received at Ship Island, MS, on 4/15/1865. Transferred to Vicksburg, MS, for exchange on 5/1/1865; Exchanged at Camp Townsend, MS, on 5/6/1865.

Elam, T.A. 3rd Lt./1st Lt., 4th Mississippi Infantry. Co. H. Federal Rolls of Prisoners of War: Captured at Blakely, AL, on 4/9/1865; Received at Ship Island, MS, on 4/15/1865. Transferred to Vicksburg, MS, for exchange on 4/28/1865; Confined at New Orleans, LA, on 4/30/1865. Exchanged at Camp Townsend, MS, on 5/6/1865.

Eldridge, Elijah T. Pvt., 35th Mississippi Infantry. Co. A. Federal Rolls of Prisoners of War: Captured at Blakely, AL, on 4/9/1865; Received at Ship Island, MS, on 4/15/1865. Transferred to Vicksburg, MS, for exchange on 5/1/1865; Exchanged at Camp Townsend, MS, on 5/6/1865.

Eldridge, George L. (AKA E.L.) Pvt., 1st Mississippi Light Artillery. Co. G. Federal Rolls of Prisoners of War: Captured at Blakely, AL, on 4/9/1865; Received at Ship Island, MS, on 4/15/1865. Transferred to Vicksburg, MS, for exchange on 5/1/1865; Exchanged at Camp Townsend, MS, on 5/6/1865.

Ellen, W. Pvt., 46th Mississippi Infantry. Co. __. Federal Rolls of Prisoners of War: Captured at Blakely, AL, on 4/9/1865; Received at Ship Island, MS, on 4/15/1865. Transferred to Vicksburg, MS, for exchange on 5/1/1865; Exchanged at Camp Townsend, MS, on 5/6/1865.

Ellett, H.T., Jr. Pvt., 1st Mississippi Light Artillery. Co. K. Federal Rolls of Prisoners of War: Captured at Blakely, AL, on 4/9/1865; Received at Ship Island, MS, on 4/15/1865. Transferred to Vicksburg, MS, for exchange on 5/1/1865; Exchanged at Camp Townsend, MS, on 5/6/1865.

Ellis, George W. Pvt., 39th Mississippi Infantry. Co. I. Federal Rolls of Prisoners of War: Captured at Blakely, AL, on 4/9/1865; Received at Ship Island, MS, on 4/15/1865. Transferred to Vicksburg, MS, for exchange on 5/1/1865; Exchanged at Camp Townsend, MS, on 5/6/1865.

Ellis, John W. Pvt./Sgt., 7th Mississippi Battalion Infantry. Co. E. Federal Rolls of Prisoners of War: Captured at Blakely, AL, on 4/9/1865; Received at Ship Island, MS, on 4/15/1865. Transferred to Vicksburg, MS, for exchange on 5/1/1865; Exchanged at Camp Townsend, MS, on 5/6/1865.

Elloyne, Larry Pvt., 35th Mississippi Infantry. Co. F. Federal Rolls of Prisoners of War: Captured at Blakely, AL, on 4/9/1865; Received at Ship Island, MS, on 4/15/1865. Transferred to Vicksburg, MS, for exchange on 5/1/1865; Exchanged at Camp Townsend, MS, on 5/6/1865.

Ellzy, John E. Pvt., 7th Mississippi Battalion Infantry. Co. B. Federal Rolls of Prisoners of War: Captured at Blakely, AL, on 4/9/1865; Received at Ship Island, MS, on 4/15/1865. Transferred to Vicksburg, MS, for exchange on 5/1/1865; Exchanged at Camp Townsend, MS, on 5/6/1865.

Elmore, Thomas J. Sgt./Capt., 4th Mississippi Infantry. Co. __. Federal Rolls of Prisoners of War: Captured at Blakely, AL, on 4/9/1865; Received at Ship Island, MS, on 4/15/1865. Transferred to Vicksburg, MS, for exchange on 4/28/1865; Confined at New Orleans, LA, on 4/30/1865. Exchanged at Camp Townsend, MS, on 5/6/1865.

Enochs, E.B. 1st Lt./Capt., 4th Mississippi Infantry. Co. F. Federal Rolls of Prisoners of War: Captured at Blakely, AL, on 4/9/1865; Received at Ship Island, MS, on 4/15/1865. Transferred to Vicksburg, MS, for exchange on 4/28/1865; Confined at New Orleans,

LA, on 4/30/1865. Exchanged at Camp Townsend, MS, on 5/6/1865.

Enochs, J.V. (AKA I.V.) Sgt./Capt., 36th Mississippi Infantry. Co. B. Federal Rolls of Prisoners of War: Captured at Blakely, AL, on 4/9/1865; Received at Ship Island, MS, on 4/15/1865. Transferred to Vicksburg, MS, for exchange on 4/28/1865; Confined at New Orleans, LA, on 4/30/1865. Exchanged at Camp Townsend, MS, on 5/6/1865.

Erickson, John (AKA Ericson) Pvt., 18th Mississippi Infantry. Co. C. Federal Rolls of Prisoners of War: Captured at Pass Manchac, LA, on 9/11/1864; Received at Ship Island, MS, on 10/7/1864. Transferred to Fort Columbus, New York Harbor, NY, on 11/5/1864.

Erskins, J. (AKA Erskin) Pvt., 18th Mississippi Infantry. Federal Rolls of Prisoners of War: Captured at Pass Manchac, LA, on 9/11/1864; Received at Ship Island, MS, from New Orleans, LA, on 10/7/1864. Transferred to Fort Columbus, New York Harbor, NY, on 11/5/1864.

Ervin, J.H. Pvt., 1st Mississippi Light Artillery. Co. __. Federal Rolls of Prisoners of War: Captured at Blakely, AL, on 4/9/1865; Received at Ship Island, MS, on 4/15/1865. Transferred to Vicksburg, MS, for exchange on 5/1/1865; Exchanged at Camp Townsend, MS, on 5/6/1865.

Everett, J.C. Pvt., 1st Mississippi Light Artillery. Co. __. Federal Rolls of Prisoners of War: Captured at Blakely, AL, on 4/9/1865; Received at Ship Island, MS, on 4/15/1865. Transferred to Vicksburg, MS, for exchange on 5/1/1865; Exchanged at Camp Townsend, MS, on 5/6/1865.

Everett, T.J. Pvt., 1st Mississippi Light Artillery. Co. __. Federal Rolls of Prisoners of War: Captured at Blakely, AL, on 4/9/1865; Received at Ship Island, MS, on 4/15/1865. Transferred to Vicksburg, MS, for exchange on 5/1/1865; Exchanged at Camp Townsend, MS, on 5/6/1865.

Fairley, Hugh S. Pvt., 1st Mississippi Light Artillery. Co. K. Federal Rolls of Prisoners of War: Captured at Blakely, AL, on 4/9/1865; Received at Ship Island, MS, on 4/15/1865. Transferred to Vicksburg, MS, for exchange on 5/1/1865; Exchanged at Camp Townsend, MS, on 5/6/1865. Born: 1829 at Jefferson County, MS. Died: 1903.

Fairman, Julian O. Pvt., 1st Mississippi Light Artillery. Co. F. Federal Rolls of Prisoners of War: Captured at Blakely, AL, on 4/9/1865; Received at Ship Island, MS, on 4/15/1865. Transferred to Vicksburg, MS, for exchange on 5/1/1865; Exchanged at Camp Townsend, MS, on 5/6/1865. Confederate Widows Pension Application dated 1909 on file at the Mississippi Department of Archives and History. Target Name: Fairman, Kate. County: Lincoln.

Fauville, Edwin K. (AKA Fenville, E.R.) Pvt., 1st Mississippi Light Artillery. Co. D. Federal Rolls of Prisoner of War: Captured at Blakely, AL, on 4/9/1865; Received at Ship Island, MS, on 4/15/1865. Transferred to Vicksburg, MS, for exchange on 5/1/1865; Exchanged at Camp Townsend, MS, on 5/6/1865.

Ferguson, S.P. (AKA Furgurson) Pvt., 39th Mississippi Infantry. Co. F. Federal Rolls of Prisoners of War: Captured at Blakely, AL, on 4/9/1865; Received at Ship Island, MS, on 4/15/1865. Transferred to Vicksburg, MS, for exchange on 5/1/1865; Exchanged at Camp Townsend, MS, on 5/6/1865.

Fielder, J.R. Pvt., 4th Mississippi Infantry. Co. I. Federal Rolls of Prisoners of War: Captured at Blakely, AL, on 4/9/1865; Received at Ship Island, MS, on 4/15/1865. Transferred to Vicksburg, MS, for exchange on 5/1/1865; Exchanged at Camp Townsend, MS, on 5/6/1865. Confederate Pension Application dated 1904 on file at the Mississippi Department of Archives and History. Target Name: Fielder, J.R. County: Chickasaw.

Finley, B.D. Pvt./Sgt., 39th Mississippi Infantry. Co. E. Federal Rolls of Prisoners of War: Captured at Blakely, AL, on 4/9/1865; Received at Ship Island, MS, on 4/15/1865. Transferred to Vicksburg, MS, for exchange on 5/1/1865; Exchanged at Camp Townsend, MS, on 5/6/1865.

Finley, W. (AKA Findley) Pvt., 35th Mississippi Infantry. Co. I. Federal Rolls of Prisoners of War: Captured at Blakely, AL, on 4/9/1865; Received at Ship Island, MS, on 4/15/1865. Transferred to Vicksburg, MS, for exchange on 5/1/1865; Exchanged at Camp Townsend, MS, on 5/6/1865.

Fisher, Archibald (AKA Archer) Pvt., 1st Mississippi Light Artillery. Co. D. Federal Rolls of Prisoners of War: Captured at Blakely, AL, on 4/9/1865; Received at Ship Island, MS, on 4/15/1865. Transferred to Vicksburg, MS, for exchange on 5/1/1865; Exchanged at Camp Townsend, MS, on 5/6/1865.

Fleming, James Pvt., 7th Mississippi Battalion Infantry. Co. D. Federal Rolls of Prisoners of War: Captured at Blakely, AL, on 4/9/1865; Received at Ship Island, MS, on 4/15/1865. Transferred to Vicksburg, MS, for exchange on 5/1/1865; Exchanged at Camp Townsend, MS, on 5/6/1865.

Fleming, John G. Pvt., 7th Mississippi Battalion Infantry. Co. D. Federal Rolls of Prisoners of War: Captured at Blakely, AL, on 4/9/1865; Received at Ship Island, MS, on 4/15/1865. Transferred to Vicksburg, MS, for exchange on 5/1/1865; Exchanged at Camp Townsend, MS, on 5/6/1865.

Fletcher, William Helveston (AKA Buck) Pvt., Mississippi Home Guard (Gillis's). Federal Rolls of Prisoners of War: Received at Ship Island, MS. Born: 3/17/1819. Married: Sarah Havens. Children: 7. Died: 9/4/1899. Buried: Fletcher Family Cemetery located at Jackson County, MS, in an unmarked grave. Wife born: 2/25/1821 in Mississippi. Wife died: 6/3/1860.

Flint, F.M.C. Pvt., 7th Mississippi Battalion Infantry. Co. G. Federal Rolls of Prisoners of War: Captured at Blakely, AL, on 4/9/1865; Received at Ship Island, MS, on 4/15/1865. Transferred to Vicksburg, MS, for exchange on 5/1/1865; Exchanged at Camp Townsend, MS, on 5/6/1865.

Floyd, F. Pvt., 4th Mississippi Infantry. Co. G. Federal Rolls of Prisoners of War: Captured in Alabama on 4/1/1865; Received at Ship Island, MS. Transferred to Vicksburg, MS, for exchange on 5/1/1865; Exchanged at Camp Townsend, MS, on 5/6/1865.

Flynn, J. (AKA J.B., J.T., J.F.) Pvt./Sgt., Powers Cavalry Regiment. Co. F. Federal Rolls of Prisoners of War: Captured at Clinton, LA, on 8/25/1864; Received at Ship Island, MS, from New Orleans, LA, on 10/7/1864. Transferred to Fort Columbus, New York Harbor, NY, on 11/5/1864.

Folkes, Augustus A. Pvt./Cpl., 1st Mississippi Light Artillery. Co. G. Federal Rolls of Prisoners of War:

Captured at Blakely, AL, on 4/9/1865; Received at Ship Island, MS, on 4/15/1865. Transferred to Vicksburg, MS, for exchange on 5/1/1865; Exchanged at Camp Townsend, MS, on 5/6/1865.

Fortenberry, John T. (AKA Fortenbery) Pvt., 20th Mississippi Infantry. Co. I. Died: 12/15/1864 at Ship Island, MS, due to chronic dysentery. Buried: Ship Island, MS, Cemetery in Grave #92.

Fox, J.T. Pvt., 35th Mississippi Infantry. Co. C. Federal Rolls of Prisoners of War: Captured at Blakely, AL, on 4/9/1865; Received at Ship Island, MS, on 4/15/1865. Transferred to Vicksburg, MS, for exchange on 5/1/1865; Exchanged at Camp Townsend, MS, on 5/6/1865.

Frazier, J. Pvt., 35th Mississippi Infantry. Co. __. Federal Rolls of Prisoners of War: Captured at Blakely, AL, on 4/9/1865; Received at Ship Island, MS, on 4/15/1865. Transferred to Vicksburg, MS, for exchange on 5/1/1865; Exchanged at Camp Townsend, MS, on 5/6/1865.

Frazier, James H. Pvt./Cpl., 1st Mississippi Light Artillery. Co. B. Federal Rolls of Prisoners of War: Captured at Blakely, AL, on 4/9/1865; Received at Ship Island, MS, on 4/15/1865. Transferred to Vicksburg, MS, for exchange on 5/1/1865; Exchanged at Camp Townsend, MS, on 5/6/1865.

Freeman, J.W. Pvt., 1st Mississippi Light Artillery. Co. __. Federal Rolls of Prisoners of War: Captured at Blakely, AL, on 4/9/1865; Received at Ship Island, MS, on 4/15/1865. Transferred to Vicksburg, MS, for exchange on 5/1/1865; Exchanged at Camp Townsend, MS, on 5/6/1865.

Freeman, James H. Artificer, 1st Mississippi Light Artillery. Co. K. Federal Rolls of Prisoners of War: Captured at Blakely, AL, on 4/9/1865; Received at Ship Island, MS, on 4/15/1865. Transferred to Vicksburg, MS, for exchange on 5/1/1865; Exchanged at Camp Townsend, MS, on 5/6/1865.

Fuller, Ambus J. Pvt., 36th Mississippi Infantry. Co. A. Federal Rolls of Prisoners of War: Captured at Blakely, AL, on 4/9/1865; Received at Ship Island, MS, on 4/15/1865. Transferred to Vicksburg, MS, for exchange on 5/1/1865; Exchanged at Camp Townsend, MS, on 5/6/1865.

Fuller, Robert R. (AKA R.P.) Pvt., 39th Mississippi Infantry. Co. E. Federal Rolls of Prisoners of War: Captured at Blakely, AL, on 4/9/1865; Received at Ship Island, MS, on 4/15/1865. Transferred to Vicksburg, MS, for exchange on 5/1/1865; Exchanged at Camp Townsend, MS, on 5/6/1865. Confederate Pension Application dated 1921 on file at the Mississippi Department of Archives and History. Target Name: Fuller, R.P. County: Copiah.

Fuller, William Pvt., 1st Mississippi Light Artillery. Co. F. Federal Rolls of Prisoners of War: Captured at Blakely, AL, on 4/9/1865; Received at Ship Island, MS, on 4/15/1865. Transferred to Vicksburg, MS, for exchange on 5/1/1865; Exchanged at Camp Townsend, MS, on 5/6/1865. Born: 1829. Died: 1901. Buried: Weir Cemetery located at McRae, White County, AR.

Gallagher, C.W. Capt., 39th Mississippi Infantry. Cos. A & D. Federal Rolls of Prisoners of War: Captured at Blakely, AL, on 4/9/1865; Received at Ship Island, MS, on 4/15/1865. Transferred to Vicksburg, MS, for exchange on 4/28/1865; Confined at New Orleans, LA, on 4/30/1865. Exchanged at Camp Townsend, MS, on 5/6/1865.

Gallaspy, Garland M. (AKA Gallespie) 2nd Lt./Capt., 36th Mississippi Infantry. Co. C. Federal Rolls of Prisoners of War: Captured at Blakely, AL, on 4/9/1865; Received at Ship Island, MS, on 4/15/1865. Transferred to Vicksburg, MS, for exchange on 4/28/1865; Confined at New Orleans, LA, on 4/30/1865. Exchanged at Camp Townsend, MS, on 5/6/1865.

Garner, C.D. Pvt., 1st Mississippi Light Artillery. Co. B. Federal Rolls of Prisoners of War: Captured at Blakely, AL, on 4/9/1865; Received at Ship Island, MS, on 4/15/1865. Transferred to Vicksburg, MS, for exchange on 5/1/1865; Exchanged at Camp Townsend, MS, on 5/6/1865. Confederate Pension Application dated 1921 on file at the Mississippi Department of Archives and History. Target Name: Garner, C.D. County: Forrest. Also a Confederate Widows Pension Application dated 1935 on file. Target Name: Garner, Roxie. County: Lowndes.

Garner, E.T. (AKA E.Y.) Pvt., 35th Mississippi Infantry. Co. C. Federal Rolls of Prisoners of War: Captured at Blakely, AL, on 4/9/1865; Received at Ship Island, MS, on 4/15/1865. Transferred to Vicksburg, MS, for exchange on 5/1/1865; Exchanged at Camp Townsend, MS, on 5/6/1865.

Garner, J.P. Pvt., 35th Mississippi Infantry. Co. I. Federal Rolls of Prisoners of War: Captured at Blakely, AL, on 4/9/1865; Received at Ship Island, MS, on 4/15/1865. Transferred to Vicksburg, MS, for exchange on 5/1/1865; Exchanged at Camp Townsend, MS, on 5/6/1865.

Garrison, James B. (AKA John) Pvt., 35th Mississippi Infantry. Co. H. Federal Rolls of Prisoners of War: Captured at Blakely, AL, on 4/9/1865; Received at Ship Island, MS, on 4/15/1865. Transferred to Vicksburg, MS, for exchange on 5/1/1865; Exchanged at Camp Townsend, MS, on 5/6/1865.

Gibbons, Seth Pvt., 35th Mississippi Infantry. Co. C. Federal Rolls of Prisoners of War: Captured at Blakely, AL, on 4/9/1865; Received at Ship Island, MS, on 4/15/1865. Transferred to Vicksburg, MS, for exchange on 5/1/1865; Exchanged at Camp Townsend, MS, on 5/6/1865.

Gibson, Demetrius D. Pvt./Cpl., 36th Mississippi Infantry. Co. __. Federal Rolls of Prisoners of War: Captured at Blakely, AL, on 4/9/1865; Received at Ship Island, MS, on 4/15/1865. Transferred to Vicksburg, MS, for exchange on 5/1/1865; Exchanged at Camp Townsend, MS, on 5/6/1865.

Gibson, William A. Pvt., 35th Mississippi Infantry. Co. H. Federal Rolls of Prisoners of War: Captured at Blakely, AL, on 4/9/1865; Received at Ship Island, MS, on 4/15/1865. Transferred to Vicksburg, MS, for exchange on 5/1/1865; Exchanged at Camp Townsend, MS, on 5/6/1865. Confederate Pension Application dated 1917 on file at the Mississippi Department of Archives and History. Target Name: Gibson, W.A. County: Lowndes.

Gieger, Jesse, Jr. (AKA Gigger) Pvt., 7th Mississippi Battalion Infantry. Co. G. Federal Rolls of Prisoners of War: Captured at Blakely, AL, on 4/9/1865; Received at Ship Island, MS, on 4/15/1865. Transferred to Vicksburg, MS, for exchange on 5/1/1865; Exchanged at Camp Townsend, MS, on 5/6/1865.

Gilbert, J. Pvt., 35th Mississippi Infantry. Co. __.

Federal Rolls of Prisoners of War: Captured at Blakely, AL, on 4/9/1865; Received at Ship Island, MS, on 4/15/1865. Transferred to Vicksburg, MS, for exchange on 5/1/1865; Exchanged at Camp Townsend, MS, on 5/6/1865.

Gilles, Elisha M. Pvt., 36th Mississippi Infantry. Co. K. Federal Rolls of Prisoners of War: Captured at Blakely, AL, on 4/9/1865; Received at Ship Island, MS, on 4/15/1865. Transferred to Vicksburg, MS, for exchange on 5/1/1865; Exchanged at Camp Townsend, MS, on 5/6/1865.

Girault, John M. Pvt./Sgt., 1st Mississippi Light Artillery. Co. K. Federal Rolls of Prisoners of War: Captured at Blakely, AL, on 4/9/1865; Received at Ship Island, MS, on 4/15/1865. Transferred to Vicksburg, MS, for exchange on 5/1/1865; Exchanged at Camp Townsend, MS, on 5/6/1865.

Girault, Matthew A. Pvt./Cpl., 1st Mississippi Light Artillery. Co. K. Federal Rolls of Prisoners of War: Captured at Blakely, AL, on 4/9/1865; Received at Ship Island, MS, on 4/15/1865. Transferred to Vicksburg, MS, for exchange on 5/1/1865; Exchanged at Camp Townsend, MS, on 5/6/1865.

Gober, Elijah C. Pvt., 1st Mississippi Light Artillery. Co. I. Federal Rolls of Prisoners of War: Captured at Blakely, AL, on 4/9/1865; Received at Ship Island, MS, on 4/15/1865. Transferred to Vicksburg, MS, for exchange on 5/1/1865; Exchanged at Camp Townsend, MS, on 5/6/1865.

Godfrey, T.W. Pvt., 36th Mississippi Infantry. Co. F. Federal Rolls of Prisoners of War: Captured at Blakely, AL, on 4/9/1865; Received at Ship Island, MS, on 4/15/1865. Transferred to Vicksburg, MS, for exchange on 5/1/1865; Exchanged at Camp Townsend, MS, on 5/6/1865.

Godley, James (AKA Joseph) Pvt., 14th Mississippi Cavalry. Co. B. Federal Rolls of Prisoners of War: Captured near Washington County, MS, on 11/19/1864; Received at Ship Island, MS, from New Orleans, LA, on 1/25/1865. Transferred to Vicksburg, MS, for exchange on 5/1/1865; Exchanged at Camp Townsend, MS, on 5/6/1865.

Goff, A.K. Pvt., 1st Mississippi Light Artillery. Co. K. Federal Rolls of Prisoners of War: Captured at Blakely, AL, on 4/9/1865; Received at Ship Island, MS, on 4/15/1865. Transferred to Vicksburg, MS, for exchange on 5/1/1865; Exchanged at Camp Townsend, MS, on 5/6/1865.

Goff, Moses J. (AKA M.L.) Pvt., 1st Mississippi Light Artillery. Co. K. Federal Rolls of Prisoners of War: Captured at Blakely, AL, on 4/9/1865; Received at Ship Island, MS, on 4/15/1865. Transferred to Vicksburg, MS, for exchange on 5/1/1865; Exchanged at Camp Townsend, MS, on 5/6/1865.

Gonday, J.H. Pvt., 1st Mississippi Light Artillery. Co. K. Federal Rolls of Prisoners of War: Captured at Blakely, AL, on 4/9/1865; Received at Ship Island, MS, on 4/15/1865. Transferred to Vicksburg, MS, for exchange on 5/1/1865; Exchanged at Camp Townsend, MS, on 5/6/1865.

Goodwin, Jeff Pvt., 1st Mississippi Light Artillery. Co. K. Federal Rolls of Prisoners of War: Captured at Blakely, AL, on 4/9/1865; Received at Ship Island, MS, on 4/15/1865. Transferred to Vicksburg, MS, for exchange on 5/1/1865; Exchanged at Camp Townsend, MS, on 5/6/1865.

Gough, William G. 1st Lt., 7th Mississippi Battalion Infantry. Co. E. Federal Rolls of Prisoners of War: Captured at Blakely, AL, on 4/9/1865; Received at Ship Island, MS, on 4/15/1865. Transferred to Vicksburg, MS, for exchange on 4/28/1865; Confined at New Orleans, LA, on 4/30/1865. Exchanged at Camp Townsend, MS, on 5/6/1865.

Grady, Curtis D. (AKA C.T.) Pvt., 35th Mississippi Infantry. Co. A. Federal Rolls of Prisoners of War: Captured at Blakely, AL, on 4/9/1865; Received at Ship Island, MS, on 4/15/1865. Transferred to Vicksburg, MS, for exchange on 5/1/1865; Exchanged at Camp Townsend, MS, on 5/6/1865.

Graham, A. Pvt., 1st Mississippi Light Artillery. Co. __. Federal Rolls of Prisoners of War: Captured at Blakely, AL, on 4/9/1865; Received at Ship Island, MS, on 4/15/1865. Transferred to Vicksburg, MS, for exchange on 5/1/1865; Exchanged at Camp Townsend, MS, on 5/6/1865.

Grant, Robert C. Pvt., 1st Mississippi Light Artillery. Co. G. Federal Rolls of Prisoners of War: Captured at Blakely, AL, on 4/9/1865; Received at Ship Island, MS, on 4/15/1865. Transferred to Vicksburg, MS, for exchange on 5/1/1865; Exchanged at Camp Townsend, MS, on 5/6/1865. Born: 1848 at Warren County, MS. Died: 1904.

Grantham, E.J. (AKA Ed) Pvt., 46th Mississippi Infantry. Co. D. Federal Rolls of Prisoners of War: Captured at Blakely, AL, on 4/9/1865; Received at Ship Island, MS, on 4/15/1865. Transferred to Vicksburg, MS, for exchange on 5/1/1865; Exchanged at Camp Townsend, MS, on 5/6/1865.

Grantham, Maston Pvt., 7th Mississippi Battalion Infantry. Co. A. Federal Rolls of Prisoners of War: Captured at Blakely, AL, on 4/9/1865; Received at Ship Island, MS, on 4/15/1865. Transferred to Vicksburg, MS, for exchange on 5/1/1865; Exchanged at Camp Townsend, MS, on 5/6/1865.

Gray, James Lafayette Pvt., 1st Mississippi Light Artillery. Cos. A & F. Federal Rolls of Prisoners of War: Captured at Blakely, AL, on 4/9/1865; Received at Ship Island, MS, on 4/15/1865. Transferred to Vicksburg, MS, for exchange on 5/1/1865; Exchanged at Camp Townsend, MS, on 5/6/1865. Born: 1845 Died: 1938. Buried: Covington County, MS.

Green, E.J. (AKA Greer) Pvt., 1st Mississippi Light Artillery. Co. B. Federal Rolls of Prisoners of War: Captured at Blakely, AL, on 4/9/1865; Received at Ship Island, MS, on 4/15/1865. Transferred to Vicksburg, MS, for exchange on 5/1/1865; Exchanged at Camp Townsend, MS, on 5/6/1865.

Green, J.H. (AKA Greer) Sgt., 35th Mississippi Infantry. Co. K. Federal Rolls of Prisoners of War: Captured at Blakely, AL, on 4/9/1865; Received at Ship Island, MS, on 4/15/1865. Transferred to Vicksburg, MS, for exchange on 5/1/1865; Exchanged at Camp Townsend, MS, on 5/6/1865.

Green, Stephen Pvt., 36th Mississippi Infantry. Co. K. Federal Rolls of Prisoners of War: Captured at Blakely, AL, on 4/9/1865; Received at Ship Island, MS, on 4/15/1865. Transferred to Vicksburg, MS, for exchange on 5/1/1865; Exchanged at Camp Townsend, MS, on 5/6/1865.

Gregg, R. Pvt., 4th Mississippi Infantry. Co. G. Federal Rolls of Prisoners of War: Captured at Blakely, AL, on 4/9/1865; Received at Ship Island, MS, on

4/15/1865. Transferred to Vicksburg, MS, for exchange on 5/1/1865; Exchanged at Camp Townsend, MS, on 5/6/1865.

Grey, T.A. Pvt., 9th Mississippi Cavalry (Millen's). Co. A. Federal Rolls of Prisoners of War: Captured at Jackson County, MS, on 12/11/1864; Received at Ship Island, MS, from New Orleans, LA, on 1/25/1865. Transferred to Vicksburg, MS, for exchange on 5/1/1865; Exchanged at Camp Townsend, MS, on 5/1/1865.

Griffin, A.J. Pvt., 1st Mississippi Light Artillery. Co. __. Federal Rolls of Prisoners of War: Captured at Blakely, AL, on 4/9/1865; Received at Ship Island, MS, on 4/15/1865. Transferred to Vicksburg, MS, for exchange on 5/1/1865; Exchanged at Camp Townsend, MS, on 5/6/1865.

Griffin, Asa J. Pvt., 35th Mississippi Infantry. Co. D. Federal Rolls of Prisoners of War: Captured at Blakely, AL, on 4/9/1865; Received at Ship Island, MS, on 4/15/1865. Transferred to Vicksburg, MS, for exchange on 5/1/1865; Exchanged at Camp Townsend, MS, on 5/6/1865.

Griffin, John A. Pvt., 36th Mississippi Infantry. Co. E. Federal Rolls of Prisoners of War: Captured at Blakely, AL, on 4/9/1865; Received at Ship Island, MS, on 4/15/1865. Transferred to Vicksburg, MS, for exchange on 5/1/1865; Exchanged at Camp Townsend, MS, on 5/6/1865. Confederate Pension Application dated 1902 on file at the Mississippi Department of Archives and History. Target Name: Griffin, John A. County: Copiah.

Griffin, Richard Pvt./Artificer, 1st Mississippi Light Artillery. Co. B. Federal Rolls of Prisoners of War: Captured at Blakely, AL, on 4/9/1865; Received at Ship Island, MS, on 4/15/1865. Transferred to Vicksburg, MS, for exchange on 5/1/1865; Exchanged at Camp Townsend, MS, on 5/6/1865.

Griffin, Thomas R. Pvt., 1st Mississippi Light Infantry. Co. I. Federal Rolls of Prisoners of War: Captured at Blakely, AL, on 4/9/1865; Received at Ship Island, MS, on 4/15/1865. Transferred to Vicksburg, MS, for exchange on 5/1/1865; Exchanged at Camp Townsend, MS, on 5/6/1865.

Guice, David W. Pvt., 1st Mississippi Light Artillery. Co. K. Federal Rolls of Prisoners of War: Captured at Blakely, AL, on 4/9/1865; Received at Ship Island, MS, on 4/15/1865. Transferred to Vicksburg, MS, for exchange on 5/1/1865; Exchanged at Camp Townsend, MS, on 5/6/1865.

Guinn, J.H. Pvt., 1st Mississippi Light Artillery. Co. __. Federal Rolls of Prisoners of War: Captured at Blakely, AL, on 4/9/1865; Received at Ship Island, MS, on 4/15/1865. Transferred to Vicksburg, MS, for exchange on 5/1/1865; Exchanged at Camp Townsend, MS, on 5/6/1865.

Gulledge, R.W. Pvt., 4th Mississippi Infantry. Co. G. Federal Rolls of Prisoners of War: Captured at Blakely, AL, on 4/9/1865; Received at Ship Island, MS, on 4/15/1865. Transferred to Vicksburg, MS, for exchange on 5/1/1865; Exchanged at Camp Townsend, MS, on 5/6/1865.

Gunner, B.C. Pvt., 36th Mississippi Infantry. Co. __. Federal Rolls of Prisoners of War: Captured at Blakely, AL, on 4/9/1865; Received at Ship Island, MS, on 4/15/1865. Transferred to Vicksburg, MS, for exchange on 5/1/1865; Exchanged at Camp Townsend, MS, on 5/6/1865.

Haigwood, Edward Pvt., 4th Mississippi Infantry. Co. G. Federal Rolls of Prisoners of War: Captured in Alabama on 4/1/1865; Received at Ship Island, MS, on 5/1/1865. Transferred to Vicksburg, MS, for exchange on 5/1/1865; Exchanged at Camp Townsend, MS, on 5/6/1865.

Haigwood, M. Pvt., 4th Mississippi Infantry. Co. G. Federal Rolls of Prisoners of War: Captured in Alabama on 4/1/1865; Received at Ship Island, MS. Transferred to Vicksburg, MS, for exchange on 5/1/1865; Exchanged at Camp Townsend, MS, on 5/6/1865.

Haley, Merrill T. (AKA Holly) Pvt., 36th Mississippi Infantry. Co. B. Federal Rolls of Prisoners of War: Captured at Blakely, AL, on 4/9/1865; Received at Ship Island, MS, on 4/15/1865. Transferred to Vicksburg, MS, for exchange on 5/1/1865; Exchanged at Camp Townsend, MS, on 5/6/1865. Confederate Widows Pension Application dated 1926 on file at the Mississippi Department of Archives and History. Target Name: Haley, Mrs. Merrill T. County: Smith.

Hall, C.G. (AKA D.G.) Pvt., 46th Mississippi Infantry. Co. B. Federal Rolls of Prisoners of War: Captured at Blakely, AL, on 4/9/1865; Received at Ship Island, MS, on 4/15/1865. Transferred to Vicksburg, MS, for exchange on 5/1/1865; Exchanged at Camp Townsend, MS, on 5/6/1865.

Halsell, Thomas Pvt., 39th Mississippi Infantry. Co. D. Federal Rolls of Prisoners of War: Captured at Blakely, AL, on 4/9/1865; Received at Ship Island, MS, on 4/15/1865. Transferred to Vicksburg, MS, for exchange on 5/1/1865; Exchanged at Camp Townsend, MS, on 5/6/1865.

Hamel, J.J. Pvt., 1st Mississippi Light Artillery. Co. I. Federal Rolls of Prisoners of War: Captured at Blakely, AL, on 4/9/1865; Received at Ship Island, MS, on 4/15/1865. Transferred to Vicksburg, MS, for exchange on 5/1/1865; Exchanged at Camp Townsend, MS, on 5/6/1865.

Hamel, William Pvt., 1st Mississippi Light Artillery. Co. I. Federal Rolls of Prisoners of War: Captured at Blakely, AL, on 4/9/1865; Received at Ship Island, MS, on 4/15/1865. Transferred to Vicksburg, MS, for exchange on 5/1/1865; Exchanged at Camp Townsend, MS, on 5/6/1865. Born: 1843. Died: 1925. Buried: Yazoo County, MS.

Hamilton, C.S. (AKA C.J.) Sgt., 35th Mississippi Infantry. Co. __. Federal Rolls of Prisoners of War: Captured at Blakely, AL, on 4/9/1865; Received at Ship Island, MS, on 4/15/1865. Transferred to Vicksburg, MS, for exchange on 5/1/1865; Exchanged at Camp Townsend, MS, on 5/6/1865.

Hamilton, H.M. Pvt., 4th Mississippi Infantry. Co. C. Federal Rolls of Prisoners of War: Captured at Blakely, AL, on 4/9/1865; Received at Ship Island, MS, on 4/15/1865. Transferred to Vicksburg, MS, for exchange on 5/1/1865; Exchanged at Camp Townsend, MS, on 5/6/1865.

Hamilton, James D. Pvt., 2nd Mississippi Militia. Federal Rolls of Prisoners of War: Captured at Ascension Parish, LA, on 12/14/1864; Received at Ship Island, MS, from New Orleans, LA, on 1/25/1865. Transferred to New Orleans, LA, on 3/31/1865.

Hammond, S.P. (AKA S.B.) Pvt., 39th Mississippi Infantry. Co. D. Federal Rolls of Prisoners of War: Captured at Blakely, AL, on 4/9/1865; Received at

Ship Island, MS, on 4/15/1865. Transferred to Vicksburg, MS, for exchange on 5/1/1865; Exchanged at Camp Townsend, MS, on 5/6/1865.

Hamplin, Robert Pvt./Sgt., 35th Mississippi Infantry. Co. K. Federal Rolls of Prisoners of War: Captured at Blakely, AL, on 4/9/1865; Received at Ship Island, MS, on 4/15/1865. Transferred to Vicksburg, MS, for exchange on 5/1/1865; Exchanged at Camp Townsend, MS, on 5/6/1865.

Hand, John Cpl./Pvt., 1st Mississippi Light Artillery. Co. G. Federal Rolls of Prisoners of War: Captured at Blakely, AL, on 4/9/1865; Received at Ship Island, MS, on 4/15/1865. Transferred to Vicksburg, MS, for exchange on 5/1/1865; Exchanged at Camp Townsend, MS, on 5/6/1865.

Hansford, D.C. (AKA B.C.) Pvt., 39th Mississippi Infantry. Co. D. Federal Rolls of Prisoners of War: Captured at Blakely, AL, on 4/9/1865; Received at Ship Island, MS, on 4/15/1865. Transferred to Vicksburg, MS, for exchange on 5/1/1865; Exchanged at Camp Townsend, MS, on 5/6/1865.

Hardin, John M. Pvt., 4th Mississippi Light Artillery. Co. F. Federal Rolls of Prisoners of War: Captured at Blakely, AL, on 4/9/1865; Received at Ship Island, MS, on 4/15/1865. Transferred to Vicksburg, MS, for exchange on 5/1/1865; Exchanged at Camp Townsend, MS, on 5/6/1865.

Hardy, Robert Sgt./2nd Lt., 35th Mississippi Infantry. Co. C. Federal Rolls of Prisoners of War: Captured at Fort Gaines, AL, on 8/8/1864; Received at Ship Island, MS, from New Orleans, LA, on 10/25/1864. Exchanged on 1/4/1865.

Harndon, Charles S. Pvt./Sgt., 35th Mississippi Infantry. Co. H. Federal Rolls of Prisoners of War: Captured at Blakely, AL, on 4/9/1865; Received at Ship Island, MS, on 4/15/1865. Transferred to Vicksburg, MS, for exchange on 5/1/1865; Exchanged at Camp Townsend, MS, on 5/6/1865.

Harper, Levi Pvt., 36th Mississippi Infantry. Co. F. Federal Rolls of Prisoners of War: Captured at Blakely, AL, on 4/9/1865; Received at Ship Island, MS, on 4/15/1865. Transferred to Vicksburg, MS, for exchange on 5/1/1865; Exchanged at Camp Townsend, MS, on 5/6/1865.

Harper, R.B. Pvt./Cpl., 39th Mississippi Infantry. Co. B. Federal Rolls of Prisoners of War: Captured at Blakely, AL, on 4/9/1865; Received at Ship Island, MS, on 4/15/1865. Transferred to Vicksburg, MS, for exchange on 5/1/1865; Exchanged at Camp Townsend, MS, on 5/6/1865.

Harrel, Wesley S. (AKA Harrol) Pvt./Cpl., 35th Mississippi Infantry. Co. G. Federal Rolls of Prisoners of War: Captured at Blakely, AL, on 4/9/1865; Received at Ship Island, MS, on 4/15/1865. Transferred to Vicksburg, MS, for exchange on 5/1/1865; Exchanged at Camp Townsend, MS, on 5/6/1865.

Harrington, M. Pvt., 7th Mississippi Battalion Infantry. Co. __. Federal Rolls of Prisoners of War: Captured at Blakely, AL, on 4/9/1865; Received at Ship Island, MS, on 4/15/1865. Transferred to Vicksburg, MS, for exchange on 5/1/1865; Exchanged at Camp Townsend, MS, on 5/6/1865.

Harrington, P. Pvt., 35th Mississippi Infantry. Co. __. Federal Rolls of Prisoners of War: Captured at Blakely, AL, on 4/9/1865; Received at Ship Island, MS, on 4/15/1865. Transferred to Vicksburg, MS, for exchange on 5/1/1865; Exchanged at Camp Townsend, MS, on 5/6/1865.

Harrington, T.J. Sgt., 35th Mississippi Infantry. Co. __. Federal Rolls of Prisoners of War: Captured at Blakely, AL, on 4/9/1865; Received at Ship Island, MS, on 4/15/1865. Transferred to Vicksburg, MS, for exchange on 5/1/1865; Exchanged at Camp Townsend, MS, on 5/6/1865.

Harris, E.F. Pvt., 46th Mississippi Infantry. Co. __. Federal Rolls of Prisoners of War: Captured at Blakely, AL, on 4/9/1865; Received at Ship Island, MS, on 4/15/1865. Transferred to Vicksburg, MS, for exchange on 5/1/1865; Exchanged at Camp Townsend, MS, on 5/6/1865.

Harris, J.W. Pvt., 1st Mississippi Light Artillery. Co. F. Federal Rolls of Prisoners of War: Captured at Blakely, AL, on 4/9/1865; Received at Ship Island, MS, on 4/15/1865. Transferred to Vicksburg, MS, for exchange on 5/1/1865; Exchanged at Camp Townsend, MS, on 5/6/1865.

Harris, Richard Pvt./Cpl., 1st Mississippi Light Artillery. Co. G. Federal Rolls of Prisoners of War: Captured at Blakely, AL, on 4/9/1865; Received at Ship Island, MS, on 4/15/1865. Transferred to Vicksburg, MS, for exchange on 5/1/1865; Exchanged at Camp Townsend, MS, on 5/6/1865. Born: 1838. Died: 1898. Buried: Warren County, MS.

Harris, William A. Pvt./Sgt., 36th Mississippi Infantry. Co. E. Federal Rolls of Prisoners of War: Captured at Blakely, AL, on 4/9/1865; Received at Ship Island, MS, on 4/15/1865. Transferred to Vicksburg, MS, for exchange on 5/1/1865; Exchanged at Camp Townsend, MS, on 5/6/1865.

Harrison, Benjamin F. Pvt., 36th Mississippi Infantry. Co. B. Federal Rolls of Prisoners of War: Captured at Blakely, AL, on 4/9/1865; Received at Ship Island, MS, on 4/15/1865. Transferred to Vicksburg, MS, for exchange on 5/1/1865; Exchanged at Camp Townsend, MS, on 5/6/1865.

Harrison, Jeptha R. Cpl./2nd Lt., 4th Mississippi Infantry. Co. B. Federal Rolls of Prisoners of War: Captured at Fort Gaines, AL, on 8/8/1864; Received at Ship Island, MS, from New Orleans, LA, on 10/25/1864. Exchanged on 1/4/1865.

Harrison, John Pvt., 1st Mississippi Light Artillery. Co. G. Federal Rolls of Prisoners of War: Captured at Blakely, AL, on 4/9/1865; Received at Ship Island, MS, on 4/15/1865. Transferred to Vicksburg, MS, for exchange on 5/1/1865; Exchanged at Camp Townsend, MS, on 5/6/1865.

Hart, James B., Sr. 2nd Lt./Captain, 46th Mississippi Infantry. F & S. Federal Rolls of Prisoners of War: Captured at Blakely, AL, on 4/9/1865; Received at Ship Island, MS, on 4/15/1865. Transferred to Vicksburg, MS, for exchange on 4/28/1865; Confined at New Orleans, LA, on 4/30/1865. Exchanged at Camp Townsend, MS, on 5/6/1865. Confederate Widows Pension Application dated 1916 on file at the Mississippi Department of Archives and History. Target Name: Hart, Mrs.J.B. County: Yazoo.

Hatten, William W. (AKA Hatton) 2nd Lt., 7th Mississippi Battalion Infantry. Cos. C & G. Federal Rolls of Prisoners of War: Captured at Fort Gaines, AL, on 8/8/1864; Received at Ship Island, MS, from New Orleans, LA, on 10/25/1864. Exchanged on 1/4/1865. Confederate Widows Pension Application dated

1902 on file at the Mississippi Department of Archives and History. Target Name: Hatton, Eliza. County: Covington.

Hawley, A.P. Pvt., 1st Mississippi Light Artillery. Co. Cowan's. Federal Rolls of Prisoners of War: Captured at Blakely, AL, on 4/9/1865; Received at Ship Island, MS, from New Orleans, LA, on 4/15/1865. Transferred to Vicksburg, MS, for exchange on 5/1/1865; Exchanged at Camp Townsend, MS, on 5/6/1865.

Haygood, Erasmus W. (AKA F.M.) Pvt., 35th Mississippi Infantry. Co. D. Federal Rolls of Prisoners of War: Captured at Blakely, AL, on 4/9/1865; Received at Ship Island, MS, on 4/15/1865. Transferred to Vicksburg, MS, for exchange on 5/1/1865; Exchanged at Camp Townsend, MS, on 5/6/1865.

Haynes, E.F. (AKA Hanes) Pvt., 46th Mississippi Infantry. Co. D. Federal Rolls of Prisoners of War: Captured at Blakely, AL, on 4/9/1865; Received at Ship Island, MS, on 4/15/1865. Transferred to Vicksburg, MS, for exchange on 5/1/1865; Exchanged at Camp Townsend, MS, on 5/6/1865.

Hazelwood, Richard B. (AKA R.D.) Pvt., 35th Mississippi Infantry. Co. G. Federal Rolls of Prisoners of War: Captured at Blakely, AL, on 4/9/1865; Received at Ship Island, MS, on 4/15/1865. Transferred to Vicksburg, MS, for exchange on 5/1/1865; Exchanged at Camp Townsend, MS, on 5/6/1865.

Helm, Green Cellus Pvt., 1st Mississippi Light Artillery. Co. B. Federal Rolls of Prisoners of War: Captured at Blakely, AL, on 4/9/1865; Received at Ship Island, MS, on 4/15/1865. Transferred to Vicksburg, MS, for exchange on 5/1/1865; Exchanged at Camp Townsend, MS, on 5/6/1865. Confederate Widows Pension Application dated 1924 on file at the Mississippi Department of Archives and History. Target Name: Helm, Amanda Irene. County: Holmes.

Henderson, R.W. Pvt., 46th Mississippi Infantry. Co. F. Federal Rolls of Prisoners of War: Captured at Blakely, AL, on 4/9/1865; Received at Ship Island, MS, on 4/15/1865. Transferred to Vicksburg, MS, for exchange on 5/1/1865; Exchanged at Camp Townsend, MS, on 5/6/1865.

Hendricks, C.L. Pvt., 1st Mississippi Light Artillery. Co. B. Federal Rolls of Prisoners of War: Captured at Blakely, AL, on 4/9/1865; Received at Ship Island, MS, on 4/15/1865. Transferred to Vicksburg, MS, for exchange on 5/1/1865; Exchanged at Camp Townsend, MS, on 5/6/1865.

Hendricks, R.H. (AKA Hendrick) Musician, 46th Mississippi Infantry. Co. E. Federal Rolls of Prisoners of War: Captured at Blakely, AL, on 4/9/1865; Received at Ship Island, MS, on 4/15/1865. Transferred to Vicksburg, MS, for exchange on 5/1/1865; Exchanged at Camp Townsend, MS, on 5/6/1865.

Hendricks, T.P. Pvt., 46th Mississippi Infantry. Co. __. Federal Rolls of Prisoners of War: Captured at Blakely, AL, on 4/9/1865; Received at Ship Island, MS, on 4/15/1865. Transferred to Vicksburg, MS, for exchange on 5/1/1865; Exchanged at Camp Townsend, MS, on 5/6/1865.

Henley, Isaac C. 1st Sgt./2nd Lt., 1st Mississippi Light Artillery. Co. B. Federal Rolls of Prisoners of War: Captured at Blakely, AL, on 4/9/1865; Received at Ship Island, MS, on 4/15/1865. Transferred to Vicksburg, MS, for exchange on 4/28/1865; Confined at New Orleans, LA, on 4/30/1865. Exchanged at Camp Townsend, MS, on 5/6/1865.

Hennington, J.R. (AKA Herrington) Pvt., 36th Mississippi Infantry. Co. D. Federal Rolls of Prisoners of War: Captured at Blakely, AL, on 4/9/1865; Received at Ship Island, MS, on 4/15/1865. Transferred to Vicksburg, MS, for exchange on 5/1/1865; Exchanged at Camp Townsend, MS, on 5/6/1865.

Hensley, Frederick B. Pvt., 36th Mississippi Infantry. Co. I. Federal Rolls of Prisoners of War: Captured at Blakely, AL, on 4/9/1865; Received at Ship Island, MS, on 4/15/1865. Transferred to Vicksburg, MS, for exchange on 5/1/1865; Exchanged at Camp Townsend, MS, on 5/6/1865. Confederate Pension Application dated 1916 on file at the Mississippi Department of Archives and History. Target Name: Hensley, F.B. County: Newton.

Herring, W.J. Pvt., 4th Mississippi Infantry. Co. E. Federal Rolls of Prisoners of War: Captured at Blakely, AL, on 4/9/1865; Received at Ship Island, MS, on 4/15/1865. Transferred to Vicksburg, MS, for exchange on 5/1/1865; Exchanged at Camp Townsend, MS, on 5/6/1865.

Herrington, J.A. Pvt., 36th Mississippi Infantry. Co. D. Federal Rolls of Prisoners of War: Captured at Blakely, AL, on 4/9/1865; Received at Ship Island, MS, on 4/15/1865. Transferred to Vicksburg, MS, for exchange on 5/1/1865; Exchanged at Camp Townsend, MS, on 5/6/1865.

Herrod, J.R. Pvt., 1st Mississippi Light Artillery. Co. F. Captured at Blakely, AL, on 4/9/1865; Received at Ship Island, MS, on 4/15/1865. Transferred to Vicksburg, MS, for exchange on 5/1/1865; Exchanged at Camp Townsend, MS, on 5/6/1865.

Herron, William H., Jr. (AKA Herrin) Pvt./Sgt., 39th Mississippi Infantry. Co. G. Federal Rolls of Prisoners of War: Captured at Blakely, AL, on 4/9/1865; Received at Ship Island, MS, on 4/15/1865. Transferred to Vicksburg, MS, for exchange on 5/1/1865; Exchanged at Camp Townsend, MS, on 5/6/1865.

Hewitt, J.A. Pvt., 1st Mississippi Light Artillery. Co. __. Federal Rolls of Prisoners of War: Captured at Blakely, AL, on 4/9/1865; Received at Ship Island, MS, on 4/15/1865. Transferred to Vicksburg, MS, for exchange on 5/1/1865; Exchanged at Camp Townsend, MS, on 5/6/1865.

Hewitt, Robert Y. (AKA Hewett) Pvt., 1st Mississippi Light Artillery. Co. D. Federal Rolls of Prisoners of War: Captured at Blakely, AL, on 4/9/1865; Received at Ship Island, MS, on 4/15/1865. Transferred to Vicksburg, MS, for exchange on 5/1/1865; Exchanged at Camp Townsend, MS, on 5/6/1865. Born: 1835. Died: 1909. Buried: Holmes County, MS.

Hickman, Jesse Pvt., 1st Mississippi Light Artillery. Co. G. Federal Rolls of Prisoners of War: Captured at Blakely, AL, on 4/9/1865; Received at Ship Island, MS, on 4/15/1865. Transferred to Vicksburg, MS, for exchange on 5/1/1865; Exchanged at Camp Townsend, MS, on 5/6/1865.

Hickman, John Pvt., 1st Mississippi Light Artillery. Co. __. Federal Rolls of Prisoners of War: Captured at Blakely, AL, on 4/9/1865; Received at Ship Island, MS, on 4/15/1865. Transferred to Vicksburg, MS, for exchange on 5/1/1865; Exchanged at Camp Townsend, MS, on 5/6/1865.

Hicks, J.R. Pvt., 1st Mississippi Light Artillery. Co. __. Federal Rolls of Prisoners of War: Captured at Blakely, AL, on 4/9/1865; Received at Ship Island, MS, on 4/15/1865. Transferred to Vicksburg, MS, for exchange on 5/1/1865; Exchanged at Camp Townsend, MS, on 5/6/1865.

Hill, J.T. Pvt., 1st Mississippi Light Artillery. Co. __. Federal Rolls of Prisoners of War: Captured at Blakely, AL, on 4/9/1865; Received at Ship Island, MS, on 4/15/1865. Transferred to Vicksburg, MS, for exchange on 5/1/1865; Exchanged at Camp Townsend, MS, on 5/6/1865.

Hilton, L.M. Pvt., 39th Mississippi Infantry. Co. F. Federal Rolls of Prisoners of War: Captured at Blakely, AL, on 4/9/1865; Received at Ship Island, MS, on 4/15/1865. Transferred to Vicksburg, MS, for exchange on 5/1/1865; Exchanged at Camp Townsend, MS, on 5/6/1865.

Hines, Richard J. Pvt., 39th Mississippi Infantry. Co. I. Federal Rolls of Prisoners of War: Captured at Blakely, AL, on 4/9/1865; Received at Ship Island, MS, on 4/15/1865. Transferred to Vicksburg, MS, for exchange on 5/1/1865; Exchanged at Camp Townsend, MS, on 5/6/1865.

Hodges, E.F. Pvt., 39th Mississippi Infantry. Co. E. Federal Rolls of Prisoners of War: Captured at Blakely, AL, on 4/9/1865; Received at Ship Island, MS, on 4/15/1865. Transferred to Vicksburg, MS, for exchange on 5/1/1865; Exchanged at Camp Townsend, MS, on 5/6/1865.

Hoffner, Rufus P. (AKA Heffner) Pvt., 1st Mississippi Light Artillery. Co. D. Federal Rolls of Prisoners of War: Captured at Blakely, AL, on 4/9/1865; Received at Ship Island, MS, on 4/15/1865. Transferred to Vicksburg, MS, for exchange on 5/1/1865; Exchanged at Camp Townsend, MS, on 5/6/1865.

Hogan, Jesse Pvt./Sgt., 8th Mississippi Cavalry. Co. H. Federal Rolls of Prisoners of War: Captured near Mobile, AL, on 12/22/1864; Received at Ship Island, MS, from New Orleans, LA, on 1/25/1865. Transferred to Vicksburg, MS, for exchange on 5/1/1865; Exchanged at Camp Townsend, MS, on 5/6/1865.

Holland, Charles 1st Sgt./Ord. Sgt., 36th Mississippi Infantry. Co. D. Federal Rolls of Prisoners of War: Captured at Blakely, AL, on 4/9/1865; Received at Ship Island, MS, on 4/15/1865. Transferred to Vicksburg, MS, for exchange on 5/1/1865; Exchanged at Camp Townsend, MS, on 5/6/1865.

Hollingsworth, Henry Pvt., 36th Mississippi Infantry. Co. D. Federal Rolls of Prisoners of War: Captured at Blakely, AL, on 4/9/1865; Received at Ship Island, MS, on 4/15/1865. Transferred to Vicksburg, MS, for exchange on 5/1/1865; Exchanged at Camp Townsend, MS, on 5/6/1865. Confederate Pension Application dated 1905 on file at the Mississippi Department of Archives and History. Target Name: Hollingsworth, Henry. County: Perry.

Hollingsworth, William M. Pvt., 36th Mississippi Infantry. Co. D. Federal Rolls of Prisoners of War: Captured at Blakely, AL, on 4/9/1865; Received at Ship Island, MS, on 4/15/1865. Transferred to Vicksburg, MS, for exchange on 5/1/1865; Exchanged at Camp Townsend, MS, on 5/6/1865.

Holmes, E.P. Pvt./Sgt., 4th Mississippi Infantry. Co. E. Federal Rolls of Prisoners of War: Captured at Blakely, AL, on 4/9/1865; Received at Ship Island, MS, on 4/15/1865. Transferred to Vicksburg, MS, for exchange on 5/1/1865; Exchanged at Camp Townsend, MS, on 5/6/1865.

Holmes, P.E. Musician, 46th Mississippi Infantry. Co. E. Federal Rolls of Prisoners of War: Captured at Blakely, AL, on 4/9/1865; Received at Ship Island, MS, on 4/15/1865. Transferred to Vicksburg, MS, for exchange on 5/1/1865; Exchanged at Camp Townsend, MS, on 5/6/1865.

Honeycutt, E.J. Pvt., 36th Mississippi Infantry. Co. H. Federal Rolls of Prisoners of War: Captured at Blakely, AL, on 4/9/1865; Received at Ship Island, MS, on 4/15/1865. Transferred to Vicksburg, MS, for exchange on 5/1/1865; Exchanged at Camp Townsend, MS, on 5/6/1865.

Honeycutt, Thomas Jefferson Pvt., 1st Mississippi Light Artillery. Co. F. Federal Rolls of Prisoners of War: Captured at Blakely, AL, on 4/9/1865; Received at Ship Island, MS, on 4/15/1865. Transferred to Vicksburg, MS, for exchange on 5/1/1865; Exchanged at Camp Townsend, MS, on 5/6/1865. Confederate Pension Application dated 1909 on file at the Mississippi Department of Archives and History. Target Name: Honeycutt, Thomas Jefferson. County: Warren.

Hood, W.H. Pvt., Powers Cavalry Regiment. Cos. A, E & G. Federal Rolls of Prisoners of War: Captured near Natchez, MS, on 9/10/1864; Transferred to Ship Island, MS, from New Orleans, LA, on 10/7/1864. Disposition unknown.

Hooter, J.W. Pvt., 4th Mississippi Infantry. Co. E. Federal Rolls of Prisoners of War: Captured in Alabama on 4/1/1865; Received at Ship Island, MS. Transferred to Vicksburg, MS, for exchange on 5/1/1865; Exchanged at Camp Townsend, MS, on 5/6/1865.

Horn, George Pvt., 8th Mississippi Cavalry. Co. __. Federal Rolls of Prisoners of War: Captured at Eva, MS, on 12/6/1864; Received at Ship Island, MS, from New Orleans, LA, on 1/25/1865. Transferred to Vicksburg, MS, for exchange on 5/1/1865; Exchanged at Camp Townsend, MS, on 5/6/1865.

Horner, John H. Pvt., 1st Mississippi Light Artillery. Co. G. Federal Rolls of Prisoners of War: Captured at Blakely, AL, on 4/9/1865; Received at Ship Island, MS, on 4/15/1865. Transferred to Vicksburg, MS, for exchange on 5/1/1865; Exchanged at Camp Townsend, MS, on 5/6/1865.

Horten, John W. (AKA Horton) Pvt., 4th Mississippi Infantry. Cos. E & G. Federal Rolls of Prisoners of War: Captured at Blakely, AL, on 4/9/1865; Received at Ship Island, MS, on 4/15/1865. Transferred to Vicksburg, MS, for exchange on 5/1/1865; Exchanged at Camp Townsend, MS, on 5/6/1865.

Horton, S.F. Pvt., 1st Mississippi Light Artillery. Co. __. Federal Rolls of Prisoners of War: Captured at Blakely, AL, on 4/9/1865; Received at Ship Island, MS, on 4/15/1865. Transferred to Vicksburg, MS, for exchange on 5/1/1865; Exchanged at Camp Townsend, MS, on 5/6/1865.

Houston, James D. Pvt., 1st Mississippi Light Artillery. Cos. D & I. Federal Rolls of Prisoners of War: Captured at Blakely, AL, on 4/9/1865; Received at Ship Island, MS, on 4/15/1865. Transferred to Vicksburg, MS, for exchange on 5/1/1865; Exchanged at Camp Townsend, MS, on 5/6/1865.

Howard, Leroy B. Pvt., 35th Mississippi Infantry. Co.

G. Federal Rolls of Prisoners of War: Captured at Blakely, AL, on 4/9/1865; Received at Ship Island, MS, on 4/15/1865. Transferred to Vicksburg, MS, for exchange on 5/1/1865; Exchanged at Camp Townsend, MS, on 5/6/1865.

Howard, Levi Pvt., 35th Mississippi Infantry. Co. B. Federal Rolls of Prisoners of War: Captured at Blakely, AL, on 4/9/1865; Received at Ship Island, MS, on 4/15/1865. Transferred to Vicksburg, MS, for exchange on 5/1/1865; Exchanged at Camp Townsend, MS, on 5/6/1865.

Howell, Benjamin F. Pvt., 39th Mississippi Infantry. Co. F. Federal Rolls of Prisoners of War: Captured at Blakely, AL, on 4/9/1865; Received at Ship Island, MS, on 4/15/1865. Transferred to Vicksburg, MS, for exchange on 5/1/1865; Exchanged at Camp Townsend, MS, on 5/6/1865.

Hudnall, Henry B. Pvt./2nd Lt., 35th Mississippi Infantry. Co. A. Federal Rolls of Prisoners of War: Captured at Fort Gaines, AL, on 8/8/1864; Received at Ship Island, MS, from New Orleans, LA, on 10/25/1864. Exchanged on 1/4/1865. Confederate Widows Pension Application dated 1920 on file at the Mississippi Department of Archives and History. Target Name: Hudnall, Sallie A. County: Kemper.

Hudson, Madison (AKA Hutson, J. M) Pvt., 39th Mississippi Infantry. Co. B. Federal Rolls of Prisoners of War: Captured at Blakely, AL, on 4/9/1865; Received at Ship Island, MS, on 4/15/1865. Transferred to Vicksburg, MS, for exchange on 5/1/1865; Exchanged at Camp Townsend, MS, on 5/6/1865.

Hughes, Thomas H. Capt., Powers Cavalry Regiment. F & S. Federal Rolls of Prisoners of War: Captured at Washington County, MS, on 11/17/1864; Received at Ship Island, MS, from New Orleans, LA, on 12/18/1864. Exchanged on 3/2/1865.

Hunter, J.T. Pvt., 46th Mississippi Infantry. Co. F. Federal Rolls of Prisoners of War: Captured at Blakely, AL, on 4/9/1865; Received at Ship Island, MS, on 4/15/1865. Transferred to Vicksburg, MS, for exchange on 5/1/1865; Exchanged at Camp Townsend, MS, on 5/6/1865.

Hunter, O. Pvt., 4th Mississippi Infantry. Co. F. Federal Rolls of Prisoners of War: Captured in Alabama on 4/1/1865; Received at Ship Island, MS. Transferred to Vicksburg, MS, for exchange on 5/1/1865; Exchanged at Camp Townsend, MS, on 5/6/1865.

Husbands, Elijah Pvt./Cpl./Sgt., 39th Mississippi Infantry. Co. __. Federal Rolls of Prisoners of War: Captured at Blakely, AL, on 4/9/1865; Received at Ship Island, MS, on 4/15/1865. Transferred to Vicksburg, MS, for exchange on 5/1/1865; Exchanged at Camp Townsend, MS, on 5/6/1865.

Hutcherson, William (AKA Hutchinson, Hutcheson) Pvt./Sgt., 35th Mississippi Infantry. Co. K. Federal Rolls of Prisoners of War: Captured at Blakely, AL, on 4/9/1865; Received at Ship Island, MS, on 4/15/1865. Transferred to Vicksburg, MS, for exchange on 5/1/1865; Exchanged at Camp Townsend, MS, on 5/6/1865.

Hutchinson, James Pvt., 35th Mississippi Infantry. Co. __. Federal Rolls of Prisoners of War: Captured at Blakely, AL, on 4/9/1865; Received at Ship Island, MS, on 4/15/1865. Transferred to Vicksburg, MS, for exchange on 5/1/1865; Exchanged at Camp Townsend, MS, on 5/6/1865.

Hyman, W.J. Pvt., 1st Mississippi Light Artillery. Co. K. Federal Rolls of Prisoners of War: Captured at Blakely, AL, on 4/9/1865; Received at Ship Island, MS, on 4/15/1865. Transferred to Vicksburg, MS, for exchange on 5/1/1865; Exchanged at Camp Townsend, MS, on 5/6/1865.

Ingram, Abijah E. Pvt., 1st Mississippi Light Artillery. Co. K. Federal Rolls of Prisoners of War: Captured at Blakely, AL, on 4/9/1865; Received at Ship Island, MS, on 4/15/1865. Transferred to Vicksburg, MS, for exchange on 5/1/1865; Exchanged at Camp Townsend, MS, on 5/6/1865. Born: 1826. Died: 1870. Buried: Copiah County.

Ingram, J.J. Pvt., 39th Mississippi Infantry. Co. __. Federal Rolls of Prisoners of War: Captured at Blakely, AL, on 4/9/1865; Received at Ship Island, MS, on 4/15/1865. Transferred to Vicksburg, MS, for exchange on 5/1/1865; Exchanged at Camp Townsend, MS, on 5/6/1865.

Irby, Thomas B. Pvt., 7th Mississippi Battalion Infantry. Co. E. Federal Rolls of Prisoners of War: Captured at Blakely, AL, on 4/9/1865; Received at Ship Island, MS, on 4/15/1865. Transferred to Vicksburg, MS, for exchange on 5/1/1865; Exchanged at Camp Townsend, MS, on 5/6/1865.

Iron, D.M. (AKA Irion) Pvt./Cpl., 35th Mississippi Infantry. Co. H. Federal Rolls of Prisoners of War: Captured at Blakely, AL, on 4/9/1865; Received at Ship Island, MS, on 4/15/1865. Transferred to Vicksburg, MS, for exchange on 5/1/1865; Exchanged at Camp Townsend, MS, on 5/6/1865.

Irwin, John Q. Pvt., 1st Mississippi Light Artillery. Co. G. Federal Rolls of Prisoners of War: Captured at Blakely, AL, on 4/9/1865; Received at Ship Island, MS, on 4/15/1865. Transferred to Vicksburg, MS, for exchange on 5/1/1865; Exchanged at Camp Townsend, MS, on 5/6/1865.

Jackson, J.H. Pvt., 36th Mississippi Infantry. Co. C. Federal Rolls of Prisoners of War: Captured at Blakely, AL, on 4/9/1865; Received at Ship Island, MS, on 4/15/1865. Transferred to Vicksburg, MS, for exchange on 5/1/1865; Exchanged at Camp Townsend, MS, on 5/6/1865.

Jackson, J.J. Pvt., 36th Mississippi Infantry. Co. __. Federal Rolls of Prisoners of War: Captured at Blakely, AL, on 4/9/1865; Received at Ship Island, MS, on 4/15/1865. Transferred to Vicksburg, MS, for exchange on 5/1/1865; Exchanged at Camp Townsend, MS, on 5/6/1865.

Jackson, T.S. Pvt., 1st Mississippi Light Artillery. Co. B. Federal Rolls of Prisoners of War: Captured at Blakely, AL, on 4/9/1865; Received at Ship Island, MS, on 4/15/1865. Transferred to Vicksburg, MS, for exchange on 5/1/1865; Exchanged at Camp Townsend, MS, on 5/6/1865.

James, Thomas W. (AKA William T.) Pvt./Cpl., 7th Mississippi Battalion Infantry. Co. E. Federal Rolls of Prisoners of War: Captured at Blakely, AL, on 4/9/1865; Received at Ship Island, MS, on 4/15/1865. Transferred to Vicksburg, MS, for exchange on 5/1/1865; Exchanged at Camp Townsend, MS, on 5/6/1865.

Jeffries, Daniel Pvt., 1st Mississippi Light Artillery. Co. I. Federal Rolls of Prisoners of War: Captured at Blakely, AL, on 4/9/1865; Received at Ship Island, MS, on 4/15/1865. Transferred to Vicksburg, MS, for

exchange on 5/1/1865; Exchanged at Camp Townsend, MS, on 5/6/1865.

Jeffries, Osborne Pvt., 1st Mississippi Light Artillery. Co. I. Federal Rolls of Prisoners of War: Captured at Blakely, AL, on 4/9/1865; Received at Ship Island, MS, on 4/15/1865. Transferred to Vicksburg, MS, for exchange on 5/1/1865; Exchanged at Camp Townsend, MS, on 5/6/1865.

Jett, W.H. Pvt., 1st Mississippi Light Artillery. Co. F. Federal Rolls of Prisoners of War: Captured at Blakely, AL, on 4/9/1865; Received at Ship Island, MS, on 4/15/1865. Transferred to Vicksburg, MS, for exchange on 5/1/1865; Exchanged at Camp Townsend, MS, on 5/6/1865.

Johnson, George W. Pvt./Cpl., 1st Mississippi Light Artillery. Cos. B & D. Federal Rolls of Prisoners of War: Captured at Blakely, AL, on 4/9/1865; Received at Ship Island, MS, on 4/15/1865. Transferred to Vicksburg, MS, for exchange on 5/1/1865; Exchanged at Camp Townsend, MS, on 5/6/1865. Buried: Johnson Chapel Cemetery at Pike County, MS.

Johnson, George W. Pvt., 1st Mississippi Light Artillery. Co. B. Federal Rolls of Prisoners of War: Captured at Blakely, AL, on 4/9/1865; Received at Ship Island, MS, on 4/15/1865. Transferred to Vicksburg, MS, for exchange on 5/1/1865; Exchanged at Camp Townsend, MS, on 5/6/1865.

Johnson, J.E. (AKA I.E.) Pvt., 1st Mississippi Infantry. Co. B. Federal Rolls of Prisoners of War: Captured at Choctaw Bend, MS, on 11/16/1864; Received at Ship Island, MS, from New Orleans, LA, on 12/13/1864. Took the U.S. Oath of Allegiance and transferred to the U.S. naval authorities at New Orleans, LA.

Johnson, J.T. Pvt., 4th Mississippi Infantry. Co. A. Federal Rolls of Prisoners of War: Captured at Blakely, AL, on 4/9/1865; Received at Ship Island, MS, on 4/15/1865. Transferred to Vicksburg, MS, for exchange on 5/1/1865; Exchanged at Camp Townsend, MS, on 5/6/1865.

Johnson, John S. Pvt., 1st Mississippi Light Artillery. Co. K. Federal Rolls of Prisoners of War: Captured at Blakely, AL, on 4/9/1865; Received at Ship Island, MS, on 4/15/1865. Transferred to Vicksburg, MS, for exchange on 5/1/1865; Exchanged at Camp Townsend, MS, on 5/6/1865.

Johnson, Joseph J. Pvt., 1st Mississippi Light Artillery. Co. K. Federal Rolls of Prisoners of War: Captured at Blakely, AL, on 4/9/1865; Received at Ship Island, MS, on 4/15/1865. Transferred to Vicksburg, MS, for exchange on 5/1/1865; Exchanged at Camp Townsend, MS, on 5/6/1865.

Johnson, Sidney E. Pvt., 7th Mississippi Battalion Infantry. Co. A. Federal Rolls of Prisoners of War: Captured at Blakely, AL, on 4/9/1865; Received at Ship Island, MS, on 4/15/1865. Transferred to Vicksburg, MS, for exchange on 5/1/1865; Exchanged at Camp Townsend, MS, on 5/6/1865.

Johnson, William Henry Pvt., 1st Mississippi Light Artillery. Co. G. Federal Rolls of Prisoners of War: Captured at Blakely, AL, on 4/9/1865; Received at Ship Island, MS, on 4/15/1865. Transferred to Vicksburg, MS, for exchange on 5/1/1865; Exchanged at Camp Townsend, MS, on 5/6/1865. Born: 1844. Died: 1900. Buried: Warren County, MS. Confederate Pension Application dated 1912 on file at the Mississippi Department of Archives and History. Target Name: Johnson, William Henry. County: Warren.

Johnston, J.H. Pvt., 36th Mississippi Infantry. Co. __. Federal Rolls of Prisoners of War: Captured at Blakely, AL, on 4/9/1865; Received at Ship Island, MS, on 4/15/1865. Transferred to Vicksburg, MS, for exchange on 5/1/1865; Exchanged at Camp Townsend, MS, on 5/6/1865.

Johnston, James H. Pvt., 1st Mississippi Light Artillery. Co. A. Federal Rolls of Prisoners of War: Captured at Blakely, AL, on 4/9/1865; Received at Ship Island, MS, on 4/15/1865. Transferred to Vicksburg, MS, for exchange on 5/1/1865; Exchanged at Camp Townsend, MS, on 5/6/1865.

Johnston, Wirt Pvt./Cpl., 1st Mississippi Light Artillery. Co. A. Federal Rolls of Prisoners of War: Captured at Blakely, AL, on 4/9/1865; Received at Ship Island, MS, on 4/15/1865. Transferred to Vicksburg, MS, for exchange on 5/1/1865; Exchanged at Camp Townsend, MS, on 5/6/1865.

Jones, Amos O. (AKA A.E.) Cpl./Pvt., 7th Mississippi Battalion Infantry. Co. B. Federal Rolls of Prisoners of War: Captured at Blakely, AL, on 4/9/1865; Received at Ship Island, MS, on 4/15/1865. Transferred to Vicksburg, MS, for exchange on 5/1/1865; Exchanged at Camp Townsend, MS, on 5/6/1865. Confederate Pension Application dated 1902 on file at the Mississippi Department of Archives and History. Target Name: Jones, A.O. County: Wayne. Also a Confederate Widows Pension on file dated 1931. Target Name: Jones, Melvina Weaver. County: Wayne.

Jones, Ferdinand Pvt., 1st Mississippi Light Artillery. Co. D. Federal Rolls of Prisoners of War: Captured at Blakely, AL, on 4/9/1865; Received at Ship Island, MS, on 4/15/1865. Transferred to Vicksburg, MS, for exchange on 5/1/1865; Exchanged at Camp Townsend, MS, on 5/6/1865.

Jones, H.J. Pvt., 1st Mississippi Light Artillery. Co. F. Federal Rolls of Prisoners of War: Captured at Blakely, AL, on 4/9/1865; Received at Ship Island, MS, on 4/15/1865. Transferred to Vicksburg, MS, for exchange on 5/1/1865; Exchanged at Camp Townsend, MS, on 5/6/1865.

Jones, J.J. Pvt., 39th Mississippi Infantry. Co. __. Federal Rolls of Prisoners of War: Captured at Blakely, AL, on 4/9/1865; Received at Ship Island, MS, on 4/15/1865. Transferred to Vicksburg, MS, for exchange on 5/1/1865; Exchanged at Camp Townsend, MS, on 5/6/1865.

Jones, Joseph C. Pvt., 1st Mississippi Light Artillery. Co. G. Federal Rolls of Prisoners of War: Captured at Blakely, AL, on 4/9/1865; Received at Ship Island, MS, on 4/15/1865. Transferred to Vicksburg, MS, for exchange on 5/1/1865; Exchanged at Camp Townsend, MS, on 5/6/1865. Born: 1829. Died 1900. Buried: Copiah County, MS.

Jones, M.D. Pvt., 1st Mississippi Light Artillery. Co. B. Federal Rolls of Prisoners of War: Captured at Blakely, AL, on 4/9/1865; Received at Ship Island, MS, on 4/15/1865. Transferred to Vicksburg, MS, for exchange on 5/1/1865; Exchanged at Camp Townsend, MS, on 5/6/1865.

Jones, P.H. Pvt., 39th Mississippi Infantry. Co. __. Federal Rolls of Prisoners of War: Captured at

Blakely, AL, on 4/9/1865; Received at Ship Island, MS, on 4/15/1865. Transferred to Vicksburg, MS, for exchange on 5/1/1865; Exchanged at Camp Townsend, MS, on 5/6/1865.

Jones, Robert E. Pvt./1st Lt., 36th Mississippi Infantry. Co. K. Federal Rolls of Prisoners of War: Captured at Blakely, AL, on 4/9/1865. Transferred to Vicksburg, MS, for exchange on 4/28/1865; Confined at New Orleans, LA, on 4/30/1865. Exchanged at Camp Townsend, MS, on 5/6/1865

Jordan, Charles Pvt./Sgt., 35th Mississippi Infantry. Co. H. Federal Rolls of Prisoners of War: Captured at Blakely, AL, on 4/9/1865; Received at Ship Island, MS, on 4/15/1865. Transferred to Vicksburg, MS, for exchange on 5/1/1865; Exchanged at Camp Townsend, MS, on 5/6/1865.

Jordan, D.H. Pvt., 4th Mississippi Infantry. Co. G. Federal Rolls of Prisoners of War: Captured at Blakely, AL, on 4/9/1865; Received at Ship Island, MS, on 4/15/1865. Transferred to Vicksburg, MS, for exchange on 5/1/1865; Exchanged at Camp Townsend, MS, on 5/6/1865.

Jordan, J.G. Pvt./Cpl., 4th Mississippi Infantry. Co. G. Federal Rolls of Prisoners of War: Captured at Blakely, AL, on 4/9/1865; Received at Ship Island, MS, on 4/15/1865. Transferred to Vicksburg, MS, for exchange on 5/1/1865; Exchanged at Camp Townsend, MS, on 5/6/1865.

Jordan, M. Pvt., 36th Mississippi Infantry. Co. __. Federal Rolls of Prisoners of War: Captured at Blakely, AL, on 4/9/1865; Received at Ship Island, MS, on 4/15/1865. Transferred to Vicksburg, MS, for exchange on 5/1/1865; Exchanged at Camp Townsend, MS, on 5/6/1865.

Jordan, W.P., Sr. Pvt., 1st Mississippi Light Artillery. Co. F. Enlisted: 1862. Federal Rolls of Prisoners of War: Captured at Blakely, AL, on 4/9/1865; Received at Ship Island, MS, on 4/15/1865. Transferred to Vicksburg, MS, for exchange on 5/1/1865; Exchanged at Camp Townsend, MS, on 5/6/1865. Born: 1/24/1830 to Hudson and Sarah May Jordan. Pre-war occupation: Farmer. Married: Susan Elizabeth Campbell in 1852 at Brookhaven, MS. Children: 6. Religion: Baptist. Died: 1915. Buried: Covington County, MS. Confederate Pension Application dated 1902 on file at the Mississippi Department of Archives and History. Target Name: Jordan, W.P. County: Covington.

Jordan, Warren W. (AKA William W.) Pvt./Cpl., 7th Mississippi Battalion Infantry. Co. __. Federal Rolls of Prisoners of War: Captured at Blakely, AL, on 4/9/1865; Received at Ship Island, MS, on 4/15/1865. Transferred to Vicksburg, MS, for exchange on 5/1/1865; Exchanged at Camp Townsend, MS, on 5/6/1865. Confederate Pension Application dated 1916 on file at the Mississippi Department of Archives and History. Target Name: Jordan, Warren W. County: Wayne.

Jordan, William A. (AKA G.S.P.) Pvt., 1st Mississippi Light Artillery. Co. B. Federal Rolls of Prisoners of War: Captured at Blakely, AL, on 4/9/1865; Received at Ship Island, MS, on 4/15/1865. Transferred to Vicksburg, MS, for exchange on 5/1/1865; Exchanged at Camp Townsend, MS, on 5/6/1865. Born: 1844. Died: 1932. Buried: Woodlawn Cemetery located in Tampa, FL. Confederate Pension Application dated 1920 on file at the Mississippi Department of Archives and History. Target Name: Jordan, G.S.P. County: Attala.

Joy, William Pvt., 35th Mississippi Infantry. Co. K. Federal Rolls of Prisoners of War: Captured at Blakely, AL, on 4/9/1865; Received at Ship Island, MS, on 4/15/1865. Transferred to Vicksburg, MS, for exchange on 5/1/1865; Exchanged at Camp Townsend, MS, on 5/6/1865.

Keathley, J.B. (AKA Kiethley) Pvt., 36th Mississippi Infantry. Co. F. Federal Rolls of Prisoners of War: Captured at Blakely, AL, on 4/9/1865; Received at Ship Island, MS, on 4/15/1865. Transferred to Vicksburg, MS, for exchange on 5/1/1865; Exchanged at Camp Townsend, MS, on 5/6/1865.

Keathley, William (AKA Keithley, Keithly) Pvt., 1st Mississippi Light Artillery. Co. K. Federal Rolls of Prisoners of War: Captured at Blakely, AL, on 4/9/1865; Received at Ship Island, MS, on 4/15/1865. Transferred to Vicksburg, MS, for exchange on 5/1/1865; Exchanged at Camp Townsend, MS, on 5/6/1865.

Kelly, Andrew J. Pvt., 7th Mississippi Battalion Infantry. Co. E. Federal Rolls of Prisoners of War: Captured at Blakely, AL, on 4/9/1865; Received at Ship Island, MS, on 4/15/1865. Transferred to Vicksburg, MS, for exchange on 5/1/1865; Exchanged at Camp Townsend, MS, on 5/6/1865.

Kelly, E. Pvt., 1st Mississippi Light Artillery. Co. F. Federal Rolls of Prisoners of War: Captured at Blakely, AL, on 4/9/1865; Received at Ship Island, MS, on 4/15/1865. Transferred to Vicksburg, MS, for exchange on 5/1/1865; Exchanged at Camp Townsend, MS, on 5/6/1865.

Kelly, James M. Pvt., 1st Mississippi Light Artillery. Co. E. Federal Rolls of Prisoners of War: Captured at Blakely, AL, on 4/9/1865; Received at Ship Island, MS, on 4/15/1865. Transferred to Vicksburg, MS, for exchange on 5/1/1865; Exchanged at Camp Townsend, MS, on 5/6/1865.

Kelly, William Pvt., 1st Mississippi Light Artillery. Co. G. Federal Rolls of Prisoners of War: Captured at Blakely, AL, on 4/9/1865; Received at Ship Island, MS, on 4/15/1865. Transferred to Vicksburg, MS, for exchange on 5/1/1865; Exchanged at Camp Townsend, MS, on 5/6/1865.

Kennedy, James C. Pvt., 36th Mississippi Infantry. Co. B. Federal Rolls of Prisoners of War: Captured at Blakely, AL, on 4/9/1865; Received at Ship Island, MS, on 4/15/1865. Transferred to Vicksburg, MS, for exchange on 5/1/1865; Exchanged at Camp Townsend, MS, on 5/6/1865.

Kerr, J.J. (AKA Kern, Kear) Pvt., 35th Mississippi Infantry. Co. F. Federal Rolls of Prisoners of War: Captured at Blakely, AL, on 4/9/1865; Received at Ship Island, MS, on 4/15/1865. Transferred to Vicksburg, MS, for exchange on 5/1/1865; Exchanged at Camp Townsend, MS, on 5/6/1865.

Key, J.W. Pvt., 1st Mississippi Light Artillery. Co. __. Federal Rolls of Prisoners of War: Captured at Blakely, AL, on 4/9/1865; Received at Ship Island, MS, on 4/15/1865. Transferred to Vicksburg, MS, for exchange on 5/1/1865; Exchanged at Camp Townsend, MS, on 5/6/1865.

Killingsworth, J.A. (AKA Killinsworth, J.H.) Pvt./2nd Lt., 35th Mississippi Infantry. Co. E. Federal Rolls of

Prisoners of War: Captured at Blakely, AL, on 4/9/1865; Received at Ship Island, MS, on 4/15/1865. Transferred to Vicksburg, MS, for exchange on 4/28/1865; Confined at New Orleans, LA, on 4/30/1865. Exchanged at Camp Townsend, MS, on 5/6/1865.

King, Louis Pvt., 1st Mississippi Light Artillery. Co. __. Federal Rolls of Prisoners of War: Captured at Blakely, AL, on 4/9/1865; Received at Ship Island, MS, on 4/15/1865. Transferred to Vicksburg, MS, for exchange on 5/1/1865; Exchanged at Camp Townsend, MS, on 5/6/1865.

King, Thomas J. Pvt., 4th Mississippi Infantry. Cos. B & E. Federal Rolls of Prisoners of War: Captured at Blakely, AL, on 4/9/1865; Received at Ship Island, MS, on 4/15/1865. Transferred to Vicksburg, MS, for exchange on 5/1/1865; Exchanged at Camp Townsend, MS, on 5/6/1865. Confederate Widows Pension Application dated 1922 on file at the Mississippi Department of Archives and History. Target Name: King, Eliza H. County: Tallahatchie.

King, William P. Pvt., 1st Mississippi Light Artillery. Cos. F & I. Federal Rolls of Prisoners of War: Captured at Blakely, AL, on 4/9/1865; Received at Ship Island, MS, on 4/15/1865. Transferred to Vicksburg, MS, for exchange on 5/1/1865; Exchanged at Camp Townsend, MS, on 5/6/1865.

Kirklan, Richard Pvt., 39th Mississippi Infantry. Co. E. Federal Rolls of Prisoners of War: Captured at Blakely, AL, on 4/9/1865; Received at Ship Island, MS, on 4/15/1865. Transferred to Vicksburg, MS, for exchange on 5/1/1865; Exchanged at Camp Townsend, MS, on 5/6/1865.

Kirklan, Samuel Pvt., 39th Mississippi Infantry. Co. E. Federal Rolls of Prisoners of War: Captured at Blakely, AL, on 4/9/1865; Received at Ship Island, MS, on 4/15/1865. Transferred to Vicksburg, MS, for exchange on 5/1/1865; Exchanged at Camp Townsend, MS, on 5/6/1865.

Kirkpatrick, T.N. (AKA T.W.) Sgt., 4th Mississippi Infantry. Co. __. Federal Rolls of Prisoners of War: Captured at Blakely, AL, on 4/9/1865; Received at Ship Island, MS, on 4/15/1865. Transferred to Vicksburg, MS, for exchange on 5/1/1865; Exchanged at Camp Townsend, MS, on 5/6/1865.

Knight, P.B.H. Pvt., 1st Mississippi Light Artillery. Cos. D & F. Federal Rolls of Prisoners of War: Captured at Blakely, AL, on 4/9/1865; Received at Ship Island, MS, on 4/15/1865. Transferred to Vicksburg, MS, for exchange on 5/1/1865; Exchanged at Camp Townsend, MS, on 5/6/1865. Confederate Pension Application dated 1916 on file at the Mississippi Department of Archives and History. Target Name: Knight, P.B. County: Copiah.

Knight, Paul Pvt., 36th Mississippi Infantry. Co. __. Federal Rolls of Prisoners of War: Captured at Blakely, AL, on 4/9/1865; Received at Ship Island, MS, on 4/15/1865. Transferred to Vicksburg, MS, for exchange on 5/1/1865; Exchanged at Camp Townsend, MS, on 5/6/1865.

Lacey, Louis J. (AKA Lacy) Pvt., 1st Mississippi Light Artillery. Co. K. Federal Rolls of Prisoners of War: Captured at Blakely, AL, on 4/9/1865; Received at Ship Island, MS, on 4/15/1865. Transferred to Vicksburg, MS, for exchange on 5/1/1865; Exchanged at Camp Townsend, MS, on 5/6/1865. Born: 1837. Died: 1893. Buried: Jefferson County.

Lacey, W.H. (AKA Lacy) Pvt., 36th Mississippi Infantry. Co. C. Federal Rolls of Prisoners of War: Captured at Blakely, AL, on 4/9/1865; Received at Ship Island, MS, on 4/15/1865. Transferred to Vicksburg, MS, for exchange on 5/1/1865; Exchanged at Camp Townsend, MS, on 5/6/1865. Born: 1846 in Mississippi. Died: 1912. Buried: State Cemetery located in Austin, Texas.

Lally, Albert Pvt., 35th Mississippi Infantry. Co. A. Federal Rolls of Prisoners of War: Captured at Blakely, AL, on 4/9/1865; Received at Ship Island, MS, on 4/15/1865. Transferred to Vicksburg, MS, for exchange on 5/1/1865; Exchanged at Camp Townsend, MS, on 5/6/1865.

Lamkin, D. Washington Q.M. Sgt./2nd Lt., 1st Mississippi Light Artillery. F & S. Federal Rolls of Prisoners of War: Captured at Blakely, AL, on 4/9/1865; Received at Ship Island, MS, on 4/15/1865. Transferred to Vicksburg, MS, for exchange on 4/28/1865; Confined at New Orleans, LA, on 4/30/1865. Exchanged at Camp Townsend, MS, on 5/6/1865.

Lancaster, L. (AKA S, J) Pvt., 46th Mississippi Infantry. Co. G. Federal Rolls of Prisoners of War: Captured in Alabama on 4/1/1865; Received at Ship Island, MS. Transferred to Vicksburg, MS, for exchange on 5/1/1865; Exchanged at Camp Townsend, MS, on 5/6/1865.

Landfair, J.W. Pvt., 4th Mississippi Infantry. Co. G. Federal Rolls of Prisoners of War: Captured at Blakely, AL, on 4/9/1865; Received at Ship Island, MS, on 4/15/1865. Transferred to Vicksburg, MS, for exchange on 5/1/1865; Exchanged at Camp Townsend, MS, on 5/6/1865.

Landruth, T.M. Pvt., 4th Mississippi Infantry. Co. __. Federal Rolls of Prisoners of War: Captured at Blakely, AL, on 4/9/1865; Received at Ship Island, MS, on 4/15/1865. Transferred to Vicksburg, MS, for exchange on 5/1/1865; Exchanged at Camp Townsend, MS, on 5/6/1865.

Lane, Bryant Pvt., 35th Mississippi Infantry. Co. B. Federal Rolls of Prisoners of War: Captured at Blakely, AL, on 4/9/1865; Received at Ship Island, MS, on 4/15/1865. Transferred to Vicksburg, MS, for exchange on 5/1/1865; Exchanged at Camp Townsend, MS, on 5/6/1865.

Lang, Enoch Pvt., 35th Mississippi Infantry. Co. A. Federal Rolls of Prisoners of War: Captured at Blakely, AL, on 4/9/1865; Received at Ship Island, MS, on 4/15/1865. Transferred to Vicksburg, MS, for exchange on 5/1/1865; Exchanged at Camp Townsend, MS, on 5/6/1865. Confederate Pension Application dated 1916 on file at the Mississippi Department of Archives and History. Target Name: Lang, Enoch. County: Smith. Also a Confederate Widows Pension on file dated 1924. Target Name: Lang, Nancy E. County: Smith.

Lang, Simeon Pvt., 35th Mississippi Infantry. Co. B. Federal Rolls of Prisoners of War: Captured at Blakely, AL, on 4/9/1865; Received at Ship Island, MS, on 4/15/1865. Transferred to Vicksburg, MS, for exchange on 5/1/1865; Exchanged at Camp Townsend, MS, on 5/6/1865.

Lang, Wiley Pvt., 35th Mississippi Infantry. Co. B. Federal Rolls of Prisoners of War: Captured at Blakely, AL, on 4/9/1865; Received at Ship Island, MS, on 4/15/1865. Transferred to Vicksburg, MS, for

exchange on 5/1/1865; Exchanged at Camp Townsend, MS, on 5/6/1865.

Lanier, W. Pvt., 36th Mississippi Infantry. Co. __. Federal Rolls of Prisoners of War: Captured at Blakely, AL, on 4/9/1865; Received at Ship Island, MS, on 4/15/1865. Transferred to Vicksburg, MS, for exchange on 5/1/1865; Exchanged at Camp Townsend, MS, on 5/6/1865.

Lassiter, John G. Pvt., 35th Mississippi Infantry. Co. B. Federal Rolls of Prisoners of War: Captured at Blakely, AL, on 4/9/1865; Received at Ship Island, MS, on 4/15/1865. Transferred to Vicksburg, MS, for exchange on 5/1/1865; Exchanged at Camp Townsend, MS, on 5/6/1865.

Lassiter, William M. Pvt., 35th Mississippi Infantry. Co. B. Federal Rolls of Prisoners of War: Captured at Blakely, AL, on 4/9/1865; Received at Ship Island, MS, on 4/15/1865. Transferred to Vicksburg, MS, for exchange on 5/1/1865; Exchanged at Camp Townsend, MS, on 5/6/1865.

Latimer, J.F. (AKA J.H.) Pvt., 39th Mississippi Infantry. Co. E. Federal Rolls of Prisoners of War: Captured at Blakely, AL, on 4/9/1865; Received at Ship Island, MS, on 4/15/1865. Transferred to Vicksburg, MS, for exchange on 5/1/1865; Exchanged at Camp Townsend, MS, on 5/6/1865.

Lawrence, J.W. Pvt., 4th Mississippi Infantry. Co. H. Federal Rolls of Prisoners of War: Captured at Blakely, AL, on 4/9/1865; Received at Ship Island, MS, on 4/15/1865. Transferred to Vicksburg, MS, for exchange on 5/1/1865; Exchanged at Camp Townsend, MS, on 5/6/1865.

Lawrence, John H. (AKA O.S.) Sgt., 1st Mississippi Light Artillery. Co. D. Federal Rolls of Prisoners of War: Captured at Blakely, AL, on 4/9/1865; Received at Ship Island, MS, on 4/15/1865. Transferred to Vicksburg, MS, for exchange on 5/1/1865; Exchanged at Camp Townsend, MS, on 5/6/1865. Confederate Widows Pension Application dated 1908 on file at the Mississippi Department of Archives and History. Target Name: Lawrence, T.L. County: Noxubee.

Ledbetter, Alex H. Sgt./1st Lt., 35th Mississippi Infantry. Co. F. Federal Rolls of Prisoners of War: Captured at Blakely, AL, on 4/9/1865; Received at Ship Island, MS, on 4/15/1865. Transferred to Vicksburg, MS, for exchange on 4/28/1865; Confined at New Orleans, LA, on 4/30/1865. Exchanged at Camp Townsend, MS, on 5/6/1865.

Lee, H.F. Cpl./Pvt., 39th Mississippi Infantry. Co. A. Federal Rolls of Prisoners of War: Captured at Blakely, AL, on 4/9/1865; Received at Ship Island, MS, on 4/15/1865. Transferred to Vicksburg, MS, for exchange on 5/1/1865; Exchanged at Camp Townsend, MS, on 5/6/1865.

Lee, Joseph D. Pvt., 4th Mississippi Infantry. Co. I. Federal Rolls of Prisoners of War: Captured at Blakely, AL, on 4/9/1865; Received at Ship Island, MS, on 4/15/1865. Transferred to Vicksburg, MS, for exchange on 5/1/1865; Exchanged at Camp Townsend, MS, on 5/6/1865.

Lee, N.J. Pvt., 39th Mississippi Infantry. Co. A. Federal Rolls of Prisoners of War: Captured at Blakely, AL, on 4/9/1865; Received at Ship Island, MS, on 4/15/1865. Transferred to Vicksburg, MS, for exchange on 5/1/1865; Exchanged at Camp Townsend, MS, on 5/6/1865.

Lee, S.A. Pvt./Sgt., 36th Mississippi Infantry. Co. F. Federal Rolls of Prisoners of War: Captured at Blakely, AL, on 4/9/1865; Received at Ship Island, MS, on 4/15/1865. Transferred to Vicksburg, MS, for exchange on 5/1/1865; Exchanged at Camp Townsend, MS, on 5/6/1865.

Lee, Thomas Pvt., 1st Mississippi Light Artillery. Co. K. Federal Rolls of Prisoners of War: Captured at Blakely, AL, on 4/9/1865; Received at Ship Island, MS, on 4/15/1865. Transferred to Vicksburg, MS, for exchange on 5/1/1865; Exchanged at Camp Townsend, MS, on 5/6/1865. Born: 1831. Died: 1923. Buried: Sarepta Baptist Church Cemetery located in Franklin County, MS.

Lee, W.L. (AKA Leigh, Larkin) Pvt./Cpl., 7th Mississippi Battalion Infantry. Co. E. Federal Rolls of Prisoners of War: Captured at Blakely, AL, on 4/9/1865; Received at Ship Island, MS, on 4/15/1865. Transferred to Vicksburg, MS, for exchange on 5/1/1865; Exchanged at Camp Townsend, MS, on 5/6/1865.

Lee, W.T. Pvt., 46th Mississippi Infantry. Cos. G & H. Federal Rolls of Prisoners of War: Captured at Blakely, AL, on 4/9/1865; Received at Ship Island, MS, on 4/15/1865. Transferred to Vicksburg, MS, for exchange on 5/1/1865; Exchanged at Camp Townsend, MS, on 5/6/1865.

Legg, Daniel Mayo Cpl./Pvt., 1st Mississippi Light Artillery. Co. G. Federal Rolls of Prisoners of War: Captured at Blakely, AL, on 4/9/1865; Received at Ship Island, MS, on 4/15/1865. Transferred to Vicksburg, MS, for exchange on 5/1/1865; Exchanged at Camp Townsend, MS, on 5/6/1865. Born: 1827. Died: 1901. Buried: Warren County, MS.

Leigh, J.C. (AKA Lloyd) Sgt., 36th Mississippi Infantry. Co. __. Federal Rolls of Prisoners of War: Captured at Blakely, AL, on 4/9/1865; Received at Ship Island, MS, on 4/15/1865. Transferred to Vicksburg, MS, for exchange on 5/1/1865; Exchanged at Camp Townsend, MS, on 5/6/1865.

Lemons, James P. (AKA Lemoyne) Pvt./Sgt., 36th Mississippi Infantry. Co. F. Federal Rolls of Prisoners of War: Captured at Blakely, AL, on 4/9/1865; Received at Ship Island, MS, on 4/15/1865. Transferred to Vicksburg, MS, for exchange on 5/1/1865; Exchanged at Camp Townsend, MS, on 5/6/1865.

Lewis, John F. Pvt., 36th Mississippi Infantry. Co. B. Federal Rolls of Prisoners of War: Captured at Blakely, AL, on 4/9/1865; Received at Ship Island, MS, on 4/15/1865. Transferred to Vicksburg, MS, for exchange on 5/1/1865; Exchanged at Camp Townsend, MS, on 5/6/1865.

Lewis, Tavner J. (AKA Tabner) Pvt., 36th Mississippi Infantry. Co. B. Federal Rolls of Prisoners of War: Captured at Blakely, AL, on 4/9/1865; Received at Ship Island, MS, on 4/15/1865. Transferred to Vicksburg, MS, for exchange on 5/1/1865; Exchanged at Camp Townsend, MS, on 5/6/1865. Confederate Widows Pension Application dated 1924 on file at the Mississippi Department of Archives and History. Target Name: Lewis, Margarett. County: Walthall .

Lewis, W.A.L. Pvt./Asst. Surg., 36th Mississippi Infantry. Co. D. Federal Rolls of Prisoners of War: Captured at Blakely, AL, on 4/9/1865; Received at Ship Island, MS, on 4/15/1865. Transferred to Vicksburg, MS, for exchange on 4/28/1865; Confined at New Orleans, LA, on 4/30/1865. Exchanged at Camp Townsend, MS, on 5/6/1865.

Lide, Alexander Sparks Sgt./Pvt., 35th Mississippi Infantry. Co. C. Federal Rolls of Prisoners of War: Captured at Blakely, AL, on 4/9/1865; Received at Ship Island, MS, on 4/15/1865. Transferred to Vicksburg, MS, for exchange on 5/1/1865; Exchanged at Camp Townsend, MS, on 5/6/1865. Confederate Widows Pension Application dated 1922 on file at the Mississippi Department of Archives and History. Target Name: Lide, Emma K. County: Lowndes.

Liles, George W.S. Pvt., 39th Mississippi Infantry. Co. B. Federal Rolls of Prisoners of War: Captured at Blakely, AL, on 4/9/1865; Received at Ship Island, MS, on 4/15/1865. Transferred to Vicksburg, MS, for exchange on 5/1/1865; Exchanged at Camp Townsend, MS, on 5/6/1865.

Lindsey, J.E. Pvt., 36th Mississippi Infantry. Co. __. Federal Rolls of Prisoners of War: Captured at Blakely, AL, on 4/9/1865; Received at Ship Island, MS, on 4/15/1865. Transferred to Vicksburg, MS, for exchange on 5/1/1865; Exchanged at Camp Townsend, MS, on 5/6/1865.

Little, T.T. (AKA J.J.) Pvt., 36th Mississippi Infantry. Co. __. Federal Rolls of Prisoners of War: Captured at Blakely, AL, on 4/9/1865; Received at Ship Island, MS, on 4/15/1865. Transferred to Vicksburg, MS, for exchange on 5/1/1865; Exchanged at Camp Townsend, MS, on 5/6/1865.

Little, Thomas C. Pvt., 36th Mississippi Infanry. Co. A. Federal Rolls of Prisoners of War: Captured at Blakely, AL, on 4/9/1865; Received at Ship Island, MS, on 4/15/1865. Transferred to Vicksburg, MS, for exchange on 5/1/1865; Exchanged at Camp Townsend, MS, on 5/6/1865.

Lloyd, Evan S. Pvt., 36th Mississippi Infantry. Co. K. Federal Rolls of Prisoners of War: Captured at Blakely, AL, on 4/9/1865; Received at Ship Island, MS, on 4/15/1865. Transferred to Vicksburg, MS, for exchange on 5/1/1865; Exchanged at Camp Townsend, MS, on 5/6/1865.

Lloyd, Samuel H. Pvt., 4th Mississippi Infantry. Co. A. Federal Rolls of Prisoners of War: Captured at Blakely, AL, on 4/9/1865; Received at Ship Island, MS, on 4/15/1865. Transferred to Vicksburg, MS, for exchange on 5/1/1865; Exchanged at Camp Townsend, MS, on 5/6/1865.

Lockhart, B.A. (AKA R.A.) Sgt., 1st Mississippi Light Artillery. Co. D. Federal Rolls of Prisoners of War: Captured at Blakely, AL, on 4/9/1865; Received at Ship Island, MS, on 4/15/1865. Transferred to Vicksburg, MS, for exchange on 5/1/1865; Exchanged at Camp Townsend, MS, on 5/6/1865.

Lockhart, Thomas J. Cpl., 1st Mississippi Light Artillery. Co. D. Federal Rolls of Prisoners of War: Captured at Blakely, AL, on 4/9/1865; Received at Ship Island, MS, on 4/15/1865. Transferred to Vicksburg, MS, for exchange on 5/1/1865; Exchanged at Camp Townsend, MS, on 5/6/1865.

Lomax, Charles H. (AKA A.H.) Pvt., 1st Mississippi Light Artillery. Co. D. Federal Rolls of Prisoners of War: Captured at Blakely, AL, on 4/9/1865; Received at Ship Island, MS, on 4/15/1865. Transferred to Vicksburg, MS, for exchange on 5/1/1865; Exchanged at Camp Townsend, MS, on 5/6/1865.

Long, C.R. Pvt., 4th Mississippi Infantry. Co. E. Federal Rolls of Prisoners of War: Captured at Blakely, AL, on 4/9/1865; Received at Ship Island, MS, on 4/15/1865. Transferred to Vicksburg, MS, for exchange on 5/1/1865; Exchanged at Camp Townsend, MS, on 5/6/1865.

Long, James A. Pvt., 1st Mississippi Light Artillery. Co. F. Federal Rolls of Prisoners of War: Captured at Blakely, AL, on 4/9/1865; Received at Ship Island, MS, on 4/15/1865. Transferred to Vicksburg, MS, for exchange on 5/1/1865; Exchanged at Camp Townsend, MS, on 5/6/1865. Born: 1835. Died: 1897. Buried: Holmes County, MS.

Long, John C. Pvt., 4th Mississippi Infantry. Co. E. Federal Rolls of Prisoners of War: Captured at Blakely, AL, on 4/9/1865; Received at Ship Island, MS, on 4/15/1865. Transferred to Vicksburg, MS, for exchange on 5/1/1865; Exchanged at Camp Townsend, MS, on 5/6/1865. Confederate Widows Pension Application dated 1904 on file at the Mississippi Department of Archives and History. Target Name: Long, Nannie A. County: Sharkey.

Loomis, Samuel T. Pvt., 1st Mississippi Light Artillery. Co. G. Federal Rolls of Prisoners of War: Captured at Blakely, AL, on 4/9/1865; Received at Ship Island, MS, on 4/15/1865. Transferred to Vicksburg, MS, for exchange on 5/1/1865; Exchanged at Camp Townsend, MS, on 5/6/1865.

Loper, J.M. Pvt./Cpl., 39th Mississippi Infantry. Co. D. Federal Rolls of Prisoners of War: Captured at Blakely, AL, on 4/9/1865; Received at Ship Island, MS, on 4/15/1865. Transferred to Vicksburg, MS, for exchange on 5/1/1865; Exchanged at Camp Townsend, MS, on 5/6/1865.

Loper, William P. Pvt., 39th Mississippi Infantry. Co. D. Federal Rolls of Prisoners of War: Captured at Blakely, AL, on 4/9/1865; Received at Ship Island, MS, on 4/15/1865. Transferred to Vicksburg, MS, for exchange on 5/1/1865; Exchanged at Camp Townsend, MS, on 5/6/1865. Confederate Pension Application dated 1924 on file at the Mississippi Department of Archives and History. Target Name: Loper, William P. County: Scott.

Loring, J.H. (AKA Loving) Pvt., 39th Mississippi Infantry. Co. E. Federal Rolls of Prisoners of War: Captured at Blakely, AL, on 4/9/1865; Received at Ship Island, MS, on 4/15/1865. Transferred to Vicksburg, MS, for exchange on 5/1/1865; Exchanged at Camp Townsend, MS, on 5/6/1865.

Lott, Absalom Pvt., 7th Mississippi Battalion Infantry. Co. B. Federal Rolls of Prisoners of War: Captured at Blakely, AL, on 4/9/1865; Received at Ship Island, MS, on 4/15/1865. Transferred to Vicksburg, MS, for exchange on 5/1/1865; Exchanged at Camp Townsend, MS, on 5/6/1865.

Loving, J.W. Cpl., 39th Mississippi Infantry. Co. E. Federal Rolls of Prisoners of War: Captured at Blakely, AL, on 4/9/1865; Received at Ship Island, MS, on 4/15/1865. Transferred to Vicksburg, MS, for exchange on 5/1/1865; Exchanged at Camp Townsend, MS, on 5/6/1865. Confederate Widows Pension Application dated 1916 on file at the Mississippi Department of Archives and History. Target Name: Loving, Mary Jane. County: Copiah.

Luce, A. Pvt., 1st Mississippi Light Artillery. Co. B. Federal Rolls of Prisoners of War: Captured at Blakely, AL, on 4/9/1865; Received at Ship Island, MS, on 4/15/1865. Transferred to Vicksburg, MS, for exchange on 5/1/1865; Exchanged at Camp Townsend, MS, on 5/6/1865.

Luce, W.A. Pvt., 1st Mississippi Light Artillery. Co. I. Federal Rolls of Prisoners of War: Captured at Blakely, AL, on 4/9/1865; Received at Ship Island, MS, on 4/15/1865. Transferred to Vicksburg, MS, for exchange on 5/1/1865; Exchanged at Camp Townsend, MS, on 5/6/1865.

Lyndsey, James Pvt., 1st Mississippi Light Artillery. Co. G. Federal Rolls of Prisoners of War: Captured at Blakely, AL, on 4/9/1865; Received at Ship Island, MS, on 4/15/1865. Transferred to Vicksburg, MS, for exchange on 5/1/1865; Exchanged at Camp Townsend, MS, on 5/6/1865.

Lyon, G.W. Pvt., 35th Mississippi Infantry. Co. K. Federal Rolls of Prisoners of War: Captured at Blakely, AL, on 4/9/1865; Received at Ship Island, MS, on 4/15/1865. Transferred to Vicksburg, MS, for exchange on 5/1/1865; Exchanged at Camp Townsend, MS, on 5/6/1865.

Lyon, Thomas S. (AKA Lyons) Pvt., 1st Mississippi Light Artillery. Co. D. Federal Rolls of Prisoners of War: Captured at Blakely, AL, on 4/9/1865; Received at Ship Island, MS, on 4/15/1865. Transferred to Vicksburg, MS, for exchange on 5/1/1865; Exchanged at Camp Townsend, MS, on 5/6/1865. Born: 1840. Died: 1917. Buried: Holmes County, MS.

McArthur, C.N. Cpl., 46th Mississippi Infantry. Co. K. Federal Rolls of Prisoners of War: Captured at Blakely, AL, on 4/9/1865; Received at Ship Island, MS, on 4/15/1865. Transferred to Vicksburg, MS, for exchange on 5/1/1865; Exchanged at Camp Townsend, MS, on 5/6/1865. Confederate Widows Pension Application dated 1916 on file at the Mississippi Department of Archives and History. Target Name: McArthur, Mary. County: Kemper.

McCabe, Patrick Pvt./Sgt. Maj., 1st Mississippi Light Artillery. Co. K. Federal Rolls of Prisoners of War: Captured at Blakely, AL, on 4/9/1865; Received at Ship Island, MS, on 4/15/1865. Transferred to Vicksburg, MS, for exchange on 5/1/1865; Exchanged at Camp Townsend, MS, on 5/6/1865.

McCafferty, Robert Pvt., 4th Mississippi Infantry. Co. A. Federal Rolls of Prisoners of War: Captured at Blakely, AL, on 4/9/1865; Received at Ship Island, MS, on 4/15/1865. Transferred to Vicksburg, MS, for exchange on 5/1/1865; Exchanged at Camp Townsend, MS, on 5/6/1865.

McCain, William E. Cpl./Pvt., 4th Mississippi Infantry. Cos. B & D. Federal Rolls of Prisoners of War: Captured at Blakely, AL, on 4/9/1865; Received at Ship Island, MS, on 4/15/1865. Transferred to Vicksburg, MS, for exchange on 5/1/1865; Exchanged at Camp Townsend, MS, on 5/6/1865.

McCarty, John H. Pvt., 7th Mississippi Battalion Infantry. Co. A. Federal Rolls of Prisoners of War: Captured at Blakely, AL, on 4/9/1865; Received at Ship Island, MS, on 4/15/1865. Transferred to Vicksburg, MS, for exchange on 5/1/1865; Exchanged at Camp Townsend, MS, on 5/6/1865.

McCaskill, L.A. Sgt., 39th Mississippi Infantry. Co. A. Federal Rolls of Prisoners of War: Captured at Blakely, AL, on 4/9/1865; Received at Ship Island, MS, on 4/15/1865. Transferred to Vicksburg, MS, for exchange on 5/1/1865; Exchanged at Camp Townsend, MS, on 5/6/1865. Confederate Widows Pension Application dated 1923 on file at the Mississippi Department of Archives and History. Target Name: McCaskill, C.A. County: Simpson.

McClain, H.C. (AKA McClean) Pvt., 4th Mississippi Infantry. Cos. C & G. Federal Rolls of Prisoners of War: Captured at Blakely, AL, on 4/9/1865; Received at Ship Island, MS, on 4/15/1865. Transferred to Vicksburg, MS, for exchange on 5/1/1865; Exchanged at Camp Townsend, MS, on 5/6/1865.

McCone, Joel G. Pvt./Cpl., 1st Mississippi Light Artillery. Co. D. Federal Rolls of Prisoners of War: Captured at Blakely, AL, on 4/9/1865; Received at Ship Island, MS, on 4/15/1865. Transferred to Vicksburg, MS, for exchange on 5/1/1865; Exchanged at Camp Townsend, MS, on 5/6/1865.

McCray, William V. Cpl./Sgt., 1st Mississippi Light Artillery. Co. G. Federal Rolls of Prisoners of War: Captured at Blakely, AL, on 4/9/1865; Received at Ship Island, MS, on 4/15/1865. Transferred to Vicksburg, MS, for exchange on 5/1/1865; Exchanged at Camp Townsend, MS, on 5/6/1865.

McDade, Charles Alpin Pvt., 35th Mississippi Infantry. Co. B. Enlisted 12/1864. Federal Rolls of Prisoners of War: Received at Ship Island, MS. Disposition unknown. Confederate Widows Pension Application dated 1924 on file at the Mississippi Department of Archives and History. Target Name: McDade, Louisa Virginia. County: Lamar.

McDade, John A. (AKA C.A.) Pvt., 35th Mississippi Infantry. Co. B. Federal Rolls of Prisoners of War: Captured at Blakely, AL, on 4/9/1865; Received at Ship Island, MS, on 4/15/1865. Transferred to Vicksburg, MS, for exchange on 5/1/1865; Exchanged at Camp Townsend, MS, on 5/6/1865.

McDonald, Frederick W. Pvt., 1st Mississippi Light Artillery. Co. K. Federal Rolls of Prisoners of War: Captured at Blakely, AL, on 4/9/1865; Received at Ship Island, MS, on 4/15/1865. Transferred to Vicksburg, MS, for exchange on 5/1/1865; Exchanged at Camp Townsend, MS, on 5/6/1865. Confederate Pension Application dated 1909 on file at the Mississippi Department of Archives and History. Target Name: McDonald, F.W. County: Adams. Also a Confederate Widows Pension on file dated 1918. Target Name: McDonald, Fredrica. County: Adams.

McDonald, John (AKA McDonel) Pvt., 39th Mississippi Infantry. Cos. H & K. Federal Rolls of Prisoners of War: Captured at Blakely, AL, on 4/9/1865; Received at Ship Island, MS, on 4/15/1865. Transferred to Vicksburg, MS, for exchange on 5/1/1865; Exchanged at Camp Townsend, MS, on 5/6/1865.

McDonald, Robert V. (AKA McDaniel, R.P.) Cpl., 1st Mississippi Light Artillery. Co. K. Federal Rolls of Prisoners of War: Captured at Blakely, AL, on 4/9/1865; Received at Ship Island, MS, on 4/15/1865. Transferred to Vicksburg, MS, for exchange on 5/1/1865; Exchanged at Camp Townsend, MS, on 5/6/1865. Confederate Pension Application dated 19__ on file at the Mississippi Department of Archives and History. Target Name: McDonald, Laura O. County: Jefferson. Born: 1836. Died: 1917. Buried: Jefferons County, MS.

McDonald, T.W. Pvt., 1st Mississippi Light Artillery. Co. K. Federal Rolls of Prisoners of War: Captured at Blakely, AL, on 4/9/1865; Received at Ship Island, MS, on 4/15/1865. Transferred to Vicksburg, MS, for exchange on 5/1/1865; Exchanged at Camp Townsend, MS, on 5/6/1865.

McDonnell, John Pvt., 1st Mississippi Light Artillery. Co. G. Federal Rolls of Prisoners of War: Captured and paroled at Vicksburg, MS, on 7/4/1863. Federal Rolls of Prisoners of War: Captured at Blakely, AL, on 4/9/1865; Received at Ship Island, MS, on 4/15/1865. Transferred to Vicksburg, MS, for exchange on 5/1/1865; Exchanged at Camp Townsend, MS, on 5/6/1865. Born: 12/1833 at Dublin, Ireland. Occupations: Contractor and Foundry Worker. Residences: Ireland, New York City, NY, Jackson and Rodney, MS. Married: Elizabeth Muller in 1866 at Jackson, MS. Children: 9. Died: 7/4/1904 at age 70 due to paralysis. Memberships: Commander of the Robert A. Smith Camp of the United Confederate Veterans. His obituary appeared in a 1905 edition of *Confederate Veteran* magazine.

McDonnelly, John Pvt., 1st Mississippi Light Artillery. Co. G. Federal Rolls of Prisoners of War: Captured at Blakely, AL, on 4/9/1865; Received at Ship Island, MS, on 4/15/1865. Transferred to Vicksburg, MS, for exchange on 5/1/1865; Exchanged at Camp Townsend, MS, on 5/6/1865.

McDough, J.B. (AKA McDougal) Pvt., Powers Cavalry Regiment. Co. __. Federal Rolls of Prisoners of War: Captured at Natchez, MS, on 10/6/1864; Received at Ship Island, MS. Died: 2/8/1865 at Ship Island, MS, due to carcinoma. Buried: Ship Island, MS, Cemetery in Grave #135.

McGan, James Pvt., 1st Mississippi Light Artillery. Co. B. Federal Rolls of Prisoners of War: Captured at Blakely, AL, on 4/9/1865; Received at Ship Island, MS, on 4/15/1865. Transferred to Vicksburg, MS, for exchange on 5/1/1865; Exchanged at Camp Townsend, MS, on 5/6/1865.

McGuire, W.T. Pvt., 4th Mississippi Infantry. Co. F. Federal Rolls of Prisoners of War: Captured at Blakely, AL, on 4/9/1865; Received at Ship Island, MS, on 4/15/1865. Transferred to Vicksburg, MS, for exchange on 5/1/1865; Exchanged at Camp Townsend, MS, on 5/6/1865.

McHingall, J.S. Pvt., 1st Mississippi Light Artillery. Co. D. Federal Rolls of Prisoners of War: Captured at Blakely, AL, on 4/9/1865; Received at Ship Island, MS, on 4/15/1865. Transferred to Vicksburg, MS, for exchange on 5/1/1865; Exchanged at Camp Townsend, MS, on 5/6/1865.

McKee, H.K. (AKA McKiel, Kelsey) Pvt., 36th Mississippi Infantry. Co.H. Federal Rolls of Prisoners of War: Captured at Blakely, AL, on 4/9/1865; Received at Ship Island, MS, on 4/15/1865. Transferred to Vicksburg, MS, for exchange on 5/1/1865; Exchanged at Camp Townsend, MS, on 5/6/1865.

McKeel, J.L. (AKA McKiel) Pvt., 36th Mississippi Infantry. Cos. F & H. Federal Rolls of Prisoners of War: Captured at Blakely, AL, on 4/9/1865; Received at Ship Island, MS, on 4/15/1865. Transferred to Vicksburg, MS, for exchange on 5/1/1865; Exchanged at Camp Townsend, MS, on 5/6/1865.

McKnight, H.A. (AKA McCreight) 1st Lt./Capt., 35th Mississippi Infantry. Co. __. Federal Rolls of Prisoners of War: Captured at Blakely, AL, on 4/9/1865; Received at Ship Island, MS, on 4/15/1865. Transferred to Vicksburg, MS, for exchange on 4/28/1865; Confined at New Orleans, LA, on 4/30/1865. Exchanged at Camp Townsend, MS, on 5/6/1865.

McLane, William H. Pvt., 35th Mississippi Infantry. Co. B. Federal Rolls of Prisoners of War: Captured at Blakely, AL, on 4/9/1865; Received at Ship Island, MS, on 4/15/1865. Transferred to Vicksburg, MS, for exchange on 5/1/1865; Exchanged at Camp Townsend, MS, on 5/6/1865.

McLemore, H.W. Pvt., 36th Mississippi Infantry. Co. K. Federal Rolls of Prisoners of War: Captured at Blakely, AL, on 4/9/1865; Received at Ship Island, MS, on 4/15/1865. Transferred to Vicksburg, MS, for exchange on 5/1/1865; Exchanged at Camp Townsend, MS, on 5/6/1865.

McLemore, Henry R. Pvt., 39th Mississippi Infantry. Co. C. Federal Rolls of Prisoners of War: Captured at Blakely, AL, on 4/9/1865; Received at Ship Island, MS, on 4/15/1865. Transferred to Vicksburg, MS, for exchange on 5/1/1865; Exchanged at Camp Townsend, MS, on 5/6/1865.

McLeod, John J. Pvt./1st Sgt., 7th Mississippi Battalion Infantry. Co. F. Federal Rolls of Prisoners of War: Captured at Blakely, AL, on 4/9/1865; Received at Ship Island, MS, on 4/15/1865. Transferred to Vicksburg, MS, for exchange on 5/1/1865; Exchanged at Camp Townsend, MS, on 5/6/1865.

McLeod, N. Sgt., 1st Mississippi Light Artillery. Co. __. Federal Rolls of Prisoners of War: Captured at Blakely, AL, on 4/9/1865; Received at Ship Island, MS, on 4/15/1865. Transferred to Vicksburg, MS, for exchange on 5/1/1865; Exchanged at Camp Townsend, MS, on 5/6/1865.

McLeod, W.W. Pvt., 1st Mississippi Light Artillery. Co. __. Federal Rolls of Prisoners of War: Captured at Blakely, AL, on 4/9/1865; Received at Ship Island, MS, on 4/15/1865. Transferred to Vicksburg, MS, for exchange on 5/1/1865; Exchanged at Camp Townsend, MS, on 5/6/1865.

McMahon, Archibald W. (AKA McMahan, W.A.) Pvt./Cpl., 35th Mississippi Infantry. Co. __. Federal Rolls of Prisoners of War: Captured at Blakely, AL, on 4/9/1865; Received at Ship Island, MS, on 4/15/1865. Transferred to Vicksburg, MS, for exchange on 5/1/1865; Exchanged at Camp Townsend, MS, on 5/6/1865.

McMullen, T.J. (AKA McMullin) Pvt., 39th Mississippi Infantry. Co. D. Federal Rolls of Prisoners of War: Captured at Blakely, AL, on 4/9/1865; Received at Ship Island, MS, on 4/15/1865. Transferred to Vicksburg, MS, for exchange on 5/1/1865; Exchanged at Camp Townsend, MS, on 5/6/1865.

McSwain, Jonathan Pvt., 4th Mississippi Infantry. Cos. D & F. Federal Rolls of Prisoners of War: Captured at Blakely, AL, on 4/9/1865; Received at Ship Island, MS, on 4/15/1865. Transferred to Vicksburg, MS, for exchange on 5/1/1865; Exchanged at Camp Townsend, MS, on 5/6/1865. Confederate Widows Pension Application dated 1916 on file at the Mississippi Department of Archives and History. Target Name: McSwain, Margaret. County: Calhoun.

Magee, S. Pvt., 46th Mississippi Infantry. Co. G. Federal Rolls of Prisoners of War: Captured at Blakely, AL, on 4/9/1865; Received at Ship Island, MS, on 4/15/1865. Transferred to Vicksburg, MS, for exchange on 5/1/1865; Exchanged at Camp Townsend, MS, on 5/6/1865.

Mahoney, James B. Pvt., 1st Mississippi Light Artillery. Co. D. Federal Rolls of Prisoners of War: Captured at Blakely, AL, on 4/9/1865; Received at Ship Island,

MS, on 4/15/1865. Transferred to Vicksburg, MS, for exchange on 5/1/1865; Exchanged at Camp Townsend, MS, on 5/6/1865.

Mahoney, Lemuel Pvt., 1st Mississippi Light Artillery. Co. D. Federal Rolls of Prisoners of War: Captured at Blakely, AL, on 4/9/1865; Received at Ship Island, MS, on 4/15/1865. Transferred to Vicksburg, MS, for exchange on 5/1/1865; Exchanged at Camp Townsend, MS, on 5/6/1865.

Man, H.B. Pvt., 1st Mississippi Light Artillery. Co. G. Federal Rolls of Prisoners of War: Captured at Blakely, AL, on 4/9/1865; Received at Ship Island, MS, on 4/15/1865. Transferred to Vicksburg, MS, for exchange on 5/1/1865; Exchanged at Camp Townsend, MS, on 5/6/1865.

Manes, J.T. Pvt., 1st Mississippi Light Artillery. Co. __. Federal Rolls of Prisoners of War: Captured at Blakely, AL, on 4/9/1865; Received at Ship Island, MS, on 4/15/1865. Transferred to Vicksburg, MS, for exchange on 5/1/1865; Exchanged at Camp Townsend, MS, on 5/6/1865.

Manning, Wesley L. Pvt./Cpl., 39th Mississippi Infantry. Co. G. Federal Rolls of Prisoners of War: Captured at Blakely, AL, on 4/9/1865; Received at Ship Island, MS, on 4/15/1865. Transferred to Vicksburg, MS, for exchange on 5/1/1865; Exchanged at Camp Townsend, MS, on 5/6/1865. Confederate Pension Application dated 1916 on file at the Mississippi Department of Archives and History. Target Name: Manning, W.L. County: Simpson.

Marley, Walter S. Pvt., 1st Mississippi Light Artillery. Co. G. Federal Rolls of Prisoners of War: Captured at Blakely, AL, on 4/9/1865; Received at Ship Island, MS, on 4/15/1865. Transferred to Vicksburg, MS, for exchange on 5/1/1865; Exchanged at Camp Townsend, MS, on 5/6/1865.

Marson, William Pvt., 3rd Mississippi Infantry. Co. G. Federal Rolls of Prisoners of War: Captured at Gainesville, MS, on 9/12/1864; Received at Ship Island, MS, on 12/13/1864. Transferred to Vicksburg, MS, on 5/1/1865; Exchanged at Camp Townsend, MS, on 5/6/1865.

Martin, G.W. Pvt., 39th Mississippi Infantry. Co. F. Federal Rolls of Prisoners of War: Captured at Blakely, AL, on 4/9/1865; Received at Ship Island, MS, on 4/15/1865. Transferred to Vicksburg, MS, for exchange on 5/1/1865; Exchanged at Camp Townsend, MS, on 5/6/1865.

Martin, J.F. Pvt., 39th Mississippi Infantry. Co. E. Federal Rolls of Prisoners of War: Captured at Blakely, AL, on 4/9/1865; Received at Ship Island, MS, on 4/15/1865. Transferred to Vicksburg, MS, for exchange on 5/1/1865; Exchanged at Camp Townsend, MS, on 5/6/1865.

Martin, John P. Pvt., 39th Mississippi Infantry. Co. G. Federal Rolls of Prisoners of War: Captured at Blakely, AL, on 4/9/1865; Received at Ship Island, MS, on 4/15/1865. Transferred to Vicksburg, MS, for exchange on 5/1/1865; Exchanged at Camp Townsend, MS, on 5/6/1865.

Martin, Judson J. Pvt./Cpl., 1st Mississippi Light Artillery. Co. K. Federal Rolls of Prisoners of War: Captured at Blakely, AL, on 4/9/1865; Received at Ship Island, MS, on 4/15/1865. Transferred to Vicksburg, MS, for exchange on 5/1/1865; Exchanged at Camp Townsend, MS, on 5/6/1865.

Martin, L.B. Pvt., 4th Mississippi Infantry. Co. B. Federal Rolls of Prisoners of War: Captured at Blakely, AL, on 4/9/1865; Received at Ship Island, MS, on 4/15/1865. Transferred to Vicksburg, MS, for exchange on 5/1/1865; Exchanged at Camp Townsend, MS, on 5/6/1865.

Martin, Osqua C. Pvt., 7th Mississippi Battalion Infantry. Co. A. Federal Rolls of Prisoners of War: Captured at Blakely, AL, on 4/9/1865; Received at Ship Island, MS, on 4/15/1865. Transferred to Vicksburg, MS, for exchange on 5/1/1865; Exchanged at Camp Townsend, MS, on 5/6/1865. Confederate Pension Application dated 1916 on file at the Mississippi Department of Archives and History. Target Name: Martin, Louisa. County: Smith.

Martin, W.J. Sgt./2nd Lt., 36th Mississippi Infantry. Co. B. Federal Rolls of Prisoners of War: Captured at Blakely, AL, on 4/9/1865; Received at Ship Island, MS, on 4/15/1865. Transferred to Vicksburg, MS, for exchange on 4/28/1865; Confined at New Orleans, LA, on 4/30/1865. Exchanged at Camp Townsend, MS, on 5/6/1865.

Martin, William J. Pvt., 1st Mississippi Light Artillery. Co. K. Federal Rolls of Prisoners of War: Captured at Blakely, AL, on 4/9/1865; Received at Ship Island, MS, on 4/15/1865. Transferred to Vicksburg, MS, for exchange on 5/1/1865; Exchanged at Camp Townsend, MS, on 5/6/1865. Confederate Widows Pension Application dated 1916 on file at the Mississippi Department of Archives and History. Target Name: Martin, Eliza M. County: Hinds.

Mathews, W.B. Pvt., 1st Mississippi Light Artillery. Co. G. Federal Rolls of Prisoners of War: Captured at Blakely, AL, on 4/9/1865; Received at Ship Island, MS, on 4/15/1865. Transferred to Vicksburg, MS, for exchange on 5/1/1865; Exchanged at Camp Townsend, MS, on 5/6/1865.

Matkins, W.T. Pvt., 35th Mississippi Infantry. Co. C. Federal Rolls of Prisoners of War: Captured at Blakely, AL, on 4/9/1865; Received at Ship Island, MS, on 4/15/1865. Transferred to Vicksburg, MS, for exchange on 5/1/1865; Exchanged at Camp Townsend, MS, on 5/6/1865.

Matthews, J.B.T. Sgt., 4th Mississippi Infantry. Co. F. Federal Rolls of Prisoners of War: Captured at Blakely, AL, on 4/9/1865; Received at Ship Island, MS, on 4/15/1865. Transferred to Vicksburg, MS, for exchange on 5/1/1865; Exchanged at Camp Townsend, MS, on 5/6/1865.

Maxey, John J. Pvt., 8th Mississippi Cavalry. Co. B. Federal Rolls of Prisoners of War: Captured at Milton, FL, on 10/28/1864; Received at Ship Island, MS, on 12/13/1864. Transferred to Vicksburg, MS, for exchange on 5/1/1865; Exchanged at Camp Townsend, MS, on 5/6/1865.

Merphee, F.M. (AKA Murphree) Pvt., 4th Mississippi Infantry. Co. F. Federal Rolls of Prisoners of War: Captured at Blakely, AL, on 4/9/1865; Received at Ship Island, MS, on 4/15/1865. Transferred to Vicksburg, MS, for exchange on 5/1/1865; Exchanged at Camp Townsend, MS, on 5/6/1865.

Meyers, H.B. (AKA Myers) Pvt./Sgt., 39th Mississippi Infantry. Co. B. Federal Rolls of Prisoners of War: Captured at Blakely, AL, on 4/9/1865; Received at Ship Island, MS, on 4/15/1865. Transferred to Vicksburg, MS, for exchange on 5/1/1865; Exchanged at Camp Townsend, MS, on 5/6/1865.

Michaus, F.W. Pvt., Powers Cavalry Regiment. Co. B. Federal Rolls of Prisoners of War: Captured at Liberty, MS, on 11/16/1864; Received at Ship Island, MS, from New Orleans, LA, on 12/13/1864. Transferred to Vicksburg, MS, for exchange on 5/1/1865; Exchanged at Camp Townsend, MS, on 5/6/1865.

Middleton, R.H. Pvt./Sgt., 1st Mississippi Light Artillery. Co. B. Federal Rolls of Prisoners of War: Captured at Blakely, AL, on 4/9/1865; Received at Ship Island, MS, on 4/15/1865. Transferred to Vicksburg, MS, for exchange on 5/1/1865; Exchanged at Camp Townsend, MS, on 5/6/1865.

Miggins, William Pvt., 39th Mississippi Infantry. Co. B. Federal Rolls of Prisoners of War: Captured at Blakely, AL, on 4/9/1865; Received at Ship Island, MS, on 4/15/1865. Transferred to Vicksburg, MS, for exchange on 5/1/1865; Exchanged at Camp Townsend, MS, on 5/6/1865.

Miles, John (AKA Joshua) Pvt., 35th Mississippi Infantry. Co. G. Federal Rolls of Prisoners of War: Captured at Blakely, AL, on 4/9/1865; Received at Ship Island, MS, on 4/15/1865. Transferred to Vicksburg, MS, for exchange on 5/1/1865; Exchanged at Camp Townsend, MS, on 5/6/1865.

Miles, Wiley Pvt., 35th Mississippi Infantry. Co. G. Federal Rolls of Prisoners of War: Captured at Blakely, AL, on 4/9/1865; Received at Ship Island, MS, on 4/15/1865. Transferred to Vicksburg, MS, for exchange on 5/1/1865; Exchanged at Camp Townsend, MS, on 5/6/1865. Confederate Pension Application dated 1903 on file at the Mississippi Department of Archives and History. Target Name: Miles, Wiley. County: Webster. Also a Confederate Widows Pension on file dated 1910. Target Name: Miles, Clara. County: Webster.

Miller, Andrew J. Pvt./Cpl., 7th Mississippi Battalion Infantry. Co. D. Federal Rolls of Prisoners of War: Captured at Blakely, AL, on 4/9/1865; Received at Ship Island, MS, on 4/15/1865. Transferred to Vicksburg, MS, for exchange on 5/1/1865; Exchanged at Camp Townsend, MS, on 5/6/1865.

Miller, F.C. Pvt., 1st Mississippi Light Artillery. Co. K. Federal Rolls of Prisoners of War: Captured at Blakely, AL, on 4/9/1865; Received at Ship Island, MS, on 4/15/1865. Transferred to Vicksburg, MS, for exchange on 5/1/1865; Exchanged at Camp Townsend, MS, on 5/6/1865.

Miller, G.W. Pvt., 1st Mississippi Light Artillery. Co. D. Federal Rolls of Prisoners of War: Captured at Blakely, AL, on 4/9/1865; Received at Ship Island, MS, on 4/15/1865. Transferred to Vicksburg, MS, for exchange on 5/1/1865; Exchanged at Camp Townsend, MS, on 5/6/1865.

Miller, Henry E. Artificer/Pvt., 1st Mississippi Light Artillery. Co. I. Federal Rolls of Prisoners of War: Captured at Blakely, AL, on 4/9/1865; Received at Ship Island, MS, on 4/15/1865. Transferred to Vicksburg, MS, for exchange on 5/1/1865; Exchanged at Camp Townsend, MS, on 5/6/1865. Born: 1829. Died: 1885. Buried: Yazoo County, MS. Confederate Widows Pension Application dated 1925 on file at the Mississippi Department of Archives and History. Target Name: Miller, Caroline. County: Yazoo.

Millsap, Thomas E. Sgt./2nd Lt., 36th Mississippi Infantry. Co. G. Federal Rolls of Prisoners of War: Captured at Blakely, AL, on 4/9/1865; Received at Ship Island, MS, on 4/15/1865. Transferred to Vicksburg, MS, for exchange on 4/28/1865; Confined at New Orleans, LA, on 4/30/1865. Exchanged at Camp Townsend, MS, on 5/6/1865

Minga, Henry F. Pvt., 1st Mississippi Light Artillery. Co. D. Federal Rolls of Prisoners of War: Captured at Blakely, AL, on 4/9/1865; Received at Ship Island, MS, on 4/15/1865. Transferred to Vicksburg, MS, for exchange on 5/1/1865; Exchanged at Camp Townsend, MS, on 5/6/1865.

Minter, J.B. Pvt., 4th Mississippi Infantry. Co. H. Federal Rolls of Prisoners of War: Captured at Blakely, AL, on 4/9/1865; Received at Ship Island, MS, on 4/15/1865. Transferred to Vicksburg, MS, for exchange on 5/1/1865; Exchanged at Camp Townsend, MS, on 5/6/1865.

Mitchel, Charles T. (AKA Mitchell) Sgt./Pvt., 35th Mississippi Infantry. Co. F. Federal Rolls of Prisoners of War: Captured at Blakely, AL, on 4/9/1865; Received at Ship Island, MS, on 4/15/1865. Transferred to Vicksburg, MS, for exchange on 5/1/1865; Exchanged at Camp Townsend, MS, on 5/6/1865.

Mitchell, J.M. Pvt., 35th Mississippi Infantry. Co. C. Federal Rolls of Prisoners of War: Captured at Blakely, AL, on 4/9/1865; Received at Ship Island, MS, on 4/15/1865. Transferred to Vicksburg, MS, for exchange on 5/1/1865; Exchanged at Camp Townsend, MS, on 5/6/1865.

Mitchell, L.E. Pvt., 39th Mississippi Infantry. Co. I. Federal Rolls of Prisoners of War: Captured at Blakely, AL, on 4/9/1865; Received at Ship Island, MS, on 4/15/1865. Transferred to Vicksburg, MS, for exchange on 5/1/1865; Exchanged at Camp Townsend, MS, on 5/6/1865.

Mitchell, William W. (AKA W.M.) Pvt., 7th Mississippi Battalion Infantry. Co. E. Federal Rolls of Prisoners of War: Captured at Blakely, AL, on 4/9/1865; Received at Ship Island, MS, on 4/15/1865. Transferred to Vicksburg, MS, for exchange on 5/1/1865; Exchanged at Camp Townsend, MS, on 5/6/1865.

Mixon, J.H. Pvt., 7th Mississippi Battalion Infantry. Co. F. Federal Rolls of Prisoners of War: Captured at Blakely, AL, on 4/9/1865; Received at Ship Island, MS, on 4/15/1865. Transferred to Vicksburg, MS, for exchange on 5/1/1865; Exchanged at Camp Townsend, MS, on 5/6/1865.

Mixon, John H., Sr. Pvt., 7th Mississippi Battalion Infantry. Co. F. Federal Rolls of Prisoners of War: Captured at Blakely, AL, on 4/9/1865; Received at Ship Island, MS, on 4/15/1865. Transferred to Vicksburg, MS, for exchange on 5/1/1865; Exchanged at Camp Townsend, MS, on 5/6/1865. Confederate Widows Pension Application dated 1915 on file at the Mississippi Department of Archives and History. Target Name: Mixon, Martha J. County: Forrest.

Mobley, James R. Pvt., 35th Mississippi Infantry. Co. B. Federal Rolls of Prisoners of War: Captured at Blakely, AL, on 4/9/1865; Received at Ship Island, MS, on 4/15/1865. Transferred to Vicksburg, MS, for exchange on 5/1/1865; Exchanged at Camp Townsend, MS, on 5/6/1865.

Mobly, Ephraim M. (AKA Mobley) Pvt., 39th Mississippi Infantry. Co. C. Federal Rolls of Prisoners of War: Captured at Blakely, AL, on 4/9/1865; Received at Ship Island, MS, on 4/15/1865. Transferred to Vicksburg, MS, for exchange on 5/1/1865; Exchanged at Camp Townsend, MS, on 5/6/1865.

Monroe, J.P. Pvt., 39th Mississippi Infantry. Co. D. Federal Rolls of Prisoners of War: Captured at Blakely, AL, on 4/9/1865; Received at Ship Island, MS, on 4/15/1865. Transferred to Vicksburg, MS, for exchange on 5/1/1865; Exchanged at Camp Townsend, MS, on 5/6/1865.

Monroe, J.T. Pvt., 39th Mississippi Infantry. Co. __. Federal Rolls of Prisoners of War: Captured at Blakely, AL, on 4/9/1865; Received at Ship Island, MS, on 4/15/1865. Transferred to Vicksburg, MS, for exchange on 5/1/1865; Exchanged at Camp Townsend, MS, on 5/6/1865.

Moore, D.B. Cpl., 36th Mississippi Infantry. Co. __. Federal Rolls of Prisoners of War: Captured at Blakely, MS, on 4/9/1865; Received at Ship Island, MS, on 4/15/1865. Transferred to Vicksburg, MS, for exchange on 5/1/1865; Exchanged at Camp Townsend, MS, on 5/6/1865.

Moore, J.E. Pvt., 1st Mississipi Light Artillery. Co. K. Federal Rolls of Prisoners of War: Captured at Blakely, AL, on 4/9/1865; Received at Ship Island, MS, on 4/15/1865. Transferred to Vicksburg, MS, for exchange on 5/1/1865; Exchanged at Camp Townsend, MS, on 5/6/1865.

Moore, W.H. Pvt., 1st Mississippi Light Artillery. Co. ___. Federal Rolls of Prisoners of War: Captured at Blakely, AL, on 4/9/1865; Received at Ship Island, MS, on 4/15/1865. Transferred to Vicksburg, MS, for exchange on 5/1/186; Exchanged at Camp Townsend, MS, on 5/6/1865.

Morgan, William J. Pvt., 35th Mississippi Infantry. Co. K. Federal Rolls of Prisoners of War: Captured at Blakely, AL, on 4/9/1865; Received at Ship Island, MS, on 4/15/1865. Transferred to Vicksburg, MS, for exchange on 5/1/1865; Exchanged at Camp Townsend, MS, on 5/6/1865.

Morrel, Jackson Pvt./1st Lt., 36th Mississippi Infantry. Co. I. Federal Rolls of Prisoners of War: Captured at Blakely, AL, on 4/9/1865; Received at Ship Island, MS, on 4/15/1865. Transferred to Vicksburg, MS, for exchange on 4/28/1865; Confined at New Orleans, LA, on 4/30/1865. Exchanged at Camp Townsend, MS, on 5/6/1865.

Morris, Abner Butler Pvt., 1st Mississippi Light Artillery. Co. D. Federal Rolls of Prisoners of War: Captured at Blakely, AL, on 4/9/1865; Received at Ship Island, MS, on 4/15/1865. Transferred to Vicksburg, MS, for exchange on 5/1/1865; Exchanged at Camp Townsend, MS, on 5/6/1865. Confederate Widows Pension Application dated 1922 on file at the Mississippi Department of Archives and History. Target Name: Morris, Huanna. County: Lafayette.

Morris, C.L. Pvt., 39th Mississippi Infantry. Co. C. Federal Rolls of Prisoners of War: Captured at Blakely, AL, on 4/9/1865; Received at Ship Island, MS, on 4/15/1865. Transferred to Vicksburg, MS, for exchange on 5/1/1865; Exchanged at Camp Townsend, MS, on 5/6/1865.

Morris, J.C. Pvt., 4th Mississippi Infantry. Co. G. Federal Rolls of Prisoners of War: Captured at Blakely, AL, on 4/9/1865; Received at Ship Island, MS, on 4/15/1865. Transferred to Vicksburg, MS, for exchange on 5/1/1865; Exchanged at Camp Townsend, MS, on 5/6/1865.

Morris, James W. Pvt., 4th Mississippi Infantry. Co. G. Federal Rolls of Prisoners of War: Captured at Blakely, AL, on 4/9/1865; Received at Ship Island, MS, on 4/15/1865. Transferred to Vicksburg, MS, for exchange on 5/1/1865; Exchanged at Camp Townsend, MS, on 5/6/1865.

Morris, Luther A. Pvt., 35th Mississippi Infantry. Co. B. Federal Rolls of Prisoners of War: Captured at Blakely, AL, on 4/9/1865; Received at Ship Island, MS, on 4/15/1865. Transferred to Vicksburg, MS, for exchange on 5/1/1865; Exchanged at Camp Townsend, MS, on 5/6/1865.

Morse, J.N. Pvt., 1st Mississippi Light Artillery. Co. D. Federal Rolls of Prisoners of War: Captured at Blakely, AL, on 4/9/1865; Received at Ship Island, MS, on 4/15/1865. Transferred to Vicksburg, MS, for exchange on 5/1/1865; Exchanged at Camp Townsend, MS, on 5/6/1865.

Morse, James W. Pvt., 36th Mississippi Infantry. Co. F. Federal Rolls of Prisoners of War: Captured at Blakely, AL, on 4/9/1865; Received at Ship Island, MS, on 4/15/1865. Transferred to Vicksburg, MS, for exchange on 5/1/1865; Exchanged at Camp Townsend, MS, on 5/6/1865.

Morse, W.H. Pvt., 36th Mississippi Infantry. Co. __. Federal Rolls of Prisoners of War: Captured at Blakely, AL, on 4/9/1865; Received at Ship Island, MS, on 4/15/1865. Transferred to Vicksburg, MS, for exchange on 5/1/1865; Exchanged at Camp Townsend, MS, on 5/6/1865.

Mosley, Robert J. Pvt., 35th Mississippi Infantry. Co. A. Federal Rolls of Prisoners of War: Captured at Blakely, AL, on 4/9/1865; Received at Ship Island, MS, on 4/15/1865. Transferred to Vicksburg, MS, for exchange on 5/1/1865; Exchanged at Camp Townsend, MS, on 5/6/1865.

Mosley, William C. Pvt., 35th Mississippi Infantry. Co. A. Federal Rolls of Prisoners of War: Captured at Blakely, AL, on 4/9/1865; Received at Ship Island, MS, on 4/15/1865. Transferred to Vicksburg, MS, for exchange on 5/1/1865; Exchanged at Camp Townsend, MS, on 5/6/1865.

Murphy, William R. Pvt., 1st Mississippi Light Artillery. Co. G. Federal Rolls of Prisoners of War: Captured at Blakely, AL, on 4/9/1865; Received at Ship Island, MS, on 4/15/1865. Transferred to Vicksburg, MS, for exchange on 5/1/1865; Exchanged at Camp Townsend, MS, on 5/6/1865.

Murrell, J.D. Q.M. Sgt., 1st Mississippi Light Artillery. F & S. Federal Rolls of Prisoners of War: Captured at Blakely, AL, on 4/9/1865; Received at Ship Island, MS, on 4/15/1865. Transferred to Vicksburg, MS, for exchange on 5/1/1865; Exchanged at Camp Townsend, MS, on 5/6/1865.

Muse, J.S. Pvt., 39th Mississippi Infantry. Co. F. Federal Rolls of Prisoners of War: Captured at Blakely, AL, on 4/9/1865; Received at Ship Island, MS, on 4/15/1865. Transferred to Vicksburg, MS, for exchange on 5/1/1865; Exchanged at Camp Townsend, MS, on 5/6/1865.

Nations, F.M. Sgt., 4th Mississippi Infantry. Co. D. Federal Rolls of Prisoners of War: Captured at Blakely, AL, on 4/9/1865; Received at Ship Island, MS, on 4/15/1865. Transferred to Vicksburg, MS, for exchange on 5/1/1865; Exchanged at Camp Townsend, MS, on 5/6/1865.

Neal, A.J. Sgt./Pvt., 1st Mississippi Light Artillery. Co. F. Federal Rolls of Prisoners of War: Captured at Blakely, AL, on 4/9/1865; Received at Ship Island, MS, on 4/15/1865. Transferred to Vicksburg, MS, for exchange on 5/1/1865; Exchanged at Camp Townsend, MS, on 5/6/1865.

Neal, L.S. (AKA G.S.) Pvt., 8th Mississippi Cavalry. Co. G. Federal Rolls of Prisoners of War: Captured at Milton, FL, on 10/25/1864; Received at Ship Island, MS, on 12/13/1864. Transferred to Vicksburg, MS, for exchange on 5/1/1865; Exchanged at Camp Townsend, MS, on 5/6/1865.

Neely, John W. Pvt., 1st Mississippi Light Artillery. Co. G. Federal Rolls of Prisoners of War: Captured at Blakely, AL, on 4/9/1865; Received at Ship Island, MS, on 4/15/1865. Transferred to Vicksburg, MS, for exchange on 5/1/1865; Exchanged at Camp Townsend, MS, on 5/6/1865.

Neely, Samuel C. (AKA Neelly) Pvt., 1st Mississippi Light Artillery. Co. G. Federal Rolls of Prisoners of War: Captured at Blakely, AL, on 4/9/1865; Received at Ship Island, MS, on 4/15/1865. Transferred to Vicksburg, MS, for exchange on 5/1/1865; Exchanged at Camp Townsend, MS, on 5/6/1865. Born: 1832. Died: 1890. Buried: Warren County, MS.

Neil, William M. (AKA Neel) Pvt., 1st Mississippi Light Artillery. Cos. I & K. Federal Rolls of Prisoners of War: Captured at Blakely, AL, on 4/9/1865; Received at Ship Island, MS, on 4/15/1865. Transferred to Vicksburg, MS, for exchange on 5/1/1865; Exchanged at Camp Townsend, MS, on 5/6/1865.

Nelson, C. Pvt., 1st Mississippi Light Artillery. Co. I. Federal Rolls of Prisoners of War: Captured at Blakely, AL, on 4/9/1865; Received at Ship Island, MS, on 4/15/1865. Transferred to Vicksburg, MS, for exchange on 5/1/1865; Exchanged at Camp Townsend, MS, on 5/6/1865.

Nelson, Lemuel D. Pvt., 36th Mississippi Infantry. Co. I. Federal Rolls of Prisoners of War: Captured at Blakely, AL, on 4/9/1865; Received at Ship Island, MS, on 4/15/1865. Transferred to Vicksburg, MS, for exchange on 5/1/1865; Exchanged at Camp Townsend, MS, on 5/6/1865.

Nelson, T.P. Capt./Maj., 4th Mississippi Infantry. Co. G. Federal Rolls of Prisoners of War: Captured at Blakely, AL, on 4/9/1865; Received at Ship Island, MS, on 4/15/1865. Transferred to Vicksburg, MS, for exchange on 4/28/1865; Confined at New Orleans, LA, on 4/30/1865. Exchanged at Camp Townsend, MS, on 5/6/1865.

Newell, David Pvt., 35th Mississippi Infantry. Co. B. Federal Rolls of Prisoners of War: Captured at Blakely, AL, on 4/9/1865; Received at Ship Island, MS, on 4/15/1865. Transferred to Vicksburg, MS, for exchange on 5/1/1865; Exchanged at Camp Townsend, MS, on 5/6/1865.

Newell, John J. (AKA A.J.) Pvt., 35th Mississippi Infantry. Co. B. Federal Rolls of Prisoners of War: Captured at Blakely, AL, on 4/9/1865; Received at Ship Island, MS, on 4/15/1865. Transferred to Vicksburg, MS, for exchange on 5/1/1865; Exchanged at Camp Townsend, MS, on 5/6/1865.

Newman, C.R. Surgeon, 39th Mississippi Infantry. F & S. Federal Rolls of Prisoners of War: Captured at Blakely, AL, on 4/9/1865; Received at Ship Island, MS, on 4/15/1865. Transferred to Vicksburg, MS, for exchange on 4/28/1865; Confined at New Orleans, LA, on 4/30/1865. Exchanged at Camp Townsend, MS, on 5/6/1865.

Newman, Oscar S. Pvt., 1st Mississippi Light Artillery. Co. K. Federal Rolls of Prisoners of War: Captured at Blakely, AL, on 4/9/1865; Received at Ship Island, MS, on 4/15/1865. Transferred to Vicksburg, MS, for exchange on 5/1/1865; Exchanged at Camp Townsend, MS, on 5/6/1865.

Nichols, J.J. (AKA Nicholds) Pvt., 35th Mississippi Infantry. Co. C. Federal Rolls of Prisoners of War: Captured at Blakely, AL, on 4/9/1865; Received at Ship Island, MS, on 4/15/1865. Transferred to Vicksburg, MS, for exchange on 5/1/1865; Exchanged at Camp Townsend, MS, on 5/6/1865.

Nix, L.B. Pvt., 1st Mississippi Light Artillery. Co. G. Federal Rolls of Prisoners of War: Captured at Blakely, AL, on 4/9/1865; Received at Ship Island, MS, on 4/15/1865. Transferred to Vicksburg, MS, for exchange on 5/1/1865; Exchanged at Camp Townsend, MS, on 5/6/1865.

Nolans, W.T. (AKA W.M.) Sgt., 4th Mississippi Infantry. Co. __. Federal Rolls of Prisoners of War: Captured at Blakely, AL, on 4/9/1865; Received at Ship Island, MS, on 4/15/1865. Transferred to Vicksburg, MS, for exchange on 5/1/1865; Exchanged at Camp Townsend, MS, on 5/6/1865.

Norman, B.F. Pvt., 39th Mississippi Infantry. Co. D. Federal Rolls of Prisoners of War: Captured at Blakely, AL, on 4/9/1865; Received at Ship Island, MS, on 4/15/1865. Transferred to Vicksburg, MS, for exchange on 5/1/1865; Exchanged at Camp Townsend, MS, on 5/6/1865.

Norman, C.R. Pvt./Surgeon, 39th Mississippi Infantry. Co. G. Federal Rolls of Prisoners of War: Captured at Blakely, AL, on 4/9/1865; Received at Ship Island, MS, on 4/15/1865. Transferred to Vicksburg, MS, for exchange on 4/28/1865; Confined at New Orleans, LA, on 4/30/1865. Exchanged at Camp Townsend, MS, on 5/6/1865.

Norris, E.S. Pvt., 1st Mississippi Light Artillery. Co. G. Federal Rolls of Prisoners of War: Captured at Blakely, AL, on 4/9/1865; Received at Ship Island, MS, on 4/15/1865. Transferred to Vicksburg, MS, for exchange on 5/1/1865; Exchanged at Camp Townsend, MS, on 5/6/1865.

Norwood, William S. Pvt./Cpl., 4th Mississippi Infantry. Co. K. Federal Rolls of Prisoners of War: Captured at Blakely, AL, on 4/9/1865; Received at Ship Island, MS, on 4/15/1865. Transferred to Vicksburg, MS, for exchange on 5/1/1865; Exchanged at Camp Townsend, MS, on 5/6/1865. Buried: North Union Cemetery located in Attala County, MS.

O'Connor, Patrick Pvt., 1st Mississippi Light Artillery. Co. G. Federal Rolls of Prisoners of War: Captured at Blakely, AL, on 4/9/1865; Received at Ship Island, MS, on 4/15/1865. Transferred to Vicksburg, MS, for exchange on 5/1/1865; Exchanged at Camp Townsend, MS, on 5/6/1865.

O'Reilly, J.R.M. Pvt., 1st Mississippi Light Artillery.

Co. __. Federal Rolls of Prisoners of War: Captured at Blakely, AL, on 4/9/1865; Received at Ship Island, MS, on 4/15/1865. Transferred to Vicksburg, MS, for exchange on 5/1/1865; Exchanged at Camp Townsend, MS, on 5/6/1865.

O'Reilly, Thomas Pvt., 1st Mississippi Light Artillery. Co. G. Federal Rolls of Prisoners of War: Captured at Blakely, AL, on 4/9/1865; Received at Ship Island, MS, on 4/15/1865. Transferred to Vicksburg, MS, for exchange on 5/1/1865; Exchanged at Camp Townsend, MS, on 5/6/1865.

Oden, Elias M. Pvt., 35th Mississippi Infantry. Co. B. Federal Rolls of Prisoners of War: Captured at Blakely, AL, on 4/9/1865; Received at Ship Island, MS, on 4/15/1865. Transferred to Vicksburg, MS, for exchange on 5/1/1865; Exchanged at Camp Townsend, MS, on 5/6/1865.

Oden, George H. Pvt., 35th Mississippi Infantry. Co. B. Federal Rolls of Prisoners of War: Captured at Blakely, AL, on 4/9/1865; Received at Ship Island, MS, on 4/15/1865. Transferred to Vicksburg, MS, for exchange on 5/1/1865; Exchanged at Camp Townsend, MS, on 5/6/1865.

Oden, George W. 2nd Lt./Captain, 35th Mississippi Infantry. Co. B. Federal Rolls of Prisoners of War: Captured at Blakely, AL, on 4/9/1865; Received at Ship Island, MS, on 4/15/1865. Transferred to Vicksburg, MS, for exchange on 4/28/1865; Confined at New Orleans, LA, on 4/30/1865. Exchanged at Camp Townsend, MS, on 5/6/1865. Confederate Widows Pension Application dated 1917 on file at the Mississippi Department of Archives and History. Target Name: Oden, Berline K. County: Jones.

Oliver, Francis D. Sgt./Pvt., 35th Mississippi Infantry. Co. A. Federal Rolls of Prisoners of War: Captured at Blakely, AL, on 4/9/1865; Received at Ship Island, MS, on 4/15/1865. Transferred to Vicksburg, MS, for exchange on 5/1/1865; Exchanged at Camp Townsend, MS, on 5/6/1865.

Osteen, Thomas B. Pvt., 36th Mississippi Infantry. Co. B. Federal Rolls of Prisoners of War: Captured at Blakely, AL, on 4/9/1865; Received at Ship Island, MS, on 4/15/1865. Transferred to Vicksburg, MS, for exchange on 5/1/1865; Exchanged at Camp Townsend, MS, on 5/6/1865.

Overstreet, Daniel C. Pvt., 36th Mississippi Infantry. Co. I. Federal Rolls of Prisoners of War: Captured at Blakely, AL, on 4/9/1865; Received at Ship Island, MS, on 4/15/1865. Transferred to Vicksburg, MS, for exchange on 5/1/1865; Exchanged at Camp Townsend, MS, on 5/6/1865.

Owens, Louis (AKA Owen, W.L.) Pvt., 7th Mississippi Battalion Infantry. Co. C. Federal Rolls of Prisoners of War: Captured at Blakely, AL, on 4/9/1865; Received at Ship Island, MS, on 4/15/1865. Transferred to Vicksburg, MS, for exchange on 5/1/1865; Exchanged at Camp Townsend, MS, on 5/6/1865.

Pace, J.P. Pvt., 36th Mississippi Infantry. Co. F. Federal Rolls of Prisoners of War: Captured at Blakely, AL, on 4/9/1865; Received at Ship Island, MS, on 4/15/1865. Transferred to Vicksburg, MS, for exchange on 5/1/1865; Exchanged at Camp Townsend, MS, on 5/6/1865.

Pace, W. Pvt., 46th Mississippi Infantry. Co. __. Federal Rolls of Prisoners of War: Captured in MS on 12/6/1864; Received at Ship Island, MS, from New Orleans, LA, on 1/25/1865. Transferred to Vicksburg, MS, for exchange on 5/1/1865; Exchanged at Camp Townsend, MS, on 5/6/1865.

Page, A.M. Pvt., 35th Mississippi Infantry. Co. K. Federal Rolls of Prisoners of War: Captured at Blakely, AL, on 4/9/1865; Received at Ship Island, MS, on 4/15/1865. Transferred to Vicksburg, MS, for exchange on 5/1/1865; Exchanged at Camp Townsend, MS, on 5/6/1865.

Paramore, W.R. Pvt., 35th Mississippi Infantry. Co. C. Federal Rolls of Prisoners of War: Captured at Blakely, AL, on 4/9/1865; Received at Ship Island, MS, on 4/15/1865. Transferred to Vicksburg, MS, for exchange on 5/1/1865; Exchanged at Camp Townsend, MS, on 5/6/1865. Born: 1837 at Clayton County, MS. Died: 1911 at Kemp County, MS.

Park, G.W. Pvt., 1st Mississippi Light Artillery. Co. A. Federal Rolls of Prisoners of War: Captured at Blakely, AL, on 4/9/1865; Received at Ship Island, MS, on 4/15/1865. Transferred to Vicksburg, MS, for exchange on 5/1/1865; Exchanged at Camp Townsend, MS, on 5/6/1865.

Parker, Marquis L. Pvt., 7th Mississippi Battalion Infantry. Co. A. Federal Rolls of Prisoners of War: Captured at Blakely, AL, on 4/9/1865; Received at Ship Island, MS, on 4/15/1865. Transferred to Vicksburg, MS, for exchange on 5/1/1865; Exchanged at Camp Townsend, MS, on 5/6/1865.

Parker, P.H. (AKA O.H.) Pvt., 36th Mississippi Infantry. Co. F. Federal Rolls of Prisoners of War: Captured at Blakely, AL, on 4/9/1865; Received at Ship Island, MS, on 4/15/1865. Transferred to Vicksburg, MS, for exchange on 5/1/1865; Exchanged at Camp Townsend, MS, on 5/6/1865.

Parker, Willis J. (AKA M.J.) Pvt., 7th Mississippi Battalion Infantry. Co. B. Federal Rolls of Prisoners of War: Captured at Blakely, AL, on 4/9/1865; Received at Ship Island, MS, on 4/15/1865. Transferred to Vicksburg, MS, for exchange on 5/1/1865; Exchanged at Camp Townsend, MS, on 5/6/1865.

Parker, William Watson Pvt., 46th Mississippi Infantry. Co. G. Federal Rolls of Prisoners of War: Captured at Blakely, AL, on 4/9/1865; Received at Ship Island, MS, on 4/15/1865. Transferred to Vicksburg, MS, for exchange on 5/1/1865; Exchanged at Camp Townsend, MS, on 5/6/1865. Confederate Widows Pension Application dated 1903 on file at the Mississippi Department of Archives and History. Target Name: Parker, Harriet Jarina. County: Hinds.

Parks, G.W. Pvt., 35th Mississippi Infantry. Co. __. Federal Rolls of Prisoners of War: Captured at Blakely, AL, on 4/9/1865; Received at Ship Island, MS, on 4/15/1865. Transferred to Vicksburg, MS, for exchange on 5/1/1865; Exchanged at Camp Townsend, MS, on 5/6/1865.

Parks, J.P. Pvt., 39th Mississippi Infantry. Co. D. Federal Rolls of Prisoners of War: Captured at Blakely, AL, on 4/9/1865; Received at Ship Island, MS, on 4/15/1865. Transferred to Vicksburg, MS, for exchange on 5/1/1865; Exchanged at Camp Townsend, MS, on 5/6/1865.

Parish, John W. (AKA J.B.) Pvt., 35th Mississippi Infantry. Co. B. Federal Rolls of Prisoners of War: Captured at Blakely, AL, on 4/9/1865; Received at Ship Island, MS, on 4/15/1865. Transferred to Vicksburg, MS, for exchange on 5/1/1865; Exchanged at Camp Townsend, MS, on 5/6/1865.

Parrish, Benjamin James Pvt./Cpl., 35th Mississippi Infantry. Co. K. Federal Rolls of Prisoners of War: Captured at Blakely, AL, on 4/9/1865; Received at Ship Island, MS, on 4/15/1865. Transferred to Vicksburg, MS, for exchange on 5/1/1865; Exchanged at Camp Townsend, MS, on 5/6/1865. Confederate Widows Pension Application dated 1922 on file at the Mississippi Department of Archives and History. Target Name: Parrish, Lula E. County: Oktibbhea.

Partin, Charles P. Capt./Maj., 36th Mississippi Infantry. Co. C. Federal Rolls of Prisoners of War: Captured at Blakely, AL, on 4/9/1865; Received at Ship Island, MS, on 4/15/1865. Transferred to Vicksburg, MS, for exchange on 4/28/1865; Confined at New Orleans, LA, on 4/30/1865. Exchanged at Camp Townsend, MS, on 5/6/1865. Confederate Widows Pension Application dated 1916 on file at the Mississippi Department of Archives and History. Target Name: Partin, Almeda Jane. County: Newton.

Patterson, Isaac N. Pvt./Sgt., 4th Mississippi Infantry. Cos. I & H. Federal Rolls of Prisoners of War: Captured at Blakely, AL, on 4/9/1865; Received at Ship Island, MS, on 4/15/1865. Transferred to Vicksburg, MS, for exchange on 5/1/1865; Exchanged at Camp Townsend, MS, on 5/6/1865. Confederate Pension Application dated 1916 on file at the Mississippi Department of Archives and History. Target Name: Patterson, I.N. County: Calhoun.

Patterson, John T. Pvt./2nd Lt., 4th Mississippi Infantry. Co. I. Federal Rolls of Prisoners of War: Captured at Blakely, AL, on 4/9/1865; Received at Ship Island, MS, on 4/15/1865. Transferred to Vicksburg, MS, for exchange on 4/28/1865; Confined at New Orleans, LA, on 4/30/1865. Exchanged at Camp Townsend, MS, on 5/6/1865. Confederate Pension Application dated 1916 on file at the Mississippi Department of Archives and History. Target Name: Patterson, John T. County: Stone.

Patterson, W.H. Pvt., 1st Mississippi Light Artillery. Cos. F & I. Federal Rolls of Prisoners of War: Captured at Blakely, AL, on 4/9/1865; Received at Ship Island, MS, on 4/15/1865. Transferred to Vicksburg, MS, for exchange on 5/1/1865. Federal Rolls of Prisoners of War: Captured at Blakely, AL, on 4/9/1865; Received at Ship Island, MS, on 4/15/1865. Transferred to Vicksburg, MS, for exchange on 5/1/1865; Exchanged at Camp Townsend, MS, on 5/6/1865.

Patterson, W.P. (AKA N.P.) Pvt., 1st Mississippi Light Artillery. Co. __. Federal Rolls of Prisoners of War: Captured at Blakely, AL, on 4/9/1865; Received at Ship Island, MS, on 4/15/1865. Transferred to Vicksburg, MS, for exchange on 5/1/1865; Exchanged at Camp Townsend, MS, on 5/6/1865.

Patten, James R. Cpl./Pvt., 4th Mississippi Infantry. Co. D. Federal Rolls of Prisoners of War: Captured at Blakely, AL, on 4/9/1865; Received at Ship Island, MS, on 4/15/1865. Transferred to Vicksburg, MS, for exchange on 5/1/1865; Exchanged at Camp Townsend, MS, on 5/6/1865.

Patton, John Sgt./Lt., 1st Mississippi Light Artillery. Co. I. Federal Rolls of Prisoners of War: Captured at Blakely, AL, on 4/9/1865; Received at Ship Island, MS, on 4/15/1865. Transferred to Vicksburg, MS, for exchange on 4/28/1865; Confined at New Orleans, LA, on 4/30/1865; Exchanged at Camp Townsend, MS, on 5/6/1865.

Payne, George T. (AKA G.L.) Pvt., 1st Mississippi Light Artillery. Co. A. Federal Rolls of Prisoners of War: Captured at Blakely, AL, on 4/9/1865; Received at Ship Island, MS, on 4/15/1865. Transferred to Vicksburg, MS, for exchange on 5/1/1865; Exchanged at Camp Townsend, MS, on 5/6/1865.

Pearce, Levine (AKA Pierce) Cpl., 35th Mississippi Infantry. Co. G. Federal Rolls of Prisoners of War: Captured at Blakely, AL, on 4/9/1865; Received at Ship Island, MS, on 4/15/1865. Transferred to Vicksburg, MS, for exchange on 5/1/1865; Exchanged at Camp Townsend, MS, on 5/6/1865.

Penn, John A. Pvt., Powers Cavalry Regiment. Co. __. Federal Rolls of Prisoners of War: Captured near Clinton, LA, on 8/25/1864; Forwarded to Ship Island, MS, from New Orleans, LA, on 10/7/1864. Exchanged on 1/4/1865. Confederate Pension Application dated 1910 on file at the Mississippi Department of Archives and History. Target Name: Penn, John A. County: Lincoln. Also a Confederate Widows Pension Application dated 1922 on file. Target Name: Penn, Mrs. Jno.A. County: Lincoln.

Pepper, J.F. (AKA F.J.) Pvt., 1st Mississippi Light Artillery. Cos. B & K. Federal Rolls of Prisoners of War: Captured at Blakely, AL, on 4/9/1865; Received at Ship Island, MS, on 4/15/1865. Transferred to Vicksburg, MS, for exchange on 5/1/1865; Exchanged at Camp Townsend, MS, on 5/6/1865. Confederate Pension Application dated 1922 on file at the Mississippi Department of Archives and History. Target Name: Pepper, F.J. County: Yazoo.

Pepper, J.J. Pvt., 1st Mississippi Light Artillery. Cos. B & D. Federal Rolls of Prisoners of War: Captured at Blakely, AL, on 4/9/1865; Received at Ship Island, MS, on 4/15/1865. Transferred to Vicksburg, MS, for exchange on 5/1/1865; Exchanged at Camp Townsend, MS, on 5/6/1865.

Perkins, Melvin N. (AKA M.M.) Pvt./Cpl., 1st Mississippi Light Artillery. Cos. D & K. Federal Rolls of Prisoners of War: Captured at Blakely, AL, on 4/9/1865; Received at Ship Island, MS, on 4/15/1865. Transferred to Vicksburg, MS, for exchange on 5/1/1865; Exchanged at Camp Townsend, MS, on 5/6/1865.

Perkins, Than M. Pvt., 1st Mississippi Light Artillery. Co. K. Federal Rolls of Prisoners of War: Captured at Blakely, AL, on 4/9/1865; Received at Ship Island, MS, on 4/15/1865. Transferred to Vicksburg, MS, for exchange on 5/1/1865; Exchanged at Camp Townsend, MS, on 5/6/1865.

Permenter, James D. Pvt., 36th Mississippi Infantry. Co. H. Federal Rolls of Prisoners of War: Captured at Blakely, AL, on 4/9/1865; Received at Ship Island, MS, on 4/15/1865. Transferred to Vicksburg, MS, for exchange on 4/28/1865; Exchanged at Camp Townsend, MS, on 5/6/1865.

Philan, J.D. (AKA Phelan) Pvt., 46th Mississippi Infantry. Co. __. Federal Rolls of Prisoners of War: Captured at Blakely, AL, on 4/9/1865; Received at Ship Island, MS, on 4/15/1865. Transferred to Vicksburg, MS, for exchange on 5/1/1865; Exchanged at Camp Townsend, MS, on 5/6/1865.

Phillips, Green Pvt., 35th Mississippi Infantry. Co. __. Federal Rolls of Prisoners of War: Captured at Blakely, AL, on 4/9/1865; Received at Ship Island, MS, on 4/15/1865. Transferred to Vicksburg, MS, for

exchange on 5/1/1865; Exchanged at Camp Townsend, MS, on 5/6/1865.

Phillips, Zack Pvt., 35th Mississippi Infantry. Co. __. Federal Rolls of Prisoners of War: Captured at Blakely, AL, on 4/9/1865; Received at Ship Island, MS, on 4/15/1865. Transferred to Vicksburg, MS, for exchange on 5/1/1865; Exchanged at Camp Townsend, MS, on 5/6/1865.

Pickett, Seaborn R. Pvt., 1st Mississippi Light Artillery. Co. D. Federal Rolls of Prisoners of War: Captured at Blakely, AL, on 4/9/1865; Received at Ship Island, MS, on 4/15/1865. Transferred to Vicksburg, MS, for exchange on 5/1/1865; Exchanged at Camp Townsend, MS, on 5/6/1865.

Pierce, J.C. Pvt., 1st Mississippi Light Artillery. Co. D. Federal Rolls of Prisoners of War: Captured at Blakely, AL, on 4/9/1865; Received at Ship Island, MS, on 4/15/1865. Transferred to Vicksburg, MS, for exchange on 5/1/1865; Exchanged at Camp Townsend, MS, on 5/6/1865.

Pierce, W. Randal Pvt., 36th Mississippi Infantry. Co. A. Federal Rolls of Prisoners of War: Captured at Blakely, AL, on 4/9/1865; Received at Ship Island, MS, on 4/15/1865. Transferred to Vicksburg, MS, for exchange on 5/1/1865; Exchanged at Camp Townsend, MS, on 5/6/1865.

Pippin, Franklin G. Pvt., 1st Mississippi Light Artillery. Co. D. Federal Rolls of Prisoners of War: Captured at Blakely, AL, on 4/9/1865; Received at Ship Island, MS, on 4/15/1865. Transferred to Vicksburg, MS, for exchange on 5/1/1865; Exchanged at Camp Townsend, MS, on 5/6/1865.

Polk, John Pvt., 39th Mississippi Infantry. Cos. F & G. Federal Rolls of Prisoners of War: Captured at Blakely, AL, on 4/9/1865; Received at Ship Island, MS, on 4/15/1865. Transferred to Vicksburg, MS, for exchange on 5/1/1865; Exchanged at Camp Townsend, MS, on 5/6/1865.

Poole, J.M. Pvt., 35th Mississippi Infantry. Co. __. Federal Rolls of Prisoners of War: Captured at Blakely, AL, on 4/9/1865; Received at Ship Island, MS, on 4/15/1865. Transferred to Vicksburg, MS, for exchange on 5/1/1865; Exchanged at Camp Townsend, MS, on 5/6/1865.

Pope, Hugh Pvt., 35th Mississippi Infantry. Co. C. Federal Rolls of Prisoners of War: Captured at Blakely, AL, on 4/9/1865; Received at Ship Island, MS, on 4/15/1865. Transferred to Vicksburg, MS, for exchange on 5/1/1865; Exchanged at Camp Townsend, MS, on 5/6/1865.

Porter, James H. (AKA J.M.) Cpl., 39th Mississippi Infantry. Co. C. Federal Rolls of Prisoners of War: Captured at Blakely, AL, on 4/9/1865; Received at Ship Island, MS, on 4/15/1865. Transferred to Vicksburg, MS, for exchange on 5/1/1865; Exchanged at Camp Townsend, MS, on 5/6/1865.

Porter, John M. Pvt., 39th Mississippi Infantry. Co. C. Federal Rolls of Prisoners of War: Captured at Blakely, AL, on 4/9/1865; Received at Ship Island, MS, on 4/15/1865. Transferred to Vicksburg, MS, for exchange on 5/1/1865; Exchanged at Camp Townsend, MS, on 5/6/1865. Confederate Pension Application dated 1900 on file at the Mississippi Department of Archives and History. Target Name: Porter, John M. County: Hinds.

Porter, William Pvt., 4th Mississippi Infantry. Cos. F & I. Federal Rolls of Prisoners of War: Captured at Blakely, AL, on 4/9/1865; Received at Ship Island, MS, on 4/15/1865. Transferred to Vicksburg, MS, for exchange on 5/1/1865; Exchanged at Camp Townsend, MS, on 5/6/1865.

Powell, T.D. Pvt., 4th Mississippi Infantry. Co. E. Federal Rolls of Prisoners of War: Captured at Blakely, AL, on 4/9/1865; Received at Ship Island, MS, on 4/15/1865. Transferred to Vicksburg, MS, for exchange on 5/1/1865; Exchanged at Camp Townsend, MS, on 5/6/1865.

Price, Archibald Pvt., 36th Mississippi Infantry. Co. B. Federal Rolls of Prisoners of War: Captured at Blakely, AL, on 4/9/1865; Received at Ship Island, MS, on 4/15/1865. Transferred to Vicksburg, MS, for exchange on 5/1/1865; Exchanged at Camp Townsend, MS, on 5/6/1865.

Priggett, Alexander (AKA Pridget) Pvt., 39th Mississippi Infantry. Co. B. Federal Rolls of Prisoners of War: Captured at Blakely, AL, on 4/9/1865; Received at Ship Island, MS, on 4/15/1865. Transferred to Vicksburg, MS, for exchange on 5/1/1865; Exchanged at Camp Townsend, MS, on 5/6/1865.

Pritchard, Thomas J. Pvt., 1st Mississippi Light Artillery. Co. K. Federal Rolls of Prisoners of War: Captured at Blakely, AL, on 4/9/1865; Received at Ship Island, MS, on 4/15/1865. Transferred to Vicksburg, MS, for exchange on 5/1/1865; Exchanged at Camp Townsend, MS, on 5/6/1865.

Pruitt, R.K. (AKA Prewitt) Sgt./2nd Lt., 4th Mississippi Infantry. Co. __. Federal Rolls of Prisoners of War: Captured at Blakely, AL, on 4/9/1865; Received at Ship Island, MS, on 4/15/1865. Transferred to Vicksburg, MS, for exchange on 4/28/1865; Confined at New Orleans, LA, on 4/30/1865. Exchanged at Camp Townsend, MS, on 5/6/1865.

Quimby, John B. Pvt., 1st Mississippi Light Artillery. Co. B. Federal Rolls of Prisoners of War: Captured at Blakely, AL, on 4/9/1865; Received at Ship Island, MS, on 4/15/1865. Transferred to Vicksburg, MS, for exchange on 5/1/1865; Exchanged at Camp Townsend, MS, on 5/6/1865.

Raines, B.F. (AKA Rinns) Pvt., 1st Mississippi Light Artillery. Co. F. Federal Rolls of Prisoners of War: Captured at Blakely, AL, on 4/9/1865; Received at Ship Island, MS, on 4/15/1865. Transferred to Vicksburg, MS, for exchange on 5/1/1865; Exchanged at Camp Townsend, MS, on 5/6/1865.

Raley, Andrew J. Pvt., 7th Mississippi Battalion Infantry. Co. D. Federal Rolls of Prisoners of War: Captured at Blakely, AL, on 4/9/1865; Received at Ship Island, MS, on 4/15/1865. Transferred to Vicksburg, MS, for exchange on 5/1/1865; Exchanged at Camp Townsend, MS, on 5/6/1865.

Raley, Calvin C. Sgt./Pvt., 1st Mississippi Light Artillery. Co. D. Federal Rolls of Prisoners of War: Captured at Blakely, AL, on 4/9/1865; Received at Ship Island, MS, on 4/15/1865. Transferred to Vicksburg, MS, for exchange on 5/1/1865; Exchanged at Camp Townsend, MS, on 5/6/1865.

Rand, R.E. Pvt., 1st Mississippi Light Artillery. Co. __. Federal Rolls of Prisoners of War: Captured at Blakely, AL, on 4/9/1865; Received at Ship Island, MS, on 4/15/1865. Transferred to Vicksburg, MS, for exchange on 5/1/1865; Exchanged at Camp Townsend, MS, on 5/6/1865.

Rasberry, John T. Pvt., 1st Mississippi Light Artillery. Co. I. Federal Rolls of Prisoners of War: Captured at Blakely, AL, on 4/9/1865; Received at Ship Island, MS, on 4/15/1865. Transferred to Vicksburg, MS, for exchange on 5/1/1865; Exchanged at Camp Townsend, MS, on 5/6/1865.

Rassen, John (AKA Rosson, Rawson) Pvt., 46th Mississippi Infantry. Co. A. Federal Rolls of Prisoners of War: Captured at Blakely, AL, on 4/9/1865; Received at Ship Island, MS, on 4/15/1865. Transferred to Vicksburg, MS, for exchange on 5/1/1865; Exchanged at Camp Townsend, MS, on 5/6/1865.

Rawls, Benjamin F. Sgt./2nd Lt., 7th Mississippi Battalion Infantry. Co. B. Federal Rolls of Prisoners of War: Captured at Blakely, AL, on 4/9/1865; Received at Ship Island, MS, on 4/15/1865. Transferred to Vicksburg, MS, for exchange on 4/28/1865; Confined at New Orleans, LA, on 4/30/1865. Exchanged at Camp Townsend, MS, on 5/6/1865.

Ray, E. Pvt., 1st Mississippi Light Artillery. Co. B. Federal Rolls of Prisoners of War: Captured at Blakely, AL, on 4/9/1865; Received at Ship Island, MS, on 4/15/1865. Transferred to Vicksburg, MS, for exchange on 5/1/1865; Exchanged at Camp Townsend, MS, on 5/6/1865.

Ray, John F. Pvt., 1st Mississippi Light Artillery. Co. B. Federal Rolls of Prisoners of War: Captured at Blakely, AL, on 4/9/1865; Received at Ship Island, MS, on 4/15/1865. Transferred to Vicksburg, MS, for exchange on 5/1/1865; Exchanged at Camp Townsend, MS, on 5/6/1865. Confederate Widows Pension Application dated 1913 on file at the Mississippi Department of Archives and History. Target Name: Ray, Martha C. County—Madison.

Rayburn, W.R. (AKA Rayben, N.R.) Pvt., 39th Mississippi Infantry. Co. __. Federal Rolls of Prisoners of War: Captured at Blakely, AL, on 4/9/1865; Received at Ship Island, MS, on 4/15/1865. Transferred to Vicksburg, MS, for exchange on 5/1/1865; Exchanged at Camp Townsend, MS, on 5/6/1865.

Read, John L. (AKA Reed) Pvt., 35th Mississippi Infantry. Co. D. Federal Rolls of Prisoners of War: Captured at Blakely, AL, on 4/9/1865; Received at Ship Island, MS, on 4/15/1865. Transferred to Vicksburg, MS, for exchange on 5/1/1865; Exchanged at Camp Townsend, MS, on 5/6/1865.

Rear, W.T. (AKA Reed) Pvt., 46th Mississippi Infantry. Co. F. Federal Rolls of Prisoners of War: Captured in Alabama on 4/1/1865; Received at Ship Island, MS. Transferred to Vicksburg, MS, for exchange on 5/1/1865; Exchanged at Camp Townsend, MS, on 5/6/1865.

Reddell, I.F. Pvt., Powers Cavalry Regiment. Co. C. Federal Rolls of Prisoners of War: Captured at Liberty, MS, on 11/19/1864; Received at Ship Island, MS, from New Orleans, LA, on 12/13/1864. Transferred to Vicksburg, MS, for exchange on 5/1/1865; Exchanged at Camp Townsend, MS, on 5/6/1865.

Reddell, J.T. Pvt., Powers Cavalry Regiment. Co. C. Federal Rolls of Prisoners of War: Captured at Liberty, MS, on 11/19/1864; Received at Ship Island, MS, from New Orleans, LA, on 12/13/1864. Transferred to Vicksburg, MS, for exchange on 5/1/1865; Exchanged at Camp Townsend, MS, on 5/6/1865.

Reed, George Pvt., 35th Mississippi Infantry. Co. G. Federal Rolls of Prisoners of War: Captured at Blakely, AL, on 4/9/1865; Received at Ship Island, MS, on 4/15/1865. Transferred to Vicksburg, MS, for exchange on 5/1/1865; Exchanged at Camp Townsend, MS, on 5/6/1865.

Reed, Wiley W. (AKA Reid) Pvt., 35th Mississippi Infantry. Co. G. Federal Rolls of Prisoners of War: Captured at Blakely, AL, on 4/9/1865; Received at Ship Island, MS, on 4/15/1865. Transferred to Vicksburg, MS, for exchange on 5/1/1865; Exchanged at Camp Townsend, MS, on 5/6/1865.

Reese, A.H. Cpl./2nd Lt., 35th Mississippi Infantry. Co. C. Federal Rolls of Prisoners of War: Captured at Blakely, AL, on 4/9/1865; Received at Ship Island, MS, on 4/15/1865. Transferred to Vicksburg, MS, for exchange on 4/28/1865; Confined at New Orleans, LA, on 4/30/1865. Exchanged at Camp Townsend, MS, on 5/6/1865.

Reeves, J.B. (AKA Reaves) Pvt., 7th Mississippi Battalion Infantry. Co. F. Enlisted: 1862 at Quitman, MS. Federal Rolls of Prisoners of War: Captured at Blakely, AL, on 4/9/1865; Received at Ship Island, MS, on 4/15/1865. Transferred to Vicksburg, MS, for exchange on 5/1/1865; Exchanged at Camp Townsend, MS, on 5/6/1865. Wounded in the leg at Franklin, TN. Born: 1844 in Georgia. Pre-war occupation: Farmer. Married: N.M. Buchanan on 10/14/1869 in Jones County, MS. Children: 2. Post-war occupation: Farmer. Religion: Presbyterian. Died: 1913. Buried: Covington County, MS. Confederate Widows Pension Application dated 1916 on file at the Mississippi Department of Archives and History. Target Name: Reeves, Melissa. County: Covington.

Reid, Luther R. Pvt., 1st Mississippi Light Artillery. Co. G. Federal Rolls of Prisoners of War: Captured at Blakely, AL, on 4/9/1865; Received at Ship Island, MS, on 4/15/1865. Transferred to Vicksburg, MS, for exchange on 5/1/1865; Exchanged at Camp Townsend, MS, on 5/6/1865.

Reush, E.T. (AKA Kersh) Cpl., 39th Mississippi Infantry. Co. G. Federal Rolls of Prisoners of War: Captured at Blakely, AL, on 4/9/1865; Received at Ship Island, MS, on 4/15/1865. Transferred to Vicksburg, MS, for exchange on 5/1/1865; Exchanged at Camp Townsend, MS, on 5/6/1865.

Reynolds, C.T.W. Pvt., 1st Mississippi Light Artillery. Co. D. Federal Rolls of Prisoners of War: Captured at Blakely, AL, on 4/9/1865; Received at Ship Island, MS, on 4/15/1865. Transferred to Vicksburg, MS, for exchange on 5/1/1865; Exchanged at Camp Townsend, MS, on 5/6/1865.

Reynolds, Lewis Pvt., 7th Mississippi Battalion Infantry. Co. C. Federal Rolls of Prisoners of War: Captured at Blakely, AL, on 4/9/1865; Received at Ship Island, MS, on 4/15/1865. Transferred to Vicksburg, MS, for exchange on 5/1/1865; Exchanged at Camp Townsend, MS, on 5/6/1865.

Reynolds, T.C. (AKA I . C.) Pvt., 1st Mississippi Light Artillery. Co. I. Federal Rolls of Prisoners of War: Captured at Blakely, AL, on 4/9/1865; Received at Ship Island, MS, on 4/15/1865. Transferred to Vicksburg, MS, for exchange on 5/1/1865; Exchanged at Camp Townsend, MS, on 5/6/1865.

Reynolds, Thomas W. (AKA Eggleston, Stephen A.) Pvt., 1st Mississippi Light Artillery. Co. I. Federal Rolls of Prisoners of War: Captured at Blakely, AL, on 4/9/

1865; Received at Ship Island, MS, on 4/15/1865. Transferred to Vicksburg, MS, for exchange on 5/1/1865; Exchanged at Camp Townsend, MS, on 5/6/1865.

Rhodes, Samuel D. 2nd Lt., 39th Mississippi Infantry. Co. B. Federal Rolls of Prisoners of War: Captured at Blakely, AL, on 4/9/1865; Received at Ship Island, MS, on 4/15/1865. Transferred to Vicksburg, MS, for exchange on 4/28/1865; Confined at New Orleans, LA, on 4/30/1865. Exchanged at Camp Townsend, MS, on 5/6/1865.

Rhymes, James A. (AKA Rinns, Rimes) Pvt., 36th Mississippi Infantry. Co. B. Federal Rolls of Prisoners of War: Captured at Blakely, AL, on 4/9/1865; Received at Ship Island, MS, on 4/15/1865. Transferred to Vicksburg, MS, for exchange on 5/1/1865; Exchanged at Camp Townsend, MS, on 5/6/1865.

Richardson, Thomas Clark Pvt./Sgt., 1st Mississippi Light Artillery. Cos. F & I. Federal Rolls of Prisoners of War: Captured at Blakely, AL, on 4/9/1865; Received at Ship Island, MS, on 4/15/1865. Transferred to Vicksburg, MS, for exchange on 5/1/1865; Exchanged at Camp Townsend, MS, on 5/6/1865. Born: 1836. Died: 1904. Buried: Warren County, MS. Confederate Pension Application dated 1903 on file at the Mississippi Department of Archives and History. Target Name: Richardson, Thomas Clark. County: Warren. Also a Confederate Widows Pension Application dated 1916 on file. Target Name: Richardson, V.I. County: Warren.

Richardson, W.G. Pvt., 1st Mississippi Light Artillery. Co. I. Federal Rolls of Prisoners of War: Captured at Blakely, AL, on 4/9/1865; Received at Ship Island, MS, on 4/15/1865. Transferred to Vicksburg, MS, for exchange on 5/1/1865; Exchanged at Camp Townsend, MS, on 5/6/1865.

Richmond, J.S. Pvt., 1st Mississippi Light Artillery. Co F. Federal Rolls of Prisoners of War: Captured at Blakely, AL, on 4/9/1865; Received at Ship Island, MS, on 4/15/1865. Transferred to Vicksburg, MS, for exchange on 5/1/1865; Exchanged at Camp Townsend, MS, on 5/6/1865.

Riddell, J.E. Pvt., 4th Mississippi Infantry. Co. G. Federal Rolls of Prisoners of War: Captured at Blakely, AL, on 4/9/1865; Received at Ship Island, MS, on 4/15/1865. Transferred to Vicksburg, MS, for exchange on 5/1/1865; Exchanged at Camp Townsend, MS, on 5/6/1865.

Ridley, Robert C. Pvt./Sgt., 4th Mississippi Infantry. Co. A. Federal Rolls of Prisoners of War: Captured at Blakely, AL, on 4/9/1865; Received at Ship Island, MS, on 4/15/1865. Transferred to Vicksburg, MS, for exchange on 5/1/1865; Exchanged at Camp Townsend, MS, on 5/6/1865.

Rimes, James A. (AKA Rhymes) Pvt., 36th Mississippi Infantry. Co. B. Federal Rolls of Prisoners of War: Captured at Blakely, AL, on 4/9/1865; Received at Ship Island, MS, on 4/15/1865. Transferred to Vicksburg, MS, for exchange on 5/1/1865; Exchanged at Camp Townsend, MS, on 5/6/1865.

Riner, C.F. Pvt., 36th Mississippi Infantry. Co. __. Federal Rolls of Prisoners of War: Captured at Blakely, AL, on 4/9/1865; Received at Ship Island, MS, on 4/15/1865. Transferred to Vicksburg, MS, for exchange on 5/1/1865; Exchanged at Camp Townsend, MS, on 5/6/1865.

Rivers, H.P. Pvt., 1st Mississippi Light Artillery. Co. D. Federal Rolls of Prisoners of War: Captured at Blakely, AL, on 4/9/1865; Received at Ship Island, MS, on 4/15/1865. Transferred to Vicksburg, MS, for exchange on 5/1/1865; Exchanged at Camp Townsend, MS, on 5/6/1865.

Rivers, James S. Pvt., 36th Mississippi Infantry. Co. B. Federal Rolls of Prisoners of War: Captured at Blakely, AL, on 4/9/1865; Received at Ship Island, MS, on 4/15/1865. Transferred to Vicksburg, MS, for exchange on 5/1/1865; Exchanged at Camp Townsend, MS, on 5/6/1865.

Rivers, T.R. Pvt., 36th Mississippi Infantry. Co. __. Federal Rolls of Prisoners of War: Captured at Blakely, AL, on 4/9/1865; Received at Ship Island, MS, on 4/15/1865. Transferred to Vicksburg, MS, for exchange on 5/1/1865; Exchanged at Camp Townsend, MS, on 5/6/1865.

Roach, John D. Pvt., 1st Mississippi Light Artillery. Cos. A & F. Federal Rolls of Prisoners of War: Captured at Blakely, AL, on 4/9/1865; Received at Ship Island, MS, on 4/15/1865. Transferred to Vicksburg, MS, for exchange on 5/1/1865; Exchanged at Camp Townsend, MS, on 5/6/1865.

Robert, A.J. (AKA Roberts) Pvt., 46th Mississippi Infantry. Co. G. Federal Rolls of Prisoners of War: Captured at Blakely, AL, on 4/9/1865; Received at Ship Island, MS, on 4/15/1865. Transferred to Vicksburg, MS, for exchange on 5/1/1865; Exchanged at Camp Townsend, MS, on 5/6/1865.

Roberts, George W. Pvt., 1st Mississippi Light Artillery. Co. E. Federal Rolls of Prisoners of War: Captured at Blakely, AL, on 4/9/1865; Received at Ship Island, MS, on 4/15/1865. Transferred to Vicksburg, MS, for exchange on 5/1/1865; Exchanged at Camp Townsend, MS, on 5/6/1865.

Roberts, James S. Pvt./Cpl., 1st Mississippi Light Artillery. Co. I. Federal Rolls of Prisoners of War: Captured at Blakely, AL, on 4/9/1865; Received at Ship Island, MS, on 4/15/1865. Transferred to Vicksburg, MS, for exchange on 5/1/1865; Exchanged at Camp Townsend, MS, on 5/6/1865. Born: 1829. Died: 1901. Buried: Yazoo County, MS.

Roberts, Leroy Pvt., 1st Mississippi Light Artillery. Co. I. Federal Rolls of Prisoners of War: Captured at Blakely, AL, on 4/9/1865; Received at Ship Island, MS, on 4/15/1865. Transferred to Vicksburg, MS, for exchange on 5/1/1865; Exchanged at Camp Townsend, MS, on 5/6/1865.

Roberts, Walter J. Pvt./Sgt., 39th Mississippi Infantry. Co. C. Federal Rolls of Prisoners of War: Captured at Blakely, AL, on 4/9/1865; Received at Ship Island, MS, on 4/15/1865. Transferred to Vicksburg, MS, for exchange on 5/1/1865; Exchanged at Camp Townsend, MS, on 5/6/1865.

Robertson, H.H. Pvt., 4th Mississippi Infantry. Co. G. Federal Rolls of Prisoners of War: Captured at Blakely, AL, on 4/9/1865; Received at Ship Island, MS, on 4/15/1865. Transferred to Vicksburg, MS, for exchange on 5/1/1865; Exchanged at Camp Townsend, MS, on 5/6/1865.

Robertson, John W. (AKA Robinson) Pvt., 36th Mississippi Infantry. Co. G. Federal Rolls of Prisoners of War: Captured at Blakely, AL, on 4/9/1865; Received at Ship Island, MS, on 4/15/1865. Transferred to Vicksburg, MS, for exchange on 5/1/1865; Exchanged at Camp Townsend, MS, on 5/6/1865.

Robertson, William T. Sgt., 39th Mississippi Infantry. Co. C. Federal Rolls of Prisoners of War: Captured at Blakely, AL, on 4/9/1865; Received at Ship Island, MS, on 4/15/1865. Transferred to Vicksburg, MS, for exchange on 5/1/1865; Exchanged at Camp Townsend, MS, on 5/6/1865.

Robinett, William Pvt., 1st Mississippi Light Artillery. Co. F. Federal Rolls of Prisoners of War: Captured at Blakely, AL, on 4/9/1865; Received at Ship Island, MS, on 4/15/1865. Transferred to Vicksburg, MS, for exchange on 5/1/1865; Exchanged at Camp Townsend, MS, on 5/6/1865.

Robinson, L.D. Pvt., 1st Mississippi Light Artillery. Co. D. Federal Rolls of Prisoners of War: Captured at Blakely, AL, on 4/9/1865; Received at Ship Island, MS, on 4/15/1865. Transferred to Vicksburg, MS, for exchange on 5/1/1865; Exchanged at Camp Townsend, MS, on 5/6/1865.

Rodgers, James Pvt., 36th Mississippi Infantry. Co. F. Federal Rolls of Prisoners of War: Captured at Blakely, AL, on 4/9/1865; Received at Ship Island, MS, on 4/15/1865. Transferred to Vicksburg, MS, for exchange on 5/1/1865; Exchanged at Camp Townsend, MS, on 5/6/1865.

Rodgers, W.W. (AKA Rogers) Pvt., 39th Mississippi Infantry. Co. G. Federal Rolls of Prisoners of War: Captured at Blakely, AL, on 4/9/1865; Received at Ship Island, MS, on 4/15/1865. Transferred to Vicksburg, MS, for exchange on 5/1/1865; Exchanged at Camp Townsend, MS, on 5/6/1865.

Rodgers, William Pvt., 36th Mississippi Infantry. Co. F. Federal Rolls of Prisoners of War: Captured at Blakely, AL, on 4/9/1865; Received at Ship Island, MS, on 4/15/1865. Transferred to Vicksburg, MS, for exchange on 5/1/1865; Exchanged at Camp Townsend, MS, on 5/6/1865.

Rogers, G.R. Pvt., 4th Mississippi Infantry. Co. G. Federal Rolls of Prisoners of War: Captured at Blakely, AL, on 4/9/1865; Received at Ship Island, MS, on 4/15/1865. Transferred to Vicksburg, MS, for exchange on 5/1/1865; Exchanged at Camp Townsend, MS, on 5/6/1865.

Rogers, J.D. Pvt., 4th Mississippi Infantry. Co. G. Federal Rolls of Prisoners of War: Captured at Blakely, AL, on 4/9/1865; Received at Ship Island, MS, on 4/15/1865. Transferred to Vicksburg, MS, for exchange on 5/1/1865; Exchanged at Camp Townsend, MS, on 5/6/1865.

Rogers, W.H. Pvt., 4th Mississippi Infantry. Co. E. Federal Rolls of Prisoners of War: Captured at Blakely, AL, on 4/9/1865; Received at Ship Island, MS, on 4/15/1865. Transferred to Vicksburg, MS, for exchange on 5/1/1865; Exchanged at Camp Townsend, MS, on 5/6/1865.

Rowe, George W. Pvt., 35th Mississippi Infantry. Co. B. Federal Rolls of Prisoners of War: Captured at Blakely, AL, on 4/9/1865; Received at Ship Island, MS, on 4/15/1865. Transferred to Vicksburg, MS, for exchange on 5/1/1865; Exchanged at Camp Townsend, MS, on 5/6/1865.

Rowe, J.L. (AKA J.S.) Pvt., 1st Mississippi Light Artillery. Co. __. Federal Rolls of Prisoners of War: Captured at Blakely, AL, on 4/9/1865; Received at Ship Island, MS, on 4/15/1865. Transferred to Vicksburg, MS, for exchange on 5/1/1865; Exchanged at Camp Townsend, MS, on 5/6/1865.

Rowland, A.S. Pvt., 4th Mississippi Infantry. Cos. E & G. Federal Rolls of Prisoners of War: Captured at Blakely, AL, on 4/9/1865; Received at Ship Island, MS, on 4/15/1865. Transferred to Vicksburg, MS, for exchange on 5/1/1865; Exchanged at Camp Townsend, MS, on 5/6/1865.

Rumpt, J.W. Cpl./Sgt., 36th Mississippi Infantry. Co. G. Federal Rolls of Prisoners of War: Captured at Blakely, AL, on 4/9/1865; Received at Ship Island, MS, on 4/15/1865. Transferred to Vicksburg, MS, for exchange on 5/1/1865; Exchanged at Camp Townsend, MS, on 5/6/1865.

Runnells, James F. (AKA Runels) Pvt., 39th Mississippi Infantry. Co. F. Enlisted: 1862 at Siloam, MS. Federal Rolls of Prisoners of War: Captured at Blakely, AL, on 4/9/1865; Received at Ship Island, MS, on 4/15/1865. Transferred to Vicksburg, MS, for exchange on 5/1/1865; Exchanged at Camp Townsend, MS, on 5/6/1865. Born: 12/21/1844 to Elias Runnells and Patience Floyd Runnells at Simpson County, MS. Pre-war occupation: Farmer. Married: Lucinda Rankin on 2/15/1866 at Simpson County, MS. Children: 6. Religion: Protestant Methodist. Post-war occupation: Milling and Farming.

Rush, Benjamin F. 1st Lt./Captain, 35th Mississippi Infantry. Co. A. Federal Rolls of Prisoners of War: Captured at Blakely, AL, on 4/9/1865; Received at Ship Island, MS, on 4/15/1865. Transferred to Vicksburg, MS, for exchange on 4/28/1865; Confined at New Orleans, LA, on 4/30/1865. Exchanged at Camp Townsend, MS, on 5/6/1865.

Rush, E.T. Cpl., 39th Mississippi Infantry. Co. __. Federal Rolls of Prisoners of War: Captured at Blakely, AL, on 4/9/1865; Received at Ship Island, MS, on 4/15/1865. Transferred to Vicksburg, MS, for exchange on 5/1/1865; Exchanged at Camp Townsend, MS, on 5/6/1865.

Rush, James H. Sgt., 35th Mississippi Infantry. Co. A. Federal Rolls of Prisoners of War: Captured at Blakely, AL, on 4/9/1865; Received at Ship Island, MS, on 4/15/1865. Transferred to Vicksburg, MS, for exchange on 5/1/1865; Exchanged at Camp Townsend, MS, on 5/6/1865.

Rush, S.R. Pvt., 36th Mississippi Infantry. Co. C. Federal Rolls of Prisoners of War: Captured at Blakely, AL, on 4/9/1865; Received at Ship Island, MS, on 4/15/1865. Transferred to Vicksburg, MS, for exchange on 5/1/1865; Exchanged at Camp Townsend, MS, on 5/6/1865.

Russell, Franklin Pvt., 39th Mississippi Infantry. Co. D. Federal Rolls of Prisoners of War: Captured at Blakely, AL, on 4/9/1865; Received at Ship Island, MS, on 4/15/1865. Transferred to Vicksburg, MS, for exchange on 5/1/1865; Exchanged at Camp Townsend, MS, on 5/6/1865.

Russell, H.J. Pvt., 4th Mississippi Infantry. Co. H. Federal Rolls of Prisoners of War: Captured at Blakely, AL, on 4/9/1865; Received at Ship Island, MS, on 4/15/1865. Transferred to Vicksburg, MS, for exchange on 5/1/1865; Exchanged at Camp Townsend, MS, on 5/6/1865. Confederate Pension Application dated 1916 on file at the Mississippi Department of Archives and History. Target Name: Russell, H.J. County: Montgomery.

Russell, J.N. (AKA J.W.) Pvt./Cpl., 4th Mississippi Infantry. Cos. A & H. Federal Rolls of Prisoners of

War: Captured at Blakely, AL, on 4/9/1865; Received at Ship Island, MS, on 4/15/1865. Transferred to Vicksburg, MS, for exchange on 5/1/1865; Exchanged at Camp Townsend, MS, on 5/6/1865.

Russell, W.A. Sgt./Pvt., 36th Mississippi Infantry. Co. D. Federal Rolls of Prisoners of War: Captured at Blakely, AL, on 4/9/1865; Received at Ship Island, MS, on 4/15/1865. Transferred to Vicksburg, MS, for exchange on 5/1/1865; Exchanged at Camp Townsend, MS, on 5/6/1865.

Ryan, Z.J. Pvt./2nd Lt., 4th Mississippi Infantry. Co. F. Federal Rolls of Prisoners of War: Captured at Blakely, AL, on 4/9/1865; Received at Ship Island, MS, on 4/15/1865. Transferred to Vicksburg, MS, for exchange on 4/28/1865; Confined at New Orleans, LA, on 4/30/1865. Exchanged at Camp Townsend, MS, on 5/6/1865.

Sandifer, James C. Pvt., 1st Mississippi Light Artillery. Co. D. Federal Rolls of Prisoners of War: Captured at Blakely, AL, on 4/9/1865; Received at Ship Island, MS, on 4/15/1865. Transferred to Vicksburg, MS, for exchange on 5/1/1865; Exchanged at Camp Townsend, MS, on 5/6/1865. Born: 1842. Died: 1871. Buried: Holmes County, MS.

Sanford, B.O. Pvt., 46th Mississippi Infantry. Co. K. Federal Rolls of Prisoners of War: Captured at Blakely, AL, on 4/9/1865; Received at Ship Island, MS, on 4/15/1865. Transferred to Vicksburg, MS, for exchange on 5/1/1865; Exchanged at Camp Townsend, MS, on 5/6/1865.

Sanford, G.P. (AKA Stanford) Pvt., 46th Mississippi Infantry. Co. K. Federal Rolls of Prisoners of War: Captured at Blakely, AL, on 4/9/1865; Received at Ship Island, MS, on 4/15/1865. Transferred to Vicksburg, MS, for exchange on 5/1/1865; Exchanged at Camp Townsend, MS, on 5/6/1865.

Saucier, David Cpl./Sgt., 3rd Mississippi Infantry. Co. H. Federal Rolls of Prisoners of War: Captured at Pass Christian, MS, on 11/2/1864; Received at Ship Island, MS, from New Orleans, LA, on 12/13/1864. Transferred to Vicksburg, MS, for exchange on 5/1/1865; Exchanged at Camp Townsend, MS, on 5/6/1865.

Saunders, Maston Rush Artificer, 1st Mississippi Light Artillery. Co. A. Federal Rolls of Prisoners of War: Captured at Blakely, AL, on 4/9/1865; Received at Ship Island, MS, on 4/15/1865. Transferred to Vicksburg, MS, for exchange on 5/1/1865; Exchanged at Camp Townsend, MS, on 5/6/1865.

Scarborough, Richmond C. Cpl./Pvt., 36th Mississippi Infantry. Co. I. Federal Rolls of Prisoners of War: Captured at Blakely, AL, on 4/9/1865; Received at Ship Island, MS, on 4/15/1865. Transferred to Vicksburg, MS, for exchange on 5/1/1865; Exchanged at Camp Townsend, MS, on 5/6/1865.

Scott, Almanzor W. (AKA A.U.) Pvt./Sgt., 36th Mississippi Infantry. Co. A. Federal Rolls of Prisoners of War: Captured at Blakely, AL, on 4/9/1865; Received at Ship Island, MS, on 4/15/1865. Transferred to Vicksburg, MS, for exchange on 5/1/1865; Exchanged at Camp Townsend, MS, on 5/6/1865.

Scott, E.W. Pvt., 1st Mississippi Light Artillery. Co. Cowan's. Federal Rolls of Prisoners of War: Captured at Blakely, AL, on 4/9/1865; Received at Ship Island, MS, on 4/15/1865. Transferred to Vicksburg, MS, for exchange on 5/1/1865; Exchanged at Camp Townsend, MS, on 5/6/1865.

Scott, George W. Pvt., 1st Mississippi Light Artillery. Cos. I & K. Federal Rolls of Prisoners of War: Captured at Blakely, AL, on 4/9/1865; Received at Ship Island, MS, on 4/15/1865. Transferred to Vicksburg, MS, for exchange on 5/1/1865; Exchanged at Camp Townsend, MS, on 5/6/1865.

Scott, J.J. Pvt., 1st Mississippi Light Artillery. Co. D. Federal Rolls of Prisoners of War: Captured at Blakely, AL, on 4/9/1865; Received at Ship Island, MS, on 4/15/1865. Transferred to Vicksburg, MS, for exchange on 5/1/1865; Exchanged at Camp Townsend, MS, on 5/6/1865.

Scott, W.P. Pvt., 35th Mississippi Infantry. Co. ___. Federal Rolls of Prisoners of War: Captured at Blakely, AL, on 4/9/1865; Received at Ship Island, MS, on 4/15/1865. Transferred to Vicksburg, MS, for exchange on 5/1/1865; Exchanged at Camp Townsend, MS, on 5/6/1865.

Scott, William R. Pvt., 1st Mississippi Light Artillery. Co. K. Federal Rolls of Prisoners of War: Captured at Blakely, AL, on 4/9/1865; Received at Ship Island, MS, on 4/15/1865. Transferred to Vicksburg, MS, for exchange on 5/1/1865; Exchanged at Camp Townsend, MS, on 5/6/1865.

Scrimpshire, N.M.B. (AKA Srumpshire) Pvt., 7th Mississippi Battalion Infantry. Co. E. Federal Rolls of Prisoners of War: Captured at Blakely, AL, on 4/9/1865; Received at Ship Island, MS, on 4/15/1865. Transferred to Vicksburg, MS, for exchange on 5/1/1865; Exchanged at Camp Townsend, MS, on 5/6/1865. Confederate Pension Application dated 1900 on file at the Mississippi Department of Archives and History. Target Name: Scrimpshire, N.B. County: Clarke.

Selby, Daniel H. (AKA Selly) Pvt., 35th Mississippi Infantry. Co. A. Federal Rolls of Prisoners of War: Captured at Blakely, AL, on 4/9/1865; Received at Ship Island, MS, on 4/15/1865. Transferred to Vicksburg, MS, for exchange on 5/1/1865; Exchanged at Camp Townsend, MS, on 5/6/1865. Confederate Widows Pension Application dated 1924 on file at the Mississippi Department of Archives and History. Target Name: Selby, Elizabeth H. County: Yazoo.

Selby, J.H. Pvt., 2nd Mississippi Militia (State Troops). Co. D. Federal Rolls of Prisoners of War: Captured near Mobile, AL, on 12/6/1864; Received at Ship Island, MS, from New Orleans, LA, on 1/25/1864. Transferred to Vicksburg, MS, for exchange on 5/1/1865; Exchanged at Camp Townsend, MS, on 5/6/1865.

Selby, William C. Pvt./Sgt., 35th Mississippi Infantry. Co. A. Federal Rolls of Prisoners of War: Captured at Blakely, AL, on 4/9/1865; Received at Ship Island, MS, on 4/15/1865. Transferred to Vicksburg, MS, for exchange on 5/1/1865; Exchanged at Camp Townsend, MS, on 5/6/1865. Confederate Pension Application dated 1916 on file at the Mississippi Department of Archives and History. Target Name: Selby, W.C. County: Yazoo.

Selina, H.B. (AKA Selma) Pvt., 36th Mississippi Infantry. Co. ___. Federal Rolls of Prisoners of War: Captured at Blakely, AL, on 4/9/1865; Received at Ship Island, MS, on 4/15/1865. Transferred to Vicksburg, MS, for exchange on 5/1/1865; Exchanged at Camp Townsend, MS, on 5/6/1865.

Sexton, John F. Pvt., 1st Mississippi Light Artillery.

Co. F. Federal Rolls of Prisoners of War: Captured at Blakely, AL, on 4/9/1865; Received at Ship Island, MS, on 4/15/1865. Transferred to Vicksburg, MS, for exchange on 5/1/1865; Exchanged at Camp Townsend, MS, on 5/6/1865.

Shaffer, G.W. Pvt., 35th Mississippi Infantry. Co. G. Federal Rolls of Prisoners of War: Captured at Blakely, AL, on 4/9/1865; Received at Ship Island, MS, on 4/15/1865. Transferred to Vicksburg, MS, for exchange on 5/1/1865; Exchanged at Camp Townsend, MS, on 5/6/1865.

Shaffer, John F. Pvt./Cpl., 35th Mississippi Infantry. Co. C. Federal Rolls of Prisoners of War: Captured at Blakely, AL, on 4/9/1865; Received at Ship Island, MS, on 4/15/1865. Transferred to Vicksburg, MS, for exchange on 5/1/1865; Exchanged at Camp Townsend, MS, on 5/6/1865.

Shaw, John A. Pvt., 46th Mississippi Infantry. Co. A. Federal Rolls of Prisoners of War: Captured at Blakely, AL, on 4/9/1865; Received at Ship Island, MS, on 4/15/1865. Transferred to Vicksburg, MS, for exchange on 5/1/1865; Exchanged at Camp Townsend, MS, on 5/6/1865.

Sheilds, John W. Pvt., 35th Mississippi Infantry. Co. D. Federal Rolls of Prisoners of War: Captured at Blakely, AL, on 4/9/1865; Received at Ship Island, MS, on 4/15/1865. Transferred to Vicksburg, MS, for exchange on 5/1/1865; Exchanged at Camp Townsend, MS, on 5/6/1865.

Shelton, Henry M. Cpl./Sgt., 1st Mississippi Light Artillery. Co. D. Federal Rolls of Prisoners of War: Captured at Blakely, AL, on 4/9/1865; Received at Ship Island, MS, on 4/15/1865. Transferred to Vicksburg, MS, for exchange on 5/1/1865; Exchanged at Camp Townsend, MS, on 5/6/1865. Born: 1844. Died: 1917. Buried: Gurley Cemetery located at Gurley, AL.

Sheppard, T.G. Pvt., 1st Mississippi Light Artillery. Co. D. Federal Rolls of Prisoners of War: Captured at Blakely, AL, on 4/9/1865; Received at Ship Island, MS, on 4/15/1865. Transferred to Vicksburg, MS, for exchange on 5/1/1865; Exchanged at Camp Townsend, MS, on 5/6/1865.

Sherdin, W.A. Pvt., 35th Mississippi Infantry. Co. C. Federal Rolls of Prisoners of War: Captured at Blakely, AL, on 4/9/1865; Received at Ship Island, MS, on 4/15/1865. Transferred to Vicksburg, MS, for exchange on 5/1/1865; Exchanged at Camp Townsend, MS, on 5/6/1865.

Sheron, R.A. (AKA Shearon, Sherron) Pvt., 36th Mississippi Infantry. Co. C. Federal Rolls of Prisoners of War: Captured at Blakely, AL, on 4/9/1865; Received at Ship Island, MS, on 4/15/1865. Transferred to Vicksburg, MS, for exchange on 5/1/1865; Exchanged at Camp Townsend, MS, on 5/6/1865.

Sherrod, W. Pvt., 35th Mississippi Infantry. Co. I. Federal Rolls of Prisoners of War: Captured at Blakely, AL, on 4/9/1865; Received at Ship Island, MS, on 4/15/1865. Transferred to Vicksburg, MS, for exchange on 5/1/1865; Exchanged at Camp Townsend, MS, on 5/6/1865.

Sherwood, J.J. Pvt., 7th Mississippi Battalion Infantry. Co. __. Federal Rolls of Prisoners of War: Captured at Blakely, AL, on 4/9/1865; Received at Ship Island, MS, on 4/15/1865. Transferred to Vicksburg, MS, for exchange on 5/1/1865; Exchanged at Camp Townsend, MS, on 5/6/1865.

Shields, S.N. Pvt., 1st Mississippi Light Artillery. Co. __. Federal Rolls of Prisoners of War: Captured at Blakely, AL, on 4/9/1865; Received at Ship Island, MS, on 4/15/1865. Transferred to Vicksburg, MS, for exchange on 5/1/1865; Exchanged at Camp Townsend, MS, on 5/6/1865.

Shipley, Thomas J. Sgt./Pvt., 36th Mississippi Infantry. Co. H. Federal Rolls of Prisoners of War: Captured at Blakely, AL, on 4/9/1865; Received at Ship Island, MS, on 4/15/1865. Transferred to Vicksburg, MS, for exchange on 5/1/1865; Exchanged at Camp Townsend, MS, on 5/6/1865.

Shiver, Ed.E. (AKA Sluter, Slude) Pvt., 35th Mississippi Infantry. Co. H. Federal Rolls of Prisoners of War: Captured at Blakely, AL, on 4/9/1865; Received at Ship Island, MS, on 4/15/1865. Transferred to Vicksburg, MS, for exchange on 5/1/1865; Exchanged at Camp Townsend, MS, on 5/6/1865.

Shoemaker, Benjamin Pvt., 46th Mississippi Infantry. Co. E. Federal Rolls of Prisoners of War: Captured at Blakely, AL, on 4/9/1865; Received at Ship Island, MS, on 4/15/1865. Transferred to Vicksburg, MS, for exchange on 5/1/1865; Exchanged at Camp Townsend, MS, on 5/6/1865.

Shoemaker, D. Pvt., 46th Mississippi Infantry. Co. E. Federal Rolls of Prisoners of War: Captured at Blakely, AL, on 4/9/1865; Received at Ship Island, MS, on 4/15/1865. Transferred to Vicksburg, MS, for exchange on 5/1/1865; Exchanged at Camp Townsend, MS, on 5/6/1865.

Simons, M.B. Pvt., 2nd Mississippi Cavalry. Co. __. Federal Rolls of Prisoners of War: Captured at East Baton Rouge, LA, on 12/13/1864; Received at Ship Island, MS, from New Orleans, LA, on 1/25/1865. Transferred to Vicksburg, MS, for exchange on 5/1/1865; Exchanged at Camp Townsend, MS, on 5/6/1865.

Sims, C.A. Pvt., 39th Mississippi Infantry. Co. D. Federal Rolls of Prisoners of War: Captured at Blakely, AL, on 4/9/1865; Received at Ship Island, MS, on 4/15/1865. Transferred to Vicksburg, MS, for exchange on 5/1/1865; Exchanged at Camp Townsend, MS, on 5/6/1865.

Sims, G.R. Pvt., 39th Mississippi Infantry. Co. D. Federal Rolls of Prisoners of War: Captured at Blakely, AL, on 4/9/1865; Received at Ship Island, MS, on 4/15/1865. Transferred to Vicksburg, MS, for exchange on 5/1/1865; Exchanged at Camp Townsend, MS, on 5/6/1865. Confederate Pension Application dated 1916 on file at the Mississippi Department of Archives and History. Target Name: Sims, G.R. County: Newton.

Sims, J.H. Pvt., 46th Mississippi Infantry. Co. G. Federal Rolls of Prisoners of War: Captured at Blakely, AL, on 4/9/1865; Received at Ship Island, MS, on 4/15/1865. Disposition unknown.

Singleton, J.E. Pvt., 46th Mississippi Infantry. Co. __. Federal Rolls of Prisoners of War: Captured at Blakely, AL, on 4/9/1865; Received at Ship Island, MS, on 4/15/1865. Transferred to Vicksburg, MS, for exchange on 5/1/1865; Exchanged at Camp Townsend, MS, on 5/6/1865.

Skinner, P.J. Pvt., 1st Mississippi Light Artillery. Co. I. Federal Rolls of Prisoners of War: Captured at Blakely, AL, on 4/9/1865; Received at Ship Island, MS, on 4/15/1865. Transferred to Vicksburg, MS, for

exchange on 5/1/1865; Exchanged at Camp Townsend, MS, on 5/6/1865.

Slay, Nathan G. (AKA H.G.) Pvt./Sgt., 36th Mississippi Infantry. Co. B. Federal Rolls of Prisoners of War: Captured at Blakely, AL, on 4/9/1865; Received at Ship Island, MS, on 4/15/1865. Transferred to Vicksburg, MS, for exchange on 5/1/1865; Exchanged at Camp Townsend, MS, on 5/6/1865.

Sluter, E.E. (AKA Sluder) Pvt., 35th Mississippi Infantry. Co. H. Federal Rolls of Prisoners of War: Captured at Blakely, AL, on 4/9/1865; Received at Ship Island, MS, on 4/15/1865. Transferred to Vicksburg, MS, for exchange on 5/1/1865; Exchanged at Camp Townsend, MS, on 5/6/1865.

Smith, A.V. Pvt., 1st Mississippi Light Artillery. Co. F. Federal Rolls of Prisoners of War: Captured at Blakely, AL, on 4/9/1865; Received at Ship Island, MS, on 4/15/1865. Transferred to Vicksburg, MS, for exchange on 5/1/1865; Exchanged at Camp Townsend, MS, on 5/6/1865.

Smith, Angus W. Pvt., 1st Mississippi Light Artillery. Cos. E & K. Federal Rolls of Prisoners of War: Captured at Blakely, AL, on 4/9/1865; Received at Ship Island, MS, on 4/15/1865. Transferred to Vicksburg, MS, for exchange on 5/1/1865; Exchanged at Camp Townsend, MS, on 5/6/1865. Born: 1843. Died: 1928. Buried: Jefferson County, MS.

Smith, Bailey H. Pvt., 36th Mississippi Infantry. Co. A. Federal Rolls of Prisoners of War: Captured at Blakely, AL, on 4/9/1865; Received at Ship Island, MS, on 4/15/1865. Transferred to Vicksburg, MS, for exchange on 5/1/1865; Exchanged at Camp Townsend, MS, on 5/6/1865.

Smith, Benjamin L. Pvt., 35th Mississippi Infantry. Co. A. Federal Rolls of Prisoners of War: Captured at Blakely, AL, on 4/9/1865; Received at Ship Island, MS, on 4/15/1865. Transferred to Vicksburg, MS, for exchange on 5/1/1865; Exchanged at Camp Townsend, MS, on 5/6/1865.

Smith, Daniel Pvt., 39th Mississippi Infantry. Co. A. Federal Rolls of Prisoners of War: Captured at Blakely, AL, on 4/9/1865; Received at Ship Island, MS, on 4/15/1865. Transferred to Vicksburg, MS, for exchange on 5/1/1865; Exchanged at Camp Townsend, MS, on 5/6/1865.

Smith, Eson A., Sr. Pvt., 7th Mississippi Battalion Infantry. Co. F. Federal Rolls of Prisoners of War: Captured at Blakely, AL, on 4/9/1865; Received at Ship Island, MS, on 4/15/1865. Transferred to Vicksburg, MS, for exchange on 5/1/1865; Exchanged at Camp Townsend, MS, on 5/6/1865.

Smith, Irwin Pvt., Mississippi Militia. Co. F. Federal Rolls of Prisoners of War: Captured at Franklin, MS, on 11/18/1864; Received at Ship Island, MS, from New Orleans, LA, on 12/13/1864. Transferred to Vicksburg, MS, for exchange on 5/1/1865; Exchanged at Camp Townsend, MS, on 5/6/1865.

Smith, J.A. Pvt./Cpl., 1st Mississippi Light Artillery. Co. F. Federal Rolls of Prisoners of War: Captured at Blakely, AL, on 4/9/1865; Received at Ship Island, MS, on 4/15/1865. Transferred to Vicksburg, MS, for exchange on 5/1/1865; Exchanged at Camp Townsend, MS, on 5/6/1865.

Smith, J.M. (AKA J.N.) Pvt., 39th Mississippi Infantry. Co. A. Enlisted: 1862 at Jackson, MS. Federal Rolls of Prisoners of War: Captured at Blakely, AL, on 4/9/1865; Received at Ship Island, MS, on 4/15/1865. Transferred to Vicksburg, MS, for exchange on 5/1/1865; Exchanged at Camp Townsend, MS, on 5/6/1865. Born: 1/20/1842 in North Carolina to Daniel Smith and Nancy Wilkinson Smith. Pre-war occupation: Farmer. Married: Ellen McRaney in 1870 at Covington County, MS. Children: 7. Religion: Presbyterian. Post-war occupation: Farmer.

Smith, J.R. Pvt., 7th Mississippi Battalion Infantry. Co. A. Federal Rolls of Prisoners of War: Captured at Blakely, AL, on 4/9/1865; Received at Ship Island, MS, on 4/15/1865. Transferred to Vicksburg, MS, for exchange on 5/1/1865; Exchanged at Camp Townsend, MS, on 5/6/1865.

Smith, James W. Pvt., 35th Mississippi Infantry. Co. H. Federal Rolls of Prisoners of War: Captured at Blakely, AL, on 4/9/1865; Received at Ship Island, MS, on 4/15/1865. Transferred to Vicksburg, MS, for exchange on 5/1/1865; Exchanged at Camp Townsend, MS, on 5/6/1865.

Smith, Martin Thomas (AKA Marin) 2nd Cpl./Sgt., 1st Mississippi Light Artillery. Co. B. Federal Rolls of Prisoners of War: Captured at Blakely, AL, on 4/9/1865; Received at Ship Island, MS, on 4/15/1865. Transferred to Vicksburg, MS, for exchange on 5/1/1865; Exchanged at Camp Townsend, MS, on 5/6/1865. Born: 1833. Died: 1914. Buried: Yazoo County, MS. Confederate Widows Pension Application dated 1924 on file at the Mississippi Department of Archives and History. Target Name: Smith, Emily M. County: Yazoo.

Smith, Moutford Street Pvt., 7th Mississippi Infantry. Co. E. Federal Rolls of Prisoners of War: Captured at Blakely, AL, on 4/9/1865; Received at Ship Island, MS, on 4/15/1865. Transferred to Vicksburg, MS, for exchange on 5/1/1865; Exchanged at Camp Townsend, MS, on 5/6/1865.

Smith, S. Pvt., 1st Mississippi Light Artillery. Co. F. Federal Rolls of Prisoners of War: Captured at Blakely, AL, on 4/9/1865; Received at Ship Island, MS, on 4/15/1865. Transferred to Vicksburg, MS, for exchange on 5/1/1865; Exchanged at Camp Townsend, MS, on 5/6/1865.

Smith, Samuel G. Sgt., 1st Mississippi Light Artillery. Co. I. Federal Rolls of Prisoners of War: Captured at Blakely, AL, on 4/9/1865; Received at Ship Island, MS, on 4/15/1865. Transferred to Vicksburg, MS, for exchange on 5/1/1865; Exchanged at Camp Townsend, MS, on 5/6/1865.

Smith, Samuel L. Cpl./1st Lt., 36th Mississippi Infantry. Co. D. Federal Rolls of Prisoners of War: Captured at Blakely, AL, on 4/9/1865; Received at Ship Island, MS, on 4/15/1865. Transferred to Vicksburg, MS, for exchange on 4/28/1865; Confined at New Orleans, LA, on 4/30/1865. Exchanged at Camp Townsend, MS, on 5/6/1865.

Smith, Theodore (AKA Buie, R.M.) Pvt., 1st Mississippi Light Artillery. Co. K. Federal Rolls of Prisoners of War: Captured at Blakely, AL, on 4/9/1865; Received at Ship Island, MS, on 4/15/1865. Transferred to Vicksburg, MS, for exchange on 5/1/1865; Exchanged at Camp Townsend, MS, on 5/6/1865.

Smith, W.L. Pvt., 7th Mississippi Battalion Infantry. Co. F. Federal Rolls of Prisoners of War: Captured at Blakely, AL, on 4/9/1865; Received at Ship Island, MS, on 4/15/1865. Transferred to Vicksburg, MS, for

exchange on 5/1/1865; Exchanged at Camp Townsend, MS, on 5/6/1865.

Smith, W.M. (AKA M.W.) Pvt., 1st Mississippi Light Artillery. Co. F. Federal Rolls of Prisoners of War: Captured at Blakely, AL, on 4/9/1865; Received at Ship Island, MS, on 4/15/1865. Transferred to Vicksburg, MS, for exchange on 5/1/1865; Exchanged at Camp Townsend, MS, on 5/6/1865.

Smith, William J. Pvt., 36th Mississippi Infantry. Co. G. Federal Rolls of Prisoners of War: Captured at Blakely, AL, on 4/9/1865; Received at Ship Island, MS, on 4/15/1865. Transferred to Vicksburg, MS, for exchange on 5/1/1865; Exchanged at Camp Townsend, MS, on 5/6/1865.

Smith, William M. Cpl./Bugler, 1st Mississippi Light Artillery. Co. F. Federal Rolls of Prisoners of War: Captured at Blakely, AL, on 4/9/1865; Received at Ship Island, MS, on 4/15/1865. Transferred to Vicksburg, MS, for exchange on 5/1/1865; Exchanged at Camp Townsend, MS, on 5/6/1865.

Sorrels, G. Pvt., 1st Mississippi Light Artillery. Co. F. Federal Rolls of Prisoners of War: Captured at Blakely, AL, on 4/9/1865; Received at Ship Island, MS, on 4/15/1865. Transferred to Vicksburg, MS, for exchange on 5/1/1865; Exchanged at Camp Townsend, MS, on 5/6/1865.

Sorrels, H.O. Pvt., 1st Mississippi Light Artillery. Co. I. Federal Rolls of Prisoners of War: Captured at Blakely, AL, on 4/9/1865; Received at Ship Island, MS, on 4/15/1865. Transferred to Vicksburg, MS, for exchange on 5/1/1865; Exchanged at Camp Townsend, MS, on 5/6/1865.

Sparks, ? Pvt., 1st Mississippi Light Artillery. Co. __. Federal Rolls of Prisoners of War: Captured at Blakely, AL, on 4/9/1865; Received at Ship Island, MS, on 4/15/1865. Transferred to Vicksburg, MS, for exchange on 5/1/1865; Exchanged at Camp Townsend, MS, on 5/6/1865.

Speaks, Benjamin Pvt., 39th Mississippi Infantry. Co. B. Federal Rolls of Prisoners of War: Captured at Blakely, AL, on 4/9/1865; Received at Ship Island, MS, on 4/15/1865. Transferred to Vicksburg, MS, for exchange on 5/1/1865; Exchanged at Camp Townsend, MS, on 5/6/1865.

Sproles, Samuel W. Pvt./Sgt., 1st Mississippi Light Artillery. Co. D. Federal Rolls of Prisoners of War: Captured at Blakely, AL, on 4/9/1865; Received at Ship Island, MS, on 4/15/1865. Transferred to Vicksburg, MS, for exchange on 5/1/1865; Exchanged at Camp Townsend, MS, on 5/6/1865.

Stafford, William J. Pvt., 39th Mississippi Infantry. Co. I. Federal Rolls of Prisoners of War: Captured at Blakely, AL, on 4/9/1865; Received at Ship Island, MS, on 4/15/1865. Transferred to Vicksburg, MS, for exchange on 5/1/1865; Exchanged at Camp Townsend, MS, on 5/6/1865.

Staggs, A. Pvt., 2nd Mississippi Cavalry. Co. __. Federal Rolls of Prisoners of War: Captured at Green County, MS, on 12/11/1864; Received at Ship Island, MS, from New Orleans, LA, on 1/25/1865. Transferred to Vicksburg, MS, for exchange on 5/1/1865; Exchanged at Camp Townsend, MS, on 5/6/1865.

Standard, Jesse F. Pvt., 1st Mississippi Light Artillery. Co. G. Federal Rolls of Prisoners of War: Captured at Blakely, AL, on 4/9/1865; Received at Ship Island, MS, on 4/15/1865. Transferred to Vicksburg, MS, for exchange on 5/1/1865; Exchanged at Camp Townsend, MS, on 5/6/1865.

Stanton, E.G. Pvt., 8th Mississippi Cavalry. Co. H. Federal Rolls of Prisoners of War: Captured at Milton, FL, on 10/25/1864; Received at Ship Island, MS, from New Orleans, LA, on 10/25/1864. Transferred to Vicksburg, MS, for exchange on 5/1/1865; Exchanged at Camp Townsend, MS, on 5/6/1865.

Starke, J.R. (Stark) Pvt./Sgt. Maj., 35th Mississippi Infantry. Co. K. Federal Rolls of Prisoners of War: Captured at Blakely, AL, on 4/9/1865; Received at Ship Island, MS, on 4/15/1865. Transferred to Vicksburg, MS, for exchange on 5/1/1865; Exchanged at Camp Townsend, MS, on 5/6/1865.

Steed, P.M. Pvt., 36th Mississippi Infantry. Co. F. Federal Rolls of Prisoners of War: Captured at Blakely, AL, on 4/9/1865; Received at Ship Island, MS, on 4/15/1865. Transferred to Vicksburg, MS, for exchange on 5/1/1865; Exchanged at Camp Townsend, MS, on 5/6/1865.

Stenner, William (AKA Stinner, Stemmer) Pvt., 46th Mississippi Infantry. Co. A. Federal Rolls of Prisoners of War: Captured at Blakely, AL, on 4/9/1865; Received at Ship Island, MS, on 4/15/1865. Transferred to Vicksburg, MS, for exchange on 5/1/1865; Exchanged at Camp Townsend, MS, on 5/6/1865.

Stephens, J.J. Sgt., 1st Mississippi Light Artillery. Co. F. Federal Rolls of Prisoners of War: Captured at Blakely, AL, on 4/9/1865; Received at Ship Island, MS, on 4/15/1865. Transferred to Vicksburg, MS, for exchange on 5/1/1865; Exchanged at Camp Townsend, MS, on 5/6/1865.

Stephens, M.H. Pvt., 1st Mississippi Light Artillery. Co. F. Federal Rolls of Prisoners of War: Captured at Blakely, AL, on 4/9/1865; Received at Ship Island, MS, on 4/15/1865. Transferred to Vicksburg, MS, for exchange on 5/1/1865; Exchanged at Camp Townsend, MS, on 5/6/1865.

Stevens, John W. Pvt., 1st Mississippi Light Artillery. Co. D. Federal Rolls of Prisoners of War: Captured at Blakely, AL, on 4/9/1865; Received at Ship Island, MS, on 4/15/1865. Transferred to Vicksburg, MS, for exchange on 5/1/1865; Exchanged at Camp Townsend, MS, on 5/6/1865.

Stevens, T.L. Pvt., 1st Mississippi Light Artillery. Co. F. Federal Rolls of Prisoners of War: Captured at Blakely, AL, on 4/9/1865; Received at Ship Island, MS, on 4/15/1865. Transferred to Vicksburg, MS, for exchange on 5/1/1865; Exchanged at Camp Townsend, MS, on 5/6/1865.

Stevenson, Henry C. Pvt., 35th Mississippi Infantry. Co. A. Federal Rolls of Prisoners of War: Captured at Blakely, AL, on 4/9/1865; Received at Ship Island, MS, on 4/15/1865. Transferred to Vicksburg, MS, for exchange on 5/1/1865; Exchanged at Camp Townsend, MS, on 5/6/1865.

Steward, Moses P. (AKA Stuart) Pvt., 46th Mississippi Infantry. Co. G. Federal Rolls of Prisoners of War: Captured at Blakely, AL, on 4/9/1865; Received at Ship Island, MS, on 4/15/1865. Transferred to Vicksburg, MS, for exchange on 5/1/1865; Exchanged at Camp Townsend, MS, on 5/6/1865.

Stewart, William H. 1st Sgt./Ord. Sgt., 1st Mississippi Light Artillery. Co. H. Federal Rolls of Prisoners of War: Captured at Spanish Fort, AL, on 4/8/1865; Received at Ship Island, MS, on 4/10/1865. Transferred to Vicksburg, MS, for exchange on 5/1/1865; Exchanged at Camp Townsend, MS, on 5/6/1865.

Stone, A.C. Pvt./Cpl., 35th Mississippi Infantry. Co. I. Federal Rolls of Prisoners of War: Captured at Blakely, AL, on 4/9/1865; Received at Ship Island, MS, on 4/15/1865. Transferred to Vicksburg, MS, for exchange on 5/1/1865; Exchanged at Camp Townsend, MS, on 5/6/1865.

Stovall, W.D. Pvt./Asst. Surg., 4th Mississippi Infantry. F & S. Federal Rolls of Prisoners of War: Captured at Blakely, AL, on 4/9/1865; Received at Ship Island, MS, on 4/15/1865. Transferred to Vicksburg, MS, for exchange on 4/28/1865; Confined at New Orleans, LA, on 4/30/1865. Exchanged at Camp Townsend, MS, on 5/6/1865.

Street, A.L. Pvt., 1st Mississippi Light Artillery. Co. I. Federal Rolls of Prisoners of War: Captured at Blakely, AL, on 4/9/1865; Received at Ship Island, MS, on 4/15/1865. Transferred to Vicksburg, MS, for exchange on 5/1/1865; Exchanged at Camp Townsend, MS, on 5/6/1865.

Street, William Pvt., 1st Mississippi Light Artillery. Co. B. Federal Rolls of Prisoners of War: Captured at Blakely, AL, on 4/9/1865; Received at Ship Island, MS, on 4/15/1865. Transferred to Vicksburg, MS, for exchange on 5/1/1865; Exchanged at Camp Townsend, MS, on 5/6/1865.

Stringer, W.M. (AKA Stinger) Pvt., 7th Mississippi Infantry. Co. A. Federal Rolls of Prisoners of War: Captured at Blakely, AL, on 4/9/1865; Received at Ship Island, MS, on 4/15/1865. Transferred to Vicksburg, MS, for exchange on 5/1/1865; Exchanged at Camp Townsend, MS, on 5/6/1865.

Strong, J.W. Pvt., 1st Mississippi Light Artillery. Co. K. Federal Rolls of Prisoners of War: Captured at Blakely, AL, on 4/9/1865; Received at Ship Island, MS, on 4/15/1865. Transferred to Vicksburg, MS, for exchange on 5/1/1865; Exchanged at Camp Townsend, MS, on 5/6/1865. Confederate Pension Application dated 1907 on file at the Mississippi Department of Archives and History. Target Name: Strong, J.W. County: Hinds.

Strother, James Thomas Pvt., 1st Mississippi Light Artillery. Cos. H & I. Federal Rolls of Prisoners of War: Captured at Blakely, AL, on 4/9/1865; Received at Ship Island, MS, on 4/15/1865. Transferred to Vicksburg, MS, for exchange on 5/1/1865; Exchanged at Camp Townsend, MS, on 5/6/1865. Confederate Pension Application dated 1912 on file at the Mississippi Department of Archives and History. Target Name: Strother, James Thomas. County: Warren. Also a Confederate Widows Pension Application dated 1924 on file. Target Name: Strother, J.F. County: Warren.

Strout, John N. (AKA Strait) Pvt., 35th Mississippi Infantry. Co. E. Federal Rolls of Prisoners of War: Captured at Blakely, AL, on 4/9/1865; Received at Ship Island, MS, on 4/15/1865. Transferred to Vicksburg, MS, for exchange on 5/1/1865; Exchanged at Camp Townsend, MS, on 5/6/1865.

Stuart, J.W. (AKA J.N.) Pvt., 35th Mississippi Infantry. Co. __. Federal Rolls of Prisoners of War: Captured at Blakely, AL, on 4/9/1865; Received at Ship Island, MS, on 4/15/1865. Transferred to Vicksburg, MS, for exchange on 5/1/1865; Exchanged at Camp Townsend, MS, on 5/6/1865.

Sturgeon, Hiram Pvt., Powers Cavalry Regiment. Co. E. Federal Rolls of Prisoners of War: Captured at Woodville, MS, on 10/8/1864; Received at Ship Island, MS, from New Orleans, LA, on 10/21/1864. Transferred to Fort Columbus, New York Harbor, NY, on 11/5/1864.

Sullivan, E. Pvt., 46th Mississippi Infantry. Co. __. Federal Rolls of Prisoners of War: Captured at Blakely, AL, on 4/9/1865; Received at Ship Island, MS, on 4/15/1865. Transferred to Vicksburg, MS, for exchange on 5/1/1865; Exchanged at Camp Townsend, MS, on 5/6/1865.

Sullivan, J.J. Pvt., 39th Mississippi Infantry. Co. E. Federal Rolls of Prisoners of War: Captured at Blakely, AL, on 4/9/1865; Received at Ship Island, MS, on 4/15/1865. Transferred to Vicksburg, MS, for exchange on 5/1/1865; Exchanged at Camp Townsend, MS, on 5/6/1865.

Sullivan, Thomas J.H. (AKA T.G.H.) Pvt., 46th Mississippi Infantry. Co. B. Federal Rolls of Prisoners of War: Captured at Blakely, AL, on 4/9/1865; Received at Ship Island, MS, on 4/15/1865. Transferred to Vicksburg, MS, for exchange on 5/1/1865; Exchanged at Camp Townsend, MS, on 5/6/1865.

Swain, Samuel R. Pvt., 1st Mississippi Light Artillery. Co. D. Federal Rolls of Prisoners of War: Captured at Blakely, AL, on 4/9/1865; Received at Ship Island, MS, on 4/15/1865. Transferred to Vicksburg, MS, for exchange on 5/1/1865; Exchanged at Camp Townsend, MS, on 5/6/1865.

Swayze, Hardy S. Cpl./Sgt., 1st Mississippi Light Artillery. Co. B. Federal Rolls of Prisoners of War: Captured at Blakely, AL, on 4/9/1865; Received at Ship Island, MS, on 4/15/1865. Transferred to Vicksburg, MS, for exchange on 5/1/1865; Exchanged at Camp Townsend, MS, on 5/6/1865. Confederate Widows Pension Application dated 1928 on file at the Mississippi Department of Archives and History. Target Name: Swayze, Janie H. County: Yazoo.

Swayze, Orange H. Pvt., 1st Mississippi Light Artillery. Co. B. Federal Rolls of Prisoners of War: Captured at Blakely, AL, on 4/9/1865; Received at Ship Island, MS, on 4/15/1865. Transferred to Vicksburg, MS, for exchange on 5/1/1865; Exchanged at Camp Townsend, MS, on 5/6/1865. Born: 1844. Died: 1917. Buried: Yazoo County, MS.

Swisher, A. Pvt., 1st Mississippi Light Artillery. Co. I. Federal Rolls of Prisoners of War: Captured at Blakely, AL, on 4/9/1865; Received at Ship Island, MS, on 4/15/1865. Transferred to Vicksburg, MS, for exchange on 5/1/1865; Exchanged at Camp Townsend, MS, on 5/6/1865.

Taylor, A. Pvt., 35th Mississippi Infantry. Co. I. Federal Rolls of Prisoners of War: Captured at Blakely, AL, on 4/9/1865; Received at Ship Island, MS, on 4/15/1865. Transferred to Vicksburg, MS, for exchange on 5/1/1865; Exchanged at Camp Townsend, MS, on 5/6/1865.

Taylor, James Kurtis Cpl., 4th Mississippi Infantry. Co. F. Federal Rolls of Prisoners of War: Captured and paroled at Vicksburg, MS, on 7/4/1863. Federal Rolls of Prisoners of War: Captured at Blakely, AL, on 4/9/1865; Received at Ship Island, MS, on 4/15/1865. Transferred to Vicksburg, MS, for exchange on 5/1/1865; Exchanged at Camp Townsend, MS, on 5/6/1865. Died: 1922 at Beauvoir Confederate

Soldier's Home located at Biloxi, MS. Buried: Evergreen Cemetery located at North Carrollton, MS.

Taylor, L.R. Pvt., 36th Mississippi Infantry. Co. F. Federal Rolls of Prisoners of War: Captured at Spanish Fort, AL, on 4/8/1865; Received at Ship Island, MS, on 4/10/1865. Transferred to Vicksburg, MS, for exchange on 5/1/1865; Exchanged at Camp Townsend, MS, on 5/6/1865.

Taylor, Peter Pvt./Asst. Surg., 46th Mississippi Infantry. Co. A. Federal Rolls of Prisoners of War: Captured at Blakely, AL, on 4/9/1865; Received at Ship Island, MS, on 4/15/1865. Transferred to Vicksburg, MS, for exchange on 4/28/1865; Confined at New Orleans, LA, on 4/30/1865. Exchanged at Camp Townsend, MS, on 5/6/1865.

Templeton, J.F. Pvt., 1st Mississippi Light Artillery. Co. G. Federal Rolls of Prisoners of War: Captured at Blakely, AL, on 4/9/1865; Received at Ship Island, MS, on 4/15/1865. Transferred to Vicksburg, MS, for exchange on 5/1/1865; Exchanged at Camp Townsend, MS, on 5/6/1865.

Templeton, S.A. Pvt./Sgt., 35th Mississippi Infantry. Co. C. Federal Rolls of Prisoners of War: Captured at Blakely, AL, on 4/9/1865; Received at Ship Island, MS, on 4/15/1865. Transferred to Vicksburg, MS, for exchange on 5/1/1865; Exchanged at Camp Townsend, MS, on 5/6/1865.

Templeton, S.W. Pvt., 39th Mississippi Infantry. Co. E. Federal Rolls of Prisoners of War: Captured at Blakely, AL, on 4/9/1865; Received at Ship Island, MS, on 4/15/1865. Transferred to Vicksburg, MS, for exchange on 5/1/1865; Exchanged at Camp Townsend, MS, on 5/6/1865.

Terry, B.T. Pvt., 35th Mississippi Infantry. Co. C. Federal Rolls of Prisoners of War: Captured at Blakely, AL, on 4/9/1865; Received at Ship Island, MS, on 4/15/1865. Transferred to Vicksburg, MS, for exchange on 5/1/1865; Exchanged at Camp Townsend, MS, on 5/6/1865.

Terry, John Pvt., 1st Mississippi Light Artillery. Co. G. Federal Rolls of Prisoners of War: Captured at Blakely, AL, on 4/9/1865; Received at Ship Island, MS, on 4/15/1865. Transferred to Vicksburg, MS, for exchange on 5/1/1865; Exchanged at Camp Townsend, MS, on 5/6/1865.

Terry, Roland G. (AKA R.J.) Pvt./Cpl., 36th Mississippi Infantry. Co. B. Federal Rolls of Prisoners of War: Captured at Spanish Fort, AL, on 4/8/1865; Received at Ship Island, MS, on 4/10/1865. Transferred to Vicksburg, MS, for exchange on 5/1/1865; Exchanged at Camp Townsend, MS, on 5/6/1865. Confederate Pension Application dated 1912 on file at the Mississippi Department of Archives and History. Target Name: Terry, Roland G. County: Pike.

Thomas, B.B. Pvt., 35th Mississippi Infantry. Co. H. Federal Rolls of Prisoners of War: Captured at Blakely, AL, on 4/9/1865; Received at Ship Island, MS, on 4/15/1865. Transferred to Vicksburg, MS, for exchange on 5/1/1865; Exchanged at Camp Townsend, MS, on 5/6/1865.

Thomas, F.M. (AKA L.M.) 1st Lt., 39th Mississippi Infantry. Co. E. Federal Rolls of Prisoners of War: Captured at Blakely, AL, on 4/9/1865; Received at Ship Island, MS, on 4/15/1865. Transferred to Vicksburg, MS, for exchange on 4/28/1865; Confined at New Orleans, LA, on 4/30/1865. Exchanged at Camp Townsend, MS, on 5/6/1865.

Thompsen, Benjamin (AKA Thompson) Pvt., 1st Mississippi Light Artillery. Co. G. Federal Rolls of Prisoners of War: Captured at Blakely, AL, on 4/9/1865; Received at Ship Island, MS, on 4/15/1865. Transferred to Vicksburg, MS, for exchange on 5/1/1865; Exchanged at Camp Townsend, MS, on 5/6/1865.

Thompson, A.H.S. Pvt., 7th Mississippi Battalion Infantry. Co. A. Federal Rolls of Prisoners of War: Captured at Blakely, AL, on 4/9/1865; Received at Ship Island, MS, on 4/15/1865. Transferred to Vicksburg, MS, for exchange on 5/1/1865; Exchanged at Camp Townsend, MS, on 5/6/1865.

Thornton, Moses Pvt., 36th Mississippi Infantry. Co. D. Federal Rolls of Prisoners of War: Captured at Spanish Fort, AL, on 4/8/1865; Received at Ship Island, MS, on 4/10/1865. Transferred to Vicksburg, MS, for exchange on 5/1/1865; Exchanged at Camp Townsend, MS, on 5/6/1865.

Tidwell, Levi N. Pvt., 35th Mississippi Infantry. Co. E. Federal Rolls of Prisoners of War: Captured at Blakely, AL, on 4/9/1865; Received at Ship Island, MS, on 4/15/1865. Transferred to Vicksburg, MS, for exchange on 5/1/1865; Exchanged at Camp Townsend, MS, on 5/6/1865. Confederate Widows Pension Application dated 1916 on file at the Mississippi Department of Archives and History. Target Name: Tidwell, Louiza. County: Neshoba.

Tiller, Oscar S. Pvt., 1st Mississippi Light Artillery. Co. I. Federal Rolls of Prisoners of War: Captured at Blakely, AL, on 4/9/1865; Received at Ship Island, MS, on 4/15/1865. Transferred to Vicksburg, MS, for exchange on 5/1/1865; Exchanged at Camp Townsend, MS, on 5/6/1865.

Tims, John W. Pvt., 7th Mississippi Battalion Infantry. Cos. D & E. Federal Rolls of Prisoners of War: Captured at Blakely, AL, on 4/9/1865; Received at Ship Island, MS, on 4/15/1865. Transferred to Vicksburg, MS, for exchange on 5/1/1865; Exchanged at Camp Townsend, MS, on 5/6/1865. Confederate Widows Pension Application on file dated 1915 at the the Mississippi Department of Archives and History. Target Name: Tims, Martha. County: Clarke.

Tinsley, Burrell Pvt./3rd Lt., 35th Mississippi Infantry. Co. A. Federal Rolls of Prisoners of War: Captured at Blakely, AL, on 4/9/1865; Received at Ship Island, MS, on 4/15/1865. Transferred to Vicksburg, MS, for exchange on 4/28/1865; Confined at New Orleans, LA, on 4/30/1865. Exchanged at Camp Townsend, MS, on 5/6/1865.

Tobin, J.W. (AKA J.N.) Pvt., 46th Mississippi Infantry. Co. __. Federal Rolls of Prisoners of War: Captured at Blakely, AL, on 4/9/1865; Received at Ship Island, MS, on 4/15/1865. Transferred to Vicksburg, MS, for exchange on 5/1/1865; Exchanged at Camp Townsend, MS, on 5/6/1865.

Torry, James A. (AKA Torrey) Pvt., 1st Mississippi Light Artillery. Co. K. Federal Rolls of Prisoners of War: Captured at Blakely, AL, on 4/9/1865; Received at Ship Island, MS, on 4/15/1865. Transferred to Vicksburg, MS, for exchange on 5/1/1865; Exchanged at Camp Townsend, MS, on 5/6/1865. Confederate Widows Pension Application dated 1920 on file at the Mississippi Department of Archives and History. Target Name: Torrey, Elizabeth A. County: Franklin.

Towle, S.C. Pvt., 16th Mississippi Infantry. Co. D. Federal Rolls of Prisoners of War: Captured at Brookhaven, MS, on 11/18/1864; Transferred to Ship Island, MS, from New Orleans, LA, on 12/13/1864. Transferred to Vicksburg, MS, for exchange on 5/1/1865; Exchanged at Camp Townsend, MS, on 5/6/1865.

Trainor, Thomas (AKA Trainer) Pvt., 1st Mississippi Light Artillery. Co. G. Federal Rolls of Prisoners of War: Captured at Blakely, AL, on 4/9/1865; Received at Ship Island, MS, on 4/15/1865. Transferred to Vicksburg, MS, for exchange on 5/1/1865; Exchanged at Camp Townsend, MS, on 5/6/1865.

Travis, Thomas Pvt., 4th Mississippi Infantry. Co. G. Federal Rolls of Prisoners of War: Captured at Blakely, AL, on 4/9/1865; Received at Ship Island, MS, on 4/15/1865. Transferred to Vicksburg, MS, for exchange on 5/1/1865; Exchanged at Camp Townsend, MS, on 5/6/1865.

Treadway, David C. Pvt., 35th Mississippi Infantry. Co. B. Federal Rolls of Prisoners of War: Captured at Blakely, AL, on 4/9/1865; Received at Ship Island, MS, on 4/15/1865. Transferred to Vicksburg, MS, for exchange on 5/1/1865; Exchanged at Camp Townsend, MS, on 5/6/1865.

Tribble, Robert E. Pvt./Cpl., 1st Mississippi Light Artillery. Co. G. Federal Rolls of Prisoners of War: Captured at Blakely, AL, on 4/9/1865; Received at Ship Island, MS, on 4/15/1865. Transferred to Vicksburg, MS, for exchange on 5/1/1865; Exchanged at Camp Townsend, MS, on 5/6/1865.

Trigg, William A. (AKA W.I.) Pvt./Sgt., 46th Mississippi Infantry. Co. A. Federal Rolls of Prisoners of War: Captured at Blakely, AL, on 4/9/1865; Received at Ship Island, MS, on 4/15/1865. Transferred to Vicksburg, MS, for exchange on 5/1/1865; Exchanged at Camp Townsend, MS, on 5/6/1865.

Trotter, W.A. Capt., 7th Mississippi Battalion Infantry. Co. D. Federal Rolls of Prisoners of War: Captured at Blakely, AL, on 4/9/1865; Received at Ship Island, MS, on 4/15/1865. Transferred to Vicksburg, MS, for exchange on 4/28/1865; Confined at New Orleans, LA, on 4/30/1865. Exchanged at Camp Townsend, MS, on 5/6/1865

Tucker, Hardy G. Pvt., 39th Mississippi Infantry. Co. G. Federal Rolls of Prisoners of War: Captured at Blakely, AL, on 4/9/1865; Received at Ship Island, MS, on 4/15/1865. Transferred to Vicksburg, MS, for exchange on 5/1/1865; Exchanged at Camp Townsend, MS, on 5/6/1865.

Tucker, J.H. Pvt., 39th Mississippi Infantry. Co. __. Federal Rolls of Prisoners of War: Captured at Blakely, AL, on 4/9/1865; Received at Ship Island, MS, on 4/15/1865. Transferred to Vicksburg, MS, for exchange on 5/1/1865; Exchanged at Camp Townsend, MS, on 5/6/1865.

Tucker, James J. Pvt., 39th Mississippi Infantry. Co. G. Federal Rolls of Prisoners of War: Captured at Blakely, AL, on 4/9/1865; Received at Ship Island, MS, on 4/15/1865. Transferred to Vicksburg, MS, for exchange on 5/1/1865; Exchanged at Camp Townsend, MS, on 5/6/1865.

Tucker, John Pvt., 1st Mississippi Light Artillery. Co. K. Federal Rolls of Prisoners of War: Captured at Blakely, AL, on 4/9/1865; Received at Ship Island, MS, on 4/15/1865. Transferred to Vicksburg, MS, for exchange on 5/1/1865.

Turnage, William B. Pvt., 1st Mississippi Light Artillery. Co. D. Federal Rolls of Prisoners of War: Captured at Blakely, AL, on 4/9/1865; Received at Ship Island, MS, on 4/15/1865. Transferred to Vicksburg, MS, for exchange on 5/1/1865; Exchanged at Camp Townsend, MS, on 5/6/1865.

Turner, A.A. Cpl., 7th Mississippi Battalion Infantry. Co. __. Federal Rolls of Prisoners of War: Captured at Blakely, AL, on 4/9/1865; Received at Ship Island, MS, on 4/15/1865. Transferred to Vicksburg, MS, for exchange on 5/1/1865; Exchanged at Camp Townsend, MS, on 5/6/1865.

Turner, Tom Pvt., 1st Mississippi Light Infantry. Co. G. Federal Rolls of Prisoners of War: Captured at Blakely, AL, on 4/9/1865; Received at Ship Island, MS, on 4/15/1865. Transferred to Vicksburg, MS, for exchange on 5/1/1865; Exchanged at Camp Townsend, MS, on 5/6/1865.

Turner, W.S. Pvt./Sgt., 39th Mississippi Infantry. Co. I. Federal Rolls of Prisoners of War: Captured at Blakely, AL, on 4/9/1865; Received at Ship Island, MS, on 4/15/1865. Transferred to Vicksburg, MS, for exchange on 5/1/1865; Exchanged at Camp Townsend, MS, on 5/6/1865. Confederate Pension Application dated 1922 on file at the Mississippi Department of Archives and History. Target Name: Turner, W.S. County: Carroll.

Turnipseed, D.B. Pvt., 36th Mississippi Infantry. Co. D. Federal Rolls of Prisoners of War: Captured at Spanish Fort, AL, on 4/8/1865; Received at Ship Island, MS, on 4/10/1865. Transferred to Vicksburg, MS, for exchange on 5/1/1865; Exchanged at Camp Townsend, MS, on 5/6/1865.

Tuttle, John Pvt., 1st Mississippi Light Artillery. Co. G. Federal Rolls of Prisoners of War: Captured at Blakely, AL, on 4/9/1865; Received at Ship Island, MS, on 4/15/1865. Transferred to Vicksburg, MS, for exchange on 5/1/1865; Exchanged at Camp Townsend, MS, on 5/6/1865.

Tuttle, R.E. Cpl., 1st Mississippi Light Artillery. Co. G. Federal Rolls of Prisoners of War: Captured at Blakely, AL, on 4/9/1865; Received at Ship Island, MS, on 4/15/1865. Transferred to Vicksburg, MS, for exchange on 5/1/1865; Exchanged at Camp Townsend, MS, on 5/6/1865.

Tutton, John M. Pvt., 35th Mississippi Infantry. Co. F. Federal Rolls of Prisoners of War: Captured at Blakely, AL, on 4/9/1865; Received at Ship Island, MS, on 4/15/1865. Transferred to Vicksburg, MS, for exchange on 5/1/1865; Exchanged at Camp Townsend, MS, on 5/6/1865.

Tye, John Fletcher, Sr. 2nd Lt./1st Lt., 1st Mississippi Light Artillery. Co. I. Federal Rolls of Prisoners of War: Captured at Blakely, AL, on 4/9/1865; Received at Ship Island, MS, on 4/15/1865. Transferred to Vicksburg, MS, for exchange on 4/281865; Confined at New Orleans, LA, on 4/30/1865. Exchanged at Camp Townsend, MS, on 5/6/1865. Born: 1832 in North Carolina. Died: 1907 at Holmes County, MS.

Tyler, Louis Pvt., 36th Mississippi Infantry. Co. __. Federal Rolls of Prisoners of War: Captured at Spanish Fort, AL, on 4/8/1865; Received at Ship Island, MS, on 4/10/1865. Transferred to Vicksburg, MS, for exchange on 5/1/1865; Exchanged at Camp Townsend, MS, on 5/6/1865.

Vance, Jim Neely Pvt., 4th Mississippi Infantry. Cos.

F & H. Federal Rolls of Prisoners of War: Captured at Blakely, AL, on 4/9/1865; Received at Ship Island, MS, from New Orleans, LA, on 4/15/1865. Transferred to Vicksburg, MS, for exchange on 5/1/1865; Exchanged at Camp Townsend, MS, on 5/6/1865. Confederate Pension Application dated 1921 on file at the Mississippi Department of Archives and History. Target Name: Vance, Jim Neely. County: Calhoun.

Vandervier, J.G. (AKA Vanderver, S.G.) Pvt., 1st Mississippi Light Artillery. Co. B. Federal Rolls of Prisoners of War: Captured at Blakely, AL, on 4/9/1865; Received at Ship Island, MS, from New Orleans, LA, on 4/15/1865. Transferred to Vicksburg, MS, for exchange on 5/1/1865; Exchanged at Camp Townsend, MS, on 5/6/1865.

VanDevender, R.W. Pvt., 46th Mississippi Infantry. Co. K. Federal Rolls of Prisoners of War: Captured at Blakely, AL, on 4/9/1865; Received at Ship Island, MS, on 4/15/1865. Transferred to Vicksburg, MS, for exchange on 5/1/1865; Exchanged at Camp Townsend, MS, on 5/6/1865.

Varnell, D.F. Pvt., 1st Mississippi Light Artillery. Co. F. Federal Rolls of Prisoners of War: Captured at Blakely, AL, on 4/9/1865; Received at Ship Island, MS, on 4/15/1865. Transferred to Vicksburg, MS, for exchange on 5/1/1865; Exchanged at Camp Townsend, MS, on 5/6/1865.

Vaughn, John N. (AKA Vann) Pvt., 7th Mississippi Battalion Infantry. Co. E. Federal Rolls of Prisoners of War: Captured at Blakely, AL, on 4/9/1865; Received at Ship Island, MS, on 4/15/1865. Transferred to Vicksburg, MS, for exchange on 5/1/1865; Exchanged at Camp Townsend, MS, on 5/6/1865.

Vaughn, Taylor Pvt., 35th Mississippi Infantry. Co. K. Age at enlistment: 16. Federal Rolls of Prisoners of War: Captured at Blakely, AL, on 4/9/1865; Received at Ship Island, MS, on 4/15/1865. Transferred to Vicksburg, MS, for exchange on 5/1/1865; Exchanged at Camp Townsend, MS, on 5/6/1865. Born: 5/5/1846 at Double Springs, MS; Orphaned at age 7 and raised by his brother, George. Married: Emma Jane Gregg in 1866; Mary Francis Cannon in 1909. Children: 2—1 son and 1 daughter. Died: 8/19/1918 at Sherman, TX. Buried: Stringtown, OK, under a Masonic marker. A synopsis of his life appeared in *Confederate Veteran Magazine* in 1918.

Vincent, G.W. (AKA Vinson, J.W.) Pvt., 46th Mississippi Infantry. Co. G. Federal Rolls of Prisoners of War: Captured at Blakely, AL, on 4/9/1865; Received at Ship Island, MS, on 4/15/1865. Transferred to Vicksburg, MS, for exchange on 5/1/1865; Exchanged at Camp Townsend, MS, on 5/6/1865.

Wadsworth, W.R. Pvt., 1st Mississippi Light Artillery. Co. __. Federal Rolls of Prisoners of War: Captured at Blakely, AL, on 4/9/1865; Received at Ship Island, MS, on 4/15/1865. Transferred to Vicksburg, MS, for exchange on 5/1/1865; Exchanged at Camp Townsend, MS, on 5/6/1865.

Wafford, Jefferson L. (AKA Wofford, J.D.) Capt./Major, 1st Mississippi Light Artillery. Co. D. Federal Rolls of Prisoners of War: Captured at Blakely, AL, on 4/9/1865; Received at Ship Island, MS, on 4/15/1865. Transferred to Vicksburg, MS, for exchange on 4/28/1865; Confined at New Orleans, LA, on 4/30/1865. Exchanged at Camp Townsend, MS, on 5/6/1865.

Wages, John G. Pvt., 39th Mississippi Infantry. Co. A. Federal Rolls of Prisoners of War: Captured at Blakely, AL, on 4/9/1865; Received at Ship Island, MS, on 4/15/1865. Transferred to Vicksburg, MS, for exchange on 5/1/1865; Exchanged at Camp Townsend, MS, on 5/6/1865.

Walden, T.B. (AKA Walder) Pvt., 46th Mississippi Infantry. Co. G. Federal Rolls of Prisoners of War: Captured at Blakely, AL, on 4/9/1865; Received at Ship Island, MS, on 4/15/1865. Transferred to Vicksburg, MS, for exchange on 5/1/1865; Exchanged at Camp Townsend, MS, on 5/6/1865. Confederate Pension Application dated 1916 at the Mississippi Department of Archives and History. Target Name: Walden, T.B. County: Jones.

Walden, W.W. Pvt., 46th Mississippi Infantry. Co. G. Federal Rolls of Prisoners of War: Captured in Alabama on 4/1/1865; Received at Ship Island, MS. Transferred to Vicksburg, MS, for exchange on 5/1/1865; Exchanged at Camp Townsend, MS, on 5/6/1865.

Walker, Daniel Pvt., 36th Mississippi Infantry. Co. __. Federal Rolls of Prisoners of War: Captured at Blakely, AL, on 4/9/1865; Received at Ship Island, MS, on 4/15/1865. Transferred to Vicksburg, MS, for exchange on 5/1/1865; Exchanged at Camp Townsend, MS, on 5/6/1865.

Walker, James Pvt., 36th Mississippi Infantry. Co. I. Federal Rolls of Prisoners of War: Captured at Blakely, AL, on 4/9/1865; Received at Ship Island, MS, on 4/15/1865. Transferred to Vicksburg, MS, for exchange on 5/1/1865; Exchanged at Camp Townsend, MS, on 5/6/1865.

Wall, James A. 3rd Lt./Pvt., 36th Mississippi Infantry. Co. I. Federal Rolls of Prisoners of War: Captured at Blakely, AL, on 4/9/1865; Received at Ship Island, MS, on 4/15/1865. Transferred to Vicksburg, MS, for exchange on 5/1/1865. Born: 1831 at Newton County, MS. Died: 1910. Buried: Newton County, MS.

Waller, William W. Pvt., 1st Mississippi Light Artillery. Co __. Federal Rolls of Prisoners of War: Captured at Blakely, AL, on 4/9/1865; Received at Ship Island, MS, on 4/15/1865. Transferred to Vicksburg, MS, for exchange on 5/1/1865; Exchanged at Camp Townsend, MS, on 5/6/1865. Born: 1845 at Yazoo County, MS. Died: 1935. Buried: Yazoo County, MS.

Wane, R.G. Pvt., 36th Mississippi Infantry. Co. __. Federal Rolls of Prisoners of War: Captured at Blakely, AL, on 4/9/1865; Received at Ship Island, MS, on 4/15/1865. Transferred to Vicksburg, MS, for exchange on 5/1/1865; Exchanged at Camp Townsend, MS, on 5/6/1865.

Ward, A.W. (AKA Ware) Pvt., 39th Mississippi Infantry. Co. F. Federal Rolls of Prisoners of War: Captured at Blakely, AL, on 4/9/1865; Received at Ship Island, MS, on 4/15/1865. Transferred to Vicksburg, MS, for exchange on 5/1/1865; Exchanged at Camp Townsend, MS, on 5/6/1865.

Ward, G.W. (AKA Ware) Pvt., 39th Mississippi Infantry. Co. F. Federal Rolls of Prisoners of War: Captured at Blakely, AL, on 4/9/1865; Received at Ship Island, MS, on 4/15/1865. Transferred to Vicksburg, MS, for exchange on 5/1/1865; Exchanged at Camp Townsend, MS, on 5/6/1865.

Ward, Jesse Pvt., 1st Mississippi Light Artillery. Co. I.

Federal Rolls of Prisoners of War: Captured at Blakely, AL, on 4/9/1865; Received at Ship Island, MS, on 4/15/1865. Transferred to Vicksburg, MS, for exchange on 5/1/1865; Exchanged at Camp Townsend, MS, on 5/6/1865.

Ward, W.A. Pvt./3rd Lt., 35th Mississippi Infantry. Co. G. Federal Rolls of Prisoners of War: Captured at Blakely, AL, on 4/9/1865; Received at Ship Island, MS, on 4/15/1865. Transferred to Vicksburg, MS, for exchange on 4/28/1865; Confined at New Orleans, LA, on 4/30/1865. Exchanged at Camp Townsend, MS, on 5/6/1865.

Ware, A.W. Pvt., 39th Mississippi Infantry. Co. F. Federal Rolls of Prisoners of War: Captured at Blakely, AL, on 4/9/1865; Received at Ship Island, MS, on 4/15/1865. Transferred to Vicksburg, MS, for exchange on 5/1/1865; Exchanged at Camp Townsend, MS, on 5/6/1865.

Ware, G.W. Pvt., 39th Mississippi Infantry. Co. F. Federal Rolls of Prisoners of War: Captured at Blakely, AL, on 4/9/1865; Received at Ship Island, MS, on 4/15/1865. Transferred to Vicksburg, MS, for exchange on 5/1/1865; Exchanged at Camp Townsend, MS, on 5/6/1865.

Warren, David Pvt., 46th Mississippi Infantry. Co. G. Federal Rolls of Prisoners of War: Captured in Alabama on 4/1/1865; Received at Ship Island, MS. Transferred to Vicksburg, MS, for exchange on 5/1/1865; Exchanged at Camp Townsend, MS, on 5/6/1865.

Warren, J.W. Pvt., 36th Mississippi Infantry. Co. __. Federal Rolls of Prisoners of War: Captured at Blakely, AL, on 4/9/1865; Received at Ship Island, MS, on 4/15/1865. Transferred to Vicksburg, MS, for exchange on 5/1/1865; Exchanged at Camp Townsend, MS, on 5/6/1865.

Warren, L.B. Pvt./2nd Lt., 1st Mississippi Light Artillery. Co. B. Federal Rolls of Prisoners of War: Captured at Blakely, AL, on 4/9/1865; Received at Ship Island, MS, on 4/15/1865. Transferred to Vicksburg, MS, for exchange on 4/28/1865; Confined at New Orleans, LA, on 4/30/1865. Exchanged at Camp Townsend, MS, on 5/6/1865.

Waters, Peter B. Pvt., 39th Mississippi Infantry. Co. C. Federal Rolls of Prisoners of War: Captured at Blakely, AL, on 4/9/1865; Received at Ship Island, MS, on 4/15/1865. Transferred to Vicksburg, MS, for exchange on 5/1/1865; Exchanged at Camp Townsend, MS, on 5/6/1865.

Watkins, E.D. (AKA E.K.) Cpl., 36th Mississippi Infantry. Co. __. Federal Rolls of Prisoners of War: Captured at Blakely, AL, on 4/9/1865; Received at Ship Island, MS, on 4/15/1865. Transferred to Vicksburg, MS, for exchange on 5/1/1865; Exchanged at Camp Townsend, MS, on 5/6/1865.

Watson, I.J. Pvt., 39th Mississippi Infantry. Co. E. Federal Rolls of Prisoners of War: Captured at Blakely, AL, on 4/9/1865; Received at Ship Island, MS, on 4/15/1865. Transferred to Vicksburg, MS, for exchange on 5/1/1865; Exchanged at Camp Townsend, MS, on 5/6/1865.

Weatherby, H.F. Pvt., 4th Mississippi Infantry. Co. G. Federal Rolls of Prisoners of War: Captured at Blakely, AL, on 4/9/1865; Received at Ship Island, MS, on 4/15/1865. Transferred to Vicksburg, MS, for exchange on 5/1/1865; Exchanged at Camp Townsend, MS, on 5/6/1865. Confederate Widows Pension Application dated 1916 on file at the Mississippi Department of Archives and History. Target Name: Weatherby, M.J. County: Clarke.

Weaver, Romandus F. (AKA Richard) 2nd Lt., 36th Mississippi Infantry. Co. H. Federal Rolls of Prisoners of War: Captured at Blakely, AL, on 4/8/1865; Received at Ship Island, MS, on 4/15/1865. Transferred to Vicksburg, MS, for exchange on 4/28/1865; Confined at New Orleans, LA, on 4/30/1865. Exchanged at Camp Townsend, MS, on 5/6/1865.

Webb, A.H. Pvt., 35th Mississippi Infantry. Co. H. Federal Rolls of Prisoners of War: Captured at Blakely, AL, on 4/9/1865; Received at Ship Island, MS, on 4/15/1865. Transferred to Vicksburg, MS, for exchange on 5/1/1865; Exchanged at Camp Townsend, MS, on 5/6/1865.

Webb, John Addison Pvt., 4th Mississippi Infantry. Co G. Federal Rolls of Prisoners of War: Captured at Blakely, AL, on 4/9/1865; Received at Ship Island, MS, on 4/15/1865. Transferred to Vicksburg, MS, for exchange on 5/1/1865; Exchanged at Camp Townsend, MS, on 5/6/1865. Born: 1843 in Virginia. Died: 1924 at Hinds County, MS. Conedarate Pension Application dated 1922 on file at the Mississippi Department of Archives and History. Target Name: Webb, John A. County: Hinds.

Webb, Peyton S. (AKA Payton) Pvt., 4th Mississippi Infantry. Co. E. Federal Rolls of Prisoners of War: Captured at Blakely, AL, on 4/9/1865; Received at Ship Island, MS, on 4/15/1865. Transferred to Vicksburg, MS, for exchange on 5/1/1865; Exchanged at Camp Townsend, MS, on 5/6/1865. Born: 1837 in Tennessee. Died: 1934 at Montgomery County, MS. Confederate Pension Application dated 1916 on file at the Mississippi Department of Archives and History. Target Name: Webb, Payton S. County: Montgomery.

Webb, William Henry Pvt., 4th Mississippi Infantry. Co. E. Federal Rolls of Prisoners of War: Captured at Blakely, AL, on 4/9/1865; Received at Ship Island, MS, on 4/15/1865. Transferred to Vicksburg, MS, for exchange on 5/1/1865; Exchanged at Camp Townsend, MS, on 5/6/1865. Confederate Pension Application dated 1915 on file at the Mississippi Department of Archives and History. Target Name: Webb, William Henry. County: Leflore.

Week, James M. Cpl., 36th Mississippi Infantry. Co. __. Federal Rolls of Prisoners of War: Captured at Blakely, AL, on 4/9/1865; Received at Ship Island, MS, on 4/15/1865. Transferred to Vicksburg, MS, for exchange on 5/1/1865; Exchanged at Camp Townsend, MS, on 5/6/1865. Confederate Widows Pension Application dated 1916 on file at the Mississippi Department of Archives and History. Target Name: Week, Catherine. County: Copiah.

Weems, James M. Pvt./Sgt., 4th Mississippi Infantry. Co. G. Federal Rolls of Prisoners of War: Captured at Blakely, AL, on 4/9/1865; Received at Ship Island, MS, on 4/15/1865. Transferred to Vicksburg, MS, for exchange on 5/1/1865. Born: 1809 at Holmes County, MS. Died: 1873 at Holmes County, MS.

Welch, Joseph M. (AKA Welsh) Pvt., 7th Mississippi Battalion Infantry. Co. G. Enlisted: 7/1863 at Williamsburg, MS. Federal Rolls of Prisoners of War: Captured at Blakely, AL, on 4/9/1865; Received at Ship Island, MS, on 4/15/1865. Transferred to Vicksburg, MS, for exchange on 5/1/1865; Exchanged at Camp Townsend, MS, on 5/6/1865. Born: 7/1845 at Covington County, MS, to James Welch and Martha Holbert Hill Welch. Pre-war occupation: Farmer. Married: Nancy E. Rogers on 8/14/1880. Children: 3. Post-war occupation: Farmer. Religion: Baptist. Died: 1927 at Covington County, MS. Buried: Covington County, MS. Confederate Widows Pension Application dated 1927 on file at the Mississippi Department of Archives and History. Target Name: Welch, Nancy E. County: Covington.

Welsh, A.G. Pvt., 1st Mississippi Light Artillery. Co. G. Federal Rolls of Prisoners of War: Captured at Blakely, AL, on 4/9/1865; Received at Ship Island, MS, on 4/15/1865. Transferred to Vicksburg, MS, for exchange on 5/1/1865; Exchanged at Camp Townsend, MS, on 5/6/1865.

Welsh, Ransom J. (AKA Welch, Ranson) Pvt./Sgt., 7th Mississippi Battalion Infantry. Co. G. Enlisted: 5/12/1862 at Williamsburg, MS. Federal Rolls of Prisoners of War: Captured at Blakely, AL, on 4/9/1865; Received at Ship Island, MS, on 4/15/1865. Transferred to Vicksburg, MS, for exchange on 5/1/1865; Exchanged at Camp Townsend, MS, on 5/6/1865. Born: 2/2/1841 at Covington County, MS, to James Welsh and Martha Holbert Hill Welsh. Pre-war occupations: Farmer and stock raising. Married: Francis D. Rogers on 12/29/1869 at Covington County, MS. Children: 5. Religion: Baptist. Died: 1910. Buried: Covington County, MS. Confederate Pension Application dated 1915 on file at the Mississippi Department of Archives and History. Target Name: Welch, Ransom J. County: Covington. Also a Confederate Widows Pension Application dated 1918 on file. Target Name: Welch, Frances C. County: Covington.

West, E.A. (AKA Albert L.) Pvt./Cpl., 36th Mississippi Infantry. Co. G. Federal Rolls of Prisoners of War: Captured at Blakely, AL, on 4/9/1865; Received at Ship Island, MS, on 4/15/1865. Transferred to Vicksburg, MS, for exchange on 5/1/1865; Exchanged at Camp Townsend, MS, on 5/6/1865.

Wheeling, T.E. Sgt., 36th Mississippi Infantry. Co. I. Federal Rolls of Prisoners of War: Captured at Blakely, AL, on 4/9/1865; Received at Ship Island, MS, on 4/15/1865. Transferred to Vicksburg, MS, for exchange on 5/1/1865; Exchanged at Camp Townsend, MS, on 5/6/1865.

Whienberg, H. Pvt., 1st Mississippi Light Artillery. Co. __. Federal Rolls of Prisoners of War: Captured at Blakely, AL, on 4/9/1865; Received at Ship Island, MS, on 4/15/1865. Transferred to Vicksburg, MS, for exchange on 5/1/1865; Exchanged at Camp Townsend, MS, on 5/6/1865.

White, F.M. (AKA T.M.) Pvt./Sgt., 4th Mississippi Infantry. Co.C. Federal Rolls of Prisoners of War: Captured at Blakely, AL, on 4/9/1865; Received at Ship Island, MS, on 4/15/1865. Transferred to Vicksburg, MS, for exchange on 5/1/1865; Exchanged at Camp Townsend, MS, on 5/6/1865. Born: 1839 at Holmes County, MS. Died: 1924 at Holmes County, MS. Confederate Pension Application dated 1917 on file at the Mississippi Department of Archives and History. Target Name: White, F.M. County: Holmes.

White, John A. Pvt., 35th Mississippi Infantry. Co. A. Federal Rolls of Prisoners of War: Captured at Blakely, AL, on 4/9/1865; Received at Ship Island, MS, on 4/15/1865. Transferred to Vicksburg, MS, for exchange on 5/1/1865; Exchanged at Camp Townsend, MS, on 5/6/1865.

Whitehead, William Henry Pvt., 39th Mississippi Infantry. Co. E. Federal Rolls of Prisoners of War: Captured at Blakely, AL, on 4/9/1865; Received at Ship Island, MS, on 4/15/1865. Transferred to Vicksburg, MS, for exchange on 5/1/1865; Exchanged at Camp Townsend, MS, on 5/6/1865. Born: 1837 at Copiah County, MS. Died: 1912 at Franklin County, MS. Buried: Mt. Carmel Cemetery located at Franklin County, MS. Confederate Pension Application dated 1902 on file at the Mississippi Department of Archives and History. Target Name: Whitehead, W.H. County: Franklin. Also a Confederate Widows Pension Application dated 1912 on file. Target Name: Whitehead, Rebecca. County: Franklin.

Whitman, R. Pvt., 1st Mississippi Light Artillery. Co. __. Federal Rolls of Prisoners of War: Captured at Blakely, AL, on 4/9/1865; Received at Ship Island, MS, on 4/15/1865. Transferred to Vicksburg, MS, for exchange on 5/1/1865; Exchanged at Camp Townsend, MS, on 5/6/1865.

Whittaker, John Pvt., 1st Mississippi Light Artillery. Co. G. Federal Rolls of Prisoners of War: Captured at Blakely, AL, on 4/9/1865; Received at Ship Island, MS, on 4/15/1865. Transferred to Vicksburg, MS, for exchange on 5/1/1865; Exchanged at Camp Townsend, MS, on 5/6/1865.

Whittaker, Warden G. (AKA W.J.) Pvt., 1st Mississippi Light Artillery. Co. G. Federal Rolls of Prisoners of War: Captured at Blakely, AL, on 4/9/1865; Received at Ship Island, MS, on 4/15/1865. Transferred to Vicksburg, MS, for exchange on 5/1/1865; Exchanged at Camp Townsend, MS, on 5/6/1865.

Wiggins, Benjamin F. (AKA B.Y.) Pvt./Cpl., 1st Mississippi Light Artillery. Co. G. Federal Rolls of Prisoners of War: Captured at Blakely, AL, on 4/9/1865; Received at Ship Island, MS, on 4/15/1865. Transferred to Vicksburg, MS, for exchange on 5/1/1865; Exchanged at Camp Townsend, MS, on 5/6/1865.

Wildy, H.H. 1st Lt./Ensign, 46th Mississippi Infantry. Co. E. Federal Rolls of Prisoners of War: Captured at Blakely, AL, on 4/9/1865; Received at Ship Island, MS, on 4/15/1865. Transferred to Vicksburg, MS, for exchange on 5/1/1865; Exchanged at Camp Townsend, MS.

Williams, Benjamin Pvt., 39th Mississippi Infantry. Co. I. Federal Rolls of Prisoners of War: Captured at Blakely, AL, on 4/9/1865; Received at Ship Island, MS, on 4/15/1865. Transferred to Vicksburg, MS, for exchange on 5/1/1865; Exchanged at Camp Townsend, MS, on 5/6/1865.

Williams, J.M. Pvt., 46th Mississippi Infantry. Co. G. Federal Rolls of Prisoners of War: Captured in Alabama on 4/1/1865; Received at Ship Island, MS. Transferred to Vicksburg, MS, for exchange on 5/1/1865; Exchanged at Camp Townsend, MS, on 5/6/1865.

Williams, James Cpl., 7th Mississippi Battalion Infantry. Co. E. Federal Rolls of Prisoners of War: Captured at Blakely, AL, on 4/9/1865; Received at Ship Island, MS, on 4/15/1865. Transferred to Vicksburg, MS, for

exchange on 5/1/1865; Exchanged at Camp Townsend, MS, on 5/6/1865.

Williams, Jefferson Winston Pvt./ Sgt., 1st Mississippi Light Artillery. Co. D. Enlisted: 4/10/1862 at Lexington, MS, on for the war. On Hospital Register at Marion, AL, where he remained until 9/1864. Federal Rolls of Prisoners of War: Captured at Blakely, AL, on 4/9/1865; Received at Ship Island, MS, on 4/15/1865. Transferred to Vicksburg, MS, for exchange on 5/1/1865; Exchanged at Camp Townsend, MS, on 5/6/1865. Born: 1827 in Lawrence County, MS. Married: (1) Mary Susan Morris, (2) Harriet Amanda Morris and (3) Julia Horten, whom he married in Holmes County, GA. after 1865. Children: 14. Residence after war: Holmes County, MS. Died: 1897. Buried: Mississippi with family.

Williams, John Pvt., 36th Mississippi Infantry. Co. __. Federal Rolls of Prisoners of War: Captured at Blakely, AL, on 4/9/1865; Received at Ship Island, MS, on 4/15/1865. Transferred to Vicksburg, MS, for exchange on 5/1/1865; Exchanged at Camp Townsend, MS, on 5/6/1865.

Williams, Mart S. Pvt., 35th Mississippi Infantry. Co. C. Federal Rolls of Prisoners of War: Captured at Blakely, AL, on 4/9/1865; Received at Ship Island, MS, on 4/15/1865. Transferred to Vicksburg, MS, for exchange on 5/1/1865; Exchanged at Camp Townsend, MS, on 5/6/1865.

Williams, R.J. Pvt./Cpl., 39th Mississippi Infantry. Co. E. Federal Rolls of Prisoners of War: Captured at Blakely, AL, on 4/9/1865; Received at Ship Island, MS, on 4/15/1865. Transferred to Vicksburg, MS, for exchange on 5/1/1865; Exchanged at Camp Townsend, MS, on 5/6/1865.

Williams, William Pvt., 36th Mississippi Infantry. Co. __. Federal Rolls of Prisoners of War: Captured at Blakely, AL, on 4/9/1865; Received at Ship Island, MS, on 4/15/1865. Transferred to Vicksburg, MS, for exchange on 5/1/1865; Exchanged at Camp Townsend, MS, on 5/6/1865.

Williams, Willam Sgt., 36th Mississippi Infantry. Co. __. Federal Rolls of Prisoners of War: Captured at Blakely, AL, on 4/9/1865; Received at Ship Island, MS, on 4/15/1865. Transferred to Vicksburg, MS, for exchange on 5/1/1865; Exchanged at Camp Townsend, MS, on 5/6/1865.

Williams, William M. Pvt., 46th Mississippi Infantry. Co. C. Federal Rolls of Prisoners of War: Captured in Alabama on 4/1/1865; Received at Ship Island, MS. Transferred to Vicksburg, MS, for exchange on 5/1/1865; Exchanged at Camp Townsend, MS, on 5/6/1865.

Williamson, Allen Sgt./Pvt., 8th Mississippi Infantry. Cos. G & I. Federal Rolls of Prisoners of War: Captured at Milton, FL, on 10/25/1864; Received at Ship Island, MS, from New Orleans, LA, on 12/13/1864. Transferred to Vicksburg, MS, for exchange on 5/1/1865; Exchanged at Camp Townsend, MS, on 5/6/1865.

Williamson, S.P. Pvt., 39th Mississippi Infantry. Co. D. Federal Rolls of Prisoners of War: Captured at Blakely, AL, on 4/9/1865; Received at Ship Island, MS, on 4/15/1865. Transferred to Vicksburg, MS, for exchange on 5/1/1865; Exchanged at Camp Townsend, MS, on 5/6/1865. Confederate Widows Pension Application dated 1916 on file at the Mississippi Department of Archives and History. Target Name: Williamson, Harriett. County: Covington.

Williamson, W.H. (AKA Williams) Pvt., 39th Mississippi Infantry. Co. D. Federal Rolls of Prisoners of War: Captured at Blakely, AL, on 4/9/1865; Received at Ship Island, MS, on 4/15/1865. Transferred to Vicksburg, MS, for exchange on 5/1/1865; Exchanged at Camp Townsend, MS, on 5/6/1865.

Willis, Joseph B. Pvt./Sgt., 1st Mississippi Light Artillery. Co. G. Federal Rolls of Prisoners of War: Captured at Blakely, AL, on 4/9/1865; Received at Ship Island, MS, on 4/15/1865. Transferred to Vicksburg, MS, for exchange on 5/1/1865; Exchanged at Camp Townsend, MS, on 5/6/1865.

Willis, Thomas B. Pvt., 1st Mississippi Light Artillery. Co. G. Federal Rolls of Prisoners of War: Captured at Blakely, AL, on 4/9/1865; Received at Ship Island, MS, on 4/15/1865. Transferred to Vicksburg, MS, for exchange on 5/1/1865; Exchanged at Camp Townsend, MS, on 5/6/1865.

Willis, W.F. Pvt./Cpl., 4th Mississippi Infantry. Co. C. Federal Rolls of Prisoners of War: Captured at Blakely, AL, on 4/9/1865; Received at Ship Island, MS, on 4/15/1865. Transferred to Vicksburg, MS, for exchange on 5/1/1865; Exchanged at Camp Townsend, MS, on 5/6/1865.

Wilson, J.R. Pvt., 1st Mississippi Light Artillery. Co. __. Federal Rolls of Prisoners of War: Captured at Blakely, AL, on 4/9/1865; Received at Ship Island, MS, on 4/15/1865. Transferred to Vicksburg, MS, for exchange on 5/1/1865; Exchanged at Camp Townsend, MS, on 5/6/1865.

Wilson, Joseph T. Pvt., 35th Mississippi Infantry. Co. B. Federal Rolls of Prisoners of War: Captured at Blakely, AL, on 4/9/1865; Received at Ship Island, MS, on 4/15/1865. Transferred to Vicksburg, MS, for exchange on 5/1/1865; Exchanged at Camp Townsend, MS, on 5/6/1865.

Wilson, W.A. (AKA M.A.) Pvt., 39th Mississippi Infantry. Co. G. Federal Rolls of Prisoners of War: Captured at Blakely, AL, on 4/9/1865; Received at Ship Island, MS, on 4/15/1865. Transferred to Vicksburg, MS, for exchange on 5/1/1865; Exchanged at Camp Townsend, MS, on 5/6/1865. Confederate Widows Pension Application dated 1916 on file at the Mississippi Department of Archives and History. Target Name: Wilson, Carrie. County: Lauderdale.

Wilson, William Pvt., 39th Mississippi Infantry. Co. D. Federal Rolls of Prisoners of War: Captured at Blakely, AL, on 4/9/1865; Received at Ship Island, MS, on 4/15/1865. Transferred to Vicksburg, MS, for exchange on 5/1/1865; Exchanged at Camp Townsend, MS, on 5/6/1865.

Wimberly, J.A. Pvt., 4th Mississippi Infantry. Co. G. Federal Rolls of Prisoners of War: Captured at Blakely, AL, on 4/9/1865; Received at Ship Island, MS, on 4/15/1865. Transferred to Vicksburg, MS, for exchange on 5/1/1865; Exchanged at Camp Townsend, MS, on 5/6/1865.

Windham, Milton Pvt., 36th Mississippi Infantry. Co. K. Federal Rolls of Prisoners of War: Captured at Blakely, AL, on 4/9/1865; Received at Ship Island, MS, on 4/15/1865. Transferred to Vicksburg, MS, for exchange on 5/1/1865; Exchanged at Camp Townsend, MS, on 5/6/1865.

Windham, W.J. Pvt., 46th Mississippi Infantry. Co. G.

Federal Rolls of Prisoners of War: Captured in Alabama on 4/1/1865; Received at Ship Island, MS. Transferred to Vicksburg, MS, for exchange on 5/1/1865; Exchanged at Camp Townsend, MS, on 5/6/1865.

Windham, Warren T. Pvt./Cpl., 7th Mississippi Battalion Infantry. Co. G. Federal Rolls of Prisoners of War: Captured at Blakely, AL, on 4/9/1865; Received at Ship Island, MS, on 4/15/1865. Transferred to Vicksburg, MS, for exchange on 5/1/1865; Exchanged at Camp Townsend, MS, on 5/6/1865.

Winston, Samuel L. Lt., Powers Cavalry Regiment. Co. __. Federal Rolls of Prisoners of War: Captured at Washington, MS, on 11/11/1864; Forwarded to Ship Island, MS, from New Orleans, LA, on 12/18/1864. Exchanged on 3/2/1865.

Witset, J. Pvt., 35th Mississippi Infantry. Co. __. Federal Rolls of Prisoners of War: Captured at Blakely, AL, on 4/9/1865; Received at Ship Island, MS, on 4/15/1865. Transferred to Vicksburg, MS, for exchange on 5/1/1865; Exchanged at Camp Townsend, MS, on 5/6/1865.

Wood, D.M. Pvt., 46th Mississippi Infantry. Co. G. Federal Rolls of Prisoners of War: Captured in Alabama on 4/1/1865; Received at Ship Island, MS. Transferred to Vicksburg, MS, for exchange on 5/1/1865; Exchanged at Camp Townsend, MS, on 5/6/1865.

Wood, James T. (AKA Woods, J.F.) Pvt., 1st Mississippi Light Artillery. Co. G. Federal Rolls of Prisoners of War: Captured at Blakely, AL, on 4/9/1865; Received at Ship Island, MS, on 4/15/1865. Transferred to Vicksburg, MS, for exchange on 5/1/1865; Exchanged at Camp Townsend, MS, on 5/6/1865.

Woodward, Isaac Pvt., 35th Mississippi Infantry. Co. I. Federal Rolls of Prisoners of War: Captured at Blakely, AL, on 4/9/1865; Received at Ship Island, MS, on 4/15/1865. Transferred to Vicksburg, MS, for exchange on 5/1/1865; Exchanged at Camp Townsend, MS, on 5/6/1865.

Worsham, W.D. Pvt., 8th Mississippi Cavalry. Co. G. Federal Rolls of Prisoners of War: Captured at Weldon, FL, on 10/25/1864; Received at Ship Island, MS, from New Orleans, LA, on 12/13/1864. Transferred to Vicksburg, MS, for exchange on 5/1/1865; Exchanged at Camp Townsend, MS, on 5/6/1865.

Yerger, D.D. Pvt., 1st Mississippi Light Artillery. Co. G. Federal Rolls of Prisoners of War: Captured at Blakely, AL, on 4/9/1865; Received at Ship Island, MS, on 4/15/1865. Transferred to Vicksburg, MS, for exchange on 5/1/1865; Exchanged at Camp Townsend, MS, on 5/6/1865.

Young, Henry T. (AKA H.F.) Pvt., 1st Mississippi Light Artillery. Co. G. Federal Rolls of Prisoners of War: Captured at Blakely, AL, on 4/9/1865; Received at Ship Island, MS, on 4/15/1865. Transferred to Vicksburg, MS, for exchange on 5/1/1865; Exchanged at Camp Townsend, MS, on 5/6/1865.

Young, S.C. Asst. Surg., 1st Mississippi Light Artillery. Co. K. Federal Rolls of Prisoners of War: Captured at Blakely, AL, on 4/9/1865; Received at Ship Island, MS, on 4/15/1865. Transferred to Vicksburg, MS, for exchange on 4/28/1865; Confined at New Orleans, LA, on 4/30/1865. Exchanged at Camp Townsend, MS, on 5/6/1865.

Missouri Prisoners of War

Adams, J.D. Cpl., 3rd & 5th Missouri Infantry (Consolidated). Co. __. Federal Rolls of Prisoners of War: Captured at Blakely, AL, on 4/9/1865; Received at Ship Island, MS, on 4/15/1865. Transferred to Vicksburg, MS, for exchange on 5/1/1865; Exchanged at Camp Townsend, MS, on 5/6/1865.

Adams, S.W. Pvt., 3rd & 5th Missouri Infantry (Consolidated). Co. __. Federal Rolls of Prisoners of War: Captured at Blakely, AL, on 4/9/1865; Received at Ship Island, MS, on 4/15/1865. Transferred to Vicksburg, MS, for exchange on 5/1/1865; Exchanged at Camp Townsend, MS, on 5/6/1865.

Adams, V.P. Pvt., 3rd & 5th Missouri Infantry (Consolidated). Co. __. Federal Rolls of Prisoners of War: Captured at Blakely, AL, on 4/9/1865; Received at Ship Island, MS, on 4/15/1865. Transferred to Vicksburg, MS, for exchange on 5/1/1865; Exchanged at Camp Townsend, MS, on 5/6/1865.

Adams, William L. Pvt., 1st & 3rd Missouri Cavalry (Consolidated). Co. __. Federal Rolls of Prisoners of War: Captured at Blakely, AL, on 4/9/1865; Received at Ship Island, MS, on 4/15/1865. Transferred to Vicksburg, MS, for exchange on 5/1/1865; Exchanged at Camp Townsend, MS, on 5/6/1865.

Algeo, Charles (AKA Algo) 1st Sgt., 1st & 3rd Missouri Cavalry (Consolidated). Co. H. Federal Rolls of Prisoners of War: Captured at Blakely, AL, on 4/9/1865; Received at Ship Island, MS, on 4/15/1865. Transferred to Vicksburg, MS, for exchange on 5/1/1865; Exchanged at Camp Townsend, MS, on 5/6/1865.

Allen, A.D. Pvt., 3rd & 5th Missouri Infantry (Consolidated). Co. __. Federal Rolls of Prisoners of War: Captured at Blakely, AL, on 4/9/1865; Received at Ship Island, MS, on 4/15/1865. Transferred to Vicksburg, MS, for exchange on 5/1/1865; Exchanged at Camp Townsend, MS, on 5/6/1865.

Allen, Albert O., Sr. Sgt./Ord. Sgt., 3rd & 5th Missouri Infantry (Consolidated). Co. __. Enlisted: 7/1861 at New Madrid, MO. Federal Rolls of Prisoners of War: Captured at Blakely, AL, on 4/9/1865; Received at Ship Island, MS, on 4/15/1865. Transferred to Vicksburg, MS, for exchange on 5/1/1865; Exchanged at Camp Townsend, MS, on 5/6/1865. Rolls of Prisoners of War, C.S.A: Surrendered at Citronelle, AL, on 5/4/1865; Paroled at Jackson, MS, on 5/12/1865. Soldier also served as a Pvt. with the 1st Missouri Infantry. Co.F. Born: 12/12/1841 to N.B. Allen and Sarah Bollinger near Fredricktown, MO. Married: Laura Watson in 1881. Children: 4 —1 son and 3 daughters. Occupations: Owner of the weekly Record newspaper, first school commissioner of New Madrid County, MO, and Missouri State Legislator. Memberships: Mason at the Knights of Templar Lodge at Jefferson City, MO, for 59 years. Died: 4/4/1926 at the home of his daughter, Mrs.M.D. Reilly, Jr., at Omaha, NE.

Allen, Isaac Cpl., 1st & 3rd Missouri Cavalry (Consolidated). Co. D. Enlisted: 12/24/1861 at Albany, MO. Age at enlistment: 17. Residence at enlistment: Ray County, MO. Federal Rolls of Prisoners of War: Captured at Blakely, AL, on 4/9/1865; Received at Ship Island, MS, on 4/15/1865. Transferred to Vicksburg, MS, for exchange on 5/1/1865; Exchanged at Camp Townsend, MS, on 5/6/1865.

Althison, J. Pvt., 3rd & 5th Missouri Infantry (Consolidated). Co. __. Federal Rolls of Prisoners of War: Captured at Blakely, AL, on 4/9/1865; Received at Ship Island, MS, on 4/15/1865. Transferred to Vicksburg, MS, for exchange on 5/1/1865; Exchanged at Camp Townsend, MS, on 5/6/1865.

Anderson, Joseph E. Pvt., 1st & 3rd Missouri Cavalry (Consolidated). Co. E. Federal Rolls of Prisoners of War: Captured at Blakely, AL, on 4/9/1865; Received at Ship Island, MS, on 4/15/1865. Transferred to Vicksburg, MS, for exchange on 5/1/1865; Exchanged at Camp Townsend, MS, on 5/6/1865.

Anderson, W. Pvt., 3rd & 5th Missouri Infantry (Consolidated). Co. __. Federal Rolls of Prisoners of War: Captured at Blakely, AL, on 4/9/1865; Received at Ship Island, MS, on 4/15/1865. Transferred to Vicksburg, MS, for exchange on 5/1/1865; Exchanged at Camp Townsend, MS, on 5/6/1865.

Archer, Thomas B. Pvt., 2nd & 6th Missouri Infantry (Consolidated). Co. C. Federal Rolls of Prisoners of War: Captured at Blakely, AL, on 4/9/1865; Received at Ship Island, MS, on 4/15/1865. Transferred to Vicksburg, MS, for exchange on 5/1/1865; Exchanged at Camp Townsend, MS, on 5/6/1865.

Asben, W.N. (AKA Asbell) Pvt., 3rd & 5th Missouri Infantry (Consolidated). Co. __. Federal Rolls of Prisoners of War: Captured at Blakely, AL, on 4/9/1865; Received at Ship Island, MS, on 4/15/1865. Transferred to Vicksburg, MS, for exchange on 5/1/1865; Exchanged at Camp Townsend, MS, on 5/6/1865.

Ashford, Randolph Pvt., 1st & 3rd Missouri Cavalry (Consolidated). Co. E. Federal Rolls of Prisoners of War: Captured at Blakely, AL, on 4/9/1865; Received at Ship Island, MS, on 4/15/1865. Transferred to Vicksburg, MS, for exchange on 5/1/1865; Exchanged at Camp Townsend, MS, on 5/6/1865.

Askew, Clark (AKA Pascal C.) Pvt., 2nd & 6th Missouri Infantry (Consolidated). Co. H. Federal Rolls of Prisoners of War: Captured at Blakely, AL, on 4/9/1865; Received at Ship Island, MS, on 4/15/1865. Transferred to Vicksburg, MS, for exchange on 5/1/1865; Exchanged at Camp Townsend, MS, on 5/6/1865.

Babel, Benjamin F. (AKA Baber) Pvt./Cpl., 3rd & 5th Missouri Infantry (Consolidated). Co. A. Federal Rolls of Prisoners of War: Captured at Blakely, AL, on 4/9/1865; Received at Ship Island, MS, on 4/15/1865. Transferred to Vicksburg, MS, for exchange on 5/1/1865; Exchanged at Camp Townsend, MS, on 5/6/1865.

Babnight, R. Pvt., 3rd & 5th Missouri Infantry (Consolidated). Co. __. Federal Rolls of Prisoners of War: Captured at Blakely, AL, on 4/9/1865; Received at Ship Island, MS, on 4/15/1865. Transferred to Vicksburg, MS, for exchange on 5/1/1865; Exchanged at Camp Townsend, MS, on 5/6/1865.

Backer, Jacob Pvt., 1st & 3rd Missouri Cavalry (Consolidated). Co. B. Federal Rolls of Prisoners of War: Captured at Blakely, AL, on 4/9/1865; Received at Ship Island, MS, on 4/15/1865. Transferred to Vicksburg, MS, for exchange on 5/1/1865; Exchanged at Camp Townsend, MS, on 5/6/1865.

Backer, John A.C. Pvt., 1st & 3rd Missouri Cavalry (Consolidated). Co. B. Federal Rolls of Prisoners of War: Captured at Blakely, AL, on 4/9/1865; Received at Ship Island, MS, on 4/15/1865. Transferred to Vicksburg, MS, for exchange on 5/1/1865; Exchanged at Camp Townsend, MS, on 5/6/1865.

Badger, John L.T. Pvt., 1st & 3rd Missouri Cavalry (Consolidated). Co. B. Federal Rolls of Prisoners of War: Captured at Blakely, AL, on 4/9/1865; Received at Ship Island, MS, on 4/15/1865. Transferred to Vicksburg, MS, for exchange on 5/1/1865; Exchanged at Camp Townsend, MS, on 5/6/1865.

Bailey, J.P. Pvt., 1st & 3rd Missouri Cavalry (Consolidated). Co. __. Federal Rolls of Prisoners of War: Captured at Blakely, AL, on 4/9/1865; Received at Ship Island, MS, on 4/15/1865. Transferred to Vicksburg, MS, for exchange on 5/1/1865; Exchanged at Camp Townsend, MS, on 5/6/1865.

Baldock, Richard Pvt./Musician, 3rd & 5th Missouri Infantry (Consolidated). Co. B. Federal Rolls of Prisoners of War: Captured at Blakely, AL, on 4/9/1865; Received at Ship Island, MS, on 4/15/1865. Transferred to Vicksburg, MS, for exchange on 5/1/1865; Exchanged at Camp Townsend, MS, on 5/6/1865.

Barbee, James D. Pvt., 1st & 3rd Missouri Cavalry (Consolidated). Co. I. Enlisted: 1/1/1863 at Weston, MO. Age at enlistment: 34. Residence at enlistment: Platte County, MO. Federal Rolls of Prisoners of War: Captured at Blakely, AL, on 4/9/1865; Received at Ship Island, MS, on 4/15/1865. Transferred to Vicksburg, MS, for exchange on 5/1/1865; Exchanged at Camp Townsend, MS, on 5/6/1865.

Barbee, William T. Pvt., 1st & 3rd Missouri Cavalry (Consolidated). Co. I. Federal Rolls of Prisoners of War: Captured at Blakely, AL, on 4/9/1865; Received at Ship Island, MS, on 4/15/1865. Transferred to Vicksburg, MS, for exchange on 5/1/1865; Exchanged at Camp Townsend, MS, on 5/6/1865. Rolls of Prisoners of War, C.S.A: Surrendered at Citronelle, AL, on 5/4/1865; Paroled at Jackson, MS, on 5/13/1865. Residence at parole: Copiah County, MS.

Barker, John D. Pvt., 1st & 3rd Missouri Cavalry (Consolidated). Co. __. Federal Rolls of Prisoners of War: Captured at Blakely, AL, on 4/9/1865; Received at Ship Island, MS, on 4/15/1865. Transferred to Vicksburg, MS, for exchange on 5/1/1865; Exchanged at Camp Townsend, MS, on 5/6/1865.

Barnard, John Pvt., 2nd & 6th Missouri Infantry (Consolidated). Co. F. Federal Rolls of Prisoners of War: Captured at Blakely, AL, on 4/9/1865; Received at Ship Island, MS, on 4/15/1865. Transferred to Vicksburg, MS, for exchange on 5/1/1865; Exchanged at Camp Townsend, MS, on 5/6/1865.

Barroll, Charles E. Drum Major, 3rd & 5th Missouri Infantry (Consolidated). Co. __. Federal Rolls of Prisoners of War: Captured at Blakely, AL, on 4/9/1865; Received at Ship Island, MS, on 4/15/1865. Transferred to Vicksburg, MS, for exchange on 5/1/1865; Exchanged at Camp Townsend, MS, on 5/6/1865.

Baxter, W.M. (AKA Bustin) Pvt., 1st & 3rd Missouri Cavalry (Consolidated). Co. __. Federal Rolls of Prisoners of War: Captured at Blakely, AL, on 4/9/1865; Received at Ship Island, MS, on 4/15/1865. Transferred to Vicksburg, MS, for exchange on 5/1/1865; Exchanged at Camp Townsend, MS, on 5/6/1865.

Beadle, W.P. (AKA Beagle) Sgt., 1st & 3rd Missouri Cavalry (Consolidated). Co. __. Federal Rolls of Prisoners of War: Captured at Blakely, AL, on 4/9/1865; Received at Ship Island, MS, on 4/15/1865. Transferred to Vicksburg, MS, for exchange on 5/1/1865; Exchanged at Camp Townsend, MS, on 5/6/1865.

Beas, Thomas Pvt., 2nd Missouri Cavalry. Co. __. Federal Rolls of Prisoners of War: Captured at Greene County, MS, on 12/13/1864; Received at Ship Island, MS, on 1/25/1865. Transferred to Vicksburg, MS, for exchange on 5/1/1865; Exchanged at Camp Townsend, MS, on 5/6/1865.

Beeley, T.J. (AKA F.J.) Pvt., 1st & 3rd Missouri Cavalry (Consolidated). Co. __. Federal Rolls of Prisoners of War: Captured at Blakely, AL, on 4/9/1865; Received at Ship Island, MS, on 4/15/1865. Transferred to Vicksburg, MS, for exchange on 5/1/1865; Exchanged at Camp Townsend, MS, on 5/6/1865.

Bell, Samuel A. Pvt., 1st & 3rd Missouri Cavalry (Consolidated). Co. B. Federal Rolls of Prisoners of War: Captured at Blakely, AL, on 4/9/1865; Received at Ship Island, MS, on 4/15/1865. Transferred to Vicksburg, MS, for exchange on 5/1/1865; Exchanged at Camp Townsend, MS, on 5/6/1865.

Bell, William C. (AKA Belle) Pvt., 1st & 3rd Missouri

Cavalry (Consolidated). Co. K. Federal Rolls of Prisoners of War: Captured at Blakely, AL, on 4/9/1865; Received at Ship Island, MS, on 4/15/1865. Transferred to Vicksburg, MS, for exchange on 5/1/1865; Exchanged at Camp Townsend, MS, on 5/6/1865. Rolls of Prisoners of War, C.S.A: Surrendered at Citronelle, AL, on 5/4/1865; Paroled at Meridian, MS, in 5/1865. Confederate Pension Application on file at the Tennessee State Library and Archives. Target Name: Bell, William C. Application Number: S10553. County: Cannon.

Bently, James R. Pvt., 3rd & 5th Missouri Infantry (Consolidated). Co. __. Federal Rolls of Prisoners of War: Captured at Blakely, AL, on 4/9/1865; Received at Ship Island, MS, on 4/15/1865. Transferred to Vicksburg, MS, for exchange on 5/1/1865; Exchanged at Camp Townsend, MS, on 5/6/1865.

Berryhill, Benjamin F. (AKA Berrihill, Frank) Pvt., 3rd & 5th Missouri Infantry (Consolidated). Co. G. Federal Rolls of Prisoners of War: Captured at Blakely, AL, on 4/9/1865; Received at Ship Island, MS, on 4/15/1865. Transferred to Vicksburg, MS, for exchange on 5/1/1865; Exchanged at Camp Townsend, MS, on 5/6/1865.

Bertin, G. Pvt., 1st & 3rd Missouri Cavalry (Consolidated). Co. __. Federal Rolls of Prisoners of War: Captured at Blakely, AL, on 4/9/1865; Received at Ship Island, MS, on 4/15/1865. Transferred to Vicksburg, MS, for exchange on 5/1/1865; Exchanged at Camp Townsend, MS, on 5/6/1865.

Black, Adam Sgt., 1st & 3rd Missouri Cavalry (Consolidated). Co. E. Federal Rolls of Prisoners of War: Captured at Blakely, AL, on 4/9/1865; Received at Ship Island, MS, on 4/15/1865. Transferred to Vicksburg, MS, for exchange on 5/1/1865; Exchanged at Camp Townsend, MS, on 5/6/1865. Rolls of Prisoners of War, C.S.A: Surrendered at Citronelle, AL, on 5/4/1865; Paroled at Meridian, MS, in 5/1865.

Black, Anderson Pvt., 1st & 3rd Missouri Cavalry (Consolidated). Co. H. Enlisted: 12/29/1861 at Grant's Hill, MO. Age at enlistment: 22. Residence at enlistment: Worth County, MO. Wounded at Franklin, TN. Federal Rolls of Prisoners of War: Captured at Blakely, AL, on 4/9/1865; Received at Ship Island, MS, on 4/15/1865. Transferred to Vicksburg, MS, for exchange on 5/1/1865; Exchanged at Camp Townsend, MS, on 5/6/1865.

Blackburn, James R. Sgt., 1st & 3rd Missouri Cavalry (Consolidated). Co. B. Federal Rolls of Prisoners of War: Captured at Blakely, AL, on 4/9/1865; Received at Ship Island, MS, on 4/15/1865. Transferred to Vicksburg, MS, for exchange on 5/1/1865; Exchanged at Camp Townsend, MS, on 5/6/1865.

Blain, James W. Pvt., 1st & 3rd Missouri Cavalry (Consolidated). Co. D. Enlisted: 12/24/1861 at Camden, MO. Age at enlistment: 17. Residence at enlistment: Ray County, MO. Federal Rolls of Prisoners of War: Captured and paroled at Corinth, MS. Rolls for 2/1863 through 6/1863: Absent, in hospital at Enterprise, MS. Federal Rolls of Prisoners of War: Captured at Blakely, AL, on 4/9/1865; Received at Ship Island, MS, on 4/15/1865. Transferred to Vicksburg, MS, for exchange on 5/1/1865; Exchanged at Camp Townsend, MS, on 5/6/1865.

Blakely, Robert A. Pvt., 1st & 3rd Missouri Infantry (Consolidated). Co. E. Federal Rolls of Prisoners of War: Captured at Blakely, AL, on 4/9/1865; Received at Ship Island, MS, on 4/15/1865. Transferred to Vicksburg, MS, for exchange on 5/1/1865; Exchanged at Camp Townsend, MS, on 5/6/1865.

Blanks, Marble (AKA Myrtle) Pvt., 2nd & 6th Missouri Infantry (Consolidated). Co. C. Federal Rolls of Prisoners of War: Captured at Blakely, AL, on 4/9/1865; Received at Ship Island, MS, on 4/15/1865. Transferred to Vicksburg, MS, for exchange on 5/1/1865; Exchanged at Camp Townsend, MS, on 5/6/1865.

Bledsoe, W.H. Pvt., 3rd & 5th Missouri Infantry (Consolidated). Co. __. Federal Rolls of Prisoners of War: Captured at Blakely, AL, on 4/9/1865; Received at Ship Island, MS, on 4/15/1865. Transferred to Vicksburg, MS, for exchange on 5/1/1865; Exchanged at Camp Townsend, MS, on 5/6/1865.

Bondaure, Marshall (AKA Bondaue) Pvt., 3rd & 5th Missouri Infantry (Consolidated). Co. __. Federal Rolls of Prisoners of War: Captured at Blakely, AL, on 4/9/1865; Received at Ship Island, MS, on 4/15/1865. Transferred to Vicksburg, MS, for exchange on 5/1/1865; Exchanged at Camp Townsend, MS, on 5/6/1865.

Bowers, T.M. (AKA Bower, F.M.) Pvt., 3rd & 5th Missouri Infantry (Consolidated). Co. __. Federal Rolls of Prisoners of War: Captured at Blakely, AL, on 4/9/1865; Received at Ship Island, MS, on 4/15/1865. Transferred to Vicksburg, MS, for exchange on 5/1/1865; Exchanged at Camp Townsend, MS, on 5/6/1865.

Bradford, William L. Pvt./Cpl., 1st & 3rd Missouri Cavalry (Consolidated). Co. K. Enlisted: 1/1/1863 at Rolla, MO. Age at enlistment: 22. Residence at enlistment: Phelps County, MO. Federal Rolls of Prisoners of War: Captured at Blakely, AL, on 4/9/1865; Received at Ship Island, MS, on 4/15/1865. Transferred to Vicksburg, MS, for exchange on 5/1/1865; Exchanged at Camp Townsend, MS, on 5/6/1865.

Bradley, James M. (AKA J.W.) Pvt., 3rd & 5th Missouri Infantry (Consolidated). Co. K. Federal Rolls of Prisoners of War: Captured at Blakely, AL, on 4/9/1865; Received at Ship Island, MS, on 4/15/1865. Transferred to Vicksburg, MS, for exchange on 5/1/1865; Exchanged at Camp Townsend, MS, on 5/6/1865.

Bradley, John A. (AKA Bradly) 3rd Sgt., 1st & 3rd Missouri Cavalry (Consolidated). Co. I. Enlisted: 1/1/1862 at Westport, MO. Age at enlistment: 26. Residence at enlistment: Jackson County, MO. Wounded at Franklin, TN. Federal Rolls of Prisoners of War: Captured at Blakely, AL, on 4/9/1865; Received at Ship Island, MS, on 4/15/1865. Transferred to Vicksburg, MS, for exchange on 5/1/1865; Exchanged at Camp Townsend, MS, on 5/6/1865.

Bradley, John W. (AKA Brady) Sgt., 1st & 3rd Missouri Cavalry (Consolidated). Co. I. Federal Rolls of Prisoners of War: Captured at Blakely, AL, on 4/9/1865; Received at Ship Island, MS, on 4/15/1865. Transferred to Vicksburg, MS, for exchange on 5/1/1865; Exchanged at Camp Townsend, MS, on 5/6/1865.

Bradley, Samuel M. Sgt., 3rd & 5th Missouri Infantry (Consolidated). Co. H. Federal Rolls of Prisoners of War: Captured at Blakely, AL, on 4/9/1865; Received at Ship Island, MS, on 4/15/1865. Transferred to Vicksburg, MS, for exchange on 5/1/1865; Exchanged at Camp Townsend, MS, on 5/6/1865.

Brady, John W. 5th Sgt., 1st & 3rd Missouri Cavalry

(Consolidated). Co. I. Enlisted: 1/1/1862 at Platte City, MO. Age at enlistment: 21. Residence at enlistment: Platte County, MO. Federal Rolls of Prisoners of War: Captured at Blakely, AL, on 4/9/1865; Received at Ship Island, MS, on 4/15/1865. Transferred to Vicksburg, MS, for exchange on 5/1/1865; Exchanged at Camp Townsend, MS, on 5/6/1865.

Bragg, B.H. Pvt., 3rd & 5th Missouri Infantry (Consolidated). Co. __. Federal Rolls of Prisoners of War: Captured at Blakely, AL, on 4/9/1865; Received at Ship Island, MS, on 4/15/1865. Transferred to Vicksburg, MS, for exchange on 5/1/1865; Exchanged at Camp Townsend, MS, on 5/6/1865.

Branch, Loid Pvt., 3rd & 5th Missouri Infantry (Consolidated). Co. __. Federal Rolls of Prisoners of War: Captured at Blakely, AL, on 4/9/1865; Received at Ship Island, MS, on 4/15/1865. Transferred to Vicksburg, MS, for exchange on 5/1/1865; Exchanged at Camp Townsend, MS, on 5/6/1865.

Bratten, William (AKA Bratton) Pvt., 3rd & 5th Missouri Infantry (Consolidated). Co. G. Federal Rolls of Prisoners of War: Captured at Blakely, AL, on 4/9/1865; Received at Ship Island, MS, on 4/15/1865. Transferred to Vicksburg, MS, for exchange on 5/1/1865; Exchanged at Camp Townsend, MS, on 5/6/1865.

Bridgefort, R.T. (AKA Bridgeport) Pvt., 3rd & 5th Missouri Infantry (Consolidated). Co. __. Federal Rolls of Prisoners of War: Captured at Blakely, AL, on 4/9/1865; Received at Ship Island, MS, on 4/15/1865. Transferred to Vicksburg, MS, for exchange on 5/1/1865; Exchanged at Camp Townsend, MS, on 5/6/1865.

Bridges, Blackburn Pvt., 1st & 3rd Missouri Cavalry (Consolidated). Cos. F & I. Federal Rolls of Prisoners of War: Captured at Blakely, AL, on 4/9/1865; Received at Ship Island, MS, on 4/15/1865. Transferred to Vicksburg, MS, for exchange on 5/1/1865; Exchanged at Camp Townsend, MS, on 5/6/1865.

Briscoe, Joseph Sgt., 3rd & 5th Missouri Infantry. (Consolidated). Co. __. Federal Rolls of Prisoners of War: Captured at Blakely, AL, on 4/9/1865; Received at Ship Island, MS, on 4/15/1865. Transferred to Vicksburg, MS, for exchange on 5/1/1865; Exchanged at Camp Townsend, MS, on 5/6/1865.

Brown, F. Pvt., 1st & 3rd Missouri Cavalry (Consolidated). Co. __. Federal Rolls of Prisoners of War: Captured at Blakely, AL, on 4/9/1865; Received at Ship Island, MS, on 4/15/1865. Transferred to Vicksburg, MS, for exchange on 5/1/1865; Exchanged at Camp Townsend, MS, on 5/6/1865.

Brown, Felix C. Sgt., 1st & 3rd Missouri Cavalry (Consolidated). Co. H. Enlisted: 12/31/1861. Age at enlistment: 29. Federal Rolls of Prisoners of War: Captured at Blakely, AL, on 4/9/1865; Received at Ship Island, MS, on 4/15/1865. Transferred to Vicksburg, MS, for exchange on 5/1/1865; Exchanged at Camp Townsend, MS, on 5/6/1865.

Brown, G.W. Pvt., 2nd & 6th Missouri Infantry (Consolidated). Co. __. Federal Rolls of Prisoners of War: Captured at Blakely, AL, on 4/9/1865; Received at Ship Island, MS, on 4/15/1865. Transferred to Vicksburg, MS, for exchange on 5/1/1865; Exchanged at Camp Townsend, MS, on 5/6/1865.

Brown, J.W. Cpl., 3rd & 5th Missouri Infantry (Consolidated). Co. G. Federal Rolls of Prisoners of War: Captured at Blakely, AL, on 4/9/1865; Received at Ship Island, MS, on 4/15/1865. Transferred to Vicksburg, MS, for exchange on 5/1/1865; Exchanged at Camp Townsend, MS, on 5/6/1865.

Browning, Daniel B. Pvt., 3rd & 5th Missouri Infantry (Consolidated). Co. I. Federal Rolls of Prisoners of War: Captured at Blakely, AL, on 4/9/1865; Received at Ship Island, MS, on 4/15/1865. Transferred to Vicksburg, MS, for exchange on 5/1/1865; Exchanged at Camp Townsend, MS, on 5/6/1865.

Buford, William S. Pvt., 2nd & 6th Missouri Infantry (Consolidated). Co. G. Federal Rolls of Prisoners of War: Captured at Blakely, AL, on 4/9/1865; Received at Ship Island, MS, on 4/15/1865. Transferred to Vicksburg, MS, for exchange on 5/1/1865; Exchanged at Camp Townsend, MS, on 5/6/1865.

Burden, Henry C. (AKA Burdell) Pvt., 3rd & 5th Missouri Infantry (Consolidated). Co. D. Federal Rolls of Prisoners of War: Captured at Blakely, AL, on 4/9/1865; Received at Ship Island, MS, on 4/15/1865. Transferred to Vicksburg, MS, for exchange on 5/1/1865; Exchanged at Camp Townsend, MS, on 5/6/1865.

Burton, Thomas Pvt., 3rd & 5th Missouri Infantry (Consolidated). Co. __. Federal Rolls of Prisoners of War: Captured at Blakely, AL, on 4/9/1865; Received at Ship Island, MS, on 4/15/1865. Transferred to Vicksburg, MS, for exchange on 5/1/1865; Exchanged at Camp Townsend, MS, on 5/6/1865.

Bybee, F.E. Pvt., 3rd & 5th Missouri Infantry (Consolidated). Co. __. Federal Rolls of Prisoners of War: Captured at Blakely, AL, on 4/9/1865; Received at Ship Island, MS, on 4/15/1865. Transferred to Vicksburg, MS, for exchange on 5/1/1865; Exchanged at Camp Townsend, MS, on 5/6/1865.

Bybee, James Pvt., 1st & 3rd Missouri Cavalry (Consolidated). Co. I. Enlisted: 3/2/1862 at Weston, MO. Age at enlistment: 34. Residence at enlistment: Platte County, MO. Federal Rolls of Prisoners of War: Captured at Blakely, AL, on 4/9/1865; Received at Ship Island, MS, on 4/15/1865. Transferred to Vicksburg, MS, for exchange on 5/1/1865; Exchanged at Camp Townsend, MS, on 5/6/1865.

Byrne, Edward F.V. (AKA Burnes, Edward F.D.) Sgt., 2nd & 6th Missouri Infantry (Consolidated). Co. K. Federal Rolls of Prisoners of War: Captured at Blakely, AL, on 4/9/1865; Received at Ship Island, MS, on 4/15/1865. Transferred to Vicksburg, MS, for exchange on 5/1/1865; Exchanged at Camp Townsend, MS, on 5/6/1865.

Cain, Thomas Pvt., 1st & 3rd Missouri Cavalry (Consolidated). Co. __. Federal Rolls of Prisoners of War: Captured at Blakely, AL, on 4/9/1865; Received at Ship Island, MS, on 4/15/1865. Transferred to Vicksburg, MS, for exchange on 5/1/1865; Exchanged at Camp Townsend, MS, on 5/6/1865.

Caldwell, C.T. Pvt., 3rd & 5th Missouri Infantry (Consolidated). Co. __. Federal Rolls of Prisoners of War: Captured at Blakely, AL, on 4/9/1865; Received at Ship Island, MS, on 4/15/1865. Transferred to Vicksburg, MS, for exchange on 5/1/1865; Exchanged at Camp Townsend, MS, on 5/6/1865.

Callaghan, William (AKA Callahan) Pvt./Cpl., 1st & 3rd Missouri Cavalry (Consolidated). Co. E. Enlisted: 12/16/1861 at Platte City, MO. Age at enlistment: 30. Residence at enlistment: Platte County, MO.

Wounded at Vicksburg, MS, and Franklin, TN. Federal Rolls of Prisoners of War: Captured at Blakely, AL, on 4/9/1865; Received at Ship Island, MS, on 4/15/1865. Transferred to Vicksburg, MS, for exchange on 5/1/1865; Exchanged at Camp Townsend, MS, on 5/6/1865.

Camlin, Green B. (AKA Camblin, Greenberry) Pvt., 1st & 3rd Missouri Cavalry (Consolidated). Co. __. Enlisted: 12/7/1861 at Callaway County. Age at enlistment: 26. Transferred from Co. B on 1/1/1862. Wounded at New Hope Church, TN. Federal Rolls of Prisoners of War: Captured at Blakely, AL, on 4/9/1865; Received at Ship Island, MS, on 4/15/1865. Transferred to Vicksburg, MS, for exchange on 5/1/1865; Exchanged at Camp Townsend, MS, on 5/6/1865.

Canter, William J. Pvt., 1st & 3rd Missouri Cavalry (Consolidated). Co. __. Federal Rolls of Prisoners of War: Captured at Blakely, AL, on 4/9/1865; Received at Ship Island, MS, on 4/15/1865. Transferred to Vicksburg, MS, for exchange on 5/1/1865; Exchanged at Camp Townsend, MS, on 5/6/1865.

Carter, John D. Cpl./1st Lt., 3rd & 5th Missouri Infantry (Consolidated). Co. E. Federal Rolls of Prisoners of War: Captured at Blakely, AL, on 4/9/1865; Received at Ship Island, MS, on 4/15/1865. Transferred to Vicksburg, MS, for exchange on 4/28/1865; Confined at New Orleans, LA, on 4/30/1865. Exchanged at Camp Townsend, MS, on 5/6/1865.

Carter, Thomas Miller Capt./Lt. Col., 2nd & 6th Missouri Infantry (Consolidated). Co. C. Federal Rolls of Prisoners of War: Captured at Blakely, AL, on 4/9/1865; Received at Ship Island, MS, on 4/15/1865. Transferred to Vicksburg, MS, for exchange on 4/28/1865; Confined at New Orleans, LA, on 4/30/1865. Exchanged at Camp Townsend, MS, on 5/6/1865.

Carver, J.R. Sgt., 3rd & 5th Missouri Infantry (Consolidated). Co. __. Federal Rolls of Prisoners of War: Captured at Blakely, AL, on 4/9/1865; Received at Ship Island, MS, on 4/15/1865. Transferred to Vicksburg, MS, for exchange on 5/1/1865; Exchanged at Camp Townsend, MS, on 5/6/1865.

Casebolt, Eli (AKA Caseboult) Pvt., 1st & 3rd Missouri Cavalry (Consolidated). Co. E. Federal Rolls of Prisoners of War: Captured at Blakely, AL, on 4/9/1865; Received at Ship Island, MS, on 4/15/1865. Transferred to Vicksburg, MS, for exchange on 5/1/1865; Exchanged at Camp Townsend, MS, on 5/6/1865.

Casey, Rives Pvt., 3rd & 5th Missouri Infantry (Consolidated). Co. __. Federal Rolls of Prisoners of War: Captured at Blakely, AL, on 4/9/1865; Received at Ship Island, MS, on 4/15/1865. Transferred to Vicksburg, MS, for exchange on 5/1/1865; Exchanged at Camp Townsend, MS, on 5/6/1865.

Champlin, Hugh L. Pvt., 1st & 3rd Missouri Cavalry (Consolidated). Co. K. Federal Rolls of Prisoners of War: Captured at Blakely, AL, on 4/9/1865; Received at Ship Island, MS, on 4/15/1865. Transferred to Vicksburg, MS, for exchange on 5/1/1865; Exchanged at Camp Townsend, MS, on 5/6/1865.

Chance, Alexander Cpl./Sgt., 1st & 3rd Missouri Cavalry (Consolidated). Co. C. Enlisted: 12/24/1861 at Holt County, MO. Age at enlistment: 17. Promoted to Sgt. in 9/1863. Federal Rolls of Prisoners of War: Captured at Blakely, AL, on 4/9/1865; Received at Ship Island, MS, on 4/15/1865. Transferred to Vicksburg, MS, for exchange on 5/1/1865; Exchanged at Camp Townsend, MS, on 5/6/1865.

Chapman, John T. Cpl./Pvt., 2nd & 6th Missouri Infantry (Consolidated). Co. K. Federal Rolls of Prisoners of War: Captured at Blakely, AL, on 4/9/1865; Received at Ship Island, MS, on 4/15/1865. Transferred to Vicksburg, MS, for exchange on 5/1/1865; Exchanged at Camp Townsend, MS, on 5/6/1865.

Cherry, S.C. Pvt., 3rd & 5th Missouri Infantry (Consolidated). Co. __. Federal Rolls of Prisoners of War: Captured at Blakely, AL, on 4/9/1865; Received at Ship Island, MS, on 4/15/1865. Transferred to Vicksburg, MS, for exchange on 5/1/1865; Exchanged at Camp Townsend, MS, on 5/6/1865.

Chism, Jacob Pvt., 3rd & 5th Missouri Infantry (Consolidated). Co. __. Federal Rolls of Prisoners of War: Captured at Blakely, AL, on 4/9/1865; Received at Ship Island, MS, on 4/15/1865. Transferred to Vicksburg, MS, for exchange on 5/1/1865; Exchanged at Camp Townsend, MS, on 5/6/1865.

Clark, August C. Pvt., 2nd & 6th Missouri Infantry (Consolidated). Co. I. Federal Rolls of Prisoners of War: Captured at Blakely, AL, on 4/9/1865; Received at Ship Island, MS, on 4/15/1865. Transferred to Vicksburg, MS, for exchange on 5/1/1865; Exchanged at Camp Townsend, MS, on 5/6/1865.

Clark, D.C. Sgt., 1st & 3rd Missouri Cavalry (Consolidated). Co. H. Federal Rolls of Prisoners of War: Captured at Blakely, AL, on 4/9/1865; Received at Ship Island, MS, on 4/15/1865. Transferred to Vicksburg, MS, for exchange on 5/1/1865; Exchanged at Camp Townsend, MS, on 5/6/1865.

Clemons, Henry N. (AKA Clemens, H.M.) Cpl., 1st & 3rd Missouri Cavalry (Consolidated). Co. I. Enlisted: 12/16/1861 at Independence, Jackson County, MO. Age at enlistment: 47. Wounded on 7/4/1864. Federal Rolls of Prisoners of War: Captured at Blakely, AL, on 4/9/1865; Received at Ship Island, MS, on 4/15/1865. Transferred to Vicksburg, MS, for exchange on 5/1/1865; Exchanged at Camp Townsend, MS, on 5/6/1865.

Cleveland, Charles Boarman 1st Sgt./1st Lt./Adjt., 1st & 3rd Missouri Cavalry (Consolidated). Co. K/F & S. Enlisted: 12/5/1861 at Huntsville, MO. Age at enlistment: 20. Residence at enlistment: Randolph County, MO. Federal Rolls of Prisoners of War: Captured and paroled at Vicksburg, MS, on 7/4/1863. Promoted to Regtl. Adjt. on 2/22/1864 until the return of Adjutant Clewell. Federal Rolls of Prisoners of War: Captured at Blakely, AL, on 4/9/1865; Received at Ship Island, MS, on 4/15/1865. Transferred to Vicksburg, MS, for exchange on 5/1/1865; Exchanged at Camp Townsend, MS, on 5/6/1865. Rolls of Prisoners of War, C.S.A: Surrendered at Citronelle, AL, on 5/4/1865; Paroled at Jackson, MS, on 5/15/1865. Born: 5/13/1840 at Randolph County, MO, to William Cleveland of Maryland and Jane Elizabeth Abell of Charleston, VA. Education: Mount Pleasant Academy, Huntsville, MO, and the U.S. Naval Academy at Annapolis, MD. Married: Lizzie Houston Woolf in 1872. Children: 5 — 3 sons and 2 daughters. Occupations: School Teacher and Clerk of the Circuit Court of Marengo County, AL. Residences: Birmingham, AL, and spent winters in Florida. Memberships: Mason in the Knights of

Pythias, and Adjutant of the Archibald Gracie Camp of the United Confederate Veterans at Marengo, County AL. Religion: Episcopal. Died: 5/11/1916 at Miami, FL. Buried: Elmwood Cemetery, Birmingham, AL.

Clewell, Frank C. (AKA Clewall) Sgt. Maj./Lt./Adjt., 1st & 3rd Missouri Cavalry (Consolidated). Co. I/F & S. Enlisted: 12/16/1861 at Platte City, MO. Age at enlistment: 22. Residence at enlistment: Platte County, MO. Promoted to Regtl. Adjt. in 4/1863. Federal Rolls of Prisoners of War: Captured at Big Black River Bridge, MS. Federal Rolls of Prisoners of War: Captured at Blakely, AL, on 4/9/1865; Received at Ship Island, MS, on 4/15/1865. Transferred to Vicksburg, MS, for exchange on 5/1/1865; Exchanged at Camp Townsend, MS, on 5/6/1865.

Clifford, J.D. Pvt., 3rd & 5th Missouri Infantry (Consolidated). Co. A. Federal Rolls of Prisoners of War: Captured at Blakely, AL, on 4/9/1865; Received at Ship Island, MS, on 4/15/1865. Transferred to Vicksburg, MS, for exchange on 5/1/1865; Exchanged at Camp Townsend, MS, on 5/6/1865.

Cline, Henry Pvt., 3rd & 5th Missouri Infantry (Consolidated). Co. __. Federal Rolls of Prisoners of War: Captured at Blakely, AL, on 4/9/1865; Received at Ship Island, MS, on 4/15/1865. Transferred to Vicksburg, MS, for exchange on 5/1/1865; Exchanged at Camp Townsend, MS, on 5/6/1865.

Coburn, S.A. (AKA L.A.) Pvt., 3rd & 5th Missouri Infantry (Consolidated). Co. __. Federal Rolls of Prisoners of War: Captured at Blakely, AL, on 4/9/1865; Received at Ship Island, MS, on 4/15/1865. Transferred to Vicksburg, MS, for exchange on 5/1/1865; Exchanged at Camp Townsend, MS, on 5/6/1865.

Cochran, M. Pvt., 3rd & 5th Missouri Infantry (Consolidated). Co. __. Federal Rolls of Prisoners of War: Captured at Blakely, AL, on 4/9/1865; Received at Ship Island, MS, on 4/15/1865. Transferred to Vicksburg, MS, for exchange on 5/1/1865; Exchanged at Camp Townsend, MS, on 5/6/1865.

Cockrell, W.D. Pvt., 3rd & 5th Missouri Infantry (Consolidated). Co. __. Federal Rolls of Prisoners of War: Captured at Blakely, AL, on 4/9/1865; Received at Ship Island, MS, on 4/15/1865. Transferred to Vicksburg, MS, for exchange on 5/1/1865; Exchanged at Camp Townsend, MS, on 5/6/1865.

Colley, John Pvt., 3rd & 5th Missouri Infantry (Consolidated). Co. __. Federal Rolls of Prisoners of War: Captured at Blakely, AL, on 4/9/1865; Received at Ship Island, MS, on 4/15/1865. Transferred to Vicksburg, MS, for exchange on 5/1/1865; Exchanged at Camp Townsend, MS, on 5/6/1865.

Collins, Patrick W. Sgt./2nd Lt., 1st & 4th Missouri Infantry (Consolidated). Co. D. Federal Rolls of Prisoners of War: Captured at Blakely, AL, on 4/9/1865; Received at Ship Island, MS, on 4/15/1865. Transferred to Vicksburg, MS, for exchange on 5/1/1865; Exchanged at Camp Townsend, MS, on 5/6/1865.

Compton, J.W. Pvt., 3rd & 5th Missouri Infantry (Consolidated). Co. __. Federal Rolls of Prisoners of War: Captured at Blakely, AL, on 4/9/1865; Received at Ship Island, MS, on 4/15/1865. Transferred to Vicksburg, MS, for exchange on 5/1/1865; Exchanged at Camp Townsend, MS, on 5/6/1865.

Conner, Stanfield Pvt., 1st & 3rd Missouri Cavalry (Consolidated). Co. H. Enlisted: 12/27/1861 at Litsville, MO. Age at enlistment: 23. Residence at enlistment: Nodaway County, MO. Federal Rolls of Prisoners of War: Captured at Blakely, AL, on 4/9/1865; Received at Ship Island, MS, on 4/15/1865. Transferred to Vicksburg, MS, for exchange on 5/1/1865; Exchanged at Camp Townsend, MS, on 5/6/1865.

Cooke, Matthew Pvt., 1st & 3rd Missouri Cavalry (Consolidated). Co. D. Enlisted: 12/24/1861 at Camden, MO. Age at enlistment: 17. Residence at enlistment: Ray County, MO. Wounded at Vicksburg, MS. Federal Rolls of Prisoners of War: Captured at Blakely, AL, on 4/9/1865; Received at Ship Island, MS, on 4/15/1865. Transferred to Vicksburg, MS, for exchange on 5/1/1865; Exchanged at Camp Townsend, MS, on 5/6/1865.

Corkery, J.J. Sgt./Pvt., 3rd & 5th Missouri Infantry (Consolidated). Co. __. Federal Rolls of Prisoners of War: Captured at Blakely, AL, on 4/9/1865; Received at Ship Island, MS, on 4/15/1865. Transferred to Vicksburg, MS, for exchange on 5/1/1865; Exchanged at Camp Townsend, MS, on 5/6/1865.

Corney, James B. (AKA Carney) 2nd Lt., 3rd & 5th Missouri Infantry (Consolidated). Co. B. Federal Rolls of Prisoners of War: Captured at Blakely, AL, on 4/9/1865; Received at Ship Island, MS, on 4/15/1865. Transferred to Vicksburg, MS, for exchange on 4/28/1865; Confined at New Orleans, LA, on 4/30/1865. Exchanged at Camp Townsend, MS, on 5/6/1865.

Crismon, John Pvt., 1st & 3rd Missouri Cavalry (Consolidated). Co. B. Federal Rolls of Prisoners of War: Captured at Blakely, AL, on 4/9/1865; Received at Ship Island, MS, on 4/15/1865. Transferred to Vicksburg, MS, for exchange on 5/1/1865; Exchanged at Camp Townsend, MS, on 5/6/1865. Residence at exchange: Maries County, MO.

Cruse, R.M. Pvt., 3rd & 5th Missouri Infantry (Consolidated). Co. __. Federal Rolls of Prisoners of War: Captured at Blakely, AL, on 4/9/1865; Received at Ship Island, MS, on 4/15/1865. Transferred to Vicksburg, MS, for exchange on 5/1/1865; Exchanged at Camp Townsend, MS, on 5/6/1865.

Cruther, G. Pvt., 2nd & 6th Missouri Infantry (Consolidated). Co. H. Federal Rolls of Prisoners of War: Captured at Blakely, AL, on 4/9/1865; Received at Ship Island, MS, on 4/15/1865. Transferred to Vicksburg, MS, for exchange on 5/1/1865; Exchanged at Camp Townsend, MS, on 5/6/1865.

Cunningham, James H. Pvt., 2nd & 6th Missouri Infantry (Consolidated). Co. F. Federal Rolls of Prisoners of War: Captured at Blakely, AL, on 4/9/1865; Received at Ship Island, MS, on 4/15/1865. Transferred to Vicksburg, MS, for exchange on 5/1/1865; Exchanged at Camp Townsend, MS, on 5/6/1865.

Daggett, J. Pvt., 1st & 3rd Missouri Cavalry (Consolidated). Co. __. Federal Rolls of Prisoners of War: Captured at Blakely, AL, on 4/9/1865; Received at Ship Island, MS, on 4/15/1865. Transferred to Vicksburg, MS, for exchange on 5/1/1865; Exchanged at Camp Townsend, MS, on 5/6/1865.

Dale, John D. Pvt., 3rd & 5th Missouri Infantry (Consolidated). Co. I. Federal Rolls of Prisoners of War: Captured at Blakely, AL, on 4/9/1865; Received at Ship Island, MS, on 4/15/1865. Transferred to Vicksburg,

MS, for exchange on 5/1/1865; Exchanged at Camp Townsend, MS, on 5/6/1865.

Daniels, Hiram Martin Pvt., 2nd & 6th Missouri Infantry (Consolidated). Co. I. Federal Rolls of Prisoners of War: Captured at Blakely, AL, on 4/9/1865; Received at Ship Island, MS, on 4/15/1865. Transferred to Vicksburg, MS, for exchange on 5/1/1865; Exchanged at Camp Townsend, MS, on 5/6/1865.

Dannaberry, A.C. (AKA H.C.) Pvt., 3rd & 5th Missouri Infantry (Consolidated). Co. __. Federal Rolls of Prisoners of War: Captured at Blakely, AL, on 4/9/1865; Received at Ship Island, MS, on 4/15/1865. Transferred to Vicksburg, MS, for exchange on 5/1/1865; Exchanged at Camp Townsend, MS, on 5/6/1865.

Dark, R.H. Pvt., 3rd & 5th Missouri Infantry (Consolidated). Co. __. Federal Rolls of Prisoners of War: Captured at Blakely, AL, on 4/9/1865; Received at Ship Island, MS, on 4/15/1865. Transferred to Vicksburg, MS, for exchange on 5/1/1865; Exchanged at Camp Townsend, MS, on 5/6/1865.

David, Marks Pvt., 3rd & 5th Missouri Infantry (Consolidated). Co. B. Federal Rolls of Prisoners of War: Captured at Blakely, AL, on 4/9/1865; Received at Ship Island, MS, on 4/15/1865. Transferred to Vicksburg, MS, for exchange on 5/1/1865; Exchanged at Camp Townsend, MS, on 5/6/1865.

Davidson, John (AKA Davison) Pvt., 3rd & 5th Missouri Infantry (Consolidated). Cos. A, C & G. Federal Rolls of Prisoners of War: Captured at Blakely, AL, on 4/9/1865; Received at Ship Island, MS, on 4/15/1865. Transferred to Vicksburg, MS, for exchange on 5/1/1865; Exchanged at Camp Townsend, MS, on 5/6/1865.

Davis, Albert Cpl., 3rd & 5th Missouri Infantry (Consolidated). Co. __. Federal Rolls of Prisoners of War: Captured at Blakely, AL, on 4/9/1865; Received at Ship Island, MS, on 4/15/1865. Transferred to Vicksburg, MS, for exchange on 5/1/1865; Exchanged at Camp Townsend, MS, on 5/6/1865.

Davis, J.C. Pvt., 3rd & 5th Missouri Infantry (Consolidated). Co. E. Federal Rolls of Prisoners of War: Captured at Blakely, AL, on 4/9/1865; Received at Ship Island, MS, on 4/15/1865. Transferred to Vicksburg, MS, for exchange on 5/1/1865; Exchanged at Camp Townsend, MS, on 5/6/1865.

Davis, William C. (AKA Davies) Pvt., 3rd & 5th Missouri Infantry (Consolidated). Co. A. Federal Rolls of Prisoners of War: Captured at Blakely, AL, on 4/9/1865; Received at Ship Island, MS, on 4/15/1865. Transferred to Vicksburg, MS, for exchange on 5/1/1865; Exchanged at Camp Townsend, MS, on 5/6/1865.

Day, Elbert F. (AKA Ebon) Pvt., 3rd & 5th Missouri Infantry (Consolidated). Co. I. Federal Rolls of Prisoners of War: Captured at Blakely, AL, on 4/9/1865; Received at Ship Island, MS, on 4/15/1865. Transferred to Vicksburg, MS, for exchange on 5/1/1865; Exchanged at Camp Townsend, MS, on 5/6/1865.

Dearing, James R. (AKA Deering) Cpl., 1st & 3rd Missouri Cavalry (Consolidated). Co. G. Enlisted: 12/31/1861 at Gallatin, MO. Age at enlistment: 28. Residence at enlistment: Daviess County, MO. Wounded at Corinth, MS, and Franklin, TN. Federal Rolls of Prisoners of War: Captured at Blakely, AL, on 4/9/1865; Received at Ship Island, MS, on 4/15/1865. Transferred to Vicksburg, MS, for exchange on 5/1/1865; Exchanged at Camp Townsend, MS, on 5/6/1865.

Dearing, Jesse Pvt., 1st & 3rd Missouri Cavalry (Consolidated). Co. B. Federal Rolls of Prisoners of War: Captured at Blakely, AL, on 4/9/1865; Received at Ship Island, MS, on 4/15/1865. Transferred to Vicksburg, MS, for exchange on 5/1/1865; Exchanged at Camp Townsend, MS, on 5/6/1865.

Deats, Conrad (AKA Deaty, Dietz) Pvt., 1st & 3rd Missouri Cavalry (Consolidated). Co. F. Enlisted: 9/1/1862 at Lindon, MO. Age at enlistment: 19. Residence at enlistment: Atchison County, MO. Wounded at Big Black River Bridge, MS, in 5/1863. Federal Rolls of Prisoners of War: Captured at Blakely, AL, on 4/9/1865; Received at Ship Island, MS, on 4/15/1865. Transferred to Vicksburg, MS, for exchange on 5/1/1865; Exchanged at Camp Townsend, MS, on 5/6/1865.

Dell, William Pvt., 3rd & 5th Missouri Infantry (Consolidated). Co. __. Federal Rolls of Prisoners of War: Captured at Blakely, AL, on 4/9/1865; Received at Ship Island, MS, on 4/15/1865. Transferred to Vicksburg, MS, for exchange on 5/1/1865; Exchanged at Camp Townsend, MS, on 5/6/1865.

Devinney, James Louis Pvt., 3rd Missouri Battalion Cavalry. Co. F. Enlisted: 12/24/1861 at Springfield, MO. Federal Rolls of Prisoners of War: Captured at Blakely, AL, on 4/9/1865; Received at Ship Island, MS, on 4/15/1865. Transferred to Vicksburg, MS, for exchange on 5/1/1865; Exchanged at Camp Townsend, MS, on 5/6/1865. Rolls of Prisoners of War, C.S.A: Surrendered at Citronelle, AL, on 5/4/1865; Paroled at Jackson, MS, in 5/1865. Wounded: 3 times. Born: 7/11/1845 at Louisville, Jefferson County, KY. Married: Almyra Jane Forsyth. Children: 6. Residences: St. Joseph, MO, in 1870. Died: 8/19/1915 at Ripley, Lauderdale County, TN. Buried: Ripley, TN.

Dillard, Robert T. (AKA R.J.) Pvt., 1st & 3rd Missouri Cavalry (Consolidated). Co. K. Enlisted: 12/5/1861 at Shamrock, MO. Age at enlistment: 16. Residence at enlistment: Callaway County, MO. Federal Rolls of Prisoners of War: Captured at Blakely, AL, on 4/9/1865; Received at Ship Island, MS, on 4/15/1865. Transferred to Vicksburg, MS, for exchange on 5/1/1865; Exchanged at Camp Townsend, MS, on 5/6/1865.

Diring, J.S. Pvt., 1st & 3rd Missouri Cavalry (Consolidated). Co. __. Federal Rolls of Prisoners of War: Captured at Blakely, AL, on 4/9/1865; Received at Ship Island, MS, on 4/15/1865. Transferred to Vicksburg, MS, for exchange on 5/1/1865; Exchanged at Camp Townsend, MS, on 5/6/1865.

Dixon, Robert Pvt., 1st & 3rd Missouri Cavalry (Consolidated). Co. K. Federal Rolls of Prisoners of War: Captured at Blakely, AL, on 4/9/1865; Received at Ship Island, MS, on 4/15/1865. Transferred to Vicksburg, MS, for exchange on 5/1/1865; Exchanged at Camp Townsend, MS, on 5/6/1865.

Dodson, Benjamin G. (AKA Dotson) Pvt., 2nd & 6th Missouri Infantry (Consolidated). Co. K. Federal Rolls of Prisoners of War: Captured at Blakely, AL, on 4/9/1865; Received at Ship Island, MS, on 4/15/1865. Transferred to Vicksburg, MS, for exchange on 5/1/1865; Exchanged at Camp Townsend, MS, on 5/6/1865.

Donovan, Joseph T. Pvt., 3rd & 5th Missouri Infantry (Consolidated). Co. __. Federal Rolls of Prisoners of War: Captured at Blakely, AL, on 4/9/1865; Received at Ship Island, MS, on 4/15/1865. Transferred to Vicksburg, MS, for exchange on 5/1/1865; Exchanged at Camp Townsend, MS, on 5/6/1865.

Dorsey, William H. (AKA Dossy) Pvt., 3rd & 5th Missouri Infantry (Consolidated). Co. H. Federal Rolls of Prisoners of War: Captured at Blakely, AL, on 4/9/1865; Received at Ship Island, MS, on 4/15/1865. Transferred to Vicksburg, MS, for exchange on 5/1/1865; Exchanged at Camp Townsend, MS, on 5/6/1865.

Doty, J.H. Pvt., 3rd & 5th Missouri Infantry (Consolidated). Co. __. Federal Rolls of Prisoners of War: Captured at Blakely, AL, on 4/9/1865; Received at Ship Island, MS, on 4/15/1865. Transferred to Vicksburg, MS, for exchange on 5/1/1865; Exchanged at Camp Townsend, MS, on 5/6/1865.

Douglas, Andrew J. Pvt., 2nd & 6th Missouri Infantry (Consolidated). Co. E. Federal Rolls of Prisoners of War: Captured at Blakely, AL, on 4/9/1865; Received at Ship Island, MS, on 4/15/1865. Transferred to Vicksburg, MS, for exchange on 5/1/1865; Exchanged at Camp Townsend, MS, on 5/6/1865.

Douglass, James B. Pvt., 2nd & 6th Missouri Infantry (Consolidated). Co. K. Federal Rolls of Prisoners of War: Captured at Blakely, AL, on 4/9/1865; Received at Ship Island, MS, on 4/15/1865. Transferred to Vicksburg, MS, for exchange on 5/1/1865; Exchanged at Camp Townsend, MS, on 5/6/1865.

Drake, N.B. Pvt., 3rd & 5th Missouri Infantry (Consolidated). Co. __. Federal Rolls of Prisoners of War: Captured at Blakely, AL, on 4/9/1865; Received at Ship Island, MS, on 4/15/1865. Transferred to Vicksburg, MS, for exchange on 5/1/1865; Exchanged at Camp Townsend, MS, on 5/6/1865.

Dunn, John Levi Pvt., 2nd & 6th Missouri Infantry (Consolidated). Co. I. Federal Rolls of Prisoners of War: Captured at Blakely, AL, on 4/9/1865; Received at Ship Island, MS, on 4/15/1865. Transferred to Vicksburg, MS, for exchange on 5/1/1865; Exchanged at Camp Townsend, MS, on 5/6/1865.

Dysart, J. Sprague (AKA J.L.) Ord. Sgt., 3rd & 5th Missouri Infantry (Consolidated). Co. __. Federal Rolls of Prisoners of War: Captured and paroled at Vicksburg, MS, on 7/4/1863. Federal Rolls of Prisoners of War: Captured at Blakely, AL, on 4/9/1865; Received at Ship Island, MS, on 4/15/1865. Transferred to Vicksburg, MS, for exchange on 5/1/1865; Exchanged at Camp Townsend, MS, on 5/6/1865. Soldier also served as a Pvt. with the Missouri State Guard. Born: 2/13/1832 to John Dysart and Matilda Brooks at Howard County, MO. Married: Mollie J. Spary. Children: 2.

Eastford, Frank Pvt., 3rd & 5th Missouri Infantry (Consolidated). Co. __. Federal Rolls of Prisoners of War: Captured at Blakely, AL, on 4/9/1865; Received at Ship Island, MS, on 4/15/1865. Transferred to Vicksburg, MS, for exchange on 5/1/1865; Exchanged at Camp Townsend, MS, on 5/6/1865.

Eaton, Alfred Pvt., 2nd & 6th Missouri Infantry (Consolidated). Co. A. Federal Rolls of Prisoners of War: Captured at Blakely, AL, on 4/9/1865; Received at Ship Island, MS, on 4/15/1865. Transferred to Vicksburg, MS, for exchange on 5/1/1865; Exchanged at Camp Townsend, MS, on 5/6/1865.

Eaton, Edward Pvt./Cpl., 2nd & 6th Missouri Infantry (Consolidated). Co. A. Federal Rolls of Prisoners of War: Captured at Blakely, AL, on 4/9/1865; Received at Ship Island, MS, on 4/15/1865. Transferred to Vicksburg, MS, for exchange on 5/1/1865; Exchanged at Camp Townsend, MS, on 5/6/1865.

Eaton, Jeremiah, Sr. 2nd Lt./1st Lt., 3rd & 5th Missouri Infantry (Consolidated). Co. H. Federal Rolls of Prisoners of War: Captured at Blakely, AL, on 4/9/1865; Received at Ship Island, MS, on 4/15/1865. Transferred to Vicksburg, MS, for exchange on 4/28/1865; Confined at New Orleans, LA, on 4/30/1865. Exchanged at Camp Townsend, MS, on 5/6/1865.

Edgar, John H. Pvt., 3rd & 5th Missouri Infantry (Consolidated). Co. I. Federal Rolls of Prisoners of War: Captured at Blakely, AL, on 4/9/1865; Received at Ship Island, MS, on 4/15/1865. Transferred to Vicksburg, MS, for exchange on 5/1/1865; Exchanged at Camp Townsend, MS, on 5/6/1865.

Edmondson, Charles L. Capt., 1st & 4th Missouri Infantry (Consolidated). Cos. B & K. Federal Rolls of Prisoners of War: Captured at Blakely, AL, on 4/9/1865; Received at Ship Island, MS, on 4/15/1865. Transferred to Vicksburg, MS, for exchange on 4/28/1865; Confined at New Orleans, LA, on 4/30/1865. Exchanged at Camp Townsend, MS, on 5/6/1865.

Elliott, William H. Pvt., 1st & 3rd Missouri Cavalry (Consolidated). Co. A. Federal Rolls of Prisoners of War: Captured at Blakely, AL, on 4/9/1865; Received at Ship Island, MS, on 4/15/1865. Transferred to Vicksburg, MS, for exchange on 5/1/1865; Exchanged at Camp Townsend, MS, on 5/6/1865.

England, Ambrose D. Pvt., 2nd & 6th Missouri Infantry (Consolidated). Co. H. Federal Rolls of Prisoners of War: Captured at Blakely, AL, on 4/9/1865; Received at Ship Island, MS, on 4/15/1865. Transferred to Vicksburg, MS, for exchange on 5/1/1865; Exchanged at Camp Townsend, MS, on 5/6/1865.

Erwin, J.A. (AKA Ervin) Pvt., 3rd & 5th Missouri Infantry (Consolidated). Co. __. Federal Rolls of Prisoners of War: Captured at Blakely, AL, on 4/9/1865; Received at Ship Island, MS, on 4/15/1865. Transferred to Vicksburg, MS, for exchange on 5/1/1865; Exchanged at Camp Townsend, MS, on 5/6/1865.

Evans, Henry J. 2nd Lt., 1st & 3rd Missouri Cavalry (Consolidated). Co. I. Federal Rolls of Prisoners of War: Captured at Blakely, AL, on 4/9/1865; Received at Ship Island, MS, on 4/15/1865. Transferred to Vicksburg, MS, for exchange on 4/28/1865; Confined at New Orleans, LA, on 4/30/1865. Exchanged at Camp Townsend, MS, on 5/6/1865.

Ewing, George S. Cpl./Sgt., 3rd & 5th Missouri Infantry (Consolidated). Co. C. Federal Rolls of Prisoners of War: Captured at Blakely, AL, on 4/9/1865; Received at Ship Island, MS, on 4/15/1865. Transferred to Vicksburg, MS, for exchange on 5/1/1865; Exchanged at Camp Townsend, MS, on 5/6/1865.

Fagan, James Pvt., 2nd & 6th Missouri Infantry (Consolidated). Co. __. Federal Rolls of Prisoners of War: Captured at Blakely, AL, on 4/9/1865; Received at Ship Island, MS, on 4/15/1865. Transferred to Vicksburg, MS, for exchange on 5/1/1865; Exchanged at Camp Townsend, MS, on 5/6/1865.

Farley, Thaddeus (AKA Thadeus, Thadeoas, Thadious)

Pvt., 1st & 3rd Missouri Cavalry (Consolidated). Co. I. Enlisted: 12/16/1861 at Farley, MO. Age at enlistment: 19. Residence at enlistment: Platte County, MO. Wounded at Kennesaw Mountain, GA. Federal Rolls of Prisoners of War: Captured at Blakely, AL, on 4/9/1865; Received at Ship Island, MS, on 4/15/1865. Transferred to Vicksburg, MS, for exchange on 5/1/1865; Exchanged at Camp Townsend, MS, on 5/6/1865.

Farris, W. Pvt., 1st & 3rd Missouri Cavalry (Consolidated). Co. __. Federal Rolls of Prisoners of War: Captured at Blakely, AL, on 4/9/1865; Received at Ship Island, MS, on 4/15/1865. Transferred to Vicksburg, MS, for exchange on 5/1/1865; Exchanged at Camp Townsend, MS, on 5/6/1865.

Fentrall, W.E. Pvt., 3rd & 5th Missouri Infantry (Consolidated). Co. __. Federal Rolls of Prisoners of War: Captured at Blakely, AL, on 4/9/1865; Received at Ship Island, MS, on 4/15/1865. Transferred to Vicksburg, MS, for exchange on 5/1/1865; Exchanged at Camp Townsend, MS, on 5/6/1865.

Fields, Jonathan G. Pvt., 1st & 3rd Missouri Cavalry (Consolidated). Co. F. Federal Rolls of Prisoners of War: Captured at Blakely, AL, on 4/9/1865; Received at Ship Island, MS, on 4/15/1865. Transferred to Vicksburg, MS, for exchange on 5/1/1865; Exchanged at Camp Townsend, MS, on 5/6/1865.

Fisher, William H. Pvt., 1st Missouri Light Artillery. Federal Rolls of Prisoners of War: Captured at Bruinsville, TX, on 3/15/1864; Received at Ship Island, MS. Died: 12/15/1864 at Ship Island, MS, due to chronic dysentery. Buried: Ship Island, MS, Cemetery in Grave #118.

Flack, A.P. Pvt., 1st & 3rd Missouri Cavalry (Consolidated). Co. __. Federal Rolls of Prisoners of War: Captured at Blakely, AL, on 4/9/1865; Received at Ship Island, MS, on 4/15/1865. Transferred to Vicksburg, MS, for exchange on 5/1/1865; Exchanged at Camp Townsend, MS, on 5/6/1865.

Fleming, James B. Pvt., 1st & 3rd Missouri Cavalry (Consolidated). Co. I. Federal Rolls of Prisoners of War: Captured at Blakely, AL, on 4/9/1865; Received at Ship Island, MS, on 4/15/1865. Transferred to Vicksburg, MS, for exchange on 5/1/1865; Exchanged at Camp Townsend, MS, on 5/6/1865.

Fletcher, T. Pvt., 2nd & 6th Missouri Infantry (Consolidated). Co. __. Federal Rolls of Prisoners of War: Captured at Blakely, AL, on 4/9/1865; Received at Ship Island, MS, on 4/15/1865. Transferred to Vicksburg, MS, for exchange on 5/1/1865; Exchanged at Camp Townsend, MS, on 5/6/1865.

Fletcher, Thomas J. Pvt./1st Lt., 3rd & 5th Missouri Infantry (Consolidated). Co. B. Federal Rolls of Prisoners of War: Captured at Blakely, AL, on 4/9/1865; Received at Ship Island, MS, on 4/15/1865. Transferred to Vicksburg, MS, for exchange on 4/28/1865; Confined at New Orleans, LA, on 4/30/1865. Exchanged at Camp Townsend, MS, on 5/6/1865.

Flourney, Peter C. (AKA Flournoy) Capt./Col., 2nd & 6th Missouri Infantry (Consolidated). Co. K. Federal Rolls of Prisoners of War: Captured at Blakely, AL, on 4/9/1865; Received at Ship Island, MS, on 4/15/1865. Transferred to Vicksburg, MS, for exchange on 4/28/1865; Confined at New Orleans, LA, on 4/30/1865. Exchanged at Camp Townsend, MS, on 5/6/1865.

Foster, Richard Pvt., 3rd & 5th Missouri Infantry (Consolidated). Co. __. Federal Rolls of Prisoners of War: Captured at Blakely, AL, on 4/9/1865; Received at Ship Island, MS, on 4/15/1865. Transferred to Vicksburg, MS, for exchange on 5/1/1865; Exchanged at Camp Townsend, MS, on 5/6/1865.

Franklin, William E. Asst. Surg., 2nd & 6th Missouri Infantry (Consolidated). Co. B. Federal Rolls of Prisoners of War: Captured at Blakely, AL, on 4/9/1865; Received at Ship Island, MS, on 4/15/1865. Transferred to Vicksburg, MS, for exchange on 4/28/1865; Confined at New Orleans, LA, on 4/30/1865. Exchanged at Camp Townsend, MS, on 5/6/1865.

Fray, James M. Pvt., 3rd & 5th Missouri Infantry (Consolidated). Co. K. Federal Rolls of Prisoners of War: Captured at Blakely, AL, on 4/9/1865; Received at Ship Island, MS, on 4/15/1865. Transferred to Vicksburg, MS, for exchange on 5/1/1865; Exchanged at Camp Townsend, MS, on 5/6/1865.

Frazier, Stephen 3rd Cpl., 1st & 3rd Missouri Cavalry (Consolidated). Co. D. Enlisted: 12/24/1861 at Camden, MO. Age at enlistment: 35. Residence at enlistment: Ray County, MO. Federal Rolls of Prisoners of War: Captured at Blakely, AL, on 4/9/1865; Received at Ship Island, MS, on 4/15/1865. Transferred to Vicksburg, MS, for exchange on 5/1/1865; Exchanged at Camp Townsend, MS, on 5/6/1865.

Freeman, Frederick (AKA Fryman, I.F.) Pvt., 2nd & 6th Missouri Infantry (Consolidated). Co. E. Federal Rolls of Prisoners of War: Captured at Blakely, AL, on 4/9/1865; Received at Ship Island, MS, on 4/15/1865. Transferred to Vicksburg, MS, for exchange on 5/1/1865; Exchanged at Camp Townsend, MS, on 5/6/1865.

Friend, J.B. Sgt., 1st & 3rd Missouri Cavalry (Consolidated). Co. K. Federal Rolls of Prisoners of War: Captured at Blakely, AL, on 4/9/1865; Received at Ship Island, MS, on 4/15/1865. Transferred to Vicksburg, MS, for exchange on 5/1/1865; Exchanged at Camp Townsend, MS, on 5/6/1865. Rolls of Prisoners of War, C.S.A: Surrendered at Citronelle, AL, on 5/4/1865; Paroled at Jackson, MS, on 5/13/1865. Residence at parole: Carthage, Jasper County, MO.

Fuller, Thomas K. (AKA T.R.) Pvt., 1st & 3rd Missouri Cavalry (Consolidated). Co. I. Federal Rolls of Prisoners of War: Captured at Blakely, AL, on 4/9/1865; Received at Ship Island, MS, on 4/15/1865. Transferred to Vicksburg, MS, for exchange on 5/1/1865; Exchanged at Camp Townsend, MS, on 5/6/1865.

Gates, Elijah Col., 1st & 3rd Missouri Cavalry (Consolidated). F & S. Enlisted: 12/26/1861 at Buchanan County, MO. Elected Col. on 12/31/1861 at Easton, MO. Age at enlistment: 32. Federal Rolls of Prisoners of War: Captured at Big Black River Bridge, MS; Escaped and rejoined command after 7/4/1863. Wounded at Atlanta, GA, and in both arms at Franklin, TN, resulting in amputation of left arm. Federal Rolls of Prisoners of War: Captured at Blakely, AL, on 4/9/1865; Confined one day at Spanish Fort, AL. Received at Ship Island, MS, on 4/16/1865; Transferred to Vicksburg, MS, for exchange on 4/28/1865. Confined at New Orleans, LA, on 4/30/1865; Exchanged at Camp Townsend, MS, on 5/6/1865. Rolls of Prisoners of War, C.S.A: Surrendered at Citronelle, AL, on 5/4/1865; Paroled at Jackson, MS, on 5/15/1865. Soldier also served as a 1st

Sgt./Capt./Lt. Col. with the Missouri State Guard. Enlisted: 5/1861. Received the United Daughters of the Confederacy Cross of Honor for his wartime service. Born: 12/17/1827 to John and Mary Maupine Gates at Lancaster, Garrard County, KY. Married: Maria Stamper on 4/1/1865. Children: 12. Occupations: Sheriff of Buchanan County, MO, and elected Missouri State Treasurer in 1876. Died: 3/4/1915 at St. Joseph, MO. Wife born: 11/25/1827 at Livingston County, MO. Wife died: 12/24/1898 at St. Joseph, MO.

Gentry, Thomas J. Pvt., 1st & 3rd Missouri Infantry (Consolidated). Co. K. Federal Rolls of Prisoners of War: Captured at Blakely, AL, on 4/9/1865; Received at Ship Island, MS, on 4/15/1865. Transferred to Vicksburg, MS, for exchange on 5/1/1865; Exchanged at Camp Townsend, MS, on 5/6/1865.

Gentry, W. Pvt., 3rd & 5th Missouri Infantry (Consolidated). Co. I. Federal Rolls of Prisoners of War: Captured at Blakely, AL, on 4/9/1865; Received at Ship Island, MS, on 4/15/1865. Transferred to Vicksburg, MS, for exchange on 5/1/1865; Exchanged at Camp Townsend, MS, on 5/6/1865.

German, William T. (AKA W.Y.) Pvt., 3rd & 5th Missouri Infantry (Consolidated). Co. G. Federal Rolls of Prisoners of War: Captured at Blakely, AL, on 4/9/1865; Received at Ship Island, MS, on 4/15/1865. Transferred to Vicksburg, MS, for exchange on 5/1/1865; Exchanged at Camp Townsend, MS, on 5/6/1865.

Gibson, J. Pvt., 3rd & 5th Missouri Infantry (Consolidated). Co. __. Federal Rolls of Prisoners of War: Captured at Blakely, AL, on 4/9/1865; Received at Ship Island, MS, on 4/15/1865. Transferred to Vicksburg, MS, for exchange on 5/1/1865; Exchanged at Camp Townsend, MS, on 5/6/1865.

Giddings, W.B. Pvt., 3rd & 5th Missouri Cavalry (Consolidated). Co. __. Federal Rolls of Prisoners of War: Captured at Blakely, AL, on 4/9/1865; Received at Ship Island, MS, on 4/15/1865. Transferred to Vicksburg, MS, for exchange on 5/1/1865; Exchanged at Camp Townsend, MS, on 5/6/1865.

Gillmore, T.H. Pvt., 3rd & 5th Missouri Infantry (Consolidated). Co. __. Federal Rolls of Prisoners of War: Captured at Blakely, AL, on 4/9/1865; Received at Ship Island, MS, on 4/15/1865. Transferred to Vicksburg, MS, for exchange on 5/1/1865; Exchanged at Camp Townsend, MS, on 5/6/1865.

Gittleens, James Pvt., 1st & 3rd Missouri Cavalry (Consolidated). Co. B. Federal Rolls of Prisoners of War: Captured at Blakely, AL, on 4/9/1865; Received at Ship Island, MS, on 4/15/1865. Transferred to Vicksburg, MS, for exchange on 5/1/1865; Exchanged at Camp Townsend, MS, on 5/6/1865. Rolls of Prisoners of War, C.S.A: Surrendered at Citronelle, AL, on 5/4/1865; Paroled at Meridian, MS, in 5/1865.

Glenn, John M. Pvt., 3rd & 5th Missouri Infantry (Consolidated). Co. __. Federal Rolls of Prisoners of War: Captured at Blakely, AL, on 4/9/1865; Received at Ship Island, MS, on 4/15/1865. Transferred to Vicksburg, MS, for exchange on 5/1/1865; Exchanged at Camp Townsend, MS, on 5/6/1865.

Goen, E.B. (AKA E.J.) Pvt., 1st & 3rd Missouri Infantry (Consolidated). Co. K. Federal Rolls of Prisoners of War: Captured at Blakely, AL, on 4/9/1865; Received at Ship Island, MS, on 4/15/1865. Transferred to Vicksburg, MS, for exchange on 5/1/1865; Exchanged at Camp Townsend, MS, on 5/6/1865.

Goodyear, T.F. Pvt., 3rd & 5th Missouri Infantry (Consolidated). Co. __. Federal Rolls of Prisoners of War: Captured at Blakely, AL, on 4/9/1865; Received at Ship Island, MS, on 4/15/1865. Transferred to Vicksburg, MS, for exchange on 5/1/1865; Exchanged at Camp Townsend, MS, on 5/6/1865.

Gordon, Joseph H. Pvt., 3rd & 5th Missouri Infantry (Consolidated). Co. F. Federal Rolls of Prisoners of War: Captured at Blakely, AL, on 4/9/1865; Received at Ship Island, MS, on 4/15/1865. Transferred to Vicksburg, MS, for exchange on 5/1/1865; Exchanged at Camp Townsend, MS, on 5/6/1865.

Gordon, William A. Surg., 1st & 3rd Missouri Cavalry (Consolidated). F & S. Enlisted: 1/1/1863 at Lexington, MO. Age at enlistment: 40. Residence at enlistment: Lafayette County, MO. Isolated from regiment at Baker's Creek, MS, but later rejoined; Left with wounded at Allatoona, GA, but rejoined regiment on 2/7/1865. Federal Rolls of Prisoners of War: Captured at Blakely, AL, on 4/9/1865; Confined one day at Spanish Fort, AL. Received at Ship Island, MS, on 4/16/1865; Transferred to Vicksburg, MS, for exchange on 4/28/1865. Confined at New Orleans, LA, on 4/30/1865; Exchanged at Camp Townsend, MS, on 5/6/1865.

Gotcher, Nathaniel P. Pvt., 1st & 3rd Missouri Cavalry (Consolidated). Co. K. Federal Rolls of Prisoners of War: Captured at Blakely, AL, on 4/9/1865; Received at Ship Island, MS, on 4/15/1865. Transferred to Vicksburg, MS, for exchange on 5/1/1865; Exchanged at Camp Townsend, MS, on 5/6/1865.

Grant, Joseph P. Pvt., 1st & 3rd Missouri Cavalry (Consolidated). Co. __. Federal Rolls of Prisoners of War: Captured at Blakely, AL, on 4/9/1865; Received at Ship Island, MS, on 4/15/1865. Transferred to Vicksburg, MS, for exchange on 5/1/1865; Exchanged at Camp Townsend, MS, on 5/6/1865.

Gray, J.M. Cpl., 3rd & 5th Missouri Infantry (Consolidated). Co. __. Federal Rolls of Prisoners of War: Captured at Blakely, AL, on 4/9/1865; Received at Ship Island, MS, on 4/15/1865. Transferred to Vicksburg, MS, for exchange on 5/1/1865; Exchanged at Camp Townsend, MS, on 5/6/1865.

Greathouse, John F. Pvt., 1st & 3rd Missouri Cavalry (Consolidated). Co. K. Enlisted: 12/25/1861 at Platte City, Platte County, MO. Age at enlistment: 21. Federal Rolls of Prisoners of War: Captured at Blakely, AL, on 4/9/1865; Received at Ship Island, MS, on 4/15/1865. Transferred to Vicksburg, MS, for exchange on 5/1/1865; Exchanged at Camp Townsend, MS, on 5/6/1865.

Green, Abe Pvt., 3rd & 5th Missouri Infantry (Consolidated). Co. __. Federal Rolls of Prisoners of War: Captured at Blakely, AL, on 4/9/1865; Received at Ship Island, MS, on 4/15/1865. Transferred to Vicksburg, MS, for exchange on 5/1/1865; Exchanged at Camp Townsend, MS, on 5/6/1865.

Greene, J.B. (AKA Greeny) Pvt., 3rd & 5th Missouri Infantry (Consolidated). Co. __. Federal Rolls of Prisoners of War: Captured at Blakely, AL, on 4/9/1865; Received at Ship Island, MS, on 4/15/1865. Transferred to Vicksburg, MS, for exchange on 5/1/1865; Exchanged at Camp Townsend, MS, on 5/6/1865.

Greenwell, John Pvt., 1st & 3rd Missouri Cavalry (Consolidated). Co. B. Enlisted: 12/11/1861 at High Hill, Montgomery County, MO. Age at enlistment: 21. Federal Rolls of Prisoners of War: Captured at Blakely, AL, on 4/9/1865 while wounded; Received at Ship Island, MS, on 4/15/1865. Transferred to Vicksburg, MS, for exchange on 5/1/1865; Exchanged at Camp Townsend, MS, on 5/6/1865.

Guthrie, O.T. (AKA O.F.) Lt., 1st & 3rd Missouri Cavalry (Consolidated). Co. H. Federal Rolls of Prisoners of War: Captured at Blakely, AL, on 4/9/1865; Received at Ship Island, MS, on 4/15/1865. Transferred to Vicksburg, MS, for exchange on 4/28/1865; Confined at New Orleans, LA, on 4/30/1865. Exchanged at Camp Townsend, MS, on 5/6/1865.

Guthrie, R.B. (AKA R.E.) Capt., 3rd & 5th Missouri Infantry (Consolidated). Co. C. Federal Rolls of Prisoners of War: Captured at Blakely, AL, on 4/9/1865; Received at Ship Island, MS, on 4/15/1865. Transferred to Vicksburg, MS, for exchange on 4/28/1865; Confined at New Orleans, LA, on 4/30/1865. Exchanged at Camp Townsend, MS, on 5/6/1865.

Hackley, George Pvt., 3rd & 5th Missouri Infantry (Consolidated). Co. __. Federal Rolls of Prisoners of War: Captured at Blakely, AL, on 4/9/1865; Received at Ship Island, MS, on 4/15/1865. Transferred to Vicksburg, MS, for exchange on 5/1/1865; Exchanged at Camp Townsend, MS, on 5/6/1865.

Hall, John M. (AKA J.H.) Pvt., 3rd & 5th Missouri Infantry (Consolidated). Co. G. Federal Rolls of Prisoners of War: Captured at Blakely, AL, on 4/9/1865; Received at Ship Island, MS, on 4/15/1865. Transferred to Vicksburg, MS, for exchange on 5/1/1865; Exchanged at Camp Townsend, MS, on 5/6/1865.

Halloway, Churchill H. (AKA Holloway) Pvt./Sgt. Maj., 2nd & 6th Missouri Infantry (Consolidated). Co. B. Federal Rolls of Prisoners of War: Captured at Blakely, AL, on 4/9/1865; Received at Ship Island, MS, on 4/15/1865. Transferred to Vicksburg, MS, for exchange on 5/1/1865; Exchanged at Camp Townsend, MS, on 5/6/1865.

Hamlet, J. Pvt., 3rd & 5th Missouri Infantry (Consolidated). Co. __. Federal Rolls of Prisoners of War: Captured at Blakely, AL, on 4/9/1865; Received at Ship Island, MS, on 4/15/1865. Transferred to Vicksburg, MS, for exchange on 5/1/1865; Exchanged at Camp Townsend, MS, on 5/6/1865.

Hanley, John Pvt., 2nd & 6th Missouri Infantry (Consolidated). Co. __. Federal Rolls of Prisoners of War: Captured at Blakely, AL, on 4/9/1865; Received at Ship Island, MS, on 4/15/1865. Transferred to Vicksburg, MS, for exchange on 5/1/1865; Exchanged at Camp Townsend, MS, on 5/6/1865.

Hardin, J Pvt., 1st & 3rd Missouri Cavalry (Consolidated). Co. __. Federal Rolls of Prisoners of War: Captured at Blakely, AL, on 4/9/1865; Received at Ship Island, MS, on 4/15/1865. Transferred to Vicksburg, MS, for exchange on 5/1/1865; Exchanged at Camp Townsend, MS, on 5/6/1865.

Harmon, John Philip Sgt./Lt., 3rd & 5th Missouri Infantry (Consolidated). Co. I. Federal Rolls of Prisoners of War: Captured at Blakely, AL, on 4/9/1865; Received at Ship Island, MS, on 4/15/1865. Transferred to Vicksburg, MS, for exchange on 4/28/1865; Confined at New Orleans, LA, on 4/30/1865. Exchanged at Camp Townsend, MS, on 5/6/1865

Harris, Adelbert Pvt./Ord. Sgt., 1st & 3rd Missouri Cavalry (Consolidated). Co. I/F & S. Enlisted: 12/16/1861 at Weston, Platte County, MO. Age at enlistment: 20. Federal Rolls of Prisoners of War: Captured at Blakely, AL, on 4/9/1865; Received at Ship Island, MS, on 4/15/1865. Transferred to Vicksburg, MS, for exchange on 5/1/1865; Exchanged at Camp Townsend, MS, on 5/6/1865.

Harris, John E. Sgt., 3rd & 5th Missouri Infantry (Consolidated). Co. __. Federal Rolls of Prisoners of War: Captured at Blakely, AL, on 4/9/1865; Received at Ship Island, MS, on 4/15/1865. Transferred to Vicksburg, MS, for exchange on 5/1/1865; Exchanged at Camp Townsend, MS, on 5/6/1865.

Harvey, J.L. Sgt., 3rd & 5th Missouri Infantry (Consolidated). Co. __. Federal Rolls of Prisoners of War: Captured at Blakely, AL, on 4/9/1865; Received at Ship Island, MS, on 4/15/1865. Transferred to Vicksburg, MS, for exchange on 5/1/1865; Exchanged at Camp Townsend, MS, on 5/6/1865.

Hatton, John A (AKA Hatten) Pvt., 1st & 3rd Missouri Cavalry (Consolidated). Co. C. Enlisted: 12/6/1861 at Oregon, Holt County, MO. Age at enlistment: 19. Federal Rolls of Prisoners of War: Captured at Blakely, AL, on 4/9/1865; Received at Ship Island, MS, on 4/15/1865. Transferred to Vicksburg, MS, for exchange on 5/1/1865; Exchanged at Camp Townsend, MS, on 5/6/1865.

Haugh, W.J. (AKA N.J.) Pvt., 3rd & 5th Missouri Infantry (Consolidated). Co. __. Federal Rolls of Prisoners of War: Captured at Blakely, AL, on 4/9/1865; Received at Ship Island, MS, on 4/15/1865. Transferred to Vicksburg, MS, for exchange on 5/1/1865; Exchanged at Camp Townsend, MS, on 5/6/1865.

Hawkins, John Pvt., 3rd & 5th Missouri Infantry (Consolidated). Co. __. Federal Rolls of Prisoners of War: Captured at Blakely, AL, on 4/9/1865; Received at Ship Island, MS, on 4/15/1865. Transferred to Vicksburg, MS, for exchange on 5/1/1865; Exchanged at Camp Townsend, MS, on 5/6/1865.

Haynes, J.W. (AKA J.N.) Pvt., 3rd & 5th Missouri Infantry (Consolidated). Co. __. Federal Rolls of Prisoners of War: Captured at Blakely, AL, on 4/9/1865; Received at Ship Island, MS, on 4/15/1865. Transferred to Vicksburg, MS, for exchange on 5/1/1865; Exchanged at Camp Townsend, MS, on 5/6/1865.

Hearn, Campbell S. Pvt., 3rd & 5th Missouri Infantry (Consolidated). Co. D. Federal Rolls of Prisoners of War: Captured at Blakely, AL, on 4/9/1865; Received at Ship Island, MS, on 4/15/1865. Transferred to Vicksburg, MS, for exchange on 5/1/1865; Exchanged at Camp Townsend, MS, on 5/6/1865.

Hearn, J.L. (AKA J.S.) Pvt., 3rd & 5th Missouri Infantry (Consolidated). Co. __. Federal Rolls of Prisoners of War: Captured at Blakely, AL, on 4/9/1865; Received at Ship Island, MS, on 4/15/1865. Transferred to Vicksburg, MS, for exchange on 5/1/1865; Exchanged at Camp Townsend, MS, on 5/6/1865.

Hearn, Robert S. 2nd Lt./1st Lt., 3rd & 5th Missouri Infantry (Consolidated). Co. D. Federal Rolls of Prisoners of War: Captured at Blakely, AL, on 4/9/1865; Received at Ship Island, MS, on 4/15/1865.

Transferred to Vicksburg, MS, for exchange on 4/28/1865; Confined at New Orleans, LA, on 4/30/1865. Exchanged at Camp Townsend, MS, on 5/6/1865.

Hedderbrand, Charles Pvt., 2nd & 6th Missouri (Consolidated). Co. __. Federal Rolls of Prisoners of War: Captured at Blakely, AL, on 4/9/1865; Received at Ship Island, MS, on 4/15/1865. Transferred to Vicksburg, MS, for exchange on 5/1/1865; Exchanged at Camp Townsend, MS, on 5/6/1865.

Hedrick, W.C. Cpl., 3rd & 5th Missouri Infantry (Consolidated). Co. __. Federal Rolls of Prisoners of War: Captured at Blakely, AL, on 4/9/1865; Received at Ship Island, MS, on 4/15/1865. Transferred to Vicksburg, MS, for exchange on 5/1/1865; Exchanged at Camp Townsend, MS, on 5/6/1865.

Hempstead, Samuel Pvt., 2nd & 6th Missouri Infantry (Consolidated). Co. D. Federal Rolls of Prisoners of War: Captured at Blakely, AL, on 4/9/1865; Received at Ship Island, MS, on 4/15/1865. Transferred to Vicksburg, MS, for exchange on 5/1/1865; Exchanged at Camp Townsend, MS, on 5/6/1865.

Henderson, Albert S. (AKA H.S.) Pvt., 1st & 3rd Missouri Cavalry (Consolidated). Co. I. Enlisted: 1/1/1863 at Rolla, Phelps County, MO. Age at enlistment: 25. Federal Rolls of Prisoners of War: Captured at Big Black River Bridge, MS, in 1863. Federal Rolls of Prisoners of War: Captured at Blakely, AL, on 4/9/1865; Received at Ship Island, MS, on 4/15/1865. Transferred to Vicksburg, MS, for exchange on 5/1/1865; Exchanged at Camp Townsend, MS, on 5/6/1865.

Henley, James A. 2nd Sgt., 1st & 3rd Missouri Cavalry (Consolidated). Co. K. Enlisted: 12/5/1861 at Montgomery City, Montgomery County, MO. Age at enlistment: 22. Wounded at Allatoona, GA, in 1864. Federal Rolls of Prisoners of War: Captured at Blakely, AL, on 4/9/1865; Received at Ship Island, MS, on 4/15/1865. Transferred to Vicksburg, MS, for exchange on 5/1/1865; Exchanged at Camp Townsend, MS, on 5/6/1865.

Herbert, Horatio Samuel Sgt., 1st & 3rd Missouri Cavalry (Consolidated). Co. E. Wounded at Allatoona, GA, in 1864. Federal Rolls of Prisoners of War: Captured at Blakely, AL, on 4/9/1865; Received at Ship Island, MS, on 4/15/1865. Transferred to Vicksburg, MS, for exchange on 5/1/1865; Exchanged at Camp Townsend, MS, on 5/6/1865. Born: 12/25/1837 to Rev. James Herbert and Harriet Weston Herbert at Erie, PA. Married: Innie A. Hooker. Children: 2. Occupations: Owner and editor of the Rolla, MO, Herald newspaper. Wife born: 9/15/1860.

Hestler, William Pvt., 3rd & 5th Missouri Infantry (Consolidated). Co. __. Federal Rolls of Prisoners of War: Captured at Blakely, AL, on 4/9/1865; Received at Ship Island, MS, on 4/15/1865. Transferred to Vicksburg, MS, for exchange on 5/1/1865; Exchanged at Camp Townsend, MS, on 5/6/1865.

Higgason, W.S. Pvt., 1st & 3rd Missouri Cavalry (Consolidated). Co. __. Federal Rolls of Prisoners of War: Captured at Blakely, AL, on 4/9/1865; Received at Ship Island, MS, on 4/15/1865. Transferred to Vicksburg, MS, for exchange on 5/1/1865; Exchanged at Camp Townsend, MS, on 5/6/1865.

Higgason, William L. (AKA Hickerson) Pvt., 1st & 3rd Missouri Cavalry (Consolidated). Co. K. Federal Rolls of Prisoners of War: Captured at Blakely, AL, on 4/9/1865; Received at Ship Island, MS, on 4/15/1865. Transferred to Vicksburg, MS, for exchange on 5/1/1865; Exchanged at Camp Townsend, MS, on 5/6/1865.

Hill, Daniel P. Pvt./Cpl., 3rd & 5th Missouri Infantry (Consolidated). Co. H. Federal Rolls of Prisoners of War: Captured at Blakely, AL, on 4/9/1865; Received at Ship Island, MS, on 4/15/1865. Transferred to Vicksburg, MS, for exchange on 5/1/1865; Exchanged at Camp Townsend, MS, on 5/6/1865.

Hill, Isaac W. Pvt./Cpl., 3rd & 5th Missouri Infantry (Consolidated). Co. H. Federal Rolls of Prisoners of War: Captured at Blakely, AL, on 4/9/1865; Received at Ship Island, MS, on 4/15/1865. Transferred to Vicksburg, MS, for exchange on 5/1/1865; Exchanged at Camp Townsend, MS, on 5/6/1865.

Hill, James P. Pvt., 3rd & 5th Missouri Infantry (Consolidated). Co. __. Federal Rolls of Prisoners of War: Captured at Blakely, AL, on 4/9/1865; Received at Ship Island, MS, on 4/15/1865. Transferred to Vicksburg, MS, for exchange on 5/1/1865; Exchanged at Camp Townsend, MS, on 5/6/1865.

Hinton, James M. Pvt., 1st & 3rd Missouri Cavalry (Consolidated). Co. E. Federal Rolls of Prisoners of War: Captured at Blakely, AL, on 4/9/1865; Received at Ship Island, MS, on 4/15/1865. Transferred to Vicksburg, MS, for exchange on 5/1/1865; Exchanged at Camp Townsend, MS, on 5/6/1865.

Hinton, John R. Pvt., 1st & 3rd Missouri Cavalry (Consolidated). Co. E. Federal Rolls of Prisoners of War: Captured at Blakely, AL, on 4/9/1865; Received at Ship Island, MS, on 4/15/1865. Transferred to Vicksburg, MS, for exchange on 5/1/1865; Exchanged at Camp Townsend, MS, on 5/6/1865.

Hodges, Hiram (AKA H.H.) Pvt., 3rd & 5th Missouri Infantry (Consolidated). Co. __. Federal Rolls of Prisoners of War: Captured at Blakely, AL, on 4/9/1865; Received at Ship Island, MS, on 4/15/1865. Transferred to Vicksburg, MS, for exchange on 5/1/1865; Exchanged at Camp Townsend, MS, on 5/6/1865.

Holder, Alexander Pvt., 1st & 3rd Missouri Cavalry (Consolidated). Co. C. Enlisted: 12/6/1861 at Oregon, Holt County, MO. Age at enlistment: 20. Federal Rolls of Prisoners of War: Captured at Blakely, AL, on 4/9/1865; Received at Ship Island, MS, on 4/15/1865. Transferred to Vicksburg, MS, for exchange on 5/1/1865; Exchanged at Camp Townsend, MS, on 5/6/1865.

Holiday, Walter Cpl., 3rd & 5th Missouri Infantry (Consolidated). Co. __. Federal Rolls of Prisoners of War: Captured at Blakely, AL, on 4/9/1865; Received at Ship Island, MS, on 4/15/1865. Transferred to Vicksburg, MS, for exchange on 5/1/1865; Exchanged at Camp Townsend, MS, on 5/6/1865.

Holland, Christopher Columbus Pvt., 1st & 3rd Missouri Cavalry (Consolidated). Co. E. Enlisted: 12/27/1861 at Platte River, Buchanan County, MO. Age at enlistment: 25. Federal Rolls of Prisoners of War: Captured at Blakely, AL, on 4/9/1865; Received at Ship Island, MS, on 4/15/1865. Transferred to Vicksburg, MS, for exchange on 5/1/1865; Exchanged at Camp Townsend, MS, on 5/6/1865.

Holland, John E.C. Pvt., 1st & 3rd Missouri Cavalry (Consolidated). Cos. A & E. Enlisted: 12/7/1861 at

Andrew County, MO. Age at enlistment: 27. Transferred to Co. E while at Corinth, MS. Federal Rolls of Prisoners of War: Captured at Blakely, AL, on 4/9/1865; Received at Ship Island, MS, on 4/15/1865. Transferred to Vicksburg, MS, for exchange on 5/1/1865; Exchanged at Camp Townsend, MS, on 5/6/1865.

Hollis, Charles P. Pvt., 3rd & 5th Missouri Infantry (Consolidated). Co. __. Federal Rolls of Prisoners of War: Captured at Blakely, AL, on 4/9/1865; Received at Ship Island, MS, on 4/15/1865. Transferred to Vicksburg, MS, for exchange on 5/1/1865; Exchanged at Camp Townsend, MS, on 5/6/1865.

Holmes, C.G. (AKA Helmer) Pvt., 1st & 3rd Missouri Cavalry (Consolidated). Co. __. Federal Rolls of Prisoners of War: Captured at Blakely, AL, on 4/9/1865; Received at Ship Island, MS, on 4/15/1865. Transferred to Vicksburg, MS, for exchange on 5/1/1865; Exchanged at Camp Townsend, MS, on 5/6/1865.

Holt, William H. Pvt., 1st & 3rd Missouri Cavalry (Consolidated). Co. K. Enlisted: 12/5/1861 at Williamsburg, Callaway County, MO. Age at enlistment: 20. Federal Rolls of Prisoners of War: Captured at Blakely, AL, on 4/9/1865; Received at Ship Island, MS, on 4/15/1865. Transferred to Vicksburg, MS, for exchange on 5/1/1865; Exchanged at Camp Townsend, MS, on 5/6/1865. Rolls of Prisoners of War, C.S.A: Surrendered at Citronelle, AL, on 5/4/1865; Paroled at Meridian, MS, in 5/1865.

Hooper, A.W. Pvt., 3rd & 5th Missouri Infantry (Consolidated). Co. __. Federal Rolls of Prisoners of War: Captured at Blakely, AL, on 4/9/1865; Received at Ship Island, MS, on 4/15/1865. Transferred to Vicksburg, MS, for exchange on 5/1/1865; Exchanged at Camp Townsend, MS, on 5/6/1865.

Hopkins, George W. (AKA G.N.) Pvt., 3rd & 5th Missouri Infantry (Consolidated). Co. H. Federal Rolls of Prisoners of War: Captured at Blakely, AL, on 4/9/1865; Received at Ship Island, MS, on 4/15/1865. Transferred to Vicksburg, MS, for exchange on 5/1/1865; Exchanged at Camp Townsend, MS, on 5/6/1865.

Hornback, Silas H.F. Pvt./Jr. 2nd Lt., 2nd & 6th Missouri Infantry (Consolidated). Co. A. Federal Rolls of Prisoners of War: Captured at Blakely, AL, on 4/9/1865; Received at Ship Island, MS, on 4/15/1865. Transferred to Vicksburg, MS, for exchange on 4/28/1865; Confined at New Orleans, LA, on 4/30/1865. Exchanged at Camp Townsend, MS, on 5/6/1865.

Horton, John J. Sgt., 1st & 3rd Missouri Cavalry (Consolidated). Co. I. Federal Rolls of Prisoners of War: Captured at Blakely, AL, on 4/9/1865; Received at Ship Island, MS, on 4/15/1865. Transferred to Vicksburg, MS, for exchange on 5/1/1865; Exchanged at Camp Townsend, MS, on 5/6/1865.

Houston, Benton F. (AKA Huston) Pvt., 2nd & 6th Missouri Infantry (Consolidated). Co. C. Federal Rolls of Prisoners of War: Captured at Blakely, AL, on 4/9/1865; Received at Ship Island, MS, on 4/15/1865. Transferred to Vicksburg, MS, for exchange on 5/1/1865; Exchanged at Camp Townsend, MS, on 5/6/1865.

Hudgens, Humphrey D. Pvt., 1st & 3rd Missouri Cavalry (Consolidated). Co. A. Enlisted: 12/7/1861 at Utica, Livingston County, MO. Age at enlistment: 29. Federal Rolls of Prisoners of War: Captured at Blakely, AL, on 4/9/1865; Received at Ship Island, MS, on 4/15/1865. Transferred to Vicksburg, MS, for exchange on 5/1/1865; Exchanged at Camp Townsend, MS, on 5/6/1865.

Huff, William H. Pvt./2nd Lt., 2nd & 6th Missouri Infantry (Consolidated). Co. E. Enlisted: 1/21/1862 at Lone Jack, MO. Age at enlistment: 26. Resident at enlistment: Lone Jack, MO. Federal Rolls of Prisoners of War: Captured at Blakely, AL, on 4/9/1865; Received at Ship Island, MS, on 4/15/1865. Transferred to Vicksburg, MS, for exchange on 4/28/1865; Confined at New Orleans, LA, on 4/30/1865. Exchanged at Camp Townsend, MS, on 5/6/1865.

Huffaker, H.C. (AKA Huffaxer, A.C.) Pvt., 1st & 3rd Missouri Cavalry (Consolidated). Co. G. Federal Rolls of Prisoners of War: Captured at Blakely, AL, on 4/9/1865; Received at Ship Island, MS, on 4/15/1865. Transferred to Vicksburg, MS, for exchange on 5/1/1865; Exchanged at Camp Townsend, MS, on 5/6/1865.

Hugan, Humphrey D. Pvt., 1st & 3rd Missouri Cavalry (Consolidated). Co. __. Federal Rolls of Prisoners of War: Captured at Blakely, AL, on 4/9/1865; Received at Ship Island, MS, on 4/15/1865. Transferred to Vicksburg, MS, for exchange on 5/1/1865; Exchanged at Camp Townsend, MS, on 5/6/1865.

Hunt, D. Pvt., 3rd & 5th Missouri Infantry (Consolidated). Co. B. Federal Rolls of Prisoners of War: Captured at Blakely, AL, on 4/9/1865; Received at Ship Island, MS, on 4/15/1865. Transferred to Vicksburg, MS, for exchange on 5/1/1865; Exchanged at Camp Townsend, MS, on 5/6/1865.

Hunter, Duke W. Pvt./Surg., 2nd & 6th Missouri Infantry (Consolidated). F & S. Enlisted 1/1862 at Springfield, MO. Age at enlistment: 30. Federal Rolls of Prisoners of War: Captured at Blakely, AL, on 4/9/1865; Received at Ship Island, MS, on 4/15/1865. Transferred to Vicksburg, MS, for exchange on 4/28/1865; Confined at New Orleans, LA, on 4/30/1865. Exchanged at Camp Townsend, MS, on 5/6/1865.

Hurt, James C. Pvt., 1st & 3rd Missouri Cavalry (Consolidated). Co. A. Federal Rolls of Prisoners of War: Captured at Blakely, AL, on 4/9/1865; Received at Ship Island, MS, on 4/15/1865. Transferred to Vicksburg, MS, for exchange on 5/1/1865; Exchanged at Camp Townsend, MS, on 5/6/1865.

Hutchinson, John Pvt./Cpl., 3rd & 5th Missouri Infantry (Consolidated). Co. H. Federal Rolls of Prisoners of War: Captured at Blakely, AL, on 4/9/1865; Received at Ship Island, MS, on 4/15/1865. Transferred to Vicksburg, MS, for exchange on 5/1/1865; Exchanged at Camp Townsend, MS, on 5/6/1865.

Jackson, Joseph P. (AKA J.F.) Pvt., 1st & 3rd Missouri Cavalry (Consolidated). Co. __. Federal Rolls of Prisoners of War: Captured at Blakely, AL, on 4/9/1865; Received at Ship Island, MS, on 4/15/1865. Transferred to Vicksburg, MS, for exchange on 5/1/1865; Exchanged at Camp Townsend, MS, on 5/6/1865.

James, A. Pvt., 3rd & 5th Missouri Infantry (Consolidated). Co. __. Federal Rolls of Prisoners of War: Captured at Blakely, AL, on 4/9/1865; Received at Ship Island, MS, on 4/15/1865. Transferred to Vicksburg, MS, for exchange on 5/1/1865; Exchanged at Camp Townsend, MS, on 5/6/1865.

James, Joel P. Pvt., 1st & 3rd Missouri Cavalry (Consolidated). Co. K. Enlisted: 12/5/1861 at High Hill, Montgomery County, MO. Age at enlistment: 24. Federal Rolls of Prisoners of War: Captured at Baker's Creek, MS; Exchanged on 10/29/1864. Federal Rolls of Prisoners of War: Captured at Blakely, AL, on 4/9/1865; Received at Ship Island, MS, on 4/15/1865. Transferred to Vicksburg, MS, for exchange on 5/1/1865; Exchanged at Camp Townsend, MS, on 5/6/1865.

James, John B. Pvt., 1st & 3rd Missouri Cavalry (Consolidated). Co. K. Enlisted: 9/18/1863 at New Florence, Montgomery County, AL. Age at enlistment: 28. Federal Rolls of Prisoners of War: Captured at Blakely, AL, on 4/9/1865; Received at Ship Island, MS, on 4/15/1865. Transferred to Vicksburg, MS, for exchange on 5/1/1865; Exchanged at Camp Townsend, MS, on 5/6/1865. Rolls of Prisoners of War, C.S.A: Surrendered at Citronelle, AL, on 5/4/1865; Paroled at Meridian, MS, in 5/1865.

James, Lycurgus (AKA Lyerirgus) Pvt., 1st & 3rd Missouri Cavalry (Consolidated). Co. K. Enlisted: 5/16/1862 at Rocheport, Boone County, MO. Age at enlistment: 21. Federal Rolls of Prisoners of War: Captured at Big Black River Bridge, MS; Exchanged on 10/29/1864. Federal Rolls of Prisoners of War: Captured at Blakely, AL, on 4/9/1865; Received at Ship Island, MS, on 4/15/1865. Transferred to Vicksburg, MS, for exchange on 5/1/1865; Exchanged at Camp Townsend, MS, on 5/6/1865.

James, Silvannus S. (AKA Stokes) Pvt., 3rd & 5th Missouri Infantry (Consolidated). Co. B. Federal Rolls of Prisoners of War: Captured at Blakely, AL, on 4/9/1865; Received at Ship Island, MS, on 4/15/1865. Transferred to Vicksburg, MS, for exchange on 5/1/1865; Exchanged at Camp Townsend, MS, on 5/6/1865.

Jarrett, R.F. Pvt., 3rd & 5th Missouri Infantry (Consolidated). Co. __. Federal Rolls of Prisoners of War: Captured at Blakely, AL, on 4/9/1865; Received at Ship Island, MS, on 4/15/1865. Transferred to Vicksburg, MS, for exchange on 5/1/1865; Exchanged at Camp Townsend, MS, on 5/6/1865.

Jeger, H. Pvt., 3rd & 5th Missouri Infantry (Consolidated). Co. __. Federal Rolls of Prisoners of War: Captured at Blakely, AL, on 4/9/1865; Received at Ship Island, MS, on 4/15/1865. Transferred to Vicksburg, MS, for exchange on 5/1/1865; Exchanged at Camp Townsend, MS, on 5/6/1865.

Jenkins, Joseph M. Pvt., 3rd & 5th Missouri Infantry (Consolidated). Cos. F & K. Federal Rolls of Prisoners of War: Captured at Blakely, AL, on 4/9/1865; Received at Ship Island, MS, on 4/15/1865. Transferred to Vicksburg, MS, for exchange on 5/1/1865; Exchanged at Camp Townsend, MS, on 5/6/1865.

Jett, Benjamin D. Pvt./Cpl., 3rd & 5th Missouri Infantry (Consolidated). Co. H. Federal Rolls of Prisoners of War: Captured at Blakely, AL, on 4/9/1865; Received at Ship Island, MS, on 4/15/1865. Transferred to Vicksburg, MS, for exchange on 5/1/1865; Exchanged at Camp Townsend, MS, on 5/6/1865.

Johnson, Edwin P. Sgt./Sgt. Maj., 1st & 3rd Missouri Cavalry (Consolidated). Co. __. Federal Rolls of Prisoners of War: Captured at Blakely, AL, on 4/9/1865; Received at Ship Island, MS, on 4/15/1865. Transferred to Vicksburg, MS, for exchange on 5/1/1865; Exchanged at Camp Townsend, MS, on 5/6/1865.

Johnson, J.W. Cpl., 1st & 3rd Missouri Cavalry (Consolidated). Co. __. Federal Rolls of Prisoners of War: Captured at Blakely, AL, on 4/9/1865; Received at Ship Island, MS, on 4/15/1865. Transferred to Vicksburg, MS, for exchange on 5/1/1865; Exchanged at Camp Townsend, MS, on 5/6/1865.

Johnson, R.W. Pvt., 3rd & 5th Missouri Infantry (Consolidated). Co. A. Federal Rolls of Prisoners of War: Captured at Blakely, AL, on 4/9/1865; Received at Ship Island, MS, on 4/15/1865. Transferred to Vicksburg, MS, for exchange on 5/1/1865; Exchanged at Camp Townsend, MS, on 5/6/1865.

Johnson, Wade Pvt., 1st & 3rd Missouri Cavalry (Consolidated). Co. __. Federal Rolls of Prisoners of War: Captured at Blakely, AL, on 4/9/1865; Received at Ship Island, MS, on 4/15/1865. Transferred to Vicksburg, MS, for exchange on 5/1/1865; Exchanged at Camp Townsend, MS, on 5/6/1865.

Johnston, H.H. Pvt., 3rd & 5th Missouri Infantry (Consolidated). Co. __. Federal Rolls of Prisoners of War: Captured at Blakely, AL, on 4/9/1865; Received at Ship Island, MS, on 4/15/1865. Transferred to Vicksburg, MS, for exchange on 5/1/1865; Exchanged at Camp Townsend, MS, on 5/6/1865.

Jones, John Pvt., 3rd & 5th Missouri Infantry (Consolidated). Co. __. Federal Rolls of Prisoners of War: Captured at Blakely, AL, on 4/9/1865; Received at Ship Island, MS, on 4/15/1865. Transferred to Vicksburg, MS, for exchange on 5/1/1865; Exchanged at Camp Townsend, MS, on 5/6/1865.

Jones, W. Pvt., 3rd & 5th Missouri Infantry (Consolidated). Co. __. Federal Rolls of Prisoners of War: Captured at Blakely, AL, on 4/9/1865; Received at Ship Island, MS, on 4/15/1865. Transferred to Vicksburg, MS, for exchange on 5/1/1865; Exchanged at Camp Townsend, MS, on 5/6/1865.

Kavenaugh, William H. Pvt., 3rd & 5th Missouri Infantry (Consolidated). Co. I. Federal Rolls of Prisoners of War: Captured at Blakely, AL, on 4/9/1865; Received at Ship Island, MS, on 4/15/1865. Transferred to Vicksburg, MS, for exchange on 5/1/1865; Exchanged at Camp Townsend, MS, on 5/6/1865.

Keifer, E. Pvt., 3rd & 5th Missouri Infantry (Consolidated). Co. __. Federal Rolls of Prisoners of War: Captured at Blakely, AL, on 4/9/1865; Received at Ship Island, MS, on 4/15/1865. Transferred to Vicksburg, MS, for exchange on 5/1/1865; Exchanged at Camp Townsend, MS, on 5/6/1865.

Kelly, John W. (AKA J.M.) Cpl./Pvt., 3rd & 5th Missouri Infantry (Consolidated). Co. D. Federal Rolls of Prisoners of War: Captured at Blakely, AL, on 4/9/1865; Received at Ship Island, MS, on 4/15/1865. Transferred to Vicksburg, MS, for exchange on 5/1/1865; Exchanged at Camp Townsend, MS, on 5/6/1865.

Kemp, Anthony N. (AKA A.M.) Pvt., 3rd & 5th Missouri Infantry (Consolidated). Co. H. Federal Rolls of Prisoners of War: Captured at Blakely, AL, on 4/9/1865; Received at Ship Island, MS, on 4/15/1865. Transferred to Vicksburg, MS, for exchange on 5/1/1865; Exchanged at Camp Townsend, MS, on 5/6/1865.

Kennedy, D.N. Pvt., 3rd & 5th Missouri Infantry

(Consolidated). Co. __. Federal Rolls of Prisoners of War: Captured at Blakely, AL, on 4/9/1865; Received at Ship Island, MS, on 4/15/1865. Transferred to Vicksburg, MS, for exchange on 5/1/1865; Exchanged at Camp Townsend, MS, on 5/6/1865.

Kennedy, John Sgt., 3rd & 5th Missouri Infantry (Consolidated). Co. __. Federal Rolls of Prisoners of War: Captured at Blakely, AL, on 4/9/1865; Received at Ship Island, MS, on 4/15/1865. Transferred to Vicksburg, MS, for exchange on 5/1/1865; Exchanged at Camp Townsend, MS, on 5/6/1865.

Kennedy, Matthew Pvt., 3rd & 5th Missouri Infantry (Consolidated). Co. F. Federal Rolls of Prisoners of War: Captured at Blakely, AL, on 4/9/1865; Received at Ship Island, MS, on 4/15/1865. Transferred to Vicksburg, MS, for exchange on 5/1/1865; Exchanged at Camp Townsend, MS, on 5/6/1865.

Kerr, Henry Clay Pvt., 1st & 3rd Missouri Cavalry (Consolidated). Co. G. Federal Rolls of Prisoners of War: Captured at Blakely, AL, on 4/9/1865; Received at Ship Island, MS, on 4/15/1865. Transferred to Vicksburg, MS, for exchange on 5/1/1865; Exchanged at Camp Townsend, MS, on 5/6/1865.

Kerr, N.E. Pvt., 3rd & 5th Missouri Infantry (Consolidated). Co. __. Federal Rolls of Prisoners of War: Captured at Blakely, AL, on 4/9/1865; Received at Ship Island, MS, on 4/15/1865. Transferred to Vicksburg, MS, for exchange on 5/1/1865; Exchanged at Camp Townsend, MS, on 5/6/1865.

Ketchum, Charles Pvt., 3rd & 5th Missouri Infantry (Consolidated). Co. __. Federal Rolls of Prisoners of War: Captured at Blakely, AL, on 4/9/1865; Received at Ship Island, MS, on 4/15/1865. Transferred to Vicksburg, MS, for exchange on 5/1/1865; Exchanged at Camp Townsend, MS, on 5/6/1865.

Kincaid, R. Pvt., 3rd & 5th Missouri Infantry (Consolidated). Co. __. Federal Rolls of Prisoners of War: Captured at Blakely, AL, on 4/9/1865; Received at Ship Island, MS, on 4/15/1865. Transferred to Vicksburg, MS, for exchange on 5/1/1865; Exchanged at Camp Townsend, MS, on 5/6/1865.

King, William Pvt., 3rd & 5th Missouri Infantry (Consolidated). Co. K. Federal Rolls of Prisoners of War: Captured at Blakely, AL, on 4/9/1865; Received at Ship Island, MS, on 4/15/1865. Transferred to Vicksburg, MS, for exchange on 5/1/1865; Exchanged at Camp Townsend, MS, on 5/6/1865.

Kirby, W.C. (AKA Kerby) Pvt., 3rd & 5th Missouri Infantry (Consolidated). Co. F. Federal Rolls of Prisoners of War: Captured at Blakely, AL, on 4/9/1865; Received at Ship Island, MS, on 4/15/1865. Transferred to Vicksburg, MS, for exchange on 5/1/1865; Exchanged at Camp Townsend, MS, on 5/6/1865.

Lacy, Gordon Pvt., 2nd & 6th Missouri Infantry (Consolidated). Co. __. Federal Rolls of Prisoners of War: Captured at Blakely, AL, on 4/9/1865; Received at Ship Island, MS, on 4/15/1865. Transferred to Vicksburg, MS, for exchange on 5/1/1865; Exchanged at Camp Townsend, MS, on 5/6/1865.

Lanter, Davis Capt., 1st & 3rd Missouri Cavalry (Consolidated). Co. C. Enlisted: 12/20/1861 at Platte City, MO. Age at enlistment: 40. Federal Rolls of Prisoners of War: Captured at Blakely, AL, on 4/9/1865; Confined at Spanish Fort, AL, for one day. Received at Ship Island, MS, on 4/16/1865; Transferred to Vicksburg, MS, for exchange on 4/28/1865. Confined at New Orleans, LA, on 4/30/1865; Exchanged at Camp Townsend, MS, on 5/6/1865.

Lara, James Pvt., 2nd & 6th Missouri Infantry (Consolidated). Co. __. Federal Rolls of Prisoners of War: Captured at Blakely, AL, on 4/9/1865; Received at Ship Island, MS, on 4/15/1865. Transferred to Vicksburg, MS, for exchange on 5/1/1865; Exchanged at Camp Townsend, MS, on 5/6/1865.

Lee, Albert Cpl., 3rd & 5th Missouri Infantry (Consolidated). Co. __. Federal Rolls of Prisoners of War: Captured at Blakely, AL, on 4/9/1865; Received at Ship Island, MS, on 4/15/1865. Transferred to Vicksburg, MS, for exchange on 5/1/1865; Exchanged at Camp Townsend, MS, on 5/6/1865.

Lewis, J.P. Cpl., 3rd & 5th Missouri Infantry (Consolidated). Co. __. Federal Rolls of Prisoners of War: Captured at Blakely, AL, on 4/9/1865; Received at Ship Island, MS, on 4/15/1865. Transferred to Vicksburg, MS, for exchange on 5/1/1865; Exchanged at Camp Townsend, MS, on 5/6/1865.

Lewis, Nat Cpl., 3rd & 5th Missouri Infantry (Consolidated). Co. __. Federal Rolls of Prisoners of War: Captured at Blakely, AL, on 4/9/1865; Received at Ship Island, MS, on 4/15/1865. Transferred to Vicksburg, MS, for exchange on 5/1/1865; Exchanged at Camp Townsend, MS, on 5/6/1865.

Link, August Pvt., 3rd & 5th Missouri Infantry (Consolidated). Co. B. Federal Rolls of Prisoners of War: Captured at Blakely, AL, on 4/9/1865; Received at Ship Island, MS, on 4/15/1865. Transferred to Vicksburg, MS, for exchange on 5/1/1865; Exchanged at Camp Townsend, MS, on 5/6/1865.

Locke, Robert A. (AKA Lock) Sgt., 1st & 3rd Missouri Cavalry (Consolidated). Co. I. Enlisted: 12/16/1861 at Independence, MO. Age at enlistment: 22. Residence at enlistment: Jackson County, MO. Federal Rolls of Prisoners of War: Captured at Big Black River Bridge, MS; Exchanged on 2/13/1865. Federal Rolls of Prisoners of War: Captured at Blakely, AL, on 4/9/1865; Received at Ship Island, MS, on 4/15/1865. Transferred to Vicksburg, MS, for exchange on 5/1/1865; Exchanged at Camp Townsend, MS, on 5/6/1865.

Logan, Diraly (AKA Denaly) Cpl., 3rd & 5th Missouri Infantry (Consolidated). Co. __. Federal Rolls of Prisoners of War: Captured at Blakely, AL, on 4/9/1865; Received at Ship Island, MS, on 4/15/1865. Transferred to Vicksburg, MS, for exchange on 5/1/1865; Exchanged at Camp Townsend, MS, on 5/6/1865.

Long, Robert Joshua Pvt., 1st & 3rd Missouri Cavalry (Consolidated). Co. K. Wounded at New Hope Church, GA. Federal Rolls of Prisoners of War: Captured at Blakely, AL, on 4/9/1865; Received at Ship Island, MS, on 4/15/1865. Transferred to Vicksburg, MS, for exchange on 5/1/1865; Exchanged at Camp Townsend, MS, on 5/6/1865. Received the United Daughters of the Confederacy Cross of Honor for his wartime service. Born: 3/20/1834 to Alexander Ewing Long and Matilda Owings at Montgomery County, KY. Married: Mary Elizabeth Burge. Children: 1 son — David Ewing Long. Wife born: 10/23/1847. Wife died: 1/17/1932.

Lowe, Andrew J. (AKA Low) Pvt., 1st & 3rd Missouri Cavalry (Consolidated). Co. F. Enlisted: 12/25/1861 at Oregon, MO. Age at enlistment: 17. Residence at enlistment: Holt County, MO. Federal Rolls of Prisoners of War: Captured at Blakely, AL, on 4/9/1865; Received at Ship Island, MS, on 4/15/1865. Transferred to Vicksburg, MS, for exchange on 5/1/1865; Exchanged at Camp Townsend, MS, on 5/6/1865.

Lowe, John P. (AKA Low) Pvt., 1st & 3rd Missouri Cavalry (Consolidated). Co. F. Enlisted: 12/6/1861 at Savannah, MO. Age at enlistment: 25. Residence at enlistment: Andrew County, MO. Federal Rolls of Prisoners of War: Captured at Blakely, AL, on 4/9/1865; Received at Ship Island, MS, on 4/15/1865. Transferred to Vicksburg, MS, for exchange on 5/1/1865; Exchanged at Camp Townsend, MS, on 5/6/1865.

Lyon, Samuel B. Pvt., 2nd & 6th Missouri Infantry (Consolidated). Co. __. Enlisted: 12/1861 at St. Clair County, MO. Age at enlistment: 24. Federal Rolls of Prisoners of War: Captured at Blakely, AL, on 4/9/1865; Received at Ship Island, MS, on 4/15/1865. Transferred to Vicksburg, MS, for exchange on 5/1/1865; Exchanged at Camp Townsend, MS, on 5/6/1865.

McCall, John P. Pvt., 1st & 3rd Missouri Cavalry (Consolidated). Co. B. Enlisted: 12/11/1861 at Readsville, MO. Age at enlistment: 18. Residence at enlistment: Callaway County, MO. Federal Rolls of Prisoners of War: Captured at Blakely, AL, on 4/9/1865; Received at Ship Island, MS, on 4/15/1865. Transferred to Vicksburg, MS, for exchange on 5/1/1865; Exchanged at Camp Townsend, MS, on 5/6/1865.

McCarty, D.A. Pvt., 1st & 3rd Missouri Cavalry (Consolidated). Co. __. Federal Rolls of Prisoners of War: Captured at Blakely, AL, on 4/9/1865; Received at Ship Island, MS, on 4/15/1865. Transferred to Vicksburg, MS, for exchange on 5/1/1865; Exchanged at Camp Townsend, MS, on 5/6/1865.

McCauley, Arthur (AKA McCarley, McCawley) 2nd Lt./1st Lt., 1st & 3rd Missouri Cavalry (Consolidated). Co. I. Enlisted: 5/13/1862 at Corinth, MS. Residence at enlistment: Crystal Springs, MS. Elected 2nd Lt. on 6/15/1862; Promoted to 1st Lt. on 10/3/1862. Federal Rolls of Prisoners of War: Captured at Blakley, AL, on 4/9/1865; Received at Ship Island, MS, on 4/15/1865. Transferred to Vicksburg, MS, for exchange on 4/28/1865; Confined at New Orleans, LA, on 4/30/1865. Exchanged at Camp Townsend, MS, on 5/6/1865.

McClellan, A. Lt., Missouri Artillery Battery (Brown's). Federal Rolls of Prisoners of War: Captured at Blakely, AL, on 4/9/1865; Received at Ship Island, MS, on 4/15/1865. Transferred to Vicksburg, MS, for exchange on 4/28/1865; Confined at New Orleans, LA, on 4/30/1865. Exchanged at Camp Townsend, MS, on 5/6/1865.

McClure, John S. Pvt., 2nd & 6th Missouri Infantry (Consolidated). Co. C. Enlisted: 12/2/1861 at St. Clair, MO. Wounded at Corinth, MS. Federal Rolls of Prisoners of War: Captured at Blakely, AL, on 4/9/1865; Received at Ship Island, MS, on 4/15/1865. Transferred to Vicksburg, MS, for exchange on 5/1/1865; Exchanged at Camp Townsend, MS, on 5/6/1865.

McCorkle, Christopher Columbus Pvt., 1st & 3rd Missouri Cavalry (Consolidated). Cos. D & E. Enlisted: 5/15/1862 at Plattsburg, MO. Age at enlistment: 20. Residence at enlistment: Clay County, MO. Federal Rolls of Prisoners of War: Captured in Missouri in 9/1862; Exchanged in 6/1863. Severely wounded at Allatoona, GA. Federal Rolls of Prisoners of War: Captured at Blakely, AL, on 4/9/1865; Received at Ship Island, MS, on 4/15/1865. Transferred to Vicksburg, MS, for exchange on 5/1/1865; Exchanged at Camp Townsend, MS, on 5/6/1865. Born: 12/16/1842 near Mosby, MO. Memberships: Mason, charter member of the Odd Fellows Lodge, and adjutant of the Winnie Davis Camp of United Confederate Veterans. Religion: Presbyterian. Died: 6/22/913 at Clay County, MO. Buried: Van Alstyne Cemetery located at Clay County, MO. His obituary appeared in a 1913 edition of *Confederate Veteran* magazine.

McFerson, Barton (AKA McPherson) Pvt., 1st & 3rd Missouri Cavalry (Consolidated). Co. H. Enlisted 9/1/1862 at Newton County, MO. Age at enlistment: 18. Residence at enlistment: Stockton, MO. Federal Rolls of Prisoners of War: Captured at Blakely, AL, on 4/9/1865; Received at Ship Island, MS, on 4/15/1865. Transferred to Vicksburg, MS, for exchange on 5/1/1865; Exchanged at Camp Townsend, MS, on 5/6/1865.

McGlothen, G.C. Pvt., 1st & 3rd Missouri Cavalry (Consolidated). Co. B. Federal Rolls of Prisoners of War: Captured at Blakely, AL, on 4/9/1865; Received at Ship Island, MS, on 4/15/1865. Transferred to Vicksburg, MS, for exchange on 5/1/1865; Exchanged at Camp Townsend, MS, on 5/6/1865.

McHugh, Charles (AKA McCue) Pvt., 3rd & 5th Missouri Infantry (Consolidated). Co. H. Enlisted: 12/1861 at Springfield, MO. Age at enlistment: 18. Residence at enlistment: Jamesport, MO. Federal Rolls of Prisoners of War: Captured at Blakely, AL, on 4/9/1865; Received at Ship Island, MS, on 4/15/1865. Transferred to Vicksburg, MS, for exchange on 5/1/1865; Exchanged at Camp Townsend, MS, on 5/6/1865.

McHugh, Peter Pvt., 3rd & 5th Missouri Infantry (Consolidated). Co. __. Federal Rolls of Prisoners of War: Captured at Blakely, AL, on 4/9/1865; Received at Ship Island, MS, on 4/15/1865. Transferred to Vicksburg, MS, for exchange on 5/1/1865; Exchanged at Camp Townsend, MS, on 5/6/1865.

McKee, David Pvt., 3rd & 5th Missouri Infantry (Consolidated). Cos. D & F. Federal Rolls of Prisoners of War: Captured at Blakely, AL, on 4/9/1865; Received at Ship Island, MS, on 4/15/1865. Transferred to Vicksburg, MS, for exchange on 5/1/1865; Exchanged at Camp Townsend, MS, on 5/6/1865.

McKinney, William Pvt., 1st & 3rd Missouri Cavalry (Consolidated). Co. __. Federal Rolls of Prisoners of War: Captured at Blakely, AL, on 4/9/1865; Received at Ship Island, MS, on 4/15/1865. Transferred to Vicksburg, MS, for exchange on 5/1/1865; Exchanged at Camp Townsend, MS, on 5/6/1865.

McKinney, Willis Pvt., 2nd & 6th Missouri Infantry (Consolidated). Co. G. Wounded at Baker's Creek, MS. Federal Rolls of Prisoners of War: Captured at Blakely, AL, on 4/9/1865; Received at Ship Island, MS, on 4/15/1865. Transferred to Vicksburg, MS, for exchange on 5/1/1865; Exchanged at Camp Townsend, MS, on 5/6/1865.

McMillion, James Sgt., 1st & 3rd Missouri Cavalry

(Consolidated). Co. G. Enlisted: 12/31/1861 at Pattonsburg, Daviess County, MO. Age at enlistment: 25. Wounded at Franklin, TN. Federal Rolls of Prisoners of War: Captured at Blakely, AL, on 4/9/1865; Received at Ship Island, MS, on 4/15/1865. Transferred to Vicksburg, MS, for exchange on 5/1/1865; Exchanged at Camp Townsend, MS, on 5/6/1865.

McNeely, John Pvt., 3rd & 5th Missouri Infantry (Consolidated). Co. B. Federal Rolls of Prisoners of War: Captured at Blakely, AL, on 4/9/1865; Received at Ship Island, MS, on 4/15/1865. Transferred to Vicksburg, MS, for exchange on 5/1/1865; Exchanged at Camp Townsend, MS, on 5/6/1865.

McTirf, J.D. Pvt., 1st & 3rd Missouri Cavalry (Consolidated). Co. K. Enlisted: 1/1/1863 at St. Joseph, MO. Age at enlistment: 21. Residence at enlistment: Buchanan County, MO. Federal Rolls of Prisoners of War: Captured at Blakely, AL, on 4/9/1865; Received at Ship Island, MS, on 4/15/1865. Transferred to Vicksburg, MS, for exchange on 5/1/1865; Exchanged at Camp Townsend, MS, on 5/6/1865. Rolls of Prisoners of War, C.S.A: Surrendered at Citronelle, AL, on 5/4/1865; Paroled at Meridian, MS, in 5/1865.

Madole, Frank R. (AKA T.R.) Cpl./Sr. 2nd Lt., 2nd & 6th Missouri Infantry (Consolidated). Co. D. Federal Rolls of Prisoners of War: Captured at Blakely, AL, on 4/9/1865; Received at Ship Island, MS, on 4/15/1865. Transferred to Vicksburg, MS, for exchange on 4/28/1865; Confined at New Orleans, LA, on 4/30/1865. Exchanged at Camp Townsend, MS, on 5/6/1865.

Mahone, John F. Sgt./Jr. 2nd Lt., 1st & 3rd Missouri Cavalry (Consolidated). Co. A. Federal Rolls of Prisoners of War: Captured at Blakely, AL, on 4/9/1865; Received at Ship Island, MS, on 4/15/1865. Transferred to Vicksburg, MS, for exchange on 4/28/1865; Confined at New Orleans, LA, on 4/30/1865. Exchanged at Camp Townsend, MS, on 5/6/1865.

Malloy, Phillip Y. (AKA Molloy, P.T.) Drum Major, 3rd & 5th Missouri Infantry (Consolidated). Co. C. Enlisted: 6/2/1861. Federal Rolls of Prisoners of War: Captured at Blakely, AL, on 4/9/1865; Received at Ship Island, MS, on 4/15/1865. Transferred to Vicksburg, MS, for exchange on 5/1/1865; Exchanged at Camp Townsend, MS, on 5/6/1865.

Marmaduke, Thaddeus S., Jr. 2nd Lt./2nd Lt., 3rd & 5th Missouri Infantry (Consolidated). Co. B. Enlisted: 12/1/1861 at Osage River, MO. Residence at enlistment: Bloomington, MO. Elected Jr. 2nd Lt. on 11/6/1862. Federal Rolls of Prisoners of War: Captured at Blakely, AL, on 4/9/1865; Received at Ship Island, MS, on 4/15/1865. Transferred to Vicksburg, MS, for exchange on 4/28/1865; Confined at New Orleans, LA, on 4/30/1865. Exchanged at Camp Townsend, MS, on 5/6/1865.

Marsh, S.H. (AKA Harrison) Pvt., 1st & 3rd Missouri Cavalry (Consolidated). Co. __. Federal Rolls of Prisoners of War: Captured at Blakely, AL, on 4/9/1865; Received at Ship Island, MS, on 4/15/1865. Transferred to Vicksburg, MS, for exchange on 5/1/1865; Exchanged at Camp Townsend, MS, on 5/6/1865.

Marshall, Henry S. Pvt./Cpl., 3rd & 5th Missouri Infantry (Consolidated). Co. I. Enlisted: 12/7/1861 at St. Clair, MO. Federal Rolls of Prisoners of War: Captured at Blakely, AL, on 4/9/1865; Received at Ship Island, MS, on 4/15/1865. Transferred to Vicksburg, MS, for exchange on 5/1/1865; Exchanged at Camp Townsend, MS, on 5/6/1865.

Martin, Edward Pvt., 3rd & 5th Missouri Infantry (Consolidated). Co. __. Federal Rolls of Prisoners of War: Captured at Blakely, AL, on 4/9/1865; Received at Ship Island, MS, on 4/15/1865. Transferred to Vicksburg, MS, for exchange on 5/1/1865; Exchanged at Camp Townsend, MS, on 5/6/1865.

Martin, Jasper Pvt., 3rd & 5th Missouri Infantry (Consolidated). Co. __. Federal Rolls of Prisoners of War: Captured at Blakely, AL, on 4/9/1865; Received at Ship Island, MS, on 4/15/1865. Transferred to Vicksburg, MS, for exchange on 5/1/1865; Exchanged at Camp Townsend, MS, on 5/6/1865.

Martin, Josiah Green Pvt., 2nd & 6th Missouri Infantry (Consolidated). Co. H. Enlisted: 6/1861 at Chariton County, MO. Wounded at Kennesaw Mountain, GA, and hospitalized at Marietta, GA. Federal Rolls of Prisoners of War: Captured at Blakely, AL, on 4/9/1865; Received at Ship Island, MS, on 4/15/1865. Transferred to Vicksburg, MS, for exchange on 5/1/1865; Exchanged at Camp Townsend, MS, on 5/6/1865. Received the United Daughters of the Confederacy Cross of Honor for his wartime service. Born: 1/14/1840 to John Martin and Eliza G. Adams at Meade County, KY. Married: Susan Staples. Children: 1 son — John Martin, born 2/14/1876. Died: 3/7/1899 at Keytesville, MO. Wife born: 8/3/1850 in Kentucky. Wife died: 2/27/1890 at Keytesville, MO.

Martin, Thomas Benton Pvt./Cpl., 3rd & 5th Missouri Infantry (Consolidated). Co. G. Enlisted: 1/1/1862 at Springfield, MO. Age at enlistment: 18. Residence at enlistment: Smithton, Pettis County, MO. Federal Rolls of Prisoners of War: Captured and paroled at Vicksburg, MS, on 7/4/1863. Federal Rolls of Prisoners of War: Captured at Blakely, AL, on 4/9/1865; Received at Ship Island, MS, on 4/15/1865. Transferred to Vicksburg, MS, for exchange on 5/1/1865; Exchanged at Camp Townsend, MS, on 5/6/1865. Rolls of Prisoners of War, C.S.A: Surrendered at Citronelle, AL, on 5/4/1865; Paroled at Jackson, MS, on 5/12/1865. Soldier also served as a Pvt. with the Missouri State Guard. Enlisted: 8/11/1861 at Warrensburg, MO. Born: 12/23/1842 to William Martin and Martha E. Merrell at Athens, AL. Married: Mary E. Herrin. Children: 3 —1 son and 2 daughters.

Matthews, James Pvt./Cpl., 1st & 3rd Missouri Cavalry (Consolidated). Co. G. Federal Rolls of Prisoners of War: Captured at Blakely, AL, on 4/9/1865; Received at Ship Island, MS, on 4/15/1865. Transferred to Vicksburg, MS, for exchange on 5/1/1865; Exchanged at Camp Townsend, MS, on 5/6/1865.

Mead, William Pvt., 1st & 3rd Missouri Cavalry (Consolidated). Co. G. Enlisted: 12/31/1861 at Springfield, MO. Age at enlistment: 24. Residence at enlistment: Daviess County, MO. Federal Rolls of Prisoners of War: Captured at Blakely, AL, on 4/9/1865; Received at Ship Island, MS, on 4/15/1865. Transferred to Vicksburg, MS, for exchange on 5/1/1865; Exchanged at Camp Townsend, MS, on 5/6/1865.

Meagher, Pat Pvt., 3rd & 5th Missouri Infantry (Consolidated). Co. __. Federal Rolls of Prisoners of War: Captured at Blakely, AL, on 4/9/1865; Received at

Ship Island, MS, on 4/15/1865. Transferred to Vicksburg, MS, for exchange on 5/1/1865; Exchanged at Camp Townsend, MS, on 5/6/1865.

Meeks, G.C. (AKA Meaks) Pvt., 2nd & 6th Missouri Infantry (Consolidated). Co. __. Federal Rolls of Prisoners of War: Captured at Blakely, AL, on 4/9/1865; Received at Ship Island, MS, on 4/15/1865. Transferred to Vicksburg, MS, for exchange on 5/1/1865; Exchanged at Camp Townsend, MS, on 5/6/1865.

Meeks, Lewis C. Pvt., 3rd & 5th Missouri Infantry (Consolidated). Co. D. Federal Rolls of Prisoners of War: Captured at Blakely, AL, on 4/9/1865; Received at Ship Island, MS, on 4/15/1865. Transferred to Vicksburg, MS, for exchange on 5/1/1865; Exchanged at Camp Townsend, MS, on 5/6/1865.

Mercer, Levi Pvt., 1st & 3rd Missouri Cavalry (Consolidated). Co. K. Enlisted: 4/1/1863 at Big Black, MS. Age at enlistment: 46. Residence at enlistment: Portland, MO. Served in the 1st Missouri Cavalry from 12/5/1861 through 3/25/1863 when discharged as over age. Federal Rolls of Prisoners of War: Captured at Blakely, AL, on 4/9/1865; Received at Ship Island, MS, on 4/15/1865. Transferred to Vicksburg, MS, for exchange on 5/1/1865; Exchanged at Camp Townsend, MS, on 5/6/1865.

Merryweather, W.D. Pvt., 2nd & 6th Missouri Infantry (Consolidated). Co. I. Federal Rolls of Prisoners of War: Captured at Blakely, AL, on 4/9/1865; Received at Ship Island, MS, on 4/15/1865. Transferred to Vicksburg, MS, for exchange on 5/1/1865; Exchanged at Camp Townsend, MS, on 5/6/1865.

Miles, Nicholas V. Cpl., 2nd & 6th Missouri Infantry (Consolidated). Co. D. Enlisted: 1/3/1862 at New Madrid, MO. Age at enlistment: 25. Residence at enlistment: St. Louis, MO. Wounded at Port Gibson, MS, in 1863, and at Allatoona, GA, in 1864. Federal Rolls of Prisoners of War: Captured at Blakely, AL, on 4/9/1865; Received at Ship Island, MS, on 4/15/1865. Transferred to Vicksburg, MS, for exchange on 5/1/1865; Exchanged at Camp Townsend, MS, on 5/6/1865.

Miller, Andrew J. Pvt./Sgt., 1st & 3rd Missouri Cavalry (Consolidated). Co. G. Enlisted: 1/11/1862 at Springfield, MO. Age at enlistment: 22. Residence at enlistment: California, MO. Federal Rolls of Prisoners of War: Captured at Blakely, AL, on 4/9/1865; Received at Ship Island, MS, on 4/15/1865. Transferred to Vicksburg, MS, for exchange on 5/1/1865; Exchanged at Camp Townsend, MS, on 5/6/1865.

Miller, H. Pvt., 3rd & 5th Missouri Infantry (Consolidated). Co. __. Federal Rolls of Prisoners of War: Captured at Blakely, AL, on 4/9/1865; Received at Ship Island, MS, on 4/15/1865. Transferred to Vicksburg, MS, for exchange on 5/1/1865; Exchanged at Camp Townsend, MS, on 5/6/1865.

Miller, Thomas W. (AKA S.W.) Pvt., 3rd & 5th Missouri Infantry (Consolidated). Co. I. Federal Rolls of Prisoners of War: Captured at Blakely, AL, on 4/9/1865; Received at Ship Island, MS, on 4/15/1865. Transferred to Vicksburg, MS, for exchange on 5/1/1865; Exchanged at Camp Townsend, MS, on 5/6/1865.

Minshall, John E., Sr. 2nd Lt./Adjt., 3rd & 5th Missouri Infantry (Consolidated). Co. H. Enlisted: 1/1/862 at Springfield, MO. Age at enlistment: 24. Residence at enlistment: Chillicothe, MO. Elected 2nd Lt. on 1/16/1862; Promoted to Adjutant on 5/8/1862. Federal Rolls of Prisoners of War: Captured at Blakely, AL, on 4/9/1865; Received at Ship Island, MS, on 4/15/1865. Transferred to Vicksburg, MS, for exchange on 4/28/1865; Confined at New Orleans, LA, on 4/30/1865. Exchanged at Camp Townsend, MS, on 5/6/1865.

Minter, John A., Jr. 2nd Lt./2nd Lt., 1st & 3rd Missouri Cavalry (Consolidated). Co. F. Enlisted: 12/27/1861 at Greene County, MO. Age at enlistment: 42. Residence at enlistment: St. Joseph, MO. Elected Jr. 2nd Lt. on 1/15/1862; Promoted to Sr. 2nd Lt. on 11/8/1862. Federal Rolls of Prisoners of War: Captured at Blakely, AL, on 4/9/1865; Received at Ship Island, MS, on 4/15/1865. Transferred to Vicksburg, MS, for exchange on 4/28/1865; Confined at New Orleans, LA, on 4/30/1865. Exchanged at Camp Townsend, MS, on 5/6/1865.

Mitchell, A.C. (AKA A.E.) Pvt., 3rd & 5th Missouri Infantry (Consolidated). Co. __. Federal Rolls of Prisoners of War: Captured at Blakely, AL, on 4/9/1865; Received at Ship Island, MS, on 4/15/1865. Transferred to Vicksburg, MS, for exchange on 5/1/1865; Exchanged at Camp Townsend, MS, on 5/6/1865.

Mitchell, Benjamin L. 1st Sgt./3rd Lt./Jr. 2nd Lt., 3rd & 5th Missouri Infantry (Consolidated). Co. C. Enlisted: 1/11/1862 at Bolivar, MO. Age at enlistment: 19. Residence at enlistment: Bolivar, MO. Promoted to 3rd Lt. on 11/26/1862. Federal Rolls of Prisoners of War: Captured at Blakely, AL, on 4/9/1865; Received at Ship Island, MS, on 4/15/1865. Transferred to Vicksburg, MS, for exchange on 4/28/1865; Confined at New Orleans, LA, on 4/30/1865. Exchanged at Camp Townsend, MS, on 5/6/1865.

Monkers, William Thomas (AKA Munkres) Pvt., 1st & 3rd Missouri Cavalry (Consolidated). Co. E. Enlisted: 4/14/1862 at Platte River, Buchanan County, MO. Age at enlistment: 21. Residence at enlistment: Buchanan County, MO. Federal Rolls of Prisoners of War: Captured at Baker's Creek, MS, on 5/15/1863. Federal Rolls of Prisoners of War: Captured at Blakely, AL, on 4/9/1865; Received at Ship Island, MS, on 4/15/1865. Transferred to Vicksburg, MS, for exchange on 5/1/1865; Exchanged at Camp Townsend, MS, on 5/6/1865.

Montgomery, Elliott Pvt., 3rd & 5th Missouri Infantry (Consolidated). Co. __. Federal Rolls of Prisoners of War: Captured at Blakely, AL, on 4/9/1865; Received at Ship Island, MS, on 4/15/1865. Transferred to Vicksburg, MS, for exchange on 5/1/1865; Exchanged at Camp Townsend, MS, on 5/6/1865.

Montgomery, Simeon J. Pvt., 1st & 3rd Missouri Cavalry (Consolidated). Co. K. Federal Rolls of Prisoners of War: Captured at Blakely, AL, on 4/9/1865; Received at Ship Island, MS, on 4/15/1865. Transferred to Vicksburg, MS, for exchange on 5/1/1865; Exchanged at Camp Townsend, MS, on 5/6/1865.

Moore, Eli Pvt., 1st & 3rd Missouri Cavalry (Consolidated). Co. H. Federal Rolls of Prisoners of War: Captured at Blakely, AL, on 4/9/1865; Received at Ship Island, MS, on 4/15/1865. Transferred to Vicksburg, MS, for exchange on 5/1/1865; Exchanged at Camp Townsend, MS, on 5/6/1865.

Moore, Thomas L. Pvt., 1st & 3rd Missouri Cavalry (Consolidated). Co. I. Enlisted: 12/16/1861 at Farley, Platte County, MO. Age at enlistment: 20. Federal Rolls of Prisoners of War: Captured at Blakely, AL, on 4/9/1865; Received at Ship Island, MS, on 4/15/1865. Transferred to Vicksburg, MS, for exchange on 5/1/1865; Exchanged at Camp Townsend, MS, on 5/6/1865.

Moreland, Francis M. (AKA Morland) Pvt., 1st & 3rd Missouri Cavalry (Consolidated). Co. E. Enlisted: 12/15/1861 at Camden Point, Platte County, MO. Age at enlistment: 22. Wounded at Corinth, MS. Federal Rolls of Prisoners of War: Captured at Blakely, AL, on 4/9/1865; Received at Ship Island, MS, on 4/15/1865. Transferred to Vicksburg, MS, for exchange on 5/1/1865; Exchanged at Camp Townsend, MS, on 5/6/1865.

Morning, John Pvt., 2nd & 6th Missouri Infantry (Consolidated). Co. __. Federal Rolls of Prisoners of War: Captured at Blakely, AL, on 4/9/1865; Received at Ship Island, MS, on 4/15/1865. Transferred to Vicksburg, MS, for exchange on 5/1/1865; Exchanged at Camp Townsend, MS, on 5/6/1865.

Morris, Elijah C. (AKA Eli) Pvt., 2nd & 6th Missouri Infantry (Consolidated). Co. H. Federal Rolls of Prisoners of War: Captured at Blakely, AL, on 4/9/1865; Received at Ship Island, MS, on 4/15/1865. Transferred to Vicksburg, MS, for exchange on 5/1/1865; Exchanged at Camp Townsend, MS, on 5/6/1865.

Morris, J.N. Cpl., 3rd & 5th Missouri Infantry (Consolidated). Co. __. Federal Rolls of Prisoners of War: Captured at Blakely, AL, on 4/9/1865; Received at Ship Island, MS, on 4/15/1865. Transferred to Vicksburg, MS, for exchange on 5/1/1865; Exchanged at Camp Townsend, MS, on 5/6/1865.

Morris, James Pvt., 3rd & 5th Missouri Infantry (Consolidated). Co. __. Federal Rolls of Prisoners of War: Captured at Blakely, AL, on 4/9/1865; Received at Ship Island, MS, on 4/15/1865. Transferred to Vicksburg, MS, for exchange on 5/1/1865; Exchanged at Camp Townsend, MS, on 5/6/1865.

Morris, Lorenzo Pvt./Sgt., 1st & 3rd Missouri Cavalry (Consolidated). Co. H. Federal Rolls of Prisoners of War: Captured at Blakely, AL, on 4/9/1865; Received at Ship Island, MS, on 4/15/1865. Transferred to Vicksburg, MS, for exchange on 5/1/1865; Exchanged at Camp Townsend, MS, on 5/6/1865. Residence at exchange: Anderson County, MO.

Morrison, S.W. Pvt., 3rd & 5th Missouri Infantry (Consolidated). Co. __. Federal Rolls of Prisoners of War: Captured at Blakely, AL, on 4/9/1865; Received at Ship Island, MS, on 4/15/1865. Transferred to Vicksburg, MS, for exchange on 5/1/1865; Exchanged at Camp Townsend, MS, on 5/6/1865.

Morrison, W.B. Pvt., 3rd & 5th Missouri Infantry (Consolidated). Co. __. Federal Rolls of Prisoners of War: Captured at Blakely, AL, on 4/9/1865; Received at Ship Island, MS, on 4/15/1865. Transferred to Vicksburg, MS, for exchange on 5/1/1865; Exchanged at Camp Townsend, MS, on 5/6/1865.

Mulhouse, ? Pvt., 3rd & 5th Missouri Infantry (Consolidated). Co. __. Federal Rolls of Prisoners of War: Captured at Blakely, AL, on 4/9/1865; Received at Ship Island, MS, on 4/15/1865. Transferred to Vicksburg, MS, for exchange on 5/1/1865; Exchanged at Camp Townsend, MS, on 5/6/1865.

Mullins, John Pvt., 3rd & 5th Missouri Infantry (Consolidated). Co. F. Federal Rolls of Prisoners of War: Captured at Blakely, AL, on 4/9/1865; Received at Ship Island, MS, on 4/15/1865. Transferred to Vicksburg, MS, for exchange on 5/1/1865; Exchanged at Camp Townsend, MS, on 5/6/1865.

Murphy, M.F. (AKA F.M.) Pvt., 3rd & 5th Missouri Infantry (Consolidated). Co. __. Federal Rolls of Prisoners of War: Captured at Blakely, AL, on 4/9/1865; Received at Ship Island, MS, on 4/15/1865. Transferred to Vicksburg, MS, for exchange on 5/1/1865; Exchanged at Camp Townsend, MS, on 5/6/1865.

Nealy, J. (AKA Neely) Pvt., 3rd & 5th Missouri Infantry (Consolidated). Co. __. Federal Rolls of Prisoners of War: Captured at Blakely, AL, on 4/9/1865; Received at Ship Island, MS, on 4/15/1865. Transferred to Vicksburg, MS, for exchange on 5/1/1865; Exchanged at Camp Townsend, MS, on 5/6/1865.

Nees, G.T. Pvt., 1st & 3rd Missouri Cavalry (Consolidated). Co. H. Federal Rolls of Prisoners of War: Captured at Blakely, AL, on 4/9/1865; Received at Ship Island, MS, on 4/15/1865. Transferred to Vicksburg, MS, for exchange on 5/1/1865; Exchanged at Camp Townsend, MS, on 5/6/1865.

Nerbert, H.S. (AKA Nerhert) Sgt., 1st & 3rd Missouri Cavalry (Consolidated). Co. __. Federal Rolls of Prisoners of War: Captured at Blakely, AL, on 4/9/1865; Received at Ship Island, MS, on 4/15/1865. Transferred to Vicksburg, MS, for exchange on 5/1/1865; Exchanged at Camp Townsend, MS, on 5/6/1865.

Netherton, Daniel 4th Sgt., 1st & 3rd Missouri Cavalry (Consolidated). Co. G. Enlisted: 12/31/1861 at Salem, MO. Age at enlistment: 19. Residence at enlistment: Daviess County, MO. Federal Rolls of Prisoners of War: Captured at Blakely, AL, on 4/9/1865; Received at Ship Island, MS, on 4/15/1865. Transferred to Vicksburg, MS, for exchange on 5/1/1865; Exchanged at Camp Townsend, MS, on 5/6/1865.

Nevins, Peter (AKA Nevens) Pvt., 1st & 3rd Missouri Cavalry (Consolidated). Co. A. Enlisted: 12/7/1861 at Easton, MO. Age at enlistment: 25. Residence at enlistment: Buchanan County, MO. Federal Rolls of Prisoners of War: Captured at Blakely, AL, on 4/9/1865; Received at Ship Island, MS, on 4/15/1865. Transferred to Vicksburg, MS, for exchange on 5/1/1865; Exchanged at Camp Townsend, MS, on 5/6/1865.

Newland, W.F. Pvt., 3rd & 5th Missouri Infantry. Co. __. Federal Rolls of Prisoners of War: Captured at Blakely, AL, on 4/9/1865; Received at Ship Island, MS, on 4/15/1865. Transferred to Vicksburg, MS, for exchange on 5/1/1865; Exchanged at Camp Townsend, MS, on 5/6/1865.

Newman, John K. Sgt. Maj., 3rd & 5th Missouri Infantry (Consolidated). Co. __. Federal Rolls of Prisoners of War: Captured at Blakely, AL, on 4/9/1865; Received at Ship Island, MS, on 4/15/1865. Transferred to Vicksburg, MS, for exchange on 5/1/1865; Exchanged at Camp Townsend, MS, on 5/6/1865.

Nicholas, William Pvt., 3rd & 5th Missouri Infantry (Consolidated). Co. __. Federal Rolls of Prisoners of War: Captured at Blakely, AL, on 4/9/1865; Received at Ship Island, MS, on 4/15/1865. Transferred to Vicksburg, MS, for exchange on 5/1/1865; Exchanged at Camp Townsend, MS, on 5/6/1865.

Nichols, James Pvt., 3rd & 5th Missouri Infantry (Consolidated). Co. __. Federal Rolls of Prisoners of War: Captured at Blakely, AL, on 4/9/1865; Received at Ship Island, MS, on 4/15/1865. Transferred to Vicksburg, MS, for exchange on 5/1/1865; Exchanged at Camp Townsend, MS, on 5/6/1865.

Nichols, Reuben A. Pvt., 1st & 3rd Missouri Cavalry (Consolidated). Co. E. Federal Rolls of Prisoners of War: Captured at Blakely, AL, on 4/9/1865; Received at Ship Island, MS, on 4/15/1865. Transferred to Vicksburg, MS, for exchange on 5/1/1865; Exchanged at Camp Townsend, MS, on 5/6/1865.

Nichols, Robert Allen Pvt., 1st & 3rd Missouri Cavalry (Consolidated). Co. E. Enlisted: 12/25/1861. Age at enlistment: 19. Wounded on 2/3/1865. Federal Rolls of Prisoners of War: Captured at Blakely, AL, on 4/9/1865; Received at Ship Island, MS, on 4/15/1865. Transferred to Vicksburg, MS, for exchange on 5/1/1865; Exchanged at Camp Townsend, MS, on 5/6/1865.

Norbert, H.L. (AKA H.S.) Sgt., 1st & 3rd Missouri Cavalry (Consolidated). Co. __. Federal Rolls of Prisoners of War: Captured at Blakely, AL, on 4/9/1865; Received at Ship Island, MS, on 4/15/1865. Transferred to Vicksburg, MS, for exchange on 5/1/1865; Exchanged at Camp Townsend, MS, on 5/6/1865.

Norrell, D.A. (AKA Norvell) Sgt., 3rd & 5th Missouri Infantry (Consolidated). Co. __. Federal Rolls of Prisoners of War: Captured at Blakely, AL, on 4/9/1865; Received at Ship Island, MS, on 4/15/1865. Transferred to Vicksburg, MS, for exchange on 5/1/1865; Exchanged at Camp Townsend, MS, on 5/6/1865.

Norris, P. Pvt., 1st & 3rd Missouri Cavalry (Consolidated). Co. __. Federal Rolls of Prisoners of War: Captured at Blakely, AL, on 4/9/1865; Received at Ship Island, MS, on 4/15/1865. Transferred to Vicksburg, MS, for exchange on 5/1/1865; Exchanged at Camp Townsend, MS, on 5/6/1865.

O'Brien, J. (AKA O'Brian) Pvt., 1st & 3rd Missouri Cavalry (Consolidated). Co. B. Federal Rolls of Prisoners of War: Captured at Blakely, AL, on 4/9/1865; Received at Ship Island, MS, on 4/15/1865. Transferred to Vicksburg, MS, for exchange on 5/1/1865; Exchanged at Camp Townsend, MS, on 5/6/1865.

O'Dell, Joel R. (AKA D.) Pvt., 1st & 3rd Missouri Cavalry (Consolidated). Co. F. Federal Rolls of Prisoners of War: Captured at Blakely, AL, on 4/9/1865; Received at Ship Island, MS, on 4/15/1865. Transferred to Vicksburg, MS, for exchange on 5/1/1865; Exchanged at Camp Townsend, MS, on 5/6/1865.

O'Neill, Chris Pvt., 3rd & 5th Missouri Infantry (Consolidated). Co. G. Federal Rolls of Prisoners of War: Captured at Blakely, AL, on 4/9/1865; Received at Ship Island, MS, on 4/15/1865. Transferred to Vicksburg, MS, for exchange on 5/1/1865; Exchanged at Camp Townsend, MS, on 5/6/1865.

Ogle, Benjamin F. (AKA B.T.) Pvt./Musician, 2nd & 6th Missouri Infantry (Consolidated). Co. A. Federal Rolls of Prisoners of War: Captured at Blakely, AL, on 4/9/1865; Received at Ship Island, MS, on 4/15/1865. Transferred to Vicksburg, MS, for exchange on 5/1/1865; Exchanged at Camp Townsend, MS, on 5/6/1865.

Osborn, John Pvt., 1st & 3rd Missouri Cavalry (Consolidated). Co. G. Federal Rolls of Prisoners of War: Captured at Blakely, AL, on 4/9/1865; Received at Ship Island, MS, on 4/15/1865. Transferred to Vicksburg, MS, for exchange on 5/1/1865; Exchanged at Camp Townsend, MS, on 5/6/1865. Residence at exchange: Andrew County, MO.

Otho, Frederick Pvt., 2nd & 6th Missouri Infantry (Consolidated). Co. G. Federal Rolls of Prisoners of War: Captured at Blakely, AL, on 4/9/1865; Received at Ship Island, MS, on 4/15/1865. Transferred to Vicksburg, MS, for exchange on 5/1/1865; Exchanged at Camp Townsend, MS, on 5/6/1865.

Owens, David T. (AKA Owen) Pvt., 1st & 3rd Missouri Cavalry (Consolidated). Co. K. Enlisted: 3/20/1862 at Williamsburg, MO. Age at enlistment: 23. Residence at enlistment: Callaway County, MO. Federal Rolls of Prisoners of War: Captured at Blakely, AL, on 4/9/1865; Received at Ship Island, MS, on 4/15/1865. Transferred to Vicksburg, MS, for exchange on 5/1/1865; Exchanged at Camp Townsend, MS, on 5/6/1865.

Pafor, J.W. Pvt., 3rd & 5th Missouri Infantry (Consolidated). Co. __. Federal Rolls of Prisoners of War: Captured at Blakely, AL, on 4/9/1865; Received at Ship Island, MS, on 4/15/1865. Transferred to Vicksburg, MS, for exchange on 5/1/1865; Exchanged at Camp Townsend, MS, on 5/6/1865.

Paine, Henry M. (AKA Payne, A.M.) Pvt., 2nd & 6th Missouri Infantry (Consolidated). Co. A. Federal Rolls of Prisoners of War: Captured at Blakely, AL, on 4/9/1865; Received at Ship Island, MS, on 4/15/1865. Transferred to Vicksburg, MS, for exchange on 5/1/1865; Exchanged at Camp Townsend, MS, on 5/6/1865.

Painter, Henry Clay (AKA A.C.) Pvt., 2nd & 6th Missouri Infantry (Consolidated). Co. C. Federal Rolls of Prisoners of War: Captured at Blakely, AL, on 4/9/1865; Received at Ship Island, MS, on 4/15/1865. Transferred to Vicksburg, MS, for exchange on 5/1/1865; Exchanged at Camp Townsend, MS, on 5/6/1865.

Palmerty, Dane Pvt., 3rd & 5th Missouri Infantry (Consolidated). Co. __. Federal Rolls of Prisoners of War: Captured at Blakely, AL, on 4/9/1865; Received at Ship Island, MS, on 4/15/1865. Transferred to Vicksburg, MS, for exchange on 5/1/1865; Exchanged at Camp Townsend, MS, on 5/6/1865.

Parbetry, Henry E. Pvt., 1st & 3rd Missouri Cavalry (Consolidated). Co. I. Federal Rolls of Prisoners of War: Captured at Blakely, AL, on 4/9/1865; Received at Ship Island, MS, on 4/15/1865. Transferred to Vicksburg, MS, for exchange on 5/1/1865; Exchanged at Camp Townsend, MS, on 5/6/1865. Residence at exchange: Springfield, MO.

Parker, William Sgt., 3rd & 5th Missouri Infantry (Consolidated). Co. __. Federal Rolls of Prisoners of War: Captured at Blakely, AL, on 4/9/1865; Received at Ship Island, MS, on 4/15/1865. Transferred to Vicksburg, MS, for exchange on 5/1/1865; Exchanged at Camp Townsend, MS, on 5/6/1865.

Patterson, Abraham W. Sgt., 3rd & 5th Missouri Infantry (Consolidated). Co. K. Federal Rolls of Prisoners of War: Captured at Blakely, AL, on 4/9/1865; Received at Ship Island, MS, on 4/15/1865. Transferred to Vicksburg, MS, for exchange on 5/1/

1865; Exchanged at Camp Townsend, MS, on 5/6/1865.

Patton, William Cpl., 1st & 3rd Missouri Cavalry (Consolidated). Co. E. Federal Rolls of Prisoners of War: Captured at Blakely, AL, on 4/9/1865; Received at Ship Island, MS, on 4/15/1865. Transferred to Vicksburg, MS, for exchange on 5/1/1865; Exchanged at Camp Townsend, MS, on 5/6/1865.

Pearce, J.N. (AKA J.V.) Pvt., 1st & 3rd Missouri Cavalry (Consolidated). Co. __. Federal Rolls of Prisoners of War: Captured at Blakely, AL, on 4/9/1865; Received at Ship Island, MS, on 4/15/1865. Transferred to Vicksburg, MS, for exchange on 5/1/1865; Exchanged at Camp Townsend, MS, on 5/6/1865.

Peck, Charles Pvt., 3rd & 5th Missouri Infantry (Consolidated). Co. __. Federal Rolls of Prisoners of War: Captured at Blakely, AL, on 4/9/1865; Received at Ship Island, MS, on 4/15/1865. Transferred to Vicksburg, MS, for exchange on 5/1/1865; Exchanged at Camp Townsend, MS, on 5/6/1865.

Pemberton, J.R. Sgt., 3rd & 5th Missouri Infantry (Consolidated). Co. __. Federal Rolls of Prisoners of War: Captured at Blakely, AL, on 4/9/1865; Received at Ship Island, MS, on 4/15/1865. Transferred to Vicksburg, MS, for exchange on 5/1/1865; Exchanged at Camp Townsend, MS, on 5/6/1865.

Pentorry, John (AKA Pentery) Pvt., 3rd & 5th Missouri Infantry (Consolidated). Co. __. Federal Rolls of Prisoners of War: Captured at Blakely, AL, on 4/9/1865; Received at Ship Island, MS, on 4/15/1865. Transferred to Vicksburg, MS, for exchange on 5/1/1865; Exchanged at Camp Townsend, MS, on 5/6/1865.

Perry, Thomas C. Pvt., 3rd & 5th Missouri Infantry (Consolidated). Co. H. Federal Rolls of Prisoners of War: Captured at Blakely, AL, on 4/9/1865; Received at Ship Island, MS, on 4/15/1865. Transferred to Vicksburg, MS, for exchange on 5/1/1865; Exchanged at Camp Townsend, MS, on 5/6/1865.

Peterman, F.B.A. Cpl., 3rd & 5th Missouri Infantry (Consolidated). Co. __. Federal Rolls of Prisoners of War: Captured at Blakely, AL, on 4/9/1865; Received at Ship Island, MS, on 4/15/1865. Transferred to Vicksburg, MS, for exchange on 5/1/1865; Exchanged at Camp Townsend, MS, on 5/6/1865.

Phelps, W.J. Pvt., 3rd & 5th Missouri Infantry (Consolidated). Co. __. Federal Rolls of Prisoners of War: Captured at Blakely, AL, on 4/9/1865; Received at Ship Island, MS, on 4/15/1865. Transferred to Vicksburg, MS, for exchange on 5/1/1865; Exchanged at Camp Townsend, MS, on 5/6/1865.

Piefey, G.W. (AKA Piejey) Pvt., 1st & 3rd Missouri Cavalry (Consolidated). Co. __. Federal Rolls of Prisoners of War: Captured at Blakely, AL, on 4/9/1865; Received at Ship Island, MS, on 4/15/1865. Transferred to Vicksburg, MS, for exchange on 5/1/1865; Exchanged at Camp Townsend, MS, on 5/6/1865.

Plaster, Frank Pvt., 3rd & 5th Missouri Infantry (Consolidated). Co. __. Federal Rolls of Prisoners of War: Captured at Blakely, AL, on 4/9/1865; Received at Ship Island, MS, on 4/15/1865. Transferred to Vicksburg, MS, for exchange on 5/1/1865; Exchanged at Camp Townsend, MS, on 5/6/1865.

Plunket, John Pvt., 3rd & 5th Missouri Infantry (Consolidated). Co. __. Federal Rolls of Prisoners of War: Captured at Blakely, AL, on 4/9/1865; Received at Ship Island, MS, on 4/15/1865. Transferred to Vicksburg, MS, for exchange on 5/1/1865; Exchanged at Camp Townsend, MS, on 5/6/1865.

Pollard, E.T. Pvt., 3rd & 5th Missouri Infantry (Consolidated). Co. __. Federal Rolls of Prisoners of War: Captured at Blakely, AL, on 4/9/1865; Received at Ship Island, MS, on 4/15/1865. Transferred to Vicksburg, MS, for exchange on 5/1/1865; Exchanged at Camp Townsend, MS, on 5/6/1865.

Porter, Francis E. Pvt., 3rd & 5th Missouri Infantry (Consolidated). Cos. A & G. Federal Rolls of Prisoners of War: Captured at Blakely, AL, on 4/9/1865; Received at Ship Island, MS, on 4/15/1865. Transferred to Vicksburg, MS, for exchange on 5/1/1865; Exchanged at Camp Townsend, MS, on 5/6/1865.

Pratt, J.C. Pvt., 3rd & 5th Missouri Infantry (Consolidated). Co. __. Federal Rolls of Prisoners of War: Captured at Blakely, AL, on 4/9/1865; Received at Ship Island, MS, on 4/15/1865. Transferred to Vicksburg, MS, for exchange on 5/1/1865; Exchanged at Camp Townsend, MS, on 5/6/1865.

Price, Charles B. Pvt., 1st & 3rd Missouri Cavalry (Consolidated). Co. B. Enlisted: 1/8/1862 at Carrollton, MO. Age at enlistment: 23. Residence at enlistment: Carroll County, MO. Wounded at Allatoona, GA. Federal Rolls of Prisoners of War: Captured at Blakely, AL, on 4/9/1865; Received at Ship Island, MS, on 4/15/1865. Transferred to Vicksburg, MS, for exchange on 5/1/1865; Exchanged at Camp Townsend, MS, on 5/6/1865.

Price, William Cpl., 3rd & 5th Missouri Infantry (Consolidated). Co. __. Federal Rolls of Prisoners of War: Captured at Blakely, AL, on 4/9/1865; Received at Ship Island, MS, on 4/15/1865. Transferred to Vicksburg, MS, for exchange on 5/1/1865; Exchanged at Camp Townsend, MS, on 5/6/1865.

Pryor, John W. Pvt., 1st & 3rd Missouri (Consolidated). Co. E. Enlisted: 12/15/1861 at Osceola, MO. Wounded at Vicksburg, MS, on 5/22/1863. Federal Rolls of Prisoners of War: Captured and paroled at Vicksburg, MS, on 7/4/1863. Federal Rolls of Prisoners of War: Captured at Blakely, AL, on 4/9/1865; Received at Ship Island, MS, on 4/15/1865. Transferred to Vicksburg, MS, for exchange on 5/1/1865; Exchanged at Camp Townsend, MS, on 5/6/1865. Rolls of Prisoners of War, C.S.A: Surrendered at Citronelle, AL, on 5/4/1865; Paroled at Jackson, MS, on 5/12/1865. Born: 5/10/1840 to Silas H. Pryor and Lavinia Fulton at Chillicothe, OH. Married: Mahala J. Hale. Children: 1 son and 2 daughters. Wife born: 2/6/1846 at Andrew County, MO. Wife died: 12/13/1888 at St. Joseph, MO.

Pugh, Joseph B. Pvt., 2nd & 6th Missouri Infantry (Consolidated). Co. I. Federal Rolls of Prisoners of War: Captured at Blakely, AL, on 4/9/1865; Received at Ship Island, MS, on 4/15/1865. Transferred to Vicksburg, MS, for exchange on 5/1/1865; Exchanged at Camp Townsend, MS, on 5/6/1865.

Purnell, J.M. Pvt., 3rd & 5th Missouri Infantry (Consolidated). Co. __. Federal Rolls of Prisoners of War: Captured at Blakely, AL, on 4/9/1865; Received at Ship Island, MS, on 4/15/1865. Transferred to Vicksburg, MS, for exchange on 5/1/1865; Exchanged at Camp Townsend, MS, on 5/6/1865.

Quarles, William M. Pvt./Ensign/Lt., 3rd & 5th Missouri Infantry (Consolidated). Cos. A & C. Federal

Rolls of Prisoners of War: Captured at Blakely, AL, on 4/9/1865; Received at Ship Island, MS, on 4/15/1865. Transferred to Vicksburg, MS, for exchange on 4/28/1865; Confined at New Orleans, LA, on 4/30/1865. Exchanged at Camp Townsend, MS, on 5/6/1865.

Randolph, A.J. Pvt., 3rd & 5th Missouri Infantry (Consolidated). Co. __. Federal Rolls of Prisoners of War: Captured at Blakely, AL, on 4/9/1865; Received at Ship Island, MS, on 4/15/1865. Transferred to Vicksburg, MS, for exchange on 5/1/1865; Exchanged at Camp Townsend, MS, on 5/6/1865.

Ray, Hamilton J. Cpl./Sgt., 1st & 3rd Missouri Cavalry (Consolidated). Co. A. Federal Rolls of Prisoners of War: Captured at Blakely, AL, on 4/9/1865; Received at Ship Island, MS, on 4/15/1865. Transferred to Vicksburg, MS, for exchange on 5/1/1865; Exchanged at Camp Townsend, MS, on 5/6/1865.

Ray, William Pvt., 3rd & 5th Missouri Infantry (Consolidated). Co. __. Federal Rolls of Prisoners of War: Captured at Blakely, AL, on 4/9/1865; Received at Ship Island, MS, on 4/15/1865. Transferred to Vicksburg, MS, for exchange on 5/1/1865; Exchanged at Camp Townsend, MS, on 5/6/1865.

Redman, James B. Sgt., 1st & 3rd Missouri Cavalry (Consolidated). Co. I. Enlisted: 12/16/1861 at Platte City, MO. Age at enlistment: 22. Residence at enlistment: Platte County, MO. Rolls for 5/1863 through 8/1863: Absent, sick. Federal Rolls of Prisoners of War: Captured at Blakely, AL, on 4/9/1865; Received at Ship Island, MS, on 4/15/1865. Transferred to Vicksburg, MS, for exchange on 5/1/1865; Exchanged at Camp Townsend, MS, on 5/6/1865.

Redmond, Edward (AKA Redman) Pvt., 1st & 3rd Missouri Cavalry (Consolidated). Co. I. Enlisted: 12/16/1861 at Kansas City, MO. Age at enlistment: 31. Residence at enlistment: Jackson County, MO. Wounded at Corinth, MS, on 10/5/1862. Federal Rolls of Prisoners of War: Captured at Blakely, AL, on 4/9/1865; Received at Ship Island, MS, on 4/15/1865. Transferred to Vicksburg, MS, for exchange on 5/1/1865; Exchanged at Camp Townsend, MS, on 5/6/1865.

Redmond, John 2nd Lt./1st Lt., 3rd & 5th Missouri Infantry (Consolidated). Cos. B, D & E. Federal Rolls of Prisoners of War: Captured at Blakely, AL, on 4/9/1865; Received at Ship Island, MS, on 4/15/1865. Transferred to Vicksburg, MS, for exchange on 4/28/1865; Confined at New Orleans, LA, on 4/30/1865. Exchanged at Camp Townsend, MS, on 5/6/1865.

Reed, James Pvt., 1st & 3rd Missouri Cavalry (Consolidated). Co. E. Federal Rolls of Prisoners of War: Captured at Blakely, AL, on 4/9/1865; Received at Ship Island, MS, on 4/15/1865. Transferred to Vicksburg, MS, for exchange on 5/1/1865; Exchanged at Camp Townsend, MS, on 5/6/1865.

Reeves, Francis (AKA Reaves) 2nd Lt., 3rd & 5th Missouri Infantry. Co. __. Federal Rolls of Prisoners of War: Captured at Blakely, AL, on 4/9/1865; Received at Ship Island, MS, on 4/15/1865. Transferred to Vicksburg, MS, for exchange on 4/28/1865; Confined at New Orleans, LA, on 4/30/1865. Exchanged at Camp Townsend, MS, on 5/6/1865.

Renick, James W. Pvt., 1st & 4th Missouri Infantry (Consolidated). Cos. C & E. Enlisted: 1/8/1862 at Springfield, MO. Federal Rolls of Prisoners of War: Captured and paroled at Vicksburg, MS, on 7/4/1863. Wounded in left arm at Corinth, MS, and right arm at Kennesaw Mountain, GA. Federal Rolls of Prisoners of War: Captured at Blakely, AL, on 4/9/1865; Received at Ship Island, MS, on 4/15/1865. Transferred to Vicksburg, MS, for exchange on 5/1/1865; Exchanged at Camp Townsend, MS, on 5/6/1865. Received the United Daughters of the Confederacy Cross of Honor for his wartime service. Born: 10/4/1842 to Andrew Renick and Sabina Livesay near Wellington, MO. Married: Sallie A. Greenwell. Children: 6 — 4 sons and 2 daughters. Died: 10/29/1923. Wife born: 1855 at Columbus, Johnson County, MO.

Reynolds, Joseph F. Pvt., 3rd & 5th Missouri Infantry (Consolidated). Co. __. Federal Rolls of Prisoners of War: Captured at Blakely, AL, on 4/9/1865; Received at Ship Island, MS, on 4/15/1865. Transferred to Vicksburg, MS, for exchange on 5/1/1865; Exchanged at Camp Townsend, MS, on 5/6/1865.

Rhoades, W.F. Pvt., 3rd & 5th Missouri Infantry (Consolidated). Co. __. Federal Rolls of Prisoners of War: Captured at Blakely, AL, on 4/9/1865; Received at Ship Island, MS, on 4/15/1865. Transferred to Vicksburg, MS, for exchange on 5/1/1865; Exchanged at Camp Townsend, MS, on 5/6/1865.

Riddle, Thomas F. Pvt., 2nd & 6th Missouri Infantry (Consolidated). Co. C. Federal Rolls of Prisoners of War: Captured at Blakely, AL, on 4/9/1865; Received at Ship Island, MS, on 4/15/1865. Transferred to Vicksburg, MS, for exchange on 5/1/1865; Exchanged at Camp Townsend, MS, on 5/6/1865.

Riley, John T. 1st Sgt., 1st & 3rd Missouri Cavalry (Consolidated). Co. H. Enlisted: 12/27/1861. Age at enlistment: 35. Federal Rolls of Prisoners of War: Captured at Baker's Creek, MS, on 5/15/1865; Exchanged on 11/25/1864. Wounded on 2/4/1865. Federal Rolls of Prisoners of War: Captured at Blakely, AL, on 4/9/1865; Received at Ship Island, MS, on 4/15/1865. Transferred to Vicksburg, MS, for exchange on 5/1/1865; Exchanged at Camp Townsend, MS, on 5/6/1865.

Ritchie, William Pvt., 3rd & 5th Missouri Infantry (Consolidated). Co. E. Federal Rolls of Prisoners of War: Captured at Blakely, AL, on 4/9/1865; Received at Ship Island, MS, on 4/15/1865. Transferred to Vicksburg, MS, for exchange on 5/1/1865; Exchanged at Camp Townsend, MS, on 5/6/1865.

Robb, J. Pvt., 3rd & 5th Missouri Infantry (Consolidated). Co. __. Federal Rolls of Prisoners of War: Captured at Blakely, AL, on 4/9/1865; Received at Ship Island, MS, on 4/15/1865. Transferred to Vicksburg, MS, for exchange on 5/1/1865; Exchanged at Camp Townsend, MS, on 5/6/1865.

Roberts, G.W. (AKA G.N.) Pvt., 3rd & 5th Missouri Infantry (Consolidated). Co. __. Federal Rolls of Prisoners of War: Captured at Blakely, AL, on 4/9/1865; Received at Ship Island, MS, on 4/15/1865. Transferred to Vicksburg, MS, for exchange on 5/1/1865; Exchanged at Camp Townsend, MS, on 5/6/1865.

Robertson, Andrus Malankton 3rd Lt./Sr. 2nd Lt., 3rd & 5th Missouri Infantry (Consolidated). Co. D. Federal Rolls of Prisoners of War: Captured at Blakely, AL, on 4/9/1865; Received at Ship Island, MS, on 4/15/1865. Transferred to Vicksburg, MS, for exchange on 4/28/1865; Confined at New Orleans, LA, on 4/30/1865. Exchanged at Camp Townsend, MS, on 5/6/1865.

Robertson, Eli C. Pvt., 1st & 3rd Missouri Cavalry (Consolidated). Co. B. Enlisted: 12/31/1861 at Gentryville, MO. Age at enlistment: 20. Residence at enlistment: Gentry County, MO. Federal Rolls of Prisoners of War: Captured at Blakely, AL, on 4/9/1865; Received at Ship Island, MS, on 4/15/1865. Transferred to Vicksburg, MS, for exchange on 5/1/1865; Exchanged at Camp Townsend, MS, on 5/6/1865.

Robertson, J. Pvt., 3rd & 5th Missouri Infantry (Consolidated). Co. __. Federal Rolls of Prisoners of War: Captured at Blakely, AL, on 4/9/1865; Received at Ship Island, MS, on 4/15/1865. Transferred to Vicksburg, MS, for exchange on 5/1/1865; Exchanged at Camp Townsend, MS, on 5/6/1865.

Robertson, William Pvt., 1st & 3rd Missouri Cavalry (Consolidated). Co. G. Federal Rolls of Prisoners of War: Captured at Blakely, AL, on 4/9/1865; Received at Ship Island, MS, on 4/15/1865. Transferred to Vicksburg, MS, for exchange on 5/1/1865; Exchanged at Camp Townsend, MS, on 5/6/1865.

Robertson, Willis Pvt., 1st & 3rd Missouri Cavalry (Consolidated). Co. E. Federal Rolls of Prisoners of War: Captured at Blakely, AL, on 4/9/1865; Received at Ship Island, MS, on 4/15/1865. Transferred to Vicksburg, MS, for exchange on 5/1/1865; Exchanged at Camp Townsend, MS, on 5/6/1865. Residence at exchange: Maries County, MO. Soldier also served as a Pvt. with the 10th Missouri Infantry.

Rose, E. Pvt., 3rd & 5th Missouri Infantry (Consolidated). Co. __. Federal Rolls of Prisoners of War: Captured at Blakely, AL, on 4/9/1865; Received at Ship Island, MS, on 4/15/1865. Transferred to Vicksburg, MS, for exchange on 5/1/1865; Exchanged at Camp Townsend, MS, on 5/6/1865.

Rush, Martin Pvt., 2nd & 6th Missouri Infantry (Consolidated). Co. __. Federal Rolls of Prisoners of War: Captured at Blakely, AL, on 4/9/1865; Received at Ship Island, MS, on 4/15/1865. Transferred to Vicksburg, MS, for exchange on 5/1/1865; Exchanged at Camp Townsend, MS, on 5/6/1865.

St. Clair, Charles Edward Pvt., 2nd & 6th Missouri Infantry (Consolidated). Co. B. Enlisted: 4/1862 at Corinth, MS. Federal Rolls of Prisoners of War: Captured and paroled at Vicksburg, MS, on 7/4/1863. Federal Rolls of Prisoners of War: Captured at Blakely, AL, on 4/9/1865; Received at Ship Island, MS, on 4/15/1865. Transferred to Vicksburg, MS, for exchange on 5/1/1865; Exchanged at Camp Townsend, MS, on 5/6/1865. Rolls of Prisoners of War, C.S.A: Surrendered at Citronelle, AL, on 5/4/1865; Paroled at Jackson, MS, on 5/13/1865. Received the United Daughters of the Confederacy Cross of Honor for his wartime service. Born: 6/5/1835 to Robert St. Clair and Elmyra Hewitt at Roanoke County, VA. Married: Mary Lauretta Mann. Children: 2 daughters, Minnie Ethel and Elmyra Letholz. Wife born: 7/8/1846 at Loudoun County, VA.

Salmons, William Pvt., 2nd & 6th Missouri Infantry (Consolidated). Co. __. Federal Rolls of Prisoners of War: Captured at Blakely, AL, on 4/9/1865; Received at Ship Island, MS, on 4/15/1865. Transferred to Vicksburg, MS, for exchange on 5/1/1865; Exchanged at Camp Townsend, MS, on 5/6/1865.

Saylor, John R. Pvt., 3rd & 5th Missouri Infantry (Consolidated). Co. __. Federal Rolls of Prisoners of War: Captured at Blakely, AL, on 4/9/1865; Received at Ship Island, MS, on 4/15/1865. Transferred to Vicksburg, MS, for exchange on 5/1/1865; Exchanged at Camp Townsend, MS, on 5/6/1865.

Scoggins, W.J. Pvt., 3rd & 5th Missouri Infantry (Consolidated). Co. __. Federal Rolls of Prisoners of War: Captured at Blakely, AL, on 4/9/1865; Received at Ship Island, MS, on 4/15/1865. Transferred to Vicksburg, MS, for exchange on 5/1/1865; Exchanged at Camp Townsend, MS, on 5/6/1865.

Scott, James T. Pvt., 2nd & 6th Missouri Infantry (Consolidated). Co. __. Federal Rolls of Prisoners of War: Captured at Blakely, AL, on 4/9/1865; Received at Ship Island, MS, on 4/15/1865. Transferred to Vicksburg, MS, for exchange on 5/1/1865; Exchanged at Camp Townsend, MS, on 5/6/1865.

Shackleford, John H. (AKA Shackelford) Pvt., 3rd & 5th Missouri Infantry (Consolidated). Co. H. Federal Rolls of Prisoners of War: Captured at Blakely, AL, on 4/9/1865; Received at Ship Island, MS, on 4/15/1865. Transferred to Vicksburg, MS, for exchange on 5/1/1865; Exchanged at Camp Townsend, MS, on 5/6/1865.

Shafer, Thomas H. (AKA Shaeffer) Pvt., 2nd & 6th Missouri Infantry (Consolidated). Co. H. Federal Rolls of Prisoners of War: Captured at Blakely, AL, on 4/9/1865; Received at Ship Island, MS, on 4/15/1865. Transferred to Vicksburg, MS, for exchange on 5/1/1865; Exchanged at Camp Townsend, MS, on 5/6/1865.

Shanks, A.M. Cpl., 3rd & 5th Missouri Infantry (Consolidated). Co. E. Federal Rolls of Prisoners of War: Captured at Blakely, AL, on 4/9/1865; Received at Ship Island, MS, on 4/15/1865. Transferred to Vicksburg, MS, for exchange on 5/1/1865; Exchanged at Camp Townsend, MS, on 5/6/1865.

Shelton, A.H. Pvt., 3rd & 5th Missouri Infantry (Consolidated). Co. __. Federal Rolls of Prisoners of War: Captured at Blakely, AL, on 4/9/1865; Received at Ship Island, MS, on 4/15/1865. Transferred to Vicksburg, MS, for exchange on 5/1/1865; Exchanged at Camp Townsend, MS, on 5/6/1865.

Shelton, James Pvt., 2nd & 6th Missouri Infantry (Consolidated). Co. __. Federal Rolls of Prisoners of War: Captured at Blakely, AL, on 4/9/1865; Received at Ship Island, MS, on 4/15/1865. Transferred to Vicksburg, MS, for exchange on 5/1/1865; Exchanged at Camp Townsend, MS, on 5/6/1865.

Shelton, W.L. Pvt., 3rd & 5th Missouri Infantry (Consolidated). Co. __. Federal Rolls of Prisoners of War: Captured at Blakely, AL, on 4/9/1865; Received at Ship Island, MS, on 4/15/1865. Transferred to Vicksburg, MS, for exchange on 5/1/1865; Exchanged at Camp Townsend, MS, on 5/6/1865.

Shultz, George E. (AKA Schultz) 1st Sgt., 1st & 3rd Missouri Cavalry (Consolidated). Co. G. Enlisted: 12/31/1861 at Pattonsburg, MO. Age at enlistment: 25. Residence at enlistment: Davies County, MO. Federal Rolls of Prisoners of War: Captured at Baker's Creek, MS, on 5/15/1863. Federal Rolls of Prisoners of War: Captured at Blakely, AL, on 4/9/1865; Received at Ship Island, MS, on 4/15/1865. Transferred to Vicksburg, MS, for exchange on 5/1/1865; Exchanged at Camp Townsend, MS, on 5/6/1865.

Simons, J.B. Sgt., 2nd & 6th Missouri Infantry (Consolidated). Co. __. Federal Rolls of Prisoners of War:

Captured at Blakely, AL, on 4/9/1865; Received at Ship Island, MS, on 4/15/1865. Transferred to Vicksburg, MS, for exchange on 5/1/1865; Exchanged at Camp Townsend, MS, on 5/6/1865.

Simpson, Albert W. Sgt./Lt., 3rd & 5th Missouri Infantry (Consolidated). Co. E. Federal Rolls of Prisoners of War: Captured at Blakely, AL, on 4/9/1865; Received at Ship Island, MS, on 4/15/1865. Transferred to Vicksburg, MS, for exchange on 4/28/1865; Confined at New Orleans, LA, on 4/30/1865. Exchanged at Camp Townsend, MS, on 5/6/1865.

Simpson, C.S. Pvt., 3rd & 5th Missouri Infantry (Consolidated). Co. __. Federal Rolls of Prisoners of War: Captured at Blakely, AL, on 4/9/1865; Received at Ship Island, MS, on 4/15/1865. Transferred to Vicksburg, MS, for exchange on 5/1/1865; Exchanged at Camp Townsend, MS, on 5/6/1865.

Slemmons, Joseph Martin (AKA Martain) Pvt., 1st & 3rd Missouri Cavalry (Consolidated). Co. C. Enlisted: 12/24/1861 at Iowa Point, MO. Age at enlistment: 22. Residence at enlistment: Doniphan County, IO. Wounded at Elkhorn Tavern, AR. Federal Rolls of Prisoners of War: Captured at Blakely, AL, on 4/9/1865; Received at Ship Island, MS, on 4/15/1865. Transferred to Vicksburg, MS, for exchange on 5/1/1865; Exchanged at Camp Townsend, MS, on 5/6/1865.

Smith, Anderson C. (AKA A.R.) Capt., 3rd & 5th Missouri Infantry (Consolidated). Co. E. Federal Rolls of Prisoners of War: Captured at Blakely, AL, on 4/9/1865; Received at Ship Island, MS, on 4/15/1865. Transferred to Vicksburg, MS, for exchange on 4/28/1865; Confined at New Orleans, LA, on 4/30/1865. Exchanged at Camp Townsend, MS, on 5/6/1865.

Smith, Albert W. Pvt., 3rd & 5th Missouri Infantry (Consolidated). Co. __. Federal Rolls of Prisoners of War: Captured at Blakely, AL, on 4/9/1865; Received at Ship Island, MS, on 4/15/1865. Transferred to Vicksburg, MS, for exchange on 5/1/1865; Exchanged at Camp Townsend, MS, on 5/6/1865.

Smith, Andrew J. Pvt., 1st & 3rd Missouri Cavalry (Consolidated). Co. H. Enlisted: 12/31/1861 at Grant's Hill, MO. Age at enlistment: 26. Residence at enlistment: Worth County, MO. Federal Rolls of Prisoners of War: Captured at Franklin, TN. Federal Rolls of Prisoners of War: Captured at Blakely, AL, on 4/9/1865; Received at Ship Island, MS, on 4/15/1865. Transferred to Vicksburg, MS, for exchange on 5/1/1865; Exchanged at Camp Townsend, MS, on 5/6/1865.

Smith, Benjamin F. Pvt., 1st & 3rd Missouri Cavalry (Consolidated). Co. C. Enlisted: 12/3/1861 at Oregon, MO. Age at enlistment: 18. Residence at enlistment: Holt County, MO. Federal Rolls of Prisoners of War: Captured at Blakely, AL, on 4/9/1865; Received at Ship Island, MS, on 4/15/1865. Transferred to Vicksburg, MS, for exchange on 5/1/1865; Exchanged at Camp Townsend, MS, on 5/6/1865.

Smith, Francis Marion Pvt., 3rd & 5th Missouri Infantry (Consolidated). Co. D. Federal Rolls of Prisoners of War: Captured at Blakely, AL, on 4/9/1865; Received at Ship Island, MS, on 4/15/1865. Transferred to Vicksburg, MS, for exchange on 5/1/1865; Exchanged at Camp Townsend, MS, on 5/6/1865.

Smith, James R. Pvt./Cpl., 3rd & 5th Missouri Infantry (Consolidated). Co. G. Federal Rolls of Prisoners of War: Captured at Blakely, AL, on 4/9/1865; Received at Ship Island, MS, on 4/15/1865. Transferred to Vicksburg, MS, for exchange on 5/1/1865; Exchanged at Camp Townsend, MS, on 5/6/1865.

Smith, John Pvt., 1st & 3rd Missouri Cavalry (Consolidated). Co. H. Federal Rolls of Prisoners of War: Captured at Blakely, AL, on 4/9/1865; Received at Ship Island, MS, on 4/15/1865. Transferred to Vicksburg, MS, for exchange on 5/1/1865; Exchanged at Camp Townsend, MS, on 5/6/1865.

Smith, R.F. Pvt., 3rd & 5th Missouri Infantry (Consolidated). Co. __. Federal Rolls of Prisoners of War: Captured at Blakely, AL, on 4/9/1865; Received at Ship Island, MS, on 4/15/1865. Transferred to Vicksburg, MS, for exchange on 5/1/1865; Exchanged at Camp Townsend, MS, on 5/6/1865.

Smith, S.H. Pvt., 1st & 3rd Missouri Cavalry (Consolidated). Co. __. Federal Rolls of Prisoners of War: Captured at Blakely, AL, on 4/9/1865; Received at Ship Island, MS, on 4/15/1865. Transferred to Vicksburg, MS, for exchange on 5/1/1865; Exchanged at Camp Townsend, MS, on 5/6/1865.

Smith, Sanford Pvt., 3rd & 5th Missouri Infantry (Consolidated). Co. __. Federal Rolls of Prisoners of War: Captured at Blakely, AL, on 4/9/1865; Received at Ship Island, MS, on 4/15/1865. Transferred to Vicksburg, MS, for exchange on 5/1/1865; Exchanged at Camp Townsend, MS, on 5/6/1865.

Smith, William G. (AKA W.C.) Pvt., 1st & 3rd Missouri Cavalry (Consolidated). Co. E. Federal Rolls of Prisoners of War: Captured at Blakely, AL, on 4/9/1865; Received at Ship Island, MS, on 4/15/1865. Transferred to Vicksburg, MS, for exchange on 5/1/1865; Exchanged at Camp Townsend, MS, on 5/6/1865.

Snead, James T. Pvt., 2nd & 6th Missouri Infantry (Consolidated). Co. H. Federal Rolls of Prisoners of War: Captured at Blakely, AL, on 4/9/1865; Received at Ship Island, MS, on 4/15/1865. Transferred to Vicksburg, MS, for exchange on 5/1/1865; Exchanged at Camp Townsend, MS, on 5/6/1865.

Snyder, Charles B. Pvt., 2nd & 6th Missouri Infantry (Consolidated). Co. __. Federal Rolls of Prisoners of War: Captured at Blakely, AL, on 4/9/1865; Received at Ship Island, MS, on 4/15/1865. Transferred to Vicksburg, MS, for exchange on 5/1/1865; Exchanged at Camp Townsend, MS, on 5/6/1865.

Sparkman, John Pvt., 3rd & 5th Missouri Infantry (Consolidated). Co. __. Federal Rolls of Prisoners of War: Captured at Blakely, AL, on 4/9/1865; Received at Ship Island, MS, on 4/15/1865. Transferred to Vicksburg, MS, for exchange on 5/1/1865; Exchanged at Camp Townsend, MS, on 5/6/1865.

Speaks, William H. Pvt., 1st & 3rd Missouri Cavalry (Consolidated). Co. K. Enlisted: 1/1/1863 at Columbia, MO. Age at enlistment: 23. Residence at enlistment: Boone County, MO. Federal Rolls of Prisoners of War: Captured at Big Black River Bridge, MS, in 5/1863; Exchanged in 2/1864. Federal Rolls of Prisoners of War: Captured at Blakely, AL, on 4/9/1865; Received at Ship Island, MS, on 4/15/1865. Transferred to Vicksburg, MS, for exchange on 5/1/1865; Exchanged at Camp Townsend, MS, on 5/6/1865.

Spencer, George W. Pvt., 1st & 3rd Missouri Cavalry (Consolidated). Co. E. Enlisted: 1/1/1863 at Haynesville, Claiborne Parish, LA; Joined Co. E at

Demopolis, AL, on 10/1/1863. Age at enlistment: 18. Federal Rolls of Prisoners of War: Captured at Blakely, AL, on 4/9/1865; Received at Ship Island, MS, on 4/15/1865. Transferred to Vicksburg, MS, for exchange on 5/1/1865; Exchanged at Camp Townsend, MS, on 5/6/1865.

Spencer, William J. (AKA W.T.) Pvt., 1st & 3rd Missouri Cavalry (Consolidated). Co. E. Enlisted: 5/1/1862 at Haynesville, Claiborne Parish, LA; Joined Co. E at Demopolis, AL, on 8/1/1863. Age at enlistment: 18. Federal Rolls of Prisoners of War: Captured at Blakely, AL, on 4/9/1865; Received at Ship Island, MS, on 4/15/1865. Transferred to Vicksburg, MS, for exchange on 5/1/1865; Exchanged at Camp Townsend, MS, on 5/6/1865. Soldier also served as a Pvt. with the 31st Louisiana Infantry. Co. E for 13 months.

Stamper, John Thomas Pvt., 1st & 3rd Missouri Cavalry (Consolidated). Co. A. Enlisted: 4/1861. Federal Rolls of Prisoners of War: Captured at Blakely, AL, on 4/9/1865; Received at Ship Island, MS, on 4/15/1865. Transferred to Vicksburg, MS, for exchange on 5/1/1865; Exchanged at Camp Townsend, MS, on 5/6/1865. Rolls of Prisoners of War, C.S.A: Surrendered at Citronelle, AL, on 5/4/1865; Paroled at Jackson, MS, on 5/11/1865. Received the United Daughters of the Confederacy Cross of Honor for his wartime service. Born: 3/26/1837 to Larkin Stamper and Emily Maupin at Livingston County, MO. Married: Aelia Meadows. Died: 3/28/1919 near Saxton, MO. Wife born: 9/18/1836. Wife died: 11/2/1905.

Stanley, James M. (AKA Standley) Pvt., 2nd & 6th Missouri Infantry (Consolidated). Co. H. Federal Rolls of Prisoners of War: Captured at Blakely, AL, on 4/9/1865; Received at Ship Island, MS, on 4/15/1865. Transferred to Vicksburg, MS, for exchange on 5/1/1865; Exchanged at Camp Townsend, MS, on 5/6/1865.

Stanley, John W. (AKA James W.) 5th Sgt., 1st & 3rd Missouri Cavalry (Consolidated). Co. D. Enlisted: 2/24/1862 at Albany, MO. Age at enlistment: 23. Residence at enlistment: Gentry County, MO. Federal Rolls of Prisoners of War: Captured at Blakely, AL, on 4/9/1865; Received at Ship Island, MS, on 4/15/1865. Transferred to Vicksburg, MS, for exchange on 5/1/1865; Exchanged at Camp Townsend, MS, on 5/6/1865.

Stapleton, H. Pvt., 3rd & 5th Missouri Infantry (Consolidated). Co. __. Federal Rolls of Prisoners of War: Captured at Blakely, AL, on 4/9/1865; Received at Ship Island, MS, on 4/15/1865. Transferred to Vicksburg, MS, for exchange on 5/1/1865; Exchanged at Camp Townsend, MS, on 5/6/1865.

Statham, B.T. Pvt., 3rd & 5th Missouri Infantry (Consolidated). Co. __. Federal Rolls of Prisoners of War: Captured at Blakely, AL, on 4/9/1865; Received at Ship Island, MS, on 4/15/1865. Transferred to Vicksburg, MS, for exchange on 5/1/1865; Exchanged at Camp Townsend, MS, on 5/6/1865.

Steel, David (AKA Steele) Pvt., 1st & 3rd Missouri Cavalry (Consolidated). Co. I. Federal Rolls of Prisoners of War: Captured at Blakely, AL, on 4/9/1865; Received at Ship Island, MS, on 4/15/1865. Transferred to Vicksburg, MS, for exchange on 5/1/1865; Exchanged at Camp Townsend, MS, on 5/6/1865.

Stiles, E.J. Sgt., 3rd & 5th Missouri Infantry (Consolidated). Co. __. Federal Rolls of Prisoners of War: Captured at Blakely, AL, on 4/9/1865; Received at Ship Island, MS, on 4/15/1865. Transferred to Vicksburg, MS, for exchange on 5/1/1865; Exchanged at Camp Townsend, MS, on 5/6/1865.

Stiles, Samuel M. Pvt., 1st & 3rd Missouri Cavalry (Consolidated). Co. H. Enlisted: 12/29/1861 at Grant's Hill, MO. Age at enlistment: 23. Residence at enlistment: Worth County, MO. Wounded at Baker's Creek, MS, and Franklin, TN. Federal Rolls of Prisoners of War: Captured at Blakely, AL, on 4/9/1865; Received at Ship Island, MS, on 4/15/1865. Transferred to Vicksburg, MS, for exchange on 5/1/1865; Exchanged at Camp Townsend, MS, on 5/6/1865.

Stock, J.M. (AKA Stack) Pvt., 3rd & 5th Missouri Infantry (Consolidated). Co. E. Federal Rolls of Prisoners of War: Captured at Blakely, AL, on 4/9/1865; Received at Ship Island, MS, on 4/15/1865. Transferred to Vicksburg, MS, for exchange on 5/1/1865; Exchanged at Camp Townsend, MS, on 5/6/1865.

Stone, John B. 2nd. Lt., 2nd & 6th Missouri Infantry (Consolidated). Co. G. Federal Rolls of Prisoners of War: Captured at Blakely, AL, on 4/9/1865; Received at Ship Island, MS, on 4/15/1865. Transferred to Vicksburg, MS, for exchange on 4/28/1865; Confined at New Orleans, LA, on 4/30/1865. Exchanged at Camp Townsend, MS, on 5/6/1865.

Stoney, John T. (AKA Story) Cpl./Sgt., 3rd & 5th Missouri Infantry (Consolidated). Co. B. Federal Rolls of Prisoners of War: Captured at Blakely, AL, on 4/9/1865; Received at Ship Island, MS, on 4/15/1865. Transferred to Vicksburg, MS, for exchange on 5/1/1865; Exchanged at Camp Townsend, MS, on 5/6/1865.

Strong, Andrew Jackson Pvt./2nd Lt., 1st & 3rd Missouri Cavalry (Consolidated). Co. B. Enlisted: 12/11/1861 at Stringtown, MO. Age at enlistment: 23. Residence at enlistment: Cole County, MO. Elected 2nd Lt. on 11/20/1862. Wounded at Baker's Creek, MS, and Jonesboro, GA. Federal Rolls of Prisoners of War: Captured at Blakely, AL, on 4/9/1865; Received at Ship Island, MS, on 4/15/1865. Transferred to Vicksburg, MS, for exchange on 4/28/1865; Confined at New Orleans, LA, on 4/30/1865. Exchanged at Camp Townsend, MS, on 5/6/1865.

Stull, John D. Pvt., 1st & 3rd Missouri Cavalry (Consolidated). Co. B. Enlisted: 12/11/1861 at Callaway County, MO. Age at enlistment: 19. Wounded on 8/9/1864. Federal Rolls of Prisoners of War: Captured at Blakely, AL, on 4/9/1865; Received at Ship Island, MS, on 4/15/1865. Transferred to Vicksburg, MS, for exchange on 5/1/1865; Exchanged at Camp Townsend, MS, on 5/6/1865.

Summers, F.M. Pvt., 3rd & 5th Missouri Infantry (Consolidated). Co. H. Federal Rolls of Prisoners of War: Captured at Blakely, AL, on 4/9/1865; Received at Ship Island, MS, on 4/15/1865. Transferred to Vicksburg, MS, for exchange on 5/1/1865; Exchanged at Camp Townsend, MS, on 5/6/1865.

Sutton, John P. Pvt., 2nd & 6th Missouri Infantry (Consolidated). Co. A. Federal Rolls of Prisoners of War: Captured at Blakely, AL, on 4/9/1865; Received at Ship Island, MS, on 4/15/1865. Transferred to Vicksburg, MS, for exchange on 5/1/1865; Exchanged at Camp Townsend, MS, on 5/6/1865.

Talifero, P. Pvt., 3rd & 5th Missouri Infantry (Consolidated). Co. __. Federal Rolls of Prisoners of War:

Captured at Blakely, AL, on 4/9/1865; Received at Ship Island, MS, on 4/15/1865. Transferred to Vicksburg, MS, for exchange on 5/1/1865; Exchanged at Camp Townsend, MS, on 5/6/1865.

Tannehill, Carlton J. (AKA Carleton) Pvt., 1st & 3rd Missouri Cavalry (Consolidated). Co. B. Enlisted: 12/11/1861 at High Hill, MO. Age at enlistment: 25. Residence at enlistment: Montgomery County, MO. Wounded at Corinth, MS, Peachtree Creek, GA, and Franklin, TN. Federal Rolls of Prisoners of War: Captured at Blakely, AL, on 4/9/1865; Received at Ship Island, MS, on 4/15/1865. Transferred to Vicksburg, MS, for exchange on 5/1/1865; Exchanged at Camp Townsend, MS, on 5/6/1865.

Tanner, Henry C. Pvt., 2nd & 6th Missouri Infantry (Consolidated). Co. C. Federal Rolls of Prisoners of War: Captured at Blakely, AL, on 4/9/1865; Received at Ship Island, MS, on 4/15/1865. Transferred to Vicksburg, MS, for exchange on 5/1/1865; Exchanged at Camp Townsend, MS, on 5/6/1865.

Taylor, J. Pvt., 3rd & 5th Missouri Infantry (Consolidated). Co. __. Federal Rolls of Prisoners of War: Captured at Blakely, AL, on 4/9/1865; Received at Ship Island, MS, on 4/15/1865. Transferred to Vicksburg, MS, for exchange on 5/1/1865; Exchanged at Camp Townsend, MS, on 5/6/1865.

Taylor, Obadiah 2nd Lt./Capt., 3rd & 5th Missouri Infantry (Consolidated). Co. A. Federal Rolls of Prisoners of War: Captured at Blakely, AL, on 4/9/1865; Received at Ship Island, MS, on 4/15/1865. Transferred to Vicksburg, MS, for exchange on 4/28/1865; Confined at New Orleans, LA, on 4/30/1865. Exchanged at Camp Townsend, MS, on 5/6/1865.

Taylor, Wesley Pvt., 3rd & 5th Missouri Infantry (Consolidated). Co. H. Federal Rolls of Prisoners of War: Captured at Blakely, AL, on 4/9/1865; Received at Ship Island, MS, on 4/15/1865. Transferred to Vicksburg, MS, for exchange on 5/1/1865; Exchanged at Camp Townsend, MS, on 5/6/1865.

Terrell, Whitfield Price (AKA Terrill) Pvt./Cpl., 3rd & 5th Missouri Infantry (Consolidated). Co. H. Federal Rolls of Prisoners of War: Captured at Blakely, AL, on 4/9/1865; Received at Ship Island, MS, on 4/15/1865. Transferred to Vicksburg, MS, for exchange on 5/1/1865; Exchanged at Camp Townsend, MS, on 5/6/1865.

Thatcher, Charles Pvt., 1st & 3rd Missouri Cavalry (Consolidated). Co. __. Federal Rolls of Prisoners of War: Captured at Blakely, AL, on 4/9/1865; Received at Ship Island, MS, on 4/15/1865. Transferred to Vicksburg, MS, for exchange on 5/1/1865; Exchanged at Camp Townsend, MS, on 5/6/1865.

Thomas, Caleb Pvt., 2nd & 6th Missouri Infantry (Consolidated). Co. C. Enlisted: 5/1861 at Boonesboro, MO. Federal Rolls of Prisoners of War: Captured and paroled at Vicksburg, MS, on 7/4/1863. Federal Rolls of Prisoners of War: Captured at Franklin, TN, in 11/1864; Received at Camp Douglas, IL. Exchanged in 2/1865. Federal Rolls of Prisoners of War: Captured at Blakely, AL, on 4/9/1865; Received at Ship Island, MS, on 4/15/1865. Transferred to Vicksburg, MS, for exchange on 5/1/1865; Exchanged at Camp Townsend, MS, on 5/6/1865. Received the United Daughters of the Confederacy Cross of Honor in 1905 for his wartime service. Born: 1/11/1843 to Lorenzo Dow Thomas and Rebecca Thomas at Somerset, Pulaski County, KY. Married: Mary E. Yelton on 11/19/1866. Children: 10. Occupation: President of the Peoples Bank, Glasgow, MO. Buried: Richland Christian Church Cemetery in Missouri. Wife died: 11/23/1927.

Thomas, O. Pvt., 3rd & 5th Missouri Infantry (Consolidated). Co. __. Federal Rolls of Prisoners of War: Captured at Blakely, AL, on 4/9/1865; Received at Ship Island, MS, on 4/15/1865. Transferred to Vicksburg, MS, for exchange on 5/1/1865; Exchanged at Camp Townsend, MS, on 5/6/1865.

Thompson, Harry D. Cpl./2nd Lt., 1st & 4th Missouri Infantry (Consolidated). Co. F. Federal Rolls of Prisoners of War: Captured at Blakely, AL, on 4/9/1865; Received at Ship Island, MS, on 4/15/1865. Transferred to Vicksburg, MS, for exchange on 4/28/1865; Confined at New Orleans, LA, on 4/30/1865. Exchanged at Camp Townsend, MS, on 5/6/1865.

Thompson, William H. Hosp. Stew./Pvt., 2nd & 6th Missouri Infantry (Consolidated). Co. __. Federal Rolls of Prisoners of War: Captured at Blakely, AL, on 4/9/1865; Received at Ship Island, MS, on 4/15/1865. Transferred to Vicksburg, MS, for exchange on 5/1/1865; Exchanged at Camp Townsend, MS, on 5/6/1865.

Thurmond, John T. (AKA Thurman, J.H.) Pvt./Sgt., 3rd & 5th Missouri Infantry (Consolidated). Co. E. Federal Rolls of Prisoners of War: Captured at Blakely, AL, on 4/9/1865; Received at Ship Island, MS, on 4/15/1865. Transferred to Vicksburg, MS, for exchange on 5/1/1865; Exchanged at Camp Townsend, MS, on 5/6/1865.

Tidwell, C.K. Pvt., 3rd & 5th Missouri Infantry (Consolidated). Co. __. Federal Rolls of Prisoners of War: Captured at Blakely, AL, on 4/9/1865; Received at Ship Island, MS, on 4/15/1865. Transferred to Vicksburg, MS, for exchange on 5/1/1865; Exchanged at Camp Townsend, MS, on 5/6/1865.

Tillford, Thomas Pvt., 3rd & 5th Missouri Infantry. Co. __. Federal Rolls of Prisoners of War: Captured at Blakely, AL, on 4/9/1865; Received at Ship Island, MS, on 4/15/1865. Transferred to Vicksburg, MS, for exchange on 5/1/1865; Exchanged at Camp Townsend, MS, on 5/6/1865.

Tobin, James M. Pvt., 1st & 3rd Missouri Cavalry (Consolidated). Co. E. Enlisted: 3/22/1862 at Platte River, MO. Age at enlistment: 24. Residence at enlistment: Buchanan County, MO. Federal Rolls of Prisoners of War: Captured at Allatoona, GA, while severely wounded. Federal Rolls of Prisoners of War: Captured at Blakely, AL, on 4/9/1865; Received at Ship Island, MS, on 4/15/1865. Transferred to Vicksburg, MS, for exchange on 5/1/1865; Exchanged at Camp Townsend, MS, on 5/6/1865.

Todd, Albert H. 2nd Lt., 1st & 3rd Missouri Cavalry (Consolidated). Co. I. Enlisted: 12/16/1861 at Platte City, MO. Age at enlistment: 18. Residence at enlistment: Platte County, MO. Wounded at Allatoona, GA, resulting in left arm amputation. Federal Rolls of Prisoners of War: Captured at Blakely, AL, on 4/9/1865; Confined one day near Spanish Fort, AL. Received at Ship Island, MS, on 4/16/1865; Transferred to Vicksburg, MS, for exchange on 4/28/1865. Confined at New Orleans, LA, on 4/30/1865; Exchanged at Camp Townsend, MS, on 5/6/1865.

Todd, Marcus L., Jr. 2nd Lt., 1st & 3rd Missouri

Cavalry (Consolidated). Co. I. Enlisted: 12/16/1861 at Platte City, MO. Age at enlistment: 26. Residence at enlistment: Platte County, MO. Federal Rolls of Prisoners of War: Captured at Big Black River Bridge, MS, in 5/1863; Exchanged in 1865. Federal Rolls of Prisoners of War: Captured at Blakely, AL, on 4/9/1865; Confined one day near Spanish Fort, AL. Received at Ship Island, MS, on 4/16/1865; Transferred to Vicksburg, MS, for exchange on 4/28/1865. Confined at New Orleans, LA, on 4/30/1865; Exchanged at Camp Townsend, MS, on 5/6/1865.

Townsend, Edmund L. Pvt./Sgt., 3rd & 5th Missouri Infantry (Consolidated). Co. __. Federal Rolls of Prisoners of War: Captured at Blakely, AL, on 4/9/1865; Received at Ship Island, MS, on 4/15/1865. Transferred to Vicksburg, MS, for exchange on 5/1/1865; Exchanged at Camp Townsend, MS, on 5/6/1865.

Trimble, John A. Pvt., 1st & 3rd Missouri Cavalry (Consolidated). Co. D. Enlisted: 12/24/1861 at Albany, MO. Age at enlistment: 24. Residence at enlistment: Ray County, MO. Slightly wounded at Kennesaw Mountain, GA, and Franklin, TN. Federal Rolls of Prisoners of War: Captured at Blakely, AL, on 4/9/1865; Received at Ship Island, MS, on 4/15/1865. Transferred to Vicksburg, MS, for exchange on 5/1/1865; Exchanged at Camp Townsend, MS, on 5/6/1865.

Tuif, J.D. Pvt., 1st & 3rd Missouri Cavalry (Consolidated). Co. __. Federal Rolls of Prisoners of War: Captured at Blakely, AL, on 4/9/1865; Received at Ship Island, MS, on 4/15/1865. Transferred to Vicksburg, MS, for exchange on 5/1/1865; Exchanged at Camp Townsend, MS, on 5/6/1865.

Tunnel, E.C. Pvt., 2nd & 6th Missouri Infantry (Consolidated). Co. G. Federal Rolls of Prisoners of War: Captured at Blakely, AL, on 4/9/1865; Received at Ship Island, MS, on 4/15/1865. Transferred to Vicksburg, MS, for exchange on 5/1/1865; Exchanged at Camp Townsend, MS, on 5/6/1865.

Turner, Lynch Sgt./Pvt., 3rd & 5th Missouri Infantry (Consolidated). Co. C. Federal Rolls of Prisoners of War: Captured at Blakely, AL, on 4/9/1865; Received at Ship Island, MS, on 4/15/1865. Transferred to Vicksburg, MS, for exchange on 5/1/1865; Exchanged at Camp Townsend, MS, on 5/6/1865.

Tuttle, James Pvt., 2nd & 6th Missouri Infantry (Consolidated). Co. F. Federal Rolls of Prisoners of War: Captured at Blakely, AL, on 4/9/1865; Received at Ship Island, MS, on 4/15/1865. Transferred to Vicksburg, MS, for exchange on 5/1/1865; Exchanged at Camp Townsend, MS, on 5/6/1865.

Upton, John G. Cpl./Pvt., 3rd & 5th Missouri Infantry (Consolidated). Co. A. Federal Rolls of Prisoners of War: Captured at Blakely, AL, on 4/9/1865; Received at Ship Island, MS, on 4/15/1865. Transferred to Vicksburg, MS, for exchange on 5/1/1865; Exchanged at Camp Townsend, MS, on 5/6/1865.

Utterback, W.F. Sgt., 3rd & 5th Missouri Infantry (Consolidated). Co. __. Federal Rolls of Prisoners of War: Captured at Blakely, AL, on 4/9/1865; Received at Ship Island, MS, on 4/15/1865. Transferred to Vicksburg, MS, for exchange on 5/1/1865; Exchanged at Camp Townsend, MS, on 5/6/1865.

Vandiver, Elijah M. (AKA Vandivier) Pvt., 1st & 3rd Missouri Cavalry (Consolidated). Co. B. Enlisted: 12/11/1861 at Reform, MO. Age at enlistment: 26. Residence at enlistment: Callaway County, MO. Federal Rolls of Prisoners of War: Captured at Blakely, AL, on 4/9/1865; Received at Ship Island, MS, on 4/15/1865. Transferred to Vicksburg, MS, for exchange on 5/1/1865; Exchanged at Camp Townsend, MS, on 5/6/1865.

Vaughn, W.E. Pvt., 3rd & 5th Missouri Infantry (Consolidated). Co. __. Federal Rolls of Prisoners of War: Captured at Blakely, AL, on 4/9/1865; Received at Ship Island, MS, on 4/15/1865. Transferred to Vicksburg, MS, for exchange on 5/1/1865; Exchanged at Camp Townsend, MS, on 5/6/1865.

Vernon, J.M. Pvt., 3rd & 5th Missouri Infantry (Consolidated). Co. __. Federal Rolls of Prisoners of War: Captured at Blakely, AL, on 4/9/1865; Received at Ship Island, MS, on 4/15/1865. Transferred to Vicksburg, MS, for exchange on 5/1/1865; Exchanged at Camp Townsend, MS, on 5/6/1865.

Walden, William Pvt., 1st & 3rd Missouri Cavalry (Consolidated). Co. K. Federal Rolls of Prisoners of War: Captured at Blakely, AL, on 4/9/1865; Received at Ship Island, MS, on 4/15/1865. Transferred to Vicksburg, MS, for exchange on 5/1/1865; Exchanged at Camp Townsend, MS, on 5/6/1865.

Walker, Joseph W. (AKA Joel) Pvt., 2nd & 6th Missouri Infantry (Consolidated). Co. C. Federal Rolls of Prisoners of War: Captured at Blakely, AL, on 4/9/1865; Received at Ship Island, MS, on 4/15/1865. Transferred to Vicksburg, MS, for exchange on 5/1/1865; Exchanged at Camp Townsend, MS, on 5/6/1865.

Walker, William Young Pvt., 2nd & 6th Missouri Infantry (Consolidated). Co. I. Federal Rolls of Prisoners of War: Captured at Blakely, AL, on 4/9/1865; Received at Ship Island, MS, on 4/15/1865. Transferred to Vicksburg, MS, for exchange on 5/1/1865; Exchanged at Camp Townsend, MS, on 5/6/1865.

Wallace, R. Pvt., 3rd & 5th Missouri Infantry (Consolidated). Co. __. Federal Rolls of Prisoners of War: Captured at Blakely, AL, on 4/9/1865; Received at Ship Island, MS, on 4/15/1865. Transferred to Vicksburg, MS, for exchange on 5/1/1865; Exchanged at Camp Townsend, MS, on 5/6/1865.

Welch, J.C. Pvt., 3rd & 5th Missouri Infantry (Consolidated). Co. __. Federal Rolls of Prisoners of War: Captured at Blakely, AL, on 4/9/1865; Received at Ship Island, MS, on 4/15/1865. Transferred to Vicksburg, MS, for exchange on 5/1/1865; Exchanged at Camp Townsend, MS, on 5/6/1865.

Wells, Pat Pvt., 3rd & 5th Missouri Infantry (Consolidated). Co. __. Federal Rolls of Prisoners of War: Captured at Blakely, AL, on 4/9/1865; Received at Ship Island, MS, on 4/15/1865. Transferred to Vicksburg, MS, for exchange on 5/1/1865; Exchanged at Camp Townsend, MS, on 5/6/1865.

Whaley, Maston Pvt., 1st & 3rd Missouri Cavalry (Consolidated). Co. B. Federal Rolls of Prisoners of War: Captured at Blakely, AL, on 4/9/1865; Received at Ship Island, MS, on 4/15/1865. Transferred to Vicksburg, MS, for exchange on 5/1/1865; Exchanged at Camp Townsend, MS, on 5/6/1865. Residence at exchange: Washington County, MO.

Wiley, T.J. Pvt., 3rd & 5th Missouri Infantry (Consolidated). Co. __. Federal Rolls of Prisoners of War: Captured at Blakely, AL, on 4/9/1865; Received at Ship

Island, MS, on 4/15/1865. Transferred to Vicksburg, MS, for exchange on 5/1/1865; Exchanged at Camp Townsend, MS, on 5/6/1865.

Williams, J.R. Pvt., 1st & 3rd Missouri Cavalry (Consolidated). Co. __. Federal Rolls of Prisoners of War: Captured at Blakely, AL, on 4/9/1865; Received at Ship Island, MS, on 4/15/1865. Transferred to Vicksburg, MS, for exchange on 5/1/1865; Exchanged at Camp Townsend, MS, on 5/6/1865.

Williams, James S. Pvt., 2nd & 6th Missouri Infantry (Consolidated). Co. A. Federal Rolls of Prisoners of War: Captured at Blakely, AL, on 4/9/1865; Received at Ship Island, MS, on 4/15/1865. Transferred to Vicksburg, MS, for exchange on 5/1/1865; Exchanged at Camp Townsend, MS, on 5/6/1865.

Williams, M.B. Pvt., 3rd & 5th Missouri Infantry (Consolidated). Co. __. Federal Rolls of Prisoners of War: Captured at Blakely, AL, on 4/9/1865; Received at Ship Island, MS, on 4/15/1865. Transferred to Vicksburg, MS, for exchange on 5/1/1865; Exchanged at Camp Townsend, MS, on 5/6/1865.

Williams, Merritt Cpl., 3rd & 5th Missouri Infantry (Consolidated). Co. F. Federal Rolls of Prisoners of War: Captured at Blakely, AL, on 4/9/1865; Received at Ship Island, MS, on 4/15/1865. Transferred to Vicksburg, MS, for exchange on 5/1/1865; Exchanged at Camp Townsend, MS, on 5/6/1865.

Williams, Thomas Pvt., 3rd & 5th Missouri Infantry (Consolidated). Co. D. Federal Rolls of Prisoners of War: Captured at Blakely, AL, on 4/9/1865; Received at Ship Island, MS, on 4/15/1865. Transferred to Vicksburg, MS, for exchange on 5/1/1865; Exchanged at Camp Townsend, MS, on 5/6/1865.

Wilson, J.R. Pvt., 1st & 3rd Missouri Cavalry (Consolidated). Co. __. Federal Rolls of Prisoners of War: Captured at Blakely, AL, on 4/9/1865; Received at Ship Island, MS, on 4/15/1865. Transferred to Vicksburg, MS, for exchange on 5/1/1865; Exchanged at Camp Townsend, MS, on 5/6/1865.

Wilson, James A. Pvt./Cpl., 2nd & 6th Missouri Infantry (Consolidated). Co. __. Federal Rolls of Prisoners of War: Captured at Blakely, AL, on 4/9/1865; Received at Ship Island, MS, on 4/15/1865. Transferred to Vicksburg, MS, for exchange on 5/1/1865; Exchanged at Camp Townsend, MS, on 5/6/1865.

Wilson, John Pvt., 3rd & 5th Missouri Infantry (Consolidated). Cos. E & H. Federal Rolls of Prisoners of War: Captured at Blakely, AL, on 4/9/1865; Received at Ship Island, MS, on 4/15/1865. Transferred to Vicksburg, MS, for exchange on 5/1/1865; Exchanged at Camp Townsend, MS, on 5/6/1865.

Winn, John W. Pvt., 1st & 3rd Missouri Cavalry (Consolidated). Co. G. Federal Rolls of Prisoners of War: Captured at Blakely, AL, on 4/9/1865; Received at Ship Island, MS, on 4/15/1865. Transferred to Vicksburg, MS, for exchange on 5/1/1865; Exchanged at Camp Townsend, MS, on 5/6/1865.

Wise, John Pvt., 2nd & 6th Missouri Infantry (Consolidated). Co. __. Federal Rolls of Prisoners of War: Captured at Blakely, AL, on 4/9/1865; Received at Ship Island, MS, on 4/15/1865. Transferred to Vicksburg, MS, for exchange on 5/1/1865; Exchanged at Camp Townsend, MS, on 5/6/1865.

Withers, John A. (AKA J.H.) Pvt., 3rd & 5th Missouri Infantry (Consolidated). Cos. D & F. Federal Rolls of Prisoners of War: Captured at Blakely, AL, on 4/9/1865; Received at Ship Island, MS, on 4/15/1865. Transferred to Vicksburg, MS, for exchange on 5/1/1865; Exchanged at Camp Townsend, MS, on 5/6/1865.

Wolfe, Daniel Henry (AKA Woolf) Pvt., 3rd & 5th Missouri Infantry (Consolidated). Co. __. Federal Rolls of Prisoners of War: Captured at Blakely, AL, on 4/9/1865; Received at Ship Island, MS, on 4/15/1865. Transferred to Vicksburg, MS, for exchange on 5/1/1865; Exchanged at Camp Townsend, MS, on 5/6/1865.

Wolfe, W.H. (AKA H.A.) Pvt./Hosp. Stew., 3rd & 5th Missouri Infantry (Consolidated). F & S. Federal Rolls of Prisoners of War: Captured at Blakely, AL, on 4/9/1865; Received at Ship Island, MS, on 4/15/1865. Transferred to Vicksburg, MS, for exchange on 5/1/1865; Exchanged at Camp Townsend, MS, on 5/6/1865.

Wood, John M. Pvt., 3rd & 5th Missouri Infantry (Consolidated). Co. __. Federal Rolls of Prisoners of War: Captured at Blakely, AL, on 4/9/1865; Received at Ship Island, MS, on 4/15/1865. Transferred to Vicksburg, MS, for exchange on 5/1/1865; Exchanged at Camp Townsend, MS, on 5/6/1865.

Wright, Charles A. Pvt., 1st & 3rd Missouri Cavalry (Consolidated). Co. K. Enlisted: 12/5/1861 at Mexico, MO. Age at enlistment: 23. Residence at enlistment: Audrain County, MO. Federal Rolls of Prisoners of War: Captured at Big Black River Bridge, MS, in 5/1863. Federal Rolls of Prisoners of War: Captured at Blakely, AL, on 4/9/1865; Received at Ship Island, MS, on 4/15/1865. Transferred to Vicksburg, MS, for exchange on 5/1/1865; Exchanged at Camp Townsend, MS, on 5/6/1865.

Wright, S.M. Pvt., 1st & 3rd Missouri Cavalry (Consolidated). Co. H. Enlisted: 12/29/1861 at Alanthus Grove, MO. Age at enlistment: 41. Residence at enlistment: Gentry County, MO. Federal Rolls of Prisoners of War: Captured and paroled at Vicksburg, MS, on 7/4/1863. Federal Rolls of Prisoners of War: Captured at Blakely, AL, on 4/9/1865; Received at Ship Island, MS, on 4/15/1865. Transferred to Vicksburg, MS, for exchange on 5/1/1865; Exchanged at Camp Townsend, MS, on 5/6/1865.

Wyatt, Richard Pvt., 2nd & 6th Missouri Infantry (Consolidated). Co. __. Federal Rolls of Prisoners of War: Captured at Blakely, AL, on 4/9/1865; Received at Ship Island, MS, on 4/15/1865. Transferred to Vicksburg, MS, for exchange on 5/1/1865; Exchanged at Camp Townsend, MS, on 5/6/1865.

North Carolina Prisoners of War

Allen, A.A. Pvt., 29th North Carolina Infantry. Co. K. Federal Rolls of Prisoners of War: Captured at Spanish Fort, AL, on 4/8/1865; Received at Ship Island, MS, on 4/10/1865. Transferred to Vicksburg, MS, for exchange on 5/1/1865; Exchanged at Camp Townsend, MS, on 5/6/1865.

Allen, Henry H. Pvt., 29th North Carolina Infantry. Co. E. Enlisted: 10/25/1864 for the duration of the war. Federal Rolls of Prisoners of War: Captured at Spanish Fort, AL, on 4/8/1865; Received at Ship Island, MS, on 4/10/1865. Transferred to Vicksburg, MS, for exchange on 5/1/1865; Exchanged at Camp Townsend, MS, on 5/6/1865.

Anderson, William T. 1st Lt., 39th North Carolina Infantry. Co. B. Enlisted: 10/19/1861 at Macon County, NC. Age at enlistment: 28. Rolls for 1/1863 through 2/1863: Wounded in shoulder and groin at Murfreesboro, TN, on 12/31/1862; Returned to duty in 2/1863. Rolls for 2/1863 through 2/1864: Present. Federal Rolls of Prisoners of War: Captured at Spanish Fort, AL, on 4/8/1865; Received at Ship Island, MS, on 4/10/1865. Transferred to Vicksburg, MS, for exchange on 4/28/1865; Confined at New Orleans, LA, on 4/30/1865. Exchanged at Camp Townsend, MS, on 5/6/1865. Born: 2/2/1832 at Blount County, TN, to Mansfield and Hannah T. Black Anderson. Married: Martha A. Thomas on 5/19/1864 at Macon County, NC. Died: 6/30/1884 at Macon County, NC. Burial: Coweeta Baptist Cemetery at Smithbridge Township, Macon County, NC.

Angel, Daniel W. Cpl./3rd Lt./Capt., 29th North Carolina Infantry. Co. B. Enlisted: 7/3/1861. Age at enlistment: 23. Residence at enlistment: Yancey County, NC. Appointed 3rd Lt. on 5/2/1862 and Capt. on 4/25/1863. Wounded in hand at Chickamauga, GA, on 9/19/1863. Federal Rolls of Prisoners of War: Captured at Spanish Fort, AL, on 4/5/1865; Received at Ship Island, MS, on 4/10/1865. Transferred to Vicksburg, MS, for exchange on 4/28/1865; Confined at New Orleans, LA, on 4/30/1865. Exchanged at Camp Townsend, MS, on 5/6/1865.

Ashworth, Jonathan Pvt., 29th North Carolina Infantry. Co. H. Enlisted: 9/11/1861. Age at enlistment: 17. Residence at enlistment: Buncombe County, NC. Federal Rolls of Prisoners of War: Captured near Murfreesboro, TN, on 2/5/1863 while wounded in the head; Received at Nashville, TN. Transferred to Louisville, KY, on 4/20/1863; Forwarded to Fort McHenry, MD. Paroled at Fort McHenry, MD, on 4/30/1863; Transferred to City Point, VA, for exchange on 5/2/1863. Federal Rolls of Prisoners of War: Captured at Spanish Fort, AL, on 4/8/1865; Received at Ship Island, MS, on 4/10/1865. Transferred to Vicksburg, MS, for exchange on 5/1/1865; Exchanged at Camp Townsend, MS, on 5/6/1865.

Becker, John Pvt., 39th North Carolina Infantry. Co. H. Federal Rolls of Prisoners of War: Captured at Spanish Fort, AL, on 4/8/1865; Received at Ship Island, MS, on 4/10/1865. Transferred to Vicksburg, MS, for exchange on 5/1/1865; Exchanged at Camp Townsend, MS, on 5/6/1865.

Biers, L. (AKA Biens) Pvt./Sgt., 39th North Carolina Infantry. Co. D. Federal Rolls of Prisoners of War: Captured at Spanish Fort, AL, on 4/8/1865; Received at Ship Island, MS, on 4/10/1865. Transferred to Vicksburg, MS, for exchange on 5/1/1865; Exchanged at Camp Townsend, MS, on 5/6/1865.

Bird, Carmine S. Pvt./Hosp. Stew., 39th North Carolina Infantry. Co. B. Enlisted: 3/1/1863 at Macon County, NC, for the duration of the war. Age at enlistment: 18. Rolls for 4/1863 through 2/1864: Present, promoted to Hospital Steward. Federal Rolls of Prisoners of War: Captured at Spanish Fort, AL, on 4/8/1865; Received at Ship Island, MS, on 4/10/1865. Transferred to Vicksburg, MS, for exchange on 5/1/1865; Exchanged at Camp Townsend, MS, on 5/6/1865.

Black, W.D. Pvt., 29th North Carolina Infantry. Co. C. Enlisted: 10/29/1864. Federal Rolls of Prisoners of War: Captured at Spanish Fort, AL, on 4/8/1865; Received at Ship Island, MS, on 4/10/1865. Transferred to Vicksburg, MS, for exchange on 5/1/1865; Exchanged at Camp Townsend, MS, on 5/6/1865.

Blackwell, S. Pvt., 39th North Carolina Infantry. Co. G. Federal Rolls of Prisoners of War: Captured at Spanish Fort, AL, on 4/8/1865; Received at Ship Island, MS, on 4/10/1865. Transferred to Vicksburg,

MS, for exchange on 5/1/1865; Exchanged at Camp Townsend, MS, on 5/6/1865.

Block, W.H. Pvt., 29th North Carolina Infantry. Co. K. Federal Rolls of Prisoners of War: Captured at Spanish Fort, AL, on 4/8/1865; Received at Ship Island, MS, on 4/10/1865. Transferred to Vicksburg, MS, for exchange on 5/1/1865; Exchanged at Camp Townsend, MS, on 5/6/1865.

Bovin, R.J. (AKA Bovim) Pvt., 29th North Carolina Infantry. Co. F. Federal Rolls of Prisoners of War: Captured at Spanish Fort, AL, on 4/8/1865; Received at Ship Island, MS, on 4/10/1865. Transferred to Vicksburg, MS, for exchange on 5/1/1865; Exchanged at Camp Townsend, MS, on 5/6/1865.

Boyd, Samuel M. Pvt., 29th North Carolina Infantry. Co. F. Enlisted: 8/31/1861. Age at enlistment: 24. Residence at enlistment: Jackson County, NC. Federal Rolls of Prisoners of War: Captured at Spanish Fort, AL, on 4/8/1865; Received at Ship Island, MS, on 4/10/1865. Transferred to Vicksburg, MS, for exchange on 5/1/1865; Exchanged at Camp Townsend, MS, on 5/6/1865. Rolls of Prisoners of War, C.S.A: Surrendered at Citronelle, AL, on 5/4/1865; Paroled at Meridian, MS, on 5/11/1865.

Bradley, B.G. Pvt., 29th North Carolina Infantry. Co. A. Federal Rolls of Prisoners of War: Captured at Spanish Fort, AL, on 4/8/1865; Received at Ship Island, MS, on 4/10/1865. Transferred to Vicksburg, MS, for exchange on 5/1/1865; Exchanged at Camp Townsend, MS, on 5/6/1865. Soldier also served as a Pvt. with Mallett's North Carolina Infantry Battalion. Co. D.

Bradley, Jere W. Pvt., 29th North Carolina Infantry. Co. D. Enlisted: 8/13/1861. Age at enlistment: 20. Residence at enlistment: Madison County, NC. Wounded in 1863. Federal Rolls of Prisoners of War: Captured at Spanish Fort, AL, on 4/8/1865; Received at Ship Island, MS, on 4/10/1865. Transferred to Vicksburg, MS, for exchange on 5/1/1865; Exchanged at Camp Townsend, MS, on 5/6/1865. Confederate Pension Application on file at the North Carolina State Archives. Target Name: Bradley, Jere W.

Brindal, F. Sgt., 39th North Carolina Infantry. Co. H. Federal Rolls of Prisoners of War: Captured at Spanish Fort, AL, on 4/8/1865; Received at Ship Island, MS, on 4/10/1865. Transferred to Vicksburg, MS, for exchange on 5/1/1865; Exchanged at Camp Townsend, MS, on 5/6/1865.

Brown, John Pvt., 39th North Carolina Infantry. Co. H. Federal Rolls of Prisoners of War: Captured at Spanish Fort, AL, on 4/8/1865; Received at Ship Island, MS, on 4/10/1865. Transferred to Vicksburg, MS, for exchange on 5/1/1865; Exchanged at Camp Townsend, MS, on 5/6/1865.

Brown, W.E. Sgt., 29th North Carolina Infantry. Co. K. Federal Rolls of Prisoners of War: Captured at Spanish Fort, AL, on 4/8/1865; Received at Ship Island, MS, on 4/10/1865. Transferred to Vicksburg, MS, for exchange on 5/1/1865; Exchanged at Camp Townsend, MS, on 5/6/1865.

Byrd, W.A. Pvt., 29th North Carolina Infantry. Co. B. Wounded on 6/24/1864. Federal Rolls of Prisoners of War: Captured at Spanish Fort, AL, on 4/8/1865; Received at Ship Island, MS, on 4/10/1865. Transferred to Vicksburg, MS, for exchange on 5/1/1865; Exchanged at Camp Townsend, MS, on 5/6/1865. Rolls of Prisoners of War, C.S.A: Surrendered at Citronelle, AL, on 5/4/1865; Paroled at Meridian, MS, on 5/11/1865. Residence at parole: Yancey County, NC. Confederate Pension Application on file at the North Carolina State Archives. Target Name: Byrd, W.A.

Cabe, Leander F. (AKA Calie) Pvt., 39th North Carolina Infantry. Co. I. Federal Rolls of Prisoners of War: Captured at Spanish Fort, AL, on 4/8/1865; Received at Ship Island, MS, on 4/10/1865. Transferred to Vicksburg, MS, for exchange on 5/1/1865; Exchanged at Camp Townsend, MS, on 5/6/1865. Soldier also served as a Pvt. with Mallett's North Carolina Battalion Infantry.

Cacey, J.T. (AKA Case) Pvt., 39th North Carolina Infantry. Co. D. Enlisted: 5/1863 at Buncombe County, NC. Age at enlistment: 18. Federal Rolls of Prisoners of War: Captured at Spanish Fort, AL, on 4/8/1865; Received at Ship Island, MS, on 4/10/1865. Transferred to Vicksburg, MS, for exchange on 5/1/1865; Exchanged at Camp Townsend, MS, on 5/6/1865. Confederate Pension Application on file at the North Carolina State Archives. Target Name: Case, J.T.

Cacey, James M. (AKA Case) Pvt., 39th North Carolina Infantry. Co. D. Enlisted: 3/1/1863 at Buncombe County, NC, for the duration of the war. Age at enlistment: 18. Rolls for 5/1863 through 6/1863: Present. Rolls for 9/1863 through 10/1863: Present. Rolls for 1/1864 through 2/1864: Present. Federal Rolls of Prisoners of War: Captured at Spanish Fort, AL, on 4/8/1865; Received at Ship Island, MS, on 4/10/1865. Transferred to Vicksburg, MS, for exchange on 5/1/1865; Exchanged at Camp Townsend, MS, on 5/6/1865.

Cacey, William B. (AKA Case) Pvt./Cpl., 39th North Carolina Infantry. Co. D. Enlisted: 10/28/1861 at Buncombe County, NC. Age at enlistment: 18. Rolls for 2/1862 through 4/1862: Present. Rolls for 11/1862 through 6/1863: Present. Wounded at Chickamauga, GA, on 9/19/1863 and absent through 2/1864. Federal Rolls of Prisoners of War: Captured at Spanish Fort, AL, on 4/8/1865; Received at Ship Island, MS, on 4/10/1865. Transferred to Vicksburg, MS, for exchange on 5/1/1865; Exchanged at Camp Townsend, MS, on 5/6/1865.

Cagle, Henry W. Cpl./1st Sgt./2nd Lt., 39th North Carolina Infantry. Co. D. Enlisted: 10/28/1861 at Buncombe County, NC. Age at enlistment: 29. Rolls for 11/1862 through 12/1862: Present, wounded in arm at Murfreesboro, TN, on 12/31/1862. Rolls for 1/1863 through 6/1863: Present. Elected 2nd Lt. on on 8/10/1863. Federal Rolls of Prisoners of War: Captured at Spanish Fort, AL, on 4/8/1865; Received at Ship Island, MS, on 4/10/1865. Transferred to Vicksburg, MS, for exchange on 4/28/1865; Confined at New Orleans, LA, on 4/30/1865. Exchanged at Camp Townsend, MS, on 5/6/1865. Rolls of Prisoners of War, C.S.A: Surrendered at Citronelle, AL, on 5/4/1865; Paroled at Meridian, MS, on 5/12/1865.

Carlton, C.B. Pvt., 29th North Carolina Infantry. Co. K. Federal Rolls of Prisoners of War: Captured at Spanish Fort, AL, on 4/8/1865; Received at Ship Island, MS, on 4/10/1865. Transferred to Vicksburg, MS, for exchange on 5/1/1865; Exchanged at Camp Townsend, MS, on 5/6/1865.

Casey, J.M. Pvt., 39th North Carolina Infantry. Co. D. Federal Rolls of Prisoners of War: Captured at Spanish Fort, AL, on 4/8/1865; Received at Ship Island, MS, on 4/10/1865. Transferred to Vicksburg, MS, for exchange on 5/1/1865; Exchanged at Camp Townsend, MS, on 5/6/1865.

Casey, W.B. Pvt., 39th North Carolina Infantry. Co. D. Federal Rolls of Prisoners of War: Captured at Spanish Fort, AL, on 4/8/1865; Received at Ship Island, MS, on 4/10/1865. Transferred to Vicksburg, MS, for exchange on 5/1/1865; Exchanged at Camp Townsend, MS, on 5/6/1865.

Cody, William A. (AKA Gody) Pvt., 29th North Carolina Infantry. Co. B. Enlisted: 7/3/1861. Age at enlistment: 26. Residence at enlistment: Yancey County, NC. Deserted on 11/13/1861; Returned to duty. Wounded on 10/4/1864. Federal Rolls of Prisoners of War: Captured at Spanish Fort, AL, on 4/8/1865; Received at Ship Island, MS, on 4/10/1865. Transferred to Vicksburg, MS, for exchange on 5/1/1865; Exchanged at Camp Townsend, MS, on 5/6/1865. Confederate Pension Application on file at the North Carolina State Archives. Target Name: Gody, William A.

Conner, Samuel P. (AKA Connor) Pvt., 29th North Carolina Infantry. Co. F. Enlisted: 8/31/1861. Age at enlistment: 18. Residence at enlistment: Jackson County, NC. Federal Rolls of Prisoners of War: Captured at Spanish Fort, AL, on 4/8/1865; Received at Ship Island, MS, on 4/10/1865. Transferred to Vicksburg, MS, for exchange on 5/1/1865; Exchanged at Camp Townsend, MS, on 5/6/1865.

Coon, John Pvt., 29th North Carolina Infantry. Co. H. Federal Rolls of Prisoners of War: Captured at Spanish Fort, AL, on 4/8/1865; Received at Ship Island, MS, on 4/10/1865. Transferred to Vicksburg, MS, for exchange on 5/1/1865; Exchanged at Camp Townsend, MS, on 5/6/1865. Rolls of Prisoners of War, C.S.A: Surrendered at Citronelle, AL, on 5/4/1865; Paroled at Meridian, MS, on 5/11/1865. Residence at parole: Buncombe County, NC.

Crane, A.J. (AKA Crain) Pvt., 29th North Carolina Infantry. Co. G. Enlisted: 9/5/1861. Federal Rolls of Prisoners of War: Captured at Spanish Fort, AL, on 4/8/1865; Received at Ship Island, MS, on 4/10/1865. Transferred to Vicksburg, MS, for exchange on 5/1/1865; Exchanged at Camp Townsend, MS, on 5/6/1865.

Crawford, James G. Capt., 39th North Carolina Infantry. Co. I. Enlisted: Macon County, NC; Elected Capt. on 3/25/1862. Age at enlistment: 29. Occupation at enlistment: Sheriff of Macon County, NC. Rolls for 11/1862 through 6/1863: Present. Rolls for 9/1863 through 10/1863: Present. Furloughed on 2/2/1864. Rolls for 3/1864 through 4/1864: Absent, on Court Martial duty. Wounded in right hand near Atlanta, GA, during the Summer of 1864. Federal Rolls of Prisoners of War: Captured at Spanish Fort, AL, on 4/8/1865; Received at Ship Island, MS, on 4/10/1865. Transferred to Vicksburg, MS, for exchange on 4/28/1865; Confined at New Orleans, LA, on 4/30/1865. Exchanged at Camp Townsend, MS, on 5/6/1865. Born: Macon County, NC.

Crockett, B.F. Pvt., 29th North Carolina Infantry. Co. K. Federal Rolls of Prisoners of War: Captured at Spanish Fort, AL, on 4/8/1865; Received at Ship Island, MS, on 4/10/1865. Transferred to Vicksburg, MS, for exchange on 5/1/1865; Exchanged at Camp Townsend, MS, on 5/6/1865.

Curtis, J.A. Pvt., 39th North Carolina Infantry. Co. B. Federal Rolls of Prisoners of War: Captured at Spanish Fort, AL, on 4/8/1865; Received at Ship Island, MS, on 4/10/1865. Transferred to Vicksburg, MS, for exchange on 5/1/1865; Exchanged at Camp Townsend, MS, on 5/6/1865.

Davis, C.J. Pvt., 39th North Carolina Infantry. Co. D. Federal Rolls of Prisoners of War: Captured at Spanish Fort, AL, on 4/8/1865; Received at Ship Island, MS, on 4/10/1865. Transferred to Vicksburg, MS, for exchange on 5/1/1865; Exchanged at Camp Townsend, MS, on 5/6/1865.

Davis, Chesley, J. Pvt., 39th North Carolina Infantry. Co. D. Enlisted: 11/7/1861 at Henderson County, NC. Age at enlistment: 30. Rolls for 2/1862 through 4/1862: Present. Rolls for 6/1862 through 7/1862: Absent, without leave. Rolls for 9/1863 through 10/1863: Present, under arrest. Rolls for 1/1864 through 2/1864: Present. Federal Rolls of Prisoners of War: Captured at Spanish Fort, AL, on 4/8/1865; Received at Ship Island, MS, on 4/10/1865. Transferred to Vicksburg, MS, for exchange on 5/1/1865; Exchanged at Camp Townsend, MS, on 5/6/1865.

Dayton, Jackson (AKA Deyton) Pvt., 29th North Carolina Infantry. Co. __. Enlisted: 7/26/1861. Age at enlistment: 20. Residence at enlistment: Yancey County, NC. Federal Rolls of Prisoners of War: Captured at Spanish Fort, AL, on 4/8/1865; Received at Ship Island, MS, on 4/10/1865. Transferred to Vicksburg, MS, for exchange on 5/1/1865; Exchanged at Camp Townsend, MS, on 5/6/1865.

Drake, F. Pvt., 29th North Carolina Infantry. Co. D. Federal Rolls of Prisoners of War: Captured at Spanish Fort, AL, on 4/8/1865; Received at Ship Island, MS, on 4/10/1865. Transferred to Vicksburg, MS, for exchange on 5/1/1865; Exchanged at Camp Townsend, MS, on 5/6/1865.

Drake, John Pvt., 29th North Carolina Infantry. Co. D. Federal Rolls of Prisoners of War: Captured at Spanish Fort, AL, on 4/8/1865; Received at Ship Island, MS, on 4/10/1865. Transferred to Vicksburg, MS, for exchange on 5/1/1865; Exchanged at Camp Townsend, MS, on 5/6/1865.

Ducker, John H. Pvt., 39th North Carolina Infantry. Co. D. Enlisted: 11/7/1861 at Buncombe County, NC. Age at enlistment: 26. Rolls for 2/1862 through 4/1862: Present. Rolls for 2/1863 through 4/1863: Absent, detached as Teamster. Rolls for 5/1863 through 6/1863: Present. Returned to duty on 1/1/1863 after being absent without leave for 57 days. Rolls for 9/1863 through 10/1863: Present, under arrest. Rolls for 1/1864 through 2/1864: Present. Federal Rolls of Prisoners of War: Captured at Spanish Fort, AL, on 4/8/1865; Received at Ship Island, MS, on 4/10/1865. Transferred to Vicksburg, MS, for exchange on 5/1/1865; Exchanged at Camp Townsend, MS, on 5/6/1865.

Duncan, David W. Pvt., 29th North Carolina Infantry. Co. K. Enlisted: 9/14/1864 for the duration of the war. Age at enlistment: 17. Residence at enlistment: Yancey County, NC. Federal Rolls of Prisoners of War: Captured at Spanish Fort, AL, on 4/8/1865; Received at Ship Island, MS, on 4/10/1865. Transferred to Vicksburg, MS, for exchange on 5/1/1865; Exchanged at Camp Townsend, MS, on 5/6/1865.

Duncan, William Sgt., 29th North Carolina Infantry. Co. K. Federal Rolls of Prisoners of War: Captured at Spanish Fort, AL, on 4/8/1865; Received at Ship Island, MS, on 4/10/1865. Transferred to Vicksburg, MS, for exchange on 5/1/1865; Exchanged at Camp Townsend, MS, on 5/6/1865.

Duvall, William W. Pvt., 39th North Carolina Infantry. Co. I. Enlisted: 3/25/1862 at Macon County, NC. Age at enlistment: 27. Rolls for 3/25/1862 through 4/1862: Present. Rolls for 11/1862 through 6/1863: Present. Rolls for 9/1863 through 10/1863: Present. Rolls for 1/1864 through 4/1864: Present. Wounded at New Hope Church, GA. Federal Rolls of Prisoners of War: Captured at Spanish Fort, AL, on 4/8/1865; Received at Ship Island, MS, on 4/10/1865. Transferred to Vicksburg, MS, for exchange on 5/1/1865; Exchanged at Camp Townsend, MS, on 5/6/1865.

Dwyer, Ellis Pvt., 39th North Carolina Infantry. Co. B. Federal Rolls of Prisoners of War: Captured at Spanish Fort, AL, on 4/8/1865; Received at Ship Island, MS, on 4/10/1865. Transferred to Vicksburg, MS, for exchange on 5/1/1865; Exchanged at Camp Townsend, MS, on 5/6/1865.

Elliott, Kinchen C. Pvt./Sgt. Maj., 29th North Carolina Infantry. Co. E/F & S. Federal Rolls of Prisoners of War: Captured at Spanish Fort, AL, on 4/8/1865; Received at Ship Island, MS, on 4/10/1865. Transferred to Vicksburg, MS, for exchange on 5/1/1865; Exchanged at Camp Townsend, MS, on 5/6/1865.

Endy, R. Pvt., 29th North Carolina Infantry. Co. F. Federal Rolls of Prisoners of War: Captured at Spanish Fort, AL, on 4/8/1865; Received at Ship Island, MS, on 4/10/1865. Transferred to Vicksburg, MS, for exchange on 5/1/1865; Exchanged at Camp Townsend, MS, on 5/6/1865.

Endy, W.R. Pvt., 29th North Carolina Infantry. Co. E. Federal Rolls of Prisoners of War: Captured at Spanish Fort, AL, on 4/8/1865; Received at Ship Island, MS, on 4/10/1865. Transferred to Vicksburg, MS, for exchange on 5/1/1865; Exchanged at Camp Townsend, MS, on 5/6/1865.

Foster, James Pvt., 29th North Carolina Infantry. Co. C. Enlisted: 8/6/1861. Age at enlistment: 21. Residence at enlistment: Buncombe County, NC. Federal Rolls of Prisoners of War: Captured at Spanish Fort, AL, on 4/8/1865; Received at Ship Island, MS, on 4/10/1865. Transferred to Vicksburg, MS, for exchange on 5/1/1865; Exchanged at Camp Townsend, MS, on 5/6/1865.

Frady, John J. (AKA Fraday) Drummer/Pvt., 39th North Carolina Infantry. Co. I. Enlisted: 3/25/1862 at Macon County, NC. Age at enlistment: 23. Rolls for 11/1862 through 4/1863: Present, reduced to Pvt. On Register of Canton, MS, Hospital: Admitted on 6/16/1863. Wounded at Chickamauga, GA, on 9/19/1863. Rolls for 10/1863 through 4/1864: Present. Federal Rolls of Prisoners of War: Captured at Spanish Fort, AL, on 4/8/1865; Received at Ship Island, MS, on 4/10/1865. Transferred to Vicksburg, MS, for exchange on 5/1/1865; Exchanged at Camp Townsend, MS, on 5/6/1865.

Frances, W. (AKA Francis) Pvt., 29th North Carolina Infantry. Co. E. Federal Rolls of Prisoners of War: Captured at Spanish Fort, AL, on 4/8/1865; Received at Ship Island, MS, on 4/10/1865. Transferred to Vicksburg, MS, for exchange on 5/1/1865; Exchanged at Camp Townsend, MS, on 5/6/1865.

Franklin, W.R. Pvt., 29th North Carolina Infantry. Co. F. Residence at enlistment: Jackson County, NC. Federal Rolls of Prisoners of War: Captured at Spanish Fort, AL, on 4/8/1865; Received at Ship Island, MS, on 4/10/1865. Transferred to Vicksburg, MS, for exchange on 5/1/1865; Exchanged at Camp Townsend, MS, on 5/6/1865. Rolls of Prisoners of War, C.S.A: Surrendered at Citronelle, AL, on 5/4/1865; Paroled at Meridian, MS, on 5/11/1865.

Franks, Isham D. Pvt., 39th North Carolina Infantry. Co. B. Enlisted: 3/1/1863 at Macon County, NC, for the duration of the war. Age at enlistment: 36. Hospitalized on 7/10/1863. Rolls for 1/1864 through 2/1864: Absent, on detached service. Federal Rolls of Prisoners of War: Captured at Spanish Fort, AL, on 4/8/1865; Received at Ship Island, MS, on 4/10/1865. Transferred to Vicksburg, MS, for exchange on 5/1/1865; Exchanged at Camp Townsend, MS, on 5/6/1865.

Franks, J.D. Pvt., 39th North Carolina Infantry. Co. D. Federal Rolls of Prisoners of War: Captured at Spanish Fort, AL, on 4/8/1865; Received at Ship Island, MS, on 4/10/1865. Transferred to Vicksburg, MS, for exchange on 5/1/1865; Exchanged at Camp Townsend, MS, on 5/6/1865.

Fulcher, James B. Pvt., 39th North Carolina Infantry. Co. D. Enlisted: 11/15/1861 at Macon County, NC. Age at enlistment: 19. Rolls for 2/1862 through 4/1862: Present. Rolls for 11/1862 through 4/1863: Present. Rolls for 5/1863 through 6/1863: Absent, detached as Hospital Nurse at Yazoo City, MS. Rolls for 9/1863 through 10/1863: Present. Rolls for 1/1864 through 2/1864: Absent, on detached service. Federal Rolls of Prisoners of War: Captured at Spanish Fort, AL, on 4/8/1865; Received at Ship Island, MS, on 4/10/1865. Transferred to Vicksburg, MS, for exchange on 5/1/1865; Exchanged at Camp Townsend, MS, on 5/6/1865.

Garrett, T.L. Pvt., 39th North Carolina Infantry. Co. A. Federal Rolls of Prisoners of War: Captured at Spanish Fort, AL, on 4/8/1865; Received at Ship Island, MS, on 4/10/1865. Transferred to Vicksburg, MS, for exchange on 5/1/1865; Exchanged at Camp Townsend, MS, on 5/6/1865.

Gibson, Franklin Pvt., 39th North Carolina Infantry. Co. H. Federal Rolls of Prisoners of War: Captured at Spanish Fort, AL, on 4/8/1865; Received at Ship Island, MS, on 4/10/1865. Transferred to Vicksburg, MS, for exchange on 5/1/1865; Exchanged at Camp Townsend, MS, on 5/6/1865.

Gibson, Stephen Pvt., 29th North Carolina Infantry. Co. F. Federal Rolls of Prisoners of War: Captured at Spanish Fort, AL, on 4/8/1865; Received at Ship Island, MS, on 4/10/1865. Transferred to Vicksburg, MS, for exchange on 5/1/1865; Exchanged at Camp Townsend, MS, on 5/6/1865.

Gillespie, James A. Pvt./Sgt., 29th North Carolina Infantry. Co. H. Enlisted: 9/11/1861. Age at enlistment: 28. Residence at enlistment: Buncombe County, NC. Federal Rolls of Prisoners of War: Captured at Spanish Fort, AL, on 4/8/1865; Received at Ship Island, MS, on 4/10/1865. Transferred to

Vicksburg, MS, for exchange on 5/1/1865; Exchanged at Camp Townsend, MS, on 5/6/1865.

Glidwell, J.H. Pvt., 39th North Carolina Infantry. Co. D. Federal Rolls of Prisoners of War: Captured at Spanish Fort, AL, on 4/8/1865; Received at Ship Island, MS, on 4/10/1865. Transferred to Vicksburg, MS, for exchange on 5/1/1865; Exchanged at Camp Townsend, MS, on 5/6/1865.

Godforth, John W. Pvt., 29th North Carolina Infantry. Co. K. Enlisted: 1864 for the duration of the war. Age at enlistment: 19. Federal Rolls of Prisoners of War: Captured at Spanish Fort, AL, on 4/8/1865; Received at Ship Island, MS, on 4/10/1865. Transferred to Vicksburg, MS, for exchange on 5/1/1865; Exchanged at Camp Townsend, MS, on 5/6/1865.

Grant, Henry Pvt., 29th North Carolina Infantry. Co. H. Enlisted: 5/13/1862 for the duration of the war. Age at enlistment: 18. Residence at enlistment: Buncombe County, NC. Wounded at Kennesaw Mountain, GA, on 4/25/1864. Federal Rolls of Prisoners of War: Captured at Spanish Fort, AL, on 4/8/1865; Received at Ship Island, MS, on 4/10/1865. Transferred to Vicksburg, MS, for exchange on 5/1/1865; Exchanged at Camp Townsend, MS, on 5/6/1865. Confederate Pension Application on file at the North Carolina State Archives. Target Name: Grant, Henry.

Grant, Thomas Pvt., 29th North Carolina Infantry. Co. H. Enlisted: 9/11/1861. Age at enlistment: 25. Residence at enlistment: Buncombe County, NC. Federal Rolls of Prisoners of War: Captured and paroled at Yazoo City, MS, on 7/13/1863. Federal Rolls of Prisoners of War: Captured at Spanish Fort, AL, on 4/8/1865; Received at Ship Island, MS, on 4/10/1865. Transferred to Vicksburg, MS, for exchange on 5/1/1865; Exchanged at Camp Townsend, MS, on 5/6/1865. Confederate Pension Application on file at the North Carolina State Archives. Target Name: Grant, Thomas.

Gribble, Elijah Pvt., 39th North Carolina Infantry. Co. I. Enlisted: 3/25/1862 at Macon County, NC. Age at enlistment: 21. Rolls for 3/25/1862 through 4/1862: Present. Rolls for 11/1862 through 6/1863: Present. Wounded at Chickamauga, GA, on 9/19/1863; Returned to duty on 11/1/1863. Rolls for 1/1864 through 4/1864: Present. Federal Rolls of Prisoners of War: Captured near Atlanta, GA, on 7/10/1864; Received at Louisville, KY, on 8/5/1864. Transferred to Camp Chase, OH, on 8/6/1864; Transferred to City Point, VA, for exchange on 3/4/1865. Exchanged at Boulware Wharf, James River, VA, on 3/10/1865. Federal Rolls of Prisoners of War: Captured at Spanish Fort, AL, on 4/8/1865; Received at Ship Island, MS, on 4/10/1865. Transferred to Vicksburg, MS, for exchange on 5/1/1865; Exchanged at Camp Townsend, MS, on 5/6/1865.

Grindstaff, Isaac Pvt., 29th North Carolina Infantry. Co. I. Enlisted: 6/12/1862 as a substitution for the duration of the war. Age at enlistment: 17. Federal Rolls of Prisoners of War: Captured at Murfreesboro, TN, on 12/31/1862 while wounded in the knee; Transferred to Nashville, TN, on 1/5/1863. Received at Camp Morton, IN; Forwarded to City Point, VA, for exchange on 4/22/1863. Federal Rolls of Prisoners of War: Captured at Spanish Fort, AL, on 4/8/1864; Received at Ship Island, MS, on 4/10/1864. Transferred to Vicksburg, MS, for exchange on 5/1/1865; Exchanged at Camp Townsend, MS, on 5/6/1865. Rolls of Prisoners of War, C.S.A: Surrendered at Citronelle, AL, on 5/4/1865; Paroled at Meridian, MS, on 5/11/1865.

Guthrie, Ervin Pvt., 29th North Carolina Infantry. Co. D. Enlisted: 8/13/1861. Age at enlistment: 16. Residence at enlistment: Madison County, NC. Wounded near Atlanta, GA, in 8/1864. Federal Rolls of Prisoners of War: Captured at Spanish Fort, AL, on 4/8/1865; Received at Ship Island, MS, on 4/10/1865. Transferred to Vicksburg, MS, for exchange on 5/1/1865; Exchanged at Camp Townsend, MS, on 5/6/1865. Confederate Pension Application on file at the North Carolina State Archives. Target Name: Guthrie, Ervin.

Hamper, F.C. Pvt., 29th North Carolina Infantry. Co. H. Federal Rolls of Prisoners of War: Captured at Spanish Fort, AL, on 4/8/1865; Received at Ship Island, MS, on 4/10/1865. Transferred to Vicksburg, MS, for exchange on 5/1/1865; Exchanged at Camp Townsend, MS, on 5/6/1865.

Hampton, John J. Pvt., 39th North Carolina Infantry. Cos. B & D. Enlisted: 10/28/1861. Age at enlistment: 23. Rolls for 11/1861 through 2//1862: Present. Rolls for 11/1862 through 12/1862: Absent, without leave. Rolls for 1/1863 through 2/1863: Deserted. Rolls for 3/1863 through 4/1863: Present, returned to duty on 3/14/1863. Rolls for 9/1863 through 10/1863: Present. Rolls for 1/1864 through 2/1864: Present. Federal Rolls of Prisoners of War: Captured at Spanish Fort, AL, on 4/8/1865; Received at Ship Island, MS, on 4/10/1865. Transferred to Vicksburg, MS, for exchange on 5/1/1865; Exchanged at camp Townsend, MS, on 5/6/1865.

Haney, J.W. Pvt., 39th North Carolina Infantry. Co. A. Federal Rolls of Prisoners of War: Captured at Spanish Fort, AL, on 4/8/1865; Received at Ship Island, MS, on 4/10/1865. Transferred to Vicksburg, MS, for exchange on 5/1/1865; Exchanged at Camp Townsend, MS, on 5/6/1865.

Haney, Levi (AKA Hainey) Pvt., 39th North Carolina Infantry. Co. D. Federal Rolls of Prisoners of War: Captured at Spanish Fort, AL, on 4/8/1865; Received at Ship Island, MS, on 4/10/1865. Transferred to Vicksburg, MS, for exchange on 5/1/1865; Exchanged at Camp Townsend, MS, on 5/6/1865.

Harris, James W. Pvt., 29th North Carolina Infantry. Co. B. Enlisted: 7/3/1861. Age at enlistment: 25. Residence at enlistment: Yancey County, NC. Deserted on 9/6/1863; Returned to duty. Wounded at Nashville, TN, in 1/1864. Federal Rolls of Prisoners of War: Captured at Spanish Fort, AL, on 4/8/1865; Received at Ship Island, MS, on 4/10/1865. Transferred to Vicksburg, MS, for exchange on 5/1/1865; Exchanged at Camp Townsend, MS, on 5/6/1865. Confederate Pension Application on file at the North Carolina State Archives. Target Name: Harris, James W.

Harris, Nelson Pvt., 29th North Carolina Infantry. Co. B. Enlisted: 7/3/1861. Age at enlistment: 19. Residence at enlistment: Yancey County, NC. Federal Rolls of Prisoners of War: Captured at Spanish Fort, AL, on 4/8/1865; Received at Ship Island, MS, on 4/10/1865. Transferred to Vicksburg, MS, for exchange on 5/1/1865; Exchanged at Camp Townsend, MS, on 5/6/1865.

Henry, Harvey M. Pvt., 29th North Carolina Infantry. Co. E. Enlisted: 11/6/1862 for the duration of the war.

Age at enlistment: 18. Residence at enlistment: Haywood County, NC. Wounded in chest at Murfreesboro, TN, on 12/31/1862. Federal Rolls of Prisoners of War: Captured at Spanish Fort, AL, on 4/8/1865; Received at Ship Island, MS, on 4/10/1865. Transferred to Vicksburg, MS, for exchange on 5/1/1865; Exchanged at Camp Townsend, MS, on 5/6/1865.

Hicks, W.M. (AKA Hix) Pvt., 29th North Carolina Infantry. Co. B. Federal Rolls of Prisoners of War: Captured at Spanish Fort, AL, on 4/8/1865; Received at Ship Island, MS, on 4/10/1865. Transferred to Vicksburg, MS, for exchange on 5/1/1865; Exchanged at Camp Townsend, MS, on 5/6/1865.

Hill, William A. Pvt./Sgt., 39th North Carolina Infantry. Co. D. Federal Rolls of Prisoners of War: Captured at Spanish Fort, AL, on 4/8/1865; Received at Ship Island, MS, on 4/10/1865. Transferred to Vicksburg, MS, for exchange on 5/1/1865; Exchanged at Camp Townsend, MS, on 5/6/1865.

Howey, Joseph W. Pvt., 39th North Carolina Infantry. Co. A. Enlisted: Mallett's North Carolina Battalion Infantry. Co. B; Transferred to the 39th North Carolina Infantry. Co. A on 6/6/1864. Federal Rolls of Prisoners of War: Captured at Spanish Fort, AL, on 4/8/1865; Received at Ship Island, MS, on 4/10/1865. Transferred to Vicksburg, MS, for exchange on 5/1/1865; Exchanged at Camp Townsend, MS, on 5/6/1865.

Hunter, D.V. Pvt., 29th North Carolina Infantry. Co. B. Enlisted: 1/2/1863 for the duration of the war. Age at enlistment: 19. Wounded at Kennesaw Mountain, GA, on 7/2/1864. Federal Rolls of Prisoners of War: Captured at Spanish Fort, AL, on 4/8/1865; Received at Ship Island, MS, on 4/10/1865. Transferred to Vicksburg, MS, for exchange on 5/1/1865; Exchanged at Camp Townsend, MS, on 5/6/1865. Confederate Pension Application on file at the North Carolina State Archives. Target Name: Hunter, D.V.

Ingle, D.M. Pvt., 29th North Carolina Infantry. Co. B. Federal Rolls of Prisoners of War: Captured at Spanish Fort, AL, on 4/8/1865; Received at Ship Island, MS, on 4/10/1865. Transferred to Vicksburg, MS, for exchange on 5/1/1865; Exchanged at Camp Townsend, MS, on 5/6/1865.

Ingle, E.S. Pvt., 29th North Carolina Infantry. Co. C. Federal Rolls of Prisoners of War: Captured at Spanish Fort, AL, on 4/8/1865; Received at Ship Island, MS, on 4/10/1865. Transferred to Vicksburg, MS, for exchange on 5/1/1865; Exchanged at Camp Townsend, MS, on 5/6/1865.

Ingle, J.S. Pvt., 29th North Carolina Infantry. Co. A. Enlisted: 10/1862 for the duration of the war. Age at enlistment: 16. Federal Rolls of Prisoners of War: Captured at Spanish Fort, AL, on 4/8/1865 while wounded; Received at Ship Island, MS, on 4/10/1865. Transferred to Vicksburg, MS, for exchange on 5/1/1865; Exchanged at Camp Townsend, MS, on 5/6/1865.

Johnson, A.L. Pvt., 29th North Carolina Infantry. Co. B. Federal Rolls of Prisoners of War: Captured at Spanish Fort, AL, on 4/8/1865; Received at Ship Island, MS, on 4/10/1865. Transferred to Vicksburg, MS, for exchange on 5/1/1865; Exchanged at Camp Townsend, MS, on 5/6/1865.

Jones, Eli H. Pvt., 39th North Carolina Infantry. Co. D. Enlisted: 5/1/1863 at Buncombe County, NC, for the duration of the war. Age at enlistment: 20. Rolls for 5/1863 through 6/1863: Present. Rolls for 9/1863 through 10/1863: Present. Rolls for 1/1864 through 2/1864: Present. Federal Rolls of Prisoners of War: Captured at Spanish Fort, AL, on 4/8/1865; Received at Ship Island, MS, on 4/10/1865. Transferred to Vicksburg, MS, for exchange on 5/1/1865; Exchanged at Camp Townsend, MS, on 5/6/1865.

Jones, Hiram Pvt., 29th North Carolina Infantry. Co. G. Enlisted: 5/1/1862 for the duration of the war. Age at enlistment: 26. Federal Rolls of Prisoners of War: Captured at Spanish Fort, AL, on 4/8/1865; Received at Ship Island, MS, on 4/10/1865. Transferred to Vicksburg, MS, for exchange on 5/1/1865; Exchanged at Camp Townsend, MS, on 5/6/1865.

Jones, J.J. Pvt., 39th North Carolina Infantry. Co. B. Enlisted: 9/1/1862 at Macon County, NC, for the duration of the war. Age at enlistment: 24. Rolls for 11/1862 through 2/1863: Present. Rolls for 1/1863 through 4/1863: Absent, detailed as Teamster. Rolls for 5/1863 through 6/1863: Present. Rolls for 9/1863 through 10/1863: Present, wounded at Chickamauga, GA, on 9/20/1863. Rolls for 1/1864 through 2/1864: Absent, on detached service. Wounded in right knee near Atlanta, GA, in 7/1864. Federal Rolls of Prisoners of War: Captured at Spanish Fort, AL, on 4/8/1865; Received at Ship Island, MS, on 4/10/1865. Transferred to Vicksburg, MS, for exchange on 5/1/1865; Exchanged at Camp Townsend, MS, on 5/6/1865. Confederate Pension Application on file at the North Carolina State Archives. Target Name: Jones, J.J.

Jones, James Wesley Pvt./Cpl./Sgt., 39th North Carolina Infantry. Co. H. Enlisted: 2/25/1862 at Buncombe County, NC. Age at enlistment: 24. Rolls for 3/1862 through 4/1862: Present. Rolls for 11/1862 through 12/1862: Present. Rolls for 1/1863 through 6/1863: Present, promoted to Cpl. Promoted to Sgt. on 10/1/1863. Rolls for 1/1864 through 2/1864: Absent, on furlough. Federal Rolls of Prisoners of War: Captured at Spanish Fort, AL, on 4/8/1865; Received at Ship Island, MS, on 4/10/1865. Transferred to Vicksburg, MS, for exchange on 5/1/1865; Exchanged at Camp Townsend, MS, on 5/6/1865.

Jones, John Sgt., 39th North Carolina Infantry. Co. D. Federal Rolls of Prisoners of War: Captured at Spanish Fort, AL, on 4/8/1865; Received at Ship Island, MS, on 4/10/1865. Transferred to Vicksburg, MS, for exchange on 5/1/1865; Exchanged at Camp Townsend, MS, on 5/6/1865.

Jones, R.P. Pvt., 39th North Carolina Infantry. Co. D. Enlisted: 3/11/1864 for the duration of the war. Age at enlistment: 20. Wounded at Spanish Fort, AL, on 2/20/1865. Federal Rolls of Prisoners of War: Captured at Spanish Fort, AL, on 4/8/1865; Received at Ship Island, MS, on 4/10/1865. Transferred to Vicksburg, MS, for exchange on 5/1/1865; Exchanged at Camp Townsend, MS, on 5/6/1865. Confederate Pension Application on file at the North Carolina State Archives. Target name: Jones, R.P.

Jones, Stephen A. Pvt., 39th North Carolina Infantry. Co. D. Enlisted: 2/25/1862 at Buncombe County, NC. Age at enlistment: 22. Rolls for 2/1862 through 4/1862: Present. Rolls for 11/1862 through 6/1863: Present. Rolls for 9/1863 through 10/1863: Present, under arrest. Rolls for 1/1864 through 2/1864: Present. Federal Rolls of Prisoners of War: Captured at Spanish Fort, AL, on 4/8/1865; Received at Ship Island, MS, on 4/10/1865. Transferred to Vicksburg, MS, for exchange on 5/1/1865; Exchanged at Camp Townsend, MS, on 5/6/1865.

Kinsey, Elisha L. Pvt., 39th North Carolina Infantry. Co. B. Enlisted: 10/19/1861 at Macon County, NC. Age at enlistment: 27. Rolls for 2/1862 through 4/1862: Present. Rolls for 11/1862 through 2/1863: Present. Rolls for 4/1863 through 2/1864: Absent, detailed as Teamster. Wounded in right shoulder at Allatoona, GA, on 10/5/1864. Federal Rolls of Prisoners of War: Captured at Spanish Fort, AL, on 4/8/1865; Received at Ship Island, MS, on 4/10/1865. Transferred to Vicksburg, MS, for exchange on 5/1/1865; Exchanged at Camp Townsend, MS, on 5/6/1865.

Lance, A.H. Pvt., 39th North Carolina Infantry. Co. D. Federal Rolls of Prisoners of War: Captured at Spanish Fort, AL, on 4/8/1865; Received at Ship Island, MS, on 4/10/1865. Transferred to Vicksburg, MS, for exchange on 5/1/1865; Exchanged at Camp Townsend, MS, on 5/6/1865.

Lance, James M. Pvt., 39th North Carolina Infantry. Co. H. Enlisted: 10/28/1861 at Buncombe County, NC. Age at enlistment: 18. Rolls for 2/1862 through 4/1862: Present. Rolls for 11/1862 through 6/1863: Present. Rolls for 9/1863 through 10/1863: Present, under arrest. Rolls for 1/1864 through 2/1864: Present. Federal Rolls of Prisoners of War: Captured at Spanish Fort, AL, on 4/8/1865; Received at Ship Island, MS, on 4/10/1865. Transferred to Vicksburg, MS, for exchange on 5/1/1865; Exchanged at Camp Townsend, MS, on 5/6/1865.

Lanning, James Riley Pvt./Color Bearer, 29th North Carolina Infantry. Co. C. Enlisted: 1/27/1862. Participated in the battles of Big Bethel, Murfreesboro, Chickamauga, Latimer Hill, Allatoona and Nashville. Federal Rolls of Prisoners of War: Captured at Spanish Fort, AL, on 4/8/1865; Received'at Ship Island, MS, on 4/10/1865. Transferred to Vicksburg, MS, for exchange on 5/1/1865; Exchanged at Camp Townsend, MS, on 5/6/1865. On Register of U.S.A. General Hospital # 1, Vicksburg, MS: Admitted on 5/3/1865 due to chronic diarrhea. Wounded in hand at Latimer Hill, GA, while carrying the regimental flag. Named to the Confederate Roll of Honor for his actions at the Battle of Murfreesboro, TN. Soldier also served as a Pvt. with the 1st North Carolina Infantry. Co.E. Married: Atlanta McFalls. Occupation after war: Farmer. Children: 11. Residence after war: Asheville, NC, area.

Lowe, Andrew P. (AKA Law) Pvt., 39th North Carolina Infantry. Co. B. Enlisted: 10/19/1861 at Macon County, NC. Age at enlistment: 19. Rolls for 1/1862 through 4/1862: Present. Wounded in the back at Murfreesboro, TN, on 12/31/1862. Rolls for 3/1863 through 6/1863: Present. Rolls for 9/1863 through 10/1863: Present. Rolls for 1/1864 through 2/1864: Present. Federal Rolls of Prisoners of War: Captured at Spanish Fort, AL, on 4/8/1865; Received at Ship Island, MS, on 4/10/1865. Transferred to Vicksburg, MS, for exchange on 5/1/1865; Exchanged at Camp Townsend, MS, on 5/6/1865.

McCorkle, M.G. Pvt., 39th North Carolina Infantry. Co. A. Enlisted: Mallett's North Carolina Battalion Infantry. Co. B; Transferred to the 39th North Carolina Infantry. Co. A on 6/6/1864. Federal Rolls of Prisoners of War: Captured at Spanish Fort, AL, on 4/8/1865; Received at Ship Island, MS, on 4/10/1865. Transferred to Vicksburg, MS, for exchange on 5/1/1865; Exchanged at Camp Townsend, MS, on 5/6/1865.

McCracken, W.L. Pvt., 29th North Carolina Infantry. Co. E. Federal Rolls of Prisoners of War: Captured at Spanish Fort, AL, on 4/8/1865; Received at Ship Island, MS, on 4/10/1865. Transferred to Vicksburg, MS, for exchange on 5/1/1865; Exchanged at Camp Townsend, MS, on 5/6/1865.

McDaniel, S.L. Pvt., 29th North Carolina Infantry. Co. E. Federal Rolls of Prisoners of War: Captured at Spanish Fort, AL, on 4/8/1865; Received at Ship Island, MS, on 4/10/1865. Transferred to Vicksburg, MS, for exchange on 5/1/1865; Exchanged at Camp Townsend, MS, on 5/6/1865.

McGrient, A.J. (AKA McGwier) Pvt., 39th North Carolina Infantry. Co. A. Federal Rolls of Prisoners of War: Captured at Spanish Fort, AL, on 4/8/1865; Received at Ship Island, MS, on 4/10/1865. Transferred to Vicksburg, MS, for exchange on 5/1/1865; Exchanged at Camp Townsend, MS, on 5/6/1865.

McIntyre, J. (AKA McIntire) Pvt., 29th North Carolina Infantry. Co. B. Federal Rolls of Prisoners of War: Captured at Spanish Fort, AL, on 4/8/1865; Received at Ship Island, MS, on 4/10/1865. Transferred to Vicksburg, MS, for exchange on 5/1/1865; Exchanged at Camp Townsend, MS, on 5/6/1865.

McMahon, Jackson (AKA McMahan) Pvt., 29th North Carolina Infantry. Co. B. Enlisted: 7/3/1861. Age at enlistment: 19. Residence at enlistment: Yancey County, NC. Federal Rolls of Prisoners of War: Captured at Spanish Fort, AL, on 4/8/1865; Received at Ship Island, MS, on 4/10/1865. Transferred to Vicksburg, MS, for exchange on 5/1/1865; Exchanged at Camp Townsend, MS, on 5/6/1865.

Marcay, John Asst. Surg., 39th North Carolina Infantry. F & S. Federal Rolls of Prisoners of War: Captured at Spanish Fort, AL, on 4/8/1865; Received at Ship Island, MS, on 4/10/1865. Transferred to Vicksburg, MS, for exchange on 4/28/1865; Exchanged at Camp Townsend, MS, on 5/6/1865.

Mars, G.L. Pvt., 39th North Carolina Infantry. Co. A. Federal Rolls of Prisoners of War: Captured at Spanish Fort, AL, on 4/8/1865; Received at Ship Island, MS, on 4/10/1865. Transferred to Vicksburg, MS, for exchange on 5/1/1865; Exchanged at Camp Townsend, MS, on 5/6/1865.

Marshall, William Pvt., 29th North Carolina Infantry. Co. H. Enlisted: 10/8/1863 at Camp Vance, NC, for the duration of the war. Federal Rolls of Prisoners of War: Captured at Spanish Fort, AL, on 4/8/1865; Received at Ship Island, MS, on 4/10/1865. Transferred to Vicksburg, MS, for exchange on 5/1/1865; Exchanged at Camp Townsend, MS, on 5/6/1865.

Martin, James Pvt., 29th North Carolina Infantry. Co. F. Federal Rolls of Prisoners of War: Captured at Spanish Fort, AL, on 4/8/1865; Received at Ship Island, MS, on 4/10/1865. Transferred to Vicksburg, MS, for exchange on 5/1/1865; Exchanged at Camp Townsend, MS, on 5/6/1865.

Martin, W.A. Sgt., 29th North Carolina Infantry. Co. F. Federal Rolls of Prisoners of War: Captured at Spanish Fort, AL, on 4/8/1865; Received at Ship

Island, MS, on 4/10/1865. Transferred to Vicksburg, MS, for exchange on 5/1/1865; Exchanged at Camp Townsend, MS, on 5/6/1865.

Mason, W.C. Pvt., 39th North Carolina Infantry. Co. B. Enlisted: 4/1864 for the duration of the war. Age at enlistment: 17. Wounded at Spanish Fort, AL, in 3/1865. Federal Rolls of Prisoners of War: Captured at Spanish Fort, AL, on 4/8/1865; Received at Ship Island, MS, on 4/10/1865. Transferred to Vicksburg, MS, for exchange on 5/1/1865; Exchanged at Camp Townsend, MS, on 5/6/1865. Confederate Pension Application on file at the North Carolina State Archives. Target Name: Mason, W.C.

Mathew, E.R. (AKA Matthews, E.K.) Pvt., 29th North Carolina Infantry. Co. D. Residence at enlistment: Buncombe County, NC. Federal Rolls of Prisoners of War: Captured at Spanish Fort, AL, on 4/8/1865; Received at Ship Island, MS, on 4/10/1865. Transferred to Vicksburg, MS, for exchange on 5/1/1865; Exchanged at Camp Townsend, MS, on 5/6/1865.

Messer, Lawson Pvt., 29th North Carolina Infantry. Co. E. Federal Rolls of Prisoners of War: Captured at Spanish Fort, AL, on 4/8/1865; Received at Ship Island, MS, on 4/10/1865. Transferred to Vicksburg, MS, for exchange on 5/1/1865; Exchanged at Camp Townsend, MS, on 5/6/1865. Confederate Pension Application on file at the North Carolina State Archives. Target Name: Messer, Lawson.

Mintz, John M. (AKA Mince) Pvt., 29th Carolina Infantry. Co. H. Federal Rolls of Prisoners of War: Captured at Spanish Fort, AL, on 4/8/1865; Received at Ship Island, MS, on 4/10/1865. Transferred to Vicksburg, MS, for exchange on 5/1/1865; Exchanged at Camp Townsend, MS, on 5/6/1865.

Mintz, John Zebedee (AKA Mince, J.Y.) Pvt., 29th North Carolina Infantry. Co. H. Federal Rolls of Prisoners of War: Captured at Spanish Fort, AL, on 4/8/1865; Received at Ship Island, MS, on 4/10/1865. Transferred to Vicksburg, MS, for exchange on 5/1/1865; Exchanged at Camp Townsend, MS, on 5/6/1865. Born: 2/12/1842. Died: 2/23/1931. Buried: Leanna Cemetery located at Neosho County, KS.

Moore, T.F. Pvt., 29th North Carolina Infantry. Co. A. Federal Rolls of Prisoners of War: Captured at Spanish Fort, AL, on 4/8/1865; Received at Ship Island, MS, on 4/10/1865. Transferred to Vicksburg, MS, for exchange on 5/1/1865; Exchanged at Camp Townsend, MS, on 5/6/1865. Soldier also served as a Pvt. with Mallett's North Carolina Infantry Battalion. Co.D.

Morgan, J.W. Pvt./Sgt., 39th North Carolina Infantry. Co. B. Enlisted: 10/19/1861 at Macon County, NC. Age at enlistment: 19. Federal Rolls of Prisoners of War: Captured at Spanish Fort, AL, on 4/8/1865; Received at Ship Island, MS, on 4/10/1865. Transferred to Vicksburg, MS, for exchange on 5/1/1865; Exchanged at Camp Townsend, MS, on 5/6/1865.

Murray, James F. Pvt., 29th North Carolina Infantry. Co. E. Federal Rolls of Prisoners of War: Captured at Spanish Fort, AL, on 4/8/1865; Received at Ship Island, MS, on 4/10/1865. Transferred to Vicksburg, MS, for exchange on 5/1/1865; Exchanged at Camp Townsend, MS, on 5/6/1865.

Norman, S.S. Pvt., 39th North Carolina Infantry. Co. H. Federal Rolls of Prisoners of War: Captured at Spanish Fort, AL, on 4/8/1865; Received at Ship Island, MS, on 4/10/1865. Transferred to Vicksburg, MS, for exchange on 5/1/1865; Exchanged at Camp Townsend, MS, on 5/6/1865.

Padgett, James H. (AKA Padget) Pvt., 29th North Carolina Infantry. Co. H. Enlisted: 9/11/1861. Age at enlistment: 25. Residence at enlistment: Buncombe County, NC. Federal Rolls of Prisoners of War: Captured at Spanish Fort, AL, on 4/8/1865; Received at Ship Island, MS, on 4/10/1865. Transferred to Vicksburg, MS, for exchange on 5/1/1865; Exchanged at Camp Townsend, MS, on 5/6/1865.

Parker, Silas Pvt., 29th North Carolina Infantry. Co. K. Enlisted: 9/16/1861. Age at enlistment: 18. Residence at enlistment: Yancey County, NC. Deserted on 9/24/1863; Returned to duty. Federal Rolls of Prisoners of War: Captured at Spanish Fort, AL, on 4/8/1865; Received at Ship Island, MS, on 4/10/1865. Transferred to Vicksburg, MS, for exchange on 5/1/1865; Exchanged at Camp Townsend, MS, on 5/6/1865.

Payne, Hazel Pvt., 39th North Carolina Infantry. Co. C. Federal Rolls of Prisoners of War: Captured at Spanish Fort, AL, on 4/8/1865; Received at Ship Island, MS, on 4/10/1865. Transferred to Vicksburg, MS, for exchange on 5/1/1865; Exchanged at Camp Townsend, MS, on 5/6/1865.

Penland, Noble Z. Cpl./2nd Lt., 29th North Carolina Infantry. Co. K. Federal Rolls of Prisoners of War: Captured at Spanish Fort, AL, on 4/8/1865; Received at Ship Island, MS, on 4/10/1865. Transferred to Vicksburg, MS, for exchange on 4/28/1865; Confined at New Orleans, LA, on 4/30/1865. Exchanged at Camp Townsend, MS, on 5/6/1865.

Pettigrew, G.W. Pvt., 29th North Carolina Infantry. Co. A. Enlisted: 11/1/1862 for the duration of the war. Residence at enlistment: Alamance County, NC. Federal Rolls of Prisoners of War: Captured at Spanish Fort, AL, on 4/8/1865; Received at Ship Island, MS, on 4/10/1865. Transferred to Vicksburg, MS, for exchange on 5/1/1865; Exchanged at Camp Townsend, MS, on 5/6/1865.

Phillips, A.E. Pvt., 29th North Carolina Infantry. Co. B. Federal Rolls of Prisoners of War: Captured at Spanish Fort, AL, on 4/8/1865; Received at Ship Island, MS, on 4/10/1865. Transferred to Vicksburg, MS, for exchange on 5/1/1865; Exchanged at Camp Townsend, MS, on 5/6/1865.

Potts, J.S. Pvt., 39th North Carolina Infantry. Co. B. Federal Rolls of Prisoners of War: Captured at Spanish Fort, AL, on 4/8/1865; Received at Ship Island, MS, on 4/10/1865. Transferred to Vicksburg, MS, for exchange on 5/1/1865; Exchanged at Camp Townsend, MS, on 5/6/1865.

Randolph, J. Pvt., 29th North Carolina Infantry. Co. A. Federal Rolls of Prisoners of War: Captured at Spanish Fort, AL, on 4/8/1865; Received at Ship Island, MS, on 4/10/1865. Transferred to Vicksburg, MS, for exchange on 5/1/1865; Exchanged at Camp Townsend, MS, on 5/6/1865.

Reed, Joseph M. (AKA Reid) Pvt./Sgt., 39th North Carolina Infantry. Co. C. Enlisted: 3/25/1862 at Macon County, NC. Age at enlistment: 26. Rolls for 3/25/1862 through 4/1862: Present. Rolls for 11/1862 through 6/1863: Present, promoted to Sgt. on 11/20/1862. Rolls for 9/1863 through 10/1863: Present. Rolls for 1/1864 through 2/1864: Present. Federal Rolls of Prisoners of War: Captured at Spanish Fort, AL, on 4/8/1865; Received at Ship Island, MS, on 4/10/1865. Transferred to Vicksburg, MS, for exchange on 5/1/1865; Exchanged at Camp Townsend, MS, on 5/6/1865.

Rhoades, David (AKA Rhodes) Pvt., 29th North Carolina Infantry. Co. H. Federal Rolls of Prisoners of War: Captured at Spanish Fort, AL, on 4/8/1865; Received at Ship Island, MS, on 4/10/1865. Transferred to Vicksburg, MS, for exchange on 5/1/1865; Exchanged at Camp Townsend, MS, on 5/6/1865.

Rhodes, Thomas Wilburn Cpl./Pvt., 39th North Carolina Infantry. Co. B. Enlisted: 10/19/1861 at Macon County, NC, for 12 months. Age at enlistment: 16. Rolls for 2/1862 through 4/1862: Present, reduced from Cpl. to Pvt. Discharged on 11/10/1862 but re-enlisted. Federal Rolls of Prisoners of War: Captured at Spanish Fort, AL, on 4/8/1865; Received at Ship Island, MS, on 4/10/1865. Transferred to Vicksburg, MS, for exchange on 5/1/1865; Exchanged at Camp Townsend, MS, on 5/6/1865. Born: 12/27/1845 at Haywood, NC, to Milton Rhodes and Mary Norris. Married: Twice — Margaret M. Carpenter on 6/20/1865 and Mary Ann Telitha Carpenter. Died: 4/27/1936 at Macon County, NC.

Robertson, M. Pvt., 29th North Carolina Infantry. Co. B. Federal Rolls of Prisoners of War: Captured at Spanish Fort, AL, on 4/8/1865; Received at Ship Island, MS, on 4/10/1865. Transferred to Vicksburg, MS, for exchange on 5/1/1865; Exchanged at Camp Townsend, MS, on 5/6/1865. Confederate Pension Application on file at the North Carolina State Archives. Target Name: Robertson, M.

Roland, G.M. (AKA Rolnet) Pvt., 39th North Carolina Infantry. Co. E. Federal Rolls of Prisoners of War: Captured at Spanish Fort, AL, on 4/8/1865; Received at Ship Island, MS, on 4/10/1865. Transferred to Vicksburg, MS, for exchange on 5/1/1865; Exchanged at Camp Townsend, MS, on 5/6/1865.

Rone, S.M. Pvt., 39th North Carolina Infantry. Co. A. Federal Rolls of Prisoners of War: Captured at Spanish Fort, AL, on 4/8/1865; Received at Ship Island, MS, on 4/10/1865. Transferred to Vicksburg, MS, for exchange on 5/1/1865; Exchanged at Camp Townsend, MS, on 5/6/1865.

Russell, John M. Pvt., 39th North Carolina Infantry. Cos. B & I. Federal Rolls of Prisoners of War: Captured at Spanish Fort, AL, on 4/8/1865; Received at Ship Island, MS, on 4/10/1865. Transferred to Vicksburg, MS, for exchange on 5/1/1865; Exchanged at Camp Townsend, MS, on 5/6/1865.

Sanders, J.L. Pvt., 39th North Carolina Infantry. Co. B. Federal Rolls of Prisoners of War: Captured at Spanish Fort, AL, on 4/8/1865; Received at Ship Island, MS, on 4/10/1865. Transferred to Vicksburg, MS, for exchange on 5/1/1865; Exchanged at Camp Townsend, MS, on 5/6/1865.

Scott, Thomas J. Pvt./Sgt., 29th North Carolina Infantry. Co. D. Federal Rolls of Prisoners of War: Captured at Spanish Fort, AL, on 4/8/1865; Received at Ship Island, MS, on 4/10/1865. Transferred to Vicksburg, MS, for exchange on 5/1/1865; Exchanged at Camp Townsend, MS, on 5/6/1865.

Shuler, J.M. (AKA Sheeler) Pvt., 29th North Carolina Infantry. Co. F. Enlisted: 9/1/1864 for the duration of the war. Age at enlistment: 17. Residence at enlistment: Jackson County, NC. Federal Rolls of Prisoners of War: Captured at Spanish Fort, AL, on 4/8/1865; Received at Ship Island, MS, on 4/10/1865. Transferred to Vicksburg, MS, for exchange on 5/1/1865; Exchanged at Camp Townsend, MS, on 5/6/1865. Rolls of Prisoners of War, C.S.A: Surrendered at Citronelle, AL, on 5/4/1865; Paroled at Meridian, MS, on 5/11/1865.

Silvers, Thomas B. (AKA Silver, T.D.) Pvt., 29th North Carolina Infantry. Co. B. Enlisted: 7/3/1861. Age at enlistment: 17. Residence at enlistment: Yancey County, NC. Wounded in left shoulder at Murfreesboro, TN, on 12/31/1862. Federal Rolls of Prisoners of War: Captured at Spanish Fort, AL, on 4/8/1865; Received at Ship Island, MS, on 4/10/1865. Transferred to Vicksburg, MS, for exchange on 5/1/1865; Exchanged at Camp Townsend, MS, on 5/6/1865.

Sluder, William (AKA Swider) Pvt., 29th North Carolina Infantry. Co. C. Federal Rolls of Prisoners of War: Captured at Spanish Fort, AL, on 4/8/1865; Received at Ship Island, MS, on 4/10/1865. Transferred to Vicksburg, MS, for exchange on 5/1/1865; Exchanged at Camp Townsend, MS, on 5/6/1865.

Smith, John A. Pvt., 29th North Carolina Infantry. Co. D. Residence at enlistment: Madison County, NC. Federal Rolls of Prisoners of War: Captured at Spanish Fort, AL, on 4/8/1865; Received at Ship Island, MS, on 4/10/1865. Transferred to Vicksburg, MS, for exchange on 5/1/1865; Exchanged at Camp Townsend, MS, on 5/6/1865.

Sorrells, David S. Pvt./Cpl., 39th North Carolina Infantry. Co. I. Enlisted: 3/25/1862 at Macon County, NC. Age at enlistment: 17. Rolls for 3/25/1862 through 4/1862: Present. Rolls for 11/1862 through 6/1863: Present, promoted to Cpl. on 4/1/1863. Rolls for 9/1863 through 10/1863: Present. Rolls for 1/1864 through 4/1864: Present. Federal Rolls of Prisoners of War: Captured at Spanish Fort, AL, on 4/8/1865; Received at Ship Island, MS, on 4/10/1865. Transferred to Vicksburg, MS, for exchange on 5/1/1865; Exchanged at Camp Townsend, MS, on 5/6/1865.

Spirey, Benjamin F. Pvt., 29th North Carolina Infantry. Co. C. Enlisted: 5/1/1863 for the duration of the war. Age at enlistment: 37. Residence at enlistment: Buncombe County, NC. Federal Rolls of Prisoners of War: Captured at Spanish Fort, AL, on 4/8/1865; Received at Ship Island, MS, on 4/10/1865. Transferred to Vicksburg, MS, for exchange on 5/1/1865; Exchanged at Camp Townsend, MS, on 5/6/1865.

Starnes, W.L. Pvt., 39th North Carolina Infantry. Co. A. Enlisted: Mallett's North Carolina Battalion Infantry. Co. B; Transferred to the 39th North Carolina Infantry. Co. A on 6/6/1864. Federal Rolls of Prisoners of War: Captured at Spanish Fort, AL, on 4/8/1865; Received at Ship Island, MS, on 4/10/1865. Transferred to Vicksburg, MS, for exchange on 5/1/1865; Exchanged at Camp Townsend, MS, on 5/6/1865.

Stepleton, S.B. Pvt., 29th North Carolina Infantry. Co. F. Federal Rolls of Prisoners of War: Captured at Spanish Fort, AL, on 4/8/1865; Received at Ship Island, MS, on 4/10/1865. Transferred to Vicksburg, MS, for exchange on 5/1/1865; Exchanged at Camp Townsend, MS, on 5/6/1865.

Steppe, Henry Pvt., 39th North Carolina Infantry. Co. D. Enlisted: 11/16/1861 at Buncombe County, NC.

Age at enlistment: 19. Residence at enlistment: Henderson County, NC. Deserted at Lenoir Station, TN, on 11/25/1862; Returned to duty. Federal Rolls of Prisoners of War: Captured at Spanish Fort, AL, on 4/8/1865; Received at Ship Island, MS, on 4/10/1865. Transferred to Vicksburg, MS, for exchange on 5/1/1865; Exchanged at Camp Townsend, MS, on 5/6/1865.

Stroup, John M. (AKA Strop) Pvt., 29th North Carolina Infantry. Cos. G & H. Enlisted: 9/11/1861. Age at enlistment: 17. Residence at enlistment: Buncombe County, NC. Wounded in foot at Murfreesboro, TN, on 12/31/1862. Transferred to the 14th North Carolina Battalion Cavalry on 6/6/1864; Transferred back to the 29th North Carolina Infantry on 9/20/1864. Federal Rolls of Prisoners of War: Captured at Spanish Fort, AL, on 4/8/1865; Received at Ship Island, MS, on 4/10/1865. Transferred to Vicksburg, MS, for exchange on 5/1/1865; Exchanged at Camp Townsend, MS, on 5/6/1865.

Sumter, John Pvt., 39th North Carolina Infantry. Co. F. Federal Rolls of Prisoners of War: Captured at Spanish Fort, AL, on 4/8/1865; Received at Ship Island, MS, on 4/10/1865. Transferred to Vicksburg, MS, for exchange on 5/1/1865; Exchanged at Camp Townsend, MS, on 5/6/1865.

Sumter, Lee Pvt./Sgt., 39th North Carolina Infantry. Cos. A & F. Federal Rolls of Prisoners of War: Captured at Spanish Fort, AL, on 4/8/1865; Received at Ship Island, MS, on 4/10/1865. Transferred to Vicksburg, MS, for exchange on 5/1/1865; Exchanged at Camp Townsend, MS, on 5/6/1865.

Suthards, W.G. Pvt., 39th North Carolina Infantry. Co. B. Federal Rolls of Prisoners of War: Captured at Spanish Fort, AL, on 4/8/1865; Received at Ship Island, MS, on 4/10/1865. Transferred to Vicksburg, MS, for exchange on 5/1/1865; Exchanged at Camp Townsend, MS, on 5/6/1865.

Tathum, Thomas N. (AKA Tatham) Pvt., 39th North Carolina Infantry. Co. K. Enlisted: Thomas' Legion. Co. A; Transferred to the 39th North Carolina Infantry. Co. K in 11/1862. Rolls for 1/1863 through 6/1863: Present. Rolls for 9/1863 through 10/1863: Present, seriously wounded in the face and blinded in one eye at Kennesaw Mountain, GA, on 6/18/1864. Federal Rolls of Prisoners of War: Captured at Spanish Fort, AL, on 4/8/1865; Received at Ship Island, MS, on 4/10/1865. Transferred to Vicksburg, MS, for exchange on 5/1/1865; Exchanged at Camp Townsend, MS, on 5/6/1865. Confederate Pension Application on file at the North Carolina State Archives. Target Name: Tatham, Thomas N.

Truett, Silas M. Cpl./Pvt./2nd Lt./1st Lt., 39th North Carolina Infantry. Co. I. Enlisted: Thomas' Legion. Co. A as a Cpl.; Transferred to the 39th North Carolina Infantry. Co. I in 11/1862 as a Pvt. Elected 2nd Lt. on 8/13/1863 and 1st Lt. on 10/31/1863. Federal Rolls of Prisoners of War: Captured at Spanish Fort, AL, on 4/8/1865; Received at Ship Island, MS, on 4/10/1865. Transferred to Vicksburg, MS, for exchange on 4/28/1865; Confined at New Orleans, LA, on 4/30/1865. Exchanged at Camp Townsend, MS, on 5/6/1865.

Umphis, James Pvt., 39th North Carolina Infantry. Co. G. Federal Rolls of Prisoners of War: Captured at Spanish Fort, AL, on 4/8/1865; Received at Ship Island, MS, on 4/10/1865. Transferred to Vicksburg, MS, for exchange on 5/1/1865; Exchanged at Camp Townsend, MS, on 5/6/1865.

Vanhook, William T. Pvt., 39th North Carolina Infantry. Co. B. Federal Rolls of Prisoners of War: Captured at Spanish Fort, AL, on 4/8/1865; Received at Ship Island, MS, on 4/10/1865. Transferred to Vicksburg, MS, for exchange on 5/1/1865; Exchanged at Camp Townsend, MS, on 5/6/1865.

Varner, W.A Pvt., 29th North Carolina Infantry. Co. D. Federal Rolls of Prisoners of War: Captured at Spanish Fort, AL, on 4/8/1865; Received at Ship Island, MS, on 4/10/1865. Transferred to Vicksburg, MS, for exchange on 5/1/1865; Exchanged at Camp Townsend, MS, on 5/6/1865.

Warlick, David M. (AKA Warlock) Pvt., 39th North Carolina Infantry. Co. A. Enlisted: 12/16/1861 at Cherokee County, NC. Age at enlistment: 20. Residence at enlistment: Buncombe County, NC. Rolls for 2/1862 through 4/1862: Present. Rolls for 11/1862 through 2/1863: Present. Rolls for 3/1863 through 6/1863: Absent, in hospital at Rome, GA. Rolls for 9/1863 through 10/1863: Present. Federal Rolls of Prisoners of War: Captured at Spanish Fort, AL, on 4/8/1865; Received at Ship Island, MS, on 4/10/1865. Transferred to Vicksburg, MS, for exchange on 5/1/1865; Exchanged at Camp Townsend, MS, on 5/6/1865.

Warlick, Manuel A. (AKA Warnick, Worleck, Mamiel) Pvt., 39th North Carolina Infantry. Co. A. Enlisted: 12/1863 for the duration of the war. Age at enlistment: 18. Wounded in the chest at Resaca, GA, in 5/1864. Federal Rolls of Prisoners of War: Captured at Spanish Fort, AL, on 4/8/1865; Received at Ship Island, MS, on 4/10/1865. Transferred to Vicksburg, MS, for exchange on 5/1/1865; Exchanged at Camp Townsend, MS, on 5/6/1865. Confederate Pension Application on file at the North Carolina State Archives. Target Name: Warlick, Manuel A.

Watts, William A. Pvt./Sgt., 39th North Carolina Infantry. Co. C. Federal Rolls of Prisoners of War: Captured at Spanish Fort, AL, on 4/8/1865; Received at Ship Island, MS, on 4/10/1865. Transferred to Vicksburg, MS, for exchange on 5/1/1865; Exchanged at Camp Townsend, MS, on 5/6/1865.

Wells, Julius D. Pvt., 29th North Carolina Infantry. Co. C. Federal Rolls of Prisoners of War: Captured and paroled at Yazoo City, MS, on 7/13/1863. Federal Rolls of Prisoners of War: Captured at Spanish Fort, AL, on 4/8/1865; Received at Ship Island, MS, on 4/10/1865. Transferred to Vicksburg, MS, for exchange on 5/1/1865; Exchanged at Camp Townsend, MS, on 5/6/1865.

Wells, Julius M. Sgt., 29th North Carolina Infantry. Co. H. Federal Rolls of Prisoners of War: Captured at Spanish Fort, AL, on 4/8/1865; Received at Ship Island, MS, on 4/10/1865. Transferred to Vicksburg, MS, for exchange on 5/1/1865; Exchanged at Camp Townsend, MS, on 5/6/1865.

Whitaker, Harrison Benjamin Pvt./Sgt./2nd Lt., 39th North Carolina Infantry. Co. __. Enlisted: 3/30/1862 at Cherokee County, NC. Age at enlistment: 22. Residence at enlistment: Cherokee County, NC. Rolls for 3/1862 through 5/1862: Present, promoted to Sgt. on 5/19/1862. Rolls for 1/1863 through 2/1863: Absent, sick at hospital in Atlanta, GA, since 1/22/1863. Rolls for 3/1863 through 8/1863: Present, promoted to Sgt. on 8/31/1863. Elected 2nd Lt. in 1/1864. Federal Rolls of Prisoners of War: Captured at Spanish Fort, AL, on 4/8/1865; Received at Ship Island, MS, on 4/10/1865. Transferred to Vicksburg, MS, for exchange on 4/28/1865; Confined at New Orleans, LA, on 4/30/1865. Exchanged at Camp Townsend, MS, on 5/6/1865. Rolls of Prisoners of War, C.S.A: Surrendered at Citronelle, AL, on 5/4/1865; Paroled at Meridian, MS, on 5/9/1865.

Whittaker, J.L. Pvt./Sgt. Maj., 39th North Carolina Infantry. Co. C/F & S. Federal Rolls of Prisoners of War: Captured at Spanish Fort, AL, on 4/8/1865; Received at Ship Island, MS, on 4/10/1865. Transferred to Vicksburg, MS, for exchange on 5/1/1865; Exchanged at Camp Townsend, MS, on 5/6/1865.

Wild, Posey C. Pvt./1st Sgt./3rd Lt./2nd Lt., 39th North Carolina Infantry. Co. I. Enlisted: 3/25/1862 at Macon County, NC. Age at enlistment: 25. Rolls for 11/1862 through 6/1863: Present, promoted to Sgt. on 11/8/1862 and 1st Sgt. on 2/8/1863. Rolls for 9/1863 through 10/1863: Absent, on furlough; Elected 3rd Lt. on 8/10/1863. Rolls for 1/1864 through 4/1864: Present. Federal Rolls of Prisoners of War: Captured at Spanish Fort, AL, on 4/8/1865; Received at Ship Island, MS, on 4/10/1865. Transferred to Vicksburg, MS, for exchange on 4/28/1865; Confined at New Orleans, LA, on 4/30/1865. Exchanged at Camp Townsend, MS, on 5/6/1865.

Willis, Stephen Morgan Pvt., 29th North Carolina Infantry. Co. I. Enlisted: 4/10/1862 at Mitchell County, NC. Federal Rolls of Prisoners of War: Captured at Spanish Fort, AL, on 4/8/1865; Received at Ship Island, MS, on 4/10/1865. Transferred to Vicksburg, MS, for exchange on 5/1/1865; Exchanged at Camp Townsend, MS, on 5/6/1865. Born: 6/10/1849. Died: 2/28/1934.

Wilson, Madison D. Sgt., 29th North Carolina Infantry. Co. I. Enlisted: 7/11/1861. Age at enlistment: 19. Residence at enlistment: Mitchell County, NC. Deserted on 9/27/1862; Returned to duty. Wounded in knee at Nashville, TN, in 12/1864. Federal Rolls of Prisoners of War: Captured at Spanish Fort, AL, on 4/8/1865; Received at Ship Island, MS, on 4/10/1865. Transferred to Vicksburg, MS, for exchange on 5/1/1865; Exchanged at Camp Townsend, MS, on 5/6/1865. Confederate Pension Application on file at the North Carolina State Archives. Target Name: Wilson, Madison D.

Woodfin, William A. Pvt./Cpl., 39th North Carolina Infantry. Co. I. Enlisted: 3/25/1862 at Macon County, NC. Age at enlistment: 17. Rolls for 3/25/1862 through 4/1862: Present. Rolls for 9/1862 through 2/1863: Absent, without leave. Detailed for hospital duty on 4/23/1863 to extend through 10/1863. Rolls for 1/1864 through 4/1864: Present, promoted to Cpl. on 4/30/1864. Federal Rolls of Prisoners of War: Captured at Spanish Fort, AL, on 4/8/1865; Received at Ship Island, MS, on 4/10/1865. Transferred to Vicksburg, MS, for exchange on 5/1/1865; Exchanged at Camp Townsend, MS, on 5/6/1865.

South Carolina Prisoners of War

Aiken, Edward Pvt., 3rd South Carolina Light Artillery (Culpepper's). Co. C. Federal Rolls of Prisoners of War: Captured at Fort Gaines, AL, on 8/8/1864; Received at Ship Island, MS, from New Orleans, LA, on 10/25/1864. Transferred to Vicksburg, MS, for exchange on 1/4/1865; Exchanged at Camp Townsend, MS, on 5/6/1865.

Aiken, John D. (AKA Askins) 3rd South Carolina Light Artillery (Culpepper's). Co. C. Federal Rolls of Prisoners of War: Captured at Fort Gaines, AL, on 8/8/1864; Received at Ship Island, MS, from New Orleans, LA, on 10/25/1864. Transferred to Vicksburg, MS, for exchange on 1/4/1865; Exchanged at Camp Townsend, MS, on 5/6/1865

Ardis, Abraham P. (AKA Artis) Pvt., 3rd South Carolina Light Artillery (Culpepper's). Co. C. Federal Rolls of Prisoners of War: Captured at Blakely, AL, on 4/9/1865; Received at Ship Island, MS, on 4/15/1865. Transferred to Vicksburg, MS, for exchange on 5/1/1865; Exchanged at Camp Townsend, MS, on 5/6/1865.

Ardis, John W. (AKA Artis) Pvt., 3rd South Carolina Light Artillery (Culpepper's). Co. C. Federal Rolls of Prisoners of War: Captured at Blakely, AL, on 4/9/1865; Received at Ship Island, MS, on 4/15/1865. Transferred to Vicksburg, MS, for exchange on 5/1/1865; Exchanged at Camp Townsend, MS, on 5/6/1865.

Ardis, William J. (AKA Artis) Pvt., 3rd South Carolina Light Artillery (Culpepper's). Co. C. Federal Rolls of Prisoners of War: Captured at Blakely, AL, on 4/9/1865; Received at Ship Island, MS, on 4/15/1865. Transferred to Vicksburg, MS, for exchange on 5/1/1865; Exchanged at Camp Townsend, MS, on 5/6/1865.

Brown, D.W. Pvt./Bugler, 3rd South Carolina Light Artillery (Culpepper's). Co. C. Federal Rolls of Prisoners of War: Captured at Fort Gaines, AL, on 8/8/1864; Received at Ship Island, MS, from New Orleans, LA, on 10/25/1864. Exchanged on 1/4/1865.

Brown, George M. Pvt., 3rd South Carolina Light Artillery (Culpepper's). Co. C. Federal Rolls of Prisoners of War: Captured at Fort Gaines, AL, on 8/8/1864; Received at Ship Island, MS, from New Orleans, LA, on 10/29/1864. Exchanged on 1/4/1865. Confederate Pension Application dated 5/5/1919 on file at the South Carolina Department of Archives and History. Target Name: Brown, George M. Series: S126088. Item Number: 03842. Residence: Friendfield, Florence County, SC.

Chresman, J.M. Pvt., 3rd South Carolina Light Artillery (Culpepper's). Co. C. Federal Rolls of Prisoners of War: Captured at Blakely, AL, on 4/9/1865; Received at Ship Island, MS, on 4/15/1865. Transferred to Vicksburg, MS, for exchange on 5/1/1865; Exchanged at Camp Townsend, MS, on 5/6/1865.

Cohen, Arthur M. Pvt., 3rd South Carolina Light Artillery (Culpepper's). Co. C. Federal Rolls of Prisoners of War: Captured at Blakely, AL, on 4/9/1865; Received at Ship Island, MS, on 4/15/1865. Transferred to Vicksburg, MS, for exchange on 5/1/1865; Exchanged at Camp Townsend, MS, on 5/6/1865.

Cole, H.H. (AKA Hale) Pvt., 3rd South Carolina Light Artillery (Culpepper's). Co. C. Federal Rolls of Prisoners of War: Captured at Fort Gaines, AL, on 8/8/1865; Received at Ship Island, MS, from New Orleans, LA, on 10/25/1864. Exchanged on 1/4/1865.

Cook, J.C. Pvt., 3rd South Carolina Light Artillery (Culpepper's). Co. C. Federal Rolls of Prisoners of War: Captured at Blakely, AL, on 4/9/1865; Received at Ship Island, MS, on 4/15/1865. Transferred to Vicksburg, MS, for exchange on 5/1/1865; Exchanged at Camp Townsend, MS, on 5/6/1865.

Coward, James A. Sgt./1st Sgt., 3rd South Carolina Light Artillery (Culpepper's). Co. C. Federal Rolls of Prisoners of War: Captured at Fort Gaines, AL, on 8/8/1864; Received at Ship Island, MS, from New Orleans, LA, on 10/25/1864. Exchanged on 1/4/1865.

Cox, G.E.G. Pvt., 3rd South Carolina Light Artillery (Culpepper's). Co. C. Federal Rolls of Prisoners of War: Captured at Blakely, AL, on 4/9/1865; Received at Ship Island, MS, on 4/15/1865. Transferred to Vicksburg, MS, for exchange on 5/1/1865; Exchanged at Camp Townsend, MS, on 5/6/1865.

Culpepper, James F. (AKA Culpeper) Capt., 3rd South Carolina Light Artillery (Culpepper's). Co. C. Federal Rolls of Prisoners of War: Captured at Blakely, AL, on 4/9/1865; Received at Ship Island, MS, on

4/15/1865. Transferred to Vicksburg, MS, for exchange on 4/28/1865; Confined at New Orleans, LA, on 4/30/1865. Exchanged at Camp Townsend, MS, on 5/6/1865.

Davis, H.H. Pvt., 3rd South Carolina Light Artillery (Culpepper's). Co. C. Federal Rolls of Prisoners of War: Captured at Fort Gaines, AL, on 8/8/1864; Received at Ship Island, MS, from New Orleans, LA, on 10/25/1864. Exchanged on 1/4/1865.

Dean, J.F. Pvt., 3rd South Carolina Light Artillery (Culpepper's). Co. C. Federal Rolls of Prisoners of War: Captured at Blakely, AL, on 4/9/1865; Received at Ship Island, MS, on 4/15/1865. Transferred to Vicksburg, MS, for exchange on 5/1/1865; Exchanged at Camp Townsend, MS, on 5/6/1865.

Delorme, Henry B. Pvt., 3rd South Carolina Light Artillery (Culpepper's). Co. C. Federal Rolls of Prisoners of War: Captured at Blakely, AL, on 4/9/1865; Received at Ship Island, MS, on 4/15/1865. Transferred to Vicksburg, MS, on 5/1/1865; Exchanged at Camp Townsend, MS, on 5/6/1865. Soldier also served with the 1st Mississippi Cavalry.

Farmer, J.H. Pvt., 3rd South Carolina Light Artillery (Culpepper's). Co. C. Federal Rolls of Prisoners of War: Captured at Fort Gaines, AL, on 8/8/1864; Received at Ship Island, MS, from New Orleans, LA, on 10/25/1864. Exchanged on 1/4/1865.

Giddings, J.S. (AKA Geddings) Pvt., 3rd South Carolina Light Artillery (Culpepper's). Co. C. Federal Rolls of Prisoners of War: Captured at Blakely, AL, on 4/9/1865; Received at Ship Island, MS, on 4/15/1865. Transferred to Vicksburg, MS, for exchange on 5/1/1865; Exchanged at Camp Townsend, MS, on 5/6/1865.

Giddings, Job M. (AKA Geddings, M.) Pvt., 3rd South Carolina Light Artillery (Culpepper's). Co. C. Federal Rolls of Prisoners of War: Captured at Blakely, AL, on 4/9/1865; Received at Ship Island, MS, on 4/15/1865. Transferred to Vicksburg, MS, for exchange on 5/1/1865; Exchanged at Camp Townsend, MS, on 5/6/1865.

Giddings, Peter J. (AKA Geddings) Pvt., 3rd South Carolina Light Artillery (Culpepper's). Co. C. Federal Rolls of Prisoners of War: Captured at Blakely, AL, on 4/9/1865; Received at Ship Island, MS, on 4/15/1865. Transferred to Vicksburg, MS, for exchange on 5/1/1865; Exchanged at Camp Townsend, MS, on 5/6/1865.

Giddings, Thomas G.W. (AKA Geddings) Pvt., 3rd South Carolina Light Artillery (Culpepper's). Co. C. Federal Rolls of Prisoners of War: Captured at Blakely, AL, on 4/9/1865. Transferred to Vicksburg, MS, for exchange on 5/1/1865; Exchanged at Camp Townsend, MS, on 5/6/1865.

Gregg, R.L. Pvt., 3rd South Carolina Light Artillery (Culpepper's). Co. C. Federal Rolls of Prisoners of War: Captured at Blakely, AL, on 4/9/1865; Received at Ship Island, MS, on 4/15/1865. Transferred to Vicksburg, MS, for exchange on 5/1/1865; Exchanged at Camp Townsend, MS, on 5/6/1865.

Grimsley, A.P. Cpl., 3rd South Carolina Light Artillery (Culpepper's). Co. C. Federal Rolls of Prisoners of War: Captured at Blakely, AL, on 4/9/1865; Received at Ship Island, MS, on 4/15/1865. Transferred to Vicksburg, MS, for exchange on 5/1/1865; Exchanged at Camp Townsend, MS, on 5/6/1865.

Ham, H. Pvt., 3rd South Carolina Light Artillery (Culpepper's). Co. C. Federal Rolls of Prisoners of War: Captured at Blakely, AL, on 4/9/1865; Received at Ship Island, MS, on 4/15/1865. Transferred to Vicksburg, MS, for exchange on 5/1/1865; Exchanged at Camp Townsend, MS, on 5/6/1865.

Hancock, John S. (AKA S.) Pvt., 3rd South Carolina Light Artillery (Culpepper's). Co. C. Federal Rolls of Prisoners of War: Captured at Fort Gaines, AL, on 8/8/1864; Transferred to Ship Island, MS, from New Orleans, LA, on 10/25/1864. Exchanged on 1/4/1865.

Hatchell, F. Pvt., 3rd South Carolina Light Artillery (Culpepper's). Co. C. Federal Rolls of Prisoners of War: Captured at Blakely, AL, on 4/9/1865; Received at Ship Island, MS, on 4/15/1865. Transferred to Vicksburg, MS, for exchange on 5/1/1865; Exchanged at Camp Townsend, MS, on 5/6/1865.

Hatchell, J.B. Pvt., 3rd South Carolina Light Artillery (Culpepper's). Co. C. Federal Rolls of Prisoners of War: Captured at Blakely, AL, on 4/9/1865; Received at Ship Island, MS, on 4/15/1865. Transferred to Vicksburg, MS, for exchange on 5/1/1865; Exchanged at Camp Townsend, MS, on 5/6/1865.

Hatchell, R.E.T. Pvt., 3rd South Carolina Light Artillery (Culpepper's). Co. C. Federal Rolls of Prisoners of War: Captured at Blakely, AL, on 4/9/1865; Received at Ship Island, MS, on 4/15/1865. Transferred to Vicksburg, MS, for exchange on 5/1/1865; Exchanged at Camp Townsend, MS, on 5/6/1865. Confederate Widows Pension Application dated 12/18/1919 on file at the South Carolina Department of Archives and History. Target Name: Hatchell, Mary Jane. Series: S126088. Item Number: 03907. Residence: Effingham, Florence County, SC.

Hatchell, S.B. (AKA Hathell) Pvt., 3rd South Carolina Light Artillery (Culpepper's). Co. C. Federal Rolls of Prisoners of War: Captured at Fort Gaines, AL, on 8/8/1864; Received at Ship Island, MS, from New Orleans, LA, on 10/25/1864. Died: 12/5/1864 at Ship Island, MS, due to chronic dysentery. Buried: Ship Island, MS, Cemetery in Grave #65.

Hatchell, W.G. Pvt., 3rd South Carolina Light Artillery (Culpepper's). Co. C. Federal Rolls of Prisoners of War: Captured at Blakely, AL, on 4/9/1865; Received at Ship Island, MS, on 4/15/1865. Transferred to Vicksburg, MS, for exchange on 5/1/1865; Exchanged at Camp Townsend, MS, on 5/6/1865.

Hodge, Elijah J. Pvt., 3rd South Carolina Light Artillery (Culpepper's). Co. C. Federal Rolls of Prisoners of War: Captured at Blakely, AL, on 4/9/1865; Received at Ship Island, MS, on 4/15/1865. Transferred to Vicksburg, MS, for exchange on 5/1/1865; Exchanged at Camp Townsend, MS, on 5/6/1865.

Hudson, J.P. Pvt., 3rd South Carolina Light Artillery (Culpepper's). Co. C. Federal Rolls of Prisoners of War: Captured at Blakely, AL, on 4/9/1865; Received at Ship Island, MS, on 4/15/1865. Transferred to Vicksburg, MS, for exchange on 5/1/1865; Exchanged at Camp Townsend, MS, on 5/6/1865.

Hudson, John Wesley Pvt., 3rd South Carolina Light Artillery (Culpepper's). Co. C. Federal Rolls of Prisoners of War: Captured at Blakely, AL, on 4/9/1865; Received at Ship Island, MS, on 4/15/1865. Transferred to Vicksburg, MS, for exchange on 5/1/1865; Exchanged at Camp Townsend, MS, on 5/6/1865.

Born: 9/29/1836 at Darlington, SC. Died: 10/9/1924 at Camden, SC. Married: Charity McRoy. Children: 6. Religion: Methodist. Pre-war and post-war occupation: Farmer.

Humphreys, Thomas H.D. (AKA Humphries) Pvt., 3rd South Carolina Light Artillery (Culpepper's). Co. C. Federal Rolls of Prisoners of War: Captured at Blakely, AL, on 4/9/1865; Received at Ship Island, MS, on 4/15/1865. Transferred to Vicksburg, MS, for exchange on 5/1/1865; Exchanged at Camp Townsend, MS, on 5/6/1865.

James, Simon Pvt., 3rd South Carolina Light Artillery (Culpepper's). Co. C. Federal Rolls of Prisoners of War: Captured at Fort Gaines, AL, on 8/8/1864; Received at Ship Island, MS, from New Orleans, LA, on 10/25/1864. Died: 11/27/1864 at Ship Island, MS, due to dysentery. Buried: Ship Island, MS, Cemetery in Grave #44.

Jeffords, E.G. Cpl./Sgt., 3rd South Carolina Light Artillery (Culpepper's). Co. C. Federal Rolls of Prisoners of War: Captured at Blakely, AL, on 4/9/1865; Received at Ship Island, MS, on 4/15/1865. Transferred to Vicksburg, MS, for exchange on 5/1/1865; Exchanged at Camp Townsend, MS, on 5/6/1865.

Jeffords, S.K. Pvt., 3rd South Carolina Light Artillery (Culpepper's). Co. C. Federal Rolls of Prisoners of War: Captured at Blakely, AL, on 4/9/1865; Received at Ship Island, MS, on 4/15/1865. Transferred to Vicksburg, MS, for exchange on 5/1/1865; Exchanged at Camp Townsend, MS, on 5/6/1865.

Jeffords, Thomas Pvt., 3rd South Carolina Light Artillery (Culpepper's). Co. C. Federal Rolls of Prisoners of War: Captured at Blakely, AL, on 4/9/1865; Received at Ship Island, MS, on 4/15/1865. Transferred to Vicksburg, MS, for exchange on 5/1/1865; Exchanged at Camp Townsend, MS, on 5/6/1865.

Jennings, Richard Pvt., 3rd South Carolina Light Artillery (Culpepper's). Co. C. Federal Rolls of Prisoners of War: Captured at Blakely, AL, on 4/9/1865; Received at Ship Island, MS, on 4/15/1865. Transferred to Vicksburg, MS, on 5/1/1865; Exchanged at Camp Townsend, MS, on 5/6/1865. Born: 11/29/1845 at Sumter County, SC. Died: Orangeburg, SC. Married: Mary Melissa Byrd. Children: 8. Religion: Methodist. Post-war occupation: Stone Cutter. Buried: Sunnyside Cemetery located at Orangeburg, SC. Confederate Soldiers Pension Application on file dated 1901 at the South Carolina Archives. Target Name: Jennings, Richard.

Kenney, Daniel (AKA Kenny) Pvt., 3rd South Carolina Light Artillery (Culpepper's). Co. C. Federal Rolls of Prisoners of War: Captured at Blakely, AL, on 4/9/1865; Received at Ship Island, MS, on 4/15/1865. Transferred to Vicksburg, MS, for exchange on 5/1/1865; Exchanged at Camp Townsend, MS, on 5/6/1865.

Kesterson, W. Pvt., 3rd South Carolina Light Artillery (Culpepper's). Co. C. Federal Rolls of Prisoners of War: Captured at Blakely, AL, on 4/9/1865; Received at Ship Island, MS, on 4/15/1865. Transferred to Vicksburg, MS, for exchange on 5/1/1865; Exchanged at Camp Townsend, MS, on 5/6/1865.

Kiel, B. Pvt., 3rd South Carolina Light Artillery (Culpepper's). Co. C. Federal Rolls of Prisoners of War: Captured at Blakely, AL, on 4/9/1865; Received at Ship Island, MS, on 4/15/1865. Transferred to Vicksburg, MS, for exchange on 5/1/1865; Exchanged at Camp Townsend, MS, on 5/6/1865.

King, H. Pvt., 3rd South Carolina Light Artillery (Culpepper's). Co. C. Federal Rolls of Prisoners of War: Captured at Blakely, AL, on 4/9/1865; Received at Ship Island, MS, on 4/15/1865. Transferred to Vicksburg, MS, for exchange on 5/1/1865; Exchanged at Camp Townsend, MS, on 5/6/1865.

Kingrey, William Pvt., 3rd South Carolina Light Artillery (Culpepper's). Co. C. Federal Rolls of Prisoners of War: Captured at Blakely, AL, on 4/9/1865; Received at Ship Island, MS, on 4/15/1865. Transferred to Vicksburg, MS, for exchange on 5/1/1865; Exchanged at Camp Townsend, MS, on 5/6/1865.

Kirby, John M. Pvt./Cpl., 3rd South Carolina Light Artillery (Culpepper's). Co. C. Federal Rolls of Prisoners of War: Captured at Blakely, AL, on 4/9/1865; Received at Ship Island, MS, on 4/15/1865. Transferred to Vicksburg, MS, for exchange on 5/1/1865; Exchanged at Camp Townsend, MS, on 5/6/1865.

Kirby, William Isaiah (AKA W.J.) Pvt., 3rd South Carolina Light Artillery (Culpepper's). Co. C. Federal Rolls of Prisoners of War: Captured at Fort Gaines, AL, on 8/8/1864; Received at Ship Island from New Orleans, LA, on 10/25/1864. Died: 12/24/1864 at Ship Island, MS. Buried: Ship Island, MS, Cemetery. Born: 1835 in Darlington County, SC, to John Kirby and Susannah Nettles. Married: Martha Abergail Daniels in 1857.

Kirby, William Mahoney (AKA W.J.) Pvt., 3rd South Carolina Light Artillery (Culpepper's). Co. C. Federal Rolls of Prisoners of War: Captured at Fort Gaines, AL, on 8/8/1864; Received at Ship Island, MS, from New Orleans, LA, on 10/25/1864. Died: 12/24/1864 at Ship Island, MS, due to dysentery. Buried: Ship Island, MS, Cemetery in Grave #109. Confederate Widows Pension Application dated 9/23/1919 on file at the South Carolina Department of Archives and History. Target Name: Kirby, Mattie Nettles. Series: S126088. Item Number: 07484. Residence: Lynchburg, Lee County, SC.

Kyle, D.H. Pvt., 3rd South Carolina Light Artillery (Culpepper's). Co. C. Federal Rolls of Prisoners of War: Captured at Blakely, AL, on 4/9/1865; Received at Ship Island, MS, on 4/15/1865. Transferred to Vicksburg, MS, for exchange on 5/1/1865; Exchanged at Camp Townsend, MS, on 5/6/1865.

Lackey, William R. Pvt., 3rd South Carolina Light Artillery (Culpepper's). Co. C. Federal Rolls of Prisoners of War: Captured at Blakely, AL, on 4/9/1865; Received at Ship Island, MS, on 4/15/1865. Transferred to Vicksburg, MS, for exchange on 5/1/1865; Exchanged at Camp Townsend, MS, on 5/6/1865.

Langston, Robert R. Pvt./Bugler, 3rd South Carolina Light Artillery (Culpepper's). Co. C. Federal Rolls of Prisoners of War: Captured at Fort Gaines, AL, on 8/8/1864; Received at Ship Island, MS, from New Orleans, LA, on 10/25/1864. Exchanged on 1/4/1865.

Laughlin, T. (AKA S.) Pvt., 3rd South Carolina Light Artillery (Culpepper's). Co. C. Federal Rolls of Prisoners of War: Captured at Blakely, AL, on 4/9/1865; Received at Ship Island, MS, on 4/15/1865. Transferred to Vicksburg, MS, for exchange on 5/1/1865; Exchanged at Camp Townsend, MS, on 5/6/1865.

Lawrence, James P. Pvt., 3rd South Carolina Light Artillery (Culpepper's). Co. C. Federal Rolls of

Prisoners of War: Captured at Blakely, AL, on 4/9/1865; Received at Ship Island, MS, on 4/15/1865. Transferred to Vicksburg, MS, for exchange on 5/1/1865; Exchanged at Camp Townsend, MS, on 5/6/1865.

Lawrence, John A. Pvt., 3rd South Carolina Light Artillery (Culpepper's). Co. C. Federal Rolls of Prisoners of War: Captured at Fort Gaines, AL, on 8/8/1864; Received at Ship Island, MS, from New Orleans, LA, on 10/25/1864. Exchanged on 1/4/1865.

Lee, John R. Pvt./Cpl., 3rd South Carolina Light Artillery (Culpepper's). Co. C. Federal Rolls of Prisoners of War: Captured at Blakely, AL, on 4/9/1865; Received at Ship Island, MS, on 4/15/1865. Transferred to Vicksburg, MS, for exchange on 5/1/1865; Exchanged at Camp Townsend, MS, on 5/6/1865. Confederate Widows Pension Application dated 12/12/1919 on file at the South Carolina Department of Archives and History. Target Name: Lee, Frances. Series: S126088. Item Number: 03944. Residence: Lake City, Florence County, SC.

Lee, William Pvt., 3rd South Carolina Light Artillery (Culpepper's). Co. C. Federal Rolls of Prisoners of War: Captured at Blakely, AL, on 4/9/1865; Received at Ship Island, MS, on 4/15/1865. Transferred to Vicksburg, MS, for exchange on 5/1/1865; Exchanged at Camp Townsend, MS, on 5/6/1865.

Lloyd, G.F. Pvt., 3rd South Carolina Light Artillery (Culpepper's). Co. C. Federal Rolls of Prisoners of War: Captured at Blakely, AL, on 4/9/1865; Received at Ship Island, MS, on 4/15/1865. Transferred to Vicksburg, MS, for exchange on 5/1/1865; Exchanged at Camp Townsend, MS, on 5/6/1865.

Lloyd, J.W. Pvt., 3rd South Carolina Light Artillery (Culpepper's). Co. C. Federal Rolls of Prisoners of War: Captured at Blakely, AL, on 4/9/1865; Received at Ship Island, MS, on 4/15/1865. Disposition unknown.

Lloyd, William (AKA J.W.) Pvt., 3rd South Carolina Light Artillery (Culpepper's). Co. C. Federal Rolls of Prisoners of War: Captured at Blakely, AL, on 4/9/1865; Received at Ship Island, MS, on 4/15/1865. Transferred to Vicksburg, MS, for exchange on 5/1/1865; Exchanged at Camp Townsend, MS, on 5/6/1865.

McAfee, R. Pvt., 3rd South Carolina Light Artillery (Culpepper's). Co. C. Federal Rolls of Prisoners of War: Captured at Blakely, AL, on 4/9/1865; Received at Ship Island, MS, on 4/15/1865. Transferred to Vicksburg, MS, for exchange on 5/1/1865; Exchanged at Camp Townsend, MS, on 5/6/1865.

McAllister, W.J. Pvt., 3rd South Carolina Light Artillery (Culpepper's). Co. C. Federal Rolls of Prisoners of War: Captured at Blakely, AL, on 4/9/1865; Received at Ship Island, MS, on 4/15/1865. Transferred to Vicksburg, MS, for exchange on 5/1/1865; Exchanged at Camp Townsend, MS, on 5/6/1865.

McCord, S.B. Cpl., 3rd South Carolina Light Artillery (Culpepper's). Co. C. Federal Rolls of Prisoners of War: Captured at Blakely, AL, on 4/9/1865; Received at Ship Island, MS, on 4/15/1865. Transferred to Vicksburg, MS, for exchange on 5/1/1865; Exchanged at Camp Townsend, MS, on 5/6/1865.

McCrory, W.H. (AKA McRoy) Pvt./Cpl., 3rd South Carolina Light Artillery (Culpepper's). Co. C. Federal Rolls of Prisoners of War: Captured at Fort Gaines, AL, on 8/8/1864; Received at Ship Island, MS, from New Orleans, LA, on 10/25/1864. Exchanged on 1/4/1865.

McGee, P.A.W. Pvt., 3rd South Carolina Light Artillery (Culpepper's). Co. C. Federal Rolls of Prisoners of War: Captured at Blakely, AL, on 4/9/1865; Received at Ship Island, MS, on 4/15/1865. Transferred to Vicksburg, MS, for exchange on 5/1/1865; Exchanged at Camp Townsend, MS, on 5/6/1865.

McLeod, Richard T. (AKA McLaid, R.) Pvt., 3rd South Carolina Light Artillery (Culpepper's). Co. C. Federal Rolls of Prisoners of War: Captured at Blakely, AL, on 4/9/1865; Received at Ship Island, MS, on 4/15/1865. Transferred to Vicksburg, MS, for exchange on 5/1/1865; Exchanged at Camp Townsend, MS, on 5/6/1865. Confederate Pension Application dated 9/24/1919 on file at the South Carolina Department of Archives and History. Target Name: McLeod, Richard T. Series: S126088. Item Number: 11215. Residence: Tindals, Sumter County, SC.

Mathews, J.M. Pvt., 3rd South Carolina Light Artillery (Culpepper's). Co. C. Federal Rolls of Prisoners of War: Captured at Blakely, AL, on 4/9/1865; Received at Ship Island, MS, on 4/15/1865. Transferred to Vicksburg, MS, for exchange on 5/1/1865; Exchanged at Camp Townsend, MS, on 5/6/1865.

Matthews, Andrew (AKA Mathews) Pvt., 3rd South Carolina Light Artillery (Culpepper's). Co. C. Federal Rolls of Prisoners of War: Captured at Blakely, AL, on 4/9/1865; Received at Ship Island, MS, on 4/15/1865. Transferred to Vicksburg, MS, for exchange on 5/1/1865; Exchanged at Camp Townsend, MS, on 5/6/1865. Confederate Pension Application dated 4/7/1919 on file at the South Carolina Department of Archives and History. Target Name: Matthews, Andrew. Series: S126088. Item Number: 03953. Residence: Effingham, Florence County, SC.

Matthews, S.P. (AKA Mathewes) Pvt., 3rd South Carolina Light Artillery (Culpepper's). Co. C. Federal Rolls of Prisoners of War: Captured at Blakely, AL, on 4/9/1865; Received at Ship Island, MS, on 4/15/1865. Transferred to Vicksburg, MS, for exchange on 5/1/1865; Exchanged at Camp Townsend, MS, on 5/6/1865.

Moses, David L. Pvt., 3rd South Carolina Light Artillery (Culpepper's). Co. C. Federal Rolls of Prisoners of War: Captured at Blakely, AL, on 4/9/1865; Received at Ship Island, MS, on 4/15/1865. Transferred to Vicksburg, MS, for exchange on 5/1/1865; Exchanged at Camp Townsend, MS, on 5/6/1865.

Nesbit, Stuart E. Pvt., 3rd South Carolina Light Artillery (Culpepper's). Co. C. Federal Rolls of Prisoners of War: Captured at Blakely, AL, on 4/9/1865; Received at Ship Island, MS, on 4/15/1865. Transferred to Vicksburg, MS, for exchange on 5/1/1865; Exchanged at Camp Townsend, MS, on 5/6/1865.

Newman, John W. Pvt., 3rd South Carolina Light Artillery (Culpepper's). Co. C. Federal Rolls of Prisoners of War: Captured at Blakely, AL, on 4/9/1865; Received at Ship Island, MS, on 4/15/1865. Transferred to Vicksburg, MS, for exchange on 5/1/1865; Exchanged at Camp Townsend, MS, on 5/6/1865.

Nichols, John M. Pvt./Cpl., 3rd South Carolina Light Artillery (Culpepper's). Co. C. Federal Rolls of Prisoners of War: Captured at Fort Gaines, AL, on 8/8/1864; Received at Ship Island, MS, from New Orleans, LA, on 10/25/1864. Exchanged on 1/4/1865.

O'Pry, Erwin G. (AKA G.E.) Pvt., 3rd South Carolina Light Artillery (Culpepper's). Co. C. Federal Rolls of Prisoners of War: Captured at Fort Gaines, AL, on 8/8/1864; Received at Ship Island, MS, from New Orleans, LA, on 10/25/1864. Died: 12/2/1864 at Ship Island, MS, due to dysentery. Buried: Ship Island, MS, Cemetery in Grave #57.

O'Pry, Sidney Pvt., 3rd South Carolina Light Artillery (Culpepper's). Co. C. Federal Rolls of Prisoners of War: Captured at Fort Gaines, AL, on 8/8/1864; Received at Ship Island, MS, from New Orleans, LA, on 10/25/1864. Died: 12/2/1864 at Ship Island, MS, due to chronic dysentery. Buried: Ship Island, MS, Cemetery.

Oliver, J.H. Pvt., 3rd South Carolina Light Artillery (Culpepper's). Co. C. Federal Rolls of Prisoners of War: Captured at Fort Gaines, AL, on 8/8/1864; Received at Ship Island, MS, from New Orleans, LA, on 10/25/1864. Exchanged on 1/4/1865.

Osteen, John M. (AKA O'Steen) Pvt., 3rd South Carolina Light Artillery (Culpepper's). Co. C. Federal Rolls of Prisoners of War: Captured at Fort Gaines, AL, on 8/8/1864; Received at Ship Island, MS, from New Orleans, LA, on 10/25/1864. Exchanged on 1/4/1865.

Pervis, James N. Cpl., 3rd South Carolina Light Artillery (Culpepper's). Co. C. Federal Rolls of Prisoners of War: Captured at Blakely, AL, on 4/9/1865; Received at Ship Island, MS, on 4/15/1865. Transferred to Vicksburg, MS, for exchange on 5/1/1865; Exchanged at Camp Townsend, MS, on 5/6/1865.

Pervis, R.N. (AKA Purvis) 3rd South Carolina Light Artillery (Culpepper's). Co. C. Federal Rolls of Prisoners of War: Captured at Blakely, AL, on 4/9/1865; Received at Ship Island, MS, on 4/15/1865. Transferred to Vicksburg, MS, for exchange on 5/1/1865; Exchanged at Camp Townsend, MS, on 5/6/1865.

Phillips, B. Pvt., 3rd South Carolina Light Artillery (Culpepper's). Co. C. Federal Rolls of Prisoners of War: Captured at Blakely, AL, on 4/9/1865; Received at Ship Island, MS, on 4/15/1865. Transferred to Vicksburg, MS, for exchange on 5/1/1865; Exchanged at Camp Townsend, MS, on 5/6/1865.

Rallings, R.J. (AKA Rollings) Pvt., 3rd South Carolina Light Artillery (Culpepper's). Co. C. Federal Rolls of Prisoners of War: Captured at Blakely, AL, on 4/9/1865; Received at Ship Island, MS, on 4/15/1865. Transferred to Vicksburg, MS, for exchange on 5/1/1865; Exchanged at Camp Townsend, MS, on 5/6/1865.

Reddick, J.E. Pvt., 3rd South Carolina Light Artillery (Culpepper's). Co. C. Federal Rolls of Prisoners of War: Captured at Blakely, AL, on 4/9/1865; Received at Ship Island, MS, on 4/15/1865. Transferred to Vicksburg, MS, for exchange on 5/1/1865; Exchanged at Camp Townsend, MS, on 5/6/1865. Confederate Widows Pension Application dated 1/5/1923 on file at the South Carolina Department of Archives and History. Target Name: Reddick, Caroline. Series: S126088. Item Number: 10174. Residence: Eau Claire, Richland County, SC.

Robertson, H.C. Pvt., 3rd South Carolina Light Artillery (Culpepper's). Co. C. Federal Rolls of Prisoners of War: Captured at Blakely, AL, on 4/9/1865; Received at Ship Island, MS, on 4/15/1865. Transferred to Vicksburg, MS, for exchange on 5/1/1865; Exchanged at Camp Townsend, MS, on 5/6/1865.

Ruer, Daniel Pvt., 3rd South Carolina Light Artillery (Culpepper's). Co. C. Federal Rolls of Prisoners of War: Captured at Blakely, AL, on 4/9/1865; Received at Ship Island, MS, on 4/15/1865. Transferred to Vicksburg, MS, for exchange on 5/1/1865; Exchanged at Camp Townsend, MS, on 5/6/1865.

Scurry, John J. Pvt., 3rd South Carolina Light Artillery (Culpepper's). Co. C. Federal Rolls of Prisoners of War: Captured at Blakely, AL, on 4/9/1865; Received at Ship Island, MS, on 4/15/1865. Transferred to Vicksburg, MS, for exchange on 5/1/1865; Exchanged at Camp Townsend, MS, on 5/6/1865.

Severance, Thomas B. (AKA Leverance, Saverance, T.G.) Pvt., 3rd South Carolina Light Artillery (Culpepper's). Co. C. Federal Rolls of Prisoners of War: Captured at Fort Gaines, AL, on 8/8/1864; Received at Ship Island, MS, from New Orleans, LA, on 10/24/1864. Died: 12/27/1864 at Ship Island, MS, due to chronic dysentery. Buried: Ship Island, MS, Cemetery in Grave #116.

Simon, James Pvt., 3rd South Carolina Light Artillery (Culpepper's). Co. C. Died: 11/27/1864 at Ship Island, MS, due to dysentery. Buried: Ship Island, MS, Cemetery in Grave #44.

Sims, James C. (AKA Simms, J.E.) Pvt., 3rd South Carolina Light Artillery (Culpepper's). Co. C. Federal Rolls of Prisoners of War: Captured at Fort Gaines, AL, on 8/8/1864; Received at Ship Island, MS, from New Orleans, LA, on 10/24/1865. Exchanged on 1/4/1865.

Sims, M.P. Sgt., 3rd South Carolina Light Artillery (Culpepper's). Co. C. Federal Rolls of Prisoners of War: Captured at Blakely, AL, on 4/9/1865; Received at Ship Island, MS, on 4/15/1865. Transferred to Vicksburg, MS, for exchange on 5/1/1865; Exchanged at Camp Townsend, MS, on 5/6/1865.

Spencer, A.J. Asst. Surg., 3rd South Carolina Light Artillery (Culpepper's). F & S. Federal Rolls of Prisoners of War: Captured at Blakely, AL, on 4/9/1865; Received at Ship Island, MS, on 4/15/1865. Transferred to Vicksburg, MS, for exchange on 4/28/1865; Confined at New Orleans, LA, on 4/30/1865. Exchanged at Camp Townsend, MS, on 5/6/1865.

Spinks, J.M. Pvt., 3rd South Carolina Light Artillery (Culpepper's). Co. C. Federal Rolls of Prisoners of War: Captured at Blakely, AL, on 4/9/1865; Received at Ship Island, MS, on 4/15/1865. Transferred to Vicksburg, MS, for exchange on 5/1/1865; Exchanged at Camp Townsend, MS, on 5/6/1865.

Swails, Morgan Pvt., 3rd South Carolina Light Artillery (Culpepper's). Co. C. Federal Rolls of Prisoners of War: Captured at Blakely, AL, on 4/9/1865; Received at Ship Island, MS, on 4/15/1865. Transferred to Vicksburg, MS, for exchange on 5/1/1865; Exchanged at Camp Townsend, MS, on 5/6/1865.

Taulman, F.A. Pvt., 3rd South Carolina Light Artillery (Culpepper's). Co. C. Federal Rolls of Prisoners of War: Captured at Blakely, AL, on 4/9/1865; Received at Ship Island, MS, on 4/15/1865. Transferred to Vicksburg, MS, for exchange on 5/1/1865; Exchanged at Camp Townsend, MS, on 5/6/1865.

Taylor, J.S. Pvt., 3rd South Carolina Light Artillery (Culpepper's). Co. C. Federal Rolls of Prisoners of War: Captured at Blakely, AL, on 4/9/1865; Received at Ship Island, MS, on 4/15/1865. Transferred to Vicksburg, MS, for exchange on 5/1/1865; Exchanged at Camp Townsend, MS, on 5/6/1865.

Taylor, W.E. Pvt., 3rd South Carolina Light Artillery (Culpepper's). Co. C. Federal Rolls of Prisoners of War: Captured at Blakely, AL, on 4/9/1865; Received at Ship Island, MS, on 4/15/1865. Transferred to Vicksburg, MS, for exchange on 5/1/1865; Exchanged at Camp Townsend, MS, on 5/6/1865.

Tedder, Richard F. Pvt., 3rd South Carolina Light Artillery (Culpepper's). Co. C. Federal Rolls of Prisoners of War: Captured at Blakely, AL, on 4/9/1865; Received at Ship Island, MS, on 4/15/1865. Transferred to Vicksburg, MS, for exchange on 5/1/1865; Exchanged at Camp Townsend, MS, on 5/6/1865.

Turner, Erasmus J. Pvt., 3rd South Carolina Light Artillery (Culpepper's). Co. C. Federal Rolls of Prisoners of War: Captured at Blakely, AL, on 4/9/1865; Received at Ship Island, MS, on 4/15/1865. Transferred to Vicksburg, MS, for exchange on 5/1/1865; Exchanged at Camp Townsend, MS, on 5/6/1865.

Turner, John Pvt., 3rd South Carolina Light Artillery (Culpepper's). Co. C. Federal Rolls of Prisoners of War: Captured at Blakely, AL, on 4/9/1865; Received at Ship Island, MS, on 4/15/1865. Transferred to Vicksburg, MS, for exchange on 5/1/1865; Exchanged at Camp Townsend, MS, on 5/6/1865.

Turner, Rasmus J. Pvt., 3rd South Carolina Light Artillery (Culpepper's). Co. C. Federal Rolls of Prisoners of War: Captured at Fort Gaines, AL, on 8/8/1864; Received at Ship Island, MS, from New Orleans, LA, on 10/25/1864. Exchanged on 1/4/1865. Confederate Pension Application dated 10/29/1919 on file at the South Carolina Department of Archives and History. Target Name: Turner, Rasmus J. Series: S126088. Item Number: 04011. Residence: Coward, Florence County, SC.

Vestz, W. Pvt., 3rd South Carolina Light Artillery (Culpepper's). Co. C. Federal Rolls of Prisoners of War: Captured at Blakely, AL, on 4/9/1865; Received at Ship Island, MS, on 4/15/1865. Transferred to Vicksburg, MS, for exchange on 5/1/1865; Exchanged at Camp Townsend, MS, on 5/6/1865.

Weeks, Augustus S. Pvt., 3rd South Carolina Light Artillery (Culpepper's). Co. C. Federal Rolls of Prisoners of War: Captured at Blakely, AL, on 4/9/1865; Received at Ship Island, MS, on 4/15/1865. Transferred to Vicksburg, MS, for exchange on 5/1/1865; Exchanged at Camp Townsend, MS, on 5/6/1865.

White, James G. Pvt., 3rd South Carolina Light Artillery (Culpepper's). Co. C. Federal Rolls of Prisoners of War: Captured at Blakely, AL, on 4/9/1865; Received at Ship Island, MS, on 4/15/1865. Transferred to Vicksburg, MS, for exchange on 5/1/1865; Exchanged at Camp Townsend, MS, on 5/6/1865.

Whitworth, P.H. Pvt., 3rd South Carolina Light Artillery (Culpepper's). Co. C. Federal Rolls of Prisoners of War: Captured at Blakely, AL, on 4/9/1865; Received at Ship Island, MS, on 4/15/1865. Transferred to Vicksburg, MS, for exchange on 5/1/1865; Exchanged at Camp Townsend, MS, on 5/6/1865.

Tennessee Prisoners of War

Baker, Joseph E. Pvt./Cpl./2nd Sgt., Winston's Light Artillery Battery (Belmont Battery). Enlisted: 8/10/1863 at Decatur, GA, for the duration of the war. Rolls for 8/1863 through 10/1863: Present, appointed Cpl. on 9/1/1863. Rolls for 11/1863 through 12/1863: Absent, on 10 day furlough since 12/29/1863. Rolls for 1/1864 through 2/1864: Present, appointed 2nd Sgt. on 1/1/1864. Rolls for 5/1864 through 8/1864: Absent, on picket duty with Lt. Alonzo Pillow; Lost 1 horse bridle valued at $12.00. Federal Rolls of Prisoners of War: Captured at Blakely, AL, on 4/9/1865; Received at Ship Island, MS, on 4/15/1865. Transferred to Vicksburg, MS, for exchange on 5/1/1865; Exchanged at Camp Townsend, MS, on 5/6/1865. Rolls of Prisoners of War, C.S.A: Surrendered at Citronelle, AL, on 5/4/1865; Paroled at Jackson, MS, on 5/12/1865. Residence at parole: Nashville, TN.

Barker, Edward Pvt./2nd Sgt., Winston's Light Artillery Battery (Belmont Battery). Enlisted: 3/12/1862 at Memphis, TN, for the duration of the war. Federal Rolls of Prisoners of War: Captured at Island No. 10 on 4/8/1862; Received at Camp Douglas, IL. Transferred to Vicksburg, MS, for exchange on 9/6/1862. Rolls for 8/1862 through 4/1863: Present. Rolls for 5/1863 through 6/1863: Absent, on detached service at Mobile, AL. Rolls for 7/1863 through 8/1864: Present. Federal Rolls of Prisoners of War: Captured at Blakely, AL, on 4/9/1865; Received at Ship Island, MS, on 4/15/1865. Transferred to Vicksburg, MS, for exchange on 5/1/1865; Exchanged at Camp Townsend, MS, on 5/6/1865. Rolls of Prisoners of War, C.S.A: Surrendered at Citronelle, AL, on 5/4/1865; Paroled at Jackson, MS, on 5/12/1865. Residence at parole: Memphis, TN.

Barnard, James N. Pvt., Winston's Light Artillery Battery (Belmont Battery). Federal Rolls of Prisoners of War: Captured at Blakely, AL, on 4/9/1865; Received at Ship Island, MS, on 4/15/1865. Transferred to Vicksburg, MS, for exchange on 5/1/1865; Exchanged at Camp Townsend, MS, on 5/6/1865.

Barnes, A.J. (AKA Barnard) Pvt., Winston's Light Artillery Battery (Belmont Battery). Enlisted: 1/10/1863 at Bradley County, TN, as a conscript from the Camp of Instruction at Knoxville, TN, for the duration of the war. Rolls for 1/1863 through 2/1863: Present. Rolls for 3/1863 through 4/1863: Absent, on detached service with the Whitworth gun since 3/25/1863 by order of Brig. Gen. James E. Slaughter. Rolls for 5/1863 through 6/1863: Present. Rolls for 7/1863 through 8/1863: Absent, sick in hospital at Mobile, AL. Rolls for 9/1863 through 8/1864: Present. On Register of Ross Hospital, Mobile, AL: Admitted on 9/26/1864 due to febris intermittens quot; Returned to duty on 10/2/1864. On Register of Ross Hospital, Mobile, AL: Admitted on 10/11/1864 due to chronic diarrhea; Returned to duty on 10/16/1864. Federal Rolls of Prisoners of War: Captured at Blakely, AL, on 4/9/1865; Received at Ship Island, MS, on 4/15/1865. Transferred to Vicksburg, MS, for exchange on 5/1/1865; Exchanged at Camp Townsend, MS, on 5/6/1865. Rolls of Prisoners of War, C.S.A: Surrendered at Citronelle, AL, on 5/4/1865; Paroled at Jackson, MS, on 5/12/1865. Residence at parole: Bradley County, TN. Wounded: Yes, right hip and right shoulder at Blakely, AL. Born: 1841 at Bradley County, TN. Married: Yes. Children: 2 daughters. Residence after war: Bradley County, TN. Occupation after war: Hireland. Ailments after war: Rheumatism and neuralgia in shoulder and hip. Confederate Pension Application dated 6/7/1902 on file at the Tennessee State Library and Archives. Target Name: Barnes, A.J. Application Number: S4294. County: Bradley. Disposition: Approved.

Bennett, Fielding 2nd Cpl./5th Sgt./Pvt., Winston's Light Artillery Battery (Belmont Battery). Enlisted: 3/14/1862 at Memphis, TN, for the duration of the war. Federal Rolls of Prisoners of War: Captured at Island No. 10 on 4/8/1862; Received at Camp Douglas, IL. Transferred to Vicksburg, MS, for exchange on 9/8/1862. On Register of U.S.A. Prison Hospital, Camp Douglas, IL: Admitted on 4/20/1862 due to debilitas; Released on 5/17/1862. Rolls for 10/1862 through 2/1863: Present, appointed 5th Sgt. on 2/1/1863. Rolls for 3/1863 through 4/1863: Absent, on detached service with the Whitworth gun since 3/25/1863 by order of Brig. Gen. James E. Slaughter. Rolls for 5/1863 through 2/1864: Present, reduced from Sgt. to Pvt. on 1/1/1864. Rolls for 5/1864 through 8/1864: Absent, on picket duty with Lt. Alonzo Pillow. On Register of Ross Hospital, Mobile, AL: Admitted on 1/5/1865 due to chronic syphilis; Returned to duty on 3/12/1865. Remarks: Shows complaint of gonorrhea and syphilis. Federal Rolls of Prisoners of War: Captured at Blakely, AL, on 4/9/1865; Received at Ship Island, MS, on 4/15/1865. Transferred to Vicksburg, MS, for exchange on 5/1/1865; Exchanged at Camp Townsend, MS, on 5/6/1865. Rolls of Prisoners of War, C.S.A: Surrendered at Citronelle, AL, on 5/4/1865; Paroled at Jackson, MS, while hospitalized on 5/12/1865. Residence at parole: Memphis, TN.

Bird, L. (AKA Byrd) Pvt., Winston's Light Artillery Battery (Belmont Battery). Federal Rolls of Prisoners of War: Captured at Blakely, AL, on 4/9/1865; Received at Ship Island, MS, on 4/15/1865. Transferred to Vicksburg, MS, for exchange on 5/1/1865; Exchanged at Camp Townsend, MS, on 5/6/1865.

Bowles, E. (AKA Bolles, Boller) Pvt., Winston's Light Artillery Battery (Belmont Battery). Federal Rolls of Prisoners of War: Captured at Blakely, AL, on 4/9/1865; Received at Ship Island, MS, on 4/15/1865. Transferred to Vicksburg, MS, for exchange on 5/1/1865; Exchanged at Camp Townsend, MS, on 5/6/1865.

Brooks, J.E. Pvt., Winston's Light Artillery Battery (Belmont Battery). Federal Rolls of Prisoners of War: Captured at Blakely, AL, on 4/9/1865; Received at Ship Island, MS, on 4/15/1865. Transferred to Vicksburg, MS, for exchange on 5/1/1865; Exchanged at Camp Townsend, MS, on 5/6/1865.

Brown, George W. (AKA G.N.) Pvt., Barry's Light Artillery Battery (Lookout Battery). Enlisted: 10/1/1862 at Knoxville, TN, for 3 years. Rolls for 10/1862 through 10/1864: Present. Federal Rolls of Prisoners of War: Captured at Spanish Fort, AL, on 4/8/1865; Received at Ship Island, MS, on 4/10/1865. Transferred to Vicksburg, MS, for exchange on 5/1/1865; Exchanged at Camp Townsend, MS, on 5/6/1865. Soldier also served as a Pvt. with Ragsdale's Cavalry Company. Born: 7/10/1842 at Hamilton County, TN. Married: Yes, wife died in 1905. Children: Yes, 2 sons and 1 daughter. Residence after war: Chattanooga, TN. Occupation after war: Carpenter. Property after war: Small house and lot at Highland Park valued at $800. Ailments after war: Arteriosclerosis and general debility. Died: 1/15/1912. Confederate Pension Application dated 4/13/1909 on file at the Tennessee State Library and Archives. Target Name: Brown, George W. Application Number: S11134. County: Hamilton. Disposition: Approved. Amount of pension: $25 quarterly.

Brown, William C. Pvt., Barry's Light Artillery Battery (Lookout Battery). Enlisted: 10/1/1862 at Knoxville, TN, for 3 years. Rolls for 10/1862 through 4/1863: Present. Rolls for 5/1863 through 5/1863: Sick in quarters. Rolls for 9/1863 through 4/1864: Present. Rolls for 9/1864 through 10/1864: Present, on daily duty as Commissary Sgt. Federal Rolls of Prisoners of War: Captured at Spanish Fort, AL, on 4/8/1865; Received at Ship Island, MS, on 4/10/1865. Transferred to Vicksburg, MS, for exchange on 5/1/1865; Exchanged at Camp Townsend, MS, on 5/6/1865. Wounded: Yes, flesh wound in the neck at Spanish Fort, AL. Soldier also served as a Pvt. with Ashby's Cavalry. Born: 1835 at Blount County, TN. Married: Yes. Residence after war: Hampton, Carter County, TN. Property after war: House and lot in Hampton, TN, valued at $150. Confederate Pension Application dated 8/15/1900 on file at the Tennessee State Library and Archives. Target Name: Brown, William C. Application Number: S2973. County: Carter. Disposition: Rejected.

Buckall, H.H. (AKA Buckalee) Pvt., Winston's Light Artillery Battery (Belmont Battery). Federal Rolls of Prisoners of War: Captured at Blakely, AL, on 4/9/1865; Received at Ship Island, MS, from New Orleans, LA, on 4/15/1865. Transferred to Vicksburg, MS, for exchange on 5/1/1865.

Buff, James Pvt., Barry's Light Artillery Battery (Lookout Battery). Enlisted: 5/12/1862 at Chattanooga, TN, for 2 years. Rolls for 5/1862 through 2/1863: Present. Rolls for 3/1863 through 6/1863: Present, on extra daily duty as Blacksmith. Rolls for 9/1863 through 10/1863: Absent, sent to hospital at Newton, MS, on 9/7/1863. Rolls for 11/1863 through 12/1863: Present. Rolls for 3/1864 through 10/1864: Present, detailed as Blacksmith. Federal Rolls of Prisoners of War: Captured at Spanish Fort, AL, on 4/8/1865; Received at Ship Island, MS, on 4/10/1865. Transferred to Vicksburg, MS, for exchange on 5/1/1865; Exchanged at Camp Townsend, MS, on 5/6/1865.

Bulger, E.P. (AKA Bolger) Pvt., Winston's Light Artillery Battery (Belmont Battery). Federal Rolls of Prisoners of War: Captured at Blakely, AL, on 4/9/1865; Received at Ship Island, MS, on 4/15/1865. Transferred to Vicksburg, MS, for exchange on 5/1/1865; Exchanged at Camp Townsend, MS, on 5/6/1865.

Cady, Timothy (AKA Jim) Pvt., Winston's Light Artillery Battery (Belmont Battery). Enlisted: 6/6/1861 at Nashville, TN, for 12 months. Federal Rolls of Prisoners of War: Captured at Island No. 10 on 4/8/1862; Received at Camp Douglas, IL. Transferred to Vicksburg, MS, for exchange on 9/8/1862. Rolls for 10/1862 through 12/1862: Present, re-enlisted. Rolls for 1/1863 through 12/1863: Present. Rolls for 1/1864 through 2/1864: Present, sick in camp. Rolls for 5/1864 through 8/1864: Absent, sick in General Hospital at Mobile, AL, due to slight wounds received at Cassville, GA. Federal Rolls of Prisoners of War: Captured at Blakely, AL, on 4/9/1865; Received at Ship Island, MS, on 4/15/1865. Transferred to Vicksburg, MS, for exchange on 5/1/1865; Exchanged at Camp Townsend, MS, on 5/6/1865. Rolls of Prisoners of War, C.S.A: Surrendered at Citronelle, AL, on 5/4/1865; Paroled at Jackson, MS, on 5/12/1865. Residence at parole: Nashville, TN. Took the U.S. Oath of Allegiance at Nashville, TN, on 6/5/1865. Description at oath: Eyes: grey. Hair: dark. Complexion: fair. Height: 5'4½". Residence at oath: Davidson County, TN.

Calhoun, B. Pvt., Winston's Light Artillery Battery (Belmont Battery). Federal Rolls of Prisoners of War: Captured at Blakely, AL, on 4/9/1865; Received at Ship Island, MS, on 4/15/1865. Transferred to Vicksburg, MS, for exchange on 5/1/1865; Exchanged at Camp Townsend, MS, on 5/6/1865.

Calhoun, James B. Pvt., Winston's Light Artillery

Battery (Belmont Battery). Federal Rolls of Prisoners of War: Captured on 4/9/1865 at Blakely, AL; Sent to Ship Island, MS, on 4/15/1865. Transferred to Vicksburg, MS, for exchange on 5/1/1865; Exchanged at Camp Townsend, MS, on 5/6/1865. Soldier also served as a Pvt. in the 6th Alabama Cavalry. Co. E. Born: 1845 at Henry County, AL. Soldier is recorded on the 1907 Census of Alabama Confederate Veterans. Residence: Henry County, AL.

Campbell, Henry E. (AKA Campble) Pvt., Barry's Light Artillery Battery (Lookout Battery). Enlisted: 4/4/1862 at Chattanooga, TN, for 3 years. Occupation at enlistment: Hospital Nurse. Rolls for 4/1862 through 6/1862: Present. Rolls for 7/1862 through 8/1862: Absent, sick. Rolls for 9/1862 through 10/1863: Present. Rolls for 11/1863 through 12/1863: Present, on daily duty as Hospital Nurse. Rolls for 3/1864 through 4/1864: Present, on daily duty as Hospital Nurse. Rolls for 9/1864 through 10/1864: Absent, sent to hospital in Atlanta, GA, on 7/4/1864. Federal Rolls of Prisoners of War: Captured at Spanish Fort, AL, on 4/8/1865; Received at Ship Island, MS, on 4/10/1865. Transferred to Vicksburg, MS, for exchange on 5/1/1865; Exchanged at Camp Townsend, MS, on 5/6/1865.

Carle, Thomas (AKA Carroll, Carleton) Pvt., Winston's Light Artillery Battery (Belmont Battery). Federal Rolls of Prisoners of War: Captured at Blakely, AL, on 4/9/1865; Received at Ship Island, MS, on 4/15/1865. Transferred to Vicksburg, MS, for exchange on 5/1/1865; Exchanged at Camp Townsend, MS, on 5/6/1865.

Casey, Patrick Pvt., Winston's Light Artillery Battery. (Belmont Battery). Enlisted: 5/13/1861 at Nashville, TN, for 12 months. Age at enlistment: 40. Federal Rolls of Prisoners of War: Captured at Island No. 10 on 4/8/1862; Received at Camp Douglas, IL. Transferred to Vicksburg, MS, for exchange on 9/6/1862. Rolls for 9/1862 through 11/1862: Discharged due to being overage at Jackson, MS, on 10/18/1862. Rolls for 11/1862 through 12/1862: Present, substitution. Rolls for 1/1863 through 2/1863: Present, re-enlisted as a conscript from the Camp of Instruction at Knoxville, TN, for the duration of the war. Rolls for 3/1863 through 6/1863: Absent, on detached service at Mobile, AL, since 4/25/1863. Rolls for 7/1863 through 8/1863: Absent, sick in hospital at Mobile, AL. Rolls for 9/1863 through 2/1864: Present. Rolls for 5/1864 through 8/1864: Present, sick in camp. Federal Rolls of Prisoners of War: Captured at Blakely, AL, on 4/9/1865; Received at Ship Island, MS, on 4/15/1865. Transferred to Vicksburg, MS, for exchange on 5/1/1865; Exchanged at Camp Townsend, MS, on 5/6/1865. Rolls of Prisoners of War, C.S.A: Surrendered at Citronelle, AL, on 5/4/1865; Paroled at Jackson, MS, on 5/12/1865. Took the U.S. Oath of Allegiance at Nashville, TN, on 5/24/1865. Residence at oath: Davidson County, TN. Description at oath: Eyes: blue. Hair: dark. Complexion: fair. Height: 5'6".

Chalker, C.A. Pvt., Winston's Light Artillery Battery (Belmont Battery). Federal Rolls of Prisoners of War: Captured at Blakely, AL, on 4/9/1865; Received at Ship Island, MS, on 4/15/1865. Transferred to Vicksburg, MS, for exchange on 5/1/1865; Exchanged at Camp Townsend, MS, on 5/6/1865.

Chalker, W.D. Pvt., Winston's Light Artillery Battery (Belmont Battery). Federal Rolls of Prisoners of War: Captured at Blakely, AL, on 4/9/1865; Received at Ship Island, MS, on 4/15/1865. Transferred to Vicksburg, MS, for exchange on 5/1/1865; Exchanged at Camp Townsend, MS, on 5/6/1865.

Chancellor, William Pvt., Winston's Light Artillery Battery (Belmont Battery). Federal Rolls of Prisoners of War: Captured at Blakely, AL, on 4/9/1865; Received at Ship Island, MS, on 4/15/1865. Transferred to Vicksburg, MS, for exchange on 5/1/1865; Exchanged at Camp Townsend, MS, on 5/6/1865.

Claffey, James (AKA Coffey) Pvt., Winston's Light Artillery Battery (Belmont Battery). Enlisted: 6/6/1861 at Nashville, TN. Age at enlistment: 35. Federal Rolls of Prisoners of War: Captured at Island No. 10 on 4/8/1862; Received at Camp Douglas, IL. Transferred to Vicksburg, MS, for exchange on 9/6/1862. Rolls for 8/1862 through 2/1864: Present. Rolls for 5/1864 through 8/1864: Present, sick in camp. On Register of Ross Hospital, Mobile, AL: Admitted on 8/5/1864 due to febris remittens; Returned to duty on 8/30/1864. On Register of Ross Hospital, Mobile, AL: Admitted on 3/6/1865 due to febris remittens; Returned to duty on 3/13/1865. Federal Rolls of Prisoners of War: Captured at Blakely, AL, on 4/9/1865; Received at Ship Island, MS, on 4/15/1865. Transferred to Vicksburg, MS, for exchange on 5/1/1865; Exchanged at Camp Townsend, MS, on 5/6/1865. Rolls of Prisoners of War, C.S.A: Surrendered at Citronelle, AL, on 5/4/1865; Paroled at Jackson, MS, on 5/12/1865. Residence at parole: Nashville, TN.

Connelly, William (AKA Connely) Pvt./2nd Cpl., Winston's Light Artillery Battery (Belmont Battery). Enlisted: 6/1/1861 at Nashville, TN, for 12 months. Rolls for 8/1862 through 2/1863: Present. Rolls for 3/1863 through 4/1863: Absent, on detached service at Mobile, AL, since 4/25/1863. Rolls for 5/1863 through 2/1864: Present, appointed 2nd Cpl. on 7/1/1863. Rolls for 5/1864 through 8/1864: Absent, on picket duty with Lt. Pillow. On Return dated 12/1864, Department of the Gulf: Detached to Lt. Col. Huger on line of city redoubts as Instructor of Heavy Artillery. Federal Rolls of Prisoners of War: Captured at Blakely, AL, on 4/9/1865; Received at Ship Island, MS, on 4/15/1865. Transferred to Vicksburg, MS, for exchange on 5/1/1865; Exchanged at Camp Townsend, MS, on 5/6/1865. Rolls of Prisoners of War, C.S.A: Surrendered at Citronelle, AL, on 5/4/1865; Paroled at Jackson, MS, on 5/12/1865. Residence at parole: Nashville, TN. Took the U.S. Oath of Allegiance at Nashville, TN, on 6/5/1865. Description at oath: Eyes: grey. Hair: dark. Complexion: dark. Height: 5'6".

Conners, Michael (AKA Connors, Conors) Pvt., Winston's Light Artillery Battery (Belmont Battery). Enlisted: 12/1/1862 at Mobile, AL, as a substitution for Robert William Lawler for the duration of the war. Occupation at enlistment: Laborer. Rolls for 12/1862 through 2/1863: Present. Rolls for 3/1863 through 4/1863: Absent, on detached service at Mobile, AL, since 4/25/1863. Rolls for 5/1863 through 8/1864: Present. On Descriptive List dated 6/11/1863: Age: 46. Eyes: hazel. Hair: dark. Complexion: fair. Height: 5'6". Federal Rolls of Prisoners of War: Captured at Blakely, AL, on 4/9/1865; Received at Ship

Island, MS, on 4/15/1865. Transferred to Vicksburg, MS, for exchange on 5/1/1865; Exchanged at Camp Townsend, MS, on 5/6/1865. Rolls of Prisoners of War, C.S.A: Surrendered at Citronelle, AL, on 5/4/1865; Paroled at Jackson, MS, on 5/12/1865. Residence at parole: Nashville, TN. Born: Kilkenny, Ireland.

Connolly, James (AKA Connelly) Pvt., Winston's Light Artillery Battery (Belmont Battery). Enlisted: 3/28/1863 at Mobile, AL, as a substitution for George W. Campbell for the duration of the war. Occupation at enlistment: Laborer. Rolls for 3/1863 through 4/1863: Present. Rolls for 5/1863 through 6/1863: Absent, on detached service at Mobile, AL. On Descriptive List dated 6/11/1863: Age: 50. Eyes: blue. Hair: grey. Complexion: dark. Height: 5'6". Rolls for 7/1863 through 8/1864: Present. On Register of Ross Hospital, Mobile, AL: Admitted on 9/19/1864 due to febris intermittens quot.; Returned to duty on 10/2/1864. On Register of Ross Hospital, Mobile, AL: Admitted on 11/13/1864 due to febris intermittens tert.; Returned to duty on 12/5/1864. Federal Rolls of Prisoners of War: Captured at Blakely, AL, on 4/9/1865; Received at Ship Island, MS, on 4/15/1865. Transferred to Vicksburg, MS, for exchange on 5/1/1865; Exchanged at Camp Townsend, MS, on 5/6/1865. Rolls of Prisoners of War, C.S.A: Surrendered at Citronelle, AL, on 5/4/1865; Paroled at Jackson, MS, on 5/12/1865. Residence at parole: Nashville, TN. Born: Galway, Ireland.

Corbett, Matthew (AKA Corbitt) Pvt., Winston's Light Artillery Battery (Belmont Battery). Enlisted: 1/13/1863 at Mobile, AL, for the duration of the war. Occupation at enlistment: Laborer. Rolls for 1/1863 through 8/1864: Present. On Descriptive List dated 6/11/1863: Age: 50. Eyes: blue. Hair: dark. Complexion: fair. Height: 5'8". Federal Rolls of Prisoners of War: Captured at Blakely, AL, on 4/9/1865; Received at Ship Island, MS, on 4/15/1865. Transferred to Vicksburg, MS, for exchange on 5/1/1865; Exchanged at Camp Townsend, MS, on 5/6/1865. Rolls of Prisoners of War, C.S.A: Surrendered at Citronelle, AL, on 5/4/1865; Paroled at Jackson, MS, on 5/12/1865. Residence at parole: Mobile, AL. Born: Clare, Ireland.

Craddock, L. Pvt., Winston's Light Artillery Battery (Belmont Battery). Federal Rolls of Prisoners of War: Captured at Blakely, AL, on 4/9/1865; Received at Ship Island, MS, on 4/15/1865. Transferred to Vicksburg, MS, for exchange on 5/1/1865; Exchanged at Camp Townsend, MS, on 5/6/1865.

Cullan, Hugh (AKA Crillen, Cullen, Cullin, Cullian, Cullam, Cullom) Pvt./6th Cpl., Winston's Light Artillery Battery (Belmont Battery). Enlisted: 6/6/1861 at Nashville, TN. Age at enlistment: 20. Rolls for 11/1861 through 3/1862: Present. Federal Rolls of Prisoners of War: Captured at Island No. 10 on 4/8/1862; Received at Camp Douglas, IL. Transferred to Vicksburg, MS, for exchange on 9/6/1862. Rolls for 10/1862 through 2/1863: Present. Rolls for 3/1863 through 4/1863: Absent, on detached service with the Whitworth gun since 3/25/1863. Rolls for 5/1863 through 8/1864: Present, appointed 6th Cpl. on 8/1/1863. On Return dated 12/1864, Department of the Gulf: Detached with lieutenants Lindsay and Thomas, with section reporting to Brig. Gen. St. John R. Liddell on eastern shore. Federal Rolls of Prisoners of War: Captured at Blakely, AL, on 4/9/1865; Received at Ship Island, MS, on 4/15/1865. Transferred to Vicksburg, MS, for exchange on 5/1/1865; Exchanged at Camp Townsend, MS, on 5/6/1865. Rolls of Prisoners of War, C.S.A: Surrendered at Citronelle, AL, on 5/4/1865; Paroled at Jackson, MS, on 5/12/1865. Residence at parole: Nashville, TN. Took the U.S. Oath of Allegiance at Nashville, TN, on 6/5/1865. Description at oath: Eyes: hazel. Hair: dark. Complexion: dark. Height: 5'8".

Cunelon, S. Pvt., Winston's Light Artillery Battery (Belmont Battery). Federal Rolls of Prisoners of War: Captured at Blakely, AL, on 4/9/1865; Received at Ship Island, MS, on 4/15/1865. Transferred to Vicksburg, MS, for exchange on 5/1/1865; Exchanged at camp Townsend, MS, on 5/6/1865.

Dalton, Colby T. (AKA Coby) Pvt., Winston's Light Artillery Battery (Belmont Battery). Enlisted: 1/16/1863 at Granger County, TN, as a conscript from the Camp of Instruction at Knoxville, TN, for the war. Rolls for 1/1863 through 2/1863: Present. Rolls for 3/1863 through 4/1863: Absent, on detached service at Mobile, AL, since 4/25/1863. Rolls for 5/1863 through 6/1863: Absent, without leave since 6/21/1863. Rolls for 7/1863 through 8/1863: Present, attempted desertion on 6/21/1863 but captured near Selma, AL, on 7/1/1863. Released on President's Proclamation. Rolls for 9/1863 through 2/1864: Present. Rolls for 5/1864 through 8/1864: Absent, sick in hospital at Mobile, AL. On Register of Ross Hospital, Mobile, AL: Admitted on 8/7/1864 due to febris remittens; Returned to duty on 8/10/1864. On Register of Ross Hospital, Mobile, AL: Admitted on 8/22/1864 due to febris remittens; Returned to duty on 9/8/1864. Name on Regimental Return dated 12/1864, Department of the Gulf: Detached with lieutenants Lindsay and Thomas, with section reporting to Brig. Gen. St. John R. Liddell on eastern shore. Federal Rolls of Prisoners of War: Captured at Blakely, AL, on 4/9/1865; Received at Ship Island, MS, on 4/15/1865. Transferred to Vicksburg, MS, for exchange on 5/1/1865; Exchanged at Camp Townsend, MS, on 5/6/1865. Rolls of Prisoners of War, C.S.A: Surrendered at Citronelle, AL, on 5/4/1865; Paroled at Jackson, MS, on 5/12/1865. Remarks: Left sick at Vicksburg, MS. On Register of U.S.A. Prison Hospital, Vicksburg, MS: Admitted on 5/5/1865 due to acute diarrhea; Returned to duty on 5/25/1865 and released by the U.S. Provost Marshall. Soldier also served as a Pvt. with the 26th Tennessee Infantry. Co.D. Wounded: No, but contracted chronic conjunctivitis while a prisoner of war at Ship Island, MS. Born: 1841 at Grainger County, TN. Married: Yes. Children: 1 son. Occupation: Farmer. Residence after war: Idol, Grainger County, TN. Property after war: Household and kitchen furniture, 2 pigs, 1 cow and 1 calf valued at $50. Ailments after war: Chronic conjunctivitis, asthma, and right inguinal hernia. Confederate Pension Application dated 8/1904 on file at the Tennessee State Library and Archives. Target Name: Dalton, Colby. Application Number: S6347. County: Grainger. Disposition: Approved.

Day, William Pvt., Winston's Light Artillery Battery (Belmont Battery). Federal Rolls of Prisoners of War:

Captured at Blakely, AL, on 4/9/1865; Received at Ship Island, MS, on 4/15/1865. Transferred to Vicksburg, MS, for exchange on 5/1/1865.

Dean, William Pvt., Winston's Light Artillery Battery (Belmont Battery). Federal Rolls of Prisoners of War: Captured in Alabama on 3/24/1865; Received at Ship Island, MS. Transferred to Vicksburg, MS, for exchange on 5/1/1865.

Devaney, Martin (AKA Derany, Deveny) Pvt., Winston's Light Artillery Battery (Belmont Battery). Enlisted: 4/19/1863 at Mobile, AL, as a substitution for William B. Jones for the duration of the war. Occupation at enlistment: Laborer. Rolls for 4/1863 through 6/1863: Absent, on detached service at Mobile, AL, since 4/25/1863. Rolls for 7/1863 through 2/1864: Present. Rolls for 5/1864 through 8/1864: Absent, on picket duty with Lt. Alonzo Pillow. Federal Rolls of Prisoners of War: Captured at Blakely, AL, on 4/9/1865; Received at Ship Island, MS, on 4/15/1865. Transferred to Vicksburg, MS, for exchange on 5/1/1865; Exchanged at Camp Townsend, MS, on 5/6/1865. Rolls of Prisoners of War, C.S.A: Surrendered at Citronelle, AL, on 5/4/1865; Paroled at Jackson, MS, on 5/12/1865. Age at parole: 46. Residence at parole: New Orleans, LA. Description at parole: Eyes: blue. Hair: light. Complexion: florid. Height: 5'7". Born: Galway, Ireland.

Donovan, Michael 1st Cpl./2nd Sgt./Pvt., Winston's Light Artillery Battery (Belmont Battery). Enlisted: 5/17/1861 at Nashville, TN, for 12 months. Age at enlistment: 30. Rolls for 11/1861 through 3/1862: Present. Federal Rolls of Prisoners of War: Captured at Island No. 10 on 4/8/1862; Received at Camp Douglas, IL. Transferred to Vicksburg, MS, for exchange on 9/6/1862. Rolls for 10/1862 through 12/1863: Present, re-enlisted. Rolls for 1/1863 through 2/1863: Present. Rolls for 3/1863 through 4/1863: Present, reduced from 2nd Sgt. to Pvt. on 3/4/1863. Rolls for 5/1863 through 2/1864: Present. Rolls for 5/1864 through 8/1864: Absent, on picket duty with Lt. Alonzo Pillow. Federal Rolls of Prisoners of War: Captured at Blakely, AL, on 4/9/1865; Received at Ship Island, MS, on 4/15/1865. Transferred to Vicksburg, MS, for exchange on 5/1/1865; Exchanged at Camp Townsend, MS, on 5/6/1865. Rolls of Prisoners of War, C.S.A: Surrendered at Citronelle, AL, on 5/4/1865; Paroled at Jackson, MS, on 5/12/1865.

Duffy, Robert (AKA Duffie) Pvt./Cpl./Pvt., Winston's Light Artillery Battery (Belmont Battery). Enlisted: 3/10/1862 at Memphis, TN, for the duration of the war. Federal Rolls of Prisoners of War: Captured at Island No. 10 on 4/8/1862; Received at Camp Douglas, IL. Transferred to Vicksburg, MS, for exchange on 9/6/1862. Rolls for 10/1862 through 12/1862: Present, re-enlisted. Rolls for 1/1863 through 8/1863: Present, appointed Cpl. on 7/1/1863. Rolls for 9/1863 through 12/1863: Present, reduced from Cpl. to Pvt. on 12/23/1863. Rolls for 1/1864 through 2/1864: Present. Rolls for 5/1864 through 8/1864: Absent, on picket duty with Lt. Alonzo Pillow. On Register of Ross Hospital Mobile, AL: Admitted on 9/19/1864 due to febris intermittens; Returned to duty on 9/30/1864. Federal Rolls of Prisoners of War: Captured at Blakely, AL, on 4/9/1865; Received at Ship Island, MS, on 4/15/1865. Transferred to Vicksburg, MS, for exchange on 5/1/1865; Exchanged at Camp Townsend, MS, on 5/6/1865. Rolls of Prisoners of War, C.S.A: Surrendered at Citronelle, AL, on 5/4/1865; Paroled at Jackson, MS, on 5/12/1865.

Duncan, Thomas A. (AKA Dunkin) Pvt., Barry's Light Artillery Battery (Lookout Battery). Enlisted: 4/4/1862 at Chattanooga, TN, for 3 years. Rolls for 5/15/1862 through 12/1863: Present. Rolls for 3/1864 through 4/1864: Present, returned from hospital on 3/18/1864. Rolls for 9/1864 through 10/1864: Present. Federal Rolls of Prisoners of War: Captured at Spanish Fort, AL, on 4/8/1865; Received at Ship Island, MS, on 4/10/1865. Transferred to Vicksburg, MS, for exchange on 5/1/1865; Exchanged at Camp Townsend, MS, on 5/6/1865.

Elliott, H. Pvt., Winston's Light Artillery Battery (Belmont Battery). Federal Rolls of Prisoners of War: Captured at Blakely, AL, on 4/9/1865; Received at Ship Island, MS, on 4/15/1865. Transferred to Vicksburg, MS, for exchange on 5/1/1865; Exchanged at Camp Townsend, MS, on 5/6/1865.

Fassett, J.D. Pvt., Winston's Light Artillery Battery (Belmont Battery). Federal Rolls of Prisoners of War: Captured at Blakely, AL, on 4/9/1865; Received at Ship Island, MS, on 4/15/1865. Transferred to Vicksburg, MS, for exchange on 5/1/1865; Exchanged at Camp Townsend, MS, on 5/6/1865.

Faust, Samuel (AKA Faist, Foust) Pvt., Winston's Light Artillery Battery (Belmont Battery). Enlisted: 1/21/1863 at Carter County, TN, as a conscript from the Camp of Instruction at Knoxville, TN, for the duration of the war. Rolls for 1/1863 through 2/1863: Present. Rolls for 3/1863 through 8/1863: Absent, on detached service at the floating battery by order of Brig. Gen. James E. Slaughter. Rolls for 9/1863 through 12/1863: Present. Rolls for 1/1864 through 2/1864: Present, sick in camp. Rolls for 5/1864 through 8/1864: Present. Federal Rolls of Prisoners of War: Captured at Blakely, AL, on 4/9/1865; Received at Ship Island, MS, on 4/15/1865. Transferred to Vicksburg, MS, for exchange on 5/1/1865; Exchanged at Camp Townsend, MS, on 5/6/1865. Rolls of Prisoners of War, C.S.A: Surrendered at Citronelle, AL, on 5/4/1865; Paroled at Jackson, MS, on 5/12/1865.

Felkins, William M. (AKA Feister, Filkins) Pvt., Barry's Light Artillery Battery (Lookout Battery). Enlisted: 3/11/1863 at Knoxville, TN, for 2 years as a substitute for J.B. Hall; Transferred from the Camp of Instruction. Rolls for 3/1863 through 4/1864: Present. Rolls for 9/1864 through 10/1864: Absent, wounded and sent to hospital in Atlanta, GA, on 8/6/1864. On Register of Ocmulgee Hospital, Macon, GA: Admitted on 8/11/1864 due to head fracture; Furloughed on 10/7/1864. Federal Rolls of Prisoners of War: Captured at Spanish Fort, AL, on 4/8/1865; Received at Ship Island, MS, on 4/10/1865. Transferred to Vicksburg, MS, for exchange on 5/1/1865; Exchanged at Camp Townsend, MS, on 5/6/1865.

Fisher, T.L. (AKA J.S., T.S.) Pvt., Winston's Light Artillery Battery (Belmont Battery). Federal Rolls of Prisoners of War: Captured at Blakely, AL, on 4/9/1865; Received at Ship Island, MS, on 4/15/1865. Transferred to Vicksburg, MS, for exchange on 5/1/1865; Exchanged at Camp Townsend, MS, on 5/6/1865.

Fluker, J.F. Pvt., Winston's Light Artillery Battery

(Belmont Battery). Federal Rolls of Prisoners of War: Captured at Blakely, AL, on 4/9/1865; Received at Ship Island, MS, on 4/15/1865. Transferred to Vicksburg, MS, for exchange on 5/1/1865; Exchanged at Camp Townsend, MS, on 5/6/1865.

Ford, Benjamin C. Pvt./Cpl./Sgt., Winston's Light Artillery Battery (Belmont Battery). Enlisted: 10/30/1863 at Decatur, GA, for the duration of the war. Rolls for 11/1863 through 12/1863: Present, appointed Cpl. on 11/1/1863. Rolls for 1/1864 through 2/1864: Present, appointed Sgt. on 1/1/1864. Rolls for 5/1864 through 8/1864: Absent, sick in General Hospital Moore since 8/26/1864. On Register of Ross Hospital, Mobile, AL: Admitted on 9/27/1864 due to febris intermittens; Returned to duty on 10/2/1864. On Return dated 12/1864, Department of the Gulf: Detached with lieutenants Lindsay and Thomas with section reporting to Brig. Gen. St. John R. Liddell on eastern shore. Federal Rolls of Prisoners of War: Captured at Blakely, AL, on 4/9/1865; Received at Ship Island, MS, on 4/15/1865. Transferred to Vicksburg, MS, for exchange on 5/1/1865; Exchanged at Camp Townsend, MS, on 5/6/1865. Rolls of Prisoners of War, C.S.A: Surrendered at Citronelle, AL, on 5/4/1865; Paroled while hospitalized at Jackson, MS, on 5/12/1865. Took the U.S. Oath of Allegiance on 8/18/1865 at Nashville, TN. Residence at oath: Davidson County, TN. Description at oath: Eyes: grey. Hair: light. Complexion: fair. Height: 5'10½".

Fortner, Wiley Pvt., Barry's Light Artillery Battery (Lookout Battery). Enlisted: 10/4/1862 at Knoxville, TN, for 3 years. Rolls for 10/1862 through 10/1864: Present. Federal Rolls of Prisoners of War: Captured at Spanish Fort, AL, on 4/8/1865; Received at Ship Island, MS, on 4/10/1865. Transferred to Vicksburg, MS, for exchange on 5/1/1865; Exchanged at Camp Townsend, MS, on 5/6/1865. Born: 1830 at Green County, TN. Married: Yes. Children: 6 daughters. Residence after war: Old Fort, Polk County, TN. Property after war: 100 acres of upland valued at $150. Ailments after war: tumor in posterior triangle of left side of neck the size of a lemon, right inguinal scrotal hernia, prinpura hemorrhagia and rheumatism. Confederate Pension Application dated 5/9/1903 on file at the Tennessee State Library and Archives. Target Name: Fortner, Wiley. Application Number: S4990. County: Polk. Disposition: Rejected.

Francis, John Pvt., Winston's Light Artillery Battery (Belmont Battery). Enlisted: 6/10/1861 at Nashville, TN. Age at enlistment: 20. Rolls for 8/1861 through 3/1862: Present. Federal Rolls of Prisoners of War: Captured at Island No. 10 on 4/8/1862; Received at Camp Douglas, IL. Transferred to Vicksburg, MS, for exchange on 9/6/1862. Rolls for 10/1862 through 12/1862: Present, re-enlisted. Rolls for 1/1863 through 2/1863: Present. Rolls for 3/1863 through 4/1863: Absent, on detached service with the Whitworth gun since 4/10/1863. Rolls for 5/1863 through 8/1864: Present. Federal Rolls of Prisoners of War: Captured at Blakely, AL, on 4/9/1865; Received at Ship Island, MS, on 4/15/1865. Transferred to Vicksburg, MS, for exchange on 5/1/1865; Exchanged at Camp Townsend, MS, on 5/6/1865. Rolls of Prisoners of War, C.S.A: Surrendered at Citronelle, AL, on 5/4/1865; Paroled at Jackson, MS, on 5/12/1865. Took the U.S. Oath of Allegiance on 6/13/1865 at Nashville, TN. Residence at oath: Jefferson County, KY. Description at oath: Eyes: hazel. Hair: dark. Complexion: dark. Height: 5'5".

George, James M. Pvt., Winston's Light Artillery Battery (Belmont Battery). Enlisted: 1/21/1863 at Blount County, TN, as a conscript from the Camp of Instruction at Knoxville, TN, for the duration of the war. Rolls for 1/1863 through 2/1863: Present. Rolls for 3/1863 through 4/1863: Absent, on detached service at Mobile, AL, since 4/25/1863. Rolls for 5/1863 through 8/1864: Present. On Register of Ross Hospital, Mobile, AL: Admitted on 8/22/1864 due to febris intermittens tert.; Returned to duty on 8/25/1864. Federal Rolls of Prisoners of War: Captured at Blakely, AL, on 4/9/1865; Received at Ship Island, MS, on 4/15/1865. Transferred to Vicksburg, MS, for exchange on 5/1/1865; Exchanged at Camp Townsend, MS, on 5/6/1865. Rolls of Prisoners of War, C.S.A: Surrendered at Citronelle, AL, on 5/4/1865; Paroled at Jackson, MS, on 5/12/1865.

Gibson, Elias P. (AKA Gileson) Pvt., Winston's Light Artillery Battery (Belmont Battery). Enlisted: 1/10/1863 at Bradley County, TN, as a conscript from the Camp of Instruction at Knoxville, TN, for the duration of the war. Rolls for 1/1863 through 2/1863: Present. Rolls for 3/1863 through 4/1863: Absent, on detached service with the Whitworth gun since 3/25/1863. Rolls for 5/1863 through 10/1863: Present. Rolls for 11/1863 through 12/1863: Absent, sick in hospital at Spring Hill, AL. Rolls for 1/1864 through 2/1864: Present. Rolls for 5/1864 through 8/1864: Absent, on picket duty with Lt. Alonzo Pillow. Federal Rolls of Prisoners of War: Captured at Blakely, AL, on 4/9/1865; Received at Ship Island, MS, on 4/15/1865. Transferred to Vicksburg, MS, for exchange on 5/1/1865; Exchanged at Camp Townsend, MS, on 5/6/1865. Rolls of Prisoners of War, C.S.A: Surrendered at Citronelle, AL, on 5/4/1865; Paroled at Jackson, MS, on 5/12/1865. Wounded: Yes, hit with a spent minié ball but not injured seriously. Born: Garrett County, KY. Married: Yes. Children: None. Occupation: Farmer. Residence after war: Englewood, McMinn County, TN. Property after war: Horse and buggy valued at $125, household goods valued at $150, and 188 acres of land valued at $900. Ailments after war: heart insufficience due to fatty degeneration. Confederate Pension Application dated 8/15/1911 on file at the Tennessee State Library and Archives. Target Name: Gibson, Elias P. Application Number: S13126. County: McMinn. Disposition: Approved.

Gleason, J.W. (AKA Glisson) Pvt., Winston's Light Artillery Battery (Belmont Battery). Federal Rolls of Prisoners of War: Captured at Blakely, AL, on 4/9/1865; Received at Ship Island, MS, on 4/15/1865. Transferred to Vicksburg, MS, for exchange on 5/1/1865; Exchanged at Camp Townsend, MS, on 5/6/1865.

Grace, James Pvt., Winston's Light Artillery Battery (Belmont Battery). Enlisted: 5/20/1861 at Nashville, TN. Rolls for 11/1861 through 3/1862: Present. Federal Rolls of Prisoners of War: Captured at Island No. 10 on 4/8/1862; Received at Camp Douglas, IL. Transferred to Vicksburg, MS, for exchange on 9/6/1862. Rolls for 10/1862 through 12/1862: Present, re-enlisted. Rolls for 1/1863 through 6/1863: Present.

Rolls for 7/1863 through 8/1863: Deserted on 7/20/1863. Rolls for 9/1863 through 10/1863: Absent, was returned from desertion under guard on 9/15/1863 and is now in the Provost Guard House under charges. Rolls for 11/1863 through 12/1863: Absent, under going sentence imposed by a Military Court of 12 months at hard labor administered on 11/19/1863. Rolls for 1/1864 through 2/1864: Present, released from arrest and returned to duty by order of Maj. Gen. Dabney H. Maury. Rolls for 5/1864 through 8/1864: Present. On Register of Ross Hospital, Mobile, AL: Admitted on 9/17/1864 due to febris intermittens quot; Returned to duty on 9/25/1864. Federal Rolls of Prisoners of War: Captured at Blakely, AL, on 4/9/1865; Received at Ship Island, MS, on 4/15/1865. Transferred to Vicksburg, MS, for exchange on 5/1/1865. Rolls of Prisoners of War, C.S.A: Surrendered at Citronelle, AL, on 5/4/1865; Paroled at Jackson, MS, on 5/12/1865. Remarks: Left sick at Vicksburg, MS. On Register of U.S.A. Prison Hospital, Vicksburg, MS: Admitted on 5/5/1865 due to chronic diarrhea; Released on 5/25/1865.

Grooms, Thomas S. (AKA Groomes) Pvt./Artificer, Winston's Light Artillery Battery (Belmont Battery). Enlisted: 12/14/1862 at Hamilton County, TN, for the duration of the war. Rolls for 12/1862 through 6/1863: Absent, on detached service at Chattanooga, TN, by order of Brig. Gen. Benjamin H. Helm since since 12/19/1862. Rolls for 7/1863 through 8/1863: Present, returned from detached service at Chattanooga, TN, on 8/24/1863. Rolls for 9/1863 through 8/1864: Present, appointed Artificer on 10/1/1863. On Register of Ross Hospital, Mobile, AL: Admitted on 9/26/1864 due to febris intermittens quot.; Returned to duty on 9/30/1864. Federal Rolls of Prisoners of War: Captured at Blakely, AL, on 4/9/1865; Received at Ship Island, MS, on 4/15/1865. Transferred to Vicksburg, MS, for exchange on 5/1/1865; Exchanged at Camp Townsend, MS, on 5/6/1865. Rolls of Prisoners of War, C.S.A: Surrendered at Citronelle, AL, on 5/4/1865; Paroled at Jackson, MS, on 5/12/1865.

Guinn, Harvey (AKA Gwinn, Gwynn) Pvt./Sgt., Winston's Light Artillery Battery (Belmont Battery). Enlisted: 1/7/1863 at Roane County, TN, as a conscript from the Camp of Instruction at Knoxville, TN, for the duration of the war. Rolls for 1/1863 through 2/1863: Present. Rolls for 3/1863 through 4/1863: Absent, on detached service at Mobile, AL, since 4/25/1863. Rolls for 5/1863 through 12/1863: Present. Rolls for 1/1864 through 2/1864: Present, lost horse bridle valued at $12.00 and 2 horse halters valued at $12.00. Rolls for 5/1864 through 8/1864: Deserted on 5/15/1864. Took the U.S. Oath of Allegiance on 6/2/1864 at Chattanooga, TN. Residence at oath: Rowland County, TN. Description at oath: Eyes: grey. Hair: dark. Complexion: dark. Height: 5'7". Federal Rolls of Prisoners of War: Captured at Blakely, AL, on 4/9/1865; Received at Ship Island, MS, on 4/15/1865. Transferred to Vicksburg, MS, for exchange on 5/1/1865; Exchanged at Camp Townsend, MS, on 5/6/1865.

Hampton, John Pvt., Winston's Light Artillery Battery (Belmont Battery). Enlisted: 1/10/1863 at Decatur County, TN, as a conscript from the Camp of Instruction at Knoxville, TN, for the duration of the war. Rolls for 1/1863 through 4/1863: Present. Rolls for 5/1863 through 6/1863: Absent, sick in General Hospital. Rolls for 7/1863 through 8/1864: Present. On Register of Ross Hospital, Mobile, AL: Admitted on 8/12/1864 due to febris intermittens tertian; Returned to duty on 8/19/1864. Federal Rolls of Prisoners of War: Captured at Blakely, AL, on 4/9/1865; Received at Ship Island, MS, on 4/15/1865. Transferred to Vicksburg, MS, for exchange on 5/1/1865; Exchanged at Camp Townsend, MS, on 5/6/1865. Rolls of Prisoners of War, C.S.A: Surrendered at Citronelle, AL, on 5/4/1865; Paroled at Jackson, MS, on 5/12/1865. Residence at parole: Decatur County, TN.

Hatley, Uriah (AKA Hattley, Harley, Rye) Pvt., Winston's Light Artillery Battery (Belmont Battery). On Return dated 12/1864, Department of the Gulf: Detached to Lt. Col. Huger on line of city redoubts as Instructor of Heavy Artillery. Federal Rolls of Prisoners of War: Captured at Blakely, AL, on 4/9/1865; Received at Ship Island, MS, on 4/15/1865. Transferred to Vicksburg, MS, for exchange on 5/1/1865; Exchanged at Camp Townsend, MS, on 5/6/1865. Rolls of Prisoners of War, C.S.A: Surrendered at Citronelle, AL, on 5/4/1865; Paroled at Jackson, MS, on 5/12/1865. Residence at parole: Dixon County, TN.

Hatter, Moody Pvt., Winston's Light Artillery Battery (Belmont Battery). Federal Rolls of Prisoners of War: Captured at Blakely, AL, on 4/9/1865; Received at Ship Island, MS, on 4/15/1865. Transferred to Vicksburg, MS, for exchange on 5/1/1865; Exchanged at Camp Townsend, MS, on 5/6/1865.

Horan, Martin (AKA Haran, Horn, Horne, Horin, Mart, W.) Pvt./4th Cpl./3rd Cpl., Winston's Light Artillery Battery (Belmont Battery). Enlisted: 5/21/1861 at Nashville, TN. Age at enlistment: 28. Rolls for 8/1861 through 3/1862: Present. Federal Rolls of Prisoners of War: Captured at Island No. 10 on 4/8/1862; Received at Camp Douglas, IL. Transferred to Vicksburg, MS, for exchange on 9/6/1862. Rolls for 10/1862 through 6/1863: Absent, on detached service at Mobile, AL. Rolls for 7/1863 through 10/1863: Absent, reduced to Pvt. from Cpl. on 7/1/1863 and now in Provost Guard House under charges. Rolls for 11/1863 through 2/1864: Absent, sick in hospital at Spring Hill, AL. Rolls for 5/1864 through 8/1864: Present. On Register of Ross Hospital, Mobile, AL: Admitted on 8/22/1864 due to febris intermittens quot.; Returned to duty on 8/26/1864. On Return dated 12/1864, Department of the Gulf: Detached to Lt. Col. Huger on line of city redoubts as Instructor of Heavy Artillery. Federal Rolls of Prisoners of War: Captured at Blakely, AL, on 4/9/1865; Received at Ship Island, MS, on 4/15/1865. Transferred to Vicksburg, MS, for exchange on 5/1/1865; Exchanged at Camp Townsend, MS, on 5/6/1865. Rolls of Prisoners of War, C.S.A: Surrendered at Citronelle, AL, on 5/4/1865; Paroled at Jackson, MS, on 5/12/1865. Residence at parole: Nashville, TN.

Horton, Joseph W. Pvt., Winston's Light Artillery Battery (Belmont Battery). Enlisted: 3/14/1864 at Pollard, AL, for the duration of the war. Rolls for 5/1864 through 8/1864: Present, sick in camp. Federal Rolls of Prisoners of War: Captured at Blakely, AL, on 4/9/1865; Received at Ship Island, MS, on 4/15/1865. Transferred to Vicksburg, MS, for exchange on 5/1/

1865; Exchanged at Camp Townsend, MS, on 5/6/1865. Rolls of Prisoners of War, C.S.A: Surrendered at Citronelle, AL, on 5/4/1865; Paroled at Jackson, MS, on 5/12/1865. Residence at parole: Nashville, TN. Took the U.S. Oath of Allegiance at Nashville, TN, on 5/24/1865. Residence at oath: Davidson County, TN. Description at oath: Eyes: grey. Hair: grey. Complexion: fair. Height: 6'2".

Iceberg, Simeon (AKA Iceburg, Icenburg, L.) Pvt., Winston's Light Artillery Battery (Belmont Battery). Enlisted: 1/21/1863 at Hawkins County, TN, as a conscript from the Camp of Instruction at Knoxville, TN, for the duration of the war. Rolls for 1/1863 through 2/1863: Present. Rolls for 3/1863 through 8/1863: Absent, on detached service on the floating battery by order of Brig. Gen. James E. Slaughter. Rolls for 9/1863 through 10/1863: Absent, returned from detached service on the floating battery on 10/20/1863 but sick in hospital at Mobile, AL. Rolls for 11/1863 through 12/1863: Absent, sick in hospital at Spring Hill, AL. Rolls for 1/1864 through 2/1864: Present, sick in camp; Lost a horse saddle and two horse bridles valued at $69.00. Rolls for 5/1864 through 8/1864: Absent, on picket duty with Lt. Alonzo Pillow. Federal Rolls of Prisoners of War: Captured at Blakely, AL, on 4/9/1865; Received at Ship Island, MS, on 4/15/1865. Transferred to Vicksburg, MS, for exchange on 5/1/1865; Exchanged at Camp Townsend, MS, on 5/6/1865.

Jackson, C.M. Pvt., Winston's Light Artillery Battery (Belmont Battery). Federal Rolls of Prisoners of War: Captured at Blakely, AL, on 4/9/1865; Received at Ship Island, MS, on 4/15/1865. Transferred to Vicksburg, MS, for exchange on 5/1/1865; Exchanged at Camp Townsend, MS, on 5/6/1865.

Jackson, William Pvt., Winston's Light Artillery Battery (Belmont Battery). Enlisted: 12/28/1863 at Demopolis, AL, for the duration of the war. Rolls for 1/1864 through 2/1864: Present. Rolls for 5/1864 through 8/1864: Absent, sick in hospital at Mobile, AL. On Return dated 12/1864, Department of the Gulf: Absent, on short leave since 12/29/1864. Federal Rolls of Prisoners of War: Captured at Blakely, AL, on 4/9/1865; Received at Ship Island, MS, on 4/15/1865. Transferred to Vicksburg, MS, for exchange on 5/1/1865; Exchanged at Camp Townsend, MS, on 5/6/1865. Rolls of Prisoners of War, C.S.A: Surrendered at Citronelle, AL, on 5/4/1865; Paroled at Meridian, MS, on 5/9/1865.

Joslyn, John H. (AKA Joslin, Jocelyn) Pvt./Sgt., Winston's Light Artillery Battery (Belmont Battery). Enlisted: 5/20/1861 at Nashville, TN. Rolls for 8/1861 through 3/1862: Present. Federal Rolls of Prisoners of War: Captured at Island No. 10 on 4/8/1862; Received at Camp Douglas, IL. Transferred to Vicksburg, MS, for exchange on 9/5/1862. Rolls for 10/1862 through 2/1863: Present. Rolls for 3/1863 through 4/1863: Absent, on detached service at Mobile, AL, on 4/25/1863. Rolls for 5/1863 through 12/1863: Present. Rolls for 1/1864 through 2/1864: Present, lost a valise valued at $7.00. Rolls for 5/1864 through 8/1864: Present. On Register of Ross Hospital, Mobile, AL: Admitted on 8/17/1864 due to febris cont.; Returned to duty on 8/21/1864. On Register of Ross Hospital, Mobile, AL: Admitted on 9/14/1864 due to febris remittens; Returned to duty on 9/19/1864. On Return dated 12/1864, Department of the Gulf: Detached to Lt. Col. Huger on line of city redoubts as Instructor of Heavy Artillery. Federal Rolls of Prisoners of War: Captured at Blakely, AL, on 4/9/1865; Received at Ship Island, MS, on 4/15/1865. Transferred to Vicksburg, MS, for exchange on 5/1/1865; Exchanged at Camp Townsend, MS, on 5/6/1865. Rolls of Prisoners of War, C.S.A: Surrendered at Citronelle, AL, on 5/4/1865; Paroled at Meridian, MS, on 5/9/1865.

King, J.G. Pvt., Winston's Light Artillery Battery (Belmont Battery). Federal Rolls of Prisoners of War: Captured at Blakely, AL, on 4/9/1865; Received at Ship Island, MS, on 4/15/1865. Transferred to Vicksburg, MS, for exchange on 5/1/1865; Exchanged at Camp Townsend, MS, on 5/6/1865.

Lapsley, Norvell A. (AKA Norrell, W.A.) Asst. Surg., Winston's Light Artillery Battery (Belmont Battery). Federal Rolls of Prisoners of War: Captured at Blakely, AL, on 4/9/1865; Received at Ship Island, MS, on 4/16/1865. Transferred to Vicksburg, MS, for exchange on 4/28/1865; Confined at New Orleans, LA, on 4/30/1865. Exchanged at Camp Townsend, MS, on 5/6/1865. Rolls of Prisoners of War, C.S.A: Surrendered at Citronelle, AL, on 5/4/1865; Paroled at Jackson, MS, on 5/15/1865. Took the U.S. Oath of Allegiance at Nashville, TN, on 6/2/1865. Residence at oath: Smith County, TN. Description at oath: Eyes: hazel. Hair: dark. Complexion: fair. Height: 5'8½".

Lee, M.T. (AKA M.F.) Sgt., Winston's Light Artillery Battery (Belmont Battery). Federal Rolls of Prisoners of War: Captured at Blakely, AL, on 4/9/1865; Received at Ship Island, MS, on 4/15/1865. Transferred to Vicksburg, MS, for exchange on 5/1/1865; Exchanged at Camp Townsend, MS, on 5/6/1865.

Lindsey, John W. 1st Sgt./Sr. 1st Lt., Winston's Light Artillery Battery (Belmont Battery). Enlisted: 10/1/1861 at Nashville, TN, in Capt. Anglade's Co. as a 1st Sgt.; Transferred on 1/15/1862 as 1st Sgt. Rolls for 11/1861 through 3/1862: Present. Federal Rolls of Prisoners of War: Captured at Island No. 10 on 4/8/1862; Received at Camp Chase, OH. Transferred to Johnson's Island, OH, on 4/26/1862; Received at Camp Chase, OH, on 7/4/1862 and exchanged on 8/25/1862. Rolls for 9/1862 through 2/1863: Present, elected 1st Lt. on 10/7/1862. Rolls for 3/1863 through 4/1863: Absent, on detached service at Mobile, AL, since 4/25/1863. Rolls for 5/1863 through 8/1864: Present. On Return dated 12/1864, Department of the Gulf: Detached with lieutenants Lindsay and Thomas with section reporting to Brig. Gen. St. John R. Liddell on eastern shore since 12/15/1864. Federal Rolls of Prisoners of War: Captured at Blakely, AL, on 4/9/1865; Received at Ship Island, MS, on 4/15/1865. Transferred to Vicksburg, MS, for exchange on 4/28/1865; Confined at New Orleans, LA, on 4/30/1865. Exchanged at Camp Townsend, MS, on 5/6/1865. Rolls of Prisoners of War, C.S.A: Surrendered at Citronelle, AL, on 5/4/1865; Paroled at Jackson, MS, on 5/15/1865. Took the U.S. Oath of Allegiance at Nashville, TN, on 5/31/1865. Residence at oath: Davidson County, TN. Description at oath: Eyes: blue. Hair: light. Complexion: fair. Height: 5'8".

Lock, Joe E. Pvt., Winston's Light Artillery Battery

(Belmont Battery). Federal Rolls of Prisoners of War: Captured at Blakely, AL, on 4/9/1865; Received at Ship Island, MS, on 4/15/1865. Transferred to Vicksburg, MS, for exchange on 5/1/1865; Exchanged at Camp Townsend, MS, on 5/6/1865.

Loflin, William Pvt., Winston's Light Artillery Battery (Belmont Battery). Federal Rolls of Prisoners of War: Captured at Blakely, AL, on 4/9/1865; Received at Ship Island, MS, on 4/15/1865. Transferred to Vicksburg, MS, for exchange on 5/1/1865; Exchanged at Camp Townsend, MS, on 5/6/1865.

Lyle, J.D. Pvt., Winston's Light Artillery Battery (Belmont Battery). Enlisted: 12/16/1862 at Hamilton County, TN, for the duration of the war. Rolls for 12/1862 through 8/1863: Absent, on detached service at Chattanooga, TN, by order of Brig. Gen. Benjamin H. Helm since 12/1862. Rolls for 7/1863 through 2/1864: Present, returned from detached service at Chattanooga, TN, on 8/24/1863. Rolls for 5/1864 through 8/1864: Absent, on picket duty with Lt. Alonzo Pillow and on extra daily duty as Wheelwright. On Return dated 12/1864, Department of the Gulf: On extra daily duty as Wheelwright. Federal Rolls of Prisoners of War: Captured at Blakely, AL, on 4/9/1865; Received at Ship Island, MS, on 4/15/1865. Transferred to Vicksburg, MS, for exchange on 5/1/1865; Exchanged at Camp Townsend, MS, on 5/6/1865. Rolls of Prisoners of War, C.S.A: Surrendered at Citronelle, AL, on 5/4/1865; Paroled at Jackson, MS, on 5/12/1865. Wounded: Yes, struck across top of head with a musket by a Federal soldier resulting in a 1 to 2 inch gash after surrendering at Blakely, AL. Born: 6/10/1837 at Jefferson County, TN. Married: Yes, wife died in 1890. Children: 3 sons. Residence after war: Calhoun, McMinn County, TN. Property after war: None. Ailments after war: Lower third of left arm amputated, scar on side of head, enlarged prostate, kidney disease, cistetis, and weak back. Died: 11/23/1908. Confederate Pension Application dated 4/14/1903 on file at the Tennessee State Library and Archives. Target Name: Lyle, J.D. Application Number: S4867. County: McMinn. Disposition: Approved.

McCullough, A. Pvt., Winston's Light Artillery Battery (Belmont Battery). Federal Rolls of Prisoners of War: Captured at Blakely, AL, on 4/9/1865; Received at Ship Island, MS, on 4/15/1865. Transferred to Vicksburg, MS, for exchange on 5/1/1865; Exchanged at Camp Townsend, MS, on 5/6/1865. Born: 5/15/1849 near Manlyville, Henry County, TN. Married: Eudora Jane "Dora" Clements on 11/9/1881 by H.P. Lowry at his home in Henry County, TN. Died: 11/29/1930 at the West Tennessee Asylum in Bolivar, TN, due to cerebral hemorrhage and senile psychosis. Buried: Henry County, TN. Wife born: 9/15/1855 at Manlyville, Henry County, TN. Wife's property: 80 acres of land valued at $800. Wife died: 3/29/1932. Confederate Widows Pension Application dated 12/17/1930 on file at the Tennessee State Library and Archives. Target Name: McCullough, Eudora Jane. Application Number: W10011. County: Henry. Disposition: Approved.

McDonald, James Pvt., Winston's Light Artillery Battery (Belmont Battery). Enlisted: 6/14/1861 at Nashville, TN, for 12 months. Rolls for 8/1861 through 11/1861: Present. Federal Rolls of Prisoners of War: Captured at Island No. 10 on 4/8/1862; Received at Camp Douglas, IL. Transferred to Vicksburg, MS, for exchange on 9/6/1862. Rolls for 9/1862 through 10/1862: Discharged at Jackson, MS, on 10/17/1862 due to being overage and Final Statement given. Rolls for 11/1862 through 2/1863: Present, re-enlisted on 11/3/1862 at Mobile, AL, for the duration of the war. Rolls for 3/1863 through 4/1863: Absent, on detached service at Mobile, AL, since 4/25/1863. Rolls for 5/1863 through 8/1864: Present. On Register of Ross Hospital, Mobile, AL: Admitted on 8/16/1864 due to febris remittens; Returned to duty on 8/22/1864. Federal Rolls of Prisoners of War: Captured at Blakely, AL, on 4/9/1865; Received at Ship Island, MS, on 4/15/1865. Transferred to Vicksburg, MS, for exchange on 5/1/1865; Exchanged at Camp Townsend, MS, on 5/6/1865. Rolls of Prisoners of War, C.S.A: Surrendered at Citronelle, AL, on 5/4/1865; Paroled while hospitalized at Jackson, MS, on 5/12/1865. Took the U.S. Oath of Allegiance at Nashville, TN, on 5/24/1865. Residence at oath: Humphries County, TN. Description at oath: Eyes: grey. Hair: dark. Complexion: dark. Height: 5'5".

McGuinn, J. Pvt., Winston's Light Artillery Battery (Belmont's). Federal Rolls of Prisoners of War: Captured at Blakely, AL, on 4/9/1865; Received at Ship Island, MS, on 4/15/1865. Transferred to Vicksburg, MS, for exchange on 5/1/1865; Exchanged at Camp Townsend, MS, on 5/6/1865.

McNilly, William M. (AKA McNally, McNealy, McNelly, A.M.) Pvt., Barry's Light Artillery Battery (Lookout Battery). Enlisted: 2/1/1863 at Knoxville, TN, for 3 years. Transferred from the Camp of Instruction. Rolls for 2/1863 through 10/1864: Present. Federal Rolls of Prisoners of War: Captured at Spanish Fort, AL, on 4/8/1865; Received at Ship Island, MS, on 4/10/1865. Transferred to Vicksburg, MS, for exchange on 5/1/1865; Exchanged at Camp Townsend, MS, on 5/6/1865. Rolls of Prisoners of War, C.S.A: Surrendered at Decatur, AL, on 5/17/1865; Took the U.S. Oath of Allegiance at Nashville, TN, on 5/22/1865. Description at oath: Eyes: blue. Hair: light. Complexion: fair. Height: 5'9". Residence at oath: McMinn County, TN.

McQuinn, J. Pvt., Winston's Light Artillery Battery (Belmont Battery). Federal Rolls of Prisoners of War: Captured at Blakely, AL, on 4/9/1865; Received at Ship Island, MS, on 4/15/1865. Transferred to Vicksburg, MS, for exchange on 5/1/1865; Exchanged at Camp Townsend, MS, on 5/6/1865.

Maher, N. Pvt., Winston's Light Artillery Battery (Belmont Battery). Federal Rolls of Prisoners of War: Captured at Blakely, AL, on 4/9/1865; Received at Ship Island, MS, on 4/15/1865. Transferred to Vicksburg, MS, for exchange on 5/1/1865; Exchanged at Camp Townsend, MS, on 5/6/1865.

Mock, L.L. Pvt., Winston's Light Artillery Battery (Belmont Battery). Federal Rolls of Prisoners of War: Captured at Blakely, AL, on 4/9/1865; Received at Ship Island, MS, on 4/15/1865. Transferred to Vicksburg, MS, for exchange on 5/1/1865; Exchanged at Camp Townsend, MS, on 5/6/1865.

Moore, T. Pvt., Winston's Light Artillery Battery (Belmont Battery). Federal Rolls of Prisoners of War: Captured at Blakely, AL, on 4/9/1865; Received at Ship Island, MS, on 4/15/1865. Transferred to Vicksburg,

MS, for exchange on 5/1/1865; Exchanged at Camp Townsend, MS, on 5/6/1865.

Moran, Thomas Pvt./4th Cpl., Winston's Light Artillery Battery (Belmont Battery). Enlisted: 12/17/1862 at Mobile, AL, as a substitution for William H. Sanders for the duration of the war. Occupation at enlistment: Laborer. Rolls for 12/1862 through 2/1863: Present. Rolls for 3/1863 through 4/1863: Absent, on detached service at Mobile, AL. Rolls for 5/1863 through 8/1864: Present, appointed 4th Cpl. on 3/1/1864. On Register of Ross Hospital, Mobile, AL: Admitted on 9/9/1864 due to syphilis primition; Transferred to Greenville, AL, General Hospital on 9/13/1864. On Return dated 12/1864, Department of the Gulf: Absent, sick. Federal Rolls of Prisoners of War: Captured at Blakely, AL, on 4/9/1865; Received at Ship Island, MS, on 4/15/1865. Transferred to Vicksburg, MS, for exchange on 5/1/1865; Exchanged at Camp Townsend, MS, on 5/6/1865. Rolls of Prisoners of War, C.S.A: Surrendered at Citronelle, AL, on 5/4/1865; Paroled at Jackson, MS, on 5/12/1865. Age at parole: 39. Born: Roscomonan, Ireland.

Morris, Samuel Pvt., Winston's Light Artillery Battery (Belmont Battery). Enlisted: 1/10/1863 at Blount County, TN, as a conscript from the Camp of Instruction at Knoxville, TN, for the duration of the war. Rolls for 1/1863 through 2/1863: Present. Rolls for 3/1863 through 4/1863: Absent, on detached service with the Whitworth gun since 4/10/1863. Rolls for 5/1863 through 6/1863: Absent, without leave since 6/21/1863. Rolls for 7/1863 through 8/1863: Present, attempted desertion on 6/25/1863 but caught near Selma, AL, on 7/1/1863; Released on the President's Proclamation. Rolls for 9/1863 through 8/1864: Present. Federal Rolls of Prisoners of War: Captured at Blakely, AL, on 4/9/1865; Received at Ship Island, MS, on 4/15/1865. Transferred to Vicksburg, MS, for exchange on 5/1/1865; Exchanged at Camp Townsend, MS, on 5/6/1865. Rolls of Prisoners of War, C.S.A: Surrendered at Citronelle, AL, on 5/4/1865; Paroled at Jackson, MS, on 5/12/1865.

Moyat, B. Eugene Pvt./Bugler, Winston's Light Artillery Battery (Belmont Battery). Enlisted: 10/23/1863 at Mobile, AL, as a substitution for J.B. Calf for the duration of the war. Rolls for 9/1863 through 12/1863: Present, appointed Bugler on on 10/23/1863. Rolls for 1/1864 through 2/1864: Present, lost horse saddle valued at $45.00 and horse bridle valued at $12.00. Rolls for 5/1864 through 8/1864: Present. Federal Rolls of Prisoners of War: Captured at Blakely, AL, on 4/9/1865; Received at Ship Island, MS, on 4/15/1865. Transferred to Vicksburg, MS, for exchange on 5/1/1865; Exchanged at Camp Townsend, MS, on 5/6/1865. Rolls of Prisoners of War, C.S.A: Surrendered at Citronelle, AL, on 5/4/1865; Paroled at Jackson, MS, on 5/12/1865. Age at parole: 42. Residence at parole: Houma, LA. Description at parole: Eyes: grey. Hair: auburn. Complexion: dark. Height: 5'7". Name on Register of Paroled Prisoners at Terrebonne Parish, LA.

Parnell, E. Pvt., Winston's Light Artillery Battery (Belmont Battery). Federal Rolls of Prisoners of War: Captured at Blakely, AL, on 4/9/1865; Received at Ship Island, MS, on 4/15/1865. Transferred to Vicksburg, MS, for exchange on 5/1/1865; Exchanged at Camp Townsend, MS, on 5/6/1865.

Peet, H. Pvt., Winston's Light Artillery Battery (Belmont Battery). Federal Rolls of Prisoners of War: Captured at Blakely, AL, on 4/9/1865; Received at Ship Island, MS, on 4/15/1865. Transferred to Vicksburg, MS, for exchange on 5/1/1865; Exchanged at Camp Townsend, MS, on 5/6/1865.

Perry, Frank Pvt., Winston's Light Artillery Battery (Belmont Battery). Federal Rolls of Prisoners of War: Captured at Blakely, AL, on 4/9/1865; Received at Ship Island, MS, on 4/15/1865. Transferred to Vicksburg, MS, for exchange on 5/1/1865; Exchanged at Camp Townsend, MS, on 5/6/1865.

Presnell, Caleb Cpl., Winston's Light Artillery Battery (Belmont Battery). Federal Rolls of Prisoners of War: Captured at Blakely, AL, on 4/9/1865; Received at Ship Island, MS, on 4/15/1865. Transferred to Vicksburg, MS, for exchange on 5/1/1865; Exchanged at Camp Townsend, MS, on 5/6/1865.

Riley, A.K. Pvt., Winston's Light Artillery Battery (Belmont Battery). Federal Rolls of Prisoners of War: Captured at Blakely, AL, on 4/9/1865; Received at Ship Island, MS, on 4/15/1865. Transferred to Vicksburg, MS, for exchange on 5/1/1865; Exchanged at Camp Townsend, MS, on 5/6/1865.

Roberts, James M. Pvt., Barry's Light Artillery Battery (Lookout Battery). Enlisted: 5/31/1862 at Chattanooga, TN, for 2 years. Transferred from the 26th Tennessee Infantry. Co.B. Rolls for 7/1862 through 12/1863: Present. On Register of 1st Mississippi C.S.A. Hospital, Jackson, MS: Admitted on 2/16/1864 due to debilitas; Returned to duty on 2/24/1864. Rolls for 3/1864 through 10/1864: Present. Federal Rolls of Prisoners of War: Captured at Spanish Fort, AL, on 4/8/1865; Received at Ship Island, MS, on 4/10/1865. Transferred to Vicksburg, MS, for exchange on 5/1/1865; Exchanged at Camp Townsend, MS, on 5/6/1865.

Rogers, John Pvt., Winston's Light Artillery Battery (Belmont Battery). Federal Rolls of Prisoners of War: Captured at Blakely, AL, on 4/9/1865; Received at Ship Island, MS, on 4/15/1865. Transferred to Vicksburg, MS, for exchange on 5/1/1865; Exchanged at Camp Townsend, MS, on 5/6/1865.

Rowe, William H. Pvt., Winston's Light Artillery Battery (Belmont Battery). Enlisted: 1/21/1863 at Hawkins County, TN, as a conscript from the Camp of Instruction at Knoxville, TN, for the duration of the war. Rolls for 1/1863 through 2/1863: Present. Rolls for 3/1863 through 4/1863: Absent, on detached service with the Whitworth gun since 3/25/1863. Rolls for 5/1863 through 2/1864: Present. Rolls for 5/1864 through 8/1864: Present, sick in camp. On Register of Ross Hospital, Mobile, AL: Admitted on 11/20/1864 due to febris intermittens quot.; Returned to duty on 11/26/1864. Federal Rolls of Prisoners of War: Captured at Blakely, AL, on 4/9/1865; Received at Ship Island, MS, on 4/15/1865. Transferred to Vicksburg, MS, for exchange on 5/1/1865; Exchanged at Camp Townsend, MS, on 5/6/1865. Rolls of Prisoners of War, C.S.A: Surrendered at Citronelle, AL, on 5/4/1865; Paroled at Jackson, MS, on 5/12/1865. Residence at parole: Carter County, TN.

Rowe, William Henry Harrison Pvt., Winston's Light Artillery Battery (Belmont Battery). Federal Rolls of Prisoners of War: Captured at Spanish Fort, AL, on 4/8/1865; Received at Ship Island, MS, on 4/10/1865.

Transferred to Vicksburg, MS, for exchange on 5/1/1865; Exchanged at Camp Townsend, MS, on 5/6/1865. Wounded: No, but contracted mumps and rheumatism. Born: 3/8/1820 at Carter County, TN. Married: Yes. Children: None. Occupation: Corn Mill Tender. Residence after war: Johnson City, TN. Property after war: None. Ailments after war: Chronic muscular rheumatism. Died: 3/2/1919 at Unicoi County, TN. Confederate Pension Application dated 5/25/1906 on file at the Tennessee State Library and Archives. Target Name: Rowe, William Henry Harrison. Application Number: S8226. County: Unicoi. Disposition: Approved.

Scally, James (AKA Scalley, Sealy, Seally, Skally, Skelly) Pvt./5th Cpl./2nd Sgt., Winston's Light Artillery Battery (Belmont Battery). Enlisted: 6/1/1861 at Nashville, TN, for 12 months. Age at enlistment: 24. Rolls for 11/1861 through 3/1862: Present. Federal Rolls of Prisoners of War: Captured at Island No. 10 on 4/8/1862; Received at Camp Douglas, IL. Transferred to Vicksburg, MS, for exchange on 9/6/1862. Rolls for 10/1862 through 12/1862: Present, re-enlisted. Rolls for 1/1863 through 6/1863: Present, appointed 5th Cpl. on 2/1/1863. Rolls for 7/1863 through 8/1864: Present, appointed 2nd Sgt. on 7/1/1863. On Return dated 12/1864, Department of the Gulf: Detached to Lt. Col. Huger on line of city redoubts as Instructor of Heavy Artillery. Federal Rolls of Prisoners of War: Captured at Blakely, AL, on 4/9/1865; Received at Ship Island, MS, on 4/15/1865. Transferred to Vicksburg, MS, for exchange on 5/1/1865; Exchanged at Camp Townsend, MS, on 5/6/1865. Rolls of Prisoners of War, C.S.A: Surrendered at Citronelle, AL, on 5/4/1865; Paroled at Jackson, MS, on 5/12/1865.

Scott, Milo W. Pvt., Barry's Light Artillery Battery (Lookout Battery). Enlisted: 7/28/1862 at Chattanooga, TN, for 3 years. Paid $50.00 bounty. Rolls for 7/1862 through 8/1862: Present. Rolls for 9/1862 through 10/1862: Absent, sick at Chattanooga, TN, through 12/1862. Rolls for 1/1863 through 4/1864: Present. Rolls for 9/1864 through 10/1864: Absent, in hospital at Atlanta, GA, since 8/26/1864. On Register of Ocmulgee Hospital, Macon, GA: Admitted on 8/29/1864 due to diarrhea; Transferred to Blackie Hospital, Augusta, GA. Federal Rolls of Prisoners of War: Captured at Spanish Fort, AL, on 4/8/1865; Received at Ship Island, MS, on 4/10/1865. Transferred to Vicksburg, MS, for exchange on 5/1/1865; Exchanged at Camp Townsend, MS, on 5/6/1865.

Shelton, James K.P. Pvt., Winston's Light Artillery Battery (Belmont Battery). Federal Rolls of Prisoners of War: Captured at Blakely, AL, on 4/9/1865; Received at Ship Island, MS, on 4/15/1865. Transferred to Vicksburg, MS, for exchange on 5/1/1865; Exchanged at Camp Townsend, MS, on 5/6/1865. Wounded: No. Born: 1844 at Rutherford County, TN. Married: Yes, Sophia Keele on 1/10/1866 at Coffee County, TN, by Rev. Carroll Haley. Children: 4 — 2 sons and 2 daughters. Occupation: Farmer. Residence after war: Gould, Coffee County, TN. Property after war: 10 acres of land valued at $50. Ailments after war: kidney trouble, heart trouble and rheumatism. Died: 10/15/1908 at Coffee County, TN. Wife Born: 1839 in Alabama. Confederate Pension Application dated 3/3/1903 on file at the Tennessee State Library and Archives. Target Name: Shelton, J.P. County: Coffee. Disposition: Approved. Also a Confederate Widows Pension Application dated 10/27/1908 on file. Target Name: Shelton, Sophia. Application Number: W2144. County: Coffee. Disposition: Approved.

Slover, Albert M. (AKA Sleuer) Pvt., Barry's Light Artillery Battery (Lookout Battery). Enlisted: 10/14/1862 at Knoxville, TN, for 3 years. Transferred from the Camp of Instruction. Rolls for 10/1862 through 10/1864: Present. Federal Rolls of Prisoners of War: Captured at Spanish Fort, AL, on 4/8/1865; Received at Ship Island, MS, on 4/10/1865. Transferred to Vicksburg, MS, for exchange on 5/1/1865; Exchanged at Camp Townsend, MS, on 5/6/1865.

Slover, James E. (AKA Sleuer) Pvt., Barry's Light Artillery Battery (Lookout Battery). Enlisted: 10/17/1862 at Knoxville, TN, for 3 years. Rolls for 10/1862 through 10/1864: Present. Federal Rolls of Prisoners of War: Captured at Spanish Fort, AL, on 4/8/1865; Received at Ship Island, MS, on 4/10/1865. Transferred to Vicksburg, MS, for exchange on 5/1/1865; Exchanged at Camp Townsend, MS, on 5/6/1865.

Smith, H. Pvt., Winston's Light Artillery Battery (Belmont Battery). Federal Rolls of Prisoners of War: Captured at Blakely, AL, on 4/9/1865; Received at Ship Island, MS, on 4/15/1865. Transferred to Vicksburg, MS, for exchange on 5/1/1865; Exchanged at Camp Townsend, MS, on 5/6/1865.

Stephens, William K. (AKA Stevens, W.R.) Pvt., Barry's Light Artillery Battery (Lookout Battery). Enlisted: 2/3/1863 at Knoxville, TN, for 3 years. Transferred from the Camp of Instruction. Rolls for 2/1863 through 4/1863: Present. Rolls for 5/1863 through 10/1863: Absent, in hospital at Jackson, MS, since 5/31/1863. Rolls for 11/1863 through 10/1864: Present. Federal Rolls of Prisoners of War: Captured at Spanish Fort, AL, on 4/8/1865; Received at Ship Island, MS, on 4/10/1865. Transferred to Vicksburg, MS, for exchange on 5/1/1865; Exchanged at Camp Townsend, MS, on 5/6/1865. Rolls of Prisoners of War, C.S.A: Surrendered at Decatur, AL, on 5/17/1865; Took the U.S. Oath of Allegiance at Nashville, TN, on 5/22/1865. Description at oath: Eyes: gray. Hair: light. Complexion: fair. Height: 5'11". Residence at oath: Meigs County, TN.

Stewart, J.T. Pvt., Winston's Light Artillery Battery (Belmont Battery). Federal Rolls of Prisoners of War: Captured at Blakely, AL, on 4/9/1865; Received at Ship Island, MS, on 4/15/1865. Transferred to Vicksburg, MS, for exchange on 5/1/1865; Exchanged at Camp Townsend, MS, on 5/6/1865.

Sullivan, John Pvt., Winston's Light Artillery Battery (Belmont Battery). Enlisted: 3/2/1863 at Mobile, AL, for the duration of the war. Rolls for 5/1863 through 8/1864: Present. Federal Rolls of Prisoners of War: Captured at Blakely, AL, on 4/9/1865; Received at Ship Island, MS, on 4/15/1865. Transferred to Vicksburg, MS, for exchange on 5/1/1865; Exchanged at Camp Townsend, MS, on 5/6/1865. Rolls of Prisoners of War, C.S.A: Surrendered at Citronelle, AL, on 5/4/1865; Paroled at Jackson, MS, on 5/12/1865. Residence at parole: Mobile, AL.

Tate, Perryman M. Pvt., Barry's Light Artillery Battery (Lookout Battery). Enlisted: 1/19/1863 at Chattanooga, TN, for 3 years. Rolls for 1/1863 through

2/1863: Present. Rolls for 3/1863 through 6/1863: Absent, in hospital at Greenville, AL. Rolls for 9/1863 through 10/1863: Present. Rolls for 11/1863 through 4/1864: Present, on extra duty making oil for harness. Rolls for 9/1864 through 10/1864: Present. Federal Rolls of Prisoners of War: Captured at Spanish Fort, AL, on 4/8/1865; Received at Ship Island, MS, on 4/10/1865. Transferred to Vicksburg, MS, for exchange on 5/1/1865; Exchanged at Camp Townsend, MS, on 5/6/1865.

Thomas, David Dyre Pvt./Cpl., Barry's Light Artillery Battery (Lookout Battery). Enlisted: 5/15/1862 at Chattanooga, TN, for 3 years. Rolls for 5/1862 through 1/1864: Present. On Register of Loring's Division Hospital, Marion, AL: Admitted on 2/24/1864; Returned to duty on 3/18/1864. Rolls for 4/1864 through 10/1864: Present. Federal Rolls of Prisoners of War: Captured at Spanish Fort, AL, on 4/8/1865; Received at Ship Island, MS, on 4/10/1865. Transferred to Vicksburg, MS, for exchange on 5/1/1865; Exchanged at Camp Townsend, MS, on 5/6/1865.

Thomas, John B. Pvt./1st Sgt./Jr. 2nd Lt., Winston's Light Artillery Battery (Belmont Battery). Enlisted: 3/15/1862 at Memphis, TN, for the duration of the war. Federal Rolls of Prisoners of War: Captured at Island No. 10 on 4/8/1862; Received at Camp Douglas, IL. Transferred to Vicksburg, MS, for exchange on 9/8/1862. On Register of U.S.A. Prison Hospital, Camp Douglas, IL: Admitted on 6/20/1862 due to typhoid fever; Released on 7/12/1863. Rolls for 10/1862 through 8/1863: Present, appointed 1st Sgt. on 10/7/1862 and elected Jr. 2nd Lt. on 7/20/1863. Rolls for 9/1863 through 10/1863: Absent, sick in hospital at Spring Hill, AL, since 10/27/1863. Rolls for 11/1863 through 2/1864: Present. Rolls for 5/1864 through 8/1864: Absent, on picket duty with Lt. Alonzo Pillow on the East Fowl River. On Return dated 12/1864, Department of the Gulf: On detached service with Lt. Lindsay in command of section on the eastern shore. Federal Rolls of Prisoners of War: Captured at Blakely, AL, on 4/9/1865; Received at Ship Island, MS, on 4/16/1865. Confined at New Orleans, LA, on 4/30/1865; Transferred to Vicksburg, MS, for exchange on 4/28/1865. Exchanged at Camp Townsend, MS, on 5/6/1865. Rolls of Prisoners of War, C.S.A: Surrendered at Citronelle, AL, on 5/4/1865; Paroled at Jackson, MS, on 5/15/1865.

Thomas, John C. Asst. Surg., 41st Tennessee Infantry. F & S. Federal Rolls of Prisoners of War: Captured in front of Blakely, AL, on 4/1/1865; Received at Ship Island, MS, on 4/4/1865. Transferred to Vicksburg, MS, for exchange on 4/28/1865; Confined at New Orleans, LA, on 4/30/1865. Exchanged at Camp Townsend, MS, on 5/6/1865. Rolls of Prisoners of War, C.S.A: Surrendered at Citronelle, AL, on 5/4/1865; Paroled at Meridian, MS, on 5/11/1865.

Thomas, N.E. Pvt., Winston's Light Artillery Battery (Belmont Battery). Federal Rolls of Prisoners of War: Captured at Blakely, AL, on 4/9/1865; Received at Ship Island, MS, on 4/15/1865. Transferred to Vicksburg, MS, for exchange on 5/1/1865; Exchanged at Camp Townsend, MS, on 5/6/1865.

Traynor, James P. Pvt., Barry's Light Artillery Battery (Lookout Battery). Enlisted: 7/27/1862 at Chattanooga, TN, for 3 years. Rolls for 8/1862 through 2/1863: Present. Rolls for 3/1863 through 4/1863: Present, sick in quarters. Rolls for 5/1863 through 10/1863: Present. Rolls for 11/1863 through 12/1863: Present, on duty at Way's Bluff. Rolls for 3/1864 through 10/1864: Present. Federal Rolls of Prisoners of War: Captured at Spanish Fort, AL, on 4/8/1865; Received at Ship Island, MS, on 4/10/1865. Transferred to Vicksburg, MS, for exchange on 5/1/1865; Exchanged at Camp Townsend, MS, on 5/6/1865.

Wade, William H. Pvt./Cpl./Artificer, Winston's Light Artillery Battery (Belmont Battery). Enlisted: 4/1/1863 at Mobile, AL, for the duration of the war. Rolls for 4/1863 through 6/1863: Present. Rolls for 7/1863 through 8/1863: Absent, sick in hospital at Mobile, AL; Appointed Cpl. on 7/1/1863. Rolls for 9/1863 through 10/1863: Present, appointed Artificer on 10/1/1863. Rolls for 11/1863 through 8/1864: Present. On Register of Ross Hospital, Mobile, AL: Admitted on 8/5/1864 due to febris intermittens tert.; Returned to duty on 8/9/1864. On Register of Ross Hospital, Mobile, AL: Admitted on 9/9/1864 due to febris intermittens tert.; Returned to duty on 9/16/1864. Federal Rolls of Prisoners of War: Captured at Blakely, AL, on 4/9/1865; Received at Ship Island, MS, on 4/15/1865. Transferred to Vicksburg, MS, for exchange on 5/1/1865; Exchanged at Camp Townsend, MS, on 5/6/1865. Rolls of Prisoners of War, C.S.A: Captured at Citronelle, AL, on 5/4/1865; Paroled at Jackson, MS, on 5/12/1865. Remarks: Left sick on the road between Vicksburg, MS, and Jackson, MS. On Register of U.S.A. Post Hospital, Jackson, MS: Admitted on 5/14/1865 due to bulbo syphilis; Released on 6/12/1865.

Walker, James Sgt., Winston's Light Artillery Battery (Belmont Battery). Federal Rolls of Prisoners of War: Captured at Blakely, AL, on 4/9/1865; Received at Ship Island, MS, on 4/15/1865. Transferred to Vicksburg, MS, for exchange on 5/1/1865; Exchanged at Camp Townsend, MS, on 5/6/1865.

Warnick, Edward A. (AKA Warnek, Warneke) Pvt., Barry's Light Artillery Battery (Lookout Battery). Enlisted: 5/14/1862 at Chattanooga, TN, for 3 years. Paid $50.00 bounty. Rolls for 5/1862 through 10/1864: Present. Federal Rolls of Prisoners of War: Captured at Spanish Fort, AL, on 4/8/1865; Received at Ship Island, MS, on 4/10/1865. Transferred to Vicksburg, MS, for exchange on 5/1/1865; Exchanged at Camp Townsend, MS, on 5/6/1865.

Weishampt, Jacob Pvt., Barry's Light Artillery Battery (Lookout Battery). Enlisted: 2/1/1863 at Knoxville, TN, for 3 years. Transferred from the Camp of Instruction. Rolls for 2/1863 through 12/1863: Present. Rolls for 3/1864 through 4/1864: Present, sick in quarters. Rolls for 9/1864 through 10/1864: Present. Federal Rolls of Prisoners of War: Captured at Spanish Fort, AL, on 4/8/1865; Received at Ship Island, MS, on 4/10/1865. Transferred to Vicksburg, MS, for exchange on 5/1/1865; Exchanged at Camp Townsend, MS, on 5/6/1865. Rolls of Prisoners of War, C.S.A: Surrendered at Decatur, AL, on 5/17/1865; Took the U.S. Oath of Allegiance at Chattanooga, TN, on 5/27/1865. Description at oath: Eyes: blue. Hair: dark. Complexion: dark. Height: 5'5".

Wheatley, H. (AKA Whatley) Pvt., 55th Tennessee Infantry. Co. A. Enlisted: 10/1/1861 at Trenton, TN, for 1 year. Age at enlistment: 22. Federal Rolls of

Prisoners of War: Captured at Island No. 10 on 4/8/1862; Received at Camp Randall, WI, on 5/13/1862. Forwarded to Camp Douglas, IL; Transferred to Vicksburg, MS, for exchange on 9/4/1862. On Register of Breckinridge's Division Hospital, Lauderdale Springs, MS: Present on detached service from 7/1863 through 8/1863 by order of Surgeon J.W. Thompson. Federal Rolls of Prisoners of War: Captured at Gravel Hill, Alabama on 3/24/1865; Received at Ship Island, MS, on 4/4/1865. Transferred to Vicksburg, MS, for exchange on 5/1/1865; Exchanged at Camp Townsend, MS, on 5/6/1865.

Whitehead, W.D. Cpl., Winston's Light Artillery Battery (Belmont Battery). Federal Rolls of Prisoners of War: Captured at Blakely, AL, on 4/9/1865; Received at Ship Island, MS, on 4/15/1865. Transferred to Vicksburg, MS, for exchange on 5/1/1865; Exchanged at Camp Townsend, MS, on 5/6/1865.

Wiggins, Joseph O. Pvt., Winston's Light Artillery Battery (Belmont Battery). Federal Rolls of Prisoners of War: Captured at Blakely, AL, on 4/9/1865; Received at Ship Island, MS, on 4/15/1865. Transferred to Vicksburg, MS, for exchange on 5/1/1865; Exchanged at Camp Townsend, MS, on 5/6/1865.

Winston, George A. Sgt. Maj./5th Sgt./1st Sgt., Winston's Light Artillery Battery (Belmont Battery). F & S. Enlisted: 12/30/1861 at Nashville, TN, for 12 months in the 44th Tennessee Infantry; Transferred on 3/15/1863 and appointed Sgt. Major same day. Rolls for 3/1863 through 2/1864: Present, promoted from 5th Sgt. to 1st Sgt. on 7/20/1863. Rolls for 5/1864 through 8/1864: Present, sick in camp. On Return dated 12/1864, Department of the Gulf: On detached service with Lt. Lindsay. Federal Rolls of Prisoners of War: Captured at Blakely, AL, on 4/9/1865; Received at Ship Island, MS, on 4/15/1865. Transferred to Vicksburg, MS, for exchange on 4/28/1865; Exchanged at Camp Townsend, MS, on 5/6/1865. Rolls of Prisoners of War, C.S.A: Surrendered at Citronelle, AL, on 5/4/1865; Paroled while hospitalized at Jackson, MS, on 5/12/1865.

Winston, William C. 2nd Lt./1st Lt./Capt., Winston's Light Artillery Battery (Belmont Battery). Enlisted: 5/25/1861 at Nashville, TN; Elected 1st Lt. at reorganization of company on 10/7/1862. Rolls for 11/1861 through 3/1862: Present. Federal Rolls of Prisoners of War: Captured at Island No. 10 on 4/7/1862; Received at Johnson's Island, OH, on 5/16/1862. Transferred to Vicksburg, MS, for exchange on 9/1/1862. Rolls for 11/1862 through 12/1862: Absent, ordered to Tennessee on recruiting service. Rolls for 1/1863 through 6/1863: Present, returned from Tennessee on 1/19/1863. Rolls for 7/1863 through 8/1863: Present, promoted to Capt. on 7/16/1863 by order of Brig. Gen. James E. Slaughter to date from 5/15/1863. Rolls for 9/1863 through 10/1863: Present, sick in camp. Rolls for 11/1863 through 8/1864: Present. Federal Rolls of Prisoners of War: Captured at Blakely, AL, on 4/9/1865; Received at Ship Island, MS, on 4/16/1865. Transferred to Vicksburg, MS, for exchange on 4/28/1865; Confined at New Orleans, LA, on 4/30/1865. Exchanged at Camp Townsend, MS, on 5/6/1865.

Winter, J.C. Pvt., Winston's Light Artillery Battery (Belmont Battery). Federal Rolls of Prisoners of War: Captured at Blakely, AL, on 4/9/1865; Received at Ship Island, MS, on 4/15/1865. Transferred to Vicksburg, MS, for exchange on 5/1/1865; Exchanged at Camp Townsend, MS, on 5/6/1865.

Wofford, Mark J. Pvt./Artificer, Barry's Light Artillery Battery (Lookout Battery). Enlisted: 4/4/1862 at Chattanooga, TN, for 3 years. Rolls for 5/1862 through 10/1863: Present. Rolls for 11/1863 through 12/1863: Present, on duty at Way's Bluff. Rolls for 3/1864 through 10/1864: Present. Federal Rolls of Prisoners of War: Captured at Spanish Fort, AL, on 4/8/1865; Received at Ship Island, MS, on 4/10/1865. Transferred to Vicksburg, MS, for exchange on 5/1/1865; Exchanged at Camp Townsend, MS, on 5/6/1865. Wounded: No. Born: Spartanburg, SC. Married: Yes. Children: 3—1 son and 2 daughters. Occupation: Farmer. Residence after war: District 15, Hamilton County, TN. Property after war: Farming tools valued at $7.50. Ailments after war: diabetes and varicose veins below right knee. Confederate Pension Application dated 2/4/1902 on file at the Tennessee State Library and Archives. Target Name: Wofford, Mark J. Application Number: S3959. County: Hamilton.

Texas Prisoners of War

Abothnot, R.B. (AKA Abathnot, R.T., R.F.) Pvt., 1st Field Battery Texas Light Artillery (Edgar's). Federal Rolls of Prisoners of War: Captured at Greensburg, LA, on 10/7/1864; Received at Ship Island, MS. Died: 11/20/1864 at Ship Island, MS, due to pneumonia. Buried: Ship Island, MS, Cemetery in Grave #29.

Agnew, James C. Pvt., 14th Texas Cavalry (Dismounted). Co. E. Federal Rolls of Prisoners of War: Captured at Spanish Fort, AL, on 4/8/1865; Received at Ship Island, MS, on 4/10/1865. Transferred to Vicksburg, MS, for exchange on 5/1/1865; Exchanged at Camp Townsend, MS, on 5/6/1865.

Akin, W.D. Pvt., 32nd Texas Cavalry (Dismounted). Co. C. Federal Rolls of Prisoners of War: Captured at Spanish Fort, AL, on 4/8/1865; Received at Ship Island, MS, on 4/10/1865. Transferred to Vicksburg, MS, for exchange on 5/1/1865; Exchanged at Camp Townsend, MS, on 5/6/1865.

Anderson, A.A. Pvt., 12th Texas Cavalry. Co. G. Mustered into service: 10/1861. Rolls for 7/1862 through 11/1862: Present. On Register of Houston, TX, General Hospital: Admitted on 2/28/1862 due to typhoid fever; Returned to duty: 3/7/1862. Rolls for 9/1863 through 1/1864: Absent. Federal Rolls of Prisoners of War: Captured during the Red River Campaign in 1864. On Register of St. Louis U.S.A. General Hospital, New Orleans, LA: Admitted on 9/27/1864 as a prisoner of war; Returned to duty: 10/5/1864. On Report of Prisoners of War Confined at Steam Levee Press #4, New Orleans, LA: Sent to hospital. Federal Rolls of Prisoners of War: Captured at Morganza, LA, on 8/8/1864; Received at Ship Island, MS, from New Orleans, LA, on 10/7/1864. Transferred to Fort Columbus, New York Harbor, NY, on 11/5/1864; Forwarded to Elmira, NY, on 11/19/1864. Transferred to James River, VA, for exchange on 2/20/1865. On Register of General Hospital #9, Richmond VA: Admitted on 2/28/1865; Transferred to Camp Lee, VA, on 3/1/1865. On Register of General Hospital #9, Richmond, VA: Admitted on 3/5/1865.

Anderson, E.L. (AKA E.D.) Pvt., 32nd Texas Cavalry (Dismounted). Co. D. Federal Rolls of Prisoners of War: Captured at Spanish Fort, AL, on 4/8/1865; Received at Ship Island, MS, on 4/10/1865. Transferred to Vicksburg, MS, for exchange on 5/1/1865; Exchanged at Camp Townsend, MS, on 5/6/1865.

Andrews, Ed. Pvt., 32nd Texas Cavalry (Dismounted). Co. D. Federal Rolls of Prisoners of War: Captured at Spanish Fort, AL, on 4/8/1865; Received at Ship Island, MS, on 4/10/1865. Transferred to Vicksburg, MS, for exchange on 5/1/1865; Exchanged at Camp Townsend, MS, on 5/6/1865.

Atteberry, Charles (AKA Atterberry) Pvt., 2nd Texas Cavalry (Mounted Rifles). Co. __. Federal Rolls of Prisoners of War: Captured on 9/19/1864; Received at Ship Island, MS, on 10/21/1864. Exchanged on 1/4/1865.

Austin, G.M. (AKA Aston) Sgt./Pvt., 9th Texas Infantry (Young's). Co. C. Federal Rolls of Prisoners of War: Captured at Spanish Fort, AL, on 4/8/1865; Received at Ship Island, MS, on 4/10/1865. Transferred to Vicksburg, MS, for exchange on 5/1/1865; Exchanged at Camp Townsend, MS, on 5/6/1865.

Baldwin, John B. Pvt., 9th Texas Infantry (Young's). Co. C. Enlisted: 10/4/1861 at Sherman, Grayson County, Texas. Age at enlistment: 16. Federal Rolls of Prisoners of War: Captured at Spanish Fort, AL, on 4/8/1865; Received at Ship Island, MS, on 4/10/1865. Transferred to Vicksburg, MS, for exchange on 5/1/1865; Exchanged at Camp Townsend, MS, on 5/6/1865.

Bearden, J.J. Pvt., 32nd Texas Cavalry (Dismounted). Co. B. Federal Rolls of Prisoners of War: Captured at Spanish Fort, AL, on 4/8/1865; Received at Ship Island, MS, on 4/10/1865. Transferred to Vicksburg, MS, for exchange on 5/1/1865; Exchanged at Camp Townsend, MS, on 5/6/1865.

Belguard, A. (AKA Belgard) Pvt. Robertson's Cavalry Squad. Co. B. Federal Rolls of Prisoners of War: Captured at Mobile Bay, AL, on 8/5/1864; Received at Ship Island, MS. Died: 10/31/1864 at Ship Island, MS, due to measles and chronic diarrhea. Buried: Ship Island, MS, Cemetery in Grave #5.

Beornard, J.C. (AKA Bernard) Pvt., 32nd Texas Cavalry (Dismounted). Co. I. Federal Rolls of Prisoners of War: Captured at Spanish Fort, AL, on 4/8/1865; Received at Ship Island, MS, on 4/10/1865. Transferred to Vicksburg, MS, for exchange on 5/1/1865; Exchanged at Camp Townsend, MS, on 5/6/1865.

Booty, A.J., Jr. 2nd Lt./Capt., 10th Texas Cavalry (Locke's). Co. F. Federal Rolls of Prisoners of War: Captured at Tensas Parish, LA; Received at Ship Island, MS, from New Orleans, LA, on 11/25/1864. Transferred to Fort Columbus, New York Harbor, NY, in 11/1864. Died: 8/17/1882. Buried: Booty Cemetery at Natchitoches, Natchitoches Parish, LA.

Box, James Robert Sgt., 14th Texas Cavalry (Dismounted). Co. D. Enlisted: 4/1861. Federal Rolls of Prisoners of War: Captured at Spanish Fort, AL, on 4/8/1865; Received at Ship Island, MS, on 4/10/1865. Transferred to Vicksburg, MS, for exchange on 5/1/1865; Exchanged at Camp Townsend, MS, on 5/6/1865. Born: 7/28/1835 at Benton County, AL, to George Box and Salina Sue Jones Box. Married: Sarah Margaret Elliott on 12/23/1866 at Rusk County, TX. Children: 9. Occupation: Farmer. Died: 12/7/1915 at Hayden Community, Van Zandt County, TX. Buried: Myrtle Springs Cemetery, Myrtle Springs, Van Zandt County, TX. Wife born: 11/13/1844 at Williamson County, TN. Wife died: 1/30/1918 at Van Zandt County, TX. Confederate Pension Application on file at the Texas State Library and Archives. Target name: Box, James Robert. Application Number: 34469. County: Van Zandt.

Brock, M.V. Pvt., 32nd Texas Cavalry (Dismounted). Co. B. Federal Rolls of Prisoners of War: Captured at Spanish Fort, AL, on 4/8/1865; Received at Ship Island, MS, on 4/10/1865. Transferred to Vicksburg, MS, for exchange on 5/1/1865; Exchanged at Camp Townsend, MS, on 5/6/1865.

Burdett, John C. 3rd Lt./Capt., 32nd Texas Cavalry (Dismounted). Co. F. Federal Rolls of Prisoners of War: Captured at Spanish Fort, AL, on 4/8/1865; Received at Ship Island, MS, on 4/10/1865. Transferred to Vicksburg, MS, for exchange on 4/28/1865; Confined at New Orleans, LA, on 4/30/1865. Exchanged at Camp Townsend, MS, on 5/6/1865.

Byers, Lafayette (AKA Bias) Pvt., 32nd Texas Cavalry (Dismounted). Cos. E & K. Federal Rolls of Prisoners of War: Captured at Spanish Fort, AL, on 4/8/1865; Received at Ship Island, MS, on 4/10/1865. Transferred to Vicksburg, MS, for exchange on 5/1/1865; Exchanged at Camp Townsend, MS, on 5/6/1865.

Byrd, James F. Pvt., Waul's Texas Legion (Cavalry). Co. F. Enlisted: 1862 at Gonzales, TX. Escaped from Ship island, MS, by volunteering to load a boat, then joining the prisoners that were to be exchanged. Born: 12/18/1844. Married: Eliza Elizabeth May. Died: 6/9/1915. Buried: Harick Cemetery located 4 miles east of Robert Lee on TX State Hwy. 158, turn left on the dirt road and travel 4.3 miles.

Callender, Curtis B. (AKA Calender) Pvt., 4th Texas Cavalry. Co. C. Federal Rolls of Prisoners of War: Captured at Plaquemine Parish, LA, on 11/17/1864; Received at Ship Island, MS, from New Orleans, LA, on 12/13/1864. Transferred to New Orleans, LA, for exchange on 3/31/1865.

Carlton, C.B. Pvt., 10th Texas Cavalry (Locke's). Co. I. Federal Rolls of Prisoners of War: Captured at Spanish Fort, AL, on 4/8/1865; Received at Ship Island, MS, on 4/10/1865. Transferred to Vicksburg, MS, for exchange on 5/1/1865; Exchanged at Camp Townsend, MS, on 5/6/1865.

Chapman, Robert Pvt., 12th Texas Cavalry. Co. F. Federal Rolls of Prisoners of War: Captured at Concordia Parish, LA, on 8/26/1864; Received at Ship Island, MS. Died: 10/17/1864 at Ship Island, MS, due to consumption. Buried: Ship Island, MS, Cemetery in Grave #2.

Clay, William H. Pvt., 10th Texas Cavalry (Locke's). Co. E. Federal Rolls of Prisoners of War: Captured at Spanish Fort, AL, on 4/8/1865; Received at Ship Island, MS, on 4/10/1865. Transferred to Vicksburg, MS, for exchange on 5/1/1865; Exchanged at Camp Townsend, MS, on 5/6/1865.

Cobb, T.M. Pvt., 10th Texas Cavalry (Locke's). Co. G. Federal Rolls of Prisoners of War: Captured at Flintday, AL, on 3/25/1865; Received at Ship Island, MS. Transferred to Vicksburg, MS, for exchange on 5/1/1865; Exchanged at Camp Townsend, MS, on 5/6/1865.

Cox, James Pvt., 16th Texas Infantry. Co. A. Died: 11/19/1864 at Ship Island, MS, due to scurvy. Buried: Ship Island, MS, Cemetery in Grave #26.

Creekmore, Henry Clay (AKA Creekmine) Pvt./Sgt., 32nd Texas Cavalry (Dismounted). Co. C. Federal Rolls of Prisoners of War: Captured at Spanish Fort, AL, on 4/8/1865; Received at Ship Island, MS, on 4/10/1865. Transferred to Vicksburg, MS, for exchange on 5/1/1865; Exchanged at Camp Townsend, MS, on 5/6/1865. Confederate Pension Application on file at the Texas State Library and Archives. Target Name: Creekmore, Henry Clay. Application Number: 19720. County: Bowie. Also a Confederate Widows Pension on file. Target Name: Creekmore, Elizabeth Francis. Application Number: 21439. County: Bowie.

Dawson, Benjamin F. Pvt., 32nd Texas Cavalry (Dismounted). Co. D. Federal Rolls of Prisoners of War: Captured at Morganza, LA, on 8/25/1864; Received at Ship Island, MS, from New Orleans, LA, on 10/7/1864. Transferred to Fort Columbus, New York Harbor, NY, on 11/5/1864. Soldier also served with the 1st Texas Battalion Infantry. Co. A.

Day, John M. Pvt., 11th Texas Cavalry. Co. C. Federal Rolls of Prisoners of War: Captured at Cane River, LA, on 4/25/1864; Received at Ship Island, MS, from New Orleans, LA, on 10/7/1864. Transferred to Fort Columbus, New York Harbor, NY, in 11/1864.

Dill, Elijah O. (AKA Elijah C, D.O.) Pvt., 14th Texas Cavalry. Co. H. Enlisted: 3/1/1862. Federal Rolls of Prisoners of War: Captured at Spanish Fort, AL, on 4/8/1865; Received at Ship Island, MS, on 4/10/1865. Transferred to Vicksburg, MS, for exchange on 5/1/1865; Exchanged at Camp Townsend, MS, on 5/6/1865. Born: 2/4/1843. Died: 3/12/1893. Buried: Marlow City Cemetery, Stephens County, Oklahoma. Married: Martha M. Huckaby. Wife born: 6/9/1865. Wife Died: 3/21/1936.

Dorris, E.B. Pvt., 32nd Texas Cavalry (Dismounted). Co. I. Enlisted: Jeff, TX. Federal Rolls of Prisoners of War: Captured at Blakely, AL, on 4/9/1865; Received at Ship Island, MS, on 4/15/1865. Transferred to Vicksburg, MS, for exchange on 5/1/1865; Exchanged at Camp Townsend, MS, on 5/6/1865. Residence at exchange: Huckaby, TX. Soldier also served as a Pvt. with the 9th Kentucky Infantry. Co. H.

Douglas, W. Pvt., 32nd Texas Cavalry (Dismounted). Co. __. Federal Rolls of Prisoners of War: Captured at Cane River, LA, on 4/25/1864; Received at Ship Island, MS, from New Orleans, LA, on 10/7/1864. Transferred to Fort Columbus, New York Harbor, NY, on 11/5/1864.

Duncan, C. Pvt./Lt., 9th Texas Cavalry (Dismounted). Co. C. Federal Rolls of Prisoners of War: Captured at Choctaw Bend, MS, on 8/11/1864; Received at Ship Island, MS, from New Orleans, LA, on 12/11/1864. Transferred to New Orleans, LA, for exchange on 3/2/1865.

Estes, Benjamin T. (AKA B.F.) Capt., 32nd Texas Cavalry (Dismounted). Co. H. Federal Rolls of Prisoners of War: Captured at Spanish Fort, AL, on 4/8/1865; Received at Ship Island, MS, on 4/10/1865. Transferred to Vicksburg, MS, for exchange on 4/28/1865; Confined at New Orleans, LA, on 4/30/1865. Exchanged at Camp Townsend, MS, on 5/6/1865. Occupation after war: Judge of the 5th Judicial District from 1877 through 1885, and President of the Texarkana National Bank until his death in 1902.

Fennelly, W.A. (AKA Finley, W.O.) Pvt., 32nd Texas Cavalry (Dismounted). Co. B. Federal Rolls of Prisoners of War: Captured at Spanish Fort, AL, on 4/8/1865; Received at Ship Island, MS, on 4/10/1865. Transferred to Vicksburg, MS, for exchange on 5/1/1865; Exchanged at Camp Townsend, MS, on 5/6/1865.

Ferguson, W.H. (AKA Furgerson) Pvt., 32nd Texas Cavalry (Dismounted). Co. G. Federal Rolls of Prisoners of War: Captured at Spanish Fort, AL, on 4/8/1865; Received at Ship Island, MS, on 4/10/1865. Transferred to Vicksburg, MS, for exchange on 5/1/1865; Exchanged at Camp Townsend, MS, on 5/6/1865.

Ferrell, Solomon L. Cpl./Pvt., 14th Texas Cavalry. Co. I. Federal Rolls of Prisoners of War: Captured at Spanish Fort, AL, on 4/8/1865; Received at Ship Island, MS, on 4/10/1865. Transferred to Vicksburg, MS, for exchange on 5/1/1865; Exchanged at Camp Townsend, MS, on 5/6/1865.

Fowler, T.A. Pvt./Sgt., 32nd Texas Cavalry (Dismounted). Co. F. Federal Rolls of Prisoners of War: Captured at Spanish Fort, AL, on 4/8/1865; Received at Ship Island, MS, on 4/10/1865. Transferred to Vicksburg, MS, for exchange on 5/1/1865; Exchanged at Camp Townsend, MS, on 5/6/1865.

Glaze, J.B. Cpl./Pvt., 32nd Texas Cavalry (Dismounted). Co. C. Federal Rolls of Prisoners of War: Captured at Spanish Fort, AL, on 4/8/1865; Received at Ship Island, MS, on 4/10/1865. Transferred to Vicksburg, MS, for exchange on 5/1/1865; Exchanged at Camp Townsend, MS, on 5/6/1865. Confederate Pension Application on file at the Texas State Library and Archives. Target Name: Glaze, J.B. . Application Number: 41865. County: Ward.

Gourly, Robert Pvt./Sgt., 14th Texas Cavalry (Dismounted). Co. B. Federal Rolls of Prisoners of War: Captured at Spanish Fort, AL, on 4/8/1865; Received at Ship Island, MS, on 4/10/1865. Transferred to Vicksburg, MS, for exchange on 5/1/1865; Exchanged at Camp Townsend, MS, on 5/6/1865.

Grey, S.B. (AKA Gray) Pvt., 32nd Texas Cavalry (Dismounted). Cos. I & K. Federal Rolls of Prisoners of War: Captured at Spanish Fort, AL, on 4/8/1865; Received at Ship Island, MS, on 4/10/1865. Transferred to Vicksburg, MS, for exchange on 5/1/1865; Exchanged at Camp Townsend, MS, on 5/6/1865.

Hall, Harvey J. (AKA Hill) Pvt., 14th Texas Cavalry (Dismounted). Co. C. Federal Rolls of Prisoners of War: Captured at Spanish Fort, AL, on 4/8/1865; Received at Ship Island, MS, on 4/10/1865. Transferred to Vicksburg, MS, for exchange on 5/1/1865; Exchanged at Camp Townsend, MS, on 5/6/1865.

Hancock, John M. Pvt., 32nd Texas Cavalry (Dismounted). Co. G. Federal Rolls of Prisoners of War: Captured at Spanish Fort, AL, on 4/8/1865; Received at Ship Island, MS, on 4/10/1865. Transferred to Vicksburg, MS, for exchange on 5/1/1865; Exchanged at Camp Townsend, MS, on 5/6/1865.

Harrington, G.L. Pvt., 1st Texas Regiment. Co. __. Federal Rolls of Prisoners of War: Captured at Morganza, LA, on 7/31/1864; Received at Ship Island, MS, from New Orleans, LA, on 10/28/1864. Transferred to Fort Columbus, New York Harbor, NY, on 11/5/1864.

Harris, W.H. Sgt., 9th Texas Cavalry. Co. D. Federal Rolls of Prisoners of War: Captured at Spanish Fort, AL, on 4/8/1865; Received at Ship Island, MS, on 4/10/1865. Transferred to Vicksburg, MS, for exchange on 5/1/1865; Exchanged at Camp Townsend, MS, on 5/6/1865.

Hart, H.J. Pvt., 9th Texas Cavalry. Co. C. Federal Rolls of Prisoners of War: Captured at Catfish Point, MS, on 11/16/1864; Received at Ship Island, MS, from New Orleans, LA, on 12/13/1864. Transferred to New Orleans, LA, for exchange on 3/21/1865.

Hart, W.J. Pvt., 14th Texas Cavalry. Co. C. Federal Rolls of Prisoners of War: Captured at Spanish Fort, AL, on 4/8/1865; Received at Ship Island, MS, on 4/10/1865. Transferred to Vicksburg, MS, for exchange on 5/1/1865; Exchanged at Camp Townsend, MS, on 5/6/1865.

Heath, W.C. Pvt., 32nd Texas Cavalry (Dismounted). Co. C. Federal Rolls of Prisoners of War: Captured at Spanish Fort, AL, on 4/8/1865; Received at Ship Island, MS, on 4/10/1865. Transferred to Vicksburg, MS, for exchange on 5/1/1865; Exchanged at Camp Townsend, MS, on 5/6/1865.

Henly, J. Pvt., 32nd Texas Cavalry (Dismounted). Co. F. Federal Rolls of Prisoners of War: Captured at Spanish Fort, AL, on 4/8/1865; Received at Ship Island, MS, on 4/10/1865. Transferred to Vicksburg, MS, for exchange on 5/1/1865; Exchanged at Camp Townsend, MS, on 5/6/1865.

Hines, William M. Pvt., 32nd Texas Cavalry (Dismounted). Co. I. Federal Rolls of Prisoners of War: Captured at Spanish Fort, AL, on 4/8/1865; Received at Ship Island, MS, on 4/10/1865. Transferred to Vicksburg, MS, for exchange on 5/1/1865; Exchanged at Camp Townsend, MS, on 5/6/1865.

Hinton, F.J. Pvt., 9th Texas Cavalry (Dismounted). Co. C. Federal Rolls of Prisoners of War: Captured at Catfish Point, MS, on 11/16/1864; Received at Ship Island, MS, from New Orleans, LA, on 12/13/1864. Transferred to New Orleans, LA, for exchange on 3/21/1865.

Holmes, Stephen J. Pvt., 14th Texas Cavalry (Dismounted). Co. E. Federal Rolls of Prisoners of War:

Captured at Spanish Fort, AL, on 4/8/1865; Received at Ship Island, MS, on 4/10/1865. Transferred to Vicksburg, MS, for exchange on 5/1/1865; Exchanged at Camp Townsend, MS, on 5/6/1865.

Inzer, Edwin H. (AKA Inge, Juge) Sgt., 9th Texas Cavalry (Dismounted). Co. C. Federal Rolls of Prisoners of War: Captured at Catfish Point, MS, on 11/16/1864; Received at Ship Island, MS, from New Orleans, LA, on 12/13/1864. Died: 4/23/1865 at Ship Island, MS, due to a gunshot wound by a sentinel who thought he was signaling for an escape attempt by shaking sand from his blanket. Buried: Ship Island, MS, Cemetery in Grave #149.

Johnson, Jesse W. Pvt., 14th Texas Cavalry (Dismounted). Co. B. Federal Rolls of Prisoners of War: Captured at Spanish Fort, AL, on 4/8/1865; Received at Ship Island, MS, on 4/10/1865. Transferred to Vicksburg, MS, for exchange on 5/1/1865; Exchanged at Camp Townsend, MS, on 5/6/1865.

Jones, J.H. Pvt., 14th Texas Cavalry (Dismounted). Co. G. Federal Rolls of Prisoners of War: Captured at Spanish Fort, AL, on 4/8/1865; Received at Ship Island, MS, on 4/10/1865. Transferred to Vicksburg, MS, for exchange on 5/1/1865; Exchanged at Camp Townsend, MS, on 5/6/1865.

Jones, Samuel Pvt., 32nd Texas Cavalry (Dismounted). Co. I. Federal Rolls of Prisoners of War: Captured at Spanish Fort, AL, on 4/8/1865; Received at Ship Island, MS, on 4/10/1865. Transferred to Vicksburg, MS, for exchange on 5/1/1865; Exchanged at Camp Townsend, MS, on 5/6/1865. Born: 6/4/1832 to John and Mary Jones in Columbiana, Shelby County, AL. Married: 12/3/1867 Margaret Missouri Slappey in Salem, AL. Buried: Mount Olive Cemetery, Opelika, AL. Wife Born: 10/14/1842 in Russell County, AL. Wife Died: 11/20/1923 at Opelika, AL. Wife Buried: Mount Olive Cemetery, Opelika, AL.

Leeders, George Pvt., 32nd Texas Cavalry (Dismounted). Co. F. Federal Rolls of Prisoners of War: Captured at Black River, LA, on 11/30/1864; Received at Ship Island, MS, from New Orleans, LA, on 12/13/1864. Transferred to Vicksburg, MS, for exchange on 5/1/1865; Exchanged at Camp Townsend, MS, on 5/6/1865.

Lloyd, Thomas Brown Pvt./2nd Lt./1st Lt., 10th Texas Cavalry. Co. E. Promoted to 2nd Lt. on 8/22/1863. Wounded in left leg at Murfreesboro, TN, on 12/31/1862. Federal Rolls of Prisoners of War: Captured at Rodney, MS, on 7/19/1864; Received at Ship Island, MS, from New Orleans, LA, on 11/25/1864. Transferred to Fort Columbus, New York Harbor, NY, in 11/1864; Released from New York on 6/12/1865. Born: 7/12/1836. Died: 11/15/1889. Buried: Lloyd Cemetery at Rusk County, TX.

Long, R. Pvt., 9th Texas Cavalry (Dismounted). Cos. C & K. Federal Rolls of Prisoners of War: Captured at Spanish Fort, AL, on 4/8/1865; Received at Ship Island, MS, on 4/10/1865. Transferred to Vicksburg, MS, for exchange on 5/1/1865; Exchanged at Camp Townsend, MS, on 5/6/1865.

McDavid, John M. Pvt., 14th Texas Cavalry (Dismounted). Co. D. Federal Rolls of Prisoners of War: Captured at Spanish Fort, AL, on 4/8/1865; Received at Ship Island, MS, on 4/10/1865. Transferred to Vicksburg, MS, for exchange on 5/1/1865; Exchanged at Camp Townsend, MS, on 5/6/1865.

Martin, A. Sgt., 32nd Texas Cavalry (Dismounted). Co. D. Federal Rolls of Prisoners of War: Captured at Spanish Fort, AL, on 4/8/1865; Received at Ship Island, MS, on 4/10/1865. Transferred to Vicksburg, MS, for exchange on 5/1/1865; Exchanged at Camp Townsend, MS, on 5/6/1865.

Martin, Mathew D. Sgt./Pvt., 14th Texas Cavalry (Dismounted). Co. G. Federal Rolls of Prisoners of War: Captured at Spanish Fort, AL, on 4/8/1865; Received at Ship Island, MS, on 4/10/1865. Transferred to Vicksburg, MS, for exchange on 5/1/1865; Exchanged at Camp Townsend, MS, on 5/6/1865.

Mims, Henry A. Pvt., 32nd Texas Cavalry (Dismounted). Co. D. Federal Rolls of Prisoners of War: Captured at Spanish Fort, AL, on 4/8/1865; Received at Ship Island, MS, on 4/10/1865. Transferred to Vicksburg, MS, for exchange on 5/1/1865; Exchanged at Camp Townsend, MS, on 5/6/1865. Confederate Pension Application on file at the Texas State Library and Archives. Target Name: Mims, Henry A. Application Number: 19703. County: Marion. Also a Confederate Widows Pension Application on file. Target Name: Mims, Mrs. Henry A. Application Number: 33790. County: Cass.

Moore, George W. Pvt., 10th Texas Cavalry (Dismounted). Co. G. Federal Rolls of Prisoners of War: Captured at Spanish Fort, AL, on 4/8/1865; Received at Ship Island, MS, on 4/10/1865. Transferred to Vicksburg, MS, for exchange on 5/1/1865; Exchanged at Camp Townsend, MS, on 5/6/1865.

Pass, William Cpl./Pvt., 14th Texas Cavalry (Dismounted). Co. B. Federal Rolls of Prisoners of War: Captured at Spanish Fort, AL, on 4/8/1865; Received at Ship Island, MS, on 4/10/1865. Transferred to Vicksburg, MS, for exchange on 5/1/1865; Exchanged at Camp Townsend, MS, on 5/6/1865.

Patterson, William B. Pvt., 18th Texas Cavalry. Co. E. Federal Rolls of Prisoners of War: Captured at Point Coupée Parish, LA, on 10/22/1864; Received at Ship Island, MS, from New Orleans, LA, on 10/28/1864. Transferred to Fort Columbus, New York Harbor, NY, on 11/5/1864.

Phenix, C.L. Pvt., 32nd Texas Cavalry (Dismounted). Co. F. Federal Rolls of Prisoners of War: Captured at Spanish Fort, AL, on 4/8/1865; Received at Ship Island, MS, on 4/10/1865. Transferred to Vicksburg, MS, for exchange on 5/1/1865; Exchanged at Camp Townsend, MS, on 5/6/1865.

Pickering, W.H. (AKA H.W.) Pvt., 12th Texas Cavlary. Co. F. Federal Rolls of Prisoners of War: Captured at Concordia Parish, LA, on 8/26/1864; Received at Ship Island, MS, from New Orleans, LA, on 10/7/1864. Transferred to Fort Columbus, NY, Harbor, New York on 11/5/1864.

Reno, F.M. Pvt., 32nd Texas Cavalry (Dismounted). Co. K. Federal Rolls of Prisoners of War: Captured at Spanish Fort, AL, on 4/8/1865; Received at Ship Island, MS, on 4/10/1865. Transferred to Vicksburg, MS, for exchange on 5/1/1865; Exchanged at Camp Townsend, MS, on 5/6/1865.

Richardson, Y.D. Pvt., 1st Texas Cavalry. Co. ___. Federal Rolls of Prisoners of War: Captured at Concordia Parish, LA, on 8/26/1864; Received at Ship Island, MS, from New Orleans, LA, on 10/7/1864. Transferred to Fort Columbus, New York Harbor, NY, on 11/5/1864.

Robbins, W.G. Pvt., 1st Texas Cavalry. Co. __. Federal Rolls of Prisoners of War: Captured at Williamsport, LA, on 8/1/1864; Received at Ship Island, MS, on 10/7/1864. Transferred to Fort Columbus, New York Harbor, NY, on 11/5/1864.

Rockmore, J.R. (AKA Rockmine) Pvt., 32nd Texas Cavalry (Dismounted). Co. C. Federal Rolls of Prisoners of War: Captured at Spanish Fort, AL, on 4/8/1865; Received at Ship Island, MS, on 4/10/1865. Transferred to Vicksburg, MS, for exchange on 5/1/1865; Exchanged at Camp Townsend, MS, on 5/6/1865.

Rushing, Benjamin Franklin Pvt., 10th Texas Cavalry (Dismounted). Co. E. Federal Rolls of Prisoners of War: Captured at Spanish Fort, AL, on 4/8/1865; Received at Ship Island, MS, on 4/10/1865. Transferred to Vicksburg, MS, for exchange on 5/1/1865; Exchanged at Camp Townsend, MS, on 5/6/1865. Confederate Pension Application on file at the Texas State Library and Archives. Target Name: Rushing, Benjamin Franklin. Application Number: 39248. County: Franklin. Also a Confederate Widows Pension Application on file. Target Name: Rushing, Mrs. Benjamin Franklin. Application Number: 50416. County: Kaufman.

Scoggins, F. Pvt., 23rd Texas Cavalry. Co. __. Federal Rolls of Prisoners of War: Captured at Simsport, LA, on 8/1/1864; Received at Ship Island, MS, from New Orleans, LA, on 10/7/1864. Transferred to Fort Columbus, New York Harbor, NY, on 11/5/1864.

Smith, A.J. Pvt., 8th Texas Cavalry. Co. __. Federal Rolls of Prisoners of War: Captured at Arangus Pass, TX, on 9/2/1864; Received at Ship Island, MS, from New Orleans, LA, on 10/7/1864. Transferred to Fort Columbus, New York Harbor, NY, on 11/5/1864.

Snodgrass, James Pvt., 9th Texas Infantry. Co. H. Enlisted: 10/14/1861 at Fannin County, TX. Age at enlistment: 22. Federal Rolls of Prisoners of War: Captured at Spanish Fort, AL, on 4/8/1865; Received at Ship Island, MS, on 4/10/1865. Transferred to Vicksburg, MS, for exchange on 5/1/1865; Exchanged at Camp Townsend, MS, on 5/6/1865. Confederate Widows Pension Application on file at the Texas State Library and Archives. Target Name: Snodgrass, Mrs.A.D. Application Number: 38745. County: Dickens.

Sparks, Tilman Pvt., Waller's Cavalry Regiment. Co. __. Federal Rolls of Prisoners of War: Captured at Concordia Parish, LA, on 7/31/1864; Received at Ship Island, MS, from New Orleans, LA, on 10/7/1864. Transferred to Fort Columbus, New York Harbor, NY, on 11/5/1864. Born: 7/24/1837 at Hot Springs, AR. Married: Elsie Peaveyhouse on 5/13/1861 at Falls County, TX. Died: 10/23/1912 at Parker County, TX. Confederate Pension Application on file at the Texas State Library and Archives. Target Name: Sparks, Tilman. Application Number: 16297. County: Parker. Also a Confederate Widows Pension Application on file. Target Name: Sparks, Elsy. Application Number: 22091. County: Parker.

Taylor, Robert W. Pvt./Sgt., 1st Texas Infantry. Co. I. Federal Rolls of Prisoners of War: Captured at Simsport, LA, on 9/27/1864; Received at Ship Island, MS, from New Orleans, LA, on 10/21/1864. Transferred to Fort Columbus, New York Harbor, NY, on 11/5/1864.

Thompson, G. Pvt., Texas Cavalry. Co. __. Federal Rolls of Prisoners of War: Captured at Red River, LA, on 9/29/1864; Received at Ship Island, MS, from New Orleans, LA, on 10/28/1864. Transferred to Fort Columbus, New York Harbor, NY, on 11/5/1864.

Thompson, S.M. Pvt., 12th Texas Cavalry. Co. F. Federal Rolls of Prisoners of War: Captured at Bruinsburg, LA, on 9/20/1864; Received at Ship Island, MS, from New Orleans, LA, on 10/21/1864. Transferred to Fort Columbus, New York Harbor, NY, on 11/5/1864.

Trimble, W.W. Pvt./Cpl., 32nd Texas Cavalry (Dismounted). Co. C. Federal Rolls of Prisoners of War: Captured at Spanish Fort, AL, on 4/8/1865; Received at Ship Island, MS, on 4/10/1865. Transferred to Vicksburg, MS, for exchange on 5/1/1865; Exchanged at Camp Townsend, MS, on 5/6/1865. Confederate Pension Application on file at the Texas State Library and Archives. Target Name: Trimble, W.W. . Application Number: 17507. County: Comanche.

Tulley, William Pvt., 1st Texas Heavy Artillery. Co. __. Federal Rolls of Prisoners of War: Captured at Fort Gaines, AL, on 8/8/1864; Received at Ship Island, MS, from New Orleans, LA, on 10/25/1864. Exchanged on 1/4/1865.

Wells, J.T. Pvt., 32nd Texas Cavalry (Dismounted). Co. D. Federal Rolls of Prisoners of War: Captured at Spanish Fort, AL, on 4/8/1865; Received at Ship Island, MS, on 4/10/1865. Transferred to Vicksburg, MS, for exchange on 5/1/1865; Exchanged at Camp Townsend, MS, on 5/6/1865. Confederate Pension Application on file at the Texas State Library and Archives. Target Name: Wells, J.T. Application Number: 03413. County: Rains.

White, John C. Capt./2nd Lt., 32nd Texas Cavalry (Dismounted). Co. C. Federal Rolls of Prisoners of War: Captured at Spanish Fort, AL, on 4/8/1865; Received at Ship Island, MS, on 4/10/1865. Transferred to Vicksburg, MS, for exchange on 4/28/1865; Confined at New Orleans, LA, on 4/30/1865. Exchanged at Camp Townsend, MS, on 5/6/1865. Confederate Widows Pension Application on file at the Texas State Library and Archives. Target Name: White, Martha. Application: Rejected. County: Travis.

Williams, J.A. Pvt., 32nd Texas Cavalry (Dismounted). Co. D. Federal Rolls of Prisoners of War: Captured at Spanish Fort, AL, on 4/8/1865; Received at Ship Island, MS, on 4/10/1865. Transferred to Vicksburg, MS, for exchange on 5/1/1865; Exchanged at Camp Townsend, MS, on 5/6/1865.

Wilson, G.W. Pvt., 32nd Texas Cavalry (Dismounted). Co. A. Federal Rolls of Prisoners of War: Captured at Spanish Fort, AL, on 4/8/1865; Received at Ship Island, MS, on 4/10/1865. Transferred to Vicksburg, MS, for exchange on 5/1/1865; Exchanged at Camp Townsend, MS, on 5/6/1865.

Woodard, Pleasant Washington Pvt., 32nd Texas Cavalry (Dismounted). Co. H. Enlisted: 9/15/1861 in the 9th Kentucky Mounted Infantry. Co. H; Transferred to the 32nd Texas Cavalry on 5/2/1863. Rolls for 5/1863 through 4/1864: Present. Federal Rolls of Prisoners of War: Captured at Spanish Fort, AL, on 4/8/1865; Received at Ship Island, MS, on 4/10/1865. Transferred to Vicksburg, MS, for exchange on 5/1/1865; Exchanged at Camp Townsend, MS, on

5/6/1865. Rolls of Prisoners of War, C.S.A: Surrendered at Citronelle, AL, on 5/4/1865; Paroled at Meridian, MS, on 5/11/1865. Born: 1/18/1838 to William Woodward and Sarah Drinkard Woodward. Married: Etta Jospehine Martin on 1/12/1868 at Bowie County, TX. Children: 5. Died: 1/6/1890 at Bowie County, TX. Buried: Woodstock Cemetery at Bowie County, TX. Soldier also served as a Pvt. with the 9th Kentucky Mounted Infantry. Co. H. Confederate Widows Pension Application on file at the Texas State Library and Archives. Target Name: Woodard, Etta J. Application Number: 32801. County: Bowie.

Confederate Navy Prisoners of War

Adams, B.F. Pvt., C.S.A. Navy (Ram Tennessee). Federal Rolls of Prisoners of War: Captured at Mobile Bay, AL, on 8/5/1864; Received at Ship Island, MS, from New Orleans, LA, on 10/28/1864. Disposition unknown.

Adams, F.H. Pvt., C.S.A. Marine Corps. Co. D. Federal Rolls of Prisoners of War: Captured at Blakely, AL, on 4/9/1864; Received at Ship Island, MS, from New Orleans, LA, on 4/15/1864. Exchanged on 3/1/1865.

Adams, William Lt., C.S.A. Navy (Ram Tennessee). Age at enlistment: 32. Description at enlistment: Eyes: grey. Hair: dark. Complexion: dark. Federal Rolls of Prisoners of War: Captured at Mobile Bay, AL, on 8/5/1864; Received at Ship Island, MS, from New Orleans, LA, on 10/28/1864. Exchanged on 3/1/1865.

Alexander, William Landsman, C.S.A. Navy (Ram Tennessee). Age at enlistment: 31. Description at enlistment: Eyes: grey. Hair: dark. Complexion: dark. Occupation at enlistment: Sailor. Federal Rolls of Prisoners of War: Captured at Mobile Bay, AL, on 8/5/1864; Received at Ship Island, MS, from New Orleans, LA, on 10/28/1864. Exchanged on 3/1/1865. Born: Scotland.

Alsbroke, D.M. (AKA G.M.) Landsman, C.S.A. Navy (Ram Tennessee). Age at enlistment: 28. Description at enlistment: Eyes: light blue. Hair: dark. Complexion: light. Occupation at enlistment: Farmer. Federal Rolls of Prisoners of War: Captured at Mobile Bay, AL, on 8/5/1864; Received at Ship Island, MS, from New Orleans, LA, on 10/28/1864. Died: 12/6/1864 at Ship Island, MS. Buried: Ship Island, MS, Cemetery. Born: Tennessee.

Bailey, Robert Landsman/Lead Seaman, C.S.A. Navy (Steamer Selma). Federal Rolls of Prisoners of War: Captured at Mobile Bay, AL, on 8/5/1864; Received at Ship Island, MS, from New Orleans, LA, on 12/13/1864. Died: 1/17/1865 at Ship Island, MS, due to typhoid pneumonia. Buried: Ship Island, MS, Cemetery in Grave #132.

Barnes, William Landsman, C.S.A. Navy (Ram Tennessee). Age at enlistment: 30. Description at enlistment: Eyes: blue. Hair: dark. Complexion: florid. Occupation at enlistment: Laborer. Federal Rolls of Prisoners of War: Captured at Fort Gaines, AL, on 8/8/1864; Received at Ship Island, MS, from New Orleans, LA, on 10/28/1864. Exchanged on 3/2/1865. Remarks: Deserted on 4/9/1865. Born: Ireland.

Barry, R. Pvt., C.S.A. Marine Corps. Co. D. Federal Rolls of Prisoners of War: Captured at Blakely, AL, on 4/9/1865; Received at Ship Island, MS, on 4/15/1865. Transferred to Vicksburg, MS, for exchange on 5/1/1865; Exchanged at Camp Townsend, MS, on 5/6/1865.

Barry, R.F. Pvt., C.S.A. Marine Corps. Co. D. Federal Rolls of Prisoners of War: Captured at Mobile Bay, AL, on 8/5/1864; Received at Ship Island, MS, from New Orleans, LA, on 10/28/1864. Exchanged on 3/2/1865.

Bassett, H. Pvt., C.S.A. Marine Corps. Co. D. Federal Rolls of Prisoners of War: Captured at Blakely, AL, on 4/9/1865; Received at Ship Island, MS, on 4/15/1865. Transferred to Vicksburg, MS, for exchange on 5/1/1865; Exchanged at Camp Townsend, MS, on 5/6/1865.

Bateman, William. Pvt., C.S.A. Navy (Steamer Selma). Federal Rolls of Prisoners of War: Captured at Mobile Bay, AL, on 8/5/1864; Received at Ship Island, MS, from New Orleans, LA, on 10/28/1864. Took the U.S. Oath of Allegiance and transferred to the U.S. naval authorities at New Orleans, LA, on 1/2/1865.

Baylor, R.H. (AKA Bayler) Landsman/Surg. Steward, C.S.A. Navy (Steamer Selma). Federal Roll of Prisoners of War: Captured at Mobile Bay, AL, on 8/5/1864; Received at Ship Island, MS, from New Orleans, LA, on 10/28/1864. Transferred to New Orleans, LA, on 4/11/1865; Released on the U.S. Oath of Allegiance on 4/11/1865 by order of Maj. Gen. E.R.S. Canby. Residence at release: Wythe County, VA. Description at release: Eyes: blue. Hair: sandy. Complexion: light. Height: 5'4".

Beckman, Henry (AKA Beatman) Fireman, C.S.A. Navy (Ram Tennessee). Age at enlistment: 32. Description at enlistment: Eyes: blue. Hair: light. Complexion: light. Federal Rolls of Prisoners of War: Captured at Mobile Bay, AL, on 8/5/1864;

Received at Ship Island, MS, from New Orleans, LA, on 10/28/1864. Took the U.S. Oath of Allegiance and transferred to the U.S. naval authorities at New Orleans, LA, on 1/2/1865. Born: Germany.

Beckwith, H. Landsman/Fireman, C.S.A. Navy (Ram Tennessee). Age at enlistment: 18. Description at enlistment: Eyes: dark. Hair: dark. Complexion: dark. Occupation at enlistment: Farmer. Federal Rolls of Prisoners of War: Captured at Mobile Bay, AL, on 8/5/1864; Received at Ship Island, MS, from New Orleans, LA, on 10/28/1864. Exchanged on 3/2/1865. Born: Germany.

Belcher, H (AKA Butcher, K., R.) Carpenter, C.S.A. Navy (Steamer Selma). Federal Rolls of Prisoners of War: Captured at Mobile Bay, AL, on 8/5/1864; Received at Ship Island, MS, from New Orleans, LA, on 10/28/1864. Exchanged on 3/2/1865.

Black, James P. Landsman, C.S.A. Navy (Ram Tennessee). Federal Rolls of Prisoners of War: Captured at Mobile Bay, AL, on 8/5/1864; Received at Ship Island, MS, from New Orleans, LA, on 10/28/1864. Transferred to Vicksburg, MS, for exchange on 5/1/1865; Exchanged at Camp Townsend, MS, on 5/6/1865.

Blackey, Mark Landsman, C.S.A. Navy (Steamer Selma). Federal Rolls of Prisoners of War: Captured at Mobile Bay, AL, on 8/5/1864; Received at Ship Island, MS, from New Orleans, LA, on 10/28/1864. Exchanged on 3/2/1865.

Brackey, Jacob (AKA Brockey) 2nd Class Boy/1st Class Boy, C.S.A. Navy (Steamer Selma). Federal Rolls of Prisoners of War: Captured at Mobile Bay, AL, on 8/5/1864; Received at Ship Island, MS, from New Orleans, LA, on 10/28/1864. Exchanged on 3/2/1865.

Brady, John Fireman, C.S.A. Navy (Ram Tennessee). Age at enlistment: 36. Description at enlistment: Eyes: blue. Hair: light. Complexion: light. Federal Rolls of Prisoners of War: Captured at Mobile Bay, AL, on 8/5/1864; Received at Ship Island, MS, from New Orleans, LA, on 10/28/1864. Transferred to Vicksburg, MS, for exchange on 5/1/1865; Exchanged at Camp Townsend, MS, on 5/6/1865. Born: Ireland.

Bragg, John A. Landsman, C.S.A. Navy (Ram Tennessee). Transferred to the C.S.A. Naval service in 8/1863 at Mobile, AL. Federal Rolls of Prisoners of War: Captured at Mobile Bay, AL, on 8/5/1864; Received at Ship Island, MS, from New Orleans, LA, on 10/28/1864. Exchanged on 3/2/1865. Born: 1/1/1837 at Sumter County, AL, to Alexander Jackson Bragg and Mary Ann Southall Bragg. Soldier also served as a Pvt. with the 1st Alabama Infantry.

Brassell, H. Pvt., C.S.A. Marine Corps. Co. D. Federal Rolls of Prisoners of War: Captured at Mobile Bay, AL, on 8/5/1864; Received at Ship Island, MS, from New Orleans, LA, on 10/28/1864. Exchanged on 3/2/1865.

Brogan, Thomas Pvt., C.S.A. Marine Corps. Co. D. Federal Rolls of Prisoners of War: Captured at Mobile Bay, AL, on 8/5/1864; Received at Ship Island, MS, from New Orleans, LA, on 10/28/1864. Took the U.S. Oath of Allegiance and transferred to the U.S. naval authorities at New Orleans, LA, on 1/21/1865.

Brown, Charles 2nd Mate, C.S.A. Navy (Ram Tennessee). Age at enlistment: 36. Description at enlistment: Eyes: grey. Hair: dark. Complexion: fair. Federal Rolls of Prisoners of War: Captured at Mobile Bay, AL, on 8/5/1864; Received at Ship Island, MS, from New Orleans, LA, on 10/28/1864. Exchanged on 3/2/1865. Born: Norway.

Brown, John (AKA James) 2nd Class Fireman, C.S.A. Navy (Ram Tennessee). Age at enlistment: 27. Description at enlistment: Eyes: blue. Hair: brown. Complexion: dark. Federal Rolls of Prisoners of War: Captured at Fort Gaines, AL, on 8/8/1864; Received at Ship Island, MS, from New Orleans, LA, on 10/28/1864. Exchanged on 3/2/1865. Born: Ireland.

Bryant, James Seaman, C.S.A. Navy (Ram Tennessee). Age at enlistment: 22. Description at enlistment: Eyes: grey. Hair: brown. Complexion: fair. Federal Rolls of Prisoners of War: Captured at Mobile Bay, AL, on 8/5/1864; Received at Ship Island, MS, from New Orleans, LA, on 10/28/1864. Exchanged on 3/2/1865. Born: Georgia.

Buller, T.M. Landsman, C.S.A. Navy (Ram Tennessee). Age at enlistment: 19. Description at enlistment: Eyes: grey. Hair: dark. Complexion: fair. Federal Rolls of Prisoners of War: Captured at Mobile Bay, AL, on 8/5/1864; Received at Ship Island, MS, from New Orleans, LA, on 10/28/1864. Exchanged on 3/2/1865. Born: Tennessee.

Burke, Peter Cook, C.S.A. Navy (Steamer Selma). Federal Rolls of Prisoners of War: Captured at Mobile Bay, AL, on 8/5/1864; Received at Ship Island, MS, from New Orleans, LA, on 10/28/1864. Exchanged on 3/2/1865.

Busby, B.F. Landsman, C.S.A. Navy (Steamer Selma). Federal Rolls of Prisoners of War: Captured at Mobile Bay, AL, on 8/5/1864; Received at Ship Island, MS, from New Orleans, LA, on 10/28/1864. Exchanged on 3/2/1865.

Butcher, Henry Carpenter's Mate, C.S.A. Navy (Steamer Selma). Federal Rolls of Prisoners of War: Captured at Mobile Bay, AL, on 8/5/1864; Received at Ship Island, MS, from New Orleans, LA, on 10/28/1864. Exchanged on 3/2/1865.

Caliman, Dennis Seaman/Landsman, C.S.A. Navy (Ram Tennessee). Age at enlistment: 29. Description at enlistment: Eyes: grey. Hair: light. Complexion: fair. Federal Rolls of Prisoners of War: Captured at Mobile Bay, AL, on 8/5/1864; Received at Ship Island, MS, from New Orleans, LA, on 12/13/1864. Exchanged on 3/2/1865. Born: Ireland.

Casey, J. Landsman, C.S.A. Marine Corps. Co. D. Federal Rolls of Prisoners of War: Captured at Blakely, AL, on 4/9/1865; Received at Ship Island, MS, on 4/15/1865. Transferred to Vicksburg, MS, for exchange on 5/1/1865; Exchanged at Camp Townsend, MS, on 5/6/1865.

Cohen, J.H. Paymaster Clerk, C.S.A. Navy. Federal Rolls of Prisoners of War: Captured at Mobile Bay, AL, on 8/5/1864; Received at Ship Island, MS, from New Orleans, LA, on 11/25/1864. Exchanged on 3/2/1865.

Courtney, William Seaman, C.S.A. Navy (Ram Tennessee). Enlisted: 7/6/1864 at Mobile Bay, AL. Federal Rolls of Prisoners of War: Captured on 8/5/1864 at Mobile Bay, AL, with powder burns to face and eyes; Received at Ship Island, MS, from New Orleans, LA, on 10/28/1864. Disposition unknown. Married: Rachel __ on 12/25/1866 at Holmes County, FL. Died: 10/16/1899 at Elro, Washington County, FL.

Wife Born: 1846. Confederate Widows Pension Application dated 1899 on file at the Florida State Library and Archives. Target Name: Courtney, Rachel. Application Number: A11677. County: Washington.

Danfield, John Ordinary Seaman, C.S.A. Navy (Steamer Selma). Federal Rolls of Prisoners of War: Captured at Fort Gaines, AL, on 8/8/1864; Received at Ship Island, MS, from New Orleans, LA, on 10/28/1864. Transferred to Vicksburg, MS, for exchange on 5/1/1865; Exchanged at Camp Townsend, MS, on 5/6/1865.

Daniels, Henry Landsman, C.S.A. Navy (Ram Tennessee). Age at enlistment: 19. Description at enlistment: Eyes: grey. Hair: dark. Complexion: ruddy. Federal Rolls of Prisoners of War: Captured at Fort Gaines, AL, on 8/8/1864; Received at Ship Island, MS, from New Orleans, LA, on 10/28/1864. Exchanged on 3/2/1865. Born: South Carolina.

Davidson, John W. Landsman, C.S.A. Navy (Ram Tennessee). Age at enlistment: 22. Description at enlistment: Eyes: dark. Hair: dark. Complexion: dark. Federal Rolls of Prisoners of War: Captured at Fort Gaines, AL, on 8/8/1864; Received at Ship Island, MS, from New Orleans, LA, on 10/28/1864. Transferred to Vicksburg, MS, for exchange on 5/1/1865; Exchanged at Camp Townsend, MS, on 5/6/1865. Born: Tennessee.

Davis, G.W. Landsman, C.S.A. Navy (Ram Tennessee). Age at enlistment: 40. Description at enlistment: Eyes: blue. Hair: dark. Complexion: ruddy. Federal Rolls of Prisoners of War: Captured at Fort Gaines, AL, on 8/8/1864; Received at Ship Island, MS, from New Orleans, LA, on 10/28/1864. Exchanged on 3/2/1865. Born: London, England.

Desporte, H. Ordinary Seaman, C.S.A. Navy (Steamer Selma). Federal Rolls of Prisoners of War: Captured at Fort Gaines, AL, on 8/8/1864; Received at Ship Island, MS, from New Orleans, LA, on 10/28/1864. Transferred to Vicksburg, MS, for exchange on 5/1/1865; Exchanged at Camp Townsend, MS, on 5/6/1865.

Diamond, John Sgt., C.S.A. Marine Corps. Co. D. Federal Rolls of Prisoners of War: Captured at Mobile Bay, AL, on 8/5/1864; Received at Ship Island, MS, from New Orleans, LA, on 10/29/1864. Transferred to Vicksburg, MS, for exchange on 5/1/1865; Exchanged at Camp Townsend, MS, on 5/6/1865.

Dodge, John Coal Heaver, C.S.A. Navy (Steamer Selma). Federal Rolls of Prisoners of War: Captured at Mobile Bay, AL, on 8/5/1864; Received at Ship Island, MS, from New Orleans, LA, on 10/28/1864. Exchanged on 3/2/1865.

Donahue, J.K. (AKA J.H., J.R.) Pvt., C.S.A. Navy. Federal Rolls of Prisoners of War: Captured at Mobile Bay, AL, on 8/5/1864; Received at Ship Island, MS, from New Orleans, LA, on 11/25/1864. Exchanged on 3/2/1865.

Dorgan, John Pvt., C.S.A. Marine Corps. Co. D. Federal Rolls of Prisoners of War: Captured at Fort Gaines, AL, on 8/8/1864; Received at Ship Island, MS, from New Orleans, LA, on 10/28/1864. Took the U.S. Oath of Allegiance and transferred to the U.S. naval authorities at New Orleans, LA, on 1/2/1865.

Douglas, W.B. Landsman, C.S.A. Navy (Steamer Selma). Federal Rolls of Prisoners of War: Captured at Mobile Bay, AL, on 8/5/1864; Received at Ship Island, MS, from New Orleans, LA, on 10/28/1864. Exchanged on 3/2/1865.

Drumskey, J. Pvt., C.S.A. Marine Corps. Co. D. Federal Rolls of Prisoners of War: Captured at Blakely, AL, on 4/9/1865; Received at Ship Island, MS, on 4/15/1865. Transferred to Vicksburg, MS, for exchange on 5/1/1865; Exchanged at Camp Townsend, MS, on 5/6/1865.

Dunn, Michael. Pvt., C.S.A. Marine Corps. Co. D. Federal Rolls of Prisoners of War: Captured at Fort Gaines, AL, on 8/8/1864; Received at Ship Island, MS, from New Orleans, LA, on 10/25/1865. Took the U.S. Oath of Allegiance and transferred to the U.S. naval authorities at New Orleans, LA, on 1/2/1865. Residence at oath: Buffalo, NY. Description at oath: Eyes: blue. Hair: black. Complexion: dark. Height: 5'5".

Edgar, H. (AKA W., N.) Ordinary Seaman, C.S.A. Navy (Steamer Selma). Federal Rolls of Prisoners of War: Captured at Mobile Bay, AL, on 8/5/1864; Received at Ship Island, MS, from New Orleans, LA, on 10/28/1864. Transferred to Vicksburg, MS, for exchange on 5/1/1865; Exchanged at Camp Townsend, MS, on 5/6/1865.

Elden, Peter (AKA Eldon) Ordinary Seaman/2nd Mate, C.S.A. Navy (Steamer Selma). Federal Rolls of Prisoners of War: Captured at Mobile Bay, AL, on 8/5/1864; Received at Ship Island, MS, from New Orleans, LA, on 10/28/1864. Transferred to Vicksburg, MS, for exchange on 5/1/1865; Exchanged at Camp Townsend, MS, on 5/6/1865.

Finley, Francis Pvt., C.S.A. Marine Corps. Co. D. Federal Rolls of Prisoners of War: Captured at Mobile Bay, AL, on 8/5/1864; Received at Ship Island, MS, from New Orleans, LA, on 10/28/1864. Exchanged on 3/2/1865.

Flehan, C. Pvt., C.S.A. Marine Corps. Co. D. Federal Rolls of Prisoners of War: Captured at Blakely, AL, on 4/9/1865; Received at Ship Island, MS, on 4/15/1865. Transferred to Vicksburg, MS, for exchange on 5/1/1865; Exchanged at Camp Townsend, MS, on 5/6/1865.

Flynn, Dennis (AKA Flinn, Fynn) Landsman, C.S.A. Navy (Ram Tennessee). Age at enlistment: 25. Description at enlistment: Eyes: blue. Hair: dark. Complexion: light. Occupation at enlistment: Boatman. Federal Rolls of Prisoners of War: Captured at Mobile Bay, AL, on 8/5/1864; Received at Ship Island, MS, from New Orleans, LA, on 10/28/1864. Died: 3/7/1865 at Ship Island, MS, due to pthisis pulmonary. Buried: Ship Island, MS, Cemetery in Grave #138. Born: Ireland.

Fraler, H.T. (AKA Frader, H.G.) Ordinary Seaman, C.S.A. Navy (Steamer Selma). Federal Rolls of Prisoners of War: Captured at Mobile Bay, AL, on 8/5/1864; Received at Ship Island, MS, from New Orleans, LA, on 10/28/1864. Exchanged on 3/2/1865.

Fralick, J.H. (AKA I.H.) Landsman, C.S.A. Navy (Steamer Selma). Federal Rolls of Prisoners of War: Captured at Mobile Bay, AL, on 8/5/1864; Received at Ship Island, MS, from New Orleans, LA, on 10/28/1864. Exchanged on 3/2/1865.

Franklich, Thomas (AKA Frankledge) Landsman/2nd Mate, C.S.A. Navy (Ram Tennessee). Age at enlistment: 40. Description at enlistment: Eyes: black.

Hair: gray. Federal Rolls of Prisoners of War: Captured at Fort Gaines, AL, on 8/8/1864; Received at Ship Island, MS, from New Orleans, LA, on 10/28/1864. Exchanged on 3/2/1865. Buried: Magnolia Cemetery located at Mobile, AL. Born: Hungary.

Frazier, Alex Pvt., C.S.A. Marine Corps. Co. D. Federal Rolls of Prisoners of War: Captured at Mobile Bay, AL, on 8/5/1864; Received at Ship Island, MS, from New Orleans, LA, on 10/28/1864. Exchanged on 3/2/1865.

Frazier, B.F. Landsman, C.S.A. Navy (Steamer Selma). Federal Rolls of Prisoners of War: Captured at Mobile Bay, AL, on 8/5/1864; Received at Ship Island, MS, from New Orleans, LA, on 10/28/1864. Exchanged on 3/2/1865.

Frazier, W. Pvt., C.S.A. Marine Corps. Co. D. Federal Rolls of Prisoners of War: Captured at Blakely, AL, on 4/9/1865; Received at Ship Island, MS, on 4/15/1865. Transferred to Vicksburg, MS, for exchange on 5/1/1865; Exchanged at Camp Townsend, MS, on 5/6/1865.

Gardiner, F. (AKA T.) Sgt., C.S.A. Marine Corps. Co. D. Federal Rolls of Prisoners of War: Captured at Blakely, AL, on 4/9/1865; Received at Ship Island, MS, from New Orleans, LA, on 4/15/1865. Transferred to Vicksburg, MS, for exchange on 5/1/1865; Exchanged at Camp Townsend, MS, on 5/6/1865.

Gilliland, John (AKA Gilleland) Seaman/Cook, C.S.A. Navy (Steamer Selma). Federal Rolls of Prisoners of War: Captured at Mobile Bay, AL, on 8/5/1864, where he was wounded. Received at Ship Island, MS, from New Orleans, LA, on 10/28/1864. Took the U.S. Oath of Allegiance and transferred to the U.S. naval authorities at New Orleans, LA, on 1/2/1865.

Gommons, Thomas (AKA Gemmon, Gommow) Seaman/1st Mate, C.S.A. Navy (Steamer Selma). Federal Rolls of Prisoners of War: Captured at Mobile Bay, AL, on 8/5/1864; Received at Ship Island, MS, from New Orleans, LA, on 10/28/1864. Died: 12/3/1864 at Ship Island, MS, due to chronic dysentery. Buried: Ship Island, MS, Cemetery in Grave #62.

Graham, Charles F. Landsman, C.S.A. Navy (Ram Tennessee). Federal Rolls of Prisoners of War: Captured at Fort Gaines, AL, on 8/8/1864; Received at Ship Island, MS, from New Orleans, LA, on 10/28/1864. Exchanged on 3/2/1865.

Graham, Thomas Pvt., C.S.A. Navy (Ram Tennessee). Federal Rolls of Prisoners of War: Captured at Mobile Bay, AL, on 8/5/1864; Received at Ship Island, MS, from New Orleans, LA, on 10/28/1864. Disposition unknown.

Grant, J.N. Landsman, C.S.A. Navy (Steamer Selma). Federal Rolls of Prisoners of War: Captured at Mobile Bay, AL, on 8/5/1864; Received at Ship Island, MS, from New Orleans, LA, on 10/28/1864. Exchanged on 3/2/1865.

Hagarty, John (AKA Hagy) Landsman, C.S.A. Navy (Ram Tennessee). Age at enlistment: 21. Description at enlistment: Eyes: dark. Hair: dark. Complexion: dark. Occupation at enlistment: Farmer. Federal Rolls of Prisoners of War: Captured at Fort Gaines, AL, on 8/8/1864; Received at Ship Island, MS, from New Orleans, LA, on 10/28/1864. Escaped on 1/13/1865. Born: Ohio.

Harlan, Jeff Pvt., C.S.A. Marine Corps. Co. D. Federal Rolls of Prisoners of War: Captured at Fort Gaines, AL, on 8/8/1864; Received at Ship Island, MS, from New Orleans, LA, on 10/28/1864. Transferred to Vicksburg, MS, for exchange on 5/1/1865; Exchanged at Camp Townsend, MS, on 5/6/1865.

Harris, C.B. Pvt., C.S.A. Marine Corps. Co. D. Federal Rolls of Prisoners of War: Captured at Blakely, AL, on 4/9/1865; Received at Ship Island, MS, on 4/15/1865. Transferred to Vicksburg, MS, for exchange on 5/1/1865; Exchanged at Camp Townsend, MS, on 5/6/1865.

Harrison, Thomas Landsman, C.S.A. Navy (Steamer Selma). Federal Rolls of Prisoners of War: Captured at Mobile Bay, AL, on 8/5/1864; Received at Ship Island, MS, from New Orleans, LA, on 10/28/1864. Exchanged on 3/2/1865.

Harrod, John (AKA Harrold) Landsman, C.S.A. Navy (Ram Tennessee). Age at enlistment: 30. Description at enlistment: Eyes: black. Hair: dark. Complexion: dark. Occupation at enlistment: Farmer. Federal Rolls of Prisoners of War: Captured at Fort Gaines, AL, on 8/8/1864; Received at Ship Island, MS, from New Orleans, LA, on 10/28/1864. Transferred to Vicksburg, MS, for exchange on 5/1/1865; Exchanged at Camp Townsend, MS, on 5/6/1865. Born: Kentucky.

Hart, W. Pvt., C.S.A. Marine Corps. Co. D. Federal Rolls of Prisoners of War: Captured at Blakely, AL, on 4/9/1865; Received at Ship Island, MS, on 4/15/1865. Transferred to Vicksburg, MS, for exchange on 5/1/1865; Exchanged at Camp Townsend, MS, on 5/6/1865.

Henderson, G.W. Pvt., C.S.A Navy (Ram Tennessee). Federal Rolls of Prisoners of War: Captured at Mobile Bay, AL, on 8/5/1864; Received at Ship Island, MS, from New Orleans, LA, on 10/28/1864. Exchanged on 3/2/1865.

Hicks, A. Pvt., C.S.A. Marine Corps. Co. D. Federal Rolls of Prisoners of War: Captured at Blakely, AL, on 4/9/1865; Received at Ship Island, MS, on 4/15/1865. Transferred to Vicksburg, MS, for exchange on 5/1/1865; Exchanged at Camp Townsend, MS, on 5/6/1865.

Holley, John (AKA Holly) Landsman, C.S.A. Navy (Steamer Selma). Federal Rolls of Prisoners of War: Captured at Mobile Bay, AL, on 8/5/1864; Received at Ship Island, MS, from New Orleans, LA, on 10/28/1864. Exchanged on 3/2/1865.

Holst, John Landsman, C.S.A. Navy (Ram Tennessee). Age at enlistment: 29. Description at enlistment: Eyes: dark. Hair: dark. Complexion: dark. Federal Rolls of Prisoners of War: Captured at Fort Gaines, AL, on 8/8/1864; Received at Ship Island, MS, from New Orleans, LA, on 10/28/1864. Exchanged on 3/2/1865.

Hughes, B.F. Capt., C.S.A. Marine Corps. Co. D. Federal Rolls of Prisoners of War: Captured at Blakely, AL, on 4/9/1865; Received at Ship Island, MS, on 4/15/1865. Transferred to Vicksburg, MS, for exchange on 4/28/1865; Confined at New Orleans, LA, on 4/30/1865. Exchanged at Camp Townsend, MS, on 5/6/1865.

Insley, S.P. Landsman/2nd Mate, C.S.A. Navy (Ram Tennessee). Age at enlistment: 42. Description at enlistment: Eyes: grey. Hair: light. Complexion: light. Federal Rolls of Prisoners of War: Captured at Mobile Bay, AL, on 8/5/1864; Received at Ship Island,

MS, from New Orleans, LA, on 10/28/1864. Exchanged on 3/2/1865. Born: Maryland.

Jenkins, E.B. Landsman, C.S.A. Navy (Steamer Selma). Federal Rolls of Prisoners of War: Captured at Mobile Bay, AL, on 8/5/1864; Received at Ship Island, MS, from New Orleans, LA, on 10/29/1864. Exchanged on 3/2/1865.

Jeniran, I.N. (AKA I. A) Pvt., C.S.A. Marine Corps. Co. D. Federal Rolls of Prisoners of War: Captured at Mobile Bay, AL, on 8/5/1864; Received at Ship Island, MS, from New Orleans, LA, on 10/29/1864. Transferred to Vicksburg, MS, for exchange on 5/1/1865; Exchanged at Camp Townsend, MS, on 5/6/1865.

Johnson, A.B. Pvt., C.S.A. Marine Corps. Co. D. Federal Rolls of Prisoners of War: Captured at Mobile Bay, AL, on 8/5/1864; Received at Ship Island, MS, from New Orleans, LA, on 10/28/1864. Transferred to Vicksburg, MS, for exchange on 5/1/1865; Exchanged at Camp Townsend, MS, on 5/6/1865.

Johnson, Napoleon B. Pvt., C.S.A. Marine Corps. Co. D. Enlisted: 1/1/1863 at Talladega, AL; Transferred for duty on the C.S.S. Tennessee on 3/15/1864. Federal Rolls of Prisoners of War: Captured at Mobile Bay, AL, on 8/5/1864; Received at Ship Island, MS, from New Orleans, LA, on 10/28/1864. Exchanged on 3/2/1865. Confederate Widows Pension Application dated 1914 on file at the Alabama Dept. of Archives and History. Target Name: Johnson, Mrs.M.A. County: Shelby. Buried: Rocky Ridge Cemetery located at Shelby County, AL.

Kape, J.C. (AKA Kupe, J.O.) Pvt., C.S.A. Marine Corps. Co. D. Federal Rolls of Prisoners of War: Captured at Fort Gaines, AL, on 8/8/1864; Received at Ship Island, MS, from New Orleans, LA, on 10/28/1864. Took the U.S. Oath of Allegiance and transferred to the U.S. naval authorities at New Orleans, LA, on 1/2/1865.

Kelly, Daniel Landsman, C.S.A. Navy (Steamer Selma). Federal Rolls of Prisoners of War: Captured at Mobile Bay, AL, on 8/5/1864; Received at Ship Island, MS, from New Orleans, LA, on 10/28/1864. Exchanged on 3/2/1865.

Kender, Isham Landsman, C.S.A. Navy (Steamer Selma). Federal Rolls of Prisoners of War: Captured at Mobile Bay, AL, on 8/5/1864; Recevied at Ship Island, MS, from New Orleans, LA, on 10/28/1864. Exchanged on 3/2/1865.

Kennedy, John Pvt., C.S.A. Marine Corps. Co. D. Federal Rolls of Prisoners of War: Captured at Fort Gaines, AL, on 8/8/1864; Received at Ship Island, MS, from New Orleans, LA, on 10/25/1864. Took the U.S. Oath of Allegiance and transferred to the U.S. naval authorities at New Orleans, LA, on 1/2/1865. Residence at oath: New Orleans, LA. Description at oath: Eyes: grey. Hair: black. Complexion: dark. Height: 5'7". Sailor also served as a Fireman on the C.S.S. Baltic.

King, Frank Landsman, C.S.A. Navy (Ram Tennessee). Age at enlistment: 20. Description at enlistment: Eyes: grey. Hair: dark. Complexion: light. Occupation at enlistment: Farmer. Federal Rolls of Prisoners of War: Captured at Mobile Bay, AL, on 8/5/1864; Received at Ship Island, MS, from New Orleans, LA, on 10/28/1864. Took the U.S. Oath of Allegiance and transferred to the U.S. naval authorities at New Orleans, LA, on 1/2/1865. Born: Alabama.

Kinley, James 3rd Mate, C.S.A. Navy (Ram Tennessee). Federal Rolls of Prisoners of War: Captured at Mobile Bay, AL, on 8/5/1864; Received at Ship Island, MS, from New Orleans, LA, on 10/28/1864. Exchanged on 3/2/1865.

Lambert, James Pvt., C.S.A. Marine Corps. Co. D. Federal Rolls of Prisoners of War: Captured at Mobile Bay, AL, on 8/5/1864; Received at Ship Island, MS, from New Orleans, LA, on 10/28/1864. Exchanged on 3/2/1865.

Lancaster, A. (AKA U.) Pvt., C.S.A. Marine Corps. Co. D. Federal Rolls of Prisoners of War: Captured at Blakely, AL, on 4/9/1865; Received at Ship Island, MS, on 4/15/1865. Transferred to Vicksburg, MS, for exchange on 5/1/1865; Exchanged at Camp Townsend, MS, on 5/6/1865.

Lancaster, William F. Pvt., C.S.A. Marine Corps. Co. D. Enlisted: Mobile, AL. Federal Rolls of Prisoners of War: Captured at Blakely, AL, on 4/9/1865; Received at Ship Island, MS, on 4/15/1865. Transferred to Vicksburg, MS, for exchange on 5/1/1865; Exchanged at Camp Townsend, MS, on 5/6/1865. Born: 1841.

Lance, W.L. (AKA Land, N., S.) Pvt., C.S.A. Marine Corps. Co. D. Federal Rolls of Prisoners of War: Captured at Mobile Bay, AL, on 8/5/1864; Received at Ship Island, MS, from New Orleans, LA, on 10/28/1864. Transferred to Vicksburg, MS, for exchange on 5/1/1865; Exchanged at Camp Townsend, MS, on 5/6/1865.

Langdon, George Barnemus Moore Seaman/2nd Engineer, C.S.A. Navy (Steamer Selma). Enlisted: 12/29/1862 in the C.S.A. Navy; Appointed 2nd Asst. Engineer on 5/21/1863 on the C.S.S. Tuscaloosa. Residence at enlistment: St. Louis, MO. Federal Rolls of Prisoners of War: Captured at Mobile Bay, AL, on 8/5/1864; Received at Ship Island, MS, from New Orleans, LA, on 10/28/1864. Transferred to Vicksburg, MS, for exchange on 4/28/1865; Confined at New Orleans, LA, on 4/30/1865. Exchanged at Camp Townsend, MS, on 5/6/1865. Description at exchange: Eyes: brown. Hair: brown. Complexion: light. Height: 5'3". Sailor also served as a Pvt. with the Missouri State Guards and as a Sgt. with the Missouri Light Artillery Battery (Walsh's). Enlisted: 1861 at Monroe Station, MO. Born: 9/27/1828 to George W. Langdon and Sarah Russell at Sackett Harbor, NY. Married: Levicia Ann Parker. Children: 1 son, Loomis Wiley Langdon. Died: 12/6/1897 at Hannibal, MO. Son born: 2/10/1867. Son died: 8/21/1881. Wife born: 12/1/1839 at Lewis County, MO. Wife died: 11/18/1910 at Hannibal, MO.

Laughlin, M. Coal Heaver, C.S.A. Navy (Steamer Selma). Federal Rolls of Prisoners of War: Captured at Mobile Bay, AL, on 8/5/1864; Received at Ship Island, MS, from New Orleans, LA, on 10/28/1864. Took the U.S. Oath of Allegiance and transferred to the U.S. naval authorities at New Orleans, LA.

Lewis, William Pvt., C.S.A. Marine Corps. Co. D. Federal Rolls of Prisoners of War: Captured at Mobile Bay, AL, on 8/5/1864; Received at Ship Island, MS, from New Orleans, LA, on 10/28/1864. Exchanged on 3/2/1865.

Loflin, John Landsman, C.S.A. Navy (Steamer Selma).

Federal Rolls of Prisoners of War: Captured at Mobile Bay, AL, on 8/5/1864; Received at Ship Island, MS, from New Orleans, LA, on 10/28/1864. Exchanged on 3/2/1865.

Lorring, George Engineer, C.S.A. Navy. Federal Rolls of Prisoners of War: Captured at Mobile Bay, AL, on 8/5/1864; Received at Ship Island, MS, from New Orleans, LA, on 11/25/1864. Exchanged on 3/2/1865.

McBright, J. (AKA McBride) Coal Heaver, C.S.A. Navy (Ram Tennessee). Age at enlistment: 24. Description at enlistment: Eyes: blue. Hair: dark. Complexion: dark. Occupation at enlistment: Blacksmith. Federal Rolls of Prisoners of War: Captured at Mobile Bay, AL, on 8/5/1864; Received at Ship Island, MS, from New Orleans, LA, on 10/28/1864. Exchanged on 3/2/1865. Born: New York.

McCann, James (AKA Can) Seaman, C.S.A. Navy (Steamer Selma). Federal Rolls of Prisoners of War: Captured at Mobile Bay, AL, on 8/5/1864; Received at Ship Island, MS, from New Orleans, LA, on 10/28/1864. Died: 3/18/1865 at Ship Island, MS, due to dropsy. Buried: Ship Island, MS, Cemetery in Grave #142.

McCarty, John (AKA McCarthy) Fireman, C.S.A. Navy (Ram Tennessee). Age at enlistment: 30. Description at enlistment: Eyes: grey. Hair: light. Complexion: fair. Federal Rolls of Prisoner of War: Captured at Mobile Bay, AL, on 8/5/1864; Received at Ship Island, MS, from New Orleans, LA, on 10/28/1864. Exchanged on 3/2/1865. Born: Ireland.

McFarlough, George B. (AKA McFarland) Seaman, C.S.A. Navy (Ram Tennessee). Age at enlistment: 25. Description at enlistment: Eyes: blue. Hair: unknown. Complexion: dark. Occupation at enlistment: Sailor. Federal Rolls of Prisoners of War: Captured at Mobile Bay, AL, on 8/5/1864; Received at Ship Island, MS, from New Orleans, LA, on 10/28/1864. Transferred to Vicksburg, MS, for exchange on 5/1/1865; Exchanged at Camp Townsend, MS, on 5/6/1865. Born: Ireland.

McKinney, L.M. Pvt., C.S.A. Marine Corps. Co. D. Federal Rolls of Prisoners of War: Captured at Mobile Bay, AL, on 8/5/1864; Received at Ship Island, MS, from New Orleans, LA, on 10/28/1864. Exchanged on 3/2/1865.

McLaughlin, Michael Cpl., C.S.A. Marine Corps. Co. D. Federal Rolls of Prisoners of War: Captured at Mobile Bay, AL, on 8/5/1864; Received at Ship Island, MS, from New Orleans, LA, on 10/28/1864. Took the U.S. Oath of Allegiance and transferred to the U.S. naval authorities at New Orleans, LA, on 1/2/1865.

McManning, A. (AKA McHanning) Seaman, C.S.A. Navy. Federal Rolls of Prisoners of War: Captured at Mobile Bay, AL, on 8/5/1864; Received at Ship Island, MS, from New Orleans, LA, on 1/25/1865. Transferred to Vicksburg, MS, for exchange on 5/1/1865; Exchanged at Camp Townsend, MS, on 5/6/1865.

McNamara, M. Pvt., C.S.A. Marine Corps. Co. D. Federal Rolls of Prisoners of War: Captured at Fort Gaines, AL, on 8/8/1864; Received at Ship Island, MS, from New Orleans, LA, on 10/25/1864. Took the U.S. Oath of Allegiance and transferred to the U.S. naval authorities at New Orleans, LA, on 1/2/1865.

Martin, B.F. (AKA B.S., B.J.) Landsman, C.S.A. Navy (Ram Tennessee). Age at enlistment: 23. Description at enlistment: Eyes: blue. Hair: light. Complexion: light. Occupation at enlistment: Farmer. Federal Rolls of Prisoners of War: Captured at Mobile Bay, AL, on 8/5/1864; Received at Ship Island, MS, from New Orleans, LA, on 10/28/1864. Took the U.S. Oath of Allegiance and transferred to the U.S. naval authorities at New Orleans, LA, on 1/2/1865. Born: Kentucky.

Miller, Phillip Pvt., C.S.A. Marine Corps. Co. D. Federal Rolls of Prisoners of War: Captured at Mobile Bay, AL, on 8/5/1864; Received at Ship Island, MS, from New Orleans, LA, on 10/28/1864. Exchanged on 3/2/1865.

Moffit, Joshua Landsman, C.S.A. Navy (Ram Tennessee). Age at enlistment: 25. Description at enlistment: Eyes: blue. Hair: dark. Complexion: fair. Federal Rolls of Prisoners of War: Captured at Mobile Bay, AL, on 8/5/1864; Received at Ship Island, MS, from New Orleans, LA, on 10/28/1864. Transferred to Vicksburg, MS, for exchange on 5/1/1865; Exchanged at Camp Townsend, MS, on 5/6/1865. Born: North Carolina.

Montanara, H. Pvt., C.S.A. Marine Corps. Co. D. Federal Rolls of Prisoners of War: Captured at Mobile Bay, AL, on 8/5/1864; Received at Ship Island, MS, from New Orleans, LA, on 10/28/1864. Took the U.S. Oath of Allegiance and transferred to the U.S. naval authorities at New Orleans, LA, on 1/2/1865.

Montgomery, I.E. Comm., C.S.A. Navy. Federal Rolls of Prisoners of War: Captured at Choctaw Bend, MS, on 11/16/1864; Received at Ship Island, MS, from New Orleans, LA, on 12/18/1864. Exchanged on 3/2/1865.

Moran, James 3rd Cabin Boy, C.S.A. Navy (Steamer Selma). Federal Rolls of Prisoners of War: Captured at Mobile Bay, AL, on 8/5/1864; Received at Ship Island, MS, from New Orleans, LA, on 10/28/1864. Exchanged on 3/2/1865.

Murphy, John Ordinary Seaman, C.S.A Navy (Ram Tennessee). Age at enlistment: 24. Description at enlistment: Eyes: blue. Hair: dark brown. Complexion: light. Federal Rolls of Prisoners of War: Captured at Mobile Bay, AL, on 8/5/1864; Received at Ship Island, MS, from New Orleans, LA, on 10/28/1864. Exchanged on 3/2/1865. Born: Ireland.

Murphy, P. Pvt., C.S.A. Marine Corps. Co. D. Federal Rolls of Prisoners of War: Captured at Fort Gaines, AL, on 8/8/1864; Received at Ship Island, MS, from New Orleans, LA, on 10/28/1864. Exchanged on 3/2/1865.

Murray, John R. Seaman/Acting Masters Mate, C.S.A. Navy (Steamer Selma). Federal Rolls of Prisoners of War: Captured at Mobile Bay, AL, on 8/5/1864; Received at Ship Island, MS, from New Orleans, LA, on 10/28/1864. Exchanged on 3/2/1865.

Nash, J.D. (AKA Nas) Landsman, C.S.A. Navy (Ram Tennessee). Federal Rolls of Prisoners of War: Captured at Mobile Bay, AL, on 8/5/1864; Received at Ship Island, MS, from New Orleans, LA, on 10/28/1864. Transferred to Vicksburg, MS, for exchange on 5/1/1865; Exchanged at Camp Townsend, MS, on 5/6/1865.

O'Conner, John 2nd Assistant Engineer, C.S.A. Navy. Federal Rolls of Prisoners of War: Captured at Mobile Bay, AL, on 8/5/1864; Received at Ship Island,

MS, from New Orleans, LA, on 10/25/1864. Exchanged on 3/2/1865.

O'Connor, Charles Seaman, C.S.A. Navy (Steamer Selma). Enlisted: 5/8/1862 at Mobile, AL, for service on the CSS *Selma*. Federal Rolls of Prisoners of War: Captured at Mobile Bay, AL, on 8/5/1864; Received at Ship Island, MS, from New Orleans, LA, on 10/28/1864. Transferred to the C.S.A. Army in Brig. Gen. Randall L. Gibson's Brigade at Mobile, AL, on 2/9/1865 for secret duty at Spanish Fort, AL. Born: 10/21/1824 in County Cork, Ireland. Residence: Pensacola, FL, in 1902. Confederate Pension Application dated 1902 on file at the Florida State Library and Archives. Name: O'Connor, Charles. Application Number: A12749. County: Escambia.

O'Donnell, W. Landsman, C.S.A. Navy (Ram Tennessee). Age at enlistment: 19. Description at enlistment: Eyes: blue. Hair: dark. Complexion: ruddy. Federal Rolls of Prisoners of War: Captured at Mobile Bay, AL, on 8/5/1864; Received at Ship Island, MS, from New Orleans, LA, on 10/28/1864. Exchanged on 3/2/1865. Born: Arkansas.

O'Keefe, James Pvt., C.S.A. Marine Corps. Co. D. Federal Rolls of Prisoners of War: Captured at Fort Gaines, AL, on 8/8/1864; Received at Ship Island, MS, from New Orleans, LA, on 10/25/1864. Took the U.S. Oath of Allegiance and transferred to the U.S. naval authorities at New Orleans, LA, on 1/2/1865.

Olly, W.P. Pvt., C.S.A. Marine Corps. Co. D. Federal Rolls of Prisoners of War: Captured at Mobile Bay, AL, on 8/5/1864; Received at Ship Island, MS, from New Orleans, LA, on 10/28/1864. Transferred to Vicksburg, MS, for exchange on 5/1/1865; Exchanged at Camp Townsend, MS, on 5/6/1865.

Osbrook, D. (AKA Oabrook) Landsman, C.S.A. Navy (Ram Tennessee). Federal Rolls of Prisoners of War: Captured at Mobile Bay, AL, on 8/5/1864; Received at Ship Island, MS, from New Orleans, LA, on 11/25/1864. Died: 12/6/1864 at Ship Island, MS, due to typhoid fever. Buried: Ship Island, MS, Cemetery in Grave #70.

Palmer, John Pvt., C.S.A. Marine Corps. Co. D. Federal Rolls of Prisoners of War: Captured at Mobile Bay, AL, on 8/5/1864; Received at Ship Island, MS, from New Orleans, LA, on 10/28/1864. Exchanged on 3/2/1865.

Parsons, C.H. (AKA Parsens, E.H.) Coal Heaver, C.S.A. Navy (Steamer Selma). Federal Rolls of Prisoners of War: Captured at Mobile Bay, AL, on 8/5/1864; Received at Ship Island, MS, from New Orleans, LA, on 10/28/1864. Transferred to Vicksburg, MS, for exchange on 5/1/1865; Exchanged at Camp Townsend, MS, on 5/6/1865.

Patterson, W.B. (AKA N.B.) 2nd Asst. Engineer, C.S.A. Navy. Federal Rolls of Prisoners of War: Captured at Mobile Bay, AL, on 8/5/1864; Received at Ship Island, MS, from New Orleans, LA, on 10/25/1864. Exchanged on 3/2/1865.

Perrins, H.C. Arty. Mate, C.S.A. Navy (Steamer Selma). Federal Rolls of Prisoners of War: Captured at Mobile Bay, AL, on 8/5/1864; Received at Ship Island, MS, from New Orleans, LA, on 10/25/1864. Exchanged on 3/2/1865.

Piles, A.J. Landsman, C.S.A. Navy (Ram Tennessee). Federal Rolls of Prisoners of War: Captured at Mobile Bay, AL, on 8/5/1864; Received at Ship Island, MS, from New Orleans, LA, on 10/28/1864. Took the U.S. Oath of Allegiance and transferred to the U.S. naval authorities at New Orleans, LA, on 1/2/1865.

Pitts, A.J. (AKA Piles) Landsman, C.S.A. Navy (Ram Tennessee). Federal Rolls of Prisoners of War: Captured at Mobile Bay, AL, on 8/5/1864; Received at Ship Island, MS, from New Orleans, LA, on 10/28/1864. Took the U.S. Oath of Allegiance and transferred to the U.S. naval authorities at New Orleans, LA, on 1/2/1865.

Post, A.P. Pilot, C.S.A. Navy. Federal Rolls of Prisoners of War: Captured at Mobile Bay, AL, on 8/5/1864; Received at Ship Island, MS, from New Orleans, LA, on 10/25/1864. Exchanged on 3/2/1865.

Powers, John H. 1st Class Fireman, C.S.A. Navy (Ram Tennessee). Age at enlistment: 36. Description at enlistment: Eyes: grey. Hair: black and gray. Complexion: ruddy. Federal Rolls of Prisoners of War: Captured at Mobile Bay, AL, on 8/5/1864; Received at Ship Island, MS, from New Orleans, LA, on 10/28/1864. Took the U.S. Oath of Allegiance and transferred to the U.S. naval authorities at New Orleans, LA, on 1/2/1865. Born: Ireland.

Price, Thomas Pvt., C.S.A. Navy (Ram Tennessee). Federal Rolls of Prisoners of War: Captured at Mobile Bay, AL, on 8/5/1864; Received at Ship Island, MS, from New Orleans, LA, on 12/13/1864. Exchanged on 3/2/1865.

Quinn, Ed Pvt., C.S.A. Marine Corps. Co. D. Federal Rolls of Prisoners of War: Captured at Fort Gaines, AL, on 8/8/1864; Received at Ship Island, MS, from New Orleans, LA, on 10/28/1864. Exchanged on 3/2/1865.

Quinn, John Landsman, C.S.A. Navy (Ram Tennessee). Age at enlistment: 32. Description at enlistment: Eyes: brown. Hair: dark. Complexion: dark. Occupation at enlistment: Laborer. Federal Rolls of Prisoners of War: Captured at Fort Gaines, AL, on 8/8/1864; Received at Ship Island, MS, from New Orleans, LA, on 10/28/1864. Exchanged on 3/2/1865. Born: Ireland.

Rap, John 2nd Engineer, C.S.A. Navy (Ram Tennessee). Federal Rolls of Prisoners of War: Captured at Mobile Bay, AL, on 8/5/1864; Received at Ship Island, MS, from New Orleans, LA, on 10/28/1864. Exchanged on 3/2/1865.

Rasmuson, A. (AKA Rossmorsson) 2nd Mate/Quartermaster, C.S.A. Navy (Ram Tennessee). Age at enlistment: 32. Description at enlistment: Eyes: blue. Hair: light. Complexion: fair. Federal Rolls of Prisoners of War: Captured at Mobile Bay, AL, on 8/5/1864 while wounded; Received at Ship Island, MS, from New Orleans, LA, on 10/28/1864. Exchanged on 3/2/1865. Born: Denmark.

Reynolds, John Pvt., C.S.A. Marine Corps. Co. D. Federal Rolls of Prisoners of War: Captured at Fort Gaines, AL, on 8/8/1864; Received at Ship Island, MS, from New Orleans, LA, on 10/25/1864. Took the U.S. Oath of Allegiance and transferred to the U.S. naval authorities at New Orleans, LA, on 1/2/1865.

Rich, Francis (AKA Frank) Seaman, C.S.A. Navy (Ram Tennessee). Age at enlistment: 29. Description at enlistment: Eyes: blue. Hair: light. Complexion: fair. Federal Rolls of Prisoners of War: Captured at Mobile Bay, AL, on 8/5/1864; Received at Ship Island, MS, from New Orleans, LA, on 10/28/1864. Exchanged on 3/2/1865. Born: Ireland.

Riley, John Landsman, C.S.A. Navy (Ram Tennessee). Age at enlistment: 49. Description at enlistment: Eyes: blue. Hair: dark. Complexion: ruddy. Occupation at enlistment: Fireman. Federal Rolls of Prisoners of War: Captured at Mobile Bay, AL, on 8/5/1864. Received at Ship Island, MS, from New Orleans, LA, on 10/28/1864. Exchanged on 3/2/1865. Born: Ireland.

Rogers, William 3rd Asst. Engineer/2nd Asst. Engineer, C.S.A. Navy. Federal Rolls of Prisoners of War: Captured at Mobile Bay, AL, on 8/5/1864; Received at Ship Island, MS, from New Orleans, LA, on 10/25/1864. Exchanged on 3/2/1865.

Scott, David Seaman, C.S.A. Navy (Steamer Selma). Federal Rolls of Prisoners of War: Captured at Mobile Bay, AL, on 8/5/1864; Received at Ship Island, MS, from New Orleans, LA, on 10/28/1864. Transferred to Vicksburg, MS, for exchange on 5/1/1865; Exchanged at Camp Townsend, MS, on 5/6/1865.

Seymour, Charles Coal Heaver/Landsman, C.S.A. Navy (Ram Tennessee). Age at enlistment: 27. Description at enlistment: Eyes: hazel. Hair: dark. Complexion: dark. Federal Rolls of Prisoners of War: Captured at Mobile Bay, AL, on 8/5/1864; Received at Ship Island, MS, from New Orleans, LA, on 10/28/1864. Exchanged on 3/2/1865. Born: New Orleans, LA.

Shea, Daniel (AKA Shay) Fireman, C.S.A. Navy (Ram Tennessee). Age at enlistment: 45. Description at enlistment: Eyes: blue. Hair: dark. Complexion: fair. Federal Rolls of Prisoners of War: Captured at Mobile Bay, AL, on 8/5/1864; Received at Ship Island, MS, from New Orleans, LA, on 10/28/1864. Transferred to New Orleans, LA, on 2/15/1865. Born: Ireland.

Sheridan, Thomas J. Landsman, C.S.A. Navy (Ram Tennessee). Age at enlistment: 20. Description at enlistment: Eyes: dark. Hair: dark. Complexion light. Occupation: Carpenter. Federal Rolls of Prisoners of War: Captured at Mobile Bay, AL, on 8/5/1864; Received at Ship Island, MS, from New Orleans, LA, on 10/28/1864. Exchanged on 3/2/1865. Born: Mobile, AL.

Shields, John P. Landsman, C.S.A. Navy (Ram Tennessee). Age at enlistment: 19. Description at enlistment: Eyes: blue. Hair: brown. Complexion: dark. Federal Rolls of Prisoners of War: Captured at Mobile Bay, AL, on 8/5/1864; Received at Ship Island, MS, from New Orleans, LA, on 10/28/1864. Exchanged on 3/2/1865. Born: Mobile, AL.

Shroeder, John 1st Chief Fireman, C.S.A. Navy (Steamer Selma). Federal Rolls of Prisoners of War: Captured at Mobile Bay, AL, on 8/5/1864; Received at Ship Island, MS, from New Orleans, LA, on 10/28/1864. Transferred to Vicksburg, MS, for exchange on 5/1/1865; Exchanged at Camp Townsend, MS, on 5/6/1865.

Sill, Joseph Landsman/Coal Heaver C.S.A. Navy (Steamer Selma). Federal Rolls of Prisoners of War: Captured at Mobile Bay, AL, on 8/5/1864; Received at Ship Island, MS, from New Orleans, LA, on 10/28/1864. Exchanged on 3/2/1865.

Simmons, Charles 2nd Gunner/Seaman, C.S.A. Navy. Federal Rolls of Prisoners of War: Captured at Mobile Bay, AL, on 8/5/1864; Received at Ship Island, MS, from New Orleans, LA, on 10/28/1864. Transferred to Vicksburg, MS, for exchange on 5/1/1865; Exchanged at Camp Townsend, MS, on 5/6/1865.

Sims, W. Pvt., C.S.A. Marine Corps. Co. D. Federal Rolls of Prisoners of War: Captured at Blakely, AL, on 4/9/1865; Received at Ship Island, MS, on 4/15/1865. Transferred to Vicksburg, MS, for exchange on 5/1/1865; Exchanged at Camp Townsend, MS, on 5/6/1865.

Smith, G.A. Pvt., C.S.A. Marine Corps. Co. D. Federal Rolls of Prisoners of War: Captured at Fort Gaines, AL, on 8/8/1864; Received at Ship Island, MS, from New Orleans, LA, on 10/29/1864. Transferred to Vicksburg, MS, for exchange on 5/1/1865; Exchanged at Camp Townsend, MS, on 5/6/1865.

Smith, H.S. (AKA H.T.) Gunner, C.S.A. Navy. Federal Rolls of Prisoners of War: Captured at Mobile Bay, AL, on 8/5/1864; Received at Ship Island, MS, from New Orleans, LA, on 11/25/1864. Exchanged on 3/2/1865.

Smith, J.W. Landsman, C.S.A. Navy (Steamer Selma). Federal Rolls of Prisoners of War: Captured at Mobile Bay, AL, on 8/5/1864; Received at Ship Island, MS, from New Orleans, LA, on 11/25/1864. Died: 2/27/1865 at Ship Island, MS, due to carcinoma. Buried: Ship Island, MS, Cemetery in Grave #137.

Smith, James W. Seaman, C.S.A. Navy (Ram Tennessee). Age at enlistment: 24. Description at enlistment: Eyes: grey. Hair: dark. Complexion: light. Federal Rolls of Prisoners of War: Captured at Mobile Bay, AL, on 8/5/1864; Received at Ship Island, MS, from New Orleans, LA, on 10/28/1864. Died: Ship Island, MS, on 2/27/1865 due to hepatitis. Buried: Ship Island, MS, Cemetery in Grave #137. Born: Tennessee.

Smith, John A. Seaman, C.S.A. Navy (Ram Tennessee). Age at enlistment: 39. Description at enlistment: Eyes: grey. Hair: dark. Complexion: dark. Federal Rolls of Prisoners of War: Captured at Mobile Bay, AL, on 8/5/1864; Received at Ship Island, MS, from New Orleans, LA, on 10/28/1864. Died: 2/27/1865 at Ship Island, MS. Buried: Ship Island, MS, Cemetery.

Spriggs, George (AKA John) Landsman, C.S.A. Navy (Ram Tennessee). Age at enlistment: 30. Description at enlistment: Eyes: blue. Hair: dark. Complexion: ruddy. Occupation at enlistment: Boatman. Federal Rolls of Prisoners of War: Captured at Mobile Bay, AL, on 8/5/1864; Received at Ship Island, MS, from New Orleans, LA, on 10/28/1864. Exchanged on 3/2/1865. Born: Ireland.

Staff, Oliver Mess Boy/Seaman, C.S.A. Navy (Ram Tennessee). Federal Rolls of Prisoners of War: Captured at Mobile Bay, AL, on 8/5/1864; Received at Ship Island, MS, from New Orleans, LA, on 11/25/1864. Died: 11/30/1864 at Ship Island, MS, due to dysentery. Buried: Ship Island, MS, Cemetery in Grave #55.

Stoker, John (AKA Stroker) Pvt., C.S.A. Marine Corps. Co. D. Federal Rolls of Prisoners of War: Captured at Fort Gaines, AL, on 8/8/1864; Received at Ship Island, MS, from New Orleans, LA, on 10/28/1864. Transferred to Vicksburg, MS, for exchange on 5/1/1865; Exchanged at Camp Townsend, MS, on 5/6/1865.

Stone, J. Pvt., C.S.A. Marine Corps. Co. D. Federal Rolls of Prisoners of War: Captured at Blakely, AL, on 4/9/1865; Received at Ship Island, MS, on 4/15/1865. Transferred to Vicksburg, MS, for exchange on 5/1/1865; Exchanged at Camp Townsend, MS, on 5/6/1865.

Straub, W.J. (AKA Straul) Pvt., C.S.A. Marine Corps. Co. D. Federal Rolls of Prisoners of War: Captured at Fort Gaines, AL, on 8/8/1864; Received at Ship Island, MS, from New Orleans, LA, on 10/28/1864. Exchanged on 3/2/1865.

Sutton, James Pilot, C.S.A. Navy. Federal Rolls of Prisoners of War: Captured at Mobile Bay on 8/5/1864; Received at Ship Island, MS, from New Orleans, LA, on 11/25/1864. Exchanged on 3/2/1865.

Tanning, J. (AKA I.) Seaman, C.S.A. Navy. Federal Rolls of Prisoners of War: Captured at Mobile Bay, AL, on 8/5/1864; Received at Ship Island, MS, from New Orleans, LA, on 1/25/1865. Transferred to Vicksburg, MS, for exchange on 5/1/1865; Exchanged at Camp Townsend, MS, on 5/6/1865.

Taylor, J.B. (AKA I.B.) Pvt., C.S.A. Marine Corps. Co. D. Federal Rolls of Prisoners of War: Captured at Fort Gaines, AL, on 8/8/1864; Received at Ship Island, MS, from New Orleans, LA, on 10/28/1864. Exchanged on 3/2/1865.

Taylor, J.W. (AKA J.R.) Landsman, C.S.A. Navy (Ram Tennessee). Age at enlistment: 22. Description at enlistment: Eyes: grey. Hair: light. Complexion: light. Occupation at enlistment: Farmer. Federal Rolls of Prisoners of War: Captured at Fort Gaines, AL, on 8/8/1864; Received at Ship Island, MS, from New Orleans, LA, on 10/28/1864. Exchanged on 3/2/1865. Born: Mississippi.

Tennent, Samuel (AKA Tenant) Seaman, C.S.A. Navy (Ram Tennessee). Age at enlistment: 45. Description at enlistment: Eyes: grey. Hair: auburn. Complexion: light. Occupation at enlistment: Butcher. Federal Rolls of Prisoners of War: Captured at Fort Gaines, AL, on 8/8/1864; Received at Ship Island, MS, from New Orleans, LA, on 10/28/1864. Exchanged on 3/2/1865. Born: Rhode Island.

Thomason, M.D. (AKA Tomason) Ordinary Seaman, C.S.A. Navy (Ram Tennessee). Description at enlistment: Eyes: brown. Hair: black. Complexion: dark. Federal Rolls of Prisoners of War: Captured at Fort Gaines, AL, on 8/8/1864; Received at Ship Island, MS, from New Orleans, LA, on 10/28/1864. Exchanged on 3/2/1865. Born: Mobile, AL.

Thompson, Pat Ordinary Seaman, C.S.A. Navy (Ram Tennessee). Age at enlistment: 35. Description at enlistment: Eyes: blue. Hair: dark. Complexion: fair. Federal Rolls of Prisoners of War: Captured at Fort Gaines, AL, on 8/8/1864; Received at Ship Island, MS, from New Orleans, LA, on 10/28/1864. Exchanged on 3/2/1865. Born: Ireland.

Tobin, Richard Landsman, C.S.A. Navy (Ram Tennessee). Age at enlistment: 27. Description at enlistment: Eyes: hazel. Hair: dark. Complexion: fair. Occupation at enlistment: Laborer. Federal Rolls of Prisoners of War: Captured at Fort Gaines, AL, on 8/8/1864; Received at Ship Island, MS, from New Orleans, LA, on 10/28/1864. Exchanged on 3/2/1865. Born: Ireland.

Tomney, Patrick (AKA Tunnally) Landsman, C.S.A. Navy (Ram Tennessee). Age at enlistment: 34. Description at enlistment: Eyes: blue. Hair: dark. Complexion: fair. Federal Rolls of Prisoners of War: Captured at Fort Gaines, AL, on 8/8/1864; Received at Ship Island, MS, from New Orleans, LA, on 10/28/1864. Exchanged on 3/2/1865. Born: Ireland.

Tucker, J.C. (AKA I.C.) Landsman, C.S.A. Navy (Ram Tennessee). Federal Rolls of Prisoners of War: Captured at Fort Gaines, AL, on 8/8/1864; Received at Ship Island, MS, from New Orleans, LA, on 10/28/1864. Exchanged on 3/2/1865.

Viler, Charles Pvt., C.S.A. Marine Corps. Co. D. Federal Rolls of Prisoners of War: Captured at Fort Gaines, AL, on 8/8/1864; Received at Ship Island, MS, from New Orleans, LA, on 10/25/1864. Took the U.S. Oath of Allegiance and transferred to the U.S. naval authorities at New Orleans, LA, on 1/2/1865.

Villas, Charles Seaman, C.S.A. Navy (Steamer Selma). Federal Rolls of Prisoners of War: Captured at Mobile Bay, AL, on 8/5/1864; Received at Ship Island, MS, from New Orleans, LA, on 10/28/1864. Took the U.S. Oath of Allegiance and transferred to the U.S. naval authorities at New Orleans, LA, on 1/2/1865.

Volkhart, J.M. (AKA I.M.) Pvt., C.S.A. Marine Corps. Co. D. Federal Rolls of Prisoners of War: Captured at Fort Gaines, AL, on 8/8/1864; Received at Ship Island, MS, from New Orleans, LA, on 10/28/1864. Transferred to Vicksburg, MS, for exchange on 5/1/1865; Exchanged at Camp Townsend, MS, on 5/6/1865.

Waggonbrunner, M. (AKA Wagontrenes) Landsman, C.S.A. Navy (Ram Tennessee). Age at enlistment: 41. Description at enlistment: Eyes: blue. Hair: light. Complexion: fair. Federal Rolls of Prisoners of War: Captured at Mobile Bay, AL, on 8/5/1864; Received at Ship Island, MS, from New Orleans, LA, on 10/28/1864. Exchanged on 3/2/1865. Born: Germany.

Walker, R. Pvt., C.S.A. Marine Corps. Co. D. Federal Rolls of Prisoners of War: Captured at Blakely, AL, on 4/9/1865; Received at Ship Island, MS, on 4/15/1865. Transferred to Vicksburg, MS, for exchange on 5/1/1865; Exchanged at Camp Townsend, MS, on 5/6/1865.

Wallace, B.T. Landsman, C.S.A. Navy (Ram Tennessee). Age at enlistment: 27. Description at enlistment: Eyes: blue. Hair: dark. Complexion: fair. Federal Rolls of Prisoners of War: Captured at Fort Gaines, AL, on 8/8/1864; Received at Ship Island, MS, from New Orleans, LA, on 10/28/1864. Exchanged on 3/2/1865. Born: Virginia.

Ward, C. Pvt., C.S.A. Marine Corps. Co. D. Federal Rolls of Prisoners of War: Captured at Blakely, AL, on 4/9/1865; Received at Ship Island, MS, from New Orleans, LA, on 4/15/1865. Transferred to Vicksburg, MS, for exchange on 5/1/1865; Exchanged at Camp Townsend, MS, on 5/6/1865.

Ward, H. Pvt., C.S.A. Marine Corps. Co. D. Federal Rolls of Prisoners of War: Captured at Fort Gaines, AL, on 8/8/1864; Received at Ship Island, MS, from New Orleans, LA, on 10/28/1864. Exchanged on 3/2/1865.

Ward, John Pvt., C.S.A. Marine Corps. Co. D. Federal Rolls of Prisoners of War: Captured at Fort Gaines, AL, on 8/8/1864; Received at Ship Island, MS, from New Orleans, LA, on 10/28/1864. Exchanged on 3/2/1865.

Whelan, James (AKA Whaler) 2nd Fireman, C.S.A. Navy (Ram Tennessee). Age at enlistment: 38. Description at enlistment: Eyes: hazel. Hair: black and gray. Complexion: ruddy. Federal Rolls of Prisoners of War: Captured at Fort Gaines, AL, on 8/8/1864; Received at Ship Island, MS, from New Orleans, LA, on 10/28/1864. Transferred to Vicksburg, MS, for exchange on 5/1/1865; Exchanged at Camp Townsend, MS, on 5/6/1865. Born: Ireland.

Wheeler, Chris Pvt., C.S.A. Marine Corps. Co. D. Federal Rolls of Prisoners of War: Captured at Fort Gaines, AL, on 8/8/1864; Received at Ship Island, MS, from New Orleans, LA, on 10/28/1864. Exchanged on 3/2/1865.

White, William 2nd Gunner, C.S.A. Navy (Ram Tennessee). Age at enlistment: 29. Description at enlistment: Eyes: hazel. Hair: dark brown. Complexion: dark. Federal Rolls of Prisoners of War: Captured at Mobile Bay, AL, on 8/5/1864; Received at Ship Island, MS, from New Orleans, LA, on 10/28/1864. Exchanged on 3/2/1865. Born: New York.

Williams, D. Landsman, C.S.A. Navy (Ram Tennessee). Federal Rolls of Prisoners of War: Captured at Fort Gaines, AL, on 8/8/1864; Received at Ship Island, MS, from New Orleans, LA, on 10/28/1864. Exchanged on 3/2/1865.

Williams, E. Pvt., C.S.A. Marines Corps. Co. D. Federal Rolls of Prisoners of War: Captured at Blakely, AL, on 4/9/1865; Received at Ship Island, MS, from New Orleans, LA, on 4/15/1865. Transferred to Vicksburg, MS, for exchange on 5/1/1865; Exchanged at Camp Townsend, MS, on 5/6/1865.

Confederate Staff and Regular Prisoners of War

Allen, Riley Sgt., 20th Confederate Cavalry. Co. C. Federal Rolls of Prisoners of War: Captured at Liberty, MS, on 11/16/1864; Received at Ship Island, MS, from New Orleans, LA, on 12/13/1864. Transferred to Vicksburg, MS, for exchange on 5/1/1865; Exchanged at Camp Townsend, MS, on 5/6/1865.

Amos, J.W. (AKA Ames, Amet) Sgt., 15th Confederate Cavalry. Co. E. Federal Rolls of Prisoners of War: Captured near Pensacola, FL, on 11/17/1864; Received at Ship Island, MS, from New Orleans, LA, on 12/13/1864. Transferred to Vicksburg, MS, for exchange on 5/1/1865; Exchanged at Camp Townsend, MS, on 5/6/1865.

Anderson, Charles D. Col. (Commander of Fort Gaines). Federal Rolls of Prisoners of War: Captured at Fort Gaines, AL, on 8/8/1864; Received at Ship Island, MS, from New Orleans, LA, on 10/25/1864. Exchanged on 1/4/1865.

Anding, W.D. (AKA W.G.) Pvt., 20th Confederate Cavalry. Co. K. Federal Rolls of Prisoners of War: Captured at Liberty, MS, on 11/16/1864; Received at Ship Island, MS, from New Orleans, LA, on 12/13/1864. Transferred to Vicksburg, MS, for exchange on 5/1/1865; Exchanged at Camp Townsend, MS, on 5/6/1865.

Atkinson, John Pvt., 15th Confederate Cavalry. Co. I. Federal Rolls of Prisoners of War: Captured in Alabama on 4/1/1865; Received at Ship Island, MS. Transferred to Vicksburg, MS, for exchange on 5/1/1865; Exchanged at Camp Townsend, MS, on 5/6/1865.

Babb, John Pvt., 20th Confederate Cavalry. Co. __. Federal Rolls of Prisoners of War: Captured at Liberty, MS, on 11/15/1864; Received at Ship Island, MS, from New Orleans, LA, on 12/13/1864. Transferred to Vicksburg, MS, for exchange on 5/1/1865; Exchanged at Camp Townsend, MS, on 5/6/1865.

Baker, Beverly Pvt./1st Sgt., 15th Confederate Cavalry. Co. B. Enlisted: 3/30/1861 at Marianna, FL, in the 1st Florida Infantry. Co. E. Age at enlistment: 19. Rolls for 3/30/1861 through 3/30/1862: Present, promoted to 1st Sgt. on 11/1/1861. Soldier also served as a Pvt. with Capt. R.L. Smith's Cavalry Company (Florida). Enlisted: 4/20/1862 at Marianna, FL. Promoted to Sgt. prior to 8/30/1862. Company merged into the 15th Confederate Cavalry. Co. B on 9/24/1863. Federal Rolls of Prisoners of War: Captured at Mount Pleasant, AL, on 4/11/1865; Received at Ship Island, MS. Transferred to Vicksburg, MS, for exchange on 5/1/1865; Exchanged at Camp Townsend, MS, on 5/6/1865. Married: Jennie DeRoulhac on 12/14/1876 at Jackson County, FL. Died: 12/9/1895 at Jackson County, FL. Confederate Widows Pension Application dated 1925 on file at the Florida State Library and Archives. Target Name: DeRoulhac, Jennie. Application Number: A02572. County: Escambia.

Baker, George Pvt., 15th Confederate Cavalry. Co. E. Federal Rolls of Prisoners of War: Received at Ship Island, MS, as a prisoner of war.

Baldridge, William Pvt., 20th Confederate Cavalry. Co. K. Federal Rolls of Prisoners of War: Captured at Liberty, MS, on 11/16/1864; Received at Ship Island, MS, from New Orleans, LA, on 12/13/1864. Transferred to Vicksburg, MS, for exchange on 5/1/1865; Exchanged at Camp Townsend, MS, on 5/6/1865.

Bankhead, J. (AKA I.) Sgt., C.S.A. Signal Corps. Federal Rolls of Prisoners of War: Captured at Fort Gaines, AL, on 8/8/1864; Received at Ship Island, MS, from New Orleans, LA, on 10/25/1864. Exchanged on 1/4/1865.

Barber, M. (AKA Barbour) Pvt., 20th Confederate Cavalry. Co. E. Federal Rolls of Prisoners of War: Captured at Liberty, MS, on 11/16/1864; Received at Ship Island, MS, on 12/13/1864. Transferred to Vicksburg, MS, for exchange on 5/1/1865; Exchanged at Camp Townsend, MS, on 5/6/1865.

Barberot, Phillip (AKA Barburan, N.) Pvt., C.S.A. Engineer Corps. Federal Rolls of Prisoners of War: Captured at Fort Gaines, AL, on 8/8/1864; Received at Ship Island, MS, from New Orleans, LA, on 10/25/1864. Died: Ship Island, MS, on 11/28/1864 due to dysentery. Buried: Ship Island, MS, Cemetery in Grave #50.

Beince, A. Pvt., 15th Confederate Cavalry. Co. C. Federal Rolls of Prisoners of War: Received at Ship Island, MS, as a prisoner of war.

Bennett, Joseph Pvt., 15th Confederate Cavalry. Co. E. Federal Rolls of Prisoners of War: Received at Ship Island, MS, as a prisoner of war.

Berry, J.P. Pvt., 20th Confederate Cavalry. Co. C. Federal Rolls of Prisoners of War: Captured at Liberty, MS, on 11/15/1864; Received at Ship Island, MS, from New Orleans, LA, on 12/13/1864. Transferred to Vicksburg, MS, for exchange on 5/1/1865; Exchanged at Camp Townsend, MS, on 5/6/1865.

Bethia, J.H. (AKA Berthea, Betha, Bethier) Pvt., 20th Confederate Cavalry. Co. I. Federal Rolls of Prisoners of War: Captured at Liberty, MS, on 11/15/1864; Received at Ship Island, MS, from New Orleans, LA, on 12/13/1864. Died: 3/12/1865 at Ship Island, MS, due to dysentery. Buried: Ship Island, MS, Cemetery in Grave #139.

Blake, Samuel H. (AKA Blanc, L.H.) Cpl., 15th Confederate Cavalry. Co. E. Federal Rolls of Prisoners of War: Captured near Pensacola, FL, on 11/17/1864; Received at Ship Island, MS, from New Orleans, LA, on 12/13/1864. Transferred to Vicksburg, MS, for exchange on 5/1/1865; Exchanged at Camp Townsend, MS, on 5/6/1865. Born: 7/30/1838. Died: 1/18/1890. Confederate Widows Pension Application dated 1903 on file at the Florida State Library and Archives. Target Name: Blake, L.L. Application Number: A11882. County: Santa Rosa.

Bonnett, P.A. Pvt., 15th Confederate Cavalry. Co. G. Federal Rolls of Prisoners of War: Received at Ship Island, MS, as a prisoner of war.

Boswell, James (AKA Baswell) Pvt., 15th Confederate Cavalry. Co. __. Federal Rolls of Prisoners of War: Captured at Pine Barren, FL, on 11/17/1864; Received at Ship Island, MS, from New Orleans, LA, on 12/13/1864. Transferred to Vicksburg, MS, for exchange on 5/1/1865; Exchanged at Camp Townsend, MS, on 5/6/1865.

Bowen, W.H. Pvt., 20th Confederate Cavalry. Co. H. Federal Rolls of Prisoners of War: Captured at Liberty, MS, on 11/16/1864; Received at Ship Island, MS, from New Orleans, LA, on 12/13/1864. Transferred to Vicksburg, MS, for exchange on 5/1/1865; Exchanged at Camp Townsend, MS, on 5/6/1865.

Brent, W.D. Pvt., 15th Confederate Cavalry. Co. D. Federal Rolls of Prisoners of War: Received at Ship Island, MS, as a prisoner of war.

Brock, J.W. Pvt., 15th Confederate Cavalry. Co. I. Federal Rolls of Prisoners of War: Received at Ship Island, MS, as a prisoner of war.

Brown, E. Lt., 20th Confederate Cavalry. Co. __. Federal Rolls of Prisoners of War: Captured at Liberty, MS, on 11/16/1864; Received at Ship Island, MS, from New Orleans, LA, on 12/18/1864. Exchanged on 3/2/1865.

Brown, S.T. Pvt., 15th Confederate Cavalry. Co. I. Federal Rolls of Prisoners of War: Received at Ship Island, MS, as a prisoner of war.

Buggs, William (AKA Biggs) Pvt., C.S.A. Signal Corps. Federal Rolls of Prisoners of War: Captured at Fort Gaines, AL, on 8/8/1864; Received at Ship Island, MS, from New Orleans, LA, on 10/25/1864. Exchanged on 1/4/1865.

Burgerot, Phillip Pvt., C.S.A. Engineer Corps. Died: 11/29/1864 at Ship Island, MS, due to dysentery. Buried: Ship Island, MS, Cemetery in Grave #51.

Burgess, Jerome Pvt., 15th Confederate Cavalry. Co. C. Enlisted: 5/17/1864 at Camp Powell, AL. Federal Rolls of Prisoners of War: Received at Ship Island, MS, as a prisoner of war.

Callahan, Mathew (AKA, Callowho, Calhoun, W.) Pvt., C.S.A. Engineer Corps. Federal Rolls of Prisoners of War: Captured at Fort Gaines, AL, on 8/8/1864; Transferred to Ship Island, MS, from New Orleans, LA, on 10/25/1864. Died: 12/3/1864 at Ship Island, MS, due to chronic dysentery. Buried: Ship Island, MS, Cemetery in Grave #60.

Campbell, Charles Edward Pvt., 15th Confederate Cavalry. Co. E. Federal Rolls of Prisoners of War: Received at Ship Island, MS, as a prisoner of war. Married: Jane A. Hart on 12/12/1862. Died: 5/16/1907 in Santa Rosa County, FL. Confederate Widows Pension Application dated 1902 at the Florida State Library and Archives. Target Name: Hart, Jane. Application Number: A01047. County: Santa Rosa.

Carley, J.T. (AKA Carlie) Pvt., 15th Confederate Cavalry. Co. H. Enlisted: 3/11/1863 at Mobile, AL. Federal Rolls of Prisoners of War: Captured in Mississippi on 12/6/1864; Received at Ship Island, MS, from New Orleans, LA, on 1/25/1865. Transferred to Vicksburg, MS, for exchange on 5/1/1865; Exchanged at Camp Townsend, MS, on 5/6/1865.

Cawthorn, Lafayette F. Pvt., 15th Confederate Cavalry. Co. I. Enlisted: 4/21/1864. Federal Rolls of Prisoners of War: Received at Ship Island, MS, as a prisoner of war. Married: Nancy McSwain on 3/1/1858 at Walton County, FL. Died: 5/3/1911 in Alabama. Confederate Widows Pension Application dated 1917 on file at the Florida State Library and Archives. Target Name: McSwain, Nancy. Application Number: A01938. County: Walton.

Cawthorn, William J. (AKA Cawthon) Pvt., 15th Confederate Cavalry. Co. I. Enlisted: 4/1864 at Santa Rosa County, FL. Federal Rolls of Prisoners of War: Captured at Shoal River, FL, on 9/22/1864; Received at Ship Island, MS. Transferred to Fort Columbus, New York Harbor, NY. Died: 2/26/1865 at Elmira, NY, due to typhoid fever. Buried: Woodlawn National Cemetery, Chemung County, NY. Confederate Widows Pension Application dated 1917 on file at the Florida State Library and Archives. Target Name: McSwain, Charlotte. Application Number: A01956. County: Walton.

Clark, John Capt., Ambassador John Slidell's Staff. Federal Rolls of Prisoners of War: Captured at Blakely, AL, on 4/9/1865; Received at Ship Island, MS, on 4/15/1865. Transferred to Vicksburg, MS, for exchange on 4/28/1865; Confined at New Orleans, LA, on 4/30/1865. Exchanged at Camp Townsend, MS, on 5/6/1865.

Clark, T.B. Telegrapher, Ambassador John Slidell's Staff. Federal Rolls of Prisoners of War: Captured at Blakely, AL, on 4/9/1865; Received at Ship Island, MS, on 4/15/1865. Transferred to Vicksburg, MS, for exchange on 5/1/1865; Exchanged at Camp Townsend, MS, on 5/6/1865.

Clements, J.M. Cpl./Sgt., 15th Confederate Cavalry. Co. E. Federal Rolls of Prisoners of War: Received at Ship Island, MS, as a prisoner of war.

Cooper, Jesse Byrd Sgt., 15th Confederate Cavalry.

Co. D. Federal Rolls of Prisoners of War: Captured at Pine Barren, FL, on 11/17/1864; Received at Ship Island, MS, from New Orleans, LA, on 12/13/1864. Transferred to Vicksburg, MS, for exchange on 5/1/1865; Exchanged at Camp Townsend, MS, on 5/6/1865. Born: 1839. Died: 1911. Buried: Vaughn Cemetery located at Molino, Escambia County, Florida.

Crosby, Daniel Pvt., C.S.A. Engineer Corps. Federal Rolls of Prisoners of War: Captured at Fort Gaines, AL, on 8/8/1864; Received at Ship Island, MS, from New Orleans, LA, on 10/25/1864. Died: 12/16/1864 at Ship Island, MS, due to chronic dysentery. Buried: Ship Island, MS, Cemetery in Grave #94.

Daniel, D. Pvt., 15th Confederate Cavalry. Co. __. Federal Rolls of Prisoners of War: Captured at Shoal River, FL, on 9/22/1864; Received at Ship Island, MS, from New Orleans, LA, on 10/21/1864. Transferred to Fort Columbus, New York Harbor, NY, in 11/1864.

Daniels, Lawson Pvt./4th Cpl./Pvt., 15th Confederate Cavalry. Co. B. Enlisted: 3/14/1862 at Jackson County, FL. Occupation at enlistment: Farmer. Promoted to 4th Cpl. in mid–1862. Resigned in 11/1862. Federal Rolls of Prisoners of War: Captured at Marianna, FL, on 9/27/1864; Sent to Fort Pickens, FL. Forwarded to New Orleans, LA, on 10/8/1864; Received at Ship Island, MS, on 10/24/1864. Transferred to Fort Columbus, New York Harbor, NY, on 11/5/1864; Forwarded to Elmira, NY, on 11/20/1864. Died: 4/14/1865 at Elmira, NY, due to general debility. Buried: Woodlawn National Cemetery, Chemung County, NY. Age at capture: 46. Born: 12/18/1819 at Dale County, AL. Married: Emeline Tabor on 2/10/1841 at Orange Hill, Washington County, FL. Children: 8.

Davis, Hugh L. Lt. (Brig. Gen. George B. Hodges Staff). Federal Rolls of Prisoners of War: Captured at Liberty, MS, on 8/11/1864; Received at Ship Island, MS, from New Orleans, LA, on 12/11/1864. Exchanged on 3/2/1865.

Dillard, William J. Pvt., C.S.A. Signal Corps. Federal Rolls of Prisoners of War: Captured at Mobile Bay, AL, on 8/5/1864; Received at Ship Island, MS. Died: 1/26/1865 at Ship Island, MS, due to typhoid fever. Buried: Ship Island, MS, Cemetery in Grave #131.

Dolife, Rufus F. (AKA Dolive, Ruffin) Sgt., 15th Confederate Cavalry. Co. F. Federal Rolls of Prisoners of War: Captured in Alabama on 4/1/1865; Received at Ship Island, MS. Transferred to Vicksburg, MS, for exchange on 5/1/1865; Exchanged at Camp Townsend, MS, on 5/6/1865. Died: 4/5/1910 at Loxley, AL. Confederate Widows Pension Application dated 5/19/1928 on file at the Alabama Department of Archives and History. Target Name: Dolive, Angela. County: Baldwin.

Dolife, S. (AKA Dolive) Pvt., 15th Confederate Cavalry. Co. C. Enlisted: 4/9/1862 at Blakely, AL. Federal Rolls of Prisoners of War: Captured in Alabama on 4/1/1865; Received at Ship Island, MS. Transferred to Vicksburg, MS, for exchange on 5/1/1865; Exchanged at Camp Townsend, MS, on 5/6/1865.

Duarte, D. Pvt. (Lt. Gen. Richard Taylor's Staff). Federal Rolls of Prisoners of War: Captured near Franklin, LA, on 11/25/1863; Received at Ship Island, MS, from New Orleans, LA, on 11/25/1864. Transferred to Fort Columbus, New York Harbor, NY, in 11/1864.

Duffy, C. (AKA Duff) Pvt., C.S.A. Engineers Corps. Federal Rolls of Prisoners of War: Captured at Fort Gaines, AL, on 8/8/1864; Received at Ship Island, MS, from New Orleans, LA, on 10/25/1864. Exchanged on 1/4/1865.

Durden, James F. (AKA Darden) Pvt., 15th Confederate Cavalry. Co. D. Federal Rolls of Prisoners of War: Captured at Escambia County, FL; Received at Ship Island, MS, from New Orleans, LA, on 1/25/1865. Transferred to Vicksburg, MS, for exchange on 5/1/1865; Exchanged at Camp Townsend, MS, on 5/6/1865.

Farragut, N.G. Pvt., 15th Confederate Cavalry. Co. G. Federal Rolls of Prisoners of War: Received at Ship Island, MS, as a prisoner of war.

Fleming, Robert P. (AKA Flemming) Pvt., 15th Confederate Cavalry. Co. E. Federal Rolls of Prisoners of War: Captured at Pine Barren, FL, on 11/17/1864; Received at Ship Island, MS, from New Orleans, LA, on 12/13/1864. Transferred to Vicksburg, MS, for exchange on 5/1/1865; Exchanged at Camp Townsend, MS, on 5/6/1865. Born: 2/4/1838 at Conecuh, AL. Confederate Pension Application dated 1908 on file at the Florida State Library and Archives. Target Name: Fleming, Robert P. Application Number: A11020. County: Escambia.

Flemming, Aden Lucius (AKA Fleming, Lucious) Pvt./Capt., 15th Confederate Cavalry. Co. E. Federal Rolls of Prisoners of War: Captured at Pine Barren, FL, on 11/17/1864; Received at Ship Island, MS, from New Orleans, LA, on 12/13/1864. Transferred to Vicksburg, MS, for exchange on 4/28/1865; Confined at New Orleans, LA, on 4/30/1865. Exchanged at Camp Townsend, MS, on 5/6/1865. Confederate Pension Application dated 1907 on file at the Florida State Library and Archives. Target Name: Fleming, Aden Lucius. Application Number: A07605. County: Santa Rosa.

Fortenberry, John Pvt., 20th Confederate Cavalry. Co. I. Federal Rolls of Prisoners of War: Captured at Brookhaven, MS, on 11/17/1864; Received at Ship Island, MS, on 12/13/1864. Transferred to Vicksburg, MS, for exchange on 5/1/1865; Exchanged at Camp Townsend, MS, on 5/6/1865.

Frater, John W. (AKA Frader) Pvt./Cpl., 15th Confederate Cavalry. Co. E. Federal Rolls of Prisoners of War: Captured at Pine Barren, FL, on 11/17/1864; Received at Ship Island, MS, from New Orleans, LA, on 12/13/1864. Transferred to Vicksburg, MS, for exchange on 5/1/1865; Exchanged at Camp Townsend, MS, on 5/6/1865.

Frederick, A. Pvt., C.S.A. Engineer Corps. Federal Rolls of Prisoners of War: Captured at Fort Gaines, AL, on 8/8/1864; Received at Ship Island, MS, from New Orleans, LA, on 10/25/1864. Refused to be exchanged on 1/4/1865.

Gardable, E. (AKA Gardeble) Pvt., 2nd Confederate Engineer Troops. Co. A. Federal Rolls of Prisoners of War: Captured at Fort Gaines, AL, on 8/8/1864; Received at Ship Island, MS, from New Orleans, LA, on 10/25/1864. Exchanged on 1/4/1865.

Garner, W.J. Cpl./Sgt., 15th Confederate Cavalry. Co. D. Federal Rolls of Prisoners of War: Received at Ship Island, MS, as a prisoner of war.

Garrison, Ebonezar Artificer/Pvt., 2nd Confederate Engineer Troops. Co. C. Federal Rolls of Prisoners of War: Captured in Alabama on 3/23/1865; Received at Ship Island, MS. Transferred to Vicksburg, MS, for exchange on 5/1/1865; Exchanged at Camp Townsend, MS, on 5/6/1865.

Gerold, Thomas Pvt., 20th Confederate Cavalry. Co. K. Federal Rolls of Prisoners of War: Captured at Liberty, MS, on 11/16/1864; Received at Ship Island, MS, from New Orleans, LA, on 12/13/1864. Transferred to Vicksburg, MS, for exchange on 5/1/1865; Exchanged at Camp Townsend, MS, on 5/6/1865.

Gilbert, B.T. (AKA B.F.) Pvt., 15th Confederate Cavalry. Co. K. Enlisted: 3/17/1862 at Washington County, AL. Age at enlistment: 33. Federal Rolls of Prisoners of War: Received at Ship Island, MS, as a prisoner of war.

Godwin, James M. Pvt., 15th Confederate Cavalry. Co. D. Federal Rolls of Prisoners of War: Received at Ship Island, MS, as a prisoner of war. Confederate Widows Pension Application on file at the Alabama Department of Archives and History. Target Name: Godwin, Francis A. Application Number: 31949. County: Escambia.

Goff, L.P. Pvt., 15th Confederate Cavalry. Co. K. Federal Rolls of Prisoners of War: Captured at Jackson, MS, on 12/15/1864; Received at Ship Island, MS, from New Orleans, LA, on 1/25/1865. Transferred to Vicksburg, MS, for exchange on 5/1/1865; Exchanged at Camp Townsend, MS, on 5/6/1865.

Gonzales, C.B. Pvt., 15th Confederate Cavalry. Co. D. Federal Rolls of Prisoners of War: Received at Ship Island, MS, as a prisoner of war.

Gould, L.D. Pvt., 15th Confederate Cavalry. Co. F. Federal Rolls of Prisoners of War: Received at Ship Island, MS, as a prisoner of war.

Green, George S. Sgt./Ord. Sgt., 20th Confederate Cavlary. Co. K. Federal Rolls of Prisoners of War: Captured at Liberty, MS, on 11/16/1864; Received at Ship Island, MS, from New Orleans, LA, on 12/13/1864. Exchanged on 3/2/1865.

Green, Lee Pvt., 20th Confederate Cavalry. Cos. H & K. Federal Rolls of Prisoners of War: Captured at Liberty, MS, on 11/16/1864; Received at Ship Island, MS, from New Orleans, LA, on 12/13/1864. Exchanged on 3/2/1865.

Guinn, John (AKA Gwinn) Pvt., 20th Confederate Cavalry. Co. K. Federal Rolls of Prisoners of War: Captured at Liberty, MS, on 11/16/1864; Received at Ship Island, MS, from New Orleans, LA, on 12/13/1864. Transferred to Vicksburg, MS, for exchange on 5/1/1865; Exchanged at Camp Townsend, MS, on 5/6/1865.

Hamilton, T.N. (AKA F.N., T.W.) Sgt., 14th Confederate Cavalry. Co. C. Federal Rolls of Prisoners of War: Captured near Summit, MS, on 11/18/1864; Received at Ship Island, MS, from New Orleans, LA, on 12/13/1864. Transferred to Vicksburg, MS, for exchange on 5/1/1865; Exchanged at Camp Townsend, MS, on 5/6/1865.

Harrison, J.T. Pvt., 15th Confederate Cavalry. Co. K. Federal Rolls of Prisoners of War: Received at Ship Island, MS, as a prisoner of war.

Hart, Abraham Pvt., 15th Confederate Cavalry. Co. I. Wounded at the battle of Cleburne, AL. Federal Rolls of Prisoners of War: Received at Ship Island, MS, as a prisoner of war. Confederate Pension Application on file at the Alabama Department of Archives and History. Target Name: Hart, Abraham. Application Number: 11117. County: Covington.

Hart, David Pvt., 15th Confederate Cavalry. Co. A. Federal Rolls of Prisoners of War: Received at Ship Island, MS, as a prisoner of war.

Hart, Z. Pvt., C.S.A. Engineer Corps. Federal Rolls of Prisoners of War: Captured at Fort Gaines, AL, on 8/8/1864; Transferred to Ship Island, MS, from New Orleans, LA, on 10/25/1864. Refused to be exchanged.

Harvey, James H. Pvt., 15th Confederate Cavalry. Co. B. Federal Rolls of Prisoners of War: Received at Ship Island, MS, as a prisoner of war.

Hatch, F.M. Pvt., 20th Confederate Cavalry. Co. F. Federal Rolls of Prisoners of War: Captured at Liberty, MS, on 11/11/1864; Received at Ship Island, MS, from New Orleans, LA, on 12/13/1864. Transferred to Vicksburg, MS, for exchange on 5/1/1865; Exchanged at Camp Townsend, MS, on 5/6/1865.

Hawthorn, J.R. Pvt., 15th Confederate Cavalry. Cos. E & A. Federal Rolls of Prisoners of War: Captured near Pensacola, FL, on 11/17/1864; Received at Ship Island, MS, from New Orleans, LA, on 12/13/1864. Transferred to Vicksburg, MS, for exchange on 5/1/1865; Exchanged at Camp Townsend, MS, on 5/6/1865.

Hayden, G.B. Hosp. Stew., 15th Confederate Cavalry, F & S. Federal Rolls of Prisoners of War: Captured at Blakely, AL, on 4/9/1865; Received at Ship Island, MS, on 4/15/1865. Transferred to Vicksburg, MS, for exchange on 5/1/1865; Exchanged at Camp Townsend, MS, on 5/6/1865.

Hazard, Alfred Capt., C.S.A. Retired List. Federal Rolls of Prisoners of War: Captured in East Louisiana on 11/20/1864; Received at Ship Island, MS, from New Orleans, LA, on 12/18/1864. Exchanged on 3/2/1865.

Henderson D.F. Pvt., 20th Confederate Cavalry. Cos. E & F. Federal Rolls of Prisoners of War: Captured at Liberty, MS, on 11/16/1864; Received at Ship Island, MS, from New Orleans, LA, on 12/13/1864. Transferred to Vicksburg, MS, for exchange on 5/1/1865; Exchanged at Camp Townsend, MS, on 5/6/1865.

Henry, Francis Pvt., C.S.A. Engineer Corps. Federal Rolls of Prisoners of War: Captured at Fort Gaines, AL, on 8/8/1864; Received at Ship Island, MS, from New Orleans, LA, on 10/25/1864. Died: 12/5/1864 at Ship Island, MS, due to typhoid fever. Buried: Ship Island, MS, Cemetery in Grave #68.

Hetzler, Peter (AKA Hetzell) Pvt., 15th Confederate Cavalry. Co. F. Federal Rolls of Prisoners of War: Captured at Blakely, AL, on 4/9/1865; Received at Ship Island, MS, on 4/15/1865. Transferred to Vicksburg, MS, for exchange on 5/1/1865; Exchanged at Camp Townsend, MS, on 5/6/1865.

Holden, B. Pvt., C.S.A. Engineer Corps. Federal Rolls of Prisoners of War: Captured at Fort Gaines, AL, on 8/8/1864; Transferred to Ship Island, MS, from New Orleans, LA, on 10/25/1864. Exchanged on 1/4/1865.

Hughes, Tyria M. Pvt., 15th Confederate Cavalry. Co. E. Federal Rolls of Prisoners of War: Captured at Pensacola, FL, on 11/17/1864; Received at Ship Island, MS, from New Orleans, LA, on 12/13/1864. Transferred to Vicksburg, MS, for exchange on 5/1/1865; Exchanged at Camp Townsend, MS, on 5/6/1865. Died: 9/24/1906. Confederate Widows Pension Application on file dated 6/16/1908 at the Alabama Department of Archives and History. Target Name: Hughes, L.N. Application Number: 24776. County: Butler

Hughes, William (AKA Bill) Pvt., 15th Confederate Cavalry. Co. __. Federal Rolls of Prisoners of War: Captured near Pensacola, FL, on 11/17/1864; Received at Ship Island, MS, from New Orleans, LA, on 12/13/1864. Transferred to Vicksburg, MS, for exchange on 5/1/1865; Exchanged at Camp Townsend, MS, on 5/6/1865.

Johnson, B.M. Cpl., 15th Confederate Cavalry. Co. E. Federal Rolls of Prisoners of War: Captured at Pine Barren, FL, on 11/17/1864; Received at Ship Island, MS, from New Orleans, LA, on 12/13/1864. Transferred to Vicksburg, MS, for exchange on 5/1/1865; Exchanged at Camp Townsend, MS, on 5/6/1865.

Johnson, Caleb A. Pvt., 15th Confederate Cavalry. Co. D. Federal Rolls of Prisoners of War: Captured at Pine Barren, FL, on 11/17/1864; Received at Ship Island, MS, from New Orleans, LA, on 12/13/1864. Transferred to Vicksburg, MS, for exchange on 5/1/1865; Exchanged at Camp Townsend, MS, on 5/6/1865.

Johnson, D. Cpl., 20th Confederate Cavalry. Co. G. Federal Rolls of Prisoners of War: Captured near Liberty, MS, on 11/17/1864; Received at Ship Island, MS, from New Orleans, LA, on 12/13/1864. Transferred to Vicksburg, MS, for exchange on 5/1/1865; Exchanged at Camp Townsend, MS, on 5/6/1865.

Johnson, R.S. Pvt., 15th Confederate Cavalry. Co. D. Federal Rolls of Prisoners of War: Received at Ship Island, MS, as a prisoner of war.

Johnson, William J. (AKA J.W. Pvt., 15th Confederate Cavalry. Co. E. Federal Rolls of Prisoners of War: Captured in Florida on 12/24/1864; Received at Ship Island, MS, from New Orleans, LA, on 1/25/1865. Transferred to Vicksburg, MS, for exchange on 5/1/1865; Exchanged at Camp Townsend, MS, on 5/6/1865.

Jordan, Thomas E. Pvt., 15th Confederate Cavalry. Co. D. Federal Rolls of Prisoners of War: Captured at Pollard, AL, on 12/15/1864; Received at Ship Island, MS, from New Orleans, LA, on 1/25/1865. Exchanged on 1/3/1865.

Kelley, William J. (AKA Joseph, J.W.) Pvt., 15th Confederate Cavalry. Co. D. Enlisted: 5/10/1864 at Milton, FL. Federal Rolls of Prisoners of War: Captured at Mount Pleasant, AL, on 4/11/1865; Received at Ship Island, MS. Transferred to Vicksburg, MS, for exchange on 5/1/1865; Exchanged at Camp Townsend, MS, on 5/6/1865.

Kelly, Edward Pvt., 15th Confederate Cavalry. Co. E. Federal Rolls of Prisoners of War: Captured at Mount Pleasant, AL, on 4/11/1865; Received at Ship Island, MS, as a prisoner of war.

Kennedy, John Pvt., 20th Confederate Cavalry. Co. E. Federal Rolls of Prisoners of War: Captured at Liberty, MS, on 11/11/1864; Received at Ship Island, MS, from New Orleans, LA, on 12/13/1864. Transferred to Vicksburg, MS, for exchange on 5/1/1865; Exchanged at Camp Townsend, MS, on 5/6/1865.

Kimbro, Stephen (AKA Kimbrol) Pvt., 20th Confederate Cavalry. Co. E. Federal Rolls of Prisoners of War: Captured at Liberty, MS, on 11/17/1864; Received at Ship Island, MS, from New Orleans, LA, on 12/13/1864. Transferred to Vicksburg, MS, for exchange on 5/1/1865; Exchanged at Camp Townsend, MS, on 5/6/1865.

Leigh, George M. (AKA Lee) Pvt., 15th Confederate Cavalry. Co. E. Enlisted: 11/1863 at Mobile, AL. Federal Rolls of Prisoners of War: Captured at Pine Barren, FL, on 11/17/1864; Received at Ship Island, MS, from New Orleans, LA, on 12/13/1864. Transferred to Vicksburg, MS, for exchange on 5/1/1865; Exchanged at Camp Townsend, MS, on 5/6/1865. Born: 1846 at Brooklyn, Conecuh County, AL. Residence after war: Geneva County, AL. Confederate Widows Pension Application on file at the Alabama Department of Archives and History. Target Name: Leigh, Kate. Application Number: 33286. County: Geneva.

Lewis, C. Pvt., 15th Confederate Cavalry. Co. C. Federal Rolls of Prisoners of War: Captured in Alabama on 3/25/1865; Received at Ship Island, MS. Transferred to Vicksburg, MS, for exchange on 5/1/1865. Disposition unknown.

Lewis, G.W. Pvt., 15th Confederate Cavalry. Co. E. Federal Rolls of Prisoners of War: Captured at Pine Barren, FL, on 11/17/1864; Received at Ship Island, MS, from New Orleans, LA, on 12/13/1864. Transferred to Vicksburg, MS, for exchange on 5/1/1865; Exchanged at Camp Townsend, MS, on 5/6/1865.

Lewis, James F. Pvt./Cpl., 15th Confederate Cavalry. Co. D. Federal Rolls of Prisoners of War: Captured at Liberty, MS, on 11/18/1864; Received at Ship Island, MS, from New Orleans, LA, on 12/13/1864. Transferred to Vicksburg, MS, for exchange on 5/1/1865; Exchanged at Camp Townsend, MS, on 5/6/1865.

Lewis, T.C. Pvt., 20th Confederate Cavalry. Co. E. Federal Rolls of Prisoners of War: Captured at Liberty, MS, on 11/16/1864; Received at Ship Island, MS, from New Orleans, LA, on 12/13/1864. Transferred to Vicksburg, MS, for exchange on 5/1/1865; Exchanged at Camp Townsend, MS, on 5/6/1865.

Lundy, W.G. (AKA W.C.) Pvt., 15th Confederate Cavalry. Co. C. Federal Rolls of Prisoners of War: Captured in Alabama on 3/22/1865; Received at Ship Island, MS. Transferred to Vicksburg, MS, for exchange on 5/1/1865; Exchanged at Camp Townsend, MS, on 5/6/1865.

Mason, A.W. Pvt., 15th Confederate Cavalry. Co. E. Federal Rolls of Prisoners of War: Captured at Pollard, AL, on 12/14/1864; Received at Ship Island, MS, from New Orleans, LA, on 1/25/1865. Transferred to Vicksburg, MS, for exchange on 5/1/1865; Exchanged at Camp Townsend, MS, on 5/6/1865.

Mason, N.M (AKA Mayson, M.M.) Pvt., 15th Confederate Cavalry. Co. E. Federal Rolls of Prisoners of War: Received at Ship Island, MS, as a prisoner of war.

McDavid, A.J. (AKA A.S.) Pvt., 15th Confederate Cavalry. Co. C. Federal Rolls of Prisoners of War: Received at Ship Island, MS, as a prisoner of war.

McKnight, Isaac Pvt., 20th Confederate Cavalry. Co. E. Federal Rolls of Prisoners of War: Captured at Liberty, MS, on 11/17/1864; Received at Ship Island, MS, from New Orleans, LA, on 12/13/1864. Transferred to Vicksburg, MS, for exchange on 5/1/1865; Exchanged at Camp Townsend, MS, on 5/6/1865.

McQuillan, W.J. Pvt., C.S.A. Engineers Corps. Federal Rolls of Prisoners of War: Captured at Fort

Gaines, AL, on 8/8/1864; Received at Ship Island, MS, from New Orleans, LA, on 10/28/1864. Exchanged on 1/4/1865.

McRae, William D. Pvt., 1st Confederate Cavalry. Co. E. Federal Prisoners of War: Captured in AR on 7/27/1864; Received at Ship Island, MS, from New Orleans, LA, on 12/13/1864. Transferred to New Orleans, LA, on 3/31/1865; Remarks: Guerilla.

McVoy, Thomas (AKA McVay) Pvt., 15th Confederate Cavalry. Co. A. Federal Rolls of Prisoners of War: Captured at Pine Barren, FL, on 11/17/1864; Received at Ship Island, MS, from New Orleans, LA, on 12/13/1864. Transferred to Vicksburg, MS, for exchange on 5/1/1865; Exchanged at Camp Townsend, MS, on 5/6/1865. Married: Indiana Hernandez. Died: 7/29/1885 at Escambia County, FL. Confederate Widows Pension Application dated 1906 on file at the Florida State Library and Archives. Target Name: Hernandez, Indiana. Application Number: A11411. County: Escambia.

McWhorter, C.J. (AKA C.I.) Pvt., 15th Confederate Cavalry. Co. H. Federal Rolls of Prisoners of War: Captured at Mount Pleasant, AL, on 4/11/1865; Received at Ship Island, MS. Transferred to New Orleans, LA, for exchange on 6/8/1865.

Miller, T.R. Pvt., 15th Confederate Cavalry. Co. E. Federal Rolls of Prisoners of War: Captured near Pensacola, FL, on 11/17/1864; Received at Ship Island, MS, from New Orleans, LA, on 12/13/1864. Transferred to Vicksburg, MS, for exchange on 5/1/1865; Exchanged at Camp Townsend, MS, on 5/6/1865.

Mints, J.J. (AKA Mims) Pvt., 15th Confederate Cavalry. Co. E. Federal Rolls of Prisoners of War: Captured at Pine Barren, FL, on 11/17/1864; Received at Ship Island, MS, from New Orleans, LA, on 12/13/1864. Transferred to Vicksburg, MS, for exchange on 5/1/1865; Exchanged at Camp Townsend, MS, on 5/6/1865.

Mitternight, Christopher Columbus (AKA Christian C.) Pvt., 15th Confederate Cavalry. Co. E. Enlisted: 1861 at Mobile, AL, in the 12th Alabama Infantry. Co. I. Federal Rolls of Prisoners of War: Captured near Pollard, AL, on 12/18/1864; Received at Ship Island, MS, from New Orleans, LA, on 1/25/1865. Transferred to Vicksburg, MS, for exchange on 5/1/1865; Exchanged at Camp Townsend, MS, on 5/6/1865.

Mobley, William M. Asst. Surg., 15th Confederate Cavalry, F & S. Federal Rolls of Prisoners of War: Captured at Blakely, AL, on 4/9/1865; Received at Ship Island, MS, on 4/15/1865. Transferred to Vicksburg, MS, for exchange on 4/28/1865; Confined at New Orleans, LA, on 4/30/1865. Exchanged at Camp Townsend, MS, on 5/6/1865.

Moore, D.S. (AKA D.L.) Pvt., 15th Confederate Cavalry. Co. E. Federal Rolls of Prisoners of War: Captured near Pensacola, FL, on 11/17/1864; Received at Ship Island, MS, from New Orleans, LA, on 12/13/1864. Transferred to Vicksburg, MS, for exchange on 5/1/1865; Exchanged at Camp Townsend, MS, on 5/6/1865.

Morgan, Samuel Pvt., 15th Confederate Cavalry. Co. D. Federal Rolls of Prisoners of War: Captured at Pine Barren, FL, on 11/17/1864; Received at Ship Island, MS, from New Orleans, LA, on 12/13/1864. Transferred to Vicksburg, MS, for exchange on 5/1/1865; Exchanged at Camp Townsend, MS, on 5/6/1865.

Morrison, B. Pvt., 15th Confederate Cavalry. Co. C. Federal Rolls of Prisoners of War: Captured near Summit, MS, on 11/18/1864; Received at Ship Island, MS, from New Orleans, LA, on 12/13/1864. Transferred to Vicksburg, MS, on 5/1/1865; Exchanged at Camp Townsend, MS, on 5/6/1865.

Newton, Charles A. Pvt./Bugler, 15th Confederate Cavalry. Co. E. Federal Rolls of Prisoners of War: Received at Ship Island, MS, as a prisoner of war. Born: 1836. See sketch of Charles A. Newton in Memorial Record of Alabama (1893). Volume I. Pages 717–719 at the Alabama Department of Archives and History.

Norton, D.C. Sgt., 15th Confederate Cavalry. Co. H. Enlisted: 9/4/1862 at Mobile, AL. Federal Rolls of Prisoners of War: Captured at Blakely, AL, on 4/9/1865; Received at Ship Island, MS, on 4/15/1865. Transferred to Vicksburg, MS, for exchange on 5/1/1865; Exchanged at Camp Townsend, MS, on 5/6/1865.

Odom, Aaron J. (AKA Odam) Pvt., 15th Confederate Cavalry. Co. E. Federal Rolls of Prisoners of War: Captured near Pensacola, FL, on 11/17/1864; Received at Ship Island, MS, from New Orleans, LA, on 12/13/1864. Transferred to Vicksburg, MS, for exchange on 5/1/1865; Exchanged at Camp Townsend, MS, on 5/6/1865.

Parker, George M. Pvt., 15th Confederate Cavalry. Co. E. Federal Rolls of Prisoners of War: Captured at Pine Barren, FL, on 11/17/1864; Received at Ship Island, MS, from New Orleans, LA, on 12/13/1864. Transferred to Vicksburg, MS, for exchange on 5/1/1865; Exchanged at Camp Townsend, MS, on 5/6/1865.

Parker, John W. (AKA J.W.D.) Pvt., 15th Confederate Cavalry. Co. E. Federal Rolls of Prisoners of War: Captured at Pine Barren, FL, on 11/17/1864; Received at Ship Island, MS, from New Orleans, LA, on 12/13/1864. Transferred to Vicksburg, MS, for exchange on 5/1/1865; Exchanged at Camp Townsend, MS, on 5/6/1865

Parker, P.T. Pvt., 15th Confederate Cavalry. Co. E. Federal Rolls of Prisoner of War: Received at Ship Island, MS, as a prisoner of war.

Parker, W.M. (AKA W.A.) Pvt., 15th Confederate Cavalry. Co. E. Federal Rolls of Prisoners of War: Captured near Pollard, AL, on 12/15/1864; Received at Ship Island, MS, from New Orleans, LA, on 1/25/1865. Transferred to Vicksburg, MS, for exchange on 5/1/1865; Exchanged at Camp Townsend, MS, on 5/6/1865.

Penny, Frank Pvt., C.S.A. Engineers Corps. Federal Rolls of Prisoners of War: Received at Ship Island, MS, as a prisoner of war.

Pitts, John Pvt., 15th Confederate Cavalry. Co. I. Federal Rolls of Prisoners of War: Captured at Marianna, FL, on 9/27/1864; Sent to Fort Pickens, AL. Forwarded to New Orleans, LA; Received at Ship Island, MS, on 10/24/1864. Died: 11/22/1864 at Ship Island, MS, due to pneumonia. Buried: Ship Island, MS, Cemetery in Grave #33.

Preslar, W.A. Pvt., 15th Confederate Cavalry. Co. E. Federal Rolls of Prisoners of War: Captured at Pine Barren, FL, on 11/17/1864; Received at Ship Island,

MS, from New Orleans, LA, on 12/13/1864. Transferred to Vicksburg, MS, for exchange on 5/1/1865; Exchanged at Camp Townsend, MS, on 5/6/1865.

Price, John Civilian, C.S.A. Government Employee. Federal Rolls of Prisoners of War: Captured at St. Joseph, LA, on 8/20/1864; Received at Ship Island, MS, from New Orleans, LA, on 12/13/1864. Transferred to Vicksburg, MS, for exchange on 5/1/1865; Exchanged at Camp Townsend, MS, on 5/6/1865.

Purvis, G.M. Pvt., 15th Confederate Cavalry. Co. G. Federal Rolls of Prisoners of War: Captured at Pine Barren, FL, on 11/17/1864; Received at Ship Island, MS, from New Orleans, LA, on 12/13/1864. Transferred to Vicksburg, MS, for exchange on 5/1/1865; Exchanged at Camp Townsend, MS, on 5/6/1865.

Ratcliff, H.B. Pvt., 20th Confederate Cavalry. Co. K. Federal Rolls of Prisoners of War: Captured at Clinton, LA, on 11/16/1864; Received at Ship Island, MS, from New Orleans, LA, on 12/13/1864. Transferred to Vicksburg, MS, for exchange on 5/1/1865; Exchanged at Camp Townsend, MS, on 5/6/1865.

Redman, D.M. (AKA Redmond) Cpl./Sgt., 14th Confederate Cavalry. Co. F. Federal Rolls of Prisoners of War: Captured at Liberty, MS, on 11/16/1864; Received at Ship Island, MS, from New Orleans, LA, on 12/13/1864. Transferred to Vicksburg, MS, for exchange on 5/1/1865; Exchanged at Camp Townsend, MS, on 5/6/1865.

Reed, T.W. Pvt., 20th Confederate Cavalry. Co. A. Federal Rolls of Prisoners of War: Captured at Brookhaven, MS, on 11/18/1864; Received at Ship Island, MS, from New Orleans, LA, on 12/13/1864. Transferred to Vicksburg, MS, for exchange on 5/1/1865; Exchanged at Camp Townsend, MS, on 5/6/1865.

Register, Ezekiel A. Pvt., 15th Confederate Cavalry. Co. B. Federal Rolls of Prisoners of War: Received at Ship Island, MS, as a prisoner of war.

Renfroe, J.G. Pvt., 15th Confederate Cavalry. Co. E. Federal Rolls of Prisoners of War: Captured near Pollard, AL, on 12/14/1864; Received at Ship Island, MS, from New Orleans, LA, on 1/25/1865. Transferred to Vicksburg, MS, for exchange on 5/1/1865; Exchanged at Camp Townsend, MS, on 5/6/1865.

Reynolds, B.A. 1st Lt., C.S.A. Engineer Corps. Federal Rolls of Prisoners of War: Captured at Fort Gaines, AL, on 8/8/1864; Received at Ship Island, MS, from New Orleans, LA, on 10/25/1864. Exchanged on 1/4/1865.

Rhodes, Newton M. (AKA Rhoades, Rhode, N.M.) Pvt., 15th Confederate Cavalry. Co. E. Federal Rolls of Prisoners of War: Captured at Pine Barren, FL, on 11/17/1864; Received at Ship Island, MS, from New Orleans, LA, on 12/13/1864. Transferred to Vicksburg, MS, for exchange on 5/1/1865; Exchanged at Camp Townsend, MS, on 5/6/1865.

Riley, W.J. Pvt., 15th Confederate Cavalry. Co. I. Federal Rolls of Prisoners of War: Captured in Alabama on 4/1/1865; Received at Ship Island, MS. Transferred to Vicksburg, MS, for exchange on 5/1/1865; Exchanged at Camp Townsend, MS, on 5/6/1865.

Robertson, Joel Pvt., 20th Confederate Cavalry. Co. E. Federal Rolls of Prisoners of War: Captured at Liberty, MS, on 11/16/1864; Received at Ship Island, MS, from New Orleans, LA, on 12/13/1864. Transferred to Vicksburg, MS, for exchange on 5/1/1865; Exchanged at Camp Townsend, MS, on 5/6/1865.

Robins, T.A. Pvt., 15th Confederate Cavalry. Co. E. Federal Rolls of Prisoners of War: Captured at Pine Barren, FL, on 11/17/1864; Received at Ship Island, MS, from New Orleans, LA, on 12/13/1864. Died: 3/28/1865.

Rochester, L.M. (AKA S.M.) Pvt., C.S.A. Signal Corps. Federal Rolls of Prisoners of War: Captured at Jackson Parish, LA, on 10/27/1864; Received at Ship Island, MS, from New Orleans, LA, on 12/13/1864. Disposition unknown.

Rogers, J.F. Pvt., 15th Confederate Cavalry. Co. E. Federal Rolls of Prisoners of War: Captured at Pine Barren, FL, on 11/17/1864; Received at Ship Island, MS, from New Orleans, LA, on 12/13/1864. Transferred to Vicksburg, MS, for exchange on 5/1/1865; Exchanged at Camp Townsend, MS, on 5/6/1865.

Rogers, William D. Pvt., 15th Confederate Cavalry. Co. E. Federal Rolls of Prisoners of War: Captured at Escambia County, FL, on 11/17/1864; Received at Ship Island, MS. Died: 3/28/1865 at Ship Island, MS, due to dysentery. Buried: Ship Island, MS, Cemetery in Grave #143. Soldier also served as a Pvt. with the 1st Florida Infantry. (The Florida State Library and Archives has a series of letters written by Rogers in Manuscript Collection M89–22).

Roulhac, Joseph B.G. (AKA Roulhack) 1st Lt., 15th Confederate Cavalry. Co. B. Enlisted: 3/14/1862 at Jackson County, FL, in a C.S.A. unit; Dropped from Rolls in 10/1862. Wounded at Santa Rosa Island, FL, on 10/9/1861. Federal Rolls of Prisoners of War: Captured at Marianna, FL, on 9/27/1864; Sent to Fort Pickens, FL. Forwarded to New Orleans, LA, on 10/8/1864; Received at Ship Island, MS, on 10/24/1864. Transferred to Fort Columbus, New York Harbor, NY, on 11/5/1864; Forwarded to Elmira, NY, on 11/20/1864. Paroled at Elmira, NY, on 12/12/1864. Age at parole: 39. Description at parole: Hair: dark. Complexion: light. Height: 5'9½". Occupation at parole: Manager of buggy factory. Born: 3/13/1825 in North Carolina. Candidate for the U.S. Congress in 1856. Died: 6/5/1865 after being released from Elmira, NY, due to hardships during imprisonment. Buried: Episcopal Cemetery located at Marianna, Jackson County, FL.

Ruggles, E.J. Lt., C.S.A. Signal Corps. Federal Rolls of Prisoners of War: Captured at Fort Adams, __ on 10/13/1864; Received at Ship Island, MS, from New Orleans, LA, on 10/25/1864. Transferred to New York in 11/1864.

St. Martin, E. Pvt., C.S.A. Signal Corps. Federal Rolls of Prisoners of War: Captured at Bayou Conway, LA, on 1/5/1865; Received at Ship Island, MS, from New Orleans, LA, on 1/25/1865. Transferred to Vicksburg, MS, for exchange on 5/1/1865; Exchanged at Camp Townsend, MS, on 5/6/1865.

Sabler, C. Pvt., C.S.A. Engineers Corps. Federal Rolls of Prisoners of War: Captured at Fort Gaines, AL, on 8/8/1864; Received at Ship Island, MS, from New Orleans, LA, on 10/24/1864. Exchanged on 1/4/1865.

Sarter, W.C. (AKA Sartor) Pvt., 15th Confederate Cavalry. Co. E. Federal Rolls of Prisoners of War: Captured at Pine Barren, FL, on 11/17/1864; Received at Ship Island, MS, from New Orleans, LA, on 12/13/1864. Transferred to Vicksburg, MS, for exchange on 5/1/1865; Exchanged at Camp Townsend, MS, on 5/6/1865.

Saunders, D.L. (AKA B.L.) Pvt., 20th Confederate Cavalry. Co. C. Federal Rolls of Prisoners of War: Captured at Liberty, MS, on 11/16/1864; Received at Ship Island, MS, from New Orleans, LA, on 12/13/1864. Exchanged on 3/2/1865.

Scarborough, H (AKA Scarbrough) Pvt., 20th Confederate Cavalry. Co. A. Federal Rolls of Prisoners of War: Captured at Liberty, MS, on 11/16/1864; Received at Ship Island, MS, from New Orleans, LA, on 12/13/1864. Exchanged on 3/2/1865.

Scurlock, T.O. (AKA Scarlock) Pvt., 20th Confederate Cavalry. Co. C. Federal Rolls of Prisoners of War: Captured at Liberty, MS, on 11/16/1864; Received at Ship Island, MS, from New Orleans, LA, on 12/13/1864. Exchanged on 3/2/1865.

Sermon, William Pvt., 20th Confederate Cavalry. Co. K. Federal Rolls of Prisoners of War: Captured at Liberty, MS, on 11/16/1864; Received at Ship Island, MS, from New Orleans, LA, on 12/13/1864. Exchanged on 3/2/1865.

Simpson, Elisha Pvt., 15th Confederate Cavalry. Co. K. Federal Rolls of Prisoners of War: Received at Ship Island, MS, as a prisoner of war.

Smith, C.A. Sgt., 14th Confederate Cavalry. Co. __. Federal Rolls of Prisoners of War: Captured at Brookhaven, MS, on 11/18/1864; Received at Ship Island, MS, from New Orleans, LA, on 12/13/1864. Transferred to Vicksburg, MS, for exchange on 5/1/1865; Exchanged at Camp Townsend, MS, on 5/6/1865.

Smith, H.P. Pvt., 15th Confederate Cavalry. Co. E. Federal Rolls of Prisoners of War: Received at Ship Island, MS, as a prisoner of war.

Smith, Nicholas Pvt., 20th Confederate Cavalry. Co. K. Federal Rolls of Prisoners of War: Captured at Liberty, MS, on 11/18/1864; Received at Ship Island, MS, from New Orleans, LA, on 12/13/1864. Transferred to Vicksburg, MS, for exchange on 5/1/1865; Exchanged at Camp Townsend, MS, on 5/6/1865.

Smith, R.A. Pvt., 14th Confederate Cavalry. Co. F. Federal Rolls of Prisoners of War: Captured at Liberty, MS, on 11/17/1864; Received at Ship Island, MS, from New Orleans, LA, on 12/13/1864. Transferred to Vicksburg, MS, for exchange on 5/1/1865; Exchanged at Camp Townsend, MS, on 5/6/1865.

Spier, W.T. (AKA Spin.W.F.) Pvt., 15th Confederate Cavalry. Co. E. Federal Rolls of Prisoners of War: Captured near Pensacola, FL, on 11/17/1864; Received at Ship Island, MS, from New Orleans, LA, on 12/13/1864. Transferred to Vicksburg, MS, for exchange on 5/1/1865; Exchanged at Camp Townsend, MS, on 5/6/1865.

Stephens, T.J. (AKA Stevens) Pvt., 20th Confederate Cavalry. Co. F. Federal Rolls of Prisoners of War: Captured at Liberty, MS, on 11/11/1864; Received at Ship Island, MS, from New Orleans, LA, on 12/13/1864. Exchanged on 3/2/1865.

Stevens, Burrel Pvt., 15th Confederate Cavalry. Co. D. Federal Rolls of Prisoners of War: Received at Ship Island, MS, as a prisoner of war.

Stewart, J.K. Pvt., C.S.A. Signal Corps. Federal Rolls of Prisoners of War: Captured at Woodville, MS, on 10/13/1864; Received at Ship Island, MS, from New Orleans, LA, on 10/21/1864. Transferred to Fort Columbus, New York Harbor, NY, on 11/5/1864.

Stroud, James S. Pvt., 14th Confederate Cavalry. Co. F. Federal Rolls of Prisoners of War: Captured at Liberty, MS, on 11/16/1864; Received at New Orleans, LA, on 12/13/1864. Transferred to Vicksburg, MS, for exchange on 5/1/1865; Exchanged at Camp Townsend, MS, on 5/6/1865.

Sunday, J.W. Pvt., 15th Confederate Cavalry. Co. E. Federal Rolls of Prisoners of War: Captured at Pine Barren, FL, on 11/17/1864; Received at Ship Island, MS, from New Orleans, LA, on 12/13/1864. Transferred to Vicksburg, MS, for exchange on 5/1/1865; Exchanged at Camp Townsend, MS, on 5/6/1865.

Taylor, W.R. Pvt., 15th Confederate Cavalry. Co. A. Federal Rolls of Prisoners of War: Received at Ship Island, MS, as a prisoner of war.

Thompson, E.E. Pvt., C.S.A. Signal Corps. Federal Rolls of Prisoners of War: Captured at Fort Gaines, AL, on 8/8/1864; Received at Ship Island, MS, from New Orleans, LA, on 10/25/1864. Exchanged on 1/4/1865.

Tonart, William (AKA Tuart) Pvt., 15th Confederate Cavalry. Co. D. Federal Rolls of Prisoners of War: Received at Ship Island, MS, as a prisoner of war.

Townsend, William 2nd Lt., 15th Confederate Cavalry. Co. E. Federal Rolls of Prisoners of War: Captured at Pine Barren, FL, in 9/1864; Received at Ship Island, MS. Transferred to Vicksburg, MS, for exchange on 5/1/1865; Exchanged at Camp Townsend, MS, on 5/6/1865

Traywick, Robert H. Pvt., 15th Confederate Cavalry. Co. I. Federal Rolls of Prisoners of War: Received at Ship Island, MS, as a prisoner of war.

Tucker, F.A. Pvt., C.S.A. Engineer Corps. Federal Rolls of Prisoners of War: Captured at Fort Gaines, AL, on 8/8/1864; Received at Ship Island, MS, from New Orleans, LA, on 12/13/1864. Exchanged on 1/4/1865.

Tucker, Joel H. Pvt., 15th Confederate Cavalry. Co. A. Federal Rolls of Prisoners of War: Received at Ship Island, MS, as a prisoner of war.

Turvin, D.J. (AKA Terwin) Pvt., 15th Confederate Cavalry. Co. E. Federal Rolls of Prisoners of War: Captured at Pine Barren, FL, on 11/17/1864; Received at Ship Island, MS, from New Orleans, LA, on 12/13/1864. Transferred to Vicksburg, MS, for exchange on 5/1/1865; Exchanged at Camp Townsend, MS, on 5/6/1865.

Wade, S.J. Pvt., 20th Confederate Cavalry. Cos. G & I. Federal Rolls of Prisoners of War: Captured at Brookhaven, MS, on 11/17/1864; Received at Ship Island, MS, from New Orleans, LA, on 12/13/1864. Transferred to Vicksburg, MS, for exchange on 5/1/1865; Exchanged at Camp Townsend, MS, on 5/6/1865.

Ward, D.J. Pvt., C.S.A. Signal Corps. Federal Rolls of Prisoners of War: Captured at Fort Gaines, AL, on 8/8/1864; Received at Ship Island, MS, from New Orleans, LA, on 10/25/1864. Exchanged on 1/4/1865.

Weekley, W.B. (AKA W.E.) Cpl., 15th Confederate Cavalry. Co. C. Federal Rolls of Prisoners of War: Received at Ship Island, MS, as a prisoner of war.

Wells, William (AKA Welles) Pvt., 20th Confederate Cavalry. Co. K. Federal Rolls of Prisoners of War: Captured at Liberty, MS, on 11/16/1864; Received at Ship Island, MS, from New Orleans, LA, on 12/13/1864. Transferred to Vicksburg, MS, for exchange on 5/1/1865; Exchanged at Camp Townsend, MS, on 5/6/1865.

White, J.B. Pvt., 20th Confederate Cavalry. Co. K. Federal Rolls of Prisoners of War: Captured at Liberty, MS, on 11/16/1864; Received at Ship Island, MS, from New Orleans, LA, on 12/13/1864. Transferred to Vicksburg, MS, for exchange on 5/1/1865; Exchanged at Camp Townsend, MS, on 5/6/1865.

Williams, A. Pvt., 15th Confederate Cavalry. Co. E. Federal Rolls of Prisoners of War: Captured near Mobile, AL, on 12/18/1864; Received at Ship Island, MS, from New Orleans, LA, on 1/25/1865. Transferred to Vicksburg, MS, for exchange on 5/1/1865; Exchanged at Camp Townsend, MS, on 5/6/1865.

Williams, I.G. (AKA J.G.) Pvt., 15th Confederate Cavalry. Co. __. Federal Rolls of Prisoners of War: Captured at Weldon, FL, on 10/25/1864; Received at Ship Island, MS, from New Orleans, LA, on 12/13/1864. Transferred to Vicksburg, MS, for exchange on 5/1/1865; Exchanged at Camp Townsend, MS, on 5/6/1865.

Williamson, Allen Pvt., 15th Confederate Cavalry. Co. E. Federal Rolls of Prisoners of War: Captured at Pine Barren, FL, on 11/17/1864; Received at Ship Island, MS, from New Orleans, LA, on 12/13/1864. Transferred to Vicksburg, MS, for exchange on 5/1/1865; Exchanged at Camp Townsend, MS, on 5/6/1865. Married: Vicey Williamson.

Woodall, J.M. Pvt., 20th Confederate Cavalry. Co. C. Federal Rolls of Prisoners of War: Captured at Spanish Fort, AL, on 4/8/1865; Received at Ship Island, MS, on 4/10/1865. Transferred to Vicksburg, MS, for exchange on 5/1/1865; Exchanged at Camp Townsend, MS, on 5/6/1865.

Woodcock, T.S. Pvt., 15th Confederate Cavalry. Co. G. Federal Rolls of Prisoners of War: Captured near Pollard, AL, on 12/18/1864; Received at Ship Island, MS, from New Orleans, LA, on 1/25/1865. Transferred to Vicksburg, MS, for exchange on 5/1/1865; Exchanged at Camp Townsend, MS, on 5/6/1865.

Citizen Prisoners of War

Albritton, Thomas (AKA Alberton) Citizen (Clinton, LA). Federal Rolls of Prisoners of War: Captured at Clinton, LA, on 8/25/1864; Received at Ship Island, MS. Died: 2/6/1865 at Ship Island, MS, due to asthma. Buried: Ship Island, MS, Cemetery in Grave #134.

Andrews, John W., Judge Citizen (New Orleans, LA). Arrested for exhibiting a Cross in the Louisiana Club at New Orleans that he claimed was made from the bones of a Union soldier. Sentenced to 2 years at hard labor in solitary confinement on the Ship Island, MS, fortifications by Maj. Gen. Benjamin F. Butler on 6/30/1862. Released on 9/18/1862.

Batchelder, James C. Citizen (New Orleans, LA). Sentenced to imprisonment at Ship Island, MS, by Maj. Gen. Benjamin F. Butler for offensive language; Received at Ship Island, MS, on 8/7/1862. Released by order of Maj. Gen. Nathaniel P. Banks on 12/30/1862.

Beckimer, Fred Citizen (New Orleans, LA). Sentenced to 1 month imprisonment at Ship Island, MS, by Maj. Gen. Benjamin F. Butler for an unknown offense; Received at Ship Island, MS, on 9/18/1862.

Beggs, James Citizen (New Orleans, LA). Sentenced to imprisonment at Ship Island, MS, by Maj. Gen. Benjamin F. Butler for an unknown offense; Received at Ship Island, MS, on 8/7/1862. Released on the U.S. Oath of Allegiance by Maj. Gen. Nathaniel P. Banks on 12/30/1862.

Biggs, James Citizen (New Orleans, LA). Sentenced to imprisonment at Ship Island, MS, by Maj. Gen. Benjamin F. Butler for an unknown offense; Received at Ship Island, MS, on 6/7/1862. Released by order of Maj. Gen. Nathaniel P. Banks on 12/30/1862.

Bloom, Joseph Citizen (New Orleans, LA). Sentenced to imprisonment at Ship Island, MS, by Maj. Gen. Benjamin F. Butler for an unknown offense; Received at Ship Island, MS, on 11/11/1862. Released by order of Maj. Gen. Nathaniel P. Banks on 12/30/1862.

Boyer, Ernest Citizen (New Orleans, LA). Sentenced to imprisonment at Ship Island, MS, by Maj. Gen. Benjamin F. Butler for an unknown offense; Received at Ship Island, MS, on 9/18/1862. Released on 10/5/1862.

Breckle, John Citizen (New Orleans, LA). Sentenced to 2 months imprisonment at Ship Island, MS, by Maj. Gen. Benjamin F. Butler for an unknown offense; Received at Ship Island, MS, on 9/18/1862.

Brown, James George (AKA J.M.) Citizen, (New Orleans, LA). A private secretary of Maj. Gen. Benjamin F. Butler, he was sentenced to imprisonment at Ship Island, MS, by Butler on charges of betraying official business confided to him on 12/5/1862. Released by Maj. Gen. Nathaniel P. Banks on 8/15/1863. Brown was also a fledgling Union spy-for-hire.

Burkett, ?, Mrs. (AKA Berkett) Citizen (New Orleans, LA). Sentenced to imprisonment at Ship Island, MS, by Maj. Gen. Benjamin F. Butler for carrying Rebel correspondence between the lines on 8/3/1862. Released by Maj. Gen. Benjamin F. Butler on 8/30/1862.

Campbell, Arch Citizen (New Orleans, LA). Sentenced to 6 months imprisonment at Ship Island, MS, by Maj. Gen. Benjamin F. Butler for an unknown offense; Received at Ship Island, MS, on 9/18/1862.

Carpenter, Thomas Citizen (Liberty, MS). Federal Rolls of Prisoners of War: Captured at Liberty, MS; Received at Ship Island, MS; Released on 1/21/1865 by order of Maj. Gen.E.R.S. Canby. Residence at release: East Baton Rouge Parish, LA. Description at release: Eyes: blue. Hair: light. Complexion: light. Height: 5'11".

Carroll, C.F. (AKA C.T.) Citizen Telegrapher (Pollard, AL). Federal Rolls of Prisoners of War: Captured at Pollard, AL, on 12/16/1864; Received at Ship Island, MS, from New Orleans, LA, on 1/25/1865. Transferred to Vicksburg, MS, for exchange on 5/1/1865; Exchanged at Camp Townsend, MS, on 5/6/1865.

Casey, Patrick Citizen (New Orleans, LA). Sentenced to 6 months imprisonment at Ship Island, MS, by Maj. Gen. Benjamin F. Butler for disguising Rebels as steamboat workers and landing them behind Confederate lines; Received at Ship Island, MS, on 10/5/1862.

Chappothine, Charles Citizen (New Orleans, LA). Sentenced to 3 months imprisonment at Ship Island, MS, by Maj. Gen. Benjamin F. Butler for an unknown offense; Received at Ship Island, MS, on 10/5/1862.

Cogan, James Citizen (New Orleans, LA). Sentenced to 6 months imprisonment at Ship Island, MS, by Maj. Gen. Benjamin F. Butler for an unknown offense; Received at Ship Island, MS, on 8/21/1862.

Cooney, John Citizen (New Orleans, LA). Sentenced to imprisonment at Ship Island, MS, by Maj. Gen. Benjamin F. Butler for selling liquor to U.S. soldiers; Received at Ship Island, MS, on 8/22/1862. Released by order of Maj. Gen. Nathaniel P. Banks on 11/22/1863.

Cowen, ?, Mrs. Citizen (New Orleans, LA). Sentenced to imprisonment at Ship Island, MS, by Maj. Gen. Benjamin F. Butler for an unknown offense; Received at Ship Island, MS, on 8/20/1862. Released on 9/1/1862.

Dale, Aaron H. Citizen (New Orleans, LA). Sentenced to imprisonment at Ship Island, MS, by Maj. Gen. Benjamin F. Butler for an unknown offense; Received at Ship Island, MS, on 9/24/1862. Released by order of Maj. Gen. Nathaniel P. Banks on 12/30/1862.

Davis, C.H. Citizen (Tensas Parish, LA). Federal Rolls of Prisoners of War: Captured at Tensas Parish, LA, on 9/19/1864; Received at Ship Island, MS, from New Orleans, LA, on 10/7/1864. Transferred to Fort Columbus, New York Harbor, NY, on 11/3/1864.

Davis, J. Citizen (Mississippi). Federal Rolls of Prisoners of War: Captured at East Pascagoula, MS, on 4/19/1865; Received at Ship Island, MS. Transferred to Vicksburg, MS, for exchange on 5/1/1865; Exchanged at Camp Townsend, MS, on 5/6/1865.

Davis, R.L. Citizen (Alabama). Federal Rolls of Prisoners of War: Captured in Alabama on 3/24/1865; Received at Ship Island, MS. Transferred to Vicksburg, MS, for exchange on 5/1/1865; Exchanged at Camp Townsend, MS, on 5/6/1865.

DeFerat, G. Citizen (New Orleans, LA). Sentenced to 3 months imprisonment at Ship Island, MS, by Maj. Gen. Benjamin F. Butler for writing and publishing seditious articles; Received at Ship Island, MS, on 10/16/1862.

Dodge, L.J. Citizen (New Orleans, LA). Sentenced to imprisonment at Ship Island, MS, by Maj. Gen. Benjamin F. Butler for an unknown offense; Received at Ship Island, MS, on 11/8/1862. Released by order of Maj. Gen. Nathaniel P. Banks on 12/30/1862.

Donnelly, J. (AKA Donnally) Citizen. Federal Rolls of Prisoners of War: Captured in Alabama on 3/24/1865; Received at Ship Island, MS. Transferred to Vicksburg, MS, for exchange on 5/1/1865; Exchanged at Camp Townsend, MS, on 5/6/1865.

Doyle, Daniel Citizen (New Orleans, LA). A paroled Confederate Prisoner of War that was captured at the fall of Forts Jackson and St. Philip, he and five other paroled prisoners formed themselves into a military company named the Monroe Life Guard, in honor of imprisoned New Orleans Mayor John T. Monroe. The six conspired to force their way through the Union lines surrounding New Orleans in order to join the Confederate army at Corinth, MS. Tried and found guilty before a Union military commission on 5/31/1862, they were sentenced to die by hanging on 6/7/1862. Their sentence was commuted to hard labor at Ship Island, MS, on 6/4/1862 by order of Maj. Gen. Benjamin F. Butler. Received at Ship Island, MS, on 6/16/1862; Released by order of Maj. Gen. Nathaniel P. Banks on 8/15/1863. Served as a Pvt. with the 1st Louisiana Heavy Artillery (Regulars). Co. D. Enlisted: 3/14/1861 at New Orleans, LA. Rolls for 3/1861 through 2/1862: Present, on extra duty as a Carpenter.

Dubois, Henry Citizen (New Orleans, LA). Sentenced to imprisonment at Ship Island, MS, by Maj. Gen. Benjamin F. Butler for an unknown offense; Received at Ship Island, MS, on 9/24/1862. Released on 12/6/1862.

Duchine, Loran Citizen (New Orleans, LA). Sentenced to 2 months imprisonment at Ship Island, MS, by Maj. Gen. Benjamin F. Butler for an unknown offense; Received at Ship Island, MS, on 9/6/1862.

Dumas, E. Citizen. Federal Rolls of Prisoners of War: Captured at Pollard, AL, on 12/16/1864; Received at Ship Island, MS, from New Orleans, LA, on 1/25/1865. Transferred to Vicksburg, MS, for exchange on 5/1/1865; Exchanged at Camp Townsend, MS, on 5/6/1865.

Dunoy, R.F. Citizen (New Orleans, LA). Sentenced to imprisonment at Ship Island, MS, by Maj. Gen. Benjamin F. Butler for an unknown offense; Received at Ship Island, MS, on 8/20/1862.

Durand, Joseph Citizen (New Orleans, LA). Sentenced to 2 months imprisonment at Ship Island, MS, by Maj. Gen. Benjamin F. Butler for an unknown offense; Received at Ship Island, MS, on 9/6/1862.

Easten, Edward R. Citizen (New Orleans, LA). Sentenced to imprisonment at Ship Island, MS, by Maj. Gen. Benjamin F. Butler for refusing to take the U.S. Oath of Allegiance; Received at Ship Island, MS, on 9/18/1862. Released by order of Maj. Gen. Nathaniel P. Banks on 12/21/1862.

Edwards, Charles Citizen (Alabama). Federal Rolls of Prisoners of War: Captured in Alabama on 3/26/1865; Received at Ship Island, MS. Transferred to Vicksburg, MS, for exchange on 5/1/1865.

Exodus Negro Citizen (New Orleans, LA). Sentenced to life imprisonment at Ship Island, MS, by Maj. Gen. Nathaniel P. Banks for murder; Received at Ship Island, MS, on 11/16/1863. Confined in the Ship Island, MS, stockade.

French, Robert Citizen. Died: 4/23/1865 at Ship Island, MS, due to cancer. Buried: Ship Island, MS, Cemetery.

Fuller, Levett Negro Citizen (New Orleans, LA). Sentenced as a U.S. Military Convict to imprisonment in the Ship Island, MS, stockade by Maj. Gen. Nathaniel P. Banks for an unknown offense; Received at Ship Island, MS, on 12/7/1863. Died: 6/1864 at Ship Island, MS. Buried: Ship Island, MS, Cemetery.

Gaspard, Eugene Citizen (New Orleans, LA). Sentenced to imprisonment at Ship Island, MS, by Maj. Gen. Benjamin F. Butler for an unknown offense; Received at Ship Island, MS, on 10/31/1862. Released by order of Maj. Gen. Nathaniel P. Banks on 5/1/1863.

Gillis, Marcellus Citizen (New Orleans, LA). Sentenced to imprisonment at Ship Island, MS, by Maj. Gen. Benjamin F. Butler for an unknown offense; Received at Ship Island, MS, on 8/14/1862.

Graves, George H. Citizen (New Orleans, LA). Sentenced to imprisonment at Ship Island, MS, by Maj. Gen. Benjamin F. Butler for an unknown offense; Received at Ship Island, MS, on 11/25/1862. Released by order of Maj. Gen. Nathaniel P. Banks on 2/25/1863.

Hamberger, M. Citizen (Alabama). Federal Rolls of Prisoners of War: Captured in Alabama on 4/1/1865; Received at Ship Island, MS. Transferred to New Orleans, LA, for exchange on 6/5/1865.

Haney, C.W. (Henry, C.H.) Citizen (Telegraph Operator). Federal Rolls of Prisoners of War: Captured at Brookhaven, MS, on 11/18/1864; Received at Ship island, MS, from New Orleans, LA, on 12/13/1864. Exchanged on 3/2/1865.

Hearn, W.S. Citizen (Alabama). Federal Rolls of Prisoners of War: Captured in Alabama on 3/24/1865; Received at Ship Island, MS. Transferred to Vicksburg, MS, for exchange on 5/1/1865; Exchanged at Camp Townsend, MS, on 5/6/1865.

Hebard, B.W. Citizen (New Orleans, LA). Sentenced to imprisonment at Ship Island, MS, by Maj. Gen. Benjamin F. Butler for an unknown offense; Received at Ship Island, MS, on 10/16/1862. Released by order of Maj. Gen. Nathaniel P. Banks on 11/16/1863.

Howard, Charles Citizen (New Orleans, LA). Sentenced to imprisonment at Ship Island, MS, by Maj. Gen. Nathaniel P. Banks for an unknown offense; Received at Ship Island, MS, on 9/18/1863. Transferred to Fort Jefferson, Dry Tortugas Islands on 10/31/1863.

Hunt, H.J. Citizen (Alabama). Federal Rolls of Prisoners of War: Captured in Alabama on 3/29/1865; Received at Ship Island, MS. Transferred to Vicksburg, MS, for exchange on 5/1/1865; Exchanged at Camp Townsend, MS, on 5/6/1865.

Israel, Max Citizen (New Orleans, LA). Sentenced to imprisonment at Ship Island, MS, by Maj. Gen. Benjamin F. Butler for an unknown offense; Received at Ship Island, MS. Released on 10/1/1862.

Johnson, Samuel Citizen (New Orleans, LA). Sentenced to imprisonment at Ship Island, MS, by Maj. Gen. Benjamin F. Butler for an unknown offense; Received at Ship Island, MS, on 12/11/1862.

Johnston, Samuel Citizen (New Orleans, LA). Sentenced to imprisonment at Ship Island, MS, by Maj. Gen. Benjamin F. Butler for an unknown offense; Received at Ship Island, MS, on 12/5/1862. Released by order of Maj. Gen. Nathaniel P. Banks on 4/5/1863.

Jones, Madison Negro Citizen (New Orleans, LA). Sentenced to imprisonment in the Ship Island, MS, stockade as a U.S. Military Convict by Maj. Gen. Benjamin F. Butler for an unknown offense; Received at Ship Island, MS, on 12/5/1862. Died: 1/7/1863 at Ship Island, MS. Buried: Ship Island, MS, Cemetery.

Joseph, Joseph Citizen (New Orleans, LA). Sentenced to imprisonment at Ship Island, MS, by Maj. Gen. Nathaniel P. Banks for an unknown offense; Received at Ship Island, MS, on 1/31/1863. Released by order of Maj. Gen. Nathaniel P. Banks on 7/31/1863.

Kane, Patrick (AKA Cain) Citizen (New Orleans, LA). A paroled Confederate Prisoner of War that was captured at the fall of Forts Jackson and St. Philip, he and five other paroled prisoners formed themselves into a military company named the Monroe Life Guard, in honor of imprisoned New Orleans Mayor John T. Monroe. The six conspired to force their way through the Union lines surrounding New Orleans in order to join the Confederate army at Corinth, MS. Tried and found guilty before a Union military commission on 5/31/1862, they were sentenced to die by hanging on 6/7/1862. Their sentence was commuted to hard labor at Ship Island, MS, on 6/4/1862 by order of Maj. Gen. Benjamin F. Butler. Received at Ship Island, MS, on 6/16/1862; Released by order of Maj. Gen. Nathaniel P. Banks on 8/15/1863. Soldier served as a Pvt. with the 1st Louisiana Heavy Artillery (Regulars). Co. H. Enlisted: 5/24/1861 at New Orleans, LA. Rolls for 5/24/1861 through 2/1862: Present.

Kane, Thomas Citizen (New Orleans, LA). Sentenced to imprisonment at Ship Island, MS, by Maj. Gen. Nathaniel P. Banks for an unknown offense; Received at Ship Island, MS, on 2/6/1863. Released by order of Maj. Gen. Nathaniel P. Banks on 3/16/1863.

Keller, A.J. Citizen (New Orleans, LA). Sentenced to imprisonment at Ship Island, MS, by Maj. Gen. Benjamin F. Butler for an unknown offense; Received at Ship Island, MS, on 10/5/1862. Released by order of Maj. Gen. Nathaniel P. Banks on 1/5/1863.

Keller, Fidel Citizen (New Orleans, LA). A New Orleans bookseller, he displayed a human skeleton with a sign around its neck reading "Chickahominy" in his bookshop window, suggesting that the skeleton was a Union soldier that had died in that battle. He was sentenced on 6/30/1862 to 2 years at hard labor on Ship Island, MS, by Maj. Gen. Benjamin F. Butler and ordered to have no communications with anyone besides fellow prisoner Mrs. Phillips. He was unaware that Mrs. Eugenia Phillips had been sentenced to Ship Island the same day, and thought the Mrs. Phillips to whom Butler was referring was Matilda Phillips, the owner of a local brothel. He requested that the order of communicating with Mrs. Phillips be countermanded, in fear that it would distress his wife. Butler consented to his request, and he was ordered to have no contact with anyone on the island. The bones which he was displaying were purchased from a Mexican Consul for usage by a local medical student, and were not a Union soldier. Released from Ship Island, MS, on 11/3/1862.

Kendricks, David Citizen (Mobile, AL). Federal Rolls of Prisoners of War: Captured at Blakely, AL, on 4/9/1865; Received at Ship Island, MS, on 4/15/1865. Died: 4/16/1865 at Ship Island, MS, due to dysentery. Buried: Ship Island, MS, Cemetery in Grave #147.

King, P. Citizen (Louisiana). Federal Rolls of Prisoners of War: Captured at Bayou Lafourche, LA, on 5/5/1864; Sent to Ship Island, MS. Forwarded to Fort Columbus, New York Harbor, NY, on 11/16/1864; Transferred to Elmira, NY, on 11/19/1864.

LaRue, Anna Citizen (New Orleans, LA). The wife of New Orleans gambler John LaRue, she was arrested on 7/10/1862 for inciting a riot by wearing a secession badge on her bosom in front of the St. Charles Hotel in New Orleans that resulted in the wounding of a Union soldier. Sent to Ship Island, MS, by order of Maj. Gen. Benjamin F. Butler and ordered to be isolated from the other women on the island. Released from Ship Island, MS, on 8/6/1862. Her husband was a prisoner at the time of her arrest at Fort Jackson, LA, by order of Gen. Butler for being a vagrant with no known occupation other than playing cards.

LeBeau, Edgar Citizen (New Orleans, LA). Sentenced to imprisonment at Ship Island, MS, for one year on 8/21/1862 by Maj. Gen. Benjamin F. Butler due to conspiring to conceal weapons belonging to the Confederacy in order to prevent their capture by Union forces. Released on 9/28/1862.

LeBeau, Edward Citizen (New Orleans, LA). Sentenced to imprisonment at Ship Island, MS, for one year on 8/21/1862 by Maj. Gen. Benjamin F. Butler due to conspiring to conceal weapons belonging to the Confederacy in order to prevent their capture by Union forces. Released on 9/28/1862.

Lee, Charles H. Citizen (New Orleans, LA). Sentenced to imprisonment at Ship Island, MS, by Maj. Gen. Benjamin F. Butler for an unknown offense; Received at Ship Island, MS. Released by order of Maj. Gen. Benjamin F. Butler on 10/5/1862.

Lieb, Theodore Citizen (New Orleans, LA). Arrested on 6/15/1862 for membership in an 8 member gang of thieves consisting of former Union soldiers and New Orleans citizens that impersonated Federal soldiers in order to enter homes to steal. Sentenced to death along with his 7 accomplices, his sentence was commuted to hard labor on Ship Island, MS, by Maj. Gen. Benjamin F. Butler due to his youthful age of 18. Received at Ship Island, MS, on 7/3/1862; Transferred to Fort Jefferson, Dry Tortugas Islands on 10/31/1863.

Losberg, Fred Citizen (New Orleans, LA). Sentenced to imprisonment at Ship Island, MS, by Maj. Gen. Benjamin F. Butler for an unknown offense; Received at Ship Island, MS, on 8/7/1862. Released by order of Maj. Gen. Nathaniel P. Banks on 12/30/1862.

McLane, Abraham (AKA Abram) Citizen (New Orleans, LA). A paroled Confederate Prisoner of War that was captured at the fall of forts Jackson and St. Philip, he and five other paroled prisoners formed themselves into a military company named the Monroe Life Guard, in honor of imprisoned New Orleans Mayor John T. Monroe. The six conspired to force their way through the Union lines surrounding New Orleans in order to join the Confederate army at Corinth, MS. Tried and found guilty before a Union military commission on 5/31/1862, they were sentenced to die by hanging on 6/7/1862. Their sentence was commuted to hard labor at Ship Island, MS, on 6/4/1862 by order of Maj. Gen. Benjamin F. Butler. Received at Ship Island, MS, on 6/16/1862; Released by order of Maj. Gen. Nathaniel P. Banks on 8/15/1863. Soldier served as a Pvt. with the 23rd Louisiana Infantry. Co. I. Enlisted: 8/15/1861 at New Orleans, LA. Rolls for 11/1861 through 2/1862: Present, sick in hospital.

Malley, T.O. Citizen (New Orleans, LA). Sentenced to imprisonment at Ship Island, MS, by Maj. Gen. Benjamin F. Butler for selling liquor to U.S. troops; Received at Ship Island, MS, on 10/6/1862.

Marshall, William H. Citizen (New Orleans, LA). Sentenced to imprisonment at Ship Island, MS, by Maj. Gen. Benjamin F. Butler for trading with Confederates; Received at Ship Island, MS, on 10/26/1862. Released by order of Maj. Gen. Nathaniel P. Banks on 8/15/1863.

Mensmen, George Citizen (New Orleans, LA). Sentenced to imprisonment at Ship Island, MS, by Maj. Gen. Benjamin F. Butler for an unknown offense; Received at Ship Island, MS, on 9/24/1862.

Minnett, Thomas Citizen (New Orleans, LA). Sentenced to imprisonment at Ship Island, MS, by Maj. Gen. Benjamin F. Butler for robbery; Received at Ship Island, MS, on 7/3/1862. Transferred to Fort Jefferson, Dry Tortugas Islands by order of Maj. Gen. Nathaniel P. Banks on 10/31/1863.

Mitchell, N. Citizen. Federal Rolls of Prisoners of War: Captured in Alabama on 4/1/1865; Received at Ship Island, MS. Transferred to Vicksburg, MS, for exchange on 5/1/1865; Exchanged at Camp Townsend, MS, on 5/6/1865.

Moore, F.W. Citizen (New Orleans, LA). Sentenced to imprisonment at Ship Island, MS, by Maj. Gen. Benjamin F. Butler for an unknown offense; Received at Ship Island, MS, on 9/4/1862. Released by order of Maj. Gen. Nathaniel P. Banks on 3/4/1863.

Morris, Eugene Citizen (New Orleans, LA). Sentenced to imprisonment at Ship Island, MS, by Maj. Gen. Benjamin F. Butler for disguising Rebels as steamboat workers and landing them behind Confederate lines; Received at Ship Island, MS, on 10/5/1862. Released by order of Maj. Gen. Nathaniel P. Banks on 12/30/1862.

Murphy, Michael Citizen (New Orleans, LA). Sentenced to imprisonment at Ship Island, MS, by Maj. Gen. Benjamin F. Butler for being a Confederate officer and spy; Received at Ship Island, MS, on 9/18/1862. Released on the U.S. Oath of Allegiance by order of Maj. Gen. Nathaniel P. Banks on 12/30/1862.

O'Brien, John Citizen (New Orleans, LA). Sentenced to imprisonment at Ship Island, MS, by Maj. Gen. Edward R.S. Canby for an unknown offense; Received at Ship Island, MS, on 4/13/1866. Died: 7/11/1866.

O'Brien, John M. Citizen (New Orleans, LA). Sentenced to imprisonment at Ship Island, MS, by Maj. Gen. Benjamin F. Butler for boasting that he had not taken the U.S. Oath of Allegiance; Received at Ship Island, MS, on 9/18/1862. Released by order of Maj. Gen. Nathaniel P. Banks on 12/21/1862.

O'Connor, Smyth Citizen (New Orleans, LA). Sentenced to imprisonment at Ship Island, MS, by Maj. Gen. Nathaniel P. Banks for assault and battery; Received at Ship Island, MS, on 12/24/1862. Released by order of Maj. Gen. Nathaniel P. Banks on 8/24/1863.

Patterson, William Citizen (New Orleans, LA). Sentenced to imprisonment at Ship Island, MS, by Maj. Gen. Nathaniel P. Banks for an unknown offense; Received at Ship Island, MS, on 12/30/1862. Released by order of Maj. Gen. Nathaniel P. Banks on 6/30/1863.

Payne, J.G. Citizen. Federal Rolls of Prisoners of War: Captured in Alabama on 3/28/1865; Received at Ship Island, MS. Transferred to Vicksburg, MS, for exchange on 5/1/1865; Exchanged at Camp Townsend, MS, on 5/6/1865.

Penvett, Alonzo A. Citizen (New Orleans, LA). Sentenced to imprisonment at Ship Island, MS, by Maj. Gen. Benjamin F. Butler for an unknown offense; Received at Ship Island, MS. Released by order of Maj. Gen. Benjamin F. Butler on 10/5/1862.

Perry, B.F. Citizen (New Orleans, LA). Sentenced to imprisonment at Ship Island, MS, by Maj. Gen. Benjamin F. Butler for an unknown offense; Received at Ship Island, MS, on 11/4/1862. Released by order of Maj. Gen. Nathaniel P. Banks on 12/30/1862.

Phillips, Eugenia, Mrs. Citizen (New Orleans, LA). Arrested on 6/28/1862, she was sent to Ship Island, MS, on 6/30/1862 by order of Maj. Gen. Benjamin F. Butler in consequence of laughing at Union Lt. George C. Dekay's funeral procession at New Orleans, LA, on 6/27/1862. Released on the U.S. Oath of Allegiance on 9/14/1862 due to the appeals of her husband, former Alabama U.S. Congressman Philip Phillips, to Gen. Butler. She moved to Mobile, AL, after her release and became a symbol of Confederate defiance to the Union occupation of New Orleans.

Preston, W.B. (AKA W.N.) Citizen. Federal Rolls of Prisoners of War: Captured in Alabama on 3/24/1865; Received at Ship Island, MS. Transferred to Vicksburg, MS, for exchange on 5/1/1865; Exchanged at Camp Townsend, MS, on 5/6/1865.

Riley, John H. Citizen. Federal Rolls of Prisoners of War: Captureed at Clinton, LA, on 11/16/1864; Received at Ship Island, MS, from New Orleans, LA, on 12/13/1864. Transferred to Vicksburg, MS, for exchange on 5/1/1865; Exchanged at Camp Townsend, MS, on 5/6/1865.

Riley, W.B. Citizen. Federal Rolls of Prisoners of War: Captured in Alabama on 3/24/1865; Received at Ship Island, MS. Transferred to Vicksburg, MS, for exchange on 5/1/1865; Exchanged at Camp Townsend, MS, on 5/6/1865.

Roberts, Stephen Citizen (Baton Rouge, LA). Arrested for wounding U.S. Colonel James W. McMillan on 6/9/1862 for pursuing his furloughed son, Lt. Josiah Roberts, to the threshold of his home. Sent to Fort Jackson, LA; Forwarded to Ship Island, MS. An account of the shooting is recorded in the 10/27/1865 edition of the Baton Rouge, LA, newspaper Tri-Weekly Advocate.

Robinson, E.T. (AKA C.T.) Citizen (Montgomery, AL). Federal Rolls of Prisoners of War: Captured near Pollard, AL, on 11/16/1864; Received at Ship Island, MS, from New Orleans, LA, on 1/25/1865. Transferred to New Orleans, LA, for exchange on 6/5/1865.

Rosegue, J. (AKA Rosegice) Citizen. Federal Rolls of Prisoners of War: Captured in Alabama on 3/24/1865; Received at Ship Island, MS. Transferred to Vicksburg, MS, for exchange on 5/1/1865; Exchanged at Camp Townsend, MS, on 5/6/1865.

Royal, Edward Citizen (New Orleans, LA). Sentenced to imprisonment at Ship Island, MS, by Maj. Gen. Benjamin F. Butler for an unknown offense; Received at Ship Island, MS, on 9/18/1862. Released by order of Maj. Gen. Nathaniel P. Banks on 7/31/1863.

Santen, A. Citizen (New Orleans, LA). Sentenced to imprisonment at Ship Island, MS, by Maj. Gen. Benjamin F. Butler for circulating a false story; Received at Ship Island, MS, on 9/18/1862. Released by order of Maj. Gen. Nathaniel P. Banks on 12/21/1862.

Sewall, M.N. Citizen. Federal Rolls of Prisoners of War: Captured at Atchafalya, LA, on 12/30/1864; Received at Ship Island, MS, from New Orleans, LA, on 1/25/1865. Transferred to New Orleans, LA, for exchange on 3/30/1865.

Sheppard, William H. (AKA Shepphard) Citizen (New Orleans, LA). Sentenced to imprisonment at hard labor at Ship Island, MS, by Maj. Gen. Benjamin F. Butler until he produced a stolen box; Received at Ship Island, MS, on 9/29/1862. Released by order of Maj. Gen. Nathaniel P. Banks on 12/30/1862.

Smith, Edward C. Citizen (New Orleans, LA). A paroled Confederate Prisoner of War that was captured at the fall of Forts Jackson and St. Philip, he and five other paroled prisoners formed themselves into a military company named the Monroe Life Guard, in honor of imprisoned New Orleans Mayor John T. Monroe. The six conspired to force their way through the Union lines surrounding New Orleans in order to join the Confederate army at Corinth, MS. Tried and found guilty before a Union military commission on 5/31/1862, they were sentenced to die by hanging on 6/7/1862. Their sentence was commuted to hard labor at Ship Island, MS, on 6/4/1862 by order of Maj. Gen. Benjamin F. Butler. Received at Ship Island, MS, on 6/16/1862; Released by order of Maj. Gen. Nathaniel P. Banks on 8/15/1863. Soldier served as a Pvt./Cpl. with the 1st Louisiana Heavy Artillery (Regulars). Co. B. Enlisted: 3/4/1861 at New Orleans, LA. Rolls for 3/4/1861 through 2/1862: Present.

Stanley, William Citizen (New Orleans, LA). A paroled Confederate Prisoner of War that was captured at the fall of Forts Jackson and St. Philip, he and five other paroled prisoners formed themselves into a military company named the Monroe Life Guard, in honor of imprisoned New Orleans Mayor John T. Monroe. The six conspired to force their way through the Union lines surrounding New Orleans in order to join the Confederate army at Corinth, MS. Tried and found guilty before a Union military commission on 5/31/1862, they were sentenced to die by hanging on 6/7/1862. Their sentence was commuted to hard labor at Ship Island, MS, on 6/4/1862 by order of Maj. Gen. Benjamin F. Butler. Received at Ship Island, MS, on 6/16/1862; Released by order of Maj. Gen. Nathaniel P. Banks on 8/15/1863. Soldier served as a Sgt./Pvt. with the 1st Louisiana Heavy Artillery (Regulars). Co. B. Enlisted: 2/28/1861 at New Orleans, LA. Rolls for 3/1861 through 4/1861: Present, elected Sgt. on 3/12/1861. Rolls for 5/1861 through 6/1861: Present, reduced to Pvt. from Sgt. on 6/5/1861. Rolls for 7/1861 through 8/1861: Present. Rolls for 9/1861 through 12/1861: Present, on extra duty as Ordnance Man, working in the powder magazine. Rolls for 1/1862 through 2/1862: Present. Regimental Return for 3/1862: Detailed in Magazine.

Stein, John Citizen, (Louisiana). Federal Rolls of Prisoners of War: Captured on 8/19/1864; Received at Fort Columbus, New York Harbor, NY, from Ship Island, MS, on 11/16/1864. Transferred to Elmira, NY, on 11/18/1864.

Sykes, George Citizen (New Orleans, LA). Sentenced to imprisonment at Ship Island, MS, by Maj. Gen. Benjamin F. Butler for an unknown offense; Received at Ship Island, MS, on 8/29/1862. Released by order of Maj. Gen. Nathaniel P. Banks on 2/28/1863.

Tablon, Charles E. Citizen (New Orleans, LA). Sentenced to imprisonment at Ship Island, MS, by Maj. Gen. Benjamin F. Butler for an unknown offense; Received at Ship Island, MS, on 11/25/1862. Released by order of Maj. Gen. Nathaniel P. Banks on 2/25/1863.

Taylor, Hamilton Citizen. Federal Rolls of Prisoners of War: Captured at Harrison County, MS, on 11/2/1864; Received at Ship Island, MS, from New Orleans, LA, on 12/13/1864. Transferred to Vicksburg, MS, for exchange on 5/1/1865; Exchanged at Camp Townsend, MS, on 5/6/1865.

Taylor, Frederick A. Citizen (New Orleans, LA). Sentenced to 6 months imprisonment at Ship Island, MS, by Maj. Gen. Benjamin F. Butler for an unknown offense; Received at Ship Island, MS, on 10/5/1862. Released on the U.S. Oath of Allegiance by order of Maj. Gen. Nathaniel P. Banks on 12/30/1862.

Trephagen, H.S. (AKA Traphagen) Citizen (New Orleans, LA). Sentenced to imprisonment at Ship Island, MS, by Maj. Gen. Benjamin F. Butler for inciting people to take up arms against the U.S. authorities while on parole; Released by order of Maj. Gen. Benjamin F. Butler on 9/18/1862.

Ure, James H. Citizen (New Orleans, LA). Sentenced to imprisonment at Ship Island, MS, by Maj. Gen. Benjamin F. Butler for an unknown offense; Received at Ship Island, MS, on 9/24/1862. Released by order of Maj. Gen. Nathaniel P. Banks on 12/25/1862.

Wagner, E. Citizen, (Blockade Runner). Federal Rolls of Prisoners of War: Captured at Lake Maurepas, LA, on 12/21/1864; Received at Ship Island, MS, from New Orleans, LA, on 1/25/1865. Transferred to Vicksburg, MS, for exchange on 5/1/1865; Exchanged at Camp Townsend, MS, on 5/6/1865.

Walker, Alexander Citizen/Journalist (New Orleans, LA). Sentenced to imprisonment at Ship Island, MS, for one year by Maj. Gen. Benjamin F. Butler due to criticizing the Union occupation of New Orleans, LA. Received at Ship Island, MS, on 8/13/1862.

Weltz, P.E., Jr. Citizen (New Orleans, LA). Sentenced to imprisonment at Ship Island, MS, by Maj. Gen. Benjamin F. Butler for an unknown offense; Received at Ship Island, MS, on 10/28/1862. Released by order of Maj. Gen. Nathaniel P. Banks on 12/30/1862.

Williams, George L. Citizen (New Orleans, LA). A paroled Confederate Prisoner of War that was captured at the fall of Forts Jackson and St. Philip, he and five other paroled prisoners formed themselves into a military company named the Monroe Life Guard, in honor of imprisoned New Orleans Mayor John T. Monroe. The six conspired to force their way through the Union lines surrounding New Orleans in order to join the Confederate army at Corinth, MS. Tried and found guilty before a Union military commission on 5/31/1862, they were sentenced to die by hanging on 6/7/1862. Their sentence was commuted to hard labor at Ship Island, MS, on 6/4/1862 by order of Maj. Gen. Benjamin F. Butler. Received at Ship Island, MS, on 6/16/1862; Released by order of Maj. Gen. Nathaniel P. Banks on 8/15/1863. Soldier served as a Pvt. with the 1st Louisiana Heavy Artillery (Regulars). Co. F. Enlisted: 3/28/1861 at New Orleans, LA. Rolls for 3/28/1861 through 4/1861: Present. Rolls for 5/1861 through 2/1862: Present, working in Magazine. Regimental Return for 3/1862: Assigned to Ordnance.

Williams, W. Citizen (New Orleans, LA). Sentenced to imprisonment at Ship Island, MS, by Maj. Gen. Benjamin F. Butler for an unknown offense; Received at Ship Island, MS, on 11/22/1862. Released by order of Maj. Gen. Nathaniel P. Banks on 3/12/1863.

Wiltz, P.E., Jr. Citizen (New Orleans, LA). Sentenced to imprisonment at Ship Island, MS, by Maj. Gen. Benjamin F. Butler for an unknown offense; Released on the U.S. Oath of Allegiance by order of Maj. Gen. Nathaniel P. Banks on 12/30/1862.

Wright, H.M. Citizen (New Orleans, LA). Sentenced to imprisonment at Ship Island, MS, by Maj. Gen. Benjamin F. Butler for an unknown offense; Received at Ship Island, MS, on 10/15/1862. Released by order of Maj. Gen. Nathaniel P. Banks on 12/25/1862.

Chapter Notes

Chapter One

1. National Park Service, *Gulf Islands National Seashore Publication* (2004).
2. Richard P. Weinert, "Neglected Key to the Gulf Coast," *Journal of Mississippi History* 31 (November 1969): 269; National Park Service, *Gulf Islands National Seashore Publication* (2004).
3. Richebourg Gaillard McWilliams, *Pierre LeMoyne d'Iberville, d'Iberville's Journal* (Tuscaloosa: University of Alabama, 1981), 3.
4. Isaac Joslin Cox, *The Journeys of Rene Robert Cavelier: Sieur de La Salle* (New York: Allerton Book Company, 1906), 2:126–127, 159–160; Robert Lowry and William H. McCardle, *History of Mississippi* (Spartanburg, SC: Reprint Company Publishers, 1998), 16.
5. Cox, *The Journeys of Rene Robert Cavelier: Sieur de La Salle*, 2:241–242; Dunbar Rowland, *History of Mississippi, Heart of the South* (Chicago: S.J. Clarke Publishing Company, 1925), 1:135; Richebourg Gaillard McWilliams, *Pierre LeMoyne d'Iberville, d'Iberville's Journal* (Tuscaloosa: University of Alabama, 1981), 1; Edwin C. Bearss, *Historic Resource Study: Ship Island, Harrison County, Mississippi, Gulf Islands National Seashore, Florida/Mississippi* (Denver: 1984), 13.
6. McWilliams, *Pierre LeMoyne d'Iberville, d'Iberville's Journal*, 3.
7. McWilliams., 32–33; Rowland, *History of Mississippi, Heart of the South*, 1:140; Bearss, *Historic Resource Study: Ship Island*, 13.
8. Bearss, *Historic Resource Study: Ship Island*, 36–38.
9. M. Lepage DuPratz, *History of Louisiana* (New Orleans: Pelican Press, Inc., 1947), 16.
10. J.F.H. Claiborne, *Mississippi as a Province, Territory and State* (Jackson: Power and Barksdale, 1879), 18.
11. McWilliams, *Pierre LeMoyne d'Iberville, d'Iberville's Journal*, 43–44.
12. McWilliams, 59; Claiborne, *Mississippi as a Province, Territory and State*, 19; Rowland, *History of Mississippi, Heart of the South*, 1:143;
13. Claiborne, 16, 19.
14. McWilliams, *Pierre LeMoyne d'Iberville, d'Iberville's Journal*, 89; Rowland, *History of Mississippi, Heart of the South*, 1:133–134.
15. Rowland, 1:143.
16. Claiborne, *Mississippi as a Province, Territory and State*, 19; Richard A. McLemore, *History of Mississippi* (Jackson: Jackson University and College Press of Mississippi, 1973), 1:116; Rowland, *History of Mississippi, Heart of the South*, 1:145–149, 181.
17. Rowland, *History of Mississippi, Heart of the South*, 1:146–147, 149; Claiborne, *Mississippi as a Province, Territory and State*, 20.
18. Rowland, *History of Mississippi, Heart of the South*, 1:150, 173; George W. Brown, ed. *Dictionary of Canadian Biography* (Toronto: University of Toronto Press, 1966), 2:396; Richard P. Weinert, "Neglected Key to the Gulf Coast," *Journal of Mississippi History* 31:271 (November 1969); McWilliams, *Pierre LeMoyne d'Iberville, d'Iberville's Journal*, 92.
19. Claiborne, *Mississippi as a Province, Territory and State*, 19.
20. Richebourg Gaillard McWilliams, *Fleur de Lys and Calumet, Being the Penicaut Narrative of French Adventures in Louisiana* (Baton Rouge: Louisiana State University Press, 1953) 2–3.
21. Rowland, *History of Mississippi, Heart of the South*, 1: 172.
22. Ibid., 172.
23. McWilliams, *Pierre LeMoyne d'Iberville, d'Iberville's Journal*, 8.
24. Ibid.
25. Brown, ed., *Dictionary of Canadian Biography*, 2:396; McWilliams, *Pierre LeMoyne d'Iberville, d'Iberville's Journal*, 10.
26. McWilliams, *Pierre LeMoyne d'Iberville, d'Iberville's Journal*, 11; Claiborne, *Mississippi as a Province, Territory and State*, 27; DuPratz, *History of Louisiana* (New Orleans: Pelican Press, Inc., 1947) 24–25.
27. McWilliams, *Pierre LeMoyne d'Iberville, d'Iber-*

ville's Journal, 159–160; Claiborne, *Mississippi as a Province, Territory and State*, 27; Bearss, *Historic Resource Study: Ship Island*, 17.

28. Rowland, *History of Mississippi, Heart of the South*, 1:187–189.

29. McWilliams, *Pierre LeMoyne d'Iberville, d'Iberville's Journal*, 12–13; Claiborne, *Mississippi as a Province, Territory and State*, 29.

30. Bearss, *Historic Resource Study: Ship Island*, 19; Rowland, *History of Mississippi, Heart of the South*, 1:52, 192, 199.

31. Richard P. Weinert, "The Neglected Key to the Gulf Coast," 273; Claiborne, *Mississippi as a Province, Territory and State*, 35; Rowland, *History of Mississippi, Heart of the South*, 1:197; Bearss, *Historic Resource Study: Ship Island*, 19.

32. Weinert, "The Neglected Key to the Gulf Coast," 273.

33. Weinert, 275; Claiborne, *Mississippi as a Province, Territory and State* 35, 38; Rowland, *History of Mississippi, Heart of the South*, 1:199–206, 212, 217, 219.

34. Rowland, *History of Mississippi, Heart of the South*, 1: 211–212, 215.

35. *Ibid.*, 218.

36. *Ibid.*, 210.

37. Weinert, "The Neglected Key to the Gulf Coast," 277–278.

38. Weinert, 277; Claiborne, *Mississippi as a Province, Territory and State*, 35; Bearss, *Historic Resource Study: Ship Island*, 27–29.

39. Zed Burns, *Confederate Forts* (Natchez: Southern Historical Publishing Company, 1977), 43; Weinert, "The Neglected Key to the Gulf Coast," 278; McLemore, *History of Mississippi*, 1:127.

40. Paul S. Boyer, ed., *The Oxford Companion to United States History* (New York: Oxford University Press, Inc., 2001), 814; Bearss, *Historic Resource Study: Ship Island*, 33–34.

41. *Ibid.*, 551, 814.

42. National Park Service, *Gulf Islands National Seashore Publication*, Mississippi District, May, 2004.

43. National Park Service, *Gulf Islands National Seashore Publication*, Mississippi District, June, 2004.

44. *Ibid.*

45. John A. Garraty and Mark C. Carnes, *American National Biography* (New York: Oxford University Press, 1999), 3:690–693.

46. Margaret E. Wagner, ed., *Library of Congress Civil War Desk Reference* (New York: Simon and Schuster, 2002), 130–131; Paul S. Boyer, ed., *Oxford Companion to United States History* (New York: Oxford University Press, Inc., 2001), 192, 714.

47. Rowland, *History of Mississippi, Heart of the South*, 1: 773.

48. Wagner, ed., *Library of Congress Civil War Desk Reference*, 143.

49. Rowland, *History of Mississippi, Heart of the South*, 1:776, 778.

50. Roy P. Basler, ed., *The Collected Works of Abraham Lincoln* (New Brunswick: Rutgers University Press, 1953), vol. 4, *1860–1861*, 261.

51. Rowland, *History of Mississippi, Heart of the South*, 1:741.

52. *The Natchez Daily Courier*, January 18, 1861; H. Grady Howell, Jr., *To Live and Die in Dixie* (Jackson: Chickasaw Bayou Press, 1991), 21.

53. *Official Records of the War of the Rebellion* (Harrisburg, PA: The National Historical Society, 1985), series 1, vol. 1:329.

54. McCabe to Pettus letter, January 20, 1861, Mississippi Dept. of Archives and History, RG 27; Dunbar Rowland, *Military History of Mississippi 1803–1898* (Spartanburg, SC: Reprint Company Publishers, 1999), 35; Elmer to Pettus letter, February 28, 1861, Mississippi Department of Archives and History, RG 27.

55. *Official Records of the War of the Rebellion*, series 1, vol. 63:681, 683–686.

56. *Ibid.*, series 1, vol. 62, part 2:80.

57. *Ibid.*, series 1, vol. 63:708–709.

58. *Ibid.*, 703.

59. *Ibid.*, 699.

60. *Official Records of the Union and Confederate Navies in the War of the Rebellion* (Harrison, PA: The National Historical Society, 1985), series 1, vol. 16:560; Zed Burns, *Fort Massachusetts*, 45; *Official Records of the War of the Rebellion*, series 1, vol. 63:703; *Confederate Military History* (Wilmington, NC: Broadfoot Publishing Company, 1987), vol. 9:67.

61. Peggy Robbins, "When the Rebels Lost Ship Island," *Civil War Times Illustrated* 17:42 (January 1979).

62. Reverend J. William Jones, ed., *Southern Historical Society Papers* (Millwood, NY: Kraus Reprint Company, 1977), vol. 1, no. 5.

63. *Official Records of the Union and Confederate Navies in the War of the Rebellion*, series 1, vol. 16: 581–582; Burns, *Fort Massachusetts*, 46; *Confederate Military History* (Wilmington, NC: Broadfoot Publishing, 1987), 9:67.

64. *Official Records of the War of the Rebellion*, series 1, vol. 63:690.

65. *Official Records of the War of the Rebellion*, series 1, vol. 63:706; *Official Records of the Union and Confederate Navies in the War of the Rebellion* (Harrison, PA: The National Historical Society, 1985), series 1, vol. 16:581.

66. *Ibid.*, 581.

67. *Ibid.*, 602–603.

68. *Official Records of the War of the Rebellion*, series 1, vol. 63:720.

69. *Official Records of Union and Confederate Navies in the War of the Rebellion*, 615.

70. *Ibid.*, 616–617.

71. *Official Records of the War of the Rebellion*, series 1, vol. 16:644.

72. Peggy Robbins, "When the Rebels Lost Ship Island," *Civil War Times Illustrated*, vol. 17, no. 9 (January1979), 45; *Official Records of the Union and Confederate Navies in the War of the Rebellion*, series 1, vol. 16:644.

73. *Official Records of the War of the Rebellion*, series 1, vol. 6:730–731.

74. *Ibid.*, 730–734.

75. *Ibid.*, 733.

76. *Ibid.*, 734–736.

77. *Ibid.*, 730.

78. *Ibid.*, 738.

79. *Ibid.*, series 1, vol. 63:739.
80. *Official Records of the Union and Confederate Navies in the War of the Rebellion,* series 1, vol. 16: 678–679.
81. Robbins, "When the Rebels Lost Ship Island," 45.
82. *Ibid.,* 44.
83. *Official Records of the Union and Confederate Navies in the War of the Rebellion,* series 1, vol. 16:740.
84. *Ibid.,* 739–745.
85. *Ibid.,* 639–640.
86. *Ibid.,* 753; Robbins, "When the Rebels Lost Ship Island," 45.

Chapter Two

1. *Official Records of the War of the Rebellion* (Harrisburg, PA: The National Historical Society, 1985), series 1, vol. 16:677–678.
2. *Ibid.,* series 3, vol. 1:826.
3. Benjamin F. Butler, *Autobiography and Personal Reminiscences of Major-General Benj. F. Butler* (Boston: A.M. Thayer & Company, 1892), 297, 312; Jesse Ames Marshall, ed., *Private and Official Correspondence of Gen. Benjamin F. Butler,* 5 vols. (Self Published, 1917), 1:264; James Parton, *General Butler in New Orleans* (New York: 1864), chapter 11; *Official Records of the War of the Rebellion,* series 3, vol. 1: 819–866.
4. Richard S. West Jr., *Lincoln's Scapegoat General: A Life of Benjamin F. Butler, 1818–1893* (Boston: Houghton Mifflin Company, 1965), 113; Gideon Welles, "Admiral Farragut and New Orleans," *The Galaxy: An Illustrated Magazine of Entertaining Reading* 12 (November-December 1871), 677.
5. Loyall Farragut, *The Life of David Glasgow Farragut: First Admiral of the U.S. Navy* (New York: 1879), 9–11.
6. Marshall, ed., *Private and Official Correspondence of Gen. Benjamin F. Butler,* vol. 1:318; James G. Hollandsworth, "What a Hell of a Place to Send 2000 Men 3000 Miles": Union Soldiers on Ship Island During the Civil War," *The Journal of Mississippi History* 62 (Spring 2000), 124.
7. *Ibid.,* 124.
8. Charles L. Dufour, *The Night the War Was Lost* (Garden City, NY: Doubleday, 1960), 122.
9. U.S. Department of the Interior, National Park Service, *Gulf Islands National Seashore Park* (Ocean Springs, MS, 2000).
10. *Ibid.*
11. Civil War letter of Albert A. Andrews, The Connecticut Historical Society Museum, Hartford, CT.
12. Dufour, *The Night the War Was Lost,* 122; *New Orleans Daily-Crescent,* December 18, 1861; *Harper's Weekly,* December 1861.
13. *Official Records of the War of the Rebellion,* series 1, vol. 6:790.
14. Marshall, ed., *Private and Official Correspondence of Gen. Benjamin F. Butler,* vol. 1:318.
15. *Ibid.,* 319.
16. *Official Records of the War of the Rebellion,* series 3, vol. 1:862.
17. *Ibid.,* 863.
18. Marshall, ed., *Private and Official Correspondence of Gen. Benjamin F. Butler,* vol. 1:332, 341; West, *Lincoln's Scapegoat General,* 115.
19. *Ibid.,* 116–118.
20. Marshall, ed., *Private and Official Correspondence of Gen. Benjamin F. Butler,* vol. 1:360–362; *Official Records of the War of the Rebellion,* series 3, vol. 4:694–695.
21. Benjamin F. Butler, *Autobiography and Personal Reminiscences of Major-General Benj. F. Butler* (Boston: A. M. Thayer & Company, 1892), 336; Dufour, *The Night the War Was Lost,* 160–161.
22. *Ibid.*
23. Marshall, ed., *Private and Official Correspondence of Gen. Benjamin F. Butler,* vol.1:365, 367; *Official Records of the War of the Rebellion,* series 1, vol. 6:701; West, *Lincoln's Scapegoat General: A Life of Benjamin F. Butler, 1818–1893,* 119–120.
24. Marshall, ed., *Private and Official Correspondence of Gen. Benjamin F. Butler,* vol.1:382–383.
25. Butler, *Autobiography and Personal Reminiscences,* 355.
26. *Official Records of the War of the Rebellion,* series 1, vol. 6:832–833.
27. West, *Lincoln's Scapegoat General,* 122–123.
28. Richard B. Graham, "Civil War Post Office at Ship Island, MS," *Linn's Stamp News* (March 4, 2002).
29. *Official Records of the Union and Confederate Navies in the War of the Rebellion,* series 1, vol.18:28, 30, 31, 33, 34.
30. *Ibid.,* 35; Loyall Farragut, *The Life of David Glasgow Farragut,* 212; Charles Lee Lewis, *David Glasgow Farragut: Our First Admiral* (Annapolis: U.S. Naval Institute, 1943), 28.
31. Dufour, *The Night the War Was Lost,* 208–209.
32. Edwin B. Lufkin, *History of the Thirteenth Maine Regiment* (Bridgton, ME: H.A. Shorey & Son, Publishers, 1898), chapter 3.
33. *Official Records of the Union and Confederate Navies in the War of the Rebellion* (Harrison, PA: The National Historical Society, 1985), series 1, vol.18:90.
34. *Ibid.,* 14–23; Chester G. Hearn, *Admiral David Glasgow Farragut: The Civil War Years* (Annapolis: Naval Institute Press, 1998), 75–80; *Official Records of the War of the Rebellion,* series 1, vol. 6: 685.
35. *Official Records of the Union and Confederate Navies in the War of the Rebellion,* series 1, vol.18:86, 87, 91; James Parton, *General Butler in New Orleans* (New York: 1864), 213; Edwin C. Bearss, *Historic Resource Study: Ship Island, Harrison County, Mississippi, Gulf Islands National Seashore, Florida/Mississippi* (Denver: 1984) 130–131; *Official Records of the War of the Rebellion,* series 1, vol. 6:707–708.
36. *Official Records of the Union and Confederate Navies in the War of the Rebellion,* series 1, vol.18:131, 132, 133, 362.
37. *Ibid.,* 160; West, *Lincoln's Scapegoat General,* 125.
38. Butler, *Autobiography and Personal Reminiscences,* 366.
39. *Official Records of the Union and Confederate Navies in the War of the Rebellion,* series 1, vol.18:283, 284, 302, 307, 372.

40. Marshall, ed., *Private and Official Correspondence of Gen. Benjamin F. Butler*, vol.1:422–423; West, *Lincoln's Scapegoat General*, 126.
41. *Ibid.*, 423.
42. West, *Lincoln's Scapegoat General*, 127.
43. *Ibid.*, 128; *Official Records of the War of the Rebellion*, series 1, vol.6:716–717; Bearss, *Historic Resource Study: Ship Island*, 143–144.
44. *New Orleans Bee*, May 14, 1862; *Official Records of the War of the Rebellion*, series 2, vol. 3:616–717; vol.5:848–849.
45. Edwin B. Lufkin, *History of the Thirteenth Maine Regiment from Its Organization in 1861 to Its Muster Out in 1865* (Bridgton, ME: 1898), 17–18.
46. *Ibid.*, 28; *Official Records of the War of the Rebellion*, series 1, vol.15:619–620.
47. *Ibid.*, 29.
48. *Ibid.*, 29–30, 112; John M. Stanyan, *A History of the Eighth Regiment of New Hampshire Volunteers in the Civil War of 1861–1865* (Concord, NH: 1892), 121–122.
49. Bearss, *Historic Resource Study: Ship Island*, 155–158.
50. Marshall, ed., *Private and Official Correspondence of Gen. Benjamin F. Butler*, vol. 2:24; *Official Records of the War of the Rebellion*, series 2, vol. 4:105.
51. *Ibid.*, 24; 105; *New Orleans Daily Picayune*, July 3, 1862; Bearss, *Historic Resource Study: Ship Island*, 157.
52. Marshall, ed., *Private and Official Correspondence of Gen. Benjamin F. Butler*, vol. 2:25.
53. Bearss, *Historic Resource Study: Ship Island*, 158.
54. *Ibid.*, 159–160.
55. *Ibid.*, 161, 164; Marshall, ed., *Private and Official Correspondence of Gen. Benjamin F. Butler*, vol. 2:25.
56. *Official Records of the War of the Rebellion*, series 2, vol. 4: 880–881.
57. Bearss, *Historic Resource Study: Ship Island*, 167–168.
58. *Ibid.*, 196–197; *Official Records of the War of the Rebellion*, series 1, vol. 15:590, 613.
59. Andrew M. Sherman, *In the Lowlands of Louisiana in 1863: An Address Delivered by Rev. Andrew M. Sherman at the Forty-second Reunion of the Twenty-third Conn. Regimental Association* (Morristown, NJ: 1908), 10.
60. Bearss, *Historic Resource Study: Ship Island*, 197–198.
61. Marshall, ed., *Private and Official Correspondence of Gen. Benjamin F. Butler*, vol. 2: 461; West, *Lincoln's Scapegoat General*, 202.
62. *Harper's Weekly*, December 1862.
63. *New York Times*, December 19, 1862.

Chapter Three

1. Edwin C. Bearss, *Historic Resource Study: Ship Island, Harrison County, Mississippi, Gulf Islands National Seashore, Florida/Mississippi* (Denver: 1984), 201–203; James G. Hollandsworth, *The Louisiana Native Guards: The Black Military Experience During the Civil War* (Baton Rouge: Louisiana State University Press, 1995), 39.

2. *Ibid.*, 211–212.
3. Bearss, *Historic Resource Study: Ship Island*, 271.
4. *Ibid.*, 213–214; *New Orleans L'Union*, April 14, 1863; Hollandsworth, *The Louisiana Native Guards*, 46–47.
5. Military Record of Colonel Nathan W. Daniels, 74th United States Colored Troops, National Archives and Records Administration RG 94; Special Order Number 384, U.S. War Department, August 27, 1863, National Archives and Records Administration, 74th United States Colored Troops Regimental Papers.
6. *Official Records of the War of the Rebellion* (Harrisburg, PA: The National Historical Society, 1985), series 1, vol. 26, part 1:689; 74th United States Colored Troops Regimental Papers and Muster Rolls and Returns, National Archives and Records Administration, RG 94; Ship Island, Mississippi Post Returns, July 1863, National Archives and Records Administration, Microfilm M-617; U.S. Department of the Gulf, Special Order Number 265, October 23, 1863, National Archives and Records Administration, RG 393; Register of Prisoners Confined at Ship Island, Mississippi, 1862–1870, National Archives and Records Administration, RG 393.
7. Andrew M. Sherman, *In the Lowlands of Louisiana in 1863: An Address Delivered by Rev. Andrew M. Sherman at the Forty-second Reunion of the Twenty-third Conn. Regimental Association* (Morristown, NJ: 1908), Addenda, 36–38.
8. Bearss, *Historic Resource Study: Ship Island*, 219–222; Hollandsworth, *The Louisiana Native Guards*, 80–81.
9. *Official Records of the War of the Rebellion*, series 3, vol. 4:164–165, 214–264; U.S. War Department General Order Number 17, July 7, 1864, 74th United States Colored Troops Regimental Papers, National Archives and Records Administration, RG 94.
10. *Ibid.*, series 1, vol. 34, part 3:331–333, 408–409, 490–492; part 1:212; series 1, vol. 36:409.
11. Bearss, *Historic Resource Study: Ship Island*, 271–274.
12. *Ibid.*, 274–278.
13. John A. Bragg Narrative, Henry S. Halbert Papers, LPR147, Alabama Department of Archives and History.
14. Report of a Medical Inspection, Surgeon F.M. Getty, October 29, 1864, National Archives and Records Administration, RG 249, Letters Received.
15. *Ibid.*, Hartz to Holmstedt, November 21, 1864; *Official Records of the War of the Rebellion*, series 2, vol. 7:1258–1260.
16. Special Inspection Report of the Ship Island Garrison, Lt. Colonel W.D. Smith, October 19, 1864, National Archives and Records Administration, RG 94.
17. Special Inspection Report of the Ship Island Garrison, Lt. Colonel W.D. Smith, January 3, 1865, National Archives and Records Administration, RG 94.
18. *Ibid.*
19. *Ibid.*
20. *Official Records of the War of the Rebellion*, series 1, vol. 61, part 4:819–820, 942; Bearss, *Historic Resource Study: Ship Island*, 296–298.

21. *Ibid.*, series 2, vol. 8:62.
22. *Ibid.*, series 2, vol. 7:1246.
23. Kate Cumming, *Kate: The Journal of a Confederate Nurse*, edited by Richard Barksdale Harwell (Baton Rouge: Louisiana State University Press, 1987), 250-251.
24. James A.P. Braxley and William A. Gibson Narratives, Henry S. Halbert Papers, LPR147, Alabama Department of Archives and History.
25. Cumming, *Kate,* 250.
26. James A.P. Braxley Narrative, Henry S. Halbert Papers.
27. *Official Records of the War of the Rebellion*, series 1, vol. 61, part 1:207-208; Bearss, *Historic Resource Study: Ship Island,* 315-316.
28. Alden M'Lellan, "Vivid Reminiscences of War Times," *Confederate Veteran* (Wilmington, NC: Broadfoot Publishing, 1986) Vol. 14:264-266.
29. William A. Gibson Narrative, Henry S. Halbert Papers, LPR147, Alabama Department of Archives and History.
30. *Official Records of the War of the Rebellion* (Harrisburg, PA: The National Historical Society, 1985), series 2, vol. 8, part 1:156, 490-491, 499, 518.
31. Bearss, *Historic Resource Study: Ship Island,* 321-322.
32. M'Lellan, "Vivid Reminiscences of War Times," *Confederate Veteran* (Wilmington, NC: Broadfoot Publishing, 1986), vol. 14:264-266.
33. W.M. Buster, "Experiences in Escaping Prison Life," *Confederate Veteran* (Wilmington, NC: Broadfoot Publishing, 1986), vol. 15:378.
34. *Official Records of the War of the Rebellion,* series 2, vol. 8, part 1:549.
35. *Ibid.*, 551, 556.
36. Bearss, *Historic Resource Study: Ship Island,* 323-324.

Chapter Four

1. Returns from United States Military Posts, 1800-1916: Ship Island, Mississippi, National Archives and Records Administration, Microfilm M-617; Returns from Regular U.S. Army Infantry Regiments: June, 1821-December, 1916, National Archives and Records Administration, Microfilm M-665.
2. Letters Received, District of Louisiana, Headquarters, Fifth Military District to Headquarters, Department of Louisiana, April 6, 1867, National Archives and Records Administration, RG 393; Edwin C. Bearss, *Historic Resource Study: Ship Island, Harrison County, Mississippi, Gulf Islands National Seashore, Florida/Mississippi* (Denver: 1984), 327-328.
3. Letters Received—1868-1870, Colonel Joseph A. Mower to Commanding Officer, Department of the Gulf, June 16, 1868, National Archives and Records Administration, RG 393.
4. Returns from Regular U.S. Army Infantry Regiments: June, 1821-December, 1916, National Archives and Records Administration, Microfilm M-665.
5. Returns from United States Military Posts, 1800-1916: Ship Island, Mississippi, National Archives and Records Administration, Microfilm M-617; Bearss, *Historic Resource Study: Ship Island,* 329-330.
6. Letters sent 1868-1870, Colonel Joseph A. Mower, Dept. of Louisiana, to Adjutant-General, U.S. War Department, December 14, 1869, National Archives and Records Administration, RG 393; Letters sent 1868-1870, Colonel Charles H. Smith, Dept. of Louisiana, to Military Division of the South, January 24 and February 16, 1870, National Archives and Records Administration, RG 393.
7. Letters sent 1868-1870, Colonel Charles H. Smith, Dept. of Louisiana, to Bvt. Brigadier-General Calvin H. Frederick, Chief Quartermaster, Dept. of Louisiana, March 19, 1870, National Archives and Records Administration, RG 393; Letters sent 1868-1870, Colonel Charles H. Smith, Dept. of Louisiana, to Warden, Arkansas State Penitentiary, Little Rock, Arkansas, March 19, 1870, National Archives and Records Administration, RG 393; Register of Prisoners Confined on Ship Island, Mississippi, 1862-1870, National Archives and Records Administration, RG 393; Letters sent 1868-1870, Colonel Charles H. Smith, Dept. of Louisiana, to Lieutenant-Colonel Edward W. Hincks, National Archives and Records Administration, RG 393.
8. Bearss, *Historic Resource Study: Ship Island,* 354.
9. *Ibid.*, 355-356.
10. *Ibid.*, 357-359.
11. Lieutenant George B. Oldham to Quartermaster-General Montgomery C. Meigs, May 24, 1866, Quartermaster-General Cemeterial Files: Ship Island, Mississippi, National Archives and Records Administration, RG 92.
12. Captain Charles Barnard to Quartermaster-General Montgomery C. Meigs, May 25, 1867, Quartermaster-General Cemeterial Files: Ship Island, Mississippi, National Archives and Records Administration, RG 92.
13. Bearss, *Historic Resource Study: Ship Island,* 362-363.
14. Quartermaster-General Samuel B. Holabird to Major E.R. Kirk, June 25, 1885, Quartermaster-General Cemeterial Files: Ship Island, Mississippi, National Archives and Records Administration, RG 92; Chalmette National Cemetery Superintendent J.A. Commerford to Major E.R. Kirk, July 6, 1885, Quartermaster-General Cemeterial Files: Ship Island, Mississippi, National Archives and Records Administration, RG 92.
15. Chalmette National Cemetery Superintendent J.A. Commerford to Major E.R. Kirk, July 6, 1885, Quartermaster-General Cemeterial Files: Ship Island, Mississippi, National Archives and Records Administration, RG 92.
16. Quartermaster-General Samuel B. Holabird to Major E.R. Kirk, July 18, 1885, Quartermaster-General Cemeterial Files: Ship Island, Mississippi, National Archives and Records Administration, RG 92.
17. Ralph C. Williams, *The United States Public Health Service, 1798-1950* (Washington: 1951), 73-76; *Annual Report of the National Board of Health for Fiscal Year 1882* (Washington: 1883), 18 22.

18. *Annual Report of the National Board of Health for Fiscal Year 1879* (Washington: 1880), 467–468.

19. *Annual Report of the National Board of Health for Fiscal Year 1880* (Washington: 1881), 603.

20. *Annual Report of the National Board of Health for Fiscal Year 1881* (Washington: 1882), 273–274; *Annual Report of the National Board of Health for Fiscal Year 1882* (Washington: 1883), 465–469; Williams, *The United States Public Health Service, 1798–1950* (Washington: 1951), 77–79; *Annual Report of the Surgeon-General of the Marine-Hospital Service of the United States for Fiscal Year 1883* (Washington: 1883), 58–90; *Annual Report of the Supervisory Surgeon-General of the Marine-Hospital Service of the United States for Fiscal Year 1896* (Washington: 1896), 852; *Annual Report of the Supervisory Surgeon-General of the Marine-Hospital Service of the United States for Fiscal Year 1884* (Washington: 1884), 37.

21. *Annual Report of the Supervisory Surgeon-General of the Marine-Hospital Service of the United States for Fiscal Year 1888* (Washington: 1888), 23; *Annual Report of the Supervisory Surgeon-General of the Marine-Hospital Service of the United States for Fiscal Year 1896* (Washington: 1896), 852–853; *Annual Report of the Supervisory Surgeon-General of the Marine-Hospital Service of the United States for Fiscal Year 1889* (Washington: 1889), 111; *Annual Report of the Supervisory Surgeon-General of the Marine-Hospital Service of the United States for Fiscal Year 1891* (Washington: 1891), 46–47; *Annual Report of the Supervisory Surgeon-General of the Marine-Hospital Service of the United States for Fiscal Year 1893* (Washington: 1893), 256–258.

22. *Annual Report of the Supervisory Surgeon-General of the Marine-Hospital Service of the United States for Fiscal Year 1894* (Washington: 1894), 216–218.

23. *Annual Report of the Supervisory Surgeon-General of the Marine-Hospital Service of the United States for Fiscal Year 1907* (Washington: 1908), 96; *Annual Report of the Surgeon-General of the Public Health Service of the United States for Fiscal Year 1916* (Washington: 1916), 133; *Annual Report of the Surgeon-General of the Public Health Service of the United States for Fiscal Year 1917* (Washington: 1917), 97.

24. Bearss, *Historic Resource Study: Ship Island Light House Station, Harrison County, Mississippi, Gulf Islands National Seashore, Florida/Mississippi*, Light House Station section (Denver: 1984), 12–14.

25. Ibid., 31–44.

26. Description of Ship Island Light Station, Site File, National Archives and Records Administration, RG 26; Superintendent of Lighthouses to Commissioner of Lighthouses, October 14, 1930, Bureau of Lighthouses Correspondence File, National Archives and Records Administration, RG 26; Francis Ross Arnold, *America's Lighthouses: Their Illustrated History Since 1719* (New York: Penguin Group USA, 1981), 38; *Notice To Mariners*, Numbers 1–26, Notice Number 1482, March 11, 1950; *Biloxi-Gulfport Daily Herald*, June 28, 1972; *United States Coast Pilot: Gulf Coast, Puerto Rico and Virgin Islands* (Washington: 1958), 111.

27. United States Coast Guard 8th District Files: Ship Island Light Station, Revocable License to Licensee Philip M. Duvic, September 25, 1959; Edwin .C. Bearss, *Historic Resource Study: Ship Island, Harrison County, Mississippi, Gulf Islands National Seashore, Florida/Mississippi*, Light House Station section (Denver: 1984), 61–65; United States Coast Guard 8th District Files: Ship Island Light Station, Announcement of Sale of Ship Island Day Beacon, May 5, 1965; *Biloxi-Gulfport Daily Herald*, June 23 and 28, 1972.

28. *Lighthouse Digest*, May 2000.

29. Lieutenant Edward P. Nones to Chief of Ordnance Adelbert Buffington, Document Number 26478a, June 8, 1901, Ordnance Department General Correspondence: 1894–1913, National Archives and Records Administration, RG 156; Chief of Ordnance Adelbert Buffington to Lieutenant Edward P. Nones, Document Number 26478a, June 14, 1901, Ordnance Department General Correspondence: 1894–1913, National Archives and Records Administration, RG 156.

30. Edwin C. Bearss, *Historic Structure Report: Fort on Ship Island (Fort Massachusetts) 1857–1935, Harrison County, Mississippi, Gulf Islands National Seashore, Florida/Mississippi* (Denver: 1984), 259–260.

31. Ibid., 268, 271–272; Public Law Number 60, Seventy-third Session of the United States Congress, June 15, 1933, National Archives and Records Administration, RG 92, General Correspondence, File Number 602.2; Luther W. Maples to United States War Department, June 25, 1932, National Archives and Records Administration, RG 92, General Correspondence 1922–1935, File Number 680.44.

32. Lieutenant-Colonel M.D. Wheeler, Assistant Quartermaster to Joe Graham Post 119, American Legion, March 7, 1934, National Archives and Records Administration, RG 92, General Correspondence 1922–1935, File Number 602.2; Public Law Number 414, Seventh-Fourth Session of the United States Congress, National Archives and Records Administration, RG 49, Abandoned Military Reservations File: Ship Island; Lieutenant-Colonel M.D. Wheeler, Assistant Quartermaster to Luther W. Maples, November 18, 1935, National Archives and Records Administration, RG 92, General Correspondence 1922–1935, File Number 602.2; Luther W. Maples to Lieutenant-Colonel M. D. Wheeler, Assistant Quartermaster, December 16, 1935, National Archives and Records Administration, RG 92, General Correspondence 1922–1935, File Number 602.2.

33. *Gulfport Daily-Herald*, September 22, 1947.

34. Ibid.

35. *Gulf Islands National Seashore Files*, Ocean Springs, MS.

36. Mrs. Rogers Winter, "The Memorial at Ship Island," *Confederate Veteran* 38:284–286.

Bibliography

Bearss, Edwin Cole. *Historic Resource Study: Ship Island, Harrison County, Mississippi-Gulf Islands National Seashore-Florida/Mississippi.* U.S. Dept. of the Interior, National Park Service: Denver Service Center, 1984.

_____. *Historic Structure Report: Fort on Ship Island (Fort Massachusetts).* U.S. Dept. of the Interior, National Park Service: Denver Service Center, 1986.

Beers, Henry Putney. *French and Spanish Records of Louisiana.* Baton Rouge: Louisiana State University Press, 1989.

Bettersworth, John K. *Confederate Mississippi: The People and Policies of a Cotton State in Wartime.* Baton Rouge: Louisiana University Press, 1943.

Booth, Andrew B. *Records of Louisiana Soldiers and Louisiana Commands.* Vols. 1–3. Spartanburg, SC: The Reprint Company Publishers, 1984.

Boyer, Paul S., ed. *The Oxford Companion to United States History.* New York: Oxford University Press, 2001.

Brown, George W., ed. *Dictionary of Canadian Biography.* Vol. 1. Toronto: University of Toronto Press, 1966.

Burns, Zed H. *Confederate Forts.* Natchez, MS: Southern Historical Publishing Company, 1977.

Calore, Paul. *Naval Campaigns of the Civil War.* Jefferson, NC: McFarland, 2002.

Chamber, Julius. *The Mississippi River and Its Wonderful Valley: Twenty-Seven Hundred and Seventy Five Miles from Source to Sea.* New York: G.P. Putnam's Sons, 1910.

Claiborne, John Francis Hamtramck. *Mississippi as a Province, Territory and State.* Jackson: Power and Barksdale, 1879.

Confederate Veteran. Vols. 1–40. Wilmington, NC: Broadfoot Publishing, 1986.

Coombe, Jack D. *Gunfire Around the Gulf.* New York: Bantam Books, 1999.

Cox, Isaac Joslin. *The Journeys of Rene Robert Cavelier: Sieur de La Salle.* New York: Allerton Book Company, 1906.

Donnelly, Ralph W. *The Confederate States Marine Corps, The Rebel Leathernecks.* Shippensburg, PA: White Mane Publishing Company, Inc., 1989.

Dupratz, M. Lepage. *History of Louisiana.* New Orleans: Pelican Press, Inc., 1947.

Fowler Jr., William M. *Under Two Flags: The American Navy in the Civil War.* New York: W.W. Norton & Company, 1990.

Garraty, John, and Mark C. Carnes. *American National Biography.* Vol. 20. New York: Oxford University Press, 1999.

Garrison, Webb. *The Encyclopedia of Civil War Usage: An Illustrated Compendium of the Everyday Language of Soldiers and Civilians.* Nashville: Cumberland House, 2001.

Geus, Theodor. *The Mississippi.* Lexington: University Press of Kentucky, 1989.

Giraud, Marcel. *A History of French Louisiana.* Vol. 1, *The Reign of Louis XIV, 1698–1715.* Baton Rouge: Louisiana State University Press, 1993.

Green, Arthur E. *Southerners at War: The 38th Alabama Infantry Volunteers.* Shippensburg, PA: Burd Street Press, 1999.

_____. *Too Little, Too Late: Compiled Military Service Records of the 63rd Alabama Infantry, CSA.* Heritage Books, Inc: Bowie, MD, 2001.

Hearn, Chester G. *Admiral David Glasgow Farragut: The Civil War Years.* Annapolis: Naval Institute Press, 1998.

_____. *The Capture of New Orleans 1862.* Baton Rouge: Louisiana State University Press, 1995.

Hollandsworth Jr., James G. *The Louisiana Native Guards: The Black Military Experience During the Civil War.* Baton Rouge: Louisiana State University Press, 1995.

_____. *Pretense of Glory.* Baton Rouge: Louisiana State University Press, 1998.

Howell Jr., H. Grady. *To Live and Die in Dixie: The Third Mississippi Infantry, C.S.A.* Jackson, MS: Chickasaw Bayou Press, 1991.

Latour, Arsene LaCarriere. *Historical Memoir of the War in West Florida and Louisiana in 1814–1815.* Gainesville: University Press of Florida, 1999.

———. *The War in West Florida and Louisiana in 1814–1815.* New Orleans: Historic New Orleans Collection and Gainesville: University Press of Florida, 1999.

Lemore-Jackson, Richard Aubrey. *History of Mississippi.* Vols. 1 & 2. Jackson: Jackson University and College Press of Mississippi, 1973.

Lewis, Charles Lee. *David Glasgow Farragut: Our First Admiral.* Annapolis: United States Naval Institute, 1943.

Logan, William Bryant. *The Smithsonian Guide to Historic America.* New York: Workman Publishing Company, 1989.

Lowry, Robert, and William H. McCardle. *History of Mississippi.* Spartanburg, SC: Reprint Company Publishers, 1998.

Maples, Luther. *Camp Fires of Ship Island.* Gulfport, MS: Gulfport Printing Company, 1957.

McWilliams, Richebourg. *Pierre LeMoyne d'Iberville: d'Iberville's Gulf Journals.* Edited by Gaillard McWilliams. Tuscaloosa: University of Alabama Press, 1981.

Musicant, Ivan. *Divided Waters.* New York: Harper Collins Publishers, 1995.

Page, David. *Ships Versus Shore: Civil War Engagements Along Southern Shores and Rivers.* Nashville: Rutledge Hill Press, 1994.

Riley, Franklin L., ed. *Publications of the Mississippi Historical Society.* Vol. 6. Oxford: Mississippi Historical Society, 1902.

Robertson, James Alexander. *Louisiana under Spain, France and the United States, 1785–1807.* Cleveland: A.H. Clark Company, 1911.

Rowland, Dunbar. *History of Mississippi, Heart of the South.* Chicago: S.J. Clarke Publishing Company, 1925.

———. *A Military History of Mississippi, 1803–1898.* Spartanburg, SC: Reprint Company Publishers, 1988.

———. *Mississippi Provincial Archives, 1763–1766, English Dominion.* Vol. 1. Nashville: Press of Brandon Printing Company, 1911.

Rowland, Dunbar, and A.G. Sanders. *Mississippi Provincial Archives, French Dominion, 1729–1748.* Vol. 4. Revised and edited by Patricia Kay Galloway. Baton Rouge: Louisiana State University Press, 1984.

Scriber, Terry, G. *Twenty-Seventh Louisiana Volunteer Infantry.* Gretna, LA: Pelican Publishing Company, 2006.

Scriber, Terry G., and Theresa A. Scriber. *The Fourth Louisiana Battalion in the Civil War: A History and Roster.* Jefferson, NC: McFarland, 2007.

Speer, Lonnie R. *Portals to Hell: Military Prisons of the Civil War.* Mechanicsburg, PA: Stackpole Books, 1997.

Wagner, Margaret E., ed. *The Library of Congress Civil War Desk Reference.* New York: Simon and Schuster, 2002.

Warner, Ezra J. *Generals in Blue.* Baton Rouge: Louisiana State University Press, 1964.

———. *Generals in Gray.* Baton Rouge: Louisiana State University Press, 1959.

Weaver, C.P. *Thank God My Regiment an African One.* Baton Rouge: Louisiana State University Press, 1998.

Welcher, Frank J. *The Union Army 1861–1865: The Western Theater.* Vol. 2. Bloomington: Indiana University Press, 1993.

West Jr., Richard S. *Lincoln's Scapegoat General: A Life of Benjamin F. Butler, 1818–1893.* Boston: Houghton, Mifflin Company, 1965.

Williams, George F. *The Memorial War Book.* New York: Lovell Brothers Company, 1894.

Woodward, Joseph Janiver (Surgeon, U.S. Army). *Medical and Surgical History of the Civil War.* Vol. 3. Wilmington, NC: Broadfoot Publishing Company, 1990

Microfilm

Descriptive Lists of Confederate Prisoners and Deserters Released on Taking the Oath of Allegiance. Compiled by the Office of the Commissary General of Prisoners. National Archives and Records Administration: M598, Roll 8, Vols. 10–11.

Register of Confederate Prisoners at Ship Island, Mississippi. National Archives and Records Administration: M598, Roll 136, Vol. 406.

Register of Deaths of Prisoners 1862–1865. Compiled by the Office of the Commissary General of Prisoners. National Archives and Records Administration: M598, Rolls 5–7, Vols. 5–6.

Registers of Deaths of Prisoners—Mississippi, Arkansas, and Tennessee 1862–1865. Compiled by the Surgeon General's Office. National Archives and Records Administration: M598, Rolls 10–11, Vols. 18–19.

Periodicals

Biloxi-Gulfport Daily Herald
Natchez Daily Courier
New Orleans Bee
New Orleans Commercial-Bulletin
New Orleans Daily Crescent
New Orleans Daily-Picayune
New Orleans L'Union
New Orleans Times-Democrat
New York Herald
New York Times

Index

Abbay, George F. 291
Abbay, Sidney M. 291
Abby, W.C. 67
Abercrombie, Peter F. 225
Abercrombie, William A. 225
Able, Dan 74
Abothnot, R.B. 401
Abvitton, A.I. 234
Achord, J.C. 234
Acker, J.N. 121
Ackley, John 234
Acree, Alfred W. 121
Acton, J.G. 121
Acton, J.V. 121
Adair, F.M. 291
Adams, A.B. 121
Adams, B.F. 407
Adams, Charles F. 291
Adams, F.H. 407
Adams, Fletcher C. 291
Adams, J.D. 343
Adams, Jesse W. 121
Adams, M. 121
Adams, Monroe C. 291
Adams, Newton A. 121
Adams, S.W. 343
Adams, Samuel 234
Adams, Samuel H. 121
Adams, Spencer 291
Adams, V.P. 343
Adams, W.H. 234
Adams, William 407
Adams, William L. 343
Adams, Zacariah T. 121
Adcock, J.P. 291
Adcock, John C. 121
Addesholt, M. 121
Addington, W. 122
Addison, D.H. 234
Adduck, T.F. 122
Aderton, William 106
Agely, H.K. 122
Agnew, J.W. 291
Agnew, James C. 401
Aiken, E.T. 122
Aiken, Edward 382

Aiken, John D. 382
Ajaley, John 291
Akin, W.D. 401
Alabama, state of 21, 22, 70, 89; congressman from 47; soldiers of 74
Alabama Reserves 70
Albritton, A.J. 234
Albritton, Thomas, citizen 426
Aldridge, J.K. 122
Aldridge, James L. 122
Aldridge, John H. 291
Alexander, A.J. 291
Alexander, E.S. 122
Alexander, G. 234
Alexander, J.J. 291
Alexander, Thaddeus L. 291
Alexander, William 122, 407
Alford, Alexander 292
Alford, William B. 234
Alford, Y.N. 233
Algeo, Charles 343
Algiers, Louisiana 43
Allain, David J. 235
Allain, E.J. 235
Allan, A.D. 122, 343
Allen, A.A. 371
Allen, Albert O. Sr., ordnance sergeant 343
Allen, Clement S. 292
Allen, Columbus H. 235
Allen, D.J. 235
Allen, David J. 235
Allen, George W. 122
Allen, Green B. 122
Allen, Henry H. 371
Allen, Henry Watkins, lieutenant-colonel 25, 27, 28
Allen, Isaac 343
Allen, Lewis T. 106
Allen, Riley 417
Allen, W.F. 235
Allen, W.S. 122
Allen, William 106, 122
Allen, Y.M. 122
Alley, John 225

Allgood, Wyatt 292
Allison, Adam Lafayette 292
Allison, John Davis 292
Allrest, J. 122
Alsbroke, D.M. 407
Alstead, John 225
Althison, J. 343
Ambrose, W. 235
Ambrose, William 235
America, continent of 10
American Legion 96
Ames, Oliver 235
Amite River 14
Amos, J.W. 417
Anderson, A.A. 235, 401
Anderson, A.W. 292
Anderson, C.D. 67, 122
Anderson, C.K. 122
Anderson, Charles D., colonel 417
Anderson, E.L. 401
Anderson, Frank M. 292
Anderson, H.H. 292
Anderson, Henry J. 292
Anderson, I.C. 235
Anderson, J. 12
Anderson, J.C. 235
Anderson, James C. 123
Anderson, John C. 225
Anderson, John P. 123
Anderson, Pvt. Joseph E. 343
Anderson, Lt. 76
Anderson, R.F.B. 123
Anderson, W. 343
Anderson, W.C. 292
Anderson, William 292
Anderson, William D. 292
Anderson, William T. 371
Anding, W.D. 417
Andrew, John Albion, governor 30, 34
Andrews, Albert A. 33, 106
Andrews, Ed. 401
Andrews, George Leonard, brigadier-general 72
Andrews, James H. 106
Andrews, John 106, 426

Andrews, John W. judge, 48, 49, 51
Andrews, M.J. 106
Andrews, Rapson K. 235
Andrews, T.L. 235
Andrews, Wade L. 123
Angel, Daniel W., captain 371
Angle, William J. 292
Anglin, W.H. 123
Annapolis, Maryland 97
Annie, sloop 85, 87
Anselm, Benoit B. 235
Ansley, Henry G. 292
Apalachee River 70
Appalachian Mountains 16
Appomattox Court House, Virginia 77
Archer, C.B. 123
Archer, John H. 292
Archer, Joseph F. 292
Archer, Thomas B. 343
Archibald, C.H. 123
Archibald, Edwin M. 123
Ardis, Abraham P. 382
Ardis, John W. 382
Ardis, William J. 382
Arkansas: state of 10, 81; natives of 70
Arkansas State Penitentiary 81
Armistead, B.B. 123
Armstead, I.M. 123
Armstrong, Charles 106
Armstrong, Elias, mechanic 123
Armstrong, James, captain 123
Armstrong, Stephen Francis 123
Armstrong, William 124
Army of the Gulf (U.S.) 54
Army of the Potomac (U.S.) 40
Arnold, Felix B. 293
Arnold, Felix M. 293
Arnold, Fletcher P. 293
Arnold, Henry 124
Arnold, W.H. 293
Arnold, Wiley F. 293
Aroine, J., mechanic 236
Artus, M., commandant 18
Asben, W.N. 344
Ash, Matt P., hospital steward 293
Ashford, Randolph 344
Ashley, J.H. 293
Ashworth, Jonathan 371
Askew, Clark 344
Askew, Duke 293
Askew, Samuel H. 124
Atkins, Thomas J. 124
Atkinson, James W. 236
Atkinson, John 417
Atkinson, Samuel A. 124
Atlantic Ocean, coast of 31, 35
Atteberry, Charles 401
Atteburg, Charles 236
Aubert, F.H. 124
Aucoin, Franklin 236
Augusta, Maine, mentioned in letter 39
Austin, G.M. 401
Austin, John 225
Auter, Albert F. 293
Auter, Solomon B. 293

Averett, A.M. 124
Averheart, T.M. 124
Avery, William 124
Axis 97
Aycock, R.W. 236
Ayer, B.H. 124
Aymes, O. 236

Baar, J.M. 236
Babb, John 417
Babb, John M. 293
Babel, Benjamin F. 344
Babers, A.J. 293
Babnight, R. 344
Bachelder, James P. 106
Bachelor, J. 124
Bachelor, T.J. 124
Backer, Jacob 344
Backer, John A.C. 344
Badger, John L.T. 344
Badger, William S. 124
Le Badine, frigate 11
Baggett, H.P. 124
Baggett, John D.I. 124
Baggett, Julius C.A. 124
Bailey, J.A. 124
Bailey, J.P. 344
Bailey, Pvt. J. Taylor 125
Bailey, Jeremiah W. 125, 293
Bailey, Robert 407
Bailey, W.G. 125
Bailey, William B. 236
Baily, J.F. 125
Baily, U.J. 125
Baird, H. 293
Bairfield, A.D. 125
Baker, Allen 125
Baker, Beverly 417
Baker, George 236, 417
Baker, George Franklin 125
Baker, Joseph E. 388
Baker, O.H.P. 125
Balcom, Charles 106
Baldock, Richard 344
Baldridge, John S. 293
Baldridge, William 417
Baldwin, John 236
Baldwin, John B. 401
Baldwyn, Ralph P. 125
La Baleine, ship 19
Ball, C. 293
Balson, F.W. 225
Baltimore, Maryland 20
Baltzell, Thomas W. 225
Banc, Louis, captain 15
Bank of New Orleans 50
Bankhead, J. 417
Banks, Nathaniel Prentiss, major-general 51, 53, 54, 55, 56, 57, 58
Banks, Robert 125
Barbee, James D. 344
Barbee, William T. 344
Barber, M. 417
Barberot, Phillip 417
Barker, Edward 388
Barker, John D. 344
Barklay, J.W. captain, 71
Barkley, F.M. 125
Barksdale, C.H. 125

Barksdale, John C. 293
Barksdale, W.B. 125
Barley, I. 125
Barnabus, Gabel 125
Barnard, Charles, captain 85
Barnard, James N. 388
Barnard, John 344
Barnard, John G., brigadier-general 40
Barnes, A.J. 388
Barnes, Calvin 106
Barnes, J. 293
Barnes, John E. 96
Barnes, Thomas J. 125
Barnes, William 407
Barnett, James Madison 125
Barnett, James W. 126
Barnett, S.C. 126
Barnett, William Franklin 126
Barneycastle, Henry 126
Baronne Street, New Orleans 73
Barr, George W. 126
Barr, James M. 126
Barret, John W. 126
Barrett, A.C. 236
Barrett, Alonzo 106
Barrett, Charles C. 236
Barrett, G.D. 126
Barrett, V. 236
Barroll, Charles E. 344
Barron, James P. 126
Barron, John W. 126
Barry, Barry R. 407
Barry, R.F. 407
Barry, William S. 293
Barry's Mississippi Brigade 70
Barstow, Edwin F., captain 79
Baskins, Peter B. 126
Bassett, H. 407
Bassett, John A. 126
Basye, Smith 294
Batchelder, Charles H. 294
Batchelder, James C., citizen 426
Bateman, William 407
Baton Rouge Arsenal 82
Baton Rouge, Louisiana 14, 48, 79; penitentiary at 81
Battery Gladden 70
Battle, R.R., Jr. 126
Baunett, J.C. 237
Baxley, John P. 126
Baxter, W.M. 344
Bay St. Louis, Mississippi 14, 46
Baylor, R.H., surgeon steward 407
Bayogoulas Indians 13
Bazer, Jerry E. 237
Beadle, W.P. 344
Beal, F.M. 294
Beall, James R. 294
Bean, Bartlett M. 126
Bean, Carlostian J. 107
Beard, David J. 127
Beard, J.A. 127
Bearden, J.J. 401
Beas, Thomas 344
Beasley, James 127
Beauchamp, James T. 237
Beaupeurt, J.C.C. 237

Beauregard, Pierre Gustave Toutant, general 41, 45
Becker, John 371
Beckham, T.W. 127
Beckimer, Fred, citizen 426
Beckman, Henry 407
Beckwith, H. 408
Becnel, F. 237
Beeley, T.J. 344
Beftin, Gustav 237
Beggs, James, citizen 426
Beince.A. 418
Belcher, H. 408
Belcher, J.H. 127
Belcher, W.E. 127
Belguard, A. 401
Belk, Simeon T. 294
Bell, A.N., inspector 88, 89
Bell, B.C. 294
Bell, C.W. 237
Bell, Edward 127
Bell, J.R. 294
Bell, J.T. 127
Bell, John W. 127
Bell, Samuel A. 344
Bell, S.W. 127
Bell, William C. 344
Bell, William H. 127
Bell, William J. 294
Belsom, Phil 237
Bemiss, Dr.Samuel M. 89
Benbow, Richard N. 127
Benefield, James A. 127
Benjamin, Judah P., secretary of war (C.S.) 34
Bennett, Alexander 294
Bennett, Fielding 388
Bennett, Joseph 418
Bennett, Joshua S. 294
Bennett, William R. 294
Benson, A. 294
Benson, R.P. 127
Bently, James R. 345
Benton, Thomas 237
Benton, Thomas H. 294
Beornard, J.C. 401
Berdaux, J.W. 127
Berden, William T. 294
Bergere, Sister 19
Bergeron, Omer 237
Bernard, E. 237
Berry, Charles 294
Berry, Harry B. 128
Berry, J.P. 418
Berry, James L. 107
Berry, Seth 294
Berry, William E. 128
Berry, William M. 294
Berryhill, Benjamin F. 345
Bertin, G. 345
Bertin, Gustave 237
Berton, A. 237
Bertram, Henry, colonel 76
Besley, John 128
Best, George M. 128
Betat, Charles 237
Bethia, J.H. 418
Betts, William H. 128
Beville, R.W. 128

Bide, J.H. 128
Bienville, Jean Baptiste Lemoyne, Sieur 11, 12, 13, 14, 15, 16, 17, 18, 19, 86
Biers, L. 371
Big Black River 74
Big Black River Bridge 73
Biggs, Eleazor 294
Biggs, James, citizen 426
Billings, Adonirum J. 107
Billingslea, D.F.C. 294
Billington, John Webster 295
Biloxi Bay 14, 15
Biloxi Indians 14
Biloxi, Mississippi: 23, 41, 85, 87, 91, 97; settlement at 14, 15, 16, 17, 18, 19, 20, 86
Biloxi Rifle Guard 22
Binford, John M. 128
Binford, Peter, assistant surgeon 128
Bird, Carmine S., hospital steward 371
Bird, John C. 295
Bird, Joseph 295
Bird, L. 389
Bird, William F. 107
Bishop, John A. 128
Bishop, John F. 295
Bishop, J. Uriah 128
Bishop, Reuben 128
Bishop, Robert A. 128
Bishop, William 128
Bithune, W.L. 295
Blache, C. 238
Black, Adam 345
Black, Anderson 345
Black, David 295
Black, James P. 408
Black Joker, blockade runner 41
Black, Oliver 107
Black, W.D. 371
Black Prince, ship 36
Blackburn, J.J. 128
Blackburn, James R. 345
Blackburn, T.C. 128
Blackburn, Thomas J. 128
Blackburn, William Pinkney 128
Blackey, Mark 408
Blackman, Theophilus B. 128
Blackshire, W.A. 129
Blackstone, John H. 238
Blackwell, S. 371
Blackwood, Alexander S. 129
Blain, James W. 345
Blair, D.S. 295
Blair, James 129
Blake, Samuel H. 418
Blakely, Robert A. 345
Blakenship, William 129
Blanchard, Robert 295
Bland, Thomas G. 238
Blaney, John J. 225
Blanks, Marble 345
Bledsoe, N.S. 129
Bledsoe, W.H. 345
Bliss, Zenas, major 80, 81
Block, W.H. 372
Blodgett, George, lieutenant 49

Bloom, Joseph, citizen 426
Blundell, J.R. 295
Bobbits, James J. 295
Boman, John F. 129
Bond, J.A. 129
Bond, John Frank 129
Bondaure, Marshall 345
Bonds, J.A. 129
Bonds, S.A. 295
Bonduler, Champ D. 295
Boney, Green L. 295
Bonifay, George 129
Bonner, William 295
Bonnett, P.A. 418
Bonney, John 107
Boone, Samuel D. 129
Booth, William 129
Booth, William S. 238
Booty, A.J., Jr., captain 402
Boozman, H. 295
Borden, Warren L. 107
Borken, Thomas 295
Bosman, Jeff R. 295
Bostick, J.W. 295
Boston Common 31
Boston Harbor 31
Boston, Massachusetts 30, 34, 36
Boswell, James 418
Bouden, Henry 129
Boudreaux, Jules 238
Bourg, T.V. 238
Bourgeois, Adam 238
Bourgeois, Theogene 238
Bourgin, Gustave Adolphe 238
Bovard, William 239
Bovin, R.J. 372
Bowden, Andrew Jackson 239
Bowden, Littlebery B. 296
Bowen, L.M. 239
Bowen, W.H. 418
Bower, Edward L., captain 296
Bowers, James 129
Bowers, T.M. 345
Bowie, John H. 296
Bowler, J.W. 129
Bowles, E. 389
Bowlin, William 225
Bowman, Edwin 129
Bowman, F.W. 239
Bowman, G.S. 130
Bowman, John W. 296
Bowman, William M., captain 239
Bowry, F.B. 239
Box, James R. 130
Box, James Robert 402
Boyd, Henry 239
Boyd, J.C. 130
Boyd, Samuel M. 372
Boydston, Benjamin L. 296
Boyer, Ernest, citizen 426
Boykin, W.C. 296
Boyles, Jesse Ransom 130
Bozeman, Alex C. 296
Bracken, Thomas O. 239
Brackey, Jacob 408
Bradbury, William S. 107
Bradfield, James R. 130
Bardford, J.A. 130
Bradford, J.L., captain 74

Index

Bradford, William L. 345
Bradley, B.G. 372
Bradley, George 107
Bradley, Irwin P. 130
Bradley, James M. 345
Bradley, Jere W. 372
Bradley, John A. 345
Bradley, John W. 345
Bradley, Samuel M. 345
Bradshaw, S. 130
Brady, John 408
Brady, John W. 345
Bragg, B.H. 346
Bragg, J.R. 296
Bragg, John A. 59, 408
Brainard, Herbert T.N. 107
Bramer, Eli 296
Branch, John 130
Branch, Loid 346
Brandon, C.C. 296
Brannin, Seabron R. 130
Brant, Lafayette 107
Brashears, W.F. 239
Brassell, H. 408
Brassfield, Levi 296
Braswell, Eli 130
Braswell, S.S. 296
Bratten, William 346
Braxley, James A.P. 67, 68, 69
Brazell, John D. 130
Brazier, Wyatt 296
Breckinridge Democrat 37
Breckle, John, citizen 426
Breed, A.N. 130
Breed, J.W. 130
Brent, F.C. 130
Brent, W.D. 418
Brest, France 11
Brewer, Drew M.E. 130
Brewer, Edmond H. 131
Brewer, G.W. 296
Brewer, Lucius L. 131
Bridgefort, R.T. 346
Bridgeforth, William M. 296
Bridges, Blackburn 346
Bridges, Parham Plummer 296
Briggs, George 239
Briggs, J.P. 296
Briggs, James H. 296
Brill, Charles 239
Brinberry, John F. 240
Brindal, F. 372
Brinsbergm, F.F. 240
Brinson, William C. 131
Briscoe, Joseph 346
Britton, Rich, pilot 74
Britton, William M. 296
Britton, William S. 297
Broadus, Moses 131
Broadway, Jesse W. 297
Brock, J.W. 418
Brock, M.V. 402
Brock, N.P. 131
Broder, John 240
Brogan, Thomas 408
Brogden, Joseph 240
Brooks, G.E. 131
Brooks, G.L. 131
Brooks, J.E. 389

Brooks, John S. 107
Brooks, William C. 131
Brooks, William E. 107
Brother, John 240
Broughton, A. Benjamin, adjutant 240
Brown, B. 131
Brown, Charles 408
Brown, D.W. 382
Brown, E. 418
Brown, F. 346
Brown, Felix C. 346
Brown, G.W. 346
Brown, George M. 382
Brown, George W. 107, 389
Brown, J.H. 131
Brown, J.W. 346
Brown, James George, citizen 426
Brown, Jeff 297
Brown, Joel M. 226
Brown, John 372
Brown, John, abolitionist 21
Brown, John, fireman 408
Brown, John Mordichai 131
Brown, Oakley 131
Brown, Oliver 21
Brown, Owen 21
Brown, Robert 297
Brown, Ruth Mills 21
Brown, S.T. 418
Brown, T. 297
Brown, W.E. 240, 372
Brown, W.J. 131
Brown, Watson 21
Brown, William 240
Brown, William C. 389
Brown, William R. 297
Brown, William S. 297
Browning, Daniel B. 346
Bruce, A.B. 240
Brunson, William R. 297
Bryan, William F. 132
Bryant, Frank 131
Bryant, J. 132
Bryant, J.W. 132
Bryant, James 408
Bryant, Samuel 132
Buckall, H.H. 389
Buckingham, William Alfred, governor 30
Buckley, J.E. 297
Budershan, Joseph S. 132
Buff, James 389
Buffington, Adelbert, ordnance-chief 94
Buford, William S. 346
Buggs, William 418
Bulger, E.P. 389
Bullen, Randal G. 297
Buller, T.M. 408
Bullock, C.M. 240
Bunch, S. 297
Bunelon, J.C. 132
Buntyn, George M. 132
Burch, John W. 240
Burchmore, F., adjutant 57
Burck, J.W. 132
Burden, Henry C. 346
Burdett, John C. 402

Burgerot, Phillip 418
Burgess, Jerome 418
Burke, A. 132
Burke, Daniel B. 108
Burke, Peter 408
Burkett, Joshua 132
Burkett, Mrs. 426
Burlington, Maine 87
Burnes, Samuel 240
Burnett, E.M. 226
Burnett, J.A. 297
Burney, Marshall D. 132
Burns, James J. 297
Burton, John H. 132
Burton, Thomas 346
Busby, B.F. 408
Busby, S.A. 132
Bush, Albert G. 226
Bush, Allen Henry 226
Bush, Americus B., Jr. 132
Bush, Herbert H. 132
Bush, John E. 132
Bush, Ryan O. 133
Buster, W.M. 76, 77
Butcher, Henry 408
Butler, Andrew 34, 36, 39
Butler, Benjamin Franklin, major-general 30, 31, 34, 35, 36, 37, 38, 39, 40, 41, 42, 43, 45, 46, 47, 48, 49, 50, 51, 53, 54, 55, 56, 86
Butler, Daniel B. 108
Butler, George W. 297
Butler, Sarah 35, 36, 38, 41, 45
Butts, Phillips Adam 133
Buzzell, Solon D. 108
Bybee, F.E. 346
Bybee, James 346
Byers, Lafayette 402
Byrd, J.F. 240
Byrd, James F. 402
Byrd, W.A. 372
Byrne, Edward F.V. 346
Byrnes, William 297

Cabbrett, G.M. 297
Cabbrett, W.N. 297
Cabe, Leander F. 372
Cacey, J.T. 372
Cacey, James M. 372
Cacey, William B. 372
Cadillac, Antoine de la Motte 17
Cady, Timothy 389
Caffee, J.C. 133
Cagle, Henry W. 372
Cailey, William 241
Cain, F.M. 297
Cain, Jessee T. 133
Cain, Thomas 346
Caistis, George 241
Caldwell, C.T. 346
Caldwell, H.D. 297
Caldwell, H.M. 133
Caldwell, M.J. 133
Caldwell, W. 133
Calhoun, B. 389
Calhoun, Evander M. 133
Calhoun, James B. 133, 389
Calhoun, Thomas J. 133
Caliman, Dennis 408

Callaghan, William 346
Callahan, J.W. 133
Callahan, Mathew 418
Callaway, Zachary T. 133
Callender, Curtis B. 402
Calloway, George A. 133
Cameron, Finaly 108
Cameron, Simon, secretary of war (U.S.) 30
Camle, G.S. 108
Camlin, Green B. 347
Camp Chase 30
Camp Street, New Orleans 76
Camp Walker 23
Campbell, A.D. 297
Campbell, Arch, citizen 426
Campbell, Charles Edward 418
Campbell, Daniel W. 133
Campbell, Eugene 241
Campbell, Henry E. 390
Campbell, J.A. 134
Campbell, John A. 134
Campbell, John B. 241
Campbell, Thomas B. 134
Campbell, W.B. 134
Campeen, W.S. 298
Canal Street, New Orleans 50
Canarny, James 134
Canby, Edward Richard Sprigg, major-general 58, 66, 69, 72, 73, 77
Cane, S.P. 134
Canerghton, James B. 134
Canfield, A.R., surgeon 298
Canfield, J.O. 298
Cannan, Stephen 134
Canney, William E. 241
Canon, P.J. 134
Canter, William J. 347
Cape Fear 35
Capps, D.C. 134
Caraway, R.A. 298
Careter, George 241
Carey, F.S. 241
Carle, Thomas 390
Carlee, T.E. 134
Carlen, John G. 134
Carleton, Eugene 298
Carleton, J. 134
Carley, J.T. 418
Carley, John 134
Carley, William 241
Carlisle, E.T. 134
Carlisle, S.B. 134
Carlton, C.B. 372, 402
Carlton, William C. 226
Carmena, Leroy 241
Carmichael, Daniel 298
Carmichael, John 298
Carmichael, John B. 298
Carmichael, John Duncan 134
Carmichael, M.M.C. 298
Carmichael, Michael 298
Carmouche, Alcide 241
Carmonche, Avelaid 241
Carondelet Street, New Orleans 58, 73
Carothers, Richard S. 298
Carpenter, Francis N. 108

Carpenter, Nathan M., captain 134
Carpenter, Thomas, citizen 426
Carr, Cicero A. 298
Carr, E.T. 134
Carr, James D. 298
Carr, John N. 298
Carr, W.S. 134
Carr, William S. 135
Carraway, Lelan 226
Carraway, Richard Thomas Adam 298
Carrington, Algernon S., captain 135
Carrington, John 135
Carrington, Lester 135
Carroll, C.F., citizen telegrapher 426
Carroll, Daniel 135
Carroll, John 298
Carroll, John A. 135
Carroll, John L. 135
Carroll, R. Thomas 135
Carson, Levi C. 108
Carter, Alden G. 108
Carter, Andrew D. 298
Carter, Charles W. 135
Carter, E.L. 135
Carter, H.R. Dr. 89
Carter, James M. 299
Carter, John D. 347
Carter, M.D. 241
Carter, Thomas Miller, colonel 347
Carter, Thomas W. 135
Carter, W.R. 135
Carty, Thomas 241
Carver, Hiram H. 242
Carver, J.R. 347
Case, T.J. 299
Casebolt, Eli 347
Casey, J. 135, 408
Casey, J.M. 373
Casey, Patrick 390
Casey, Patrick, citizen 426
Casey, Rives 347
Casey, W.A. 135
Casey, W.B. 373
Casket Girls 17
Cason, Benton W. 242
Cason, Daniel M. 135
Cass County, Nebraska 77
Cast, Robert 135
Cat Island 9, 12, 19, 20, 21, 24, 27, 28, 86; lighthouse station at 91
Cater, N.S. 299
Cates, John M. 135
Cates, Sewell L. 108
Causey, William H. 299
Cawley, John 135
Cawthorn, Lafayette F. 418
Cawthorn, William J. 418
Cedar Point, Alabama 65
Ceres, steamer 51
Chaddock, Isaac 242
Chaitan, C.B. 135
Chalker, C.A. 390
Chalker, W.D. 390
Chalker, William D. 136
Chalmers, William E., Jr. 136

Chalmette, Louisiana 20, 87, 88
Chalmette National Cemetery 85, 86, 87, 88
Chamber, D. 299
Chambers, James 299
Chambliss, Phil S. 136
Champion, C.C. 299
Champion, James A. 299
Champion, Lorenzo Richard 136
Champlin, A. Parker, Dr. 90
Champlin, George W. 108
Champlin, Hugh L. 347
Chamsen, D. 299
Chance, Alexander 347
Chancellor, William 390
Chancey, R.L. 242
Chandeleur Island 9, 16, 26, 89; light at 25; station at 90
Chandler, D. 242
Chandler, James Samuel 242
Chandler, S.J. 136
Chandler, T.S. 136
Chaney, Levy R. 242
Chapman, A.J. 136
Chapman, B.D. 226
Chapman, E. 136
Chapman, Jacob P. 108
Chapman, John T. 347
Chapman, Robert 402
Chapman, W.A. 136
Chapman, W.T. 136
Chapman, William S. 108
Chappell, Robert W. 299
Chappothine, Charles, citizen 426
Charles Henry, sloop 26
Charleston, South Carolina 21
Charlestown, Virginia 21
Chase, Braddock R. 108
Chase, John 108
Chason, John 226
Chateague, de 17
Chateaumerant, M. Marquis de 11
Chattanooga, Tennessee 68
Che Kiang, transport 51
Cherry, Algernon H. 299
Cherry, John H. 299
Cherry, Joshua 299
Cherry, S.C. 347
Cherry, Thomas J. 299
Cherub, frigate 31
Chesser, T.N. 136
Chestnut, Samuel 136
Chevalier, James L. 299
Chickahominy, sign reading 48
Childers, Paul A. 136
Chisholm, R.G. 299
Chism, Jacob 347
Chresman, J.M. 382
Christian, John M. 136
Christin, Ernest F. 243
Church, Morris 108
City Hall, New Orleans 50
Claffey, James 390
Clampett, William 243
Clancy, P.D. 136
Clapton, David 136
Clarisse, Lighthouse Keeper Peter 91, 96
Clark, A.O. 299

Clark, August C. 347
Clark, D.C. 347
Clark, Daniel 299
Clark, Elijah Thomas 300
Clark, F.P. 136
Clark, J. 136
Clark, James 137
Clark, James M. 300
Clark, John, captain 418
Clark, John Isaac 137
Clark, J.T. 137
Clark, L. 243
Clark, Norman 109
Clark, R.H. 137
Clark, Stephen B. 109
Clark, T.B., telegrapher 418
Clark, T.M. 300
Clark, W.H. 243
Clark, William A. 300
Clarke, Edward A. 226
Clarke, J.T. 137
Clarke, James I. 137
Clarke, William L. 243
Clawson, William M. 300
Clay, William H. 402
Clayton, Webster Henry 137
Clayton, William T. 226
Cleary, Inspector 87
Clements, A. 137
Clements, A.R., ordnance sergeant 137
Clements, Charles 137
Clements, J.M. 418
Clements, Joshua W. 137
Clemons, Henry N. 347
Cleveland, Charles Boarman, adjutant 347
Cleveland, President Grover 89
Cleveland, J.H. 137
Clewell, Frank C., adjutant 348
Clifford, Charles F. 300
Clifford, George T. 137
Clifford, J.D. 348
Clifton, William 300
Cline, Henry 348
Clinton, W. 137
Closson, Joel 109
Coast Survey (U.S.) 38
Coats, William P. 300
Cobb, John N. 137
Cobb, T.M. 402
Cobb, William 137
Coburn, S.A. 348
Coburn, Stanley D. 137
Cochran, Sir Alexander, admiral 20
Cochran, M. 348
Cockerel, J.M. 300
Cockrell, F.M., brigadier-general 70
Cockrell, L.D. 137
Cockrell, T.J. 243
Cockrell, W.D. 348
Cody, William A. 243, 373
Coff, W. 243
Cogan, James, citizen 427
Cogburn, Samuel H. 137
Coggins, V.S. 300
Cohen, Arthur M. 382

Cohen, J.H., paymaster clerk 408
Coker, J.L.F. 300
Coker, John 138
Coker, Thomas 138
Colburn, C.C. 138
Colburn, W.J. 300
Colby, F.M. 138
Cole, Pvt. H.H. 382
Cole, J.S. 300
Cole, Marquis L., Jr., captain 300
Coleman, Abner N. 138
Coleman, C.F. 138
Coleman, W.S. 138
Coleson, D.R. 243
Colley, John 348
Colley, Robert N. 109
Collins, G.W. 138
Collins, James R. 300
Collins, Patrick W. 348
Collins, Paul William 243
Collum, J.M. 138
Columbus, Mississippi 71
Colson, Aaron 109
Comeau, Louis O. 243
Comfort, Charles L. 243
Commerford, J.A., superintendent 87, 88
Company of the Indies 19
Compton, J.W. 348
Coney, W.C. 138
Confederate States of America 22
Confederate Veteran, magazine 55
Conklin, James W. 300
Connally, John W. 138
Connecticut, state of 30, 33
Connelly, William 390
Conner, John M. 300
Conner, Samuel P. 373
Conner, Stanfield 348
Conners, Michael 390
Connolly, James 391
Conold, R.O. 138
Constitution, steamer 31, 32, 34, 37
Cook, J.C. 382
Cook, J.R. 138
Cook, Marion 300
Cook, William 244
Cook, William Brown 300
Cook, William C. 138, 244
Cooke, Matthew 348
Coolidge, Calvin, president 96
Coon, John 373
Cooney, John, citizen 427
Cooper, J.B. 244
Cooper, Jesse Byrd 418
Cooper, Joseph 138
Cooper, L.L. 301
Cooper, R.L. 301
Cooper, Samuel, adjutant-general 23, 24, 28
Cooper, Wesley A. 138
Cooty, Thomas 244
Copeland, Eugenius W. 138
Copeland, Hilliard A. 138
Copeland, J.D. 139
Corbett, Matthew 391
Corcom, John 244
Corinth, Mississippi 45

Corkern, John 244
Corkery, J.J. 348
Corley, P.J. 139
Corn, James 301
Corney, James B. 348
Corntings, J.B. 139
Corps d'Afrique 56
Corps of Artillery (C.S.) 27
Corps of Engineers (C.S.) 28
Corson, Levi S. 109
Cort, J.B. 139
Cortiss, George 244
Cosby, Pvt. 139
Costello, John C. 244
Couisinard, Charles 244
Coulter, E.D. 301
Coulton, N.J. 301
Council, John Cecil 226
Council of Commerce of Louisiana 18
Courcey, J.W. 244
Courtney, Henry S. 244
Courtney, William 408
Cousins, Richard M. 244
Cowan, James J., captain 301
Cowan, Ludwell B., Jr. 301
Cowan, Warren 301
Coward, James A. 382
Cowart, Alford Johnson 139
Cowen, Mrs. 427
Cox, Austin 301
Cox, Daniel C. 301
Cox, F.N. 301
Cox, G.E.G. 382
Cox, J.L. 244
Cox, James 402
Cox, James E. 139
Cox, John J. 244
Cox, Taylor 139
Cox, Thomas J. 139
Cox, Willie H. 301
Coy, James A. 139
Coyle, W.H. 244
Cozby, N.W. 139
Cozzens, Richard M. 245
Craddock, Benjamin F. 139
Craddock, L. 391
Craig, Robert D. 139
Crain, Joseph 139
Craine, John 140
Crane, A.J. 373
Crane, William J. 140
Cranfield, W.G.S. 140
Crans, Edward 109
Craps, P. 140
Craven, John 140
Craven, Thomas T., captain 38
Crawford, H.A. 140
Crawford, J.N. 301
Crawford, James G., captain 373
Crawford, John 245
Crawson, B.C. 140
Crayon, William 245
Creed, Cornelius 301
Creekmore, Henry Clay 402
Creel, B. 301
Creel, John W. 140
Cregg, R. 140
Crenshaw, A.D. 301

Crenshaw, James Arnet 140
Crenshaw, M.V., captain 140
Crenshaw, William L. 140
Creole, steamer 46
Cresswell, R.W. 301
Crews, Frank L. 140
Crews, Henry C. 301
Crickenones, H.C. 245
Crider, Henry 140
Crimson, John 348
Crocker, W.S. 140
Crockett, B.F. 245, 373
Crole, J.A. 140
Crooks, L.M. 140
Crosby, Daniel 419
Crosby, John 140
Crosby, William 140
Cross, Albion P. 109
Cross, J. Wesley 140
Cross of the Order of St. Louis 14, 18
Crouch, Charles 74
Crow, G.L. 301
Crow, J.A. 140
Crowell, Sanford 109
Crowell, Silas T. 109
Crowson, Zachariah C. 140
Crozat, Antoine, Marquis du Chatel 17, 18
Crump, Robert W. 245
Crumpton, M.M. 141
Crune, W.J. 141
Cruse, R.M. 348
Cruther, G. 348
C.S.S. *A.G. Brown* 28
C.S.S. *Arrow* 26
C.S.S. *Florida* 29
C.S.S. *Grey Cloud* 25, 28
C.S.S. *Ocean Springs* 28
C.S.S. *Oregon* 24, 25, 26, 28
C.S.S. *Selma* 59
C.S.S. *Swain* 25
C.S.S. *Tennessee* 59
Culberson, James 141
Culbertson, C.W. 245
Culbertson, John T. 301
Cullan, Hugh 391
Culpepper, J.B. 141
Culpepper, James F., captain 382
Cummings, Dennis Flynn 141
Cummings, Kate, nurse 67
Cummings, Pvt. Thomas 141
Cummins, S. 141
Cunelon, S. 391
Cunningham, James H. 348
Cupps, R.W. 302
Curl, Cullin 226
Currey, I.M. 245
Currin, S. 109
Curry, John M. 245
Curtis, Capt. 33
Curtis, J.A. 302, 373
Curtis, J.W. 302
Curtis, John Robert 141
Curtis, S.N. 302
Curtiss, W.H. 302
Cushing, Ira W. 109
Cutts, R.W. 302

Dabney, T.G. 302
Dabney, William Presley T. 302
Daggett, J. 348
Dahm, Michael 245
Daigle, Aristide 245
Daigre, Aristide 246
Daigree, Aristide 246
Dailey, William G. 141
Daily, W.F. 141
Daimand, Pvt. F. 246
Dale, Aaron H., citizen 427
Dale, John D. 348
Dalton, Colby T. 391
Dalton, Perry W. 141
Dana, Napoleon Jackson Tecumseh, major-general 77
Danfield, John 409
Danico, George E. 109
Daniel, Christopher Columbus 302
Daniel, D. 419
Daniel, William 226
Daniels, C.C. 302
Daniels, Henry 409
Daniels, Hiram Martin 349
Daniels, Lawson 419
Daniels, Nathan W., colonel 55, 56
Dannaberry, A.C. 349
Danneburg, A.C. 141
Danner, A.C., captain 70
Dansby, A. 141
Danzey, S.W. 141
Daprie, O.P. 246
Darby, Thomas J. 226
Dark, R.H. 349
D'Armond, Frank Kenneth 246
Datin, William S. 302
Daudrille, John E. 302
Daudrille, William J. 302
Daugherty, A. 141
David, Charles King 246
David, Isaac Johnson 246
David, Josiah R. 109
David, Marks 349
Davidson, Henry 141
Davidson, John 349
Davidson, John W. 409
Dauphin Island 12, 16, 17, 18
Davis, Albert 349
Davis, C.H., citizen 427
Davis, C.J. 373
Davis, C.J., sergeant 302
Davis, Capers L. 302
Davis, Chesley J. 373
Davis, Edward L.H. 302
Davis, Ellis Fairbanks 227
Davis, G.W. 409
Davis, Gales A. 302
Davis, George 303
Davis, Green H. 303
Davis, H.C. 142
Davis, H.H. 383
Davis, Henry M. 303
Davis, Hugh H., Sr. 246
Davis, Hugh L. 419
Davis, J., citizen 427
Davis, J.C. 349
Davis, J.P. 303

Davis, J.T. 142
Davis, J.W. 142
Davis, James J. 303
Davis, Jefferson 142
Davis, Jefferson: president 22, 23, 24, 30, 51, 77, 97; secretary of war (C.S.) 20
Davis, John Chappel 246
Davis, John D. 142
Davis, John E. 142
Davis, John P. 142
Davis, John W. 303
Davis, Joseph C. 142
Davis, Joshua D. 303
Davis, Josiah R. 109
Davis, Luther 303
Davis, O. 246
Davis, R.L., citizen 427
Davis, Thomas J. 303
Davis, W.A., Jr. 142
Davis, W.B. 142
Davis, William 246
Davis, William C. 349
Dawson, Benjamin F. 402
Dawson, William T. 303
Day, B.M. 246
Day, Elbert F. 349
Day, John H. 247
Day, John M. 402
Day, William 391
Day, William O. 303
Dayton, Jackson 373
Dean, J.F. 383
Dean, William 392
Dear, Hardy C. 303
Dearing, James R. 349
Dearing, Jesse 349
Dearman, S. 142
Deas, Francis H. 303
Deas, Slater Allen 303
Deason, John 142
Deats, Conrad 349
DeBerry, W.S. 142
Decoration Day 87
Dedlake, James William 303
Deer Island 14
Dees, J.A. 142
DeFerat, G., citizen 427
DeJames, C.R. 142
DeKay, George 47, 48, 49
de la Fosse, frigate 17
Delery, I.D. 247
Delery, W.S. 142
Dell, William 349
DeLoach, S. Wesley 142
Delorme, Henry B. 383
Democratic National Convention 21
Demony, William 143
Demouliin, Augustin 247
Denley, John 303
Dennis, James 143
Dennis, Patrick C. 143
Dennison, J.W. 303
Denson, James N. 303
Dent, Richard H. 143
Denton, William M. 303
Denty, J.M. 143
Denwitt, J.A. 143

Department of Alabama, Mississippi and East Louisiana (C.S.) 72
Department of Arkansas (U.S.) 58
Department of Louisiana (U.S.) 80, 81
Department of New England (U.S.) 30
Department of the Gulf (U.S.) 35, 39, 41, 50, 51, 54, 55, 56, 58, 79, 84, 85
Deshazo, T.L. 143
Desport, H. 409
Devaney, Martin 392
DeVaughn, John 143
Devinney, James Louis 349
Dewart, J.D. 247
Diamond, John 409
Diamond, William A. 143
D'Iberville, Pierre Lemoyne 9, 10, 11, 12, 13, 14, 15, 16, 17, 86
Dicheny, Francis 247
Dicheny, H. 247
Dickens, Hampton 143
Dickens, R.D. 303
Dickins, J.N. 143
Dickinson, B.L. 143
Dickson, John B. 247
Dickson, John J. 227
Dieherman, Joseph 247
Dieman, J. 247
Dill, Elijah O. 402
Dillard, Allan 303
Dillard, Robert T. 349
Dillard, William J. 419
Dimitry, Theodore J. 247
Dinsmore, Orin A. 109
Diring, J.S. 349
Dismukes, G.W. 143
District of South Alabama (U.S.) 65
Division of West Mississippi (U.S.) 58
Dixon, Robert 349
Dixon, William P. 247
Dodds, Charles A. 143
Dodge, John, coal heaver 409
Dodge, L.J., citizen 427
Dodson, Benjamin G. 349
Dodson, G.W. 143
Dog Keys 87
Dog River 28
Doggett, George W. 143
Doherty, Peter 247
Doherty, Stephen C. 247
Dolife, Rufus F. 419
Dolife, S. 419
Dollar, Elisha 143
Dollar, W.H. 144
Dominick, J.L. 144
Dominick, W.D. 144
Donahue, J.K. 409
Donald, Henry 304
Donald, William 144
Donaldsonville Cannoneers 24
Donehue, Barney A. 304
Donnell, W.P. 304
Donnelly, J., citizen 427
Donovan, David S. 304
Donovan, Joseph T. 350

Donovan, Michael 392
Dorgan, James 110
Dorgan, John 409
Dorris, E.B. 402
Dorsey, George H. 304
Dorsey, George W. 304
Dorsey, William H. 350
Doss, F. 144
Dotson, James L. 304
Dotson, John H. 304
Doty, J.H. 350
Douay, Father Anastase 11, 13
Dougherty, A.R. 248
Dougherty, J.M. 304
Douglas, Albert B. 304
Douglas, Andrew J. 350
Douglas, S.W. 144
Douglas, Stephen Arnold 21
Douglas, W. 403
Douglas, W.B. 409
Douglas, Walton 144
Douglas, William E. 144
Douglass, James B. 350
Dow, Neal, brigadier-general 50, 51; colonel, 45, 46
Dowling, J.C. 144
Dowling, W.T. 144
Downey, John 144
Downey, William J. 144
Downing, Daniel Whitaker 304
Downing, W.B. 304
Downs, Willis A. 144
Doyle, Daniel 45
Doyle, Daniel, citizen 427
Drafton, Harrison 110
Drake, F. 373
Drake, John 373
Drake, N.B. 350
Draper, J. 144
Draper, P.M. 144
Driver, W.T. 144
Drummond, W.H. 144
Drummonds, Benjamin F. 145
Drumsky, J. 409
Dry Tortugas 57, 65
Duarte, D. 419
Duberry, Thomas 145
DuBoise, C.B. 145
Duboise, Charles 110
Dubois, Henry, citizen 427
Dubose, L.L. 304
Duchine, Loran, citizen 427
Ducker, John H. 373
Duffie, E.W. 304
Duffy, C. 419
Duffy, Robert 392
Duggan, Patrick 145
Duggans, Thomas 227
Duggar, Francis James 227
Duggar, Jonathan Wesley 227
Dugger, Thomas O. 227
Duite, W.G.B. 145
Duke, J.H. 145
Dumas, E., citizen 427
Dunaway, Jesse M. 145
Duncan, C. 403
Duncan, David W. 373
Duncan, Johnson Kelly: brigadier-general 41; colonel 27, 28, 29

Duncan, Rhodes 145
Duncan, Thomas A. 392
Duncan, William 374
Dunklin, Joseph C. 66, 67, 68, 145
Dunlap, Ezekiel H. 145
Dunn, J.A. 145, 304
Dunn, John B. 145
Dunn, John Levi 350
Dunn, Michael 409
Dunn, policeman 50
Dunn, William J. 145
Dunn, William L. 248
Dunnam, E.C. 145
Dunnard, F.M. 145
Dunnaway, Jesse W. 145
Dunoy, R.F., citizen 427
DuPratz, Antoine Simon Le Page, quote of 79
Dupuy, Paul Adonis 248
Durand, Joseph, citizen 427
Durden, James F. 419
Durell, Henry E. 110
Durham, Dewitt Clinton, captain 304
Durrett, N.B. 145
Durrive, Ed, major 70
Duvall, William W. 374
Duvic, Philip M. 93
Duvio, Octave 248
Dwyer, Ellis 374
Dykes, James C. 305
Dysart, J. Sprague, ordnance sergeant 350

Eaken, Moses R. 305
Earl, Silas 305
Earle, Joseph W. 110
Early, William G. 145
East, Benjamin R. 145
East Pascagoula, Mississippi 56, 65
East Pass, Santa Rosa Island 41
East Point 46
East Ship Island 97
Easten, Edward R., citizen 427
Eastern Bay State Regiment 34
Eastford, Frank 350
Eastman, Daniel E. 110
Eaton, Alfred 350
Eaton, Edward 350
Eaton, Jeremiah, Sr. 350
Eaves, S.G. 305
Eaves, William 305
Echols, Benson W. 146
Echols, John H., lieutenant-colonel 146
Edgar, A.A. 146
Edgar, H. 146, 409
Edgar, J. 146
Edgard, John H. 350
Edings, S.A. 146
Edmonds, R.S. 146
Edmonds, S.P., captain 97
Edmondson, Charles L., captain 350
Edmundson, J. 146
Edwards, Alva C. 146
Edwards, Benjamin 146
Edwards, Benjamin C. 305
Edwards, Charles, citizen 427

Edwards, J. 248
Edwards, J.F. 305
Edwards, John J. 305
Edwards, T.B. 248
Edwards, W. 146
Edwins, A.W. 305
Eggleston, Lewis H. 110
Eighteenth New York Battery 51
Eighteenth New York Cavalry 72
Eighth New Hampshire Infantry 35
Eighth Vermont Infantry 35, 45
Eisland, George W. 146
Elam, J.W. 146
Elam, John F. 248
Elam, T.A. 305
Elden, Peter 409
Eldridge, Elijah T. 305
Eldridge, George L. 305
Elfair, Eugene 248
Ella, ship 80
Ellen, W. 305
Ellett, H.T., Jr. 305
Elliott, Charles 146
Elliott, H. 392
Elliott, J.M. 146
Elliott, Kinchen C. 374
Elliott, Samuel J. 146
Elliott, William H. 350
Ellis, Benjamin Franklin 147
Ellis, E. 147
Ellis, George W. 305
Ellis, J., hospital steward 147
Ellis, J.F. 147
Ellis, John W. 305
Ellis, S.L. 147
Ellis, Thomas J. 147
Ellison, Samuel 147
Elloyne, Larry 305
Ellzy, John E. 305
Elmore, Mark 227
Elmore, Thomas J., captain 305
Elmwood, Nebraska 77
Elysian Fields Street 73
Elysian Fields Street Depot, New Orleans 73
Emmerson, F.H. 147
Endy, R. 374
Endy, W.R. 374
England 20
England, Ambrose D. 350
English, Alfred 147
Enochs, E.B., captain 305
Enochs, J.B., captain 306
Enzor, Henry 147
Epler, Rufus 224
Erickson, John 306
Erskins, J. 306
Erskins, William 248
Ervin, J.H. 306
Erwin, J.A. 350
Essan, W.J. 248
Essels, Andus 147
Essex, frigate 31
Essman, Charles E. 147
Estes, Benjamin T., captain 403
Etheredge, J.W. 147
Etheredge, S.E. 147
Ethcredge, W.J. 147

Etheridge, E.T. 147
Eubanks, J.P. 147
Euzon, A. 147
Evans, Fielden 148
Evans, Henry J. 350
Evans, John T. 148
Evans, Thomas 148
Everett, Capt., battery of 41
Everett, J.C. 306
Everett, Miles 227
Everett, T.J. 306
Evers, David K. 227
Ewing, George S. 350
Ewing, J. 148
Exodus, negro citizen 427
Ezell, G.W. 148

Faber, Phillip 148
Fagan, Edward A. 148
Fagan, James 350
Fagan, Michael 110
Fails, G.B. 148
Fair, A.J. 148
Fair, G.W. 148
Fairbanks, Erastus, governor 30
Fairchild, J.F. 248
Fairley, Hugh S. 306
Fairman, Julien O. 306
Fall, Isaac R. 110
Fanchee, U. 249
Farber, Phillip 148
Farley, P. 148
Farley, Robert J. 148
Farley, Thaddeus 350
Farmer, J.H. 383
Farmer, T.J. 148
Farmer, W.C. 148
Farnott, S. 249
Farr, James L. 148
Farragut, David Glasgow, captain 31, 34, 36, 37, 38, 40, 41, 42, 43, 45, 86
Farragut, N.G. 419
Farrell, John 249
Farrinas, William 149
Farrington, J.D. 149
Farrior, James L. 149
Farris, W. 351
Fassett, J.D. 392
Faucher, J. 249
Faulk, J.P. 149
Faulk, W.W. 149
Faulkner, Larkin C. 149
Faulkner, Richard 149
Faur, J.J. 149
Faust, Samuel 392
Fauville, Edwin K. 306
Favrot, St. Clair 249
Fayssoux, C.I., captain 76
Fazende, Numa 249
Fecel, Jules N. 249
Feldue, A.G. 249
Felkins, William M. 392
Fellows, Samuel 249
Fennelly, W.A. 403
Fenner, James W. 224
Fentrall, W.E. 351
Fentrell, William E. 149
Ferdon, George W. 110

Ferguay, Calvin D. 149
Ferguson, A.J. 149
Ferguson, J.M. 149
Ferguson, S.P. 306
Ferguson, W.H. 403
Fernald, Joseph R. 110
Ferrell, Solomon L. 403
Ferriott, H. 249
Fettus, Jesse, captain 79
Fielder, J.R. 306
Fields, John C. 149
Fields, Jonathan G. 351
Fifteenth Maine Infantry 35, 85
Fifth Military District (U.S.) 79, 85
Fifty-Second Massachusetts Infantry 51
Fikes, T. 149
Finch, P.A. 149
Fincher, A.M. 149
Fincher, Elijah 149
Fincher, J.T. 149
Fincher, P.H. 149
Finchols, A. 149
Finley, B.D. 306
Finley, Francis 409
Finley, James 150
Finley, Patrick 150
Finley, W. 306
First District Lock-Up, New Orleans 50
First Louisiana Heavy Artillery 27
First Maine Artillery Battery 45
First Mississippi Light Artillery 70
First Missouri Cavalry 71, 74
Fisher, Archibald 306
Fisher, Belle 58
Fisher, T.L. 392
Fisher, William H. 351
Fitzgerald, A.C. 150
Flack, A.P. 351
Flanagan, F.L. 150
Flavin, James 249
Flehan, C. 409
Flemens, F.A. 249
Fleming, H.S. 150
Fleming, James 306
Fleming, James B. 351
Fleming, John G. 306
Fleming, Robert P. 419
Flemming, Aden Lucius, captain 419
Fletcher, T. 351
Fletcher, Thomas J. 351
Fletcher, William Helveston 306
Flincher, E. 150
Flint, F.M.C. 306
Florida: coast of 15, 31; state of 21, 22, 96; territory of 11, 16
Florida Keys 31
Flourney, Peter C., colonel 351
Floyd, F. 306
Floyd, John A., captain 150
Fluker, J.F. 392
Fluker, J.S. 150
Fly, Alfred W. 110
Flynn, Dennis 409
Flynn, J. 306
Folkes, Augustus A. 306

Follansbee, George R. 110
Forbes, Alexander Ambrose 249
Force, Francis M. 150
Ford, Ben 249
Ford, Benjamin C. 393
Ford, Thomas 110
Forestier, Urbin 250
Forshee, J.N. 150
Fort Blakely 68, 69, 70, 71, 76, 77
Fort Gaines 65, 67, 69
Fort Jackson 31, 35, 37, 40, 41, 42, 43, 45, 46, 50, 56, 81
Fort Jefferson 57, 65
Fort Louis 19
Fort Macomb 45, 46, 58
Fort Maurepas 14, 16
Fort Massachusetts 65, 80, 81, 84, 89, 94, 96, 97
Fort McHenry 20
Fort Pickens 35
Fort Pike 46, 56, 57, 58, 79, 80, 81
Fort St. Louis de la Mobile 17
Fort St. Philip 31, 35, 37, 40, 41, 42, 43, 45, 46, 81, 96
Fort Sumter 23
Fort Twiggs 27, 28
Fortenberry, John 419
Fortenberry, John T. 307
Fortieth United States Infantry 80
Fortlouis, Leopold, driver 250
Fortlouis, Michel Louis 250
Fortner, Wiley 393
Fortress Monroe 31, 34
Foss, Samuel F. 110
Foster, James 374
Foster, Jesse M. 250
Foster, N.H. 250
Foster, Richard 351
Foster, William H. 250
Fountain, H.T. 150
Fourteenth Maine Infantry 35
Fourth Louisiana Infantry 24, 25
Fourth Massachusetts Light Artillery 31
Fourth Wisconsin Infantry 35
Fowler, D.W. 150
Fowler, Orrin 111
Fowler, T.A. 403
Fox, J.T. 307
Frady, John J. 374
Frails, G.B. 150
Fraler, H.T. 409
Fralick, J.H. 409
France 10, 13, 14, 15, 16, 17, 18, 19, 20
Frances, W. 374
Francis, John 393
Franklich, Thomas 409
Franklin, W.R. 374
Franklin, William E., assistant surgeon 351
Franks, Isham D. 374
Franks, J.D. 374
Frasier, E.P. 150
Frater, John W. 419
Fray, James M. 351
Frazier, Alex 410
Frazier, B.F. 410
Frazier, J. 307

Frazier, James H. 307
Frazier, Stephen 351
Frazier, W. 410
Frederick, A. 419
Frederick, Calvin H., brevet brigadier-general 81
Freeman, Frederick 351
Freeman, J.W. 307
Freeman, James H., artificer 307
Freeman, John 150
Freeman, Newton 150
French, Charles Hannibal 111
French, Jonas H., colonel 34
French, Robert 25
French, Robert, citizen 427
French Quarter, New Orleans 45, 54
Fridge, John D. 250
Friend, J.B. 351
Friends of Gulf Islands National Seashore 93
Frying Pan Shoals 35
Fulcher, James B. 374
Fulford, J.B. 150
Fuller, Ambus J. 307
Fuller, Levett, negro citizen 427
Fuller, Robert R. 307
Fuller, Thomas K. 351
Fuller, Thomas S. 150
Fuller, W.D. 150
Fuller, William 307
Fuller, William C. 150
Fulmer, W.F. 150
Fulton, William B., captain 150

Gabble, J. 250
Gaines, D. 251
Gallagher, C.W., captain 307
Gallaspy, Garland M., captain 307
Gallaway, Eli 151
Gallaway, George W. 251
Gallespie, Wesley 151
Galloway, Eli 151
Galloway, Francis M. 151
Galloway, R.C. 151
Gamble, W.T. 151
Gammell, John W. 151
Gammons, Samuel B. 227
Ganett, J.S. 251
Gansolus, Abner 111
Gantray, Benjamin J. 151
Gantray, William T. 151
Gardable, E. 419
Gardiner, F. 410
Gardiner, Richard H. 251
Gardner, Richard H. 251
Garner, C.D. 307
Garner, E.T. 307
Garner, John 151
Garner, J.P. 307
Garner, W.J. 419
Garrett, H.H. 151
Garrett, Isaiah, 251
Garrett, J.F. 151
Garrett, J.W. 151
Garrett, T.L. 374
Garris, William A. 151
Garrison, Andrew J. 151
Garrison, Ebonezar 419

Garrison, James B. 307
Garrity, Patrick 151
Gaspard, Eugene, citizen 427
Gasque, Wilson H. 251
Gatchell, Roswell E. 111
Gately, Thomas 251
Gates, Elijah, colonel 70, 74, 351
Gaudin, C.A. 251
Gautreau, Richard 251
Gay, Andrew Hynes 251
Geary, James 251
General Banks, steamer 56
Genine, Patrick 111
Genright, John 151
Gentry, Thomas J. 352
Gentry, W. 352
George, James M. 393
George, King II 20
George, Paul R., captain 34, 37, 39
Georgia, state of 21, 22, 24
Gerard, Joseph W. 252
German, William T. 352
Gerold, Thomas 420
Gertrude, Sister 19
Getty, F.M., surgeon 63; report of 64
Ghent, Belgium 20
Gholson, Samuel Jameson, attorney 22
Gholston, Thomas Marion 151
Gibbons, Seth 307
Gibbs, A.W. 151
Gibson, C. 152
Gibson, Demetrious D. 307
Gibson, Edward M. 111
Gibson, Elias P. 393
Gibson, Emanual Mercer 224
Gibson, Franklin 374
Gibson, J. 352
Gibson, Stephen 374
Gibson, William A. 67, 71, 307
Giddings, J.S. 383
Giddings, Job M. 383
Giddings, Peter J. 383
Giddings, Thomas G.W. 383
Giddings, W.B. 352
Giddons, P. 152
Giddons, W.C. 152
Gieger, Jesse, Jr. 307
Gihon, John H., assistant surgeon 57, 58, 64
Gilbert, B.T. 420
Gilbert, J. 307
Gilbert, John 152
Gilbert, William 111
Gilder, Joseph 152
Gill, Charles 152
Gilland, James P. 152
Gilles, Elijah M. 308
Gillespie, James A. 374
Gilliland, A.J. 152
Gilliland, John 410
Gillis, Marcellus, citizen 427
Gillmore, T.H. 352
Gilmore, A.A. 152
Gilmore, J.M. 152
Gilmore, J.W. 152
Gilpin, Thomas B. 252
Girard, J. 252

Girault, John M. 308
Girault, Matthew A. 308
La Gironde, ship 15, 19
Gittleens, James 352
Glass, M. 152
Glass, W.R. 152
Glasscock, James P. 252
Glaze, J.B. 403
Glaze, J.M. 152
Gleason, J.W. 393
Glenn, Adolphus 152
Glenn, John M. 352
Glidwell, J.H. 375
Glosson, James M. 152
Gober, Elijah C. 308
Godforth, John W. 375
Godfrey, John, assistant surgeon 89
Godfrey, T.W. 308
Godley, James 308
Godsey, Madison M. 152
Godwin, David 153
Godwin, Henry J. 153
Godwin, J.K. 153
Godwin, James M. 420
Goen, E.B. 352
Goff, A.K. 308
Goff, L.P. 420
Goff, Moses J. 308
Golson, John N. 153
Gommons, Thomas 410
Gonday, J.H. 308
Gonzales, C.B. 420
Gonzalez, John B. 153
Goodall, William S. 153
Goode, D.W. 153
Goode, Robert 153
Goodhue, John 111
Gooding, D.W. 153
Goodloe, Charles H. 153
Goodman, D. 252
Goodwin, Elisha 153
Goodwin, J. 153
Goodwin, James 153
Goodwin, Jeff 308
Goodwin, William W. 153
Goodwyn, D. 153
Goodwyn, J.F. 153
Goodyear, T.F. 352
Gordon, E.W. 111
Gordon, Joseph H. 352
Gordon, P.L. 111
Gordon, William A., surgeon 352
Gordy, W.F. 153
Gotcher, Nathaniel P. 352
Gough, William G. 308
Gouint, Sieur 19
Gould, L.D. 420
Gould, Mrs. Lydia 85
Gourly, Robert 403
Grace, Baylis E. 154
Grace, George T. 154
Grace, James 393
Gracey, William C. 154
Grady, Curtis D. 308
Grady, J. 154
Grady, N.A. 154
Graff, Capt. Lawrence de 11
Graham, A. 308

Graham, Charles F. 410
Graham, Daniel 154
Graham, H. 154
Graham, J.H. 252
Graham, J.P. 154
Graham, Thomas 410
Graham, Walter 154
Grand Bay 24
Grandchampt, E. 252
Granger, Gordon, major-general 65, 66
Grant, George A. 111
Grant, Henry 375
Grant, J.N. 410
Grant, John C. 154
Grant, Joseph P. 352
Grant, P.F. 154
Grant, Robert C. 308
Grant, Thomas 375
Grant, William F.B. 111
Grant, William H. 111
Grantham, A.A. 154
Grantham, E.J. 308
Grantham, Maston 308
Grantham, T.W. 154
Grass, George Edward 111
Gratix, Robert 154
Graves, George H., citizen 427
Graves, J.T.J. 154
Graves, William 252
Gray, Charles B. 154
Gray, J.M. 352
Gray, James Lafayette 308
Gray, John 154
Gray, John J. 155
Gray, Oliver Crosby, captain 224
Gray, Reuben 111
Gray, Samuel 155
Gray, T.A. 309
Gray, T.J. 155
Grayson, Y.W. 155
Greathouse, John F. 352
Green, A.T. 155
Green, Abe 352
Green, Charles 155
Green, E.J. 308
Green, George S. 420
Green, J.H. 308
Green, James T. 155
Green, John 252
Green, John Herbert 252
Green, John M. 252
Green, Lee 420
Green, R. 111
Green, Stephen 308
Green, Thomas R. 155
Green, W.J. 155
Green Mountains 86
Greene, J.B. 352
Greenville, Louisiana 66, 79
Greenwell, John 353
Greenwood, Alabama 70
Greer, Daniel C. 155
Gregg, R. 308
Gregg, R.L. 383
Gregory, W.H. 155
Grenshaw, James 155
Grey, S.B. 403
Grey, T.A. 309

Gribble, Elijah 375
Grice, Hansel 227
Griffin, A.J. 309
Griffin, Asa J. 309
Griffin, John 252
Griffin, John A. 309
Griffin, R.C. 155
Griffin, Richard, artificer 309
Griffin, T.R. 155
Griffin, Thomas R. 309
Griffin, William A. 155
Griffing, Stephen Henry 67, 68, 155
Griffith, John W. 111
Grimes, J.E. 155
Grimes, Joseph E. 253
Grimsley, A.P. 383
Grindstaff, Isaac 375
Groce, David 155
Grogan, Patrick T. 155
Groom, William E. 156
Grooms, Thomas S., artificer 394
Grose, G.S. 155
Grosvenor, William M., colonel 57, 58
Grount, William 253
Grout, Horace V.B. 111
Grover, Adelbert 111
Grover, Cuvier, brigadier-general 53
Guedry, Jules 253
Guice, David W. 309
Guinn, Harvey 394
Guinn, J.H. 309
Guinn, John 420
Gulf Blockading Squadron 26, 29
Gulf Coast 10, 16, 17, 19, 20, 24, 31, 54, 65, 69, 93, 94, 97; cities of 37, 90
Gulf Islands National Seashore 97
Gulf of Mexico 9, 10, 11, 12, 16, 19, 20, 21, 29, 31, 34, 36, 38, 43, 45, 51, 53, 56, 58, 77, 78, 86, 88, 93, 97; quarantine station in 89, 90
Gulfport Channel Outer Range Rear Light 91
Gulfport, Mississippi 90, 96, 97
Gulledge, R.W. 309
Gum, John 253
Gunn, George W. 156
Gunn, James H. 156
Gunn, Marshall H. 112
Gunner, B.C. 309
Gutherie, O.F. 74
Guthrie, Benjamin J. 156
Guthrie, Ervin 375
Guthrie, O.T. 353
Guthrie, R.B., captain 353
Guthrie, William T. 156
Guy, James M. 156
Guymor, James O. 156

Hackley, George 353
Hadden, John T. 156
Hadley, Thomas 156
Hagaman, Tappen 156
Hagarty, John 410
Haigwood, Edward 309
Haigwood, M. 309

Haisley, A.J. 156
Halbertson, J.H. 224
Hale, James 156
Hale, Merrill T. 309
Hall, Alfred G., lieutenant-colonel 56, 57, 58
Hall, C.G. 309
Hall, Charles, ordnance sergeant 82
Hall, E. 156
Hall, H.F. 156
Hall, Harvey J. 403
Hall, Hopewell 253
Hall, Horace 112
Hall, J.P. 156
Hall, John 156
Hall, John M. 353
Hall, Lafayette 156
Hall, M.W. 156
Hallmark, Claborn W. 157
Halloway, Churchill H. 353
Halsell, Thomas 309
Ham, H. 383
Hamberger, M., citizen 428
Hambright, Hugh 157
Hamel, J.J. 309
Hamel, William 309
Hamer, John Smith 157
Hamilton, C.S. 309
Hamilton, E.J. 157
Hamilton, Erastus H. 112
Hamilton, F.J. 157
Hamilton, H.M. 309
Hamilton, Henry 253
Hamilton, Henry Clay 157
Hamilton, J.C. 157
Hamilton, J.S. 253
Hamilton, James D. 309
Hamilton, L.W. 112
Hamilton, Robert 157
Hamilton, T.N. 420
Hamlet, A.B. 157
Hamlet, J. 353
Hammett, G. 157
Hammond, S.P. 309
Hammond, Thomas 253
Hammonds, H.K.P. 157
Hamner, W.J. 157
Hamper, F.C. 375
Hamplin, J.J. 253
Hamplin, Robert 310
Hampton, John 394
Hampton, John J. 375
Hampton Roads 35
Hancock, John M. 403
Hancock, John S. 383
Hand, John 310
Hand, Neil 157
Hand, Robert M. 157
Hand, W.W. 157
Handsboro, Mississippi 23
Hanes, B.F. 157
Haney, C.W., citizen telegrapher 428
Haney, J.W. 375
Haney, L. 253
Haney, Levi 375
Hanley, Francis H. 157
Hanley, John 353

Hannelly, A.O. 157
Hannelly, John 157
Hanning, Amos 112
Hansford, D.C. 310
Hanson, Benjamin 112
Hanson, D.C. 157
Hanson, William Rodford 158
Hanwell, Robert R. 158
Happell, Thomas J. 158
Hardee, William Joseph 24
Hardeman, W.J. 158
Harden, John G. 158
Hardin, Cuvier G. 112
Hardin, J. 353
Hardin, John M. 310
Hardwick, John G. 158
Hardy, Robert 310
Hargis, R.W. 158
Hargrove, W.F. 158
Harlan, Jeff 410
Harley, David 253
Harmon, John Philip 353
Harndon, Charles S. 310
Harper, A.T. 158
Harper, Levi 310
Harper, R.B. 310
Harpers Ferry, Virginia 21, 22
Harrel, Wesley S. 310
Harrelson, J. Samuel 253
Harrick, E.G. 253
Harries, George P. 253
Harriman, Sylvester 112
Harrington, G.L. 403
Harrington, M. 310
Harrington, P. 310
Harrington, T.J. 310
Harris, Adelbert, ordnance sergeant 353
Harris, B.F. 158
Harris, C.B. 410
Harris, Charles 253
Harris, E.F. 310
Harris, E.H. 112
Harris, Eli 158
Harris, George W. 158
Harris, J. 158
Harris, J.W. 310
Harris, James T. 158
Harris, James W. 375
Harris, John 159, 254
Harris, John E. 353
Harris, Joseph 254
Harris, Nelson 375
Harris, Richard 310
Harris, Simeon B. 159
Harris, T.H. 159
Harris, W. 159
Harris, W.H. 403
Harris, W.J. 159
Harris, William A. 310
Harris, William G. 159
Harrison, Benjamin F. 310
Harrison, Sen. Byron Patton "Pat" 96
Harrison, C.J. 31
Harrison, Edward 159
Harrison, G.W. 159
Harrison, J. 159
Harrison, J.A. 159

Harrison, Jeptha R. 310
Harrison, J.T. 420
Harrison, John 310
Harrison, Morris 159
Harrison, Samuel 159
Harrison, Thomas 410
Harrison County, Mississippi 96
Harrod, John 410
Harrod, Walter 254
Harrold, Burrel W. 159
Harrolson, James M. 159
Hart, Abraham 420
Hart, Allen Thomas 159
Hart, David 420
Hart, Elisha 160
Hart, H.F. 160
Hart, H.J. 403
Hart, Henry 76
Hart, James B., Sr., captain 310
Hart, R.T. 254
Hart, Thomas 254
Hart, W. 410
Hart, W.J. 403
Hart, Z. 420
Hartley, J.K. 160
Hartley, William E. 160
Hartsfield, John W. 227
Harvard, W. 254
Harvell, William Castle 254
Harvey, E.W. 160
Harvey, J.L. 353
Harvey, James H. 420
Harwell, E.W. 160
Harwell, Robert R. 160
Hatch, Colin C. 112
Hatch, F.M. 420
Hatchell, F. 383
Hatchell, J.B. 383
Hatchell, R.E.T. 383
Hatchell, S.B. 383
Hatchell, W.G. 383
Hatley, Uriah 394
Hatten, William W. 310
Hatter, Moody 394
Hatteras Inlet 35
Hatton, John A. 353
Hatton, T.J. 160
Hatton, William L. 227
Haugh, W.J. 353
Haupt, James E. 160
Havana, Cuba 17, 18, 36
Hawkins, John 353
Hawkins, W.A. 160
Hawley, A.P. 311
Hawthorn, J.R. 420
Hay, A.J. 160
Hayden, G.B., hospital steward 420
Hayes, M.V.B. 160
Hayes, Rutherford B., president 88
Hayes, William 160
Hayford, Rufus S. 112
Haygood, Erasmus W. 311
Haynes, E.F. 311
Haynes, J.M. 160
Haynes, J.W. 353
Hays, Andrew W. 160
Hays, Charles W. 29

Hays, Jesse 160
Hays, John N. 160
Hays, L.F. 160
Hays, N.H. 160
Hays, R.D. 160
Hays, William 160
Haywood, T.B. 228
Hazard, Alfred, captain 420
Hazelwood, Richard B. 311
Hazes, J.F. 161
Head, R.A. 161
Head, William R., captain 161
Head of Passes 38, 40
Healey, P.B. 161
Heard, John F.M. 161
Hearn, C.C. 161
Hearn, Campbell S. 353
Hearn, J.L. 353
Hearn, N.G. 161
Hearn, Mr. 46
Hearn, Robert S., lieutenant 353
Hearn, W.S., citizen 428
Heath, M.T. 161
Heath, W.C. 403
Heath, W.H. 161
Heatherington, William H. 254
Heatherton, E. 161
Hebard, B.W., citizen 428
Hebert, A.J. 254
Hebert, Adrien 254
Hebert, J. Grey 254
Hebert, Jules A., Sr. 254
Hedderbrand, Charles 354
Hedrick, W.C. 354
Height, H. 161
Heite, H.U. 161
Hellington, F.K. 161
Helm, Green Cellus 311
Helm, L.R. 255
Hempstead, Samuel 354
Henderson, Albert S. 354
Henderson, B.F. 255
Henderson, B.S. 161
Henderson, Charles 161
Henderson, D.F. 420
Henderson, G.W. 410
Henderson, James D. 255
Henderson, R.W. 311
Henderson, S.M. 161
Hendley, J.W. 161
Hendrick, A.J. 255
Hendricks, C.L. 311
Hendricks, R.H. 311
Hendricks, T.P. 311
Hendricks, W.J. 161
Hendriks, David 161
Henford, Pvt. 161
Henley, Hezekiah 162
Henley, Isaac C. 311
Henley, J.P. 162
Henley, James A. 354
Henly, J. 403
Henning, Elisha 162
Hennington, J.R. 311
Henry, August J. 255
Henry, Francis 420
Henry, Harvey M. 375
Henry, Joseph Oscar 255
Hensley, Frederick B. 311

Henson, J.B. 255
Henson, James M. 162
Henson, John 162
Henson, William R. 162
Hentz, Dr. Thaddeus H. 228
Herard, W. 255
Herbert, Horatio Samuel 354
Hercomb, James 162
Hermes, launch 90
Herring, Elisha 162
Herring, Emanuel 162
Herring, W.J 311
Herrington, J.A. 311
Herrod, J.R. 311
Herron, Stephen W. 162
Herron, William H., Jr. 311
Herzey, P. 162
Hestler, William 354
Hetzler, Peter 420
Heustis, H.M. 162
Hewitt, J.A. 311
Hewitt, Robert Y. 311
Hice, George W. 112
Hickman, Jesse 311
Hickman, John 311
Hickman, Josiah A. 255
Hicks, A. 410
Hicks, F.N. 162
Hicks, J.R. 312
Hicks, John T. 162
Hicks, W.M. 376
Hicks, Walter W. 162
Hide, Jesse 255
Higgason, W.S. 354
Higgason, William L. 354
Higgins, Edward, captain 25
Hightower, A.W. 162
Hill, Daniel P. 354
Hill, G.B. 162
Hill, George W. 162
Hill, Henry J. 162
Hill, Isaac W. 354
Hill, J.T. 162, 312
Hill, James P. 354
Hill, Robert D. 162
Hill, William A. 376
Hill, William M. 163
Hilton, George W. 112
Hilton, L.M. 312
Hilton, Thomas 163
Hilton, V.A. 163
Hinckell, John 163
Hincks, Edward W., lieutenant-colonel 80, 81
Hines, Richard J. 312
Hines, William M. 403
Hinson, Edward 163
Hinton, F.J. 403
Hinton, James M. 354
Hinton, John R. 354
Hinton, John S. 163
Hinton, W.H. 163
Hirrick, T. 163
Hitchings, Charles F. 112
Hitt, J.A. 163
Hixon, Daniel A. 163
Hode, James A. 163
Hodge, Elijah J. 383
Hodges, E.F. 312

Hodges, Henry, chief quartermaster 84
Hodges, Hiram 354
Hoffman, George 113
Hoffner, Rufus P. 312
Hogan, Jesse 312
Hogan, Michael 255
Hogan, W.R. 163
Holabird, Samuel Beckley, quartermaster-general 87, 88
Holden, B. 420
Holder, Alexander 354
Holdridge, Palmer B. 113
Holdsworth, William 163
Holiday, Walter 354
Holifield, Joel 163
Hollace, J.E. 163
Holland, Brit 163
Holland, Charles, ordnance sergeant 312
Holland, Christopher Columbus 354
Holland, Ebinezer H. 255
Holland, John E.C. 354
Holley, A. 163
Holley, John 410
Holley, Milton 163
Holley, William J. 163
Hollingshead, J.W. 163
Hollingsworth, George W. 163
Hollingswoth, Henry 312
Hollingsworth, William M. 312
Hollis, Charles P. 355
Holly, Amond D. 163
Holly, George 61
Holly, Thomas R. 164
Holly, W.J. 256
Holmes, B.R. 164
Holmes, C.G. 355
Holmes, Daniel 113
Holmes, E.P. 312
Holmes, Edward 256
Holmes, P.E 312
Holmes, Stephen J. 403
Holmes, William McC. 256
Holmstedt, Ernest, colonel 58, 59, 61, 63, 64, 65, 66, 67, 69, 72, 73
Holst, John 410
Holstein, D.C. 256
Holt, A.D. 164
Holt, William H. 355
Holtree, Richard J. 256
Holtzclaw's Brigade 70
Homburger, J. 256
Homstedt, D.O. 256
Honeycutt, E.J. 312
Honeycutt, Thomas Jefferson 312
Honeycutt, William L. 164
Honipson, T. 113
Honnelly, John 164
Honning, Amos 113
Hood, W.H. 312
Hooker, James 256
Hooper, A.W. 355
Hooper, Caleb S. 113
Hooper, Orlando 113
Hooter, J.W. 312
Hopkins, George W. 355
Horan, Martin 394

Index

Hording, Henry 113
Horgan, Michael 256
Horn, George 312
Horn Island 12, 17, 24, 29, 56, 87
Hornback, Silas H.F. 355
Hornberger, I. 256
Horne, William H. 164
Horner, John H. 312
Hornipson, S. 113
Horr, John 256
Horten, John W. 312
Horton, John J. 355
Horton, Joseph W. 394
Horton, S.F. 312
Houston, Benton F. 355
Houston, James D. 312
Houston, W.T. 164
Howard, Capt. 22, 23
Howard, Charles, citizen 428
Howard, G.W. 164
Howard, Harris 164
Howard, J.M. 164
Howard, John 164
Howard, L.A. 164
Howard, Leroy B. 312
Howard, Levi 313
Howe, Edward 256
Howell, Benjamin F. 313
Howell, James 164
Howell, Phil M. 164
Howey, Joseph W. 376
Howze, Morris 256
Hubbard, M.A. 164
Hubbard, W.L. 164
Huckaby, G.J. 164
Huckaby, R.P. 164
Huckaby, Robert 164
Huckaby, W.B. 164
Hucker, J.S. 256
Hudgens, Humphrey D. 355
Hudnall, Henry B. 313
Hudson, Burrell 164
Hudson, J.P. 383
Hudson, J.W. 165
Hudson, John Wesley 383
Hudson, Madison 313
Hudson, Thomas A. 165
Huey, Samuel B. 165
Huey, S.H. 165
Huff, John J., captain 79
Huff, John M. 165
Huff, William H. 355
Huffaker, H.C. 355
Huffman, J.R. 165
Hugan, Humphrey D. 355
Huger, Capt. 25
Hughes, B.F., captain 410
Hughes, Thomas H., captain 313
Hughes, Tyria M. 420
Hughes, William 421
Hull, Hopewell 256
Humphrey, George W. 113
Humphreys, Thomas H.D. 384
Humphries, H.M. 256
Hunt, D. 355
Hunt, H.J., citizen 428
Hunt, J.H. 258
Hunt, Thomas 257
Hunt, William 165

Hunter, D.V. 376
Hunter, Duke W., surgeon 355
Hunter, J.T. 313
Hunter, Pvt.O. 313
Hurlbut, Stephen Augustus, major-general 66
Hurley, Daniel 257
Hurricane Camille 93, 97
Hurricane Georges 97
Hurricane Katrina 94, 97
Hurt, James C. 355
Husbands, Elijah 313
Hutcherson, William 313
Hutches, James 257
Hutchings, Charles F. 113
Hutchings, George T. 165
Hutchins, H.C. 165
Hutchinson, J.P. 257
Hutchinson, James 313
Hutchinson, John 355
Hutchinson, Joseph 257
Hyce, James 257
Hyman, W.J. 313

Iceberg, Simeon 395
Illinois, transport 51
L'Imitation de Notre Seigneur, prayer book 13
India Company 17
Ingle, D.M. 376
Ingle, E.S. 376
Ingle, J.S. 376
Ingraham, T.E.R. 165
Ingram, Abijah E. 313
Ingram, J.J. 313
Insley, S.P. 410
Inzer, Edward H. 67
Inzer, Edwin H. 404
Irby, Thomas B. 313
Iron, D.M. 313
Irvin, J.J. 257
Irvin, John J. 257
Irvin, W. 257
Irwin, Freeman B. 228
Irwin, John Q. 313
Isle aux Chats 15
Isle aux Chevreuil 14, 15
Isle aux Vassieux 13
Isle of Orleans 20
Isle Surgeres 12, 15, 16
Israel, Clement B. 257
Israel, Max, citizen 428
Istrouma, marker named 14

Jackson, A.E. 257
Jackson, Andrew, general 20; statue of, 54
Jackson, C.M. 395
Jackson, Daniel S. 165
Jackson, J.F. 165
Jackson, J.H. 313
Jackson, J.J. 313
Jackson, J.W. 165
Jackson, Joseph A.T. 165
Jackson, Joseph P. 355
Jackson, M.H. 165
Jackson, Mississippi 22, 74
Jackson, Shields 165
Jackson, T.S. 313

Jackson, William 395
Jackson, William P. 258
Jackson Barracks, Louisiana 80, 81
Jackson Square, New Orleans 54
James, A. 355
James, C.A. 165
James, Joel P. 356
James, John B. 356
James, Lycurgus 356
James, Silvannus S. 356
James, Simon 384
James, Thomas W. 313
James, William 113
Janvasett, A. 165
Jaramey, E. 165
Jarman, John L. 165
Jarome, E. 165
Jarrard, J.T. 165
Jarrett, R.F. 356
Jeffords, E.G. 384
Jeffords, S.K. 384
Jeffords, Thomas 384
Jeffries, Daniel 313
Jeffries, Osborne 314
Jeger, H. 356
Jeniran, I.N. 411
Jenkins, E.B. 411
Jenkins, Joseph M. 356
Jennery, J.H. 166
Jennings, H. 166
Jennings, J.W. 166
Jennings, Richard 384
Jett, Benjamin D. 356
Jett, W.H. 314
Joe Graham American Legion Post 96, 97
Joel, Moses 258
Joey, N. 166
Joffrion, Ernest J. 258
Johns, E.N. 166
Johns, Shadrick 228
Johnson, A.B. 411
Johnson, A.L. 376
Johnson, Andrew S., surgeon 113
Johnson, B.M. 421
Johnson, Caleb A. 421
Johnson, Charles Moore 166
Johnson, D. 421
Johnson, Edwin P. 356
Johnson, F.C. 166
Johnson, George W. 314
Johnson, Herbert P. 166
Johnson, J.E. 314
Johnson, J.H. 166
Johnson, J.T. 314
Johnson, J.W. 356
Johnson, Jesse W. 404
Johnson, John S. 314
Johnson, Joseph F. 113
Johnson, Joseph J. 314
Johnson, M.A. 166
Johnson, Napoleon B. 411
Johnson, R.S. 421
Johnson, R.W. 166, 356
Johnson, Richard 113
Johnson, Robert 166
Johnson, S.L. 258
Johnson, Samuel, citizen 428
Johnson, Sidney E. 314

Johnson, T. 166
Johnson, Thomas J. 166
Johnson, Wade 356
Johnson, William 166
Johnson, William Henry 314
Johnson, William J. 421
Johnston, Charles B., major 166
Johnston, David 166
Johnston, H.H. 356
Johnston, J.H. 314
Johnston, James H. 314
Johnston, James P. 166
Johnston, John W. 166
Johnston, Joseph Eggleston, general, surrender of 77
Johnston, Samuel, citizen 428
Johnston, Wirt 314
Joliet, Louis 10
Jones, A.J. 166
Jones, Amos O. 314
Jones, C.C. 166
Jones, C.M. 167
Jones, D. 167
Jones, Edward F., colonel 32
Jones, Eli H. 376
Jones, Enoch 228
Jones, F.J. 167
Jones, Ferdinand 314
Jones, H.J. 314
Jones, Henry M. 167
Jones, Hiram 376
Jones, J.H. 404
Jones, J.J. 314, 376
Jones, J.K. 167
Jones, James 167
Jones, James K. 167
Jones, James L. 167
Jones, James Wesley 376
Jones, John 356, 376
Jones, John A. 167
Jones, Joseph C. 314
Jones, M.D. 314
Jones, Madison, negro citizen 428
Jones, O.H. 167
Jones, P.H. 314
Jones, R.P. 376
Jones, Robert E. 315
Jones, Samuel 404
Jones, Stephen A. 376
Jones, W. 356
Jones, W.E. 167
Jones, W.J. 167
Jones, W.P. 167
Jones, W.R. 167
Jones, William Blunt 228
Jordan, Charles 315
Jordan, D.H. 315
Jordan, Eleazer W. 113
Jordan, G.M. 167
Jordan, J.G. 315
Jordan, M. 315
Jordan, Ralph T. 113
Jordan, Thomas E. 421
Jordan, W.P., Sr. 315
Jordan, Warren W. 315
Jordan, William A. 315
Jordan River 46
Joseph, Joseph, citizen 428
Joslyn, John H. 395

Joy, William 315
Justiss, J.B. 228

Kain, G.W. 167
Kane, Patrick 45, 428
Kane, Thomas, citizen 428
Kape, J.C. 411
Kaplan, H.C. 167
Kasson, Leverett 258
Kates, H. 167
Kavenaugh, William H. 356
Keane, John, major-general 20
Keath, Joseph 167
Keathley, J.B. 315
Keathley, William 315
Keel, James F. 167
Keely, John T. 167
Keifer, E. 356
Keifer, J.M. 167
Keller, A.J. citizen, 428
Keller, Fidel, bookseller 48, 49, 428
Kelley, William J. 421
Kellum, William Allen 168
Kelly, Andrew J. 315
Kelly, Berry 168
Kelly, Daniel 411
Kelly, E. 315
Kelly, E.D. 168
Kelly, Edward 421
Kelly, G.P. 168
Kelly, Henry 168
Kelly, James M. 315
Kelly, John W. 356
Kelly, Thomas 258
Kelly, W.R. 168
Kelly, William 315
Kemp, Anthony N. 356
Kemp, James 168
Kemp, Joy 258
Kender, Isham 411
Kendricks, David, citizen 428
Kenerson, David C. 113
Kennedy, D.N. 356
Kennedy, Daniel 168
Kennedy, Edward 168
Kennedy, Edward M. 168
Kennedy, Edward W. 168
Kennedy, James C. 315
Kennedy, John 357, 411, 421
Kennedy, Matthew 357
Kennedy, S.R. 168
Kennedy, W.L. 168
Kennedy, Walton 168
Kennedy, William W. 168
Kennerly, J.C. 258
Kenney, Daniel 384
Kenney, W.J. 168
Kent, W.P. 168
Kentland, W. 168
Kentucky, state of 77
Kerr, Henry Clay 357
Kerr, J.J. 315
Kerr, N.E. 357
Kersey, David Emanuel 228
Kesterson, W. 384
Ketchum, Charles 357
Ketchum, D. 169
Key, Cornelius N. 258

Key, J.W. 315
Key West, Florida 35, 38
Kiel, B. 384
Kiel, Mathney 228
Kiffer, James M. 169
Killaugh, Martin 169
Killian, John D. 258
Killingsworth, J.A. 315
Killingsworth, J.J. 169
Kilpatrick, Alick H. 169
Kilpatrick, James E. 169
Kimball, W.H. 228
Kimbro, Stephen, 421
Kimbrough, Mrs. 98
Kincaid, R. 357
Kinchen, H. 259
Kinchen, John W. 259
Kinchen, N. 259
King, E.L. 97
King, Frank 411
King, George D. 169
King, H. 384
King, J.G. 395
King, Louis 316
King, P., citizen 428
King, Thomas 169
King, Thomas J. 316
King, William 357
King, William P. 316
Kingfisher, ship 32
Kingrey, William 384
Kinley, James 411
Kinsey, Elisha L. 377
Kintland, W. 169
Kirby, James W. 169
Kirby, John M. 384
Kirby, W.C. 357
Kirby, William 259
Kirby, William Isaiah 384
Kirby, William Mahoney 384
Kirkham, H.H. 169
Kirklan, Richard 316
Kirklan, Samuel 316
Kirkland, William J. 169
Kirkpatrick, T.N. 316
Kittrell, G. 259
Kline, George A. 169
Klinet, Crawford W. 169
Kling, Bernard L. 259
Kling, Cyrille 259
Knight, Charles M. 113
Knight, James M. 169
Knight, John J. 170
Knight, P.B.H. 316
Knight, Paul 316
Knight, Streeter 114
Knotts, J.D. 170
Knowland, John 170
Knowles, Raymond 170
Knox, J.H. 170
Kolb, Andrew 170
Kyle, D.H. 384
Kyle, Willie D. 170
Kyles, J.B. 170
Kyles, W.H. 170
Kyzer, Z.E. 170

LaBlanc, Dosite 259
LaBlanc, E. 259

LaBlanc, Jackson 259
Lacey, Louis J. 316
Lacey, Thomas A. 170
Lacey, W.H. 316
Lacey, William E. 170
Lackey, William R. 384
Lacock, H. 259
Lacy, Gordon 357
Lagrone, William S. 170
Lagrove, J.G. 170
La Habana 18, 41
Lake Champlain 20
Lake Maurepas 14
Lake Pontchartrain 14
Lakin, Newell J. 114
Lally, Albert 316
La Maisonnoeruve, Officer, death of 18
Lamb, Charles S. 114
Lambert, Frank 170
Lambert, J. Edgar, captain 259
Lambert, James 411
Lambert, John C. 259
Lambert, William 170
Lambreth, Z.T. 170
Lamkin, D. Washington 316
Lancaster, A. 411
Lancaster, John M. 171
Lancaster, L. 316
Lancaster, William F. 411
Lance, A.H. 377
Lance, James M. 377
Lance, W.L. 411
Landfair, J.W. 316
Landreth, John 171
Landrum, Samuel W., captain 171
Landruth, T.M. 316
Landsden, J.A. 171
Landsdon, J.A. 171
Landsford, J.P. 171
Lane, Alexander 171
Lane, Bryant 316
Lane, J.H. 171
Lane, J.M. 171
Lane, John J. 171
Lane, Kingsbury 260
Lanehart, Jacob E. 260
Lang, Enoch 316
Lang, Simeon 316
Lang, Wiley 316
Langdon, George Barnemus Moore, engineer 411
Langlett, Charles 260
Langlois, J.V. 260
Langston, Robert R. 384
Lanie, A.R., captain 260
Lanie, C.A. 260
Lanier, A.J. 229
Lanier, R.J. 260
Lanier, W. 317
Lannery, J.R. 171
Lanning, James Riley, color-bearer 377
Lanter, Davis, captain 357
Lapsley, Norvell A., assistant-surgeon 395
Lara, James 357
LaRochelle, France 11, 16
LaRue, Anna 50, 428

LaRue, John 50
LaSalle, Bertrand 260
LaSalle, Rene Robert Cavalier 10, 13, 17; expedition of 11
Lashly, William 260
Lassiter, James 171
Lassiter, John G. 317
Lassiter, William M. 317
Laterriere, Charles 260
Latimer, J.F. 317
Latimer, M. 171
Laughlin, M., coal-heaver 411
Laughlin, T. 384
Laurent, A. 261
Lavener, J.R. 171
Lavergne, Seymour L. 261
Law, J.A., lieutenant-colonel 172
Law, John 17, 18
Lawler, Nicholas, ordnance sergeant 114
Lawless, Caleb R. 172
Lawless, E. 172
Lawrence, A.J. 172
Lawrence, J.W. 317
Lawrence, James P. 384
Lawrence, John A. 385
Lawrence, John H. 317
Lawrence, Joseph F. 261
Lawrence, Robert 114
Lawson, Aaron 172
Lawson, J.M. 172
Lay, E.C. 172
Lay, J.S. 172
Layet, Adolphe 172
Laynard, E.W. 233
Leach, Hugh A. 172
Leach, M. 261
League, R.M. 172
Leap, William E. 172
Leavens, E.B. 172
Leavens, I.F. 172
LeBeau, Edgar, citizen 429
LeBeau, Edward, citizen 429
LeBlance, E. 261
LeClercq, A. 261
Ledbetter, Alex H. 317
Ledlow, J.W. 172
Lee, A.V., captain 172
Lee, Albert 357
Lee, C.S., captain 172
Lee, Charles H., citizen 429
Lee, Columbus P. 172
Lee, E.G. 261
Lee, General T. 172
Lee, H.F. 317
Lee, J. 173
Lee, J.W. 261
Lee, John R. 385
Lee, Joseph D. 317
Lee, Lawrence 261
Lee, M.T. 395
Lee, N.J. 317
Lee, Robert E.: colonel 21; general, surrender of 77
Lee, S.A. 317
Lee, T.N. 173
Lee, Thomas 317
Lee, W.L. 317
Lee, W.T. 317

Lee, William 173, 385
Leeders, George 404
Leely, S.C. 114
Lees, Thomas 173
Le Francois 11
Legg, Daniel Mayo 317
Leicank, Joseph 261
Leigh, George M. 421
Leigh, J.C. 317
Leister, E.F. 173
Lejeune, Theodule 262
Lemoine, Cesaire 262
Lemons, James P. 317
Le Moyne, Charles 10
Lemp, John 262
Lenville, W.W. 173
Leonard, Thomas 173
Leopold, William 262
L'Epinay, Jean-Michel de 17, 18
Lester, William A. 173
Letain, Edward 262
Leverett, John D. 173
Lewis, steamer 41
Lewis, C. 421
Lewis, Daniel 262
Lewis, F.M. 173
Lewis, G.W. 421
Lewis, Henry H. 262
Lewis, J.J. 173
Lewis, J.P. 357
Lewis, James F. 421
Lewis, John, ordnance sergeant 81
Lewis, John F. 317
Lewis, Nat 357
Lewis, T. 262
Lewis, T.C. 421
Lewis, Tavner J. 317
Lewis, W.A.L., assistant surgeon 317
Lewis, William 411
Libby, Alvarado L. 114
Libby, George H. 114
Lide, Alexander Sparks 318
Lidell, Robert F. 173
Liddell, St. John Richardson, brigadier-general 70
Liddell, William 173
Lieb, Theodore, citizen 429
Lightfoot, Allen 173
Lightfoot, James Henry 173
Liles, George W.S. 318
Lilly, A.K. 262
Lincoln, Abraham: administration of 31; assassination of 67, 71; president 22, 24, 30, 34, 35, 51, 58
Lindsey, J.E. 318
Lindsey, John W. 395
Lindsley, George J. 114
Lingo, B. 174
Link, August 357
Links, R. 262
Linville, W.W. 174
Lisbony, Auguste R. 262
Lisenby, Anthony L. 174
Little, H.B. 174
Little, James M.K. 174
Little, Jefferson J. 174
Little, T.T. 318

Little, Thomas C. 318
Little Rock, Arkansas, penitentiary at 81
Littlefield, George W. 114
Littlejohn, William 174
Lloyd, Evans S. 318
Lloyd, G.F. 385
Lloyd, J.W. 385
Lloyd, Jesse C. 174
Lloyd, Samuel H. 318
Lloyd, Thomas Brown 404
Lloyd, William 385
Lobell, L. 263
Lobell, S. 263
Lock, Joe E. 395
Locke, Robert A. 357
Lockhart, B.A. 318
Lockhart, Thomas J. 318
Lockhart's Battalion Infantry 63, 66, 67
Loflin, James 263
Loflin, John 411
Loflin, William 396
Loftin, Thomas Green 174
Loftis, Samuel 174
Logan, Diraly 357
Logan, N.H. 174
Logan, Samuel H. 174
Lomax, Charles H. 318
Lombard, Edward Homer 263
Long, C.R. 318
Long, Felix H.G. 229
Long, James A. 318
Long, John C. 318
Long, Marcellus J. 114
Long, N.L. 174
Long, Nicholas A. 229
Long, R. 404
Long, Robert Joshua 357
Long, Thomas A. 174
Long, Washburn 114
Loomis, Samuel T. 318
Loper, J.M. 318
Loper, William P. 318
Lorieum, J.N. 174
Loring, J.H. 318
Lorio, Leonce 263
Lorring, George, engineer 412
Losberg, Fred, citizen 429
Lott, Absalom 318
Lott, F.M. 263
Lott, Heuston Alexander 174
Louis, John J. 174
Louis XIV, King 10, 16, 17
Louise, Sister 19
Louisiana: deltas of 36; natives of 45; state of 21, 22, 23, 37, 38, 58, 89; territory of 10, 14, 16, 17, 18, 19, 86
Louisiana Club 48, 49
Louisiana Purchase 20
Louisiana Rigolets 46, 56
Louisiana State Board of Health 89
Lounan, G.F. 175
Lovell, Mansfield, major-general 29, 34, 36, 45
Lovett, John B. 263
Loving, J.W. 318

Lowary, H. 175
Lowe, Andrew J. 357
Lowe, Andrew P. 377
Lowe, J.D. 175
Lowe, John P. 358
Lowell, Massachusetts 30
Loyal, James 175
Lucas, J.N. 175
Luce, A. 318
Luce, John T. 114
Luce, W.A. 319
Lufkin, Edwin B. 39
Lugenbuhl, Peter 263
Lundy, W.G. 421
Lunsford, W.N. 175
Luten, Lewis 175
Lyden, P.O. 263
Lyens, J.M. 175
Lyle, J.D. 396
Lyles, John 175
Lynch, Patrick 175
Lynch, S.P. 263
Lyndsey, James 319
Lynn, J.M. 175
Lynn, W.B. 175
Lyon, G.W. 319
Lyon, Samuel B. 358
Lyon, Thomas S. 319
Lyrio, Leonce 263

Mack, Peter 265
Madden, John 114
Maddox, W. 179
Madison, A. 179
Madison, Alexander 179
Madison, James 179
Madison, James, president 20
Madole, Frank R. 359
Magazine Street, New Orleans 76, 81
Magee, S. 320
Magoran, James 265
Maguire, John P. 179
Mahearn, J.A. 179
Maher, N. 396
Mahone, John F. 359
Mahoney, Emanuel 321
Mahoney, James B. 320
Mahoney, John 179
Maine: soldiers of 35, 50, 55, 56; state of 30
Majors, Edward 179
Malbouchia River 13
Malley, T.O., citizen 429
Malloy, E.J. 180
Malloy, Phillip Y. 359
Man, H.B. 321
Manberet, A. 265
Manchac, Louisiana 14
Manchew, J. 180
Manes, J.T. 321
Mann, Isaac B. 114
Mann, J.W. 180
Manning, Amos 114
Manning, John H. 115
Manning, Thomas 180
Manning, Wesley L. 321
Manor, J.D. 180
Mansfield, John 115

Maples, Luther W. 96
Maples, Simeon 180
Marcay, John, assistant surgeon 377
Marcy, Randolph B. 35
Mardi Gras 14
Maria A. Wood, schooner 41
Marie, Jean 265
Marigny Street, New Orleans 73
Le Marin, frigate 11, 15
Marion, Jerome 180
Marley, Walter S. 321
Marmaduke, Thaddeus S. Jr. 359
Maroney, Thomas 115
Marquette, Père Jacques 10
Marrs, J.L. 265
Mars, G.L. 377
Marsh, S.H. 359
Marshal, S.J. 180
Marshall, H.S. 115
Marshall, Henry S. 359
Marshall, J.S. 180
Marshall, William 377
Marshall, William H., citizen 429
Marson, William 321
Marston, Matthew Randall, captain 58
Marten, Davis 265
Martin, A. 180, 404
Martin, Adam A. 265
Martin, B.F. 412
Martin, C.L. 180
Martin, Charles W., captain 180
Martin, Edward 180, 359
Martin, G.M. 265
Martin, George M. 265
Martin, G.W. 265, 321
Martin, I.W. 265
Martin, J.A. 265
Martin, J.F. 321
Martin, J.W. 265
Martin, James 377
Martin, Jasper 359
Martin, John E.A. 266
Martin, John P. 321
Martin, Josiah Green 359
Martin, Judson J. 321
Martin, Julius A. 266
Martin, L.B. 321
Martin, M.M. 180
Martin, Mathew D. 404
Martin, Osqua C. 321
Martin, Ransom H. 180
Martin, Sanders 180
Martin, Thomas Benton 359
Martin, W. 180
Martin, W.A. 377
Martin, W.F. 180
Martin, W.J. 321
Martin, W.H. 181
Martin, William J. 321
Martin, William M. 181
Martins, T.P. 181
Marx, A. 94
Maryland, state of 29, 30
Mask, Dudley 181
Mask, Phil 181
Mason, A.W. 421
Mason, Arthur W. 115

Mason, J.C. 181
Mason, N.M. 421
Mason, Robert 181
Mason, W.C. 378
Massachusetts: regiments from 34; state of 30, 36, 37, 51
Massacre Island 12, 16, 17
Matanzas, ship 40
Mather, James 266
Mathew, E.R. 378
Mathews, G.W. 181
Mathews, J. 266
Mathews, J.M. 385
Mathews, Thomas 266
Mathews, Thompson B. 266
Mathews, W.B. 321
Mathews, William 229
Matkins, R. 181
Matkins, W.T. 321
Maton, Robert 181
Matthews, Andrew 385
Matthews, J.B.T. 321
Matthews, James 359
Matthews, S.P. 385
Mattison, B.S. 181
Maunels Canal 43
Maxey, John J. 321
May, Benjamin H. 181
May, C.E., manager 96, 97
May, F.T. 181
May, John D. 181
May, M.M. 181
May, Peter D. 181
Maynor, J.T. 181
McAfee, R. 385
McAffee, Henry 175
McAllister, T.H. 175
McAllister, W.J. 385
McArthur, C.N. 319
McBride, Patrick 175
McBright, Israel 229
McBright, J., coal-heaver 412
McCabe, James, ordnance sergeant 83, 87, 88
McCabe, John, colonel 23
McCabe, Patrick, major 319
McCafferty, Robert 319
McCain, George H. 175
McCain, William E. 319
McCall, James 175
McCall, John P. 358
McCall, John W. 175
McCall, R.L. 175
McCane, George 175
McCann, James 412
McCant, G.C. 263
McCardley, Calvin M. 175
McCarey, B.S. 176
McCarley, S.A. 176
McCarthy, D.A. 176
McCartney, M.E. 176
McCartney, Thomas N. 176
McCarty, D.A. 358
McCarty, J.D. 176
McCarty, John 412
McCarty, John H. 319
McCarty, Officer, death of 18
McCarty, S.B. 176
McCaskill, L.A. 319

McCauley, Arthur 358
McCauley, Felix M. 176
McChein, R. 263
McClain, H.C. 319
McClain, J.S. 176
McClain, William F. 176
McClan, J.M. 176
McClellan, A. 358
McClellan, George B., general 34, 35, 50
McClure, John S. 358
McClusky, James H. 176
McColl, Dan, Ship Island lighthouse keeper, 87, 91
McCollars, Benjamin B. 176
McCone, Joel G. 319
McConnelly, J.C. 176
McCord, S.B. 385
McCorkle, Christopher Columbus 358
McCorkle, M.G. 377
McCormick, B.B. 264
McCormick, W.J. 176
McCowan, James 176
McCoy, John 177
McCracken, W.L. 377
McCrae, steamer 25
McCray, William V. 319
McCrory, R. 177
McCrory, Robert P. 264
McCrory, T.M. 177
McCrory, W.H. 385
McCullough, A. 396
McCullough, David S. 177
McCurdy, A.J. 177
McDade, Charles Alpin 319
McDade, John A. 319
McDaniel, David 177
McDaniel, John G. 177
McDaniel, S.L. 377
McDaniel, W.A. 177
McDaniels, David 115
McDavid, A.J. 421
McDavid, John M. 404
McDermott, Patrick C. 115
McDonald, B.H. 177
McDonald, Frederick W. 319
McDonald, J.B. 264
McDonald, J.H. 264
McDonald, James 396
McDonald, John 319
McDonald, Robert V. 319
McDonald, T.W. 319
McDonald, Thomas 177
McDonald, William 177
McDonald, William A. 177
McDonnell, John 320
McDonnelly, John 320
McDonnica, William 177
McDough, J.B. 320
McDuffie, W.K. 177
McElhaney, W.T. 177
McElrath, S.B. 177
McFarland, Amos 115
McFarlough, George B. 412
McFerson, Barton 358
McGan, James 320
McGee, P.A.W. 385
McGinnis, Thomas 177

McGlothen, G.C. 358
McGowan, James 264
McGowans, I. 264
McGrient, A.J. 377
McGriff, R. 177
McGriff, Richard Patrick 177
McGuinn, J. 396
McGuinty, James A. 177
McGuire, W.T. 320
McHatton, Robert E. 264
McHethey, R. 264
McHingall, J.S. 320
McHugh, Charles 358
McHugh, Peter 358
McInnis, M. 178
McIntyre, J. 377
McKean, William W., flag-officer 27, 28, 29
McKee, David 358
McKee, George W. 83, 84
McKee, H.K. 320
McKee, J.L. 320
McKeithern, J.S. 178
McKenin, J.P. 178
McKenny, S.J. 178
McKenzie, Aaron 178
McKim, J.W., captain 39
McKinney, James M. 178
McKinney, L.M. 412
McKinney, William 358
McKinney, Willis 358
McKissick, William 178
McKnight, H.A., captain 320
McKnight, Isaac 421
McLane, Abraham 45, 429
McLane, W. 264
McLane, William H. 320
McLarney, Frank H. 178
McLaughlin, Michael 412
McLaughlin, William D. 178
McLean, J.M. 264
McLean, S.S. 178
McLean, William, captain 264
McLellan, Alden 70, 73, 76
McLellan, C.W., captain 76
McLellan, Mrs. George 73
McLellan, William H. 76
McLemore, H.W. 320
McLemore, Henry R. 320
McLeod, John J. 320
McLeod, N. 320
McLeod, Richard T. 385
McLeod, W.W. 320
McLinn, H. 264
McMahon, Archibald W. 320
McMahon, Jackson 377
McManning, A. 412
McMath, W. 178
McMillan, J.A. 178
McMillion, James 358
McMullen, T.J. 320
McNair, Charles T. 178
McNair, J.F. 178
McNamara, M. 412
McNeely, John 359
McNeely, M.A. 264
McNeil, Alex 73
McNilly, William M. 396
McQuillan, Michael 115

McQuillan, W.J. 421
McQuinn, J. 396
McQuote, Lillie 178
McRae, Alex 178
McRae, Christopher C. 178
McRae, Daniel A. 179
McRae, James, captain 179
McRae, P. 179
McRae, William 179
McRae, William D. 422
McRae, William N. 179
McRee, Mark C. 179
McRessick, W.F. 179
McSwain, Jonathan 320
McTirf, J.D. 359
McToohey, M. 264
McVay, F.S. 265
McVea, Thomas Scott 265
McVey, H. 179
McVey, Robert, ordnance sergeant 82, 83, 85
McVoy, M.W. 179
McVoy, Thomas 422
McWhorter, C.J. 422
McWhorter, Eliphalet A., major 179
Mead, William 359
Meadows, Daniel P. 181
Meadows, William S. 181
Meager, Pat 359
Meeks, G.C. 360
Meeks, Lewis C. 360
Meeks, William S. 229
Meggingon, D.A. 182
Meigs, Montgomery Cunningham, quartermaster-general 85
Melton, Albert L. 182
Melton, James H. 182
Mensmen, George, citizen 429
Mercer, Levi 360
Merchant, William H. 115
Meredith, E.C. 182
Meredith, P. 182
Meredith, Samuel 182
Meridian, Mississippi 69, 76
Merle, Ernest 266
Merphee, F.M. 321
Merrett, Marion 266
Merriam, Frank, officer 28
Merrill, Benjamin 182
Merrill, G. 182
Merritt, Alexander S. 229
Merritt, J.F. 182
Merritt, Marion 182
Merryweather, W.D. 360
Mervine, William M., flag-officer 26, 27
Messer, Lawson 378
Messer, Peter 182
Messerory, Alonzo 115
Messor, Alex 182
Mexican War 24, 29, 31
Mexico, invasion of 80
Meyers, H.B. 321
Michael, D.L. 182
Michaus, F.W. 322
Michaux, Frank W. 266
Middleton, R.H. 322
Middleton, W.E. 182

Miggins, William 322
Miles, John 322
Miles, Nicholas V. 360
Miles, W.R., colonel 76
Miles, Wiley 322
Millener, Jeff 266
Miller, A.J. 182
Miller, Andrew J. 322, 360
Miller, Eliphalet 87, 88, 115
Miller, F.C. 322
Miller, G.W. 322
Miller, H. 360
Miller, Henry E., artificer 322
Miller, J.R. 182, 266
Miller, James R. 266
Miller, Julius A. 182
Miller, M.D.L. 182
Miller, Nathaniel 229
Miller, Perkins Poole 267
Miller, Phillip 412
Miller, R. 267
Miller, R.B. 183
Miller, T. 183
Miller, T.R. 422
Miller, Thomas W. 360
Miller, W.D.L. 183
Miller, Warren P. 183
Millett, William E. 115
Milley, N.H. 183
Millner, W.A. 183
Millsap, T.E. 183
Millsap, Thomas E. 322
Milneburg, Louisiana 73
Milstead, W.H.C. 183
Milton, John L. 183
Mims, Hames M., adjutant 183
Mims, Henry A. 404
Minga, Henry F. 322
Minnett, Thomas, citizen 429
Minor, Pickens 183
Minshall, John E. Sr., adjutant 360
Minter, J.B. 322
Minter, John A., Jr. 360
Mints, J.J. 422
Mintz, John M. 378
Mintz, John Zebedee 378
Mississippi: gulf coast of 9, 22, 70, 85; state of 20, 21, 22, 23, 49, 56, 58, 89, 90, 96
Mississippi City, Mississippi 24, 33
Mississippi Company 18
Mississippi Delta 89
Mississippi River 10, 11, 13, 14, 15, 16, 18, 19, 20, 22, 24, 31, 35, 36, 37, 38, 42, 55, 72, 74, 90; basin of 17
Mississippi Sound 10, 12, 21, 24, 25, 26, 27, 29, 30, 85, 86, 90
Mississippi State Board of Health 89
Mississippi, steamer 35, 36
Mississippi Territory 20
Mississippi Valley 10, 19, 24
Missouri, state of 70, 77
Missouri, steamer 79
Mitchel, Charles T. 322
Mitchel, James 267
Mitchel, H. 267
Mitchell, A.C. 360

Mitchell, A. Landers 183
Mitchell, Benjamin 183
Mitchell, Benjamin L. 360
Mitchell, H. 183
Mitchell, Hiram 183
Mitchell, J. 183
Mitchell, J.M. 267, 322
Mitchell, James M. 267
Mitchell, Joseph A. 183
Mitchell, L.E. 322
Mitchell, N., citizen 429
Mitchell, Reuben H. 183
Mitchell, T.H. 184
Mitchell, William W. 322
Mitternight, Christopher Columbus 422
Mixon, Harvey 267
Mixon, J.H. 322
Mixon, John H., Sr. 322
Mobile, Alabama 21, 24, 26, 30, 33, 67, 68, 69, 70, 72, 74, 76, 77, 86; settlement at 9, 16, 17, 18
Mobile Bay 11, 59, 70, 73
Mobile Real Estate Association 96
Mobile River 16, 19
Mobley, James R. 322
Mobley, William M., assistant surgeon 422
Mobly, Ephraim M. 322
Mock, L.L. 396
Moffit, Joshua 412
Mollie Able, steamer 73, 74, 76
Mon, Edmond 184
Monkers, William Thomas 360
Monroe, J.P. 323
Monroe, J.T. 323
Monroe, John T., New Orleans mayor 43, 45
Monroe Guards 45
Montague, Brainard 115
Montanara, H. 412
Monteith, A. 267
Montgomery, Alabama 22, 30
Montgomery, Elliott 360
Montgomery, I.E., comm. 412
Montgomery, Simeon J. 360
Montreal, New France 10
Moody, Thomas J. 184
Mooney, J.D. 184
Mooney, J.H. 267
Mooney, James L. 267
Mooney, James W. 184
Moor, James 184
Moore, B.G., assistant surgeon 184
Moore, D.B. 323
Moore, D.S. 422
Moore, Eli 360
Moore, F.W., citizen 429
Moore, George W. 404
Moore, J.E. 323
Moore, J.H. 268
Moore, T. 396
Moore, T.F. 378
Moore, Thomas L. 361
Moore, Thomas Overton, governor of Louisiana 23, 24
Moore, W.D. 184
Moore, W.H. 323
Moore, W.W. 184

Moore, William R. 268
Mooring, Edwin W., adjutant 229
Moose, A.J. 184
Moran, Charles E. 268
Moran, James 412
Moran, Thomas 397
Moreau, F. 268
Morefield, Thomas W. 184
Moreland, Francis M. 361
Morgan, David 115
Morgan, Giles D. 184
Morgan, J.H. 268
Morgan, J.W. 378
Morgan, John 115, 268
Morgan, Samuel 422
Morgan, William J. 323
Morning, John 361
Morning Light, steamer 55
Morrel, Jackson 323
Morris, Abner Butler 323
Morris, C.L. 323
Morris, E.J. 184
Morris, Elijah C. 361
Morris, Eugene, citizen 429
Morris, I.I. 268
Morris, J.C. 323
Morris, J.L. 268
Morris, J.N. 361
Morris, J.W. 184
Morris, James 361
Morris, James W. 323
Morris, John 184
Morris, John E. 184
Morris, Lorenzo 361
Morris, Luther A. 323
Morris, Samuel 397
Morris, W.H. 184
Morrison, B. 422
Morrison, Daniel A. 184
Morrison, Edward 185
Morrison, S.W. 361
Morrison, W.B. 361
Morse, J.N. 323
Morse, James W. 323
Morse, Melville W. 116
Morse, W.H. 323
Morton, Dallas M. 185
Morton, William T. 185
Moseley, A.A. 185
Moses, David L. 385
Mosley, Robert J. 323
Mosley, William C. 323
Motley, Edwin 185
Mougoulachas Indians 13
Mount Vernon Arsenal 83
Mower, Joseph Anthony, colonel 79, 80, 81
Moyat, B. Eugene 397
Moyes, John 185
Mulhouse, ___ 361
Mullen, Thomas 268
Mullens, Thomas 268
Mullins, John 361
Mullins, William S. 185
Mumford, William B., hanging of 45
Murphey, B.J. 185
Murphy, E.G. 185
Murphy, Emanuel M. 185

Murphy, John 412
Murphy, M.F. 361
Murphy, Michael, citizen 429
Murphy, P. 412
Murphy, William R. 323
Murray, James F. 378
Murray, John R., acting masters mate 412
Murray, R.D., assistant surgeon 85, 86, 87, 89
Murrell, J.D. 323
Muse, Eli 269
Muse, J.S. 323
Myers, A.L., captain 25
Myrick, F. 185
Myrick, John T., Jr. 229

Naler, J. 185
Nash, Abner D. 185
Nash, J.D. 412
Nash, James E. 269
Nassan, steamer 55
Natchez Daily-Courier 23
Natchez, Mississippi 86
Nations, F.M. 324
Neal, A.J. 324
Neal, L.S. 324
Nealy, J. 361
Needham, George E. 116
Neely, John W. 324
Neely, Samuel C. 324
Nees, G.T. 361
Negril Bay, Jamaica 20
Neil, William M. 324
Nelms, Charles D. 185
Nelson, C. 324
Nelson, J.H. 185
Nelson, J.L. 186
Nelson, John 229
Nelson, John H. 186
Nelson, Lemuel D. 324
Nelson, T.J. 186
Nelson, T.P., major 324
Nerbert, H.S. 361
Nesbit, Stuart E. 385
Netherton, Daniel 361
Nevins, Peter 361
Nevis, island of 17
New Basin Canal, New Orleans 76
New Brunswick, ship 53, 56
New England, 36, 86; natives of 31, 32, 35, 46, 55; states of 30
New France 10
New Orleans Daily-Crescent 34
New Orleans Daily-Delta 23, 51
New Orleans Daily-Picayune 42, 50
New Orleans, Louisiana 20, 22, 23, 24, 25, 29, 30, 31, 32, 33, 34, 35, 36, 37, 38, 39, 40, 41, 42, 43, 45, 46, 47, 48, 50, 51, 53, 54, 55, 56, 57, 58, 59, 64, 66, 68, 69, 72, 73, 76, 77, 79, 80, 81, 85, 89, 93, 94; settlement at 9, 18, 19, 86
New Orleans Marine-Hospital 89
New Orleans Times-Democrat 85
New York City 29, 31, 37, 51
New York Herald 51
Newell, David 324

Newell, John J. 324
Newland, W.F. 361
Newman, C.R., surgeon 324
Newman, John K. 361
Newman, John W. 385
Newman, Oscar S. 324
Newman, William D. 186
Newson, Thomas P. 186
Newton, A. 186
Newton, C.L. 186
Newton, Charles A. 422
Newton, S.T. 186
Nicholas, William 361
Nichols, J.J. 186, 324
Nichols, James 362
Nichols, John 186
Nichols, John M. 385
Nichols, Reuben A. 362
Nichols, Robert Allen 362
Nichols, W.N. 186
Nicholson and Company 76
Nickens, Seborn 269
Nineteenth United States Infantry 81
Ninety-First United States Colored Infantry 58
Ninth Connecticut Infantry 30, 31, 33, 35, 41
Ninth Texas Cavalry (Dismounted) 67
Ninth Ward, New Orleans 80
Nix, L.B. 324
Nixon, William 186
N.O. and N.E. Railroad 73
Noble, W.A. 186
Nobles, William B. 186
Noel, J.R. 186
Nokes, Samuel 116
Nolan, P. 186
Nolan, William 186
Nolans, W.T. 324
Nones, Edward P. 94
Norbert, H.L. 362
Norfolk, Virginia 79
Norman, B.F. 324
Norman, C.R., surgeon 324
Norman, S.S. 378
Norrell, D.A. 362
Norris, C. 186
Norris, E.S. 324
Norris, Frank 186
Norris, J.B. 186
Norris, P. 362
North Carolina, state of 77, 80
North Star, ship 51, 53
Northeast Pass 38
Northup, Albert 186
Northrup, F. 186
Norton, D.C. 422
Norton, Thomas C. 186
Norwood, F. 187
Norwood, T.D. 187
Norwood, William S. 324
Notice to Mariners 91
Nowell, Charles C. 269
Noyes, Richard E. 269
N.P. Banks, steamer 76
Nunn, John A. 116
Nunn, Thomas 187

Oakley, A.P. 187
Oaks, J.D. 187
O'Banion, W.H. 269
O'Brien, Daniel 116
O'Brien, J. 362
O'Brien, John, citizen 429
O'Brien, John M., citizen 429
Ocean Springs, Mississippi 14
O'Conner, John, assistant-engineer 412
O'Connor, Charles 413
O'Connor, John F., captain 187
O'Connor, Patrick 324
O'Connor, Smyth, citizen 429
O'Daniel, William H. 270
Odel, Marcus L. 187
O'Dell, Joel R. 362
Oden, Elias M. 325
Oden, George H. 325
Oden, George W., captain 325
Oden, Thomas 187
Odom, Aaron J. 422
Odom, J.J.I. 187
O'Donnell, Jeremiah 116
O'Donnell, John 116
O'Donnell, W. 413
O'Farrell, John 270
O'Farrell, Patrick 187
Ogle, Benjamin F. 362
Ogley, Elbert 187
O'Guyon, James W. 187
O'Keefe, James 413
Old Frank, guard 61
Oldfield, George L. 187
Oldham, George B. 84, 85
Olive, George W. 187
Oliver, Charlton C. 188
Oliver, David 116
Oliver, Francis D. 325
Oliver, J.H. 386
Oliver, John 188
Oliver, Pierre D. 270
Ollie, Charles 270
Olly, W.P. 413
One-Hundred Tenth New York Infantry 64
O'Neal, James Daniel 229
O'Neill, Chris 362
O'Neill, John H. 187
O'Neill, W. 187
O'Pry, Erwin G. 386
O'Pry, Sidney 386
O'Quinn, John 187
O'Reilly, J. 187
O'Reilly, J.R.M. 324
O'Reilly, Thomas 325
Orleans Parish Prison 45, 50
Ory, James 270
Osborn, John 362
Osbrook, D. 413
Osgood, Thomas H. 116
Osteen, John M. 386
Osteen, Thomas B. 325
Otho, Frederick 362
Overstreet, B. 188
Overstreet, Daniel C. 325
Owen, A.C. 188
Owen, Edward H. 188
Owens, David T. 362

Owens, Elijah E. 188
Owens, Louis 325
Owens, W.H. 188
Owens, William 188

Pace, J.P. 325
Pace, W. 325
Pace, W.H. 188
Pacific Mail Company 31
Pack, John A. 188
Padgett, James H. 378
Pafor, J.W. 362
Page, A.M. 325
Paine, Eugene 116
Paine, Henry M. 362
Painter, Henry Clay 362
Pakenham, Sir Edward, major-general 20, 86
Palmer, J.D. 188
Palmer, James, commodore 65
Palmer, John 413
Palmer, L. 188
Palmerty, Dane 362
Paramore, W.R. 325
Parbetry, Henry E. 362
Parham, William H. 270
Paris, France 17, 19
Parish, John W. 325
Park, G.W. 325
Parker, A.E. 270
Parker, Alvis J. 188
Parker, Creach H. 188, 230
Parker, E.J. 188
Parker, Edward 188
Parker, George M. 422
Parker, Gray W. 270
Parker, H.B. 270
Parker, H.W. 189
Parker, Henry B. 270
Parker, John M.G., postmaster 37
Parker, John W. 422
Parker, Marquis L. 325
Parker, Martin V.B. 189
Parker, P.H. 325
Parker, P.T. 422
Parker, Paris 116
Parker, R.B. 189
Parker, Robert L. 270
Parker, S.J. 189
Parker, Silas 378
Parker, W.H. 189
Parker, W.M. 422
Parker, W.P.L.Q. 189
Parker, William 362
Parker, William Watson 325
Parker, Willis J. 325
Parks, G.W. 325
Parks, J.P. 325
Parmenter, Alfred 31
Parnell, E. 397
Parrish, Benjamin James 326
Parrish, J.P. 189
Parrish, Jacob 189
Parsons, C.H., coal-heaver 413
Parsons, G.B. 189
Parsons, J. 189
Parsons, J.P. 271
Parsons, R.S. 189
Parsons, W. 189

Parsons, Young 189
Parten, A.J. 189
Partin, Charles P., major 326
Parvin, Jackson L. 271
Pascagoula River 28
Pass à l'Outre 38
Pass Christian, Mississippi 46, 93
Pass, William 404
Passeuary, George 189
Pate, Howard 96, 97
Pate, John 189
Paten, Rufus, major 79
Paterson, J.P. 189
Patten, James R. 326
Patterson, Abraham W. 362
Patterson, Daniel T., commodore 20
Patterson, Pvt. Ezekiel 189
Patterson, Isaac N. 326
Patterson, John T. 326
Patterson, W.B., assistant engineer 413
Patterson, W.H. 326
Patterson, W.J. 271
Patterson, W.P. 326
Patterson, William, citizen 429
Patton, J.F. 271
Patton, John 326
Patton, William 363
Paul, W.D. 190
Payne, George T. 326
Payne, Hazel 378
Payne, J.G., citizen 429
Peabody, Ansell S. 116
Peacock, James B. 190
Pearce, A.C. 190
Pearce, J.N. 363
Pearce, James A. 190
Pearce, John T. 190
Pearce, Levine 326
Pearl River 19
Pearson, Robert H., captain 190
Pearson, W.B. 190
Peas, George A. 233
Peck, Charles 363
Peet, H. 397
Pegger, A. 271
Pelican, ship 17
Pemberton, J.R. 363
Penicaut, Andre 15
Peniston, Alma 41
Penland, Noble Z. 378
Penn, John A. 326
Penny, Frank 422
Pensacola, Florida 11, 16, 18, 20, 24, 69, 90
Pentorry, John 363
Penvett, Alonzo A., citizen 429
Pepper, J.F. 326
Pepper, J.J. 326
Perdue, J.N. 190
Perdue, John L. 190
Perkins, A.D., lieutenant-commander 56
Perkins, Melvin N. 326
Perkins, P.H. 190
Perkins, Robert D. 66, 190
Perkins, Than M. 326
Perkins, Wilson 116

462 Index

Permenter, James D. 326
Perrins, H.C., artillery mate 413
Perry, B.F., citizen 429
Perry, David D. 190
Perry, Frank 397
Perry, J. 230
Perry, John D. 190
Perry, S.K. 271
Perry, Thomas C. 363
Perryman, I.L. 271
Perryman, J.L. 271
Persky, John 190
Pervis, James N. 386
Pervis, R.N. 386
Pery, W.N. 190
Pescary, Charles W. 271
Peterman, F.B.A. 363
Peterson, Freeman F. 190
Peterson, M. 191
Peterson, Robert I. 191
Petit, John 76
Petit Bois Island 12
Pettigrew, G.W. 378
Pettus, John Jones, governor of Mississippi 22, 23
Petty, J.B. 224
Petty, T.R. 271
Peyton, George W. 271
Phelan, C. 191
Phelan, M. 191
Phelps, John Wolcott, brigadier-general 31, 32, 34, 37, 39; proclamation of 33
Phelps, W.J. 363
Phenix, C.L. 404
Philan, J.D. 326
Philan, W. Sidney 191
Philip, Prince of Orleans 18
Philips, Alfred 271
Phillip, William 272
Phillips, A.E. 378
Phillips, B. 386
Phillips, Mrs. Eugenia 47, 48, 49, 50, 51, 430
Phillips, George A. 191
Phillips, Green 326
Phillips, J.J. 191
Phillips, James Irwin 191
Phillips, Philip 48
Phillips, Mrs. Matilda 49
Phillips, W.A. 272
Phillips, William A. 272
Phillips, Zack 327
Phipps, John G. 191
Phoebe, frigate 31
Phoebe, servant 49, 50
Picayune Cotton Press, New Orleans 73
Pichard, L. 272
Pick, W.A. 272
Pickering, W.H. 404
Pickett, Abner 191
Pickett, Andrew J. 191
Pickett, J.R.W. 191
Pickett, Seaborn R. 327
Pideau, L. 272
Piefey, G.W. 363
Pierce, A.C. 191
Pierce, Franklin, president 21

Pierce, J.C. 327
Pierce, Labrazan Mitchell 192
Pierce, S.H. 192
Pierce, W. Randal 327
Pierson, William 116
Pike, George 116
Pike, M.F. 224
Piles, A.J. 413
Pillet, Archibald H. 272
Pinkard, John M. 272
Pinkham, J. 272
Pinkney, William Elder 272
Pinson, William 273
Piper, A.W. 192
Piper, Daniel 116
Pipes, Asa C. 192
Pippin, Franklin G. 327
Pistol, C.W. 192
Pitre, C.C. 273
Pitre, Leander D. 273
Pittman, Frederick R. 230
Pittman, H.R. 192
Pitts, A.J. 413
Pitts, John 192, 422
Pitts, John M. Wesley 192
Plaster, Frank 363
Platner, Albert, hospital steward 273
Platt, James S. 117
Plunket, John 363
Plymouth, England 20
Poche, A. 273
Poellnitz, Edwin A. 192
Poellnitz, James A. 192
Pogue, Isaac H. 273
Pointe Coupée Parish, Louisiana 55
Poittat, John T. 192
Poliet 61
Polk, John 327
Pollard, Alabama 69
Pollard, E.T. 363
Pollard, James M. 192
Pollet, Marie Therese 17
Ponder, Finus W. 192
Ponder, William L. 192
Pontchartrain, Louis 10
Pool, J. 192
Poole, C.F. 192
Poole, E.H. 193
Poole, J.M. 327
Poole, T.M. 193
Pope, Hugh 327
Pope, W.C. 193
Port Royal 35, 40
Port Royal Sound 35
Porter, Cmdr. David Dixon 31, 34, 37, 38, 42, 43, 45
Porter, Francis E. 363
Porter, G.W. 193
Porter, James H. 327
Porter, John M. 327
Porter, William 327
Portland, Maine 34, 88
Posey, Noah, Jr. 230
Post, A.P., pilot 413
Potter, Charles H. 117
Potts, J.S. 378
Powell, J.C. 273

Powell, J.E. 273
Powell, J.W. 193
Powell, James E. 273
Powell, John A. 273
Powell, N. 193
Powell, T.D. 327
Powell, W.C. 193
Powell, William 274
Powers, Edward A. 193
Powers, Felix F. 193
Powers, James M. 193
Powers, John H. 413
Powers, W.L. 193
Pratt, J.C. 363
Pray, Rufus L. 274
Prentiss, Charles 117
Preslar, W.A. 422
Presnell, Caleb 397
Press Street, New Orleans 73
Preston, Charles E. 85, 117
Preston, W.B., citizen 430
Prestridge, B.F. 193
Prewitt, N.C. 193
Price, Archibald 327
Price, B.F. 193
Price, Charles B. 363
Price, John, civilian 423
Price, Lewis 193
Price, M.L. 194
Price, Thomas 413
Price, William 363
Priggett, Alexander 327
Prime, Frederick Edward 23
Primot, Catherine Thierry 10
Pritchard, Hezekiah 194
Pritchard, Thomas J. 327
Pritchett, W.H. 194
Prowty, Elijah K. 56
Pruett, Darling H. 194
Pruitt, R.K. 327
Pryor, John W. 363
Puckett, Pinkney S. 194
Pugh, Joseph B. 363
Pugsley, Ira 117
Purmer, J.R. 194
Purnell, J.M. 363
Purnell, N.B. 194
Purvis, G.M. 423
Pylant, William M. 194
Pyne, Columbus C. 194

Quarantine Station 43, 46; ship island 85, 89, 90
Quarles, F.W. 194
Quarles, Thomas W. 194
Quarles, William M. 363
Quartermus, W.H. 194
Quick, James C. 274
Quimby, John B. 327
Quimby, Marshall H. 117
Quinn, Ed 413
Quinn, John 413
Quinn, R.L. 194
Quinnipesas Indians 13

Railey, Green 194
Rainer, G.C. 274
Raines, B.F. 327
Raley, Andrew J. 327

Raley, Calvin C. 327
Rallings, R.J. 386
Rand, R.E. 327
Randall, B.F. 194
Randolph, A.J. 364
Randolph, J. 378
Raney, John B. 274
Rap, John, engineer 413
Rasberry, John T. 328
Rasberry, R.H. 194
Rasmuson, A., quartermaster-sergeant 413
Rassen, John 328
Ratcliff, H.B. 423
Ratlips, J.R. 274
Rawls, Benjamin F. 328
Rawls, William S. 194
Ray, Christopher C. 195
Ray, E. 328
Ray, Hamilton J. 364
Ray, John F. 328
Ray, Marion A. 195
Ray, William 364
Rayburn, R. 195
Rayburn, W.R. 328
Rayfield, L.H. 195
Rayford, John 195
Raymond, G.C. 274
Read, Charles W., captain 25
Read, John Joseph 274
Read, John L. 328
Reader, A.J. 195
Rear, W.T. 328
Reaves, James 195
Red River Campaign 58
Reddell, I.F. 328
Reddell, J.T. 328
Reddick, J.E. 386
Reddock, William M. 195
Redman, D.M. 423
Redman, James B. 364
Redman, Thomas 274
Redmond, Edward 364
Redmond, John 364
Reed, George 328
Reed, James 364
Reed, Joseph M. 378
Reed, T.W. 423
Reed, Wiley W. 328
Reed, William F. 274
Reeks, John 274
Reese, A.H. 328
Reeves, Francis 364
Reeves, J.B. 328
Reeves, J.M. 195
Reeves, M.D. 195
Reeves, Thomas H., captain 79
Reeves, William M. 195
Reggio, Gus A. 274
Register, Ezekiel A. 423
Reid, Luther R. 328
Reil, J.R. 195
Reilly, J.C., nurse 195
Reily, F. 117
Renfroe, J.G. 423
Renfroe, W.H. 195
Renick, James W. 364
Reno, F.M. 404
Renommee, frigate 15

Rentz, J. 195
Reorganization Act 91
Reush, E.T. 328
Reyburn, George W. 195
Reynolds, B.A. 423
Reynolds, C.T.W. 328
Reynolds, Charles 117
Reynolds, Christopher 117
Reynolds, John 413
Reynolds, Joseph F. 364
Reynolds, Lewis 328
Reynolds, T.C. 328
Reynolds, Thomas W. 328
Reynolds, William H. 117
Rhoades, David 379
Rhoades, W.F. 364
Rhode, G. 196
Rhodes, B.H. 230
Rhodes, E. 196
Rhodes, I.C. 196
Rhodes, J. William 275
Rhodes, Newton M. 423
Rhodes, Samuel D. 329
Rhodes, Thomas Wilburn 379
Rhymes, James A. 329
Rice, George 66, 67
Rich, Francis 413
Richard, Cheri 275
Richards, A. 275
Richards, Thomas S., captain 196
Richardson, G.P. 275
Richardson, George P. 275
Richardson, J.Y.D. 275
Richardson, Joseph M. 117
Richardson, S.D., captain 275
Richardson, Samuel 196
Richardson, Thomas Clark 329
Richardson, W.G. 329
Richardson, Y.D. 404
Richey, B.L. 196
Richmond, J.S. 329
Richmond, Virginia 28, 34, 50, 76, 79; authorities at 36
Rickart, Henry 275
Rideau, L. 275
Riddell, J.E. 329
Riddell, Thomas F. 364
Ridley, Robert C. 329
Riggs, Calvin, 196
Rikard, William, 196
Riley, A.K. 397
Riley, George 196
Riley, George W. 196
Riley, J.A. 196
Riley, John 414
Riley, John H., citizen 430
Riley, John T. 364
Riley, Martin 196
Riley, Thomas J. 196
Riley, W. 196
Riley, W.B., citizen 430
Riley, W.J. 423
Rills, Edward H. 275
Rimes, James A. 329
Riner, C.F. 329
Ring, James W. 117
Rio Grande 88
Ripley, William P. 276
Risley, Wait 117

Ritchie, William 364
River Colbert 10
Rivers, H.P. 329
Rivers, James S. 329
Rivers, T.R. 329
Roach, John D. 329
Robb, J. 364
Robbins, W.G. 405
Roberson, Raymond 196
Robert, A.J. 329
Roberts, A.E. 276
Roberts, C. 276
Roberts, Charles A. 276
Roberts, Daniel L. 117
Roberts, E.A. 276
Roberts, G.W. 364
Roberts, George T. 197
Roberts, George W. 329
Roberts, I.W. 197
Roberts, James M. 397
Roberts, James S. 329
Roberts, Leroy 329
Roberts, Richard 197
Roberts, Stephen, citizen 430
Roberts, Walter J. 329
Robertson, Andrus Malankton 364
Robertson, D.G. 197
Robertson, Daniel S. 197
Robertson, Eli C. 365
Robertson, H.C. 386
Robertson, H.H. 329
Robertson, J. 276, 365
Robertson, Joel 423
Robertson, John Thomas 197
Robertson, John W. 329
Robertson, Leonard J. 197
Robertson, M. 379
Robertson, Simeon C. 276
Robertson, T.L. 197
Robertson, William 365
Robertson, William T. 330
Robertson, Willis 365
Robin Street, New Orleans 76
Robinette, William 330
Robins, T.A. 423
Robinson, A.K. 197
Robinson, Alexander 118
Robinson, Daniel S. 197
Robinson, Dr. 67
Robinson, E.T., citizen 430
Robinson, L.D. 330
Robinson, M.E. 197
Robinson, N.T.N., assistant commissary sergeant 276
Robinson, Richard L., major 76
Robinson, W.A. 197
Robinson, William L. 276
Robinson, Z.D. 197
Rochester, L.M. 423
Rochester, Samuel N. 276
Rockmore, J.R. 405
Rodack, J.B. 230
Rodgeres, Heptken 118
Rodgers, Baine M. 197
Rodgers, James 330
Rodgers, Robert 277
Rodgers, Thomas 197
Rodgers, W.W. 330
Rodgers, William 330

Roe, E. 277
Roe, Jacob A. 277
Roebuck, T.W. 197
Rogers, Beasley Manly 197
Rogers, G.R. 330
Rogers, J.D. 330
Rogers, J.F. 423
Rogers, James 277
Rogers, John 397
Rogers, M.W. 198
Rogers, Robert L. 198
Rogers, T.J. 198
Rogers, W.H. 330
Rogers, W.J. 198
Rogers, William, assistant engineer 414
Rogers, William A. 198
Rogers, William D. 423
Rolan, W.N. 198
Roland, A.U.B. 198
Roland, G.M. 379
Rolins, J. 198
Rondes, J.W. 277
Rone, S.M. 379
Roosevelt, Franklin Delano, president 91, 96
Roper, Dick 198
Roper, John T. 277
Rose, E. 365
Rosegue, J., citizen 430
Ross, John, hospital steward 277
Ross, T.M. 198
Ross, William 118
Roulhac, Joseph B.G. 423
Rouse, Alonzo D. 198
Rousseau, Adolphus 277
Rousseau, Sam 76
Roussell, James 277
Roussell, Thomas 277
Row, E.L. 277
Row, I.A. 277
Row, Jacob A. 278
Rowe, George W. 330
Rowe, J.L. 330
Rowe, William H. 397
Rowe, William Henry Harrison 397
Rowell, Andrew J. 198
Rowell, Robert William 198
Rowland, A.S. 330
Rowland, T.J. 198
Royal, Edward, citizen 430
Royal, F.A. 198
Royal, Moses B. 118
Royal Street, New Orleans 73
Ruer, Daniel 386
Rugeby, H.R. 198
Ruggles, E.J. 423
Ruggles, Stephen 118
Rumpt, J.W. 330
Runnells, James F. 330
Rush, Benjamin F., captain 330
Rush, E.T. 330
Rush, James H. 330
Rush, Martin 365
Rush, S.R. 330
Rushing, Benjamin Franklin 405
Russell, Benjamin 199
Russell, Franklin 330

Russell, George E. 118
Russell, H.J. 330
Russell, J.N. 330
Russell, J.P. 199
Russell, J.W. 199
Russell, John M. 379
Russell, W. 199
Russell, W.A. 331
Russoe, George 199
Rust, Henry, Jr., lieutenant-colonel 51, 53, 55
Rutherford, Eli S. 199
Rutland, Z.T. 199
Rutledge, A.B. 199
Ryals, H. 199
Ryan, Joseph Henry 199
Ryan, C.J. 331

Sabler, C. 423
Saddler, Thomas A. 199
Sadler, B.F. 278
Sadler, John 278
St. Amant, Ven, Jr. 278
St. Bernard Parish, Louisiana 85
St. Bernard, Texas 10
St. Charles Hotel, New Orleans 56
St. Charles Street, New Orleans 50
St. Charles Street Railroad Company 76
St. Clair, Pvt. Charles Edward 365
St. John, William 278
St. Joseph Street, New Orleans 73, 76
St. Louis Cathedral, New Orleans 54
St. Louis, ship 18
St. Malo, Hubert 17, 18
St. Martin, E. 423
St. Mary Street 76
Sale, R.A. 199
Sallie Robinson, steamer 46
Sally, John 199
Salmons, William 365
Salpetriere, Bishop 19
Salter, J.W. 199
Samples, William P. 200
Sanchez, Joseph 278
Sanders, Charles 200
Sanders, J.L. 379
Sanders, S. 200
Sanders, William H. 200
Sanderson, Blaney 200
Sandifer, James C. 331
Sanford, B.O. 331
Sanford, Crowell 118
Sanford, G.P. 331
Sanford, Samuel G. 200
Sangsing, J.D. 200
Santana, Charles 278
Santen, A., citizen 430
Santo Domingo 11
Sarah, steamer 81
Sarter, W.C. 423
Saucier, David 331
Saucier, Mississippi 46
Saul, Charles 278
Saunders, D.L. 424
Saunders, J.M. 200
Saunders, James 118

Saunders, James E., superintendent 21
Saunders, Matson Rush, artificer 331
Sauvenet, Charles, captain 56
Sawyer, Barney 200
Sawyer, Thomas Johnston 200
Saylor, John R. 365
Scales, Dr. T.S. 89
Scally, James 398
Scarborough, A. 278
Scarborough, E. 200
Scarborough, G.G. 200
Scarborough, H. 424
Scarborough, J. 200
Scarborough, Jepp P. 200
Scarborough, Richard C. 331
Schexnaider, Jacob 279
Schexnaider, Tonsere 278
Schexnaydre, Ozeme 279
Schwin, W.E. 200
Schwing, George B. 279
Schwing, John T. 279
Scoggins, F. 405
Scoggins, W.J. 365
Scott, Almanzor W. 331
Scott, David 414
Scott, David M. 200
Scott, E.W. 331
Scott, Edwin Allen, major 279
Scott, Em. T. 279
Scott, George W. 331
Scott, J.J. 331
Scott, James T. 365
Scott, Jeremiah 200
Scott, Milo W. 398
Scott, Thomas J. 379
Scott, W.P. 331
Scott, W.T. 200, 279
Scott, W.W. 201
Scott, William R. 331
Scott, William T. 279
Scott, Winfield 201
Scrimpshire, N.M.B. 331
Scurlock, T.O. 424
Scurry, John J. 386
Seabrook, D.O. 201
Seabrook, John P. 201
Seal, Mr. 46
Seale, H.T. 201
Seale, Littlepage B. 201
Seals, A.T. 201
Seals, Annie 96, 97
Seals, Eugene 96, 97
Seals, James 201
Searcy, Bennett 279
Seawell, Charles 201
Seay, Thomas J. 201
Second Louisiana Native Guards 55, 56
Second Ohio Battery of Light Artillery 66
Second Regiment, Corps d'Afrique 56, 57, 58
Seeders, John 279
Seeders, Robert 279
Segars, James 201
Seine, ship 19
Seitz, W.J. 201

Selby, Daniel H. 331
Selby, J.H. 331
Selby, William C. 331
Self, Elijah 201
Self, William W. 201
Selina, H.B. 331
Sells, James H. 201
Serigny, de 17
Sermon, W.H. 279
Sermon, William 424
Setton, Henry 279
Settoon, Archai 279
Seventh Vermont Infantry 35
Seventy-Eighth United States Colored Infantry 79
Seventy-Fourth United States Colored Infantry 58, 64, 66, 67
Severance, Thomas B. 386
Sevinon, W.H. 280
Sewall, Charles 201
Sewall, M.N., citizen 430
Seward, William H, secretary of state (U.S.) 34
Sewell, Alfred 201
Sexton, G.W. 202
Sexton, John F. 331
Seymour, Charles 414
Shackleford, John H. 365
Shadix, D. 202
Shafer, Thomas H. 365
Shaffer, G.W. 332
Shaffer, John F. 331
Shanks, A.M. 365
Sharp, J.J. 202
Shaw, John A. 332
Shea, Daniel 414
Shearer, E.W. 202
Sheffield, George Washington 230
Sheffield, James 202
Sheffield, John 230
Sheffield, William H. 202
Sheilds, John W. 332
Shelby, Thomas M. 202
Shell, C.D. 202
Shelton, A.H. 365
Shelton, Henry M. 332
Shelton, James 365
Shelton, James K.P. 398
Shelton, W.L. 365
Shepard, Joseph 202
Sheperd, J.A. 202
Sheperd, John J. 202
Shepley, George Foster: brigadier-general 43, 45, 50; colonel 34
Sheppard, T.G. 332
Sheppard, William H., citizen 430
Sherbert, Samuel D. 202
Sheridan, Thomas J. 414
Sheridan, W.A. 332
Sherman, Andrew 57
Sherman, Charles K., captain 202
Sherman, William Tecumseh, major-general 79
Sheron, R.A. 332
Sherrod, W. 332
Sherwood, J.J. 332
Shields, John P. 414
Shields, S.N. 332

Shieldsborough, Mississippi, wharf at 46
Shins, D. 202
Ship Island Lighthouse Station 91
Ship Island Military Reservation 96
Shipley, Thomas J. 332
Shipman, James 230
Shirley, C. 202
Shirley, W.B. 202
Shiver, Ed E. 332
Shiver, W.N.W. 230
Shoemaker, Benjamin 332
Shoemaker, D. 332
Shoemaker, James H. 203
Shorter, R.C. 203
Shortridge, George O., captain 203
Showers, James B. 203
Shroeder, John, chief fireman 414
Shropshire, Robert 203
Shrove Tuesday 14
Shuler, J.M. 379
Shultz, George E. 365
Shurer, J.G. 203
Sicard, F.C. 280
Sidebottom, James H. 203
Sigler, C.P. 203
Sill, Joseph, coal-heaver 414
Sill, Rev. 46
Silliman, R.M.E., assistant surgeon 203
Silvers, Thomas B. 379
Simmerly, T.D. 203
Simmesport, Louisiana 58
Simmons, Andrew J. 203
Simmons, Charles 414
Simmons, H.W. 203
Simmons, J.A. 203
Simmons, James R. 203
Simms, Charles W. 203
Simon, H.H. 203
Simon, James 386
Simons, J.B. 365
Simons, M.B. 332
Simonton, J.H. 203
Simpson, Albert W. 366
Simpson, C.S. 366
Simpson, Elisha 424
Simpson, George B. 280
Simpson, John J. 203
Simpson, Louis 204
Simpson, R.T., captain 204
Sims, C.A. 332
Sims, G.R. 332
Sims, J.H. 332
Sims, James C. 386
Sims, John M. 204
Sims, M.P. 386
Sims, Miles 230
Sims, Reuben 204
Sims, W. 414
Singleton, J.E. 332
Singleton, J.F. 204
Singleton, R. 204
Sixth Massachusetts Infantry 32
Sixth Michigan Infantry 35
Sixty-Third Alabama Infantry 68
Skeen, J.M. 204

Skinner, B.P. 204
Skinner, C.A. 280
Skinner, N.B. 204
Skinner, P.J. 332
Skinner, W.A. 204
Skipper, J.A. 204
Skipper, J.B. 204
Skirlock, Daniel N. 204
Skofield, James P. 280
Slaton, William 204
Slaughter, J.I. 204
Slaughter, John B. 204
Slaughter, William Shewen 280
Slay, Nathan G. 333
Slemmons, Joseph Martin 366
Slone, Dudley 280
Slover, Albert M. 398
Slover, James E. 398
Sluder, William 379
Sluter, E.E. 333
Sly, Moses 118
Small, Oscar C. 118
Smeller, J.L.H. 204
Smith, ___, hospital steward 87
Smith, A.J. 405
Smith, A.T. 204
Smith, A.V. 333
Smith, A.W. 204
Smith, Albert W. 366
Smith, Alfred H. 118
Smith, Anderson C., captain 366
Smith, Andrew J. 366
Smith, Angus W. 333
Smith, Bailey H. 333
Smith, Benjamin F. 366
Smith, Benjamin L. 333
Smith, C.A. 424
Smith, Charles H., colonel 81
Smith, D. 204
Smith, Daniel 333
Smith, Edward C. 45, 430
Smith, Eson A. Sr. 333
Smith, Felix H. 280
Smith, Francis Marion 366
Smith, G.A. 414
Smith, George 205
Smith, H. 205, 398
Smith, H.P. 424
Smith, H.S. 414
Smith, Irwin 333
Smith, J. 205
Smith, J.A. 333
Smith, J.D. 205
Smith, J.M. 333
Smith, J.R. 205, 333
Smith, J.T. 205
Smith, J.W. 280, 414
Smith, James 280
Smith, James J. 205
Smith, James R. 366
Smith, James W. 333, 414
Smith, John 280, 366
Smith, John A. 379, 414
Smith, John C. 205
Smith, John H. 205
Smith, Joseph W. 205
Smith, Martin Luther, major 28, 29
Smith, Martin Thomas 333

Smith, Melancton, commander (US) 24, 26, 27, 28, 29
Smith, Merrick M. 280
Smith, Moutford Street 333
Smith, Neil 205
Smith, Nicholas 424
Smith, R.A. 205, 424
Smith, R.F. 366
Smith, S. 333
Smith, S.H. 366
Smith, S.T. 205
Smith, Samuel G. 333
Smith, Samuel L. 333
Smith, Sanford 366
Smith, Seaborn 205
Smith, Theodore 333
Smith, W.D., lieutenant-colonel 64, 65
Smith, W.F. 205
Smith, W.L. 333
Smith, William 281
Smith, William G. 366
Smith, William H. 205
Smith, William J. 333
Smith, William M. 334
Smith, William T. 281
Smith, Z.T. 205
Smitherman, William J. 206
Smithey, Robert 206
Smoke, Robert 206
Snead, James T. 366
Snee, John T. 118
Snider, Francis 206
Snodgrass, James 405
Snow, William A. 206
Snyder, Charles B. 366
Soldier's News-Letter 37
Soloman, James A. 206
Sorrel, Green B.W. 206
Sorrells, David S. 379
Sorrels, G. 334
Sorrels, H.O. 334
South Carolina, state of 21, 22, 23
South Pass 38
Southall, John 61
Southeast Pass 38
Southwest Pass 38
Southwood, Marion, prisoner 48
Sowell, Alfred 206
Spain 18, 20
Spanish Fort 68, 69, 70
Sparkman, John 366
Sparks, ___ 334
Sparks, A.G. 281
Sparks, Charles B. 281
Sparks, Tillman 405
Speaks, Benjamin 334
Speaks, William H. 366
Spears, W.M. 281
Speigner, M. 206
Spellman, M. 281
Spencer, A.J., assistant surgeon 386
Spencer, George K. 82
Spencer, George W. 366
Spencer, Julius P. 206
Spencer, William J. 367
Spencer, William O., assistant surgeon 206

Spier, W.T. 424
Spillars, James R. 281
Spiller, J.W. 206
Spillman, M. 281
Spinger, Samuel 206
Spinks, J.M. 386
Spinks, W.H. 206
Spirey, Benjamin F. 379
Spivey, William 206
Sprayberry, Jerry P. 206
Spriggs, George 414
Springer, J. 206
Sproles, Samuel W. 334
S.R. Spaulding, ship 53
Stabler, Malachi 206
Staff, Oliver 414
Stafford, William J. 334
Staggers, D.J. 207
Staggs, A. 334
Staller, M.H. 207
Stallworth, William M., Jr. 207
Stamper, John Thomas 367
Standard, Jesse F. 334
Stanfield, James 207
Stanfield, James M. 230
Stanfield, William H. 207
Stanley, A.T. 207
Stanley, J.A. 207
Stanley, James M. 367
Stanley, John W. 367
Stanley, Stillman G. 118
Stanley, William 45, 430
Stansel, Jesse P. 207
Stansel, T.J. 207
Stanton, E.G. 334
Stanton, Edwin M., secretary of war (US) 34, 35
Staples, T.A. 207
Stapleton, H. 367
Stark, T.J. 207
Starke, J.R., major 334
Starkey, Frank A. 118
Starnes, W.L. 379
Starns, James Purnell 281
Starnes, W.L. 379
Starr, William 207
Statehouse Square, Jackson 74
Statham, B.T. 367
Steed, E.M. 334
Steel, David 367
Steele, Frederick, major-general 69, 77
Steele, W.B. 207
Stegall, Ralph 207
Steibelt, Albert 281
Stein, John, citizen 430
Steinberger, Louis 281
Stenner, William 334
Stephens, F.B. 282
Stephens, J.J. 334
Stephens, J.S. 207
Stephens, John L. 207
Stephens, L. 207
Stephens, M.H. 334
Stephens, Philip 282
Stephens, R.W. 207
Stephens, T.J. 424
Stephens, William 207
Stephens, William K. 398

Stepleton, S.B. 379
Steppe, Henry 379
Stern, Kiley 207
Stevens, Burrel 424
Stevens, H. 208
Stevens, J.N. 208
Stevens, James B. 208
Stevens, John 208
Stevens, John W. 334
Stevens, T.L. 334
Stevenson, Henry C. 334
Stevenson, J.M. 208
Steward, Moses P. 334
Stewart, Chandler 118
Stewart, J.K. 424
Stewart, J.T. 398
Stewart, John A. 208
Stewart, Samuel A. 282
Stewart, William H., ordnance sergeant 334
Stick, Leander F. 208
Stiles, E.J. 367
Stiles, Samuel M. 367
Stillwell, Pvt. G.W. 208
Stinson, C.H. 282
Stinson, Samuel N. 208
Stock, J.M. 367
Stockey, W.A. 208
Stockman, F. 208
Stockwell, F. 282
Stockwell, Thomas 282
Stoker, John 414
Stokes, C. Lester 282
Stokes, C.S. 282
Stokes, W.W. 208
Stone, A.C. 335
Stone, Howard 97
Stone, J. 415
Stone, J.D. 208
Stone, J.F. 208
Stone, John B. 367
Stone, John Bestor 208
Stone, John M. 208
Stone, W.H. 208, 282
Stones, B.F. 335
Stoney, John T. 367
Story, William L. 282
Stovall, W.D., assistant surgeon 335
Stowe, Leroy 208
Stowers, Louis Edward, captain 282
Strahan, Asa 283
Strather, John M. 209
Straub, W.J. 415
Street, A.L. 335
Street, James 283
Street, William 335
Strickland, Alsamore M. 230
Strickland, H. 209
Strickland, William 230
Stringer, W.M. 335
Stringfellow, D. 209
Stringfellow, James R. 209
Stringfellow, P.W.K. 209
Strong, Andrew Jackson 367
Strong, Edmund 118
Strong, George C., major 34, 41, 42

Strong, J.W. 335
Strong, R.R. 209
Strother, James Thomas 335
Stroud, J.L. 283
Stroud, James S. 424
Stroup, John M. 380
Strout, John N. 335
Stuart, J.E.B. 21
Stuart, J.W. 335
Stull, John D. 367
Sturgeon, Hiram 335
Sturn, Quinn 283
Sucard, F.C. 283
Suggs, John 209
Sullivan, E. 335
Sullivan, J.J. 335
Sullivan, John 398
Sullivan, O. 283
Sullivan, Thomas 283
Sullivan, Thomas J.H. 335
Sullivan, William P. 283
Summerlin, Columbus 209
Summerlin, Thomas S. 209
Summers, L.F. 209
Summers, F.M. 367
Summers, Zimri Franklin 209
Sumner, J. 209
Sumner, Truman L. 209
Sumons, A. 210
Sumter, John 380
Sumter, Lee 380
Sunday, J.W. 424
Surgère, M. le Compte de 11, 12, 15
Suthards, W.G. 380
Sutton, James, pilot 415
Sutton, John P. 367
Swails, Morgan 386
Swain, Samuel R. 335
Swayze, Hardy S. 335
Swayze, Orange H. 335
Swayze, Thomas 283
Swearingen, J.W. 210
Swisher, A. 335
Swope, W. 210
Sykes, George, citizen 430
Sylvester, William Oscar 210
Syms, M. 230

Taber, B.K. 283
Tablon, Charles E. citizen, 430
Tabor, Beverly K. 210
Tacneau, A. 283
Talbert, J. 210
Talbert, James B. 210
Talifero, P. 367
Tannehill, Carlton J. 368
Tanner, G.L. 210
Tanner, Henry C. 368
Tanning, J. 415
Tansey, John 210
Tarrant, Edward Christopher Columbus, captain 210
Tarrant, Edward William 210
Tarrant, John B. 210
Tarver, Isaac 284
Tarver, Stephen T. 210
Tate, George W. 210
Tate, J.R. 210
Tate, Perryman M. 398

Tathum, Thomas N. 380
Tatier, Beverly K. 284
Tatum, Henry 210
Taul, A.T. 210
Taulman, F.A. 386
Taylor, A. 335
Taylor, A.J. 211
Taylor, Abner R. 211
Taylor, Austin 118
Taylor, B.H. 211
Taylor, Benjamin 211
Taylor, Cary 231
Taylor, E.D. 211
Taylor, Eugene 284
Taylor, Fred, captain 284
Taylor, Frederick A., citizen 431
Taylor, H.H. 211
Taylor, Hamilton, citizen 430
Taylor, J. 368
Taylor, J.A. 211
Taylor, J.B. 415
Taylor, J.S. 386
Taylor, J.W. 415
Taylor, James Kurtis 335
Taylor, James M. 211
Taylor, John 211
Taylor, L.R. 336
Taylor, Obadiah, captain 368
Taylor, Peter, assistant surgeon 336
Taylor, R.F. 211
Taylor, Richard, lieutenant-general 72; surrender of 77
Taylor, Robert W. 405
Taylor, W.E. 387
Taylor, W.R. 424
Taylor, W.W. 211
Taylor, Wesley 368
Tchoupitoulus Street, New Orleans 94
Te Deum, singing of 14
Teadue, F.M. 211
Tearney, Barney 284
Teat, Wade Hampton 211
Tedder, Richard F. 387
Tellott, Charles L. 284
Templet, Albert 284
Templeton, J.F. 336
Templeton, S.A. 336
Templeton, S.W. 336
Templeton, W.T. 211
Tennent, Samuel 415
Tennessee, steamer 45
Tenny, William Henry 284
Tenth United States Colored Heavy Artillery 79
Terrell, Whitfield Price 368
Terry, B.T. 336
Terry, John 336
Terry, Roland 336
Texas: natives of 71, 72; state of 10, 21, 22, 54, 67
Thatcher, Charles 368
Thibodeaux, Cleber 284
Thibodeaux, Joseph 284
Thigpen, J.E. 211
Thigpen, L. Gray 211
Thigpen, S.W. 211
Third District, New Orleans 74

Third Mississippi Infantry 42
Third United States Artillery 27
Thiroux, Victor 284
Thirteenth Connecticut Infantry 33, 35, 45
Thirteenth Maine Infantry 35, 39, 40, 45, 46, 55
Thirtieth Massachusetts Infantry 35
Thirty-Fifth Mississippi Infantry 71
Thirty-First Massachusetts Infantry 35
Thirty-Ninth United States Infantry 79, 80, 85
Thomas, __ 211
Thomas, B.B. 336
Thomas, B.F. 212
Thomas, B.H. 212
Thomas, Caleb 368
Thomas, David Dyre 399
Thomas, F.M. 336
Thomas, H. 212
Thomas, J.C. 231
Thomas, J.H. 212
Thomas, James C. 212
Thomas, John B. 399
Thomas, John C., assistant surgeon 399
Thomas, John L. 212
Thomas, Lorenzo, adjutant-general 34
Thomas, M. 212
Thomas, N.E. 399
Thomas, O. 368
Thomason, M.D. 415
Thompsen, Benjamin 336
Thompson, A.H.S. 336
Thompson, Andrew J. 212
Thompson, B. 212
Thompson, B.F. 212
Thompson, E.E. 424
Thompson, Frank H. 284
Thompson, G. 405
Thompson, Harry D. 368
Thompson, James 285
Thompson, J.H. 212
Thompson, L.J. 212
Thompson, P.M. 212
Thompson, Pat 415
Thompson, Robert F. 212
Thompson, S. 212
Thompson, S.M. 405
Thompson, Samuel 118
Thompson, W.W. 213
Thompson, William H., hospital steward 368
Thopin, Sieur 18
Thornton, James T. 213
Thornton, Moses 336
Thornton, S.S. 213
Thrower, Peter J. 213
Thurmond, D. 213
Thurmond, John T. 368
Tibbets, Charles 285
Tidmore, William T. 213
Tidwell, C.K. 368
Tidwell, J.F. 21
Tidwell, Levi N. 336

Tiffith, C. 285
Tiller, Oscar S. 336
Tillford, Thomas 368
Tillman, James P. 213
Tims, John W. 336
Tingle, William P. 213
Tinsley, Burrell 336
Tippins, D.W. 231
Tippins, P.H.M. 231
Tipton, Charles G. 231
Tipton, William R. 213
Tobin, J.W. 336
Tobin, James M. 368
Tobin, Richard 415
Todd, Albert H. 368
Todd, John P. 285
Todd, M. 213
Todd, Marcus L. Jr. 368
Todd, Mr. 33
Toffier, William A. 224, 285
Tolef, J.S. 285
Tomlinson, James W. 285
Tomlinson, Jesse W. 285
Tomney, Patrick 415
Tompley, Victorine 285
Tonart, William 424
Toney, William 286
Tonti, Henry de 13, 14, 17
Tool, J.R. 213
Topographical Engineers (U.S.) 28
Torrant, S. 213
Torrington, Connecticut 21
Torry, James A. 336
Totten, Joseph Gilbert, lieutenant-colonel 22
Toulmin, John F. 213
Towle, S.C. 286, 337
Townes, Oliver, Jr. 118
Townsend, Edmund L. 369
Townsend, Phillip A. 213
Townsend, William 424
Tracy, Stephen G. 119
Trafton, Harrison 119
Train, H. 286
Trainor, Thomas 337
Trains, Henry 286
Trammell, David 213
Traphagen H.S., prisoner 51
Trask, Oliver 119
Travis, Thomas 337
Traynor, James P. 399
Traywick, Harrison 214
Traywick, Robert H. 424
Treadway, David C. 337
Treaty of Paris 20
Trennelly, C.D. 214
Trephagen, H.S., citizen 431
Tribble, Robert E. 337
Triens, F. 119
Trigg, William A. 337
Trimble, John A. 369
Trimble, W.W. 405
Trinity River, Texas 10
Triplit, C.T. 214
Troth, Robert S. 286
Trott, Wiley R. 214
Trotter, W.A., captain 337
Trotter, William John 286
Troy, R. 214

Trudeau, James, brigadier-general 23, 24
Truett, Silas M. 380
Truffey, James A. 214
Trussell, George E. 119
Tubb, Job 214
Tubb, Reuben 214
Tuck, W.T. 214
Tucker, Charles 231
Tucker, E. 214
Tucker, F.A. 424
Tucker, George W. 214
Tucker, Hardy G. 337
Tucker, J.C. 415
Tucker, J.E. 214
Tucker, J.H. 337
Tucker, James 214
Tucker, James J. 337
Tucker, Joel H. 424
Tucker, John 337
Tucker, W.S. 214
Tucker, William 214
Tuif, J.D. 369
Tullier, J.B. 286
Tully, William 405
Turbenville, J. 214
Turberville, A.H. 286
Tunnell, E.C. 369
Turnage, William B. 337
Turner, A.A. 337
Turner, Austin H. 215
Turner, E.L. 215
Turner, Erasmus J. 387
Turner, James 215
Turner, John 387
Turner, John W. 215
Turner, Lynch 369
Turner, Mark A. 215
Turner, O.N. 215
Turner, Rasmus J. 387
Turner, Sumpter 286
Turner, Theodore 119
Turner, Thomas 215
Turner, Tom 337
Turner, W.S. 337
Turner, William 215
Turnham, Joseph C. 215
Turnipseed, D.B. 337
Turvin, D.J. 424
Tussell, William L. 286
Tuttle, Alonzo 119
Tuttle, James 369
Tuttle, John 337
Tuttle, R.E. 337
Tutton, John M. 337
Twelfth Connecticut Infantry 33, 35
Twelfth Maine Infantry 34, 35, 45, 85
Twentieth United States Infantry 79
Twentieth Wisconsin Infantry 76
Twenty-Eighth Connecticut Infantry 51
Twenty-Fifth United States Infantry 80, 81
Twenty-First Alabama Infantry 67
Twenty-First Indiana Infantry 35

Twenty-Fourth Connecticut Infantry 53
Twenty-Second Maine Infantry 53
Twenty-Seven Mile Bluff 16
Twenty-Sixth Massachusetts Infantry 31, 32, 33, 35, 43, 45
Twenty-Third Connecticut Infantry 51, 57
Twiford, D. 215
Twiggs, David Emanuel, major-general 24, 25, 26, 27, 28, 29, 30
Two Brothers, ship 18
Tye, John Fletcher Sr. 337
Tyer, Benjamin 231
Tyler, John 215
Tyler, Louis 337
Tyler, R. 215
Tyus, F.J. 215

Umphis, James 380
Underwood, John 215
Union Press Building, New Orleans 58
Unsell, Alfred 287
Upton, James 215
Upton, John G. 369
United States Army 80, 81, 84, 96; ordnance department 94
United States Army Air Corps 97
United States Army Engineers 21, 23, 85
United States Bureau of Lighthouses 91
United States Coast Guard 91, 93, 94, 97
United States Colored Cavalry 58
United States Colored Heavy Artillery 58
United States Colored Infantry 58
United States Commissary-General of Prisoners 59, 66
United States Congress 20, 88, 89, 91, 96
United States Constitution 34
United States Department of Commerce 91
United States Forestry Service 94
United States Lighthouse Board 21, 91
United States Marine Hospital Service 85, 88, 89, 90
United States Mint, New Orleans 45
United States National Board of Health 88
United States National Park Service 97
United States Naval Academy 97
United States Navy 31, 35, 36, 41, 42, 56, 65; seabees 94
United States Navy Hydrographic Office 91
United States Oath of Allegiance 51, 59, 72
United States of America 20, 22, 23, 30, 72, 80, 87, 88, 97; enemies of 51; territories of 21
United States Quartermaster Department 58

United States Senate 34, 39
United States Treasury 23; secretary of 89
U.S.S. *Brooklyn* 38
U.S.S. *Cayuga* 42
U.S.S. *Colorado* 38
U.S.S. *Cuyler* 29
U.S.S. *DeSoto* 29, 32
U.S.S. *Harriet Lane* 45
U.S.S. *Hartford* 43
U.S.S. *Iroquois* 42
U.S.S. *John P. Jackson* 41, 56
U.S.S. *Kennebec* 42
U.S.S. *Kineo* 43
U.S.S. *Massachusetts* 24, 25, 26, 27, 28
U.S.S. *Metacomet* 59
U.S.S. *Miami* 43
U.S.S. *Mount Vernon* 35
U.S.S. *New London* 29, 32, 41
U.S.S. *Pensacola* 38
U.S.S. *Richmond* 38
U.S.S. *Saxon* 43
U.S.S. *Sciota* 37, 42
U.S.S. *Tecumseh* 59
U.S.S. *Vincennes* 29, 41, 65
U.S.S. *Wissahickon* 42, 43
Ure, James H., citizen 431
Utterback, W.F. 369

Valdeterre, Sieur de 18
Valparaiso, harbor at 31
Vance, Jim Neely 337
Vandervier, J.G. 338
VanDevender, R.W. 338
Vandiver, Elijah M. 369
Vanhook, William T. 380
Vann, William C.H. 215
Vanorden, Norman 119
Vanvaulkenburgh, Pvt. A.B. 119
Varnell, D.F. 338
Varner, W.A. 380
Varnon, McB. 216
Vaughn, Frederick A. 216
Vaughn, J.H. 216
Vaughn, John N. 338
Vaughn, R.E. 216
Vaughn, Taylor 338
Vaughn, W.E. 369
Vaun, W.C.H. 216
Veasey, Simon C. 216
Vermont, state of 30
Vernon, E.W. 216
Vernon, J.J. 287
Vernon, J.M. 369
Vernon, W.J. 216
Vessels, Andrew J. 216
Vestz, W. 387
Vick, J.A. 216
Vick, R.R. 216
Vickers, A. 216
Vickers, J.M. 231
Vickers, Jesse 216
Vicksburg, Mississippi 69, 72, 73, 74, 77
Vigo, Paul Joseph 287
Viler, Charles 415
Villa, J. 287

Villantray, M. de Sauvolle de la 11, 14, 15, 16
Villas, Charles 415
Villette, Sieur 19
Vincent, G.W. 338
Vines, George W. 216
Vines, J. 216
Vines, William 216
Vinson, Robert 216
Virginia, state of 21, 31, 77
Voeglin, Phillip C. 216
La Volage, ship 19
Volkhart, J.M. 415

Wade, S.J. 424
Wade, William H., artificer 399
Waddill, J.J. 287
Waddill, W. 216
Wade, Charles B. 216
Wade, F.S. 287
Wade, James 287
Wade, William A. 217
Wadsworth, J.P. 217
Wadsworth, W.R. 338
Wafford, Jefferson L., major 338
Wages, J.E. 217
Wages, John G. 338
Waggonbrunner, M. 415
Wagoner, E., citizen blockade runner 431
Wainwright, Nicholas P. 287
Walden, N. 217
Walden, T.B. 338
Walden, W.W. 338
Walden, William 369
Wales, M. 217
Walker, A.C. 217
Walker, Alexander, editor 51, 431
Walker, B.A. 287
Walker, Berry A. 231
Walker, Bryant S. 217
Walker, Daniel 338
Walker, David L. 217
Walker, George 119
Walker, J.F. 217
Walker, J.W. 217
Walker, James 338, 399
Walker, James J. 217
Walker, John M. 217
Walker, Joseph W. 369
Walker, Leroy Pope, secretary of war (C.S.) 23, 24, 26, 28
Walker, R. 415
Walker, William Young 369
Walkley, Bryant S. 217
Wall, James A. 338
Wallace, A.J. 287
Wallace, B.T. 415
Wallace, J.D. 287
Wallace, Julius Monroe 218
Wallace, R. 369
Waller, William W. 338
Walls, Robert 218
Walls, T. 218
Walsh, Robert 119
Walsh, Rufus F. 218
Walter, Henry R. 119
Walter, J. 218
Wane, R.G. 338

War Department (C.S.) 28, 29
War Department (U.S.) 56, 58, 64, 77, 81, 85, 87, 96
War of 1812 20, 24, 31
Ward, A.T. 218
Ward, A.W. 338
Ward, C. 415
Ward, Charles 218
Ward, D.A., captain 80
Ward, D.J. 424
Ward, G.W. 338
Ward, H. 415
Ward, James 218
Ward, Jesse 338
Ward, John 218, 415
Ward, M., hospital steward 218
Ward, Thomas R. 218
Ward, W.A. 339
Ware, A.W. 339
Ware, G.W. 339
Warley, Alexander F. 25, 26
Warlick, David M. 380
Warlick, Manuel A. 380
Warnick, Edward A. 399
Warren, Benjamin, captain 32
Warren, David 339
Warren, J.B. 218
Warren, J.W. 339
Warren, Johnson 218
Warren, L.B. 339
Warrior, steamer 58
Washburn, Watson J. 119
Washburn, Israel, Jr., governor 30
Washington, D.C. 20, 30, 34, 35, 48, 80
Waterbury-American 33
Waterbury, Connecticut 33
Waters, Peter B. 339
Watkins, E.D. 339
Watkins, Micajah L. 218
Watson, A.M. 218
Watson, Asa C. 288
Watson, Charles 119
Watson, Cornelius Thomas 231
Watson, G. 288
Watson, I.J. 339
Watson, James J. 231
Watson, John H. 218
Watson, Jonathan Henry 231
Wattingham, Ulysses 288
Watts, William A. 380
Weatherby, H.F. 339
Weatherly, L.F. 218
Weathers, F.M. 218
Weaver, Romandus F. 339
Webb, A.H. 339
Webb, A.T. 219
Webb, James G. 219
Webb, James T. 219
Webb, John Addison 339
Webb, Peyton S. 339
Webb, William Henry 339
Webb, William T. 219
Week, James M. 339
Weekley, W.B. 424
Weeks, Augustus S. 387
Weems, James M. 339
Weishampt, Jacob 399
Weitzel, Godfrey, brigadier-

general, lieutenant 37; mentioned in letter 40
Welch, J.C. 369
Welch, Joseph M. 339
Weldy, Edward W. 120
Welles, Gideon, secretary of the U.S.Navy 27, 29, 31, 38
Wells, J.T. 405
Wells, James M. 219
Wells, Julius D. 380
Wells, Julius M. 380
Wells, Levi B. 288
Wells, Pat 369
Wells, T.C. 288
Wells, William 424
Welsh, A.G. 340
Welsh, Ransom J. 340
Weltz, P.E., Jr., citizen 431
Wentworth, Sewall 120
Wessels, H.W., brigadier-general 66
West, Amos W. 219
West, E.A. 340
West, Henry F. 219
West End, New Orleans 76
West Florida, area of 20
West Gulf Blockading Squadron 31
West Point, Georgia 68
West Ship Island 97
Westbrook, S.J. 288
Westbrook, William M. 288
Western Company 17
Westmoreland, James 288
Whaley, Maston 369
Whatley, David A.J. 219
Whatley, S.J. 219
Whatley, W.H. 219
Wheat, Hesekiah J. 288
Wheat, William L. 219
Wheatley, H. 399
Wheatley, William 219
Wheatly, Richard, chaplain 51
Wheeler, Chris 416
Wheeler, John D. 120
Wheeles, Edward J. 219
Wheeling, T.E. 340
Whelan, James 416
Whidby, Thomas 220
Whienberg, H. 340
Whissenhunt, John F. 220
Whitaker, Harrison Benjamin 380
White, Aaron J. 288
White, Evans 288
White, F.M. 340
White, H.E. 220
White, J.B. 425
White, James Andrew 220
White, James G. 387
White, John A. 340
White, John C. 405
White, M.A. 288
White, W.T. 220
White, William 416
White, William B. 231
White, Woodbury C. 120
White House (U.S.) 20
Whitehead, W.D. 400
Whitehead, William Henry 340
Whitehurst, John B. 231

Whitman, James 220
Whitman, R. 340
Whittaker, J.L. 381
Whittaker, John 340
Whittaker, Warden G. 340
Whittle, Elisha 220
Whittle, H. 289
Whitworth, P.H. 387
Wicks, H. 220
Wiggins, Benjamin F. 340
Wiggins, Jasper W. 220
Wiggins, Joseph O. 400
Wigham, R.N. 220
Wilburn, J.D. 220
Wild, Posey C. 381
Wild Gazelle, ship 36
Wilder, Edward M. 120
Wilder, J.M. 220
Wilderness, revenue cutter 80
Wildy, H.H., ensign 340
Wiley, T.J. 369
Wilkerson, D.P. 220
Williams, A. 425
Williams, Ansel W. 120
Williams, Benjamin 340
Williams, D. 416
Williams, Daniel J. 220
Williams, David 220
Williams, E. 416
Williams, Frank M. 289
Williams, G.W. 289
Williams, George H. 120
Williams, George L. 45, 431
Williams, H.H. 221
Williams, Henry 221
Williams, I.G. 425
Williams, J.A. 405
Williams, J.J. 231, 289
Williams, J.M. 340
Williams, J.R. 370
Williams, James 340
Williams, James P. 221
Williams, James S. 370
Williams, Jefferson Winston 341
Williams, John 85, 341
Williams, John R. 232
Williams, John W. 221
Williams, M.B. 370
Williams, Mart S. 341
Williams, Merritt 370
Williams, R.J. 341
Williams, Thomas 221, 370
Williams, Thomas, brigadier-general 35
Williams, W., citizen 431
Williams, W.N.L. 221
Williams, William 341
Williams, William A. 289
Williams, William M. 341
Williams, Z. 221
Williamson, A. 232
Williamson, Allen 341, 425
Williamson, J.T.F. 221
Williamson, Monroe 221
Williamson, S.D. 221
Williamson, S.P. 341
Williamson, W.H. 341
Willis, Francis M. 221
Willis, Joseph B. 341

Willis, Stephen Morgan 381
Willis, Thomas B. 341
Willis, W.F. 341
Wilmers, A. 289
Wilmington, North Carolina 35
Wilson, Augustus 221
Wilson, D.C. 289
Wilson, G.W. 405
Wilson, H. 221
Wilson, J.R. 341, 370
Wilson, James 221
Wilson, James A. 370
Wilson, James B. 221
Wilson, Jerry 221
Wilson, John 370
Wilson, John T. 221
Wilson, Joseph 120
Wilson, Joseph H. 221
Wilson, Joseph T. 341
Wilson, Madison D. 381
Wilson, Robert 289
Wilson, S.S. 222
Wilson, V.A. 222
Wilson, W.A. 341
Wilson, William 341
Wiltz, P.E., Jr., citizen 431
Wimberly, J.A. 341
Wims, T.J. 222
Winchester, Orrin 120
Windham, Milton 341
Windham, W.J. 341
Windham, Warren T. 342
Winn, John W. 370
Winn, Moses C. 222
Winslet, A.W. 222
Winslow 29
Winston, George A. 400
Winston, James H. 289
Winston, Samuel L. 342
Winston, W.E. 222
Winston, William C., captain 400
Winter, J.C. 400
Winter, Mrs.Rogers 55, 97
Wise, John 370
Wisengur, W. 222
Witham, A.H. 120
Withers, John A. 370
Witset, J. 342
Wofford, Mark J., artificer 400
Wolf, Gustave 289
Wolf River 46
Wolfe, Daniel Henry 370
Wolfe, W.H., hospital steward 370
Womack, William 222
Wood, D.M. 342
Wood, George M. 222
Wood, James T. 342
Wood, John M. 370
Wood, Joseph F. 222
Woodall, J.M. 425
Woodard, Henry Stucky 289
Woodard, Pleasant Washington 405
Woodcock, T.S. 425
Woodfin, William A. 381
Woodman, Albert H. 120
Woods, A. 222
Woods, James 222
Woods, John W. 222

Woods, Lewis E. 290
Woods, R.Y. 222
Woodward, F.A. 222
Woodward, Isaac 342
Woodworth, John Maynard, surgeon-general 88
Woolley, Wyman Adair 222
World War II 10, 97
Worsham, Alex 290
Worsham, W.D. 342
Wright, Pvt. Charles A. 370
Wright, Charles U. 120
Wright, H.M., citizen 431
Wright, J.H. 222
Wright, James 223
Wright, S.M. 370
Wright, Thomas Harrison 223
Wright, William 120
Wyatt, H.G. 223
Wyatt, Richard 370
Wyatte, Silas M. 223
Wyman, Wallace W. 120
Wynn, William B. 232

XIII Corps (U.S.) 70
XVI Corps (U.S.) 70

Yarborough, H. 290
Yerger, D.D. 342
Young, Henry T. 342
Young, John Francis 223
Young, Levy 223
Young, S.C., assistant surgeon 342

Zachary, Bennett 290
Zimmerman, Eugene, ensign 223
Zuber, C.W.F. 223

www.ingramcontent.com/pod-product-compliance
Lightning Source LLC
Chambersburg PA
CBHW081156230426
43666CB00016B/2835